Encyclopedia of

AMERICAN

CIVIL LIBERTIES

Encyclopedia of

AMERICAN

CIVIL LIBERTIES

Volume 1
A – F
Index

Paul Finkelman
Editor

Routledge
Taylor & Francis Group
New York   London

Routledge is an imprint of the
Taylor & Francis Group, an informa business

Routledge
Taylor & Francis Group
270 Madison Avenue
New York, NY 10016

Routledge
Taylor & Francis Group
2 Park Square
Milton Park, Abingdon
Oxon OX14 4RN

© 2006 by Taylor & Francis Group, LLC
Routledge is an imprint of Taylor & Francis Group, an Informa business

Printed in the United States of America on acid-free paper
10 9 8 7 6 5 4 3 2 1

International Standard Book Number-10: 0-415-94342-6 (Hardcover)
International Standard Book Number-13: 978-0-415-94342-0 (Hardcover)

Library of Congress Cataloging-in-Publication Data

Encyclopedia of American civil liberties / Paul Finkelman, editor.
      p. cm.
    ISBN 0-415-94342-6 (set : alk. paper)
    1. Civil rights--United States--Encyclopedias. 2. Civil rights--United States--Cases. I. Finkelman, Paul, 1949-

KF4747.5.E53 2006
342.7308'503--dc22   2006045284

Visit the Taylor & Francis Web site at
http://www.taylorandfrancis.com

and the Routledge Web site at
http://www.routledge-ny.com

For Judge Avern Cohn, a friend of legal history and civil liberties.

CONTENTS

EDITOR

Paul Finkelman
President William McKinley Distinguished Professor of Law and Public Policy and Senior Fellow in the Government Law Center at Albany Law School

ASSOCIATE EDITORS

Gabriel J. Chin
Chester H. Smith Professor of Law, Professor of Public Administration, University of Arizona

Davison M. Douglas
Hanson Professor of Law, Director, Institute of Bill of Rights Law, William and Mary School of Law

Rodney A. Smolla
Dean and Allen Professor of Law, T.C. Williams School of Law, University of Richmond

Melvin I. Urofsky
Professor of Public Policy, Emeritus, Virginia Commonwealth University

Mary L. Volcansek
Dean and Professor of Political Science, Addran College of Humanities and Social Sciences, Texas Christian University

CONTRIBUTORS

Douglas E. Abrams
University of Missouri

Erin Ackerman
Johns Hopkins University

Jeffrey F. Addicott
St. Mary's University School of Law

J. Mark Alcorn
Independent Scholar

Mark C. Alexander
Seton Hall University

Azizah Y. Al-Hibri
University of Richmond

Craig H. Allen
University of Washington

Diane Marie Amann
University of California, Davis

Vikram D. Amar
University of California, Hastings College of the Law

David A. Anderson
University of Texas at Austin

Christopher J. Anderson
Drew University

Jean-Claude André
Ivey, Smith & Ramirez

Keith Aoki
University of Oregon

Annette R. Appell
University of Nevada, Las Vegas

Michael S. Ariens
St. Mary's University

Jennifer J. Ashley
Boise State University

Miriam J. Aukerman
Legal Aid of Western Michigan

Irene Segal Ayers
New York University

Paul R. Baier
Louisiana State University

Enoch W. Baker
Wayne State University

Julie A. Baker
Suffolk University

David T. Ball
Methodist Theological School

William C. Banks
Syracuse University

Judith M. Barger
Appalachian School of Law

Gordon S. Barker
College of William and Mary

Robin D. Barnes
University of Connecticut

Randy E. Barnett
Boston University

Rebecca Barnhart
City University of New York

Kathleen L. Barrett
Georgia State University

Robert F. Bauer
Perkins Coie LLP

CONTRIBUTORS

Francis J. Beckwith
Baylor University

Valena Elizabeth Beety
University of Chicago

Angela Behrens
University of Minnesota

Valerie R. Bell
Boise State University

Diane Benjamin
University of Montana

Thomas C. Berg
University of St. Thomas

Kathleen Hawkins Berkowe
Law Offices of Kathleen Hawkins Berkowe

David E. Bernstein
George Mason University

Ashutosh Bhagwat
University of California, Hastings College of the Law

Jean Binkovitz
Independent Scholar

J. Michael Bitzer
Catawba College

David Blackett
University of Arizona

G. Robert Blakey
Notre Dame University

Robert Blecker
New York Law School

Eric D. Blumenson
Suffolk University

Eli C. Bortman
Babson College

Michael W. Bowers
University of Nevada, Las Vegas

Cynthia Grant Bowman
Northwestern University

William C. Bradford
Indiana University-Purdue University

Craig M. Bradley
Indiana University

Elizabeth B. Brandt
University of Idaho

Daniel L. Brenner
National Cable TV Association

Susan W. Brenner
University of Dayton

J. Richard Broughton
Texas Wesleyan University

Todd Brower
Western State University College of Law

Geneva Brown
University of Nevada, Las Vegas

William H. Brown
North Carolina Office of Archives and History

Michael J. Broyde
Emory University

James J. Brudney
Ohio State University

Karen Bruner
Syracuse University

Michael H. Burchett
Limestone College

Alafair S. Burke
Hofstra University

John M. Burkoff
University of Pittsburgh

David D. Burnett
University of Virginia

Charles R. Calleros
Arizona State University

Clay Calvert
Pennsylvania State University

Dale Carpenter
University of Minnesota

Elizabeth S. Carpenter
Averett University

David M. Carr
Honeywell International Inc.

Nicole B. Cásarez
University of St. Thomas

John S. Celichowski
St. Benedict the Moor Ministries

Michael C. Cernovich
Law Offices of Norm Pattis

Michael Chang
Santa Clara University School of Law

Anthony Chase
Nova Southeastern University

Jim Chen
University of Minnesota

Sanjay K. Chhablani
Syracuse University

Ann B. Ching
United States Military Academy

Kathryn H. Christopher
University of Tulsa

Russell L. Christopher
University of Tulsa

Thomas K. Clancy
University of Mississippi

Jason A. Cole
University of Arizona

Ruth Colker
Ohio State University

Peter A. Collins
Boise State University

Ronald K. L. Collins
The First Amendment Center

Todd A. Collins
University of Georgia

Daniel O. Conkle
Indiana University

Beverly Blair Cook
University of Wisconsin, Milwaukee, Emeritus

Mark W. Cordes
Northern Illinois University

Ezekiel E. Cortez
Independent Scholar

Vance L. Cowden
University of South Carolina

Randall T. Coyne
University of Oklahoma

B. Keith Crew
University of Northern Iowa

David B. Cruz
University of Southern California

Larry Cunningham
Texas Tech University

Perry Dane
Rutgers University

M. K. B. Darmer
Chapman University

Brian Daugherity
College of William and Mary

James Corbett David
College of William and Mary

Martha F. Davis
Northeastern University

Louis A. Day
Louisiana State University

Dominic DeBrincat
University of Connecticut

Nora V. Demleitner
Hofstra University

George M. Dery, III
California State University

Neal Devins
College of William and Mary

Suzanne L. Diaz
University of Arizona

CONTRIBUTORS

J. Amy Dillard
American University

Michael Dimino
Widener University

Robert Dingwall
University of Nottingham

Michael Dodson
Texas Christian University

James M. Donovan
University of Georgia

Davison M. Douglas
College of William and Mary

David Dow
University of Houston

Steven B. Dow
Michigan State University

Robert E. Drechsel
University of Wisconsin, Madison

Daniel L. Dreisbach
American University

Joshua Dressler
Ohio State University

Father Robert F. Drinan, S. J.
Georgetown University

William V. Dunlap
Quinnipiac University

Philip Dynia
Loyola University

Rebecca Goodgame Ebinger
Yale University

Jane Eggers
University of Arizona

Jeannine M. Eiband
Boise State University

James W. Ely, Jr.
Vanderbilt University

Francene M. Engel
University of Maryland

Garrett Epps
Oregon University

Carl H. Esbeck
University of Missouri

Sarah Eskreis-Winkler
University of Pennsylvania

Christopher E. Everett
Nova Southeastern University

Sara Faherty
State University of New York at Buffalo

Marie A. Failinger
Hamline University

Roger A. Fairfax, Jr.
George Washington University

Daniel A. Farber
University of Minnesota

Anthony L. Fargo
University of Nevada

Anthony Paul Farley
Boston College

Stephen M. Feldman
University of Wyoming

Zanita E. Fenton
University of Miami

John M. Ferren
Senior Judge

Daniel M. Filler
University of Alabama

Michael S. Finch
Stetson University

Andrew Finkelman
University of Iowa

Paul Finkelman
Albany Law School

Edwin B. Firmage
University of Utah

Susanna Fischer
Catholic University of America

Clifford S. Fishman
Catholic University of America

Joel Fishman
Duquesne University

Roy B. Flemming
Texas A&M University

Matthew L. M. Fletcher
University of North Dakota

Patrick Flynn
University of South Carolina

James C. Foley
University of Mississippi

James C. Foster
Oregon State University - Cascades

James W. Fox, Jr.
Stetson University

Nichole H. Franklin
Boise State University

Amanda Freeman
Boise State University

Steven I. Friedland
Nova Southeastern University

Lawrence Friedman
New England School of Law

Emily R. Froimson
Arizona State University

Maryellen Fullerton
Brooklyn School of Law

Lynne Garcia
University of Maryland

James A. Gardner
University at Buffalo

Alan E. Garfield
Widener University

Scott D. Gerber
Ohio Northern University

Steven G. Gey
Florida State University

Daniel G. Gibbens
University of Oklahoma

Robert Don Gifford
Assistant United States Attorney, District of Nevada

Gary S. Gildin
University of Pennsylvania

Jean Giles-Sims
Texas Christian University

Michele Gilman
University of Baltimore

Adam Gitlin
University of Michigan

Joel K. Goldstein
Saint Louis University

Joel M. Gora
Brooklyn Law School

Mark A. Graber
University of Maryland

Lino Graglia
University of Texas at Austin

Stuart P. Green
Louisiana State University

Marcel Green
Independent Scholar

Steven K. Green
Willamette University

I. Michael Greenberger
University of Maryland

Daniel J. H. Greenwood
University of Utah

Natalie R. Gregg
Boise State University

David L. Gregory
St. John's University

Leslie C. Griffin
University of Houston

Lissa Griffin
Pace University

CONTRIBUTORS

David E. Guinn
DePaul University

Heidi Scott Giusto
Duke University

Kevin R. C. Gutzman
Western Connecticut State University

Jonathan L. Hafetz
New York University

Patrick H. Haggerty
Skadden, Arps, Slate, Meagher & Flom LLP

James Halabuk, Jr.
George Mason University

Kermit L. Hall
President, State University of New York at Albany

Timothy L. Hall
University of Mississippi

Marci A. Hamilton
Cardozo School of Law

Roberta M. Harding
University of Kentucky

Linda F. Harrison
Nova Southeastern University

Marc M. Harrold
University of Mississippi

Stephanie Roberts Hartung
Suffolk University

James G. Harwood
United States Army

Melissa Haussman
Carleton University

Cynthia G. Hawkins-León
Stetson University

Arthur S. Hayes
Fordham University

Kevin Jon Heller
University of Georgia

Craig Hemmens
Boise State University

Peter J. Henning
Wayne State University

Kay Henriksen
MacMurray College

Michael E. Herz
Cardozo School of Law

Milton Heumann
Rutgers University

Christopher Hill
Legal Services of New Jersey

B. Jessie Hill
Case Western Reserve University

Michele L. Hill
University of Richmond

Ann C. Hodges
University of Richmond

Michael H. Hoffheimer
University of Mississippi

Daniel N. Hoffman
Johnson C. Smith University

Kenneth M. Holland
Kansas State University

Bobby R. Holt
University of Tennessee

Janet Hong
University of Arizona

Chris Jay Hoofnagle
Electronic Privacy Information Center

Kevin James Houk
Drew University

Scott W. Howe
Chapman University

Stephanie Hszieh
Independent Scholar

Audrey I-Wei Huang
Suffolk University

L. Sue Hulett
Knox College

Brian M. Iannacchione
Boise State University

Randa Carolyn Issa
University of Southern California

Donald W. Jackson
Texas Christian University

Tonja Jacobi
Northwestern University

Elizabeth E. Joh
University of California, Davis

Steve R. Johnson
University of Nevada, Las Vegas

John Paul Jones
University of Richmond

Stephen Jones
Stephen Jones & Associates

Deanna Juhl
Stephen Jones & Associates

Jonathan Kahn
University of Minnesota

Thomas M. Keck
Syracuse University

Mark Kemper
Bridgewater State College

Ken I. Kersch
Princeton University

Todd Kerstetter
Texas Christian University

Kirk L. Kimber
Boise State University

Christopher D. King
Law Office of Christopher King

Jeffrey L. Kirchmeier
City University of New York

Jane E. Kirtley
University of Minnesota

Susan R. Klein
University of Texas

Helen J. Knowles
State University of New York at Oswego

Daniel T. Kobil
Capital Law School

Michael Koby
Washington University in St. Louis

Margery M. Koosed
University of Akron

Andrew Koppelman
Northwestern University

Candace Saari Kovacic-Fleischer
American University

Raymond James Krohn
Purdue University

Renée M. Landers
Suffolk University

Jefferson L. Lankford
Judge, Arizona Court of Appeals

Carlton F. W. Larson
University of California, Davis

Kenneth Lasson
University of Baltimore

Frederick M. Lawrence
Boston University

Margaret M. Lawton
Charleston School of Law

Hans Leaman
Yale University

Arthur Leavens
Western New England College of Law

Francis Graham Lee
St. Joseph's University

Donna H. Lee
City University of New York

Emery G. Lee, III
Case Western Reserve University

William E. Lee
University of Georgia

CONTRIBUTORS

Scott Lemieux
City University of New York

Arthur S. Leonard
New York Law School

Daniel Levin
University of Utah

Kay L. Levine
Emory University

Samuel J. Levine
Pepperdine Law School

David W. Levy
University of Oklahoma

Lisa Levy
Case Western Reserve University

Martin L. Levy
Texas Southern University

Bin Liang
Arizona State University

Steven Lichtman
University of Vermont

Sara E. Lindenbaum
University of Arizona

Susan E. Looper-Friedman
Capital University

María Pabón López
Indiana University-Purdue University

Aaron R. S. Lorenz
University of Massachusetts, Amherst

Jimmy Luke
Emory University

Erik Luna
University of Utah

Christopher C. Lund
University of Houston Law Center

Pamn M. Madarieta
Boise State University

Michael Madow
Brooklyn Law School

Richard Collin Mangrum
Creighton Law School

Mary K. Mankus
Syracuse University

Samuel A. Marcosson
University of Louisville

Paul Marcus
College of William and Mary

Nancy S. Marder
Chicago-Kent College of Law

Julie H. Margetta
Boston College

Karen M. Markin
University of Rhode Island

Earl F. Martin
Texas Wesleyan University

Robert W. T. Martin
Hamilton College

Gilbert D. Martinez
Texas State University, San Marcos

Calvin Massey
University of California, Hastings College of the Law

Ralph D. Mawdsley
Cleveland State University

Marilyn McAuley
Boise State University

Charles McClain
University of California, Berkeley

Celestine Richards McConville
Chapman University

David McCord
Drake University

Marthé L. McCoy
Boise State University

Janis L. McDonald
Syracuse University

Judithanne Scourfield McLauchlan
University of Florida, St. Petersburg

M. Isabel Medina
Loyola University

Daniel S. Medwed
University of Utah

Philip L. Merkel
Western State University

Bernadette Meyler
Cornell University

Alan C. Michaels
Ohio State University

Kent R. Middleton
University of Georgia

F. Thornton Miller
Missouri State University

David A. Moran
Wayne State University

Denise C. Morgan
New York Law School

Robert P. Mosteller
Duke University

Mitchell A. Mosvick
University of Virginia

Kenneth F. Mott
Gettysburg College

Kerry L. Muehlenbeck
Arizona State University

Eric L. Muller
University of North Carolina

Johann N. Neem
Western Washington University

Ronald L. Nelson
University of South Alabama

Caryn E. Neumann
Ohio State University

Joel A. Nichols
Pepperdine University

David A. Nichols
Indiana State University

John T. Nockleby
Loyola Marymount University

Lawrence D. Norden
New York University

Jerome D. O'Callaghan
State University of New York College at Cortland

J. C. Oleson
Old Dominion University

Samuel R. Olken
John Marshall Law School

Carol A. Olson
University of Akron

Kathleen K. Olson
Lehigh University

Robert M. O'Neil
University of Virginia

Melissa Ooten
University of Richmond

John V. Orth
University of North Carolina

Antony Page
Indiana University School of Law

John Gregory Palmer
Lehigh University

David Ray Papke
Marquette University

Michael S. Pardo
University of Alabama

Nicholas Parrillo
Yale University

Michael E. Parrish
University of California, San Diego

Lisa K. Parshall
Daemen College

Richard J. Peltz
University of Arkansas at Little Rock

Mary M. Penrose
University of Oklahoma

CONTRIBUTORS

Antonio F. Perez
Catholic University of America

Shawn Francis Peters
University of Wisconsin–Madison

Todd E. Pettys
University of Iowa

Tamara R. Piety
University of Tulsa

Nina Pillard
Georgetown University

Brian K. Pinaire
Lehigh University

Sherrow O. Pinder
Hobart and William Smith Colleges

Marc R. Poirier
Seton Hall University

Michael J. Polelle
John Marshall Law School

Malla Pollack
University of Idaho

Scot Powe
University of Texas at Austin

Linda Przybyszewski
University of Notre Dame

Marc Georges Pufong
Valdosta State University

Vincent L. Rabago
Office of the Arizona Attorney General

R. S. Radford
Pacific Legal Foundation

Kiran Raj
Emory University

Frank S. Ravitch
Michigan State University

Gavin J. Reddick
University of Virginia

Lee R. Remington
University of Kentucky

Jeffrey T. Renz
University of Montana

Charles W. "Rocky" Rhodes
South Texas College of Law

Thomas E. Richard
Southern University Law Center

Jef I. Richards
University of Texas at Austin

Robert D. Richards
Pennsylvania State University

James Riddlesperger
Texas Christian University

Alison P. Rivchun
University of Arizona

James E. Robertson
Minnesota State University, Mankato

Jon Roland
Constitution Society

Victor C. Romero
Pennsylvania State University

Kermit Roosevelt, III
University of Pennsylvania

William Rose
Albion College

Susan Dente Ross
Washington State University

William G. Ross
Samford University

Constance L. Rudnick
Massachusetts School of Law

David S. Rudstein
Chicago-Kent College of Law

Irma S. Russell
University of Tulsa

John Paul Ryan
Independent Consultant

Arthur J. Sabin
John Marshall Law School

Rebecca Mae Salokar
Florida International University

Lawrence G. Salzman
Pacific Legal Foundation

Vincent J. Samar
Loyola University of Chicago

Steve Sanders
University of Michigan

Stephen L. Sarazin
William Mitchell College of Law

Kevin W. Saunders
Michigan State University

Shelley Saxon
Pepperdine University

Laura J. Scalia
Independent Scholar

Michael A. Scaperlanda
University of Oklahoma

Edward J. Schoen
Rowan University

David Schultz
Hamline University

Louis N. Schulze, Jr.
Suffolk University

Aaron Schwabach
Thomas Jefferson School of Law

Herman Schwartz
American University

Martin A. Schwartz
Touro Law Center

Melissa Schwartzberg
George Washington University

Maimon Schwarzschild
University of San Diego

Judith A. M. Scully
West Virginia University

Keith E. Sealing
Syracuse University

Amy Shapiro
Syracuse University

Rebecca S. Shoemaker
Indiana State University

Salmon A. Shomade
University of Arizona

Michael R. Siebecker
Hofstra University

Mary Sigler
Arizona State University

Louis J. Sirico, Jr.
Villanova University

Christopher Slobogin
University of Florida

Steven D. Smith
University of San Diego

Rodney A. Smolla
University of Richmond

Jason M. Sokiera
University of Southern Mississippi

Daniel J. Solove
George Washington University

A. Benjamin Spencer
University of Richmond

Shaun B. Spencer
Harvard University

Clyde Spillenger
University of California, Los Angeles

Peter J. Spiro
Hofstra University

Robert Spitzer
State University of New York College at Cortland

Rick M. Steinmann
Clarion University

Jerry E. Stephens
United States Court of Appeals

Kristopher B. Stevens
Emory University

CONTRIBUTORS

Janet W. Steverson
Lewis and Clark College

Maria Stilson
Ohio State University

Cody Stoddard
Boise State University

Robert N. Strassfeld
Case Western Reserve University

Marcy Strauss
Loyola Law School

J. Thomas Sullivan
University of Arkansas at Little Rock

Kathleen S. Sullivan
Ohio University

Douglas J. Sylvester
Arizona State University

Andrew E. Taslitz
Howard University

John B. Taylor
Washington College

Gabriel H. Teninbaum
Attorney

Fernando R. Tesón
Florida State University

Joseph T. Thai
University of Oklahoma

Gerald J. Thain
University of Wisconsin

Tracy A. Thomas
University of Akron

Jay Tidmarsh
University of Notre Dame

Lee Tien
Electronic Frontier Foundation

Christopher R. Tingle
University of Southern Mississippi

Enid Trucios-Haynes
University of Kentucky

G. L. Tyler
Independent Scholar

Christopher Uggen
University of Minnesota

Laura S. Underkuffler
Duke University

Melvin I. Urofsky
Virginia Commonwealth University

Mariangela Valle-Peters
Independent Scholar

James F. Van Orden
University of North Carolina

Geiza Vargas-Vargas
Skadden, Arps, Slate, Meagher & Flom LLP

Richard L. Vining
Emory University

Robert K. Vischer
St. Thomas Law School

Mary L. Volcansek
Texas Christian University

Eugene Volokh
University of California, Los Angeles

Candice R. Voticky
Emory University

Sarah E. Waldeck
Seton Hall University

Samuel Walker
University of Nebraska at Omaha

Carol Walker
Georgia State University

E. Gregory Wallace
Campbell University

Lu-in Wang
University of Pittsburgh

Stephen Watkins
United States Army Legal Services Agency

Russell L. Weaver
University of Louisville

Mark S. Weiner
Rutgers School of Law, Newark

Alan C. Weinstein
Cleveland State University

John W. Welch
Brigham Young University

Ba-Shen Welch
Virginia Commonwealth University

Sarah N. Welling
University of Kentucky

W. Bradley Wendel
Cornell University

Stephen J. Wermiel
American University

John Wertheimer
Davidson College

Ellis M. West
University of Richmond

Keith E. Whittington
Princeton University

Garry D. Wickerd
University of Florida

William M. Wiecek
Syracuse University

Daniel R. Williams
Northeastern University

Eric J. Williams
Rutgers University

Kenneth A. Williams
Southwestern University

R. Owen Williams
Yale University

Louis E. Wolcher
University of Washington

Adam B. Wolf
American Civil Liberties Union Drug Reform Project

Kevin J. Worthen
Brigham Young University

Ronald F. Wright
Wake Forest University

Ingrid Brunk Wuerth
University of Cincinnati

Katy H. H. Yang-Page
Concord University

Tung Yin
University of Iowa

Diana H. Yoon
New York University

Gordon G. Young
University of Maryland

Susan Zaeske
University of Wisconsin

Deborah Zalesne
City University of New York

ALPHABETICAL LIST OF ENTRIES

E

M

THEMATIC LIST
OF ENTRIES

Organizations and Government Bodies

Act Up
America Online
American Anti-Slavery Society
American Civil Liberties Union
Americans United for Separation of Church
  and State
Amish and Religious Liberty
Amnesty International
Anti-Defamation League of B'nai B'rith
Burger Court
Catholics and Religious Liberty
Central Intelligence Agency
Christian Coalition
Church of Scientology and Religious Liberty
Church of the New Song and Religious Liberty
Communist Party
Department of Homeland Security
Equal Rights Amendment
Fair Labor Standards Act and Religion
Federal Communications Commission
House Un-American Activities Committee
John Birch Society
Ku Klux Klan
Lambda Legal Defense and Education Fund
Legal Aid Society of New York
Legion of Decency
Log Cabin Republicans
Mormons and Religious Liberty
National Abortion Rights Action League (NARAL)
National Association for the Advancement of
  Colored People (NAACP)
National Labor Relations Board
National Organization for Women
National Rifle Association (NRA)
Operation Rescue
Private Discriminatory Association
Puritans
Quakers and Religious Liberty
Servicemembers Legal Defense Network

Seventh Day Adventists and Religious Liberty
Southern Center for Human Rights
Southern Poverty Law Center
Warren Court

Legislation and Legislative Action, Statutes, and Acts

Abortion Laws and the Establishment Clause
Adolescent Family Life Act
Alien and Sedition Acts (1798)
American Indian Religious Freedom Act of 1978
Anti-Anarchy and Anti-Syndicalism Statutes
Antipolygamy Laws
Becker Amendment
Bills of Rights in Early State Constitutions
Bill of Rights: Structure
Blaine Amendment
Broadcast Regulation
Cable Television Regulation
Campaign Finance Reform, No. 1021
Civil Rights Act of 1866
Civil Rights Act of 1875
Civil Rights Act of 1964
Communications Decency Act (1996)
Constitutional Amendment Permitting
  School Prayer
Defense of Marriage Act
Don't Ask, Don't Tell
English Toleration Act
Equal Access Act
Equal Protection Clause and Religious Freedom
Fair Credit Reporting Act, 84 Stat. 1127 (1970)
Fair Labor Standards Act and Religion
Freedom of Access to Clinic Entrances (FACE) Act,
  108 Stat. 694 (1994)
Freedom of Information Act (1966)
Freedom of Information and Sunshine Laws
Gag Rule
Guided Discretion Statutes

Historical Overview

Biography

Cohn, Roy
Comstock, Anthony
Connor, Eugene "Bull"
Covington, Hayden
Cromwell, Oliver
Darrow, Clarence
Dawson, Joseph Martin
Debs, Eugene V.
Dees, Morris
Dershowitz, Alan
DeWitt, General John
Dies, Martin
Douglas, William Orville
Douglass, Frederick
Dworkin, Andrea
Emerson, Thomas Irwin
Estes, Billie Sol
Evers, Medgar Wiley
Falwell, Jerry
Field, Stephen J.
Flynt, Larry
Fortas, Abe
Frank, John P.
Frankfurter, Felix
Franklin, Benjamin
Freund, Paul A.
Garrison, William Lloyd
Giddings, Joshua Reed
Gideon, Clarence Earl
Gilmore, Gary
Ginsburg, Ruth Bader
Goldberg, Arthur J.
Hague, Frank
Hamilton, Alexander
Hamilton, Andrew
Hand, (Billings) Learned
Harlan, John Marshall, the Elder
Harlan, John Marshall, II
Hays, Will H.
Helper, Hinton
Hentoff, Nat
Hiss, Alger
Holmes, Oliver Wendell, Jr.
Hoover, J. Edgar
Hughes, Charles Evans
Jackson, Andrew
Jackson, Robert H.
Jefferson, Thomas
Johnson, Frank, Minis, Jr.
Johnson, Lyndon Baines
Justice, William Wayne
Kamisar, Yale
Kaufman, Irving Robert
Kendall, Amos
Kennedy, Anthony McLeod

Kevorkian, Jack
King, Martin Luther, Jr.
Kunstler, William M.
La Follette, Robert Marion, Sr.
Lilborne, John (Freeborn John)
Lincoln, Abraham
Locke, John
Long, Huey Pierce
Lovejoy, Elijah
MacKinnon, Catharine
Madison, James
Marshall, John
Marshall, Thurgood
Mason, George
McCarthy, Joseph
McCorvey, Norma (Jane Roe)
McReynolds, James C.
Meese, Edwin, III
Meiklejohn, Alexander
Mill, John Stuart
Miranda, Ernesto Arturo
Mitchell, John
Montesquieu
Murphy, Frank
Murray, John Courtney
Nixon, Richard Milhaus
O'Connor, Sandra Day
Otis, James
Paine, Thomas
Palmer, A. Mitchell
Penn, William
Phillips, Wendell
Powell, Lewis Franklin, Jr.
Prejean, Sister Helen
Quinlan, Karen Ann
Rauh, Joseph L., Jr.
Rawls, John Bordley
Rehnquist, William H.
Reno, Janet
Roberts, Owen Josephus
Roosevelt, Franklin Delano
Rorty, Richard
Rosenberg, Julius and Ethel
Rush, Benjamin
Rutledge, Wiley Blount, Jr.
Ryan, George
Sanger, Margaret Higgins
Scalia, Antonin
Schlafly, Phyllis Stewart
Shaw, Lemuel
Shepard, Matthew
Sherman, Roger
Souter, David Hackett
Stanton, Elizabeth Cady
Stevens, John Paul

Cases

Valentine v. Chrestensen, 316 U.S. 52 (1942)

Vance v. Universal Amusement Co., Inc. 445 U.S. 208 (1980)

Vernonia School District v. Acton, 515 U.S. 646 (1995)

Vidal v. Girard's Executor, 43 U.S. 127 (1844)

Virginia State Board of Pharmacy v. Virginia Citizens Consumer Council, Inc., 425 U.S. 748 (1976)

Virginia v. Black, 123 S.Ct. 1536 (2003)

Wallace v. Jaffree, 472 U.S. 38 (1985)

Walz v. Tax Commission of the City of New York, 397 U.S. 664 (1970)

Warden v. Hayden, 387 U.S. 294 (1967)

Washington v. Glucksberg, 521 U.S. 702 (1997)

Washington v. Texas, 388 U.S. 14 (1967)

Watson v. Jones, 80 U.S. 679 (1872)

Watts v. United States, 394 U.S. 705 (1969)

Webb v. Texas, 409 U.S. 95 (1972)

Webster v. Reproductive Health Services, 492 U.S. 490 (1989)

Weeks v. United States, 232 U.S. 383 (1914)

Weems v. United States, 217 U.S. 349 (1910)

West Virginia Board of Education v. Barnette, 319 U.S. 624 (1943)

Whitney v. California, 274 U.S. 357 (1927)

William Penn's Case

Wilson v. Layne, 526 U.S. 603 (1999)

Wisconsin v. Mitchell, 508 U.S. 476 (1993)

Wisconsin v. Yoder, 406 U.S. 205 (1972)

Witters v. Washington Department of Services for the Blind, 474 U.S. 481 (1986)

Wolf v. Colorado, 338 U.S. 25 (1949)

Wolman v. Walter, 433 U.S. 229 (1977)

Wong Sun v. United States, 371 U.S. 471 (1963)

Wyman v. James, 400 U.S. 309 (1971)

Wyoming v. Houghton, 526 U.S. 295 (1999)

Yates v. United States, 354 U.S. 298 (1957)

Young v. American Mini Theatres, Inc., 427 U.S. 50 (1976)

Younger v. Harris, 401 U.S. 37 (1971)

Zablocki v. Redhail, 434 U.S. 374 (1978)

Zacchini v. Scripps Howard Broadcasting Company, 433 U.S. 562 (1977)

Zelman v. Simmons-Harris, 536 U.S. 639 (2002)

Zobrest v. Catalina Foothills School District, 509 U.S. 1 (1993)

Zorach v. Clauson, 343 U.S. 306 (1952)

Zurcher v. Stanford Daily, 436 U.S. 547 (1978)

Themes, Issues, Concepts, and Events

Abolitionist Movement

Abolitionists

Abortion

Absolutism and Free Speech

Abu Ghraib

Academic Freedom

Access to Government Operations Information

Access to Judicial Records

Access to Prisons

Accommodation of Religion

Accomplice Confessions

Actual Malice Standard

Administrative Searches and Seizures

Affirmative Action

Airport Searches

American Revolution

Anne Hutchinson Trial

Anonymity and Free Speech

Anonymity in Online Communication

Anti-Abolitionist Gag Rules

Anti-Abortion Protest and Freedom of Speech

Antidiscrimination Laws

Application of First Amendment to States

Appropriation of Name or Likeness

Arraignment and Probable Cause Hearing

Arrest Warrants

Arrest without a Warrant

Assisted Suicide

Asylum, Refugees and the Convention Against Torture

Automobile Searches

Autopsies and Free Exercise Beliefs

Bad Tendency Test

Bail

Balancing Approach to Free Speech

Balancing Test

Baldus Study (Capital Punishment)

Ballot Initiatives

Baptists in Early America

Bible in American Law

Bill of Attainder

Birth Control

Blacklisting

Bloudy Tenent of Persecution for Cause of Conscience, Discussed in a Conference between Truth and Peace, The

Blue Wall of Silence

Boston Massacre Trial

Brandenburg Incitement Test

Burden of Proof: Overview

Cameras in the Courtroom

Campus Hate Speech Codes

Capital Punishment and Race Discrimination

Capital Punishment and Resentencing

Capital Punishment and the Equal Protection Clause Cases

Capital Punishment and Sentencing

Capital Punishment and the Right of Appeal

THEMATIC LIST OF ENTRIES

INTRODUCTION

The story of America is, in part, the story of civil liberties. The early settlers of Massachusetts, the Plymouth separatists—remembered as the Pilgrims—and the Massachusetts Bay Puritans came to America seeking freedom of religious worship. This was a civil liberty they sought for themselves, although not for others in their community. But by the end of the 1640s, Rhode Island offered substantial religious toleration for people of all faiths while Maryland offered toleration for most Christians. New Amsterdam would later develop a regime of toleration while Pennsylvania and South Carolina would begin as colonies open to people of all faiths. While Europeans continued to slaughter each other over matters of faith, Americans, even in the most rigid colonies, developed a sense of toleration. This was the first step towards a culture of liberties and civil liberties. Instances of religious persecution—hanging of Quakers in Boston or witches in Salem—proved to be lessons to other Americans on why civil liberties mattered.

Political struggles in the colonies helped Americans develop a growing sense of liberty. The trial of the printer John Peter Zenger in 1736 for his attacks on the governor of New York did not alter the law of libel in England or America. But the case did highlight the importance of due process, the grand jury indictment, and an impartial jury to the cause of liberty. Zenger had clearly embarrassed the governor and his administration, and under the law of the time that amounted to seditious libel. However, the grand jury refused to indict the printer, in part because what he said was substantially true. The prosecutor charged Zenger by information, bypassing the grand jury and, in the process, teaching Americans the importance of the grand jury as a buffer between the state and the individual. The prosecutor then tried to stack the jury while the judge disbarred Zenger's lawyers. Good lawyering by an appointed counsel, a clever strategy by Zenger's supporters, and an impartial jury ultimately led to an acquittal. The lesson for the colonists was that due process protections were central to a free people and civil liberties were necessary to protect the governed from the government.

The Revolutionary Era brought new civil liberties concerns. In 1776, Americans complained that the King denied them due process and fair trials. During the Revolution, Americans worried about freedom the press, bills of attainder, and the problems of creating a free society without spinning into anarchy; and about creating a stable society that avoided becoming a tyranny. Constitutional government, a bill of rights, and an expanded suffrage were designed to prevent both evils by creating stability and liberty.

Since the adoption of the Bill of Rights in 1791, Americans have often debated the meaning of civil liberties. In the 1790s, Congress passed the Fugitive Slave Law of 1793 and the Sedition Act of 1798, both of which seemed to violate provisions of the Bill of Rights. The Supreme Court did not consider the constitutionality of the first law until 1842 and never considered the constitutionality of the Sedition Act. By 1812, however, the political process and accepted political and social norms eliminated seditious libel from the American landscape, until Congress revived it during World War I. The antebellum crisis led to debates over abolitionist speech and petitions to Congress. Slavery itself was, of course, the worst violation of civil liberties in American history. But slave owners argued that their civil liberties prevented the national government from taking their property—freeing their slaves—without just compensation. The Civil War raised new questions about free speech, the suspension of habeas corpus, and the right to free slaves. The aftermath of the war led to loyalty oaths, the suspension of habeas corpus in parts of the South, and three new amendments that began to change the nature of federalism by applying the Bill of Rights and other federal protection to the states. Immigration, labor unions, anarchism, new political ideologies, the suppression of black equality, fears of pornography, feminism, and the dissemination of information about birth control all raised new civil liberties issues in the last part of the nineteenth century. World War I led to a new Sedition Act and, for the first time, the Supreme Court was forced to define the meaning of speech.

Throughout the twentieth century, the Supreme Court was at the center of the meaning of rights. The courts have protected civil liberties at times, and at others have been less protective. Most importantly, the courts have continuously expanded and reinterpreted the meaning of civil liberties. So too has popular culture. In the early nineteenth century it seemed reasonable, even within the context of freedom of speech and religion, to punish blasphemy. Today such an idea would be dismissed by almost all Americans. Early movies were often quite sexually suggestive. By the 1940s they were almost prudish. Today society tolerates almost anything in a movie, but we properly focus on who can see a movie—protecting children from sexually explicit content—rather than on the content itself.

The rights of the accused also changed over time. Since 1791, the Eighth Amendment has banned cruel and unusual punishment, and most states have had similar prohibitions in their constitutions. But until the 1960s, many police department routinely interrogated prisoners with threats, violence, sleep deprivation, and other tactics commonly called "the third degree." When the U.S. Supreme Court stopped such practices in the mid-1960s many Americans objected. They feared that the police would be unable to do their job. Two generations later, even police departments find that protecting the rights of the accused makes policing easier and is less likely to lead to false confessions. Most Americans can recite their "Miranda" rights by heart, having heard them in movies and on television over and over again. Americans know their rights and understand the value of these rights.

At the beginning of the twenty-first century, civil liberties are at the center of political discourse. The wars in Afghanistan, in Iraq and the war on terrorism have raised new questions about civil liberties in an age of what may be perpetual war or at least perpetual alerts for terrorism. Americans have to ponder how eighteenth century ideas fit into a new technological age. The Bill of Rights requires that the government may not conduct a search without a warrant, issued by a judge on the basis of probable cause. The Sixth Amendment requires a speedy trial. Can such requirements work in an age of high-tech terror? Can our democracy survive if such requirements are ignored?

With these issues in mind, Routledge publishes the *Encyclopedia of American Civil Liberties*. We have designed this work to provide a comprehensive access to the key historical and contemporary issues surrounding civil liberties in the United States. We believe that no reference work could be more timely or more vital to the nation than one on civil liberties. We hope the encyclopedia will help students, scholars, the general public, lawmakers, and government officials better understand the complexity of civil liberties and their historic role in the development of the United States.

Coverage

In addition to freedom of speech, press, religion, assembly, and petition, the encyclopedia covers topics such as privacy, property rights, the rights of the accused, and national security. Its multidisciplinary approach and breadth of scope will make it an essential library reference for lawyers, scholars, students, and general readers. The entries discuss a wide range of topics, including:

- The Constitution, the Bill of Rights, and the history of civil liberties
- Cases, trials, and important court decisions
- Associations, societies, organizations, and government bodies
- Literature, entertainment, media, and art
- Slavery, crime, and war
- Religion, censorship, and privacy
- People, places, and events

The articles are grouped into thematic entries, as follows:

Biography

Biographies cover such pioneers from Thomas Jefferson, the master stylist of American history, to Margaret Sanger, the founder of Planned Parenthood. The biography entries in this encyclopedia are focused on the social, political, and other circumstances relevant to the individual's work.

Cases

Case entries provide a clear and engaging narrative that includes the background on the case, the identification of key players, and an explanation of how the case arose. The main text of the entry should discuss the analysis, doctrine, and majority opinion vote. Case entries conclude by explaining the long-term impact of the decision, as well as the importance of the case in relation to civil liberties.

Historical Overview

Entries focus on the origin of the subject in American history and its relationship to civil liberties. The discussion includes influences (religious, philosophical, cultural, and so forth), major players and events, and long-term impact on civil liberties.

Legislation, Legislative Action, Statutes, and Acts

Entries on legislation detail the history, enactment, and current status of the law, statute, or act. This also includes precedents, actions, and events that led to its formation, cases involved in its history, and consequences or lasting impact on civil liberties.

Organizations and Government Bodies

Organizations are included that have had an impact on civil liberties in the United States. Each entry includes the organization or government body's history, key members (including founders) throughout its history, and legal implications of its impact on civil liberties.

Themes, Issues, Concepts, and Events

The focus of these entries is on the relationship between the subject and civil liberties. In addition to the basic discussion of the subject, each entry may include the following issues: history, origins, and development; legal, academic, or theoretical debates; perspectives from different fields or schools of thought; or any unresolved issues concerning the subject.

How to Use This Book

The *Encyclopedia of American Civil Liberties* contains 1423 entries of 250 to 6000 words in length. They range from biographies to thematic interpretations and analytical discussions of timely topics. As far as possible, the encyclopedia covers the history and politics of civil liberties from the time of the Founding Fathers to the present, providing the reader with a reliable, up-to-date view of the current state of scholarship on civil liberties and the meaning of freedom in American life.

Perhaps the most significant feature of the encyclopedia is the easily accessible **A to Z format**. Cross-referencing in the form of **See Alsos** at the end of most entries refer the reader to other related entries. Each article contains a list of **References and Further Reading**, including sources used by the writer and editor as well as additional items that may be of interest to the reader. Most books or articles cited are easily available through interlibrary loan services in libraries. Entries may also include a segment entitled **Cases and Statutes Cited**, which lists the citations of cases and statutes referred to in the article. **Blind Entries** direct readers to essays listed under another title. For example, the blind entry "Death Penalty" refers the reader to the article titled "Capital Punishment." A thorough, analytical index complements the accessibility of the entries, easing the reader's entry into the wealth of information provided. A **Thematic List of Entries** is also included to assist readers with research in particular areas.

Four hundred and seventy authors have contributed the entries to this encyclopedia. Contributors represent a variety of fields, among them criminal law, Constitutional law, law and religion, legal history, law and race, and reproductive rights. The expertise of a wide-ranging and diverse group of contributors will provide the reader with a broad-based overview of issues, events, and theories of the developing world.

Acknowledgments

This encyclopedia would not have been possible without the cooperation of hundreds of scholars who have written for it. My coeditors—Jack Chin, Dave Douglas, Rod Smolla, Mel Urofsky, and Mary Volcansek—have worked enormously hard in making this project happen. They have made my job as editor-in-chief a pleasure because they were such a pleasure to work with. The project began under the editorship of Sylvia Miller. I am especially grateful to Jamie Ehrlich, who has managed the project for the last year, Mark Georgiev, Mark O'Malley, Kate Aker, and Marie-Claire Antoine, and Tracy Grace for their efforts in the editorial production aspects of this encyclopedia. The creation of a reference work is a team effort, and I have been blessed with a wonderful team of scholars and publishers. I thank all of them not only for the pleasure of working together, but also for their dedication to helping all Americans learn more about our constitutional rights and our civil liberties.

Paul Finkelman

A

A BOOK NAMED "JOHN CLELAND'S MEMOIRS OF A WOMAN OF PLEASURE" v. MASSACHUSETTS, 383 U.S. 413 (1966)

A civil proceeding initiated by the Massachusetts attorney general declared *Memoirs of a Woman of Pleasure* (more commonly known as *Fanny Hill*) to be obscene. The publisher, G. P. Putman, appealed and lost. The Supreme Court, with Justice Brennan writing for a three-judge plurality (Justices Warren and Fortas joining him), reversed the lower court in a short opinion—one of three dealing with obscenity questions handed down on the same day. Justices Douglas and Black wrote opinions concurring with the judgment. Justices Clark, Harlan, and White wrote separate dissents.

The sole issue in *Memoirs* was the appellate court's application of the *Roth* (*Roth v. United States*, 354 U.S. 476, 1957) standard. Justice Brennan concluded the court erred by not applying each element separately before declaring a publication obscene. The Massachusetts appellate court in affirming the lower court decision that *Memoirs* was obscene on two of *Roth*'s criteria applied the third standard according to its view that it did "not interpret the 'social importance' test as requiring that a book which appeals to prurient interest and is patently offensive must be unqualifiedly worthless before it can be deemed obscene."

Justice Brennan disagreed and asserted that all three elements must be met. Moreover, he explained the third criterion, in accordance with his opinion in

Jacobellis v. Ohio, 378 U.S. 184 (1964), meant that the book must be "*utterly* without redeeming social value" (italics in original). The justice's restatement of this criterion had the effect of shrinking the zone of sexually explicit material that would not be protected under the First Amendment. It constituted a liberalization of this criterion in *Roth* because prosecutions for obscenity would be made more difficult.

Moreover, the social value of allegedly obscene material cannot be weighed against the other two elements; material failing any one standard, therefore, is sufficient to consider the material not obscene. Even if *Memoirs of a Woman of Pleasure* possessed "only a modicum of social value," the Massachusetts judgment would have to be reversed. Then, referring to the majority's contemporaneous decision in *Ginzburg v. United States*, 383 U.S. 463 (1966), Justice Brennan added that the circumstances of production, sale, and publicity might be pertinent when determining the obscenity of material. Commercial exploitation of the book's prurient appeal, "to the exclusion of all other values," might indicate the book lacks redeeming social importance. In this instance, however, the courts were not asked to judge *Memoirs* against this background.

In an angry dissent, Justice Clark, reporting that he supplied the deciding vote in *Roth*, complained that the "utterly without redeeming social value" standard added a new element to *Roth*. In his view, *Roth* required only that a book be judged "as a whole" and in terms of "its appeal to the prurient interest of the average person, applying contemporary community standards." Prior to *Jacobellis*, Justice Clark pointed out, no previous decisions referred to the "utterly without redeeming social value" test, and Justice Brennan's position in *Jacobellis* won only Justice Goldberg's vote, which did not give it precedential weight. Justice White, agreeing with Justice Clark, claimed that this element "is not an independent test of obscenity but is relevant only to determining the predominant prurient interest of the material." In other words, evidence of prurience implies something that is "utterly without redeeming social value."

Justice Harlan lamented that *Roth* produced "no stable approach" to the obscenity problem. Moreover, the concept of pandering, suggested first by Justice Warren in his *Roth* concurrence and subsequently adopted in *Ginzburg*, provided no more than "an uncertain . . . interpretative aid" in sorting out "this tangled state of affairs." Furthermore, Brennan's suggestion that pandering may create a context that offsets social value "wipes out any certainty the latter term might be given . . . and admits into the case highly prejudicial evidences without appropriate restrictions."

The companion cases to *Memoirs* are *Ginzburg vs. United States* and *Mishkin v. New York*, 383 U.S. 502 (1966).

ROY B. FLEMMING

Reference and Further Reading

Rembar, Charles. *The End of Obscenity: The Trials of* Lady Chatterley, Tropic of Cancer, *and* Fanny Hill. New York: Random House, 1968.

Cases and Statutes Cited

A Book Named "John Cleland's Memoirs of a Woman of Pleasure" v. Attorney General of Massachusetts, 383 U.S. 413 (1966)
Ginzburg v. United States, 383 U.S. 463 (1966)
Jacobellis v. Ohio, 378 U.S. 184 (1964)
Mishkin v. New York, 383 U.S. 502 (1966)
Roth v. United States, 354 U.S. 476 (1957)

ABINGTON TOWNSHIP SCHOOL DISTRICT v. SCHEMPP, 374 U.S. 203 (1963)

One of the two decisions known as the school prayer cases, *Abington* followed immediately in the wake of *Engel v. Vitale*, 370 U.S. 421 (1962), in which the Supreme Court declared unconstitutional the recitation in public schools of a prayer composed by the New York Board of Regents. There the Court concluded that it was "no part of the business of government to compose official prayers for any group of the American people to recite as a part of a religious program carried on by government." Unlike *Engel*, which involved the state's participation in the composition of a religious exercise, in *Abington* government acted as the sponsor rather than composer of religious exercises. The case thus posed clearly the issue of whether state-sponsored and supervised religious activities violated the First Amendment's establishment clause. A majority of the Court held that they did.

The Decision in *Abington*

At issue in *Abington* was the state-sponsored practice of beginning school days with Bible readings, selected and read by students or a teacher, and the recitation of the Lord's Prayer by students. Writing for the Court's majority, Justice Tom Clark easily concluded that the Bible readings and prayers were religious exercises. The primary defect of state-sponsored religious exercises in public schools, according to the Court's opinion, was that they offended the establishment clause's demand for neutrality on the part of government with respect to religion. The requisite constitutional neutrality was more than a mere lack of preference for one religion over another, though there was significant evidence before the Court that the religious exercises at issue preferred Christianity to Judaism. Instead, the Court characterized the necessary neutrality as one which avoided aiding or hindering religion. Justice Clark's opinion did not characterize the establishment clause in terms of a necessary separation between church and state, but it quoted favorably from previous decisions emphasizing the requirement of separation.

The decision in *Abington* did not turn on a finding that students were compelled to participate in religious exercises that offended their beliefs, since students were allowed to absent themselves from the exercises. But the Court concluded that this fact did not salvage the practices at issue, since the establishment clause required neutrality toward religion, not simply the avoidance of religious compulsion. In language that would assume even greater importance once incorporated into the three-part test of *Lemon v. Kurtzman*, 403 U.S. 602 (1971), for determining whether a government action violated the establishment clause, the Court's opinion emphasized that the requisite neutrality called for a "secular legislative purpose and a primary effect that neither advances nor inhibits religion."

Against the claim that the removal of officially sponsored prayer and Bible reading would establish a "religion of secularism," the Court denied that its decision excluded religion from schools. "Nothing we have said here," Justice Clark insisted for the majority, "indicates that . . . study of the Bible or of religion, when presented objectively as part of a secular program of education, may not be effected consistently with the First Amendment." Nor could the Court accept that its decision frustrated the free exercise of religion, an argument present by Justice Potter Stewart in a dissenting opinion. Stewart suggested that parents who wished their children to begin the school day with Bible readings and prayer had a substantial free exercise claim. If religion were excluded from public schools, then the religion would be placed at an "artificial and state-created" disadvantage. A majority of the Court, however, rejected this argument. The establishment clause meant that a local or state religious majority could not "use the machinery of the State to practice its beliefs."

Aftermath

Abington established firmly the principle that public school authorities would not be permitted to sponsor devotional religious exercises. In subsequent cases, the Court demonstrated itself to be the implacable antagonist of every attempt to makes state or local governments partners in the conduct of religious exercises or in the dissemination of religious teachings. Attempts to circumvent the holdings of *Engel* and *Abington* flourished in the decades that followed. Some states attempted to create "moments of silence" in which students might pray or meditate or do nothing, according to their individual desires. A majority of the members of the Court seemed receptive to this kind of legislative scheme, at least in some circumstances. But when evidence suggested that an Alabama statute of this nature had been passed with the purpose of restoring prayer to public schools, the Court struck the law down in *Wallace v. Jaffree*, 472 U.S. 38 (1985), as lacking a secular purpose. Since *Wallace v. Jaffree*, all lower courts have sustained these statutes as unconstitutional.

Later, when state-sponsored prayers banished from public school classrooms migrated to various paraschool functions, such as graduation ceremonies and football games, the Court responded with similar constitutional vigilance. In *Lee v. Weisman*, 505 U.S. 577 (1992), a majority of the Court held unconstitutional prayers at a middle school graduation ceremony offered by a rabbi at a school official's request. Moreover, in *Sante Fe I.S.D. v. Doe*, 530 U.S. 290 (2000), the Court struck down an arrangement

established by a school district in which students were allowed to vote on whether to have prayers at football games and to select students to offer the prayers.

The Court has also applied the essential principle of *Abington* to contexts in which religious symbols or teaching was at issue. Thus, in *Stone v. Graham*, 449 U.S. 39 (1980), the Court invalidated a school district practice of displaying the Ten Commandments in classrooms, concluding that such displays lacked a secular purpose. In *Edwards v. Aguillard*, 482 U.S. 578 (1987), the Court found a similar lack of secular purpose in a Louisiana statute providing for the teaching of "creation science" when evolution was taught.

In spite of complaints that the Court had banished religion from public schools, however, not all forms of religious devotion or even teaching about religion are excluded by the principle of *Abington*. Both the opinion for the Court and Justice William Brennan's important concurring opinion in the case emphasized the propriety of teaching about religion from an academic, rather than a devotional, standpoint. It would distort history and literature and other subjects to teach these subjects without reference to the religious experiences of humankind, and the Court hurried to acknowledge this fact. What the School Prayer cases prohibited was teaching designed to proselytize or to inculcate religious devotion. Moreover, private prayer offends no constitutional principle. Thus, in *Board of Education v. Mergens*, 496 U.S. 226 (1990), the Court refused to extend the ruling of *Engel* and *Abington* to prevent Congress from mandating equal access for religious student groups. The federal *Equal Access Act* provided that religious student groups were entitled to equal access to school facilities as enjoyed by other noncurricular groups. In *Mergens*, the Court held that this accommodation did not offend the establishment clause.

Abington acknowledged various forms of civic religiosity common in American society, including the divine invocation made a part of oaths in legal proceedings ("So help me God"), the invocation preceding the Court's sessions ("God save this honorable Court"), and civic prayers such as those offered at the beginning of congressional sessions. But Justice Clark's opinion for the majority did not seriously attempt to distinguish these aspects of public religion from the Bible readings and prayer before the Court. It would remain for future majorities to harmonize the principles articulated in *Abington* with civil religion more broadly conceived.

The School Prayer cases had a further legacy that reached outside the realm of courts into the realm of politics. After the controversy between theological liberals and fundamentalists during the early part of the twentieth century, many theological conservatives withdrew from active participation in public affairs. They focused instead on the creation of their own educational and charitable institutions rather than on political action. But the School Prayers cases of the 1960s, coupled with the Court's decision affirming a right to abortion in *Roe v. Wade*, 410 U.S. 113, in 1973, almost certainly had the effect of igniting a new wave of conservative participation in the political process. Some of this political participation took the form of advocacy of a constitutional amendment to reverse the holdings in the School Prayer cases. Although such amendments have been proposed, none has secured the measure of support necessary to win passage.

The new advocacy also turned to a variety of other political issues. In the late 1970s, for example, Baptist minister Jerry Falwell founded the Moral Majority as a political group devoted to the advocacy of conservative political policies. Although the group remained active only for a decade, it is sometimes credited with helping to elect Ronald Reagan as president of the United States. Though Falwell disbanded the organization toward the end of the following decade, Pat Robertson, a popular religious television personality and would-be candidate for the Republican nomination for president, organized the Christian Coalition to serve purposes similar to those sought by the Moral Majority. The exact political influence of these and other manifestations of what came to be known as the "Christian right" remain highly contested. But the significant presence of such groups, a presence at least partially owing its genesis to hostility to the School Prayer cases, cannot be doubted.

TIMOTHY L. HALL

References and Further Reading

Choper, Jesse H. *Securing Religious Liberty: Principles for Judicial Interpretation of the Religion Clauses*. Chicago: University of Chicago Press, 1995, 44–53.

Curry, Thomas J. *Farewell to Christendom: The Future of Church and State in America*. Oxford: Oxford University Press, 2001, 76–80.

Feldman, Stephen M. *Please Don't Wish Me a Merry Christmas: A Critical History of the Separation of Church and State*. New York: New York University Press, 1997, 233–235.

Hall, Timothy L., *Sacred Solemnity: Civic Prayer, Civil Communion, and the Establishment Clause*, Iowa Law Review 79 (1993): 44–46.

Nowak, John E., and Ronald D. Rotunda, *Constitutional Law, 1460–1465*, 7th ed. St. Paul, MN: Thompson–West, 2004.

Stone, Geoffrey R., *In Opposition to the School Prayer Amendment*, University of Chicago Law Review 50 (1983): 823–848.

Cases and Statutes Cited

Board of Education v. Mergens, 496 U.S. 226 (1990)
Engel v. Vitale, 370 U.S. 421 (1962)
Edwards v. Aguillard, 482 U.S. 578 (1987)
Everson v. Board of Education, 330 U.S. 1 (1947)
Lee v. Weisman, 505 U.S. 577 (1992)
Lemon v. Kurtzman, 403 U.S. 602 (1971)
Roe v. Wade, 410 U.S. 113 (1973)
Santa Fe Independent School Dist. v. Doe, 530 U.S. 290 (2000)
Stone v. Graham, 449 U.S. 39 (1980)
Wallace v. Jaffree, 472 U.S. 38 (1985)
Equal Access Act, 20 U.S.C. §§ 4071–74

See also **Bible Reading in Public Schools, History of before and after *Abington School District v. Schempp*; *Engel v. Vitale*, 370 U.S. 421 (1962); Legislative Prayer; *Marsh v. Chambers*, 463 U.S. 783 (1983); Prayer in Public Schools; *Santa Fe Independent School District v. Doe*, 530 U.S. 290 (2000)**

ABOLITIONIST MOVEMENT

A new and aggressive phase of American abolitionism emerged in the 1830s. Called "immediatism," the movement for the immediate, uncompensated emancipation of slaves without expatriation (which received institutional expression first from the regional New England Anti-Slavery Society, founded in 1832, then the national American Anti-Slavery Society, founded in 1833) comprised individuals regardless of race, class, or gender, a stark departure from previous efforts that were primarily gradual in scope and genteel (read elite white male) in composition. The changes signified by immediatism's seemingly sudden appearance were anything but welcomed, as evidenced by the scores of mobs that assaulted exponents of that creed; by the federal postal service's (especially its state auxiliaries in the South) effective ban of abolitionist literature from reaching a southern audience; and by the U.S. Congress's virtual stranglehold, for nearly a decade, on the voices of antislavery petitioners, preventing them from receiving an appropriate hearing in the nation's highest council.

Although those reactions constituted a curtailment of, if not utter disregard for, traditional rights as guaranteed in the state and federal constitutions—freedom of speech and of the press, the right of the people to peaceably assemble and to petition the government for a redress of grievances, according to the First Amendment to the U.S. Constitution—abolitionists, though seriously challenged, were neither thwarted nor suppressed. On the contrary, since the enjoyment of basic civil liberties was jeopardized, abolitionism actually thrived, despite and because of the animosity that immediatists directly and indirectly provoked.

Hostility and violence early greeted the abolitionist movement, as outbreaks of mob activity readily indicate. Although anti-abolitionist attacks occurred in the North throughout the three decades preceding the Civil War, the high tide of such riots took place in the years between 1834 and 1838. Too numerous to list in detail, a few incidents shall sufficiently illustrate immediatism's initial impact on northern society and reveal the difficulties that abolitionists encountered in order to broadcast their message.

In their attempts to assemble peaceably, abolitionists frequently confronted local antagonism, potentially volatile situations that sometimes threatened the safety of their very persons. For example, on October 21, 1835, an angry mob stormed a gathering of the Boston Female Anti-Slavery Society. Although concerned citizens directly targeted the meeting's invited speaker, William Lloyd Garrison, the outspoken and controversial editor of the Boston antislavery weekly, The Liberator, the society's members also confronted a raucous crowd. Yet, to protect one another from harm, white and black women marched in double-file, arm-in-arm, past protestors, a dangerous display of social equality that could have elicited unintended reactions from already belligerent demonstrators. Indeed, once the female abolitionists exited the building, the mob seized Garrison and then dragged him through the city's streets—only a night's refuge in prison protected him from additional assault.

Anti-abolitionist rioters also played havoc with the exercise of freedom of speech and of the press. Twice in July 1836 Cincinnatians sought to dissuade the southern-born former slaveholder and future Liberty Party presidential candidate James G. Birney from continuance of his abolitionist newspaper, The Philanthropist, by partial or complete destruction of his printing press. The relocated Maine native Elijah Lovejoy suffered similar opposition in the southern Illinois town of Alton. Over about a three-month period in 1837, city residents, alarmed by Lovejoy's increasing abolitionist editorial policy and his attempts to organize a state antislavery society, wrecked the press of his Presbyterian reformist paper, the Observer, three times. It was on that final and what proved to be fatal occasion, on November 7, that Lovejoy succumbed to five gunshot wounds when he, himself armed, rushed the mob that set ablaze the roof of the building that housed his press. Although some abolitionists expressed regret over Lovejoy's use of physical force in his defense, the lack of unity over faithful adherence to the movement's founding pacifistic principles gave way to near unanimity over Lovejoy's symbolic importance for abolitionism. Thus, Lovejoy was thereafter known as "the first MARTYR to American LIBERTY[,] MURDERED for asserting the FREEDOM of the PRESS."

Although riotous events concerning abolitionists were occurrences largely in free states, anti-abolitionism reared its ugly head against immediatists throughout the country. The concurrent pamphlet and petition campaigns, amplified in 1835–1836, clearly revealed that nationwide antipathy to the cause. Each initiative underscored abolitionists' faith in the redemptive power of "moral suasion," one of the movement's fundamental tenets that emphasized the demise of slaveowning and racial prejudice once their sinfulness was exposed to the American public. To achieve that much-desired end, abolitionists appealed especially to those most capable of instituting the process of emancipation: slaveholders and congressmen.

Whatever abolitionists' expectations, the reactions from those groups to their proselytizing schemes were not unlike those of the northern mobs—vitriolic and censorious. For example, when postal sacks filled with antislavery newspapers and journals (addressed to prominent citizens and not free blacks or illiterate slaves) arrived in Charleston, South Carolina, on the morning of July 29, 1835 (only a small fraction of the more than one million pieces of printed matter circulated by the American Anti-Slavery Society to points and persons across the country during the fiscal year ending in May 1836), enraged residents quickly alleviated the uncertainties that beset the city's postmaster over what to do with the troublesome material. That evening, members of the Lynch Men vigilance committee spirited away the satchels containing immediatist propaganda during a raid on the post office. The following night the abolitionist mails—as appropriately befitted what the local press called "incendiary" tracts—were ceremoniously burned, along with effigies of three leading abolitionists, before a crowd of between two and three thousand people.

Despite the swift resistance by Carolinians to outside abolitionist incursions, antislavery periodicals continued unabated. Charlestonians once more mobilized in retaliation, forming another vigilance society to search for and confiscate what were judged to be seditious publications; the committee even called upon northern state governments to legislate abolitionist organizations out of existence. Although the Charleston postmaster provided for a guarded escort for the conveyance of that dreadful material from such seemingly malignant individuals, his protection of the mails was limited to the delivery of abolitionist pamphlets to the post office only. Once there, they remained safely quarantined until orders from the postmaster general directed otherwise. The latter, Kentuckian and stalwart Jacksonian Democrat Amos Kendall, did not order a contrary course—which would have necessitated the uninhibited distribution of antislavery literature—but intimated approval, noting in correspondence that obedience to the community where one lived surpassed obligations to federal statutes.

The anti-abolitionist sentiments that the postal campaign unleashed finally reached a crescendo in December 1835, when President Andrew Jackson, in his annual message, urged Congress to enact appropriate measures against "the misguided persons [abolitionists] who have engaged in these unconstitutional and wicked attempts." The national assembly, he suggested, should pass "such a law as will prohibit, under severe penalties, the circulation in the Southern States, through the mail, of incendiary publications intended to instigate the slaves to insurrection."

Just as Carolinians prevented (extralegally if not illegally) the discussion of slavery (specifically, its abolition) at home, they sought similar action in the nation's capital. In the same month that Andrew Jackson addressed Congress, South Carolina Representative James Henry Hammond remonstrated against any further introduction of abolitionist petitions in the lower house. In so doing, he not only captured the ire and recalcitrance of his constituents in matters involving the security of the "peculiar institution," but also, by his demand that such memorials be peremptorily repudiated, initiated a debate that shifted congressional practices regarding the historic right of petition and spurred abolitionists to greater activity.

What resulted after weeks of heated deliberation was the "gag rule," which prohibited congressmen from discussing or printing the contents of any petitions that dealt with slavery. Those antislavery memorials that reached, and would soon bombard, Congress were automatically "laid on the table," with "no further action [taken] whatever." That order, adopted in May 1836 and remaining in force until 1844, did not repulse abolitionists, but rather increased their resolve. Indeed, in 1837 and 1838 alone, 412,000 antislavery petitions deluged the House, and nearly two-thirds that amount flooded the Senate. Women especially contributed to the success of such operations. They were not only active in gaining signatures—women comprised over half of the signatories—but also became more involved in public affairs and more assertive on behalf of their own, deprived, rights.

The response to abolitionism was gravely important to activists at that time, for at stake was nothing

less than the Bill of Rights. The ensuing civil liberties controversy almost instantly redounded to the benefit of an otherwise unpopular and dissenting minority portion of the citizenry. In the short run, immediatist organizations increased by more than twofold, from about two hundred in May 1835 to over five hundred the following year. To be sure, abolitionists would remain a small segment of the population throughout the antebellum period, but the struggle over the maintenance of traditional American rights, which antislavery agitation instigated, catapulted the immediatist movement and the question of slavery onto a national stage. They remained there, despite attempts to the contrary, until President Abraham Lincoln officially announced the Emancipation Proclamation on New Year's Day, 1863.

RAYMOND JAMES KROHN

References and Further Reading

Grimsted, David. *American Mobbing, 1828–1861: Toward Civil War*. New York: Oxford University Press, 1998.

Nye, Russel B. *Fettered Freedom: Civil Liberties and the Slavery Controversy, 1830–1860*. East Lansing: Michigan State College Press, 1949.

Richards, Leonard L. *Gentlemen of Property and Standing: Anti-Abolition Mobs in Jacksonian America*. New York: Oxford University Press, 1970.

Wyatt–Brown, Bertram. "The Abolitionists' Postal Campaign of 1835." *The Journal of Negro History* 50(4) (1965):227–238.

Wyly–Jones, Susan. "The 1835 Anti-Abolition Meetings in the South: A New Look at the Controversy over the Abolition Postal Campaign." *Civil War History* 47(4) (2001):289–309.

Yellin, Jean Fagan, and John C. Van Horne, eds. *The Abolitionist Sisterhood: Women's Political Culture in Antebellum America*. Ithaca, NY: Cornell University Press, 1994.

Zaeske, Susan. *Signatures of Citizenship: Petitioning, Antislavery, and Women's Political Identity*. Chapel Hill: The University of North Carolina Press, 2003.

ABOLITIONISTS

Abolitionists were individuals committed to eradicating chattel slavery in the United States. The first organized abolitionist group was the Pennsylvania Abolition Society (PAS). Dominated by socialites, politicians, businessmen, lawyers, and community leaders, its members included such prominent figures as Thomas Paine, George Washington, and Benjamin Franklin. PAS believed in the gradual abolition of slavery through legal (representing blacks in court) and political (petitioning Congress) means. PAS shunned grassroots involvement (even among African Americans) and instead focused on a strategy whereby elite white males would pursue their moral calling by working within existing institutional structures to abolish slavery.

With the surge of democratic sentiment that swept the nation in the early nineteenth century, it became obvious that PAS's conservative approach to abolitionism was outdated and ineffective. In the 1830s, the abolitionist cause moved to Massachusetts, where the emphasis was on the immediate emancipation of slaves. The movement solicited the support of the masses (including African Americans and women) through the creation of organizations and societies and the dissemination of written material (pamphlets and newspapers) in a grassroots effort to abolish slavery. Abolitionists appealed to people's emotions by emphasizing the immorality of such an "evil institution." Such was the intent of Harriet Beecher Stowe's antislavery novel, *Uncle Tom's Cabin* (1852), which was written in response to the strengthening of the *Fugitive Slave Act* of 1850.

William Lloyd Garrison's (1805–1879) newspaper, *The Liberator*, was the rallying cry for the abolitionist cause. Garrison believed not only in the immediate emancipation of slaves, but also in a commitment to treating African Americans as persons with "inherent and unalienable rights." He supported the Declaration of Independence but shunned the Constitution as a "proslavery compact," a "covenant with death," an "agreement with hell," and a "flagrant robbery of the inalienable rights of men." The Constitution, which was created at the expense of human dignity, violated the laws of God and, therefore, was null and void. Garrison detested political action and believed that abolitionism was a moral and religious crusade to open the eyes of the people to the evils of slavery.

One of the most prominent African-American abolitionists was Frederick Douglass (1818–1895), a former slave, whose autobiographies (*The Narrative of the Life of Frederick Douglass, An American Slave*, and *My Bondage, My Freedom*) revealed the details of his life as a slave and were also arguments against the institution that denied slaves their self-worth. At first Douglass supported Garrison's reading of the Constitution as a proslavery compact, but soon parted ways with Garrison when he realized that the Constitution could be interpreted to be against slavery. Douglass encouraged abolitionists to work within the system to abolish slavery by becoming active in politics and exercising their constitutional rights of speech and press, as well as voting.

The abolitionist movement began in the Revolutionary era, reached its pinnacle in the 1830s, maintained its strength in the 1850s, and continued after the Civil War until the end of Reconstruction. By 1900, slavery was completely abolished in the Western Hemisphere.

RANDA CAROLYN ISSA

References and Further Reading

Blassingame, John W., ed. *The Frederick Douglass Papers: Series One: Speeches, Debates, and Interviews*. 3 vols. New Haven and London: Yale University Press, 1979.

Cain, William E., ed. *William Lloyd Garrison and the Fight Against Slavery: Selections From* The Liberator. Boston: St. Martin's Press, 1995.

Newman, Richard S. *The Transformation of American Abolitionism: Fighting Slavery in the Early Republic*. Chapel Hill: University of North Carolina Press, 2002.

Stowe, Harriet Beecher. *Uncle Tom's Cabin*, 150th ed. Oxford: Oxford University Press, 2002.

ABOOD v. DETROIT BOARD OF EDUCATION, 431 U.S. 209 (1977)

In *Abood v. Detroit Board of Education*, the U.S. Supreme Court unanimously ruled that assessment of mandatory service charges on nonunion members in an agency shop to finance union expenditures for collective bargaining did not violate their First Amendment rights. However, the Court prohibited unions from requiring employees to contribute to the support of ideological causes to which they might be opposed as a condition of holding their jobs as public school teachers. Noting that the First Amendment safeguards the freedom to associate with others and contribute money to advance ideas and promote beliefs and that those protections are not surrendered by virtue of public employment, the Court decided compulsory contributions by union members for political purposes violate the First Amendment.

The First Amendment precludes the state from compelling association with a political point of view to retain public employment. The Court stressed, however, that the ruling did not stop the union from spending money to advance a political viewpoint or help a candidate to gain office. Rather, the First Amendment demands such political expenditures be funded by union members who neither oppose nor are forced to support those political ideas by the threat of loss of employment with the government.

By safeguarding individuals from being forced to contribute to causes they oppose as a condition of employment, *Abood* provides significant First Amendment protection against compelled financing of political or ideological speech.

EDWARD SCHOEN

References and Further Reading

Ogeka, Charles J., *Respecting Nonunion Member Employees' Rights While Avoiding a Free Ride*. Lehnert v. Ferris Faculty Ass'n, Hofstra Labor Law Journal 10 (1992): 349–373.

Schoen, Edward J. et al., *United Foods and Wileman Bros: Protection Against Compelled Commercial Speech—Now You See It, Now You Don't*, American Business Law Journal 39 (2002): 467–520.

Skaare, Jessica J., *Constitutional Law—First Amendment: University Fees Can Speak for Students: The Constitutionality of a University's Right to Fund Student Speech Via a Mandated Activities Fee*, North Dakota Law Review (2001): 549–586.

Cases and Statutes Cited

International Association of Machinists v. Street, 367 U.S. 740 (1961) (Union shops must not use compulsory assessments to support political activities against the expressed wishes of dissenting employees.)

Keller v. State Bar of California, 496 U.S. 1 (1990) (Compulsory bar association dues may not be expended to advance political causes, but may be spent for disciplining bar members or proposing ethical codes for the legal profession.)

Lehnert v. Ferris Faculty Association, 500 U.S. 507 (1991) (The state cannot compel its unionized employees to subsidize legislative lobbying or other political union activities outside the context of labor contract ratification or implementation.)

ABORTION

Prior to the middle of the nineteenth century, abortion was an issue to which men, and therefore lawmakers, judges, and politicians, paid little or no attention. With the Supreme Court's 1973 decision of *Roe v. Wade*, 410 U.S. 114 (1973), abortion became perhaps the most prominent legal and political issue of the late twentieth century and continues to be so in the twenty-first century.

In *Roe v. Wade*, the Supreme Court struck down a Texas law that prohibited all abortions except those strictly necessary to save the life of the mother. The statute in question (and similar laws in effect in a majority of states at that time) was not in fact part of the Anglo-American common law, but was of relatively recent origin. At the time at which the U.S. Constitution was ratified, there were no statutes against abortion in the United States or in England, and the English common law received by the new states recognized a crime of abortion only after "quickening"—that is, only after the movements of a fetus can be felt (generally between the fourteenth and sixteenth weeks of pregnancy). Since colonial times, early abortion was not only legal but also was widely practiced in this country, increasingly so in the early nineteenth century. Abortion services were commonly advertised in newspapers, and women's folk medicine recognized a number of traditional herbal abortifacients that were widely known. It was not until after the Civil War that criminal statutes proscribing abortion were widely adopted by the states.

Two developments in the mid-1800s may have influenced state legislatures to enact criminal sanctions against abortion. The first was the founding in 1847 of the American Medical Association (AMA), which lobbied lawmakers to enact regulations limiting the practice of medicine to professionally licensed physicians and prohibiting "irregulars," such as midwives, from providing healthcare services. In 1857, the AMA created a Committee on Ethics that launched a campaign to make all abortions illegal.

The second issue influencing the early development of abortion policy was the "first wave" feminist movement, which led many women to question their traditional roles in the family and to seek many of the social, economic, and legal privileges enjoyed by men. Abortion was seen as inimical to the proper role of women as wives and mothers. Concern for "protecting" women's traditional roles was expressed by the Supreme Court in its 1873 decision of *Bradwell v. Illinois*, 83 U.S., 16 Wall., 130 (1873), in which the Court denied women the right to practice law. The earliest state statutes generally prohibited only those abortions performed after "quickening." Not until the 1920s, during a second wave of anti-abortion legislation, did most states adopt laws proscribing abortion at all stages of pregnancy.

Abortion laws remained largely unchanged until the 1960s, when a number of events led to a reexamination of abortion policy and practice. One such event was an outbreak of German measles, which, along with the widespread use of thalidomide, resulted in an epidemic of children born with serious birth defects. Many physicians feared the criminal sanctions they risked if they performed abortions on women at risk of delivering babies with severe birth defects. Another turning point in the evolution of abortion policy was the introduction in 1960 of the first birth control pill, which launched the "sexual revolution" and the "second-wave" feminist movement. More young women began pursuing higher education, entering into traditionally male professions, and postponing motherhood or eschewing it altogether. While this new form of contraception gave women additional and more reliable control over their fertility, the option of abortion was viewed as necessary to provide complete protection from unwanted pregnancies.

As a result of these developments, many groups began to push for the liberalization of abortion laws. In 1962, the American Law Institute (ALI) introduced a Model Penal Code that recommended legalizing abortion under certain circumstances, such as when pregnancy resulted from rape or incest or when the fetus was likely to suffer from serious defects. By the time of the *Roe* decision, fourteen states had adopted some or all of the ALI's recommendations, and four states, Alaska, Hawaii, New York, and Washington, had repealed their abortion laws altogether. While some groups sought legislative reform to liberalize or repeal the old criminal laws, other groups pursued judicial recognition of a constitutionally protected civil right to reproductive autonomy that would include access to birth control and to abortion.

The Supreme Court's first foray into the issue of reproductive rights was in the case of *Griswold v. Connecticut*, 381 U.S. 479 (1965), in which the Court recognized a right of privacy within the "penumbra" of the Constitution's enumerated rights that protected the freedom of married persons to obtain contraceptives. This right of privacy was extended to unmarried persons with the Court's decision in *Eisenstadt v. Baird*, 405 U.S. 438 (1972). Justice Brennan, writing for the majority, said: "If the right of privacy means anything, it is the right of the individual, married or single, to be free from unwarranted governmental intrusion into matters so fundamentally affecting a person as the decision of whether to bear or beget a child."

These two cases set the stage for the Supreme Court's landmark decision of *Roe v. Wade*. Justice Harry Blackmun wrote the opinion for the seven-justice majority of the Court. In it he said that "the right of privacy, whether it be founded in the Fourteenth Amendment's concept of personal liberty and restrictions upon state action, as we feel it is, or . . . in the Ninth Amendment's reservation of rights to the people, is broad enough to encompass a woman's decision whether or not to terminate her pregnancy." Without resolving the question of the legal status of an unborn fetus, the Court held that the states had compelling interests in the health of the mother and the "potential human life" of the unborn. Each of these interests justifies state regulation at different stages of pregnancy. During the first trimester of pregnancy, when the Court found that abortion was medically safer than childbirth, a state has no legitimate interest in interfering with the abortion decision. After the third month of pregnancy, when the risks of abortion to the mother's health increase, the state "may, if it chooses, regulate the abortion procedure in ways that are reasonably related to maternal

health." In the third trimester, when the fetus may be viable outside the womb, the state may "regulate, or even proscribe, abortion except where it is necessary . . . for the preservation of the life or health of the mother."

While the *Roe* decision was enthusiastically embraced by most abortion rights advocates, it also provoked the formation of a "right-to-life" movement that has fought relentlessly since the day the decision was handed down to limit its application or to overturn it outright. Even those who support abortion rights have criticized the *Roe* decision on grounds ranging from its lack of textural authority to the unworkability of its trimester framework. The "pro-life" movement initially focused it efforts on the election of lawmakers who, it was hoped, would appoint judges who would limit the application of *Roe*, support laws limiting access to abortions, and even amend the Constitution to define a right to life for the unborn.

Throughout the 1970s and early 1980s, the Court continued to refine the contours of the right to abortion, but held to the position that a woman's right to terminate a pregnancy prior to fetal viability was a fundamental one and that, therefore, any state's attempt to regulate abortion was subject to "strict scrutiny." Between 1973 and 1986, the Court, using this heightened standard of judicial review, struck down state laws that required spousal consent to an abortion (*Planned Parenthood of Central Missouri v. Danforth*, 428 U.S. 52, 1976), that required a twenty-four-hour waiting period before an abortion (*Akron v. Akron Center for Reproductive Health*, 462 U.S. 416, 1983), that mandated specific information about fetal development be provided before consent would be considered "informed" (*Akron; Thornburgh v. American College of Obstetricians and Gynecologists, Pennsylvania Section*, 476 U.S. 747, 1986), that limited the methods that could be used to perform abortions (*Danforth* and *Thornburgh*), and that required a minor to notify a parent or to obtain parental consent to an abortion without providing adequate judicial bypass protections (*Bellotti v. Baird*, 443 U.S. 622, 1979; *Akron; Thornburgh*).

While the Court struck down most legislative attempts to impede or discourage abortions, it did uphold laws that reflected the government's refusal to support a woman's choice to abort. The "Hyde Amendment" enacted by Congress in 1976 to prohibit the use of Medicaid funds for abortions, along with similar state statutes, has been upheld by the Court. Many argued that these laws violated the equal protection clause by making safe abortions unavailable to poor women. But, in *Harris v. McRae*, 448 U.S. 297 (1980), that argument was rejected by the Court, which held that "although government may not place obstacles in the path of a woman's exercise of her freedom of choice, it need not remove those not of its own creation. Indigency falls in the latter category." Since the *Harris* decision, forty-seven states now prohibit the use of public funds for abortion except when the life of the mother is at risk.

The anti-abortion movement gained momentum in 1980 with the election of President Ronald Reagan, who made anti-abortion policies a top priority and vowed that he would appoint justices to the Supreme Court who would vote to overrule *Roe*. It was during this period that the abortion issue became highly politicized as the religious Right became more closely identified with the Republican administration. The Reagan years saw the passage of a number of federal laws that sought to limit access to abortion. Congress passed laws restricting access to abortions for government workers, Medicaid patients, and patients in public hospitals. "Gag rules" were imposed that prevented any facility receiving federal funds from giving women information about abortion. Reagan's administration also withheld foreign aid to countries that provided government access to abortion. But the principle focus of the Reagan and Bush administrations' anti-abortion efforts was on the Supreme Court, where views on abortion became a litmus test for judicial appointments.

When Chief Justice Warren Burger retired from the Court in 1986, Reagan appointed William Rehnquist, who had dissented in *Roe*, to fill the position. Other members of the *Roe* majority were replaced by the more conservative Justices O'Connor, Scalia, and Kennedy, each of whom had shown some degree of opposition to the right to abortion. When the case of *Webster v. Reproductive Health Services*, 492 U.S. 490 (1989), came before the Court in 1989, many believed that the Court was then poised to overturn *Roe v. Wade*.

The Court in *Webster* was asked to review a Missouri statute that declared that "the life of each human being begins at conception" and that "unborn children have protectable interest in life, health, and well being." The statute also prohibited the use of public employees or facilities for nontherapeutic abortions and required fetal viability testing for any pregnancy believed to be at twenty or more weeks. A five-justice majority upheld the statute, sustaining many restrictions on abortion that it had previously invalidated in *Thornburgh* and *Akron*. Without directly overruling the *Roe* decision, the Court effectively ceded control over abortion rights to states' regulation.

In the years following the *Webster* decision, states enacted a wide variety of laws limiting the right to abortion. One of these laws, the Pennsylvania Abortion Control Act, was brought before the Court in 1992, giving it the opportunity to clarity its *Webster* holding. In *Planned Parenthood v. Casey*, 505 U.S. 833 (1992), a plurality of the Court reaffirmed the core principles of *Roe* but abandoned the notion that abortion was a "fundamental right" that required strict scrutiny. Instead, it found that abortion was simply a "liberty claim" subject to a more deferential "undue burden" test. The Pennsylvania law, which imposed a mandatory twenty-four-hour waiting period, informed consent, and parental consent requirements, was found not to impose an undue burden on women's choice of abortion.

The *Casey* decision was disappointing to the anti-abortion movement, which had hoped that the more conservative Rehnquist Court would overturn *Roe*. Anti-abortion strategies shifted from efforts to make abortion illegal to efforts to make access to abortion inconvenient or impossible. Abortion providers suffered a plague of violent and intimidating acts, ranging from protesters attempting to block entrances to abortion clinics to the bombing, arson, and vandalism of clinics, and the murder of two physicians who performed abortions. Some states issued injunctions against anti-abortion protesters, prohibiting them from demonstrating within "buffer zones" around clinic entrances. Many of these laws were challenged as violating the First Amendment rights of the protesters. In 1997, in the case of *Schenck v. Pro-Choice Network of Western New York*, 519 U.S. 357 (1997), the Court found that the creation of "fixed" buffer zones was constitutionally valid as necessary to protect women's freedom to seek pregnancy-related services and to protect the public's safety. While the extent of the violence has been reduced by these laws, the anti-abortion movement's intimidating tactics have, nevertheless, succeeded in eliminating abortion services entirely from as many as 87 percent of all counties in the United States.

Anti-abortion legislation since *Casey* has focused primarily on outlawing certain methods of abortion, particularly dilation and evacuation (D&E) and dilation and extraction (D&X), also referred to as "partial birth" abortion. Most of these laws have been struck down because they were not limited to postviability abortions or because they failed to provide exceptions for situations when the procedure is necessary to protect the woman's life or health (*Stenberg v. Carhart*, 530 U.S. 914, 2000). Congress continues its efforts to craft legislation outlawing "partial-birth" abortions that will pass constitutional review.

The 2000 election of President George W. Bush, who is firmly dedicated to outlawing abortion entirely, puts the current status of abortion law in this country at serious risk. The resignation of Justice Sandra Day O'Connor, who was often the critical swing vote on decisions affirming the abortion right, gives President Bush the opportunity to appoint a new justice who will likely provide the fifth vote needed to overrule *Roe v. Wade*. The confirmation of O'Connor's successor was complicated by the death of Chief Justice William Rehnquist. This gave President Bush two slots to fill on the court. Abortion rights advocates opposed the confirmation of Samuel Alito, but were unsuccessful. Supporters of abortion rights were leery of John Roberts, but did not fight his confirmation as Chief Justice. At this point it is unclear whether these two justices will provide the neccessary votes to overturn *Roe*, or simply vote to uphold state legislation that limits rights of choice.

SUSAN E. LOOPER–FRIEDMAN

References and Further Reading

Ely, John Hart. *Democracy and Distrust*. 1980.
Gold, Rebecca Benson. *Abortion and Women's Health: A Turning Point for America?* 1990.
Mohr, James. *Abortion in America*. 1978.
Rubin, Eva. *Abortion, Politics, and the Courts*. 1987.
Tribe, Laurence H. *Abortion: The Clash of Absolutes*. 1990.
Wishner, Jane B., ed. *Abortion and the States: Political Change and Future Regulation*. 1993.

Cases and Statutes Cited

Akron v. Akron Center for Reproductive Health, 462 U.S. 416 (1983)
Bellotti v. Baird, 443 U.S. 622 (1979)
Bradwell v. Illinois, 83 U.S. (16 Wall.) 130 (1873)
Eisenstadt v. Baird, 405 U.S. 438 (1972)
Griswold v. Connecticut, 381 U.S. 479 (1965)
Harris v. McRae, 448 U.S. 297 (1980).
National Organization for Women v. Scheidler, 510 v. 249 (1994)
National Organization for Women v. Scheidler, 537 U.S. 393 (2003)
Planned Parenthood of Central Missouri v. Danforth, 428 U.S. 52 (1976)
Planned Parenthood of Southeastern Pennsylvania v. Casey, 505 U.S. 833 (1992)
Roe v. Wade, 410 U.S. 114 (1973)
Rust v. Sullivan, 500 U.S. 173 (1991)
Schenck v. Pro-Choice Network of Western New York, 519 U.S. 357 (1997)
Stenberg v. Carhart, 530 U.S. 914 (2000)
Thornburgh v. American College of Obstetricians and Gynecologists, Pennsylvania Section, 476 U.S. 747 (1986) (portions overruled by *Casey*)
Webster v. Reproductive Health Services, 492 U.S. 490 (1989)

ABORTION LAWS AND THE ESTABLISHMENT CLAUSE

A defining principle of the United States is the separation between church and state. This principle is embodied in the establishment clause of the First Amendment, which provides that Congress shall make no law respecting the establishment of religion. Since 1947, the prohibition has also applied to the states, and it has been interpreted to prevent the states from enacting laws that are motivated by religious purposes. When states enact laws, they must have secular purposes for doing so.

In *Roe v. Wade*, the Supreme Court ruled that the right of privacy enjoyed by all Americans protects a woman's right to decide whether to terminate a pregnancy. During the first trimester, the state may not interfere with this right at all (though in subsequent trimesters the state may impose certain restrictions). A critical premise of the Court's holding was that, at the early stages of pregnancy, the fetus is not a "person" for constitutional purposes.

This critical premise of *Roe* is obviously at odds with certain religious views, which consider a fetus a person from the moment of conception, or shortly thereafter. Indeed, in *Roe*, the Court recognized that the question of when life begins is fundamentally a religious question. In cases subsequent to *Roe*, the Court expressly held that a state is not permitted to adopt one theory of when life begins to justify its regulation of abortions (*Akron v. Akron Center for Reproductive Health, Inc.*, 462 U.S. 416, 444, 1983).

Saying that the states may not regulate abortion on the basis of religious doctrine is one thing; enforcing that prohibition is quite another. There are three reasons for the difficulty of enforcing the establishment clause norm in the abortion context. First, determining why people believe what they believe presents difficult epistemological questions; a legislator may oppose abortion because Catholic doctrine holds that a fetus is a human being, or the legislator might be a physician who has purely secular reasons for believing that a fetus possesses human qualities. Second, distinguishing religious beliefs from nonreligious beliefs presents similarly daunting difficulties. Finally, the answer to the question of when life begins may indeed have religious and nonreligious influences.

The complexity of invalidating abortion laws on the basis of the establishment clause is illustrated by *Webster v. Reproductive Health Services*, 492 U.S. 490 (1989), a case involving a challenge to a Missouri statute that placed various restrictions on the right to obtain an abortion. The preamble to the state statute asserted that life begins at conception—a statement clearly at odds with *Roe* and its progeny. Nevertheless, despite a powerful dissent from Justice Stevens that insisted that the statute reflected an "unequivocal enforcement" of religion—and was therefore in violation of the establishment clause—the

Court upheld many of the law's restrictions, reasoning that they could be justified by secular criteria unrelated to the statute's preamble.

Consequently, although *Roe*, *Akron*, and other decisions indicate that a state may not base anti-abortion legislation on religious ideology or premises, these premises are often so diffused into the secular legal culture that it is impossible to neutralize their influence. For example, in *Harris v. McRae*, 448 U.S. 297 (1980), the Supreme Court upheld the Hyde amendment, which prohibits the use of federal Medicaid funds for most abortions. Justice Stewart's opinion for the Court concluded that the attitude toward abortion reflected in the amendment could very well reflect what the Court called "traditionalist" values; these value overlap, but are not identical to, religious values.

As a matter of legal doctrine, therefore, the state may not predicate laws that interfere with a woman's right to choose on religious doctrine. At the same time, as a political matter, laws that place restrictions on abortions during the second and third trimesters will almost certainly have a strong religious influence.

DAVID R. DOW

References and Further Reading

Everson v. Board of Education, 330 U.S. 1 (1947).
Feldman, Noah, *From Liberty to Equality: The Transformation of the Establishment Clause*, Cal. Law Review 673 (2002): 90:680–700.

Cases and Statutes Cited

Akron v. Akron Center for Reproductive Health, Inc., 462 U.S. 416, 444 (1983)
Harris v. McRae, 448 U.S. 297 (1980)
Roe v. Wade, 410 U.S. 113 (1973)
Webster v. Reproductive Health Services, 492 U.S. 490 (1989)

ABORTION PROTEST CASES

In three cases, the Supreme Court has considered the rights of anti-abortion protestors outside abortion clinics. The cases have pitted free-speech values against the fundamental right to abortion declared by the Supreme Court in *Roe v. Wade*, 410 U.S. 113 (1973).

In the first of the cases, *Madsen v. Women's Health Center, Inc.*, 512 U.S. 753 (1994), anti-abortion protestors had repeatedly violated a federal court injunction against blocking access to a Florida abortion clinic and had harassed patients and doctors at the clinic and at their homes. After this defiance, the federal district court entered a broader injunction against the protestors. The new injunction prohibited

demonstrators from: (1) protesting within 36 feet of the clinic; (2) making excessive noise near the clinic by shouting and using sound devices; (3) exhibiting images observable by patients within the clinic; (4) approaching patients within 300 feet of the clinic unless the patient voluntarily indicated a desire to be approached; and (5) demonstrating within 300 feet of the home of any clinic employee.

The government defended the restrictions as necessary to protect a woman's freedom to seek medical services; to safeguard public safety and order; to keep open the free flow of traffic on streets and sidewalks; to protect private property rights; and to preserve residential privacy. The protestors complained that the restrictions were content based (and thus especially suspect under the First Amendment) and unduly restricted their free-speech rights.

The Supreme Court first held that the injunction was not content based merely because it aimed at the protestors. The nature of an injunction is to restrict only those subject to it, the Court held, and the purpose of the injunction was only to address past violations of the court's orders.

Next, the Court held that the government's interests were significant and that parts of the injunction were narrowly tailored to serve those interests. First, the Court upheld the 36-foot buffer zone as applied to the *public* property around the clinic but not the *private* property along the side and back of the clinic where there had been no showing of interference. Second, the Court upheld the ban on excessive noise near the clinic on the ground that medical recovery requires some tranquility. But the Court struck down the rest of the injunction as too broad.

The Supreme Court's next encounter with the free-speech rights of abortion-clinic protestors came three years later in *Schenck v. Pro-Choice Network*, 519 U.S. 357 (1997). In that case, several abortion clinics in upstate New York had been subjected to large-scale blockades in which protestors marched, stood, knelt, or lay in clinic parking lots and doorways. Smaller groups of protestors, called "sidewalk counselors," crowded, pushed, jostled, yelled, and spat at women entering the clinics. Police officers on the scene attempting to control the protests were also harassed verbally and by mail.

A federal district court issued an injunction against fifty individuals and three organizations (including Operation Rescue). One part of the injunction banned demonstrating within 15 feet of clinic entrances, including doorways and parking lots. The Supreme Court upheld this "fixed buffer zone" on the ground that it was necessary to prevent anti-abortion protestors from blocking entrance to and exit from the clinic.

The second part of the injunction allowed anti-abortion protestors to approach a patient to make "nonthreatening" conversation with her, but required such sidewalk counselors to withdraw a distance of 15 feet from a patient if she requested them to cease counseling her. The Court struck down this "floating buffer zone" as burdening more speech than necessary to serve the government's interests.

The third clash of abortion and free-speech rights came in *Hill v. Colorado*, 530 U.S. 703 (2000). Unlike the first two cases, *Hill* involved a statute—not a court injunction—restricting protests around abortion clinics. The Colorado law in *Hill* made it unlawful within the vicinity of a health care clinic for anyone to "knowingly approach" within 8 feet of another person, without that person's consent, "for the purpose of passing a leaflet to, displaying a sign to, or engaging in oral protest, education, or counseling" with that person. Unlike the floating buffer zone in *Schenck*, however, the statute did not require counselors to move away if a patient walked into the 8-foot zone.

The Court upheld the statute against a First Amendment free-speech challenge by anti-abortion protestors. The main issue was whether the statute was content based and thus subject to strict scrutiny, or content neutral and thus subject to lesser scrutiny. The majority held that the statute was a content-neutral regulation of the place where speech may occur. The Court observed that the statute applied equally to all demonstrators, regardless of viewpoint, and was not adopted because of the state's disagreement with the message of the anti-abortion protestors. Furthermore, the Court said, the state's interests in unimpeded access to health care and patient privacy were unrelated to the content of speech.

Justices Scalia, Thomas, and Kennedy dissented vigorously, as they had in the previous two abortion protest cases. Scalia's dissent argued that the statute was content based because it prohibited only "protest, counseling, or education," but not other speech like social or random conversation. Thus, whether a person could be prosecuted for violating the 8-foot buffer zone "depends entirely on what he intends to say once he gets there." The majority replied that the statute applied equally to all who engage in "protest, counseling, or education" speech without further regard to content.

While the dissenters agreed that the state could prohibit protestors from physically blocking access to a clinic, they chided the majority for approving a restriction on "peaceful, nonthreatening, but uninvited speech" within a distance of 8 feet from a patient entering or exiting an abortion clinic. Scalia accused the majority of distorting free-speech jurisprudence

so that it could "sustain this restriction on the free speech of abortion opponents." "Does the deck seem stacked?" he asked. "You bet."

DALE CARPENTER

Cases and Statutes Cited

Hill v. Colorado, 530 U.S. 703 (2000)
Madsen v. Women's Health Center, Inc., 512 U.S. 753 (1994)
Roe v. Wade, 410 U.S. (1973)
Schenck v. Pro-Choice Network of Western New York, 519 U.S. 357 (1997)

ABRAMS v. UNITED STATES, 250 U.S. 616 (1919)

Condemning "the hypocrisy of the United States and her allies" and denouncing President Woodrow Wilson as a hypocrite and a coward, Jacob Abrams and four associates—all five Russian-born Jews and avowed anarchists—distributed fliers on the Lower East Side of Manhattan in the summer of 1918 directing attention to U.S. efforts to halt the Bolshevik Revolution. Among other things, the fliers called for a general strike by workers to stymie the war effort against the imperial German government. Abrams and his colleagues were charged with violating the Espionage Act of 1917 (as amended in 1918), which allowed convictions for conspiring to "utter, print, write, and publish disloyal, scurrilous, and abusive language about the form of government of the United States, or language intended to bring the form of government of the United States into contempt, scorn, contumely and disrepute, or intended to incite, provoke, and encourage resistance to the United States [. . .]" Thus, the stage was set for one of the most important freedom of speech cases of the twentieth century.

One of the defendants (Joseph Schwartz) died the night before the trial started; a federal district court found the other four guilty of violating the act. At the U.S. Supreme Court, Justice John H. Clarke affirmed the convictions, emphasizing the special circumstances of wartime and the potential consequences of the dissident speech. Rooting the Court's conclusions in the recent precedent dealing with similarly "dangerous" speech—especially *Schenck v. United States*, 249 U.S. 47 (1919), *Frohwerk v. United States*, 249 U.S. 204 (1919), and *Debs v. United States*, 249 U.S. 211 (1919)—Clarke found that the plain purpose of their propaganda was to excite, at the supreme crisis of the war, disaffection, sedition, riots, and, as they hoped, revolution, in this country for the purpose of embarrassing and, if possible, defeating the military plans of the government in Europe.

13

Thus, the Court deemed that the expression in question constituted a "clear and present danger" ("whether the words are used in such circumstances and are of such a nature as to create a clear and present danger that they will bring about the substantive evils that Congress has a right to prevent")—the legal test recently implemented in the *Schenck* case—in that such advocacy may have had the tendency to inhibit the war effort, among other things. Congress was, therefore, within its authority to restrict speech in such a fashion.

Yet, *Abrams* is actually more famous for the powerful and poetic dissent authored by Justice Oliver Wendell Holmes, Jr. Though Holmes was, ironically, the one who had recently *devised* the "clear and present danger" test, he pulled back in *Abrams*, finding (with Justice Louis D. Brandeis) that the statutory requirement of "intent" had not been demonstrated in this case. More importantly, the speech at hand was not worthy of the alarm alleged by the state and accepted by the Court majority. Indeed, indicating the influences of early twentieth century philosophical pragmatism on his thinking, Holmes averred that, while one may be disturbed by or disagree with the substantive nature of such dissent, one should still be willing to subject it to the processes of inquiry, scrutiny, and significantly, "competition." The following passage portrays Holmes' famous assertion of *how* and *why* this might be done:

> But when men have realized that time has upset many fighting faiths, they may come to believe even more than they believe the very foundations of their own conduct that the ultimate good desired is better reached by free trade in ideas—that the best test for truth is the power of the thought to get itself accepted in the competition of the market; and that truth is the only ground upon which their wishes safely can be carried out. That at any rate is the theory of our Constitution. It is an experiment, as all life is an experiment.

Thus, the theory of the "marketplace of ideas" was formally articulated in American law.

While the introduction of this metaphor was significant in that it has become the predominant trope for the contemplation of free-speech issues in the United States, the *Abrams* decision was significant as well because it demonstrated the first serious challenge to the "clear and present danger" test. In essence, Holmes wondered, in this case, exactly how "clear and present" must the "danger" be in order for congressional authority to reach the situation? Estimating proximity and degree in such a way led the Court several decades later to abandon the test in favor of an evaluation of the potential for "imminent lawlessness" in *Brandenburg v. Ohio*, 395 U.S. 444 (1969).

BRIAN K. PINAIRE

References and Further Reading

Chafee, Zechariah. *Free Speech in the United States*. Cambridge, MA: Harvard University Press, 1940/1967.
Menand, Louis. *The Metaphysical Club*. New York: Farrar, Straus and Giroux, 2001.
Polenberg, Richard. *Fighting Faiths*. New York: Viking, 1987.

Cases and Statutes Cited

Brandenburg v. Ohio, 395 U.S. 444 (1969)
Debs v. United States, 249 U.S. 211 (1919)
Frohwerk v. United States, 249 U.S. 204 (1919)
Schenck v. United States, 249 U.S. 47 (1919)

See also **Freedom of Speech: Modern Period (1917–Present); Holmes, Oliver Wendell, Jr.; Marketplace of Ideas Theory;** *Schenck v. United States*, **249 U.S. 47 (1919)**

ABSOLUTISM AND FREE SPEECH

Absolutism is an approach to interpretation of the First Amendment guarantee of freedom of speech that takes literally the text of the amendment when it declares that "Congress shall make no law . . . abridging the freedom of speech." Under a theory of absolutism, Congress may not constitutionally interfere with free speech in any way; the theory would also limit the power of state and local governments, through incorporation of the First Amendment into the due process clause of the Fourteenth Amendment.

Although the U.S. Supreme Court never adopted an absolutist approach, the theory found credence in the decisions of Justice Hugo L. Black and, to a lesser degree, Justice William O. Douglas. Examining state restrictions on speech in dissent in *Beauharnais v. Illinois*, 343 U.S. 988 (1952), Black put it in simple fashion when he said, "I think the First Amendment, with the Fourteenth, 'absolutely' forbids such laws without any 'ifs' or 'buts' or 'whereases.'" Throughout the 1950s and 1960s, as the Supreme Court created new tests to balance the state's interest against free speech, Black objected. The "First Amendment's unequivocal command that there shall be no abridgment of the rights of free speech and assembly shows that the men who drafted our Bill of Rights did all the 'balancing' that was to be done in the field," Black wrote in a dissenting opinion in *Konigsberg v. State Bar of California*, 366 U.S. 36 (1961). Black's concern was that balancing tests made the importance of particular speech dependent on the value judgments of individual judges.

The views of Justice Douglas were less clear. In *Dennis v. U.S.*, 341 U.S. 494 (1951), Douglas said, "The freedom to speak is not absolute." But in *New*

York Times v. U.S., 403 U.S. 713 (1971), the Pentagon Papers case, Douglas said the guarantees of freedom of speech and of freedom of the press leave "in my view, no room for governmental restraint on the press."

Even Black's absolutism had significant definitional limits. When civil rights protesters in the 1960s argued that their demonstrations and lunch-counter sit-ins that led to their arrest were expressive conduct entitled to the protection of the First Amendment, Black drew a distinction between speech and conduct, finding the latter unprotected. Free speech, he wrote in *Cox v. Louisiana*, 379 U.S. 536 (1965), did not include the "right to engage in the conduct of picketing or patrolling, whether on publicly owned streets or on privately owned property." In *Adderly v. Florida*, 385 U.S. 39 (1966), he wrote the Court's opinion upholding the trespass convictions of students who protested outside a Florida county jail, rejecting the premise "that people who want to propagandize protests or views have a constitutional right to do so whenever and however and wherever they please." Even when the conduct was symbolic expression, Black viewed it as action that was not protected. He dissented in *Tinker v. Des Moines Indep. Community Sch. Dist.*, 393 U.S. 503 (1969), in which the Court ruled that students could wear black armbands to school as long as there was no evidence that their protest caused disruption.

STEPHEN J. WERMIEL

References and Further Reading

Meiklejohn, Alexander, *The First Amendment Is an Absolute*, 1961 Supreme Court Review (1961).
Smolla, Rodney A. *Smolla and Nimmer on Freedom of Speech*. 2005, § 2.49.
Stembridge, Patricia R., *Adjusting Absolutism: Extending First Amendment Protection for the Fringe*, B.U. Law Review 907 (2000): 80.

Cases and Statutes Cited

Adderley v. Florida, 385 U.S. 39 (1966)
Beauharnais v. Illinois, 343 U.S. 988 (1952)
Cox v. Lousiana, 379 U.S. 536 (1965)
Dennis v. U.S., 341 U.S. 494 (1951)
Konigsberg v. State Bar of California, 366 U.S. 36 (1961)
New York Times v. Sullivan, 376 U.S. 254 (1964)
New York Times v. U.S., 403 U.S. 713 (1971)
Tinker v. Des Moines Indep. Community Sch. Dist., 393 U.S. 503 (1969)

See also **Douglas, William Orville; Due Process; First Amendment and PACs; Fourteenth Amendment; Freedom of the Press: Modern Period (1917–Present); Freedom of Speech: Modern Period (1917–Present)**

ABU GHRAIB

Abu Ghraib prison was originally built in the 1960s by Western contractors but achieved notoriety during Saddam Hussein's rule as a repository for up to fifteen thousand of his political enemies. More recently, it has become infamous as the site of torture of Iraqi detainees at the hands of American soldiers.

Abu Ghraib came into American possession following the U.S.-led invasion of Iraq in March 2003. Selected by Ambassador Paul Bremer, head of the Coalition Provisional Authority that governed the country, the prison was originally to be used as a temporary facility for criminal detainees until the new Iraqi government could establish a permanent prison at another site. Rather than limiting the number of prisoners, Abu Ghraib was also designated as a detention facility for high-value security detainees. These were individuals suspected of playing a role in the growing insurgency in Iraq, who were prime targets for interrogation. Of the seventeen detention facilities in Iraq in October 2003 Abu Ghraib was the largest, holding seven thousand prisoners with a guard force of approximately ninety Americans.

The release of the infamous photographs of prisoner abuse of Iraqi detainees by U.S. soldiers in April 2004 revealed for the first time to the world that something had gone badly wrong at Abu Ghraib. From the commencement of hostilities in Afghanistan and Iraq through 2004, the United States had apprehended fifty thousand people. Three hundred allegations of abuse resulted, leading to the determination that, in sixty-six cases, prisoners under U.S. control were abused. Fifty-five of those were later found to have occurred in Iraq. The seriousness of the allegations and the horrifying scenes depicted in the pictures prompted numerous investigations. The U.S. Army dispatched Maj Gen. Antonio Taguba to report on abuse at Abu Ghraib; the Pentagon later appointed an "independent panel" to review Department of Defense detention operations and provide recommendations. These, along with reports by organizations such as the International Committee of the Red Cross ("the Red Cross") confirmed that multiple violations of international humanitarian law and the Uniform Code of Military Justice had occurred. The Taguba report cited instances of beating, terrorizing, and sodomizing detainees committed by military intelligence units and the 372nd Military Police Company.

Revelations of torture at Abu Ghraib did lasting damage to American credibility and cast doubt on the United States' respect for international law and human rights. The U.S. military responded by calling court martials for soldiers directly implicated in the abuse. However, as the Independent Panel Report makes clear, the sadistic tendencies of half-a-dozen enlisted soldiers are not alone to be blamed. Although the vast majority of detentions and prisoner interviews took place within the bounds of the law, the report points to larger systemic problems at the prison that also contributed to creating the conditions wherein such abuse was allowed to take place.

As the size and ferocity of the Iraqi insurgency grew, the inadequacies of American postwar planning became increasingly evident. Command and control structures broke down, and training of military police and interrogators proved insufficient in the face of a mounting prisoner population. A lack of understanding as to which interrogation procedures were acceptable was the result. Techniques deemed acceptable for Taliban and al Qaeda prisoners, who were found not to be entitled to protections guaranteed under the Geneva Convention of 1949, were in some cases used when questioning Iraqi detainees, who were entitled to those protections. Moreover, the presence of military intelligence operatives and the CIA, which ostensibly operated independently and had reportedly hidden "ghost detainees" during Red Cross inspections, created further confusion.

Along with an analysis of which specific decisions gave rise to conditions of lawlessness at Abu Ghraib prison, the legal community also debated the extent to which Bush administration policies with respect to domestic laws and international treaties forbidding torture played a role. Recognizing that the United States was now in a struggle against nonstate actors—terrorists who refused to abide by the laws of war—Bush administration lawyers set about providing a basis for expansive executive power in prosecuting what the President termed the Global War on Terror, or "GWOT." The lack of human intelligence on terrorist organizations gave rise to a need to extract information through interrogation. Indeed, this need proved all the more pressing at Abu Ghraib, considering that existing interrogation techniques had yielded little actionable intelligence regarding the insurgency.

A legal memorandum from Assistant Attorney General Jay S. Bybee on August 1, 2002, for example, advised Counsel to the President Alberto Gonzales that physical pain amounting to torture must be "equivalent in intensity to the pain accompanying serious physical injury such as organ failure, impairment of bodily function or even death." These and other memoranda sought to expand the range of acceptable interrogation techniques and to immunize those implementing interrogation procedures from the Convention on Torture and from U.S. law.

ANDREW FINKELMAN

References and Further Reading

Greenberg, Karen, and Joshua Dratel, eds. *The Torture Papers: The Road to Abu Ghraib*. New York: Cambridge University Press, 2005.
Independent Panel to Review DoD Detention Operations (James Schlesinger, Chairman). *Final Report of the Independent Panel to Review DoD Detention Operations*. Buffalo, NY: William Hein, 2005.

ACADEMIC FREEDOM

Origins of Academic Freedom

Academic freedom is a concept that encompasses notions of philosophy and contracts as well as civil liberties. In the United States the concept of academic freedom has developed primarily (although not exclusively) in the context of higher education. General U.S. understanding of academic freedom can be traced to two important documents published by the American Association of University Professors (AAUP). The first of these documents is the 1915 General Report of the Committee on Academic Freedom and Academic Tenure. The 1915 declaration was a manifesto on academic freedom in which the AAUP argued that academic freedom consisted of three components: the freedom of faculty to teach, to do research, and to talk and write on matters outside their disciplines. The AAUP argued that academic freedom could only be fostered in an environment of institutional neutrality.

In the second important document—the 1940 Statement of Principles on Academic Freedom and Tenure—the AAUP attempted to reduce the concept of academic freedom to a series of rule-like propositions that could guide university governance and serve as a basis for enforcing norms of academic freedom. Like the 1915 declaration, the statement of principles contains three core provisions that generally correspond with this three-part vision of research, teaching, and service responsibilities of most university professors:

> Teachers are entitled to full freedom in research and in the publication of the results, subject to the adequate performance of their other academic duties; but research for pecuniary return should be based upon an understanding with the authorities of the institution.
> Teachers are entitled to freedom in the classroom in discussing their subject, but they should be

careful not to introduce into their teaching controversial matter which has no relation to their subject. Limitations of academic freedom because of religious or other aims of the institution should be clearly stated in writing at the time of the appointment.

College and university teachers are citizens, members of a learned profession, and officers of an educational institution. When they speak or write as citizens, they should be free from institutional censorship or discipline, but their special position in the community imposes special obligations. As scholars and educational officers, they should remember that the public may judge their profession and their institution by their utterances. Hence they should at all times be accurate, should exercise appropriate restraint, should show respect for the opinions of others, and should make every effort to indicate that they are not speaking for the institution.

These provisions of the statement of principles are based on the explicit assumptions of the drafters that "institutions of higher education exist not for themselves but for the 'common good'; that academic freedom is 'essential' to that purpose; that academic tenure is 'essential' to academic freedom no less than to academic job security; and that 'academic freedom carries with it duties correlative with rights.'"

These core values of academic freedom have been secured primarily though individual and institutional commitment to them. Statements regarding academic freedom are incorporated in the handbooks and/or procedures of most American universities. Commitments regarding academic freedom are also often incorporated in contracts between university faculty and administrations. Most American schools and colleges have adopted tenure for teachers as one of the mechanisms for ensuring academic freedom.

Academic Freedom and the First Amendment

American courts have found a nexus between academic freedom and rights of free speech protected in the First Amendment. The U.S. Supreme Court, in *Keyishian v. Board of Regents*, 385 U.S. 589 (1967), has referred to academic freedom as "a special concern of the First Amendment." Yet, the scope of First Amendment protection afforded academic speech is ambiguous at best.

The first two U.S. Supreme Court cases explicitly to link academic freedom and the First Amendment were *Adler v. Board of Education*, 342 U.S. 485 (1952), and *Wieman v. Updegraff*, 344 U.S. 183 (1952). Decided during the Court's 1952 term, both cases dealt with state regulations arising from the opposition to Communism and the cold war. *Adler* involved a New York statute that required that any person espousing the use of violence or altering the form of U.S. government or belonging to a "subversive organization" that espoused such views be removed from public employment. Although the majority of the Court upheld the state law, Justice William O. Douglas dissented, reasoning that the law unreasonably infringed on the academic freedom of public school teachers by intimidating any teacher who had ever been associated with a "subversive organization" from going into teaching or voicing his or her thoughts on the topics of the day.

Wieman involved the constitutionality of a state statute requiring that state employees take a loyalty oath disclaiming affiliation with any subversive organization as a condition of state employment. In contrast to *Adler*, the majority of the Court struck down the statute. In a separate concurring opinion, Justice Felix Frankfurter reasoned that in addition to the infringement on freedom of association of state employees, the disclaimer oath would have a pernicious effect on the academic freedom of teachers.

These early cases set the stage for a series of Supreme Court decisions during the 1950s and 1960s that define the scope of First Amendment protection for teachers based on notions of academic freedom. In *Sweezy v. New Hampshire*, 354 U.S. 234 (1957), the Court addressed the question of academic freedom and the First Amendment in yet another case challenging the constitutionality of government action undertaken as part of the cold war.

In *Sweezy* a University of New Hampshire professor was charged with contempt when he refused to provide details of his lectures and political associations in answer to questions by the state attorney general as part of a state antisubversive investigation. In his concurring opinion, Justice Frankfurter said that requiring Sweezy to produce his notes violated his academic freedom rights ensured by the First Amendment. Frankfurter wrote, "[w]hen weighed against the grave harm [to academic freedom] resulting from governmental intrusion into the intellectual life of a university, [ordinary justifications] for compelling a witness to discuss the contents of his lecture [appear] grossly inadequate." Frankfurter's reasoning was based, in part, on his view that the examination of Sweezy's notes would have a chilling effect on the continued free exchange of ideas within the university.

Despite the fact that the academic freedom argument in *Sweezy* was made by an individual professor,

Justice Frankfurter's analysis was rooted significantly in the government's intrusion into the university as an institution; he characterized the government's action as an intrusion into the "intellectual life of a university," not as an intrusion into the free speech and association rights of an individual professor. Frankfurter's grand but unspecific conclusion was that a free society depends on free universities and that "this means the exclusion of governmental intervention in the intellectual life of a university."

In *Shelton v. Tucker*, 364 U.S. 479 (1960), the Court struck down an Arkansas statute requiring teachers, as a condition of employment, to submit an annual affidavit listing every organization to which they had belonged or regularly contributed for the past five years. The Court held that this requirement violated the free association rights of teachers. Although it did not base its reasoning expressly on "academic freedom" grounds, the Court quoted *Weiman* and *Sweezy*, reasoning that "[t]eachers and students must always remain free to inquire, to study and to evaluate, to gain new maturity and understanding; otherwise our civilization will stagnate and die."

The Supreme Court's majority relied on the link between free speech and academic freedom for the first time in 1967 in *Keyishian v. Board of Regents*. There the Court struck down the provisions of New York's Feinberg law that had been previously upheld in *Adler*. Writing for the majority, Justice William Brennan reasoned:

> [A]cademic freedom . . . is of transcendent value to all of us and not merely to the teachers concerned. That freedom is therefore a special concern of the First Amendment, which does not tolerate laws that cast a pall of orthodoxy over the classroom . . . . The classroom is particularly the marketplace of ideas. The Nation's future depends upon leaders trained through wide exposure to that robust exchange of ideas which discovers truth out of a multitude of tongues, [rather] than through any kind of authoritative selection.

The *Keyeshian* Court relied on the reasoning of *Sweezy* in its analysis and, as in Frankfurter's opinion in *Sweezy*, employed sweeping generalizations and avoided specific analysis. While Justice Douglas characterized academic freedom as a "transcendent value," his opinion does not shed additional light on the relationship between academic freedom and the First Amendment.

The year after *Keyishian*, Justice Douglas, writing for the majority in *Whitehill v. Elkins*, 389 U.S. 54 (1967), struck down an oath similar to that in *Wieman* on express academic freedom grounds. Continuing the sweeping, general invocation of academic freedom

without specific analysis, the Court concluded "[t]he continuing surveillance which this type of law places on teachers is hostile to academic freedom . . . . The restraints on conscientious teachers are obvious."

Individual Academic Freedom and the Public Employee Doctrine

The potentially broad reach of the First Amendment/academic freedom cases may be limited by the cases dealing with free speech of public employees. These cases define the scope of free speech rights of public employees including, arguably, teachers and faculty members at public institutions. In *Pickering v. Board of Education*, 391 U.S. 563 (1968), the Supreme Court recognized that the free speech rights of public employees may be limited when the speech interferes with the efficient operation of the government employer.

Pickering involved a teacher who was fired because he wrote a letter to a newspaper criticizing the conduct of the local board of education regarding tax increases for education. The Court held that in the absence of proof that the teacher knowingly or recklessly made false statements, he could not be fired for exercising his First Amendment rights. The *Pickering* Court did not rely on notions of academic freedom for its conclusion that the teacher's free speech rights were infringed by the school district. In fact, the Court cited *Keyishian* and *Whitehill* only for the narrower proposition that public employees do not shed the free speech rights enjoyed by all citizens simply because they are in the public's employ.

While the *Pickering* Court concluded that the teacher's free speech rights had been impermissibly invaded, the decision established a framework in which public employees' speech is subject to scrutiny when it is related to their employment or negatively affects their employer. The test adopted by the Court balances the government's interest in the efficient operation of public services and in not having those services disrupted against the speech of public employees. If the potential disruptiveness of a public employee's speech outweighs the value of that speech, the public employer may take appropriate disciplinary action against the employee.

The public employee cases—*Pickering* in particular—raise questions about the extent of First Amendment protection for individual academic freedom. While the cases certainly recognize that the speech of public employees is protected by the First Amendment, they nonetheless appear to treat the speech of teachers no differently from the speech of other public employees. It may be that *Pickering* does not reach to the speech of college and university teachers or that it only applies to the speech of teachers outside the areas of the classroom and scholarly pursuits. While the latter limitation would be inconsistent with the AAUP's conception of academic freedom, it would leave intact the reasoning of *Sweezy, Shelton, Keyishian,* and *Whitehill.*

Institutional Academic Freedom

Within this basic context, the Supreme Court has slowly articulated a limited theory of institutional academic freedom. The core principle of this theory is that public institutions involved in academic endeavors should be accorded deference in core academic decision-making, even when the decision may arguably infringe the rights of institutional participants such as students, faculty, library patrons, and researchers. Thus, for example, in *Regents of the University of Michigan v. Ewing,* 474 U.S. 214 (1985), the Court recognized that a medical student had a constitutionally protected property right in continued enrollment free from arbitrary actions of the university. Nonetheless, the Court declined to second guess the decision of a university to disqualify a medical student after he did not pass required medical boards even though most other students were given the opportunity to retake the exam. The *Ewing* Court reasoned that "[w]hen judges are asked to review the substance of a genuinely academic decision, such as this one, they should show great respect for the faculty's professional judgment."

Deference to the decision-making of educational institutions on academic questions has played a role in other decisions. For example, in *Grutter v. Bollinger,* 539 U.S. 306 (2003), in upholding the University of Michigan's admissions policy regarding affirmative action in law school admissions, Justice Sandra Day O'Connor cited *Keyishian* and *Ewing,* noting that "[o]ur holding today is in keeping with our tradition of giving a degree of deference to a university's academic decisions, within constitutionally prescribed limits." Justice O'Connor's consideration of academic freedom in university admissions paralleled Justice Lewis F. Powell's similar deference twenty-five years earlier in *Regents of the University of California v. Bakke,* 438 U.S. 265 (1978).

Likewise, in *Hazelwood School District v. Kuhlmeier,* 484 U.S. 260 (1988), the Court held that educators could exercise "editorial control over the style and content of student speech in school-sponsored expressive activities so long as their actions are reasonably related to legitimate pedagogical concerns." Although the Court did not rely on a specific academic freedom rationale, its reasoning is consistent with the developing theory of institutional academic freedom on matters of core academic concern.

Academic Freedom in the Lower Federal Courts

The lower courts struggled to make sense of the Supreme Court's approach in cases involving claims to individual academic freedom by faculty and students. While the cases rely on a number of different rationales, they consistently recognize the principle of deference to the academic decisions of educational institutions. Recently, for example, in *Brown v. Li,* 308 F. 3d 939 (9th Cir. 2002), the Ninth Circuit refused to question the University of California's decision to require excisions from a master's thesis, stating "under the Supreme Court's precedents, the curriculum of a public education institution is one means by which the institution itself expresses its policy, a policy with which others do not have a constitutional right to interfere." In *Axson–Flynn v. Johnson,* 356 F.3d 1277 (10th Cir. 2003), the Tenth Circuit similarly held that deference was due to university decision-making on curricular speech that was "reasonably related to legitimate pedagogical goals."

While a limited theory of institutional academic freedom has developed, most courts have declined to recognize an independent, constitutionally based theory of academic freedom extending to faculty or to students, particularly when the protection of faculty and/or student academic freedom interests would conflict with the policies of the academic institution. *Brown* and *Axson–Flynn,* for example, each involved claims that the First Amendment protected academic speech by students that were overridden by the Court's deference to institutional decision-making on matters of core academic concern.

In *Urofsky v. Gillmore,* 216 F. 3d 401 (4th Cir. 2001), the *en banc* panel of the Fourth Circuit expressly rejected the idea that individual faculty possess a constitutionally protected right of academic freedom separate and apart from institutional academic freedom. *Urofsky* involved a Virginia statute that prohibited state employees from accessing sexually explicit materials on state-provided computers. A number of university professors argued that the statute infringed on the free speech rights of all state employees and that, alternatively, the statute infringed on the academic freedom rights of state-employed teachers.

19

Applying *Pickering*, the Fourth Circuit found that the state did not infringe on the rights of state employees generally because states can regulate the speech of their employees undertaken in the course of the performance of their employment duties. The court also rejected the academic freedom argument stating: "[t]aking all of the cases together, the best that can be said for Appellees' claim that the Constitution protects the academic freedom of an individual professor is that teachers were the first public employees to be afforded the now-universal protection against dismissal for the exercise of First Amendment rights. Nothing in Supreme Court jurisprudence suggests that the 'right' claimed by Appellees extends any further."

Other decisions, such as *Bonnell v. Lorenzo*, 241 F. 3d 800 (6th Cir. 2001), have followed the approach of *Urofsky*, applying *Pickering* and not broader principles of academic freedom to claims advanced by individual faculty.

Academic freedom has played a role in a number of civil liberties debates arising in academic settings. In the debate about hate speech on college campuses, for example, opponents of civility and campus hate speech codes have argued that such codes violate academic freedom because they attempt to deter and sanitize protected academic speech that may be offensive. Academic freedom has also been part of the analysis of First Amendment defenses to sexual harassment claims based on a hostile educational environment. Nonetheless, cases in the hate speech and sexual harassment areas have not directly turned on the courts' analysis of academic freedom.

Despite the broad language in early Supreme Court opinions regarding academic freedom and the First Amendment, constitutional protection of academic freedom is very narrow. Courts have deferred to academic institutions on matters involving core academic decision-making. At the same time, the lower federal courts have declined to recognize an independent, constitutionally protected right of academic freedom for faculty and students, especially when the recognition of such a right would require the court to intervene in institutional academic decision-making.

ELIZABETH B. BRANDT

References and Further Reading

Byrne, J. Peter, *Academic Freedom: A "Special Concern of the First Amendment,"* Yale Law Review 99 (1989): 251–340.
Menand, Louis, ed. *The Future of Academic Tenure.* Chicago: University of Chicago Press, 1996.
Metzger, Walter P., *Profession and Constitution: Two Definitions of Academic Freedom in America*, Texas Law Review 66 (1988): 1265–1322.
Rabban, David M., *Functional Analysis of 'Individual' and 'Institutional' Academic Freedom Under the First Amendment.* Law and Contemporary Problems 53 (1990):227–301.
Van Alstyne, William W., *Academic Freedom and the First Amendment in the Supreme Court of the United States: An Unhurried Historical Review.* Law and Contemporary Problems 53 (1990):79–154.
———, ed. *Freedom and Tenure in the Academy.* Durham, NC: Duke University Press, 1993.

Cases and Statutes Cited

Adler v. Board of Education, 342 U.S. 485 (1952)
Axson–Flynn v. Johnson, 356 F.3d 1277 (10th Cir. 2003)
Bonnell v. Lorenzo, 241 F. 3d 800 (6th Cir. 2001)
Brown v. Li, 308 F. 3d 939 (9th Cir. 2002)
Grutter v. Bollinger, 539 U.S. 306 (2003)
Hazelwood School District v. Kuhlmeier, 484 U.S. 260 (1988)
Keyishian v. Board of Regents, 385 U.S. 589 (1967)
Pickering v. Board of Education, 391 U.S. 563 (1968)
Regents of the University of California v. Bakke, 438 U.S. 265 (1978)
Regents of the University of Michigan v. Ewing, 474 U.S. 214 (1985)
Shelton v. Tucker, 364 U.S. 479 (1960)
Sweezy v. New Hampshire, 354 U.S. 234 (1957)
Urofsky v. Gillmore, 216 F. 3d 401 (4th Cir. 2001)
Whitehill v. Elkins, 389 U.S. 54 (1967)
Wieman v. Updegraff, 344 U.S. 183 (1952)

See also **Campus Hate Speech Codes; Freedom of Speech and Press: Nineteenth Century; Freedom of Speech: Modern Period (1917–Present); Student Speech in Public Schools; Teacher Speech in Public Schools; Universities and Public Forums**

ACCESS TO GOVERNMENT OPERATIONS INFORMATION

In a democratic society, the informed citizen must have an affirmative right to gain access to information concerning the operations of government. Often referred to as "transparency," the public's right of access makes oversight possible and helps ensure that the government will be accountable to the people.

Access to the three branches of government varies in scope. Executive branch agencies are subject to the federal Freedom of Information and Sunshine laws, which create a presumptive right of access, subject to specific and limited exemptions. The legislative branch is generally open to public observation and review as a matter of practice and sometimes of statute. The Supreme Court declared that public and press access to criminal trials is guaranteed by the First Amendment in *Richmond Newspapers, Inc. v. Virginia*, 448 U.S. 555 (1980), and common law and court rules are designed to keep most other court proceedings open.

The rights of access to other instrumentalities of government are less clear. Although the Supreme Court has recognized that news gathering is protected by the First Amendment, the precise parameters are vague. For example, the scope of a First Amendment-based right of media access to military operations remains ill defined and a source of constant tension; competing interests of the government in maintaining operational security and the right of the public to know are imperfectly balanced. In the aftermath of 9/11 and the War on Terrorism, the government closed down access to many sources of government operations information in the name of protecting national security.

JANE E. KIRTLEY

Cases and Statutes Cited

Richmond Newspapers, Inc. v. Virginia, 448 U.S. 555 (1980)

See also **Access to Judicial Records; Freedom of Information Act (1966); Freedom of Information and Sunshine Laws; Media Access to Information; Media Access to Judicial Proceedings; Media Access to Military Operations; 9/11 and the War on Terrorism;** *Richmond Newspapers, Inc. v. Virginia*, **448 U.S. 555 (1980)**

ACCESS TO JUDICIAL RECORDS

Courts generally recognize two independent rights of public access to judicial records, one stemming from the common law and one from the First Amendment. Both are predicated on furthering government accountability.

The common law right originated before the First Amendment and is broader in scope; however, as with any common law right, it can be overridden by rule or statute. The Supreme Court recognized in *Nixon v. Warner Communications, Inc.*, 453 U.S. 589 (1978), that the common law creates a presumption of access to judicial records. But the Court denied access to White House audiotapes on grounds of supervening statute and declined to "delineate precisely the contours of the common-law right."

Common-law access is decided case by case, entrusted to the discretion of the trial court, and privileged by high deference on appeal. Access is determined by balancing public interests in disclosure, such as understanding of the judiciary or of historical events, against potential ills of disclosure, such as invasion of privacy, promotion of scandal, dissemination of defamation, or revelation of trade secrets.

The Supreme Court has not explicitly recognized a First Amendment right of access to judicial records,

but lower courts have found the right implicit in the Court's release of transcripts after access to proceedings was unconstitutionally denied in the *Press-Enterprise* cases. To analyze First Amendment access, courts employ the experience and logic test propounded in *Richmond Newspapers v. Virginia, Inc.*, 453 U.S. 589 (1978), for access to proceedings. As such, fewer records are covered. But access denial cannot be ordained by statute and merits no deference on appeal.

RICHARD J. PELTZ

Cases and Statutes Cited

Nixon v. Warner Communications, Inc., 453 U.S. 589 (1978)
Press-Enterprise Co. v. Superior Court (I), 464 U.S. 501 (1984)
Press-Enterprise Co. v. Superior Court (II), 478 U.S. 1 (1984)
Richmond Newspapers, Inc. v. Virginia, 448 U.S. 555 (1980)

See also **Cameras in the Courtroom; Discovery Materials in Court Proceedings; Duty to Obey Court Orders; Gag Orders in Judicial Proceedings; Media Access to Information; Media Access to Judicial Proceedings; Nixon, Richard Milhous;** *Richmond Newspapers, Inc. v. Virginia*, **448 U.S. 555 (1980); Right of Access to Criminal Trials; Sealed Documents in Court Proceedings; State Courts**

ACCESS TO PRISONS

In two cases decided on the same day in 1974, the U.S. Supreme Court said that state and federal prison regulations barring journalists from interviewing individual inmates did not violate the First Amendment. In *Pell v. Procunier*, 417 U.S. 817 (1974), and *Saxbe v. Washington Post*, 417 U.S. 817 (1974), the Court deferred to the judgment of prison officials who believed press interviews compromised security and discipline. The Court also said that journalists had the same right of access to prisons as the general public. Similarly, the Court in *Houchins v. KQED, Inc.*, 438 U.S. 1 (1978), rejected a television station's argument that barring cameras and sound equipment from public tours of a county jail infringed on the station's First Amendment rights as long as all members of the public faced the same restrictions.

State and federal courts consistently have found that it does not violate the First Amendment to bar the media from filming prisoner executions. In *Garrett v. Estelle*, 556 F.2d 1274 (5th Cir. 1977), a federal appellate court upheld a Texas regulation barring the filming of executions for broadcast. In 2001, a federal court in *Entertainment Network Inc. v. Lappin*, 134 F.Supp.2d 1002 (S.D. Ind. 2001), upheld a federal prison's decision to bar the Internet broadcast of an execution. However, the U.S. Court of Appeals for the Ninth Circuit said in 2002, in *California First Amendment Coalition v. Woodford*, 299 F.3d 868 (9th Cir. 2002), that California prison officials violated the First Amendment when they kept reporters and other witnesses invited to view an execution from seeing part of the lethal injection process.

ANTHONY L. FARGO

References and Further Reading

Frost, Kristen, *Case Notes and Comments: The Constitutionality of an Internet Execution*: Lappin v. Entertainment Network, Inc., DePaul–LCA Journal of Art and Entertainment Law 12 (Spring 2002): 173–216.

Levi, Nicholas, *Note: Veil of Secrecy: Public Executions, Limitations on Reporting Capital Punishment, and the Content Based Nature of Private Execution Laws*, Federal Communications Law Journal 55 (December 2002): 131–152.

Cases and Statutes Cited

California First Amendment Coalition v. Woodford, 299 F.3d 868 (9th Cir. 2002)

Entertainment Network, Inc. v. Lappin, 134 F.Supp.2d 1002 (S.D. Ind. 2001)

Garrett v. Estelle, 556 F.2d 1274 (5th Cir. 1977)

Houchins v. KQED, Inc., 438 U.S. 1 (1978)

Pell v. Procunier, 417 U.S. 817 (1974)

Saxbe v. Washington Post, 417 U.S. 843 (1974)

See also **Capital Punishment: History and Politics; Freedom of Speech and Press: Nineteenth Century; Press Clause (I): Framing and History from Colonial Period up to Early National Period; Prisoners and Freedom of Speech**

ACCOMMODATION OF RELIGION

The free exercise clause of the First Amendment is often interpreted as requiring the government to accommodate religion by refraining from applying to religious practitioners general laws that interfere with the edicts of particular religious faiths. This accommodation mandate has two aspects: the accommodation of religious belief and the accommodation of behavior motivated by religious belief. In *Reynolds v. United States* (1878), the Supreme Court's first comprehensive consideration of religious accommodation, the Court recognized that "while [laws] cannot interfere with mere religious belief and opinion, they may with practices." Even though the Court has always recognized that the law can interfere with

religiously motivated conduct, it has grappled repeatedly with the degree to which the First Amendment will permit legal interference with that conduct.

The mandatory accommodation required under the free exercise clause in some contexts is augmented by several federal and state statutes requiring accommodation of religious practitioners in other contexts. These statutes raise the issue of whether the Constitution permits government to accommodate religion in situations in which the free exercise clause does not mandate accommodation. Statutory accommodations potentially run afoul of two constitutional limits. First, to the extent that federal and state accommodation statutes provide favorable treatment to individuals based solely on religious belief, the provisions may violate the establishment clause. Second, federal statutes that require states to accommodate religion more comprehensively than the free exercise clause requires are vulnerable to the claim that Congress has exceeded its authority to remedy violations of the Fourteenth Amendment.

The History of Accommodation

For many years, courts were reluctant to require governments to accommodate religious practitioners by granting them exemptions from generally applicable laws. In *Reynolds v. United States*, 98 U.S. 145 (1878), for example, the Supreme Court refused to grant traditional Mormon practitioners an exemption from a federal statute criminalizing the practice of polygamy. Permitting individuals to avoid criminal punishment because their behavior was motivated by religious devotion, the Court held, "would be to make the professed doctrines of religious belief superior to the law of the land, and in effect to permit every citizen to become a law unto himself. Government could exist only in name under such circumstances."

This skeptical attitude characterized the Supreme Court's general approach to the issue of constitutionally mandated accommodations of religion until the early 1960s, when the Court became much more amenable to accommodation claims by religious practitioners. In 1963, the Supreme Court effectively required governments to accommodate religious practitioners in many cases in which legal obligations and religious obligations conflicted. In *Sherbert v. Verner*, 374 U.S. 398 (1963), the Court held that the state of South Carolina was required to provide unemployment benefits to a Seventh-Day Adventist woman who had been fired from her job because she had refused to work on Saturday, which was her Sabbath.

The state had refused to provide her benefits because the state unemployment statute denied benefits to anyone who refused "suitable work." The Court held that applying this provision to Sherbert forced her to "choose between following the precepts of her religion and forfeiting benefits, on the one hand, and abandoning one of the precepts of her religion in order to accept work, on the other hand." The Court held that this choice significantly burdened her free exercise of religion and could therefore only be justified by a compelling interest. Since the state had no compelling interest in refusing unemployment benefits to Sherbert while granting such benefits to others, it was required to accommodate her religious practices by providing her benefits.

The compelling interest analysis inaugurated in *Sherbert* prevailed on the Court until 1990. During this period the Court employed this analysis to require accommodations for Amish parents who sought to remove their children from school prior to the age designated in state mandatory attendance laws (*Wisconsin v. Yoder*, 406 U.S. 205, 1972), Jehovah's Witness foundry employees who refused to work on armaments production (*Thomas v. Review Board of Indiana*, 450 U.S. 707, 1971), and Native American parents whose religious beliefs prohibited them from obtaining social security numbers for their children (*Bowen v. Roy*, 476 U.S. 693, 1986).

On the other hand, the Court also refused to protect religious practitioners in a number of cases. The Court held, for example, that despite the constitutional accommodation mandate, the government could collect social security payments from Amish employers (*United States v. Lee*, 455 U.S. 252, 1982), force Jewish members of the military to refrain from wearing yarmulkes on duty (*Goldman v. Weinberger*, 475 U.S. 503, 1986), deny tax-exempt status to a religious university whose religious precepts prohibited interracial dating (*Bob Jones University v. United States*, 461 US 574, 1983), and tax the sale of religious literature (*Jimmy Swaggart Ministries v. Board of Equalization of California*, 493 U.S. 378, 1990). In short, although the Court required the government to assert a compelling interest to override the constitutional mandate of accommodation, it found that many government interests were sufficient to satisfy this standard.

Theories of Accommodation

Although the courts have focused mostly on the practical application of the accommodation mandate, judges and legal academics have also debated the theory behind religious accommodation. Proponents of accommodation argue that accommodation provides essential protection for religious minorities in a society defined by religious pluralism. Proponents of accommodation argue that the free exercise clause of the First Amendment is designed primarily to protect this culture of religious pluralism. They also argue that the theory of accommodation and religious pluralism should inform the courts' interpretation of the establishment clause. Under this approach, the need to accommodate religious practices would lead to a view of the establishment clause as fostering a spirit of what Chief Justice Warren Burger once labeled "benevolent neutrality." Granting property tax exemptions to religious organizations and permitting religious organizations to participate in government-funded social services programs are two examples of benevolent neutrality.

Proponents of accommodation also argue that accommodation is necessary to preserve the authority of religious institutions, which are (in the words of Professor Michael McConnell) "mediating structures" that provide citizens with the civic virtue necessary for successful democratic governance. Finally, proponents argue that accommodation is an overt recognition of the possibility that a supreme celestial authority exists. If God exists, they argue, then His sacred dictates must be deemed superior to those of any secular authority.

Opposition to mandatory accommodation revolves around the perceived discrimination built into the accommodation theory, which opponents believe is contrary to the underlying principles of the establishment clause. A central theme of establishment clause doctrine is that the government must be neutral toward particular religious faiths and religion in general. Mandatory accommodation rules, however, inevitably provide different levels of benefits to members of different faiths. Nonreligious individuals are automatically excluded from any accommodation regime. Members of religious groups that do not demand absolute conformity with strict behavioral decrees also will not benefit from accommodation mandates. In areas such as employment, moreover, the accommodation of religious practitioners will often have the effect of shifting burdens from one set of employees to another solely because of the employees' faith.

Under this view the internal contradictions of the oxymoron "benevolent neutrality" are evident: A system cannot be simultaneously "benevolent" and "neutral." If some citizens are given special dispensation to avoid complying with a general legal obligation based solely on their religious faith, then the system makes compliance with the law depend on one's religious faith. Such a system is not "neutral," as required by the establishment clause.

The Modern Standard

The Supreme Court has not formally adopted either position on the theory of accommodation, but in recent years the Court has significantly weakened the requirement that the government accommodate practices of religious adherents that violate otherwise applicable laws. In *Employment Division v. Smith*, 494 U.S. 872 (1990), the Supreme Court held that the First Amendment does not bar the government from applying a neutral, generally applicable law to individuals whose actions are motivated by religious faith. The Court therefore abandoned the requirement that the government must establish a compelling interest to apply general statutes to religious practitioners. The case involved the state of Oregon's refusal to grant unemployment compensation to two drug counselors who were fired from their jobs because they had used peyote in a religious ceremony conducted by the Native American Church. The Court held that the Oregon criminal law outlawing the use of peyote was not directed at members of the church. Violations of this law therefore justified denying unemployment benefits to anyone (including religious practitioners) using the prohibited substance.

After *Smith*, the Constitution requires governments to accommodate religion in only three relatively narrow circumstances: The government must (1) accommodate religion in statutes that provide benefits based on highly individualized governmental assessments of the reasons for the relevant conduct; (2) accommodate religion when the religious conduct is combined with some other constitutional right, such as free speech; and (3) still demonstrate a compelling interest before applying a statute that singles out religiously motivated practices for unfavorable treatment.

Although the Court has reduced the protection of religion through constitutionally mandated accommodation, the accommodation principle has been incorporated into several statutes protecting religious practitioners. The broadest of these statutes—the federal Religious Freedom Restoration Act—was held unconstitutional by the Supreme Court because it went beyond Congress's authority under section five of the Fourteenth Amendment. Congress subsequently enacted a narrower federal statute requiring the government to accommodate religious practitioners in the land use and prison contexts. Many states also have enacted statutes requiring the accommodation of religious practitioners, usually by reimposing the requirement that the government must prove a compelling interest before applying general legal regulations to individual actions motivated by religion. The Supreme Court has not yet ruled on the constitutionality of these statutes.

STEVEN G. GEY

References and Further Reading

Eisgruber, Christopher L., and Lawrence G. Sager, *The Vulnerability of Conscience: The Constitutional Basis for Protecting Religious Conduct*, University of Chicago Law Review 61 (1994): 1245.
Laycock, Douglas, *The Remnants of Free Exercise*, Supreme Court Review 1 (1990).
Lupu, Ira C., *Reconstructing the Establishment Clause: The Case Against the Discretionary Accommodation of Religion*, University of Pennsylvania Law Review 140 (1991): 555.
Marshall, William P., *The Case Against the Constitutionally Compelled Free Exercise Exemption*, Case Western Reserve Law Review 40 (1989–1990): 357.
McConnell, Michael W., *Accommodation of Religion*, Supreme Court Review 1 (1985).
———, *The Origins and Historical Understanding of Free Exercise of Religion*, Harvard Law Review 103 (1990): 1410.

Cases and Statutes Cited

Bob Jones University v. U.S., 461 US 574 (1983)
Bowen v. Roy, 476 U.S. 693 (1986)
Employment Division v. Smith, 494 U.S. 872 (1990)
Goldman v. Weinberger, 475 U.S. 503 (1986)
Jimmy Swaggart Ministries v. Board of Equalization of California, 493 U.S. 378 (1990)
Reynolds v. United States, 98 U.S. 145 (1878)
Sherbert v. Verner, 374 U.S. 398 (1963)
Thomas v. Review Board of Indiana, 450 U.S. 707 (1981)
United States v. Lee, 455 U.S. 252 (1982)
Wisconsin v. Yoder, 406 U.S. 205 (1972)

See also **Amish and Religious Liberty; Antipolygamy Laws; Belief–Action Distinction in Free Exercise Clause History; Conscientious Objection, the Free Exercise Clause; Exemptions for Religion Contained in Regulatory Statutes; Jehovah's Witnesses and Religious Liberty; Mormons and Religious Liberty; Release Time from Public Schools (For Religious Purposes); Religious Freedom Restoration Act; Seventh Day Adventists and Religious Liberty**

ACCOMPLICE CONFESSIONS

A defendant in a multidefendant criminal trial who confesses to illegal conduct is making a direct admission regarding his acts. This confession is admissible against the confessing defendant in court. However, when a defendant's confession also implicates a codefendant, the statement generally cannot be used as evidence in prosecuting the nonconfessing co-defendant. The confession is considered inadmissible hearsay violating the nonconfessing co-defendant's rights under the Sixth Amendment confrontation clause.

Accomplice confessions have long been an issue due to concern over how "voluntary" the confessions extracted by police really are, as well as the reliability of statements given by confessing co-defendants eager to shift blame for their criminal acts to others. The U.S. Supreme Court has addressed this issue in a number of important cases.

In *Delli Paoli v. United States* (352 U.S. 232, 1957), the Court held that a confession admitted by one defendant that also implicated a co-defendant was admissible if jurors were told to disregard that part of the confession. The *Delli Paoli* holding led the New Jersey Supreme Court Committee on Evidence to recommend that the law be changed to disallow defendant statements implicating a co-defendant, unless all references to the co-defendant could be eliminated. This recommendation was rejected and states were temporarily left to make their own decisions regarding the admissibility of such statements.

The Court readdressed the issue in *Bruton v. U.S.* (391 U.S. 123, 1968), where it overruled its holding in *Delli Paoli*. It held that jury instructions limiting the consideration of statements implicating co-defendants did not satisfy the Sixth Amendment confrontation clause. However, the Court soon relaxed its stance, finding that in certain circumstances, an error allowing such a statement (a Bruton error) could be deemed harmless and thus not amount to a breach of the Sixth Amendment's confrontation rights.

In 1970, the Court concluded that an exception to the rule against hearsay must be evaluated by the due-process standards of the Fifth and Fourteenth Amendments instead of the Sixth Amendment confrontation clause. Its reasoning was that the confrontation clause was not designed to cope with the many factors involved in passing evidentiary rules and ensuring the fairness of trials. (See *Dutton v. Evans*, 400 U.S. 74, 1970.)

One long-recognized exception to the hearsay rule was when the evidence established the existence of a conspiracy. In such cases, a statement by a co-conspirator made in furtherance of the conspiracy was admissible against other co-defendants and the declarant was not required to testify at trial. (See Rule 801 (d)(2)E, Federal Rules of Evidence.) In *Bourjaily v. U.S.*, 483 U.S. 171 (1987), and *U.S. v. Inadi*, 475 U.S. 387 (1986), the Court held that this hearsay exception did not violate the confrontation clause. The Court later expanded this exception by allowing

defendant pleas establishing the existence of a conspiracy to be admissible at trial without the declarant testifying.

EZEKIEL E. CORTEZ

References and Further Reading

Campaigne, Carol, Joanne Constantino, Glenn A. Guarino, Kathy E. Hinck, Kristin McCarthy, Kristin, Caralyn A. Irwin J. Schiffres, Melissa K. Stull, Tim A. Thomas, and Mitchell J. Waldman. 29A *American Journal* 2d Evidence § 751 (1992).

Choo, Andrew L. T. *Hearsay and Confrontation in Criminal Trials*. Oxford: Oxford University Press, 1996.

Coady, C.A.J. *Testimony: A Philosophical Study*. Oxford: Oxford University Press, 1992.

Wright, Charles Alan, and Kenneth W. Graham, Jr. 21A *Federal Practices and Procedures* 2d Evidence § 5064.1–5064.2 (West 1987).

Cases and Statutes Cited

Bourjaily v. U.S., 483 U.S. 171 (1987)
Bruton v. U.S., 391 U.S. 123 (1968)
Delli Paoli v. United States, 352 U.S. 232 (1957)
Dutton v. Evans, 400 U.S. 74 (1970)
People v. Salko, 47 NY2d 230 (1979)
U.S. v. Inadi (475 U.S. 387 (1986)
United States Constitution, Fifth Amendment
United States Constitution, Sixth Amendment
United States Constitution, Fourteenth Amendment

See also **Confrontation and Compulsory Process**

ACT UP

ACT UP—the AIDS Coalition to Unleash Power—came together in March 1987 out of the charismatic exhortations of author and playwright Larry Kramer. Already central to the creation of the Gay Men's Health Crisis, Kramer had grown impatient with the responses by the government and pharmaceutical industry to the AIDS epidemic. No longer content simply to react to the crisis, ACT UP aspired to force change through direct action, confrontation, and media-savvy street theatre.

Central to the motivational ethos of the coalition was the conviction that persons living with AIDS (PWAs) were not passive victims of a disease, but individuals who must take control of their situations through self-empowerment, demanding that bureaucracies take the problem seriously. The *Denver Principles* announced this proactive stance. Framed in 1983, the *Principles* eschewed the labels "victim" and "patient" and enumerated the rights of PWAs along with recommendations and strategies to achieve those goals. ACT UP embraced the spirit of the *Principles* and gave flesh to what had been merely abstract ideas.

The group's first demonstration took place on March 24, 1987, when it staged a protest on Wall Street over the monopoly and profiteering by Burroughs Wellcome, the manufacturer of AZT. Of the two hundred fifty participants, seventeen were arrested, launching an innovative model for activist organizing.

Although all facets of the AIDS crisis fell within the group's mission, ACT UP came to be especially associated with three broad issues. First, it effectively pressured medical corporations to develop safe and effective drug treatments and offer them at affordable prices to those who needed them. Second, activists insisted that governmental agencies, such as the Food and Drug Administration, put new AIDS drugs on a fast-track for approval. Finally, any entity perceived to be complicating the lives and treatments of PWAs was singled out for public humiliation and embarrassing publicity.

Over the years ACT UP achieved astonishing successes. It shut down the FDA to international attention (October 11, 1988), convinced the government to adopt innovative drug testing procedures (June 4–9, 1989), and pressured Burroughs Wellcome to cut the price of AZT 20 percent by interfering with trading on the floor of the New York Stock Exchange (September 14, 1989).

ACT UP's singular success relied in part on its accurate sense of how to get its message out beyond its members. Its logo—the motto "Silence = Death" in front of a pink triangle—became one of the best known symbols of the period. From its inception the group valued praxis over theory. Going far beyond the traditional protest picket lines, its actions tended to be well-conceived, high-style mediagenic events designed for visual and symbolic impact, such as the "die in" on Wall Street.

A hallmark of an ACT UP action was an intrusion into "inappropriate" spaces. These actions were known as "zaps," a term and strategy revived from earlier countercultural and gay liberationist campaigns. On the other hand, ACT UP rarely pursued its agenda in the courtroom. The few cases involving the organization more typically concerned its right to protest than AIDS issues per se.

At its height, ACT UP spawned more than seventy chapters around the country and the world. In addition, it spun off other, even more radical organizations such as Queer Nation, which fought against homophobia and assimilation of the gay community into heterosexual normalcy, and the Lesbian Avengers.

According to its own description, ACT UP is a group "united in anger." Although that visceral drive accounts for its great intensity, such emotional intensity could not be sustained over an extended period. By the 1990s, ACT UP was in decline, and today comparatively few chapters remain active. AIDS claimed many of its early charismatic leaders, and others left to pursue AIDS-related causes in more professional roles. As better drugs made AIDS more manageable for many PWAs, there was less "anger" for ACT UP to draw upon. Finally, ACT UP chapters suffered internal dissensions over whether the organization should remain with its single focus or branch out into wider issues of social justice.

Whatever the fortunes of the organization, ACT UP has an enduring legacy in its achievements to improve the lives of PWAs—in terms of quantity, through the demand for new drugs made rapidly available at affordable prices, and quality, by confronting AIDS-negative policies wherever found. Its refreshingly uninhibited and creative protests have had an enduring impact on the way ordinary citizens come together to demand recognition of their civil liberties.

JAMES M. DONOVAN

References and Further Reading

ACT UP-New York. *ACTUP Capsule History*, www.actupny.org.

Kramer, Larry. *Reports from the Holocaust: The Making of an AIDS Activist*. New York: St. Martin's Press, 1989.

Shepard, Benjamin, and Ronald Hayduk, eds. *From ACT UP to the WTO: Urban Protest and Community Building in the Era of Globalization*. London: Verso, 2002.

See also **Demonstrations and Sit-ins; Gay and Lesbian Rights**

ACTON, LORD JOHN (1834–1902)

Lord John Acton, the great liberal academic who dominated the field of history during the latter part of the Victorian Age, was born into a family of the upper echelon of society in Italy and moved to England at the age of three. There, Acton faced persecution for his Catholic religious beliefs. Lord Acton went on to become a member of the first Vatican Council, where he advocated for political and religious freedom. At times throughout his career, he was highly critical of the Vatican for intolerance and persecution. He attended university in Germany, was elected a member of the House of Commons in 1859, and acquired and was the editor of the periodical the *Rambler*, which he shaped into a liberal journal of Catholicism. In 1895, Acton was appointed the Regius Professor of Modern History at Cambridge University. He began work on a universal history that would track religious virtue and the expansion of liberty, but he died before completion.

Acton can be characterized as being critical of excessive power in only a few hands at the national level, in his Catholic Church as well as in government. Acton is best known for the famous phrase "power tends to corrupt, and absolute power corrupts absolutely." He was suspicious of unchecked nationalism, meaning a political system that governs by a general will for an entire state, since it stood to undermine traditional liberties. For example, he hailed the secession of the South from the Union in the Civil War as the realization of states' rights as the only check on absolutist rule.

Acton favored the slow evolution of institutions above broad-sweeping reactionary measures; law ought to parallel, not spur, history. He called for expanded personal freedom but viewed the central government as a hindrance to society's progress on this front. He believed that a national government must have its authority divided in order safeguard liberty, akin to checks and balances. Acton also believed that liberty encompassed the rights of minorities—persons who fall outside the so-called majority group that controls the government. Acton's views on nationalist power and liberty for all are manifest in the American system of checks and balances. This includes the Supreme Court's protection of the civil liberties of so-called minority groups from laws that persecute them, such as the Amish or Jehovah's Witnesses, while striking a necessary balance with majoritarian rule.

JAMES F. VAN ORDEN

References and Further Reading

Acton, Lord John Emerich Edward. *Lectures on Modern History*. London: Macmillan and Co., 1930.
Matthew, David. *Lord Acton and His Times*. University, Ala.: University of Alabama Press, 1968.
Watson, George. *Lord Acton's History of Liberty: A Study of His Library, with an Edited Text on His History of Liberty Notes*. Aldershot, England: Scolar Press, 1994.

ACTUAL MALICE STANDARD

In the landmark case of *The New York Times v. Sullivan*, 376 U.S. 25 (1964), the Supreme Court developed the actual malice concept. An advertisement (equivalent to a story for the Court) appeared in the Times that contained false and defamatory information about a commissioner of the city of Montgomery, Alabama. The commissioner sued, but the Supreme Court, while acknowledging the falsity and defamatory nature of the story, ruled that if the press

was to have freedom to write about public officials, it needed to be given a substantial amount of legal protection. A newspaper would only be culpable, the Court ruled, if it acted with actual malice, which the Court went on to define as "with knowledge that it [the story] was false or with reckless disregard of whether it was false or not." In *Sullivan* this applied to suits brought by public figures; the argument was that these individuals had thrust themselves into the limelight and should expect more critical stories about themselves, and that, given their public position, they would have an easier opportunity to rebut allegations and set the record straight.

In later cases the Court extended the applicability of the actual malice standard to public figures (in *Sullivan* it was limited to public officials), but it declined to extend it to public issues. Deciding who is a public figure, however, has proven to be no easy matter. It also has not proven straightforward to obtain the information necessary to determine whether a paper acted with actual malice in its reporting.

MILTON HEUMANN

References and Further Reading

O'Brien, David. *Constitutional Law and Politics*, 5th ed., vol. 2. New York: W.W. Norton and Company, 2003.
Sullivan, Kathleen, and Gerald Gunther. *Constitutional Law*, 15th ed. New York: Foundation Press, 2004.

Cases and Statutes Cited

The New York Times Company v. Sullivan, 376 U.S. 25 (1964)

See also **Freedom of the Press: Modern Period (1917–Present);** *Herbert v. Lando,* **441 U.S. 153 (1979); Public Figures; Public Officials**

ADMINISTRATIVE SEARCHES AND SEIZURES

The Fourth Amendment requires all searches and seizures to be reasonable. The Supreme Court has interpreted reasonableness to require a warrant based on probable cause, unless a recognized exception to this general rule applies. One such exception is for "administrative searches," in which the government claims that the search advances administrative interests, not traditional law enforcement objectives.

The Court first recognized an "administrative search" exception to usual Fourth Amendment rules in the 1967 companion cases of *Camara v. Municipal Court*, 387 U.S. 523, and *See v. City of Seattle*, 387

U.S. 541. At issue in the cases was the constitutionality of warrantless entries into private property to inspect for municipal housing code and fire code violations, respectively. In addressing the reasonableness of the searches, the Court treated the warrant and probable cause requirements differently. On the one hand, emphasizing the historical importance of search warrants, the Court found no justification for the government to conduct administrative inspections without a warrant, in the absence of an emergency or consent.

On the other hand, the Court reasoned that requiring the government to articulate individualized suspicion that violations existed within the areas to be searched would threaten the efficacy of an administrative inspection program designed to prevent such violations. Instead, the Court developed a standard of "probable cause" for administrative searches that requires only that the search be "reasonable." To measure reasonableness in the administrative context, the Court invoked a balancing test, weighing the government's interest in the search against the privacy expectations implicated by the search.

Since *Camara* and *See,* the Court has backed away from its insistence upon a warrant to support administrative searches, emphasizing instead the more flexible requirement of reasonableness. For example, in *New York v. Burger,* the Court upheld a state statute that authorized police to conduct warrantless searches of businesses involved in the dismantling of automobiles. The Court reasoned that in the context of a "closely regulated" industry, individuals have reduced expectations of privacy. Therefore, both the warrant and probable cause requirements have reduced application. Departing from the earlier concept of an administrative warrant, the Court held that a regulatory scheme authorizing warrantless searches of a closely regulated industry is reasonable as long as three requirements are met: (1) the government must have a substantial interest in the scheme; (2) the warrantless inspections must be necessary to further the regulatory scheme; and (3) the inspection program must provide an adequate substitute for a warrant by notifying property owners that the search is authorized and by limiting the discretion of the inspecting officers.

The Court's willingness to rely on a balancing test to determine reasonableness, rather than on the warrant and probable cause rules, is not limited to searches of closely regulated industries. More recently, the Court has recognized a "special needs" exception that applies whenever a "special need" other than the ordinary needs of law enforcement renders the warrant and/or probable cause requirements impracticable. Applying this exception, the Court has upheld,

for example, drug testing of railroad personnel to enhance railway safety, of certain U.S. Customs agents to ensure their fitness and integrity, and of public school students to detect and prevent drug use by youths.

Whether a search program advances administrative or otherwise "special" needs, as opposed to ordinary law enforcement, is not always apparent. In *Burger* (*New York v. Burger*, 482 U.S. 691, 1987), for example, the searches of automobile-dismantling businesses were conducted by police officers, and at least part of the statute's purpose was to reduce criminal activity relating to car thefts. Nevertheless, the Court treated the warrantless inspections as administrative searches of a closely inspected industry, not as traditional law enforcement searches. In doing so, the Court did not appear troubled that the state's ultimate objective may have been to reduce crime. Rather, the Court focused on the mechanism with which the state had chosen to pursue that objective, which the Court characterized as administrative.

In contrast, when the government's mechanism for pursuing its objective bears too much resemblance to traditional law enforcement, the Court will treat it as such, despite the purportedly "special" purpose that motivates it. For example, in *Ferguson v. Charleston,* 532 U.S. 67 (2001), the Court addressed the constitutionality of testing pregnant women for drugs at public hospitals in order to reduce the number of drug-influenced babies. The threat of prosecution was used as leverage to encourage women who tested positive to obtain substance abuse counseling. The government argued that the drug testing advanced a special need beyond traditional law enforcement and, therefore, could be conducted without a warrant or probable cause. The Court disagreed, emphasizing not the government's ultimate objective but the mechanism by which it had chosen to pursue that objective. Despite the government's willingness to forego criminal charges against women who obtained counseling, the "immediate objective" of the drug testing was to generate evidence for use in a potential criminal case.

Although courts and commentators often treat administrative and special needs searches separately, both lines of cases can be seen as part of the same doctrinal approach. In both contexts, the Court relaxes or does away with the usual probable cause and warrant requirements because of the nature of the governmental interest; instead, it determines "reasonableness" by the balancing test first articulated in *Camara.* Courts similarly turn to balancing, and away from warrants and probable cause requirements, to weigh the reasonableness of border searches, airport searches, and checkpoints. These lines of cases could be increasingly important as mass surveillance continues to develop as a precautionary security mechanism, testing the line between traditional law enforcement and "special" objectives.

ALAFAIR S. BURKE

References and Further Reading

Dressler, Joshua. *Understanding Criminal Procedure*, 3rd ed. New York: LexisNexis, 2002, 323–353.
Stuntz, William J., *Implicit Bargains, Government Power, and the Fourth Amendment*, Stanford Law Review 44 (1992): 553.
Sundby, Scott E., *Protecting the Citizen "Whilst He Is Quiet": Suspicionless Searches, "Special Needs" and General Warrants*, Mississippi Law Journal 74 (2004): 501.

Cases and Statutes Cited

Camara v. Municipal Court, 387 U.S. 523 (1967)
Ferguson v. Charleston, 532 U.S. 67 (2001)
New York v. Burger, 482 U.S. 691 (1987)
See v. City of Seattle, 387 U.S. 541 (1967)

See also **Airport Searches; Checkpoints (roadblocks); Drug Testing; Probable Cause; Search (General Definition); Search Warrants**

ADOLESCENT FAMILY LIFE ACT

In 1981, Congress enacted the Adolescent Family Life Demonstration Grants Act (AFLA) in response to the severe social and economic consequences that often follow pregnancy and childbirth among unmarried adolescents. The enactment of AFLA was also prompted by Congress's insight that the federal government has a responsibility to help states develop adequate approaches to the serious and increasing problems of adolescent premarital sexual relations and pregnancy.

Among the stated purposes of the AFLA is to find effective means, within the context of the family, of reaching adolescents before they become sexually active in order to promote self-discipline and other prudent approaches to the problem of adolescent premarital sexual relations and to promote adoption as an alternative to abortion. The act further indicates that since the problems of adolescent premarital sexual relations, pregnancy, and parenthood are multiple and complex, such problems are best approached through a variety of integrated and essential services provided to adolescents and their families by other family members, religious and charitable organizations, voluntary organizations, and other groups in the private sector. Furthermore, despite the fact that teenage females had, at the time, a fundamental right to an abortion, grants were to be made only to programs that did not provide abortions, abortion referrals, or abortion counseling.

The only statutory restrictions on the use of AFLA funds are that none of the AFLA grants may be used for projects that provide abortion counseling, and the grants may be made only to projects or programs that do not promote, advocate, or encourage abortion. Furthermore, AFLA funds cannot be used to provide family planning services if such services are available elsewhere in the community.

The grants endorsed by AFLA are given to organizations providing two basic kinds of services: care services and prevention services. Care services, or necessary services for the provision of care to pregnant adolescent parents and adolescent parents, include pregnancy testing; maternity counseling; adoption counseling and referral services; primary and preventive health services, including prenatal and postnatal care; nutrition information and counseling; referral to appropriate pediatric care; referral to maternity home services and mental health services; childcare sufficient to enable the adolescent parent to continue his or her education; consumer education and homemaking; and transportation. Preventive services, or necessary services to prevent adolescent sexual relations, include referral for screening and treatment of venereal disease and educational services relating to family life and problems associated with adolescent premarital sexual relations, including information on adoption, education on the responsibilities of sexuality and parenting, and assistance to parents, schools, youth agencies, and adolescents and preadolescents concerning self-discipline in human sexuality.

The seminal case dealing with AFLA is *Bowen v. Kendrick*, 108 S. Ct. 2562 (1988). In 1983, this lawsuit against the Secretary was filed in the U.S. District Court for the District of Columbia by appellees, a group of federal taxpayers, clergymen, and the American Jewish Congress. Seeking declaratory and injunctive relief, appellees challenged the constitutionality of the AFLA on the grounds that, on its face and as applied, the statute violated the religious clauses of the First Amendment. Considering the federal statute on its face and as applied, the District Court ruled that the statute violated the establishment clause of the First Amendment insofar as it provided for the involvement of religious organizations in the federally funded program.

The U.S. Supreme Court upheld the constitutionality of the AFLA. The Court found that although the AFLA provided for grants to religious and other institutions, it did not have the primary effect of advancing religion. Moreover, the Court found that the AFLA would not lead to excessive government entanglement with religion.

After protracted litigation, the parties reached a settlement agreement on January 19, 1993, which established that AFLA-funded sexuality education may not include religious references, may not be offered in a site used for religious worship services, or offered in sites with religious iconography. Moreover, the agreement established that information disbursed by the AFLA-funded programs must be medically accurate.

The effect of the AFLA on civil rights in American has the potential to restrict or hinder an adolescent's ability to make an informed choice regarding her right to have an abortion. By the language of the act, institutions that receive grants are encouraged to provide information about adoption and implicitly discouraged from providing information dealing with any aspect of the adolescent's right to an abortion. This could particularly affect segments of the population that do not have the requisite financial resources to take their pregnant adolescents to private institutions, but rather must rely on those that receive AFLA grants.

MARIANGELA VALLE–PETERS

References and Further Reading

Jones, Julie, *Money, Sex, and the Religious Right: A Constitutional Analysis of the Federally Funded Abstinence-Only-Until-Marriage Sexuality Education*, Creighton Law Review 35(2002): 1075.
Petrich, Alexandra, Bowen v. Kendrick. *Retreat from Prophylaxis in Church and State Relationships*, Hastings Constitutional Law Quarterly 16 (1989): 513.

Cases and Statutes Cited

42 U.S.C. §300z(a)(5)
42 U.S.C. §300z-1(a)(7)
42 U.S.C. §300z-1(a)(4)
42 U.S.C. §300z-1(a)(8)
42 U.S.C. §300z-1(b)(1)
42 U.S.C. §300z(b)(2)
42 U.S.C. §300z(a)(8)(A)
42 U.S.C. §300z(a)(8)(B)
42 U.S.C. §300z(10)(a)
42 U.S.C. §300z-3(b)(1)
S. Rep. No. 161, 97th Cong., 1st Sess. 20 (1981)
S. Rep. No. 161, 97th Cong., 1st Sess. 4 (1981)

See also **Abortion;** *Bowen v. Kendrick,* **487 U.S. 589 (1988)**

AFFIRMATIVE ACTION

Affirmative action has emerged as a controversial issue in American political and constitutional discourse. The phrase, which covers a range of meanings, encompasses programs designed to help women and particularly African Americans and other historically disadvantaged minorities.

Affirmative action only became a national preoccupation after the Supreme Court and Congress first took steps in the 1950s and 1960s to outlaw *de jure* discrimination. Although the Wagner Act of 1935 used the term as a remedy for unfair labor practices, President John F. Kennedy's Executive Order 10925 introduced it into civil rights discourse by directing government contractors to take "affirmative action" to employ persons without regard to "race, creed, color or national origin." This meaning of the concept, which looks to recruitment to expand applicant pools, has proved relatively uncontroversial. Yet, President Lyndon B. Johnson in his June 1965 speech at Howard University implied that more might be required. A second familiar application of affirmative action involves race-conscious decision-making that gives some degree of preference to disadvantaged minorities in college admissions, employment, or government contracting.

This latter use of the concept has proved controversial. Proponents of race-conscious programs argue that they are appropriate vehicles to remedy past discrimination against certain historically disadvantaged minorities and to create opportunity for members of those groups to succeed in America. Some, like John Hart Ely, argued that racial classifications that a white majority used to benefit minorities were of an entirely different character than those used to oppress minorities. Conversely, critics condemn affirmative action as reverse discrimination that unfairly disadvantages members of other groups who may have been innocent of any personal wrongdoing.

As a constitutional matter the issue turns in part on whether one believes that the equal protection clause of the Fourteenth Amendment forbids government from drawing racial classifications, in which case race-conscious programs are suspect, or whether it simply forbids subjugation of minority groups, in which case a constitutional distinction might be drawn between benevolent and malevolent racial classifications.

In a series of divided decisions, the Supreme Court has held that race-conscious programs must be subject to strict scrutiny that requires that any race classification be narrowly tailored to serve a compelling state interest. As such, it has refused to distinguish between race classifications that benefit or burden a disadvantaged minority. The Court has rejected redressing past societal discrimination as an interest justifying racial classification.

The Supreme Court's 2003 decisions in *Grutter v. Bollinger*, 539 U.S. 306 (2003), and *Gratz v. Bollinger*,

539 U.S. 244 (2003), addressed race preferences in university admissions. In *Grutter*, the Court held that diversity is a compelling state interest that justifies considering race as one diversity factor among others in a process that makes an individual judgment in each applicant. The Court deemed racial quotas unconstitutional but allowed schools to use numerical targets to guide decisions. *Grutter* expanded the diversity rationale by recognizing that it helped create "one nation indivisible." In *Gratz* the Court rejected a formulaic approach that awarded a specified number of points to persons based on race.

JOEL K. GOLDSTEIN

References and Further Reading

Anderson, Terry H. *The Pursuit of Fairness: A History of Affirmative Action.* Oxford: Oxford University Press, 2004.
Bowen, William G., and Derek Bok. *The Shape of the River: Long-Term Consequences of Considering Race in College and University Admissions.* Princeton, NJ: Princeton University Press, 1998.
Chin, Gabriel J., ed. *Affirmative Action and the Constitution,* 3 vols. New York: Garland Publishing, Inc., 1998.

Cases and Statutes Cited

Gratz v. Bollinger, 539 U.S. 244 (2003)
Grutter v. Bollinger, 539 U.S. 306 (2003)
Regents of the University of California v. Bakke, 438 U.S. 265 (1978)

See also **Equal Protection of Law (XIV); Fourteenth Amendment; Johnson, Lyndon Baines**

AGOSTINI v. FELTON, 521 U.S. 203 (1997)

In *Agostini v. Felton*, the U.S. Supreme Court reversed its 1985 decision in *Aguilar v. Felton*, 473 U.S. 402 (1985) (and portions of its companion decision in *School District of Grand Rapids v. Ball*, 473 U.S. 373, 1985), in which the Court had struck down government programs that provided remedial instruction in secular subjects on the grounds of religious schools. The *Agostini* decision, decided by a five-to-four vote, reflected a shift in the Court's personnel between 1985 and 1997 and the ongoing modification of the Court's strong separationist jurisprudence reflected in the two earlier decisions.

In *Aguilar*, the Court considered the constitutionality of the use of federal funds provided by Title I of the Elementary and Secondary Education Act (ESEA) to pay the salaries of public school teachers who taught remedial reading and math courses to low-income children attending parochial schools in New York City. The Court in *Aguilar* ruled in a five-to-four vote that the government's monitoring of the activities of these publicly funded teachers constituted an excessive entanglement between church and state in violation of the establishment clause.

More than a decade after the *Aguilar* decision, petitioners filed motions seeking relief from the injunction previously entered in the case that barred the use of publicly funded teachers in the parochial schools of New York City. The petitioners argued that several of the Court's more recent decisions called into question the ongoing validity of the *Aguilar* decision, especially the decision in *Zobrest v. Catalina Foothills School District*, 509 U.S. 1 (1993), in which the Court had refused to presume that a state-funded interpreter working in a religious school would engage in religious indoctrination or constituted a symbolic union of government and religion. The petitioners also noted that five of the Court's justices had expressed the view in *Board of Education, Kiryas Joel Village School District v. Grumet*, 512 U.S. 687 (1994), that *Aguilar* should be reconsidered or overruled.

The Supreme Court took the *Agostini* case and reversed. Justice Sandra Day O'Connor, who had dissented in the *Aguilar* case, wrote the opinion for the majority, finding that the provision of remedial instruction in secular subjects by publicly funded teachers did not violate the establishment clause, even if the instruction took place on the grounds of a religious school. In particular, the Court rejected the presumption of the *Aguilar* decision that a public school teacher who teaches on the property of a religious school is likely to inculcate students with the religious beliefs of that school. The *Agostini* Court also emphasized that any governmental aid under Title I comes to the religious school "only as a result of the genuinely independent and private choices" of those low-income children (and their parents) who attended a religious school. This "private choice" aspect of the Court's decision would prove important to the Court in subsequent cases.

The four dissenters sharply criticized the majority's decision. Justice David Souter, for example, claimed that "there is simply no line that can be drawn between instruction paid for at taxpayers' expense and the instruction in any subject that is not identified as formally religious."

The *Agostini* decision became an important precedent for the Court as it considered additional cases involving other forms of government aid to religious schools that involved private choice. For example, in

Zelman v. Simmons–Harris, 536 U.S. 639 (2002), the Court relied heavily on its *Agostini* decision to uphold the constitutionality of school vouchers.

DAVISON M. DOUGLAS

References and Further Reading

Bunnow, Jeremy T., *Reinventing the Lemon:* Agostini v. Felton *and the Changing Nature of Establishment Clause Jurisprudence*, Wisconsin Law Review (1998): 1133–1180.

Roberson, Doug, *Recent Development: The Supreme Court of the United States, 1996 Term: The Supreme Court's Shifting Tolerance for Public Aid to Parochial Schools and the Implications for Educational Choice:* Agostini v. Felton, *117 S. Ct. 1997 (1997)*, Harvard Journal of Law and Public Policy 21 (1998): 861–879.

Whitehead, Daniel P., *Note:* Agostini v. Felton: *Rectifying the Chaos of Establishment Clause Jurisprudence*, Capital University Law Review 27 (1999): 639–666.

Cases and Statutes Cited

Aguilar v. Felton, 473 U.S. 402 (1985)

Board of Education, Kiryas Joel Village School District v. Grumet, 512 U.S. 687 (1994)

School District of Grand Rapids v. Ball, 473 U.S. 373 (1985)

Witters v. Washington Department of Services, 474 U.S. 481 (1986)

Zelman v. Simmons–Harris, 536 U.S. 639 (2002)

Zobrest v. Catalina Foothills School District, 509 U.S. 1 (1993)

See also **Establishment Clause (I): History, Background, Framing; State Aid to Religious Schools**

AGUILAR v. FELTON, 473 U.S. 402 (1985)

In its 1985 decision in *Aguilar v. Felton*, the U.S. Supreme Court declared unconstitutional a government program that provided remedial instruction to low-income children attending parochial schools—a decision that reflected the strong separationist jurisprudence adhered to by a narrow majority of the Court's justices during that era.

Throughout the 1970s and early 1980s, the Court decided a large number of cases involving the constitutionality of various types of governmental financial assistance to religious schools. Throughout this time period, the Court assessed the constitutionality of such aid in accord with what was known as the "Lemon test," drawn from the Court's highly influential decision in *Lemon v. Kurtzman*, 403 U.S. 602 (1971). Under the Lemon test, in order for a governmental aid program to survive scrutiny under the establishment clause, (1) it must have a secular legislative purpose; (2) its principal or primary effect must be one that neither advances nor inhibits religion; and (3) it must not foster an excessive government entanglement with religion.

In *Aguilar v. Felton*, the Court determined that the aid program in question violated the third prong of the Lemon test. In this case, New York City used federal funds it received under Title I of the Elementary and Secondary Education Act (ESEA) to pay, among other things, the salaries of public school teachers who taught remedial reading and math courses to low-income children attending parochial schools in the city. To avoid an establishment clause violation, these teachers taught in special classrooms at the religious schools that were devoid of religious symbols, used secular instructional materials, and were monitored by the city through unannounced visits to make sure that they did not unwittingly inculcate their students with the religious beliefs of the parochial schools during the course of their instruction. The Supreme Court, in a five-to-four decision with Justice William Brennan writing for the majority, found that this monitoring process constituted an excessive entanglement of church and state in violation of the establishment clause.

The same day as the *Aguilar* decision, the Court decided a similar case involving the constitutionality of a state program in Michigan that also provided remedial instruction to low-income children in parochial schools. In that case, *School District of Grand Rapids v. Ball*, 473 U.S. 373 (1985), the Court, in another five-to-four decision, found that the aid program had the potential to "impermissibly advance religion" in violation of the second prong of the Lemon test because "the teachers participating in the programs may become involved in intentionally or inadvertently inculcating particular religious tenets or beliefs."

In a sense, the New York City program provided what was missing from the Michigan program: careful monitoring to make sure that such inculcation did not happen. But in *Aguilar*, the Court found that the monitoring process, which the Court described as "a permanent and pervasive state presence in the sectarian schools receiving aid," unduly entangled the government in the activities of the parochial schools in violation of the establishment clause. Therefore, both aid programs—one with governmental monitoring and one without—were unconstitutional. As a result of the *Aguilar* decision, remedial instruction to low-income parochial school children in New York City continued but at considerable public expense: typically by providing instruction in a publicly provided trailer parked near a parochial school.

The majority's decisions in *Aguilar* and *Ball* provoked bitter dissents. Chief Justice Warren Burger, for example, in his *Aguilar* dissent accused the majority of exhibiting "paranoia" and "nothing less than hostility toward religion and the children who attend church-sponsored schools." Justice Sandra Day O'Connor labeled the decision "tragic" and ridiculed the majority's notion that teachers "are likely to start teaching religion because they have walked across the threshold of a parochial school." She noted that the nineteen-year track record of the Title I program revealed not one instance in which a teacher "attempted to indoctrinate the students in particular religious tenets."

In some ways, the *Aguilar* and *Ball* decisions constituted the "high-water" mark of the Court's separationist jurisprudence. Thereafter, aided by personnel changes, the Court began to chip away at this jurisprudence and finally, in 1997, reversed the *Aguilar* and *Ball* decisions in *Agostini v. Felton*, 521 U.S. 203 (1997), in which it rejected its earlier presumption that publicly funded teachers of remedial reading and math in religious schools would inculcate their students with religious values.

DAVISON M. DOUGLAS

References and Further Reading

Roberson, Doug, *Recent Development: The Supreme Court of the United States, 1996 Term: The Supreme Court's Shifting Tolerance for Public Aid to Parochial Schools and the Implications for Educational Choice:* Agostini v. Felton, *117 S.Ct. 1997 (1997)*, Harvard Journal of Law and Public Policy 21 (1998): 861–879.
Whitehead, Daniel P., *Note:* Agostini v. Felton: *Rectifying the Chaos of Establishment Clause Jurisprudence*, Capital University Law Review 27 (1999): 639–666.

Cases and Statutes Cited

Agostini v. Felton, 521 U.S. 203 (1997)
Lemon v. Kurtzman, 403 U.S. 602 (1971)
School District of Grand Rapids v. Ball, 473 U.S. 373 (1985)

See also **Burger, Warren E.; Establishment Clause (I): History, Background, Framing;** *Lemon* **Test; State Aid to Religious Schools**

AIRPORT SEARCHES

Airplane piracy increased in occurrence and success in the 1960s, leading to the creation of a 1968 task force that developed a hijacker detection and deterrence system. The system included severe penalties for air piracy, notices to passengers of the possibility of a preboarding search, the use of a hijacker profile to identify "selectees" for further investigation, magnetometer searches, interviews with selected passengers, and frisks or searches of suspected passengers. As the program was originally crafted, passengers who triggered the magnetometer were only searched if they also were selected under the profile and could not provide sufficient identification. As a result of the government's role in requiring the search and specifying its nature, courts concluded that airport searches, even when performed by privately employed guards, are subject to the Fourth Amendment. In *United States v. Lopez*, 328 F. Supp. 1077 (E.D.N.Y. 1971), a court relied upon the then recently decided opinion in *Terry v. Ohio*, 392 U.S. 1 (1968), to deem these initial passenger searches reasonable.

In 1973, the government expanded air piracy prevention efforts by requiring electronic screening of all passengers and their carry-on items. Passengers were subject to heightened screening if they exhibited suspicious behavior or triggered the magnetometer. While subject to the Fourth Amendment, the screening did not require a warrant on account of the extreme risk presented by passengers with weapons; because advanced warning of the search was given; because the search applied to all passengers and generally lacked stigma; and because the search occurred before other passengers and airline employees, thus reducing the risk of police wrongdoing. In *United States v. Davis*, 483 F.2d 893 (9th Cir. 1973), a court determined that the new scheme was reasonable and fell under the administrative search exception to the Fourth Amendment, provided that an individual could avoid the screening by not boarding the plane. Furthermore, the screening would be unreasonable if the administrative purpose of preventing air piracy was "distorted" by other general law-enforcement objectives, such as drug interdiction or searches for large amounts of currency.

Outside the boarding context, law enforcement agents accost individuals for an investigatory stop based on "drug courier" profiling. Such profiles alone do not grant police justification to engage in an investigatory stop. However, critics have argued that the courts have effectively allowed the profiles to justify a stop. David Cole, in *No Equal Justice*, argued that the "drug courier profile is a scattershot hodgepodge of traits and characteristics so expansive that it potentially justifies stopping anybody and everybody."

The 9/11 event and the War on Terrorism focused public attention on the need to prevent air piracy, especially because the security regulations in place did not prohibit passenger possession of the box cutters and small knives used to hijack the four planes. Shortly after the attacks, the American Civil Liberties Union changed its 1973 position that the use of magnetometers violated the Fourth Amendment. The Department of Homeland Security assumed responsibility for passenger screening and implemented plans for the Enhanced Computer Assisted Passenger Prescreening System, a program to identify risky passengers, who are then subjected to heightened screening and interviews.

The agency considered a "trusted traveler" system, in which prescreened passengers could avoid the most intense screening. Checked baggage is now matched to passengers and removed from the plane if the passenger fails to board. Additionally, checked baggage is subjected to random electronic and hand searches, and dog sniffs. At times of high terrorism risk as determined by the agency, vehicles approaching airports can be subject to search as well.

CHRIS JAY HOOFNAGLE

References and Further Reading

Airline Passenger Security Screening: New Technologies and Implementation Issues. National Materials Advisory Board, National Academies Press, 1996.

Becton, Charles L., *The Drug Courier Profile: All Seems Infected That Th' Infected Spy, As All Looks Yellow to the Jaundic'd Eye*, N.C.L. Rev. 65 (1987): 417.

Brill, Steven. *After, the Rebuilding and Defending of America in the September 12 Era.* New York: Simon & Schuster, 2003.

Cole, David. *No Equal Justice, Race and Class in the American Criminal Justice System.* New York: The New Press, 1999.

LaFave, Wayne R. *Search and Seizure, a Treatise on the Fourth Amendment*, 3rd ed. St. Paul, MN: West Group 1996.

United States v. Davis, 482 F.2d 893 (9th Cir. Cal. 1973).

United States v. Lopez, 328 F. Supp. 1077 (E.D.N.Y. 1971).

Cases and Statutes Cited

United States v. Davis, 483 F.2d 893 (9th Cir. 1973) (Government's role in airport searches is dominant, subjecting such searches to the Fourth Amendment.)

United States v. Lopez, 328 F. Supp. 1077 (E.D.N.Y. 1971) (Initial passenger screening system is valid until *Terry* standard.)

See also **Administrative Searches and Seizures; American Civil Liberties Union; Department of Homeland Security; Electronic Surveillance, Technological Monitoring and Dog Sniff; 9/11 and the War on Terrorism; Profiling (including DWB); Right to Travel; Search (General Definition);** *Terry v. Ohio*, **392 U.S. 1 (1968); Warrantless Searches**

AKRON v. AKRON CENTER FOR REPRODUCTIVE HEALTH, 462 U.S. 416 (1983)

After the 1973 decision of *Roe v. Wade*, 410 U.S. 113 (1973), a myriad of legislative responses to *Roe* held that the right of privacy encompasses a woman's right to decide whether to terminate her pregnancy. In these responses the states were attempting to determine which restrictions on and regulations of abortion were constitutionally valid. A February 1978 abortion ordinance passed by the city of Akron, Ohio, was part of this wave of legislative responses. The ordinance contained seventeen provisions, five of which were at issue in *Akron v. Akron Center for Reproductive Health*. The Court, with three justices dissenting, found that all five of the provisions at issue were unconstitutional. In doing so the Court reiterated that a woman's right to an abortion is not unqualified; however, restrictive state regulations of a woman's right to choose must be supported by a compelling state interest.

The first provision of the ordinance that the Court addressed provided that abortions performed after the first trimester of pregnancy must be performed in a hospital. In finding the provision to be unconstitutional, the Court reaffirmed *Roe*'s recognition of the state's interest in a woman's health. Thus, at the end of the second trimester, the state may regulate the abortion procedure if the regulation reasonably relates to the preservation and protection of maternal health. In this case, however, the hospital requirement imposed a heavy and unnecessary burden on a woman's access to an abortion; thus, the city failed to demonstrate a compelling interest.

The requirement was heavy because an abortion at a hospital would cost twice as much as at a clinic and because the woman might need to travel to find a hospital that would perform the abortion. The requirement was unnecessary because current medical knowledge indicates that second trimester abortions have become substantially safer. Furthermore, medical evidence indicates that second trimester abortions can be performed safely in outpatient clinics.

The second provision of concern to the Court was that a physician must obtain the informed written consent of one of the parents of a minor below the age of fifteen. In reviewing this provision, the Court acknowledged that the state has an interest in encouraging parental involvement in their minor child's decision to have an abortion. However, it found the consent provision in the ordinance to be unconstitutional because, contrary to the Court's holding in *Bellotti v. Baird* (*Bellotti II*, 443 U.S. 622, 1979), the ordinance did not create any procedures for allowing a minor to avoid the consent requirement.

The third provision required an attending physician to make certain specified statements to the patient and/or her parent (if parental consent was required) to ensure that the consent for the abortion was truly informed. In considering this provision, the Court reaffirmed its previous holding in *Planned Parenthood of Central Mo. v. Danforth*, 428 U.S. 52 (1976), that a state could constitutionally require a woman to certify in writing her consent to the abortion and that her consent is informed and freely given. However, the Court found that it was the responsibility of the patient's physician to ensure that appropriate information was relayed to enable her to give informed consent. The state may not decide what information a woman must be given before she chooses to have an abortion. Furthermore, much of the information required to be given by the Akron ordinance was not designed to inform the woman, but rather to persuade her to carry the fetus to term.

In the fourth provision, a twenty-four-hour waiting period was mandated between the signing of the consent form and the performance of the abortion. The Court found that Akron failed to demonstrate that any legitimate state interest was furthered by an arbitrary and inflexible waiting period. There was no evidence that a waiting period would allow the abortion to be performed more safely or that the state's interest in the woman giving informed consent was reasonably served by the delay.

Finally, the fifth provision required that the fetal remains be disposed of in a humane and sanitary manner. The city of Akron contended that it enacted the provision to prevent the dumping of aborted fetuses on garbage piles. However, the Court found that there was uncertainty as to whether the provision had such limited intent. It was possible to interpret the statute as requiring that a decent burial be given to an embryo. The Court found that this uncertainty caused the provision to violate the due process clause in that the provision failed to give the physician the required fair notice as to what conduct was prohibited.

Although *Akron* answered a number of questions regarding the type of abortion regulations that a state could enact, it left a number of questions unanswered that would be the subject of subsequent abortion litigation.

JANET W. STEVERSON

Cases and Statutes Cited

Bellotti v. Baird, 443 U.S. 622 (1979)
Planned Parenthood of Central Mo. v. Danforth, 428 U.S. 52 (1976)
Roe v. Wade, 410 U.S. 113 (1973)

See also **Abortion;** *Planned Parenthood of Missouri v. Danforth*, **428 U.S. 52 (1976);** **Reproductive Freedom;** *Roe v. Wade*, **410 U.S. 113 (1973)**

ALCORTA v. TEXAS, 355 U.S. 28 (1957)

In *Alcorta*, the Supreme Court held that the Fourteenth Amendment due process clause bars prosecutors from knowingly presenting perjured testimony in a criminal case.

Alcorta stabbed his wife to death after finding her in a parked car with another man, Castilleja. Charged with murder, Alcorta claimed that he should be convicted of a lesser offense because he acted in the heat of passion after seeing his wife kissing Castilleja. At Alcorta's trial, Castilleja testified that his relationship with Alcorta's wife was nothing more than a casual friendship, and Alcorta was convicted of murder. After the conviction, however, Castilleja admitted that he had been engaged in a sexual relationship with Alcorta's wife and that the prosecutor had told him not to volunteer any information about that sexual relationship.

After the state courts refused to order a new trial, Alcorta appealed to the U.S. Supreme Court, which unanimously reversed. The Court observed that Castilleja's testimony gave the false impression that his relationship with Alcorta's wife was mere friendship and thereby refuted Alcorta's claim that he acted passionately after seeing his wife kissing Castilleja. Since the prosecutor knew Castilleja's testimony was false, the Court concluded that Alcorta had been denied due process. The Court's emphasis on the prosecutor's duty to avoid presenting perjured testimony, later clarified and expanded in *Napue v. Illinois*, 360 U.S. 264 (1959), laid the groundwork for later cases, such as *Brady v. Maryland*, 373 U.S. 83 (1963), and *Kyles v. Whitley*, 514 U.S. 419 (1995), which required the prosecution to disclose evidence favorable to the defendant.

DAVID A. MORAN

References and Further Reading

Imwinkelried, Edwin, and Norman Garland. *Exculpatory Evidence*, 2nd ed. Charlottesville, VA: Michie Publications, 1996.
Stacy, Tom, *The Search for Truth in Constitutional Criminal Procedure*, Columbia Law Review 91 (1991): 1369.

Cases and Statutes Cited

Brady v. Maryland, 373 U.S. 83 (1963)
Kyles v. Whitley, 514 U.S. 419 (1995)
Napue v. Illinois, 360 U.S. 264 (1959)

See also **Brady v. Maryland, 373 U.S. 83 (1963); Due Process; Fourteenth Amendment;** *Kyles v. Whitley*, **514 U.S. 419 (1995);** *Napue v. Illinois*, **360 U.S. 264 (1959)**

ALIEN AND SEDITION ACTS (1798)

Sedition may be defined as any illegal action tending to cause the disruption or overthrow of the government. In the Anglo-Saxon legal tradition, the concept of seditious libel (libel generally meaning any statement injurious of reputation) goes back to 1275, when an English statute outlawed *falsehoods* creating discord between the king and the people. By the early seventeenth century, English courts began to hold that even *true* libels could be criminally punished, since the truth of injurious statements made it much more difficult for the government to undo their harm. It became something of a maxim of English law that "the greater the truth the greater the libel."

Such statements are particularly troubling in wartime when the existence of the nation may be threatened, forcing consideration of certain fundamental and enduring questions of civil liberty. Is dissent the equivalent of disloyalty? May national security concerns justify silencing dissent? What if partisans exploit the crisis to suppress legitimate criticism of government? Who will protect valued civil liberties in such turbulent times?

These questions run throughout American history and law. The nation first confronted them in the earliest years of the republic. Abuses of civil liberties occurred, but the more enduring legacy of this troubled period remains one of the great achievements of American constitutionalism.

Background: Faction and Xenophobia

Many of the Founders were suspicious of political parties, finding their "factionalism" contrary to republican government's search for a common interest. By Washington's second term, however, two parties were alive and well; they originated in the positions taken by the main supporters and opponents of the 1787 Constitution: Federalists and Anti-Federalists, respectively.

One group had coalesced around Alexander Hamilton and called themselves Federalists; the other group, led by James Madison and Thomas Jefferson, called themselves Republicans. More telling perhaps is what they called each other: Republicans characterized their opponents as monarchists or Tories, and Federalists saw their opponents as Jacobins (the twentieth century equivalent would be "Bolsheviks") given to "licentiousness" and radical democracy instead of republicanism.

The Federalists generally represented mercantile, shipping, and financial interests, and some at least (most notably Hamilton) could even be characterized

as cryptomonarchists. Republicans distrusted executive power, felt that the people had too little power, and opposed restrictions on the liberty of the press. Federalists took opposite positions, and perhaps nowhere was the contrast more stark than about the question of political opposition. Federalists tended to deny the legitimacy of such opposition, contemptuously described as "faction." The term was Madison's, although by the 1790s Madison had come to believe that the evils of parties could be mitigated—most notably by promoting political equality to prevent any group from exerting influence beyond its numbers.

Perhaps the most significant difference was that Republicans tended to support the French Revolution, while Federalists had become bitterly hostile to it and thoroughly distrustful of France and its growing influence on the continent. Federalists wanted to strengthen ties with England. Republicans, though not unmindful of the dangers posed by France, considered British monarchism a far greater threat to the young republic.

By 1792, the French Revolution had sparked an international war, and the European nations opposing France sought to rid themselves of domestic pro-French elements (as well as any lingering reformers, republicans, or radicals). Many of these refugees fled to the neutral United States. Federalists saw in their ranks the democratic "disorganizers" that Federalists so dreaded.

In 1793, President Washington proclaimed American neutrality between France and England, incurring the wrath of both countries. The Jay Treaty of 1794 calmed Anglo–American relations, but the French only became more belligerent, launching a campaign against American shipping. (Between June 1796 and June 1797, some 316 American ships had been seized.)

The election of 1796 brought the Federalist John Adams to the presidency; Adams narrowly defeated the leader of the Republican Party, Thomas Jefferson (who under the constitutional provision then in effect became vice-president). This first contested presidential election in American history exacerbated already sharp political divisions.

Among the feared immigrants from Europe, none proved more obnoxious to the Adams administration than the Irish. In 1798, Ireland was in revolt against the British, who responded with military repression. Many Irish patriots came to the United States to avoid lengthy prison terms or the hangman. They brought with them considerable political experience and a taste for democracy coupled with a distrust of constituted authority that quickly drew them into the ranks of the Republicans. (In fairness, it should be noted that some of these refugees, particularly the aristocratic immigrants from France, were seen as threatening Republican principles.)

Meanwhile, France had not only repelled a coalition of invaders led by England but also had seized Belgium, the Rhineland, and the Italian peninsula and was threatening to invade England. In America, anti-French sentiment was enflamed by the XYZ Affair, a clumsy attempt by agents of the French foreign minister to solicit a bribe from the United States in return for further negotiations. When the administration allowed the details to be made public, in 1798, Americans were outraged at the gall of the French. Adams, riding a wave of patriotic fervor, placed the country on a war footing without ever asking for a declaration of war. Thus began America's "half war" with France.

The rancor between Federalists and Republicans came to a head in the spring of 1798 when Congress debated the President's proposed defense measures. The arguments, heard for the first time in American history, have recurred in different contexts and with different enemies up to and including the War on Terrorism. The Republicans felt Adams was overreacting to the alleged threat. The Federalists raised the specter of French invasion, abetted by French sympathizers, spies, and enemy aliens who would undermine the country's defenses (marking the first but by no means the last time that American political discourse would center on the fear of internal subversion). Ignoring the line between dissent and treason, the Federalists accused the Republicans of disloyalty or worse.

The charges of the Federalists in Congress were taken up by several of the leading Federalist newspapers, branding the Republicans as "traitors." President Adams lambasted the Republicans for supporting policies that "would sink the glory of our country and prostrate her liberties at the feet of France."

The legislative program that the Federalists would soon enact was undoubtedly meant to respond to the threat of France. But Federalists also hoped that, by becoming the party of American patriotism, they might wound, perhaps mortally, the Republican Party as well.

The Alien Acts

In times of threat from foreign powers, suspicions immediately turn to the foreigners within: resident aliens, especially enemy aliens (natives of the nation that has become the enemy). Well before the "half war," Federalists were convinced that the greatest internal danger the country faced was the wave of

foreigners—especially French, Irish, and German— who had come to America between 1790 and 1798. They were in a sense doubly dangerous: potential traitors and a source of votes for Republicans.

Congress initially attempted to reduce or even end the flow of aliens being admitted to U.S. citizenship and to prevent all foreign-born persons from voting or holding federal office. The proposal was defeated by a two-to-one majority. Ultimately, Congress enacted (though by single-vote margins in House and Senate) the Naturalization Act of June 18, 1798, which extended the period of residence required for naturalization from five years to fourteen—the longest in American history. While immigrants could vote because voter qualifications were set by the states, the Naturalization Act (repealed by the Republicans in 1802) prevented them from holding federal office until they became citizens and discouraged further immigration.

The more extreme Federalists now hoped to enact a law granting sweeping powers to the executive branch to deal with every variety of threats (from actual plots to seditious speech) from aliens and native citizens. But highly effective opposition from Albert Gallatin, a Republican leader in Congress, as well as some doubters within the ranks of the Federalists, led eventually to three separate pieces of legislation.

The Alien Enemies Act of July 6, 1798 gave the President authority—but only in the face of war or invasion—to identify citizens or subjects of a hostile nation residing in the United States and to apprehend, restrain, or remove them according to procedures in the act. This law was never used because open war with France never occurred. The approach embodied in this act has remained a part of American wartime policy to the present and arguably represents a reasonable concern about the potential for enemy aliens to act as spies or saboteurs.

On June 25, 1798, Congress approved the Alien Friends Act. It applied to all aliens, enemy or not, in times of peace or of war. Its provisions allowed the President to expel any non-naturalized foreign-born person judged by the President to be a threat to the "peace and safety" of the United States. This could be done without a hearing and without any statement of the President's reasons. Individuals who did not leave the United States within a specified time period could be imprisoned for up to three years and permanently denied American citizenship. While they were not immediately apparent, there were free speech implications to the act, since, as Geoffrey R. Stone notes in *Perilous Times*, "judgments about a person's 'dangerousness' are often predicated upon his expression, beliefs, and associations." But President Adams interpreted the act extremely narrowly; no one was deported under its provisions and it expired in June 1800.

Inevitably, though, such a fundamental assault on due process rights, right to counsel, and independent judicial review had its effects. Many French immigrants left the country, and few tried to enter. Those who remained (especially French and Irish) went to great pains to avoid public attention, and feelings of paranoia and suspicion were widespread.

Sedition Act: Theory

By far the most notorious piece of legislation introduced by the Federalists was the Sedition Act of July 14, 1798. The law made it a crime to utter or publish "any false, scandalous, and malicious writing or writings against the Government of the United States, or either House of the Congress . . . with intent to defame . . . or to bring them . . . into contempt or disrepute . . . ." Punishment was a fine (up to $2000—the 2004 equivalent of $30,000) and prison up to two years. (The blatantly political motivation behind this legislation is well illustrated by the fact that the vice-president, the Republican Thomas Jefferson, was not included in the act's coverage.)

The Sedition Act of 1798 is widely considered the first great clash between political liberties and the needs of national security in American history. Yet, as early as 1794 the Federalists had made a concerted effort to question the legitimacy of political criticism of the government by attacking the Democratic–Republican societies, groups of voluntary associations sharply critical of Federalist policy. From the Federalist perspective, these societies were illegitimate because their speech tended to foment insurrection and to undermine representative government. The Republicans, of course, insisted on the right of private citizens to organize and to criticize the actions of elected officials.

These same lines of debate surfaced in 1798, but now the Federalists were determined to pass legislation and to prosecute its violators. Given Federalist control of both houses of Congress and the presidency, even the strongest Republican arguments proved unavailing.

There is value in exploring the theoretical underpinnings of the arguments both sides presented in Congress and in the press, especially since the Federalists arguments were ultimately rejected wholeheartedly by the public and our political and legal process. The enactment of the Sedition Act, and subsequent prosecutions (discussed in the next section), proved a

Pyrrhic victory indeed and constituted a major factor in the decisive electoral defeat of the Federalists in the election of 1800.

While there were certainly public policy reasons for supporting or opposing the Sedition Act, much of the discussion centered on two essential constitutional issues:

How could a government of enumerated powers enact a law touching on seditious speech, given the absence of any such power in the text of the Constitution and what would appear to be a specific prohibition on such a law, that is, the First Amendment?

Was the law an infringement on the powers of the states, given that libel laws had traditionally been considered the exclusive concern of states and thus reserved to them by implication and by the specific text of the Tenth Amendment?

With respect to the first question, the Federalists argued that such a power in the national government could be inferred as a matter of self-preservation. All governments have a right to protect themselves from activities that might lead to their destruction. As far as the First Amendment went, the Federalists in turn argued that it did not go very far. They echoed an interpretation of English law given by William Blackstone, who argued that in England freedom of the press meant freedom from prior restraints (in essence, no governmental censorship prior to publication), but not freedom from punishment if the speech or publication proved to be criminal. For the Federalists, the First Amendment did not overturn English common law.

Instead, Republicans began to expand upon a crucial insight—the indispensability of free expression to the political process, especially one that saw governors as the servants of the people and thus subject to the people's scrutiny and criticism. To the Federalists, this was dangerous Jacobinism and mob rule undermining the policies of the enlightened ruling elite.

On the issue of state vs. federal power over sedition, the most famous statement of the Republican position came not in the congressional debates but in the Kentucky and Virginia Resolutions (drafted secretly by Thomas Jefferson and James Madison) passed by those state legislatures in the fall of 1798. The resolutions' essential argument was that the Constitution is a compact entered into by sovereign states. The federal government was limited to certain enumerated powers, and if the federal government exceeded its powers, states retained authority to protect their rights by declaring the federal action void and unenforceable. Here, the federal government had clearly exceeded its powers, since there is no enumerated power over seditious speech; there is, instead, a clear prohibition on such legislation—the First Amendment.

Sedition Act: Practice

The enmity and rancor that marked these debates continued in the prosecutions brought under the Sedition Act. The role of Grand Inquisitor was assumed by Secretary of State Thomas Pickering, one of the most extreme of the Federalists.

Seventeen indictments for seditious libel were issued; all but three were under the Sedition Act and the remaining ones were based on the common law. Pickering led the charge, mindful of the upcoming presidential election of 1800 and determined to muzzle the leading Republican newspapers. He brought charges against four of the five most important Republican newspapers as well as some lesser ones. Because of these prosecutions, two newspapers closed forever and others were forced to suspend publication until their editors were released from jail.

In the period from July 1798 until the act expired (on March 3, 1801—the last day of the Adams administration), twenty-five prominent Republicans were arrested under the act; fifteen of these arrests led to indictments and ten cases went to trial. Each resulted in a conviction. Several of the trials were presided over by Supreme Court Justice Samuel Chase (in his capacity as circuit judge) with a degree of partisan judicial improprieties not seen before in an American court and referred to as "Chase's Bloody Circuit." Other Federalist judges were almost as bad.

In November 1799, Adams sent a peace mission to Paris and gradually America's fear of Jacobinism began to dissipate. In the 1800 election, Jefferson won seventy-three electoral votes and Adams sixty-five. Republicans took control of the House by a margin of sixty-five to forty-one. The death knell of the Federalist Party was being sounded. Indeed, Republicans would dominate national politics for the next quarter-century.

In one of his first official acts as president, Jefferson pardoned all those who had been convicted under the Sedition Act and ordered the release of those still in jail, commenting, as quoted by Geoffrey R. Stone, that in his view the Sedition Act was a "nullity as absolute and as palpable as if Congress had ordered us to fall down and worship a golden image."

On July 4, 1840, Congress ordered the repayment, with interest, of all fines paid under the Sedition Act. The congressional committee report in favor of the repayment legislation said that the act was an ill-judged exercise of power, was null and void, and that its unconstitutionality had been "conclusively settled."

Lessons and Legacy

Public opinion, the "revolution of 1800" (as Jefferson described that election), the judgment of history, and the evolution of First Amendment law all contributed to the conclusive settlement of the unconstitutionality of the Sedition Act. In its landmark 1964 decision, *New York Times Co. v. Sullivan*, 376 U.S. 254 (1964), the Supreme Court for the first time in the country's history held public officials to First Amendment standards when they brought libel actions against critics of their official conduct. In the course of his opinion for the Court, Justice William J. Brennan spoke of a "profound national commitment to the principle that debate on public issues should be uninhibited, robust, and wide-open" and that such debate might include "vehement, caustic, and sometimes unpleasantly sharp attacks on government and public officials." He described the Sedition Act and the controversy it aroused as "first crystalliz[ing] a national awareness of the central meaning of the First Amendment." He noted that the Sedition Act had never been tested in the Supreme Court, but that "the court of history" clearly found it wanting.

In defending the act, Federalists celebrated it as an improvement over the English law of seditious libel because, unlike in England, the American version made malicious intent an essential element of the crime, made truth of the libel a defense, and provided that the jury rather than the judge determine an utterance's seditious tendency. Republicans found little consolation in these "liberalizing" elements, foreseeing (correctly) that juries would reflect popular hysteria even more than judges and that most of the statements prosecuted under the act would involve opinions rather than provable facts. The notion of a false political opinion is profoundly inconsistent with the First Amendment, and in 1974 in *Gertz v. Robert Welch, Inc.*, 418 U.S. 323 (1974), the Supreme Court agreed: "under the First Amendment there is no such thing as a false idea."

Political debate must indeed be vigorous, caustic, and spirited. Dissent about government policies is not the same as disloyalty. Punishing allegedly false political opinions is fundamentally incompatible with the First Amendment. These lessons of America's initial experience with seditious libel prosecutions were eloquently articulated by Jefferson in his 1801 inaugural address:

Every difference of opinion is not a difference of principle.... We are all republicans—we are all federalists.... If there be any among us who would wish to dissolve this Union or to change its republican form, let them stand undisturbed as monuments of the safety with which error of opinion may be tolerated where reason is left free to combat it.

PHILIP A. DYNIA

References and Further Reading

Chesney, Robert M., *Democratic–Republican Societies, Subversion, and the Limits of Legitimate Political Dissent in the Early Republic*, North Carolina Law Review 82 (June 2004): 1525–1579.

Curtis, Michael Kent. *Free Speech, "The People's Darling Privilege."* Durham, NC: Duke University Press, 2000.

Elkins, Stanley, and Eric McKitrick. *The Age of Federalism.* New York: Oxford University Press, 1993.

Smith, James Morton. *Freedom's Fetters.* Ithaca, NY: Cornell University Press, 1956.

Stone, Geoffrey R. *Perilous Times: Free Speech in Wartime.* New York: W.W. Norton and Company, 2004.

Cases and Statutes Cited

Gertz v. Robert Welch, Inc, 418 U.S. 323 (1974)

New York Times Co. v. Sullivan, 376 U.S. 254 (1964)

Alien Enemies Act, Act of July 6, 1798, 1 Stat 577 (1798)

Alien Friends Act, Act of June 25, 1798, 1 Stat. 570 (1798)

Naturalization Act, Act of June 18, 1798, 1 Stat. 566 (1798)

Sedition Act, Act of July 14, 1798, 1 Stat. 596 (1798)

See also **Aliens, Civil Liberties of; Bache, Benjamin Franklin; Blackstone and Common-Law Prohibition on Prior Restraints; Due Process in Immigration; Franklin, Benjamin; Freedom of Speech and Press: Nineteenth Century; Freedom of Speech and Press under the Constitution: Early History (1791–1917); Non-U.S. Citizens Civil Liberties; Philosophy and Theory of Freedom of Expression; Ratification Debate, Civil Liberties in; Theories of Civil Liberties; Zenger Trial (1735)**

ALIENS, CIVIL LIBERTIES OF

The extent to which the Constitution's Bill of Rights and other political freedoms are enjoyed by noncitizens is a question that has existed since the founding of the United States. Even prior to the ratification of the Bill of Rights, the Constitution's text distinguished between citizens of the United States and noncitizens, suggesting that the framers intended differential treatment between the groups, at the very least when it limited several federal offices to citizens. Arguably, the two most important differences wrought by citizenship status are the inability of noncitizens to vote and the fact that noncitizens are subject to exclusion and deportation.

Limits on other civil rights—such as the freedom of speech and the free exercise of religion—can be best understood by appreciating the limits on the voting rights of, and the exclusive application of immigration laws to, noncitizens. First, because noncitizens do not enjoy the right to vote, they rely upon citizens to protect their political interests, thereby limiting their ability to secure their rights. Second, because noncitizens are subject to exclusion and deportation under immigration law, their ability to exercise their civil rights in the United States may effectively be denied by removing them to their home countries. Finally, it should be noted that within the group of noncitizens, American constitutional and statutory law generally affords greater liberty and protection to lawful long-term residents than to temporary visitors or undocumented migrants.

The debate over the citizen–noncitizen divide with respect to civil liberties focuses on balancing the desire to preserve the exclusivity of citizenship as a status that ensures a person's full membership in a polity against the recognition that noncitizens are human beings deserving of a basic level of dignity and liberty. The nation's first test of the divide came with the passage of the Alien and Sedition Act of 1798. Because it permitted the president exclusive power to deport suspicious noncitizens without being subject to judicial oversight, the act pitted those committed to ensuring that noncitizens be provided the same due-process protections afforded citizens against those who believed the Constitution was created solely for the benefit of U.S. citizens.

On the one hand, Thomas Jefferson, James Madison, and other Democratic–Republicans saw the act as unconstitutionally depriving noncitizens due process of law by failing to subject their executive deportations to procedural check. On the other, Hamiltonian Federalists argued that foreign nationals were not parties to the Constitution, were not its beneficiaries, and therefore could claim no rights under it. In *Chae Chan Ping v. United States*, 130 U.S. 581 (1889), the Supreme Court sided with the Federalists by recognizing the plenary power of the federal political branches over immigration and noncitizens, citing a nation's decision to deny entry to a noncitizen as incident to its sovereignty.

Analogously, current Supreme Court jurisprudence recognizes few constitutional due-process and equal-protection limits to federal immigration power, but generally places strict restrictions on the states' powers to discriminate against noncitizens residing in the United States. Over time, the Supreme Court has reaffirmed Congress's plenary power over immigration decisions to exclude or deport noncitizens, but has also stated that noncitizens legally within the United States were entitled to a rational-basis review of federal legislation that draws alienage distinctions. Because states do not possess Congress's plenary power over immigration law, in contrast, the Court has subjected state laws that discriminate against noncitizens to strict review. The Constitution's Article VI supremacy clause also provides textual support for the idea that where the federal government has chosen to regulate a field exclusively, as it has with immigration law, then contrary state laws are preempted by the federal, rendering the former unconstitutional.

Thus, while in *Mathews v. Diaz*, 426 U.S. 67 (1976), the Court upheld a federal law limiting the grant of Medicaid benefits only to certain noncitizens, in *Graham v. Richardson*, 403 U.S. 65 (1971), the Court struck down state laws limiting public benefits to certain individuals based on citizenship. The Court's protection of noncitizens against state discrimination has extended to undocumented immigrants. In *Plyler v. Doe*, 457 U.S. 202 (1982), the Court struck down a Texas law that denied free public education to the children of undocumented migrants. The sole exception that the Court has recognized is that a state may limit certain occupations to U.S. citizens when the jobs involved go to the heart of democratic government, as in the case of state troopers (*Foley v. Connelie*, 435 U.S. 291, 1978) and public school teachers (*Ambach v. Norwich*, 441 U.S. 68, 1979).

Aside from protecting foreign nationals by employing this federal–state divide in its constitutional alienage jurisprudence, the Court has sometimes chosen to avoid interpreting the constitutionality of a federal immigration act altogether, presumably because it believes its hands are tied by the plenary power or preemption doctrines. Instead, the Court has relied on liberal interpretations of ostensibly anti-immigrant legislation, choosing to uphold and affirm the foreigner's humanity through the approval of the legislation at issue.

Thus, in *Woodby v. Immigration and Naturalization Service*, 385 U.S. 276 (1966), the Court held that the government must prove a noncitizen's deportability subject to a "clear, unequivocal, and convincing evidence" standard, which is more stringent than the "preponderance of the evidence" norm generally used in civil cases, of which deportation proceedings are a kind. Although not based on its interpretation of the Constitution, the *Woodby* court's embrace of a standard more protective of noncitizen rights suggests that the judiciary's willingness to cross Congress's constitutionally approved plenary power over noncitizens and immigration when the Court believes some

fundamental personhood norm might be violated, even if the challenged statute's language might suggest a stricter reading.

VICTOR C. ROMERO

References and Further Reading

Cole, David. *Enemy Aliens: Double Standards and Constitutional Freedoms in the War on Terrorism.* New York: New Press, 2003.
Johnson, Kevin R. *The "Huddled Masses" Myth: Immigration and Civil Rights.* Philadelphia: Temple University Press, 2004.
Motomura, Hiroshi, *Immigration Law After a Century of Plenary Power: Phantom Constitutional Norms and Statutory Interpretation*, Yale Law Journal 100 (1990): 545–613.
Neuman, Gerald L. *Strangers to the Constitution: Immigrants, Borders, and Fundamental Law.* Princeton, NJ: Princeton University Press, 1996.

Cases and Statutes Cited

Ambach v. Norwick, 441 U.S. 68 (1979)
Chae Chan Ping v. United States, 130 U.S. 581 (1889)
Foley v. Connelie, 435 U.S. 291 (1978)
Graham v. Richardson, 403 U.S. 65 (1971)
Mathews v. Diaz, 426 U.S. 67 (1976)
Plyler v. Doe, 457 U.S. 202 (1982)
Woodby v. Immigration and Naturalization Service, 385 U.S. 276 (1966)

See also **Citizenship; Equal Protection of Law (XIV)**

COUNTY OF ALLEGHENY v. ACLU, 492 U.S. 573 (1989)

In the mid-1980s, the Supreme Court first considered the constitutionality of religious holiday displays in *Lynch v. Donnelly*, 465 U.S. 668 (1984), involving a city's display of a nativity scene among other symbols of the Christmas holiday. There, a sharply divided Court upheld the display, concluding that the nativity scene, when accompanied by other, secular holiday symbols, had neither the purpose nor the effect of advancing religion and did not amount to an excessive entanglement between government and religion. Justice Sandra Day O'Connor concurred separately, suggesting that the appropriate inquiry was whether the city's action had the purpose or effect of endorsing religion. Unconstitutional endorsements of religion, according to her analysis, sent messages to those not adhering to the favored religion that they were outsiders and less than full members of the political community. In a series of concurrences in establishment clause cases following *Lynch*, O'Connor continued to argue for use of the no-endorsement test. *County of Allegheny* is significant because it was the first case in which an opinion for the Court articulated a decision in terms of O'Connor's test.

In *County of Allegheny v. ACLU*, the Court revisited the issue of religious holiday displays. The case presented the Court with two different displays. The first display included a nativity scene bearing a banner proclaiming "Gloria in Excelsis Deo!" located on the grand staircase of a county courthouse. The display was surrounded by a fence, with poinsettias eventually placed in front of the fence and small evergreen trees, with red bows, stationed at the ends of the fence. A small sign informed observers that the display had been donated by a Roman Catholic organization.

Announcing the judgment of the Court, Justice Harry Blackmun, applying the no-endorsement test, concluded that the display of the nativity scene was unconstitutional since it had the effect of endorsing religion. Blackmun noted that, unlike the nativity scene in *Lynch*, the nativity scene in the courthouse was not accompanied by other holiday emblems or symbols that might have detracted from the religious message of the scene. The poinsettias and small evergreens did not have this effect. Accordingly, he concluded, the effect of this display was one of endorsing the Christian message associated with the nativity scene.

The second display consisted of a 45-foot high Christmas tree outside one of Pittsburgh's public buildings, at the foot of which was a sign with the mayor's name titled "Salute to Liberty." Under the title the sign contained a holiday message saluting liberty and reminding observers of their "legacy of freedom." An 18-foot menorah, a symbol of the Jewish holiday Chanukah, stood beside the Christmas tree. Justice Blackmun concluded that this display did not violate the establishment clause, since its multiple symbols—partially Christian, partially Jewish, and partially secular—did not collectively convey an endorsement of Christianity and Judaism, but simply recognition of cultural diversity. Justice O'Connor concurred with both results.

Justice Kennedy, joined by Chief Justice Rehnquist and Justices White and Scalia, partially dissenting and partially concurring, concluded that both displays were constitutional. He argued that the Establishment Clause permitted "some latitude in recognizing and accommodating the central role religion plays in our society" and that a contrary view would amount to "latent hostility" toward religion. Justice Kennedy's opinion suggested an attempt to pose a new framework for understanding the essential prohibition of the establishment clause in terms only of a bar against government action coercive of religious belief or practice and action with the tendency of establishing a state religion. Justice Kennedy again emphasized the issue of coercion in *Lee v. Weisman*, 505 U.S. 577 (1992), where, writing for the Court's majority, he explained why prayers offered at a middle-school graduation ceremony violated the establishment clause.

But the notion that coercion must be a defining characteristic of establishment violations has failed to find the support of a majority of the Court. Justices Brennan and Stevens filed opinions partially concurring and partially dissenting from the judgment in the case. They, along with Justice Marshall, who joined their respective opinions, would have held both displays unconstitutional.

In terms of specific results, *County of Allegheny* reinforced the view of many observers after *Lynch v. Donnelly* that the Court had implicitly embraced what is sometimes referred to as the "reindeer rule." By this it was understood that nativity scenes would survive constitutional challenge so long as they were accompanied by secular symbols of the Christmas holiday, such as reindeer. In practice, the constitutionality of government-sponsored religious symbols has tended to turn on whether these symbols are part of a larger context that includes secular symbols as well. This judicial approach is a clear retreat from the "wall of separation" rhetoric of the Court's earlier establishment clause cases in favor of an emphasis on norms of equality. The possibility of a court finding an endorsement of religion declines as particular religious symbols take their place among other symbols.

This trend in the Court's treatment of religious symbols parallels its treatment of religious speakers during the same period. During the last two decades of the twentieth century, the Court repeatedly considered whether religious speakers were entitled to equal access to various public forums on terms comparable to those enjoyed by other speakers. The Court generally concluded that they did and, in so doing, rejected views of the establishment clause that would have denied this access as an impermissible aid to religion or as amounting to an unconstitutional breach in the wall separating government and religion. So long as religious speakers took their place in contexts with other speakers, the establishment clause did not forbid their speech and the free speech clause required that this speech be protected.

As to the Court's establishment clause jurisprudence, it appeared at the time that *County of Allegheny* might have represented a triumph of Justice O'Connor's no-endorsement test over the three-part *Lemon* test (*Lemon v. Kurtzman*, 403 U.S. 602, 1971). The case was the first in which an opinion for the Court had relied on the no-endorsement test. Subsequent cases, however, suggested that Justice O'Connor's test serves merely to supplement rather than to replace the *Lemon* test. The Court continues to examine government actions in terms of whether they have the purpose or effect of advancing religion.

TIMOTHY L. HALL

References and Further Reading

Feldman, Stephen M. *Please Don't Wish Me a Merry Christmas: A Critical History of the Separation of Church and State.* New York: New York University Press, 1997, 239–242.

Karst, Kenneth L., *Justice O'Connor and the Substance of Equal Citizenship*, Supreme Court Review 55 (2003): 357–458.

Levy, Leonard W. *The Establishment Clause: Religion and the First Amendment*, 2nd rev. ed. Chapel Hill: The University of North Carolina Press, 1994, 206–212.

Nowak, John E., and Ronald D. Rotunda. *Constitutional Law*, 7th ed. St. Paul, MN: Thompson-West, 2004, 1422–1427.

Shiffren, Steven H., *The Pluralistic Foundations of the Religion Clauses*, Cornell Law Review 90 (2004): 34–38.

Cases and Statutes Cited

Lee v. Weisman, 505 U.S. 577 (1992)
Lemon v. Kurtzman, 403 U.S. 602 (1971)
Lynch v. Donnelly, 465 U.S. 668 (1984)

See also **Lemon** Test; **Lynch v. Donnelly, 465 US 668 (1984)**; Religion in "Public Square" Debate

ALLEN v. ILLINOIS, 478 U.S. 364 (1986)

The *Allen* Court decided the issue of whether proceedings under the Illinois Sexually Dangerous Persons Act are "criminal," such that they open the door to the Fifth Amendment's protection against self-incrimination.

Allen began when the Circuit Court charged Allen with the crimes of unlawful restraint and deviate sexual assault. The State of Illinois filed a petition to have him declared a sexually dangerous person under the Illinois Dangerous Persons Act. Pursuant to the act, the Court ordered Allen to undergo two psychological evaluations. During trial, the state presented testimony about the evaluation results. Allen objected, claiming that the state elicited information from him in violation of his Fifth Amendment privilege against self-incrimination. The Court determined that Allen was a sexually dangerous person under the act.

The U.S. Supreme Court affirmed the ruling of the Illinois Supreme Court. Both courts held that the Fifth Amendment privilege was not available in sexually dangerous person proceedings because those proceedings are civil in nature and Fifth Amendment protections extend only to criminal proceedings.

However, Allen's statements to the court-ordered psychological evaluator could not be used against him in any subsequent criminal proceeding.

In examining the issue, the Court determined that the act was civil in nature because its goal was to provide treatment, not punishment, to persons whom the Court found to be "sexually dangerous." The act failed to promote retribution or deterrence, the traditional aims of punishment, and its text clearly stated that it was to be a civil act.

Illinois restricted the scope of the act by requiring the state to file criminal charges against a person before the state could file a petition asking the Court to determine whether that person was sexually dangerous. The limitation of the scope of the act to persons with criminal charges, rather than the mentally ill population at large, did not transform the civil proceeding into a criminal one. Strict procedural safeguards failed to alter the nature of the proceedings, as did the commitment of sexually dangerous persons to a maximum-security institution also housing convicts in need of psychological care. Involuntary commitment alone did not trigger criminal procedure protections, as noted in *Addington v. Texas*, 441 U.S. 418 (1979), and the state met its treatment goals by committing sexually dangerous persons to institutions designed to provide psychological care.

The Court found that the Fourteenth Amendment due process clause did not require the application of the Fifth Amendment self-incrimination privilege to be applied to the act because the constitutional purpose of the privilege was not to enhance the reliability of fact-finding determinations. Procedurally, the act satisfied the Court by requiring the state to prove more than just the commission of a sexual assault.

Allen has helped states discover the bounds of mental health proceedings. It guides them in fashioning legislation directed toward mentally ill persons, specifically sexually dangerous persons, and it further defines the scope of the Fifth Amendment privilege against self-incrimination.

ALISON P. RIVCHUN

References and Further Reading

American Bar Association. "Case Law Developments." Mental and Physical Disability Law Reporter 29 (January/February 2005):16–36.

Bilionis, Louis D., *Conservative Reformation, Popularization, and the Lessons of Reading Criminal Justice as Constitutional Law*, UCLA Law Review 52 (April 2005): 979–1060.

Blair, W. Wylie, *The Illinois Sexually Dangerous Persons Act: The Civilly Committed and Their Fifth Amendment Rights, or Lack Thereof*, Southern Illinois University Law Journal 29 (Spring 2005): 461–479.

Weitzel, Travis D., *The Constitutionality of Quasi-Convictions*, Rutgers Law Journal 36 (Spring 2005): 1029–1072.

Cases and Statutes Cited

Addington v. Texas, 441 U.S. 418 (1979)
Estelle v. Smith, 451 U.S. 454 (1981)
French v. Blackburn, 428 F. Supp. 1351 (MDNC 1977)
In re Gault, 387 U.S. 1 (1967)
Kennedy v. Mendoza–Martinez, 372 U.S. 144 (1963)
Lefkowitz v. Turley, 414 U.S. 70 (1973)
Malloy v. Hogan, 378 U.S. 1 (1964)
Mathews v. Eldridge, 424 U.S. 319 (1976)
McCarthy v. Arndstein, 266 U.S. 34 (1924)
Middendorf v. Henry, 425 U.S. 25 (1976)
Minnesota v. Murphy, 465 U.S. 420 (1984)
One Lot Emerald Cut Stones and One Ring v. U.S., 409 U.S. 232 (1972)
People v. English, 31 Ill. 2d 301 (1964)
People v. Nastasio, 19 Ill. 2d 524 (1960)
People v. Pembrock, 62 Ill. 2d 317 (1976)
Rogers v. Richmond, 365 U.S. 534 (1961)
U.S. v. Ward, 448 U.S. 242 (1980)
USCA Const. Amendment 5
725 ILCS 205 (Illinois *Sexually Dangerous Persons Act*)

*See also **In re Gault**, 387 U.S. 1 (1967)*

AMALGAMATED FOOD EMPLOYEES UNION LOCAL 590 v. LOGAN VALLEY PLAZA, 391 U.S. 308 (1968)

The conflict between the First Amendment rights of persons to speak and the rights of private property owners to exclude individuals from their property raises thorny questions at the intersection of state action doctrine and the First Amendment. *Logan Valley* concerned labor picketers who wished to inform the public of the nonunion status of a supermarket located in a large, privately owned shopping center. Accordingly, the Court needed to decide whether private property rights of the shopping center owner to declare picketers as trespassers were superior to any asserted right of the protestors to speak and to inform the public under the First and Fourteenth Amendments to the federal constitution.

The Court found that if the picketing had taken place in front of a supermarket located on the public streets, the picketers would have had a First Amendment right of access. Accordingly, the Court extended its 1946 decision in *Marsh v. Alabama*, 326 U.S. 501 (1946), concerning a company-owned town to declare that private property may under some circumstances be treated as though it were public. The Logan Valley Mall was the functional equivalent of the business block of the town in *Marsh*. Once an owner opened his property generally to the public, the more his

property rights became circumscribed by the Constitution. The difficulty of the issue is illustrated by the fact that the Court would revisit the issue four years later in *Lloyd Corp. v. Tanner*, 407 U.S. 551 (1972), and completely reverse course in *Hudgens v. NLRB*, 424 U.S. 507 (1976).

TODD BROWER

References and Further Reading

Garvey, John H. *What Are Freedoms for?* Cambridge, MA: Harvard University Press, 1996, 242–251.
Tribe, Lawrence H. *American Constitutional Law*, 2nd ed. Minneola, NY: Foundation Press, 1988, 1708–1711.

Cases and Statutes Cited

Hudgens. v. NLRB, 424 U.S. 507 (1976)
Lloyd Corp. v. Tanner, 407 U.S. 551 (1972)
Marsh v. Alabama, 326 U.S. 501 (1946)

*See also **Lloyd Corporation v. Tanner**, 407 U.S. 551 (1972)*

AMBACH v. NORWICK, 441 U.S. 68 (1979)

Interpreting the equal protection clause of the Fourteenth Amendment, the Supreme Court has generally subjected all state and local laws that discriminate on the basis of alienage to the strictest scrutiny, noting that, unlike the federal government, state entities do not have the power to regulate the admission or expulsion of noncitizens. The Court has nonetheless created a "public function" exception whereby the state is allowed to reserve certain occupations for U.S. citizens only if these jobs require their holders to perform functions intimately related to democratic self-governance. Hence, police officers exercise discretionary authority sufficiently connected to the development of state public policy that, in *Foley v. Connelie*, 435 U.S. 291 (1978), the Court upheld state laws precluding noncitizens from such service.

In *Ambach*, the Court extended this exception to uphold New York's bar against certain noncitizens who wished to become public school teachers. Citing the importance of teachers in instilling democratic values and civic virtue among their pupils, the five-person majority held that the state's decision to preclude noncitizens who were eligible but unwilling to apply for U.S. citizenship was rationally related to its goal of promoting democracy. The four dissenters questioned whether proxies for loyalty such as citizenship were rational, especially when applied against otherwise well-qualified teacher applicants. In the end, *Ambach*'s legacy may depend on the extent to which the case is limited to its facts. After all, the New York statute only precluded those who decided not to naturalize, a choice that the majority decided to hold against the noncitizens.

VICTOR C. ROMERO

References and Further Reading

Carrasco, Gilbert Paul, *Congressional Arrogation of Power: Alien Constellation in the Galaxy of Equal Protection*, Boston University Law Review 74 (1994): 591–641.

Scaperlanda, Michael A., *Partial Membership: Aliens and the Constitutional Community*, Iowa Law Review 81 (1996): 707–73.

Cases and Statutes Cited

Foley v. Connelie, 435 U.S. 291 (1978)

AMERICA ONLINE

America Online (AOL), founded in 1985 as Quantum Computer Services and since 2000 part of Time Warner, is one of the world's largest Internet service providers (ISPs). It has been involved in litigation with significant civil liberties implications.

In *Cyber Promotions v. America Online*, 948 F. Supp. 436 (E.D. Pa.1996), a mass-mailer of e-mail advertisements (a spammer) sued AOL for deliberately blocking its messages to AOL subscribers. This, the plaintiff claimed, violated its First Amendment right to have its communications delivered. A federal district court held, however, that a private ISP that is not a state actor may legally block mass-mailed e-mail messages.

The court explained that the plaintiff had not established state action under any of the three established tests: the exclusive public function test (whether the private entity has exercised powers that are traditionally the exclusive prerogative of the state); the state-assisted action test (whether the private entity has acted with the help of or in concert with state officials), or the joint participant test (whether the state has insinuated itself so far into a position of interdependence with the private entity that the state is a joint participant in the challenged activity). Similar results were reached in *Noah v. AOL Time Warner, Inc.*, 261 F. Supp. 2d 532 (E.D. Va. 2003), and *Green v. AOL*, 318 F.3d 465 (3rd Cir. 2003).

In *Zeran v. America Online*, 129 F. 3d 327 (4th Cir. 1997), AOL was sued for defamation by the victim of an Internet prank in which messages posted on an AOL bulletin board advertised T-shirts with tasteless slogans relating to the bombing of the Oklahoma City federal building. Plaintiff Ken Zeran received numerous hostile telephone calls, as well as some death threats, and claimed that AOL delayed unreasonably in removing the offending messages. The Court found that AOL was protected by the Communications Decency Act, which insulates ISPs from liability for information originating with third parties.

AARON SCHWABACH

References and Further Reading

AOL: Who We Are, http://www.corp.aol.com/whoweare/history.shtml#1985, visited August 23, 2005.

Sheridan, David R., *Zeran v. AOL and the Effect of Section 230 of the* Communications Decency Act *Upon Liability for Defamation on the Internet*, Alb. L. Rev. 61 (1997): 147.

Cases and Statutes Cited

Cyber Promotions v. America Online, 948 F. Supp. 436 (E.D. Pa.1996)

Green v. America Online, 318 F.3d 465 (3rd Cir. 2003)

In re America Online, Inc., 168 F.Supp.2d 1359 (S.D. Fla. 2001)

Noah v. AOL Time Warner, Inc., 261 F. Supp. 2d 532 (E.D. Va. 2003)

Zeran v. America Online, Inc., 129 F. 3d 327 (4th Cir. 1997)

Communications Decency Act, 47 U.S.C. sec. 230

See also **Communications Decency Act (1996); Defamation and Free Speech; State Action Doctrine; Threats and Free Speech**

AMERICAN ANTI-SLAVERY SOCIETY

At its inaugural meeting on December 4, 1833, the American Anti-Slavery Society (AASS) declared an unconditional commitment to the immediate abolition of slavery and equal rights for free black men. Loath to engage in violence and political compromise, the new organization was dedicated to "moral suasion" as a vehicle for social change. The American Colonization Society's proposals for the emancipation and resettlement of slaves in Liberia were anathema to the members of the AASS. Led by the Tappan brothers of New York and *Liberator* editor William Lloyd Garrison, the group sought to secure a perpetual place for African Americans within the United States.

In the mid-1830s, the AASS sent a seemingly endless stream of petitions to Congress, calling, most notably, for the abolition of slavery in Washington, D.C. Largely the result of female members' efforts, this campaign eventually provoked the highly controversial "gag rules," which precluded congressional debate regarding slavery until 1844. With the constitutional right to petition Congress in doubt in 1834, the AASS supplemented its petition drive by deluging southern mails with its tracts and periodicals (the *National Anti-Slavery Standard* and the *Liberator*, for example). When the first shipment of literature reached Charleston Harbor on July 29, however, it was promptly deemed "incendiary" and confiscated by the postmaster-general of the city and later destroyed by a mob of angry citizens.

Faced with this patently illegal censorship of the mails, the Jackson administration chose to turn a blind eye rather than challenge slaveholding interests. While the vast majority of white northerners opposed abolition, such repression of AASS reform efforts inspired a good deal of rights-conscious opposition from moderate and conservative northerners. Ultimately, AASS agitation laid bare the federal government's willingness to compromise such civil liberties as freedom of the press and freedom of speech on behalf of minority interests.

By 1840, the AASS faced something of an identity crisis. The role of women in the movement, its responsibility to support reforms aside from abolition, and the merits of political participation were all sources of division that ultimately led to the collapse of the organization and the end of a united national opposition to slavery. While the radical elements in the group remained loyal to Garrison, those who favored a more focused, political approach defected in 1840, forming the American and Foreign Anti-Slavery Organization.

With statements like Wendell Phillips's 1844 *The Constitution, a Proslavery Document*, the Garrisonian wing went on to assume an uncompromisingly disunionist position. It also took up the controversial cause of women's rights during the 1840s. The organization's assiduous agitation on behalf of the oppressed placed civil liberties at the center of public discourse. After its 1840 schism, AASS became the first organization in the United States actively to promote the universality of the principles enshrined in the Declaration of Independence.

JAMES CORBETT DAVID

References and Further Reading

Ericson, David F. *The Debate Over Slavery: Antislavery and Proslavery Liberalism in Antebellum America.* New York: New York University Press, 2000.
Kraditor, Aileen S. *Means and Ends in American Abolitionism: Garrison and His Critics on Strategy and Tactics, 1834–1850.* New York: Pantheon Books, 1969, c. 1967.
Jeffrey, Julie Roy. *The Great Silent Army of Abolitionism: Ordinary Women in the Antislavery Movement.* Chapel Hill: University of North Carolina Press, 1998.
Mayer, Henry. *All on Fire: William Lloyd Garrison and the Abolition of Slavery.* New York: St. Martin's Press, 1998.
Van Broekhoven, Deborah Bingham. "American Anti-Slavery Society." In *Macmillan Encyclopedia of World Slavery*, vol. 1, Paul Finkelman and Joseph C. Miller, eds. New York: Simon & Schuster and Prentice Hall International, 1998, 48.

AMERICAN BOOKSELLERS ASSOCIATION, INC. ET AL. v. HUDNUT, 771 F. 2ND 323 (1985)

The feminist movement in the 1960s and 1970s in the United States and other countries raised anew issues of discrimination and violence against women. In America, Andrea Dworkin and Catherine MacKinnon played critical intellectual and political roles in developing and pressing for a radically new perspective of how to interpret sexually explicit portrayals of women in films, books, or other works. Their ideas ignited heated debates in the United States and Canada as well as in other countries. Their perspective sparked commentary by the media, informed conferences and commission reports, and led to the passage of city ordinances in Minneapolis and Indianapolis. Their ideas also shaped an opinion of the Supreme Court of Canada ruling (*R. v. Butler*, 1 S.C.R. 452, 1992) that Canadian governments could prohibit pornography that harmed or dehumanized women through sexual depictions of their subordination or humiliation.

The Indianapolis ordinance was challenged in federal court by a large coalition of groups that also filed numerous amicus curiae briefs; the legal battle attracted national attention. The ordinance defined "pornography" very differently from how *Miller v. California*, 413 U.S. 15 (1973), identified "obscenity." Pornography, according to the ordinance, was "the graphic sexually explicit subordination of women, whether in pictures or in words" that included one or more of six different forms or portrayals of subordination. The inclusion of any of these depictions or performances in a work was sufficient to prohibit the work; the work as a whole or its artistic or scientific value was not considered. Appeals to prurient interest, patent offensiveness, or standards of the community, the three basic components of the *Miller* test, were ignored. The ordinance prohibited trafficking in pornography as defined by the ordinance, coercing others into pornographic performances, and forcing pornography onto others; anyone injured by someone who saw or read pornography had a right of action against the maker or seller of the pornographic material. *Scienter* or prior knowledge that the material was pornographic was generally not a defense.

The southern district court for Indiana in the Seventh Circuit Court of Appeals declared the ordinance was unconstitutional. A circuit court panel, whose opinion was written by Easterbrook, a Reagan appointee, affirmed the lower court's decision; the request for an *en banc* rehearing was denied. The lower court concluded the ordinance regulated speech and, accordingly, could be justified only by a compelling state interest in reducing sex discrimination, which Indianapolis did not establish. The trial judge ruled the ordinance vague, overbroad, and a prior restraint on speech.

For Easterbrook, the crux of the problem was that, given the ordinance's definition of pornography, it effectively legislated into a law a particular viewpoint: "The ordinance discriminates on the ground of the content of the speech." Depictions of women involved in sexual conduct as equals to men, regardless of the explicitness of the conduct, were lawful while portrayals of women enjoying humiliation or being submissive were unlawful without regard for the work's literary, artistic, or political qualities. "This is thought control," Easterbrook proclaimed. "It establishes an 'approved' view of women . . . Those who espouse the approved view may use sexual images; those who do not, may not."

Even if the premise underlying the ordinance is accepted—namely, that pornography is "an aspect of dominance" and that depictions of subordination tend to perpetuate subordination of women—"this simply demonstrates the power of pornography as speech." Easterbrook suggested various actions the city could take to save parts of the ordinance, but the fundamental problem, blunting these efforts, is that the law's definition of "pornography" is "defective root and branch."

ROY B. FLEMMING

References and Further Reading

Downs, Donald Alexander. *The New Politics of Pornography*. Chicago: University of Chicago Press, 1989.
Lacombe, Dany. *Blue Politics: Pornography and the Law in the Age of Feminism*. Toronto: University of Toronto Press, 1994.
MacKinnon, Catharine A. *In Harm's Way: The Pornography Civil Rights Hearings*. Cambridge, MA: Harvard University Press, 1997.

Cases and Statutes Cited

American Booksellers Association, Inc. et al. v. Hudnut, 771 F. 2nd 323 (1985)
Miller v. California, 413 U.S. 15 (1973)
R. v. Butler, 1 S.C.R. 452 (1992)

AMERICAN CIVIL LIBERTIES UNION

The American Civil Liberties Union (ACLU) is a private nonprofit organization dedicated to the defense of civil liberties. The ACLU defines civil liberties as rights enjoyed by individuals over and against the power of government. The ACLU's agenda of civil liberties issues includes First Amendment rights, including freedom of speech, press and assembly, the free exercise of religion, and a prohibition of a government establishment of religion; equal protection of the laws, including equality for racial and ethnic minorities, women, and other groups that have experienced discrimination; due process of law, including protection against unreasonable searches and seizures and protection against self-incrimination; and the right to privacy, including reproductive rights and the privacy of personal information. In addition, since the 1970s, the ACLU has fought issues related to national security and the war on terrorism that result in violations of civil liberties by the federal government.

The ACLU was founded in New York City in January 1920. It grew out of the National Civil Liberties Bureau (NCLB), which had been created in 1917 to fight the suppression of freedom of speech and other violations of civil liberties during World War I. The NCLB was founded and led by Crystal Eastman and Roger Baldwin, who were political activists opposed to the involvement of the United States in World War I. Health problems soon forced Eastman to withdraw and Baldwin became the leader of the NCLB. Following the war, Baldwin and others in the NCLB felt there was a need for a permanent organization to continue to fight for civil liberties. They created the ACLU with Baldwin as director. In 1920, the ACLU had only about 1,000 members nationwide and membership remained low for several decades.

Roger Baldwin led the organization until his retirement in 1950. Over that thirty-year period he was widely recognized as the principal advocate of civil liberties in the United States. When the ACLU was founded, the political and legal climate of the United States was extremely hostile to the idea of civil liberties. Many people associated the phrase "free speech" with disloyalty and radical political doctrines. There were no Supreme Court decisions or statutes protecting freedom of speech or other civil liberties. In a series of World War I-related cases, the Court ruled that the government could prosecute individuals for speech that posed a "clear and present danger" to society (*Schenk v. United States*, 1919). The clear and present danger test was interpreted very broadly, however, to include virtually any criticism of the government.

Faced with extreme hostility to civil liberties in the courts and in legislatures, the ACLU in its first two decades devoted its efforts primarily to public education. It issued numerous pamphlets and statements about particular controversies and occasionally staged public protests to dramatize a particular issue. During these early years the ACLU's litigation program was very limited. Much of the ACLU's work in its first years was devoted to the rights of working people and labor unions. Courts were very sympathetic to employer requests for injunctions denying workers the right to hold public demonstrations in favor of organizing labor unions.

The first case to bring the ACLU favorable national attention was the so-called "Scopes Monkey Trial" in 1925. The ACLU challenged a Tennessee law outlawing the teaching of evolution in the public schools, representing biology teacher John T. Scopes, who was prosecuted under the law. The July 1925 trial in Dayton, Tennessee, created a sensation, drawing journalists from around the world. Scopes was convicted at trial, but a state appellate court overturned the conviction because the judge erred in imposing the punishment. The state did not retry Scopes, and as a result the issues of constitutional law raised by the case never reached the U.S. Supreme Court. The Scopes case is one of the most famous trials in American history, dramatizing the issues of the freedom to teach unpopular ideas and opposition to government establishment of religion.

The Scopes case was part of the ACLU's long defense of academic freedom. It has fought attempts to have public school teachers and college professors fired because of unpopular ideas and has also fought loyalty oaths for teachers, which were widely used during the cold war period. In the 1960s, the ACLU expanded its work on academic freedom to include the rights of students. This has included the right of students to express unpopular ideas and due process rights for students facing discipline.

The ACLU enjoyed its first significant victories in the Supreme Court in 1931. The Court overturned the conviction of a California women convicted of possessing a red flag (Stromberg v. California, 283 U.S. 359, 1931) and ruled that the First Amendment prohibited prior restraint of newspapers (Near v. Minnesota, 283 U.S. 697, 1931). The Supreme Court did not begin to affirm civil liberties protections to a significant degree until the late 1930s, however. In a famous footnote in the case of U.S. v. Carolene Products, 304 U.S. 144 (1938), the Court declared that its role was to protect political and civil liberties, particularly of powerless people. In response, the ACLU altered its priorities and began to put more emphasis on litigation as a strategy for protecting civil liberties.

With the Supreme Court increasingly sympathetic to civil liberties after 1938, the ACLU exerted an enormous influence over the development of American constitutional law. One historian estimates that the ACLU was involved, directly or indirectly, in 80 percent of all recognized landmark civil liberties cases decided by the U.S. Supreme Court in the twentieth century. The ACLU initially confined its role to filing amicus ("friend of the court") briefs in court cases, addressing only the civil liberties issues involved in a case. In the 1960s, it began providing direct legal representation to its clients, handling cases at the initial trial level.

The ACLU's basic principle on free speech is that the First Amendment prohibits any restrictions on expression based on the content of the ideas expressed. Consequently, the organization has consistently defended the free-speech rights of communists and advocates of other radical political ideas. Under the same principle, the ACLU has fought censorship of literature containing allegedly offensive material. In one of its most famous cases, it overturned a U.S. Customs Bureau ban on the James Joyce novel *Ulysses*. The ACLU has also taken a broad definition of expression, arguing in cases that "expression" includes nonverbal as well as verbal expression. In 1967, the ACLU won a landmark case upholding the right of a public school student to wear an armband protesting the Vietnam War.

The ACLU defended the rights of Jehovah's Witnesses in a long series of cases and controversies from the late 1930s to the early 1950s. Because their doctrines and tactics were extremely unpopular, the Jehovah's Witnesses were subject to restrictive laws and attacks by vigilante groups. Several cases helped to define First Amendment protection for the free exercise of religion. The most famous controversy involved the refusal of public school students who were members of the Jehovah's Witnesses to participate in compulsory salutes of the American flag. In the landmark case of *West Virginia v. Barnette*, 319 U.S. 624 (1943), the Supreme Court affirmed the principle that the government cannot compel a person to express a belief that is contrary to his or her conscience.

The ACLU has been particularly controversial because of its position on the separation of church and state. The ACLU has held that the establishment clause of the First Amendment prohibits any government support or endorsement of religious activity. Since the 1925 Scopes case, the ACLU has fought other efforts to prohibit the teaching of evolution or to require the teaching of religious views of the creation of the universe. In the 1940s and 1950s, the ACLU fought government financial support for religious activities in public schools. In 1962, the

ACLU won one of its most controversial cases when the Supreme Court ruled that mandatory religious prayers in public schools violated the establishment clause of the First Amendment. The organization has also generated controversy by opposing religious displays in public buildings. The majority of these controversies involved religious displays in front of courthouses and other public buildings during the Christmas season or Christmas programs in public schools. In 2004 and 2005, the ACLU also sought to remove displays of the Ten Commandments from courthouses and public parks.

Because of its position on separation of church and state, and school prayers in particular, the ACLU has been attacked by religious conservatives as "Godless" and "antireligion." The group has responded by arguing that the free exercise of religion clause of the First Amendment protects religious expression. In addition to its support for the Jehovah's Witnesses in the 1930s and 1940s, the ACLU in the 1990s defended the right of Native Americans to use peyote, a drug that is generally illegal, in religious ceremonies. Together with many religious organizations, the ACLU supported the 1993 Religious Freedom Restoration Act designed to overturn an unfavorable Supreme Court ruling.

During World War II the ACLU defended the rights of nearly 120,000 Japanese Americans who had been evacuated from the West Coast of the United States and interned in concentration camps. Because of popular support for the war effort, the ACLU was the only national organization to provide significant support for the Japanese Americans, representing them in the major cases that reached the Supreme Court. The Court upheld the government's actions in *Hirabayashi v. United States*, 320 U.S. 81 (1943), and *Korematsu v. United States*, 323 U.S. 214 (1944), but public opinion and subsequent court cases have supported the ACLU argument that the treatment of the Japanese Americans was a gross violation of civil liberties.

The most divisive internal controversy in ACLU history occurred in 1940 when the Board of Directors adopted a policy barring individuals who belonged to totalitarian organizations from positions of leadership in the ACLU. It then expelled Elizabeth Gurley Flynn from the Board. Many dissident ACLU members accused the organization of imposing the same kind of political test that it had always opposed. The controversy simmered for many years. Eventually, in 1976, the ACLU Board, led by a new generation of civil libertarians, reinstated Flynn posthumously to the Board.

During the cold war period of the late 1940s and 1950s, the ACLU opposed many anticommunist measures as violations of freedom of belief and association. It challenged the Federal Loyalty Program created in 1947 because it barred people from federal employment simply because they had once belonged to an organization alleged to be subversive. It also called for abolition of the House Un-American Activities Committee (HUAC) because it investigated people's beliefs and associations. The ACLU opposed the 1940 Smith Act, which outlawed advocating the overthrow of the government. At the state level, ACLU affiliates opposed loyalty oaths for teachers and legislative investigations of people's beliefs and associations.

On civil rights issues, the ACLU worked closely with the NAACP from 1920 onward. In the 1920s, the ACLU called on local authorities to prevent Ku Klux Klan-led violence against African Americans, and in the 1930s joined the unsuccessful campaign for a federal law making lynching a crime. The ACLU was active in the Scottsboro case in the 1930s, which involved eight young African-American men accused of raping a white woman in Alabama. This was the first civil rights case to attract national attention. The ACLU handled two Supreme Court cases that led to landmark rulings on criminal procedure (*Powell v. Alabama*, 287 U.S. 45, 1932; *Patterson v. Alabama*, 1935). The organization also filed an amicus brief in the landmark case of *Brown v. Board of Education*, 347 U.S. 483 (1954), declaring racially segregated public schools unconstitutional. Beginning in the 1970s, the ACLU supported affirmative action programs in employment.

In the 1960s and 1970s, the ACLU's agenda expanded enormously to include new areas of civil liberties, including women's rights, prisoners' rights, children's rights, the right to abortion, the rights of lesbian and gay people, and many others. This development generated considerable controversy. Many people argued that the Constitution did not guarantee rights in these areas. Some prominent ACLU members resigned from the organization over these issues, arguing that it should adhere to its traditional role of defending First Amendment rights. In general, however, the ACLU was very successful in persuading the courts to adopt its interpretation of the Constitution. The single most important case in this regard was the 1973 decision in *Roe v. Wade*, 410 U.S. 113 (1973), holding that the constitutional right to privacy guaranteed women a right to an abortion.

The ACLU has had a major impact on the American criminal justice system. Its briefs were extremely influential in the Supreme Court cases of *Mapp v. Ohio*, 367 U.S. 643 (1961), and *Miranda v. Arizona*, 384 U.S. 436 (1966), protecting the rights of criminal suspects. The group has also supported the creation of independent agencies to review citizen complaints against police officers. ACLU attorneys brought the first prisoners' rights cases in the 1960s and in the 1970s; it created the National Prison Project, which challenged the constitutionality of prison conditions in virtually every state in the country.

The Vietnam War and the Watergate scandal led the ACLU to devote more effort to civil liberties issues related to war and national security. The organization and its affiliates brought several unsuccessful cases seeking to have the courts declare the Vietnam War unconstitutional. During the Watergate scandal, the ACLU was one of the first national organizations to call for the impeachment of President Richard Nixon because of his abuse of presidential power.

In one of the most controversial First Amendment cases in its history, the ACLU in 1977 defended the right of a small American Nazi group to hold a demonstration in the heavily Jewish community of Skokie, Illinois. The organization was heavily criticized for defending the rights of a group associated with the Holocaust and it lost many members. The ACLU replied to critics with its traditional view that restrictions on speech based on the content of the message were impermissible and that the First Amendment guarantees "freedom for the thought we hate." The federal courts eventually upheld the ACLU's position and affirmed the right of the Nazi group to hold a demonstration in Skokie.

The ACLU took up the issue of abortion rights in the 1960s and filed an amicus brief in the landmark case of *Roe v. Wade* (1973), which established a constitutional right to an abortion. In the 1970s, the ACLU created its Reproductive Rights Project, which fought to defend the *Roe* decision and worked on other related reproductive rights issues. The ACLU also created a Women's Rights Project in the early 1970s. Under the leadership of Ruth Bader Ginsburg, the project won the first important cases on women's rights in the Supreme Court, beginning with *Reed v. Reed* (1971).

In the 1970s, the ACLU began to place more emphasis on legislation as the Supreme Court became less sympathetic to civil liberties. Originally staffed by only one person, by 2005 the ACLU Washington office had a staff of over twelve full-time lobbyists. In addition, ACLU affiliates lobby in state legislatures and several affiliates employ full-time lobbyists. In the 1980s, the ACLU began to strengthen its public education program, creating a separate Public Education Department in the national office. This development reflected the belief that public opinion was increasingly hostile or indifferent to civil liberties issues.

Two former leaders of the ACLU have been appointed associate justices of the U.S. Supreme Court. Felix Frankfurter, who was among the original founders of the ACLU in 1920, was appointed to the Court in 1939 and served until 1962. Ruth Bader Ginsburg was the first director of the ACLU Women's Rights Project in the early 1970s. In that capacity she argued and won a series of landmark women's rights cases before the Court. She was appointed to the Court in 1993.

The terrorist attacks on the United States on September 11, 2001, had a dramatic effect on civil liberties. Many Americans felt that it was necessary to restrict individual liberties in order to protect against terrorism. Congress quickly passed the PATRIOT Act, which included many provisions the ACLU regarded as threats to civil liberties. Most important, the law authorized the federal government to conduct searches without notifying the person whose home or office was to be searched (so-called "sneak and peak" search warrants). The ACLU also protested interviews with Arab Americans by the Federal Bureau of Investigation, charging that the practice represented discriminatory profiling on the basis of national origins. In challenging aspects of the war on terrorism, the ACLU enjoyed significant public support. Immediately after the terrorist attacks of September 11, 2001, it developed a working coalition with conservative groups and leaders who were also concerned about expanded government powers. The membership of the ACLU grew by 30 percent between late 2001 and mid-2005.

The ACLU is a national organization with about five hundred thousand members. It maintains a national office in New York City, a legislative office in Washington, D.C., and staffed affiliate offices in all fifty states. The work of the ACLU is financed by members' dues, tax-deductible contributions, and grants to support specific projects. Grants from private foundations and donors support a series of special projects related to specific civil liberties issues. These include the Voting Rights Project, with an office in Atlanta, Georgia, the Reproductive Rights Project, the Women's Rights Project, and others.

SAMUEL WALKER

References and Further Reading

Cottrell, Robert C. *Roger Nash Baldwin and the American Civil Liberties Union*. New York: Columbia University Press, 2000.

Larson, Edward J. *Summer for the Gods: The Scopes Trial and America's Continuing Debate over Science and Religion*. New York: Basic Books, 1997.

Murphy, Paul L. *World War I and the Origin of Civil Liberties in the United States*. New York: Norton, 1979.

Walker, Samuel. *The American Civil Liberties Union: An Annotated Bibliography*. New York: Garland, 1992.

———. *In Defense of American Liberty: A History of the ACLU*, 2nd ed. Carbondale: Southern Illinois University Press, 1999.

AMERICAN COMMUNICATION ASSOCIATION v. DOUDS, 339 U.S. 382 (1950)

In 1947, Congress added Section 9(h) to the National Labor Relations Act; this section required all labor union officers to sign annual affidavits stating that they did not belong to the Communist Party or support the unlawful overthrow of the U.S. government. Unions whose officers refused to sign noncommunist affidavits were denied access to the National Labor Relations Board for relief from unfair labor practices. Congress justified the affidavit requirement as necessary to protect the free flow of Interstate Commerce from political strikes. In *American Communication Association v. Douds*, the Supreme Court upheld the statute despite noting that it "discourag[ed] the exercise of political rights protected by the First Amendment."

In an opinion written by Chief Justice Vinson, the Court concluded that the affidavit provision was designed by Congress to regulate harmful conduct in the form of political strikes, but not harmful speech. Because the statute had what the Court viewed as only an indirect effect on speech, the Court applied a balancing test, rather than the clear and present danger test, to determine the requirement's constitutional validity. After considering the competing interests, the majority concluded that protecting the national economy from disruptive political strikes outweighed any burden on the ability of a "relative handful" of union members to express their political views.

The holding's precedential value today is questionable. While not explicitly overruling *Douds*, the Court invalidated a later version of Section 9(h) as an unconstitutional bill of attainder in *United States v. Brown*, 381 U.S. 437 (1965).

NICOLE B. CÁSAREZ

References and Further Reading

Currie, David P., *The Constitution in the Supreme Court: 1946–1953*, Emory Law Journal 37 (1988): 249–294.
Kalven, Harry Jr. *A Worthy Tradition: Freedom of Speech in America*. New York: Harper & Row, 1988.

Cases and Statutes Cited

United States v. Brown, 381 U.S. 437 (1965)

See also **Balancing Approach to Free Speech; Bill of Attainder; Clear and Present Danger Test; Interstate Commerce; National Labor Relations Board; Vinson Court**

AMERICAN INDIAN RELIGIOUS FREEDOM ACT OF 1978

Congress announced that the policy of the United States was to "protect and preserve" the rights of American Indians, Alaskan Natives, and Native Hawaiians "to believe, express, and exercise" their "traditional religions" in a joint resolution adopted in 1978, now known as the American Indian Religious Freedom Act (AIRFA). The AIRFA defined the practice of "traditional religions" to include, without limitation, "access to sites, use and possession of sacred objects, the freedom to worship through ceremonials and traditional rites."

The impetus for the AIRFA was a study conducted by the House of Representatives that concluded the federal government was restricting Indian religious freedom in at least three ways. First, federal agencies such as the U.S. Forest Service, National Park Service, and the Bureau of Land Management frequently prevented Indians from entering federal land where sacred sites were located. Moreover, the agencies refused to allow the burial of tribal leaders in tribal cemeteries located on federal land. Second, federal law-enforcement officials regularly confiscated substances, such as peyote, used by Indians for religious purposes, even though federal cases had protected the use of these substances as a bona fide religious sacrament. Federal officials also confiscated the use of animal parts from endangered species, such as turkey and eagle feathers, that Indians used in religious ceremonies.

Third, the House found that federal agents directly and indirectly interfered with tribal ceremonies and religious practices. For example, federal officers had a long history of opposing and restricting the practice of tribal religions through the enforcement of Bureau of Indian Affairs-authored reservation law-and-order codes that flatly prohibited most tribal religious ceremonies. These law-and-order codes were enforced in the Courts of Indian Offenses, with judges hand-picked by federal officers. Federal courts in cases such as *United States v. Clapox*, 35 F. 575 (D. Or. 1888), upheld federal regulations, thus allowing the prosecution of Indians engaging in traditional religious practices. On-reservation federal Indian agents, as a matter of administrative practice, obstinately remained on the grounds at Rio Grande pueblos during religious ceremonies requiring that no non-Indian be present. Federal law-enforcement officers would also do little or nothing to stop unwelcome on-lookers from interfering in tribal religious ceremonies. The House also found that federal officials had directly interfered or allowed interference in tribal religious practices because the officials rejected Indian religions.

As a mere joint resolution, the AIRFA does not have the full force of federal law. Importantly, it did not include an enforcement and penalty provision. This status has undermined the effectiveness of the act in tough cases, such as *Lyng v. Northwest Indian Cemetery Protective Association*, 485 U.S. 439 (1988). There, the Supreme Court upheld a federal road project that would cut through the heart of tribal sacred sites located near the Hoopa Valley Reservation in California, even though the Ninth Circuit had determined that the project would destroy areas central to the religions of the Yurok, Karuk, and Tolowa tribes. The Court refused to enforce the act, largely because, without an enforcement clause, it had "no teeth in it."

The Court evinced greater hostility to tribal religious practices in *Employment Division v. Smith*, 494 U.S. 872 (1990). There, the state of Oregon denied unemployment benefits to individuals who had been fired for good cause. The state denied benefits to two Indians who had been fired for using peyote as a religious sacrament outside of work. The Court upheld the regulation on the theory that the regulation was a neutral law not designed to restrict religion. As such, the Court applied the rational basis test to scrutinize Oregon's action under the free exercise clause.

Congress attempted to reverse the holding in *Smith* and other freedom of religion cases by enacting the Religious Freedom Restoration Act (RFRA). This statute would require the Court to apply a compelling interest test, but the Court struck it down in *City of Boerne v. Flores*, 521 U.S. 507 (1997), as applied to state and local governments.

In 1996, President Clinton issued Executive Order No. 13007 that requires all federal agencies to accommodate access to sacred sites for Indian religious practitioners and avoid negatively affecting those sites. This executive order also does not contain an enforcement provision. In short, the AIRFA, along with Executive Order No. 13007, is little more than the imposition of a duty on federal agencies to take into consideration tribal interests, to consult with tribal leaders on the subject of Indian religion, and not to interfere with tribal religious practices.

MATTHEW L. M. FLETCHER

References and Further Reading

Carpenter, Kristen A., *A Property Rights Approach to Sacred Sites Cases: Asserting a Place for Indians as Non-owners*, UCLA Law Review 52 (2005): 4:1061–1148.

Cohen, Felix S., *The Erosion of Indian Rights, 1950-1953: A Case Study in Bureaucracy*, Yale Law Journal 62 (1953): 3:348–390.

Epps, Garrett. *To an Unknown God: Religious Freedom on Trial*. New York: St. Martin's Press, 2001.

Petoskey, John. "Indians and the First Amendment." In *American Indian Policy in the Twentieth Century*, Vine Deloria, Jr., ed. Norman: University of Oklahoma Press, 1985, 221–238.

Pevar, Stephen L. *The Rights of Indians and Tribes*, 3rd. ed., Carbondale and Edwardsville: University of Southern Illinois Press, 2002, 260–266.

Cases and Statutes Cited

City of Boerne v. Flores, 521 U.S. 507 (1997)

Employment Division v. Smith, 494 U.S. 872 (1990)

Lyng v. Northwest Indian Cemetery Protective Association, 485 U.S. 439 (1988)

Native American Church of New York v. United States, 468 F. Supp. 1247 (S.D. N.Y. 1979), aff'd, 633 F.2d 205 (2nd Cir. 1980)

People v. Woody, 61 Cal. 2d 716, 40 Cal. Rptr. 69, 394 P.2d 814 (1964)

United States v. Clapox, 35 F. 575 (D. Or. 1888)

Wilson v. Block, 708 F.2d 735 (D.C. Cir.), cert. denied, 464 U.S. 956 (1983)

American Indian Religious Freedom Act, S.J. Res. 102, Aug. 11, 1978, Pub. L. 95-341, 92 Stat. 469, codified in part 42 U.S.C. § 1996

Religious Freedom Restoration Act, 42 U.S.C. § 2000bb et seq

See also **Accommodation of Religion; *City of Boerne v. Flores*, 521 U.S. 507 (1997); Drugs, Religion, and Law; *Employment Division, Department of Human Resources v. Smith*, 494 U.S. 872 (1990); *Lyng v. Northwest Indian Cemetery Protective Association*, 485 U.S. 439 (1988); Native Americans and Religious Liberty; Religious Freedom Restoration Act**

AMERICAN REVOLUTION

The Subjects of Liberty

The words "liberty" and "rights" had far different connotations for people in the American colonies, depending on their status as slaves, free blacks, Native Americans on their homeland, women, indentured servants, loyalists, conscripted soldiers, religious dissidents, radical patriots, or propertied white males. The term "civil liberties" was not a term used in the period between 1760 and 1783. Many of the colonists depended on the rights they claimed as English citizens. For those with limited rights based on their English origins, a new understanding of rights was required; for others, the rights they claimed had far different origins in their understandings as indigenous peoples of the American or African continent.

Most of the history of the era has focused on the propertied white male colonist and his revolution against the British king and Parliament. Whether his battle was to retain rights as a citizen of the British Empire or to retain the unique habit of independence as an American colonist, he remained at the heart of the investigation of the causes of the American Revolution.

Many colonists viewed the indigenous populations as "savages" existing outside the polity of the colonial, state, or federal governments. The sovereign nations had their own views of the rights of people in relation to community. The five nations of the Haudenosaunee, in their Great Binding Law (Gayanashgowa, for example), demonstrated working concepts of confederation, and included, for example, rights of the people to deliberate and be consulted in times of dire threat to the tribes. The question of the relations between the revolutionary government and the tribal nations was not an issue of civil rights. The growing protection for colonial property rights, however, increasingly allowed the revolutionary states to encroach on Native American sovereign lands.

The free black population, particularly in the northern colonies, gradually increased as the events moved toward revolution. Slaves and free blacks expected that the cry for liberty and civil rights by the American colonists should include freedom and the end of slavery in the colonies. Petitions were sent to colonial governments seeking the end of slavery as well as, in some cases, receipt of land as compensation for involuntary servitude. While these petitions had little effect on the colonial governments, they did resonate with a number of state governments once the war began.

Between 1780 and 1804, eight states—including the fourteenth state, Vermont—abolished slavery outright or passed gradual abolition laws to end slavery over the course of the next few decades. Pennsylvania's Gradual Abolition Act of 1780 noted the inconsistency of fighting for liberty against the British while maintaining slavery. In some states, including New York, Pennsylvania, Massachusetts, and Vermont, blacks gained complete political equality; in others they gained freedom, but not the ballot. The southern states did not end slavery, but a few, such as Virginia, allowed for voluntary manumission of slaves and most reduced the harshness of punishments for slaves and free blacks.

Many black males were manumitted in exchange for long service in the continental army. Some entered military service of their own accord and others were volunteered to substitute their service for the service of their white slave owners. Many white southerners objected to allowing blacks to serve in the army. They feared uprisings among the slave population and objected to serving alongside black slaves or freedmen. In some cases the black soldiers were given service functions, such as jobs as cooks, drivers, or laborers, instead of fighting positions. Often, however, events necessitated an abandonment of this policy as the battles intensified. Black soldiers performed heroic acts in many of these battles; many had been slaves at the beginning of the Revolution and were able to gain their freedom through military service.

An undetermined number of white male indentured servants sometimes were released from their contractual bond in exchange for enlistment in the army. The rights of indentured servants were not, however, a focus of the revolutionary efforts to secure political and civil rights.

Women were represented by every possible status within the colonies, and whether they were southern female slaves or patriot or loyalist wives of propertied colonists, their plight was ignored by those who articulated the goals of the revolution. Their rights, except in the case of those included in manumissions, were not significantly improved as a result of the Revolution. The rights of white married women and widows may have diminished after the revolution as the law became more rigidly applied to their limited legal identity. Prior to and during the revolution, some of these women exercised a wider range of economic and legal power under circumstances that necessitated their action. Single women retained the power to own property, sue in court, and inherit property. However, during and after the Revolutionary period, some women, such as Mercy Otis Warren, participated in politics by writing essays and pamphlets. In New Jersey women gained the right to vote during the Revolution, although they would lose this right in the early 1800s.

The fight for liberty in the face of governmental oppression did not necessarily pertain to colonists, labeled "Tories" or "Loyalists," who refused to join the revolutionary cause. They suffered loss of life, liberty, and due-process protections at the hands of American patriots who were fighting to secure liberties for themselves. Loyalty oaths were demanded of all men over the age of sixteen. Taxes were imposed at much higher rates than those imposed on patriots. Property was confiscated; many opponents of the revolutionary cause were imprisoned, tarred and feathered, or exiled. The military and the colonial governments asserted jurisdiction to investigate, bring to trial, and punish those who spoke in support of remaining loyal to the king.

Despite the denial of due process or freedom of expression to Tories, the Revolution had a profound affect on civil liberties. Before the war, the British used arbitrary searches—writs of assistance—to look for smuggled goods and weapons. The British tried to move trials of Americans overseas, denying them access to witnesses, counsel, and juries of their peers. The war began with the British trying to seize the munitions of the Concord militia. The colonists petitioned the king, but received no response and felt cut off from having a voice in government. During the war, pamphleteers and newspaper editors pushed the patriot agenda with the printed word. These experiences led to demands after the war that culminated in the Bill of Rights, protecting the rights of petition and jury trials, banning warrantless searches, and prohibiting the federal government from disarming the state militias. Even the deprivations of Tory rights affected Americans. A number of states used bills of attainder to arrest Tories, but they did so with some discomfort, knowing that such behavior violated fundamental rights. Not surprisingly, such behavior was banned in the Constitution.

Historical Interpretations of the Revolution

Any description of liberties and rights during the period from 1760 until 1783 must take into account the different perspectives, the changes of the components of liberty and rights articulated by the people over time, and the school of historical thought reflected by the particular description of the period. Perhaps no period has received so much attention from historians with so little agreement.

During the nineteenth century George Bancroft's ten-volume *History of the United States* offered the accepted "Whig" interpretation of the American Revolution. The Whig party opposed the power of the Stuart kings in the seventeenth century on the basis that the English tradition of liberties was protected in the unwritten constitution. Bancroft and earlier historians, including Mercy Otis Warren and David Ramsay, described the Revolution as the reaction against parliamentary conspiracies to deprive the colonists of their rights as English citizens. American colonists viewed themselves as retaining the rights identified in England with the grant of the Magna Carta in 1215 and the Petition of Rights in 1628. Although not always followed by king or Parliament, these documents limited their powers and guaranteed that freemen could not be taken, imprisoned, or disseized of life, property, or liberties without due process of law.

Parliamentary actions that allowed general warrants to search any colonial home for smuggled goods (Writs of Assistance 1761) and imposed taxes and duties on commercial items including paper (The Stamp Act of 1765), sugar (The Sugar Act of 1774), and tea (The Townshend Revenue Act of 1767) pushed the colonists to articulate their right to give consent by way of proper representation in Parliament before property could be taken from them. James Otis, one of the early opponents of the use of arbitrary power against the colonists, resigned his government position in order to argue against the practice of searching homes without specific warrants. In boycotts and other acts of open defiance to taxes imposed by Parliament, the colonists vigorously objected to being deprived of property without representation and also fought to ensure their right to petition concerning their grievances against the king and Parliament. Freedom of the press was understood as an essential tool in efforts to oppose arbitrary and oppressive use of power. Free speech was an idea initially subsumed by the fight for a free press.

In response to the punitive "coercive"/"intolerable acts" of 1774, the colonists met in Philadelphia at the First Continental Congress and identified a number of the rights that were threatened by Parliament at that time. "The Declaration and Resolves" issued by the Congress on October 14, 1774, reaffirmed their belief that colonists retained all of their rights as free natural-born subjects of England, and reiterated the right not to be deprived of life, liberty, or property without consent; the right to be tried by a jury of their local peers before an independent judiciary; and the right to peaceably assemble and petition the king with their grievances. In further documents, the Congress criticized the expanded jurisdiction of admiralty and vice admiralty courts that deprived the colonists of their right to a jury trial.

The focus of this early historical interpretation pits the struggles of the enfranchised male colonist against the arbitrary exercise of power and oppression by the British Parliament and the king. The developing nationalist unified view shared by all such colonists led to the ensuing revolution and creation of the Declaration of Independence. It also fostered a sense of rights and liberties that needed protection from arbitrary and oppressive interference from government. According to this view the colonists were primarily influenced by John Locke's theories.

The arguments of the wealthy, intellectual colonists, for the most part, did not focus on the interests of the "middling" classes of artisans, tradesmen, seamen, laborers, and small rural farmers, or the increasing numbers of immigrant poor who were flocking to the cities. "New Left" historians, including Gary Nash, have described the role of the common person in the pre-Revolutionary identification of rights and liberties. The resentment toward the wealthy merchants, lawyers, and politicians grew as measures were passed ignoring the plight of the poor, the artisans, and the tradesmen while increasing the revenues for the rich colonists. In these historical accounts the poor claimed as many grievances against the wealthy colonists and their influence over government as they did against the dominance of the English parliament and king. They participated in demonstrations, uprisings, and petitions that reflected a demand for a more egalitarian society than that which existed in the goals of the elite merchants, politicians, and farmers.

As the revolution progressed, the new state governments began the task of writing their constitutions. Each of these new governments adopted its version of a declaration or bill of rights reflecting its previous colonial efforts to create written laws, its adaptations of English rights, and the unique interests of the particular state ratifying conventions. The Bay Colony reduced to writing its Massachusetts Body of Liberties in 1641 and the Laws and Liberties of Massachusetts in 1648. In 1780, their constitution began with "a declaration of the rights of the inhabitants of the Commonwealth of Massachusetts." As described by Professors Conley and Kaminski in *The Bill of Rights and the States*, when the new states prioritized the rights that were important:

> New Yorkers championed freedom of expression; Rhode Islanders passionately defended religious liberty and church–state separation; Delawareans showed an unusual preoccupation with the right to keep and bear arms; Massachusetts men stoutly objected to unreasonable searches and seizures; Vermonters led the way in abolishing slavery; Rhode Islanders and North Carolinians exalted states' rights as an antidote to centralized power; and Pennsylvanians and Virginians pioneered in asserting a broad range of individual freedoms.

Because the states were viewed as the primary protectors of the rights of citizens of the states, the Articles of Confederation did not need a declaration of rights.

Progressive historians of the early twentieth century, including Charles Beard, identified conflicting economic interests that divided classes in the colonies and motivated the colonists. These historians examined the self-interest of revolutionary leaders and eventual founding fathers of the Constitution. The economic incentives of those holding wealth and power in the colonies also pitted the Colonists against the British, particularly against Parliament's imposition of external and internal taxes. The progressive historians focused much of their attention on identifying the incentives that would protect property rights of self-interested individuals. In this explanation, the rights of the disenfranchised, those held in slavery, or other

powerless individuals were not the primary motivation of these revolutionary activities.

A major revision in the history of the causes of the American Revolution occurred with the work of Bernard Bailyn, Gordon S. Wood, and J.G.A. Pocock in what has been termed "a republican revival" or "neo-Whig" history. This interpretation agreed with the earlier Whig interpretations of history that suggested that the colonists feared conspiratorial efforts by Parliament to deprive them of their rights as English citizens. The work of Bailyn and Wood located the intellectual origins of the colonists' revolutionary rhetoric and action in seventeenth century radical Whig oppositional thought in England.

The civil rights and liberties of the revolutionary era are best understood individually as the states adopted their declarations of rights and the Constitution of 1787 was ratified with a promise of a Bill of Rights. No unified view existed, and all versions excluded many of the peoples of the new governments.

JANIS L. MCDONALD

References and Further Reading

Bailyn, Bernard. *The Ideological Origins of the American Revolution,* Cambridge, Mass.: Harvard University Press, 1967; enl. ed., Cambridge: Belknap Press, 1992.

Beard, Charles A. *An Economic Interpretation of the Constitution of the United States.* New York: Macmillan, 1913.

Bancroft, George. *History of the United States,* vols. 4–7, New York: D. Appleton, 1834–1874.

Berlin, Ira. "The Revolution in Black Life." In *The American Revolution, Explorations in the History of American Radicalism,* Alfred F. Young, ed. Dekalb: Northern Illinois University Press, 1976, 349–382.

Calhoun, Robert M. *The Loyalists in Revolutionary America, 1760–1781.* New York: Harcourt Brace Jovanovich, 1973.

Conley, Patrick T., and John P. Kaminski. *The Bill of Rights and the States, The Colonial and Revolutionary Origins of American Liberties.* Madison, WI: Madison House, 1992.

Higginbotham, Don. "Loyalist Experiences and Civil Liberties in Wartime." In *The War of American Independence: Military Attitudes, Policies, and Practice, 1763–1789.* New York: Macmillan Co., 1971.

Kerber, Linda. *Women of the Republic: Intellect and Ideology in Revolutionary America.* Chapel Hill: University of North Carolina Press, 1980.

Lemisch. "Revolution from the Bottom up." In *Towards a New Past: Dissenting Essays in American History,* Barton J. Bernstein, ed. New York: Pantheon Press, 1968.

———. "The Radicalism of the Inarticulate: Merchant Seamen in the Politics of Revolutionary America." In *Dissent: Essays in the History of American Radicalism,* Alfred F. Young, ed. Dekalb: Northern Illinois University Press, 1964.

Morgan, Edmund S., and Helen M. Morgan. *The Stamp Act Crisis: Prologue to Revolution.* Chapel Hill: University of North Carolina Press, 1953.

Nash, Gary. *Red, White and Black: The Peoples of Early America*. Englewood Cliffs, N.J.: Prentice Hall, 1974.

———. "Social Change and the Growth of Pre-Revolutionary Urban Radicalism." In *The American Revolution, Explorations in the History of American Radicalism*, Alfred F. Young, ed. Dekalb: Northern Illinois University Press, 1976, 3–36.

———. "Also There at the Creation: Going Beyond Gordon S. Wood." *WMQ*, 3d Ser., XLIV (1987), 602.

Norton, Mary Beth. *Liberty's Daughters: The Revolutionary Experience of American Women, 1750–1800*. Boston, MA: Little, Brown and Company, 1980.

Otis, James. *A Vindication of the Conduct of the House of Representatives of the Province of Massachusetts-Bay*. Boston: 1762.

———. *The Rights of the British Colonies Asserted and Proved*. Boston: 1764.

Pocock, J. G. A. *The Machiavellian Moment: Florentine Political Thought and the Atlantic Republican Tradition*. Cambridge, MA: Harvard University Press, 1975.

Potter, Janice. *The Liberty We Seek: Loyalist Ideology in Colonial New York and Massachusetts*. Cambridge, MA: Harvard University Press, 1983.

Ramsay, David. *The History of the American Revolution*, 2 vols. Foreword by Lester H. Cohen. Indianapolis, IN: Liberty Fund, 1990.

Reid, John Phillip. *Constitutional History of the American Revolution: The Authority of Rights*. Madison: The University of Wisconsin Press, 1986.

Wilson, Joan Hoff. "The Negative Impact of the American Revolution." In *Major Problems in American Women's History Series*, Mary Beth Norton, ed. Lexington, MA: D. C. Heath and Company, 1989.

Warren, Mercy Otis. *The History of the Rise, Progress, and Termination of the American Revolution, Interspersed With Biographical, Political and Moral Observations*. Boston, MA: 1814; reprinted in New York: AMS Press, 1970.

Wood, Gordon S. *The Creation of the American Republic: 1776–1787*. Chapel Hill: University of North Carolina Press, 1969.

———. *The Radicalism of the American Revolution*. New York: Alfred A. Knopf, 1992.

AMERICANS UNITED FOR SEPARATION OF CHURCH AND STATE

Americans United for Separation of Church and State (Americans United) is a Washington, D.C.-based public interest organization committed to preserving the principles of separation of church and state and religious liberty through litigation, lobbying, and public education. Americans United advocates a broad interpretation of the establishment and free exercise clauses of the First Amendment to the Constitution, sometimes described as a "strict" separationist approach. The organization's primary focus and bulk of activity have been on establishment clause issues, opposing government financial support of religious institutions—including most forms of public aid to religious schools—officially sponsored prayer and Bible reading in public schools, and the public display of religious symbols on public property. The organization publishes *Church & State* magazine.

Americans United was founded in 1947 by moderate and evangelical Protestant leaders and professional educators who became alarmed at the U.S. Supreme Court decision in *Everson v. Board of Education* (1947) upholding public payment of transportation expenses for children to attend parochial schools. The organizers also opposed President Harry S. Truman's efforts to appoint an ambassador to the Vatican, claiming that the action provided official recognition of a religious body. The organization was founded as "Protestants and Other Americans United for Separation of Church and State" (POAU), with its support coming largely from Baptist, Methodist, Presbyterian, and Seventh-Day Adventist bodies, as well as organizations such as the Baptist Joint Committee on Public Affairs, the National Association of Evangelicals, the National Education Association, and several Masonic groups. The organization's name, its primary opposition to parochial school funding, and its often highly charged rhetoric led to early claims that POAU was anti-Catholic.

In 1948, Americans United hired Glen Archer, dean of Washburn University Law School, as its first executive director. Archer, an effective public speaker and consummate fund-raiser, served as executive director for twenty-eight years, growing the membership to over two hundred thousand by the mid-1950s. Early supporters of Americans United, according to the organization, included Eleanor Roosevelt and Supreme Court Justice Hugo Black. An early affiliate of and spokesperson for Americans United was Paul Blanshard, author of the best selling *American Freedom and Catholic Power* (1949) and *God and Man in Washington* (1959), both works criticized as being anti-Catholic in orientation.

From its beginnings, Americans United has been a leading litigation organization on establishment clause issues. Americans United's earliest cases involved challenges to joint operating agreements between public and parochial schools (common in many rural areas during the 1940s and 1950s) and religiously based censorship of books and motion picture films. However, Americans United's greatest impact came through its litigation against public funding of parochial schools and religious colleges. Americans United, sometimes in conjunction with other groups, litigated several of the leading funding cases before the U.S. Supreme Court, including: *Flast v. Cohen*, 392 U.S. 83 (1968); *Lemon v. Krutzman*, 403 U.S. 602 (1971); *Tilton v. Richardson*, 403 U.S. 672 (1973); *Meek v. Pittenger*, 421 U.S. 349 (1975); *Grand Rapids School District v.*

Ball, 473 U.S. 373 (1985); *Mitchell v. Helms*, 530 U.S. 793 (2000); and *Zelman v. Simmons–Harris*, 536 U.S. 639 (2002). The only Supreme Court decision bearing its name, however, is *Valley Forge Christian College v. Americans United*, 454 U.S. 464 (1982), an Article III standing case.

By the late 1960s, Americans United had dropped its earlier name, "Protestants and Other Americans United," and its anti-Catholic rhetoric had softened, indicating developing attitudes following Vatican II. Membership declined in the 1970s and 1980s, particularly following the retirement of Glen Archer in 1976, and the organization floundered under the leadership of several short-term directors. During the 1980s, Americans United expanded its involvement in issues concerning religion and public education and the free exercise of religion. The organization also became outwardly critical of the activities of the ascending religious Right, including groups such as the Moral Majority and the Christian Coalition. Also, by the 1980s, Americans United's support base had shifted from moderate and evangelical Protestants to liberal Protestants, Unitarians, Reform Jews, and non-believers. Americans United's transformation to a secular-oriented civil rights organization was completed by the 1992 appointment of Barry Lynn, a former American Civil Liberties Union official, as executive director. Membership and name recognition subsequently grew under Lynn's directorship.

Currently, Americans United litigates and lobbies in Congress and in state legislatures on a range of church–state issues, including private school vouchers, public school prayer and Bible reading, the teaching of evolution or creationism, charitable choice (public funding of religious charities), and the official display of the Ten Commandments and other religious symbols. Americans United cosponsored litigation in various voucher cases, including *Zelman v. Simmons–Harris* (2002). The organization also supported the Religious Freedom Restoration Act (1993) and the Religious Land Use and Institutionalized Persons Act (2000).

STEVEN K. GREEN

References and Further Reading

Berg, Thomas C., *Anti-Catholicism and Modern Church-State Relations*, Loyola University Chicago Law Journal 33 (2001): 121–172.

Creedon, Lawrence P., and William D. Falcon. *United for Separation: An Analysis of POAU Assaults on Catholicism*. Milwaukee, WI: The Bruce Publishing Company, 1959.

Jeffries, John C., and James E. Ryan, *A Political History of the Establishment Clause*, Michigan Law Review 100 (2001): 279–370.

Lowell, C. Stanley. *Embattled Wall*. Washington, D.C.: Americans United, 1966.

Lowell, C. Stanley, and Herbert S. Southgate. "POAU Position on Church–State Relations." *Journal of Church and State* 5 (1963):41–60.

Salisbury, Franklin C. *The Separationist Position on Church State Relations*. Washington, D.C.: Americans United, 1965.

Stokes, Anson Phelps, and Leo Pfeffer. *Church and State in the United States*, rev. ed. New York: Harper & Row, Publishers, 1964.

Who's Who in the P.O.A.U.? Huntington, IN: Our Sunday Visitor, 1951.

Cases and Statutes Cited

Flast v. Cohen, 392 U.S. 83 (1968)
Grand Rapids School District v. Ball, 473 U.S. 373 (1985)
Lemon v. Krutzman, 403 U.S. 602 (1971)
Meek v. Pittenger, 421 U.S. 349 (1975)
Mitchell v. Helms, 530 U.S. 793 (2000)
Tilton v. Richardson, 403 U.S. 672 (1973)
Valley Forge Christian College v. Americans United, 454 U.S. 464 (1982)
Zelman v. Simmons–Harris, 536 U.S. 639 (2002)

See also **Christian Coalition;** *Zelman v. Simmons–Harris*, **536 U.S. 639 (2002)**

AMISH AND RELIGIOUS LIBERTY

The Amish seem to be an unlikely group to shape American law. These simple folk distance themselves from the trappings of modernity by living in largely isolated, rural communities. Moreover, they generally avoid relying on the courts to resolve disputes. ("Going to law," as it is called in the scriptures, is anathema to them.) Yet, remarkably, members of the faith have been at the center of several important legal cases that have helped to define the scope of judicial safeguards for religious liberty.

The Amish faith has its roots in the Reformation. Among the Protestant faiths to arise from that tumultuous period was Anabaptism, practiced by pious dissidents who made a particularly radical break with the Catholic hegemony that had long dominated political and religious life in Europe. Adhering to what might be best described as a primitive form of Christianity, they rejected infant baptism and disavowed state control of the church. In time, a group of Anabaptists who followed the teachings of Jakob Ammann splintered off and came to be known as the Amish. They followed Ammann's directives on such matters as personal adornments. Clothes were to be fastened with hooks and not buttons; beards were to be untrimmed; and hats, dresses, stockings, and other garments were to be uniformly plain.

When the Amish started flocking to the New World in the eighteenth century, they steered clear of cities and settled in rural areas. Doing so allowed the Amish to distance themselves from the innumerable perils of what they called "worldliness." For members of the faith, the call for separation from the corruption of the world at large came most clearly from Romans 12:1–2, which advises, "Be not conformed to this world, but be ye transformed by the renewing of your mind that ye may prove what is that good and acceptable and perfect will of God." No single admonition from the scriptures was more central to the lives of the Amish who fled Europe for the New World, and it would remain a basic tenet of their faith for the remainder of the millennium.

Despite their best efforts, the Amish were unable to distance themselves completely from the tentacles of state power. Throughout the early and middle parts of the twentieth century, members of Amish communities in several states—including Iowa, Kansas, Ohio, and Pennsylvania—clashed with state authorities who attempted to force them to comply with compulsory school attendance laws and related measures (such as curricula and the certification of teachers). The Amish resisted such laws in part because they seemed to threaten the faith's tradition of not sending children to school beyond the age of fourteen. Several legal cases resulted from disputes over the application of school attendance laws to the Amish, among them *Kansas v. Garber,* 419 P. 2d 896 (Kan. 1966). In that case, the Kansas Supreme Court ruled that such measures did not impose an unconstitutional burden on the religious liberty of the Amish.

A trio of Amish farmers from Wisconsin fared better than their Kansas brethren when they challenged the constitutionality of their state's school attendance law. In its landmark religious liberty opinion in *Wisconsin v. Yoder*, 406 U.S. 205 (1972), the U.S. Supreme Court held that compulsory attendance measures did in fact burden the right of the Amish to exercise their religion freely. According to Chief Justice Warren Burger, who wrote for the high court's majority striking down the application of the law on the Amish, the impact of the statute on the Amish was "not only severe, but inescapable, for the Wisconsin law affirmatively compels them, under threat of criminal sanction, to perform acts undeniably at odds with fundamental tenets of their religious beliefs."

Yoder marked in many ways a high point not only for religious liberty jurisprudence in general but also for the Amish in particular. Never again would the courts provide such stout protections for free-exercise rights. This was demonstrated in the next significant Amish case to reach the U.S. Supreme Court. *United States v. Lee,* 455 U.S. 252 (1982), involved an Amish man who claimed that he deserved a faith-based exemption to paying Social Security taxes for his employees. According to Chief Justice Burger, who wrote for the Court's majority, whereas the circumstances of *Yoder* had lent themselves to permitting a narrow accommodation for members of one particular religious group, the complexities of the tax system involved in *Lee* made providing faith-based exemptions a hopelessly complicated endeavor. "Because the broad public interest in maintaining a sound tax system is of such high order," he wrote in the Court's denial of the Amish man's claim, "religious belief in conflict with the payment of taxes affords no basis for resisting the tax."

The *Yoder* precedent proved more useful when the Amish opposed the application of state laws mandating the display of bright red and orange reflective triangles on slow-moving vehicles (SMVs). In 1996, the Wisconsin Supreme Court ruled in *Wisconsin v. Miller* (538 N.W. 2d 573, Wisc. 1995) that application of that state's SMV measure to the Amish—who had argued that placing the SMV emblem on their buggies was too "worldly"—violated their religious liberty. In determining that the state constitution's protections of conscience shielded the Amish, the court relied in part on the interpretive framework established by the U.S. Supreme Court in *Yoder* and its forebears. *Yoder* had proved similarly important in earlier SMV emblem cases in Kentucky, Ohio, and Michigan.

Such cases are all the more noteworthy because the Amish are famously hesitant to "go to law." This disinclination is rooted in large part in their adherence to the ethical principles detailed in the Sermon on the Mount. There, as he counsels meekness and nonresistance, Christ admonishes: "If any man sue you at law, and take away thy coat, let him have thy cloak also." To the Amish, being sued or prosecuted is not quite the same as suing, for defendants in legal cases typically have not chosen to invoke the law; in most instances, they have been dragged into the courts by other people. Not all members of the faith approve of these dealings with the courts, but some justify them on the grounds that the Amish typically are defendants in criminal actions rather than plaintiffs in civil matters.

SHAWN FRANCIS PETERS

References and Further Reading

Hostetler, John. *Amish Society*, 4th ed. Baltimore, Md.: Johns Hopkins University Press, 1993.

Kraybill, Donald. *The Riddle of Amish Culture*, rev. ed. Baltimore, MD: Johns Hopkins University Press, 2001.

Peters, Shawn Francis. *The* Yoder *Case: Religious Freedom, Education, and Parental Rights.* Lawrence, KS: University Press of Kansas, 2003.

Cases and Statutes Cited

Kansas v. Garber, 419 P. 2d 896 (Kan. 1966)
United States v. Lee 455 U.S. 252 (1982)
Wisconsin v. Miller 538 N.W. 2d 573 (Wisc. 1995)
Wisconsin v. Yoder, 406 U.S. 205 (1972)

AMNESTY INTERNATIONAL

Amnesty International (Amnesty), an organization dedicated to advancing human rights and ending arbitrary detention, has been active worldwide for over forty years. By the early 1990s, Amnesty had worked on behalf of 33,500 prisoners and has since added to its long list of successes. With hundreds of researchers and full-time employees combating injustice around the globe, Amnesty International has become among the world's most visible Non-Governmental Organizations (NGOs).

The group has articulated four major objectives: (1) securing the release of prisoners of conscience (Amnesty defines a prisoner of conscience as one who is imprisoned on the basis of sex, religion, national origin, or belief who has not used or advocated violence.); (2) fair trials for political prisoners; (3) an end to torture, cruel, inhuman and degrading treatment; and (4) an end to executions. It pressures governments to comply with international law obligations embodied in treaties such as the Universal Declaration of Human Rights, which nearly all nations have ratified.

Amnesty was the brainchild of Peter Benenson, a Catholic lawyer of Jewish descent. Having been previously involved in human rights advocacy, Benenson, at the age of forty, was spurred into action in 1961 at reports that two Portuguese students had been sentenced to prison for raising their glasses in public and toasting to freedom. He recruited Eric Baker, a prominent Quaker, and Louis Blom-Cooper, an internationally known lawyer, and they began an effort to pressure Portugal's Salazar regime to release the students as well as to address and publicize the status of political and religious prisoners throughout the world.

The campaign was called "An Appeal for Amnesty, 1961" and was launched when the influential liberal British Sunday newspaper *The Observer* agreed to provide a platform for an exposé highlighting the plight of eight prisoners of conscience entitled "The Forgotten Prisoners." The article attracted worldwide media attention along with a flood of letters and donations. What began as a one-year campaign soon morphed into a permanent effort. Branches soon appeared in France, Ireland, Greece, Switzerland, Norway, the United States, and others. In over 160 countries Amnesty volunteers are now working to further the organization's goals.

The group has campaigned for causes such as exposing the use of child soldiers in Africa, responsible economic development and globalization, the rights of refugees, and arms control. Amnesty was particularly active in documenting and exposing human rights abuses in Argentina during its period of military rule and in Chile under Gen. August Pinochet. More recently, it has successfully campaigned for a permanent International Criminal Court, whose statute was adopted by the U.N. General Assembly in 1998. Amnesty has assured its impartiality and independence by refusing to accept monetary contributions from governments.

Amnesty has developed a successful formula of aggressive on-site investigation to uncover abuses, followed by an intensive letter-writing campaign supplemented by posters, advertisements, and media spots designed to publicize human rights violations and to pressure governments to end them. Its efforts have paid off. In 1963, of the 770 individuals "adopted" by Amnesty International, 140 had been freed from detention. In 1975, 1,403 of its adopted prisoners had been released. In 1978, the group won the United Nations Human Rights Prize for "outstanding contributions in the field of human rights," and by 1992 its membership had exceeded one million.

The group has attracted members and publicity in innovative ways. During the 1980s, Amnesty began to organize rock concerts designed to spread awareness of human rights issues. The 1986 "Conspiracy of Hope" concert sponsored by Amnesty's U.S. section was followed in 1988 by the "Human Rights Now!" concert tour (featuring Sting, Bruce Springsteen, and others) to mark the fortieth anniversary of the Universal Declaration of Human Rights.

Although its primary focus has often been elsewhere in the world, Amnesty has been involved in the United States from the beginning. Of the eight individuals profiled in its 1961 launch piece, one of them was Ashton Jones, a sixty-five-year-old minister who had been beaten, harassed, and imprisoned several times in Louisiana and Texas for his activities in support of civil rights for African Americans.

Its activities in the United States, however, have long focused on the issue of capital punishment. In 1965, Amnesty circulated a resolution at the United Nations that sought to suspend or outright abolish executions for peacetime offenses. In 1977, the group gathered delegates from over fifty countries to Stockholm, Sweden, to denounce the death penalty, labeling it a cruel, arbitrary, and irrevocable punishment that does not deter crime. In this sense, Amnesty's opposition to the death penalty is well received by domestic opponents of capital punishment, who argue that it constitutes a type of "cruel and unusual" punishment proscribed by the Eighth Amendment. Amnesty has been particularly critical of the United States for executing child offenders—those under eighteen at the time of their crime—which Amnesty characterizes as being "in contravention of international law." Moreover, it also decries execution of criminals with histories of mental illness.

More recently, the group has been particularly vocal in denouncing U.S. government tactics in prosecuting what President George W. Bush had dubbed the Global War on Terror, or GWOT. Amnesty has focused particularly heavily on revelations of torture at the Abu Ghraib detention facility in Iraq (see Abu Ghraib entry) and has accused the American administration of sanctioning interrogation techniques that violate the Convention on Torture. The detentions of suspected terrorists in Guantánamo Bay, Cuba, has also been criticized. Although the United States maintains that detainees at the facility do not qualify for protections under the Geneva Conventions and may be held indefinitely without judicial review, Amnesty has protested the prolonged detentions without charge or access to U.S. courts. In its 2005 annual report, the organization pilloried President Bush's proposal to try certain suspects using military tribunals and has similarly denounced the practice of renditions—in which suspects in American hands are transferred to third-party countries to be interrogated and possibly tortured.

ANDREW FINKELMAN

References and Further Reading

Power, Jonathan. *Amnesty International: The Human Rights Story*. New York: McGraw–Hill, 1981.
Amnesty International Website, available at: http://www. amnesty.org.

AMSTERDAM, ANTHONY G. (1935–)

Anthony Amsterdam, law professor and opponent of the death penalty, earned an A.B. from Haverford College in 1957 and an L.L.B. in 1960 from the University of Pennsylvania. Amsterdam became an ardent opponent of capital punishment in 1963, after Justice Arthur Goldberg had written an unusual dissenting opinion on cases that had not been accepted for review. Goldberg's dissent addressed six cases in which the defendants had been sentenced to death and noted that the death penalty was barbaric and constituted excessive punishment. Amsterdam, then a University of Pennsylvania law professor, formed

a partnership with the National Association for the Advancement of Colored People Legal Defense and Education Fund to mount a challenge to the constitutionality of the death penalty.

Amsterdam successfully argued for the abolishment of the death penalty in *Furman v. Georgia*, 408 U.S. 238 (1972), when the Supreme Court ruled that the death penalty as then applied was inherently arbitrary and therefore unconstitutional. However, this moratorium on the death penalty did not last long. In 1976, the Court in *Gregg v. Georgia*, 428 U.S. 153 (1976), ruled that Georgia's new capital punishment system had sufficiently dealt with the problem of arbitrariness.

While perhaps most noted for his argument against the death penalty, Amsterdam has litigated cases involving claims of free speech and the press, privacy, and equality for racial minorities and the poor. His teaching career has included teaching positions at the University of Pennsylvania, Stanford University, and, as of 1981, New York University, where he developed the ground-breaking course Lawyering Theory Colloquium, which researches how law school experiences later affect lawyering roles and behavior. Throughout his career he has extended *pro bono* serves to numerous civil rights, legal aid, and public defender organizations. Professor Amsterdam has established himself as a leading American legal scholar by writing extensively on issues such as legal pedagogy, experimental education, and cultural influences on Supreme Court opinions and rulings.

BA-SHEN WELCH

References and Further Reading

Amsterdam, Anthony G., and Jerome Bruner. *Minding the Law*. Cambridge, MA: Harvard University Press, 2000.
Tushnet, Mark. *Constitutional Issues: The Death Penalty*. New York: Facts on File, Inc., 1994.

Cases and Statutes Cited

Furman v. Georgia, 408 U.S. 238 (1972)
Gregg v. Georgia, 428 U.S. 153 (1976)

ANARCHY

See Anti-Anarchy and Antisyndicalism Acts.

ANDERS v. CALIFORNIA, 386 U.S. 738 (1967)

In *Douglas v. California*, 372 U.S. 353 (1963), the Supreme Court held that an indigent defendant was entitled to have counsel appointed to handle the appeal of his conviction. *Anders v. California*, 386 U.S. 738 (1967), then addressed an inevitable result of *Douglas*: a situation in which assigned counsel found no meritorious issues to present on appeal.

In *Anders*, the defendant was convicted of marijuana possession and requested appointed counsel on appeal. The assigned attorney reviewed the record and consulted with his client before determining the appeal lacked merit; the lawyer advised the court by letter to this effect and asked to withdraw. The defendant's request for another attorney was denied.

The Supreme Court acknowledged that assigned counsel should be allowed to withdraw from "wholly frivolous" cases, but deemed the procedure utilized by the lawyer in this case inadequate. Rather, the Court recommended that, first, after reviewing the record and finding the case frivolous, assigned counsel should notify the court and ask to withdraw, including with that request a brief referring to anything in the record that might arguably support the appeal. Second, the court should examine the case to decide whether it is wholly frivolous. If the court concurs with the attorney's assessment, it should grant the request to withdraw and dismiss the appeal subject to certain limitations; however, if the court finds any of the legal points arguable on the merits, then it must afford the defendant with the assistance of counsel to argue the appeal.

Whereas *Anders* set in motion the procedure for grappling with a "no-merit" appeal—and states responded by creating procedures along the lines of the Court's suggestions—the case failed to offer guidance as to what constitutes a frivolous issue, leaving that question for a later day.

DANIEL S. MEDWED

References and Further Reading

Bentele, Ursula, and Eve Cary. *Appellate Advocacy: Principles and Practice*, 4th ed. 2004, 304–332.
Duggan, James E., and Andrew W. Moeller. "Make Way for the ABA: *Smith v. Robbins* Clears a Path for Anders Alternatives." *Journal of Applied Practice and Process* 3 (2001):65.
Warner, Martha C., Anders *in the Fifty States: Some Appellants' Equal Protection Is More Equal Than Others*, 23 Fla. St. U. L. Rev. 625 (1996).

Cases and Statutes Cited

Douglas v. California, 372 U.S. 353 (1963)
Ellis v. United States, 356 U.S. 674 (1958)
Eskridge v. Washington State Board, 357 U.S. 214 (1958)
Lane v. Brown, 372 U.S. 477 (1963)

See also **Due Process; Equal Protection Clause and Religious Freedom; Ineffective Assistance of Counsel; Right to Counsel**

ANNE HUTCHINSON TRIAL

The Puritans of the early Massachusetts Bay Colony formed a tightly knit community with a common belief system enforced by civil and ecclesiastical law. Yet, as the colony began to grow, divergent interpretations of scripture and the relationship between society and religion began to emerge, to the consternation of the Puritan clergy. Among the dissenters was Anne Hutchinson (1591–1643), whose radical interpretations of church doctrine directly challenged the authority of the Puritan establishment to regulate the secular and religious lives of the Massachusetts Bay settlers. Hutchinson was a follower of Minister John Cotton, whose teachings emphasized salvation by grace, bestowed directly by God upon worthy individuals, over salvation by works, which implied obedience to religious and secular authority. Hutchinson interpreted the teachings of Cotton as suggesting that those possessed with divine grace are not obligated to obey the laws of church or state. In defiance of Puritan traditions barring women from the pulpit, Hutchinson preached this doctrine, known as antinomianism, during informal meetings in her home, drawing the ire of Puritan authorities for the content of her teachings and the fact that her congregations included both men and women.

Puritan authorities first unsuccessfully tried to get Hutchinson to change her views, then arrested her brother-in-law on heresy charges. Yet Hutchinson persisted in her teachings and was arrested for heresy in November 1637 and sentenced to banishment from the Massachusetts Bay Colony, a sentence that was deferred pending an ecclesiastical trial held in March 1638. During her trial, Hutchinson befuddled her Puritan inquisitors with her intellectual acuity, engaging them in spirited theological debate for several days before declaring that her beliefs were the product of divine revelation, a clear heresy under Puritan law. She was excommunicated from the church and the sentence of banishment was imposed. A pregnant Hutchinson then fled on foot with her husband and children to the colony of Rhode Island, which had been founded by another Puritan dissenter, Roger Williams, banished from Massachusetts three years earlier under similar circumstances. There Hutchinson and her followers established a settlement that would become Portsmouth, Rhode Island. Following the death of her husband in 1642, Hutchinson moved to New York, where she and all but one of her family members were killed by Native Americans in 1643.

The trial of Anne Hutchinson is often cited as a seminal event in the shaping of American concepts of religious freedom and gender equality. By challenging the theocratic government of the Massachusetts Bay Colony, Anne Hutchinson followed in the footsteps of fellow outcast Roger Williams in questioning the relationship between church and state and the role of civil authority in regulating the private beliefs of individuals, giving rise to a longstanding debate that would inspire constitutional prohibitions of government establishment of religion in the new United States, as well as myriad legislative acts and court decisions that collectively established clear boundaries between American religious and civil institutions. By defying the circumscribed roles assigned to women in Puritan society, Hutchinson also became a pioneer in the struggle for women's rights.

MICHAEL H. BURCHETT

References and Further Reading

Battis, Emery. *Saints and Sectaries: Anne Hutchinson and the Antinomian Controversy in the Massachusetts Bay Colony*. Chapel Hill: University of North Carolina Press, 1962.

Cooper, James F., Jr. "Anne Hutchinson and the 'Lay Rebellion' against the Clergy." *The New England Quarterly* 61(3) (September 1988):381.

LaPlante, Eve. *American Jezebel: The Uncommon Life of Anne Hutchinson, the Woman who Defied the Puritans*. San Francisco: Harper San Francisco, 2004.

See also **Puritans; Quakers and Religious Liberty**

ANONYMITY AND FREE SPEECH

Anonymity has long been an important issue in American politics and jurisprudence. The key tension in American anonymity law is between the potentially chilling effects on speech stemming from compelled disclosure of identity and the desire to hold individuals accountable for harmful speech. But while early cases like *Lewis Publishing Co. v. Morgan*, 229 U.S. 288 (1913), drew this balance in favor of accountability, holding that mandatory disclosure requirements advanced knowledge by preventing deceptive propaganda, modern anonymity law strongly supports the right to speak and associate anonymously. This rich constitutional tradition of support for anonymous speech and association reflects America's historical experience with persecution and ostracism of "un-American" communists, members of disfavored religious sects, and advocates for racial equality. Today, anonymity has again become controversial with the rise of the Internet and privacy-enhancing technologies like encryption.

At its simplest, anonymous speech is speech that is not attributed to an author. But anonymity is more than the mere concealment of identity. An author might use a pseudonym to establish an identity distinct from his or her "true" identity; some individual framers of the Constitution used pseudonyms in writing the essays that later came to be known as the Federalist Papers. The U.S. Supreme Court in *McIntyre v. Ohio Elections Commission*, 514 U.S. 334 (1995), treated this aspect of anonymity—an author's choice about whether and how to identify himself or herself—as part of the "content" of the speech, subject to strict scrutiny.

In the modern era, the Supreme Court has consistently protected anonymity as an aspect of the First Amendment freedoms of speech and association. The basic theme of this jurisprudence has been the benefit of anonymity to free speech. In *Talley v. California*, 362 U.S. 60 (1960), which invalidated a state law restricting the distribution of any handbill unless it included the name and address of the person who printed, wrote, compiled, manufactured, or distributed it, the Supreme Court noted that "[a]nonymous pamphlets, leaflets, brochures and even books have played an important role in the progress of mankind," and that "identification and fear of reprisal might deter perfectly peaceful discussions of public matters of importance."

The Supreme Court has also been protective of anonymous association. In *NAACP v. Alabama ex rel. Patterson*, 357 U.S. 449 (1958), the Court refused to permit the state of Alabama to compel the state NAACP chapter to produce its membership records, saying that advocacy is "undeniably enhanced by group association," and recognizing "the vital relationship between freedom to associate and privacy in one's association." Well aware of the racial animus in the South, the Court noted that disclosure "may induce members to withdraw . . . and dissuade others from joining it because of fear of exposure of their beliefs shown through their associations and of the consequences of this exposure." Similarly, in *Shelton v. Tucker*, 364 U.S. 479 (1960), the Court invalidated an Arkansas statute requiring public school teachers to reveal to the state annually their group memberships and contributions for the previous five years, noting that "[e]ven if there were no disclosure to the general public, the pressure upon a teacher to avoid any ties which might displease those who control his professional destiny would be constant and heavy."

Today, the accountability or traceability aspect of anonymity has become more important as civil litigants and law enforcement agencies seek to discover Internet users' identities in defamation, intellectual property, and criminal cases. The law has continued to be relatively protective of anonymity; for instance, in *Columbia Insurance Co. v. Seescandy.com*, 185

F.R.D. 573 (N.D. Cal. 1999), a federal district court observed that litigants' need to seek redress "must be balanced against the legitimate and valuable right to participate in online forums anonymously or pseudonymously . . . . This ability to speak one's mind without the burden of the other party knowing all the facts about one's identity can foster open communication and robust debate. Furthermore, it permits persons to obtain information relevant to a sensitive or intimate condition without fear of embarrassment." Modern communications technology, on the other hand, tends to expose identity unless speakers take precautions such as using encryption, anonymous remailers, or anonymous proxies. Whether governments will restrict the use of such precautionary technologies remains an open question.

LEE TIEN

References and Further Reading

Froomkin, A. Michael, *Anonymity and Its Enmities*, 1995 J. Online L. art. 4.

Kreimer, Seth F., *Sunlight, Secrets, and Scarlet Letters: The Tension Between Privacy and Disclosure in Constitutional Law*, U. Pa. L. Rev. 140 (1991): 1.

Marx, Gary. "Identity and Anonymity: Some Conceptual Distinctions and Issues for Research." In *Documenting Individual Identity*, J. Caplan and J. Torpey, eds. Princeton, NJ: Princeton University Press, 2001.

Thompson, E. P. "The Crime of Anonymity." In *Albion's Fatal Tree: Crime and Society in Eighteenth-Century England*. 1975, 255.

Tien, Lee, *Who's Afraid of Anonymous Speech? McIntyre and the Internet*, Or. L. Rev. 75 (1996): 117.

Cases and Statutes Cited

Columbia Insurance Co. v. Seescandy.com, 185 F.R.D. 573 (N.D. Cal. 1999)

Lewis Publishing Co. v. Morgan, 229 U.S. 288 (1913)

McIntyre v. Ohio Elections Commission, 514 U.S. 334 (1995)

NAACP v. Alabama ex rel. Patterson, 357 U.S. 449 (1958)

Shelton v. Tucker, 364 U.S. 479 (1960)

Talley v. California, 362 U.S. 60 (1960)

Watchtower Bible and Tract Society v. Village of Stratton, 536 U.S. 150 (2002)

ANONYMITY IN ON-LINE COMMUNICATION

The current Internet architecture allows most on-line communications to be traced back to the author's computer. That tracing process depends on the cooperation of Internet Service Providers (ISPs). Changes in the Internet architecture, however, could someday end the debate over on-line anonymity, by evolving to a state of perfect identification or perfect anonymity.

Today, however, most legal challenges involving on-line anonymity involve identity seekers who demand, usually through a subpoena, that ISPs disclose identifying information about their customers. Some statutes and judicial decisions require little more than the identity seeker's signature to support its subpoena. Authors have challenged the constitutionality of such subpoenas in a variety of contexts, and a few courts have required the identity seeker to establish the merits of its claim before ordering disclosure.

Legislatures and courts considering whether to protect on-line anonymity must balance competing interests. On-line anonymity fosters free speech and association and allows authors to maintain their privacy. The Supreme Court has recognized the traditional value of anonymous speech in the United States. On the other hand, on-line anonymity can immunize authors from civil or criminal liability and can allow criminals and terrorists to communicate secretly.

Much of the justification for protecting on-line anonymity in the United States derives from the First Amendment. Other countries, however, may have different views on the value of on-line anonymity. International organizations may eventually debate whether to recognize protection for on-line anonymity, just as the United Nations and the European Union have recognized protection of privacy rights.

SHAUN B. SPENCER

References and Further Reading

Nicoll, Chris et al., eds. *Digital Anonymity and the Law: Tensions and Dimensions*. The Hague: T. M. C. Asser Press, 2003.

Sobel, David L., *The Process That "John Doe" Is Due: Addressing the Legal Challenge to Internet Anonymity*, Virginia Journal of Law & Technology 5 (2000): 3, http://www.vjolt.net/vol5/symposium/v5i1a3-Sobel.html.

Spencer, Shaun B., *CyberSLAPP Suits and John Doe Subpoenas: Balancing Anonymity and Accountability in Cyberspace*, John Marshall Journal of Computer & Information Law (2001): 493–521.

ANSLINGER, HARRY JACOB (1892–1975)

Harry Anslinger was born in Altoona, Pennsylvania, the son of an immigrant railroad worker. He earned an associate degree in engineering and business management and then went to work for the Pennsylvania Railroad as an investigator. After rising to a captain of the railroad police, he worked for a variety of military and police organizations around the world between 1917 and 1928, with a focus on stopping a growing international trade in narcotics. After a two-year tour with the Bureau of Prohibition—where Anslinger won a reputation as an honest and incorruptible agent in an agency noted for corruption—he became the first Commissioner of the Federal Bureau of Narcotics (FBN). He held that position for the next thirty-two years, a term rivaled only by J. Edgar Hoover's tenure at the FBI.

Anslinger claimed that he knew what his life's work would be from the age of twelve, when he heard the screams of a young morphine addict, screams that ended only when another boy returned from the pharmacist with more of the drug. Anslinger reported that he was appalled at how easy it was for children to secure such strong drugs.

He became an inveterate foe of all drug use, but especially of marijuana. In the 1920s, a movement of legislators, yellow journalists, and citizen groups started pressing for a federal ban on the use of marijuana, which supposedly played a major role in the corruption of youth, especially young girls. Scholars note that in addition to the moral elements of the crusade, chemical companies with an interest in eliminating hemp products, and southerners wanting to control cheap Mexican labor, also joined in the clamor.

William Randolph Hearst, whose papers led the fight, offered Anslinger space in his papers and magazines, and Anslinger gladly availed himself of the opportunity. He filled article after article with scare stories that not only warned against the alleged dangers of hemp, but also were overtly racist. "Colored students at the University of Minnesota partying with female students (white) smoking [marijuana] and getting their sympathy with stories of racial persecution. Result pregnancy." In another story he wrote that "Two Negros took a girl fourteen years old and kept her for two days under the influence of marijuana. Upon recovery she was found to be suffering from syphilis."

Medical opinion at that time did not believe marijuana to be so dangerous a drug, and some doctors argued that it had beneficial medicinal properties. Anslinger made sure that when there were legislative hearings on drug bills, at the state or the national level, members of the medical profession did not receive notice until it was too late for them to testify. When the American Medical Association (AMA) failed to appear before a congressional hearing, Anslinger lied to the committee and told them that the AMA favored strict regulation of marijuana.

In August 1937, Congress passed the Marijuana Tax Act, which provided the first block in erecting a comprehensive scheme for federal regulation of the drug. It classified marijuana as a narcotic and thus gave Anslinger's FBN still another target to go after. For the next twenty-five years Anslinger spearheaded the federal drive against drugs. Ironically, there is some evidence that in the early 1950s Anslinger secretly supplied morphine to Senator Joseph McCarthy.

Thin-skinned at all times, Anslinger did not handle criticism well and, later in his career, was reprimanded for failing to desist from harassing critics of his policies, especially Indiana University professor Alfred Lindsmith, whose books and articles attacked the war on drugs and Anslinger's leadership of it.

In 1962, Anslinger retired at the mandatory age of seventy and, for the next two years, served as a member of the American delegation to the United Nations. By then he had become completely blind and suffered from a variety of ailments, including an enlarged prostate and angina. Some thought it ironic—even hypocritical—that in his later years he became a regular user of morphine to control his pain.

MELVIN I. UROFSKY

References and Further Reading

McWilliams, John C. *The Protectors: Anslinger and the Federal Bureau of Narcotics (1930–1962)*. Newark, NJ: University of Delaware Press, 1990.

Sloman, Larry. *Reefer Madness: A History of Marijuana in America*. Indianapolis, IN: Bobbs-Merrill, 1979.

ANTHONY, SUSAN B. (1820–1906)

Susan B. Anthony, reformer and women's suffragist, was born in Adams, Massachusetts, to Daniel Anthony and Lucy Read, one of eight children. When Anthony was six, the family moved to Battenville, New York, where Daniel Anthony managed a large cotton mill. Due to Daniel Anthony's Quaker heritage, the family believed in egalitarian education for their children, and Susan attended Deborah Moulson's Female Seminary. The Anthonys prospered until the panic of 1837, when the mill closed, the children returned from boarding school, and they lost their home. Susan aided the family by teaching, but in 1845, the family moved to a farm in Rochester, New York.

After the move, Anthony taught for a decade, ending her teaching career as headmistress of the female section of Canajoharie Academy. As a teacher, Anthony enjoyed her independence but recognized the unequal pay scale between men and women. In 1849, Anthony gave her first public speech at a Daughters of Temperance meeting, starting her involvement in reform. The same year, Anthony returned to Rochester to manage the family farm and continued her involvement in temperance reform and became dedicated to the antislavery cause. Within a few years, Anthony met some of the most prominent abolitionists and women's rights advocates—Frederick Douglass, Stephen and Abby Foster, Isaac and Amy Post, and Elizabeth Cady Stanton. Stanton called the 1848 Seneca Falls Women's Rights Convention and, although a wife and mother, was dedicated to reforming laws to benefit women. Stanton and Anthony forged a friendship that would last more than fifty years.

When Anthony realized that women were welcome in the temperance movement only if they were taciturn and did not expect egalitarian treatment, she and Stanton founded the Women's State Temperance Society in 1852, but left when men voted them out of their elected positions. The two wove the women's rights and temperance movements together, going before the state legislature (the first time a women's group in the United States did this) calling for temperance laws and, later, coeducation, women's suffrage, liberal divorce laws, and married women's property rights. The women donned bloomers, an outfit associated with women radicals, and called numerous women's rights conventions. Anthony traveled extensively throughout New York, lecturing, petitioning, organizing, and fundraising. Anthony's energy never ceased; she traveled most of her next forty years, campaigning for women's rights. In 1855, she lectured at least once in each of New York's sixty-two counties and was called the movement's Napoleon.

In 1856, the American Anti-Slavery Society hired Anthony as New York's chief agent. She served the society until the Civil War, but was disheartened with the passage of the Fifteenth Amendment in 1870, which enfranchised former male slaves but ignored women. Anthony realized that women's suffrage might be won by the next generation.

Anthony worked for women's rights in numerous ways: she gave lectures; petitioned the state legislature and Congress; organized state, national, and international conventions; and formed the National Woman Suffrage Association with Stanton, which later merged with its rival, the American Woman Suffrage Association. She also wrote and distributed pamphlets, published the *Revolution* newspaper, had her biography written, and penned *History of Woman Suffrage* with Stanton and Matilda Joslyn Gage.

One of the most notable women's rights efforts consisted of women voting, in an attempt to amend laws judicially. The suffragists tested the Constitution through the Fourteenth and Fifteenth Amendments, which linked citizenship and enfranchisement. Since women were citizens, several dozen asserted their right to vote. When they were denied the right, they intended to take their case to the Supreme Court. Anthony tried the theory in 1872 and was, surprisingly, permitted to cast a ballot. Several weeks later she was arrested for violating a federal law. Anthony's trial was a sham; it was rescheduled in another county because the judge believed she prejudiced any possible jury. Judge Ward Hunt wrote his decision before the trial began and ordered the jury to find Anthony guilty. Clearly, Anthony did not have a fair trial. At its conclusion, Hunt only fined her, refusing to put the suffragist in jail. Because of this, she could not carry her case to the Supreme Court based on applying for a writ of habeas corpus. When Hunt asked if she had any comments at the end of the trial, Anthony lambasted him and refused to pay the $100 fine.

Undaunted by her trial ordeal, Anthony remained dedicated to her cause. She presided over the National-American Woman Suffrage Association from 1892 until her eightieth birthday in 1900. Anthony remained active in the women's rights movement, traveling until a month before her death in Rochester. Her legacy is documented in her speeches and books but most importantly in the passage of the Nineteenth Amendment, which granted women the right to vote, in 1920. Anthony was the first nonallegorical woman to appear on U.S. currency, with the Susan B. Anthony dollar minted from 1979 to 1981 and in 1999.

HEIDI SCOTT GIUSTO

References and Further Reading

Anthony, Katharine Susan. *Susan B. Anthony; Her Personal History and Her Era*. Garden City, NY: Doubleday, 1954.

Anthony, Susan Brownell. *An Account of the Proceedings on the Trial of Susan B. Anthony on the Charge of Illegal Voting, at the Presidential Election in November, 1872, and on the Trial of Beverly W. Jones, Edwin T. Marsh and William B. Hall*. Rochester, NY: Daily Democrat and Chronicle Book Print, 1874.

Anthony, Susan Brownell, Elizabeth Cady Stanton, and Matilda Joslyn Gage, eds. *History of Woman Suffrage*, reprint ed. Salem, NH: Ayer Co., 1985.

Barry, Kathleen. *Susan B. Anthony: A Biography of a Singular Feminist*. New York: New York University Press, 1988.

Dorr, Rheta Childe. *Susan B. Anthony, the Woman Who Changed the Mind of a Nation*. New York: Frederick A. Stokes Company, 1928.

DuBois, Ellen C., ed. *Elizabeth Cady Stanton, Susan B. Anthony, Correspondence, Writings, Speeches*. New York: Schocken Books, 1981.

Flexner, Eleanor. *Century of Struggle: The Women's Rights Movement in the United States*, rev. ed. Cambridge, MA: Harvard University Press, 1996.

Gordon, Ann D., ed. *Papers of Elizabeth Cady Stanton and Susan B. Anthony*. New Brunswick, NJ: Rutgers University Press, 1997.

Harper, Ida Husted. *Life and Work of Susan B. Anthony.* Indianapolis, IN: Hollenbeck Press, 1898–1908.
Stanton, Elizabeth Cady. *Eighty Years and More.* New York: European Publishing Company, 1898.

See also **American Anti-Slavery Society; Douglass, Frederick; Habeas Corpus: Modern History; Stanton, Elizabeth Cady**

ANTI-ABOLITIONIST GAG RULES

The First Amendment to the Constitution provides for the right of the people "to petition the Government for a redress of grievances." Starting in the 1830s, opponents of slavery inundated Congress each session with petitions seeking to end slavery wherever the federal government had jurisdiction, such as the territories and the District of Columbia. What had started as a trickle swelled to a flood, and in 1837 and 1838, abolitionists sent more than 410,000 petitions to Congress bearing more than one million signatures.

Southerners responded with outrage, and in 1836 Representative Henry L. Pinckney of South Carolina proposed a "gag rule" that provided that all petitions relating to slavery "shall, without being either printed or referred, be laid upon the table, and that no further action whatever shall be taken thereon." The rule passed by a large majority but not without opposition, especially from former president John Quincy Adams, now a congressman from Massachusetts. "I hold the resolution to be a direct violation of the Constitution," he declared, and of "the rules of this House, and the rights of my constituents."

The House renewed the Pinckney gag at each new session until 1840, when it became a standing rule. At every session, Old Man Eloquent, as Adams was nicknamed, protested, often alone, that the rule was unconstitutional. Despite threats of censure and expulsion from his proslavery colleagues, Adams gradually gained support from other northern congressmen. Adams did not agree with many of the petitions, he told the House, but he held the right to petition as one of the inalienable freedoms handed down to Americans from their English heritage. The English Bill of Rights of 1689 had confirmed this right, as had the resolutions of the Stamp Act Congress of 1765 and the First Amendment.

Finally, in 1844, Adams's perennial resolution calling for the elimination of the gag rule carried the day.

MELVIN I. UROFSKY

References and Further Reading

Bemis, Samuel Flagg. *John Quincy Adams and the Union.* New York: Knopf, 1956.

ANTI-ABORTION PROTEST AND FREEDOM OF SPEECH

The concept of a "buffer zone" was first raised in the 1990s. It was based on two things: increasingly violent and intrusive protests by anti-abortion forces and clinic actions to try to keep protesters a certain distance away from the clinics. In response, the groups filed counterchallenges in court, stating that their First Amendment rights to freedom of speech were being violated.

The central issue became one of how to differentiate between noninjurious and nonthreatening speech, which could be allowed under the First Amendment, and actions that effectively prohibited clients from entering clinics, which were outlawed under the federal FACE Act of 1994. The first Supreme Court case on the issue was *Madsen vs. Women's Health Center*, 512 U.S. 753 (1994). The case started with Operation Rescue protests at the Melbourne, Florida, Aware Woman Center for Choice in 1991. These consisted of street marches and slogans shouted through bullhorns, directly confronting clients, following clinic staff home to demonstrate against them, and blockading clinic doors (which was outlawed by the 1994 FACE Act). When the clinic applied to the state court for an injunction against such protests, the court granted it and limited demonstrators to participating outside a "buffer zone" consisting of a 36-foot radius from the clinic; they were also prohibited from making loud noises or displaying graphic images near the facility. It also prohibited protesters from approaching patients who were within 300 feet of the facility and from demonstrating within 300 feet of any clinic employee's residence, thus upholding a type of buffer zone at employees' homes as well. The court specified that it did not seek to limit protestors' First Amendment rights (Mezey, 2003, 266–268). This decision was upheld by the Florida Supreme Court in 1992.

Operation Rescue and other groups appealed the case to the Supreme Court, arguing that the restrictions were based on the content of the speech and therefore impermissible under the First Amendment. In its 1994 *Madsen* decision, the Supreme Court upheld some of the previous restrictions and struck others down. The significance of the case was found largely in its formulation of a new test for restricting public speech by court injunction based on a heightened level of constitutional scrutiny—that of a "significant" government interest. The Court did not grant Operation Rescue's desire for the highest level of constitutional scrutiny, strict scrutiny, to be used. However, the fact that the level of constitutional scrutiny was raised from the lowest, minimal level meant that speech restrictions would be harder to uphold in the future.

The new test entailed that an injunction (restriction or prohibition) against speech would be upheld unless it prevented more types of speech than necessary to promote a significant government interest (www. firstamendmentcenter.org). In this decision, the Supreme Court upheld the 36-foot buffer zone, provided it did not affect private property, and the prohibitions against loud noise within earshot of the clinic and within 300 feet of employees' homes. On the other hand, the decision struck down the previous prohibitions on displaying images outside clinics. It also significantly narrowed the restrictions concerning the 300-foot buffer zones around clinics and employees' homes, overturning the prohibitions against approaching clients within 300 feet of the clinic or "peacefully picketing" within 300 feet of employee residences. Overall, the Court stated that its decision did not impermissibly restrict speech but rather "the activities of the demonstrators who had repeatedly violated the earlier injunctions" (Mezey, 267). According to this formulation, the Court was not restricting the content of the speech and not privileging one point of view over another.

Court challenges since *Madsen* have focused on the type of activity to be prohibited, the type of buffer zone allowed (whether a fixed parameter or a "floating" one related to protesters' following a moving car or individual), and the question of whether unrelated, privately owned property such as a business or house may be included in a clinic's buffer zone against the owner's will. The 1997 Supreme Court case, *Schenk vs. Pro-Choice Network of NY*, 519 U.S. 357 (1997), focused on the first two sets of questions. This case concerned protests by Operation Rescue and affiliate organizations against physicians and clinics near Rochester and Buffalo and included the types of blockades and obstructions rendered illegal by the FACE Act of 1994. The other question had to do with the fact that the federal district court had issued an injunction against protesters' actions within a fixed 15-foot buffer zone away from the clinic as well as against their activity within a 15-foot radius from a moving car or person.

Based on the *Madsen* test, the Supreme Court found in this case that the fixed buffer zone did not "burden any more speech than necessary to serve the government interests of ensuring public safety and order and protecting women's freedom to seek abortions or other health-related services." On the other hand, the floating buffer zone was overly broad because it could include those "simply lining the sidewalks to demonstrate peacefully" and thus was struck down.

In the Supreme Court case of *Hill vs. CO*, 530 U.S. 703 (2000), the Court upheld a buffer zone passed by the Colorado Legislature in 1993 requiring protesters to remain 8 feet away from clients who were within 100 feet of the clinic. Anti-abortion activists challenged the statute three times on First Amendment grounds, losing at the Court of Appeals level in Colorado in 1997, the Colorado Supreme Court in 1999, and the U.S. Supreme Court in the 2000 case. In upholding the prohibition, the Supreme Court stated that it was not a regulation of speech but rather a "regulation of the places where some speech may occur." The Court also emphasized that the law applied to all demonstrators, regardless of viewpoint, and that other types of institutions may also show government interest in protection from protest, including schools, polling places, and courthouses.

MELISSA HAUSSMAN

References and Further Reading

Mezey, Susan Gluck. *Elusive Equality: Women's Rights, Public Policy, and the Law*. Boulder, CO: Lynne Rienner Publishers, 2003.
Websites of the First Amendment Center, www.firstamendmentcenter.org, and the Center for Reproductive Rights, www.reproductiverights.org.

ANTI-ANARCHY AND ANTI-SYNDICALISM STATUTES

From the "Salem witch trials" to the criminal prosecutions that constitute part of the government's "war on terror," American criminal law has been used to stamp out threats, perceived or actual, to federal and state governments. Federal and state legislatures have proscribed conduct that they believe could challenge their continued existence. Courts, in turn, have generally upheld the constitutionality of these statutes as legitimate exercises of legislative power.

Anarchy and syndicalism have commonly been perceived as threatening to government, and both have been regulated, not surprisingly, in federal and state criminal codes. Criminal anarchy is defined as seeking to overthrow organized government by force, violence, or other unlawful means. Criminal syndicalism is generally defined as advocating or aiding and abetting the commission of sabotage or unlawful acts of force, violence, or terrorism for the sake of accomplishing a change in industrial ownership or control. More specifically, criminal syndicalism is understood to encompass such actions when those involved intend to effect political upheaval.

The majority of federal and state criminal codes regulating anarchy and syndicalism have been enacted since the turn of the twentieth century. However, the history of anti-anarchy and anti-syndicalism statutes extends back to the founding of the country. The Sedition Act of 1798, for example, prohibited criticism of the government with the intent to bring it, or any of its high-ranking officials, into contempt or disrepute. While the constitutionality of the Sedition Act was never tested prior to its expiration in 1801, the U.S. Supreme Court has noted that "the attack upon its validity has carried the day in the court of history" (*New York Times Co. v. Sullivan*, 376 U.S. 254, 276 & n.16, 1964).

Laws such as the Sedition Act were used and threatened to be used against anarchists and syndicalists, notwithstanding the lack of an explicit prohibition on anarchy and syndicalism. Such an express prohibition against either category of conduct did not occur until the early twentieth century. As anticapitalist theories gained worldwide momentum and with the emerging domestic popularity of the Industrial Workers of the World (IWW), state governments quickly enacted laws directly targeting alleged anarchists and syndicalists. Idaho passed the nation's first antisyndicalism statute in 1917, and twenty-three other states and two territories followed suit by 1922. By 1935, twenty-two states and one territory had passed anti-anarchy statutes. Many of these states were loci of activity of the IWW. States without a significant IWW presence, on the other hand, acted out of fear of an imminent IWW organizing drive or otherwise fell within the grips of the nationwide antiradical and antilabor drives.

Simultaneously, a push for federal anti-syndicalism and anti-anarchy legislation began to take shape. Five anti-syndicalism bills were introduced before Congress in the 1920s and 1930s, only one of which made it out of committee and was subsequently passed by the Senate. This lone bill, however, never came to a vote in the House of Representatives. (Antisyndicalism provisions also found their way into at least nine broader bills [for example, sedition statutes]. However, none of these statutes was enacted.)

Efforts to ban anarchistic conduct on the federal level were more successful. On the eve of World War II, for example, Congress enacted the Alien Registration Act of 1940, 18 U.S.C. § 2385, also known as the Smith Act, which prohibited advocating for the overthrow of the government by force or violence. Upholding the constitutionality of the Smith Act, the U.S. Supreme Court noted: "That it is within the power of the Congress to protect the Government of the United States from armed rebellion is a proposition which requires little discussion . . . . No one could conceive that it is not within the power of Congress to prohibit acts intended to overthrow the Government

by force and violence" (*Dennis v. United States*, 341 U.S. 494, 501, 1951, plurality; see also *Yates v. United States*, 355 U.S. 66, 1957).

Although the Smith Act has not been repealed, it is seldom used because, after *Yates*, the government must prove that a defendant actually intended to advocate forcible overthrow of the government, a burden that is difficult, if not impossible, to satisfy in most cases. On the state side, few anti-anarchy and anti-syndicalism laws have been repealed outright, though many states have deleted provisions proscribing mere membership in an organization promoting anarchy or syndicalism. When these state laws were first challenged, ten state supreme courts and the U.S. Supreme Court upheld them as constitutional. (See, for example, *Whitney v. California*, 274 U.S. 357, 1927; *Fiske v. Kansas*, 274 U.S. 380, 1927; *Gitlow v. New York*, 268 U.S. 652, 1925; *Ex parte McDermott*, 183 P. 437, Cal. 1919, per curiam; *Berg v. State*, 233 P. 497, Ok. 1925; *State v. Moilen*, 167 N.W. 345, Minn. 1918).

Eventually, however, the judicial tide began to turn, culminating in the U.S. Supreme Court's opinion in *Brandenburg v. Ohio*, 395 U.S. 444 (1969) (per curiam). The *Brandenburg* Court reviewed the constitutionality of Ohio's criminal syndicalism act, which punished individuals who "advocate or teach the duty, necessity, or propriety of violence as a means of accomplishing industrial or political reform . . . or who voluntarily assemble with a group formed to teach or advocate the doctrines of criminal syndicalism." Striking down the statute as unconstitutional, the Court declared that "constitutional guarantees of free speech and free press do not permit a State to forbid or proscribe advocacy of the use of force or of law violation except where such advocacy is directed to inciting or producing imminent lawless action and is likely to incite or produce such action" (at 447).

In reaching this decision the court overturned the *Whitney* and *Fiske* line of cases, thereby striking a middle ground: anti-anarchy and antisyndicalism statutes may pass constitutional muster when written and construed narrowly to proscribe only conduct that was intended to, and in fact will, produce imminent lawless action.

The line between lawful advocacy and unlawful incitement is blurry and, in some cases, arbitrary. The history of anti-anarchy and anti-syndicalism acts suggests that the line between advocacy and incitement is unlikely to be tested unless and until the government believes a significant threat exists to its security. However, in light of recent attempts to combat terrorism, it is not inconceivable to imagine circumstances under which the government might employ anti-anarchy and anti-syndicalism legislation to punish potentially threatening conduct or fervent dissent.

ADAM B. WOLF

References and Further Reading

Dowell, Eldridge F. *A History of Criminal Syndicalism Legislation in the United States.* Baltimore, MD: The Johns Hopkins Press, 1939.
Stone, Geoffrey R., *War Fever*, Missouri Law Review 69 (2004): 4:1131–1155.
Whitten, Woodrow C. *Criminal Syndicalism and the Law in California: 1919–1927.* Philadelphia: The American Philosophical Society, 1969.

Cases and Statutes Cited

Brandenburg v. Ohio, 395 U.S. 444 (1969) (per curiam)
Dennis v. United States, 341 U.S. 494 (1951) (plurality)
Fiske v. Kansas, 274 U.S. 380 (1927)
Gitlow v. New York, 268 U.S. 652 (1925)
New York Times Co. v. Sullivan, 376 U.S. 254 (1964)
Whitney v. California, 274 U.S. 357 (1927)
Yates v. United States, 355 U.S. 66 (1957)
Alien Registration Act of 1940 ("Smith Act"), 18 U.S.C. § 2385

See also **Alien and Sedition Acts (1798); Freedom of Speech and Press: Nineteenth Century**

ANTI-DEFAMATION LEAGUE OF B'NAI B'RITH

The Anti-Defamation League (ADL) was founded in 1913 by Sigmund Livingston, a Chicago lawyer, to combat the anti-Semitism and discrimination against Jews that was prevalent at the time. The charter of the league states: "The immediate object of the League is to stop, by appeals to reason and conscience and, if necessary, by appeals to law, the defamation of the Jewish people. Its ultimate purpose is to secure justice and fair treatment to all citizens alike and to put an end forever to unjust and unfair discrimination against and ridicule of any sect or body of citizens." Livingston's action was in direct response to the infamous case of Leo Frank, the Jewish manager of a Georgia factory, who was falsely convicted of the murder of a young female worker and later dragged from his jail cell and lynched by a mob after the governor of Georgia announced he was commuting Frank's death sentence.

From its inception the ADL has been associated with the Independent Order of B'nai Brith, a Jewish fraternal and service organization founded in New York City in 1843. The parent organization is engaged in a wide variety of community service and welfare activities, including the promotion of human rights, assisting hospitals and victims of natural disasters, and, through the ADL, opposing anti-Semitism and other forms of racism.

In the first three decades after its founding, the ADL mission centered on combating anti-Semitism. It pursued this goal in two major ways. First, it sought to expose and counter the bigotry of groups such as the Ku Klux Klan and individuals, such as Henry Ford, whose newspaper, *The Dearborn Independent*, was notoriously anti-Semitic, even going so far as to publish the notorious Czarist anti-Semitic forgery *The Protocols of the Elders of Zion*. In the 1930s, with the ascendance of Adolf Hitler, the ADL also had to combat the rise of domestic groups eager to mimic the Nazi's anti-Semitic actions, including German-American Bund and the Christian Front, headed by Father Charles Coughlin. Second, the league combated the pervasive economic and social discrimination against Jews, as exemplified by quotas on Jewish applicants to colleges and professional schools; company, or even industry-wide, policies barring the hiring of Jews; and discrimination against Jews in hotels, restaurants, and other public accommodations.

After the Second World War, the ADL expanded its mission to include the eradication of bias and discrimination against people of all races and religions. The organization at this time began filing amicus curiae briefs in Supreme Court cases involving religious freedom and civil rights and has remained active in this area ever since. The league has, for example, filed an amicus brief in every major Supreme Court case concerning church–state separation since 1947, as well as numerous cases on affirmative action, hate crimes, and other subjects.

The positions the league has taken in its amicus briefs are generally unsurprising given its stated goals. In religion-clause cases, it has argued for a strict view of the separation of church and state, tempered by a broad view of religious accommodation in cases in which minority religions may be threatened. Thus, it opposed a Christmas display on government property in *County of Allegheny v. ACLU*, 492 U.S. 573 (1989), and the display of the Ten Commandments on such property in *Van Orden v. Perry*, 125 S.Ct. 2854 (2005), and *McCreary County v. ACLU of Kentucky*, 125 S.Ct. 2722 (2005); opposed school prayer in *Engel v. Vitale*, 370 U.S. 421 (1962), and *Santa Fe Independent School District v. Doe*, 530 U.S. 290 (2000); and opposed publicly funded tuition vouchers for religious schools in *Zelman v. Harris–Simmons*, 536 U.S. 639 (2002), and government aid in the form of instructional materials and equipment to religious schools in *Mitchell v. Helms*, 530 U.S. 793 (2000). However, the organization defended the constitutionality of a federal statute that protects the religious rights of prisoners as a valid accommodation of religion in *Cutter v. Wilkinson*, 125 S.Ct. 2113 (2005).

With the founding of the State of Israel in 1948, the ADL began combating what it viewed as anti-Zionist organizations and publications. In more recent years, the intense debate over the Palestinian–Israeli conflict has led the league to attack what it views as a new form of anti-Semitism: the claim that Jews and Jewish organizations unfairly tag any criticism of the State of Israel with an anti-Semitic label. The league has explicitly stated that criticism of specific Israeli actions or policies in and of itself does not constitute anti-Semitism, but also notes that there are those who attempt to mask anti-Semitism under the guise of criticism of Israel or Zionism.

In the 1960s, the organization became actively involved in the emerging civil rights movement and actively worked for the passage of the Civil Rights Acts of 1964 and 1968 and the Voting Rights Act of 1965—three of the most important pieces of legislation that resulted from movement. As happened with other predominantly white organizations involved in the movement, tensions emerged between the ADL and the African-American community in the 1970s and have continued to some degree to the present, in light of differing positions on affirmative action, the Israeli–Palestinian conflict, Louis Farrakhan and the Nation of Islam, and other issues. Affirmative action in education has been a major dividing point between the two groups, with the ADL filing amicus briefs opposed to racial preferences in *Bakke* (*Regents of the University of California v. Bakke*, 438 U.S. 265, 1978) and *Grutter v. Bollinger*, 539 U.S. 306 (2003). Despite these tensions, the league remains strongly committed to cooperative efforts with the African-American community in fighting racial prejudice.

In more recent years, the ADL has identified and responded to new forms of bigotry and prejudice seen from the white-supremacist movement and other domestic hate groups. The organization has also expressed grave concern about the effect that the religious Right is having in eroding what the league views as the appropriate degree of separation between church and state in the United States. Finally, the ADL has grown increasingly concerned about, and is actively seeking to combat, what it perceives as the growth of anti-Semitism on American college campuses and the efforts by evangelical Christians to bring an explicitly religious message into public schools.

ALAN C. WEINSTEIN

References and Further Reading

ADL in the Courts: Litigation Docket, Anti-Defamation League, New York 1991 through 2001.

Dinnerstein, Leonard. *The Leo Frank Case*. Athens, GA: University of Georgia Press, 1999.
Ivers, Greg. *To Build a Wall: American Jews and the Separation of Church and State*. Clinch Wise, VA: University of Virginia Press, 1995.
www.adl.org.

Cases and Statutes Cited

County of Allegheny v. ACLU, 492 U.S. 573 (1989)
Cutter v. Wilkinson, 125 S.Ct. 2113 (2005)
Engel v. Vitale, 370 U.S. 421 (1962)
Grutter v. Bollinger, 539 U.S. 306 (2003)
McCreary County v. ACLU of Kentucky, 125 S.Ct. 2722 (2005)
Mitchell v. Helms, 530 U.S. 793 (2000)
Regents of the University of California v. Bakke, 438 U.S. 265 (1978)
Santa Fe Independent School District v. Doe, 530 U.S. 290 (2000)
Van Orden v. Perry, 125 S.Ct. 2854 (2005)
Zelman v. Harris–Simmons, 536 U.S. 639 (2002)

ANTIDISCRIMINATION LAWS

Discrimination occurs when the civil rights of an individual are denied or interfered with because of the individual's membership in a particular group or class. Many statutes have been enacted to prevent discrimination on the basis of a person's race, sex, religion, age, previous condition of servitude, physical limitation, national origin, and, in some cases, sexual preference.

Congress's early foray into civil rights legislation was a series of laws—the Reconstruction Civil Rights Acts—enacted in 1866, 1870, 1871, and 1875. These laws guarantee that all persons shall have the same right in every state to make and enforce contracts, to sue, be parties, give evidence, and to the full and equal benefit of all laws. Their primary purposes were to codify the rights of former slaves guaranteed under the newly enacted Thirteenth, Fourteenth, and Fifteenth Amendments and to protect noncitizens and persons not born in the United States within its coverage.

These acts were later codified as sections 1981 through 1985. Section 1981 established the general principle that no person may be denied, on the basis of race, equal protection of the laws. Specifically enumerated rights include the right to contract and to sue, and to give evidence, but this section has also been interpreted to include the right to earn a living, to participate in public benefits programs, and to fair use and access to justice. Section 1982 guarantees the right to inherit, own, and dispose of real and personal property. Section 1983 provides a civil cause of action for denial of equal rights but is limited to public and private individuals acting under the color of state law. There is no remedy under this provision for private discrimination. Section 1985 targets conspiracies to violate civil rights.

The most prominent civil rights legislation since reconstruction is the Civil Rights Act of 1964, enacted in response to pervasive discrimination against minorities and women. Title II proscribes discrimination or segregation based on race, color, religion, or national origin in places of public accommodation; Title III makes such unlawful conduct applicable to state and local entities; Title IV applies to public education; Title V deals with the reauthorization of the Commission on Civil Rights; and Title VI applies to programs or activities receiving federal funds.

Title VII prohibits employment discrimination against applicants and employees on the basis of race or color, religion, sex, and national origin, unless the discrimination is tied to a bona fide occupational qualification or to nonfulfillment of national security requirements. Sex discrimination includes claims of discrimination on the basis of pregnancy as well as claims of sexual harassment. Title VIII, commonly known as the Federal Fair Housing Act, makes it unlawful, with some exceptions, to discriminate in the sale, rental, or advertising of a dwelling on the basis of race, color, religion, national origin, sex, familial status, or handicap, and it prohibits real estate brokers from discriminating. Title IX of the Education Amendments of 1972 prohibits discrimination or denial of benefits on the basis of sex under any educational program or activity receiving federal financial assistance. It protects employees and students and has been interpreted to encompass sexual harassment claims.

Congress has also passed federal antidiscrimination legislation to protect classes of persons other than women and minorities. The Age Discrimination in Employment Act of 1967 (ADEA) prohibits employers from discriminating against persons on the basis of age. Based on Congressional findings of marginalization and segregation of the disabled, Congress passed the Rehabilitation Act of 1973, which prohibits discrimination by any federal or federally funded program or activity, and the Americans with Disabilities Act of 1990 (ADA), guaranteeing disabled persons the same rights and benefits as nondisabled citizens.

The ADA addresses discrimination in employment, in the receipt or qualification of public benefits and services, and in the use of public accommodations and services. "Disabled" under the statute means that one or more major life activities are substantially limited by a physical or mental impairment. Major life activities include persons' abilities to care for themselves, use their hands, walk, see, hear, speak, breathe, learn, and reproduce. The Supreme Court has held that HIV/AIDS is a disability under the ADA. Discrimination within the statute encompasses not making reasonable accommodations for an individual's disability.

The constitutional authority permitting Congress to enact antidiscrimination laws derives from the commerce clause or the Fourteenth Amendment's enforcement clause. Recently, however, the Supreme Court has begun to restrict Congress's power to enact such laws. For example, in 1997, it held that the Religious Freedom Restoration Act exceeded the authority of Congress under the Fourteenth Amendment, and, in 2000, the Court held that neither the Fourteenth Amendment nor the commerce clause permitted Congress to abrogate state immunity under the ADEA and to enact a civil remedy provision within the Violence Against Women Act. For its part, Congress passed the Civil Rights Restoration Act of 1987 in order to nullify the effects of various Supreme Court decisions altering the scope and meaning of provisions in Title VI of the Civil Rights Act of 1964, the ADA, the Rehabilitation Act, and Title IX of the Education Amendments.

The struggle for equality in America suffered many setbacks until the civil rights movement in the 1950s and 1960s. After ratification of the Thirteenth Amendment, southern states enacted black codes to severely restrict African-American life. In response, Congress enacted the Fourteenth Amendment, but by the end of Reconstruction, Jim Crow laws were in full effect and the Supreme Court had upheld the idea of separate but equal. The 1950s and 1960s finally saw an end to legal discrimination and the birth of a new era for all civil liberties and rights.

DEBORAH ZALESNE

References and Further Reading

Lund, Nelson, *The Rehnquist Court's Pragmatic Approach to Civil Rights*, Northwestern University Law Review 99 (Fall 2004): 249–288.
Post, Robert C., and Reva B. Siegel, *Equal Protection by Law: Federal Anti-Discrimination Legislation After Morrison and Kimel*, Yale Law Journal 110 (December 2000): 441–526.

Cases and Statutes Cited

Age Discrimination in Employment Act of 1967, 29 U.S.C. §§ 621–634 (2000)
Americans with Disabilities Act of 1990, 42 U.S.C. §§ 12101–12213 (2000)
Civil Rights Act of 1964, 42 U.S.C. §§ 1971, 2000(a) (1994)
Civil Rights Restoration Act of 1987, Pub. L. No. 100–259 (1988)

Reconstruction Civil Rights Acts, 42 U.S.C. §§ 1981, 1982, 1983, 1984, 1985 (1866)
Rehabilitation Act of 1973, 29 U.S.C. §§ 701-797b (2004)
Religious Freedom Restoration Act of 1993, 42 U.S.C. §§ 2000bb to 2000bb-4 (1994)
Violence Against Women Act of 1994, Pub. L. No. 103–322, 108 Stat. 1902 (1994)

See also **Civil Rights Act of 1964; Religious Freedom Restoration Act; Title VII and Religious Exemptions**

ANTIPOLYGAMY LAWS

In the United States antipolygamy laws were exclusively aimed at the polygamous practices of the nineteenth-century Church of Jesus Christ of Latter-day Saints (the Mormons) which began to publicly practice and advocate polygamy in 1852.

In 1827, Joseph Smith, Jr., found and translated gold plates that became the basis of a new religion that considered itself the true version of a Christianity that had lost its way. The Mormons believed Indians were a lost Hebrew tribe that had been visited by Jesus after the crucifixion. Smith's new religion was born in an era of religious enthusiasm and revivalism centered in the northeastern part of the United States. Mormons believe all the fundamental tenets of Christianity; in addition, they believe that Native Americans are one of the lost tribes of Israel and were visited by Christ after his crucifixion, deny original sin and stress that everyone can advance to godhood, and believe that they are the only true Christians.

Although Smith, who had as many as forty-eight wives, began practicing polygamy as early as the 1835, the church did not publicly announce its advocacy of polygamy until 1852, after Brigham Young, Smith's successor after his 1844 assassination by an angry mob, had taken the Mormons to the basin of the Great Salt Lake. The antipolygamy movement, which began immediately after the announcement, was linked to the antislavery movement. Authors penned novels featuring themes of plural wives as slaves, the lust of old men for young girls, and incest in polygamous families. Scientists said that the progeny of polygamous unions carried genetic defects, as was also true of miscegenous unions; polygamy was described as an un-Christian practice found among Africans or Asians but not civilized Europeans (that is, whites).

Congress responded with a series of increasingly draconian antipolygamy laws. First, fearing that the Mormons would attempt to bring the Utah Territory into the Union as a polygamous state, Congress enacted the Morrill Act of 1862, making polygamy a crime in all territories. However, enforcement of the act was left to local probate judges and local juries, most of whom were Mormon in the Utah Territory.

In 1874, hoping to prove that polygamy was protected by the First Amendment, the Mormons set up a test case involving Brigham Young's personal secretary, George Reynolds. But in the resulting case, *United States v. Reynolds*, a unanimous Supreme Court upheld the constitutionality of the antipolygamy act against this claim, analogizing polygamy to human sacrifice in the process. Because of these enforcement problems, Congress enacted the Poland Act in 1874 to shift enforcement of the Morrill Act to federally appointed judges. The act included a variety of procedural changes that sought to guarantee successful prosecution of polygamists.

Antipolygamy sentiment continued to grow in Congress. The resulting Edmunds Act of 1882 took away past and present polygamists' right to vote and allowed prosecutors to strike potential jurors not only for being polygamists but also for espousing belief in polygamy or even refusing to discuss their marital status. In addition, the act made "unlawful cohabitation" criminal, facilitating convictions when multiple marriages could not be proven. The even harsher Edmund–Tucker Act followed in 1887. This act made unrecorded marriages felonies, forced wives to testify against husbands, disinherited children of polygamous marriages, and allowed for the confiscation of virtually all church property.

Utah legislators began drafting an antipolygamy constitution the following year. On May 19, 1890, the Court upheld the constitutionality of the government's seizure of church property in *Late Corp. of the Church of Jesus Christ of Latter-day Saints v. United States*, 136 U.S. 1 (1890).

With Congress moving towards the passage of the Cullom–Stubble Bill, which took away all the citizenship rights of Mormons, Church President Wilford Woodruff issued the "Woodruff Manifesto" outlawing polygamy in 1890. However, the practice of polygamy continued, with more than 250 secret plural marriages performed until at least 1904. Although exact numbers are impossible to determine, today there are more than thirty thousand "Mormon fundamentalists" living mostly in Utah, Arizona, and Montana and practicing polygamy. Prosecution has been sporadic, notably prior to the 2002 Salt Lake City Winter Olympics and, in one case, that of Royston Potter, who was prosecuted following an appearance on the Phil Donahue television show.

The continued practice of polygamy prompted unsuccessful congressional efforts in 1902 to amend the U.S. Constitution to ban polygamy.

The Supreme Court has not examined the constitutionality of antipolygamy laws since the 1890 *Late*

Corp. of the Church of Jesus Christ case. Under the "*Smith* test" announced in the 1990 case of *Employment Division, Department of Human Resources of Oregon v. Smith*, 494 U.S. 872 (1990), the Court held that a generally applicable criminal law was not unconstitutional even though it had a negative impact on a religious practice. Seemingly, this holding would protect antipolygamy laws from constitutional attack. However, in *Church of the Lukumi Babalu Aye v. City of Hialeah*, 508 U.S. 520 (1993), the Court found a criminal statute to be unconstitutional because, although it was of general applicability, it was *aimed at* a particular religion. This suggests the argument, untested to date, that polygamy statutes aimed at the Mormon practice could be unconstitutional.

Antipolygamy provisions are preserved in the present day state constitutions of Utah (Utah Const. art. III), Oklahoma (Okla. Const. art. I, § 2), Idaho (Idaho Const. art. I, § 4), and New Mexico (N.M. Const. art. XXI, § 1).

KEITH E. SEALING

References and Further Reading

Ostling, Richard, and Joan Ostling. *Mormon America: The Power and the Promise.* New York: Harper, 1999.
Sealing, Keith. *Polygamists out of the Closet: Statutory and State Constitutional Prohibitions Against Polygamy Are Unconstitutional Under the Free Exercise Clause*, Ga. St. U. L. Rev. 17 (2001): 691 (arguing that antipolygamy statutes are unconstitutional).
Van Wagoner, Richard. *Mormon Polygamy: A History.* Gaithersburg, MD: Signature Books, 1989.

Cases and Statutes Cited

Church of the Lukumi Babalu Aye v. City of Hialeah, 508 U.S. 520 (1993).
Davis v. Beason, 133 U.S. 333 (1890).
Employment Division, Department of Human Resources of Oregon v. Smith, 494 U.S. 872 (1990).
Late Corp. of the Church of Jesus Christ of Latter-day Saints v. United States, 136 U.S. 1 (1890).
Murphy v. Ramsey, 114 U.S. 15 (1885).
Reynolds v. United States, 98 U.S. 145 (1878).

APODACA v. OREGON, 406 U.S. 404 (1972)

In *Apodaca v. Oregon*, the U.S. Supreme Court addressed the question of whether the Sixth Amendment's right to a jury trial required a unanimous verdict. Robert Apodaca, Henry Morgan Cooper Jr., and James Arnold Madden were convicted of committing felonies by three separate Oregon juries, all of which returned less than unanimous verdicts. In a six-to-three decision, the Court denied that their convictions violated the Sixth Amendment and rejected the argument that the due process clause of the Fourteenth Amendment made the constitutional right to a jury trial applicable to the states. Specifically, it denied that the unanimity rule was essential to the function of a jury trial or necessary to support a conviction beyond a reasonable doubt.

The Court also rejected the contention that the unanimity rule was mandated by the Fourteenth Amendment's requirement that juries reflect a cross section of the community. The Court reasoned that although the Constitution forbade the systematic exclusion of specific groups from juries, defendants may not challenge the makeup of the jury simply because no member of their race is on it. The Court further rejected the idea that minority groups serving on juries would be denied the opportunity to express their opinions because it found no proof that a majority would ignore the evidence and make a decision solely on the basis of prejudice. The Court recognized that unanimous juries were more likely to result in hung juries, but nevertheless felt that the interest of the defendant would be fairly served under both situations.

RANDA CAROLYN ISSA

See also **Due Process; Jury Trial; Jury Trial Right; Jury Trials and Race**

APPLICATION OF FIRST AMENDMENT TO STATES

Those responsible for adding the Bill of Rights to the new federal constitution intended those amendments to act as limits on the national government only, a point illustrated as succinctly as possible by the opening words of the First Amendment: "*Congress* [emphasis added] shall make no law . . . ." Relying on the still recent history of the amendments' framing and ratification, Chief Justice John Marshall in *Barron v. Baltimore*, 7 Pet. (32 U.S.) 243 (1833), confirmed that understanding by rejecting a claim that the Fifth Amendment's prohibition on the taking of private property for public use without just compensation applied to state governments.

In 1868, the Fourteenth Amendment was added to the Constitution. Section 1 states (in part): "No State shall make or enforce any law which shall abridge the privileges or immunities of citizens of the United States; nor shall any State deprive any person of life, liberty, or property, without due process of law . . ." The question of whether the amendment's framers intended that one (or both) of these clauses would apply some or all of those first ten amendments to the states has been the subject of extensive scholarly and judicial commentary and controversy.

This incorporation debate (and the evolution of incorporation doctrine) need not be addressed here, except to note that, throughout the last decades of the nineteenth and early decades of the twentieth centuries, the Supreme Court read this language quite narrowly, stressing the importance of states' following due process in criminal cases. Indeed, the first case interpreting the new amendment (the *Slaughterhouse Cases*, 16 Wall., 83 U.S., 36, in 1873) read the "privileges and immunities" clause so narrowly as to in effect read it out of the Constitution (at least until the end of the twentieth century).

The majority of the justices in this era equated due process with "fundamental fairness" and with respect to Fourteenth Amendment "liberty" were far more concerned with protecting "liberty of contract" against efforts by state governments to regulate a variety of social and economic problems connected with America's rapid industrialization. The exception was Justice John Marshall Harlan (I) who, in three criminal procedures cases between 1884 and 1908, argued that the word "liberty" in the amendment was a kind of shorthand reference to the specific protections found in the Bill of Rights. (The most famous modern proponent of this "total incorporation" view was Justice Hugo Black, starting with his dissent in a 1947 case, *Adamson v. California*, 332 U.S. 46, 1947.)

Speech, Press, Assembly, and Petition

With respect to the First Amendment, an important watershed was the case of *Gitlow v. New York*, 268 U.S. 652, in 1925. In this case the defendant was charged with violating that state's Criminal Anarchy Act of 1902 by publishing several pamphlets that allegedly advocated the overthrow of New York's government by unlawful means. When Gitlow's appeal came before the Supreme Court, he argued that the New York law interfered with his freedom of speech, a "liberty" protected by the due process clause of the Fourteenth Amendment against state abridgment.

In his opinion for the Court, Justice Sanford made constitutional history when he stated (in dictum): "For present purposes we may and do assume that freedom of speech and of the press . . . are among the fundamental personal rights and 'liberties' protected by the due process clause of the Fourteenth Amendment from impairment by the States." Thus was freedom of speech "incorporated" into the Fourteenth Amendment. (The Court went on to uphold Gitlow's conviction, arguing that all constitutional liberties are subject to reasonable restrictions and that there is no

constitutional protection for speech advocating criminal activity.)

Two years later, in *Fiske v. Kansas*, 274 U.S. 380 (1927), the Court confirmed the applicability of freedom of speech to the states, with a more positive outcome for the defendant, holding that a Kansas criminal syndicalism statute as applied to Fiske violated the Constitution. Any lingering doubts about the Court's new course were further dissipated in two 1931 cases. In *Stromberg v. California*, 283 U.S. 359 (1931), the Court struck down a California law prohibiting the display of red flags. Chief Justice Charles Evans Hughes favorably cited *Gitlow* and *Fiske* and also laid the groundwork for the modern Court's "symbolic speech" cases, recognizing that certain actions can be so expressive as to constitute protected communication. In *Near v. Minnesota*, 283 U.S. 697 (1931), the Court overturned a Minnesota law as violative of freedom of the press, reaffirming that a bedrock principle of freedom of speech and the press (now also incorporated into the Fourteenth Amendment) is that governments cannot engage in "prior restraints."

Freedom of assembly was incorporated in *DeJonge v. Oregon*, 299 U.S. 353 (1937), again involving a state criminal syndicalism law. DeJonge was charged with participation in a political rally organized by the Communist Party. The evidence against DeJonge consisted solely of party literature in his possession; no illegal activity was advocated at the meeting. The Oregon Supreme Court upheld his conviction, but the U.S. Supreme Court reversed. Chief Justice Hughes argued that peaceable assembly is a "right cognate to those of free speech and free press and is equally fundamental."

While no Supreme Court case has directly held that the right to petition is incorporated into the Fourteenth Amendment, the overwhelming implication of the Court's reasoning in the cases thus far discussed must be that this right is also protected against state government infringement.

Religion

In 1934, in *Hamilton v. Regents of the University of California*, 293 U.S. 245 (1934), Justice Cardozo's concurring opinion suggests that the Fourteenth Amendment's due process clause undoubtedly includes certain religious liberties, but neither his nor the Court's opinion specifically refers to the free exercise clause. Ultimately, very much like Benjamin Gitlow, Hamilton won the battle but lost the war. He argued that his religious conviction entitled him to an exemption from the University of California's military training requirement, but the Court held that Hamilton was not compelled to attend the university. But if he did, he could be subject to the school's rules and regulations.

Thus, by the late 1930s, the speech and press and free exercise of religion components of the First Amendment had been incorporated. There were also other cases (largely involving state criminal procedures, including those in which John Marshall Harlan (I) had dissented) in which the Court refused to incorporate some element of the Bill of Rights. The time was ripe for the Court to formulate a standard that would explain these disparate outcomes, and the task fell to Justice Benjamin N. Cardozo. In *Palko v. Connecticut*, 302 U.S. 319 (1937), Cardozo explained that only those rights that were fundamental were included in Fourteenth Amendment liberty, describing them as "those fundamental principles of liberty and justice which lie at the base of all our civil and political institutions" and "rooted in the traditions and conscience of our people . . . ." For his quintessential illustration, Cardozo mentioned "freedom of thought and speech," a freedom "that is the matrix, the indispensable condition, of nearly every other form of freedom."

In 1940, building on *Hamilton v. Regents*, the Court, in *Cantwell v. Connecticut*, 310 U.S. 296 (1940), actually found in favor of the individual's claim of an infringement on free exercise. The Court held that Connecticut's conviction of a Jehovah's Witness for going door to door distributing religious literature was invalid. While the state may regulate the time, place, and manner of such solicitations, it could not forbid them entirely.

Would the Amendment's ban on establishment of religion—the only component not yet incorporated—now be added to the list of fundamental liberties applicable to the states? The answer came in a 1947 case, *Everson v. Board of Education*, 330 U.S. 1 (1947). There, speaking through Justice Black, the Court invoked Thomas Jefferson's "wall of separation between Church and State" and applied the ban on establishment of religion to state actions. At the same time, the Court decided that the wall had not been breached by the governmental action at issue in this case—New Jersey's statute authorizing boards of education to reimburse parents, including those whose children attended religious schools, for the cost of bus transportation to and from school. The Court did not see the program as prohibited aid to a specific religious institution, but rather as a general program to help all parents get their children, regardless of religion, to and from their schools.

Association

The First Amendment says nothing about "freedom of association," but in *NAACP v. Alabama*, 357 U.S. 449 (1958), the Court said that such a right was so essential to the enjoyment of rights enumerated in the amendment that it is protected against state infringements. The case must be seen, as the Court did, against the background of the struggle for civil rights for African Americans. In an attempt to frustrate the activities of the National Association for the Advancement of Colored People (NAACP) on behalf of civil rights, Alabama ordered the organization to produce a variety of its records, including its membership list. The NAACP claimed that publicizing the names of its members would inevitably lead to various reprisals, including possible violence, against those members. The Supreme Court held that the organization could assert the constitutional rights of its members, including most importantly the right to pursue lawful interests and to freely associate for the purpose of furthering such interests. The fine and contempt judgment against the NAACP by an Alabama trial court were overturned.

PHILIP A. DYNIA

References and Further Reading

Abraham, Henry J. and Barbara A. Perry. *Freedom and the Court*, 8th ed. Lawrence: University Press of Kansas, 2003.

Amar, Akhil Reed. *The Bill of Rights: Creation and Reconstruction*. New Haven, CT: Yale University Press, 1998.

Curtis, Michael Kent. *No State Shall Abridge: The 14th Amendment and the Bill of Rights*. Durham, NC: Duke University Press, 1986.

———. *Free Speech, "the People's Darling Privilege": Struggles for Freedom of Expression in American History*. Durham, NC: Duke University Press, 2000.

Cases and Statutes Cited

Adamson v. California, 332 U.S. 46 (1947)
Barron v. Baltimore, 7 Pet. (32 U.S.) 243 (1833)
Cantwell v. Connecticut, 310 U.S. 296 (1940)
DeJonge v. Oregon, 299 U.S. 353 (1937)
Everson v. Board of Education, 330 U.S. 1 (1947)
Fiske v. Kansas, 274 U.S. 380 (1927)
Gitlow v. New York, 268 U.S. 652 (1925)
Hamilton v. Regents of the University of California, 293 U.S. 245 (1934)
NAACP v. Alabama, 357 U.S. 449 (1958)
Near v. Minnesota, 283 U.S. 697 (1931)
Palko v. Connecticut, 302 U.S. 319 (1937)
Stromberg v. California, 283 U.S. 359 (1931)
Slaughterhouse Cases, 16 Wall. (83 U.S.) 36 (1873)

See also **Establishment Clause Doctrine: Supreme Court Jurisprudence; Free Exercise Clause Doctrine: Supreme Court Jurisprudence; Incorporation Doctrine; Privileges and Immunities (XIV)**

APPRENDI v. NEW JERSEY, 530 U.S. 466 (2000)

This case was designed to protect the Sixth Amendment right to a "speedy and public trial, by an impartial jury" and the right inherent in the due process clauses of the Fifth and Fourteenth Amendments to have every element of a criminal offense proven beyond a reasonable doubt. Charles Apprendi fired shots into the home of an African-American family and pleaded guilty to a number of state weapons offenses, the most serious punishable by up to ten years in prison. At sentencing, the New Jersey trial judge applied the state's statute providing for enhanced sentences for "hate crimes." Pursuant to this statute, Apprendi faced not ten but twenty years, maximum, and was sentenced to twelve years' imprisonment. The factual finding that Apprendi acted with racial animus was made by the judge, using a preponderance of evidence standard. Apprendi objected, and the U.S. Supreme Court reversed. Justice Stevens, writing for a five-member majority, declared, "Other than the fact of a prior conviction, any fact that increases the penalty for a crime beyond the prescribed statutory maximum must be submitted to a jury, and proved beyond a reasonable doubt."

In a dissent representing four justices, Justice O'Connor found the majority's holding unsupported by history, and she argued that it would disadvantage defendants and undermine three decades of sentencing reform. Under federal sentencing guidelines and state determinate sentencing regimes, judges currently make numerous factual findings that can increase a defendant's sentence for a particular offense—usually by a preponderance of the evidence standard and generally based upon certain characteristics surrounding the offense (such as whether the offense was committed with a gun) and the offender (such as the extent of his or her criminal history). The goal of the sentencing reform movement is to ensure equality of sentencing for similarly situated defendants in an efficient manner; a shift back to pure judicial discretion in sentencing or jury findings of all facts relevant to sentencing would halt this reform.

Moreover, Justice O'Connor suggested that the majority's holding amounted to a "meaningless and formalistic" rule that legislatures could easily avoid.

For example, New Jersey could increase the maximum sentence for weapons offenses from ten to twenty years' imprisonment and allow a judge to reduce the penalty to ten years by finding that the defendant did not act with racial animus. Finally, Justice O'Connor predicted that this "watershed" rule would unleash a "flood of petitions by convicted defendants seeking to invalidate their sentences."

In the years since *Apprendi* was rendered, only one of Justice O'Connor's predictions has born fruit. Though many state and federal statutes contain facts that boost maximum penalties, prosecutors have adjusted by charging those facts in the indictment and submitting them to the jury. Due to structural democratic constraints, neither Congress nor state legislatures have attempted to avoid *Apprendi*'s holding by raising statutory maximums. Likewise, *Apprendi* has not threatened completed criminal prosecutions; the vast majority of those sentences have been upheld on appeal via procedural hurdles such as harmless error, bars against successive petitions, and nonretroactivity (see *Schriro v. Summerlin*, 124 S.Ct. 2519 [2004]).

However, *Apprendi*'s negative impact on sentencing reform has been profound. In *Ring v. Arizona*, 536 U.S. 584 (2002), six justices held that because Arizona conditioned eligibility for the death penalty upon the presence of an aggravating fact that was not an element of first-degree murder, the Sixth Amendment guaranteed the defendant a right to a jury determination of that fact. This threatens the capital sentencing schemes in nine states.

In *Blakely v. Washington*, the five justices comprising the majority in *Apprendi* held that the relevant "statutory maximum" for Mr. Blakely's offense of kidnapping was the fifty-three-month sentence provided for by the Washington state sentencing guidelines and not the ten-year statutory maximum specified for the offense. Thus, the judge could not impose a ninety-month sentence based upon his finding that the defendant acted with "deliberate cruelty." This decision threatens the sentencing schemes in fourteen states and the federal system. In *United States v. Booker*, 543 U.S. (2005), five members of the Court held that the Sixth Amendment as construed by Blakely applies to judicial findings of fact under federal sentencing guidelines; however, a different five-member majority held that the remedy was not to submit those facts to the jury, but rather to transform the guidelines from mandatory rules (providing statutory maximum sentences) to advisory guidelines for federal judges.

SUSAN R. KLEIN

References and Further Reading

Bowman, Frank O., III, *Train Wreck? Or Can the Federal Sentencing System be Saved? A Plea for Rapid Reversal of* Blakely v. Washington, Am. Crim. Law Rev. 41 (2004): 215.
Chaneson, Steven L., *The Next Era of Sentencing Reform*, Emory Law Journal 54 (forthcoming 2005).
King, Nancy J., and Susan R. Klein, *Apres* Apprendi, Federal Sentencing Reporter 12 (2000): 331.
———, *Essential Elements*, Vanderbilt Law Rev. 54 (2001): 1467.
———, Apprendi *and Plea Bargaining*, Stanford Law Rev. 54 (2001): 295.
———, *Beyond* Blakely, Federal Sentencing Reporter 16 (June 2004): 413.
Klein, Susan R., and Jordan M. Steiker, *The Search for Equality in Criminal Sentencing*, Supreme Court Rev. 2002 (2003): 223.
Levine, Andrew M., *The Confounding Boundaries of "Apprendi-land": Statutory Minimums and the Federal Sentencing Guidelines*, Am. Crim. L. 29 (2002): 377.

APPROPRIATION OF NAME OR LIKENESS

Appropriation of name or likeness, the oldest and most widely recognized branch of the invasion of privacy tort, imposes liability for unauthorized use of another's name, likeness, or other identifying characteristics. Although the tort applies whenever the defendant, for his or her benefit (pecuniary or otherwise), appropriates the plaintiff's identity, the great majority of appropriation cases involve "commercial" uses like advertising or merchandising.

Although initially understood as protecting a dignitary or autonomy interest, this tort is now seen as protecting an economic interest as well. In a significant number of jurisdictions, individuals have a "right of privacy," which protects them from the indignity and embarrassment of having their personalities commercialized without their consent, and a "right of publicity," which affords them exclusive control of the commercial value of their identities. Whereas the former is a purely personal right, the latter is assignable by contract and, in many jurisdictions, descendible.

The appropriation tort's impact on the news media is limited because a news disseminator is generally privileged to use a person's name or image in connection with an article or program on a matter of public interest. This privilege, however, does not apply if there is no discernible relationship between the plaintiff and the content of the news report, if the report's content is deliberately fabricated, or if the report is a disguised advertisement. The use of a person's identity in commentary, entertainment, and creative works is ordinarily privileged as well. However, in *Zacchini v. Scripps–Howard Broadcasting Co.*, 433 U.S. 562 (1977), the Supreme Court held that the First Amendment does not bar liability for the unauthorized television news broadcast of a performer's "entire act."

MICHAEL MADOW

References and Further Reading

Keeton, W. Page et al. *Prosser and Keeton on the Law of Torts*. St. Paul, MN: West Publishing, 1984.
Madow, Michael, *Private Ownership of Public Image*, 81(1) California Law Review 125–240 (1993).
McCarthy, J. Thomas. *The Rights of Publicity and Privacy*. Eagen, MN: Thomson West, 2005.
Nimmer, Melville, *The Right of Publicity*, Law & Contemporary Problems 19 (Winter 1954): 203–223.
Prosser, William L., *Privacy*, California Law Review 48 (1960): 3:383–423.
Restatement (Second) of Torts, Sec. 652C (1976).
Warren, Samuel D. and Brandeis, Louis D., *The Right to Privacy*, Harvard Law Review 4 (1890): 5:193–220.

Cases and Statutes Cited

Zacchini v. Scripps–Howard Broadcasting Co., 433 U.S. 562 (1977)

See also **Invasion of Privacy and Free Speech; Right of Privacy**

APTHEKER v. SECRETARY OF STATE, 378 U.S. 500 (1964)

Aptheker is an important civil liberties case involving the right to travel. In *Aptheker v. Secretary of State*, 378 U.S. 500, 84 S.Ct. 1659 (1964), the U.S. Supreme Court overturned a federal law that the Court believed unconstitutionally interfered with the freedom of American citizens to travel abroad.

Herbert Aptheker (1915–2003), an historian and political activist, joined the Communist Party in 1939 and subsequently served in the U.S. military in World War II, the struggle for civil rights in the South, and the movement against the War in Vietnam. When his passport was revoked by the U.S. State Department, along with those of other Communist Party leaders, he legally challenged the governmental action.

The U.S. Supreme Court held that section 6 of the Subversive Activities Control Act, which permitted the State Department to refuse to issue or renew passports for members of communist organizations, was unconstitutional on its face. No specific circumstances surrounding application of the law could cure its constitutional infirmity since it "too broadly and indiscriminately restricts the right to travel and thereby abridges the liberty guaranteed by the Fifth Amendment." The Court had previously held the right to travel abroad was an important aspect of a citizen's liberty and that liberty was violated by a subversive activities law ignoring an "individual's knowledge, activity, commitment, and purposes in and places for travel." *Aptheker* is one of a series of cases decided by the U.S. federal courts in the beginning of the 1960s that indicated a trend away from abject judicial acquiescence in cold-war interference with civil liberty and due process.

ANTHONY CHASE

ARIZONA v. FULMINANTE, 499 U.S. 279 (1991)

Arizona v. Fulminante considered whether a state court properly found a defendant's confession was coerced in violation of the Fifth Amendment and whether admission of a coerced confession is properly evaluated using harmless error analysis.

Although the defendant was suspected of murdering his eleven-year-old stepdaughter, the state had insufficient evidence to file charges against him. While he was incarcerated in New Jersey for an unrelated felony, he was befriended by another inmate, a former officer, masquerading as an organized crime figure. The officer-turned-informant told the defendant that he knew that the defendant was "starting to get some tough treatment" from other inmates because of a rumor that he murdered a child. He offered to protect the defendant from the other inmates, but told him "You have to tell me about it, . . . for me to give you any help" (499 U.S. at 283). At that point, the defendant admitted killing and sexually assaulting the child and the confession was used to convict him for the murder.

The Court held that the state court accurately applied the "totality of the circumstances" test to determine the voluntariness of the confession (*Schneckloth v. Bustamonte*, 412 U.S. 218, 1973). Because the confession was tendered in the belief that the defendant's life was in jeopardy, the lower court appropriately found that it was "a true coerced confession in every way" (778 P.2d 602, 627, 1988).

Over the strong dissent of four justices, the majority held that harmless error analysis could be applied to admission of a coerced confession. Under this test, the state must be able to show that introduction of the confession was harmless beyond a reasonable doubt (*Chapman v. California*, 386 U.S. 18, 24, 1967). Unable to do so in this case, the Court affirmed the state court's decision to grant the defendant a new trial. By allowing the application of harmless error analysis, the Court effectively overruled the blanket exclusion of coerced confessions.

EMILY FROIMSON

Cases and Statutes Cited

Chapman v. California, 386 U.S. 18, 24 (1967)
Schneckloth v. Bustamonte, 412 U.S. 218 (1973)

See also **Coerced Confessions/Police Interrogations; Due Process**

ARIZONA v. HICKS, 480 U.S. 321 (1987)

In *Hicks*, the Supreme Court announced that probable cause is required to justify the search or seizure of items discovered in "plain view" during an unrelated search. Police entered an apartment after shots were fired through its floor, injuring a man in the apartment below. While they were searching for the shooter, weapons, and other victims, an officer noticed several pieces of expensive stereo equipment that he suspected were stolen. He read and recorded the serial numbers of all the items, moving at least one of them—a turntable—to do so. The equipment was identified by these numbers as having been stolen in an armed robbery, for which the respondent Hicks was indicted.

The state trial court and the Arizona Court of Appeals granted the respondent's motion to suppress, reasoning that the officer's obtaining the serial numbers exceeded the scope of the exigency that justified the search following the shooting. After the Arizona Supreme Court denied review, the Supreme Court granted the state's petition for certiorari.

By a vote of six to three, the Court held that the evidence should be suppressed because, although the recording of the serial numbers was not a "seizure," the moving of the turntable constituted a separate search, unrelated to the exigency justifying the officers' entry. To be reasonable under the Fourth Amendment, that separate, warrantless search required probable cause. The majority declined to adopt the dissent's suggestion that a lesser "cursory search" could be justified in connection with a plain-view inspection, holding instead that "a search is a search."

JULIE A. BAKER

References and Further Reading

Milstein, Lee C., *Note, Fortress of Solitude or Law of Malevolence? Rethinking the Desirability of Bright-Line Protection of the Home*, N.Y.U.L. Rev. 78 (2003): 1789.

Sundby, Scott C., *A Return to Fourth Amendment Basics: Undoing the Mischief of* Camara *and* Terry, Minn. L. Rev. 72 (1988): 383.
Wallin, Howard E., *Plain View Revisited*, Pace L. Rev. 22 (2002): 307.

Cases and Statutes Cited

Coolidge v. New Hampshire, 403 U.S. 443 (1971)
Illinois v. Andreas, 463 U.S. 765 (1983)
Mincey v. Arizona, 437 U.S. 385 (1978)
Payton v. New York, 445 U.S. 573 (1980)
Texas v. Brown, 460 U.S. 730 (1983)

See also **Plain View; Probable Cause; Scalia, Antonin; Search (General Definition); Seizures;** *Terry v. Ohio,* **392 U.S. 1 (1968); Warrantless Searches**

ARIZONA v. YOUNGBLOOD, 488 U.S. 51 (1988)

In *Youngblood*, a divided Supreme Court held that the Fourteenth Amendment due process clause does not require the government to preserve evidence that could conclusively prove the defendant innocent.

Weeks after a young boy was abducted and raped, Youngblood was arrested and charged with the crime after the boy picked his photo from a lineup. Youngblood maintained his innocence and requested that a semen stain on the boy's clothing be tested to determine the rapist's blood type. Unfortunately, such testing could not be performed because the police had neglected to refrigerate the stained clothing. Youngblood was convicted at trial, but an appellate court reversed the conviction because the destroyed evidence deprived Youngblood of an opportunity to prove his innocence.

The U.S. Supreme Court reinstated Youngblood's conviction by a vote of six to three. Relying on *California v. Trombetta*, the majority ruled that the government's failure to preserve potentially exculpatory evidence violates due process only if the government intentionally destroys the evidence in bad faith. Since the police did not intentionally allow the evidence to deteriorate in Youngblood's case, the Court reasoned that he was not entitled to any relief even though the police's negligence deprived him of an opportunity to establish his innocence conclusively. *Youngblood* thus sharply limits the responsibility of the government to preserve potentially exculpatory evidence for testing.

In 2000, twelve years after the Court sent Youngblood back to prison, he was exonerated when more advanced DNA testing on the stained clothing established that he was not the rapist.

DAVID A. MORAN

References and Further Reading

Imwinkelried, Edwin, and Norman Garland. *Exculpatory Evidence*, 2nd ed. Charlottesville, VA: Michie Publications, 1996.
Stacy, Tom, *The Search for Truth in Constitutional Criminal Procedure*, Columbia Law Review 91 (1991): 1369.
Whitaker, Barbara. "DNA Frees Inmate Years After Justices Rejected Plea." *The New York Times*, August 11, 2000.

Cases and Statutes Cited

California v. Trombetta, 467 U.S. 479 (1984)

See also ***California v. Trombetta*, 467 U.S. 479 (1984); Due Process; Fourteenth Amendment**

ARRAIGNMENT AND PROBABLE CAUSE HEARING

Depending on whether the crime charged is brought federally or within a state jurisdiction, an individual accused of a crime could be faced with a few different pretrial proceedings. In a federal case, once a person is arrested, the Federal Rules of Criminal Procedure mandates a defendant be brought before a magistrate judge, or other lawful substitute, without unnecessary delay and be advised of his rights and the charges alleged. Most state jurisdictions mirror this requirement. A second type of hearing, as required by the Fourth Amendment of the Constitution, requires a preliminary hearing/examination to determine whether or not there is probable cause for the underlying arrest (pre-indictment) (*Gerstein v. Pugh*, 420 U.S. 107, 1975). While each of the pretrial hearings serves separate functions, it is not unusual if they are combined and heard simultaneously in some jurisdictions.

In addition, the U.S. Supreme Court has put a time clock on the probable cause hearing so that it is to be held within forty-eight hours for those arrested without a warrant (*Riverside v. McLaughlin*, 500 U.S. 44, 1991). Furthermore, in the federal criminal system, if the defendant is determined to be a danger or a flight risk and is detained after this initial appearance, the government then has ten days to seek a grand jury indictment or a finding of "probable cause" by a magistrate judge at a preliminary hearing. If the defendant is not detained, the government then has twenty days to seek grand jury indictment. Furthermore, even a finding of "probable cause" by a federal magistrate judge does not substitute for the Fifth Amendment's requirement for indictment by a grand jury in a federal case. Thus, the case must still be presented to a grand jury. It should also be noted that states are not required to bring a criminal charge by a grand jury and therefore may generally proceed on a case with a finding of probable cause by a judge.

A preliminary hearing is the vehicle used to determine whether there is "probable cause" to believe that an offense has been committed and whether the defendant committed it. The proceeding does not establish guilt or innocence and does not preclude a subsequent grand jury from considering the same case for indictment. Therefore, even if a magistrate judge does not find probable cause to support the arrest and dismisses the complaint with a release of the accused, this does not prevent a prosecution for that same offense.

Subsequent to indictment or other charging document (for example, information), an arraignment must be held. Like the initial appearance in court after an arrest, the arraignment is merely part of the initial steps in the criminal process. At the arraignment, retained counsel represents the defendant or, if the defendant is considered indigent, court-appointed counsel is provided. In addition, the defendant is provided a copy of the charging document and asked to plead to the allegations. Normally, a defendant will initially enter a plea of "not guilty" to allow for time to receive and inspect discovery, investigate the charges, and consult with counsel. Finally, the arraignment is also significant in that it serves as a trigger for many procedural rules, such as the "speedy trial clock" (if the defendant is out of custody), discovery deadlines, and the multiple "notices," as prescribed by the procedural rules such as insanity or alibi.

ROBERT DON GIFFORD

Cases and Statutes Cited

Gerstein v. Pugh, 420 U.S. 107 (1975)
Riverside v. McLaughlin, 500 U.S. 44 (1991)

ARREST

The fact of an arrest and the definition of an arrest are of fundamental importance. An arrest is a significant intrusion upon the liberty of the person arrested. Another reason the term is important is because, when a valid arrest is made, the right of the police to search the person arrested is automatic. It is also significant because, if an arrest is made without probable cause, the subsequent seizure of evidence may be considered a fruit of that unlawful arrest and cannot be used against the suspect in a criminal trial. The timing of an arrest is also important in civil actions for claims of false arrest.

Throughout most of the history of the United States, the law of arrest was largely unregulated by the strictures of Fourth Amendment theory. There are two primary reasons for this. First, the exclusionary rule was not adopted to regulate the activities of federal authorities until the early part of the twentieth century. Only at that point, as Telford Taylor has observed, was there a "good reason" to contest the validity of a search incident to arrest. Second, law enforcement has been, and still remains, primarily a state and local issue. Given that the rule excluding illegally obtained evidence from criminal trials was not made applicable to state actors until 1961, the Fourth Amendment's requirements did not regulate the great bulk of interactions between law enforcement officials and citizens. Accordingly, the concept of an arrest developed primarily outside the body of Fourth Amendment jurisprudence.

Most of the development of the law on arrest occurred at common law. Several centuries of precedent and many commentators have produced what appear to be irreconcilable definitions of what constitutes an arrest. This is because the common law definition of arrest, like many common law principles, has proved to be very malleable and has been engrafted with factual considerations and burdened by broad generalizations. One must look beyond each factual situation and eliminate the extraneous gloss on the definition created by some authorities. Once that is done, two essential components of the common law definition of an arrest by a law enforcement officer acting pursuant to real or pretended authority emerge: (1) the officer must obtain "custody" of the suspect; and (2) the officer must intend to obtain that custody.

The concept of "custody" at common law did not require a trip to the police station, booking, or the institution of formal charges to constitute an arrest. Rather, an arrest was equated with any form of intentional detention and began at the moment of the detention. Indeed, as has been stated by Alexander in his treatise, the word arrest "is derived from the French word *arreter*, which means to stop, detain, to hinder, to obstruct." Custody occurs when the police officer physically touches the suspect with the intent to arrest him or when the suspect submits to the officer's show of authority.

Intent to arrest is the second element of the common law definition of arrest. An officer's act of obtaining custody must be intentional—that is, he or she must do the acts that would otherwise constitute an arrest with the intent to arrest the suspect. There is no required manifestation of an intent to arrest beyond the acts sufficient to obtain custody. Also, an officer must not intend to do anything with the suspect beyond the intent to detain him.

The U.S. Supreme Court has generally followed the common law rule to define an arrest. However, to permit a search incident to arrest, the Court has sometimes required more, such as an intent by the police to take the person to the police station before they are allowed to search. An arrest is justified when the police have probable cause that the person arrested has committed a crime. Probable cause is a fair probability that the person has committed the crime. In measuring probable cause, a court examines the factual and practical considerations of everyday life upon which reasonable persons act.

Modern authority to arrest is governed by statute in most jurisdictions, with each jurisdiction specifying the types of offenses that permit an arrest. Arrests are generally made for the purpose of prosecuting the person for a criminal offense. However, arrests for other purposes are also sometimes permitted, including detaining material witnesses to an offense to obtain information from them. Police officers will also exercise their authority to arrest persons for a variety of reasons, such as separating persons involved in domestic disputes or fights, but will then exercise their discretion and let the arrestees go without charging them. These are just a few of the many reasons why a large percentage of arrests do not result in prosecution.

THOMAS K. CLANCY

References and Further Reading

Alexander, C. *The Law of Arrest.* 1949 § 45.
Clancy, Thomas K., *What Constitutes an "Arrest" within the Meaning of the Fourth Amendment?* Vill. L. Rev. 48 (2003): 129.
Sherman, Lawrence W., *Defining Arrest: Practical Consequences of Agency Differences,* Crim. L. Bull. 16 (1980): 376.
Taylor, Telford. *Two Studies in Constitutional Interpretation.* 1969.

Cases and Statutes Cited

Barnhard v. State, 587 A.2d 561 (Md. App. 1991), aff'd, 602 A.2d 701 (Md. 1992)
Brinegar v. United States, 338 U.S. 160, 175 (1949)
California v. Hodari D., 499 U.S. 621 (1991)
Knowles v. Iowa, 525 U.S. 113 (1998)
Michigan v. DeFillippo, 443 U.S. 31, 37 (1979)
State v. Oquendo, 613 A.2d 1300 (Conn. 1992)
Terry v. Ohio, 392 U.S. 1 (1968)
Weeks v. United States, 232 U.S. 383 (1914)

See also **Arrest Warrants; Search (General Definition); Seizures**

ARREST WARRANTS

Law enforcement officials in America and in England in the period preceding the American Revolution did not have broad inherent authority to search and seize; such actions required authorization, and the warrant system was the primary means to confer that authority. Those were simple times and warrantless searches and seizures were virtually nonexistent. Only one type of warrantless seizure may have been common: the arrest of a suspected felon. Such arrests were rarely made except in hot pursuit of the felon. The common law also permitted warrantless arrests for misdemeanors committed in the officer's presence.

There existed at common law the legal process of obtaining an arrest warrant for criminal offenses. An arrest warrant was a command to the sheriff of the county or the marshal of the court to apprehend the suspect and bring him or her to court. This warrant was issued upon a showing of probable cause that the person had committed a felony. It was issued by the court after examining the requesting party under oath and reducing that examination to writing concerning whether a crime had been committed and the party's grounds for suspicion. The person suspected of the crime had to be named.

A similar legal process to obtain a warrant continues to this day. The contemporary authority of the police to arrest with or without warrants varies from state to state based on each state's law. Some of those considerations are whether the crime is a misdemeanor or felony and whether the crime occurred in the officer's presence.

In the twentieth century, the Supreme Court in two separate cases addressed the question of whether the Fourth Amendment required law enforcement officials to obtain a warrant before arresting a suspect. The Court made a distinction between arrests in the home and arrests in public. For arrests in a person's home, the Court in *Payton v. New York,* 445 U.S. 573 (1980), mandated that an arrest warrant was required and that that warrant carried the implicit authority to enter the home to arrest the suspect.

For arrests occurring in public, however, the Court in *United States v. Watson,* 423 U.S. 411 (1976), established that no warrant was required. The distinction between the two situations was based on the Court's view that the physical intrusion into a person's home is the "chief evil" that the Fourth Amendment is designed to prevent and that an intrusion into a home to arrest invades its sanctity and privacy. Thus, as *Payton* said, the "Fourth Amendment draws a firm line at the entrance of the house." Accordingly, absent exigent circumstances, a warrant is needed. In contrast, *Watson* relied heavily on the prevailing common law view that no warrant is needed for an arrest occurring in public.

THOMAS K. CLANCY

References and Further Reading

Clancy, Thomas K., *What Constitutes an "Arrest" within the Meaning of the Fourth Amendment*, Vill. L. Rev. 48 (2003): 129.

——, *The Role of Individualized Suspicion in Assessing the Reasonableness of Searches and Seizures*, Memphis L. Rev. 25 (1995): 483.

Coke, Edwardo. *Institutes of the Laws of England.* 1797, 177.

Davies, Thomas Y., *Recovering the Original Fourth Amendment*, Mich. L. Rev. 98 (1999): 547.

Grano, Joseph D., *Rethinking the Fourth Amendment Warrant Requirement*, Am. Crim. L. Rev. 19 (1982): 603.

Hale. *The History of the Pleas of the Crown.* 1847, 85–104.

Wasserstrom, Silas J., *The Incredible Shrinking Fourth Amendment*, Am. Crim. L. Rev. 21 (1984): 257.

Cases and Statutes Cited

Payton v. New York, 445 U.S. 573 (1980)
United States v. Watson, 423 U.S. 411 (1976)

See also **Arrest; Seizures**

ARREST WITHOUT A WARRANT

An arrest constitutes a seizure and must therefore satisfy the Fourth Amendment's requirement that all searches and seizures be reasonable. In order to be reasonable, all arrests must be supported by probable cause to believe that a crime has been committed and that the person to be arrested has committed it. A further, more difficult question is whether the determination of probable cause must be made prior to the arrest by a magistrate issuing an arrest warrant or whether police may lawfully make the arrest without a warrant so long as a magistrate subsequently finds probable cause.

The rules dictating the necessity of a warrant are best understood as not protecting the arrestee's freedom from seizure, but rather any legitimate privacy interests in the physical area that police must enter to make the arrest. Viewed from that perspective, it is not surprising that the rules governing warrants vary depending on the location of the arrest.

In *United States v. Watson*, 423 U.S. 411 (1976), the Supreme Court upheld the constitutionality of warrantless arrests made in public places. The Court's opinion in *Watson* relied heavily on a history that permitted such arrests. The common law authorized police to make warrantless arrests for misdemeanors that occurred in the officer's presence and for all felonies. The traditional common law rule became prevailing contemporary practice under federal and state laws. In light of the national consensus, the Court declined in *Watson* to impose a different rule

under the Fourth Amendment. The Court had no opportunity in *Watson* to address the constitutionality of warrantless arrests for misdemeanors committed outside a police officer's presence. However, such arrests are rare because most state statutes prohibit officers from making custodial arrests for misdemeanors unless they are committed in their presence.

Suspects who are arrested without a warrant are entitled under *Gerstein v. Pugh*, 420 U.S. 103 (1975), to a "prompt" judicial determination of probable cause following their arrest. In *Riverside v. McLaughlin*, 500 U.S. 44 (1991), the Court explained that probable cause hearings provided within forty-eight hours of arrest are presumed to be prompt, absent a contrary showing. After forty-eight hours, the burden shifts to the government to demonstrate extraordinary circumstances justifying the delay.

Despite the Court's allowance of warrantless arrests in public places, strategic or practical considerations may nevertheless persuade police to obtain an arrest warrant. For example, police may be uncertain whether their evidence amounts to probable cause. A judicial determination in advance of arrest mitigates the risk of an unlawful arrest based on the lack of probable cause. Obtaining arrest warrants and maintaining a computerized database of them also facilitates future arrests of wanted suspects during happenstance encounters such as traffic stops.

In contrast to arrests in public places, the Supreme Court has construed the Fourth Amendment to require warrants when police must search a home to make the arrest. In *Payton v. New York*, 445 U.S. 573 (1980), the Court held that the Fourth Amendment prohibits the warrantless entry into a suspect's home to make an arrest. The Court explained that its holding was not intended to protect the suspect's freedom of movement, implicated by the arrest, but rather the suspect's privacy interests in the home, implicated by the police's nonconsensual entry.

Typically, police are required to obtain a search warrant to justify entry into a person's home. A search warrant is specific about location and requires the issuing magistrate to find probable cause that the person or thing to be seized is likely to be found on the premises to be searched. An arrest warrant, in contrast, only requires probable cause to believe that the suspect has committed a crime; the magistrate makes no determination about the suspect's current location. Despite the general rule requiring search warrants, the Court held in *Payton* that a suspect's privacy interests are sufficiently protected if the police enter an arrestee's home with an arrest warrant and reason to believe that the arrestee is currently home.

If police seek to arrest a suspect in the home of a third party, however, yet another rule applies, and police must obtain a search warrant. In *Steagald v. United States*, 451 U.S. 204 (1981), the Court held that an arrest warrant for a suspect who lives elsewhere is insufficient to justify entering a third party's home to make the arrest. To protect the third party homeowner's privacy interests, police must obtain a search warrant based on probable cause to believe that the arrestee will be found on the premises.

Although the three rules established in *Watson*, *Payton*, and *Steagald* are relatively straightforward, their application can raise trickier issues. For example, it may be unclear whether the arrest is in a public place. In *United States v. Santana*, the defendant was standing directly in her open doorway at the threshold of her home. The Supreme Court noted that the doorway was private in the same sense as a defendant's yard, but nevertheless held that the defendant was in a "public place" for purposes of applying *Watson* and could be arrested without a warrant. Currently, lower courts remain divided on the question of whether the *Watson* rule or *Payton* rule applies when police arrest the suspect in a commercial establishment that is not open to the general public.

Another issue that complicates the application of the rules is the defendant's ability to challenge a violation of them. A person who challenges a police search must have a reasonable expectation of privacy in the area searched (see *Rakas v. Illinois*, 439 U.S. 128, 1978). Accordingly, if police violate *Steagald* by entering a third party's home to arrest a wanted suspect, the suspect will not be permitted to challenge the unlawful search if he or she lacks reasonable privacy expectations in the third party's home. Because the *Steagald* rule is intended to protect privacy rights and not the suspect's liberty, any challenge of the search would need to be made by a person who enjoys privacy rights in the home. If no such person has an incentive to complain, the Fourth Amendment violation may never be challenged at all.

ALAFAIR S. BURKE

References and Further Reading

Dressler, Joshua. *Understanding Criminal Procedure*, 3rd ed. Understanding Series. New York: LexisNexis, 2002.

Cases and Statutes Cited

Gerstein v. Pugh, 420 U.S. 103 (1975)
Payton v. New York, 445 U.S. 573 (1980)
Rakas v. Illinois, 439 U.S. 128 (1978)
Riverside v. McLaughlin, 500 U.S. 44 (1991)
Steagald v. United States, 451 U.S. 204 (1981)
United States v. Watson, 423 U.S. 411 (1976)

See also **Arraignment and Probable Cause Hearing; Arrest; Arrest Warrants; Probable Cause; Search (General Definition); Search Warrants; Seizures**

ASHCROFT v. FREE SPEECH COALITION, 535 U.S. 234 (2002)

Congress passed the Child Pornography Prevention Act of 1996 that, among other things, dealt with "virtual" pornographic images of minors. The act prohibited not only the production, distribution, or advertising of pornographic images of actual children but also any visual depiction of what "appears to be" or "conveys the impression" of minors engaged in sexually explicit conduct. The lead respondent, Free Speech Coalition, a lobbying group for the adult entertainment industry, challenged the law on the grounds that the two provisions were constitutionally invalid.

A federal district court for the Ninth Circuit Court of Appeals in 1997 upheld the act's constitutionality, ruling the law was content neutral and legitimately discouraged child pornography's secondary effects, like pedophilia. Two years later, a panel for the Ninth Circuit reversed the district court in a two-to-one vote. From 1999 to 2001, however, four other circuit courts sustained the validity of the act. The Supreme Court granted certiorari and declared the "appears to be" and the "conveys the impression" provisions were overbroad, affirming the Ninth Circuit's decision. Justice Kennedy wrote for Justices Stevens, Souter, Ginsburg, and Breyer. Thomas concurred with the judgment. Justice O'Connor concurred in part and dissented in part. Justices Rehnquist and Scalia dissented.

According to Justice Kennedy, "This case provides a textbook example of why we permit facial challenges to statutes that burden expression." The imposition of criminal penalties on protected speech is a "stark example of speech suppression." The law prohibited the production of images "without using any real children" and thus went beyond *New York v. Ferber*, 458 U.S. 747 (1982), which sustained state interest in preventing the exploitation of actual minors involved in pornography. Virtual images do not involve real minors nor does the production of the images harm or exploit them.

Moreover, the law made no effort to conform to *Miller v. California*, 413 U.S. 015 (1973). Materials did not have to appeal to prurient interests; depictions of sexually explicit activity, regardless of their literary, artistic, political, or scientific value, were proscribed. Also, it was not necessary for the images to be patently offensive or contravene community standards, as

Miller requires. In addition, materials or images were not considered as a whole or in their entirety; a "single graphic depiction" of sexual activity could lead to severe criminal penalties.

Finally, the Court dismissed the government's secondary effects arguments regarding child pornography. As Justice Kennedy concludes, "The Government has shown no more than a remote connection between speech that might encourage thoughts or impulses and any resulting child abuse. Without a significantly stronger, more direct connection, the Government may not prohibit speech on the ground that it may encourage pedophiles to engage in illegal conduct."

Justice Rehnquist's dissent, joined by Justice Scalia, argued that the act's explicit definition of proscribed sexual activity did not reach protected images or materials. He accordingly claimed that if properly construed, based on its definition of child pornography, the act, would reach only "computer-generated images that are virtually indistinguishable from real children engaged in sexually explicit conduct. The statute need not be read to do any more than precisely this, which is not offensive to the First Amendment."

In response to the Court's decision, Congress enacted the Prosecutorial Remedies and Other Tools to End the Exploitation of Children Today Act of 2003 (*PROTECT Act*) that adopted the dissent's language to ban some nonobscene pornography produced without an actual minor.

ROY B. FLEMMING

References and Further Reading

Jenkins, Philip. *Beyond Tolerance: Child Pornography on the Internet*. New York: New York University Press, 2003.
Kende, Mark S. "The Supreme Court's Approach to the First Amendment in Cyberspace: Free Speech as Technology's Hand-Maiden." *Constitutional Commentary* 14(3) (1997):465–480.

Cases and Statutes Cited

Ashcroft v. Free Speech Coalition, 535 U.S. 234 (2002)
Miller v. California, 413 U.S. 015 (1973)
New York v. Ferber, 458 U.S. 747 (1982)

ASHCROFT, JOHN (1942–)

John Ashcroft served as attorney general during the first term of the administration of George W. Bush, and in his last year in office analysts were terming him the worst attorney general in the nation's history. Certainly in terms of civil liberties, Ashcroft showed no sympathy for or even understanding of due process and other constitutional protections. Under the banner of the war on terrorism, Ashcroft defended every infraction as necessary for the nation's security.

Ashcroft probably would not have become attorney general except for a freak political event. A conservative and very popular with the religious Right, Ashcroft had been governor of Missouri and then in 1994 won a seat to the U.S. Senate. He ran for re-election in 2000 against the popular Democratic governor, Mel Carnahan, who was killed in a plane crash just a few weeks before the election. Too late to replace his name on the ballot, Democrats urged voters to cast their votes for Carnahan, and the lieutenant governor said he would appoint Carnahan's widow to the seat until a special election could be scheduled. Carnahan won, the first time in history that a dead man won a federal election, and Bush then named Ashcroft to head the Justice Department.

Clearly the attacks of September 11, 2001, and the resulting "war on terror" shaped Ashcroft's and the administration's policies. Historically, civil liberties have always been at risk in wartime, but this "war" took place in an era with technological possibilities of invading the privacy and rights of individuals far greater than in any previous conflict. Ashcroft determined to make full use of what he considered the unlimited power of the executive branch in wartime along with all the tools of surveillance to ferret out would-be terrorists. If he had found and prosecuted any terrorists caught in these webs, he might have offered some justification for his actions; but in fact there were none. Much of the activity in federal courts consisted of men caught in a web of often lawless tactics trying to secure minimal due process of law. As for these efforts, Ashcroft cavalierly dismissed them, saying due process in wartime could be found outside the federal court system and attacking federal judges who questioned the administration's tactics as unpatriotic and allies of the terrorists.

In the wake of 9/11, the administration rounded up hundreds of men of Arab descent and held them virtually incommunicado for weeks and months. It fought every effort by civil liberties groups to get lawyers to these men and declared that, under the war powers, so-called "enemy combatants" were not entitled to the basic constitutional protections. In the end a number of these men were deported, not for terrorist activity, but for violations of immigration law; the rest were eventually released without any charges made against them and no apology from the government. Ashcroft considered the round-up justified by the circumstances; moreover, he argued that the president's war powers allowed him to arrest and hold indefinitely not only aliens but also American citizens, and he condemned as "proterrorist wimps" those who objected to such a claim.

The bad behavior of American troops in treating prisoners in Afghanistan and Iraq eventually led journalists to discover that the Justice Department had advised the administration that in wartime it was not bound by international bans against torture. When called to testify before the Senate Judiciary Committee in June 2004, Ashcroft argued that these memoranda were nothing more than talking points and that the United States did not justify torture and the president had not ordered it. But he refused to state that torture was wrong and would never be used or justified by the administration.

Following the hurried passing of the USA PATRIOT Act in late 2001, civil libertarians warned that the broad powers given to the government in terms of surveillance posed a great threat to civil liberties. Ashcroft at the time denied that such violations would occur, but in fact they did. During his tenure, the FBI engaged in massive surveillance of suspected domestic terrorists, which included groups that had no ties to Al-Queda or other Muslim fundamentalist terror operations. Although the law established a special court to deal with requests for warrants for secret wiretaps, the Bush administration chose to bypass this tribunal and engage in illegal wiretaps on its own authority.

Even if there had been no 9/11, which some theorists believed could in fact justify the type of extralegal activities engaged in by the Bush administration, Ashcroft's record in other, nonterrorist-related areas also showed a blatant disregard for civil liberties. When he was governor of and then senator from Missouri, Ashcroft had been a strong conservative, who counted as among his strongest supporters members of the so-called Christian right. An adherent of the ultraconservative Assembly of God church, he fully shared the Christian right's opposition to abortion and their demand for greater morality in public life.

He certainly tried to impose his brand of morality while attorney general. In one of the more ludicrous policies, he insisted that a blue cloth be draped over the torso of the "Spirit of Justice" statue in the Justice Department's great hall, the place where the attorney general normally holds his or her press conferences. It appears that the bare breast of the larger-than-life statue offended his sense of morality as well as those of his religious supporters.

With his defense of antipornography legislation and other attempts by Congress to regulate the Internet, Ashcroft also kept the solicitor general busy. All were struck down by the courts as violating the First Amendment.

A long time opponent of abortion, Ashcroft paid attention to some religious anti-abortion groups who equated physician-assisted suicide with termination of pregnancy. The Supreme Court in 1990 had ruled that although there was no constitutional right to physician-assisted suicide, states were free in their power to regulate medical practice to allow such an end-of-life choice. The Court even pointed to the example of Oregon, which through a referendum had adopted a model assisted-suicide law, as one option open to the states.

But Ashcroft would have none of it, and he attempted to use provisions of the federal narcotics law to nullify the Oregon plan, even going so far as to threaten criminal prosecution of doctors who prescribed lethal drugs to qualified patients. Oregon fought back, and in the federal district court as well as in the Court of Appeals for the Ninth Circuit, the judges slapped Ashcroft down, in effect saying he was an intermeddling busybody who had no power or authority under federal law to interfere. (That case went on appeal to the U.S. Supreme Court, but Ashcroft had left office when the justices granted certiorari.)

The Ashcroft Justice Department showed little interest in civil rights, and a number of lawyers left the civil rights section in protest. Ashcroft also aroused the ire of federal attorneys when he moved to restrict their discretion in prosecuting certain types of cases. Under federal law, some offenses, such as killing a federal officer, are considered capital crimes; this means that a death penalty may be sought. Federal prosecutors often determined to allow the defendant to plea bargain down to a lesser punishment in return for cooperation, such as providing the names of drug dealers higher up in the organization. Usually, the prosecutor informs the Justice Department of his or her decision to do this, and the officials in Washington usually defer to the judgment of the attorney handling the case.

But John Ashcroft wanted federal prosecutors to go for the death penalty in every possible instance, and it would seem that he did not care at all about other matters such as ensnaring gang leaders or large drug dealers. Ashcroft's intervention in these cases, often after a judge had approved the plea bargain, brought him enormous criticism from federal attorneys and from judges as well. Upon his leaving office there was widespread anticipation that his successor, Alberto Gonzalez, would be flooded with requests to review and overturn many of Ashcroft's decisions in this area.

At the time of the terrorist attack in September 2001, many people warned that if the United States ignored its long tradition of rule by law and protection of civil liberties, it would be no better than the enemy and that, in fact, this would mean that the terrorists had won. Interestingly, when the administration began planning what powers it could utilize,

Secretary of Defense Donald Rumsfield, aware of the violations of civil liberties in previous wars, convened a panel of respected, nongovernment lawyers to advise him and the administration on what they could and could not do. They warned him against the types of orders Bush was planning to use against noncitizens before special military panels, and to assure that traditional American rights, such as trial by jury and right to counsel, were not ignored. John Ashcroft, however, intervened to make sure that these recommendations were never implemented.

MELVIN I. UROFSKY

ASSISTED SUICIDE

It was not until the last decade of the twentieth century that the U.S. Supreme Court decided three cases in which the Court began what remains a tentative exploration of whether (if at all) the U.S. Constitution guarantees a choice concerning the time and manner of one's death. The Court seemed especially concerned that it leave room for the political process to address the so-called "right to die"—a term of art, covering a broad array of factual settings raising end-of-life issues, most notably physician-assisted suicide (PAS), decisions by competent adults to refuse or remove life-sustaining treatment, and choices made on behalf of children or incompetent adults. In 2004, the nation was riveted with the Terri Schiavo case, an especially powerful illustration of the legal and political complexities that abound in this area of individual liberty.

Legal Context

American law has long recognized a constitutional right to refuse medical treatment. Like all rights, it is not absolute and subject to reasonable state regulation. As early as 1905 (*Jacobson v. Massachusetts*, 197 U.S. 11), the Supreme Court upheld a compulsory vaccination law, justified by the government's interest in stopping the spread of communicable diseases.

The first case to bring to widespread public attention the issue of hastening the death of a dying person came in 1976, when a U.S. appellate court upheld the right of close family members to allow the termination of life support for a patient, Karen Ann Quinlan, in a persistent vegetative state. Other cases soon followed and all states enacted laws recognizing the legal right to withhold or withdraw life-sustaining medical treatment. There emerged a legal consensus

on three fundamental principles: (1) Competent persons have a right to refuse medical treatment, even if the result is death; (2) persons without decision-making capacity have a right to have their family decide to withhold or withdraw treatment; (3) a "bright line" exists between "passively" hastening a person's death by withholding or withdrawing treatment and more "active" means such as assisted suicide and active euthanasia.

The U.S. Supreme Court began its tentative forays into the problem in 1990 in the case of *Cruzan v. Director, Missouri Department of Health*, 497 U.S. 261 (1990). The parents of Nancy Cruzan, who was in a persistent vegetative state with no hope of regaining consciousness, sought to terminate food and hydration, ending her life.

The Court's decision was in three parts. First, the Court said that competent adults have a constitutional right to refuse medical care. (Only Justice Antonin Scalia refused to recognize such a right.) That principle, Chief Justice William Rehnquist wrote, "may be inferred from our prior decisions." Rehnquist "assumed" that there was a right to refuse food and water and thus hasten death. Five other justices stated explicitly that such a right exists. This liberty was grounded in the due process clause of the Fourteenth Amendment. The second major portion of the opinion held that before treatment is terminated, a state may require solid evidence that a person wanted that result. The third major component of the opinion held that states have the power to prevent family members from making this decision for another. The right to end treatment is uniquely personal, and a decision by others, even close family, may not necessarily be motivated by the best interests of the patient.

Key questions were left unresolved. The right recognized here was not deemed "fundamental" and thus the opinion gave no guidance as to what level of judicial scrutiny (strict or some lower level) was appropriate. The Court also did not address what kind of proof is needed to constitute clear and convincing evidence of the person's desires in these matters. The strong implication of the Court's language was that a written "living will" would meet the test but that a state could refuse to recognize oral testimony. Finally, the Court left open the question of whether a state is or is not required to defer to the decision of a surrogate or guardian if there is "competent and probative evidence" that the patient wished that surrogate to decide.

In 1997, the Court turned its attention to PAS in two cases, *Washington v. Glucksberg*, 117 U.S. 2258 (1997), and *Vacco v. Quill*, 117 U.S. 2293 (1997). While the Court rejected facial challenges to state laws punishing persons aiding a suicide and the claim that there is a constitutional right to PAS, there was an even greater tentativeness to many of the justices' opinions than had been seen in previous cases. While the effect of the decisions was to uphold laws in forty-nine states prohibiting assisting another in committing suicide, a majority of the justices went to some pains to leave open the possibility of state laws protecting such a right consistent with the U.S. Constitution.

In *Washington v. Glucksberg*, the Court rejected the notion that the Fourteenth Amendment includes a fundamental right to assisted suicide. Reasoning that a right is fundamental under the due process clause only when grounded in history or tradition, Chief Justice Rehnquist's opinion noted that for "over 700 years" the "Anglo-American common-law tradition has punished or otherwise disapproved of both suicide and attempting suicide." Moreover, in almost every state in the United States and in most Western democracies it is a crime to assist suicide. Thus, the right is not fundamental; the Washington law could be upheld as long as it had a rational basis, which Rehnquist found in the state's concerns to preserve life, protect the integrity and ethics of the medical profession, protect vulnerable groups, and avoid the slippery slope to voluntary and possibly even involuntary euthanasia.

The constitutional issue in *Vacco v. Quill* was somewhat different: Do laws prohibiting PAS violate the equal protection clause of the Fourteenth Amendment? Rehnquist, again writing for the majority, held that such laws do not discriminate against a suspected class (for example, a racial minority) and do not violate a fundamental right, since *Glucksberg* refused to recognize the claimed right as fundamental. Under established equal protection analysis, the law must be upheld as long as it meets the rational basis test, and the state's rational interests for such laws had also been spelled out in *Glucksberg*.

States remain free to enact laws protecting this right. The Court indicated that nothing in the Constitution limits a state's ability to prohibit or allow PAS. (In 1994, the Oregon Death With Dignity Act legalized PAS for competent, terminally ill adults. Other states have considered or will consider similar laws.) Five justices in concurring opinions indicated that PAS prohibitions might be unconstitutional as applied in specific cases. Justice Sandra Day O'Connor said (several times) in her concurrence that suffering patients in the last days of their lives may have a constitutional right to relief of that suffering. Justice Stephen Breyer very clearly indicated that there may be a constitutional right to PAS in a specific case if the person's core claim is "avoidance of severe physical pain (connected with death)." He noted pointedly that the Washington and New York laws "do not prohibit doctors from providing patients with drugs sufficient to control pain despite the risk that those drugs themselves will kill."

Political Context

Against the backdrop of totalitarian abuses in Russia and Germany, post-World War II America saw a heightened concern for fundamental human rights such as equality, personal liberty, and privacy. The African-American civil rights movement and Vietnam war protests paved the way for the liberation movements of the 1970s with respect to the rights of women, gays, other racial and ethnic minorities, and people with disabilities. Starting with the Cruzan case, the 1990s brought a movement for the rights of the dying.

As often happens (for example, the right of privacy recognized in *Griswold v. Connecticut*, 381 U.S. 479 (1965), and the right to abortion in *Roe v. Wade*, 410 U.S. 113, 1973), the Supreme Court comes on the scene only after challenges to laws at the state and local level. (In 1965, every state except Connecticut recognized a right to use contraception. In 1973, most states had legalized abortion.) Thus, some of the Court's tentativeness regarding the "right to die" undoubtedly reflects a genuine desire to allow states to engage fully in the political and legal experimentation that Justice Louis D. Brandeis hailed as one of the benefits of the federal system.

Liberation movements often spark backlash; the reaction of abortion foes to *Roe v. Wade* is an especially vivid example. The "right to die" is no exception. Perhaps nothing better epitomizes the intensity of conflict in this area than the case of Terri Schiavo, which sparked in Florida "Terri's Law," arguably one of the more extreme legislative interferences (if one discounts the U.S. Congress's subsequent interjections into the Schiavo case) with the judicial process and individual rights. Many conservative groups in that state applied concerted pressure on Florida legislators to pass the law, certainly out of a concern for Schiavo, but also as a means to advance their broader prolife and anti-abortion agenda.

Shortly after Oregon's Death with Dignity law went into effect, the federal Drug Enforcement Administration threatened Oregon doctors with loss of federal prescribing privileges if they provided dying patients with services authorized by the state law. Attorney General Janet Reno ruled that this was an improper use of the federal regulations. In the midst of the 9/11 crisis, Attorney General John Ashcroft reversed his predecessor's decision. The U.S. District Court for Oregon held that Aschroft lacked authority under the federal *Controlled Substances Act* (CSA), and the Ninth Circuit affirmed. On February 22, 2005, the U.S. Supreme Court granted certiorari in *Gonzales v. Oregon* (368 F. 3d 1118, 9th Cir. 2004, cert. granted, No. 04-623, U.S. Feb. 22, 2005) and will consider whether the attorney general's interpretation of the CSA prohibiting distribution of federally controlled substances for the purpose of facilitating an individual's suicide, regardless of state law, is a permissible interpretation. A decision was expected by the end of the Court's October 2005 term.

The legal and political future of PSA and other components of "the right to die" remains an open question, one of the first great civil liberties issues of the twenty-first century.

PHILIP A. DYNIA

References and Further Reading

Allen, Michael P., *The Constitution at the Threshold of Life and Death: A Suggested Approach to Accommodate an Interest in Life and a Right to Die*, American University Law Review 53 (June 2004): 971–1021.

Glick, Henry. R. *The Right to Die: Policy Innovation and Its Consequences*. New York: Columbia University Press, 1992.

Law, Sylvia A. "Choice in Dying: A Political and Constitutional Context." In *Physician Assisted Dying*, Timothy E. Quill and Margaret P. Battin, eds. Baltimore, MD: Johns Hopkins University Press, 2004, 300–308.

Stutsman, Eli D. "Political Strategy and Legal Change." In *Physician Assisted Dying*, Timothy E. Quill and Margaret P. Battin, eds. Baltimore, MD: Johns Hopkins University Press, 2004, 300–308.

Winslade, William J. "Physician-Assisted Suicide: Evolving Public Policies." In *Physician Assisted Suicide*, Robert F. Weir, ed. Bloomington: Indiana University Press, 1997, 224–242.

Cases and Statutes Cited

Cruzan v. Director, Missouri Department of Health, 497 U.S. 261 (1990)
Gonzales v. Oregon, 368 F. 3d 1118 (9th Cir. 2004), cert. granted, No. 04-623 (U.S. Feb. 22, 2005)
Griswold v. Connecticut, 381 U.S. 479 (1965)
Jacobson v. Massachusetts, 197 U.S. 11 (1905)
Roe v. Wade, 410 U.S. 113 (1973)
Vacco v. Quill, 117 U.S. 2293 (1997)
Washington v. Glucksberg, 117 U.S. 2258 (1997)

See also **Compelling State Interest;** *Cruzan v. Missouri*, **497 U.S. 261 (1990); Gay and Lesbian Rights; Kevorkian, Jack; Privacy; Privacy, Theories of; Refusal of Medical Treatment and Religious Beliefs;** *Washington v. Glucksburg*, **521 U.S. 702 (1997)**

ASYLUM, REFUGEES, AND THE CONVENTION AGAINST TORTURE

The United States provides several forms of relief to refugees, or individuals fleeing persecution in their home country. The legal framework governing refugees derives principally from international law and has been implemented in statutes and regulations. It is the principal means by which those fleeing persecution or torture in their home countries may seek safety and possible resettlement in the United States or a third country.

Refugees may be divided into two general categories: (1) those individuals who are still outside the United States but who are seeking to resettle in the United States or another nation that receives refugees (know under U.S. law as "overseas refugees"); and (2) those individuals who have been able to reach the United States on their own and who are seeking to remain in the United States or to avoid return to their country of origin for fear of persecution (known under U.S. law as "asylum seekers"). The same definition of a "refugee" applies to both categories.

The definition of a refugee derives from the 1951 United Nations Convention Relating to the Status of Refugees and the 1967 United Nations Protocol Relating to the Status of Refugees. The 1951 refugee convention was drafted in response to atrocities that took place in Europe following World War II and was limited in both time and duration. The 1967 protocol sought to expand the protections of the 1951 convention to refugees worldwide without temporal limitations.

A refugee is defined as an individual who is outside his or her country of origin due to "a well-founded fear of being persecuted for reasons of race, religion, nationality, membership in a particular social group, or political opinion." Civil war or other internal strife does not provide a basis for establishing refugee status, unless the individual is fleeing persecution based upon one of the five protected grounds. An essentially identical definition of refugees is contained in the Refugee Act of 1980. The prohibition against returning refugees to countries where they would face persecution is known as the principle of nonrefoulement.

Persecution does not have a precise definition; it includes a wide range of harms and is not limited to threats to one's life or freedom. An applicant for asylum may establish a well-founded fear of persecution based upon persecution that occurred in the past or based upon a fear that persecution might occur in the future, as long as that fear is well founded. The Supreme Court has said that a person's fear is "well founded" if the chance of persecution is one in ten (*INS v. Cardoza–Fonseca*, 480 U.S. 421, 1987). An asylum applicant, however, must show not only that the fear of persecution is well founded but also that the persecution is on account of one of the five protected grounds. Thus, an asylum applicant must produce evidence of a persecutor's motives and not just evidence of persecution. The applicant, moreover, must show that this persecution is on account of the applicant's political opinion or other protected characteristic and not the persecutor's (*INS v. Elias–Zacharias*, 502 U.S. 478, 1992). This "nexus" requirement prevents people who fear harm or even death from establishing refugee status absent a sufficient connection to one of the five protected grounds of the refugee definition.

Of the five protected grounds, membership in a particular social group is the most fluid. It was designed to include categories of people who should be protected as refugees but who did not fall within one of the other four categories. A "particular social group" has been defined to include individuals who "share a common immutable characteristic," whether it is innate (like kinship ties) or based upon shared past experience (*Matter of Acosta*, 19 I. & N. Dec. 211, BIA 1985). Over the years, this category has been expanded to include members of certain clans, homosexuals, and women subject to female genital mutilation.

To qualify for asylum, an applicant must also establish that he is not subject to one of the statutory bars to relief, which range from convictions of certain crimes to the failure to apply for asylum within the mandated deadline. Once an individual has demonstrated his eligibility, asylum may be granted at the discretion of the agency. After an individual is granted asylum, he has the opportunity to apply for permanent residence. While in theory there is no limit to the number of individuals who may be granted asylum, in practice that number generally does not exceed fifteen thousand annually.

A second form of relief under U.S. law is known as withholding of removal, which implements the United States' duty of nonrefoulement under the refugee convention. As for asylum, an individual must demonstrate that he or she meets the definition of a refugee. But to qualify for withholding of removal, an applicant must meet a higher standard of proof and show a clear probability of persecution or that the persecution would be more likely than not to occur (*INS v. Stevic*, 467 U.S. 407, 1984). Unlike asylum, withholding of removal is mandatory for those who qualify.

A third form available to those fleeing persecution is based on the United Nations Convention Against Torture and Other Cruel, Inhuman or Degrading Treatment (commonly referred to as CAT). An individual need not meet the definition of a refugee to qualify for relief under CAT and its implementing regulations. Instead, he must show that it is more likely than not that he would be tortured if he were returned to the country from which he seeks protection. The definition of torture includes physical and mental harm, as long as that harm is intentionally inflicted and sufficiently severe. It is absolutely prohibited to return an individual who qualifies for relief under CAT. CAT has thus become an increasingly important form of relief as other avenues of obtaining relief from removal have been curtailed, particularly for individuals with criminal convictions. Unlike asylum, however, CAT provides only temporary relief from removal and does not provide a basis for obtaining permanent residence in the United States.

JONATHAN L. HAFETZ

References and Further Reading

Anker, Deborah E. *Law of Asylum in the United States*, 3rd ed. RLC Publications, 1999.
Goodwin–Gill, Guy S. *The Refugee in International Law*. Oxford: Clarendon Press, 1998.
Hathaway, James C. *The Law of Refugee Status*. Toronto: Butterworths, 1991.
Hughes, Anwen. *Asylum and Withholding of Removal—A Brief Overview of the Substantive Law*. New York: Practicing Law Institute, 2005.

Cases and Statutes Cited

INS v. Cardoza–Fonseca, 480 U.S. 421 (1987)
INS v. Elias–Zacharias, 502 U.S. 478 (1992)
INS v. Stevic, 467 U.S. 407 (1984)
Matter of Acosta, 19 I. & N. Dec. 211 (BIA 1985)
Refugee Act of 1980, Pub. L. No. 96-212, 94 Stat. 102 (1980)

See also **Aliens, Civil Liberties of; Noncitizens and Civil Liberties**

ATHEISM

Although the first two clauses of the First Amendment concern the establishment and free exercise of "religion," the amendment long has been understood to protect the liberty and equality of nonbelievers. The amendment comprehends "the infidel, the atheist" as much as "the adherent of a non-Christian faith" and "the Court has unambiguously concluded that the individual freedom of conscience protected . . . embraces the right to select any religious faith or none at all" (*Wallace v. Jaffree*, 472 U.S. 38, 1985, 52–53). The presence in the United States of a substantial minority that disclaims religious belief thus has helped maintain an expansive interpretation of the protections afforded by the amendment that extends

ATHEISM

beyond religion per se to include a broader realm of individual conscience.

The term "atheism" is a contentious one. In general, it indicates the lack of belief in God, gods, or other divine beings or principles. Its exponents range from those who actively disparage religious ideas as false and incompatible with progressive human emancipation to agnostics, who dispute the possibility of ascertaining the existence of the divine and so forswear religious belief. The U.S. Census Bureau states that, in 2001, 14 percent of respondents asked to identify their religion reported having none, a figure that would indicate a nonbelieving population of about 29.4 million. Other surveys have estimated that American atheists fall between 6 and 9 percent of the American population; a minority have offered figures as low as 3 and as high as 16 percent.

As a matter of national identity, atheists have historically held an ambiguous status. Many of the founders were deists, such as Benjamin Franklin and Thomas Jefferson, and they are claimed as ancestors of modern atheism. Moreover, the Protestant context in which American conceptions of religious liberty developed placed special emphasis on safeguarding the individual conscience as the seat of voluntary religious choice, a position favorable to the protection of atheistic belief. James Madison's "Memorial and Remonstrance" (1785) and Madison's and Jefferson's "Bill for Establishing Religious Freedom" (1786) sought to protect the free minds of nonbelievers at the same time that they protected those of Christians. Indeed, Jefferson's foundational First Amendment metaphor, that a "wall of separation" had been built between church and state, was expressed in a letter solicited by a group of Baptists in Connecticut, highlighting the alliance between Enlightenment and evangelical thinkers in their mutual efforts to protect the self from coercion.

At the same time, the United States was founded by many who were deeply committed to their faith and sought to provide religious practice with special protection—not because it was a matter of individual conscience, but rather because of its status as religion. Notably, some of the great documents of American liberty, including the "Bill for Establishing Religious Freedom," begin with an invocation of God. In this light, according to some, while the First Amendment prevents government from favoring one religious group over another, it by no means requires the state to maintain a neutral position between religion and nonbelief or to refrain from promoting religion generally. Within constitutional law, this position, labeled "nonpreferentialism" in contrast to the approach of "voluntarism and separatism," has never gained a majority on the Court, though it represents

the view of a powerful segment of the voting public, which has been inspired to organize, in part, to resist the challenge of atheism and secularization.

While atheists once were subject to some legal disabilities based on their beliefs, they never experienced the systematic persecution faced by atheists in Britain, and those disabilities were fully eliminated in principle or practice over the course of the twentieth century as the First Amendment was applied to the states through the constitutional process of incorporation. Atheists today are competent witnesses in court; they do not fear prosecution for blasphemy and they need not swear a religious oath to serve in public office. Atheists have continued, however, to challenge two forms of public expression in which government can be said to prefer religion over nonbelief in violation of the establishment clause: prayer in public schools and those appeals to religion outside the school context often labeled "ceremonial deism."

Challenges to prayer in public schools have been consistently successful. In its inaugural analysis of the issue, the Court in *Engel v. Vitale*, 370 U.S. 421 (1962), prohibited the recitation of a daily nondenominational prayer; in *Abington School District v. Schempp*, 374 U.S. 203 (1963), it struck down the reading of verses from the Bible at the opening of the school day; in *Wallace v. Jaffree* (1985), it struck down a law authorizing schools to set aside a one-minute moment of silence for "meditation or voluntary prayer"; and in *Lee v. Weisman*, 505 U.S. 577 (1992), it struck down a banally ecumenical invocation of God's blessings at a high school graduation. Similarly, in *Stone v. Graham*, 449 U.S. 39 (1980), the Court struck down a law requiring the posting of the Ten Commandments in public school classrooms, and in *Edwards v. Aguillard*, 482 U.S. 578 (1987), it struck down a law requiring the teaching of "creation science" in classrooms that also taught evolutionary biology.

Challenges to the state use of nondenominational religious appeals outside the school context have met with mixed success. Some public religious holiday displays, such as nativity scenes, have been upheld against challenge, as in *Lynch v. Donnelly*, 465 U.S. 668 (1984), while others have not, as in *County of Allegheny v. ACLU*, 492 U.S. 573 (1989). As in most First Amendment litigation, the outcome of such cases has depended heavily on close scrutiny of the factual context at issue. Challenges to traditional invocations of the deity as an aspect of national civic culture—for instance, the use of the national motto "In God We Trust" on federal currency—have failed or are highly unlikely to succeed. When upheld, such religious appeals have been said to "have lost through rote repetition any significant religious

90

content" and to be "uniquely·suited" to achieve "such wholly secular purposes as solemnizing public occasions, or inspiring commitment to meet some national challenge" (*Lynch*, 716–717).

MARK S. WEINER

References and Further Reading

Borden, Morton. *Jews, Turks, and Infidels.* Chapel Hill: University of North Carolina Press, 1984.
Dorsen, Norman, *The Religion Clauses and Nonbelievers,* William & Mary Law Review 27 (1986): 5:863–873.
Hartogensis, B.H., Denial of Equal Rights to Religious Minorities and Non-Believers in the United States, Yale Law Journal 39 (1930): 659–681.
Laycock, Douglas, *"Nonpreferential" Aid to Religion: A False Claim About Original Intent,* William & Mary Law Review 27 (1986): 5:875–923.
Zuckerman, Phil. "Atheism: Contemporary Rates and Patterns." In *The Cambridge Companion to Atheism,* Michael Martin, ed. Cambridge: Cambridge University Press, 2007.

Cases and Statutes Cited

Abington School District v. Schempp, 374 U.S. 203 (1963)
County of Allegheny v. ACLU, 492 U.S. 573 (1989)
Edwards v. Aguillard, 482 U.S. 578 (1987)
Engel v. Vitale, 370 U.S. 421 (1962)
Lee v. Weisman, 505 U.S. 577 (1992)
Lynch v. Donnelly, 465 U.S. 668 (1984)
Wallace v. Jaffree, 472 U.S. 38 (1985)

See also **American Civil Liberties Union; Americans United for Separation of Church and State; Bible Reading in Public Schools, History of before and after** *Abington School District v. Schempp***; Defining Religion; Legislative Prayer;** *Lemon* **Test; No Coercion Test; No Endorsement Test; Prayer in Public Schools; Religious Symbols on Public Property; Scopes Trial; Secular Humanism and the Public Schools; Ten Commandments on Display in Public Buildings; Wall of Separation**

AUTOMOBILE SEARCHES

The Fourth Amendment was added to the U.S. Constitution in 1791 as part of the Bill of Rights. The amendment regulates government actors and provides, in part, the "right of the people to be secure in their persons, houses, papers, and effects, against unreasonable searches and seizures." The Supreme Court, in *Weeks v. United States,* 232 U.S. 383 (1914), described the protection against unreasonable searches and seizures as recognizing the principle that "a man's house was his castle." The amendment also provides that "no warrants shall issue, but upon probable cause." In general, the Court has determined that

a search or seizure is unreasonable unless it is based on probable cause and a warrant, or probable cause and an exception to the warrant requirement.

Searches of automobiles and any containers or occupants therein implicate Fourth Amendment protections. These searches typically occur without warrants, subsequent to a traffic stop. Recognizing the difficulties in getting a warrant for a moving vehicle, the Court has fashioned an exception to the warrant clause for automobiles and containers therein. As long as police have probable cause to believe that an automobile contains an item subject to seizure, they can stop the vehicle and perform a warrantless search of the interior and any containers inside that are capable of holding the suspected item.

The Court first addressed a warrantless search of an automobile in 1925 in *Carroll v. United States,* 267 U.S. 132 (1925), a Prohibition-era case. In *Carroll,* federal agents had no warrant but did have probable cause to believe that a car contained illegal liquor. Agents stopped the car, searched its interior, and found illegal alcohol. In finding the search reasonable, the Court recognized first the inherent mobility of an automobile. The Court distinguished between a house, or other permanent structure, and an automobile; because an automobile can quickly be moved out of the jurisdiction, it is not practical for police to obtain a warrant. The Court also reasoned that one has a diminished expectation of privacy in an automobile, unlike in a house. Given these factors, the Court determined that an automobile search based upon probable cause is an exception to the warrant requirement.

In subsequent cases, the Court has developed and expanded the exception. In doing so, the Court has continued to rely on the two rationales of mobility and reduced expectation of privacy, but has found that the exception can apply even to vehicles that are stationary or are also being used as homes. In *Chambers v. Maroney,* 399 U.S. 42 (1970), pursuant to a lawful traffic stop and arrest, police drove the defendant's car back to the police station, where it was searched some time later. The Court determined the warrantless search was justified because police could have lawfully searched the car without a warrant at the scene of the arrest. In *California v. Carney,* 471 U.S. 386 (1985), police conducted a warrantless search, based upon probable cause, of a parked motor home and discovered marijuana. In finding that the search was reasonable, the Court stressed the mobility of, and the reduced expectation of privacy in, a motor home. Motor homes, like automobiles, are regulated by the government in a manner not applicable to fixed dwellings. In *Carney,* the Court noted that an objective observer could also conclude that it was being used as a vehicle and not a home.

Probable cause to search an automobile extends to any containers within the vehicle, including those belonging to passengers, that are capable of concealing the suspected item. For example, if police have probable cause to believe a vehicle contains illegal weapons, they may, without a warrant, open only those containers inside the vehicle large enough to hold such weapons.

Probable cause to believe that a container alone, not the vehicle, contains contraband or evidence does not justify a warrantless search of the entire vehicle. In such a situation, police may lawfully stop the automobile, seize the container, and search only it without a warrant. In *California v. Acevedo*, officers had probable cause to believe that a paper bag in a car's trunk contained marijuana. Without a warrant, officers stopped the vehicle, opened the trunk and the paper bag, and discovered marijuana inside the bag. The lower court held that police acted properly in seizing the bag. However, because the officers did not have probable cause to believe that the defendant's car otherwise contained contraband, the court found that the officers violated the Fourth Amendment by opening the bag without a warrant. The Supreme Court reversed and found that, while a warrantless search of the entire vehicle would have been unreasonable because there was no probable cause, the warrantless search of the bag was justified because the officers had probable cause to believe that it contained marijuana. Interpreting *Carroll* as governing all warrantless automobile cases, the Court explained that "police may search an automobile and the containers within it where they have probable cause to believe contraband or evidence is contained."

Subsequent to a lawful impoundment of a vehicle, police may also perform a warrantless search in the course of inventorying its contents. Such an inventory search, however, must be conducted in accordance with standard procedures established by the jurisdiction's law enforcement agency.

While *Carroll* set forth the rule for warrantless automobile searches, other case law controls Fourth Amendment issues surrounding warrantless searches and seizures of occupants of an automobile. If an officer lawfully stops an automobile, he or she can ask all occupants to step out of the car as a result of the lawful stop, even without any indication that the occupants are engaging in illegal activities. If the officer has probable cause to arrest an occupant of the vehicle and take that person into custody, incident to that custodial arrest, he or she can search not only the arrestee but also the passenger compartment, including any closed or open containers, without a warrant. While the arrest alone does not provide the authority for a warrantless search of the trunk, what is discovered during the search of the passenger compartment might provide the necessary justification for such a search.

MARGARET M. LAWTON

References and Further Reading

Allen, Ronald Jay, Joseph L. Hoffmann, Debra A. Livingston, and William J. Stuntz. *Comprehensive Criminal Procedure*, 2nd ed. New York: Aspen Publishers, 2005, 333–336; 489–493.

American Jurisprudence, 2nd ed., vol. 68 (*Searches and Seizures*). St. Paul, MN: West Group, 2000, sec. 268 (Vehicular Searches).

Investigation and Police Practices: Warrantless Searches and Seizures: Vehicle Searches, Container Searches, and Inventory Searches, The Georgetown Law Journal 34th Annual Review of Criminal Procedure, 91–101 (2005).

LaFave, Wayne R., Jerold Israel, and Nancy J. King. *Criminal Procedure: Criminal Practice Series*, vol. 2. St. Paul, MN: West Group, 1999, Chapter 3, sec. 2(e) and 7 (a – f).

Loewy, Arnold H., *Cops, Cars, and Citizens: Fixing the Broken Balance*, Saint John's Law Review 76 (2002): 535–581.

Cases and Statutes Cited

California v. Carney, 471 U.S. 386 (1985)
Carroll v. United States, 267 U.S. 132 (1925)
Chambers v. Maroney, 399 U.S. 42 (1970)
Florida v. Wells, 495 U.S. 1 (1990)
Knowles v. Iowa, 525 U.S. 113 (1998)
Maryland v. Wilson, 519 U.S. 408 (1997)
New York v. Belton, 453 U.S. 454 (1981)
Thornton v. United States, 541 U.S. 615 (2004)
United States v. Chadwick, 433 U.S. 1 (1977)
Weeks v. United States, 232 U.S. 383 (1914)

See also **Coolidge v. New Hampshire, 403 U.S. 443 (1971); Exclusionary Rule; *Florida v. Jimeno*, 500 U.S. 248 (1991); *Katz v. United States*, 389 U.S. 347 (1967); Plain View; Probable Cause; Search (General Definition); Seizures; *South Dakota v. Opperman*, 428 U.S. 364 (1976); *United States v. Brignoni–Ponce*, 422 U.S. 873 (1975); *United States v. Robinson*, 414 U.S. 218 (1973); *Wyoming v. Houghton*, 526 U.S. 295 (1999)**

AUTOPSIES AND FREE EXERCISE BELIEFS

As government has grown in the United States, conflicts between religious observers and the law have increased proportionately. Modern dilemmas are easy to find. Members of the Native American church seek to use peyote despite laws prohibiting its possession. Catholic churches seek to expand their sanctuaries despite historic-preservation ordinances.

One of the best illustrations of the depths to which law and religion can conflict is the class of cases involving autopsies. Autopsies are conducted by the state for many reasons, but most frequently to discover the cause of a person's death. States often have statutes requiring autopsies to be made in certain categories of cases, such as all cases of violent or sudden death.

Many religious groups, such as Orthodox Jews, Navajo Indians, the Amish, the Hmong, and several denominations of Muslims, object to autopsies. Some of these groups object to autopsies unequivocally, while others object to them only under certain circumstances. (Orthodox Jews, for example, will not generally object to autopsies conducted to detect hereditary illnesses.)

Their reasons for objecting vary as well. For Orthodox Jews, autopsies violate the Talmud's prohibitions on mutilating the dead. For the Hmong people, autopsies threaten the post-death existence of the deceased. The Hmong see funerals as times for the soul to make its way to the next life; the physical invasion inherent in an autopsy threatens that passage and can cut off the possibility of an afterlife. Indeed, it is fair to say that, for the Hmong, autopsy is the equivalent of homicide.

These objections may strike Western observers as quite foreign. For such observers, perhaps an analogy may help. Cremation is becoming increasingly popular in this country. In 1963, only 3 percent of those who died were cremated. By 1980, that number was 10 percent and, in 2005, the number is expected to be almost 30 percent. Yet, until very recently, cremation was thought to be fundamentally incompatible with Christianity. Cremation was a Roman tradition, abhorrent to the early Christians, who believed that their bodies would be physically resurrected. Indeed, it was not until 1989 that the Roman Catholic Church officially renounced its traditional opposition to cremation; the Eastern Orthodox Church continues to forbid it. If one can imagine what a governmental policy of forced cremation would mean for these Christians, then one can begin to understand the implications of forced autopsies for religious groups like Orthodox Jews and the Hmong.

In the face of this obvious conflict, one persistent question has been whether religious objectors will be exempted from mandated autopsies. The small size of these religious groups and the infrequent nature of these controversies have made these problems largely invisible to legislatures. Therefore, religious groups have turned to the courts for refuge, arguing that the free exercise clause of the Constitution entitles them to protection from forced autopsies. Until 1990, those claims might have enjoyed some success. But in 1990, the Supreme Court held that the free exercise clause does not protect religious adherents from laws that are generally applicable. The Religious Freedom Restoration Act, a federal statute designed to restore the pre-1990 standard, was passed in 1993. In 1997, however, it was declared beyond Congress's power to enact.

Since then, some similar statewide statutes have been passed. But the general rule has meant that religious objections to autopsies have generally not prevailed—even when the reasons for the autopsies are thin or almost nonexistent— as the cases cited here reflect. One example, which featured prominently in the legislative debate on the Religious Freedom Restoration Act and in the judicial opinions debating its constitutionality, was the case of *Yang v. Sturner* (728 F. Supp. 845, D.R.I., withdrawn, 750 F. Supp. 558, D.R.I. 1990). *Yang* involved the autopsy of a young Hmong man, performed over his parents' objections. The district judge who heard the case was outraged at the autopsy; he saw it as almost without purpose (given that there was no suspicion of foul play) and terribly painful for the family. But bound by the Supreme Court's 1990 opinion, the judge denied the Hmong family all relief. The judge's opinion has become a persuasive tool for those arguing for the need to accommodate autopsy objectors and religious objection more generally.

Autopsy cases are dramatic and compelling examples of religious objection in the regulatory state. But even more than that, autopsy cases encapsulate the free exercise clause; all of its complexity; all of its tensions, history, and theories can be seen through the lens of these simple cases.

Christopher C. Lund

References and Further Reading

Berg, Thomas C. *The State and Religion in a Nutshell*, 2nd ed. St. Paul, MN: West Publishing Group, 2004.

Laycock, Douglas, *The Religious Freedom Restoration Act*, Brigham Young University Law Review 3 (1993): 221–258.

Lund, Christopher C., *A Matter of Constitutional Luck: The General Applicability Requirement in Free Exercise Jurisprudence*, Harvard Journal of Law and Public Policy 26 (2003): 6:627–665.

Stern, Marc D. *Testimony on Behalf of the American Jewish Congress Before the Subcommittee on the Constitution of the Committee on the Judiciary*, Mar. 26, 1998, available at http://judiciary.house.gov/legacy/222390.htm.

Cases and Statutes Cited

City of Boerne v. Flores, 521 U.S. 507 (1997)

Employment Division, Dept. of Human Resources v. Smith, 494 U.S. 872 (1990)

Kickapoo Traditional Tribe of Texas v. Chacon, 46 F. Supp. 2d 644 (W.D. Tex. 1999)

Montgomery v. County of Clinton, Michigan, 743 F.Supp. 1253 (W.D. Mich. 1990).

United States v. Hammer, 121 F. Supp. 2d 794 (M.D. Pa. 2000).

Yang v. Sturner, 728 F. Supp. 845 (D.R.I.), withdrawn, 750 F. Supp. 558 (D.R.I. 1990).

42 U.S.C. § 2000bb (1994) (the *Religious Freedom Restoration Act*).

See also **Accommodation of Religion; Belief–Action Distinction in Free Exercise Clause History;** *City of Boerne v. Flores*, **521 U.S. 507 (1997); Conscientious Objection, the Free Exercise Clause;** *Employment Division, Department of Human Resources v. Smith*, **494 U.S. 872 (1990); Equal Protection Clause and Religious Freedom; Establishment of Religion and Free Exercise Clauses; Free Exercise Clause (I): History, Background, Framing; Free Exercise Clause Doctrine: Supreme Court Jurisprudence; Prisoners and Free Exercise Clause Rights; Refusal of Medical Treatment and Religious Beliefs; Religious Freedom Restoration Act; State Religious Freedom Statutes**

B

BACHE, BENJAMIN FRANKLIN (1769–1798)

Born the grandson of Benjamin Franklin and educated in Geneva, Benjamin Franklin Bache epitomized early America's ambivalent relationship with the press. Raised largely in France, Bache was later trained as a type founder, and his famous grandfather's contacts in Philadelphia's publishing community were critical to Bache's early career. Few publishers have been as loved and as despised as Bache; profoundly partisan, he could be vicious and unforgiving toward his political enemies.

Bache began to make a name for himself as founder and editor of Philadelphia's *General Advertiser*. Indeed, he very quickly revealed both his liberal European education and his devotion to liberty. At a time when freedom of the press was perhaps not as well developed as in the twentieth century, Bache developed a reputation as a firebrand, as revealed by his nickname, "Lightning Rod Junior." His criticisms of the first two American presidents, George Washington and John Adams, while occasionally unfair and often perceptive, meant that Bache was not popular with Federalists.

By the beginning of Washington's second term, Bache had identified him as a legitimate target of liberal criticisms. First was the perception that Washington had aristocratic tendencies. His aloofness in public as well as his inclination toward grand and ceremonial events led Bache and others to the conclusion that Washington was a monarchist in disguise. As well, Washington's position as a slaveholder and rumors of financial malfeasance in the Washington administration made him vulnerable to pointed attacks. Further, as popular devotion to Washington culminated in public celebrations of his birthday, and as Bache observed a growing opinion that Washington was somehow beyond criticism, Bache began to attack the President through his newspaper. Bache endorsed the sentiments of one of his anonymous correspondents: "Opinion has so far consecrated the President as to make it hazardous to say that he can do wrong."

As Bache's criticisms grew more pointed, Washington was forced to lead the country's young army into action to put down an insurrection in western Pennsylvania, and Bache began a sustained attack on Washington. When Washington condemned the actions of the Whiskey Rebels and the Democratic Societies he believed were responsible for the rebellion, Bache published pieces that supported the Democratic Societies' right to exist (although he condemned any violence on their part), and blamed the administration for the excise policies that motivated the rebels. A member of the Philadelphia Democratic Society himself, Bache's suspicions about Washington drove him to a near obsession with the President.

When the Washington administration entered treaty talks with Britain over what would later be known as the Jay Treaty, Bache blasted them for their secrecy and for tendencies he believed to be as anti-French as they were pro-British. He acquired a copy of the treaty before it was made public and printed it, along with a detailed criticism of its major provisions:

he hated the fact that it created a political connection between a republican government and a monarchy; he could not stand the fact that it essentially forgave the British for various wrongs committed against America; and he had a particular problem with a conflict of interest—John Jay, the primary negotiator of the treaty, could potentially have the responsibility to approve the treaty in his role as chief justice of the Supreme Court.

When Washington decided to retire after two terms, and as it became clear that John Adams would stand for president as a Federalist, Bache found himself in a dilemma: he initially saw Adams as a welcome alternative to Washington, but Thomas Jefferson had a record that more closely matched Bache's own political sensibility. His primary criticism of Adams, then, was based on his close political affiliation to Washington. Meanwhile, the *General Advertiser* had folded, and Bache founded another newspaper, the *Aurora*.

Bache had also become the exclusive publisher and distributor of Thomas Paine's *Age of Reason II*, which further alienated him from Washington. By 1798 Bache had few friends in Washington. His relentless attacks on, first Washington, and then Adams, made him an easy target for those less inclined to support universal freedom of the press. The looming military conflict with France set the stage for a final showdown between Bache and the Federalists.

When Congress passed the Alien and Sedition Acts in 1798, it was clear that some politicians had newspaper editors like Bache in mind when the bills were drafted. The provisions were vague enough, and Bache was inflammatory enough, that many insiders predicted a challenge from Bache. Even though the acts technically allowed truth as an absolute defense against prosecution under the law, Bache attacked the laws with typical enthusiasm. He published an attack on the Alien and Sedition Acts as illegal; he argued that they violated the First Amendment, and that the acts' mere existence was evidence of the Federalists' unsophisticated view of freedom of speech and press. Anticipating trouble with Bache, the Federalists had filed a libel suit against Bache even before the Alien and Sedition Acts had been passed, but their passage gave them a more powerful vehicle to quiet Bache.

Bache was arrested "on the charge of libeling the President, and the Executive Government in a manner tending to excite sedition, and opposition to the laws, by sundry publications and re-publications." While awaiting trial in a Philadelphia jail, Bache contracted yellow fever and died.

Sometimes unfair in his criticisms, Bache nonetheless saw himself as a watchdog against the intrusion of monarchy or aristocracy. He took seriously the idea of republic. He was a pioneer in the American tradition of dissent and criticism.

JAMES HALABUK, JR.

References and Further Reading

Smith, Jeffery A. *Franklin and Bache: Envisioning the Enlightened Republic.* New York: Oxford University Press, 1990.

Tagg, James. *Benjamin Franklin Bache and the Philadelphia "Aurora."* Philadelphia: University of Pennsylvania Press, 1991.

BAD TENDENCY TEST

Emerging by the early nineteenth century, the bad tendency test remained the predominant judicial approach to determining the scope of free expression for over a century. The government could not impose prior restraints on expression, but it could impose criminal penalties for speech or writing that had bad tendencies or likely harmful consequences. Many courts added that the criminal defendant, to be convicted, must also have intended harmful consequences. Even so, under the doctrine of constructive intent, the courts typically reasoned that a defendant was presumed to have intended the natural and probable consequences of his or her statements. If a defendant's expression was found to have bad tendencies, then the defendant's criminal intent would be inferred.

People v. Croswell (1804), a seditious libel prosecution arising from the criticism of public officials, manifested the bad tendency approach. *Croswell* held that such expression is protected if it is truthful and published for good motives and justifiable ends. Statements with bad tendencies, though, contravened the common good and were therefore punishable. The *Croswell* standard, in effect, took Blackstone's justification for punishing seditious libel and transformed it into the definition of seditious libel. According to Blackstone, criticism of governmental officials was subject to criminal punishment *because* of its bad or pernicious tendencies. Under the *Croswell* standard, criticism of public officials was subject to criminal punishment *if* it had bad tendencies.

In a series of unanimous U.S. Supreme Court decisions arising during the World War I era, Justice Oliver Wendell Holmes, Jr., articulated the scope of protection under the First Amendment in a variety of ways. Regardless of Holmes's precise phrasings, however, he resolved each case in accordance with the bad tendency test. In *Schenck v. United States* (1919), he used clear-and-present-danger language that in later cases would be reinterpreted more broadly: "The question in every case is whether the words used are used in such circumstances and are of such a nature as to create a clear and present danger that they will bring about the substantive evils that Congress has a right to prevent." In *Frohwerk v. United States* (1919), Holmes concluded: "[I]t is impossible to say that it might not have been found that the circulation of the paper was in quarters where a little breath would be enough to kindle a flame and that the fact was known and relied upon by those who sent the paper out." And in *Debs v. United States* (1919), Holmes approved a jury instruction that presented the bad tendency test in conventional terms: the jurors, as charged, "could not find the defendant guilty for advocacy of any of his opinions unless the words used had as their natural tendency and reasonably probable effect [to violate the law], and unless the defendant had the specific intent to do so in his mind." Moreover, Holmes added that the jury could find constructive intent. In each of these cases, then, the Court relied on the bad tendency test despite Holmes's inconsistent phrasings.

STEPHEN M. FELDMAN

References and Further Reading

Chemerinsky, Erwin. *Constitutional Law: Principles and Policies.* 2nd ed. New York: Aspen Law & Business, 2002.
Emerson, Thomas I. *The System of Freedom of Expression.* New York: Random House, 1970.
Rosenberg, Norman L. *Protecting the Best Men: An Interpretive History of the Law of Libel.* Chapel Hill: University of North Carolina Press, 1986.

Cases and Statutes Cited

Debs v. United States, 249 U.S. 211 (1919)
Frohwerk v. United States, 249 U.S. 204 (1919)
People v. Croswell, 3 Johns. Cas. 337 (N.Y. Sup. Ct. 1804)
Schenck v. United States, 249 U.S. 47 (1919)

BAIL

In 1791, the Eighth Amendment was added to the U.S. Constitution as part of the Bill of Rights for the purpose of prohibiting, among other things, the requirement of "excessive bail." As applied in the context of the American criminal justice system, "bail" refers to the security or conditions ordered by a court to ensure the appearance of an accused for all court proceedings relating to a pending criminal case. As recognized by the U.S. Supreme Court in *United States v. Salerno* (1987), "[I]n our society liberty is the norm, and detention prior to trial . . . is the carefully limited exception." This quote summarizes the fundamental notion of personal freedom embodied in the Fifth Amendment due process provisions and the Eighth Amendment prohibition against excessive bail.

History and Conception of Bail

The idea of bail can be traced back hundreds of years before the U.S. Constitution. Original theories of bail are apparent in seventh century Anglo-Saxon law, which provided that persons accused of a crime pay an amount to the family of the victim; the payment was returned if the person was eventually proven innocent.

More modern bail theory can be traced to the late ninth or early tenth century, when sheriffs were required to arrest and hold defendants until they could be brought to trial. Because it often took years before a traveling magistrate could appear for a trial, this system was unjust for the accused, whose liberty was restrained during this period of time, and was a significant imposition on the sheriff, who was often forced to detain prisoners in his own home. To remedy these deficiencies, defendants were permitted to post a monetary bond, or have friends or relatives act as sureties to ensure their appearance at trial. As such, bail was initially created to protect the liberty interests of persons accused of crimes, while ensuring their appearance at trial.

Under modern-day practices, the decisions of whether to grant bail and, if so, in what amount, are made after an individual is charged, arrested, and processed at a police station. Initial bail determinations are often made by magistrates, and may be reviewed later by the court.

History of Federal Bail Law

Congress enacted the first federal bail provision in 1789 as part of the Judiciary Act, which set the guidelines for courts in making bail decisions. The decision of whether to grant bail and the particular amount of bail were left largely to the discretion of the courts. In practice, pretrial release was not favored. There were no substantial changes to bail law until Congress passed the Bail Reform Act of 1966. Contrary to the 1789 Act, this act favored pretrial release in all non–death-penalty cases and focused mainly on the question of whether the accused was likely to flee the jurisdiction in an effort to avoid trial. The purpose of the Bail Reform Act was to eliminate unwarranted and oppressive bail conditions, especially in cases involving indigent defendants. However, many people criticized the Act because it did not address the issue of defendants committing crimes while on bail awaiting trial.

In an effort to address these public safety concerns, Congress enacted the District of Columbia Court Reform and Criminal Procedures Act of 1970. This act was the first federal law that permitted "preventive detention"—allowing courts to deny bail when an individual would pose a danger to the community if released pending trial, even if there is no evidence that the individual would flee the jurisdiction. Preventive detention is a controversial issue that continues to be hotly debated among attorneys, judges, and legal scholars. Critics of preventive detention argue that it denies defendants the presumption of innocence and allows the government to incarcerate individuals without a trial or any proof of wrongdoing, and merely on the basis of a prediction of future wrongdoing; while supporters argue that where a showing of future dangerousness is made, an individual's liberty interest is outweighed by the government's interest in ensuring community safety. In 1981, the District of Columbia Court of Appeals considered these arguments and upheld the 1970 Act in *United States v. Edwards* (1981).

Between 1970 and 1984, thirty-four states enacted statutes similar to the District of Columbia statute, all providing for preventive detention. The U.S. Supreme Court upheld constitutional challenges to many of these statutes, labeling them regulatory, rather than penal, in nature. In 1981, the U.S. Attorney General's Office released a report recommending adoption of federal preventive detention provisions. Then-Supreme Court Chief Justice Warren Burger also supported the need for more flexible bail standards that would allow courts to consider future dangerousness when making pretrial release decisions.

In response to these recommendations and rising public concern regarding crimes committed by persons released pending trial, Congress enacted the Bail Reform Act of 1984, which replaced the Bail Reform Act of 1966. Pursuant to the 1984 act, a federal court may order preventive pretrial detention of an accused if the government demonstrates that no release condition(s) will reasonably ensure the safety of other persons and the community. A federal court may also order pretrial detention if the government shows that no release conditions(s) will reasonably ensure the presence of the accused at trial. The act also set forth specific factors to be considered by the court in setting pretrial release conditions. Specifically, courts are to consider the nature and seriousness of the charged offense, the weight of the evidence against the accused, the history and characteristics of the defendant, and the nature and seriousness of the danger that would be posed to the community by releasing the accused pending trial.

In *United States v. Salerno* (1987), the Supreme Court rejected constitutional challenges to the preventive detention provisions of the 1984 Bail Reform Act, finding that such detention is consistent with both due process guarantees and protections against excessive bail embodied in the Eighth Amendment to the U.S. Constitution.

The Bail Decision

In a criminal case, bail is generally set within a very short time after arrest. Although each jurisdiction implements its own requirements and procedures for setting bail in criminal cases, many use what are commonly referred to as "bail schedules" or "master bond schedules" to set bail initially. These schedules set bail according to the offense with which a defendant is charged and do not take into account other circumstances such as a defendant's financial condition, ties to the community or prior criminal history. Some jurisdictions have discontinued the use of such schedules because they fail to take into account issues relevant to ensuring the defendant's presence at trial or assuring community safety. In *Ackies v. Purdy* (1970), a federal district court ruled that the use of a master bond list to set bail violates both the due process and equal protection rights of defendants.

Jurisdictions not using bond schedules often rely on pretrial services agencies to gather information relevant to the bail decision. Such agencies interview defendants to determine the extent of their financial resources, ties to the community, and prior criminal history. This information is then reviewed by the court to determine what amount of bail and other release conditions are necessary to ensure the defendant's appearance at trial and the safety of the community.

When setting bail, a court may consider many forms of monetary and other conditions. Monetary conditions include secured bonds, unsecured bonds, property bonds, and personal recognizance bonds. Under a personal recognizance bond, defendants are not required to submit money to secure their release but are required to pay a set amount if they fail to appear for trial. In addition to, or in lieu of, monetary requirements, defendants may be subject to release conditions such as a requirement to maintain employment, refrain from contacting the alleged victim, report to a pretrial services agency on a regular basis, submit to random drug or alcohol testing, refrain from leaving the jurisdiction, or refrain from committing any criminal acts. The Bail Reform Act includes a preference for pretrial release on personal recognizance or an unsecured appearance bond without additional conditions. Only if such release conditions will not reasonably ensure the defendant's appearance for trial or the safety of the community are other pretrial bail conditions permitted.

Defendants are permitted to request reductions in the amount of bail set or changes in the release conditions while their case is pending. Likewise, prosecutors may also request changes in a defendant's release conditions, including a request that a previously ordered bond be revoked pending trial. Generally, these requests are made in the form of a motion filed with the court before which the case is pending. However, in some circumstances, courts may allow bail reduction requests to be made orally, such as at the conclusion of a preliminary hearing or a pretrial motion to suppress evidence. Bail requests for release pending an appeal after conviction may also be made; however, such requests are rarely granted.

JUDITH M. BARGER

References and Further Reading

Dressler, Joshua. "Pretrial Release of the Defendant." In *Understanding Criminal Procedure*. 3rd ed. Newark, N.J.: LexisNexis Publishing, 2002.
Metzmeier, Kurt X., *Preventive Detention: A Comparison of Bail Refusal Practices in the United States, England, Canada and Other Common Law Nations*, Pace International Law Review 8 (1996): 399–436.
Scott, Thomas E., *Pretrial Detention Under the Bail Reform Act of 1984: An Empirical Analysis*, American Criminal Law Review 27 (1989): 1–51.
Wisotsky, Steven, *Use of a Master Bond Schedule: Equal Justice Under Law?* University of Miami Law Review 24 (1970): 808.

Cases and Statutes Cited

Ackies v. Purdy, 322 F.Supp. 38 (S.D. Fla. 1970)
United States v. Edwards, 430 A.2d 1321 (D.C. 1981)
United States v. Salerno, 481 U.S. 739 (1986)

BALANCING APPROACH TO FREE SPEECH

"Balancing" refers to a method of adjudication used by judges to reach decisions through weighing the parties' competing interests or rights. In the context of legal disputes over free speech rights, "balancing" typically means judges weighing the government's interests in restricting speech against the speaker's First Amendment free speech rights. For some courts, balancing also entails explicit cost-benefit comparisons.

Balancing approaches are usually contrasted with "categorical" approaches to free speech. Balancing requires judges to examine carefully the specific facts of each case and articulate the competing interests and rights at stake before weighing their relative strengths. In contrast, categorical approaches depend on a preestablished system of classifications or categories; judges decide which category the specific case before them belongs to, and then they apply legal rules already developed for that category. Thus, in a free speech case, the court would classify the nature of the speech as "protected" or "unprotected" by the First Amendment, categorize the setting of the speech as a "public forum" or "non-public forum" for speech, and determine whether the type of speech restriction at issue is "content based" or "content neutral." The outcome of that sequence of categorical moves would determine yet another category, the level of scrutiny ("strict" or "rational basis") that the court would apply to the government's speech restriction.

Advocates of balancing approaches believe that they ensure more nuanced, case-specific, fact-sensitive adjudication that is also more honest and transparent about the policy questions implicit in the dispute. Advocates of balancing also assert that it is more flexible and adaptable, and therefore better suited to the complexity of free speech disputes, where restrictions may not be easily classifiable as content based or content neutral, where the nature of the forum is not readily ascertainable, and where multiple speakers compete. Such complexities are often seen in cases concerning speech rights in rapidly evolving new media like cable and the Internet. See, for example, *Denver Area Educational Telecommunications Consortium, Inc. v. Federal Communications Commission* (1996) and *United States v. American Library Association* (2003).

Critics of balancing approaches argue that they are subjective, offer little predictability or certainty, and invite judges to usurp the role of legislatures by making policy determinations. Critics further charge that there is no real "weighing" because the rights and interests being compared are incommensurate. Balancing approaches have been strongly criticized in the context of free speech law for chilling speech (because speakers cannot be sure how a court would "weigh" their speech rights) and for unfairly favoring majoritarian government interests against the First Amendment rights of unpopular speakers. In this view, balancing approaches fail to safeguard speech because courts are likely to be swayed in their assessment of the government's interests by the perceived exigencies and societal fears of the day.

Justification for such criticisms of balancing can be found in a series of speech-repressive cases in the communism-phobic McCarthy era, when the U.S. Supreme Court applied the balancing approach repeatedly to find that government interests in speech restrictions outweighed the speaker's right to speak. *Dennis v. United States* (1951) is the prime example.

Balancing has been making a comeback as a legitimate approach to free speech jurisprudence. As Kathleen Sullivan, a leading constitutional scholar, and others have argued, neither balancing nor categorical approaches are inherently liberal or conservative, speech protective or speech restrictive; the approaches themselves are neutral, and not always even clearly distinguishable. Supreme Court justices who are strong proponents of balancing approaches include Justices Stevens, O'Connor, Breyer, and Souter. See, for example, Justice O'Connor's concurrence in *Rosenberger* favoring balancing over categorical approaches. A move towards balancing is evident in the Court's development of intermediate scrutiny levels, somewhere in between "strict" and "rational basis," that assess government's reasons for the speech restriction as weighed against the effects on speech. Such "heightened scrutiny" balancing has been used in commercial speech cases since *Central Hudson Gas & Electric* (1980), and in speech cases involving new technologies like cable broadcasting (for instance, *Turner Broadcasting I* [1994] and *II* [1997]).

The debate between advocates of balancing and advocates of categorizing parallels debates between advocates of "standards" and advocates of "rules."

IRENE SEGAL AYERS

References and Further Reading

Barron, Jerome A., *The Electronic Media and the Flight from First Amendment Doctrine: Justice Breyer's New Balancing Approach*, University of Michigan Journal of Law Reform 31 (1998): 817.
Huhn, Wilson R., *Assessing the Constitutionality of Laws that Are Both Content-Based and Content-Neutral: The Emerging Constitutional Calculus*, Indiana Law Journal 79 (2004): 801.
Rubenfeld, Jed, *Comment: A Reply to Posner*, Stanford Law Review 54 (2002): 753.
Schlag, Pierre, *An Attack on Categorical Approaches to Freedom of Speech*, University of California-Los Angeles Law Review 30 (1983): 671.
Smolla, Rodney A. *Smolla and Nimmer on Freedom of Speech.* Vol. 1. St. Paul, Minn.: West Group, 2003.
Sullivan, Kathleen M., *Post-Liberal Judging: The Roles of Categorization and Balancing*, University of Colorado Law Review 63 (1992): 293.

Cases and Statutes Cited

Central Hudson Gas & Electric v. Public Service Commission, 477 U.S. 557 (1980)
Dennis v. United States, 341 U.S. 494 (1951)
Denver Area Educational Telecommunications Consortium, Inc. v. Federal Communications Commission, 518 U.S. 727 (1996)
Rosenberger v. University of Virginia, 515 U.S. 819, 846–852 (1995)
Turner Broadcasting System v. FCC, 512 U.S. 622 (1994), and *Turner II*, 520 U.S. 180 (1997)
United States v. American Library Association, 539 U.S. 194 (2003)

See also **Absolutism and Free Speech; Categorical Approach to Free Speech; *Central Hudson Gas and Electric Corp. v. Public Service Commission of New York*, 477 U.S. 557 (1980); Content-Based Regulation of Speech; Content-Neutral Regulation of Speech; *Dennis v. United States*, 341 U.S. 494 (1951); Intermediate Scrutiny Test in Free Speech Cases; Public Forum Doctrines; Public/Nonpublic Forums Distinction; *Rosenberger v. Rector and Visitors of the University of Virginia*, 515 U.S. 819 (1995); *Turner Broadcasting Sys., Inc. v. FCC* (Turner I), 512 U.S. 622 (1994); 520 U.S. 180 (1997) (Turner II)**

BALANCING TEST

In constitutional adjudication, the balancing test is the predominant mode of case resolution, although major differences exist on "how to strike the balance." The balance that must be struck is between individual freedoms and societal needs such as the need to preserve order. There is only one theory of constitutional decision making in which balancing does not occupy a position—the absolutist position. Proponents—most notably Justice Hugo Black—argued that the specific provisions of the Constitution and Bill of Rights are often stated in absolute terms. For example, when the First Amendment says, "Congress shall make no law . . . abridging the freedom of speech," Justice Black was fond of saying that this meant "no" law, plain and simple. Most other justices and legal scholars, however, disagree with this absolutist position, and opt instead for balancing between individual liberties and government needs. Some would weigh equally the government's need and constitutional protections. Greater protection is given to individual freedoms in the famous "clear and present" test. Here governments are forbidden to transgress on protected liberties unless there is both a "clear" and "present" danger. Finally, even more protection is given to individual liberties by the "preferred position" rule. Under this standard, individual protections are to be given very special protection, and only substantial, grave, imminent threats justify government encroachment. Balancing becomes especially acute during crisis times. For example, does/has/should 9/11 justify tipping the scales more in the direction of government powers, trading off individual liberties to obtain a higher likelihood of safety in our society? What are the costs of these tradeoffs? Balancing allows these decisions to be made but remains silent on any hard and fast rule about how to strike the balance.

MILTON HEUMANN

References and Further Reading

Black, Hugo, *The Bill of Rights*, New York University Law Review 35 (April 1960): 865–31.
Pritchett, C. Herman. *The American Constitution.* New York: McGraw-Hill, 1968.

See also **Absolutism and Free Speech; Bad Tendency Test; Balancing Approach to Free Speech; Clear and Present Danger Test; 9/11 and The War on Terrorism**

BALDUS STUDY (CAPITAL PUNISHMENT)

The Baldus Study, conducted by Professors David Baldus, George Woodworth, and Charles Pulaski, was a sophisticated empirical analysis of 2,484 Georgia homicide cases that were charged and sentenced in the 1970s. The study found, among other results, that black defendants convicted of killing white victims were more likely to receive the death penalty than any other racial combination of defendant and victim.

The raw data showed that 11 percent of those charged with killing a white person were sentenced to death, whereas only 1 percent of those charged with killing a black person were sentenced to death. Because intraracial murders (victims and defendants of the same race) were more common than interracial murders (victims and defendants of different races), 7 percent of white defendants were sentenced to death as opposed to 4 percent of black defendants. However, death sentences resulted in 21 percent of cases involving black defendants and white victims, but only 8 percent of cases with white defendants and white victims.

The study also analyzed 230 potentially aggravating, mitigating, or evidentiary nonracial factors. Based on a regression analysis involving the most significant thirty-nine factors, the study found that death sentences were 4.3 times more likely for defendants charged with killing white rather than black victims, and that this result was largely due to the choices of prosecutors rather than juries.

The Baldus Study was presented in *McCleskey v. Kemp* to show that Georgia operated an unconstitutional racially discriminatory capital punishment system. The defendant's claims were rejected, however, on the grounds that the study failed to show either a constitutionally significant risk of racial bias in the operation of Georgia's system or a discriminatory purpose specifically in McCleskey's case.

ANTONY PAGE

References and Further Reading

Baldus, David C., George Woodworth, and Charles A. Pulaski, Jr. *Equal Justice and the Death Penalty: A Legal and Empirical Analysis.* Boston: Northeastern University Press, 1990.
Baldus, David C., George Woodworth, David Zuckerman, Neil Alan Weiner, and Barbara Broffitt, *Racial Discrimination and the Death Penalty in the Post-Furman Era: An Empirical and Legal Overview, with Recent Findings from Philadelphia*, Cornell Law Review 83 (1998): 1638–770.
Kennedy, Randall L., *McCleskey v. Kemp: Race, Capital Punishment, and the Supreme Court*, Harvard Law Review 101 (1988): 1388–433.

Cases and Statutes Cited

McCleskey v. Kemp, 481 U.S. 279 (1987)

See also **Capital Punishment; Capital Punishment and Equal Protection Clause Cases; Capital Punishment and Race Discrimination; Capital Punishment: Eighth Amendment Limits;** *Furman v. Georgia,* **408 U.S. 238 (1972);** *Gregg v. Georgia,* **428 U.S. 153 (1976);** *McCleskey v. Kemp,* **481 U.S. 277 (1987)**

BALDWIN, ROGER (1884–1981)

Roger Baldwin was the founder of the American Civil Liberties Union (ACLU) and served as its director from 1920 to 1950. He was widely recognized as the foremost advocate of civil liberties in the United States during those years.

Baldwin was born January 21, 1884, in Wellesley, Massachusetts to an old New England family that traced its roots back to the first English settlers. His father was a successful businessman in the leather goods industry. His religious background was in the Unitarian Church, and Baldwin inherited a liberal, freethinking outlook that emphasized social reform. Family members associated with prominent social and political reformers. Through his father, for example, he met attorney and future Supreme Court Justice Louis Brandeis. His uncle William Baldwin was president of the Long Island Railroad and actively involved in social reform, including child labor and racial justice. Baldwin graduated from Harvard University in 1905 and earned a graduate degree in social work the following year.

He moved to St. Louis in 1906 to take a job as a social worker and remained there until early 1917. A person of boundless energy, Baldwin immediately became a prominent social reformer whose views reflected the goals of Progressive Era reforms. In 1910, he organized and became the secretary of the St. Louis Civic League, and through this organization was involved in many social reform issues. He taught social work courses at Washington University from 1906 to 1910. He helped to establish the first juvenile court in St. Louis and co-authored with Bernard Flexner *Juvenile Courts and Probation* (1914), a detailed manual on the goals and management of a juvenile court that gained a national audience. Baldwin was also active in the National Probation Association and other national organizations. Articles by or about him appeared in national publications, and he earned a national reputation as an energetic reformer.

Despite his subsequent claims, Baldwin was not an advocate of civil liberties during his years in St. Louis. He met controversial birth control advocate Margaret Sanger and anarchist Emma Goldman when they spoke in St. Louis. Although they and other speakers faced restrictions on their right to speak, Baldwin remained a rather conventional Progressive Era reformer who optimistically believed that they could and should serve the interests of the majority of the people. He did not at this time see a fundamental conflict between government actions reflecting majority opinion and the rights of individuals or unpopular groups. Baldwin was a vigorous advocate of racial equality at a time when few whites supported the rights of African Americans. He generated controversy, for example, in presenting an African-American speaker at Washington University. Race played a significant role in moving Baldwin's political thinking in a more radical direction. A referendum in St. Louis that approved racial segregation in housing greatly disillusioned his faith in majoritarian democracy. The outbreak of war in Europe in 1914, meanwhile, shattered his optimism about social progress.

By early 1917, Baldwin was increasingly concerned about possible American entry into World War I, and in March of that year he moved to New York City to work with the American Union Against Militarism (AUAM), a pacifist organization opposing American entry into the war. He and Crystal Eastman soon established a Civil Liberties Bureau (CLB) within

the AUAM to provide assistance to young men facing military service who sought conscientious objector status. At this point Baldwin's understanding of civil liberties took shape.

After the United States declared war in April 1917, the Civil Liberties Bureau not only provided assistance to conscientious objectors but also opposed censorship of individuals and organizations opposed to the war. Eventually, the CLB's own publications were banned from the mails by the U.S. Post Office. Baldwin and Eastman's activities in this regard provoked a split within the AUAM. The organization's leaders did not want to alienate the Wilson administration in the hope that they would be able to influence the eventual peace ending the war. In July 1917, the two factions agreed to split, and Baldwin and Eastman established a separate organization, the National Civil Liberties Bureau (NCLB). The NCLB was the direct forerunner of the ACLU.

In the summer of 1918, Baldwin received notice to report for induction into the military. Although he was thirty-four years old, the draft had been extended to cover people up to age thirty-five. Opposed to conscription as a matter of principle, he refused to report for induction and was subsequently convicted and sentenced to prison. A number of prominent reformers attended his trial, and his speech to the judge setting forth the reasons for his opposition to conscription was reprinted and widely circulated around the country. Baldwin served eight months in prison in New Jersey. During this time he reflected on the issues of free speech and due process raised by the wartime repression of dissent.

Upon leaving prison in July 1919, Baldwin traveled around the country for several months, often working in blue-collar jobs and contemplating his future. This experience was his first direct contact with working people and the labor movement. Later that year, Baldwin and other former NCLB leaders concluded that a permanent organization was needed to fight for civil liberties. They established the ACLU, which was officially born in January 1920 with Baldwin as its director.

Baldwin immediately established the style of activity that he would maintain over the next thirty years as director of the ACLU. He devoted his energies primarily to public education about civil liberties, giving numerous speeches and writing many articles. Almost all of his writings were topical, addressing particular cases or controversies. Baldwin himself was not an intellectual and never wrote a complete statement of his philosophy of civil liberties. He described himself as a philosophical anarchist, but he never subscribed to any specific political doctrine. For many years, Baldwin took trips across the United

States, speaking on civil liberties and enlisting support for the ACLU. These trips helped to establish his national reputation as a civil liberties advocate.

The ACLU was governed by a board of directors that met weekly in New York City to decide on organizational policy. Although a strong advocate of democracy, Baldwin was very much an autocrat within his own organization, maintaining strong control over his own board of directors. Baldwin's major contribution to the organization was his energy and magnetic personality, which brought into the ACLU individuals who were experts in particular areas of civil liberties. These included such notable figures as future Supreme Court Justice Felix Frankfurter and the longtime co-general counsels of the ACLU, Arthur Garfield Hays and Morris Ernst. He was also able to secure contributions from wealthy individuals, many of them Quakers who provided critical financial support for the small ACLU. In its first years, the ACLU had only about a thousand members.

In 1919, Baldwin married Madeline Z. Doty, who was also a social reformer. They divorced in 1936, and Baldwin married Evelyn Preston that same year.

In the 1920s, the courts at both the state and federal levels were not sympathetic to civil liberties. Consequently, under Baldwin's leadership the ACLU gave relatively little emphasis to litigation, especially compared with later decades. Typically, the ACLU would issue a public statement regarding a particular violation of civil liberties. In this respect, Baldwin's role as speaker and writer was a major part of the ACLU's activity. Legislatures were also very hostile to civil liberties, and the ACLU devoted relatively little energy to legislation.

Baldwin involved the ACLU in numerous civil liberties issues. He was particularly concerned about the rights of working people and labor unions. During this period, courts routinely granted requests from employers to enjoin union organizers from picketing or in some instances holding meetings to discuss unionization. Baldwin was also very active in the defense of Sacco and Vanzetti, two anarchists who had been convicted of murder and whose case became a symbol of the antiradical, anti-immigrant attitudes of the 1920s. The ACLU was particularly active in fighting race discrimination, protesting mob violence against African Americans led by the Ku Klux Klan. Baldwin always arranged to have a leader of the National Association for the Advancement of Colored People (NAACP) on the ACLU board of directors.

As part of his commitment to the rights of labor, Baldwin led a demonstration in Paterson, New Jersey in 1924, protesting a court injunction prohibiting labor union picketing and meetings. Many other ACLU leaders in this period engaged in direct action in support of civil liberties. Baldwin was arrested and convicted of violating a 1796 state law against rioting that had never been previously used. In 1928, a state appeals court overturned the conviction in one of the few decisions in that decade upholding the right of freedom of assembly.

The most important ACLU case in the 1920s was a challenge to a Tennessee law prohibiting the teaching of evolution in the public schools. Baldwin placed a notice in a Tennessee newspaper indicating the ACLU's willingness to represent anyone arrested for violating the law. In this manner, the ACLU represented John T. Scopes. The 1925 trial was a national sensation that brought the first important favorable publicity to the ACLU. Baldwin himself did not play a direct role in the trial, however.

Throughout his career, Baldwin was involved with innumerable organizations and causes. The ACLU was only one of four organizations that he established in 1920 alone. One of the most important organizations Baldwin founded in the 1920s was the American Fund for Public Service (AFPS). Charles Garland inherited a large sum of money and wanted to use the money to advance social change. Baldwin convinced him to give the money to the AFPS, which he helped establish in 1922 and which was directed by Baldwin's friends and associates. Through the 1920s the Fund supported many civil liberties, liberal, and leftwing causes. The fund, for example, supported the early litigation program by the NAACP. The Depression wiped out the fund's assets after 1929 and it soon became defunct.

Baldwin always had an interest in international human rights, traveled frequently, and corresponded with rights activists in other countries. In 1927, he visited the Soviet Union, and upon his return published *Liberty Under the Soviets* (1928), a detailed account of the treatment of religious, racial, and ethnic minorities in that country.

Since its founding in 1920, Baldwin and the ACLU primarily had to fight restrictions on the free speech rights of communists and other leftwing activists. In the mid-1930s, following the rise of domestic Nazi groups, they had to confront the issue of whether the First Amendment protected the free speech rights of fascists and other advocates of totalitarianism. After a brief internal debate, Baldwin and the ACLU issued a formal statement supporting the First Amendment rights of all extremist groups, including communists and Nazis.

In the late 1930s, Baldwin's views of the federal government and civil liberties underwent a major shift. As a result of his World War I experience, he had always been extremely skeptical of virtually all government power. By the mid-1930s, however, he developed a favorable view of President Franklin D. Roosevelt's administration, seeing that some New Deal agencies, such as the new National Labor Relations Board, supported civil liberties. He immediately began to spend more time in Washington, D.C., cultivating sympathetic officials in the Roosevelt administration. This shift was prompted in part by his disillusionment with the Soviet Union under Joseph Stalin. In the early 1930s, as a result of the Depression and the rise of fascism in Europe, Baldwin became more sympathetic to radical leftwing politics. In 1933 and 1934, he made a number of statements expressing sympathy for communism that were later used by ACLU critics against him. This very radical phase was brief, however, and Baldwin soon moved to a more moderate political point of view. Along with many other liberals and leftwing activists, he was shocked by Stalin's purge of other Soviet leaders in the famous Moscow trials. In the United States, Baldwin also became disgusted with what he saw as manipulative tactics by American communists participating in the Popular Front, a coalition of liberal and leftwing organizations. As a result, Baldwin became a strong anticommunist.

Baldwin's new anticommunist outlook set the stage for the most controversial episode in his career and in the history of the ACLU. In 1940, the ACLU board of directors adopted a policy under which no supporter of totalitarian organizations could serve in an official capacity in the ACLU. Under the policy, the board then quickly removed Elizabeth Gurley Flynn from its ranks because she was a member of the Communist Party. Many critics accused the ACLU of imposing the very same kind of political test that it had long fought against, and the incident tarnished the reputation of both Baldwin and the ACLU for several decades.

Although there was no widespread suppression of dissent as there had been during the First World War, World War II presented some difficult challenges for Baldwin. He strongly opposed the evacuation and internment of the Japanese-Americans by the federal government, but a majority of the ACLU board of directors limited the terms on which the ACLU would act. The result was a major conflict within the board of directors and between the ACLU national office and the organization's affiliates in San Francisco and Los Angeles. In the end, the ACLU brought the court cases that unsuccessfully challenged the government's program (*Hirabayashi* and *Korematsu*). Baldwin played a major role in organizing the Supreme Court cases, raising necessary funds and arranging for attorneys to write the court briefs and argue the cases before the Supreme Court.

The Federal Bureau of Investigation (FBI) in 1941 secretly designated Baldwin for detention in case of a national emergency. Although his political views had become more moderate, he was still regarded as a dangerous radical by the FBI. The FBI's secret emergency detention program did not become known until the 1970s, when the Watergate scandal exposed a number of abuses of power by federal agencies. The FBI maintained extensive surveillance of Baldwin over the years. Major portions of Baldwin's FBI file were released in the 1980s and were deposited with the Baldwin and ACLU archives at Princeton University.

In one of the most curious episodes in his career, Baldwin was invited to Japan in 1947 to advise General Douglas MacArthur on developing a constitution for postwar Japan. Somewhat surprisingly, the ACLU leader and the very conservative general established a close rapport.

Baldwin's role during the Cold War has been a subject of considerable controversy. Because of the removal of Elizabeth Gurley Flynn from the ACLU board in 1940, critics accused Baldwin and the ACLU of not opposing Cold War–era restrictions on freedom of speech and association with sufficient vigor. Baldwin had formed a personal relationship with FBI Director J. Edgar Hoover when the latter was first appointed in 1924, and he remained somewhat uncritical of the Bureau in the years that followed. And while Baldwin opposed the House Un-American Activities Committee (HUAC) since it was created in 1938, some other ACLU leaders had close and private relations with the committee. Despite the criticisms, however, both Baldwin and the ACLU strongly opposed most Cold War restrictions on civil liberties, including loyalty oaths, prosecutions under the 1940 Smith Act, and blacklisting in the entertainment industry.

In 1950, the ACLU board of directors decided to remove Baldwin as director, and he was given a vague "ambassadorial" position focusing on international issues. The decision to remove him was prompted by the feeling that Baldwin had not kept up with changing times. Always an autocrat who sought to maintain strong control of the organization, Baldwin had opposed any effort to increase the ACLU's membership or to create a network of affiliates across the country. In 1950, there were about 10,000 members and four affiliates with staff members. His successor embarked on a membership and affiliate development campaign that proved to be enormously successful. This development vindicated the decision of the ACLU board in removing Baldwin as director.

After being removed as executive director, Baldwin continued to work on human rights issues for another thirty-one years, devoting most of his energies to international issues and working through the International League for the Rights of Man. In this effort, he was as tireless as he had been previously. He traveled extensively around the world, giving speeches and writing articles.

Baldwin's legacy for civil liberties is enormous. Without his energy and devotion to the organization, the ACLU probably would not have survived. Nor was there any other person who tirelessly advocated the cause of free speech and other rights during the 1920s and 1930s. The history of civil liberties in the United States would have been very different without the efforts of Roger Baldwin. President Jimmy Carter awarded Baldwin the Medal of Liberty in January 1981. Roger Baldwin died on August 26, 1981.

SAMUEL WALKER

References and Further Reading

Baldwin, Roger N. *Liberty Under the Soviets*. New York: Vanguard Press, 1928.
Cottrell, Robert C. *Roger Nash Baldwin and the American Civil Liberties Union*. New York: Columbia University Press, 2000.
Lamson, Peggy. *Roger Baldwin, Founder of the American Civil Liberties Union: A Portrait*. Boston: Little, Brown, 1976.
Walker, Samuel. *In Defense of American Liberties: A History of the ACLU*. New York: Oxford University Press, 1990.

BALLEW v. GEORGIA, 435 U.S. 223 (1978)

The manager of an adult theater was charged in a state court with distributing obscene materials, a misdemeanor. Pursuant to state law, and over his claim that the Sixth Amendment right to a jury trial required a jury of at least six members, he was tried and convicted by a jury of five people.

The purpose of a jury trial is to provide protect against government oppression by having members of the community participate in the determination of guilt, *Duncan v. Louisiana*. Although a jury traditionally comprised twelve members, the U.S. Supreme Court held in *Williams v. Florida* that the Sixth Amendment does not require a jury of that number; rather, it merely mandates a jury of sufficient size to encourage group deliberation, to shield members from outside deliberation, and to supply a representative cross-section of the community. In *Williams*, the Court concluded that a jury of six members can fulfill the functions of a jury trial, and therefore is not unconstitutional. In *Ballew v. Georgia*, however, the Supreme Court unanimously held that a five-person

jury does not comport with the requirements of the Sixth Amendment. The Court relied heavily on empirical studies raising doubts about the reliability of decisions by juries of fewer than six members, and indicating that such juries are less likely to contain members of minority groups and thus not truly represent their communities. In addition, the Court concluded that no significant state interest justified a reduction from six members to five.

DAVID S. RUDSTEIN

References and Further Reading

LaFave, Wayne R., Jerold H. Israel, and Nancy J. King. *Criminal Procedure*. 4th ed. St. Paul, Minn.: Thompson-West, 2004.
Rudstein, David S., C. Peter Erlinder, and David C. Thomas. *Criminal Constitutional Law*. Newark, N.J. and San Francisco: LexisNexis-Matthew Bender, 1990, 2004.
Singley, Carl E., *Ballew v. Georgia: Five Is Not Enough*, Temple Law Quarterly 52 (1979): 2:217–58.

Cases and Statutes Cited

Duncan v. Louisiana, 391 U.S. 145 (1968)
Williams v. Florida, 399 U.S. 78 (1970)

See also **Duncan v. Louisiana, 391 U.S. 145 (1968); Incorporation Doctrine; Jury Trial; Jury Trial Right**

BALLOT INITIATIVES

Method by which the people of various states exercise their retained right to initiate and adopt legislation directly. Proponents argue that the process is a particularly effective means of political expression, and of circumventing a legislature that is lethargic or captured by interest groups. Detractors focus on the weaknesses of the initiative process, including the misleadingly simplistic advertising used to explain complicated proposals to voters, the growing expense of getting measures on the ballot, and the related risk that the process is falling under the control of the same special interest groups it seeks to restrain.

The method of state lawmaking is not new; California, for example, adopted the process in 1911 and has deployed it with increasing frequency and importance over the last three decades. Californians have directly passed important laws doing everything from reducing local property taxes, creating new state agencies, abolishing race-based affirmative action, widening the scope of the death penalty and lifetime imprisonment, and imposing term limits on members of the state legislature. But today critics of the process, including many California voters themselves, are expressing some support for reforming the initiative process.

In states that use initiatives, to get a measure on the ballot supporters must collect a threshold number of citizen signatures, often tied to a percentage of the turnout at the last state election. The procedural details of the initiative power vary from state to state (and sometimes from locality to locality), but initiatives may be used to adopt state statutes, amendments to the state constitution, or both. States with an indirect initiative process require an intermediary step of submitting the proposed measure to the legislature. If approved by the legislature, the measure becomes law. If rejected, the measure will go to the people for their approval or rejection at the next election. By contrast, a direct initiative device allows measures to go straight onto the ballot after the signature threshold has been met and certified, without the measure having to be presented to the legislature for its consideration.

VIKRAM D. AMAR

BALTIMORE CITY DEPARTMENT OF SOCIAL SERVICES v. BOUKNIGHT, 493 U.S. 549 (1990)

Maurice M, after being hospitalized at age three months with fresh and partially healed bone fractures, was placed into shelter care by a court order but was later returned to his mother Jacqueline's custody. After a hearing, he was permitted to remain with her, provided that she complied with extensive conditions in a protective order. When Social Services later alleged that Bouknight had violated every such condition, the court granted a petition to remove Maurice from her control. Upon her repeated refusal to produce Maurice, the court ordered her imprisoned for civil contempt until she produced her son or revealed his location.

The juvenile court rejected Bouknight's later claim that the contempt order violated the Fifth Amendment's privilege against self-incrimination, which declares, "No person . . . shall be compelled in any criminal case to be a witness against himself," although the state court of appeals disagreed.

The U.S. Supreme Court reversed. The privilege applies only to the state's compelling the making of an act with a "testimonial or communicative nature" providing a link in a chain to potential criminal prosecution. Maurice's body would be physical, not testimonial, but the *act of producing* him would communicate the testimonial facts of his existence, authentic identity as Bouknight's son, and her possession of him. Nevertheless, the Court found the

privilege inapplicable, partly because it does not extend to "collective entities," like corporations, or to their representatives, such as records custodians, because they lack "private enclaves" needing protection. The *Bouknight* Court apparently viewed Bouknight as having custody of Maurice on *behalf of the state as a "collective entity."*

The Court also relied on the required records doctrine as taking the case outside the Fifth Amendment privilege. This doctrine requires first, that the purpose of government action is regulatory rather than furthering criminal investigation; and, second, that the records themselves have a "public aspect [making] them analogous to public documents," a phrase generally requiring balancing the public need against the intrusion upon the individual. Furthermore, the required records doctrine likely cannot extend to inquiries directed not at the general public but at a "highly selective group inherently suspected of criminal activities," such as requiring illegal gamblers to report their ill-gotten income to the Internal Revenue Service.

For the *Bouknight* Court, the demand to produce Maurice served the state's regulatory interest in protecting his safety, counterbalanced any intrusion upon Bouknight, and was not aimed at a "selective group inherently suspect of criminal activities" because a child may be placed by Social Services with foster parents or relatives not suspected of any crime. Without deciding the question, however, the Court noted that some privilege protection might remain for child custodians under certain circumstances.

Bouknight remained incarcerated for more than seven years after the Supreme Court's opinion. After her release, attorneys portrayed her "as a champion of civil disobedience, comparing her to the Rev. Martin Luther King Jr." State officials disagreed, adding that they feared her son was dead.

ANDREW E. TASLITZ

References and Further Reading

Merker Rosenberg, Irene, *Bouknight: On Abused Children and the Parental Privilege Against Self-Incrimination, Iowa* Law Review 76 (1991): 535.

Cases and Statutes Cited

Fisher v. United States, 425 U.S. 391 (1976)
Haynes v. United States, 390 U.S. 85 (1968)
Marchetti v. United States, 390 U.S. 39 (1948)
Shapiro v. United States, 335 U.S. 1 (1948)
United States v. Doe, 465 U.S. 605 (1984)

See also **Coerced Confessions/Police Interrogation; Self-Incrimination (V): Historical Background**

BAPTISTS IN EARLY AMERICA

From the time in the early 1600s that some of the early Puritans came to believe that infant baptism could not be justified on biblical grounds, to the final abolition of the last remaining compulsory religious taxation system in Massachusetts in 1833, the Baptists bore the brunt of the religious persecution and discrimination meted out in early American communities. The Baptists countered by waging a struggle against governmental support for established religion more persistently and effectively than any other dissenting group. While they could not have prevailed in this struggle without significant assistance from other quarters, the Baptists are to be credited with exerting unsurpassed influence on the pace and course of the emergence of religious liberty in America.

The Baptists' struggle began in the New England colonies, whose Puritan founders believed themselves to constitute the vanguard of a "New Reformation" that would complete the work that Luther and Calvin had begun by restoring the purity of the early church. The Puritans believed that theirs was the one and only true church and faith, and all New England colonists were expected to support the New Reformation project by supporting the Puritan congregations in their local communities. Any who could not bring themselves to do so were free to leave, in the eyes of the Puritan leadership. Any who would not leave were to be punished, in an effort to force the dissenters to abandon their ways and return to living in conformity with Puritan beliefs and expectations.

New England colonists who came to believe that infant baptism was illegitimate would become known to the civil authorities when they would refuse to have their own children baptized, and either turn their backs when the children of other families were being baptized or walk out of the church to avoid participating in such ceremonies. These early Baptists were then hailed into court, where they were warned, fined, or even whipped if they gave any indication that they would repeat their offending behavior. Those who refused to pay the fine were imprisoned for an indeterminate period. Church authorities would inflict a parallel process of warnings, censure, and ultimately excommunication. These early Baptists were considered social pariahs, subjected to harassment and ostracism, and they were denied the right to vote or hold office. Most either left the colony as quickly as they could or decided that they would henceforth refrain from disrupting baptism ceremonies and keep their views to themselves. To worship openly together, much less organize formally as a church, was completely out of the question.

The Puritans were committed to maintaining some connection to the Church of England, in the hope of reforming it. Roger Williams, the pastor of the Puritan church at Salem, Massachusetts, came into conflict with Puritan officials when he advocated the view that the Church of England was a false church, and that the Puritans should separate themselves from it. Although the Puritans would become known as Congregationalists for their rejection of the Church of England's system of Episcopal authority over the local congregation, they could not accept Williams's call to break from the Church of England completely. The authorities banished Williams from the Massachusetts Bay Colony in 1635, and the next year he and some friends from the Salem church founded the colony of Providence Plantations, just to the south. After a number of English Baptists migrated to Providence between 1636 and 1639, Williams and his friends re-baptized themselves by immersion and formed the first Baptist church in America, in Providence. Although Williams would himself remain a Baptist for only a few months, the church continued on after him, and a second Baptist church was founded in nearby Newport by 1644.

In 1651 John Clarke, the pastor of the Newport church, and two of its members traveled to Lynn, Massachusetts, to preach in a private home. Massachusetts authorities arrested, tried, and gave them the choice of paying a fine or being whipped. Clarke and one of the others paid the fine, but the third, Obadiah Holmes, refused. He was tied to a stake on Boston Common, stripped to the waist, and given such a severe whipping that he was unable to leave Boston for several weeks. Clarke's account of this incident was published in London a year later in an unsuccessful effort to persuade Parliament to require New England colonies to tolerate dissent.

Baptists persisted in Massachusetts, despite the persecution that they faced there. In 1654, the president of Harvard College, Henry Dunster, shocked his community when he refused to have his child baptized and publicly declared his opposition to infant baptism. When church leaders tried to persuade him of his error, Dunster responded that no support can be found for the practice of infant baptism in either the Bible or the practice of the early church. The Massachusetts legislature responded by passing a law stating that all dissenters should be removed from teaching positions at Harvard and in the public schools. Dunster was publicly admonished, required to give bond ensuring his future good behavior, and forced to resign from Harvard.

By 1665, Boston Baptists were worshipping in the home of their pastor, Thomas Goold, who along with other members of the Boston church was arrested and disenfranchised, and later imprisoned and sentenced to be banished. One of the first openings toward religious liberty in Massachusetts followed, when sixty-six residents submitted a petition asking the authorities to free and tolerate him and the others. Instead, the authorities gave Goold only a three-day release to attend to some private business. While out of prison on leave, Goold slipped away to an island where he could conduct services unmolested, until a more tolerant governor came into office in 1673, which enabled Goold to return openly to the Boston Baptist community.

When the authorities learned in 1679 that Boston's Baptists had secretly built and begun to assemble in a meetinghouse, however, the legislature passed a law making it illegal to build any church structure without its permission. The Baptists agreed to stop using their building until later that year, when a letter arrived from King Charles II expressing his support for "freedom and liberty of conscience" for all non-Catholic Christians. From that point on, the Boston Baptist church was never bothered again, and no Baptist was ever again indicted in the Massachusetts Bay Colony.

Although the overt persecution of Baptists had ended in the colony, its system of collecting taxes to support Congregationalist ministers and erect church buildings for each settlement remained in place. When Baptists would refuse to pay the tax, they were subject to imprisonment, and some of their property (for example, livestock) could be seized and sold at auction to pay the bill. In 1708, three local tax collectors (two Quakers and one Baptist) from Dartmouth were imprisoned for refusing to collect the religious tax. The governor intervened to secure their release, but when the problem erupted again in Dartmouth the Quakers presented a petition to the King and the Privy Council, which responded by exempting the residents of Dartmouth from the tax. The Privy Council decision prompted the adoption of a series of laws in Massachusetts and other New England colonies designed to exempt dissenters from the religious tax.

By 1735, the Baptists and other dissenters were more fully tolerated in New England than in England or in the southern colonies, where Anglicanism was legally established. Had the Great Awakening not burst on the New England scene in 1740, the Baptists might have remained content indefinitely with the legal status that they had achieved. The Great Awakening, however, split New England's established churches between the New Lights, who were filled with evangelical fervor, and the Old Lights, who wished to retain prevailing styles of worship and beliefs. Over a period of years, many of the New Light Congregationalists who had separated from the established churches (who thus became known

as Separates) adopted the Baptists' belief that infant baptism is illegitimate, and eventually were absorbed into the Baptist denomination (and became known as Separate-Baptists). In a series of cases during the first three decades after the Great Awakening, Massachusetts authorities cited legal technicalities in an attempt to prevent the Separate-Baptists from availing themselves of the existing exemption for Baptists from local religious taxes.

Meanwhile, beginning in about 1765 the Separate-Baptists began sending a number of evangelists into the South, especially North Carolina and Virginia. In Virginia, the authorities had been granting dissenting congregations a limited number of licenses. The Quakers, Presbyterians, and Baptists who were in Virginia prior to the Great Awakening generally complied with this law. The Separate-Baptists refused, and as a result from 1768 to 1775 about forty Separate-Baptists were jailed for preaching without a license.

The young James Madison was horrified at what he saw, but he saw little hope of redressing the situation through Virginia's colonial legislature. With the approach of the Revolutionary War, however, the tide began to turn. In 1775, with the assistance of Patrick Henry, the Virginia Baptist Association successfully petitioned for the right of Baptist ministers to minister to Baptist soldiers. In 1776, Virginia's Revolutionary Convention adopted the Virginia Declaration of Rights that, under Madison's influence, guaranteed to all "the free exercise of religion."

When war came, tax support for the Church of England was halted, and after the war the Baptists argued against the adoption of a tax system that would support religion in general. Their former ally, Patrick Henry, now led the effort to have such a system adopted. Madison credited the persuasiveness of his "Memorial and Remonstrance" for defeating the general religious assessment measure, but the signatures on petitions against the measure submitted by evangelicals, principally Baptists and Presbyterians, outnumbered those on Madison's document by five to one.

Seeing a valuable ally in Madison, John Leland, the leading Virginia Baptist champion of religious liberty, supported Madison's election to Virginia's convention to ratify the federal constitution and later to the U.S. House of Representatives in exchange for Madison's promise to secure an amendment to the federal constitution guaranteeing religious liberty. Once this was achieved, Virginia's Baptists then turned to the question of what was to be done with the property belonging to the former Church of England, now the Protestant Episcopal Church, which had been used to support its clergy. In a typical parish, this might include the parsonage and hundreds of acres of land.

For over a decade, Baptists petitioned Virginia's legislature, arguing persistently that this property belonged to all Virginians. By 1802, they had persuaded the legislature to create a system whereby this property would revert to the state as Episcopal clergy changed churches, retired, or died. This was the most sweeping social change that took place in Virginia during the Revolutionary era.

In Massachusetts, the laws exempting Baptists from religious taxation were widely accepted until 1773, when the regional Baptist association endorsed Separate-Baptist leader Isaac Backus's call for the total abolition of the religion tax system. When Backus's efforts failed to prevent Massachusetts from incorporating its religious tax system into the state constitution that it adopted post-independence to replace its colonial charter, the Baptists were left with challenging the system in court. In 1782, the Baptists succeeded in having a Bristol County court declare that the religious taxation system violated the state constitution, and by 1800 very few dissenters—whether Baptist, Universalist, Shaker, or Methodist—were being prosecuted for nonpayment of religious taxes.

The Baptists took the lead in persuading Vermont's legislature to abolish its religious tax system in 1807, and Connecticut and New Hampshire followed suit in 1818 and 1819, respectively. In Massachusetts, the Baptists had largely turned their attention away from religious liberty concerns to an ambitious program of mission and social reform efforts. In 1820, when Massachusetts called a constitutional convention to resolve the legal issues arising from the separation of Maine from Massachusetts in 1819, Baptists sought to remove the religious taxation provisions from the Massachusetts Constitution, but in the old Congregationalist elite's last stand they blocked the Baptist effort. It would be the Universalists who would eventually succeed in pushing for the abolition of Massachusetts' religious tax system in 1833.

DAVID T. BALL

References and Further Reading

Buckley, Thomas E., *Keeping Faith: Virginia Baptists and Religious Liberty*, American Baptist Quarterly 22 (2003): 421–33.
Isaac, Rhys, *Evangelical Revolt: The Nature of the Baptists' Challenge to the Traditional Order in Virginia, 1765 to 1775*, William and Mary Quarterly 31 (1974): 345–68.
McLoughlin, William G. *New England Dissent, 1630–1833: The Baptists and the Separation of Church and State.* 2 vols. Cambridge, MA: Harvard University Press, 1971.

BARCLAY v. FLORIDA, 463 U.S. 939 (1983)

Barclay was convicted of first-degree murder for his participation in the politically and racially motivated murder of a hitchhiker. After a separate sentencing hearing in which the jury recommended that Barclay be sentenced to life in prison, the trial judge imposed a death sentence. Under Florida law, a death sentence must be based on a finding of sufficient statutory aggravating circumstances that are not outweighed by any mitigating factors. Further, a jury's sentencing recommendation is only advisory; a judge may still impose a death sentence where the facts supporting it are so clear and convincing that no one could reasonably disagree.

Barclay argued that the trial judge relied on non-statutory aggravating factors in violation of Florida law and relied on statutory aggravating factors that did not apply in his case. The Court held that mere errors of state law do not ordinarily constitute a denial of due process. Because the Constitution does not require states to limit consideration of aggravating factors to those statutorily specified, the trial judge's reliance on a non-statutory factor did not violate the federal constitution. In addition, the Court determined that, despite the trial judge's improper reliance on a non-statutory aggravating factor, the Florida Supreme Court's harmless error analysis provided sufficient review of the relative weight of aggravating and mitigating factors. *Barclay* thus signals the Court's partial retreat from the demanding procedural restrictions adopted in the 1970s and the greater deference to state capital sentencing processes characteristic of its Eighth Amendment jurisprudence in the 1980s and 1990s.

MARY SIGLER

See also **Capital Punishment and Sentencing; Capital Punishment: Due Process Limits;** *Gregg v. Georgia,* **428 U.S. 153 (1976)**

BAREFOOTE v. ESTELLE, 463 U.S. 880 (1983)

Many capital punishment statutes permit jurors to consider evidence of a convicted capital murderer's "future dangerousness." In those jurisdictions, prosecutors often argue that the defendant should be executed because he is likely to commit more acts of violence and thus poses an ongoing danger to society. Evidence supporting such arguments includes such things as the defendant's recidivism, prison violence, and lack of remorse. The particular circumstances of the capital crime may suggest future dangerousness as well. But the most controversial evidence of future dangerousness is expert psychological and psychiatric testimony.

The validity of such testimony came under attack in the case of *Barefoote v. Estelle*, 463 U.S. 880 (1983). What is remarkable about the Supreme Court's opinion is that it approved of expert testimony on future dangerousness even though the overwhelming consensus among mental health experts regards such predictions as highly dubious. Most notable among the critics of future dangerousness testimony was, and still is, the American Psychiatric Association (APA). Empirical studies indicate that expert predictions of future dangerousness are wrong two out of three times. The Court brushed this and other concerns aside, reasoning instead that so long as future dangerousness is a valid factor for receiving the death penalty, jurors may hear the views of testifying mental health professionals. If lay jurors must assess future dangerousness, the Court explained, then "it makes little sense, if any, to submit that psychiatrists, out of the entire universe of persons who might have an opinion on the issue, would know so little about the subject that they should not be permitted to testify."

DANIEL R. WILLIAMS

References and Further Reading

The American Psychological Association Task Force on the Role of Psychology in the Criminal Justice System. *American Psychologist* 33 (1978): 1099. Reprinted in John Monahan, ed., *Who Is the Client? The Ethics of Psychological Intervention in the Criminal Justice System.* Washington, D.C.: American Psychological Association, 1980.
Carter, Linda E., and Ellen Kreitzberg. *Understanding Capital Punishment Law.* Newark, NJ: LexisNexis, 2004.

See also **Capital Punishment; Capital Punishment and Race Discrimination; Capital Punishment and Equal Protection Clause Cases; Capital Punishment: Eighth Amendment Limits; Capital Punishment: Due Process Limits**

BARENBLATT v. UNITED STATES, 360 U.S. 109 (1959)

In 1954, Lloyd Barenblatt was subpoenaed by the House Committee on Un-American Activities (HUAC), which was investigating communist activities and organizations. Barenblatt refused to say if he was a member of the Communist Party or had belonged to the Communist Party's Haldene Club while a graduate student at the University of Michigan. He was convicted in federal court of contempt of Congress, fined $250, and sentenced to six months in prison. He appealed the conviction, arguing that HUAC had violated his freedoms of thought, speech, press, and association. He added that, regardless of how he answered HUAC's questions, his social standing and ability to earn a living would be jeopardized. In 1959, a five-to-four majority of the Supreme Court rejected Barenblatt's arguments and reaffirmed his conviction.

The stage for the *Barenblatt* decision had been indirectly set by two 1957 decisions. In *Watkins v. United States*, the Court overturned a conviction for contempt of Congress for another communist sympathizer who had refused to answer HUAC's questions. In *Yates v. United States*, the Court ordered the acquittal of five communist defendants and sent back to the lower courts the cases of nine others in prosecutions under the federal Smith Act. Anticommunist conservatives were outraged by the decisions and dubbed June 17, 1957, the day on which both decisions were rendered, "Red Monday." Senator William Jenner of Indiana even introduced a bill to limit the Court's power to decide loyalty and subversion appeals.

The majority of the Court in *Barenblatt* retreated from *Watkins*, helped protect existing appellate jurisdiction, and to some extent defused political criticism. The authority of HUAC to conduct its investigation, Justice John Marshall Harlan II said, was unassailable, and it was indeed a violation of federal law when Barenblatt refused to answer. Furthermore, Harlan added, the balance between the individual and the government must be struck in favor of the government.

Dissenting justices were more sensitive to the civil liberties issues raised by the case. Justice Hugo Black, in a dissent joined by Chief Justice Earl Warren and Justice William O. Douglas, asserted that HUAC's goal was less investigative than judicial. HUAC wanted to try and punish suspected communists, but congressional committees did not have these judicial powers. Black also insisted that First Amendment protections were not to be balanced against government interests. "Ultimately all the questions in this case" he said, "really boil down to one—whether we as a people will try fearfully and futilely to preserve democracy by adopting totalitarian methods or whether in accordance with our traditions and our Constitution we will have the confidence and courage to be free."

In retrospect, the facts in *Barenblatt* illustrate the way that HUAC and other governmental bodies might disregard civil liberties while engaging in exposure for exposure's sake. The Supreme Court's tolerance for such activity, meanwhile, illustrates its own susceptibility to the anticommunist political hysteria of the 1950s.

DAVID RAY PAPKE

References and Further Reading

Alfange, Dean, *Congressional Investigations and the Fickle Court*, University of Cincinnati Law Review 30 (1961): 113–71.
Kutler, Stanley I. *The American Inquisition: Justice and Injustice in the Cold War*. New York: Hill & Wang, 1982.
Rohr, Marc, *Communists and the First Amendment: The Shaping of Freedom of Advocacy in the Cold War Era*, San Diego Law Review 28 (1991): 1–116.

Cases and Statutes Cited

Watkins v. United States, 354 U.S. 178 (1957)
Yates v. United States, 354 U.S. 298 (1957)

See also **Communism and the Cold War; Vagueness and Overbreadth in Criminal Statutes; Warren Court**

BARNES v. GLEN THEATRE, INC., 501 U.S. 560 (1991)

Nude dancing as an issue in earlier cases occurred in the context of alcohol regulations, such as *California v. LaRue* (1972), or zoning laws as in *Schad v. Mt. Ephraim* (1981). Although *LaRue*, in passing, suggested that nude dancing under certain circumstances might be "expressive conduct" entitled to some degree of First Amendment protection, *Barnes* is the first time that the Supreme Court directly confronted this issue. The question that emerges is whether nude dancing, if it is expressive conduct and not obscene, can be regulated without infringement on the First Amendment.

Indiana's public indecency law prohibited nudity in public places, and if individuals danced in the nude they were compelled to wear pasties and g-strings. Two establishments, The Kitty Kat Lounge and the Glen Theatre, wanted to provide totally nude dancing and together with one of the dancers challenged the law. The Court of Appeals for the Seventh Circuit declared nonobscene nude dancing performed as entertainment to be an expressive activity, protected by the First Amendment, and struck down Indiana's law.

In a five-to-four decision reversing the Court of Appeals' judgment, the members of the majority wrote three separate opinions. Rehnquist, O'Connor, and Kennedy, forming a plurality, stated that "nude dancing of the kind sought to be performed here is expressive conduct within the outer perimeters of the First Amendment, although we view it as only marginally so." As expressive conduct falling within the ambit of the First Amendment, the standard for review depended on whether the law comported with the four-part test developed in *United States v. O'Brien* (1968) that wrestled with communicative conduct (in this instance, burning a draft card) or symbolic speech that combined both speech and nonspeech. Applying this test, the three justices concluded Indiana's statute passed Constitutional muster "despite its incidental limitations on some expressive activity" because it did not target nude dancing per se and because of the state's superior interest in "protecting societal order and morality."

Scalia disagreed that Indiana's law implicated the First Amendment, and thus rejected the rationale of the plurality opinion. In his view, Indiana's law was a general law not specifically directed at expression or prohibiting conduct because of its particular communicative attributes. He favorably quotes the dissenting judge in the lower court who, arguing the law did not regulate dancing but public nudity, noted that "[a]lmost the entire domain of Indiana's statute is unrelated to expression, unless we view nude beaches and topless hot dog vendors as speech." Scalia accordingly disagreed that more than normal scrutiny of the law was required or that the O'Brien test was appropriate.

The inability of the five justices to agree on why Indiana's law was constitutional was met with confusion in the lower courts. Thus, in 2000, the Supreme Court tried a second time to gather a majority around a definitive common rule to guide states and localities on the issue of public nudity statutes. *City of Erie v. Pap's A.M* (2000) sustained *Barnes* and upheld the constitutionality of Erie's anti-nudity ordinance, which was nearly identical to Indiana's, but, once again, only a plurality (O'Connor, Rehnquist, Kennedy, and Breyer) coalesced around *Barnes* and its reasoning, while Souter, Scalia, and Thomas, the other members of the majority (Stevens and Ginsburg dissented) concurred only in the judgment.

ROY B. FLEMMING

Cases and Statutes Cited

Barnes v. Glen Theatre, Inc., 501 U.S. 560 (1991)
California v. LaRue, 409 U.S. 109 (1972)
City of Erie v. Pap's A.M, 529 U.S. 277 (2000)
Schad v. Mt. Ephraim, 452 U.S. 61 (1981)
United States v. O'Brien, 391 U.S. 367 (1968)

BARRON v. BALTIMORE, 32 U.S. 243 (1833)

Barron v. Baltimore was an appeal to the Supreme Court from the Court of Appeals of Maryland, upon a writ of error through Section 25 of the Judiciary Act of 1789, on the grounds that a state action had violated the U.S. Constitution. The suit was begun by John Barron to recover damages from the city of Baltimore, which in paving streets and diverting streams had allegedly made his wharf useless from a buildup of sand that made the water too shallow for ships. Barron claimed that Baltimore's actions violated the takings clause in the Fifth Amendment, which stated "nor shall private property be taken for public use without just compensation." This raised the question of whether the Fifth Amendment and in general the Bill of Rights restricted the states as well as the federal government.

The Marshall Court answered in the negative, denying that it had jurisdiction and stating that the Bill of Rights did not apply to the states. In the opinion of the Court, Chief Justice John Marshall reasoned first, that in America the sovereign people through state constitutions empowered and restricted state governments and through the U.S. Constitution empowered and restricted the federal government. Unless expressly stated otherwise, the Constitution, including amendments to it, referred only to the federal government. Second, through textual analysis of the Constitution, Marshall compared the Bill of Rights to Sections 9 and 10 in Article I. Section 9, which he called a brief bill of rights with restrictions on the federal government, used general language. Section 10, which earlier in *Fletcher v. Peck* he called a brief bill of rights with restrictions on the states, clearly and expressly referred to only the states with each clause beginning with "No State shall." The first ten amendments are mostly in general language similar to Section 9. Third, he observed, "it is universally understood, it is a part of the history of the day" that during the ratification debate the Anti-Federalists demanded a bill of rights, almost every ratifying convention recommended amendments, and Congress proposed and the states ratified a bill of rights with safeguards against the new federal government, not the states.

Marshall's arguments are reinforced by the speeches in the First Congress by James Madison, the main author of the Bill of Rights, who proposed that the amendments be placed within the Constitution, mostly in the Article I, Section 9 restrictions on the federal government. Also, an amendment he proposed that would expressly apply to the states, which he wanted in the Section 10 restrictions on the states, failed to pass.

While there had been some discussion prior to the case, *Barron* settled in the courts that the Bill of Rights did not apply to the states, and, despite criticism by the abolitionists, the doctrine was maintained by the Court through to the Fourteenth Amendment, which used the language in Section 10 clearly expressing, "No state shall . . . ." Through this amendment, by the Warren Court era, through a process of incorporation, the Court has applied most of the Bill of Rights to the states.

F. THORNTON MILLER

References and Further Reading

Amar, Akhil Reed. *The Bill of Rights: Creation and Reconstruction.* New Haven, CT: Yale University Press, 1998.

Ely, James W., Jr. *The Guardian of Every Other Right: A Constitutional History of Property Rights.* 2nd ed. New York: Oxford University Press, 1998.

Johnson, Herbert A. *The Chief Justiceship of John Marshall, 1801–1835.* Columbia: University of South Carolina Press, 1997.

White, G. Edward. *The Marshall Court and Cultural Change, 1815–1835.* New York: Oxford University Press, 1991.

Cases and Statutes Cited

Fletcher v. Peck, 6 Cranch 87 (1810)

See also **Abolitionists; Application of First Amendment to States; Bill of Rights: Structure; Fourteenth Amendment; Incorporation Doctrine; Madison, James; Marshall, John; Marshall Court; Takings Clause (V); Warren Court**

BARTKUS v. ILLINOIS, 359 U.S. 121 (1959)

In this decision, the Supreme Court upheld a state conviction following federal acquittal for the same crime, ruling that the so-called "double jeopardy clause" of the Fifth Amendment, which bars multiple convictions for the same crime, did not apply to the states. Alfonse Bartkus was tried in federal court for robbing a federally insured bank and acquitted, but he was later convicted in Illinois state court for the same crime and sentenced to life in prison. The defendant challenged his conviction on the grounds that the Fourteenth Amendment's due process guarantees disallowed multiple trials for the same crime. The Court declared that the Fourteenth Amendment's due process clause did not apply any of the first eight amendments to the states, and thus the ban against multiple prosecutions—the double jeopardy clause of the Fifth Amendment—did not apply to state courts. The Court relied on historical and federalist arguments that states were intended to remain separate from the federal government, beginning with their own constitutions, and their legal systems should be independent as well. Applying this "dual sovereignty" doctrine meant that the same crime could nevertheless be considered a separate offense in federal and state systems. The Court also relied on prior case law, in the Supreme Court and the states, upholding successive federal and state prosecutions, and invoked policy arguments that banning dual state and federal prosecutions would hinder states' ability to protect themselves against crime. The strong dissent in this case argued that double prosecutions are contrary to the historical and moral precedents of civilized society.

DAVID D. BURNETT

References and Further Reading

Dawson, Michael A., *Note: Popular Sovereignty, Double Jeopardy, and the Dual Sovereignty Doctrine*, Yale Law Journal 102 (1992): 46:281–303.

Lopez, Dax Eric, *Note: Not Twice for the Same: How the Dual Sovereignty Doctrine Is Used to Circumvent Non Bis In Idem*, Vanderbilt Journal of Transnational Law 33 (2000): 1263–303.

"Selective Preemption: A Preferential Solution to the Bartkus–Abbate Rule in Successive Federal–State Prosecutions." *The Notre Dame Lawyer* 57 (1981): 340–63.

See also **Double Jeopardy (V): Early History, Background, Framing; Double Jeopardy: Modern History; Due Process; Due Process of Law (V and XIV); Fourteenth Amendment; Substantive Due Process**

BARTNICKI v. VOPPER, 532 U.S. 514 (2001)

Plaintiffs, a union president and a chief negotiator, had a cellular phone conversation in which threats were made against school board members. An unknown third party intercepted and taped the conversation, and left a copy with a local activist. The activist gave copies to the local media, which disclosed the contents to the public.

Plaintiffs sued the activist and media outlets under federal and Pennsylvania wiretap laws prohibiting the disclosure of an electronic communication when a party knows or has reason to know that the communication was unlawfully intercepted. The Supreme Court assumed that the defendants violated the statutes.

The sole question was whether the First Amendment barred the statutes' application on the specific facts of these cases.

Justice Stevens, joined by five other justices, concluded that the plaintiffs' actions were barred. He began by characterizing the wiretap laws as content neutral, but then emphasized that the publication of lawfully obtained truthful information about a matter of public concern could not be punished "absent a need . . . of the highest order" (quoting *Smith v. Daily Mail Publishing Co.* [1979]). He found the government's interest in deterring unlawful interceptions to be inadequate, noting that the government could further this interest more directly by punishing interceptors and not law-abiding possessors who disclose the information. By contrast, he characterized the government's interest in protecting privacy of communication as "important," recognizing that "fear of public disclosure of private conversations might well have a chilling effect on private speech." Stevens suggested that this interest in protecting privacy and fostering private speech might justify disclosure prohibitions in most cases. But in this instance, he found the interest outweighed by the competing interest in having truthful information about a matter of public concern published. In reaching this narrow result, Stevens avoided the larger question of whether a party who himself unlawfully obtained truthful information could be punished for publishing the information and not merely for its unlawful acquisition. Justice Breyer, in a concurrence joined by Justice O'Connor, emphasized that he joined the majority's opinion only because the speakers' legitimate privacy expectations were "unusually low," and the public's interest in publication was "unusually high."

ALAN E. GARFIELD

References and Further Reading

Fishman, Clifford S., *Technology and the Internet: The Impending Destruction of Privacy by Betrayers, Grudgers, Snoops, Spammers, Corporations, and the Media*, George Washington Law Review 72 (2004): 1503.

Huhn, Wilson R., *Assessing the Constitutionality of Laws that Are Both Content-Based and Content-Neutral: The Emerging Constitutional Calculus*, Indiana Law Journal 79 (2004): 801.

Terrell, Timothy P., and Anne R. Jacobs, *Privacy, Technology, and Terrorism: Bartnicki, Kyllo, and the Normative Struggle Behind Competing Claims to Solitude and Security*, Emory Law Journal 41 (2002): 1469.

Volokh, Eugene, *Freedom of Speech and Intellectual Property: Some Thoughts After Eldred, 44 Liquormart, and Bartnicki*, Houston Law Review 40 (2003): 697.

BATES v. STATE BAR OF ARIZONA, 433 U.S. 350 (1969)

Two recent law graduates opened a law practice, which they called the "Legal Clinic of Bates and O'Steen." The lawyers placed a print ad in a local newspaper, which asked "Do You Need a Lawyer?" and offered "Legal Services at Very Reasonable Fees." The ad then listed the fees for certain routine legal services. The state bar brought a disciplinary proceeding against the two for violating a state rule of professional conduct that flatly prohibited any mass media advertising.

The Arizona Supreme Court upheld the sanction against the lawyers, reasoning that the advertising rule did not violate either federal anti-trust laws or the First Amendment (*In re Bates and O'Steen*). The U.S. Supreme Court agreed to review this decision, having decided in the previous term that a rule restricting the advertising of prescription drug prices was an unconstitutional limitation on the free flow of information about the availability and price of commercial services (*Virginia State Board of Pharmacy v. Virginia Citizens Consumer Council, Inc.*).

The Court held that the protection for commercial speech applied to advertising by lawyers, and that the Arizona rule was unconstitutionally broad. Although the law is traditionally said to be a profession, not a "mere" business, there is no reason for lawyers to pretend that they are not interested in earning fees for their work. Moreover, advertising need not be inherently misleading or deceptive. Four dissenting justices argued that there should be some distinction between advertising for products, such as prescription drugs, and professional services.

W. BRADLEY WENDEL

Cases and Statutes Cited

Bates v. Arizona State Bar, 433 U.S. 350 (1977)
In re Bates and O'Steen, 555 P.2d 640 (Ariz. 1976)
Virginia State Board of Pharmacy v. Virginia Citizens Consumer Council, Inc., 425 U.S. 748 (1976)

See also **Commercial Speech; Lawyer Advertising;** *Virginia State Board of Pharmacy v. Virginia Citizens Consumer Council, Inc.*, **425 U.S. 748 (1976)**

BATSON v. KENTUCKY, 476 U.S. 79 (1986)

In *Batson v. Kentucky*, the Supreme Court addressed how a criminal defendant can establish that a prosecutor used a peremptory challenge against a prospective juror of the defendant's race on the basis of race.

The Court had previously in a 1965 case, *Swain v. Alabama*, recognized that a state's exercise of such a race-based peremptory challenge was unconstitutional under the equal protection clause. *Swain*, however, had imposed a virtually insurmountable evidentiary burden, in that a defendant needed to show a repeated pattern of discriminatory strikes across several cases in order to prevail.

The *Batson* defendant, an African American, was convicted of burglary and receipt of stolen goods by an all-white jury. The record showed that the prosecutor had used four out of six peremptory challenges to strike all of the African Americans from the venire. The defendant had moved to discharge the jury on the basis that the prosecutor's use of peremptory challenges violated both the equal protection clause in the Fourteenth Amendment and the defendant's Sixth Amendment right to a jury drawn from a fair cross-section of the community, as incorporated against the states by the Fourteenth Amendment. The trial court denied the motion without granting a hearing, and the Kentucky Supreme Court affirmed the conviction. On appeal, the defendant conceded that *Swain* precluded an equal protection claim based only on the peremptory challenges exercised in his own case.

Justice Powell, writing for the Court, overruled this part of *Swain*. The opinion outlined a three-step procedure drawn from other equal protection cases such as *Washington v. Davis* and modeled on several state court decisions. In the first step, the defendant must raise an inference that the prosecutor exercised a peremptory challenge on the basis of race. Such an inference could be drawn from all relevant circumstances, such as the prosecutor's pattern of strikes, questions to the venire, or statements to the court.

In the second step, the burden of production—but not the burden of proof or persuasion—shifts to the prosecutor to supply a race-neutral reason. Later cases, in particular *Purkett v. Elem.*, clarified that this was a formalistic step, in that any reason, even those that are "implausible," "fantastic," "silly," or "superstitious," would be adequate to survive step two, so long as the reason was facially neutral. Mere denials of discriminatory motivation or affirmations of good faith, however, remain inadequate.

In the third step, the judge determines whether the defendant has established the prosecutor's "purposeful discrimination." Whether purposeful discrimination requires subjective discriminatory intent, and if so, whether it is sufficient, remains unclear. In any event, the Supreme Court has stated in cases such as *Miller-El v. Cockrell* that the decisive question will be the prosecutor's credibility. If the judge believes the neutral explanation, no matter how trivial, then the peremptory challenge must be sustained.

In an important concurrence, Justice Marshall objected that the Court's *Batson* framework would not end racial discrimination in jury selection. He advocated instead the complete elimination of peremptory challenges. Chief Justice Burger argued in dissent that the Court's decision had effectively ended the peremptory challenge because articulating a neutral explanation would be difficult.

The Sixth Amendment claim that a prosecutor's use of peremptory challenges might deny the defendant a jury representative of a cross-section of the community was finally rejected in *Holland v. Illinois* on the grounds that the Sixth Amendment was intended to ensure an impartial jury rather than a representative jury.

Batson was later expanded in *Powers v. Ohio* so that defendants could object to the exclusion of jurors of other races as well as their own race. *Batson* was extended to civil litigants in *Edmonson v. Leesville Concrete Co.*, criminal defense counsel in *Georgia v. McCollum*, and to prevent peremptory challenges made on the basis of gender in *J.E.B. v. Alabama ex. rel. T.B.* The Supreme Court also stated in dicta in *United States v. Martinez-Salazar* that a peremptory challenge may not be exercised on the basis of ethnic origin. As the reach of *Batson* has expanded, the Court has clarified that the primary concern is the violation of the excluded juror's equal protection right rather than solely the rights of the litigants.

The bulk of academic commentary and empirical studies suggests that *Batson* has failed to eliminate the use of race as a factor in jury selection. Much of this commentary focuses on how dishonest lawyers can easily survive a *Batson* challenge by providing false but neutral reasons for their challenges. Commentators also note that limited misuse of peremptory challenges is unlikely to be discovered. *Batson* has, however, undoubtedly reduced the most egregious uses of race and gender in jury selection.

ANTONY PAGE

References and Further Reading

Altschuler, Albert W., *The Supreme Court and the Jury: Voir Dire, Peremptory Challenges, and the Review of Jury Verdicts*, University of Chicago Law Review 56 (Winter 1989): 153–233.

Cavise, Leonard L., The Batson *Doctrine: The Supreme Court's Utter Failure to Meet the Challenge of Discrimination in Jury Selection*, Wisconsin Law Review 1999 (1999): 501–52.

Melilli, Kenneth J., Batson *in Practice: What We Have Learned About Batson and Peremptory Challenges*, Notre Dame Law Review 71 (1996): 447–503.

Muller, Eric L., *Solving the Batson Paradox: Harmless Error, Jury Representation, and the Sixth Amendment*, Yale Law Journal 106 (October 1996): 93–150.

Page, Antony, Batson's *Blind-Spot: Unconscious Stereotyping and the Peremptory Challenge*, Boston University Law Review 85 (2005): 155–263.

Cases and Statutes Cited

Batson v. Kentucky, 476 U.S. 79 (1986)
Edmonson v. Leesville Concrete Co., 500 U.S. 614 (1991)
Georgia v. McCollum, 505 U.S. 42 (1992)
Hernandez v. New York, 500 U.S. 352 (1991)
Holland v. Illinois, 493 U.S. 474 (1990)
J.E.B. v. Alabama ex. rel. T.B., 511 U.S. 127 (1994)
Miller-El v. Cockrell, 537 U.S. 322 (2003)
Powers v. Ohio, 499 U.S. 400 (1991)
Purkett v. Elem., 514 U.S. 765 (1995)
Swain v. Alabama, 380 U.S. 202 (1965)
United States v. Martinez-Salazar, 528 U.S. 304 (2000)
Washington v. Davis, 426 U.S. 229 (1976)

See also **Equal Protection of Law (XIV);** *Holland v. Illinois***, 493 U.S. 474 (1990); Jury Selection and Voir Dire; Jury Trials and Race; Race and Criminal Justice;** *Swain v. Alabama***, 380 U.S. 202 (1965)**

BEAL v. DOE, 432 U.S. 438 (1977)

Indigents who were eligible for financial assistance under Title XIX of the Social Security Act's Medicaid program challenged a Pennsylvania statute that denied funding for their desired abortions. The state law limited such support to those abortions that were certified by physicians as medically or psychiatrically necessary.

According to the U.S. Supreme Court in *Beal v. Doe*, the only question was whether Title XIX required states to fund the cost of all abortions, including those that were elective. In ruling for the state limitation, Justice Powell reasoned that the language of the congressional statute did not specifically mention abortions and did not suggest that participating states were required to fund every medical procedure. States, he said, were only required to meet certain standards for determining eligibility under a plan that was consistent with the overall objectives of Medicaid. Next, he noted that in *Roe v. Wade*, the Court had expressly recognized the "important and legitimate interest [of the state] in protecting the potentiality of human life." He also found supporting history in the fact that when Title XIX was passed in 1965, nontherapeutic abortions were illegal in most states. Finally, he deferred to the interpretation of the law by the Department of Health, Education, and Welfare, the federal agency responsible for its administration, which was akin to the Court's rendition.

Beal was one of three cases that posed direct legislative challenges to the highly controversial abortion case, *Roe v. Wade*, decided just four years earlier. One of the most direct and effective state and local strategies for curbing the availability of abortions following *Roe* was simply to deny public funding and/or the use of public hospitals and facilities for the procedure. The leading case, *Maher v. Roe*, established that although women have a fundamental constitutional right to decide whether to have an abortion, there was no corresponding obligation on the part of state and local governments to provide funding for them. *Maher* upheld Connecticut's refusal to reimburse Medicaid recipients for the cost of an abortion unless a doctor certified that it was medically or psychiatrically necessary. In the third case, *Poelker v. Doe*, the Court voted to sustain the St. Louis, Missouri, policy of denying indigent pregnant women access to nontherapeutic abortions in the city's public hospitals.

These rulings were later reaffirmed in *Harris v. McRae*, when the Court upheld congressional restrictions on federal funding for abortions, and in *Webster v. Reproductive Health Services*, sustaining Missouri's 1986 ban on the use of public hospitals, facilities, and employees for the elective procedure. After more than a decade in which the Supreme Court legitimated governmental policies denying funding and the use of public hospitals for nontherapeutic abortions, there remained, in 1989, thirteen states with no restrictions on funding. Thirty-one states passed laws denying support for indigent women.

KENNETH F. MOTT

References and Further Reading

Baer, Judith A. *Historical and Multicultural Encyclopedia of Women's Reproductive Rights in the United States*. Westport, CT: Greenwood, 2001.

Bond, Jon R., and Charles A. Johnson. "Implementing a Permissive Policy: Hospital Abortion Services after *Roe v. Wade*." *American Journal of Political Science* 26 (1982): 1–24.

Craig, Barbara Hinkson, and David M. O'Brien. *Abortion and American Politics*. Chatham, NJ: Chatham House, 1993.

Hull, N.E.H., and Peter Charles Hoffer. Roe v. Wade: *The Abortion Rights Controversy in American History*. Lawrence: University Press of Kansas, 2001.

Cases and Statutes Cited

Harris v. McRae, 448 U.S. 297 (1980)
Maher v. Roe, 432 U.S. 464 (1977)
Poelker v. Doe, 432 U.S. 519 (1977)
Roe v. Wade, 410 U.S. 113 (1973)
Webster v. Reproductive Health Services, 492 U.S. 490 (1989)

See also Harris v. McRae, 448 U.S. 297 (1980); Maher v. Roe, 432 U.S. 464 (1977); Poelker v. Doe, 432 U.S. 59 (1977); Roe v. Wade, 410 U.S. 113 (1973); Webster v. Reproductive Health Services, 492 U.S. 490 (1989)

BEAUHARNAIS v. ILLINOIS, 343 U.S. 250 (1952)

In *Beauharnais v. Illinois*, the U.S. Supreme Court upheld the validity of a 1917 Illinois group libel statute, finding that such speech fell outside the protections of the First Amendment. Speaking for a divided Court, Justice Frankfurter's majority opinion drew on the reasoning in *Chaplinsky v. New Hampshire* wherein libel was excluded from Constitutional protection, and on *Cantwell v. Connecticut* for the authority of states to punish speech that would "incite violence and breaches of the peace." Subsequent decisions, however, have cast doubt on the continuing validity of the Court's decision in *Beauharnais*.

Joseph Beauharnais, president of the While Circle League of America, was arrested and convicted for distributing leaflets calling for a halt to the "further encroachment, harassment and invasion of white people, their property, neighborhoods and persons by the Negro . . .", and further claiming that whites were in danger of being "mongrelized" by "the Negro." The Illinois law, passed against the backdrop of deadly race riots in that state, made it illegal to manufacture, sell, distribute, or exhibit anything that defames a class of citizens when such publication would expose a member of such group to "contempt, derision, or obloquy or which is productive of breach of the peace or riots."

Noting that the Illinois Supreme Court characterized Beauharnais's words as "liable to cause violence or disorder" and that one traditional basis of criminal libel law was to punish words likely to cause a breach of the peace, Justice Frankfurter's deference to the legislature in this case was colored by the state's acknowledged long history of racial strife. The opinion extended the scope of unprotected speech from libelous statements made against individuals to an entire race, class, or group of citizens, since it would be "arrant dogmatism . . . for [the Court] to deny that the Illinois legislature may warrantably believe that a man's job and his educational opportunities and the dignity accorded him may depend as much on the reputation of the racial and religious group to which he willy-nilly belongs, as on his own merits."

The majority opinion was met with four dissents, including Justice Black whose expansive interpretation of the First Amendment led him to criticize the Court's reliance on *Chaplinsky*, confining the decision to face-to-face encounters directed at individuals, and to attack the Illinois law as overly broad and tantamount to "censorship." Justice Douglas warned of the dangers of allowing legislatures to determine which kinds of speech may be proscribed, as "[t]oday a white man stands convicted for protesting in unseemly language against our decisions invalidating restrictive covenants. Tomorrow a Negro will be ha[u]led before a court for denouncing lynch law in heated terms."

Just as the Supreme Court seemed to uphold the validity of group libel laws, proponents of group libel legislation turned their focus away from prohibiting group defamation and towards bolstering freedom of expression and individual rights. The dissenters in *Beauharnais* proved to foreshadow the future direction of Supreme Court First Amendment jurisprudence, which expanded the protections afforded offensive speech in such cases as *Brandenburg v. Ohio* and *Cohen v. California*. Moreover, *New York Times Co. v. Sullivan* and *Collin v. Smith* cast doubt on the presumption of damage to the individual members of a group from criticism of a group, while the latter case also undermined the view that "fighting words need not be used in a personally abusive manner when they consist of language which defames a race or religion." As such, the *Beauharnais* decision appears eclipsed by decisions more protective of provocative speech, and its precedential value damaged if not completely diluted.

ANDREW FINKELMAN

References and Further Reading

Banks, Taunya Lovell, *What Is a Community? Group Rights and the Constitution: The Special Case of African Americans*, Margins Law Journal 1 (Spring 2001): 51.

Eastland, Terry, ed. *Freedom of Expression in the Supreme Court: The Defining Cases.* New York: Rowman & Littlefield Publishers, Inc., 2000.

Schultz, Evan P., *Group Rights, American Jews and the Failure of Group Libel Laws, 1913–1952*, Brooklyn Law Review 66 (Spring 2000): 71.

Walker, Samuel. *Hate Speech: The History of an American Controversy.* Lincoln: University of Nebraska Press, 1994.

Cases and Statutes Cited

Brandenburg v. Ohio, 395 U.S. 444 (1969)
Cantwell v. Connecticut, 310 U.S. 296 (1940)
Chaplinsky v. New Hampshire, 315 U.S. 568 (1942)
Cohen v. California, 403 U.S. 15 (1971)
Collin v. Smith, 447 F.Supp. 676 (N.D. Ill. 1978)
New York Times Co. v. Sullivan, 376 U.S. 254 (1964)

BECKER AMENDMENT

The Becker amendment was one of the more significant congressional attempts to overturn an unpopular holding of the U.S. Supreme Court. Congressman Frank Becker (R-NY) introduced the prayer and bible reading amendment of 1964, or "Becker amendment," in response to two controversial Supreme Court decisions outlawing organized prayer and Bible reading in the nation's public schools. Initially, when introduced, the Becker amendment had substantial congressional support and passage appeared likely. Ratification by three-fourths of the states seemed assured. The proposal stalled in legislative committee, however, and eventually died without a vote, primarily as a result of opposition from the religious community.

The impetus behind the Becker amendment lay in the public reaction to two Supreme Court decisions in 1962 and 1963. During the early 1960s, approximately one-half of the nation's public schools conducted either daily or weekly religious exercises, often in the form of a short reading from the Bible (usually from the Protestant King James version) and a prayer given over the schools' public address systems. Such "nonsectarian" exercises had been controversial since the mid-nineteenth century, particularly among Catholics, Jews, and other non-Protestants. Although a handful of state supreme courts had struck down such practices over the years, the majority of challenges had failed. In 1962, the U.S. Supreme Court heard a challenge to a New York law requiring public school students to repeat daily the following prayer, written by the state board of regents: "Almighty God, we acknowledge our dependence upon Thee, and we beg They blessing upon us, our parents, our teachers and our country." In an eight-to-one decision, *Engel v. Vitale*, the Court struck down the practice as a violation of the establishment clause, writing that "government should stay out of the business of writing or sanctioning official prayers and leave that purely religious function to the people themselves and to those the people choose to look to for religious guidance."

The Engel decision unleashed a public outcry, with public officials and religious leaders condemning the holding. In the weeks following the *Engel* decision, approximately seventy members of Congress, including Congressman Becker, introduced proposed constitutional amendments to permit religious exercises in public schools. The Senate Judiciary Committee held hearings on the proposals in July 1962, but took no action; by then the Court had granted review on two cases that considered the constitutionality of daily Bible readings and recitations of the Lord's Prayer. The following year, in *Abington Township School District v. Schempp* and *Murray v. Curlett*, the high court struck down the practices by the same eight-to-one vote.

The public outcry in reaction to the *Schempp* and *Murray* decisions was greater than had occurred following *Engel*. Evangelist Billy Graham and Catholic Bishop Fulton J. Sheen condemned the holdings, while Senator Strom Thurman called the decisions "another major triumph of secularism and atheism which are bent on throwing God completely our of our national life." The *Schempp* and *Murray* decisions provided renewed momentum for amendment proponents. Prior to the 1963 decisions, House Judiciary Committee Chair Emanuel Celler had opposed the proposed amendments and had refused to schedule a hearing. By the spring of 1964, Congressman Becker had gathered over 170 of the needed 218 signatures to have his proposed amendment discharged from the House Judiciary Committee, forcing Celler to hold hearings.

The final language of the Becker amendment, compiled from the various proposals, provided in part:

> Nothing in this Constitution shall be deemed to prohibit the offering, reading from, or listening to prayers or biblical scriptures, if participation therein is on a voluntary basis, in any governmental or public school. . . . Nothing in this Constitution shall be deemed to prohibit making reference to belief in, reliance upon, or invoking the aid of God or a Supreme Being in any governmental or public document, proceeding, activity, currency, school [or] institution . . .

Congressman Becker worked tirelessly to build support for the amendment, and found natural allies among evangelical groups. Groups such as the National Association of Evangelicals and the fundamentalist International Council of Christian Churches organized grassroots support and sent their officials to testify in favor of the proposed amendment. Working in Becker's favor was the fact that few members of Congress wanted to go on record as opposing prayer and Bible reading in the public schools.

Opponents of the proposed amendment, including the American Civil Liberties Union, Americans United for Separation of Church and State, the American Jewish Congress, and the Anti-Defamation League, recognized that the House Judiciary Committee would likely approve the Becker amendment if it came to a vote. These groups organized a coalition behind the public leadership of the Baptist Joint Committee on Public Affairs and the National Council of Churches (NCC). Rev. Dean Kelley of the NCC, a United Methodist minister, became the spokesperson for the coalition and quietly organized testimony from many of the nation's religious leaders, including deans of leading seminaries. Most significant, Kelley was able to obtain testimony from several religious leaders with impeccable evangelical credentials. This testimony provided political coverage to wavering members of the committee, enabling

Congressman Celler to allow the proposal to die without a committee vote. What had first appeared to be a significant threat to the First Amendment's religion clauses was diffused primarily due to the efforts of religious groups.

STEVEN K. GREEN

References and Further Reading

Alley, Robert S. *Without a Prayer: Religious Expression in Public Schools*. Amherst, NY: Prometheus Books, 1996
DelFattore, Joan. *The Fourth R: Conflicts Over Religion in America's Public Schools*. New Haven, CT: Yale University Press, 2004.
Green, Steven K. "Evangelicals and the Becker Amendment: A Lesson in Church–State Moderation." *Journal of Church and State* 33 (1991): 541–67.
Phelps Stokes, Anson, and Leo Pfeffer, *Church and State in the United States*. New York: Harper and Row, 1964.

Cases and Statutes Cited

Engel v. Vitale, 370 U.S. 421 (1962)
Murray v. Curlett, 374 U.S. 203 (1963)
School District of Abington Township, 374 U.S. 203 (1963)

See also **Abington Township School District v. Schemmp, 374 U.S. 203 (1963); Constitutional Amendment Permitting School Prayer; *Engel v. Vitale*, 370 U.S. 421 (1962)**

BELIEF–ACTION DISTINCTION IN FREE EXERCISE CLAUSE HISTORY

One of the central issues in free exercise clause jurisprudence has been the question of whether the state is obliged to give individuals exemptions from government regulations that interfere with their free exercise of religion. In resolving this issue, the U.S. Supreme Court has, for much of its history, distinguished between religious beliefs (which receive considerable protection under the free exercise clause) and religiously motivated conduct (which receives much less protection).

The Supreme Court first articulated the different constitutional protection enjoyed by religious beliefs and religiously motivated conduct in *Reynolds v. United States* (1878), a case involving the constitutionality of a congressional statute governing the Territory of Utah that made it a crime for a "person having a husband or wife living" to marry another person. Pursuant to this statute, George Reynolds, one of the leaders of the Church of Jesus Christ of Latter-Day Saints (the Mormons) whose church doctrine at that time provided that it was a "duty of male members of said church . . . to practise polygamy," was prosecuted. The question for the Court in *Reynolds* was "whether religious belief can be accepted as a justification of an overt act made criminal by the law of the land." In holding that enforcement of the criminal prohibition on plural marriage against Reynolds did not violate the free exercise clause, the Court, with Chief Justice Waite writing, cited Thomas Jefferson for his "belief–action" distinction, which provided that religious *beliefs* and *opinions* enjoy greater protection from governmental interference than do *actions* motivated by religious beliefs and opinions. In his Bill for the Establishment of Religious Freedom, Jefferson had written that to permit "the civil magistrate to intrude his powers into the field of opinion, and to restrain the profession or propagation of principles on supposition of their ill tendency, is a dangerous fallacy which at once destroys all religious liberty," but that it is legitimate for the magistrate "to interfere when principles break out into overt acts against peace and good order." The *Reynolds* Court also cited Jefferson's famous 1802 letter to the Danbury Baptists in which he wrote: "Believing with you that religion is a matter which lies solely between man and his God; . . . the legislative powers of the government reach actions only, and not opinions." The Court in *Reynolds* placed great weight on the belief–action distinction articulated by Jefferson:

> Coming as this does from an acknowledged leader of the advocates of the [free exercise clause], it may be accepted almost as an authoritative declaration of the scope and effect of the amendment thus secured. Congress was deprived of all legislative power over *mere opinion*, but was left free to reach *actions* which were in violation of social duties or subversive of good order . . . . Laws are made for the government of actions, and while they cannot interfere with mere religious *belief and opinions*, they may with *practices* . . . . [T]o permit [an exemption] would be to make the professed doctrines of religious belief superior to the law of the land, and in effect to permit every citizen to become a law unto himself [emphasis added].

Accordingly, the Court enforced the criminal sanction against *Reynolds*.

Since *Reynolds*, the Supreme Court has generally retained the distinction between beliefs and actions when deciding cases under the free exercise clause, generally striking down government regulation of religious *beliefs*. For example, in *Torcaso v. Watkins* (1961), the Court struck down a Maryland constitutional provision that required a "belief in the existence of God" in order to hold public office. The Court concluded that Maryland had "unconstitutionally

invade[d] the appellant's freedom of belief and religion" by denying him the right to hold public office on account of his nontraditional worldview.

Over the course of the twentieth century, the Court's protection of religiously motivated *conduct* has varied—at times more protective than the *Reynolds* Court and more recently, about as protective as the *Reynolds* Court.

In *Cantwell v. Connecticut* (1940), the first case in which the Court applied the free exercise clause to state and local governments, the Court, with Justice Owen Roberts writing, reasserted the distinction between "freedom to believe and freedom to act" when evaluating the constitutionality of a criminal prosecution of Jehovah's Witnesses for their aggressive proselytizing activities. "The first [freedom to believe] is absolute but, in the nature of things, the second [freedom to act] cannot be. Conduct remains subject to regulation for the protection of society." But the Court went on to say that the "power to regulate must be so exercised as not, in attaining a permissible end, unduly to infringe the protected freedom." In suggesting that some prohibitions on religiously motivated conduct might "unduly infringe" on free exercise rights, the Court invited a "weighing of two conflicting interests": the state's interest in "the preservation and protection of peace and good order" and the individual's interest in engaging in religiously motivated conduct. In sum, the Court in *Cantwell* retained the belief–action distinction, but gave actions greater protection than they had enjoyed during the nineteenth century.

During the 1960s, the Court extended the constitutional protection afforded to religiously motivated conduct under the free exercise clause. In *Sherbert v. Verner* (1963), a Seventh Day Adventist challenged a decision to deny her unemployment benefits following her termination from her job for refusing to work on Saturday, her Sabbath. The Court articulated a new test for assessing whether religiously motivated conduct should be protected under the free exercise clause. The Court determined that if the state imposed a burden on an individual's *exercise* of her religious belief—here, by denying unemployment benefits—then it must have a "compelling state interest" for so doing. The compelling state interest test offered greater protection under the free exercise clause for religiously motivated conduct than had been previously afforded by the Court. The Court retained this test until its decision in *Employment Division v. Smith* (1990).

In *Employment Division v. Smith*, the Court, in effect, jettisoned the *Sherbert v. Verner* compelling state interest test. *Smith* involved the constitutionality of the denial of unemployment benefits to Native

Americans who were fired from their job for smoking peyote as part of a religious ceremony. The *Smith* Court held that state interference with a person's religiously motivated conduct did not violate the free exercise clause so long as the interference took place pursuant to a neutral, generally applicable regulatory provision. After *Smith*, the state no longer had to justify its interference with religiously motivated conduct by demonstrating a compelling state interest. The Court continues to follow the *Smith* principle today, although both Congress and state legislatures have extended protection to religiously motivated conduct by statute in a number of areas.

Although the Court no longer speaks directly in terms of a "belief–action" distinction under the free exercise clause, it in effect maintains that distinction by affording state interferences with religious belief very high protection, while permitting state interference with religiously motivated conduct so long as the state has proceeded according to a neutral, generally applicable statute and has not acted with animus towards the religiously motivated person.

DAVISON M. DOUGLAS

References and Further Reading

Epps, Garrett, *What We Talk About When We Talk About Free Exercise*, Arizona State Law Journal 30 (1998): 563–602.
Friedelbaum, Stanley H., *Free Exercise in the States: Belief, Conduct, and Judicial Benchmarks*, Albany Law Review 63 (2000): 1059–100.

Cases and Statutes Cited

Cantwell v. Connecticut, 310 U.S. 296 (1940)
Employment Division v. Smith, 494 U.S. 872 (1990)
Reynolds v. United States, 98 U.S. 145 (1878)
Sherbert v. Verner, 374 U.S. 398 (1963)
Torcaso v. Watkins, 367 U.S. 488 (1961)

See also **Accommodation of Religion; Free Exercise Clause (I): History, Background, Framing; Jefferson Thomas; Jehovah's Witnesses and Religious Liberty; Mormons and Religious Liberty**

BELLE TERRE v. BORAAS, 416 U.S. 1 (1974)

When a local government zones, it typically classifies land uses according to use type (residential, commercial, industrial, etc.), and then regulates uses within each classification according to height and density. Residential zones are generally designated as either single-family or multi-family. Zoning ordinances therefore must define the word family for purposes of regulating the density of residential zoning districts. The Village of Belle Terre, New York, limited all development within its jurisdiction to single-family dwellings, defining the word "family" to mean "one or more persons related by blood, adoption, or marriage, living and cooking together as a single housekeeping unit, exclusive of household servants." A homeowner in the village, who was cited for violating the ordinance when he rented his house to six unrelated college students, challenged the constitutionality of the ordinance, claiming that its definition of family violated constitutional rights of equal protection, privacy, association, and travel. In *Belle Terre v. Boraas*, the Supreme Court upheld the ordinance as a reasonable means of furthering a legitimate public purpose.

Justice Douglas, writing for the majority of the Court, noted the Court's long history of deference to legislative discretion in zoning decisions, citing to its landmark decision in *Euclid v. Ambler Realty Co.*, which sustained the validity of zoning as a legitimate means of furthering the public's interest in protecting single-family uses from the threats to health and safety posed by higher-density uses. Expanding on its holding in *Berman v. Parker*, the Court said that "the police power is not confined to elimination of filth, stench, and unhealthy places"; it is also permissible for cities to "lay out zones where family values, youth values, and the blessings of quiet seclusion and clean air make the area a sanctuary for people." The Court rejected the argument of the petitioners that it should apply a heightened level of scrutiny because the ordinance infringed on fundamental constitutional rights of privacy and association. Because the Court found that the ordinance was not "aimed at transients," it concluded that no right of travel was implicated. It also found that no right of association was violated since "a 'family' may, so far as the ordinance is concerned, entertain whomever it likes." In answer to the claim that the ordinance intruded into the privacy rights of individuals by discriminating against unmarried couples, the Court found that because two unrelated persons could live together under the ordinance there was no such discrimination.

Justice Marshall dissented from the majority's opinion, believing that the ordinance did violate the plaintiff's fundamental rights of association and privacy. As such the majority's application of a rational basis test was inappropriate. Marshall argued that the ordinance could "withstand constitutional scrutiny only upon a clear showing that the burden imposed is necessary to protect a compelling and substantial governmental interest."

Although the Belle Terre Court was willing to sustain an ordinance regulating the number of unrelated persons who could constitute a "single family," two years later, in *Moore v. City of East Cleveland*, it was unwilling to allow local authorities to regulate the number of related persons who could live together in a single-family zone. In the latter case, the Court applied strict scrutiny because the "special sanctity of the family" was at stake.

SUSAN E. LOOPER-FRIEDMAN

References and Further Reading

Ginzburg, Rebecca M., *Altering 'Family': Another Look at the Supreme Court's Narrow Protection of Families in Belle Terre*, Boston University Law Review 83 (2003):2:875–96.
Juergensmeyer, Julian Conrad, and Thomas E. Roberts. *Land Use Planning and Development Regulation Law.* St. Paul, MN: Thomson West, 2003.
Mandelker, Daniel R. *Land Use Law.* 5th ed. Newark, NJ: LexisNexis Publishing, 2003.

Cases and Statutes Cited

Berman v. Parker, 348.U.S. 26 (1954)
Euclid v. Ambler Realty Co., 272 U.S. 365 (1926)
Moore v. City of East Cleveland, 431 U.S. 494 (1977)

See also **Family unity for Noncitizens; Privacy**

BELLIS v. UNITED STATES, 417 U.S. 85 (1974)

Isadore Bellis was a partner in a small law firm who received a grand jury subpoena for the financial records of the partnership and sought to resist producing them by asserting his Fifth Amendment self-incrimination privilege. While a custodian of records for a large business cannot assert the privilege after *Hale v. Henkel*, Bellis argued that the law partnership was not an organization separate from its individual partners, and, therefore, the production of the documents was the same as if he were subpoenaed personally.

The Supreme Court held that while the owner of a sole proprietorship can assert the Fifth Amendment in response to a subpoena for records of the business, a custodian of records for a collective entity who holds the documents in a representative capacity cannot assert the self-incrimination privilege. The Court applied its analysis in *United States v. White* that a collective entity is an organization that exists separately from its individual members, and must be relatively well-organized and structured and not merely a loose, informal association of individuals. The law firm had three partners and six other employees, and its records were those of the entire business and not merely of Bellis's activity alone.

The Court held that "[w]hile small, the partnership here did have an established institutional identity independent of its individual partners." The analysis in *Bellis* means that even small businesses, so long as they are not sole proprietorships, cannot refuse to produce records in response to a grand jury subpoena.

PETER J. HENNING

References and Further Reading

LaFave, Wayne R., Jerold H. Israel, and Nancy J. King. *Criminal Procedure.* Vol. 3. 2nd ed. St. Paul, MN: Thomson West, 1999.
Mosteller, Robert P., *Simplifying Subpoena Law: Taking the Fifth Amendment Seriously*, Virginia Law Review 73 (1987): 1:1–110.

Cases and Statutes Cited

Hale v. Henkel, 201 U.S. 43 (1906)
United States v. White, 322 U.S. 694 (1944)

See also **Grand Jury Investigation and Indictment;** *Hale v. Henkel,* **201 U.S. 370 (1906); Self-Incrimination (V): Historical Background**

BELLOTTI v. BAIRD, 443 U.S. 622 (1979)

As soon as the ink was dry on the Supreme Court's opinion in *Roe v. Wade,* many state legislatures passed laws to limit a woman's ability to get an abortion, or to at least place hurdles in her way. Some of these laws required that a woman seeking an abortion needed the consent of her husband, or, in the case of an unmarried minor, one or both parents.

These statutes were based on the Court's statement in *Roe* that states could impose "reasonable" regulation of the performance of abortions, given the state's "important and legitimate interest in preserving and protecting the health of the pregnant woman."

One of the first Supreme Court decisions involving this type of post-*Roe* legislation was *Planned Parenthood of Central Missouri v. Danforth,* in which the Court struck down a Missouri statute that required for a woman to get an abortion during the first 12 weeks of pregnancy she needed the consent of her spouse, or, in the case of an unmarried minor, the consent of her parents. The Court said that since *Roe v. Wade* prevented the state from interfering with the woman's right to obtain an abortion in the first 12 weeks, a state could not grant such a veto to a spouse or a parent.

A Massachusetts post-*Roe* statute provided that an unmarried pregnant minor who wanted an abortion was required to get her parents' consent. The statute provided that a minor who was unable to get that consent, or unwilling to seek that consent, could seek a court order allowing the abortion. A judge could grant permission for an abortion "for good cause shown," despite the absence of parental consent. The Court said that the minor's ability to get judicial consent was an important constitutional protection of the minor's rights. However, the Court struck down the requirement that the minor first seek parental consent as an undue burden on her rights.

The Court then distinguished between two classes of minors—those mature enough to make an informed and reasonable decision to have an abortion, and those not so mature. (The Court did not explain how to distinguish between the two.) In the case of a "mature" minor, the Court said that she needed neither her parents' consent nor that of a judge— such a minor is entitled to the full protection of *Roe v. Wade*.

Minors not mature enough to make informed decisions would be subject to a different set of proceedings. If such a minor persuaded a judge that the abortion was in her best interest, the judge could grant permission without any parental involvement. If the judge is not persuaded that an abortion is in the minor's best interest, the Court said the judge could deny consent or could require consultation with the parents before making a decision.

Since the Court's decision in *Bellotti v. Baird* did not completely foreclose parental involvement, the door was left open for further legislative efforts to limit abortions of unmarried minors.

ELI C. BORTMAN

Cases and Statutes Cited

Planned Parenthood of Central Missouri v. Danforth, 428 U.S. 52 (1976)
Roe v. Wade, 410 U.S. 113 (1973)

See also **Abortion;** *Planned Parenthood of Missouri v. Danforth,* **428 U.S. 52 (1976); Reproductive Freedom;** *Roe v. Wade,* **410 U.S. 113 (1973)**

BENTON v. MARYLAND, 395 U.S. 784 (1969)

The double jeopardy clause of the Fifth Amendment provides that no person shall "be subject for the same offense to be twice put in jeopardy of life or limb." It provides protection against a second prosecution for the same offense following either an acquittal or conviction, and protects against multiple punishments for the same offense. In *Benton v. Maryland* (1969), the Supreme Court held that the double jeopardy clause is incorporated into the due process clause of the Fourteenth Amendment and thereby made applicable to the states.

Prior to the adoption of the Fourteenth Amendment, the Supreme Court held that the specific guarantees of the Bill of Rights, the first eight amendments to the Constitution, applied only to the federal government (*Barron v. Mayor of City of Baltimore* [1833]). Thus, at this time, the Bill of Rights was not binding on state and local government. After the adoption of the Fourteenth Amendment in 1868, the question arose whether the Fourteenth Amendment incorporated any or all of the Bill of Rights. The Supreme Court has followed a process of selective incorporation pursuant to which it has determined on a case-by-case basis whether the particular right should be incorporated.

The most well-known test used to determine which rights are incorporated was articulated by Justice Cardozo in *Palko v. Connecticut* (1937). Under *Palko*, incorporation depends on whether the particular right is "of the very essence of a scheme of ordered liberty," or is "a principle or justice so rooted in the traditions and conscience of our people as to be ranked as fundamental."

The Court framed the specific issue in *Palko*: Did the state court's denial of double jeopardy protection "violate those 'fundamental principles of liberty and justice which lie at the base of all our civil and political institutions'?" The Court held that "[t]he answer surely must be 'no.'"

Three decades later, the Court in *Benton v. Maryland* reached the opposite result and overruled *Palko v. Connecticut*. By the time *Benton* was decided, the Court's approach to the incorporation issue had changed. Under *Palko* the Court made a record-specific evaluation in order to determine whether deprivation of the right in issue violated the defendant's right to due process. In later cases, however, the Court took a wholesale approach and inquired whether the right at issue should be incorporated.

The Court in *Benton* found that the Fifth Amendment protection against double jeopardy is of "the very essence of a scheme of ordered liberty," a "principle of justice so rooted in the traditions and conscience of our people as to be ranked as fundamental." In reaching this conclusion, the Court relied upon (1) the historical importance of the double jeopardy protection, as "[i]ts origins can be traced to Greek and Roman times" and was "established in the common law of England long before this Nation's independence"; (2) state practices: "every State incorporates some form of the prohibition [against double jeopardy] in its constitution or common law"; and

(3) the practical importance of the right, namely, its protection against the "embarrassment, expense and ordeal" and being compelled "to live in a continuing state of anxiety and insecurity" from multiple prosecutions for the same offense.

So, as a result of the decision in *Benton v. Maryland*, the states, like the federal government, must grant individuals protection against double jeopardy.

MARTIN A. SCHWARTZ

References and Further Reading

Chemerinsky, Erwin. *Constitutional Law: Principles and Policies*. 2nd ed. New York: Aspen Law and Business, 2002.
Rotunda, Ronald D., and John E. Nowak. *Treatise on Constitutional Law: Substance and Procedure*. 5 vols. 3rd ed. St. Paul, MN: West Group, 1999.

Cases and Statutes Cited

Barron v. Mayor of City of Baltimore, 32 U.S. 243 (1933)
Benton v. Maryland, 395 U.S. 784 (1969)
Palko v. Connecticut, 302 U.S. 319 (1937)

See also **Double Jeopardy (V): Early History, Background, Framing; Incorporation Doctrine**

BERGER v. NEW YORK, 388 U.S. 41 (1967)

Berger v. New York addressed questions pertaining to the Fourth Amendment. This decision overruled the precedent set by *Olmsteud v. United States*. This precedent established in 1928 held that a wiretap was not included in the protections of the Fourth Amendment because there was no seizure of a tangible object. *Berger* addressed this question many decades later when wiretapping was common and new technologies were being introduced.

The petitioner, Ralph Berger, was convicted of conspiracy to bribe the chairman of the New York State Liquor Authority in attempts to obtain a liquor license for a controversial arena. The charges were based on a conversation overheard on a series of telephone wiretaps placed by the District Attorney of New York County. New York State law allowed wiretaps to be placed to obtain evidence if there were reasonable grounds for suspecting evidence of a crime could be obtained. The order to place a wiretap had to specify the person whose telephone conversations were being tapped and the phone number where the wiretap was to be placed. The order would be valid for two months. Berger appealed the decision of the New York Court to the Supreme Court based on the protections of the Fourth Amendment.

The Supreme Court found the New York statute to be too broad and reversed the ruling against Berger. The Court held that authorities must have "probable cause" to obtain evidence of this nature. Authorities would have to specify the crime, place to be searched, and the conversations that needed to be seized. This decision did not seek to end electronic surveillance since it was deemed an acceptable investigation method; rather it sought to apply more supervision to this type of surveillance. After this ruling, conversations were granted the full legal protections of the Fourth Amendment.

CAROL WALKER

References and Further Reading

Pollack, Harriet, and Alexander Smith. *Civil Liberties and Civil Rights in the United States*. St. Paul, MN: West, 1978.
Powe, Lucas. *The Warren Court and American Politics*. London: Belknap, 2000.

Cases and Statutes Cited

Olmstead v. United States, 277 U.S. 438 (1928)

See also **Electronic Surveillance, Technological Monitoring, and Dog Sniffs;** *Katz v. United States,* **389 U.S. 347 (1967); Search (General Definition); Wiretapping Laws**

BERKEMER v. MCCARTY, 468 U.S. 420 (1984)

An individual is in custody, for purposes of *Miranda v. Arizona*, when a reasonable person in the suspect's position would have believed himself in custody. In *Berkemer v. McCarty*, the Supreme Court held that during a routine traffic stop a motorist is not in custody for purposes of *Miranda*. In *Berkemer*, a police officer stopped a motorist he observed swerving between lanes on a highway. The officer asked the motorist if he was intoxicated, and the motorist responded that he had consumed two beers and had smoked some marijuana. The police officer then administered a field sobriety test, and when the motorist failed the test the officer arrested him. At the police station, the officer again asked the motorist if he had consumed any alcohol or drugs and the motorist again answered in the affirmative. The officer never administered the *Miranda* warnings to the motorist. The trial court admitted both of the motorist's admissions of consuming alcohol and drugs.

As a consequence of the Supreme Court's holding in *Berkemer*, police officers do not need to administer the *Miranda* warnings during routine traffic stops before asking motorists questions. Thus, although the officer failed to provide the warnings, the Court nevertheless held that the trial court properly admitted the incriminating statements the motorist made because the interrogation was not custodial. Routine traffic stops, which are ordinarily brief and occur in the public view, do not create the police-dominated, coercive environment critical to triggering of the *Miranda* protections.

CANDICE R. VOTICKY

Cases and Statutes Cited

Miranda v. Arizona, 384 U.S. 436 (1966)

See also **Arrest; Coerced Confessions/Police Interrogations; *Miranda* Warning; Seizures; Stop and Frisk**

BETHEL SCHOOL DISTRICT v. FRASER, 478 U.S. 675 (1986)

Does the First Amendment prevent a school district from disciplining a high school student for giving a lewd speech at a school assembly?

On April 26, 1983, Matthew N. Fraser, a high school student, delivered a speech nominating a fellow student for student elective office. In attendance were about 600 high school students, some as young as fourteen years of age, and faculty. During the speech, Fraser referred to his classmate "in terms of an elaborate, graphic, and explicit sexual metaphor" according to the Court. Fraser was given a three-day suspension, and he was removed from the list of candidates to give the commencement speech. Prior to delivering the speech, Fraser had discussed the content of the speech with two of his teachers who informed him that it was "inappropriate and that he probably should not deliver it." Both teachers also told Fraser that the delivery of the speech might have "severe consequences."

The Court distinguished its earlier ruling in *Tinker v. Des Moines Independent Community School Dist.* as the lewd speech in this case was disruptive, whereas the students' actions in *Tinker* were "nondisruptive" and "passive." The Court further noted the marked distinction between the political "message" of the armbands in *Tinker* and the sexual content of Fraser's speech. The Court was careful and deliberate in distinguishing the landmark *Tinker* ruling and re-acknowledged the *Tinker* Court's famous adage that "students do not 'shed their constitutional rights to freedom of speech or expression at the schoolhouse gate.'" The Court re-affirmed the somewhat unique role of public schools within the larger constitutional framework and the burden placed on public schools to not only provide substantive education but also to inculcate students with the "fundamental values necessary to the maintenance of a democratic political system."

The Court also reaffirmed its holding in *New Jersey v. T.L.O.* that the "constitutional rights in public schools are not automatically coextensive with the rights of adults in other settings."

The Court held that the school district had not violated the First Amendment and had acted "entirely within it permissible authority" in punishing him under school disciplinary rules for his lewd and indecent speech.

Justices Brennan and Blackmun concurred with the majority opinion written by Chief Justice Burger. Justice Marshall dissented from the majority opinion in narrow fashion, asserting specifically that the school district had failed to demonstrate that Fraser's remarks were actually disruptive while agreeing in principle with Justice Brennan's concurrence.

Justice Stevens's dissent focused not on whether the school could govern the type of speech at issue in this case generally but more specifically on whether Fraser was given fair notice of the rule at issue and the consequences of his actions. Stevens's dissent addressed not the content of the speech but also its context: "It seems fairly obvious that respondent's speech would be inappropriate in certain classroom and formal social settings. On the other hand, in a locker room or perhaps in a school corridor the metaphor in the speech might be regarded as rather routine comment. If this be true, and if respondent's audience consisted almost entirely of young people with whom he conversed on a daily basis, can we—at this distance—confidently assert that he must have known that the school administration would punish him for delivering it?"

Fraser is an important case that provides some boundaries to the general notion set forth in *Tinker* that "students do not 'shed their constitutional rights to freedom of speech or expression at the schoolhouse gate.'" These boundaries take the form of the Court's attempt to balance students' right to free speech and expression with the vital need for discipline in the public school environment.

MARC M. HARROLD

References and Further Reading

Hudson, David L., and John E. Ferguson, *The Courts' Inconsistent Treatment of Bethel v. Fraser and the Curtailment of Student Rights*, John Marshall Law Review 36 (Fall 2002): 181.

Slaff, Sara, Silencing Student Speech: *Bethel School District No. 403 v. Fraser, Note,* American University Law Review 37 (Fall 1987): 203.

Cases and Statutes Cited

New Jersey v. T.L.O., 469 U.S. 325 (1985)
Tinker v. Des Moines Independent Community School Dist., 393 U.S. 503 (1969)

BETTS v. BRADY, 316 U.S. 455 (1942)

The Sixth Amendment to the U.S. Constitution provides, among other things, that "in all criminal prosecutions, the accused shall enjoy the right to have the Assistance of Counsel for his defence." The scope and nature of that right have been defined in a series of cases decided by the U.S. Supreme Court.

In *Betts v. Brady,* 316 U.S. 455 (1942), the Supreme Court was asked to decide whether the Sixth Amendment right to counsel, which applies only to the federal courts, is a "fundamental right." If the right were found to be fundamental, then it would be applicable to the states under the due process clause of the Fourteenth Amendment. That clause prohibits the states from depriving their citizens of life, liberty, or property "without Due Process of law." The Court held that the right to counsel was not a fundamental right, and therefore did not have to be honored by the state courts. In *Betts,* the defendant had been charged with robbery. Because he could not afford to pay for a lawyer he asked the court to appoint a lawyer for him. The judge refused, because in that county lawyers were only appointed at state expense for defendants charged with murder or rape. The defendant pled not guilty and chose to be tried by a judge alone, without a jury. He called some witnesses in his own defense to assert an alibi, and he cross-examined the state's witnesses. The judge found him guilty and sentenced him to eight years in prison.

The defendant brought a federal habeas corpus petition, which is the way a defendant convicted in state court can have the federal courts review that conviction under the federal Constitution. In his petition, the defendant argued that he had been deprived of federal due process of law by the court's refusal to appoint a lawyer for him, but the petition was denied. On appeal to the Supreme Court, the Court upheld the decisions of the lower courts. The Court traced the history of the right to counsel in the constitutions of the original thirteen colonies and found great diversity in the treatment of the right to counsel. It found that the right had not been treated as a fundamental one that would have to be observed by the

state courts but rather was provided to allow a defendant to appear by counsel instead of by himself. That is, the Court believed that the Sixth Amendment did not require a state ever to appoint an attorney at state expense. The Court also examined colonial statutes and found great diversity in treatment of the right. Finally, it examined the constitutions currently in force in the states and found that the issue was largely dealt with by statute and not as a constitutional issue. Thus, based on history and prevalence, the Court held that the refusal to appoint counsel for an indigent charged with a felony did not violate the "fundamental fairness" required by the due process clause.

Moreover, the Court held, under the facts of the case, the court's refusal to give the defendant a lawyer did not deprive him of due process since he did a good enough job on his own. Betts waived a trial by jury, put forth an alibi defense, and cross-examined the state's witnesses. The Court held that under the facts and circumstances of the case, the absence of a lawyer was not "so offensive to the common and fundamental ideas of fairness."

Justice Black, joined by Justices Douglas and Murphy, dissented. The dissenters would have held that the right to counsel is fundamental, that is, that the practice of trying a defendant charged with a serious crime without counsel "cannot be reconciled with common and fundamental ideas of fairness and right." The dissenters pointed to the fact that at that point in time thirty-five states had some "clear legal requirement or an established practice" that indigent defendants in serious noncapital cases be provided with lawyers when requested.

LISSA GRIFFIN

BIBLE IN AMERICAN LAW

To speak with precision of the Bible's influence on American civil liberties is impossible because of its pervasive general presence in American culture during important formative periods of its history and jurisprudence. For centuries in Western civilization and in colonial America, the Bible was considered an integral part of the law, and therefore its foundational influence was systemic, organic, and often overt.

As law and society in the American Republic increasingly drew away from its biblical roots in the nineteenth and twentieth centuries, the authority behind biblical rules and the values expressed in biblical precepts came to figure less in technical legal expressions concerning civil liberties and judicial procedures. Many biblical concepts, concerning law, ethics, human nature, civil liberties, judicial procedures, government, and society, however, continued to provide significant ingredients in the American images of justice, mercy, rights, and duties. Although clearly present, its influence on statutes, judicial opinions, or the common law in general is not always possible to document explicitly.

Sometimes the Bible can be and has been cited both for and against the same legal proposition, and postmodern culture is often in tension with biblical rubrics. While biblical provisions do not, and in many cases should not, control American law, neither can nor should they be eliminated from the realities of American law, either as a part of the common law in general or with respect to civil liberties in specific. American perceptions of civil liberties and human rights are rooted not only in the Enlightenment, but also in Greek and Roman antiquity and in the Bible.

Colonial Laws and Liberties

The Bible had extensive and direct influence on law in America during the colonial period, especially in the North. Without any doubt, the ideal notion of civic order in Puritan New England thoroughly embraced divine words and intentions as revealed in the law of Moses. The *Laws and Liberties of Massachusetts,* an early Puritan document warned, "The more any law smells of man, the more unprofitable."

Calvinism held that the judicial language in the law of Moses was binding on all people and should be incorporated into the laws of the land. Accordingly, the list of fifteen crimes punishable by death within the jurisdiction of Massachusetts (printed in 1641) was collected and crafted from the texts of the Bible and cited chapter and verse following each law. These provisions against idolatry, witchcraft, blasphemy, manslaughter, sexual offenses, kidnapping, perjury in capital cases, and subversion, offered no protections for religious liberty, freedom of speech, or rights of the accused.

Laws enacted in Massachusetts (1647), Rhode Island (1647), New Haven (1656), Pennsylvania (1681), and elsewhere selectively built upon, modified, or adapted several biblical provisions, while also adopting various regulations not prescribed by the Bible. For example, in these laws, a twofold punitive damage penalty was exacted in the case of theft of an animal (compare Exod. 22:4); when the thief could not make restitution, whipping of no more than forty lashes resulted (as in Deut. 25:3). Two or three witnesses were required in capital cases (Deut. 19:15). Debt servitude in America was limited to seven

years (compare Deut. 15:1). Examples of non-biblical "common liberties" afforded in Massachusetts (1641) included the rights of speaking in public meetings, fishing and fowling, water passage, and removing oneself and family from the jurisdiction.

Biblically motivated legal precepts and patterns had lasting influences on American jurisprudence in several ways. Religious and political institutions were seen as hand-in-hand partners, serving separate roles but working together to improve society. Lawmakers and judges cited explicit authority in support of their rulings. Biblical law was remarkable in that it expressly limited the powers of the king (see Deut. 17:14–20), a view of limited government that deeply influenced the development of constitutional law in America. As in biblical law, American law restricted the reach of governmental decisions, privileged the decisions of conscience, and guarded the basic values of individual choice. Codification, publication, and public education became parts of the fabric of committing the populace to the rule of law (compare Deut. 31:11), with Judges 21:25 being quoted in 1969 in *Barnett v. State* for the civic rule that "no individual may do simply what he will." Laws came to be seen as principles, subject to wise adaptation, paraphrase, and restatement, while the legal system still maintained the confidence that an undergirding of law itself existed and unified the nation. In addition, the biblical concept of covenant influenced the early American concepts of compact and the commonwealth, uniting God, the people, and a ruler, and this union formed the original theoretical basis of American constitutionalism.

Freedom and the American Republic

In the eighteenth century, American law began to regard and protect civil liberties and individual rights more widely. New England ministers frequently quoted Micah 4:4, "every man under his vine," in support of the right to own private property. While the Massachusetts law in 1647 had banned Jesuits from its territory and laws against Sabbath violations and heresies were common, freedom of religion soon gathered strength. The first chapter of the laws enacted in Pennsylvania in 1705, for example, was headed, "The Law concerning Liberty of Conscience." It provided that no persons, so long as they professed faith in the Trinity and acknowledged the divine inspiration of the Bible, "shall in any case be molested or prejudiced for his or her conscientious persuasion, nor shall he or she be at any time compelled to frequent or maintain any religious worship, place or ministry whatsoever, contrary to his or her mind, but shall freely and fully enjoy his or her Christian liberty in all respects, without molestation or interruption."

Americans often spoke of themselves in biblical images, as a New Israel having been delivered from the bondage of European kingship much as Israel had been delivered by Moses from slavery under the pharaohs of Egypt. Thomas Jefferson proposed a seal for the United States showing the Israelites being led by a pillar of fire, with the words "Liberty under God's law—Man's Inalienable Birthright of Freedom." An oft-cited passage used polemically in behalf of freedom was "call no man your father" (Matt. 23:9). Commissioned in 1751, the Liberty Bell bore the inscription, "And proclaim liberty throughout the land unto all the inhabitants thereof," a text from Leviticus 25:10. Flames of resistance against the Stamp Act were fanned by Galatians 5:12–13, "ye have been called unto liberty." In this spirit, Andrew Jackson called the Bible "the rock on which our Republic rests."

During the early nineteenth century, no law book was more influential in American law than was William Blackstone's often-reprinted *Commentaries*. Although offering primarily a re-statement of English common law, Blackstone drew on biblical fundamentals. For example, his justifications of the three absolute rights of personal security, liberty, and private property were based on Genesis accounts regarding Abraham, Abimelech, Isaac, and Lot.

During this era, rights were not equated with permissiveness. To the founding generation, as James Hutson has explained in *Forgotten Features of the Founding,* a right was understood in its fullest sense as a "power inherent in and owned by an individual to act in a way consistent with Christian morality." Thus, John Adams rejected Rousseau's line that Americans had given birth to the "science of rights," explaining that they had simply found their rights "in their religion."

Many biblical precepts were influential in shaping the American Republic, inspiring much of its political theory and social values. For example, several biblical passages were cited in support of the separation of church and state ("render to Caesar the things that are Caesar's," Mark 12:17). Originally, however, the separation between church and state was not as rigidly understood as it has recently become. Recent documentary research has led some to conclude that Jefferson's "wall of separation" would better be described as a "swiss cheese." At least, it should be perceived as a wall with doors and windows. This openness itself reflects various models of church–state independence and interdependence found in the Bible itself.

Because controversy existed over possible interpretations advanced by various Bible-believing churches and individuals, the Bible itself came to serve less and less in settling issues involving the public order, and legislation made little, if any, direct reference to the Bible. Formal disestablishment removed the religiously motivated Blue Laws, but court opinions continued to draw on the Bible as a source of authority. This had its upside as well as a downside, particular in the case of the debates over slavery, in which both sides invoked biblical authority in support of their views.

Twentieth Century

Well into the twentieth century, the Bible was used as a common source of legal language. In the 1920s, it went almost without saying that allusions to the Bible by legal practitioners were more frequent than to any other book outside of professional law treatises and previous case decisions. In 1943, H.B. Clark reported that "many provisions of biblical law are still seen in American statutes and court decisions."

After World War II, the concept of a legal right underwent extensive and sudden transformation. A right came to be seen as "a raw power to gratify a sweeping range of appetites in the name of vindicating individual equality and autonomy," as Hutson has described. The Bible became an influential tool in the hands of some rights advocates. In the civil rights movement in the 1960s, for example, the speeches of Martin Luther King Jr. often invoked the Bible, and sit-ins cited Exodus 1:15–22 in praise of the Egyptian midwives who disobeyed Pharaoh to save Hebrew male children.

Plentiful references to the Bible appear in judicial opinions down to the 1990s. The extensive study by Michael Medina located 150 such references in cases before 1970, 81 in the 1970s, and 115 in the 1980s. A presidential proclamation in 1983 announcing the year of the Bible extolled its role in inspiring concepts of civil government contained in the Declaration of Independence and U.S. Constitution. While it has been claimed that the Bible is the most influential book in American culture, Shakespeare is a close contender, judging by the times quoted in judicial opinions.

The Bible has been used for all kinds of judicial purposes. It has shaped substantive decisions. In *Lopez v. United States*, Chief Justice Warren took a broad meaning of the term "search" based on biblical meanings of this word. The Bible also influences interpretation, being quoted, for example, regarding the spirit and the letter of the law (2 Cor. 3:6). This rubric has had a vibrant life in the judicial rhetoric of American judges. The Bible also provides a wealth of proverbial wisdom and common sense. In cases involving conflicts of interest, judges have spoken against serving "two masters" (Matt. 6:24); see, for example, *United States v. Mississippi Valley Generating Co.* (1961) and *Brickner v. Normandy Osteopathic Hospital* (1988). American laws recognize the value of Good Samaritans.

Some parts of the Bible are quoted much more than others. Because the Bible deals with such a wide array of human concerns, it speaks to many legal issues. Even though it was not written to be read as a legal textbook or handbook, it has influenced legal opinions concerning many areas of civil liberty.

Judicial and Criminal Rights

All legal systems begin with certain rules, values, expectations, and entitlements regarding access to and treatment from the courts. By providing memorable narratives about several judicial trials, such as the proceedings involving Naboth (1 Kings 21), Boaz (Ruth 4), Jeremiah (Jeremiah 26), Susanna (Apocrypha, Daniel 13), Jesus (in the four Gospels), and Paul (Acts 21–27), the Bible shaped American social and legal expectations concerning due process, witnesses, and fairness.

The rules found in Exodus 23:1–3 and 6–9 have been styled by scholars as a decalogue for the administration of justice. These provisions require all participants in the legal process to be honest, to avoid collusion, to be impervious to social pressure, to be impartial towards the rich and the poor alike, to shun perjury, to execute none that are innocent, to take no bribes or gifts, and not to oppress a resident alien. Similar rules are found today in American codes of judicial and legal ethics. American courts, for example, *Ex parte Kurth*, have cited Deuteronomy 16:19 in support of judicial impartiality, not perverting justice nor showing favoritism.

The Bill of Rights guarantees many rights to parties accused of crimes. In some cases, these principles stem from the Bible.

The right against self-incrimination, now found in the Fifth Amendment, grew out of Roman, Canon, and Jewish law, but William Tyndale can be credited for launching its adoption into English law. His English translation of the Bible (1525) and exposition on "swear not" in Matthew 5–7 (1530) boldly asserted that scripture rejects the idea of compelling a person to bear witness against himself or herself. Following these precepts, the courageous judicial stand of John Lilbourne during the English Revolution in the early 1650s resulted in the elimination of self-incriminating oaths in the Star Chamber. The case of the adulteress in John 8 was also influential in showing that Jesus did not require her to testify for or against herself. From such developments, the right against self-incrimination found its way into the American Constitution.

In recent times, American decisions, such as *Coy v. Iowa*, have cited Paul's assertion of rights under Roman law (Acts 25:16) in support of the civil right of due process, to confront one's accusers and to answer charges with a personal defense. As legal precedent for the right to impeach accusing witnesses by separate cross-examination, Daniel's detection of false witnesses (Apocrypha, Daniel 13) has been judicially cited, as in *Virgin Islands v. Edinborough* (1980).

The presumption of innocence until proven guilty does not prevail in all legal systems. C.S. Lewis has argued that this is a distinctively Christian attitude attributable to the concept of grace found in the New Testament. The necessity of affording a full and fair defense is found in Jonah 1:5–10 and Job 31:35 ("Oh that one would hear me!"), and the rule against double jeopardy has been supported by Nahum 1:9 ("affliction shall not rise up the second time"). In *California v. Hodari D.* and other cases, Proverbs 28:1 has been used in establishing evidentiary inferences from fleeing a crime scene; *People v. Simmons* draws on the silence of Jesus before his accusers.

The right against cruel and unusual punishment is consonant with biblical scruples against vengeance (Rom. 12:19, cited in *People v. Flynn*). At the same time, the Bible is cited as authority for the legitimacy of the death penalty, especially in cases of premeditated, hateful homicide (Gen. 9:6, Exod. 21:12, Num. 35:16), although these usages are not without their conceptual difficulties and complexities, as Samuel Levine and also John Blume and Sheri Lynn Johnson have argued.

Civil Liberties

The Bible speaks powerfully of freedom, and thus it has served as a potent springboard for civil libertarianism. At the same time, this appropriation has its limitations, for freedom in the Hebrew Bible mainly means freedom from bondage, not freedom to act independently; in the New Testament freedom equates with Christ, the way that makes one free. Edward Gaffney's exposition of *The Interaction of Biblical Religion and American Constitutional Law* rightly states: "Although concerned intensely with persons, the Bible does not view them as isolated atoms, but as interrelated, socially connected parts of a whole, or as members of a community." Accordingly, freedoms in the Bible are never ends in themselves.

Freedom of speech in the Bible is not absolute, as the trial of the blasphemer in Leviticus 24 makes painfully clear. However, when Peter and John refused to be silenced by the Jerusalem Sanhedrin's charge of blasphemy ordering them to desist from speaking of or teaching in the name of Jesus (Acts 4:17), their stand became a model of free speech, echoing the bold outspokenness of the Hebrew prophets in general.

Freedom of religion is constrained in the Bible by prohibitions against idol worship. Nevertheless, the Bible grants every person freedom to choose which god to serve (Josh. 24:15). The biblical loyalty that man owes to God is absolute; political loyalties are therefore secondary and separate. This rule is seen in the courageous exercise of religious freedom by Esther and Daniel, whose examples also served as critiques of the dominance of foreign rulers.

Jesus' dictum about Caesar came to be used as an axiom of separation, but many Christian nations, especially in the Middle Ages, did not read Jesus' dictum that way. To the contrary, they saw in Isaiah 49:23 a mandate for kings and queens to be "nursing fathers and nursing mothers" to the church. Although wrongly interpreted by European monarchs from the time of John Calvin until the French Revolution, this scripture was a powerful justification for state churches and official persecution of those of other faiths.

Freedom of association is tacitly recognized in the popular assemblies that were mandated under biblical law. The New Testament presupposes the right of "two or three" to meet together for religious purposes (Matt. 18:20). Freedom of travel arises in conjunction with the Christian imperative to "go forth to every part of the world" (Mark 16:15), as exemplified by the missionary travels of Paul. Regarding the bearing of arms, Jesus warned that those who live by the sword will die by the sword, but his own disciples were armed with weapons when he was arrested on the Mount of Olives.

No issue of civil rights has been more important in American history than the question of slavery. That issue divided the nation; it also divided churches, such as the Baptists and Presbyterians. The slavery issue split the Baptists into two Conventions. Both sides grounded their views on *sola scriptura*. Although slavery in biblical times had nothing to do with race in a modern sense, biblical provisions supported various forms of slavery or servitude (Exod. 21:1–6, Lev. 25:39–55, Deut. 15:1–6, Eph. 6:5–9), economic

institutions common throughout antiquity. The case of *Pirate v. Dalby* cited Leviticus and Deuteronomy to justify slavery during Pennsylvania's period of gradual abolition. The Virginia case of *Commonwealth v. Turner* in 1827 looked to passages in Exodus 21 for guidance concerning the beating of a slave by his owner. By the 1830s, the fallacious so-called curse of Noah (Gen. 9:20–27) was used as a stock weapon by those advocating slavery; at the same time, the abolitionists drew support from biblical injunctions regarding love, justice, freedom, and release from bondage.

With various results in cases involving resident aliens, courts have referred to such passages as Leviticus 24:22, "you shall apply the same law to the alien as you do for one of your own country." See *Memorial Hospital* (1974); *Rollins* (1979); and *Bhandari* (1987).

Women and children found themselves in subordinate roles in the ancient world, and thus the Bible may be cited, on the one hand, in opposition to women's equal rights. On the other hand, courts have noted that the Bible also presents strong instances of women exercising rights in buying property (Prov. 31:16), in serving prominently in the military (Deborah, used in *Hill v. Berkman*), and in other contexts.

Family and Private Law

Biblical law extensively regulated family rights and duties in ways that supported the prevailing norms of society in biblical times. Marriage, chastity, and children were the principal areas of concern.

Marriage was complex, involving negotiation of prenuptial agreements, dowry rights, formal engagement, solemnization, and celebrations. Marriages outside the clan were at times prohibited, but marriages and sexual relations with too close of kin were also outlawed (Lev. 18:6–8). Analogously, some American courts have upheld bans on first-cousin marriages. Polygamy was allowed in Israel (Deut. 21:15), but a New Testament bishop was to have one wife (1 Tim. 3:2). Language regarding rights within marriage in American law has stemmed from the Bible concerning the husband's role as head of the family (Eph. 5:23), the right to recover consortium damages (Matt. 19:5), and spousal immunity (Gen. 2:24). The unity of person behind the concept of survivorship stems from Gen. 2:14 (see *Freeman v. Belfer*). Various statements in the Bible on divorce (Deut. 24:1, Matt. 5:32, 19:6, Luke 16:18) have been cited with legal influence in the past, such as *Wolfe v. Wolfe* (1976).

Biblical laws punishing adultery (Exod. 20:14, Deut. 22:22), incest, sodomy (Rom. 1:26–27, 1 Cor. 6:9), bestiality (Lev. 18:23), and prostitution (Deut. 23:17) have influenced American law over the years, as Patrick O'Neil demonstrates. Words such as "abominable" and "detestable crimes against nature," however, have been held to be unconstitutionally vague, as stated in *Stone v. Wainright* (1973).

The Bible grants parents rights and responsibilities over their children. American law has been heavily influenced in regard to parental education of their children (Deut. 6:7), discipline (Prov. 23:13), and child labor (a father's rights over fruits of his son's labor have been upheld, citing Gen. 12:37). At the same time, biblical law made it a capital offense for a son to strike or curse a parent (Exod. 21:15, 17), but parents lacked the power to impose such a punishment (Deut. 21:19).

The Bible protects private property from theft, but in biblical times no property concept of fee simple absolute existed, for the land belonged to God with human owners as life tenants. This concept retains vitality in the environmental duties of human stewardship over the Earth. Hebrew law prohibits usury charged to another Hebrew (Exod. 22:25), but the New Testament seems to encourage making as much money as possible, as in the parables of the talents and of the wise steward. *Klein v. Commonwealth* cited the Matthew 20:1–16 on the fairness of agreed wages.

Concepts of redemption of property in foreclosure (Lev. 25:25) and forfeiture stem from the Bible. In *United States v. Bajakajian,* the Supreme Court traced the "guilty property" theory behind *in rem* forfeiture to Exodus 21:28, "which describes property being sacrificed to God as a means of atoning for an offense." The seven-year rule for repeat bankruptcies derives from the biblical law of sabbatical release.

Reading the Bible for legal substance, however, is difficult. The Bible is not about law; it is about God. The Bible is not by people from the modern world; it must be read in historical contexts. Translating ordinary biblical passages into modern languages is hard enough; translating technical legal terms is almost impossible. Often, biblical rubrics can be cited on either side of a modern legal issue. Nevertheless, the Bible speaks profoundly on topics related to law, liberty, human nature, social predicaments, and civic obligations. It offers paradigms and precepts that have deeply influenced the development of civil rights and duties in the American experience.

JOHN W. WELCH

References and Further Reading

Blume, John H., and Sheri Lynn Johnson. "Don't Take His Eye, Don't Take His Tooth, and Don't Cast the First Stone: Limiting Religious Arguments in Capital Cases." *William & Mary Bill of Rights Journal* 9 (December 2000): 61.

Botein, Stephen. *Early American Law and Society.* New York: Knopf, 1982.

Clark, H.B. *Biblical Law.* Portland, OR: Binfords and Mort, 1943.

Falk, Ze'ev W. *Hebrew Law in Biblical Times.* 2nd ed. Provo, Utah: Brigham Young University Press, 2001.

Gaffney, Edward McGlynn, Jr. "The Interaction of Biblical Religion and American Constitutional Law." In *The Bible in American Law, Politics, and Political Rhetoric,* edited by James Turner Johnson, 81–105. Philadelphia: Fortress, 1985.

Harrelson, Walter. *The Ten Commandments and Human Rights.* Philadelphia: Fortress, 1980.

Hutson, James. *Forgotten Features of the Founding: The Recovery of Religious Themes in the Early American Republic.* Lanham, MD: Lexington Books, 2003.

Katsh, Abrham I. *The Biblical Heritage of American Democracy.* New York: Ktav Publishing House, 1977.

Levine, Samuel J., *Capital Punishment in Jewish Law and Its Application to the American Legal System: A Conceptual Overview,* St. Mary's Law Journal 29 (1998): 1037.

Medina, J. Michael, *The Bible Annotated: Use of the Bible in Reported American Decisions,* Northern Illinois University Law Review 12 (1991): 1:87–254.

Meislin, Bernard, *The Role of the Ten Commandments in American Judicial Decisions,* Jewish Law Association Studies 3 (1988): 187–209.

O'Neil, Patrick M. "Bible in American Constitutionalism," and "Bible in American Law." In *Religion and American Law: An Encyclopedia,* edited by Paul Finkelman, 29–34. New York: Garland, 2000.

Otto, Eckart. "Human Rights: The Influence of the Hebrew Bible." *Journal of Northwest Semitic Languages* 25, no. 1 (1999): 1–20.

Rogerson, John W., Margaret Davies, and M. Daniel Carroll R., eds. *The Bible in Ethics.* Sheffield: Sheffield Academic Press, 1995.

Welch, John W., *Biblical Law in America,* Brigham Young University Law Review 2002, no. 3 (2002): 611–42.

Cases and Statutes Cited

Barnett v. State, 8 Md. App. 35; 257 A. 2d 466 (1969)

Bhandari v. First Nat'l Bank of Commerce, 829 F.2d 1343 (5th Cir. 1987)

Brickner v. Normandy Osetopathic Hospital, Inc., 746 S. W.2d 108 (Mo. App. 1988)

California v. Hodari D., 499 U.S. 621 (1991)

Commonwealth v. Turner (Va. 1827)

Coy v. Iowa, 478 U.S. 1012 (1988)

Ex parte Kurth, 28 F.Supp. 258, 264 (S.D. Cal. 1939)

Freeman v. Belfer, 173 N.C. 581; 92 S.E. 486 (1917)

Hill v. Berkman, 635 F.Supp. 1228, 1238–39 (E.D.N.Y. 1986)

Klein v. Commonwealth, State Employee's Retirement System, 521 Pa. 330; 555 A.2d 1216 (1989)

Lopez v. United States, 373 U.S. 427, 459 (1963)

Memorial Hospital v. Maricopa County, 415 U.S. 250, 261 (1974)

People v. Flynn, 223 N.Y.S.2d 441, 445 (1962)

People v. Simmons, 28 Cal. 2d 699; 172 P.2d 18 (1946)

Pirate v. Dalby (Pa. 1786)

Rollins v. Proctor & Schwartz, 478 F.Supp. 1137 (D.S.C. 1979)

Stone v. Wainwright, 478 F.2d 390 (5th Cir. 1973)

United States v. Bajakajian, 524 U.S. 321 (1998)

United States v. Mississippi Valley Generating Co., 364 U.S. 520, 549 (1961)

Virgin Islands v. Edinborough, 625 F.2d 472, 473 n. 3 (3rd Cir. 1980)

Wolfe v. Wolfe, 46 Ohio St. 2d 399, 350 N.E.2d 413 (1976)

BIBLE READING IN PUBLIC SCHOOLS, HISTORY OF BEFORE AND AFTER ABINGTON SCHOOL DISTRICT v. SCHEMPP

In the eighteenth and nineteenth centuries in America, there was homogeneity among Americans in that the majority were Protestant Christians, albeit of varied denominations. Due to the variety of denominations that existed, and due to the history of religious oppression that led many to come to America, it was generally accepted that the State could not establish one denomination as a state church. Rather, all denominations should be allowed to worship as they chose. However, due to the religious homogeneity among the majority of Americans, there existed a widely held belief that America was a Christian nation and the precepts of Protestant Christianity, as taught by the Bible, were the basis of good citizenship and good government. Thus, there should be a separation of church and state, but a separation of religion (read Protestant Christianity) and state was neither necessary nor desirable.

Given the above belief and the belief that society had an obligation to inculcate its young with proper moral precepts and to teach them to be good citizens, it made sense that they be exposed to Christian precepts in school. As a result, prior to *Abington School District v. Schempp,* it was generally believed that the Bible could and should be read in public schools, as long as the passages were read without any comment or discussion. Thus, in the period before *Schempp,* there was a widespread practice of Bible reading in the public schools. Specifically, in most instances several passages of the Bible were read by the teachers to their students or, in modern times, over the public address system by a teacher or student. In fact, in 1950 the reading of the Bible was required by thirteen states and permitted in twenty-five other states. Further, in a survey conducted in 1968, 48 percent of the respondent teachers teaching before 1962 reported

that Bible selections were read in their classrooms on a daily to less than weekly basis.

The Bible that was often used for Bible reading was the King James version of the Bible, a version used by many Protestants of varying denominations, but not by Catholics, Jews, or others of different religious faiths. The reason that the Bible passages were to be read without comment was to avoid the teaching of any particular religion. It was believed that the reading of the Bible imparted general moral precepts rather than the precepts of any particular religion.

In the last three quarters of the nineteenth century and the first half of the twentieth, there raged an episodic conflict between Catholics and Protestants in many areas, including the teaching of Protestant precepts in public schools. Nevertheless, the courts, with few exceptions, upheld the reading of the Bible in the schools if the Bible was read without comment or note and if pupils who desired to avoid the reading could do so. Most held that the reading was constitutional because it was not a teaching of sectarian tenets and doctrines. Although the court holdings appear to be somewhat contradictory, they can be understood if one remembers the mindset prevailing at the time. As one commentator explains, "The Protestant position that emerged by the mid-nineteenth century was that Protestants could participate in politics and teach their religion in the schools, but that Catholics could not . . . . The key step in the Protestant argument was this: Protestants tended to assume that, whereas Catholics acted as part of a church, Protestants acted in diverse sects as individuals . . . . Thus, Catholic instruction or political action violated separation [of church and state], because it was the work of an authoritarian church, but Protestant instruction and political action did not violate separation, because it was the work of free individuals."

A few courts disagreed with this generally held view and found Bible reading in public schools to violate either the federal or a state constitution. For example, the Wisconsin Supreme Court found that the reading of the Bible, without comment, at certain times in public schools, violated the Wisconsin Constitution because such was sectarian instruction. It was sectarian instruction because each sect, with few exceptions, bases its peculiar doctrines upon some portion of the Bible, the reading of which tends to inculcate those doctrines (*State ex rel. Weiss v. District Board of School Dist. No. 8 of City of Edgerton,* 44 N.W. 967 [Wis. 1890]).

In the mid-twentieth century, the acceptance of the intertwining of religion and the state began to come undone. In 1947, the Supreme Court handed down the significant establishment clause decision of *Everson v. Board of Education.* In that case, the Supreme

Court purported to endorse a strict doctrine of separation of church and state when it stated that "[n] either a state nor the Federal Government can set up a church. Neither can pass laws which aid one religion, aid all religions, or prefer one religion over another . . . . Neither a state nor the Federal government can, openly or secretly, participate in the affairs of any religious organizations or groups and vice versa. In the words of Jefferson, the clause against establishment of religion by law was intended to erect 'a wall of separation between church and State.'" Ironically, although all of the justices concurred in the above statement, five members of the Court went on to hold that New Jersey's program of providing transportation services for non–public school children did not violate the establishment clause.

In 1963, in the *Abington School District v. Schempp* case, the Supreme Court was faced with the question of whether Bible reading in the public schools, as it was currently practiced, violated the establishment clause. The Court found that it did. The *Schempp* case involved two separate cases. The first case came from Pennsylvania where a 1959 statute required the reading of ten Bible verses, without comment, at the opening of each public school, on each school day. At the written request of a parent or guardian, however, a child could be excused from such reading. The Schempps were members of the Unitarian Church in Germantown, Pennsylvania, and two of their children attended Abington High School where such Bible reading took place. Although the school only provided copies of the King James Bible, the student doing the reading could choose any passages he liked. Thus, readings had been done from the King James, the Douay (Catholic version), and the Revised Standard versions of the Bible as well as the Jewish Holy Scriptures. In spite of the inclusiveness of the Bible readings, the Schempps brought suit to enjoin enforcement of the statute because specific religious doctrines, gleaned by a literal reading of the Bible, were contrary to their religious beliefs. Further, although the children could be excused from the reading, their father did not do this because he believed that doing so would adversely affect the relationship between the children and their classmates and teachers.

The second case in *Schempp* came to the Supreme Court from Maryland where the City of Baltimore had adopted a rule providing for the reading, without comment, of a chapter in the Holy Bible and/or a recitation of the Lord's Prayer in the Baltimore schools. The Bible used was the King James version. The Murrays, a mother and son, were atheists who sought to have the rule rescinded because it was a threat to their religious beliefs in that it placed a premium on belief as opposed to nonbelief. Further,

they felt that the Baltimore rule as practiced indicated a belief that God was the source of all moral and spiritual values, and thus such values were religious values. Such a belief rendered Petitioners' beliefs suspect and promoted doubt as to Petitioners' morality and good citizenship.

The Supreme Court struck down both the Pennsylvania statute and the Baltimore rule as violating the establishment clause. In doing so it recognized that religion was closely identified with American history and government; however, it contended that religious freedom was likewise embedded in American life. It went on to reaffirm its holding in *Everson v. Board of Education*, that the object of the First Amendment's establishment clause was "to create a complete and permanent separation of the spheres of religious activity and civil authority by comprehensively forbidding every form of public aid or support for religion" (*Everson*, 330 U.S., at 31–32). However, the establishment clause, together with the free exercise clause, mandated that a state be neutral in its relations with religious believers and nonbelievers. Thus, a state can neither favor nor disfavor religions. In the instant case, the Court found that the Bible readings were a religious ceremony. Thus, the exercises and the law requiring them violated the establishment clause. The readings were a religious ceremony because, even if the purpose of the exercise was to promote moral values, the tool used was the Bible and the Bible is an instrument of religion.

After *Schempp* was handed down, the schools in large part abided by the Court's decision. In a survey conducted in 1968 it was found that, with the exception of the South, the practice of Bible reading and prayer in public elementary schools had largely disappeared by the academic year 1964–65. Thus, a fairly entrenched practice gave way with surprising swiftness.

Like the schools, the lower courts followed the dictates of the Supreme Court and invalidated any reading of the Bible to the student body at the behest of the school or school district. Many schools, students, and parents, however, wanted the children to have some religious instruction and/or exposure to the Bible. The question then became how could children learn about the Bible without running afoul of the establishment clause. In some jurisdictions the schools allowed Bible study classes to be conducted on school grounds as part of the school curriculum. Such classes were found to be unconstitutional if they taught the Bible as religious truth. However, a Bible study class was permissible under the establishment clause if the course was secular in nature, intent, and purpose, and the effect of the course was neither to advance nor inhibit religion. Generally, a Bible study course was found to be secular if the Bible was studied from a literary and historical viewpoint, with no claims made as to its truth or falsity.

In addition to Bible study classes, some students formed voluntary Bible study clubs. In the wake of *Schempp*, the lower courts often held that such clubs could not meet on school grounds because the establishment clause required religious speech to be barred from governmental forums. However, in recent times there has been a shift away from strict separation of religion and government and a move toward accommodation of private religious activities and expression.

With regard to voluntary Bible clubs, this shift culminated in the federal Equal Access Act (EAA) enacted by Congress in 1984. Under the EAA a public secondary school that receives federal financial assistance may not deny equal access to its facilities to any students who wish to conduct a meeting within its forum on the basis of religious, political, philosophical, or other content of the speech at such meetings. This equal access requirement applies only if the school allows one or more non–curriculum-related student groups to meet on school premises during noninstructional time. Thus, the school could bar all student groups from meeting; however, if it provides an opportunity for one, it must provide an opportunity for all.

In 1990, the Supreme Court upheld the EAA in the case of *Board of Education v. Mergens*. Then, in 2001, in the case of *Good News Club v. Milford Central School*, the Court provided for equal access in elementary schools by finding that the school's authorization for a Christian children's club to meet after hours on elementary school premises did not violate the establishment clause. Thus, Bible reading can take place in public schools in the context of student-sponsored Bible clubs. However, school-sponsored clubs are prohibited.

In the future, it is likely that the Court will continue to accommodate student-initiated religious activities and speech to the extent that there is no hint of school sponsorship of such activities or speech.

JANET W. STEVERSON

References and Further Reading

Collier, James M., and John J. George. "Education and the Supreme Court." *The Journal of Higher Education* 21, no. 2 (1950): 77–83
Donovan, Matthew D., *Notes: Religion, Neutrality, and the Public School Curriculum: Equal Treatment or Separation.* Catholic Lawyer 43 (Spring 2004): 187–223.
Laycock, Douglas, *The Many Meanings of Separation.* University of Chicago Law Review 70 (Fall 2003): 1667–701.
McCarthy, Martha, *Religion and Education: Whither the Establishment Clause.* Indiana Law Journal 75 (2000): 123–66.
Valk, Rebecca A. "Note: *Good News Club v. Milford Central School*—A Critical Analysis of the Establishment Clause as Applied to Public Education." *St. John's Journal of Legal Commentary* 17 (Winter/Spring 2003): 347–98.
Way, H. Frank. "Survey Research on Judicial Decisions: The Prayer and Bible Reading Cases." *Western Political Quarterly* 21, no. 2 (1968): 189–205.

Cases and Statutes Cited

Abington School District v. Schempp, 374 U.S. 203 (1963)
Board of Education v. Mergens, 496 U.S. 226 (1990)
Equal Access Act, 20 U.S.C.A. §4071 (a)
Everson v. Board of Education, 330 U.S. 1 (1947)
Good News Club v. Milford Central School, 533 U.S. 98 (2001)
State ex rel. Weiss v. District Board of School Dist. No. 8 of City of Edgerton, 44 N.W. 967 (Wis. 1890)

BIDDLE, FRANCIS BEVERLEY (1886–1968)

Francis Biddle, the scion of a family that emigrated to America in the early seventeenth century, attended private schools, including Harvard College, from which he graduated cum laude, and the Harvard Law School, where he received an LL.B. in 1911. He then served one year as a secretary to Justice Oliver Wendell Holmes, Jr. Holmes, a fellow patrician, influenced Biddle greatly, and he claimed in his memoirs that Holmes had not only reinforced his latent sense of noblesse oblige but also turned him into a liberal. He would later write both a biography of the justice as well as a book on his legal philosophy.

In 1912, he joined the family law firm in Philadelphia, but a few years later he struck out on his own and established a new firm. A successful Philadelphia lawyer, Biddle's clients included both the Pennsylvania Railroad and labor unions, and in 1927 he published a novel, *Llanfear Pattern,* which was highly critical of Philadelphia's inbred elite society.

Nominally a Republican, he became increasingly disillusioned with the party in the 1920s. He recalled that he had seen "the dark and dismal conditions under which the miners lived, and the brutality that was dealt them if they tried to improve things." Opposed to Herbert Hoover's handling of labor issues, Biddle campaigned against him and worked for the election of Franklin Roosevelt in 1932. Roosevelt awarded him with several appointments in New Deal programs, and Biddle chaired the special commission that cleared the Tennessee Valley Authority of charges of corruption. In 1939, Roosevelt nominated him to the Court of Appeals for the Third Circuit. Within a short time Biddle grew bored with the job, and in 1940 resigned from the bench to become solicitor general. He won all fifteen cases he argued in the Supreme Court defending New Deal measures.

In 1941, Roosevelt named Robert H. Jackson to the Supreme Court and appointed Biddle to take his place as attorney general. He served in that office for four years, during which he oversaw the administration's handling of civil liberties issues during World War II.

For the most part, Biddle received good marks from civil libertarians. The Roosevelt administration, unlike that of Wilson in World War I, did not launch a wholesale attack on aliens or radicals, and did not try to either suppress radical speech or criticism of the Roosevelt administration. Moreover, Biddle took advantage of a ruling in which the Supreme Court held that federal antisubversion laws preempted state measures, and thus prevented the "little Red scares" of the 1920s.

The great failing in Biddle's administration, one that he later acknowledged, was his reluctant implementation and defense of the internment of Japanese Americans. Not until after Biddle's death in 1968 did evidence come out that middle-ranking officials in both the War Department and the Solicitor General's Office knew that the Japanese Americans posed no threat to American security, and that no proof of any sort had ever been found that they were involved in either espionage or sabotage. They deliberately withheld this information not only from the Supreme Court but from Biddle as well. A dedicated civil libertarian, it is highly unlikely that Biddle would have given his assent to the program had he been in possession of the facts.

Biddle also prosecuted several cases under the Alien Registration Act, but he refused to use it for witch-hunting of radicals, as its sponsors had hoped. While tens of thousands of German and Italian aliens were registered shortly after the United States entered the war, the Justice Department made sure that the process was carried out in such a way as to maintain the dignity of the aliens.

One should note that Biddle also knew, thanks to the work that the Federal Bureau of Investigation had done in the 1930s, just which aliens did support fascist ideology, but thanks to the FBI, practically none of them proved able to do damage to the American war effort.

With the death of Franklin Roosevelt in April 1945, Biddle's days in the Justice Department were limited, and at Harry Truman's request he resigned in June. Truman, however, then named Biddle as one of the American judges on the international tribunal that tried former Nazi leaders for "crimes against humanity." Although there has been some criticism of the Nuremburg trials as ex post facto proceedings, at the time most people believed that it was right to try to impose a rule of law on wartime atrocities. Certainly the trials provided not only a means to expose the full extent of Nazi actions, but were far better than the older method of taking the losers out into the prison yard and shooting them. At the close of the trials, Biddle recommended to Truman that provocation of aggressive wars should, in the future, be declared a crime under international law.

Truman then tried to name Biddle as the U.S. representative to United Nations Educational, Scientific and Cultural Organization (UNESCO), but the Republican-controlled Senate blocked the appointment because Biddle was considered too liberal. Rather than go through a bruising confirmation fight, which he would surely have lost, Biddle asked Truman to remove his name.

Although he never again held appointed office, Biddle remained active in politics, and chaired the liberal interest group, Americans for Democratic Action, from 1950 through 1953. During those years he was an active foe of Senator Joseph McCarthy of Wisconsin, and repeatedly denounced McCarthy and the House Committee on Un-American Activities for their witch-hunting tactics, smear campaigns, and efforts to censor school textbooks. His most cogent case against McCarthyism is in his 1951 book, *The Fear of Freedom*.

MELVIN I. UROFSKY

References and Further Reading

Biddle, Francis. *In Brief Authority*. Garden City, N.Y.: Doubleday, 1962
Murphy, Paul L. *The Constitution in Crisis Times, 1918–1969*. New York: Harper & Row, 1972.

BILL OF ATTAINDER

A bill of attainder imposes punishment on specific individuals or members of a group through an act taken by the legislature rather than a judicial trial. The U.S. Constitution prohibits bills of attainder enacted by both Congress (Art. I § 9, clause 3) and by the states (Art. I § 10). These legislative statements of guilt were used by the British parliament to punish subversive acts such as treason by sentencing alleged traitors to death. The founders believed that these acts were abused in England, as later described by Thomas Jefferson as "instruments of vengeance by a successful over a defeated party." In framing the

Constitution, the founders put their faith instead in the trial by jury in order to protect the rights of the accused against the power of the state. Bills of attainder relate closely to the heralded principle of separation of powers in the Constitution, where it is the power of the legislative branch to enact laws of general applicability, while the judiciary is to independently decide how that law should be applied in a given set of factual circumstances. During the American Revolution, the legislatures of numerous states enacted bills of attainder or bills of pains and penalties (effectively the same, but with a lower level of punishment) against persons disloyal to the Revolution. Bills of attainder were therefore prohibited in order to ensure fairness in the process of adjudicating disputes via the judicial branch, essentially safeguarding against their tyrannical use in the future as had occurred in England. The founders believed that trial by jury, not legislature, would better protect civil liberties from the whims, whether well founded or not, of the democratically elected majority.

JAMES F. VAN ORDEN

BILLS OF RIGHTS IN EARLY STATE CONSTITUTIONS

State constitution making began during the Revolution. By 1787, when delegates from twelve of the original thirteen states (Rhode Island never sent any delegates) met in Philadelphia to write the national constitution, eleven of the first thirteen states had written constitutions. What would become the fourteenth state, Vermont, had also produced a written constitution. Only Rhode Island and Connecticut failed to adopt a new constitution during or immediately after the Revolution. A number of states wrote more than one constitution in this period, refining and revising their constitutional structure. All of the constitutions dealt with the important aspects of government, such as the powers of the legislative and executive branches, the allocation of representatives, and who could vote.

Liberty, of course, had been at the center of the American Revolution. For example, the New York legislature asserted in its "Address of the Convention of the Representatives of the State of New York to Their Constituents," in 1776, that "[w]e do not fight for a few acres of land," but rather, New Yorkers and all Americans fought "for freedom—for the freedom and happiness of millions yet unborn." Similarly, Jefferson would assert in the Declaration of Independence that Americans were fighting to secure the "unalienable Rights" of "Life, Liberty, and the Pursuit of Happiness." Surprisingly, however, only five of the original states to write constitutions—Virginia, Pennsylvania, Maryland, North Carolina, and Massachusetts—actually included a bill of rights or declaration of rights in their fundamental law. On September 11, 1776, Delaware adopted a "Declaration of Rights," but this was not formally part of the state's constitution, which was adopted ten days later, on September 21. The last article of the Delaware constitution of 1776 made a reference to "the declaration of rights and fundamental rules for this State, agreed to by this convention," but the constitution did not actually contain the declaration, and it was only sometimes printed and distributed with the constitution. What would become the fourteenth state, Vermont, also had a bill of rights in its first constitution. Some of the other states did, however, offer some formal assertion of fundamental liberties. Connecticut, for example, which did not adopt a constitution (but instead simply amended its colonial charter to remove references to England and the king), passed a declaration of rights in 1784, just after the Revolution. A number of states wrote more than one constitution in this period, in the process reconsidering and refining the notion of fundamental rights.

New Hampshire, for example, did not have a declaration of rights in its constitution of 1776, but did have one in its second constitution, adopted in 1784. Georgia, on the other hand, adopted three constitutions (1777, 1789, and 1798) in this period, none of which had a bill of rights, although the constitutions did protect some civil liberties.

Most of the new state constitutions written during or after the Revolution reflected historic claims of the "rights" of Englishmen. The new states added to these rights new protections of liberty based on the events leading up the Revolution and the circumstances of the new American nation.

Religion in the State Bills of Rights

Almost every American state constitution had some provisions that dealt with religion. These provisions, either in the main body of the document or in a separate declaration of rights, are perhaps the most important differences between the rights of Englishmen and Americans. Most states provided for some form of "free exercise." New Jersey's clause in its 1776 Constitution was typical in its detail and thrust:

> That no person shall ever, within this Colony, be deprived of the inestimable privilege of worshipping Almighty God in a manner agreeable to the dictates of his own conscience; nor, under any pretence whatever,

be compelled to attend any place of worship, contrary to his own faith and judgment; nor shall any person, within this Colony, ever be obliged to pay tithes, taxes or any other rates, for the purpose of building or repairing any other church or churches, place or places of worship, or for the maintenance of any minister or ministry, contrary to what he believes to be right, or has deliberately or voluntarily engaged himself to perform.

However, the new states, including New Jersey, were ambivalent about how much political freedom members of dissenting churches should have. The first American state constitutions rejected the strict establishment of England, but at the same time the constitutions did not create and protect the religious freedom the way the U.S. Constitution and Bill of Rights would.

In England at this time an established church had special privileges and the support of the national government. The king was also the head of the church, and bishops and archbishops—princes of the Church—sat in the House of Lords. There was also a religious test for officeholding, which barred Jews, Deists, and Roman Catholics from holding office. At best England could be described as having a regime of grudging toleration for people who were not members of the Church of England. The U.S. Constitution of 1787 prohibited religious tests for officeholding, and by using the term "oath or affirmation," rather "swear an oath," opened officeholding to people of all faiths or no faith at all. The First Amendment, added to the Constitution in 1791, prohibited any establishment of religion at the national level and also guaranteed the free exercise of rights of all religions.

In this sense, the new state constitutions fell in between these two regimes, with some states being closer to the British model and some closer to what would become the American model under the Constitution and the Bill of Rights. Except for Virginia and New York, all of the first fourteen states had some form of religious test for officeholding, which was similar to what existed in England. These tests varied. Massachusetts specifically required that the governor "declare himself to be of the Christian religion," and all persons holding offices in the legislative or executive branch were required to "declare that I believe the Christian religion, and have a firm persuasion of its truth." Until 1792, Delaware required that all officeholders "profess faith in God the Father, and in Jesus Christ His only Son, and in the Holy Ghost," and that they "acknowledge" the "divine inspiration" of the Old and New Testaments. New Hampshire's constitution of 1784 required that all officeholders "shall be of the Protestant religion"—a provision that remained in place until 1877. New Jersey, North Carolina, South Carolina, and Georgia also required officeholders to be Protestants. South Carolina, which

had begun as a colony with religious freedom for all people, provided in its 1778 Constitution that "[t]he Christian Protestant religion shall be deemed, and is hereby constituted and declared to be, the established religion of this State." Until 1826, Maryland required that all officeholders be Christians. In 1867, Maryland required that all officeholders have a "belief in the existence of God." Until 1790, Pennsylvania required that officeholders believe in the divine inspiration of the Old and New Testament. In 1792, Delaware adopted such a provision. While requiring officeholders to be religious, some states did not want them to be *too* religious. Thus, Georgia, New York, North Carolina, and Tennessee all banned members of the clergy from holding public office.

Overall, the early state bills of rights show that at the time of the Revolution, the states had not fully clarified what they meant by religious freedom. For example, Section 2 of the Delaware Declaration of Rights of 1776 provided the following:

That all men have a natural and unalienable right to worship Almighty God according to the dictates of their own consciences and understandings; and that no man ought or of right can be compelled to attend any religious worship or maintain any ministry contrary to or against his own free will and consent, and that no authority can or ought to be vested in, or assumed by any power whatever that shall in any case interfere with, or in any manner controul the right of conscience in the free exercise of religious worship.

This was surely a powerful statement supporting free exercise and to some extent hostile to establishment. However, Section 3 of the same document declared "[t]hat all persons professing the Christian religion ought forever to enjoy equal rights and privileges in this state, unless, under colour of religion, any man disturb the peace, the happiness or safety of society." On top of this, as noted above, the constitution adopted a few weeks later required that all officeholders take an oath stating, "I, . . . do profess faith in God the Father, and in Jesus Christ His only Son, and in the Holy Ghost, one God, blessed for evermore; and I do acknowledge the holy scriptures of the Old and New Testament to be given by divine inspiration." Someone living in Delaware in 1777 might legitimately wonder if Unitarians or Jews were in fact full citizens of the state and entitled to freedom of worship.

Conflicting clauses like those in the Delaware Constitution (or the Protestant establishment) helped lead the framers of the U.S. Constitution to ban all religious tests for officeholding, and in the Bill of Rights to emphatically protect the "free exercise" of religion while guaranteeing that the United States could never establish any religion.

The "Palladium of Liberty"

Revolutionary-era Americans often referred to freedom of the press as the "palladium" of liberty. They understood a press that could criticize the government would be a "bulwark" (another one of their favorite terms) in preventing tyranny. Not surprisingly, most of the early state constitutions protected the press. Virginia's constitution represented the sometimes overblown language of the period: "That the freedom of the press is one of the great bulwarks of liberty, and can never be restrained but by despotic governments." Pennsylvania's language in its 1776 Constitution was more modern and more restrained: "That the people have a right to freedom of speech, and of writing, and publishing their sentiments; therefore the freedom of the press ought not to be restrained." Maryland's Constitution of 1776 was more direct: "[T]he liberty of the press ought to be inviolably preserved." Delaware's 1776 Declaration of Rights used the exact same language as Maryland. Significantly, none of these documents contained the kind of absolute prohibition on regulating a free press found in the U.S. Bill of Rights that Congress "shall make no law . . . ." Equally important, neither of these bills of rights phrased the language of a "free press" in terms that we would understand as banning a suppression of the press. The Virginia Bill of Rights, for example, says that only "despotic governments" restrain the press. The implication of this is that Virginia would be acting despotically if it did so. But, presumably the state might choose to act despotically under some circumstances. Similarly the "ought" in the Pennsylvania and Maryland documents suggests that the state "could" restrain the press, but simply should not do so. In its second constitution, adopted in 1778, South Carolina moved closer to a more affirmative protection, declaring "[t]hat the liberty of the press be inviolably preserved." Georgia's 1777 Constitution provided the most emphatic protection of the press: "[f]reedom of the press and trial by jury to remain inviolate forever." Oddly, Pennsylvania was the only state to protect freedom of speech at this time, although Maryland provided for freedom of speech for members of the state legislature, providing that "that freedom of speech and debates, or proceedings in the Legislature, ought not to be impeached in any other court or judicature." Only Pennsylvania, North Carolina, Massachusetts, and New Hampshire protected the right of assembly. A few states—New York and New Jersey, for example—did not protect freedom of the press, speech, or assembly.

One important theme in these state constitutions is the connection between liberty and the press. Without the press, the early constitution makers believed that their governments would be at risk. In an age when governments worry about a free press challenging the policies of an administration, the language of the Massachusetts Bill of Rights is particularly relevant. Written in the middle of the Revolution, the Massachusetts Bill asserted that "[t]he liberty of the press is essential to the security of freedom in a State; it ought not, therefore, to be restrained in this commonwealth." The founding generation, it seems, understood that a free press was vital to national security, because in the end, republican values and an informed citizenry was the key to a secure society.

Jury Trials and Due Process

Most of the new state constitutions had a clause protecting the rights of accused, providing for due process of law, and for preventing the adoption of arbitrary laws, such as writs of attainder or ex post facto laws. New York's first constitution declared the following:

> And this convention doth further ordain, determine, and declare, in the name and by the authority of the good people of this State, that trial by jury, in all cases in which it hath heretofore been used in the colony of New York, shall be established and remain inviolate forever. And that no acts of attainder shall be passed by the legislature of this State for crimes, other than those committed before the termination of the present war; and that such acts shall not work a corruption of blood. And further, that the legislature of this State shall, at no time hereafter, institute any new court or courts, but such as shall proceed according to the course of the common law.

New Jersey emphatically declared "that the inestimable right of trial by jury shall remain confirmed as a part of the law of this Colony, without repeal, forever." The framers in New Jersey were not yet certain if their jurisdiction was a "colony" or a state, but they understood that they wanted to be certain they would always have a trial by jury. New Jersey did not have any other protections for criminal justice or due process. South Carolina's 1776 Constitution provided for jury trials in civil suits, if either party asked for one, but not in criminal cases.

Delaware, on the other hand, provided elaborate protections for jury trials and accused criminals. Much of the language from that document would appear, almost word for word, in the Fourth, Fifth, Sixth, and Eighth Amendments to the U.S. Constitution. Delaware's 1776 Declaration of Rights prohibited "retrospective law" (what the U.S. Constitution would call ex post facto laws); and required civil trials "speedily without delay, according to the law of the land," with juries to determine the facts in all civil and criminal cases. The Delaware framers considered "that trial by jury of facts where they arise is one of the greatest securities of the lives, liberties and estates of the people." In addition, Delware's Constitution required a "speedy trial by an impartial jury" in all criminal cases, with the accused having a right to confront his accusers, subpoena witnesses, and "not be compelled to give evidence against himself." The document prohibited "excessive bail," "excessive fines," and "cruel or unusual punishments." The section on searches and seizures was particularly detailed: "That all warrants without oath to search suspected places, or to seize any person or his property, are grievous and oppressive; and all general warrants to search suspected places, or to apprehend all persons suspected, without naming or describing the place or any person in special, are illegal and ought not to be granted."

Virginia, Pennsylvania, and Maryland had similar protections of due process, often with the same language. Given the close proximity of these three states, it is not surprising that they borrowed and learned from each other in writing constitutions that protected civil liberties. Virginia's jury provision mandated that juries have twelve members and that verdicts be unanimous. Massachusetts went further than most states in its emphatic language and in its guarantees, including the right to an attorney. Thus, in 1780 the Bay State's constitution provided that:

> No subject shall be held to answer for any crimes or no offence until the same if fully and plainly, substantially and formally, described to him; or be compelled to accuse, or furnish evidence against himself; and every subject shall have a right to produce all proofs that may be favorable to him; to meet the witnesses against him face to face, and to be fully heard in his defence by himself, or his counsel at his election. And no subject shall be arrested, imprisoned, despoiled, or deprived of his property, immunities, or privileges, put out of the protection of the law, exiled or deprived of his life, liberty, or estate, but by the judgment of his peers, or the law of the land.

Fundamental Liberty

In general, the newly independent states had a sharper sense of the need to be protected from arbitrary government than they did for protecting the rights of freedom of speech, press, or religion. Yet, with one exception, nowhere in the world were civil liberties more protected than under the new constitutions of the American states. That one exception had to do with the most fundamental civil liberty of all: the right to personal autonomy as a free person.

On the eve of the Revolution, slavery was legal in all of the thirteen colonies. In explaining to the world why they were revolting, the Americans asserted "[t]hat all men are created equal; that they are endowed by their Creator with certain unalienable rights; that among these are life, liberty, and the pursuit of happiness." Yet, the man who wrote these words, Thomas Jefferson, owned about 175 slaves at the time. Many of the other signers of the Declaration were slave owners as well. Not surprisingly, there was a great conflict in the new nation between the assertions of equality and the struggle for liberty and the fact that so many leaders of the Revolution were slave owners. Not a few Englishmen and many Americans read the Declaration and wondered, as did Samuel Johnson, "How is it that we hear the loudest yelps for liberty among the drivers of negroes?" This question bothered some early constitution makers. But only three of the new states confronted the issue of slavery in their first constitutions.

Virginians borrowed some of Jefferson's language when writing their constitution. Thus, Section 1 of the Virginia Declaration of Rights began with the words, "That all men are by nature equally free and independent, and have certain inherent rights." The section ended with more language that mirrored Jefferson's Declaration, asserting that free people "cannot, by any compact, deprive or divest their posterity, namely, the enjoyment of life and liberty, with the means of acquiring and possessing property, and pursuing and obtaining happiness and safety." Had Virginia only used this language, the state's framers would have been attacking slavery directly. But, the Virginia framers were cautious and careful, and between these two clauses they inserted language designed to exclude slaves. Thus, the entire provision of Section 1 read:

> That all men are by nature equally free and independent, and have certain inherent rights, of which, when they enter into a state of society, they cannot, by any compact, deprive or divest their posterity, namely, the enjoyment of life and liberty, with the means of acquiring and possessing property, and pursuing and obtaining happiness and safety.

The phrase "when they enter into a state of society" was understood to limit the language of the document to free people. Slaves had not entered into "a state of society" but rather were property owned by people in society.

Four years later, Massachusetts began its Declaration of Rights with similar language, which did not have a proviso excluding those not "in a state of society." Article I of the Massachusetts Constitution of 1780 declared:

> All men are born free and equal, and have certain natural, essential, and unalienable rights; among which may be reckoned the right of enjoying and defending their lives and liberties; that of acquiring, possessing, and protecting property; in fine, that of seeking and obtaining their safety and happiness.

In 1781, Massachusetts courts would use this provision to declare slaves to be free, and by 1783 slavery would cease to exist in the state. In 1783, New Hampshire adopted a constitution which declared that "all men are born equal and independent," with natural rights, "among which are enjoying and defending life and liberty." This clause would be interpreted within the state to end slavery.

The remaining states did not end slavery by constitutional provision, and of course, in the southern states slavery would exist until the Civil War; the Emancipation Proclamation, and the Thirteenth Amendment ended slavery. In the North, slavery would end through gradual emancipation over a number of years. Civil liberties for blacks in the North would be slow to arrive. They would not arrive for most southern blacks until after 1865.

Despite the failure to extend civil liberty—and fundamental freedom—to all Americans, the first state constitutions were generally sensitive to individual rights, although not to the extent that the U.S. Bill of Rights would be. These first state constitutions, however, set the stage for the more expansive protection of civil liberties that James Madison would propose to Congress in 1789 and the states would ratify in 1791.

PAUL FINKELMAN

References and Further Reading

Adams, Willi Paul. *The First American Constitutions: Republican Ideology and the Making of States Constitutions in the Revolutionary Era*. Chapel Hill: University of North Carolina Press, 1980.

Conley, Patrick T., and John P. Kaminski, eds. *The Bill of Rights and the States: The Colonial and Revolutionary Origins of American Liberties*. Madison, WI: Madison House, 1992.

Rutland, Robert A. *The Birth of the Bill of Rights, 1776–1791*. Chapel Hill: University of North Carolina Press, 1955.

Wood, Gordon. *The Creation of the American Republic, 1776–1787*. Chapel Hill: University of North Carolina Press, 1969.

BILL OF RIGHTS: ADOPTION OF

The Constitution of 1787 did not contain a bill of rights, although it did have some protections for some civil liberties. The original Constitution prohibited ex post facto laws and bills of attainder, preserved the right of a jury trial in criminal cases, and banned religious tests for officeholding. The document gave life tenure to judges, which insulated them from being removed for decisions that displeased the president or other officeholders. The document provided for free speech for members of Congress but otherwise did not protect rights of expression, such as freedom of speech, press, assembly, or petition.

The lack of a bill of rights was not an oversight. On August 20, 1787, Charles Pinckney of South Carolina "submitted sundry propositions" to the Convention that were sent to the Committee on Detail. While some of Pinckney's propositions ultimately were included in the body of the Constitution, the committee ignored his proposals for a guarantee of freedom of the press and for a protection against quartering troops in private homes. On September 12, the Convention rejected Massachusetts delegate Elbridge Gerry's proposal that the right to a jury in civil cases be guaranteed by the Constitution. Virginia's George Mason then suggested that the entire Constitution be "prefaced with a Bill of Rights." He thought that "with the aid of the State declarations, a bill might be prepared in a few hours." Roger Sherman of Connecticut argued that this was unnecessary because the Constitution did not repeal the state bills of rights. Mason replied that federal laws would be "paramount to State Bills of Rights." This argument, however correct, had little effect on the Convention, which defeated Mason's motion with all states voting no.

The next day Gerry failed to get the Convention to guarantee juries for civil trials. Pinckney then joined Gerry in proposing that the Constitution have a provision that "the liberty of the Press should be inviolably observed." Roger Sherman again argued against specific protections for liberty on the ground that under a government of limited powers they were unnecessary because "[t]he power of Congress does not extend to the Press." By a vote of five states for and six against, the Convention then defeated the motion to protect "the liberty of the Press."

On Saturday, September 15, 1787, the penultimate day of the Convention, George Mason expressed his reservations about the Constitution, noting, "There is no Declaration of Rights, and the laws of the general government being paramount to the laws and Constitution of the several States, the Declaration of Rights in the separate States are no security."

Mason complained that under this Constitution, "the people" were not "secured even the enjoyment of the benefit of the common law."

Mason feared that the Senate and the president would combine "to accomplish what usurpations they pleased upon the rights and liberties of the people," while the federal judiciary would "absorb and destroy the judiciaries of the several States." He thought the expansive powers of Congress threatened the "security" of "the people for their rights." Without a bill of rights, all this was possible. He complained, "There is no declaration of any kind, for preserving the liberty of the press, or the trial by jury in civil causes; nor against the danger of standing armies in time of peace." For these reasons, Mason refused to put his signature to the new Constitution.

Another Virginian, Edmund Randolph, also refused to sign. He proposed a second Convention to consider amendments, including a bill of rights. Elbridge Gerry listed a number of problems with the Constitution, including the dangers posed by the aristocratic nature of the Senate and the centralizing tendencies of the commerce power. But, he could "get over all these" defects "if the rights of the Citizens were not rendered insecure" by the virtually unlimited power of Congress under the necessary and proper clause and the lack of a guarantee of jury trials in civil cases.

Throughout the next nine months, as the states debated the new constitution, the opponents of ratification—known as the Anti-Federalists—railed against the lack of a bill of rights in the new constitution. Many Anti-Federalists, such as Patrick Henry and Richard Henry Lee, used the bill of rights as a stalking horse for their desire to detail the entire constitution. They wanted a second convention to rewrite the entire document. Other Anti-Federalists were more sincere in their opposition. James Madison called them "honest anti-federalists," because they were not opposed to a new stronger government, but only feared that such a government would become tyrannical without a bill of rights.

Madison and other Federalists scoffed at such fears. They opposed the addition of a bill of rights, asserting that it was (1) unnecessary, (2) redundant, (3) useless, (4) actually dangerous to the liberties of the people, (5) that its presence would violate the principles of republican government embodied in the Constitution, or some combination of these.

They argued that the Constitution created a government of limited powers and thus Congress could not do anything that it was not specifically empowered to do. Personal liberty, they argued, would be protected by the states. Congress could not create a national religion or suppress freedom of the press,

they argued, because it lacked the power to do so. Thus, in the Convention, Pennsylvania's James Wilson asserted that one purpose of the states was "to preserve the rights of individuals." Oliver Ellsworth of Connecticut explained that he looked to the state governments "for the preservation of his rights." Roger Sherman argued that "the State Declarations of Rights are not repealed by this Constitution; and being in force are sufficient." He believed that the national legislature might "be safely trusted" not to interfere with the liberties of the people.

Federalists also argued that the main body of the Constitution already had some protections of liberty, such as bans on ex post facto laws or religious tests for officeholding. Thus, combined with the notion of a limited government, a bill of rights was redundant. But, Madison also argued that a Bill of Rights was useless. In a letter to Thomas Jefferson (who was in France at the time), Madison explained that there was no bill of rights because "experience proves the inefficacy of a bill of rights on those occasions when its controul is most needed. Repeated violations of these parchment barriers have been committed by overbearing majorities in every state." He noted that in Virginia he had "seen the bill of rights violated in every instance where it has been opposed to a popular current." He warned that "restrictions however strongly marked on paper will never be regarded when opposed to the decided sense of the public; and after repeated violations in extraordinary cases, they will lose even their ordinary efficacy." No bill of rights was better, in Madison's mind, than one that might be ignored.

Federalists also feared that a bill of rights would be dangerous to the liberties of the people because any rights not protected would be given up. James Wilson asked who would "be bold enough to undertake to enumerate all the rights of the people?" He thought no one could, but warned that "if the enumeration is not complete, everything not expressly mentioned will be presumed to be purposely omitted." Thus, he believed a bill of rights "not only unnecessary, but improper." Alexander Hamilton made a similar point when arguing that a bill of rights was "not only unnecessary in the proposed Constitution, but would even be dangerous. They would contain various exceptions to powers not granted; and, on this very account, would afford a colorable pretext to claim more than were granted."

Finally, some Federalists argued that under a republican government a bill of rights was unnecessary. Oliver Ellsworth, a future chief justice of the United States, argued that a bill of rights was something that the people wrested from the king; thus, in America a bill of rights was "insignificant since government is considered as originating from the people, and all the power government now has is a grant from the people." Similarly, James Wilson argued that "it would have been superfluous and absurd, to have stipulated with a federal body of our own creation, that we should enjoy those privileges, of which we are not divested." North Carolina's James Iredell maintained that in England a bill of rights was necessary because of the Crown's "usurpations" of the people's liberties. But, under the new Constitution, the people delegated power to the national government, and thus such usurpations by the national government were impossible.

The Federalists won the debate over the Constitution, and by July eleven states had ratified the document. However, five states recommended that the new government amend the new Constitution in various ways, including adding protections for civil liberties. During the ratification struggle in Virginia, James Madison argued that a bill of rights was unnecessary and sincerely believed that most of the leading Anti-Federalists were not truly interested in a bill of rights, but rather simply wanted to derail the Constitution. At the Virginia convention, he was willing to compromise by supporting the idea that the convention could recommend amendments, but only after the convention had ratified the Constitution. Madison still did not believe a bill of rights was needed, but he did believe that some amendment protecting civil liberties, if carefully framed, might not harm the Constitution. He also realized that some Virginians—especially the Baptists who were a significant force in his part of the state—supported the new form of government but nevertheless sincerely wanted a bill of rights as well.

After ratification, when campaigning for a seat in the First Congress, Madison once again considered the issue of a bill of rights. Madison discussed this in a letter to Rev. George Eve, an influential Baptist leader in his district. Madison freely admitted his disagreement with Eve in that he did not see in the Constitution "those serious dangers which have alarmed many respectable Citizens" including Eve. Thus, he told Eve that until the Constitution was ratified, he had been unwilling to support any calls for amendments, because he believed they were "calculated to throw the States into dangerous contentions, and to furnish the secret enemies of the Union with an opportunity of promoting its dissolution." However, with the Constitution ratified he was willing to support "amendments, if pursued with a proper moderation and in a proper mode" because under such circumstances they would "be not only safe, but may well serve the double purpose of satisfying the minds of well meaning opponents, and of providing additional guards in favour of liberty."

Madison told Eve that "[u]nder this change of circumstances, it is my sincere opinion that the Constitution ought to be revised, and that the first Congress meeting under it, ought to prepare and recommend to the States . . . provisions for all essential rights, particularly the rights of Conscience in the fullest latitude, the freedom of the press, trials by jury, security against general warrants, &c."

After his letter to Eve, Madison publicly declared that he would work for amendments if elected to Congress. This public support for amendments swayed the Baptists and helped secure Madison's election to Congress. Once in Congress, Madison urged the House to support a bill of rights. He still did not think one was necessary, but he told the House he was "bound in honor and in duty" to bring the amendments forward. His plan was to "advocate them until they shall be finally adopted or rejected by a constitutional majority of this House."

The Federalist leaders of the House did not want to be bothered with amendments, as they were busy creating a national government. But Madison argued that postponement would play into the hands of those extreme Anti-Federalists who had predicted that the new national government would create a tyranny. He argued that "if we continue to postpone from time to time, and refuse to let the subject come into view, it may well occasion suspicions, which, though not well founded, may tend to inflame or prejudice the public mind against our decisions." Madison feared that the "very respectable number of our constituents" who had asked for amendments might conclude that Congress was "not sincere in our desire to incorporate such amendments in the constitution as will secure those rights, which they consider as not sufficiently guarded." Although about to propose amendments, Madison was still not advocating them for their substance. Rather, he argued he had a moral obligation to present them and that it would be politically expedient for Congress to accept them. When Connecticut's Roger Sherman proposed delaying any discussion of amendments, Madison argued that it was important to consider amendments to prove to the Anti-Federalists that the supporters of the Constitution were also "sincerely devoted to liberty and a Republican Government" and not attempting to "lay the foundation of an aristocracy or despotism." He reminded the House of those who had "apprehensions" that the new government wished to "deprive them of the liberty for which they valiantly fought and honorably bled." He believed that many who had opposed the Constitution were now ready "to join their support to the cause of Federalism, if they were satisfied on this one point." Furthermore, he reminded the House that North Carolina and Rhode

Island had not yet ratified the Constitution, but that amendments might lure them into the union.

In proposing the amendments, Madison showed little passion. He told the House that he had "never considered" a bill of rights "so essential to the federal constitution" that it would have been allowed to impede ratification. But, with the Constitution ratified, Madison was willing to concede "that in a certain form and to a certain extent, such a provision was neither improper nor altogether useless." The amendments he proposed were unlikely to displease the hard-line Anti-Federalists, and in fact they did not. He proposed only amendments that were universally accepted, such as a protection of freedom of speech and freedom of worship. He noted that they were "limited to points which are important in the eyes of many and can be objectionable in those of none." Proudly he noted that "the structure & stamina of the Govt. are as little touched as possible."

Madison initially proposed that the amendments refer to specific provisions in the Constitution. So, for example, limitations on establishing religion or infringing on a free press would be inserted in Article I, Section 9 of the Constitution, which set out limits on congressional power. Fortunately, Roger Sherman prevailed upon Madison to reorganize his proposals as a series of numbered amendments that resembled the state bills of rights. This was a significant change, because it made the amendments into a coherent document as a "bill of rights."

Congress debated Madison's proposed amendments for much of the summer. Most of Madison's speeches were along the lines of his opening remarks. He wanted the amendments to eliminate the discord between those who feared the Constitution and those who supported it. But on one issue Madison became somewhat passionate. His proposed amendments had not only limited the federal government. He also proposed limits on the state governments. Two brief speeches showed that Madison remained more committed to limiting the powers of the states than to limiting the power of the national government. Thus, he passionately supported a proposal that would have prohibited the states from infringing "the equal right of conscience . . . freedom of speech or the press, . . . [and] the right of trial by jury in criminal cases." Madison thought this was "the most valuable amendment in the whole list." Although the House approved this clause, the Senate did not, and thus these rights would not become applicable to the states until after the adoption of the Fourteenth Amendment and its modern development, starting with *Gitlow v. New York* (1925). Similarly, Madison strongly opposed adding the word "expressly" to what became the Tenth Amendment. Madison thought that this would give the states too much power.

On September 24, 1789, the House and Senate agreed on twelve amendments to the Constitution. They were then sent to the states for ratification. The first two dealt with the size of the House and congressional salaries. Neither was ratified at the time. The amendment on salaries would have prevented Congress from raising its salary during any current term. Over the years, a number of states ratified this amendment, and in 1992, over two centuries after it was proposed, three-fourths of the states had ratified it and it was added to the Constitution as the Twenty-Seventh Amendment.

Nine states quickly ratified amendments three through twelve. Two states, Georgia and Connecticut, rejected the amendments, accepting the Federalist argument that they were unnecessary. Massachusetts apparently ratified the amendments, but never sent the ratification on to Congress. Before the amendments could be added to the Constitution, however, Vermont was admitted to the Union. Thus, with fourteen states, the amendments needed eleven ratifications. Vermont quickly ratified the amendments, but Virginia held out. The Anti-Federalists in the state, led by Patrick Henry, did not want the Bill of Rights ratified because they were holding out for a second convention, which would undo the Constitution and create a weaker national government. Henry understood that once a bill of rights was ratified, most opposition to the Constitution would disappear. On this point he was correct. On December 15, 1791, Virginia finally ratified the Bill of Rights. With this ratification, Anti-Federalism disappeared along with most opposition to the Constitution. Henry would in fact soon join the emerging Federalist Party and support the stronger national government. Madison would be remembered as the father of the Bill of Rights, albeit a clearly reluctant one. He never thought the nation needed a bill of rights, but in the end the document proved to be his greatest legacy and his most important contribution to American history.

PAUL FINKELMAN

References and Further Reading

Amar, Akhil. *The Bill of Rights: Creation and Reconstruction.* New Haven, CT: Yale University Press, 1998.

Cogan, Neil H. *The Complete Bill of Rights: The Drafts, Debates, Sources, and Origins.* New York: Oxford University Press, 1997.

Finkelman, Paul, *James Madison and the Bill of Rights: A Reluctant Paternity*, Supreme Court Review 1990 (1991): 301–47.

Rutland, Robert A. *The Birth of the Bill of Rights, 1776–1791*. Chapel Hill: University of North Carolina Press, 1955.

Veit, Helen E., Kenneth R. Bowling, and Charlene Bangs Bickford. *Creating the Bill of Rights: The Documentary Record of the First Federal Congress*. Baltimore: Johns Hopkins University Press, 1991.

BILL OF RIGHTS: STRUCTURE

The structure of the American Bill of Rights reflects its eighteenth-century origins. The framers of the Constitution did not include a bill of rights because they honestly believed that one was unnecessary. They understood that they were creating a government of limited powers. As Gen. Charles Cotesworth Pinckney told the South Carolina legislature after the Convention, "[I]t is admitted, on all hands, that the general government has no powers but what are expressly granted by the Constitution, and that all rights not expressed were reserved by the several states." Thus, framers like James Madison, James Wilson, and Roger Sherman argued that there was no need to prohibit the government from infringing on civil liberties because the government had no power to do so.

Tied to this structural argument was the belief that fundamental liberties, such as those in a bill or rights, had to be taken from a king or monarch. The founders took their lessons from English history. The barons at Runnymede surrounded King John I and forced him to sign the Magna Carta. In the seventeenth century, Parliament struggled with the king to gain the English Bill of Rights and other laws that protected basic liberties. The framers reasoned that Parliament or "the people" had to force the king to give them these liberties and rights. Along these lines, the framers argued that in a republic this was unnecessary because the people already had these rights and liberties. Because the government was representative, the people could never lose these rights because the government represented the people.

Anti-Federalists and even some supporters of the new Constitution did not accept these arguments. They argued that a democratically elected legislature could still take away rights from the people. They also feared that the new central government might fail to represent the interests of "the people" because the legislature was so distant from the people it represented and the terms were so long that members of the House and Senate would become estranged from their constituents. Combined with a president from far away who served for four years, the Anti-Federalists feared the new government would trample on the liberties of the people. Some Anti-Federalists feared that the president would become a king or a dictator. Thus, they demanded a bill of rights to protect their liberties.

The Bill of Rights reflected the concerns of both the Federalists and the Anti-Federalists. For the most part, the Bill of Rights did not *grant* liberties to the people but rather placed limitations on what the government could do. These amendments thus created "negative rights." Another aspect of the bill of rights was its use of general language, rather than specific details.

The First Amendment illustrates this. The amendment does not give the people the right to worship as they wish, or to speak as they wish. Rather, the amendment says that "Congress shall make no law . . . prohibiting the free exercise" of religion or "abridging the freedom of speech, press, or the right of the people to peaceably assemble and to petition the government for a redress of grievances." The amendment assumes that the people have these rights. There is no need for a toleration act in America, as there was in England. The king could in theory grant toleration to the people to worship as they wished, because the king, as the sovereign, had the right to set the religious standard for the nation. But under the American republic the people retained this right. Thus, the people did not need the permission of the government to speak or pray as they wish because the people were the sovereign, and so they had this right. Thus, under the Bill of Rights, the government was prohibited from taking these rights away from the people. Similarly, with this language the people could make no claim on Congress to facilitate these rights. Thus, for example, while Congress cannot pass laws "abridging the freedom [of] . . . the press," Congress has no obligation to provide every citizen with his or her printing press.

The only clause in the First Amendment that does not presume that the people have rights is the establishment clause. Congress could conceivably have passed a law establishing a national religion. Madison and other framers denied that Congress had the power to do this—it was not an enumerated power. But, Madison also did not have any problem adding this extra level of protection against congressional action.

Most of the rest of the Bill of Rights was also phrased in negative terms, rather than the granting of positive rights. Thus, the Second Amendment presumed that the people of the states would be able to have organized militias, as the states already had. Thus, the amendment simply said that Congress could not disband the state militias. But the Federalists who controlled Congress were not willing to go beyond the simple statement that "a well regulated militia" was "necessary to the security of a free

State." Madison and his colleagues ignored Anti-Federalists from Pennsylvania who demanded elaborate amendments setting out positive rights in great detail. This group of Pennsylvanians, who had been in the distinct minority at the state's ratifying convention, wanted amendments declaring "that the people have a right to bear arms for the defense of themselves and their own state, or the United States, or for the purpose of killing game" and that "the inhabitants of the several states shall have liberty to fowl and hunt in seasonable times, on the lands they hold, and on all other lands in the United States not enclosed, and in like manner to fish in all navigable waters, and others not private property, without being restrained therein by any laws to be passed by the legislature of the United States." Such provisions were too specific, and did not fit with the general pattern of using the Bill of Rights to place limits on Congress.

The "negative rights" or limitations on Congress in some ways provide for more universal protection of civil liberties than positive rights language might have accomplished. The Third Amendment assumed that soldiers could never be quartered in private homes except under narrowly defined circumstances created by positive law. Similarly, the Fourth Amendment "assumes" that there is a right to be secure against unreasonable searches, and so the amendment denies the government the right to conduct a search except under certain circumstances. In the same way, the Fifth Amendment declares that no one can be tried without a grand jury indictment. This limitation goes to the government action, and requires no act of enforcement by the person under investigation. Similarly, the right against self-incrimination is presumed and cannot be taken away, rather than given in the Fifth Amendment. The same is true with the Eighth Amendment's ban on cruel and unusual punishment. People are not protected from torture; rather the government simply may not use torture. A curious exception to idea of general rights is the Seventh Amendment, which provides for jury trials in civil cases where the amount at issue exceeds twenty dollars. In the modern world, this limitation is absurdly outdated.

The Sixth and Seventh Amendments contain a series of positive rights, perhaps because these rights—to a jury trial or to legal counsel—were not seen as fundamentally inherent to a nature of free political society. The rights to a speedy and public trial by an impartial jury with subpoena power, confrontation of witnesses, and an attorney are new positive rights that were not secure in English law and not fundamental to a republican society. The right to counsel was truly an innovation—something never before secured by law.

The Ninth Amendment was the most creative of all the amendments, and goes directly to the heart of the way that the framers saw positive and negative rights. Many Federalists opposed a bill of rights because they thought that it was impossible to write one. They doubted the ability of anyone to list all the rights of the people and any rights left out would be lost. This argument assumed that a complete enumeration of all rights would be impossible. Thus, in defending the Constitution in the Pennsylvania ratifying convention, James Wilson asked who would "be bold enough to undertake to enumerate all the rights of the people?" He thought no one could, but warned that "if the enumeration is not complete, everything not expressly mentioned will be presumed to be purposely omitted." He later argued that members of the Convention considered a bill of rights "not only unnecessary, but improper." Alexander Hamilton made a similar point, arguing that a bill of rights was "not only unnecessary in the proposed Constitution, but would even be dangerous. [It] would contain various exceptions to powers not granted; and, on this very account, would afford a colorable pretext to claim more than were granted." Madison agreed with this analysis. He told Jefferson that if a bill of rights were added to the Constitution, it had to "be so framed as not to imply powers not meant to be included in the enumeration."

During the debates over the Constitution, Oliver Ellsworth, who would later become chief justice of the United States, made a similar point. He noted with frustration the persistent Anti-Federalist complaint that "[t]here is no declaration of any kind to preserve the liberty of the press, etc." He answered, "Nor is liberty of conscience, or of matrimony, or of burial of the dead; it is enough that Congress have no power to prohibit either, and can have no temptation. This objection is answered in that the states have all the power originally, and Congress have only what the states grant them." In part, Ellsworth reaffirmed the impossibility of listing all the rights of the people in a bill of rights. Madison responded to this problem with the Ninth Amendment, which provides that "[t]he enumeration in [the] Constitution, of certain rights, shall not be construed to deny or disparage others retained by the people." Since the amendments listed few positive rights, Madison wanted to be sure that no one believed the government could take basic rights from the people. Thus, the Ninth Amendment preserved those rights that were either too obvious to name—such as the right "of matrimony, or of burial of the dead," and also those rights that the framers might not even have thought of. In the modern era, this amendment has helped create a right of privacy that protects reproductive rights and other kinds of personal privacy.

The Bill of Rights is a creation of the eighteenth century, written by politicians who were both pragmatists and skeptical of the power of government. Thus, it lacks large promises—such as the right to a job, housing, food, medical care, or education—which are found in some modern bills of rights. The Bill of Rights in fact makes few promises—such as that persons arrested will have fair trials, due process, and the right to an attorney. Rather, for the most part, the Bill of Rights simply limits government power so that individuals can exercise rights they presumably have always had—such as the right to speak, write, or worship as they wish, to be secure from intrusion in their homes, and to be free from being forced to incriminate themselves or face torture from their own government. While the government sometimes tried to trample their rights, most Americans, most of the time, have been able to exercise their rights without intrusion from the government. Moreover, because the rights come from what the government cannot do, for the most part Americans have been able to exercise them without having to depend on Congress or the president to vindicate their rights. Similarly, by placing a limitation on what the government can do, the Bill of Rights provided a legal claim to be taken into the courts to resist government misbehavior. Ironically, in this way the Bill of Rights has functioned to force citizens to challenge their own government, but in doing so they did not approach rights as supplicants. They did not have to ask the president or Congress for their rights, as English citizens had to ask the king for rights. Rather, they could go to the courts and demand that the national government not take away from them what they already possess, and use the explicit limitations in the Bill of Rights or the more general all-purpose limitation in the Ninth Amendment to vindicate their rights.

PAUL FINKELMAN

References and Further Reading

Amar, Akhil. *The Bill of Rights: Creation and Reconstruction*. New Haven, CT: Yale University Press, 1998.
Finkelman, Paul, *James Madison and the Bill of Rights: A Reluctant Paternity*, Supreme Court Review 1990 (1991): 301–47.
———, *The Ten Amendments as a Declaration of Rights*, Southern Illinois University Law Review 16 (1992): 351–96.
Rutland, Robert A. *The Birth of the Bill of Rights, 1776–1791*. Chapel Hill: University of North Carolina Press, 1955.
Veit, Helen E., Kenneth R. Bowling, and Charlene Bangs Bickford. *Creating the Bill of Rights: The Documentary Record of the First Federal Congress*. Baltimore: Johns Hopkins University Press, 1991.

BINGHAM, JOHN ARMOR (1815–1900)

John Armor Bingham, an Ohio lawyer, was a prominent figure in American politics and government in the latter half of the nineteenth century. He participated in many of the key events surrounding and shortly after the Civil War. Most significantly, Bingham played a pivotal role in drafting the Fourteenth Amendment. Dissenting in *Adamson v. California* (1947), Justice Hugo Black referred to Bingham as "the Madison of the first section of the Fourteenth Amendment." Bingham's views on the Fourteenth Amendment, particularly as those views pertain to whether it "incorporates" the first eight amendments of the U.S. Constitution against the states, continue to be debated.

John Bingham was born on January 21, 1815, in Mercer County, Pennsylvania. His parents were Hugh Bingham and Ester Bailey Bingham. Not much is known about his mother, who died when John was twelve. After his mother died in 1827, John relocated to Cadiz, Ohio, where he lived with his uncle, Thomas Bingham, off and on for four years. At fourteen, Bingham attended Mercer Academy, then Franklin College in New Athens, Ohio, for two years. While at Franklin College, Bingham became friends with Titus Basfield. Basfield was a former slave who became the first black person to earn a degree from an Ohio college. He and Bingham corresponded for over a quarter-century following their acquaintance at Franklin. After college, Bingham read law in Pennsylvania, the typical preparation for aspiring attorneys at the time. He studied with John J. Pearson and William Stewart, two prominent Mercer, Pennsylvania, lawyers. Bingham was admitted to practice on March 25, 1840. He returned to Cadiz that same year and four years later married his cousin Amanda Bingham (his uncle Thomas's daughter), with whom he had three children.

Abolitionist views run like a crimson thread throughout John Bingham's early life. Perhaps the most compelling indication of the influences shaping his assessment of slavery is a passing reference to his mother that he made in 1862. Calling "chattel slavery . . . an 'infernal atrocity,'" Bingham added, "I thank God that I learned to lisp it at my mother's knee." Both Hugh and Thomas Bingham were active in abolitionist political circles. Pennsylvania Governor Joseph R. Ritner, patron of John Bingham's politically active father, was an outspoken abolitionist who was described as a person "[who] appoint[ed] to high and responsible stations . . . individuals notorious for their zeal in the cause of abolition." Bingham's uncle (eventually his father-in-law), Thomas, was an associate judge of the Harrison County Court of Common

Pleas. Bingham's father and his uncle were antislavery Whigs. In time, both became "free soilers" opposing the extension of slavery to territories of the United States. Among John Bingham's childhood friends was Matthew Simpson. Simpson became a very influential bishop in the Methodist Episcopal Church in America. An advisor to President Abraham Lincoln and a close friend to Lincoln and General Ulysses S. Grant, Bishop Simpson was among those who urged Lincoln to issue the Emancipation Proclamation while the President was reluctant to do so. Simpson delivered the oration at two of President Lincoln's funerals, at the White House, and in Springfield, Illinois. Franklin College, John Bingham's alma mater, was characterized as "the fountain-head of the abolition sentiment of eastern Ohio."

Bingham's career trajectory was shaped by the antislavery convictions he developed growing up in eastern Ohio and western Pennsylvania as well as by the divisions that exploded in the Civil War. The year 1856 was a tumultuous one in American history. Foreshadowing the Civil War, the border conflict known as "Bleeding Kansas" raged with cruel atrocities on both sides. Murderous hatred stalked the halls of the Capitol, where South Carolina Congressman Preston Brooks almost beat Massachusetts Senator Charles Sumner to death with a cane after Sumner delivered a speech excoriating supporters of the pro-slavery faction in Kansas. Amid this disorder, together with his professional mentors, John J. Pearson and William Stewart, John Bingham joined the new Republican Party. Founded in 1854 in Ripon, Wisconsin, the Republican Party unsuccessfully ran John C. Fremont for president in 1856 on the slogan, "Free soil, free labor, free men." Two years previously, Republican Bingham was first elected to the U.S. House of Representatives as a member of the Thirty-fourth Congress. He served four terms until March 1863. Bingham's views during this period are illustrated by his observation on the July 21, 1861, Union defeat at the First Battle of Bull Run (Manassas): "[W]e need these reverses to bring our people up to the peril of not abolishing slavery."

Defeated in his bid for a fifth term in 1864, Bingham was appointed a major in the Union Army by President Lincoln, serving as judge advocate. Lincoln's assassination on April 15, 1865, thrust Bingham into the national spotlight. With Joseph Holt, Army judge advocate general, and Henry L. Burnett, another assistant judge advocate, Bingham argued the government's case against the eight conspirators before a nine-man military commission. Bingham culminated his extensive summation by saying, "What these conspirators did in the execution of this conspiracy by the hand of one of their co-conspirators [John Wilkes Booth] they did themselves; his act, done in the prosecution of the common design, was the act of all the parties to the treasonable combination, because done in execution and furtherance of their guilty and treasonable agreement."

Bingham was again elected to Congress in 1865. Two events dominated his second term of service: the impeachment of President Andrew Johnson and drafting of the Fourteenth Amendment. The role that Bingham played in both was defined by his participation in a group of American political figures known as Radical Republicans. These prominent members of Congress and of President Lincoln's Cabinet clashed often with Lincoln's successor, Andrew Johnson. Their fundamental difference with President Johnson revolved around the pace and direction of post-Civil War Reconstruction. For the Radical Republicans, "reconstructing" the defeated southern states required basically altering the social and political landscape of the former Confederacy in ways designed to protect the rights of former slaves—alterations they saw as the precondition for readmitting these states in rebellion to the Union. Johnson took a much more conciliatory and accommodating view. Amid a series of vitriolic clashes over three pieces of Reconstruction legislation, during which Johnson also vetoed the Civil Rights Act of 1866, he fired Radical Republican Edwin M. Stanton as secretary of war, in violation of the 1867 Tenure of Office Act. In response, the House of Representatives impeached Johnson. Bingham chaired the House Committee that argued, unsuccessfully, the articles of impeachment before the Senate.

While Radical Republicans and President Johnson locked horns over congressional Reconstruction, a Joint Committee on Reconstruction was at work on a constitutional amendment. Bingham opposed the 1866 Civil Rights Bill because he wanted the federal Bill of Rights "enforced everywhere," and he believed that this goal could be accomplished only by a constitutional amendment. As a Joint Committee member, he drafted (some say collaborating with Pennsylvania Representative Thaddeus Stevens) the first of the amendment's five sections. Section 1 reads: "All persons born or naturalized in the United States, and subject to the jurisdiction thereof, are citizens of the United States and of the State wherein they reside. No State shall make or enforce any law which shall abridge the privileges or immunities of citizens of the United States; nor shall any State deprive any person of life, liberty, or property, without due process of law; nor deny to any person within its jurisdiction the equal protection of the laws."

Writing in *McCreary County, Kentucky v. American Civil Liberties Union of Kentucky* (2005), Justice David Souter characterized the Fourteenth Amendment as "the most significant structural [constitutional] provision adopted since the original Framing." Yale Law School professor Akhil Reed Amar offers this assessment of Bingham's contribution: "It was Bingham's generation that in effect added a closing parenthesis after the first eight . . . amendments, distinguishing these amendments from all others. As a result, Americans today can lay claim to a federal Bill of Rights set apart from everything else, and symbolically first even if textually middling."

Apropos of Professor Amar's appraisal, a central controversy in the Supreme Court's interpretation of the Fourteenth Amendment involves whether its language applies all, some, or none of the first eight amendments (Bill of Rights) to the states. Under the doctrine of "selective incorporation," it is settled law that most of the specific guarantees do apply to the states. Other scholars and judges, notably adherents to the notion of a "Constitution in Exile," reject incorporation. While Bingham's speeches during congressional debate of the Fourteenth Amendment have been used by both sides in this debate, the weight of scholarly opinion supports the view that Bingham embraced incorporation.

Bingham left Congress in 1873. That year President Ulysses S. Grant appointed him envoy extraordinary and minister plenipotentiary to Japan, a post he occupied for twelve years. His appointment came at a crucial time in Japanese history, just after the Meiji restoration (1866–1869). Bingham died on March 19, 1900. He is buried in Cadiz, Ohio.

JAMES C. FOSTER

References and Further Reading

Amar, Akhil Reed. "Hero Worship and the Bill of Rights." *The American Lawyer*. December 1998, p. 66.
Aynes, Richard L., *The Continuing Importance of Congressman John A. Bingham and the Fourteenth Amendment*, Akron Law Review 36 (2003): 4:589.
———, *On Misreading John Bingham and the Fourteenth Amendment*, Yale Law Journal 103 (October 1993): 57.
Beauregard, Erving E. *Bingham of the Hills: Politician and Diplomat Extraordinary*. New York: Peter Lang, 1989.

BIRTH CONTROL

Birth control is the generic term to describe methods used to limit the number of children. These methods fall into two main categories: those that try to prevent conception, and those that terminate an embryo or fetus.

Humans seem to have utilized various forms of birth control since ancient times in almost all cultures. Common forms of birth control were non-vaginal intercourse, *coitus interruptus* (withdrawal of the penis from the vagina before the point of ejaculation), vaginal barriers or pessaries to prevent sperm from reaching the ova, and abortifacients (potions taken to induce a miscarriage in a pregnant woman).

The Catholic Church has been particularly vocal in its opposition to birth control, and cites the story of Onan and the command to be fruitful as basis for this opposition. Sexual intercourse is for procreation, and attempts to interfere in this process are viewed as contrary to God's will. Despite such opposition, evidence shows that the various forms of birth control have been widely practiced throughout the Western world.

Traditional local practice of birth control continued in the early United States, and abortion was widely practiced and accepted. Even Catholics accepted abortion before "the quickening," the point at which life was thought to begin (approximately forty days after conception). In the 1830s, an increased religiosity began to stigmatize abortion at any stage. This coincided with attempts by doctors to professionalize medicine by preventing unlicensed persons from performing medical procedures, most often abortions. This combination led the states to prohibit all abortion unless medically necessary to save the life of the mother. In 1873, Anthony Comstock persuaded Congress to pass laws defining all information about contraception as obscene and punishing anyone who disseminated such information.

Towards the end of the nineteenth century, concerns for the health risks associated with pregnancy led women's rights groups to become more vocal in their demands for access to birth control. This led to a backlash with some, including President Theodore Roosevelt, calling the practice of birth control "race suicide." The fear was that white Anglo-Saxon Protestant Americans would be outnumbered by immigrants because of their lower birth rates through practicing birth control. This tension found some resolution as many advocates of birth control also supported forcible eugenic sterilization of those deemed unfit to pass on their genes to the next generation.

One of the twentieth century's most active campaigners for birth control was Margaret Sanger, the founder of the group Planned Parenthood. She led calls for new legislation at the state and local level and also pushed for change through the courts. In *U.S. v. One Package of Japanese Pessaries* (1936), it was ruled that information about contraception was not obscene per se and that doctors could discuss contraception with their patients without fear of prosecution. In *Griswold v. Connecticut* (1965), the U.S. Supreme Court found that the penumbras of the

Fourteenth Amendment contained a right to privacy that protected married couples' use of contraceptive devices and struck down Connecticut's law prohibiting their usage. Sanger was involved in both cases. The Court later extended *Griswold* to cover unmarried couples in the case of *Eisenstadt v. Baird* (1972).

The 1960s also saw the development of the first contraceptive pill and later long-term implanted contraceptives. The contraceptive pill is credited as a leading factor in the sexual liberation experienced in the 1960s and was criticized for encouraging greater promiscuity and sexual immorality.

The awareness of the threat posed by human immunodeficiency virus/acquired immunity deficiency syndrome (HIV/AIDS) refocused the debates over birth control onto the prevention of sexually transmitted diseases. The 1980s and 1990s witnessed bitter divisions over what should be included in sex education in schools. Conservatives advocated the teaching of "abstinence only" as the only guaranteed protection against both pregnancy and infection. They resisted calls to include other methods of birth control in the curriculum for fears that greater awareness and understanding would lead to higher rates of teen sexual behavior. Others argued pragmatically that teens were likely to engage in this behavior anyway, and that other methods should be included to ensure that any sex was as safe as possible in terms of both avoiding pregnancy and preventing sexually transmitted diseases.

These debates took on an international dimension in 2001 when President George W. Bush began refusing funds for any United Nations sex education program that did not focus solely on abstinence, leading some to complain that the United States was putting its moral convictions ahead of concerns to deal with the HIV/AIDS crisis in Africa and Asia.

GAVIN J. REDDICK

References and Further Reading

Garrow, David J. *Liberty and Sexuality: The Right to Privacy and the Making of Roe v. Wade.* Berkeley: University of California Press, 1998.

Gordon, Linda. *Woman's Body, Woman's Right: Birth Control in America.* New York: Penguin Books, 1974.

———. *The Moral Property of Women: A History of Birth Control Politics in America.* Urbana: University of Illinois Press, 2002.

Kennedy, David M. *Birth Control in America: The Career of Margaret Sanger.* New Haven, CT: Yale University Press, 1970.

Noonan, John T. *Contraception: A History of Its Treatment by the Catholic Theologians and Canonists.* Cambridge, MA: Harvard University Press, 1986.

Planned Parenthood. Home Page, http://www.plannedparenthood.org.

Reed, James. *From Private Vice to Public Virtue.* New York: Basic Books, 1978.

Cases and Statutes Cited

Eisenstadt v. Baird, 405 U.S. 438 (1972)

Griswold v. Connecticut, 381 U.S. 479 (1965)

U.S. v. One Package of Japanese Pessaries, 86 F.2d 737 (1936)

See also **Abortion Laws and the Establishment Clause; Abortion Protest Cases; Anti-Abortion Protest and Freedom of Speech; *Bellotti v. Baird*, 443 U.S. 622 (1979); *Buck v. Bell*, 274 U.S. 200 (1927); Search (General Definition); Family Values Movement; Obscenity; Reproductive Freedom; *Roe v. Wade*, 410 U.S. 113 (1973)**

BIVENS v. SIX UNKNOWN NAMED AGENTS OF FEDERAL BUREAU OF NARCOTICS, 403 U.S. 388 (1971)

Bivens held, for the first time, that a federal court may hold individual government agents liable for money damages for violating a person's Fourth Amendment rights. The Supreme Court further established that the Constitution itself implies a "cause of action," that is, a right to sue, government agents responsible for conducting unreasonable searches and seizures.

Webster Bivens had committed no crime. Nevertheless, agents of the federal government ransacked his home, conducted a broad search, handcuffed him in front of his wife and children (whom they also threatened to arrest), and later strip-searched him—all without probable cause. This blatantly unconstitutional search seemed to have no redress: given that he was never prosecuted, exclusion of evidence found in the home was irrelevant. Bivens sued, seeking money damages, but the federal courts dismissed his claim, finding that there was no right to sue under the Fourth Amendment.

The Supreme Court reinstated his claim, holding that without an implicit right to sue, the Fourth Amendment would be reduced to mere words. Despite the lack of a remedy articulated by the text of the amendment, the Court nonetheless held that the Article III judicial power, as discussed in *Marbury v. Madison*, inherently includes the authority to fashion remedies (including money damages) for constitutional violations. Even though traditional state tort claims were available, the Court created a new cause of action under the Fourth Amendment, and ultimately permitted similar suits under other amendments as well.

Bivens litigation, however, is not without its difficulties. First, as a practical matter, juries are reluctant to find liability in *Bivens* actions because they perceive that the individual government agent, and not the government itself, will be made to pay. Second, subsequent Supreme Court decisions have made the *Bivens* waters far murkier. In *Bush v. Lucas, Schweiker v. Chilicky,* and *United States v. Stanley,* the Court severely restricted the analysis of whether the Constitution would imply a cause of action to particular constitutional violations. The basis for this retreat was the notion, originally detailed in Chief Justice Burger's *Bivens* dissent, that the Court must defer to the will of Congress, given the lawmaking nature of the "creation" of remedies. Thus, if Congress has not addressed a given class of grievances, or has done so without designating the remedy of money damages, the Court should recognize the doctrine of "separation of powers"—that the legislature should make law, and the courts should simply interpret it.

To counteract these problems, commentators have suggested that Congress should amend the Federal Torts Claim Act (FTCA) to waive immunity, thus permitting claimants to sue the government rather than the individual agent. Although Congress did create a statutory cause of action under the FTCA for such purposes, it intentionally excluded money damages. Thus, the *Bivens* problem still remains.

LOUIS N. SCHULZE, JR.

References and Further Reading

Bandes, Susan, *Reinventing* Bivens: *The Self-Executing Constitution,* Southern California Law Review 68 (1995): 289.

Grey, Betsy J., *Preemption of* Bivens *Claims: How Clearly Must Congress Speak?* Washington University Law Quarterly 70 (1992): 1087.

Pillard, Cornelia T.L., *Taking Fiction Seriously: The Strange Results of Public Officials' Individual Liability under Bivens,* Georgetown Law Journal 88 (1999): 65.

Thomas, Charles W., *Resolving the Problem of Qualified Immunity for Private Defendants in § 1983 and* Bivens *Damage Suits,* Louisiana Law Review 53 (1992): 449.

Cases and Statues Cited

Amos v. United States, 255 U.S. 313 (1921)
Bell v. Hood, 327 U.S. 678 (1946)
Berger v. New York, 388 U.S. 41 (1967)
Byars v. United States, 273 U.S. 28 (1927)
Gambino v. United States, 275 U.S. 310 (1927)
J.I. Case Co. v. Borak, 377 U.S. 426 (1964)
Katz v. United States, 389 U.S. 347 (1967)
Marbury v. Madison, 1 Cranch 137 (1803)
Silverman v. United States, 365 U.S. 505 (1961)
Weeks v. United States, 232 U.S. 383 (1914)

See also **Exclusionary Rule;** *Mapp v. Ohio,* **367 U.S. 643 (1961); Search (General Definition); Search Warrants; Seizures**

BLACKLEDGE v. PERRY, 417 U.S. 21 (1974)

Perry was tried and found guilty of the misdemeanor assault of a fellow inmate. When he exercised his statutory right to a new trial under North Carolina law, the prosecutor charged him with felony assault for the same conduct that had been previously charged as a less serious offense. Perry then pleaded guilty to the felony assault indictment.

Perry argued before the Supreme Court that the prosecutor's action was unconstitutional under the due process clause of the Fourteenth Amendment. The Court held that when defendants have a statutory right to a new trial, apprehension that prosecutors may retaliate by recharging with a higher offense, if they were to exercise this legal right, may impermissibly prevent defendants from ever availing themselves of a new trial. Such prosecutorial action in effect cuts off a defendant's access to the courts in violation of the due process clause. Moreover, a defendant does not have to prove that a prosecutor acted vindictively because it is the mere apprehension of retaliation that chills a defendant's assertion of the right to appeal.

Thus, absent circumstances where there is the impossibility of initially indicting on a more serious charge, prosecutors may not constitutionally bring a more serious charge against defendants who have sought new trials as of right. *Perry* therefore extended *North Carolina v. Pearce,* which held that, following a retrial, a defendant cannot receive a harsher sentence unless the trial judge sets out specific reasons.

REBECCA L. BARNHART

References and Further Reading

Breathing New Life into Prosecutorial Misconduct Doctrine, Harvard Law Review 114 (May 2001): 2074–97.

Henning, Peter J., *Prosecutorial Misconduct and Constitutional Remedies,* Washington University Law Quarterly 77 (Fall 1999): 735–46.

Cases and Statutes Cited

North Carolina v. Pearce, 395 U.S. 711 (1969)

See also **Due Process;** *North Carolina v. Pearce,* **395 U.S. 711 (1969)**

BLACKLISTING

Blacklisting is similar to blackballing. As the latter is associated with the placement of a black marble among the white ones in a bag, signifying that the applicant to a club has been denied membership by a single member, a blacklist is a powerful tool wielded by employers that denies the possibility of work to anyone whose name has been placed on a specific list. The injustice of a blacklist can be seen in its arbitrariness—just as in blackballing, where a single marble can decide one's fate, the blacklist may, over time, come to include names that no one remembers for sure how or why they got there. The Hollywood blacklist, for example, was designed to prevent left-wing film industry workers from finding employment in the American motion picture business. But because of mistaken identities, misspellings, rumor, and so forth, many individuals were not only blacklisted but effectively denied employment in spite of the fact that their names had been entered on the list through sheer inadvertence or oversight.

The Hollywood blacklist can also been seen as unfair since it targeted for reprisal as communists people whose political sympathies rarely strayed beyond that of California liberalism, and magazine subscriptions or house parties were notorious ways by which the politically naïve and socially harmless managed to get their names in a file that would follow them the rest of their lives. The canard that communists had taken over the film industry and turned the citadel of entertainment into a propaganda arm of the Soviet Union was genuinely hallucinatory in its misreading of the product that the American film industry was selling at home and abroad.

Finally, the detractors of Hollywood radicals and fellow travelers uniformly ignored the fact that without the Red Army in Europe, and the Soviet Union's "popular front" alliance with Western capitalists, Hitler's regime might never have been defeated. President Franklin Roosevelt recognized the Soviet Union as one of his first acts in office after winning the 1932 national election; that there were warm relations between Americans of all sorts and Russian communism, or its various American outposts during the 1930s and the war itself, should hardly come as a surprise nor be condemned. If even Winston Churchill could embrace Stalin, when the time was right, a Hollywood movie actor ought to be able to read a book by John Reed, or go to meetings where Reed's politics began to make increasing sense as the Great Depression deepened.

Blacklisting did not begin with the Hollywood studios. In Charles Dickens's novel *Hard Times*, his "honest-but-doomed working man," Stephen Blackpool, is blacklisted for rebellious comments that he makes to a factory owner, and his inability to find employment, crisscrossing Britain's brutal mid-nineteenth-century industrial landscape is virtually a death sentence. As labor researcher Mike Hughes documents, the rightwing Economic League operated a blacklist among British employers throughout most of the twentieth century, and was only brought to its knees by a House of Commons select committee investigation in 1990. The tale of blacklisting in American academia is a story that only a tiny handful of academics have come forward to tell. Historian Ellen Schrecker argues that, in fact, McCarthyism in the United States, whose tentacles reached well beyond the film industry and university campus, was a two-tiered process in which the success of the upper tier, led by criminal prosecutors and purveyors of rightwing political ideology, was only assured because it was founded upon a lower tier, the system of economic repression, that is, the blacklist.

Many of the same civil liberties that are at the heart of a democratic society and represent the soul of American constitutional law are the conventional victims of blacklisting—freedom of speech, association, and the press. Yet how does one campaign in the courts or march in the capital against as invisible and insidious an influence as that of a blacklist? The deprivation of civil liberties by blacklisting thus raises a special political problem and necessarily points toward hard philosophical questions about the parameters of liberty in liberal democracies. Many words have been written about the alleged superiority of negative over positive rights, the safeguards unique to negative constitutions, the essentially private and personal quality of liberty, and the transparent virtues of a government of laws and not men. The government that governs best, we are told, governs least. Lord Acton said, "Power corrupts. Absolute power corrupts absolutely." But the success of blacklisting as a political tool, the use of a discreet economic weapon for enforcing a grand public program, the destruction of civil liberties through a policy of intimidation, guilt by association, and economic strangulation—all outside the general purview of the law in liberal systems of rule—surely underscores not the strengths but the weaknesses of a politics that places economic processes, including decision making behind the blacklist, far from public regulation and the jurisdiction of the state.

Thus, a certain criticism of civil liberty itself is difficult to deflect. Civil liberty is to be enjoyed in private, but is that much more easily destroyed in private. Congress shall make no law . . . . But what if it is corporations, and other private enterprises, that rule? The state cannot force the private media to report a story or print an article or open its pages to dissident points of view. And when governments close down newspapers or television stations, it is a sure sign of the defeat of civil liberty by totalitarian tactics. But where is the freedom of speech for the citizen who does not own a newspaper or have his or her own television news station? At one level, these realities reveal fault lines separating liberty from democracy. There is "a contradiction between the sovereignty of the people and universal suffrage on the one hand, placing the fate of the nation in the hands of everyone," wrote historian Georges Lefebvre, "and the capitalist economy where the wage-earner sees his work, his wages and consequently his life in the hands of those who own the means of production."

But surely the illustration of blacklisting reveals contradictions with the system of civil liberty itself. The very private liberty that protects the right to hire and fire, the right to employ or not, the right to maneuver behind the scenes, to plan in secret, to remain silent in the face of injustice, to decline courageous action, to act on one's own prejudice without explanation, the power of joint economic activity by owners of private property—everything that makes the blacklist work is itself a right and is protected by civil liberty and by law. The house of civil liberty may not be about to fall, but it is all too easily portrayed as divided against itself.

ANTHONY CHASE

References and Further Reading

Caute, David. *The Left in Europe Since 1789*. New York: World University Library, 1966.
Hughes, Mike. *Spies at Work*. Bradford, UK: 1 in 12 Publications, 1994.
Schrecker, Ellen. *The Age of McCarthyism*. Boston: St. Martin's Press, 1994.

BLACKSTONE AND COMMON-LAW PROHIBITION ON PRIOR RESTRAINTS

In the fourth volume of his famous *Commentaries on the Laws of England*, published in 1769, William Blackstone argued that freedom of the press under the common law was limited to a prohibition on prior restraints. As Blackstone explained,

> The liberty of the press is indeed essential to the nature of a free state: but this consists in laying no *previous* restraints upon publications, and not in freedom from censure for criminal matter when published. Every freeman has an undoubted right to lay what sentiments he

pleases before the public: to forbid this, is to destroy the freedom of the press: but if he publishes what is improper, mischievous or illegal, he must take the consequences of his own temerity.

Blackstone's formulation—which imposed an absolute bar on state censorship prior to publication, but permitted punishment after the fact—was widely influential in eighteenth- and nineteenth-century America. In the 1907 case of *Patterson v. Colorado*, the Supreme Court, citing Blackstone, held that freedom of the press under the First Amendment consisted solely of a prohibition on prior restraints. In 1919, however, the Court intimated in *Schenck v. United States* that freedom of the press extended more broadly, a holding confirmed in subsequent cases.

Blackstone's denunciation of prior restraints has nonetheless remained a vital aspect of American law. In *Near v. Minnesota* (1931), the Supreme Court relied heavily on Blackstone and the prohibition on prior restraints to invalidate a Minnesota law providing for the abatement of certain newspapers as public nuisances.

CARLTON F. W. LARSON

References and Further Reading

Blackstone, William. *Commentaries on the Laws of England*. Vol. 4. Oxford: Clarendon Press, 1769.
Friendly, Fred W. *Minnesota Rag: The Dramatic Story of the Landmark Supreme Court Case that Gave New Meaning to Freedom of the Press*. New York: Random House, 1981.
Levy, Leonard. *Emergence of a Free Press*. New York: Oxford University Press, 1985.

Cases and Statutes Cited

Patterson v. Colorado, 205 U.S. 454 (1907)
Near v. Minnesota, 283 U.S. 697 (1931)
Schenck v. United States, 249 U.S. 47 (1919)

See also **Freedom of Speech and Press: Nineteenth Century; Freedom of Speech and Press under the Constitution: Early History (1791–1917)**

BLAINE AMENDMENT

The Blaine amendment was a proposed 1876 amendment to the U.S. Constitution.

Introduced by Congressman James G. Blaine in December 1875, the amendment sought to apply the First Amendment's religion clauses directly to state actions, prohibit the disbursement of public funds for parochial education, and, as revised by the Senate, forbid the exclusion of the Bible from the nation's public schools. Congress debated the measure during the heat of the 1876 summer presidential campaign, an election overshadowed by a resurgent Democratic Party and the inevitable demise of federally mandated southern reconstruction. Blaine's proposal passed a Democrat-controlled House of Representatives by an overwhelming margin, but fell four votes short in the Senate of being submitted to the states as the Sixteenth Amendment to the U.S. Constitution.

The Blaine amendment stands apart in significance from the majority of failed constitutional amendments for three reasons. First, based on the proposal's express language applying the First Amendment's religion clauses to state actions, some observers have argued that the proposal, coming eight years after the passage of the Fourteenth Amendment to the Constitution, indicates that members of Congress did not understand the due process or privileges and immunities clauses of that latter amendment to incorporate the rights contained in the Bill of Rights. Opponents of the Supreme Court's incorporation cases of the mid-twentieth century have used the Blaine amendment as one of their chief weapons. While there may be some merit to this argument, the Blaine amendment was much more expressive in its prohibition than the language of the First Amendment (and possibly differed from contemporary understandings of the establishment clause). In addition, during the debate on the measure, at least one senator referred to the Supreme Court's decision in the *Slaughterhouse Cases* (1873) rejecting the theory of incorporation under the Fourteenth Amendment as a providing a justification for the Blaine amendment. Consequently, legislators could have believed that the Blaine amendment was necessary to counteract the erroneous holding of *Slaughterhouse*.

The Blaine amendment is additionally significant as the apex of a mid-nineteenth-century controversy over the public funding of private religious schools. The "School Question" or "School Controversy," as it was popularly called, arose during the 1830s and 1840s following the creation of publicly funded "common" schools. A primary goal of the common schools was to teach republican values and integrate immigrant children into American culture. Increasingly, Catholic immigrants objected to the distinctly Protestant character of the nonsectarian curriculum of most common schools and, in turn, opted to establish Catholic parochial schools in the 1840s and 1850s. Catholic requests for pro rata shares of state school funds were regularly turned down by education officials who generally viewed parochial schools as a threat to the success of the common school movement.

After lying dormant during the Civil War and early Reconstruction years, the School Question rose to prominence as a campaign issue during the 1876 election. Some evidence suggests that Republican officials seized on the funding issue as a way of attracting anti-Catholic and anti-immigrant sentiment while seeking to align the Democratic Party with the Catholic Church. In September 1875, President Grant, hoping for a third term as president, proposed a constitutional amendment to prohibit the public funding of religious schools. James G. Blaine, also seeking the Republican presidential nomination, then introduced the amendment that bore his name:

> No State shall make any law respecting an establishment of religion, or prohibiting the free exercise thereof; and no money raised by taxation in any State for the support of public schools, or derived from any public fund therefore, not any public lands devoted thereto, shall ever be under the control of any religious sect; nor shall any money so raised or lands so devoted be divided between religious sects or denominations.

The Democrat-controlled House of Representatives overwhelmingly passed Blaine's proposal after attaching a nonenforcement provision. The Republican-controlled Senate removed the nonenforcement provision, expanded the language to prohibit the expenditure of funds derived from any source, and added a provision to preserve the reading of the Bible in the public schools, which favored Protestant interests. During the Senate debates, Democrats charged that the amendment was motivated by anti-Catholicism and would expand federal control over local educational decisions. In the end, the Senate voted along party lines to reject the Blaine amendment. As a result of the episode, many observers have charged that the Blaine amendment was motivated primarily by anti-Catholic animus. While anti-Catholicism unquestionably fueled the controversy, the Blaine amendment episode also implicated larger issues about the federal role in public education and the future and religious character of public schooling.

The Blaine amendment is also significant for its legacy. Even though Congress failed to pass the Blaine amendment in 1876, several states subsequently adopted similar non-funding provisions in their state constitutions. In 1889, Congress expressly required the states of Montana, North and South Dakota, and Washington to adopt non-funding provisions in their respective constitutions as a condition for granting statehood. Approximately two-thirds of state constitutions now contain such provisions, usually found in sections governing expenditures for public education that prohibit appropriations for the support of sectarian or denominational schools. These state "Blaine amendments" have become important because state courts have occasionally interpreted these provisions more strictly than the interpretation given to the establishment clause by the U.S. Supreme Court. For example, in 1961 the Alaska Supreme Court interpreted its non-funding provision to prohibit public reimbursement of transportation costs for children to attend religious schools, even though the U.S. Supreme Court in 1947 had upheld the constitutionality of a similar program under the federal establishment clause.

More recently, the issue of whether a stricter interpretation of a state non-funding provision might violate the free exercise and equal protection clauses came before the U.S. Supreme Court in *Locke v. Davey* (2004). Two years earlier, the Supreme Court had ruled in *Zelman v. Simmons-Harris* that a program that allows publicly financed vouchers to be used for religious school tuition does not violate the federal establishment clause. Relying on interpretations of its own constitution, however, Washington State refused to allow a student to use a publicly financed voucher to attend a religious college. The student charged that the Washington rule was unnecessarily restrictive, and that the denial infringed on his rights to free exercise and equal protection of the law. In *Locke*, however, the Supreme Court affirmed the state's decision, holding that the First Amendment allowed for "play in the joints" between the establishment and free exercise clauses, and that Washington State was free to interpret its state constitutional provisions independently of interpretations of the federal establishment clause.

STEVEN K. GREEN

References and Further Reading

DeForrest, Mark Edward, *An Overview and Evaluation of State Blaine Amendments: Origins, Scope, and First Amendment Concerns*, Harvard Journal of Law and Public Policy 26 (2003): 552–626.

Garnett, Richard W., *The Theology of the Blaine Amendments*, First Amendment Law Review 2 (2003): 23–44.

Gedicks, Frederick Mark, *Reconstructing the Blaine Amendments*, First Amendment Law Review 2 (2003): 85–106.

Feldman, Noah, *Nonsectarianism Reconsidered*, Journal of Law and Politics 18 (2002): 65–117.

Green, Steven K., *The Blaine Amendment Reconsidered*, American Journal of Legal History 36 (1992): 38–69.

———, *'Blaming Blaine': Understanding the Blaine Amendment and the 'No-Funding' Principle*, First Amendment Law Review 2 (2003): 107–52.

Hamburger, Philip. *Separation of Church and State*. Cambridge, MA: Harvard University Press, 2002.

McAfee, Ward M. *Religion, Race, and Reconstruction: The Public School in the Politics of the 1870s*. Albany: State University of New York, 1998.

Stern, Mark D., *Blaine Amendments, Anti-Catholicism, and Catholic Dogma*, First Amendment Law Review 2 (2003): 153–78.

Viteritti, Joseph P., *Blaine's Wake: School Choice, the First Amendment, and State Constitutional Law*, Harvard Journal of Law and Public Policy 26 (1998): 657–718.

Cases and Statutes Cited

Locke v. Davey, 124 S.Ct. 1307 (2004)
Slaughterhouse Cases, 83 U.S. 36 (1873)
Zelman v. Simmons-Harris, 536 U.S. 639 (2002)

See also **State Aid to Religious Schools**

BLOUDY TENENT OF PERSECUTION FOR CAUSE OF CONSCIENCE, DISCUSSED IN A CONFERENCE BETWEEN TRUTH AND PEACE, THE

Roger Williams began his religious career as a Puritan minister, and when he arrived in Massachusetts in 1630 he was initially well received. But he quickly fell into disfavor with the local leaders because of his liberal views. He changed his religious affiliation from Puritan to Baptist, and in 1639 he became a Seeker, a person who adhered to no specific religious practices. It was as a Seeker that Williams wrote "The Bloudy Tenent," while in England attempting to win back a charter for Rhode Island. The main theme of the tract, as it was of Williams's life, is that all individuals and religious bodies are entitled to religious liberty as a natural right, and that civil governments do not have the authority to enforce religious laws.

"The Bloudy Tenent" is structured as a dialogue between "Truth" (representing the orthodox views of Puritans like John Cotton) and "Peace" (representing Williams's views), and the subject of their debate is whether secular laws should favor one religion over another, and whether these laws have any basis in the Bible. Williams argued that these laws were in fact contrary to biblical teachings, and utilized the parable in Matthew 21:33–46 about the tenants who killed the son of the landowner to lay claim to his property (hence the title).

Williams used numerous biblical parables to buttress his argument that the civil authority ought not to be used to enforce religious conformity. He noted that Jesus and his disciples did not enjoy the protection of civil authority, and when he sent the disciples into the countryside to preach, he instructed them to take no food or money, but to rely on God for their needs. In the same manner, the Church of Williams's day ought to rely on spiritual authority alone, not that of the Crown.

Altogether, the prose in the tract is quite dense, and not easily read. But the message it carried could not be mistaken, and made Williams the leading champion in his time for the idea of religious liberty for both individuals and sects.

MELVIN I. UROFSKY

References and Further Reading

Morgan, Edmund S. *Roger Williams, the Church and the State*. New York: Harcourt, Brace & World, 1967.

BLUE LAWS
See Sunday Closing Cases and Laws

BLUE WALL OF SILENCE

The blue wall of silence is an unwritten code that prohibits police officers from providing adverse information against fellow officers. In essence, the code states that "cops don't tell on cops."

Officers allegedly learn about the wall of silence in the police academy when instructors inform them that all officers are "blue" (referring to the color of their uniforms) and have to protect each other no matter what. "I'll watch your back and you watch mine" is the understanding that police officers have among themselves. The problem with this philosophy is that a sense of loyalty develops that is based on relationships with other police officers rather than loyalty based on principles such as justice, fairness, and respect for human rights. Many police officers adopt this philosophy and turn a blind eye to fellow officers who engage in drug dealing, theft, assault and battery, murder, and other human rights violations.

The blue wall of silence makes it possible for police violence against citizens to be perpetuated with impunity. In one of the most egregious examples of this phenomenon, officers in the New York City Police Department failed to do or say anything to protect Abner Louima from a sadistic anal assault perpetrated by Officer Justin Volpe in a Brooklyn police station. When Volpe marched around his fellow officers waving a broken broomstick stained with Louima's blood and feces, bragging that he had "taken a man down," no police officer reported this outrageous conduct. Other egregious examples of how the blue wall of silence has operated include the cases of Rodney King (Los Angeles, Calif., 1992), Tyisha Miller (Riverside, Calif., 1998), and Amadou Diallo (New York City, 1999).

JUDITH A. M. SCULLY

References and Further Reading

Chin, Gabriel, and Scott Wells, *The Blue Wall of Silence As Evidence of Bias and Motive to Lie: A New Approach to Police Perjury*, University of Pittsburgh Law Review 59 (1998): 233.
Gallo, Gina. *Armed and Dangerous: Memoirs of a Chicago Policewoman*. New York: Forge, 2001.
Human Rights Watch. *Shielded from Justice: Police Brutality and Accountability in the United States*. Human Rights Watch Report, 1999. www.hrw.org/reports98/police/toc.htm.
Kappeler, Victor E., Richard Sluder, and Geoffrey P. Aplert. *Forces of Deviance: Understanding the Dark Side of Policing*. 2nd ed. Prospect Heights, IL.: Waveland Press, 1998.
Stamper, Norm. *Breaking Rank: A Top Cop's Expose of the Dark Side of American Policing*. New York: Nation Books, 2005.

BOARD OF EDUCATION OF THE WESTSIDE COMMUNITY SCHOOLS v. MERGENS, 496 U.S. 226 (1990)

In *Board of Education of the Westside Community Schools v. Mergens*, a public school board denied students' request to form a Christian club and meet after school on school premises. The school had created a limited open forum under the Equal Access Act (EAA) by permitting some non–curriculum-related student clubs, such as chess and stamp collecting, to meet during noninstructional time after school. The EAA, enacted by Congress in 1984, declared that once a school receiving federal financial assistance created a limited open forum, it could not discriminate against student-led clubs meeting during noninstructional time on school premises based on the "religious, political, philosophical, or other content of the speech at the meetings." The Court found that the school board's denying the Christian club the same opportunity to meet as other non–curriculum-related clubs amounted to discrimination based on the Christian club's religious speech. The Court also upheld the constitutionality of the EAA against an establishment clause claim, finding that allowing a wide range of student clubs to meet, including the Christian club, had a secular purpose and that high school students were not likely to perceive that a religious club meeting on the same basis as other clubs constituted government sponsorship of religion.

The EAA protects the right of students to meet in clubs reflecting their own interests on the same basis as any other non–curriculum-related club. Although initially applied to religious clubs, the EAA applies as well to other student interest groups, such as gay/straight clubs.

RALPH D. MAWDSLEY

References and Further Reading

Equal Access Act, 20 U.S.C. §§ 4071–4074.
Establishment Clause, U.S. Const. First Amendment.
Mawdsley, Ralph, *The Equal Access Act and Public Schools: What Are the Legal Issues Related to Recognizing Gay Student Groups?* Brigham Young University Education & Law Journal (2001): 1–33.

BOARD OF EDUCATION v. ALLEN, 392 U.S. 236 (1968)

One of the most contentious church–state issues in the United States has been the question of the constitutionality of government aid to religious schools. In *Board of Education v. Allen* (1968), the U.S. Supreme Court considered the constitutionality of a New York statute requiring public school districts to purchase and loan secular textbooks free of charge to children enrolled in both parochial and public schools. The Court, in one of its early decisions interpreting the establishment clause in the context of government aid to religious schools, sustained the constitutionality of the statute.

In 1947, the Supreme Court launched the modern establishment clause era with its decision in *Everson v. Board of Education* in which the Court narrowly sustained the constitutionality of a New Jersey law that authorized reimbursement to parents for the transportation expenses their children incurred traveling to sectarian schools. Thereafter, the Court attempted to determine what type of governmental aid to children attending private religious schools violated the establishment clause. In *Allen*, a six-to-three decision with Justice Byron White writing for the majority, the Court, conceding that "the line between state neutrality to religion and state support of religion is not easy to locate," relied on a test that it had articulated five years earlier in *Abington Township School District v. Schempp* (1963): "[W]hat are the purpose and primary effect of the enactment? If either is the advancement or inhibition of religion then the enactment exceeds the scope of legislative power as circumscribed by the Constitution."

The Court in *Allen* concluded that because the textbooks in question were secular, loaning them to children attending parochial schools did not have a "primary effect" of advancing the religious mission of the school. In reaching this conclusion, the Court concluded that "religious schools pursue two goals, religious instruction and secular education." The Court concluded that secular textbooks serve only the latter function, rejecting the plaintiffs' arguments that "all teaching in a sectarian school is religious" and that "the processes of secular and religious training are so intertwined that secular textbooks furnished to students by the public are in fact instrumental in the teaching of religion." The Court noted that there was no evidence in the record suggesting that the books in question had been used for religious instruction.

Justices Hugo Black, William Douglas, and Abe Fortas each dissented, distinguishing the bus fares at issue in *Everson* from the textbooks at issue in *Allen*. Black argued that textbooks in the hands of a sectarian school teacher would inevitably be used "to propagate the religious views of the favored sect." Aware that states were considering other forms of aid to sectarian schools, Black worried that if the Court sustained the textbook loans, "on the argument used to support this law others could be upheld providing for state or federal government funds to buy property on which to erect the buildings themselves, [or] to pay the salaries of the religious school teachers."

Although the Court sustained the textbook loan program, for the next several years it rejected various other forms of government aid to sectarian schools such as teacher salary supplements. In recent years, however, the Court has significantly liberalized its jurisprudence in this area by permitting greater government aid to religious schools.

DAVISON M. DOUGLAS

References and Further Reading

Freund, Paul, *Comment: Public Aid to Parochial Schools*, Harvard Law Review 82 (1969): 1680–92.
Futterman, David, *School Choice and the Religion Clauses: The Law and Politics of Public Aid to Private Parochial Schools*, Georgetown Law Journal 81 (1993): 711–40.

Cases and Statutes Cited

Abington Township School District v. Schempp, 374 U.S. 203 (1963)
Everson v. Board of Education, 330 U.S. 1 (1947)

See also **State Aid to Religious Schools**

BOARD OF EDUCATION v. EARLS, 536 U.S. 822 (2002) (STUDENTS)

Drug testing of students by public school officials constitutes a search that must be reasonable under the Fourth Amendment. In *Board of Education v. Earls*, the Court addressed the lawfulness of warrantless, suspicionless drug testing of students.

A school district in Pottawatomie County, Oklahoma, implemented a policy that required all students who participated in competitive extracurricular activities to submit to drug testing. Students Lindsay Earls and Daniel James, with their parents, sued the school district, arguing that the drug testing policy violated the Fourth Amendment.

The Court commenced its analysis by observing that the usual requirements of a search warrant and probable cause are uniquely situated to criminal investigations and may not be suitable for determining the reasonableness of searches intended to prevent future harms. Instead, the reasonableness of administrative searches is determined by balancing the government's legitimate interests in the search against the intrusion on individual privacy interests.

The Court had previously held that students' expectations of privacy are reduced in light of schools' responsibility for their health, education, discipline, and safety. Examining the specific policy at issue, the Court characterized the intrusion upon student privacy interests as relatively minor. Students provided urine samples in a closed restroom stall, test results were confidential, and the only consequence of a failed test was to limit the student's participation in extracurricular activities. Results did not carry academic, criminal, or other disciplinary consequences.

In contrast, the Court deemed the district's interest in drug testing as substantial. Although the government did not demonstrate a pervasive drug problem in its district, it did present evidence that some students had possessed or used drugs. Additionally, the Court noted a nationwide drug "epidemic." Weighing the intrusion on privacy interests against the government's interest in preventing and detecting drug use by schoolchildren, the Court found the policy to be reasonable.

In doing so, the Court extended its earlier ruling in *Vernonia School District v. Acton,* which applied only to school athletes. In *Vernonia,* the Court emphasized the safety hazards of drug use in athletes, as well as the reduced expectations of privacy in a locker-room atmosphere. Nevertheless, the Court found that the absence of these facts did not tip the reasonableness balance against the broader policy challenged in *Earls.*

Just as *Vernonia* did not determine the constitutionality of drug testing nonathletes, *Earls* does not resolve the constitutionality of testing students who do not participate in extracurricular activities. In its fact-specific analysis, the majority noted that students who engaged in extracurricular activities voluntarily subjected themselves to some intrusions on their privacy, and that the only consequence of a failed test was to limit participation in extracurricular activities. One member of the majority, Justice Breyer, wrote a concurring opinion emphasizing that the policy did not apply to the entire school. Four justices dissented,

reasoning that *Vernonia* was limited to athletes. Accordingly, it is possible that a majority of the Court might find unreasonable a drug testing policy that applied to all students.

ALAFAIR S. BURKE

References and Further Reading

Smiley, Jennifer E., *Comment. Rethinking the 'Special Needs' Doctrine: Suspicionless Drug Testing of High School Students and the Narrowing of Fourth Amendment Protections,* Northwestern University Law Review 95 (2001): 811.

Sundby, Scott E., *Protecting the Citizen 'Whilst He Is Quiet': Suspicionless Searches, 'Special Needs' and General Warrants,* Mississippi Law Journal 74 (2004): 501.

Cases and Statutes Cited

Vernonia School District v. Acton, 515 U.S. 646 (1995)

See also **Administrative Searches and Seizures; Drug Testing; Probable Cause; Search (General Definition); Search Warrants**

BOARD OF EDUCATION v. PICO, 457 U.S. 853 (1982)

In *Board of Education v. Pico,* the sharply divided Court held that the school board violated the students' First Amendment rights by removing from high school and junior high school libraries several books that the board found "anti-American, anti-Christian, anti-Sem[i]tic, and just plain filthy." The books were not obscene, but the board stated that "[i]t is our duty, our moral obligation, to protect the children in our schools from this moral danger as surely as from physical and medical dangers."

Justice William J. Brennan's plurality opinion (joined by Justices Thurgood Marshall and John Paul Stevens) concluded that removal of the library books implicated students' First Amendment right to "receive information and ideas." The plurality acknowledged that students' First Amendment rights must be construed "in light of the special characteristics of the school environment," but concluded that the school board denies these rights when it acts with intent to deny students access to ideas with which the board disagrees. The plurality stressed that the decision concerned only the board's authority to remove library books, which by their nature are optional rather than required reading; the decision did not concern acquisition of library books, or removal from the curriculum of required texts.

Justices Harry A. Blackmun and Byron R. White concurred. Justice Blackmun stated that "school officials may not remove books for the *purpose* of restricting access to the political ideas or social perspectives discussed in them, when that action is motivated simply by the officials' disapproval of the ideas involved" (emphasis in original). Justice White would have awaited a full trial before reaching the constitutional question.

To Chief Justice Warren E. Burger (joined by Justices William H. Rehnquist, Lewis F. Powell, Jr., and Sandra Day O'Connor), the case turned on "whether local schools are to be administered by elected school boards, or by federal judges and teenage pupils; and . . . whether the values of morality, good taste, and relevance to education are valid reasons for school board decisions concerning the contents of a school library." The chief justice wrote: "[A]s a matter of *educational policy* students should have wide access to information and ideas. But the people elect school boards, who in turn select administrators, who select the teachers, and these are the individuals best able to determine the substance of that policy" (emphasis in original).

Justice Powell accused the plurality of "reject[ing] a basic concept of public school education in our country: that the States and locally elected school boards should have the responsibility for determining the educational policy of the public schools." *Pico*, Justice Powell continued, allows "any junior high school student, by instituting a suit against a school board or teacher, [to] invite a judge to overrule an educational decision by the official body designated by the people to operate the schools."

Pico constrains the discretion of public school authorities to remove materials from school libraries. Some lower courts also cite *Pico* for a First Amendment right of students to receive information, although the right commanded only the three-justice plurality.

DOUGLAS E. ABRAMS

References and Further Reading

Chemerinsky, Erwin. *Constitutional Law: Principles and Policies*. 2nd ed. New York: Aspen, 2002.
Nowak, John E., and Ronald D. Rotunda. *Constitutional Law*. 7th ed. St. Paul, MN: Thomson West, 2004.

See also **Children and the First Amendment**

BOARD OF EDUCATION, KIRYAS JOEL SCHOOL DISTRICT v. GRUMET, 512 U.S. 687 (1994)

Kiryas Joel involved a striking fact situation: a public school district created to serve only the disabled children of an ultra-Orthodox Jewish sect. But in striking down the district under the establishment clause, the Supreme Court relied on a simple, bedrock principle: any government accommodation of religious practice must extend not only to a single sect, but to any sect engaged in a similar practice.

The Satmar Hasidim are an insular, traditionalist group who speak primarily Yiddish, permit no television or radio, wear distinctive hair and clothing, and educate their children in gender-segregated private schools permeated by religious teaching. They formed a village in upstate New York called Kiryas Joel, inhabited only by sect members. The village's disabled children, entitled to state and federal special-education assistance, at first received it in Satmar private schools, but had to switch to public schools after the Supreme Court signaled disapproval of private school aid in *Aguilar v. Felton* (1985; later overruled). The parents soon withdrew their children from public school, however, reporting that the children had been taunted by peers and traumatized by the secular atmosphere. The New York legislature then stepped in and created a special public school district tracking the lines of the village, allowing the Satmar children to receive aid in a sheltered setting, but prohibiting the district from teaching religion in its classes.

Notwithstanding the state's legitimate goal of accommodating a religious and cultural minority, the Supreme Court ruled that the creation of the district violated the establishment clause and its command of government neutrality toward varying religious views. Justice Souter's opinion for four justices, joined in part by Justice O'Connor, concluded that the Satmars had received a unique benefit, a separate school district, without any guarantee that it would be "provide[d] equally to other religious (and nonreligious) groups." The state could accommodate needs such as the Satmars', but only by a statute that did not single out one sect. Justice Scalia's dissent argued that New York had created comparable special districts before and had given no indication that it would fail to accommodate a similar group in the future.

The justices in the majority also objected to the drawing of political lines to encompass only members of one sect. Justice Souter's opinion argued that this created an improper "religious test" for membership in the district; Justice Kennedy concurred that "the Establishment Clause forbids the government to draw political boundaries on the basis of religious faith"; and Justices Stevens and Ginsburg argued even more broadly that the state cannot "affirmatively suppor[t] a religious sect's interest in segregating itself [from its] neighbors." These arguments raise interesting parallels with the Court's invalidation of race-based districting in decisions such as *Shaw v. Reno*. The arguments also touch on deep questions as to whether cultural and religious pluralism are better served by integrating and assimilating various groups or by allowing certain limited forms of "segregation" by groups, like the Satmar, that are internally non-pluralistic.

The legislature responded to the Court's holding by passing general statutes allowing the creation of smaller school districts out of larger ones under certain criteria. Two such efforts were struck down by state courts in 1997 and 1999 on the grounds that their requirements were "gerrymandered" to benefit only the Satmar. But a fourth, broader statute was upheld in 2001.

THOMAS C. BERG

References and Further Reading

Berg, Thomas C., *Slouching Toward Secularism: A Comment on* Kiryas Joel School District v. Grumet, Emory Law Journal 44 (1995): 433–99.
Boyarin, Jonathan, *Student Note: Circumscribing Constitutional Identities in* Kiryas Joel, Yale Law Journal 106 (1997): 1537–70.
Eisgruber, Christopher L., *The Constitutional Value of Assimilation*, Columbia Law Review 96 (1996): 87–103.
Greene, Abner S., Kiryas Joel *and Two Mistakes About Equality*, Columbia Law Review 96 (1996): 1–86.
Lewin, Tamar. "Controversy Over, Enclave Joins School Board Group." *New York Times*, April 20, 2002.
Lupu, Ira C., *Uncovering the Village of* Kiryas Joel, Columbia Law Review 96 (1996): 104–20.
Rosen, Jeffrey, Kiryas Joel *and* Shaw v. Reno: *A Text-Bound Interpretivist Approach*, Cumberland Law Review 26 (1996): 387–406.

Cases and Statutes Cited

Aguilar v. Felton, 473 U.S. 402 (1985)
Grumet v. Cuomo, 90 N.Y.2d 57, 681 N.E.2d 340 (1997)
Grumet v. Pataki, 93 N.Y.2d 677, 720 N.E.2d 66 (1999)
Shaw v. Reno, 509 U.S. 630 (1993)

BOB JONES UNIVERSITY v. UNITED STATES, 461 U.S. 574 (1983)

Federal law provides that "[c]orporations organized and operated exclusive for religious, charitable, or educational purposes" are entitled to tax-exempt status. But is a private school that discriminates on the basis of race entitled to federal tax-exempt status? In *Bob Jones University v. United States*, the Supreme Court concluded that racially discriminatory private school cannot receive federal tax exemptions, even if its discriminatory practices are grounded in religious belief.

Bob Jones University calls itself "the world's most unusual university." Although unaffiliated with any established church, the university is dedicated to the teaching and propagation of fundamentalist religious beliefs. In pursuit of these goals, the university dictates strict rules of conduct for its students. To enforce one such rule forbidding interracial dating and marriage, the university denies admission to applicants engaged in or known to advocate interracial dating and marriage.

The Bob Jones University controversy began in 1970, when the Internal Revenue Service (IRS) concluded that it would no longer grant tax-exempt status to schools that violate governmental policy outlawing federal funding of discriminatory institutions. After paying a portion of the federal taxes due, the university filed suit for a refund, contending that it was statutorily and constitutionally entitled to reinstatement of its tax exemption. In 1981, the Supreme Court agreed to hear *Bob Jones University* and a related case raising similar issues, *Goldsboro Christian Schools, Inc. v. United States*. At that time, *Bob Jones University* was perceived as a religious liberty lawsuit. Specifically, little attention was paid to whether or not the IRS could withhold tax breaks from segregationist academies and other racist schools; the focus of the litigation, instead, was whether First Amendment religious liberty protections would extend to a school whose discriminatory practices were tied to religious conviction.

In January 1982, however, the Reagan administration sought to moot *Bob Jones University* and *Goldsboro*. Noting that Congress never formally specified that tax-exempt organizations must conform to "public policy," the administration claimed that it lacked authority to withhold tax exemptions from racist schools. The administration's policy shift prompted a political backlash and the administration withdrew its request to have the Supreme Court declare the case moot. In May 1983, the Court, by a vote of eight to one, denied tax exemptions to the two schools. In an opinion written by Chief Justice Warren Burger, the Court held that a tax-exempt institution must confer some "public benefit" and that its purpose must not be at odds with the "common community conscience." The Court further held that the IRS has broad authority to interpret the code and to issue rulings based on its interpretation.

The Court also considered the religious liberty claims of Bob Jones University and Goldsboro Christian Schools. Noting that the "[g]overnment has a fundamental overriding interest in eradicating racial discrimination in education," the Court concluded that this governmental interest "substantially outweighs whatever burden denial of tax benefits" places on the exercise of religious belief. By holding that equality of treatment on the basis of race is the

Constitution's most essential protection, and that the government's broad interest in racial discrimination in education was at issue, the Court had little difficulty in disposing of the religious liberty claims of Bob Jones University and Goldsboro Christian Schools.

In fact, the Court devoted less than three pages of its thirty-page opinion to the religious liberty issue. Furthermore, in ruling against the two schools, the Court made no effort to distinguish Bob Jones University's prohibition of interracial dating (among a student body that included both minorities and nonminorities) from Goldsboro Christian School's refusal to admit minority students. Apparently, the Reagan policy shift had transformed *Bob Jones* from a religious liberty lawsuit into a socially significant racial discrimination lawsuit. Against this backdrop, the Court may have thought it ill advised to distinguish the social policies of one school from the admissions policies of another, preferring, instead, to speak about the evils of racial discrimination.

The Court should not be faulted for its failure to give substantial attention to religious liberty concerns. Between nondiscrimination in education and religiously inspired discrimination, the Court's endorsement of nondiscriminatory objectives is hardly surprising. Indeed, the Court broke little, if any, doctrinal ground in *Bob Jones University*. Starting with its 1982 decision in *United States v. Lee*, the Court has refused to give special exceptions to religious organizations from generally applicable eligibility schemes. *Bob Jones University*'s significance, in other words, is not tied to the case's precedential impact but to its explosive political setting.

References and Further Reading

Devins, Neal. "On Casebooks and Canons Or Why *Bob Jones University* Will Never Be Part of the Constitutional Law Canon." *Constitutional Commentary* 17, no. 2 (2000) 285–93.
Laycock, Douglas, *Tax Exemptions for Racially Discriminatory Religious Schools*, Texas Law Review 60 (1982): 1:259–77.

Case and Statutes Cited

Bob Jones University v. United States, 461 U.S. 574 (1983).
United States v. Lee, 455 U.S. 252 (1982)

CITY OF BOERNE v. FLORES, 521 U.S. 507 (1997)

The First Amendment provides that "Congress shall make no law respecting an establishment of religion, or prohibiting the free exercise thereof." The right freely to engage in the rituals and observances of the religion of one's choice, without undue governmental interference, is one of the most cherished guarantees of the Bill of Rights. Exactly what criteria courts should apply to determine when this right has been violated has been the subject of sharp controversy over the years.

The Supreme Court required strict judicial scrutiny of this issue in a 1963 free exercise case, *Sherbert v. Verner*. There, the Court held that statutes which substantially burden the practice of religion will pass constitutional muster only if they are shown to be necessary to advance some compelling governmental interest. But in 1990, the Court relaxed that standard. In *Employment Division v. Smith*, a case upholding a ban on the use of peyote, the Court held that such a law does not offend the First Amendment if the burden it imposes on the free exercise of religion is merely an incidental effect of a generally applicable measure, and the law's objective is something other than interference with religious practice.

Congress responded to the public outcry over *Smith* by enacting, by a nearly unanimous vote, the Religious Freedom Restoration Act of 1993 (RFRA). RFRA expressly codified as federal law the previous standard of constitutional protection in free exercise cases, providing that "government shall not substantially burden a person's exercise of religion" unless the burden is justified by a compelling governmental interest, and does so by the least restrictive means available.

City of Boerne presented the first major test of RFRA. P.F. Flores, as archbishop of San Antonio, applied for a building permit to enlarge St. Peter Catholic Church, a small, aging structure in the city of Boerne, Texas. The permit was denied based on the city's recent designation of a historic preservation district that included St. Peter. The archbishop sued, alleging that the permit denial violated RFRA.

It is indisputable that the city's actions would not have violated the free exercise clause under the standard established by *Employment Division v. Smith*. Nothing in the city's creation of a historic preservation district, or the denial of a permit to enlarge a structure within that district, showed an intention to restrict the practice of any religion. The historic preservation regulations applied uniformly to all properties within the designated area, regardless of their use. Thus, the church's case depended on invoking the tougher protections set out in RFRA. The city's refusal to allow any enlargement of St. Peter could be said to substantially burden the parishioners' exercise of their religion, since the record indicated that forty to sixty people per week were unable to celebrate Sunday mass at the church because of its inadequate capacity. Moreover, the denial could not be justified by a compelling governmental interest in preventing the expansion of St. Peter, nor did it meet RFRA's requirement of narrow tailoring.

In its defense, the city argued that RFRA was unconstitutional because it exceeded Congress's authority. In a majority opinion written by Justice Kennedy, the Supreme Court agreed and struck down the law as beyond Congress's enforcement powers under the Fourteenth Amendment.

The federal government has only those powers specifically granted to it by the Constitution. In enacting RFRA, Congress relied on the provision of Section 5 of the Fourteenth Amendment: "The Congress shall have power to enforce, by appropriate legislation, the provisions of this article." Justice Kennedy acknowledged that Section 5 authorizes Congress to enact laws enforcing the constitutional right of free exercise of religion, which is deemed included within the Fourteenth Amendment's guarantee of due process of law. Such laws, however, must be remedial or preventive in nature, not substantive. In determining whether legislation is within Congress's Section 5 power, the Court will look for "congruence and proportionality" between the constitutional injury Congress seeks to redress, and the means adopted to prevent or remedy it.

In this case, the Court found that RFRA restricted the states' regulatory powers even more extensively than had the test set out by *Smith*, yet Congress had articulated no history of state discrimination against religion sufficient to justify such a response. Under the doctrine of separation of powers, only the Supreme Court itself may define the substantive restrictions imposed on the states by the Fourteenth Amendment. Legislation such as RFRA that effectively alters the Court's determination of the meaning of the free exercise clause, cannot be said to be enforcing the clause, and therefore exceeds the authority granted to Congress by Section 5.

This decision is significant for its express declaration that only the judicial branch has the authority to determine what constitutes a violation of the free exercise clause—and by extension, of all other constitutional provisions incorporated into the Fourteenth Amendment. It also set out a new standard for determining whether Congress has exceeded its enforcement powers under Section 5. The Court has applied *City of Boerne*'s "congruence and proportionality" test in a variety of contexts since first enunciating it in 1997.

In response to this decision, Congress once again sought to extend heightened protection to religious liberties, this time via enactment of the Religious Land Use and Institutionalized Persons Act of 2000

(RLUIPA). Instead of broadly targeting all laws of general applicability that might burden the exercise of religion, RLUIPA targeted violations in two discrete contexts—land use controls and policies towards institutionalized persons. Like RFRA, the new law mandated strict judicial scrutiny in reviewing regulations that would substantially burden an individual's religious exercise in these contexts, but RLUIPA was buttressed with findings showing proportionality between the impact of such regulations and the need for close judicial review. Finally, congressional authority to enact RLUIPA was anchored in the Constitution's commerce and spending clauses, not the Fourteenth Amendment. Largely because of these efforts to avoid the constitutional problems identified in *City of Boerne*, the constitutionality of RLUIPA was upheld in *Cutter v. Wilkinson*.

R. S. RADFORD and NEAL DEVINS

References and Further Reading

Cookson, Catharine. *Regulating Religion: The Courts and the Free Exercise Clause*. New York: Oxford, 2001.
DeBusk, Thomas L., *RFRA Came, RFRA Went; Where Does That Leave the First Amendment? A Case Comment on* City of Boerne v. Flores, Regent University Law Review 10 (1998): 223.
Mallamud, Jonathan, *Religion, Federalism and Congressional Power: A Comment on* City of Boerne v. Flores, Capital University Law Review 26 (1997): 45.

Cases and Statutes Cited

Cutter v. Wilkinson, 125 S.Ct. 2113 (2005)
Employment Division v. Smith, 494 U.S. 872 (1990)
Religious Freedom Restoration Act of 1993, 42 U.S.C. § 2000bb et seq
Religious Land Use and Institutionalized Persons Act of 2000, 42 U.S.C. §§ 2000cc et seq
Sherbert v. Verner, 374 U.S. 398 (1963)

BOLGER v. YOUNGS DRUG PRODUCTS CORP., 463 U.S. 60 (1983)

Since the mid-1970s, it has been clear that commercial speech can be protected free speech under the First Amendment. However, it is typically accorded lesser protection than noncommercial speech. Thus, classifying a particular message as commercial or noncommercial is important. In *Bolger*, the Supreme Court developed principles relevant to such classification.

Youngs Drug Products Corporation ("Youngs") manufactured, sold, and distributed contraceptives. It publicized its products by various means, including unsolicited mass mailings to the public. The Postal Service notified Youngs that its mailings violated then existing federal statutes prohibiting the mailing of unsolicited advertisements for contraceptives. Youngs brought suit, challenging the constitutionality of the statute.

Applying its decision in *Virginia State Board of Pharmacy*, the Supreme Court held that most of the Youngs mailings were commercial speech because they were "speech which does no more than propose a commercial transaction." However, some of the Youngs materials contained discussions of important public issues such as family planning and venereal disease and so presented a closer classification question.

The *Bolger* Court offered no bright line but discussed a number of considerations. The mere fact that the pamphlets were advertising did not compel the conclusion that they were commercial speech, nor did the fact that they referred to a specific product, nor did the fact that Youngs had an economic motivation. However, the combination of *all* of those facts strongly supported the commercial nature of the speech. The Court stated that advertising is not noncommercial speech simply because it "links a product to a current public debate."

Despite characterizing Youngs's advertising as commercial speech, the Court held that the statute was unconstitutional as applied. The Court applied the *Central Hudson* four-part analysis: (1) whether the speech concerns a lawful activity and is not misleading, (2) whether the government has a substantial interest, (3) whether the regulation directly advances that interest, and (4) whether the regulation is more extensive than necessary to serve that interest.

Under this analysis, Youngs's advertising was protected. The Court noted that advertising for contraceptives entails "substantial individual and societal interests" and relates to activity that is protected from unwarranted governmental interference. Further, neither of the two interests asserted by the government justified sweeping prohibition of mailing unsolicited contraceptive advertising. First, the fact that some recipients may find the material offensive was insufficient, especially since the recipients could simply avert their eyes or dispose of the mailings. Second, aiding parents' efforts to control the manner in which their children become informed about birth control is a substantial interest. However, the marginal benefit provided by the statute in that regard came at the cost of suppressing material entirely suitable for adults. Moreover, the statute denied parents truthful information bearing on their ability to discuss birth control and to make informed decisions about it.

JANET W. STEVERSON and STEVE R. JOHNSON

References and Further Reading

Chemerinsky, Erwin, and Catherine Fisk, *What Is Commercial Speech: The Issue Not Decided in* Nike v. Kasky, Case Western Reserve Law Review 54 (2004): 4:1143–60.
Rotunda, Ronald D., and John E. Nowak. *Treatise on Constitutional Law: Substance and Procedure*. Vol. 4. 3rd ed. St. Paul, MN: West, 1999.
Tribe, Laurence H. *American Constitutional Law*. 2d ed. Mineola, NY: Foundation, 1988.

Cases and Statutes Cited

Central Hudson Gas & Electric Corp. v. Public Service Commission of New York, 447 U.S. 557 (1980)
Virginia State Board of Pharmacy v. Virginia Citizens Consumer Council, Inc., 425 U.S. 748 (1976)

See also **Free Speech in Private Corporations; *Central Hudson Gas & Electric Corp. v. Public Service Commission of New York*, 447 U.S. 557 (1980); Commercial Speech; *Virginia State Board of Pharmacy v. Virginia Citizens Consumer Council, Inc.*, 425 U.S. 748 (1976)**

BOND v. FLOYD, 385 U.S. 116 (1966)

Bond v. Floyd arose from the intersection of the struggle for civil rights and the protest movement against U.S. involvement in Vietnam, two political movements that had a dramatic impact on the United States in the 1960s. The U.S. Supreme Court faced the question whether the Georgia House of Representatives could deny a seat to the newly elected Julian Bond because of statements he made or endorsed against the Vietnam War and in support of young men who resisted the draft.

Bond, an African-American civil rights activist, came to run for the Georgia House seat because of the Supreme Court's "one man, one vote" decision in *Reynolds v. Sims*. Following that decision, a three-judge federal district court panel ordered the reapportionment of the Georgia General Assembly. Bond had been a founding member of the Student Non-Violent Coordinating Committee (SNCC), and was SNCC's director of communications, when he decided in 1965, at age twenty-five, to run for a House seat from his overwhelmingly African-American Atlanta district. He handily won in the June election and was to begin his one-year term in January 1966.

Much of SNCC's leadership strongly opposed the Vietnam War and resented the military draft, which both sent African Americans into the military and to Vietnam in disproportionate numbers and threatened to deplete the ranks of SNCC's active civil rights workers. Nonetheless, the organization hesitated to alienate the Johnson administration by officially opposing the war. Their hesitation finally evaporated after the murder of Samuel Younge, an SNCC worker and a Navy veteran, who was shot to death when he tried to use a "whites only" restroom.

In response to Younge's death, SNCC's executive committee released a statement that linked the civil rights struggle in the American South with the freedom struggles "of the colored people in . . . other countries." The statement faulted the United States for being on the wrong side in many of those struggles, noting that: "The murder of Samuel Younge in Tuskegee, Alabama is not different from the murder of people in Vietnam . . . . In each case, the U.S. government bears a great part of the responsibility for those deaths." The statement further suggested that young men should be able to choose to work in civil rights or other similar organizations as an alternative to the military draft. Finally, it expressed "sympathy" and "support" for those "who are unwilling to respond to a military draft which would compel them to contribute their lives to United States aggression in Viet Nam in the name of the 'freedom' we find so false in this country."

Bond did not have a role in drafting the statement. However, when asked about it by a radio reporter, he endorsed it and expressed his opposition to all wars as a pacifist, but to the Vietnam War in particular. Members of the Georgia House of Representatives responded by challenging Bond's right to be seated in the upcoming legislative session. Their petitions charged that Bond had violated the Selective Service laws, had given aid and comfort to the enemies of the United States and Georgia, and had brought discredit and disrespect to the House. They further contended that Bond's endorsement of the SNCC statement showed that he could not sincerely take the oath of office prescribed by the Georgia Constitution, which essentially required him to swear that he would support the Georgia and U.S. constitutions and act to promote the interests of Georgia. When the House session was called to order, Bond was not allowed to take the oath of office. After a hearing, he was denied his seat.

Bond won election two more times only to be denied his House seat, before the Supreme Court decided his case. In a unanimous opinion written by Chief Justice Warren, the Court held that the Georgia House of Representatives must allow Bond to take his oath of office and assume his seat. The Court said that neither Bond's nor SNCC's statements were punishable under the Selective Service Act because they did not expressly advocate illegal behavior. In response to the state's argument that it could bar Bond for lawful statements because it could hold its elected officials to a higher standard of loyalty than its citizens and

could, therefore, prohibit House members from saying things that ordinary citizens would have a First Amendment right to say, the Court responded that the First Amendment "requires that legislators be given the widest latitude to express their views on issues of policy."

Bond served twenty years in the Georgia General Assembly.

ROBERT N. STRASSFELD

References and Further Reading

Carson, Clayborne. *In Struggle: SNCC and the Black Awakening of the 1960s*. Cambridge, MA: Harvard University Press, 1981.
Morgan, Charles, Jr. *One Man, One Voice*. New York: Holt, Rinehart, and Winston, 1979.

Cases and Statutes Cited

Reynolds v. Sims, 377 U.S. 533 (1964)

See also **Voting Rights (Compound)**

BOOK BANNING AND BOOK REMOVALS

In *Fahrenheit 451*, Ray Bradbury wrote about a world in which the responsibility of fire fighters was to burn books rather than to extinguish fires. This radical reconceptualization of the fire fighter's role was the product of a dystopia in which all books were considered dangerous contraband. Yet the act of burning books has not been left to the imaginary worlds of science fiction writers. In Nazi Germany, for example, citizens collected books that were deemed "un-German" and burned them in great pyres on public streets. Even at the start of the twenty-first century, many seemingly well-intentioned Americans continue to wage wars on books that they think are threatening to the social order, with some even resorting to book burning escapades of their own. However, many Americans consider the burning of books—even those they strongly abhor—to be an extremely repulsive act that is normally associated with brutal totalitarian states. As a result, those who want to reduce the public's exposure to books they find dangerous have been inclined to use the less drastic—but perhaps equally effective—tactic of having the relevant books banished from public libraries and public school curriculums.

Judges have traditionally extended substantial deference to the decisions of school administrators regarding matters pertaining to the governance and general operation of public schools. This deference is most pronounced in matters regarding the school's curriculum and the books used in the teaching of that curriculum (see *Epperson v. Arkansas* [1968]). Paradoxically, this deference has in some instances resulted in outcomes that stymie the efforts of those who want to remove or ban books. For example, courts have uniformly rejected legal challenges against schools where litigants argue that books should be removed from a school's curriculum because they violate antidiscrimination laws by promoting religious/ethnic bigotry (*Rosenberg v. Board of Education of the City of New York* [1949]) and racist views (*Monteiro v. Tempe Union High School District* [1998]), or because they violate the First Amendment's establishment (*Brown v. Woodland Joint Unified School District* [1994]) and/or free exercise (*Mozert v. Hawkings County Board of Education* [1987]) clauses. In fact, the courts have recognized that students and teachers are entitled to significant First Amendment protection for the expressive acts in which they engage while on school grounds (*Tinker v. Des Moines Independent Free School District* [1969]), and that schools should not be allowed to cast a "pall of orthodoxy over the classroom" (*Keyishian v. Board of Regents* [1967]).

Nevertheless, those who want to restrict access to books in public schools have had significant success, particularly when they have been able to convince a school's administration that a book ought to be purged from the school's curriculum. Such a ban prevents the book from being used as an assigned student text in the school's curriculum, and it may—depending on its specificity—prevent teachers from discussing and presenting material from the book while teaching their classes. For example, in *Virgil v. School Board of Columbia County, Florida* (1989), the Eleventh Circuit Court of Appeals held that the school board had a reasonable basis to remove works by Aristophanes and Chaucer from its English curriculum after the Board concluded that the texts were too sexually explicit for high school students. The challenged regulation in *Virgil* allowed teachers and students to discuss the material during class discussions, and the texts were still available in the school library, but it is unclear whether any of these elements to the school's policy were required by the First Amendment. After all, the *Virgil* court relied on *Hazelwood School District v. Kuhlmeier* (1989), a Supreme Court decision that provides school administrators with the broad authority to enact any school curriculum regulations that are "reasonably related to legitimate pedagogical concerns."

First Amendment–based lawsuits against school administrators are also triggered when administrators take steps to either remove or reduce student access to particular books in school libraries. For instance, administrators might decide not to purchase certain books as part of the library's periodic efforts to gain new acquisitions. Alternatively, school officials might design policies that limit student access to currently stocked books by placing them in restricted areas of the library and by requiring parental concession before a student can gain access to the books. And, of course, administrators may decide that certain books need to be discarded entirely from the library's collection. Regardless of which method school administrators choose to employ, lower federal and state courts have been guided by the Supreme Court's conclusion in *Board of Education v. Pico* (1982) that school libraries fall outside of the school's curriculum and, consequently, that judges should provide less deference to school administrators when litigants challenge the constitutionality of library policies as opposed to curriculum policies. However, because no opinion in *Pico* garnered majority support, lower courts have emphasized that it does not constitute a binding legal precedent, but instead constitutes an important factor that judges should consider when they address school board policies that limit access to certain books in school libraries (see *Campbell v. Tammany Parish School Board* [1995]).

In *Pico*, the plurality opinion conceptualized public school libraries as environments in which students and teachers should be allowed to freely and voluntarily examine a wide array of views on those topics that they are studying—a process that is often necessary for the acquisition of human knowledge. In addition, the plurality opinion explained that students and teachers have First Amendment rights to receive information, and that administrators should not be allowed to manipulate the stock of available library materials in an attempt to promote a particular political, social, economic, or religious orthodoxy. Administrators in public schools can shape their school library's holdings, particularly when making new purchases, by considering the intellectual merit of a book, whether a book is appropriate for students of a particular age, and whether a book complements the school's curriculum. However, books currently housed in a school's library that are acceptable on these dimensions cannot be removed or restricted because administrators find them threatening to their—or the community's—ideological predispositions.

The *Pico* plurality opinion also explained that school administrators face a greater chance of running afoul of the First Amendment when they remove a book already on their school library's shelves than when they choose not to purchase a book to add to the library's existing collection. When purchasing new acquisitions for school libraries, administrators must strive to maximize, on what are normally quite limited budgets, the quality of library resources that can be provided to students and teachers. This budgetary rationale, however, is usually not available when the school attempts to remove books already sitting on its library's shelves. Since books are expensive and libraries generally prefer to have more rather than fewer titles, removing books from a library's existing stock is an inherently suspicious activity—especially when that activity prompts a lawsuit. To be sure, books can be removed from libraries for entirely legitimate reasons (for instance, they are tattered, out of date, or because room must be made for incoming new titles), but courts have nevertheless been inclined to view legal challenges to school library book removals and restrictions as more credible than challenges to administrative decisions to purchase some books but not others.

Thus, school administrators have lost most cases involving challenges to the removal or restriction of access to books in school libraries. For instance, the *Pico* Court held that the school board could not remove nine books from school libraries simply because they were considered "'anti-American, anti-Christian, anti-Sem[i]tic, and just plain filthy.'" Similarly, a federal district court overturned a school board decision that required students to gain parental consent before gaining access to books in the *Harry Potter* series that were located in the school library (*Counts v. Cedarville School District* [2003]). That court rejected the school board's argument that exposure to the *Harry Potter* books would be likely to increase student "disobedience and disrespect for authority," or that the school had an interest in preventing students from reading about "witchcraft" and "the occult." Indeed, the court considered the latter rationale indicative of the fact that school administrators were attempting to promote only traditional religious values, and thus acting in clear violation of First Amendment doctrine prohibiting viewpoint-based regulations of expression. The Ninth Circuit Court of Appeals reached the same conclusion in overturning a local school board's decision to remove a book entitled *Voodoo & Hoodoo* from all school libraries in the district (*Campbell v. Tammany Parish School Board* [1995]).

Government administrators of nonschool public libraries who have taken steps to remove or restrict access to books have frequently encountered frosty judicial receptions when their acts are challenged in court. Unlike school libraries, the policies of local and state public libraries are not entitled to any heightened judicial deference and, therefore, those officials who manage them must hew very close to traditional First Amendment free speech doctrine. For example,

a federal district court declared unconstitutional the Wichita Falls Public Library's decision to remove *Heather Has Two Mommies* and *Daddy's Roommate*—books that experts had deemed suitable for small children—from the children's section of the library and have them placed in the adult section (*Sund v. City of Wichita Falls, Texas* [2000]). Thus, nonschool public libraries are even more tightly constrained by the First Amendment than are their public school counterparts, for the efforts of library officials to remove or restrict access to books have been closely scrutinized and are rarely tolerated by the courts.

MARK KEMPER

References and Further Reading

American Library Association. Home Page. http://www.ala.org.

Cases and Statutes Cited

Board of Education, Island Trees Union School District No. 26 v. Pico, 457 U.S. 853 (1982)
Brown v. Woodland Joint Unified School District, 27 F.3d 1373 (9th Cir. 1994)
Campbell v. Tammany Parish School Board, 64 F.3d 184 (5th Cir. 1995)
Counts v. Cedarville School District, 295 F.Supp.2d 996 (W.D. Ark. 2003)
Epperson v. Arkansas, 393 U.S. 97 (1968)
Hazelwood School District v. Kuhlmeier, 484 U.S. 260 (1988)
Keyishian v. Board of Regents, 385 U.S. 589 (1967)
Monteiro v. Tempe Union High School District, 158 F.3d 1022 (9th Cir. 1998)
Mozert v. Hawkings County Board of Education, 827 F.2d 1058 (6th Cir. 1987)
Rosenberg v. Board of Education of the City of New York, 92 N.Y.S.2d 344 (1949)
Sund v. City of Wichita Falls, Texas, 121 F.Supp. 2d 530 (Fed. Dist., 2000)
Tinker v. Des Moines Independent Free School District, 393 U.S. 503 (1969)
Virgil v. School Board of Columbia County, Florida, 862 F.2d 1517 (11th Cir. 1989)

BORDENKIRCHER v. HAYES, 434 U.S. 357 (1978)

When we think of adjudicating guilt, we think of *trials*—witnesses questioned, lawyers locked in forensic combat, juries attentive to the subtleties of the case in preparation for their deliberations, and the verdict that will ultimately puncture the tension in the courtroom. The reality is that upwards of 95 percent of felony convictions are secured by the accused's own admission of guilt. These admissions of guilt in open court are the consequence of the controversial but longstanding practice of plea bargaining. The idea is simple: a criminal defendant admits guilt and thus foregoes a formal trial in exchange for sentencing leniency. Whereas the defendant benefits by the lighter punishment, society benefits by reducing the time and expense in adjudicating guilt. But are there limits to the pressure that the prosecution may apply to a defendant to induce a guilty plea?

Bordenkircher v. Hayes addresses that issue. The prosecutor offered to recommend a sentence of five years imprisonment in exchange for defendant Hayes's guilty plea to an indictment charging forgery. The prosecutor warned that he would secure another indictment if Hayes refused the plea offer, an indictment that would charge Hayes with being an "habitual offender," thus ramping up Hayes's sentencing exposure to life imprisonment. The prosecutor's motives were transparent and beyond dispute: he threatened Hayes with life imprisonment to induce him to forego his constitutional right to a jury trial. Hayes refused to plead guilty, and the prosecutor followed through on his threat, charging Hayes under the Kentucky Habitual Criminal Act. When Hayes was convicted, the judge sentenced Hayes to life imprisonment, as required by the habitual offender statute.

The Supreme Court found nothing improper with a prosecutor threatening to send a defendant to prison for life if that defendant refuses to accept a plea bargain of five years' imprisonment. The Court rooted its conclusion in the fact that plea bargaining is a form of bartering for rights, and prosecutors may legitimately drive hard bargains with the sole motive "to persuade the defendant to forgo his right to plead not guilty." That no one—not even the prosecutor himself—believed life imprisonment was the appropriate sentence for Paul Lewis Hayes was thus irrelevant to the issue of the prosecutor's ratcheting up charges in reaction to Hayes's refusal to plead guilty. *Bordenkircher* marks the triumph of plea bargaining in our system of criminal justice.

DAN R. WILLIAMS

References and Further Reading

Fisher, George, *Plea Bargaining's Triumph*, Yale Law Journal 109 (2000): 857.
Schulhofer, Stephen J., *Is Plea Bargaining Inevitable?* Harvard Law Review 97 (1984): 1037.

See also **Guilty Plea; Due Process; Plea Bargaining**

BORK, ROBERT HERON (1927–)

Noted jurist, author, and scholar, Robert Heron Bork was born in Pittsburgh, Pennsylvania. He received a B.A. from the University of Chicago in 1948 and a

J.D. in 1953. From 1954 to 1962, he worked in private practice before moving on to a professorship at Yale Law School. He served as solicitor general of the United States from 1972 to 1977 and as acting attorney general of the United States in 1973–1974. During his tenure as attorney general he became a part of the history of the Watergate scandal when he followed President's Nixon's order to fire special prosecutor Archibald Cox. Attorney General Elliot Richardson and his assistant, William Ruckelshaus, were first ordered to fire Cox, but refused to do so and resigned. Bork wished to resign as well, but Richardson and Ruckelshaus asked that he remain in order to ensure that the Justice Department continued to operate.

In 1977, Bork returned to teaching at Yale Law School. In 1982, President Ronald Reagan appointed Bork to the Court of Appeals for the District of Columbia Circuit where he established a reputation as a conservative jurist. In 1987, with the announcement of Justice Lewis Powell's retirement, President Reagan nominated Bork for the U.S. Supreme Court.

The nomination sparked a major debate because of Bork's controversial views on issues such as judicial activism, civil rights, and civil liberties. Bork advocates a strict constructionist reading of the Constitution, argues that jurists should be guided by the original intent of the founders when applying provisions of the Constitution, and maintains that judges should not legislate from the bench. This has led him to take issue with the U.S. Supreme Court and some of its decisions. For example, Bork takes aim at *Griswold v. Connecticut* (1964), a landmark case that formally established a constitutional right to privacy. Bork contends that Justice Douglas created an overall right to privacy that does not exist in the Constitution. He asserts that the judiciary erroneously utilizes the Fourteenth Amendment to create new constitutional rights. Additionally, Bork supports a more limited reading of First Amendment rights and privileges.

Bork's nomination hearings before the Senate Judiciary Committee began on September 15, 1987, and lasted twelve days. In addition to the lengthy questioning of Bork by the Committee, numerous supporters and opponents testified as well. In addition, the American Bar Association gave Bork its highest rating. However, in the end, the vote from the Judiciary Committee was nine to five against Bork. All of the Democrats voted against him, as well as one Republican, Arlen Specter. Bork's nomination was defeated in the Senate at large, mainly on party lines, by a vote of fifty-eight to forty-two. The defeat was significant because it marked a change in what was viewed as the advice and consent role of the U.S. Senate. Previously, nominees could expect to be confirmed regardless of political affiliation, as long as they were experienced and qualified.

Two months after his nomination was defeated, Bork resigned from the Court of Appeals to write and lecture at the American Enterprise Institute, where he is currently a senior fellow. He continues to research, publish, and speak on issues such as constitutional and anti-trust law, as well as American culture.

MARY K. MANKUS

References and Further Reading

Bork, Robert H. *The Tempting of America: The Political Seduction of the Law*. New York: Free Press, 1990.
———, *The Constitution, Original Intent, and Economic Rights*, San Diego Law Review 23 (1986): 823–32.
Bronner, Ethan. *Battle for Justice: How the Bork Nomination Shook America*. New York: W.W. Norton & Company, 1989.
McGuigan, Patrick B., and David M. Weyrich. *Ninth Justice: The Fight for Bork*. Washington, DC: Free Congress Research and Education Foundation, 1990.

See also **Griswold v. Connecticut, 381 U.S. 479 (1965)**

BOSTON MASSACRE TRIAL (1770)

Troops had been stationed in Boston and other cities in the colonies as a result of growing resistance by the colonists against imperial laws, especially the hated Townshend Acts. Ironically, on the same day as the Acts were repealed, March 5, 1770, a fight erupted with fatal consequences. Citizens constantly harassed the troops, and during a demonstration, a squad of British soldiers led by Captain Thomas Preston was struck by missiles thrown by the colonists. The soldiers fired into the crowd and killed five men, including an African American, Crispus Attucks, who was leading the group. Only the withdrawal of troops from Boston prevented a major riot.

The eight soldiers and their commanding officer were tried for murder and were defended by John Adams, later the second president of the United States. Adams was a leader of the popular resistance to the British government, but he did not condone violence or mob action. When Adams was asked to defend the British soldiers who were charged with murder as a result of this clash, he promptly accepted. With the help of two other lawyers, he won acquittal for all but two of the men. Those two were declared guilty of manslaughter and, after claiming benefit of clergy, were branded on the thumb.

Despite the high tensions of the period, most patriots applauded the trial as evidence that the colonists remained wedded to the rule of law, and that the right of trial by jury should not be abandoned.

MELVIN I. UROFSKY

References and Further Reading

Zobel, Hiller B. *The Boston Massacre*. New York: Norton, 1970.

BOWEN v. AMERICAN HOSPITAL ASSOCIATION, 476 U.S. 610 (1986)

Important rights and policies can be in tension when a governmental agency seeks to act on a child's behalf and parental consent has not been obtained. The conflict is heightened when the agency is part of the federal government and is attempting to regulate in an area traditionally under the control of the states. In *Bowen v. American Hospital Assn.*, the Supreme Court reined in such an attempt because it exceeded the authority conferred upon the agency by Congress.

Under Section 504 of the Rehabilitation Act of 1973, "[n]o otherwise qualified handicapped individual . . . shall, solely by reason of his handicap, be excluded from participation in, be denied the benefits of, or be subjected to discrimination under any program or activity receiving Federal financial assistance." In 1984, the Department of Health and Human Services (HHS) promulgated regulations under the act. In relevant part, the regulations established "[p]rocedures relating to health care for handicapped infants." Those procedures required the posting of informational notices, authorized expedited access to records and expedited compliance actions, and directed state child protective services agencies to "prevent instances of unlawful medical neglect of handicapped children."

Various plaintiffs, including the American Hospital Association and the American Medical Association, challenged the regulations. The lower courts held for the plaintiffs. The Supreme Court affirmed via a plurality opinion.

The plurality found that the need seen by HHS for federal monitoring of hospitals' treatment decisions rested wholly on situations in which parents refused their consent to treatment. Yet, the Court stated, a hospital's withholding treatment from a handicapped infant when the parents did not consent to treatment could not violate Section 504 of the act since—absent such consent—the infant neither is "otherwise qualified" nor has been denied care "solely by reason of his handicap."

The plurality also concluded that the regulations improperly commandeered state employees and resources. Although HHS could require state agencies to document their own compliance with Section 504, nothing in the act authorized HHS to compel state agencies to monitor and enforce compliance by other recipients (that is, the hospitals) of federal funds. The Supreme Court subsequently developed the "commandeering" principle in the *New York* and *Printz* cases.

Bowen offered important observations about the factual basis required for agency rules and about the degree of deference courts will accord to agency positions. "It is an axiom of administrative law that an agency's explanation of the basis for its decision must include a rational connection between the facts found and the choice made . . . . Agency deference has not come so far that we will uphold regulations whenever it is possible to conceive a basis for administrative action." This is particularly so when the federal agency seeks to superintend decisions "traditionally entrusted to state governance."

STEVE R. JOHNSON

References and Further Reading

"Annotation: Who is recipient of, and what constitutes program receiving, federal financial assistance for purposes of §504 of the Rehabilitation Act (29 U.S.C.A. §794), which prohibits any program or activity receiving financial assistance from discriminating on basis of disability." 160 *American Law Reports Federal* 297.

Cases and Statutes Cited

New York v. United States, 505 U.S. 144 (1992)
Printz v. United States, 521 U.S. 898 (1997)

BOWEN v. KENDRICK, 487 U.S. 589 (1988)

In *Bowen v. Kendrick*, the Court upheld the Adolescent Family Life Act (AFLA) against an establishment clause challenge. The act allowed federal grants to go to agencies that provide services related to teen sexuality and pregnancy. Both public and private agencies (including private religious organizations) were eligible for grants under the act. The act was challenged on its face, that is, it was challenged as being unconstitutional by itself, rather than as applied to various agencies. Chief Justice Rehnquist wrote the majority opinion.

The Court ostensibly applied the *Lemon* test. The *Lemon* test requires that a law have a secular purpose, a primary effect that neither advances nor inhibits religion, and that the law not excessively entangle government and religion. Yet the Court held that even though the act in some ways paralleled the views and practices of certain religions, the purpose of the act was not to promote religion, but rather to address the problems caused by teen pregnancy and sexual behavior. The Court held that the primary effect of the act did not advance religion, because the grants were available to a wide range of agencies and organizations. It was reasonable for Congress to include religious organizations in the act because such organizations can have an influence on values and family structure, and many of the religious organizations that would receive funds under the program were not "pervasively sectarian." Thus, the Court held that religion would only benefit incidentally and remotely from the act. Moreover, the Court held that the monitoring required under the act did not lead to excessive entanglement between government and religion. The Court did remand the case for a determination of whether the act violated the establishment clause as applied. This would require individual plaintiffs to challenge the program as applied to them, and thus the act could only be challenged through a patchwork of cases rather than on its face as the plaintiffs had attempted in *Bowen*.

Bowen is one of a series of cases that used the facial neutrality of a program—that is, the fact that aid was available to a wide range of providers, both religious and secular—to uphold the program despite effects that would seem to violate the *Lemon* test as applied in earlier decisions. The reasoning applied in this line of cases was expanded in *Zelman v. Simmons-Harris* (2002), a case that upheld a voucher program where the program was open to both religious and secular schools. *Bowen* might also serve as precedent for upholding "charitable choice" programs, and charitable choice proponents cite *Bowen* to support their arguments that such programs are constitutional. *Bowen*'s formalistic approach, and its language suggesting that it was reasonable for Congress to include religious organizations in AFLA since such organizations can have an influence on values and family structure, have been used by charitable choice advocates to argue that religious charities (which have an influence on helping the needy) should be allowed to receive government funding along with other charitable organizations. Yet, *Bowen* can be criticized for its formalistic reasoning and the resulting failure to seriously consider the effects of the program in question under the *Lemon* test.

FRANK S. RAVITCH

Cases and Statutes Cited

Bowen v. Kendrick, 487 U.S. 589 (1988)
Lemon v. Kurtzman, 403 U.S. 602 (1971)
Zelman v. Simmons-Harris, 536 U.S. 639 (2002)
Adolescent Family Life Act, 42 U.S.C. §§300z et. seq

BOWEN v. ROY, 476 U.S. 693 (1986)

Pursuant to federal regulations requiring social security numbers for all dependent children, Pennsylvania authorities had stopped Aid to Dependent Families and Children benefits to Stephen Roy and Karen Miller and were also taking steps to reduce food stamps. Other than failing to provide a Social Security number for their child, Little Bird of the Snow, Roy and Miller had met all other requirements. Roy based his refusal to provide a number on his Native American belief that doing so would "'rob the spirit' of his daughter and prevent her from attaining greater spiritual power." On the last day of the trial, however, it was shown that Roy had earlier obtained a Social Security number. In the face of this, Roy then claimed that since the number had not been "used," there had been no damage to her spirit.

The District Court, despite this last-minute revelation, found for Roy, holding "that the public 'interest in maintaining an efficient and fraud resistant system can be met without requiring use of a social security number . . . .'" It enjoined government from both using the existing Social Security number and denying any appropriate governmental benefits.

The Supreme Court, in an opinion by Chief Justice Warren Burger, reversed. Burger, who in *Wisconsin v. Yoder*, had surprised free exercise advocates by appearing to continue in the Warren Court's tradition by following *Sherbert v. Verner*, saw Roy's claim as involving something quite different, an effort by a free exercise claimant to dictate to government how government should conduct its own affairs. No justice explicitly disagreed with Burger on this point. Burger's refusal, however, to apply either "the least restrictive means of achieving some compelling state interest" (test of *Thomas v. Review Board*), or the test of being "essential to accomplish an overriding governmental interest" (*United State v. Lee*), led Justice Sandra Day O'Connor to issue a partial dissent, joined by Justices William Brennan and Thurgood Marshall. Justice Harry Blackmun, although not joining O'Connor's opinion—Blackmun and Justice John Paul Stevens concluded that the existing Social Security number mooted the case—agreed with O'Connor that Burger should have applied either the *Lee* or *Thomas* standards of review to the present case.

Burger, for his part, argued that when the government's burden on religion was indirect and incidental as in this situation, "The Government meets its burden when it demonstrates that a challenged requirement for government benefits, neutral and uniform in its application, is a reasonable means of promoting a legitimate public interest." If accommodations to such neutral regulations are to be made, Burger continued, that was the responsibility of the legislature. An effort to waive the Social Security number requirement was mounted in 1999, but was unsuccessful.

Four years after *Roy*, a different Court—Antonin Scalia replacing Burger and Anthony Kennedy succeeding Justice Lewis Powell—adopted a free exercise standard in *Employment Division v. Smith* that clearly owed much to Burger's opinion.

FRANCIS GRAHAM LEE

References and Further Reading

Cole, Jamie Alan, *A New Category of Free Exercise Claims: Protection for Individuals Objecting to Government Actions that Impede Their Religion*, University of Pennsylvania Law Review 135 (1987): 1557–90.
Fisher, Louis. "Statutory Exemptions for Religious Freedom." *Journal of Church and State* 44 (2002): 291–316.

Cases and Statutes Cited

Employment Division, Department of Human Resources of Oregon v. Smith, 494 U.S. 872 (1990)
Sherbert v. Verner, 374 U.S. 398 (1963)
Thomas v. Review Board of Indiana Employment Security Division, 450 U.S. 707 (1981)
United States v. Lee, 455 U.S. 252 (1982)
Wisconsin v. Yoder, 406 U.S. 205 (1972)

BOWERS v. HARDWICK, 478 U.S. 186 (1986)

When a police officer came to serve an arrest warrant upon Michael Hardwick for a citation that Hardwick had already paid, the officer found Hardwick in his bedroom engaged in consensual oral sex with another man. Hardwick was arrested and jailed for violating Georgia's sodomy law, which criminalized oral and anal sex. The American Civil Liberties Union offered to represent Hardwick and challenge the constitutionality of the sodomy law in his criminal trial. But because the Fulton County district attorney opted not to seek a jury indictment against Hardwick, the ACLU instead filed suit in federal court against Georgia Attorney General Michael Bowers. Hardwick and an anonymous married couple John and Mary Doe sought a declaration that Georgia's sodomy law unconstitutionally violated their right to privacy, which the Supreme Court had recognized in cases such as *Griswold v. Connecticut* (1965). The trial court summarily dismissed the suit, but the intermediate federal appellate court reversed, rejecting the participation of the Does but agreeing with Hardwick that Georgia's sodomy law deprived him of liberty without due process of law in violation of the Fourteenth Amendment to the U.S. Constitution.

The U.S. Supreme Court reversed, upholding Georgia's sodomy law five to four. Justices Lewis Powell, William H. Rehnquist, Sandra Day O'Connor, and Chief Justice Burger joined Justice Byron White's majority opinion. The Court commenced by framing the issue narrowly. Rather than ask whether the law violated Hardwick's fundamental right to privacy, the Court posed the threshold question as whether the Constitution "confers a fundamental right upon homosexuals to engage in sodomy," or, elsewhere, as whether under the Constitution there is "a fundamental right to engage in homosexual sodomy."

Having so narrowly framed the issue, the Court then narrowly construed its precedents. The majority refused to treat them as reflecting some abstract principle, such as the existence of a sphere of personal autonomy presumptively protected against government interference. Instead, the Court described them at a lower level of abstraction, interpreting them only as cases about discrete subjects: the opinion described the relevant cases "as dealing with child rearing and education; with family relationships; with procreation; with marriage; with contraception; and with abortion" (citations omitted). The contraception and abortion decisions might have been seen as protecting a right to engage in non-procreative sexual activity, which would then include the right to engage in oral or anal sex. The Court instead characterized them as involving only a "right to decide whether or not to beget or bear a child." The opinion contemptuously dismissed the arguments of Harvard law professor Laurence Tribe, who had joined Hardwick's counsel, as "at best, facetious." Finally, after deciding for the foregoing reasons that Georgia's law implicated no fundamental right, the Court subjected the statute to rational basis review, the form of scrutiny most deferential to legislatures, and concluded that a presumed judgment by the people of Georgia that "homosexual sodomy" was immoral was an adequate justification for its sodomy law.

Chief Justice Burger authored a concurring opinion that emphasized the long history of criminalization of sodomy as "firmly rooted in Judaeo-Christian moral and ethical standards," even going so far as to quote Blackstone's *Commentaries* assessment that sodomy was "an offense of 'deeper malignity' than

rape." Justice Powell, who later publicly stated that he thought he was probably mistaken in voting to uphold the constitutionality of Georgia's sodomy law, also wrote a concurring opinion, in which he suggested that since Hardwick had not been prosecuted, he could not raise a viable Eighth Amendment claim of cruel and unusual punishment, but that "a prison sentence for such conduct—certainly a sentence of long duration—would create a serious Eighth Amendment issue."

Justice Harry Blackmun wrote a dissenting opinion joined by Justices William Brennan, Thurgood Marshall, and John Paul Stevens. They criticized the majority for distorting the issue by its "almost obsessive focus on homosexual activity" when Georgia's ban on oral and anal sex was gender-neutral. Insisting that the Court should interpret constitutional rights with respect to their underlying purposes, the dissenters suggested that its precedents protected privacy rights "because they form so central a part of an individual's life." "[W]hat the Court really has refused to recognize is the fundamental interest all individuals have in controlling the nature of their intimate associations with others," they wrote. The dissenters argued that Georgia's law impinged upon Hardwick's "decisional privacy," or autonomy with respect to "certain decisions that are properly for the individual to make," as well as upon his "spatial privacy," for in their view, "the right of an individual to conduct intimate relationships in the intimacy of his or her own home seems . . . to be the heart of the Constitution's protection of privacy."

Justice Stevens also wrote a dissenting opinion, which was joined by Justices Brennan and Marshall. Like the Blackmun dissent, which also analogized Georgia's sodomy law to the antimiscegenation law invalidated in *Loving v. Virginia* (1967), the Stevens dissent read *Loving* as establishing that "the fact that the governing majority in a State has traditionally viewed a particular practice as immoral is not a sufficient reason for upholding a law prohibiting the practice." Invoking "our tradition of respect for the dignity of individual choice in matters of conscience," Stevens interpreted the Court's privacy decisions in cases such as *Griswold* and *Eisenstadt v. Baird* as dictating that married or unmarried different-sex couples enjoy "the right to engage in nonreproductive, sexual conduct that others may consider offensive or immoral." But because lesbian, gay, and bisexual persons have the same liberty interests as heterosexually identified people, Stevens concluded that the equal protection clause also prohibited the state from punishing same-sex sodomy. The vast majority of scholarly commentary on *Bowers v. Hardwick* holds that the dissenters had the better of the arguments.

Nevertheless, the precedent of *Bowers v. Hardwick* was used by lower courts to justify all manner of discrimination against lesbian, gay, and bisexual persons. If it is constitutional to criminalize "the conduct that defines the class," courts said, then so is subjecting same-sex couples to greater criminal punishments for engaging in sex with a minor, excluding openly lesbian/gay people from military service, and so on. For seventeen years, *Bowers* remained part of the law of the land. Finally, though, *Bowers* was overruled in 2003 by *Lawrence v. Texas*, which declared *Bowers* to be "wrong the day it was decided."

DAVID B. CRUZ

References and Further Reading

Thomas, Kendall, *Beyond the Privacy Principle*, Columbia Law Review 92 (1992): 1432.

Cases and Statutes Cited

Griswold v. Connecticut, 381 U.S. 479 (1965)
Eisenstadt v. Baird, 405 U.S. 438 (1972)
Loving v. Virginia, 388 U.S. (1967)
Lawrence v. Texas, 539 U.S. 588 (2003)

See also **Privacy; Griswold v. Connecticut, 381 U.S. 479 (1965); Lawrence v. Texas, 539 U.S. 588 (2003)**

BOY SCOUTS

See Boy Scouts of America v. Dale, 530 U.S. 640 (2000)

BOY SCOUTS OF AMERICA v. DALE, 530 U.S. 640 (2000)

The First Amendment right to free speech includes a right to associate for expressive purposes. Groups that come together to express a message cannot be compelled to include people whose presence would compromise that message. This right to expressive association can conflict with antidiscrimination laws. The task of courts in such cases is to determine whether the association has an expressive purpose, and whether forced inclusion of a particular member would undermine that purpose. *Boy Scouts of America v. Dale* presented both questions.

James Dale became a Cub Scout at the age of eight and a Boy Scout at eleven, eventually attaining the prestigious rank of Eagle Scout. In 1989, he applied for adult membership and became an assistant scoutmaster. Around the same time, after entering college, Dale first acknowledged to himself and others that he was gay.

In 1990, having apparently learned Dale's sexual orientation from a newspaper article, the Scouts revoked his membership on the grounds that the Boy Scouts "specifically forbid membership to homosexuals." In 1992, Dale filed a complaint in New Jersey state court, claiming that his expulsion violated a New Jersey statute forbidding discrimination on the basis of sexual orientation (among other traits) in any place of public accommodation. The Scouts argued that the application of this law violated their federal constitutional right to expressive association.

In the state courts, Dale ultimately prevailed. The New Jersey Supreme Court agreed that the Scouts expressed a belief in moral values and used its activities "to encourage the moral development of its members," but found itself unpersuaded that the Scouts expressed a message condemning homosexuality. Thus, it concluded, requiring the Scouts to accept Dale did not affect the Scouts' "ability to carry out their various purposes."

The Supreme Court reversed. It announced that courts in expressive association cases "must give deference to an association's assertions regarding the nature of its expression" and also to its "view of what would impair its expression." Applying the appropriate deference, the Court found that the Scouts did "teach that homosexual conduct is not morally straight" and that accepting Dale as a member would force the Scouts to send the message "that the Boy Scouts accepts homosexual conduct as a legitimate form of behavior."

The Court went on to consider whether New Jersey's interest in opposing discrimination was weighty enough to justify such an infringement on the Scouts' right to expressive association, but for practical purposes, found that the infringement was enough. The Court has never allowed an antidiscrimination law to overcome the right to expressive association if its application would seriously burden the right. *Dale* is thus doctrinally consistent both with cases that strike the down the application of antidiscrimination laws, such as *Hurley v. Irish-American Gay, Lesbian, and Bisexual Group of Boston*, and with those that allow it, such as *Roberts v. United States Jaycees* and *Runyon v. McCrary*. *Dale*'s significance lies in its announced deference to the association's assertions, which may be a departure from *Roberts* and *Runyon*.

KERMIT ROOSEVELT, III

References and Further Reading

Bernstein, David E., *Antidiscrimination Laws and the First Amendment*, Missouri Law Review 66 (2001): 83.

Koppelman, Andrew, *Signs of the Times:* Boy Scouts of America v. Dale *and the Changing Meaning of Nondiscrimination,* Cardozo Law Review 23 (2002): 1819.

Cases and Statutes Cited

Hurley v. Irish-American Gay, Lesbian, and Bisexual Group of Boston, 515 U.S. 557 (1995)
Roberts v. United States Jaycees, 468 U.S. 609 (1984)
Runyon v. McCrary, 427 U.S. 160 (1976)

See also **Antidiscrimination Laws; Freedom of Association; Gay and Lesbian Rights;** *Hurley v. Irish-American Gay, Lesbian, and Bisexual Group of Boston,* **515 U.S. 557 (1995);** *Roberts v. United States Jaycees,* **468 U.S. 609 (1984)**

BOYD v. UNITED STATES, 116 U.S. 616 (1886)

An agent of the customs department, referred to as a collector, seized thirty-five cases of plate glass in pursuance of customs law. The importer was accused of attempting to defraud the federal government of the revenues and duties normally imposed upon the goods. During the trial that followed, the government sought to obtain records of similar prior importations, specifically the receipt by the importer of twenty-nine cases of similar plate glass. A court ordered the importer to produce the invoice in question in court for governmental inspection. The production of the invoice was governed by an 1874 law (18 St. 186) that allowed the government to inspect, but not take possession of, documents of the sort requested. The 1874 legislation was enacted to revise similar past statutes (12 St. 737 and 14 St. 547), which were constitutionally objectionable; the legislation skirted constitutional questions by allowing judges to compel the production of documents without physical search or seizure. A party who refused to produce requested documents was considered guilty of the offenses that the documents may have proved.

The defense produced the requested invoice under heavy protest of Fourth and Fifth Amendment violations; they again protested during the trial when the government offered the invoice into evidence. After the trial, Boyd and unnamed companion claimants sued the government on the grounds that the statute which compelled the production of documents from the claimants was unconstitutional. They claimed that the mandatory production of documents before the court under risk of penalty constituted an illegal search. Although no government agent searched or seized evidence, the production order

was a functional equivalent of such a search. Further, assuming the guilt of a party who refused to produce requested documents before the court violated the Fifth Amendment's provision prohibiting self-incrimination.

In a lengthy legislative history reaching back to eighteenth-century British jurisprudence, Justice Bradley agrees with Boyd. He finds a strong connection between the Fourth and Fifth Amendments, writing that "they throw great light upon each other. For the 'unreasonable searches and seizures' condemned in the Fourth Amendment are almost always made for the purpose of compelling a man to give evidence against himself, which in criminal cases is condemned in the Fifth Amendment." Justice Bradley acknowledges that this breach of rights is not the most egregious example, but proposes that the Court operate under the principle of *obsta principiis* (resist the beginning) and decide this case with an eye toward more obnoxious encroachments. He writes "though the proceeding in question is divested of many of the aggravating incidents of actual search and seizure . . . it contains their substance and essence."

Boyd defines a strong relationship between the Fourth and Fifth Amendments that continues to guide the Court's deliberations in similar matters. However, the case's holding was overturned, in part, by *Warden, Md. Penitentiary v. Hayden,* which recognizes the limitations of the *Boyd* decision, most notably the production of evidence that does not serve to self-incriminate.

JOHN GREGORY PALMER

References and Further Reading

Stephens, Otis, Richard Glenn, and Donald Stephenson, eds. *Unreasonable Searches and Seizures: Rights and Liberties under the Law (America's Freedoms).* Santa Barbara, CA: ABC-CLIO, 2005.

Cases and Statutes Cited

United States of America v. E.A.B., 1–35, Thirty-five Cases of Plate Glass
Act to amend the customs revenue laws, etc., Act of June 22, 1874, 18 St. 186
An act to regulate the disposition of the proceeds of fines, penalties, and forfeitures incurred under the laws relating to the custom, and for other purposes, Act of March 2, 1867, 14 St. 547
An act to prevent and punish frauds upon the revenue, Act of March 3, 1863, 12 St. 737
Warden, Md. Penitentiary v. Hayden, 387 U.S. 294 (1967)

See also **Search (General Definition); Search Warrants; Seizures;** *Warden v. Hayden,* **387 U.S. 294 (1967)**

BOYKIN v. ALABAMA, 395 U.S. 238, 242 (1969)

The central issue in the *Boykin* case was the responsibility of a criminal court to safeguard the rights of the accused. Edward Boykin, a twenty-seven-year-old African-American man, was sentenced to death by an Alabama judge in 1966 after pleading guilty to five counts of armed robbery, at the time punishable by execution according to state law. In his automatic appeal to the Alabama Supreme Court, Boykin's attorneys argued that a death sentence for armed robbery constituted cruel and unusual punishment. The Court rejected the appeal but expressed doubts as to whether the trial judge had acted properly in accepting the defendant's guilty plea without questioning him or requiring him to address the court.

Boykin then appealed his case to the U.S. Supreme Court, which in June 1969 ruled by seven-to-two majority that the judge erred in allowing the guilty plea without requiring Boykin to confirm it himself, stating that the standards for evaluating whether a defendant knowingly and voluntarily enters a guilty plea should at least equal the standards for determining a defendant's mental competence to stand trial. Writing for the majority, Justice William O. Douglas opined that in order to meet these standards, the trial record must clearly show that the defendant personally waived his or her constitutional rights. The *Boykin* decision thus joined the *Miranda* and *Gideon* decisions in expanding and clarifying the responsibility of courts to ensure the rights of criminal defendants, thereby reinforcing constitutional guarantees of due process, trial by jury, and protection from self-incrimination.

MICHAEL H. BURCHETT

References and Further Reading

Horn, Maurita Elaine, *Confessional Stipulations: Protecting Waiver of Constitutional Rights*, University of Chicago Law Review 61 (Winter 1994): 1:225–51.
Kersch, Kenneth I. *Constructing Civil Liberties: Discontinuities in the Development of American Constitutional Law.* New York: Cambridge University Press, 2004.

Cases and Statutes Cited

Gideon v. Wainwright, 372 U.S. 335 (1963)
Miranda v. Arizona, 384 U.S. 436 (1966)

See also **Capital Punishment and Right of Appeal; Capital Punishment: Proportionality; Guilty Plea; Jury Trial Right;** *Miranda* **Warning; Plea Bargaining; Race and Criminal Justice; Self-Incrimination: Miranda and Evolution**

BRADFIELD v. ROBERTS, 175 U.S. 291 (1899)

Bradfield v. Roberts is the first of only two Supreme Court cases that have addressed whether government funding of faith-based human services programs is constitutional. In *Bradfield*, a taxpayer sued the federal government challenging a congressional appropriation that funded the construction of a hospital in the District of Columbia that was owned and operated by the Sisters of Charity, a monastic order of the Catholic Church. Pursuant to the appropriation, city officials from the District of Columbia and the hospital directors entered into an agreement providing that the hospital would care for indigent city patients in exchange for construction of the hospital and continued payments for patient care. The taxpayer alleged that the appropriation violated the establishment clause of the First Amendment, which states that "Congress shall make no law respecting an establishment of religion." In other words, the taxpayer asserted that the arrangement violated the separation between church and state.

The Court upheld the appropriation and ruled against the taxpayer. Writing for the Court, Justice Peckham reasoned that the hospital was incorporated as a secular institution. According to the Court, it was thus irrelevant that the Roman Catholic Church might influence the management of the hospital. Such influence could not "alter the legal character of the corporation" as defined in its charter. Rather, the hospital was an "ordinary private corporation" whose secular duties and rights were set forth in the legal documents of incorporation. Moreover, there was no allegation that the hospital discriminated on the basis of religion or in violation of its charter.

The Court relied on the *Bradfield* decision in 1988 in *Bowen v. Kendrick*, the only other Supreme Court decision addressing government funding of faith-based human service programs. In *Kendrick*, the Court upheld a federal statute that provided government grants to religious organizations for the counseling of pregnant teenagers. Citing to *Bradfield*, the *Kendrick* Court stated that "this Court has never held that religious institutions are disabled by the First Amendment from participating in publicly sponsored social welfare programs." The Court determined that *Bradfield* remained good law, especially given this country's long history of interdependency between the government and religious organizations in providing for the needy.

Since 1996, when the American welfare system was reformed, *Bradfield* has taken on increased importance. Among other things, the 1996 welfare legislation authorized the granting of federal funds to faith-based organizations that provide welfare-related social services. This provision is commonly called "charitable choice." Opponents of charitable choice contend that charitable choice violates the separation of church and state. Proponents of charitable choice believe that faith-based organizations are particularly effective in combating social problems, and they are seeking to expand charitable choice programs to a wide array of federal human service programs. *Bradfield* provides legal support for these charitable choice programs. However, in both *Bradfield* and *Kendrick*, the faith-based organizations at issue were not using government funds to advance their religious missions. For instance, the hospital in *Bradfield* was not conducting religious services or discriminating against nonbelievers. Thus, *Bradfield* does not answer the question as to whether a government grant for social services that also flows to religious activities is constitutional. This question remains to be resolved by the Supreme Court.

MICHELE GILMAN

References and Further Reading

Gilman, Michele, *'Charitable Choice' and the Accountability Challenge: Reconciling the Need for Regulation with the First Amendment Religion Clauses*, Vanderbilt Law Review 55 (2002): 3:799–888.
Rotunda, Ronald, and John E. Nowak. *Nowak and Rotunda's Hornbook on Constitutional Law*. 7th ed. St. Paul, MN: West, 2004.

Cases and Statutes Cited

Bowen v. Kendrick, 487 U.S. 589 (1988)
Personal Responsibility and Work Opportunity Reconciliation Act of 1996, 42 U.S.C. § 604a (charitable choice provision)

See also Bowen v. Kendrick, **487 U.S. 589 (1988)**; **Charitable Choice; Establishment Clause Doctrine: Supreme Court Jurisprudence**

BRADY v. MARYLAND, 373 U.S. 83 (1963)

In *Brady*, the Supreme Court for the first time squarely recognized that the Fourteenth Amendment due process clause guarantees criminal defendants the right to be given favorable information in the possession of the prosecution or the police.

Brady admitted at his murder trial that he had participated in the crime but claimed that his confederate, Boblit, had actually committed the killing. After Brady was convicted and sentenced to death,

his lawyers learned that the prosecution had withheld a statement Boblit made to the authorities before Brady's trial in which Boblit confirmed that he was the killer. The Maryland Court of Appeals, reasoning that Brady's admission that he had participated in the killing conclusively established his guilt, nonetheless ruled that the withheld statement was relevant to the question of punishment. Therefore, the state court granted Brady a new sentencing hearing.

Brady appealed to the U.S. Supreme Court, arguing that the withheld statement also entitled him to a new trial, but the Court rejected his argument by a vote of seven to two. The Court, however, used Brady's case to broadly hold that if the prosecution has any information favorable to the defendant and material to his or her guilt or punishment, due process requires the prosecution to turn it over to the defense. In a series of subsequent cases, including *United States v. Agurs*, *Pennsylvania v. Ritchie*, and *Arizona v. Youngblood*, the Court has reaffirmed, but also limited, the defendant's constitutional right to discovery of favorable information.

DAVID A. MORAN

References and Further Reading

Imwinkelried, Edwin, and Norman Garland, 2d ed. *Exculpatory Evidence*. Charlottesville, VA: Michie, 1996.
Stacy, Tom, *The Search for Truth in Constitutional Criminal Procedure*, Columbia Law Review 91 (1991): 1369.

Cases and Statutes Cited

Arizona v. Youngblood, 488 U.S. 51 (1988)
Pennsylvania v. Richie, 480 U.S. 39 (1987)
United States v. Agurs, 427 U.S. 97 (1976)

See also Arizona v. Youngblood, **488 U.S. 51 (1988)**; **Due Process; Fourteenth Amendment**; *United States v. Agurs*, **427 U.S. 97 (1976)**

BRANDEIS, LOUIS DEMBITZ (1856–1941)

An extremely effective lawyer and reformer in the Progressive era before Woodrow Wilson named him to the Supreme Court in 1916, Brandeis had very little if any contact with issues that would be identified as civil liberties. About the only reform that even comes close was his involvement in efforts to improve the treatment of patients in public mental asylums in the late 1890s, and that work seems to have resulted more from a request from one of his reform colleagues than from any innate personal interest.

At the time when Brandeis took his seat on the bench, the dominant issue on the Court's docket involved economic rights, primarily the protection of private property through substantive due process and the negation of protective labor legislation through the doctrine of freedom of contract. Brandeis, who as a lawyer had convinced the Court to uphold maximum hours legislation for women in *Muller v. Oregon* (1908), believed that while important rights inhered in property, they had to be subservient to the greater good. Under the states' police powers, both property rights as well as freedom of contract could be curtailed to protect workers from the harsh conditions that they faced in modern industrialized factories.

Once on the Court, Brandeis often spoke out against the conservative interpretation of property rights as a danger to the rights of others, especially workers. It is not that Brandeis did not believe in property rights; he did, but believed that when the public good required it they should be limited. He especially believed in the right of laboring people to organize into unions and to bargain collectively, although throughout the 1920s he often stood alone or with Holmes in this view, as in *Bedford Cut Stone Co. v. Journeymen Stone Cutters Association* (1927). But his most original contributions came in the areas of free speech and privacy.

In March 1919, Brandeis joined Holmes in his landmark speech decision in *Schenck v. United States* (1919), in which the Court upheld a conviction for antiwar expression under the 1917 Espionage Act. In this decision Holmes set out what would be the defining test for free speech for the next half-century: "The question in every case is whether the words are used in such circumstances and are of such a nature to create a clear and present danger that they will bring about the substantive evils that Congress has a right to prevent." Since the clear and present danger test was so highly subjective, it served as a device by which conservative judges could silence almost any unpopular opinion, a danger that civil libertarians immediately recognized. Holmes, long the darling of liberals, suddenly found himself the object of their severe criticism.

Eight months later, in *Abrams v. United States* (1919), Holmes, joined by Brandeis this time in dissent, attempted to make the clear and present danger test more speech protective, and introduced his idea of free trade in ideas, in which all ideas should be heard so that the "best test of truth is the power of the thought to get itself accepted in the competition of the market."

Brandeis would join Holmes in all of the great speech cases of the 1920s, always in dissent, but a significant difference existed between the two men in why they valued free speech. Although Holmes provided the pithy phrases, Brandeis is the one who refined the concept and who ultimately provided the arguments that remain the basis of First Amendment free speech jurisprudence to this day.

In regard to the *Schenck* opinion, Brandeis later told Felix Frankfurter that "I have never been quite happy about my concurrence . . . . I had not then thought the issues of freedom of speech out—I thought at the subject, not through it." In 1920, in his dissenting opinions in *Schaefer v. United States* (1920) and *Pierce v. United States* (1920), Brandeis, as he later recounted, began to understand the issues. Rather than list what the defendants should *not* have been allowed to say, Brandeis emphasized what they should have been allowed to say, and that would have been anything permitted in peacetime. Unlike his friend Herbert Hoover, who believed that criticism of the governmental policy ought to end at the water's shore—that is, there should be no dissent among Americans regarding foreign policy—Brandeis argued that all matters of public importance should always be open to full criticism, no matter how "radical" the speaker or how unpopular the ideas. Moreover, the test to be used in deciding whether a clear and present danger existed should not be the heightened emotional climate of wartime, but rather the quieter and presumably more rational environment of peacetime. While clearly the government could not allow war protesters to publish the times that troop ships sailed, in terms of policy criticism Brandeis would have utilized the same criteria in wartime as in peacetime, a standard that would have made convictions for seditious libel almost impossible.

In *Gilbert v. Minnesota* (1920), Brandeis and Holmes parted company over a state statute that prohibited interference with military enlistment. An official of the Nonpartisan League—hardly a radical organization—had been convicted under the law for telling a public meeting that the average citizen had not had a say in whether the United States should have entered the World War or whether Congress should have established a draft. Holmes silently concurred with McKenna's opinion for the majority that the speech constituted a clear and present danger, and that the state had the power to prevent such peril. Chief Justice White dissented on the grounds that the federal law preempted the field, grounds on which Brandeis agreed. But he apparently was very angry at his brethren who had consistently used the due process clause to strike down economic measures, but here forbore from even a rudimentary examination of a far greater imposition on civil liberties, freedom of speech. *Gilbert* is perhaps the best example that Brandeis saw a significant difference in how the

Court should approach economic measures—with judicial restraint and deferring to the elected branches' policymaking authority—and laws affecting such basic rights as speech, in which the Court should take a more strenuous approach to protect individual liberties. The dissent in *Gilbert* in many ways prefigured not only Harlan Fiske Stone's Footnote Four in *United States v. Carolene Products Co.* (1938), but also the strict scrutiny standard adopted by the Warren Court in First Amendment cases.

Brandeis's greatest contribution to free speech jurisprudence came in his concurring opinion in *Whitney v. California* (1927), which clearly delineated the differences between what one scholar has called his "republican" justification for the First Amendment and Holmes's libertarian approach.

Charlotte Anita Whitney, a niece of Justice Stephen J. Field and "a woman nearing sixty, a Wellesley graduate long distinguished in philanthropic work," had been convicted under the California Criminal Syndicalism Act of 1919 for helping to organize the Communist Labor Party in that state. The law, originally aimed at the Industrial Workers of the World, made it a felony to organize or knowingly become a member of any organization founded to advocate the commission of crimes, sabotage or violence as a means of bringing about political or industrial change. Whitney denied that the party had ever intended to become an instrument of violence and that no evidence existed to prove that it had ever engaged in criminal or violent acts. Nonetheless, the conservative majority upheld the conviction, and characterized the law as a legitimate decision by the state legislature to prevent the violent overthrow of society.

Because of technical issues (the defense had not raised the particular constitutional issue that concerned Brandeis), he chose not to dissent, but his concurrence, joined in by Holmes, provided an eloquent defense of intellectual freedom and its relation to democratic society unmatched in the annals of the Court. His opinion, which has often been cited, provides the modern basis for much of First Amendment jurisprudence.

Holmes had put forward a marketplace of ideas rationale for free speech, but it had little direct bearing upon democratic government. Holmes loved ideas, but in the abstract, and so his rationale is powerful, but in an abstract manner. His famous aphorism, that "one cannot falsely shout fire in a crowded theatre" is certainly true, but devoid of practical guidelines. Holmes cared little for the practical and dismissed reform and reformers as ineffective. The Constitution set up certain guidelines, and so long as people acted within those guidelines, he could not have cared less what they did.

For Brandeis, on the other hand, free speech constituted an essential ingredient of good government. For him, the highest calling was that of a citizen in a democracy, but the great privileges that position bestowed required corresponding responsibilities. In order to be a good citizen, one had to participate in the democratic process, to make one's voice and views known to policymakers. One could not think responsibly about complex issues if the state censored, through sedition laws and other devices, a broad spectrum of ideas. People might agree or disagree with any one view, but they had to be aware of that view in order to fulfill their obligations. Democratic government, properly conducted, provided humankind with the great opportunity for individuals to achieve their dreams. In a famous and oft-quoted passage, he wrote that:

> Those who won our independence believed that the final end of the State was to make men free to develop their faculties; and that in its government the deliberative forces should prevail over the arbitrary. They valued liberty both as an end and as a means. They believed liberty to be the secret of happiness and courage to be the secret of liberty. They believed that freedom to think as you will and to speak as you think are means indispensable to the discovery and spread of political truth; that without free speech and assembly discussion would be futile; that with them, discussion affords ordinary adequate protection against the dissemination of noxious doctrine; that the greatest menace to freedom is an inert people; that public discussion is a public duty; and that this should be a fundamental principle of the American government.

Rather than be afraid of what people might say, that radical ideas might undermine property rights, that strange ideas would yield "bad counsel," Brandeis believed that the cure for "bad speech" was not fear, but more speech. Civic virtue, that hallmark of Athenian democracy that Brandeis prized so greatly, demanded that citizens not be afraid of the different. "Men feared witches and burnt women," he noted. It is the function of speech to free men from the bondage of irrational fears.

Brandeis's tying of free speech to government has led some people to argue that the First Amendment's speech clause applies only to political speech, and that other kinds of expression do not fall within the ambit of its protection. While it is impossible to tell just how far Brandeis would have extended First Amendment protection, he clearly believed that it applied to some nonpolitical speech as well.

In *Senn v. Tile Layers Protective Union* (1937), the Court heard a challenge to a Wisconsin law that made peaceful picketing lawful, and forbade courts from issuing injunctions to prevent it. During a strike, a construction company owner tried to get an injunction to prohibit workers from peaceful picketing of his plant, on the grounds that it deprived him of his property rights. The Court, by a five-to-four vote, upheld the law, and Brandeis, in the majority opinion, intimated that picketing, aside from its value as a tool in a labor dispute, might also be a form of speech. Union members, he held, did not have to rely on statutes to make the facts of a labor dispute public, "for freedom of speech is guaranteed by the Federal Constitution." Although the Court has refused to categorize picketing per se as a protected activity, it is clear that in Brandeis's mind the First Amendment protected many forms of expression.

In his dissent in *Gilbert v. Minnesota,* Brandeis not only protested against the state sedition law but also added the following line: "I cannot believe that the liberty guaranteed by the Fourteenth Amendment includes only liberty to acquire and to enjoy property." While at the time it appeared to many as little more than a sign of the justice's frustration with his conservative brethren, in fact that sentence set in motion one of the most significant constitutional developments of the twentieth century, the incorporation of Bill of Rights protections through the due process clause of the Fourteenth Amendment so as to apply them to the states as well as to the federal government. (Ever since *Barron v. Baltimore* [1833], the Court had held that the protections in the first eight amendments to the Constitution applied only against Congress and not to the states.)

If Brandeis could have had his way, he would have wiped out the Fourteenth Amendment's due process clause completely, or else severely limited it to procedural matters. Aware that the conservatives on the Court would never allow this to happen, Brandeis wanted the same protection now given to property rights to be applied to other rights that he considered fundamental, such as speech, education, choice of profession, and travel.

Ironically, one of the Court's archconservatives first applied substantive due process to non-property rights. Justice McReynolds, in *Meyer v. Nebraska* (1922), struck down a statute that forbade teaching German in public schools. Although McReynolds used the language of property protection, he expanded it to include other rights including the raising and educating of one's children, an argument that he applied again in *Pierce v. Society of Sisters* (1925).

That same year, while the majority upheld the conviction of communist leader Ben Gitlow under New York's 1902 Criminal Anarchy Act (with Holmes and Brandeis dissenting), Justice Sanford noted, without any further elucidation, that: "For present purposes we may and do assume that freedom of speech and of the press—which are protected by the First Amendment from abridgement by Congress—are among the fundamental personal rights protected by the due process clause of the Fourteenth Amendment from impairment by the States."

Ever since that time there has been an ongoing debate over whether in fact the framers of the Fourteenth Amendment meant the Bill of Rights to apply to the states, and if so, whether only certain rights should apply (the idea of "selective incorporation" proposed by Justice Cardozo and limited to those rights deemed "fundamental") or whether all of the Bill of Rights should apply (the idea of "total incorporation" championed by Justice Black). In the end, nearly all of the rights were in fact incorporated, but through the rationale of selective incorporation. The great revolution in civil liberties in the 1960s and afterwards owed much to Brandeis.

It is difficult to know whether Brandeis would have been an advocate of selective or total incorporation. While on the bench he had the satisfaction of seeing not only speech but freedom of press incorporated, in *Near v. Minnesota* (1931), as well as right to counsel in capital cases, in *Powell v. Alabama* (1932). But in 1937 he joined in Justice Cardozo's opinion for the Court in *Palko v. Connecticut* (1937), in which Cardozo set forth his theory of selective incorporation and held that the Fifth Amendment bar against double jeopardy did not apply to the states. Brandeis had left the Court and died before Hugo Black developed his theory of total incorporation in *Adamson v. California* (1947).

Second only to Brandeis's contribution to the jurisprudence of free speech was his belief that the Constitution protected a right to privacy. Brandeis had first become interested in privacy in the 1890s, when reporters had sneaked into parties given by his socially prominent partner, Samuel D. Warren. The two men had written an article titled "The Right to Privacy" and published it in the *Harvard Law Review.* According to Dean Roscoe Pound, the article did "nothing less than add a chapter to our law." Warren and Brandeis had based their right to be let alone on common law protections, but once on the Court, Brandeis began to believe that privacy constituted such a fundamental right that—even though nowhere listed as such in the Constitution—it deserved the highest level of protection.

Brandeis found his chance to expound this idea in the first wiretapping case to come before the high court, *Olmstead v. United States* (1928). In the 1920s, technology gave the government a new tool to fight crime, the ability to listen in on the telephone conversations of alleged gangsters. By tapping Olmstead's phone, government agents secured evidence to convict him under the National Prohibition Act. He appealed on grounds that the government had not secured a warrant, and had therefore violated the Fourth Amendment. By a bare majority of five to four, the Court upheld the conviction. In a mechanistic opinion, Chief Justice Taft said that since there had been no entry into the house itself, there had been no search within the meaning of the Fourth Amendment, and therefore a warrant had not been needed.

The opinion elicited a strong dissent from four justices—Holmes, Butler, Stone, and Brandeis. Holmes condemned wiretapping as "a dirty business" and seemed to imply that gentlemen should not read other gentlemen's letters, or listen in on their conversations. Justice Butler tore apart Taft's sterile interpretation of the warrant clause, but the most impressive opinion came from Brandeis, condemning not only the action of the government but also putting forth the idea of a constitutionally protected right to privacy.

First, he considered it "less evil that some criminals should escape than that the government should play an ignoble part." The government is the great teacher in a democratic society, and if "government becomes a lawbreaker, it breeds contempt for the law."

The most noted and influential part of the dissent dealt with the question of privacy. The framers of the Constitution, he wrote, "sought to protect Americans in their beliefs, their thoughts, their emotions and their sensations. They conferred, as against the Government, the right to be let alone—the most comprehensive of rights, and the right most valued by civilized men." That passage was picked up and elaborated on until finally, in *Griswold v. Connecticut* (1965), the Court recognized privacy as a constitutionally guaranteed liberty. Although so-called originalists argue that since the Constitution does not mention privacy it cannot protect it, a majority of the Court and most of the American people have come to see privacy as Brandeis saw it—"the most comprehensive of rights, and the right most valued by civilized men."

Wiretapping itself remained legally permissible for many years, although Congress in 1934 prohibited admitting evidence obtained by wiretapping in federal courts. Not until *Berger v. New York* (1967) did the Court finally adopt Brandeis's view and bring wiretapping within the reach of the Fourth Amendment; now wiretap evidence may be introduced, but only if it has been secured after the issuance of a proper warrant.

During the 1920s and 1930s, as the Court's agenda slowly changed from concern with property rights to concern with civil liberties, Louis Brandeis clearly stood as its foremost champion of civil liberties. One

should not, however, confuse Brandeis with a modern liberal. Conservative in many ways, he was also a man of his times. He joined the majority of the Court in denying equal rights to Asiatics in *Ng Fung Ho v. White* (1922) and *Ozawa v. United States* (1922). He voted to uphold racially restrictive covenants in *Corrigan v. Buckley* (1926), and perhaps most infamously, joined in Holmes's opinion upholding forced sterilization of mentally retarded people in *Buck v. Bell* (1927).

Nonetheless, his views on speech, wiretapping, privacy, and what came to be the doctrine of incorporation, although often propounded in dissent, eventually came to be the law of the land, and forms the basis of much of today's civil liberties jurisprudence.

MELVIN I. UROFSKY

References and Further Reading

Blasi, Vincent, *The First Amendment and the Ideal of Civil Courage: The Brandeis Opinion in* Whitney v. California, William & Mary Law Review 29 (1988): 653.

Cortner, Richard C. *The Supreme Court and the Second Bill of Rights: The Fourteenth Amendment and the Nationalization of Civil Liberties.* Madison: University of Wisconsin Press, 1981.

Lahav, Pnina, *Holmes and Brandeis: Libertarian and Republican Justification for Free Speech,* Journal of Law & Politics 4 (1987): 451.

Murphy, Walter F. *Wiretapping on Trial: A Case Study in the Judicial Process.* New York: Random House, 1965.

Strum, Philippa. *Brandeis: Beyond Progressivism.* Lawrence: University Press of Kansas, 1993.

Cases and Statutes Cited

Abrams v. United States, 250 U.S. 616 (1919)
Adamson v. California, 332 U.S. 46 (1947)
Barron v. Baltimore, 7 Pet. 243 (1833)
Bedford Cut Stone Co. v. Journeymen Stone Cutters Association, 274 U.S. 37 (1927)
Berger v. New York, 388 U.S. 41 (1967)
Buck v. Bell, 274 U.S. 200 (1927)
Corrigan v. Buckley, 271 U.S. 323 (1926)
Gilbert v. Minnesota, 250 U.S. 325 (1920)
Griswold v. Connecticut, 381 U.S. 479 (1965)
Meyer v. Nebraska, 262 U.S. 390 (1922)
Muller v. Oregon, 208 U.S. 412 (1908)
Near v. Minnesota, 283 U.S. 697 (1931)
Ng Fung Ho v. White, 259 U.S. 276 (1922)
Olmstead v. United States, 277 U.S. 438 (1928)
Ozawa v. United States, 260 U.S. 178 (1922)
Palko v. Connecticut, 302 U.S. 319 (1937)
Pierce v. Society of Sisters, 268 U.S. 510 (1925)
Pierce v. United States, 252 U.S. 239 (1920)
Powell v. Alabama, 287 U.S. 45 (1932)
Schaefer v. United States, 251 U.S. 466 (1920)
Schenck v. United States, 249 U.S. 47 (1919)
Senn v. Tile Layers Protective Union, 301 U.S. 468 (1937)
United States v. Carolene Products Co., 304 U.S. 144 (1938)
Whitney v. California, 274 U.S. 357 (1927)

BRANDENBURG INCITEMENT TEST

Even though the U.S. Constitution provides strong protections for speech, in a number of early decisions, the U.S. Supreme Court gave government broad authority to prosecute those who engage in speech advocating violence or illegal activity. For example, in *Schenck v. United States* (1919), the defendants circulated a petition urging resistance to the draft during World War I. Even though the advocacy did not come close to causing the violence or illegal activity to actually happen, defendants were nevertheless convicted.

Brandenburg v. Ohio (1969) significantly altered the Court's approach to "illegal advocacy." In *Brandenburg*, members of the Klu Klux Klan (KKK) held a rally at which they made derogatory comments about African Americans and Jews, and stated that there might be a need for "revengenance" if Congress and other public officials failed to respond to KKK concerns. The Court overturned the defendant's conviction for "criminal syndicalism" (defined roughly as speech advocating the use of force or law violation), finding that the state did not have the power to prohibit the discussion of abstract principles. A criminal conviction could only be sustained if it could be shown that the advocacy was directed to inciting or producing imminent lawless conduct and is likely to produce such conduct. In the *Brandenburg* case, even though the KKK members spoke stridently, their speech was not close to causing actual violence. As a result, their convictions were reversed.

RUSSELL L. WEAVER

References and Further Reading

Weaver, Russell L., and Donald E. Lively. *Understanding the First Amendment.* Newark, NJ: LexisNexis, 2003.
Weaver, Russell L., and Arthur E. Hellman. *The First Amendment: Cases, Materials & Problems.* Newark, N.J.: LexisNexis, 2002.

BRANDENBURG v. OHIO, 395 U.S. 444 (1969)

This case originated in the state of Ohio where Clarence Brandenburg, a Ku Klux Klan leader, was convicted, fined, and sentenced to jail for having made a speech in which he suggested that if the branches of the federal government did not stop suppressing the Caucasian race, violence might be the only answer. He was charged under the Ohio criminal syndicalism statute of 1919, which punished advocacy of violence against the government.

Brandenburg appealed his conviction on the grounds that the provisions of the Ohio law were so broad that they violated freedom of speech guarantees under the First and Fourteenth Amendments. The U.S. Supreme Court, in a per curiam opinion (with concurrences by Justices Hugo L. Black and William O. Douglas) overturned Brandenburg's conviction, and in doing so significantly broadened the reach of free speech protection. The decision overturned the earlier decision in *Whitney v. California* (1927) and rejected the clear and present danger test once and for all. In a striking defense of the importance of political speech, the Court emphasized the "principle that the constitutional guarantees of free speech and free press do not permit a state to proscribe or forbid advocacy of the use of force or law violation *except* where such advocacy is directed to inciting or producing *imminent* lawless action and is likely to incite or produce such action." The decision had the effect of invalidating state and federal laws that restricted the activities of political groups, including the Smith Act of 1940.

REBECCA S. SHOEMAKER

References and Further Reading

Linde, Hans A., *'Clear and Present Danger' Reexamined: Dissonance in the Brandenburg Concerto*, Stanford Law Review 22 (June 1970): 6:1163–86.
BeVier, Lillian, *The First Amendment and Political Speech: An Inquiry into the Substance and Limits of Principle*, Stanford Law Review 30 (January 1978): 2:299–358.

Cases and Statutes Cited

Brandenburg v. Ohio 395 U.S. 444 (1969)
Whitney v. California 274 U.S. 357 (1927)

See also **Clear and Present Danger Test; Douglas, William Orville; Smith Act; *Whitney v. California*, 274 U.S. 357 (1927)**

BRANTI v. FINKEL, 445 U.S. 507 (1980)

When a newly appointed Democratic public defender discharged two assistant public defenders because they were Republicans, the discharged lawyers claimed that their First Amendment freedoms of belief and association were violated. In a prior case, *Elrod v. Burns*, the U.S. Supreme Court had held that political patronage dismissals were constitutionally valid when there is a demonstrable need for the political loyalty of employees, but that those circumstances were limited to employees who perform a policymaking function or are entrusted with confidential political information. In *Branti*, the Supreme Court broadened *Elrod* by concluding that "the ultimate inquiry is not whether the label 'policy-maker' or 'confidential' fits a particular position; rather, the question is whether the hiring authority can demonstrate that party affiliation is an appropriate requirement for the effective performance of the public office involved." The public defender could not sustain that burden because the function of assistant public defenders is to defend accused criminal defendants. Whatever policy an assistant public defender makes "relate[s] to the needs of individual clients and not to any partisan political interests," and the confidential information obtained by an assistant public defender "has no bearing whatsoever on partisan political concerns."

Later cases extended this principle. In *Rutan v. Republican Party of Illinois*, the Court applied its patronage doctrine to include sanctions short of discharge and *O'Hare Truck Services, Inc. v. City of Northlake* extended its scope to independent contractors terminated for partisan political reasons.

CALVIN MASSEY

References and Further Reading

Brinkley, Martin H., *Despoiling the Spoils:* Rutan v. Republican Party of Illinois, North Carolina Law Review 69 (1991): 719.
Johnson, Ronald N., and Gary D. Libecap, *Courts, A Protected Bureaucracy, and Reinventing Government*, Arizona Law Review 37 (1995): 791.

Cases and Statutes Cited

Elrod v. Burns, 427 U.S. 347 (1976)
O'Hare Truck Services, Inc. v. City of Northlake, 518 U.S. 712 (1996)
Rutan v. Republican Party of Illinois, 497 U.S. 62 (1990)

See also **Elrod v. Burns, 427 U.S. 347 (1976); Freedom of Association; Political Patronage and First Amendment;** *Rutan v. Republican Party of Illinois*, **497 U.S. 62 (1990)**

BRANZBURG v. HAYES, 408 U.S. 665 (1972)

In *Branzburg*, the Supreme Court confronted an issue of continuing controversy: May journalists who are called to testify before grand juries protect the identities of their confidential sources? *Branzburg* is the only case to date in which the Court has squarely addressed whether the First Amendment provides a "reporter's privilege."

The case involved a reporter from the Louisville *Courier-Journal* who had published stories about illegal drug activity, as well as journalists from the *New York Times* and a Massachusetts television station who had reported on the Black Panthers. All had been called before grand juries and asked to reveal confidential information about what they had seen or heard during their reporting.

Advocates for the reporter's privilege argue that it is grounded in the historic role of the press in holding government officials accountable and keeping citizens informed on matters of public concern. The First Amendment protects the freedom to publish and broadcast the news, but this freedom means little, advocates note, without constitutional protections for the freedom to *gather* the news.

In *Branzburg*, the Supreme Court held that the First Amendment did not provide a journalist's privilege. A plurality of four justices declined to erect what they called "a virtually impenetrable constitutional shield, beyond legislative or judicial control" by giving journalists a privilege not enjoyed by most other citizens. The Court's holding was limited to times when a news source is implicated in a crime or possesses information relevant to a grand jury's work. Justice Byron White emphasized that the decision should not threaten "the vast bulk of confidential relationships between reporters and their sources."

Justice Lewis Powell, who provided the crucial fifth vote in *Branzburg*, wrote separately to emphasize what he saw as limited scope of the Court's holding. In an important concurring opinion, Powell said that courts should balance on a case-by-case basis the rights and needs of journalists with the traditional obligation of all citizens to testify about criminal conduct. When subpoenas threaten to improperly impair the news-gathering process, Powell said, "the courts will be available to [journalists] under circumstances where legitimate First Amendment interests require protection." In dissent, Justice Potter Stewart said a reporter's constitutional right to a confidential relationship with a source stems from the broad social interest in the free flow of information. Thus, he said, the Constitution protects journalistic freedom "not for the benefit of the press so much as for the benefit of all of us."

In the years since *Branzburg*, more than half of the states have enacted statutes providing some limited form of a reporter's privilege. But there is no such federal law, and federal courts asked to shield journalists from testifying have continued to invoke *Branzburg* and hold that a reporter's privilege cannot be inferred out of the First Amendment. In a famous case in 2005, a judge jailed a *New York Times* reporter who refused to testify in an investigation concerning the leak of a CIA officer's identity by members of the George W. Bush administration.

STEVE SANDERS

References and Further Reading

Pracene, Ulan C., ed. *Journalists, Shield Laws and the First Amendment*. New York: Novinka Books, 2005.

BRASWELL v. UNITED STATES, 487 U.S. 99 (1988)

The availability of the Fifth Amendment self-incrimination privilege to resist producing documents in response to a subpoena has depended on whether the government sought the records from an individual (or sole proprietorship) or from a larger business organization. In *Fisher v. United States*, the Supreme Court held that an individual may assert the Fifth Amendment if the act of production of the records would incriminate the person. Randy Braswell, the owner of a business who received a subpoena for its records, sought to apply *Fisher*'s privilege analysis to a single-shareholder corporation.

The Supreme Court, relying on a consistent line of cases going back to its 1906 decision in *Hale v. Henkel*, reaffirmed the collective entity doctrine in *Braswell v. United States* to bar a corporation from asserting the Fifth Amendment to resist production of its records, regardless of the corporation's size or whether an owner or officer would be incriminated by the documents. The Court noted that allowing a corporation's representative to assert the self-incrimination privilege "would have a detrimental impact on the government's efforts to prosecute" white-collar crime, one of the most serious problems confronting law enforcement authorities. The Court further explained that the production of documents by the corporation's representative could not be used by the government against that person if the government charged that person with an offense in a personal capacity.

The decision to incorporate an enterprise means that it cannot assert the Fifth Amendment privilege to resist a government demand for its records.

PETER J. HENNING

References and Further Reading

LaFave, Wayne R., Jerold H. Israel, and Nancy J. King. *Criminal Procedure*. Vol. 3. 2nd ed. St. Paul, MN: Thomson West, 1999.
Mosteller, Robert P., *Simplifying Subpoena Law: Taking the Fifth Amendment Seriously*, Virginia Law Review 73 (1987): 1:1–110.
Note: Right Against Self-Incrimination—Production of Documents, Harvard Law Review 102(1988): 1:170–80.

Cases and Statutes Cited

Fisher v. United States, 425 U.S. 391 (1976)
Hale v. Henkel, 201 U.S. 43 (1906)

See also Fisher v. United States, **425 U.S. 391 (1976); Grand Jury Investigation and Indictment; Hale v. Henkel, 201 U.S. 43 (1906); Self-Incrimination (V): Historical Background**

BRAUNFELD v. BROWN, 366 U.S. 599 (1961)
See Sunday Closing Cases

BRAY v. ALEXANDRIA WOMEN'S HEALTH CLINIC, 506 U.S. 263 (1993)

In *Bray v. Alexandria Women's Health Clinic*, the Supreme Court held that the anti-conspiracy provision of the 1871 Civil Rights Act, 42 U.S.C. § 1985(3), known as the Ku Klux Klan Act, did not support a claim against an anti-abortion group's conspiracy to obstruct access to abortion clinics. Anti-abortion activists have targeted clinics, physicians, and their patients with advocacy and harassment, obstructed clinic access and, in extreme cases, bombed abortion clinics and murdered abortion providers. *Bray* challenged Operation Rescue's blockades of abortion facilities throughout the Washington, D.C. area.

Congress originally enacted Section 1985(3) to bar Ku Klux Klan–style mob violence that terrorized black people and Reconstruction supporters and impeded local officials from protecting them. The statute provides a civil cause of action against private conspiracies (1) to deprive "any person or class of persons" of the equal protection of the laws, or (2) to "prevent or hinder the constituted authorities of any State" from providing equal protection. The act applies not only to government conduct, but also to private groups like the Klan or Operation Rescue (see *Bray* and *Griffin v. Breckenridge*). To prevent Section 1985(3) from becoming "a general federal tort law," which is traditionally the province of the states, the Court had interpreted the statute's first clause—the "deprivation clause"—to impose two additional limitations: first, that "some racial, or perhaps otherwise class-based, invidiously discriminatory animus [lay] behind the conspirators' action," and, second, that the conspiracy aim to interfere with rights that are "protected against private, as well as official, encroachment" (see *Griffin,* and *Carpenters v. Scott*).

In an opinion written by Justice Scalia for a five-member majority, the Court held that the *Bray* plaintiffs had failed to meet both of those requirements. In the majority's view, the class of women as a whole was not targeted by Operation Rescue's opposition to abortion, and the subset of "women seeking abortions" is defined merely by its shared objective, making it not a statutorily protected class. In any event, the Court held, the deprivation clause does not prevent private interference with abortion, because constitutional abortion rights run only against the government. The right to interstate travel constrains private actors, but the Court viewed Operation Rescue's interference with some women's travel as a circumstantial effect rather than a purpose of the conspiracy. The majority did not rule on the belatedly raised hindrance claim.

For the four dissenters (Justices Stevens, O'Connor, Blackmun, and Souter), the case presented none of the federalism concerns that might justify restrictive interpretation of Section 1985(3). All four would have reached and sustained the plaintiffs' hindrance claim. Three dissenters concluded that obstructing women's access to abortion is sex-based "class animus" under the act, and that, unlike the deprivation clause, the hindrance clause protects the effectiveness of government and so applies even to private interference with official protection of rights like abortion. Justice Souter's separate, broader dissent questioned the narrow deprivation-clause precedents requiring class-based animus and infringement of a right guaranteed against private impairment, and would have ruled for plaintiffs on that ground as well. Justice Stevens, joined by Justice Blackmun, also would have sustained the deprivation clause claim on the more limited ground that burdening interstate travel was "one of the intended consequences of [the] conspiracy," and no specific intent to discriminate against out-of-staters should have been required.

The *Bray* majority did not foreclose litigation under the hindrance clause, and women in later cases have successfully pursued hindrance claims (see, for example, *Libertad v. Welch* and *National Abortion Federation v. Operation Rescue*), and also have gained protection under other sources of law. Partially in response to *Bray*, Congress in 1994 passed the Freedom of Access to Clinic Entrances Act (FACE), criminalizing the obstruction of clinics and the use of force to intimidate or interfere with persons seeking to provide or obtain abortions. Additionally, in *Schenck v. Pro-Choice Network of Western New York*, the Supreme Court upheld state-law buffer zones and other restrictions around abortion clinics against free speech challenges. While relief from anti-abortion protestors under RICO initially seemed promising, the Court held in *Scheidler v. NOW* that abortion protesters' interference with or shutting down of clinics did not amount to the RICO predicate act of "extortion," such that RICO did not apply.

NINA PILLARD

Cases and Statutes Cited

Carpenters v. Scott, 463 U.S. 825, 833 (1983)
Griffin v. Breckenridge, 403 U.S. 88 (1971)
Libertad v. Welch, 53 F.3d 428, 446–450 (1st Cir. 1995)
National Abortion Federation v. Operation Rescue, 8 F.3d 680 (9th Cir. 1993)
Scheidler v. NOW, 537 U.S. 393 (2003)
Schenck v. Pro-Choice Network of Western New York, 519 U.S. 357 (1997)

See also **Abortion; Operation Rescue**

BREITHAUPT v. ABRAM, 352 U.S. 432 (1957)

Breithaupt was convicted of involuntary manslaughter in New Mexico following an automobile collision resulting in three deaths. The primary evidence was a blood test showing his blood alcohol content at 0.17 percent. Breithaupt argued that this blood sample, which was obtained while he was unconscious due to his injuries, was illegally obtained and thus should have been excluded. Six justices, speaking through Justice Tom Clark, rejected this argument based on *Wolf v. Colorado*. Breithaupt also argued, on the basis of *Rochin v. California*, that the involuntary blood test "shocked the conscience," thus violating his substantive due process rights.

The Court, however, distinguished the blood test at issue in *Breithaupt* from the forceful stomach pumping at issue in *Rochin*. The majority concluded that there was nothing offensive or brutal in the taking of a blood sample, under the supervision of a physician, despite the lack of conscious consent. Instead, a blood test was part of a routine medical examination and thus not violative of a suspect's due process rights.

Chief Justice Earl Warren and Justice William O. Douglas wrote forceful dissents, both joined by Justice Hugo Black. The dissenters were especially outraged by police methods that, in Justice Douglas's words, violated "the sanctity of the person."

Breithaupt is most significant in limiting the "shocks the conscience" test elaborated in *Rochin* and in demonstrating the subjectivity involved in that test. The case was later reaffirmed in *Schmerber v. California*, decided after *Wolf* was overruled by *Mapp v. Ohio*.

EMERY G. LEE, III

References and Further Reading

LaFave, Wayne R., Jerold H. Israel, and Nancy J. King. *Criminal Procedure*. 2nd ed. St. Paul, MN: West, 1999.

Cases and Statutes Cited

Mapp v. Ohio, 367 U.S. 643 (1961)
Rochin v. California, 342 U.S. 165 (1952)
Schmerber v. California, 384 U.S. 757 (1966)
Wolf v. Colorado, (1949), *overruled by Mapp v. Ohio*, 367
    U.S. 643 (1961)

BREWER v. WILLIAMS, 430 U.S. 387 (1977)

On Christmas Eve 1968, a ten-year-old child was abducted by Williams, a recent escapee from a mental hospital. A day later, police in Davenport, Iowa, found Williams's car and located at a rest stop some of the child's clothes and the blanket in which she had been wrapped. Police initiated a search of the surrounding countryside.

Williams turned himself in on December 26 to the Davenport police. When he was formally charged, he obtained attorneys in Davenport and Des Moines who instructed the police not to question Williams during his transport to Des Moines, 160 miles away. A detective and another officer were assigned to drive Williams to Des Moines. During the car ride, the detective "delivered what [was] referred to in the briefs and oral arguments as the "Christian burial speech."

> I want to give you something to think about . . . . I want you to observe the weather conditions . . . . They are predicting several inches of snow for tonight, and I feel that you yourself are the only person that knows where this little girl's body is . . . . [T]he parents of this little girl should be entitled to a Christian burial for the little girl who was snatched away from them on Christmas (E)ve and murdered. And I feel we should stop and locate it on the way in rather than waiting until morning and trying to come back out after a snow storm and possibly not being able to find it at all.

After listening to these comments, Williams directed the police to the child's body.

During his trial, over the objections of the defense, the judge allowed the prosecution to admit Williams's highly incriminating statements to the police as to the location of the body. The jury found Williams guilty of first-degree murder.

In a five-to-four decision, the U.S. Supreme Court decided that Williams was denied his right to counsel guaranteed by the Sixth and Fourteenth Amendments. The majority said that the detective's speech constituted an interrogation outside the presence of counsel after judicial proceedings had been initiated. This conclusion was based on the admission that the detective was trying to elicit information from Williams in the car before he could re-contact his attorney in Des Moines.

The Court rejected the view that Williams had waived his Sixth Amendment right to a lawyer voluntarily during the car ride. The justices found that the prosecution had failed to meet its burden to prove that Williams affirmatively relinquished his right to counsel through a knowing and intelligent waiver. Thus, the police violated the right to counsel by eliciting incriminating statements from Williams without his counsel present.

The Court remanded the case to the Iowa courts and directed that Williams's incriminating statements and any testimony regarding the retrieval of the body be excluded from evidence at a new trial. However, the Court left open the possibility that the body, as well as its condition, could be admitted into evidence unrelated to his statement. This, in fact, occurred in the second trial where the defendant was again convicted. The Court affirmed this conviction using the so-called inevitable discovery doctrine, meaning that the confession did not affect the other evidence, as it would have been found anyway, inevitably.

PAUL MARCUS

References and Further Reading

Kamisar, Yale, Brewer v. Williams—*A Hard Look at a Discomfiting Record*, Georgetown Law Journal 66 (1977): 209.
White, Welsh S., *False Confessions and the Constitution: Safeguards Against Untrustworthy Confessions*, Harvard Civil Rights-Civil Liberties Law Review 32 (1997): 105.

See also Nix v. Williams, 467 U.S. 431 (1984); Right to Counsel; Self-Incrimination: Miranda and Evolution

BREYER, STEPHEN GERALD (1938–)

Justice Stephen Breyer, a Massachusetts Democrat, was President Bill Clinton's second and final appointment to the Court (following Ruth Bader Ginsburg in 1993). A San Francisco native and son of a lawyer for the city's school board, Breyer was educated at Stanford (1959), Oxford (1961) (where he was a Marshall Scholar), and the Harvard Law School (1964). After law school, he clerked for Supreme Court Justice Arthur Goldberg (1964–1965) and went on to a distinguished career as a professor at Harvard's law school and lecturer at its Kennedy School of Government, and a high-level congressional and Justice Department staff member—special assistant to the assistant attorney general for anti-trust (1965–1967); assistant special prosecutor, Watergate Prosecution Force (1973); special (1974–1975) and chief counsel (1979–1980), U.S. Senate Judiciary Committee); and a Carter appointee to Boston's First Circuit Court of Appeals (1980), where he ultimately served as chief judge (1990–1994).

Although Breyer clerked on the Supreme Court at the height of the Warren Court's "rights revolution," his chief scholarly interest and contribution was never in civil liberties—or even constitutional law—but rather in the law and economics of regulation. At Harvard, Breyer taught courses on anti-trust, regulatory, and administrative law. While on leave from academia, as an aide to Senator Edward Kennedy in the late 1970s, he was an influential architect of the deregulation of the airline industry. Later, as a judge, he played a major role in crafting the sentencing guidelines of the U.S. Sentencing Commission (1985–1989). In addition to many articles, Justice Breyer is the author of *Regulation and Its Reform* (1982), *Breaking the Vicious Circle: Toward Effective Risk Regulation* (1993), and co-author of a prominent administrative law casebook. That Breyer had devoted little time to contentious civil liberties and civil rights issues proved important, in the aftermath of a number of ideologically charged confirmation battles, to Clinton's decision to name him to the Court. Besides having said little about issues like abortion and affirmative action, Breyer's impressive command of economics and his understanding of (and sympathy for) business won him the goodwill of pro-business Republicans. What limited opposition there was to his appointment came from the public interest and consumer movements within the Democratic Party itself.

The texture of Justice Breyer's constitutional jurisprudence reflects his "legal process" training and longstanding interest in the design of efficient and effective regulatory systems. The style of Breyer's civil liberties opinions makes manifest his conviction that judging is a purposive task in which judges, mindful of the limits of judicial authority and expertise, collaborate with the other governmental institutions to formulate rational, goal-directed, and empirically grounded public policy. Those opinions devote relatively little time to deduction from fundamental principles and extended time to the pragmatic parsing of particular fact situations in light of purposive public policy considerations.

Since joining the Court, Justice Breyer has been called upon to apply his approach to a panoply of civil liberties issues. Despite the distinctive flavor of his analysis, in most areas of civil liberties (and civil rights), Breyer's votes have been predictably liberal, aligning fairly consistently with the votes of Justices Ginsburg, Souter, and Stevens. Justice Breyer has been a reliable supporter of the right to privacy, including expansive understandings of abortion

rights (*Stenberg v. Carhart* [2000]), the right to die (*Washington v. Glucksberg* [1997]), and gay rights (*Romer v. Evans* [1996]; *Lawrence v. Texas* [2003]). His free speech decisions are generally liberal. (See *Denver Area Educational Telecommunications Consortium v. FCC* [1995], *Ashcroft v. Free Speech Coalition* [2002], *Republican Party of Minnesota v. White* [2002], *McConnell v. Federal Elections Commission* [2003]. But see also *United States v. American Library Association* [2003]).

While maintaining a liberal predisposition, Justice Breyer has on occasion voted with the Court's conservatives in three areas of civil liberties law. While traditionally liberal in many criminal process cases involving matters such as capital punishment and other Eighth Amendment issues and the right to counsel (see, for example, *Stogner v. California* [2003], *Atkins v. Virginia* [2002], *Penry v. Johnson* [2001], *Kansas v. Hendricks* [1997]), Breyer has in some cases been more deferential to the government in search and seizure cases than quintessential constitutional liberals (*Venonia School District v. Acton* [1995], *Minnesota v. Carter* [1998], *Wyoming v. Houghton* [1999]). In a similar spirit, while evincing a quintessentially liberal concern for the civil liberties of detained persons, he has asserted that indefinite detentions might be constitutionally permissible in cases involving "terrorism or other special circumstances where special arguments might be made for forms of preventative detention and for heightened deference to the judgments of the political branches with respect to matters of national security" (*Zadvydas v. Davis* [2001]). Breyer sometimes evinces more flexibility in his establishment clause decisions than the Court's "strict separationist" justices. (Contrast *Good News Club v. Milford* [2001] and *Mitchell v. Helms* [2000], with *Rosenberger v. University of Virginia* [1995], *Zelman v. Simmons-Harris* [2002], and *Santa Fe Independent School District v. Doe* [2000].) Moreover, like many conservatives, Justice Breyer takes economic rights seriously (see *BMW v. Gore* [1996]). He nonetheless has refused to sign on to the conservative property rights jurisprudence pursuant to the Fifth Amendment's takings clause. (See *Palazzolo v. Rhode Island* [2001], *Tahoe-Sierra Preservation Council v. Tahoe Regional Planning Agency* [2002], and *Brown v. Legal Foundation of Washington* [2003].)

Perhaps the most innovative component of Justice Breyer's jurisprudence is his commitment to a belief that the Court should take greater cognizance in its decisions of the ways in which other nations and foreign and international courts have approached similar problems of law, governance, and public policy, a belief that has exerted a considerable influence on the Court's other justices. Breyer has gone so far as to suggest that this may involve American judges working to integrate the U.S. Constitution into the governing documents of other nations. He has asserted that international treaties "may eventually prove relevant" in death penalty cases, and that "the number of treaties relevant to particular domestic legal disputes seems to be growing." In *Grutter v. Bollinger* (2003), Breyer joined an opinion by Justice Ginsburg that cited international human rights agreements as authority for upholding the affirmative action policies of the University of Michigan Law School. Breyer's transnationalism is a piece with his interest in pragmatic systems building: He sees a worldwide system of governance emerging, particularly with regard to human rights, and believes that the Supreme Court has an important role to play in integrating the United States (and the U.S. Constitution) into this system. This globalist inclination could ultimately have a significant impact on the future path of the Court's civil liberties jurisprudence.

KEN I. KERSCH

References and Further Reading

Kersch, Ken I. "The Synthetic Progressivism of Stephen G. Breyer." In *Rehnquist Justice: Understanding the Court Dynamic*, edited by Earl M. Maltz. Lawrence: University Press of Kansas, 2003.
———. "Multilateralism Comes to the Courts." *The Public Interest* (Winter 2004).

BROADCAST REGULATION

The history of broadcast regulation affords a unique civil liberties perspective because it is the sole example of a government agency created to supervise the press. That agency, the Federal Communications Commission (FCC), enforced specific statutory commands, such as the requirement to give equal time to candidates for elective office or suppressing indecency, as well as created its own, such as the "fairness doctrine" and the requirement to air local programming, based on its own notions of the public interest. All of these content regulations would have been unconstitutional if applied to the print media.

Until it was repealed in 1987, the fairness doctrine was the centerpiece of broadcast regulation. It required broadcasters to give adequate coverage to significant public issues and to ensure fair coverage that accurately presents conflicting viewpoints on those issues (although not necessarily in the same program). For years the FCC and the courts could not say enough good things about the fairness doctrine; it was, the Commission said, "the single most important requirement of operation in the public interest—the

sine qua non for grant of renewal of license." No station could avoid it as the FCC made clear when it rejected a defense that opposite sides of the issues in question were fully available on other stations in the area. The FCC then proceeded to strip the license from a Philadelphia station that aired more controversial programming than any other in that market. The FCC believed that each station acting as a market (airing something of everything) was superior to having stations differentiate themselves on the basis of content. It feared that listeners would stick with a single station and thus might not be as well informed as the Commission believed they should be.

In operation the fairness doctrine proved a failure. In the days before unique formats became common, most stations would automatically do what the fairness doctrine required so that the doctrine itself should have affected only those who did not wish to comply (and those who lacked the competency to comply). Because the doctrine was triggered by complaints, however, a station in compliance could nevertheless be forced to respond to the FCC. Indeed the more controversial issues that a station covered, the more likely it was to have a complaint filed against it. Responding to a complaint—taking time from management and possibly hiring a lawyer—constituted a tax on airing controversial programming. Yet airing such programming was what the FCC claimed it desired.

Supporters of the fairness doctrine claimed that its effects were exactly those stated in its purposes: fostering coverage of controversial issues. Its repeal put the lie to that assertion. Freed from the fairness doctrine, talk radio, with its controversies, became possible and flourished. Thus, occasionally a supporter of the fairness doctrine now laments its demise and pines for the days when radio was not "uninhibited, robust, and wide open," and instead was tempered by the fairness doctrine. That, of course, is inconsistent with the premises of the First Amendment as articulated in *New York Times v. Sullivan* (1964).

In *Red Lion Broadcasting v. FCC* (1969), the Supreme Court upheld the constitutionality of the fairness doctrine. Like the FCC, the Court assumed that the doctrine was synonymous with its purposes. Further, the Court was blind to the fact that such a good doctrine could have a chilling effect on broadcast speech; if there were a chilling effect, then the FCC would take appropriate action to eliminate it.

Red Lion announced a trust hierarchy. At the top were viewers and listeners whose rights were paramount. At the bottom were broadcasters who were mere proxies for the greater good. In between were the FCC and the federal courts poised to require that broadcasters give the people their due.

The Court never knew the actual facts behind *Red Lion*. If the facts had come out, perhaps the Court would have understood that government oversight of broadcasting would operate just like the Court knows that government oversight of the print media would work. It would be partisan.

In 1963, the Democratic National Committee created an operation to monitor rightwing radio stations and harass them with equal time and fairness doctrine complaints. The expressed hope was "that challenges would be so costly to them that they would be inhibited and decide it was too expensive to continue." The monitoring did not cease with the 1964 elections and that picked up Red Lion's supposed transgression. The station, accurately sensing that it was being harassed, fought back—and lost unanimously to a Court that was sure broadcasting was unique and that the FCC was promoting the public interest.

For almost every attempt by the FCC to coerce or coax diverse programming, there is an opposite one to mandate or persuade conformity. Thus, fresh from its success in *Red Lion*, the FCC turned on popular music attempting to rid the airwaves of songs that it believed promoted the drug culture (even though such songs had peaked three years previously and the phenomenon was subsiding). A "do not play" list of twenty-two songs was produced by the Broadcast Bureau. Included were "Lucy in the Sky with Diamonds" and "With a Little Help from my Friends" by the Beatles as well as "Truckin" by the Grateful Dead. Some panicked stations ceased playing "Puff, the Magic Dragon" by Peter, Paul, and Mary.

The Commission's attention soon wandered to other issues—specifically sex and violence. Sometimes with censorship, sometimes with jawboning, the Commission attempted to return radio and television to the cultural standards of an earlier era. Like most attempts to move culture backward, this effort failed.

It has been over two decades since the Supreme Court last decided a broadcast case. Its discussions of broadcast regulation in cases involving cable and the Internet indicate that the Court recognizes its embrace of FCC actions was mistaken. Freedom of speech and the press will not blossom in an environment of government supervision. The Court knew that; broadcast regulation has proved it again.

Scot Powe

References and Further Reading

Krattenmaker, Thomas G., and Lucas A. Powe, Jr. *Regulating Broadcast Programming*. Cambridge, MA: MIT Press; Washington, D.C.: AEI Press, 1994.
Powe, Lucas A., Jr. *American Broadcasting and the First Amendment*. Berkeley: University of California Press, 1987.
Spitzer, Matthew. *Seven Dirty Words and Six Other Stories*. New Haven, Conn.: Yale University Press, 1986.

Cases and Statutes Cited

New York Times v. Sullivan, 376 U.S. 254 (1964)
Red Lion Broadcasting v. Federal Communications Commission, 395 U.S. 367 (1969)

BROOKS v. TENNESSEE, 406 U.S. 605 (1972)

In *Brooks*, the Supreme Court struck down a state statute requiring criminal defendants to testify, if at all, before any other defense witnesses take the stand. The Court concluded that such statutes violate both the Fifth Amendment self-incrimination clause and the right to counsel.

At the close of the prosecution's case in his robbery trial, Brooks's attorney requested that Brooks be allowed to testify after the other defense witnesses. Relying on a Tennessee statute requiring the defendant to testify at the beginning of the defense case or not at all, the judge refused the request. Brooks then elected to not testify, and he was convicted.

The U.S. Supreme Court reversed Brooks's conviction by vote of six to three. The Court acknowledged that the statute was intended to prevent defendants from adjusting their testimony to fit with testimony given by other defense witnesses. However, the Court held that the statute unjustifiably burdened Brooks's right not to testify because it forced him to decide whether to testify before he knew if his testimony would be necessary or helpful to his case. The Court also concluded that the statute violated Brooks's right to the effective assistance of counsel because it prevented his attorney from exercising his professional judgment as to the best time to call his client to testify.

Brooks thus holds that states may not erect arbitrary barriers that frustrate a criminal defendant's exercise of his right to testify or interfere with his attorney's ability to effectively represent him.

David A. Moran

See also **Right to Counsel; Self-Incrimination (V): Historical Background**

BROTHERHOOD OF RAILROAD TRAINMEN v. VIRGINIA EX REL. VIRGINIA STATE BAR, 377 U.S. 1 (1964)

The legal profession has traditionally exhibited antipathy toward activities that could be perceived as encouraging litigation. It has also taken a dim view of nonlawyers providing legal advice. So it is not surprising that the Virginia State Bar (and the American Bar Association, as amicus curiae) sought to prevent a labor union from operating a "department of legal counsel." This department functioned as a referral service, directing injured union members to local lawyers who could represent them in lawsuits against their employers, and also as an institutionalized warning system to employees, cautioning them not to settle injury claims without first consulting a lawyer.

The Virginia State Bar obtained an injunction against the department, contending that it constituted the unlawful solicitation of clients and the unauthorized practice of law. The U.S. Supreme Court reversed, however, on the grounds that the First Amendment's guarantees of freedom of expression, assembly, and petition gave the employees the right to associate together for the purpose of petitioning for the redress of their grievances against the railroads. The Court noted that the Virginia bar may have a legitimate interest in preventing "ambulance chasing," but that the union's interest was not commercial gain but protecting the rights of its members. One might question whether this is a tenable distinction. Plaintiffs' personal injury lawyers may be interested both in protecting the legal rights of their clients and in making money. Does one motivation diminish the other? In any event, read in conjunction with the commercial speech cases protecting most advertising by attorneys, this case is part of the foundation of the constitutional protection afforded to lawyers' commercial activities.

W. BRADLEY WENDEL

References and Further Reading

Erichson, Howard M., *Doing Good, Doing Well*, Vanderbilt Law Review 57 (2004): 2087–125.
Wolfram, Charles W. *Modern Legal Ethics*. St. Paul, Minn.: West, 1986.

See also **Freedom of Association; Lawyer Advertising;** *NAACP v. Button*, 371 U.S. 415 (1963)

BROWN v. BOARD OF EDUCATION, 347 U.S. 483 (1954)

The U.S. Supreme Court's 1954 decision in *Brown v. Board of Education*, declaring state-mandated school segregation unconstitutional, was perhaps the Court's most important decision of the twentieth century. Prior to the *Brown* decision, seventeen states (including all eleven states of the old Confederacy)

and the District of Columbia either permitted or required racial segregation in public schools. Although such segregation relegated black children to poorly funded separate schools and imposed on them the stigma of second-class citizenship, many states were determined not to allow black children to attend school with whites.

Since the 1930s, the National Association for the Advancement of Colored People (NAACP) had brought a number of lawsuits challenging various aspects of racial segregation in education. Early lawsuits included challenges to the exclusion of blacks from white state university graduate and professional schools. After the Supreme Court in 1950 held in *Sweatt v. Painter* (1950) that the exclusion of black students from the University of Texas Law School (requiring them to attend a fledgling racially separate law school) violated the equal protection clause of the Fourteenth Amendment, the NAACP brought a number of lawsuits challenging racial segregation in elementary and secondary schools. Eventually, five of these suits—filed in Delaware, Kansas, South Carolina, Virginia, and the District of Columbia—were accepted for review by the U.S. Supreme Court.

On May 17, 1954, the Supreme Court in a unanimous decision declared state-mandated school segregation unconstitutional. The unanimity was hardly a foregone conclusion. After oral argument in the cases in 1952, the Court was sharply divided and scheduled reargument for 1953. In the meantime, Chief Justice Frederick Vinson died; his replacement, Earl Warren, worked skillfully and successfully to build unanimous support for a decision striking down segregation as violating the equal protection clause.

In its decision, the Court concluded that relegating black children to racially separate schools "solely because of their race generates a feeling of inferiority as to their status in the community that may affect their hearts and minds in a way unlikely ever to be undone." Quoting from the district court in the Kansas case, the Supreme Court elaborated: "'Segregation of white and colored children in public schools has a detrimental effect upon the colored children. The impact is greater when it has the sanction of the law; for the policy of separating the races is usually interpreted as denoting the inferiority of the negro group . . . . Segregation with the sanction of law, therefore, has a tendency to [retard] the educational and mental development of negro children and to deprive them of some of the benefits they would receive in a [racially] integrated school system.'"

In issuing its landmark decision, the Court postponed for one year the question of remedy. The Court heard argument on the remedy issue and on May 31, 1955, issued a second decision in the case, a decision that came to be known as "Brown II." In this second decision, the Court directed lower courts to supervise the desegregation of southern school districts with "all deliberate speed"—a directive that some white Southerners interpreted as signaling the Court's willingness to tolerate some delay.

The *Brown* decisions did not lead to the immediate desegregation of southern school systems. Although a few communities did desegregate their schools in a token fashion within the next few years, most southern school districts refused to take any action. By the fall of 1957, only 0.15 percent of black children in the eleven states of the old Confederacy attended school with whites. Even this extraordinarily modest level of school desegregation provoked intense controversy and sometimes led to violence. For example, Arkansas Governor Orval Faubus caused a national crisis when he ordered the Arkansas National Guard to bar nine black students from desegregating Central High School in Little Rock in 1957. President Dwight Eisenhower was eventually forced to deploy federal troops to defuse the Little Rock crisis. Southern resistance would continue. On the tenth anniversary of the first *Brown* decision—May 1964—only about 1.2 percent of Southern black children attended school with white children, and in a few states, such as Mississippi, desegregation had not even begun. In the meantime, the Supreme Court, with a few exceptions, remained largely silent on the issue of enforcing the desegregation mandate of *Brown*.

After Congress passed the Civil Rights Act of 1964, which included a fund withholding provision for entities (such as southern school districts) that engaged in racial discrimination, the pace of desegregation quickened. In 1965, the Office of Education of the Department of Health, Education, and Welfare (HEW) issued a set of guidelines defining for school officials minimum desegregation standards that must be satisfied in order to retain federal funding. These guidelines, coupled with the threat of losing federal funds, contributed to an increase in school desegregation. Moreover, lower federal courts during the late 1960s began to insist that southern school districts had an affirmative duty to increase desegregation levels. In a series of decisions in the late 1960s and early 1970s, culminating in *Swann v. Charlotte-Mecklenburg Board of Education* (1971), the U.S. Supreme Court reentered the fray and insisted on significant desegregation. In the *Swann* decision, the Court legitimated the use of extensive school busing as a desegregation remedy, a decision that had an immediate and profound effect on desegregation levels across the South and in several northern and western cities as well.

Although *Brown* did not lead to the immediate desegregation of southern schools, it did contribute

to a renewed insistence among many blacks that racial segregation was morally and legally wrong and should be opposed. While the full impact of *Brown* would not be felt until after the Civil Rights Act of 1964, the decision was nevertheless a crucial event in the development of civil rights in American society. Moreover, *Brown* helped legitimate the notion that it is sometimes appropriate for courts to step in and overrule legislative bodies that have enacted laws that serve to harm racial and ethnic minorities.

DAVISON M. DOUGLAS

References and Further Reading

Cottrol, Robert J., Raymond T. Diamond, and Leland B. Ware. *Brown v. Board of Education: Caste, Culture, and the Constitution.* Lawrence: University Press of Kansas, 2003.
Klarman, Michael. *From Jim Crow to Civil Rights: The Supreme Court and the Struggle for Racial Equality.* New York: Oxford University Press, 2004.
Kluger, Richard. *Simple Justice: The History of* Brown v. Board of Education *and Black America's Struggle for Equality.* New York: Knopf, 1976.

Cases and Statutes Cited

Swann v. Charlotte-Mecklenburg Board of Education, 402 U.S. 1 (1971)
Sweatt v. Painter, 339 U.S. 629 (1950)

BROWN v. MISSISSIPPI, 279 U.S. 278 (1936)

In *Brown v. Mississippi*, the Supreme Court for the first time relied upon the due process clause of the Fourteenth Amendment to exclude a confession from evidence in a state court. *Brown* was a seminal case, because the due process doctrine then dominated the Supreme Court's confessions law jurisprudence until *Miranda v. Arizona* was decided in 1966. Even after *Miranda*, courts continue to exclude confessions extracted in violation of due process on the authority of *Brown*.

The facts of the case are appalling. *Brown* highlighted the fact that police officers in the South systematically abused black suspects in the criminal justice system during that era. A deputy sheriff, accompanied by other white men, hung defendant Ellington by a rope to a tree limb, let him down, hung him up again, and finally tied him to a tree and whipped him as the defendant protested his innocence. "[T]he signs of the rope on his neck were plainly visible during the so-called trial." After the mob released Ellington, he went home, "suffering intense pain and agony." A day or two later, the same deputy arrested Ellington and headed to a jail in an adjoining county, taking a route that went into Alabama. While in Alabama, the deputy stopped and again severely whipped Ellington, making clear that he would continue the beating until Ellington confessed. Ellington then confessed to a statement dictated by the deputy, and the deputy then took him to jail.

Two other defendants (including the named defendant Brown) were also arrested. At the same jail where Ellington was held, the deputy who had beaten Ellington was once again accompanied by a "number of white men," including an officer, and the jailer. This group forced the two defendants to strip, laid the men over chairs, and "cut to pieces" their backs with a leather strap with buckles. The deputy made clear that the beatings would continue until defendants confessed "in every matter of detail as demanded by those present." The defendants confessed, and the beating continued until the confessions conformed to the torturers' demands.

The state's only evidence against the defendants was their confessions, the circumstances of which were not disputed. Indeed, in admitting to the whipping of Ellington, the deputy stated that the severity of the beating was "'[n]ot too much for a negro; not as much as I would have done if it were left to me.'"

The Court had little trouble finding that the defendants' convictions in these circumstances violated due process. Although noting that the states have great latitude in establishing court procedures, their freedom "is the freedom of constitutional government and is limited by the requirement of due process of law." The states may not resort to torture to obtain convictions. The wrong committed in the case was "so fundamental that it made the whole proceeding a mere pretense of a trial and rendered the conviction and sentence wholly void." The Court's decision was unanimous. Professor Morgan Cloud has described *Brown* as "one of the Court's great opinions."

M. K. B. DARMER

References and Further Reading

Cloud, Morgan, *Torture and Truth*, Texas Law Review 74 (1996): 1211.
Darmer, M.K.B., *Beyond Bin Laden and Lindh: Confessions Law in an Age of Terrorism*, Cornell Journal of Law and Public Policy 12 (2003): 319–64.

Cases and Statutes Cited

Miranda v. Arizona, 384 U.S. 436 (1966)

BRUCE, LENNY (1925–1966)

Lenny Bruce is often considered the most influential figure in modern comedy, a pioneer of the acerbic social satire that would dominate the genre in the latter half of the twentieth century. His challenges to contemporary standards of artistic expression in the 1950s and 1960s also made him a target of authorities and a central figure in the debate over the limits of free speech, inspiring generations of performers and activists while exerting a substantial toll upon his own career and personal life.

Born Leonard Schneider in Long Island, New York, in 1925, Bruce began his comedy career as a vaudeville-style comedian after serving in World War II. After a brief hiatus, he returned to the stage in the early 1950s with an edgier, more experimental style heavily influenced by the emerging beat culture. His comedy routines often tested the boundaries of the decade's rigid obscenity standards with irreverent, satirical commentary on social mores and institutions, and frequently included jokes about oral sex, bodily functions, racism, and religion.

Bruce reached the peak of his mainstream success with a sold-out performance at Carnegie Hall in 1961. However, his exposure to conventional audiences resulted in a series of arrests on obscenity charges in various cities across the United States. Bruce was acquitted of some of these charges but convicted of others; he continued to perform while free on bond and refused to compromise his material despite mounting legal and financial difficulties. Meanwhile, his health—and, critics charged, the quality of his performances—began to decline under the strain of numerous trials and ongoing struggles with drug addiction.

In April 1964, during a series of performances at the Café au Go-Go in New York City, Bruce was once again arrested and charged with obscenity, inspiring outrage from the city's formidable community of artists, writers, and intellectuals. The prosecution presented a number of eyewitnesses to Bruce's Café au Go-Go performances, whose testimony included graphic descriptions of Bruce's language and gestures during the performance. The defense, spearheaded by renowned First Amendment attorney Ephriam London, countered with testimony from a series of expert witnesses, including psychiatrists, music and theater critics, and media experts, who testified that Bruce's material possessed artistic merit and was not obscene according to the community standards of the city of New York. The Court ruled that Bruce's performances were obscene, found him guilty, and sentenced him to four months of hard labor. He remained free on bond but would not live to complete the appeals process, dying of a morphine overdose in Los Angeles on August 3, 1966.

The performances and legal battles of Lenny Bruce set precedents for subsequent challenges to free speech restrictions, resulting in a gradual relaxation of obscenity standards that allowed subsequent generations of writers and performers to present content more provocative than that for which Bruce was repeatedly arrested. In 2003, in response to a petition from artists and free speech advocates, New York Governor George Pataki issued Bruce a full posthumous pardon for his 1964 conviction.

MICHAEL H. BURCHETT

References and Further Reading

Bruce, Lenny. *How to Talk Dirty and Influence People*. Rep. ed. New York: Simon & Schuster/Fireside, 1992.
Collins, Ronald K.L., *Lenny Bruce and the First Amendment: Remarks at Ohio Northern University Law School*, Ohio Northern University Law Review 30 (Winter 2004): 1:15–34.
Collins, Ronald K.L., and David, Skover. *The Trials of Lenny Bruce: The Fall and Rise of an American Icon*. Naperville, IL: Sourcebooks Mediafusion, 2002.
Saporta, Sol. *Society, Language and the University: From Lenny Bruce to Noam Chomsky*. New York: Vantage Press, 1994.

See also **Obscenity; Obscenity in History; Pardon and Commutation; Public Figures; Public Vulgarity and Free Speech; Satire and Parody and the First Amendment**

BRYAN, WILLIAM JENNINGS (1860–1925)

Perhaps best known for his famous "Cross of Gold" speech, William Jennings Bryan had a public career lasting some thirty years. He served two terms in the U.S. House of Representatives, ran for president three times, served as secretary of state under Woodrow Wilson, and had a successful career as a public speaker and attorney. He championed the causes of middle America, even when it cost him politically to do so. Yet one of his legacies is tied inextricably with the Scopes trial in 1925, and he is misunderstood and remembered as a knee-jerk fundamentalist for his role in prosecuting John Scopes for teaching evolution in Tennessee.

A believer in social contract theory, which stated that governments existed essentially to do for people what they could not do for themselves, Bryan became associated with free silver as a political issue. He preached constantly for the adoption of silver as

circulating currency, making him a populist hero for much of Midwest America. Indeed, silver became a primary issue in the 1896 election, during which Bryan ran on both the Populist and Democratic tickets and lost to William McKinley. He sought to have the gold standard repealed and replaced with silver, but many contemporary observers believed that Bryan held onto the issue far too long, even after gold supplies increased enough to make circulation of silver irrelevant.

Partly because of his devotion to temperance as a social issue, Bryan also became an outspoken supporter of women's suffrage. He, like many other suffrage activists, believed that women's votes were critical to ensure the elimination of alcoholism and its various societal problems.

Despite his having served as a soldier in the Spanish-American War, Bryan became opposed to imperialism; he had particular problems with McKinley's Philippine policies. He believed that the Philippines had the right to outright independence, as Cuba had received, rather than status as possessions of the United States. It cost the United States too much money, he argued, and led to poor relationships between the United States and Asian nations.

Bryan was also committed to reform, both economic and constitutional. He sought consumer protection against corporate excess and monopoly. He supported electoral-college reform and favored a constitutional amendment for the direct election of U.S. senators, declaring that if citizens were intelligent enough to elect representatives and the president, then they were surely smart enough to elect their senators. Nearly one hundred years before it became an issue in the 2000 and 2004 elections, Bryan called for public disclosure of campaign fundraising and spending.

The twilight of Bryan's life saw his involvement as a prosecutor in Tennessee's Scopes trial. When John Scopes was charged with violating state law, which forbade teaching evolution, Bryan found himself opposed by Scopes's attorney, Clarence Darrow (provided by the American Civil Liberties Union). The trial climaxed with Bryan himself taking the witness stand to be cross-examined by Darrow. By all accounts, Bryan was a poor witness; Darrow made Bryan admit that he believed literally in the stories from the Bible, and made it seem as if Bryan were uneducated and ignorant of scientific teachings. Bryan's team won the case, but Bryan died barely a week after it was over.

The truth about Bryan, though, was hardly that simple. Bryan's writings indicate that he supported Scopes's prosecution, not because he thought evolution had no place in schools, but because he thought that parents, not state legislatures, should decide what their children were taught in school.

Often remembered without sufficient nuance, Bryan deserves to be remembered as a defender of American civil liberties. He championed several reforms that were only accomplished after his death, and he represented the under-franchised in America.

JAMES HALABUK, JR.

References and Further Reading

Anderson, David P. *William Jennings Bryan.* Boston: Twayne Publishing, 1981.
Koenig, Louis W. *Bryan: A Political Biography of William Jennings Bryan.* New York: G.P. Putnam's Sons, 1971.
Springen, Donald K. *William Jennings Bryan: Orator of Small-Town America.* New York: Greenwood Press, 1991.

BRYANT, ANITA (1940–)

If the Stonewall riot was the event that galvanized the movement for gays' civil rights, Anita Bryant was the personality that first embodied at the national level the opposition to those rights. Her successful campaign to repeal the gay rights ordinance in Dade County, Florida, not only inflicted an enduring setback for that state and ignited copycat referenda throughout the nation, but also set the negative terms of that debate for years to come.

Born on March 25, 1940, Bryant early achieved national attention when she represented Oklahoma in the 1959 Miss America pageant. Second runner-up in that competition, she parlayed the attention into a successful recording career. Bryant would become particularly known for her rendition of the *Battle Hymn of the Republic*, a patriotic association that she would effectively exploit during later antigay campaigns. To most households, however, Anita Bryant was known simply as the Florida orange juice lady, serving for many years as the national spokeswoman for the Florida Citrus Commission. Bryant wed Bob Green in 1969, a Miami disc jockey who then served as her manager, and went on to raise four children.

On January 18, 1977, the Miami Dade Metro Commission voted to include protections for gay men and lesbians in its human rights ordinance. The amendment to Chapter 11A of the Dade County Code would have prohibited discrimination in the areas of housing, public accommodation, and employment. Bryant founded the Save Our Children, Inc. organization to spearhead a petition drive to put the ordinance on the June 7 ballot for repeal by popular vote. An overwhelming majority rejected the ordinance, setting the stage for similar repeals in Wichita, Kansas, St. Paul, Minnesota, and Eugene, Oregon.

The unprecedented battle inflicted long-term consequences on all parties. At the local level, the non-discrimination provisions were not reinstated until 1997 (Ord. 97-17, February 25, 1997). The Christian right again forced a referendum vote on September 10, 2002, which this time failed. More enduring fallout, however, includes a state law enacted in the 1977 aftermath that bans adoptions by gay persons. This policy survived a challenge in 2005 when the U.S. Supreme Court refused an appeal from the Eleventh Circuit upholding its constitutionality against equal protection claims (*Lofton v. Secretary of Dept. of Children and Family Services* [2005]).

More generally, the Dade County fight significantly altered the terms of discourse concerning gay rights. Where before the predominant stereotype had been the ineffectual poof, Bryant popularized the image of the gay "militant" bent on converting others into homosexuality, largely through child molestation. This new characterization would help give rise to the favorite myth of the right of a literal "homosexual agenda" that explicitly targets the seduction of young children.

Although her antigay movement enjoyed considerable success, Bryant herself did not. Having built her reputation on defending the family, her conservative supporters rejected her after a 1980 divorce from Green. Permanently estranged from her base, she quickly lost her association with the Citrus Commission, initiating a series of financial setbacks that included bankruptcies in 1997 and 2001. Despite the personal costs incurred by her spearheading this early campaign, recent interviews at the time of this writing have indicated no softening of her antigay position.

JAMES M. DONOVAN

References and Further Reading

Bryant, Anita. *The Anita Bryant Story: The Survival of Our Nation's Families and the Threat of Militant Homosexuality.* Old Tappan, NJ: Revell, 1977.
Nussbaum, Martha C., and Saul M. Olyan, eds. *Sexual Orientation & Human Rights in American Religious Discourse.* New York: Oxford University Press, 1998.

Cases and Statutes Cited

Lofton v. Secretary of Dept. of Children and Family Services, 358 F.3d 804 (Fla. 2004), cert. denied 125 S.Ct. 869 (2005)
Miami-Dade County Ordinance Chapter 11A

See also **Christian Coalition; Gay and Lesbian Rights; Falwell, Jerry; Family Values Movement**

BUCHANAN v. KENTUCKY, 483 U.S. 402 (1987)

David Buchanan was indicted on capital murder charges for the rape and murder of Barbel Poore. Buchanan requested that the capital portion of his charges be dropped, arguing *Enmund v. Florida* (1982) made him ineligible for the death penalty because he had neither intended to kill Poore nor had he been the gunman. This was granted. He and fellow participant Stanford were tried jointly by the state. Buchanan was found guilty and sentenced to a life sentence on the murder charge.

Following his conviction and sentence being upheld by the Kentucky Supreme Court, Buchanan appealed to the U.S. Supreme Court. Buchanan claimed that because his jury at trial had been "death qualified," he had been deprived of his Sixth Amendment right to an impartial jury of a fair cross-section of the community.

The U.S. Supreme Court disagreed, and affirmed the lower court. Death qualification of the jury was previously permitted in *Lockhart v. McCree* (1986), where the death penalty was sought for one of the defendants being tried. And in *Wainwright v. Witt* (1985), the Court ruled that "Witherspoon-excludables" did not constitute a distinctive group in regards to fair cross-section purposes. Moreover, death qualifying a jury did not make them automatically excludable for cause because the court assumes that jurors will set aside personal beliefs and make decisions based solely on case facts and the letter of the law.

NICHOLE H. FRANKLIN

Cases and Statutes Cited

Enmund v. Florida, 458 U.S. 782 (1982)
Lockhart v. McCree, 476 U.S. 162 (1986)
Wainwright v. Witt, 469 U.S. 412, 423 (1985)

BUCHANAN v. WARLEY, 245 U.S. 60 (1917)

A 1914 Louisville, Kentucky city ordinance prohibited blacks from buying houses on blocks where the majority of the residents where white, and at the same time, prohibited whites from buying houses on blocks where the majority of the residents were black. No one was forced to move under the law. In order to challenge the law, Warley, who was black, agreed to buy Buchanan's house. The contract for purchase provided that "It is understood that I am purchasing the above property for the purpose of having erected thereon a house which I propose to make my residence, and it is a distinct part of this agreement that

I shall not be required to accept a deed to the above property or to pay for said property unless I have the right under the laws of the State of Kentucky and the City of Louisville to occupy said property as a residence." After signing the contract, Warley then refused to pay for the house, asserting that the law prohibited him from doing so. This allowed Buchanan, the white seller, to sue Warley, for breach of contract. The Kentucky Supreme Court upheld the ordinance and declared that Warley did not have to pay for the house. This allowed the case to go to the U.S. Supreme Court.

This was the first case brought to the Supreme Court by the newly organized civil rights organization, the National Association for the Advancement of Colored People (NAACP). Moorfield Storey, one of the leaders of the American bar, argued the case for Buchanan. The posture of the case was of course odd. Buchanan, a white man, was suing Warley, a black, to force him to buy a house in a predominately white neighborhood. If Buchanan won, then all blacks would win.

The Supreme Court framed the question in simple terms: "May the occupancy, and, necessarily, the purchase and sale of property of which occupancy is an incident, be inhibited by the States, or by one of its municipalities, solely because of the color of the proposed occupant of the premises?" The Court refused to limit the Fourteenth Amendment to the rights of blacks or other minorities, noting that "while a principal purpose of the [Fourteenth] Amendment was to protect persons of color, the broad language used was deemed sufficient to protect all persons, white or black, against discriminatory legislation by the States." Thus, under the Fourteenth Amendment, Buchanan had just as much of a right to sell his house as Warley did to buy a house.

In upholding Buchanan's right to sell his house, and Warley's right to buy it, the Court quoted from *Strauder v. West Virginia* (1880), which had struck down a West Virginia law that prohibited blacks from serving on juries. In *Strauder*, the Court had said that the Fourteenth Amendment was "designed to assure to the colored race the enjoyment of all the civil rights that under the law are enjoyed by white persons, and to give to that race the protection of the general government, in that enjoyment, whenever it should be denied by the States. It not only gave citizenship and the privileges of citizenship to persons of color, but it denied to any State the power to withhold from them the equal protection of the laws, and authorized Congress to enforce its provisions by appropriate legislation." If this was so, then surely blacks could buy houses wherever they wanted. The Court also quoted the federal Civil Rights Act of

1866, which had specifically guaranteed that blacks would have the same right as whites to "inherit, purchase, lease, sell, hold, and convey real and personal property." Justice William Day then asked, "In the face of these constitutional and statutory provisions, can a white man be denied, consistently with due process of law, the right to dispose of his property to a purchaser by prohibiting the occupation of it for the sole reason that the purchaser is a person of color intending to occupy the premises as a place of residence?" The answer was obviously that a law could not prevent the sale of property solely on the basis of the race of the buyer or seller.

While properly understood as a civil rights case, *Buchanan* must also be seen as civil liberties case protecting the right to own and convey property. The founders saw private property as a fundamental institution in society and key to a democratic state. Many of the early states had predicated voting on property ownership because they believed that only those with a financial stake in society should be able to vote. While this theory of political participation has long been discredited, the right to own—and to buy and sell—property has been seen as a fundamental civil liberty. Here the Court accepted this notion and applied it to race discrimination.

In reaching this result, the Court rejected the idea that racial segregation, which it had approved in *Plessy v. Ferguson* (1896), applied to the sale of real estate. The Court had no difficulty distinguishing between separating the races on trains, or in schools, and the real estate transaction in this case. Here there was no attempt to mix the races in a social setting. The Court declared that it lacked any power to influence racial relations and acknowledged that the "the law is powerless to control" racial views and feelings of white superiority to blacks or white hostility to blacks. But, in upholding the right of people to buy and sell property, the Court did not see itself doing any of these things. It was merely allowing citizens to exercise "their constitutional rights and privileges" to own land.

This case did not lead to housing integration. White landowners avoided integration through restrictive covenants which the Court approved on the same theory that approved Buchanan's right to sell his land: that private individuals have a right to engage in contracts for their property. Thus, in *Corrigan v. Buckley* (1926), the Court undermined the value of *Buchanan v. Warley* by demonstrating that residential segregation could be achieved by private action—with court enforcement—even if it could not be achieved by actions of the state. *Corrigan* involved a private agreement among thirty-one landowners in Washington, DC, who all signed a restrictive covenant

that prevented them from selling law their houses or land for twenty-one years. The Court unanimously upheld the covenant, thus preventing Irene Corrigan from selling her land to a black woman. In *Shelly v. Kraemer* (1948), the Court would finally hold that restrictive covenants could not be enforced by courts because that would force the courts to violate the equal protection of citizens. Thus, after 1948 people were free to sign restrictive covenants, but they could not be enforced by courts and thus anyone would break the covenant without fear of being sued.

PAUL FINKELMAN

References and Further Reading

Vose, Clement. *Caucasians Only: The Supreme Court, The NAACP, and the Restrictive Covenant Cases.* Berkeley: University of California Press, 1959.

BUCK v. BELL, 274 U.S. 200 (1927)

In 1924, the state of Virginia passed a law granting certain state hospitals the authority to sterilize patients deemed mentally defective. After becoming pregnant out of wedlock, possibly from being raped, seventeen-year-old Carrie Buck was institutionalized by her foster parents. While institutionalized, she, like her mother before her, was deemed "feeble minded," and the hospital recommended sterilization pursuant to the new statute. This decision was upheld through a review process that included a special hospital review board, a hearing before the state trial court, and review by the state supreme court.

Under the theories of eugenic sterilization that were popular during this era, the state argued that sterilizing those with unwanted mental deficiencies would lessen the presence of these traits in future generations, save government tax dollars spent on these individuals, and allow more patients to be released from state mental hospitals. Buck's attorney argued that the statute violated her right of bodily integrity under the due process clause and cited equal protection concerns.

Based on a very limited and possibly one-sided record from the lower court, the Supreme Court found the state's arguments convincing. With only one justice dissenting without comment, the Court found that the statute provided for ample due process through the statute's review procedures and it did not violate her rights to equal protection. Justice Oliver Wendell Holmes, writing the Court's opinion, noted that since the best citizens are often required to give up their lives for the good of society, "[i]t would be strange if [the State] could not call upon those who already sap the strength of the State for these lesser sacrifices . . . in order to prevent our being swamped with incompetence." Acknowledging that other mandatory medical procedures were considered acceptable, Holmes noted, "The principle that sustains compulsory vaccination is broad enough to cover cutting the Fallopian tubes." Referring to Carrie Buck, her mother, and her newborn daughter, Holmes noted, "Three generations of imbeciles are enough."

Following the decision, several states passed similar sterilization laws and the number of sterilization procedures grew dramatically. While involuntary sterilization and the eugenics movements lost much of their support in the 1940s and 1950s, including the repeal of many states' sterilization statutes, the decision itself has never been overturned. The case has been used as valid precedent in state courts to uphold sterilization laws and was cited by the Court in *Roe v. Wade* as an example of the states' ability to limit privacy rights. However, the Court has taken some steps back from *Buck v. Bell*, such as striking down mandatory sterilization laws aimed at habitual criminals in *Skinner v. Oklahoma* and suggesting that the *Buck* decision upheld a "harsh measure" in *Board of Trustees of the University of Alabama v. Garrett*. Concurring in the 2004 case of *Tennessee v. Lane*, Justice David Souter went even further by citing *Buck* as an example of past judicial endorsement of disability discrimination. Debates over related issues, such as the sterilization of welfare recipients and criminals, whether voluntarily or involuntarily, have brought further attention to the legacy of *Buck v. Bell*, with many viewing it as one of the most intrusive encroachments into personal liberties.

TODD A. COLLINS

References and Further Reading

Berry, Roberta M., *From Involuntary Sterilization to Genetic Enhancement: The Unsettled Legacy of* Buck v. Bell, Notre Dame Journal of Law, Ethics, & Public Policy 12 (1998): 1:401–48.

Blake, Meredith, *"Welfare and Coerced Contraception: Morality Implications of State Sponsored Reproductive Control,* University of Louisville Journal of Family Law 34 (1995): 311–44.

Lombardo, Paul A., *Three Generations, No Imbeciles: New Light on* Buck v. Bell, New York University Law Review 60 (1985): 1:30–63.

Reilly, Philip. *The Surgical Solution: A History of Involuntary Sterilization in the United States.* Baltimore: John Hopkins University Press, 1991.

Cases and Statutes Cited

Board of Trustees of the University of Alabama. v. Garrett, 531 U.S. 356 (2001)

Buck v. Bell, 130 S.E. 516 (Va. 1925)
Buck v. Bell, 274 U.S. 200 (1927)
Roe v. Wade, 410 U.S. 113 (1973)
Skinner v. Oklahoma, 316 U.S. 535 (1942)
Tennessee v. Lane, 541 U.S. 509 (2004) (Souter, J., concurring)
Virginia Sterilization Act, Act of Mar. 20, 1924, c. 394, 1924 Va. Acts 569, repealed by Act of Apr. 2, 1974, c. 296, 1974 Va. Acts 445

See also **Abortion; Eugenic Sterilization;** *Jacobson v. Massachusetts,* **197 U.S. 11 (1905); Right of Privacy;** *Roe v. Wade,* **410 U.S. 113 (1973);** *Skinner v. Oklahoma,* **316 U.S. 535 (1942)**

BUCKLEY v. VALEO, 424 U.S. 1 (1976)

To appreciate the significance of *Buckley v. Valeo*, it is important to take a step back and consider the role of money in politics since the founding of the nation, but especially with the rise of the modern campaign in the twentieth century. To address the perceived abuses of money in the political system, Congress passed a series of acts throughout the 1900s, including the Tillman Act of 1907 (banning corporate contributions to presidential campaigns), the Hatch Act of 1939 (prohibiting political contributions of more than $5,000 to federal candidates or campaign committees, among other things), and the most significant of all, the Federal Election and Campaign Act (FECA). This act, passed by Congress in 1971 and amended in 1974—in the wake of the Watergate scandal and the general decline in public trust of elected officials—called for the disclosure of the sources of campaign contributions and campaign expenditures, the public funding of presidential primaries and general elections, limits on campaign expenditures for those accepting public funding, limits on expenditures from individuals' personal funds, $1,000 limitation on independent expenditures, establishment of the Federal Election Commission (FEC), and a range of contribution limits for various individuals and organizations.

Convinced that the amended act violated core First Amendment rights, a collection of individuals and groups from across the political spectrum led by Senator James L. Buckley of New York filed suit against Francis Valeo, secretary of the Senate and ex-officio member of the newly formed FEC in the U.S. District Court for the District of Columbia. This court certified the constitutional questions in the case to the D.C. Circuit Court of Appeals, which upheld virtually all of the substantive provisions of the FECA. Senator Buckley, et al., appealed the decision to the U.S. Supreme Court, which announced its decision on January 30, 1976.

The *Buckley* decision is one of the longest, most complicated, and most controversial decisions that the Court has ever produced. It is a *per curiam* opinion of the eight justices sitting at the time (Justice John Paul Stevens took no part). In essence, the Court found *constitutional* the limitations on contributions to candidates for federal office, the disclosure and recordkeeping provisions, and the public financing of presidential elections. The Court found *unconstitutional* the limitations on expenditures by candidates and their committees (except for presidential candidates accepting public funds), the $1,000 limitation on independent expenditures, the limitation on expenditures drawn from candidates' personal funds, and the method of appointment for FEC members.

The opinion, however, was quite fractured, with all the justices joining only in the "case or controversy" section of the decision. Three justices (William Brennan, Potter Stewart, and Lewis Powell) joined all parts of the decision, Justice Thurgood Marshall joined all except for the finding that limitations on expenditures by candidates from personal or family resources were unconstitutional, and Justice Harry Blackmun joined all parts except for the finding that contribution limits were constitutional. Then-Associate Justice William Rehnquist joined all parts except for the holding that public financing was constitutional with respect to the financing of nominating conventions, while Chief Justice Warren Burger joined only the sections explaining that the interest in preventing corruption was insufficient to justify expenditure limits and the section pertaining to the scope of the FEC's authority, and Justice Byron White joined only in the holding that public financing was constitutional.

While the disclosure and public funding provisions are of critical importance to the operations of modern campaigns, it was the Court's qualitative distinction drawn between campaign *expenditures* and campaign *contributions* that has had the greatest lasting significance. In its reasoning, the *per curiam* opinion held that expenditure limits violated the First Amendment, while the state's legitimate interest in preventing corruption and "the appearance of corruption" justified the limits on contributions to candidates for federal office to $1,000 for individual and groups, $5,000 for political committees, and $25,000 in total contributions during any calendar year. Further, the governmental interest in the disclosure of contributors, and amounts of $100 or more, outweighed the potential damage done to some minor parties and independent candidates. Finally, the system of public financing for presidential candidates was found to be constitutional, while the method of appointing members of the FEC was found unconstitutional.

In light of the recent abuses of public authority (that is, Watergate), the Court in this case was more prepared to accept a defense of the FECA that relied on public perceptions—whether accurate or not. As the *per curiam* opinion explained, it was not necessary to look beyond the primary purpose of the act—limiting "the actuality and appearance of corruption resulting from large individual financial contributions"—to find a constitutional justification for the contribution limits. "Under a system of private financing of elections," the opinion continued,

> [a] candidate lacking immense personal or family wealth must depend on financial contributions from others to provide the resources necessary to conduct a successful campaign . . . . To the extent that large contributions are given to secure political quid pro quo's from current and potential office holders, the integrity of our system of representative democracy is undermined. Of almost equal concern as the danger of actual quid pro quo arrangements is the impact of the *appearance of corruption* stemming from public awareness of the opportunities for abuse inherent in a regime of large individual financial contributions . . . [emphasis added].

Laws criminalizing bribery were insufficient to address these more *systemic* problems, because they addressed only the "most blatant and specific attempts of those with money to influence governmental action."

The *Buckley* decision dramatically altered American politics and shaped the nature of the modern campaign. Like water pressing against a dam, as the saying goes, money searches for a way into the political sphere and the numerous progeny since *Buckley* (dealing with limits on political action committee [PAC] spending, "hard" versus "soft" money restrictions, coordination versus correlation in a party's relationship to its candidate, etc.) indicate that the Court will continue to play a role in the superintending of campaign finance as long as the central provisions of this paradigm case are upheld.

BRIAN K. PINAIRE

References and Further Reading

Alexander, Herbert, and Brian Haggerty. *The Federal Election Campaign Act: After a Decade of Political Reform.* Los Angeles: Citizens' Research Foundation, 1981.

Polsby, Daniel. "*Buckley v. Valeo:* The Special Nature of Political Speech." In *The Supreme Court Review,* edited by Philip Kurland, 1–43. Chicago: University of Chicago Press, 1976.

Rosenkranz, E. Joshua, ed. *If Buckley Fell: A First Amendment Blueprint for Regulating Money in Politics.* New York: The Century Foundation, 1999.

Smith, Bradley. *Unfree Speech.* Princeton, N.J.: Princeton University Press, 2001.

Cases and Statutes Cited

Federal Election Campaign Act of 1971, 2 U.S.C. 441b(a); later amended in 1974, 1976, and 1979
Hatch Act of 1939, 18 U.S.C. §610
Tillman Act, ch. 420, 34 Stat. 864

See also **Burger Court; Campaign Finance Reform, No. 1021; Freedom of Speech: Modern Period (1917–Present); Politics and Money**

BULLINGTON v. MISSOURI, 451 U.S. 430 (1981)

Bullington was indicted and convicted of capital murder. Under Missouri law, this meant that he would receive either death or life imprisonment without eligibility for parole for fifty years. In addition, under Missouri law, there was a separate presentence hearing wherein the prosecutor must prove to the trial jury the existence of aggravating circumstances beyond a reasonable doubt, in order for the death penalty to be imposed. The jury imposed a life sentence. Bullington appealed and was granted a new trial because of an error in the jury selection process.

The prosecutor, then, in the second trial, sought the death penalty. Bullington objected, arguing that *Benton v. Maryland* (1969), held that the double jeopardy clause barred the seeking of the death penalty in a second trial when the first jury did not impose it. The Missouri Supreme Court agreed with the prosecutor, stating that double jeopardy did not apply in this case.

This case made its way to the Supreme Court, where the judgment of the Missouri Supreme Court was reversed. The justices felt that because the sentencing proceeding at the petitioner's first trial was like the trial of guilt or innocence, the protection of the double jeopardy clause was also available to him at retrial. This overruled *Stroud v. United States* (1919), in which the Court stated that a defendant whose conviction is reversed may receive a more severe sentence at retrial than he received at his first trial.

BRIAN M. IANNACCHIONE

Cases and Statutes Cited

Benton v. Maryland, 395 U.S. 784, 794 (1969)
Stroud v. United States, 251 U.S. 15 (1919)

See also **Capital Punishment; Double Jeopardy (V): Early History, Background, Framing**

BURDEAU v. MCDOWELL, 256 U.S. 465 (1921)

Following an internal investigation into unlawful conduct, Henry L. Doherty & Co. fired its employee, J.C. McDowell. An agent of the company took control of the office that McDowell formerly occupied, searched the office, and took possession of documents locked inside two safes and one desk; after reviewing the documents, some of which were personal, the company forwarded them to Burdeau at the Justice Department. McDowell claimed a violation of his Fourth and Fifth Amendment rights on the grounds that the documents, illegally obtained by a private entity, would have otherwise been unavailable to Burdeau and thus self-incriminated the defendant.

Overturning a lower court's decision by a seven-to-two vote (Brandeis and Holmes dissenting), the Supreme Court found no Fourth or Fifth Amendment violations. The majority opinion acknowledged that Doherty & Co.'s seizure of the documents was likely illegal, but because the search had been performed by a private party acting on its own behalf, the Fourth Amendment did not apply. The company was a private business, not working in association with the government. The Fifth Amendment question centered on whether the government may retain papers dubiously obtained by a private party for use as evidence against a criminal defendant. Writing for the majority, Justice Day reasoned that because the papers were held by a private party, the government could have legally subpoenaed the documents had they not been sent to the Justice Department. The Court held that the evidence, although stolen from McDowell by an agent of Doherty & Co., could be used in a criminal case against him.

Burdeau v. McDowell represents an articulation of the scope of the Fourth Amendment; the ruling remains standing law, allowing evidence stolen by a private party to be used against a criminal defendant.

JOHN GREGORY PALMER

BURDEN OF PROOF: OVERVIEW

If the notion of civil rights or civil liberties entails some fundamental freedoms from governmental overreaching, one of the most telling but perhaps subtle expressions of a commitment to the preservation of civil liberties is found in the legal concept of burden of proof. The burden of proof is traditionally described as a procedural device relating to the rules of engagement in the conduct of a trial. It sets out the parameters for which side should win a close case when the evidence is in equipoise or is ambiguous. However, this feature, the effect of resolving close cases, reveals that burdens of proof also have substantive effect; that is, they often represent normative judgments about who should prevail, who is more likely to be "correct," what substantive policy is to be advanced, and so forth. This aspect of burdens of proof is often obscured by the emphasis on its mechanical or procedural features, particularly when the area under examination is civil. The burden of proof as a commitment of substantive law emerges more clearly in the criminal context.

Burdens of proof are typically described, thanks to Thayer's 1890 discussion in the *Harvard Law Review*, as consisting of two parts—the burden of production, that is, who is responsible for coming up with evidence, and the burden of persuasion. Most often the burden of both production and persuasion is on the same party, usually the party bringing the suit, that is, the plaintiff, or in the case of a criminal prosecution, the prosecutor. However, this is not always the case, and sometimes meeting a production burden with respect to a particular issue allows a party to then shift the burden to his opponent, such as the duty to produce counterevidence and/or to persuade the trier of fact as to an alternative interpretation of the evidence presented.

One of the most familiar examples of this shifting of burdens is the self-defense defense to a homicide prosecution. Of course, the prosecutor has the burden of production and persuasion as to the theory of homicide. But this burden can be increased if the defendant pleads and puts on a self-defense case. Typically, the defendant bears the burden of product and some burden of persuasion that the killing with which he is charged was done in self-defense. Assuming that the defendant meets this burden, the burden would then shift back to the prosecutor to disprove the affirmative defense beyond a reasonable doubt. Because the Constitution requires that the prosecution prove its case beyond a reasonable doubt, the concept of an affirmative defense complicates the prosecutor's burden. The Model Penal Code tends to place the burden on the prosecutor to disprove any affirmative defenses. But because the task of anticipating all affirmative defenses is a daunting one, not too mention somewhat inefficient, this duty is often not triggered until the defense is raised by the defendant with the appropriate amount and quality of evidence—how much evidence the defendant must produce and the nature of his burden, whether preponderance, or some other standard, varies.

In addition, burdens of proof intersect to a large degree with yet another device with both procedural and substantive aspects—the presumption. Presumptions are evidentiary devices which require that a particular fact be assumed to be true or to exist in the absence of evidence to the contrary. Such presumptions can be conclusive or rebuttable, shifting or "bursting," but they function in much the same way as burdens of proof: to describe the contours of the way the law asserts the world should be or probably is. Thus, often discussions of burdens of proof often also involve the interaction of burdens of proof with presumptions.

A burden of proof of some kind applies to all cases, both civil and criminal. However, the *quantum* of proof that will satisfy the burden differs depending on whether a case is criminal or civil. And within the civil area the burden of proof can vary and shift depending upon the nature of the cause of action. Typically, however, in a civil case the burden, usually on the plaintiff, is a preponderance of the evidence. In certain types of cases, the burden may be the purportedly higher standard of "clear and convincing." Arguably, however, the most important and well-known burden of proof, which is relevant for purposes of civil rights and civil liberties, is the burden of proof that distinguishes most criminal cases—*beyond a reasonable doubt*.

In the area of criminal law, the burden of proof has been an issue of constitutional dimension ever since the Supreme Court's decision in *In re Winship* in 1970, although even prior to this decision, "beyond a reasonable doubt" was apparently the governing standard for criminal cases for some time, perhaps since this country's founding. The "beyond a reasonable doubt" burden applies to both state and federal criminal cases. Thus, with respect to the criminal law, the burden of proof has an explicitly substantive aspect. Academic and political commentators often view the "beyond a reasonable doubt" standard in criminal cases as a forthright acknowledgment that the playing field is not level. Like a handicap in golf, the burden of proof of "beyond a reasonable doubt" arguably represents an attempt to even out some differences in the distribution of advantages as between the state and a defendant. At a minimum, the higher standard recalibrates the array of factors that would normally heavily favor the government.

As a practical matter, the state (whether state or federal) typically has little difficulty in convincing a jury that it has met its burden, at least in the average criminal case. Nevertheless, the common perception is that placing the burden of proof on the state in criminal cases and making that burden a high one, represents a nontrivial limitation on the potential for governmental overreaching. Still, most cases do not go to trial and it can be argued that burdens of proof that apply to the conduct of trials have less impact when it comes to settlement and pleas. Given that the state's probability of prevailing is, in general, usually perceived to be fairly high, and defendants can be presumed to know that, it may be that the state is often able to use this knowledge to exert pressure on a defendant to enter a guilty plea even when the state might be at some risk if it had to go to trial. That is, the state can still use its power to bluff about its evaluation of the likelihood of prevailing in a particular case. Nevertheless, the burden of proof lurks in the background of any plea negotiations, serving as something of a counterweight, a means by which a defendant can call the state's bluff in a close case.

Apart from whether placing the burden of proof on the government at trial accomplishes the substantive goals asserted as its justification when, in fact, most cases settle, there is the issue of whether, even if a case goes to trial, the verbal formulation of "beyond a reasonable doubt" accomplishes what it is intended to do. There is some evidence from jury studies that juries do not understand this particular verbal formulation as placing the evidentiary burden on the government that lawmakers assume or intend for it to do. Indeed, such experiences led to the abandonment in the United Kingdom of this formulation in favor of one that requires a jury to be "firmly convinced" of a defendant's guilt before conviction.

Although the criminal case is the paradigmatic case of the use of a procedural device like the burden of proof to further goals related to civil liberties, its use or impact on civil liberties and civil rights is by no means limited to criminal cases. All manner of civil cases implicate important civil rights or liberties. Just a few of these are civil commitment proceedings, termination of parental rights, legitimacy proceedings, civil forfeitures, dependency proceedings, and other similar actions involving liberty, property, or family issues. In addition, there are civil causes of action that explicitly relate to civil rights such as actions under Section 1983 and Title VII. Adjustments to the burdens of proof, and shifts in understanding of who bears the burden and what sorts of evidence are necessary to meet that burden, have long been ways in which it is possible to track a strand of skepticism, perhaps even fear, in the creation of a variety of causes of action related to civil liberties and civil rights.

From time to time, burdens have been raised and shifted to suggest that claims related to civil rights or their protection have favored status, such as in *New York Times v. Sullivan* when the Supreme Court raised the burden of proof in defamation against public figures to exclude causes of action with lower burdens of proof. (Actually, the Court changed the substantive law in a way that had the *effect* of raising the burden of proof, thus providing an excellent illustration of the issue described above of the degree to

which burdens of proof implicate both substance and procedure, and presumptions and substantive evidentiary elements. What the Court did, among other things, was to rule that a presumption of damages, once a "libel per se" case had been made, was unconstitutional. One feature of this presumption was to shift the burden to the defendant to prove that his statements were true.)

In other cases, such as *Texas Department of Community Affairs v. Burdine*, changes in the understanding of who had the burden of proof have arguably signaled the shift to disfavored status for the protection of civil rights. In *Burdine*, the Supreme Court held that in a Title VII action, if an employer could prove the existence of a nondiscriminatory reason for discharge, the burden of proof shifted back to the employee/plaintiff to show that it was the *improper*, discriminatory motive that had led to the discharge, not the nondiscriminatory motive.

Tinkering with burdens of proof, either of production or persuasion, represents a way to "stack the deck" in particular kinds of cases. Thus, although facially neutral, burdens of proof can betray current normative positions about the desirability of the pursuit of a particular type of claim or of the likelihood that a particular type of claim is meritorious.

TAMARA R. PIETY

References and Further Reading

Allen, Ronald J., *Burdens of Proof, Uncertainty, and Ambiguity in Modern Legal Discourse*, Harvard Journal of Law and Public Policy 17 (1994): 627–46.

Cleary, Edward W., *Presuming and Pleading: An Essay on Juristic Immaturity*, Stanford Law Review 12 (1959): 5–28.

Jeffries, Jr., John Calvin, and Paul B. Stephan, III., *Defenses, Presumptions, and Burden of Proof in the Criminal Law*, Yale Law Journal 88 (1979): 1325–427.

Solan, Lawrence M., *Refocusing the Burden of Proof in Criminal Cases: Some Doubt About Reasonable Doubt*, Texas Law Review 78 (1999): 105–47.

Thayer, James B., *The Burdens of Proof*, Harvard Law Review 4 (1890): 45–70.

Underwood, Barbara D., *The Thumb on the Scales of Justice: Burdens of Persuasion in Criminal Cases*, Yale Law Journal 86 (1977): 1299–348.

Cases and Statutes Cited

In re Winship, 397 U.S. 358 (1970)
Texas Department of Community Affairs v. Burdine, 450 U.S. 248 (1981)
New York Times v. Sullivan, 376 U.S. 254 (1964)

See also **Due Process; *In re Winship*, 397 U.S. 358 (1970); Proof Beyond a Reasonable Doubt; Title VII and Religious Exemptions**

BURGER COURT (1969–1986)

The Burger Court was a transitional institution. It reflected the conflicting currents produced by the transition from the America of John F. Kennedy and Lyndon B. Johnson to the America of Ronald Reagan and his successors. In some areas, it ranged well beyond the civil libertarian aspects of the Warren Court. At the same time, it engendered many of the conservative tendencies that were to prevail during subsequent decades under Chief Justice William H. Rehnquist.

The composition of the Burger Court reflected its nature. In its heyday, the Warren Court had comprised Chief Justice Earl Warren leading a slim but solid liberal majority of justices made up of Hugo Black, William O. Douglas, William J. Brennan, and at different times, Arthur Goldberg, Abe Fortas, and Thurgood Marshall.

By 1972, four new justices had been appointed—Chief Justice Burger, and Justices Harry Blackmun, Lewis F. Powell, and William H. Rehnquist—replacing the liberal Warren, Fortas, and Black, and the conservative John M. Harlan, respectively. Four years later Justice Douglas left, replaced by John Paul Stevens, and in 1981 the conservative Potter Stewart was succeeded by the first female justice, Sandra Day O'Connor.

The Supreme Court of the second half of the twentieth century was thus an accurate reflection of the nation: activist liberalism led by a slim liberal majority during the 1950s and 1960s, some additional liberal advances, and a gradual movement towards conservatism in the 1970s and 1980s, and vigorous conservatism in the 1990s.

Social Issues: Abortion

The most controversial of the Burger Court decisions was *Roe v. Wade* (1973), which found that "the right of privacy founded in the Fourteenth Amendment's concept of personal liberty" barred a state's prohibiting women from terminating a pregnancy on the advice of their doctors. In a seven-to-two decision written by Justice Blackmun, with only Justices White and Rehnquist dissenting, the Court established a three trimester system: virtually no state regulation of the abortion procedure was permissible during the first trimester; "reasonable" regulation of abortion to protect the health of the mother was acceptable during the second trimester; and abortions could be prohibited during the last trimester unless the health of the mother was endangered by the pregnancy. In a companion case, *Doe v. Bolton* (1973), the same seven-to-two majority struck down state regulations of abortion that it deemed inconsistent with the right established in *Roe*.

The decision did not come out of nowhere. In 1965, the Warren Court had recognized a right of privacy for married couples to use contraceptives. *Griswold v. Connecticut* (1965). The year before *Roe*, the Court had extended the right to use contraceptives to single people in *Eisenstadt v. Baird* (1972), and for several years prior to *Roe*, lower courts and some state courts had also struck down abortion laws. Also, some states, notably California under Governor Ronald Reagan, and New York, had legislatively liberalized their abortion laws.

Nevertheless, the decision set off a firestorm of protest, particularly among some religious groups, and the Republican Party made overturning *Roe v. Wade* a central feature of its party platform. A substantial majority of the public accepted the decision, however, and wanted it retained.

Three subsidiary issues soon arose: public funding; the rights of minors to terminate a pregnancy without parental consent or notification; and state and local regulation of the abortion procedure.

Five years after *Roe*, the Court ruled that Connecticut did not have to use Medicaid funds for first trimester abortions, even if it chose to pay for childbirth or "medically necessary" abortions (*Maher v. Roe* [1977]). Three years later the Court ruled that Congress may even bar Medicaid funding for medically necessary abortions (*Harris v. McRae* [1980]).

Minors who sought to terminate their pregnancy without either notifying or obtaining the consent of either or both parents were allowed to do so, but only with court approval (*Bellotti v. Baird* [1979], *Planned Parenthood of Kansas City v. Ashcroft* [1983]).

As the abortion wars heated up and the anti-abortion forces gained strength, state and local governments adopted a wide array of regulations designed to make it more difficult for women to obtain an abortion and for abortion providers to operate. All were struck down by the Burger Court, over persistent dissents by Justices White, Rehnquist, and O'Connor, and increasingly Chief Justice Burger.

After Justice Powell's departure in 1987, the justices unhappy with *Roe v. Wade* were in the majority, and in 1992 they cut back sharply on that decision while affirming its "central holding." In *Planned Parenthood of S.E. Pa. v. Casey* (1992), Justices O'Connor, Anthony Kennedy who succeeded Justice Powell, and David Souter, who followed Justice Brennan, redefined the right established in *Roe* as the right not to be encumbered by "undue burdens" in obtaining an abortion. The state's interest in potential life from the inception of the pregnancy was recognized, and the trimester system was abandoned. The plurality and the dissenters went on to uphold five of the six state regulations limiting abortion at issue, all of which had earlier been struck down, including provisions requiring waiting periods, favoring childbirth over abortion, and "informed consent;" only the requirement that a spouse be notified before an abortion was struck down. As of 2005, over four hundred state and local laws designed to make an abortion more difficult to provide and to obtain have been enacted.

Social Issues: Homosexual Intercourse

During these years, homosexuals, among the most oppressed of American minorities, also tried to free themselves from the legal burdens they faced, especially laws that made sexual intercourse between members of the same sex a criminal offense. These laws were rarely enforced but could be used for blackmail and to justify employment and other disabilities.

By the mid-1980s, some twenty-six states no longer had such laws. Nevertheless, in 1986, the last year of Chief Justice Burger's tenure, a five-to-four majority of the Court refused to strike down a Georgia sodomy statute (*Bowers v. Hardwick* [1986]).

Bowers remained the law for seventeen years. During this period, many states repealed such laws or had them struck down by their highest courts. Finally, in 2003, the Court overruled *Bowers* and struck down a Texas law on due process grounds (*Lawrence v. Texas* [2003]).

Religion: The Establishment Clause

Religion has always played a central role in American life and politics. At the same time, the Constitution mandates a separation between church and state. Reconciling these two forces has resulted in a complex, often baffling series of Supreme Court decisions, a high proportion of which were issued during the Burger Court.

The difficulties and resulting inconsistencies appeared in the Supreme Court's first decision on the use of public funds for aid to religious schools. In *Everson v. Board of Education* (1947), the Court, speaking through Justice Black, erected a "wall of separation between church and state" as a result of which, "[n]either [a state nor the federal government] can aid one religion, aid all religions, or prefer one religion over another." Despite the apparent comprehensiveness of that statement, a five-to-four majority

of the Court went on to approve New Jersey's willingness to fund bus transportation for children attending religious schools. That inconsistency pervaded the many subsequent separation decisions.

Guiding principles were announced early in the life of the Burger Court by the Chief Justice in *Lemon v. Kurtzman* (1971): "First, the statute must have a secular legislative purpose; second, its principal or primary effect must be one that neither advances nor inhibits religion; finally, the statute must not foster 'an excessive government entanglement with religion.'" In *Lemon*, the Court ruled that government may not fund salary supplements for teachers of secular subjects at religious schools or pay for their secular textbooks or other instructional materials or services, because that would "excessively entangle" the government in the administrative affairs of the church in order to ensure that the grant was not used for religious purposes. The chief justice also raised the dangers of political divisiveness because of religious strife over aid.

Although Chief Justice Burger sought to weaken the "wall of separation" metaphor by calling it "blurred, indistinct and variable," the Court initially took a strong separationist position, holding that the Constitution bars the loan of maps, magazines, tape recorders, and laboratory equipment to parochial schools (*Meek v. Pittinger* [1975], *Wolman v. Walter* [1977]), as well as remedial and therapeutic services on parochial school premises (*Aguilar v. Felton* [1984]). The Rehnquist Court later overruled these decisions in *Mitchell v. Helms* (2000) and *Agostini v. Felton* (1995). The Burger Court did, however, allow the state to provide standardized testing and diagnostic services even when done on religious school premises in *Wolman*. In *Committee for Public Education v. Nyquist* (1973), the Court had also refused to allow government-funded tuition rebates and tax deductions for attendance at nonpublic schools. Ten years later, however, in *Mueller v. Allen* (1983), a five-to-four majority held that a tax deduction for parents of children in *all* schools (public and nonpublic) for tuition, textbooks, and transportation was constitutionally permissible. Writing for the Court, then-Justice Rehnquist stressed that the aid was "channel [ed]" through the parents for the benefit of the child, rather than given to the schools, and was "neutrally available" to a broad spectrum of citizens. The prospect of religious strife was disparaged and the fact that 96 percent of the nonpublic schoolchildren went to religious schools was deemed irrelevant. In succeeding years, individual choice and neutrality became key factors.

With respect to higher education, the Burger Court took a less restrictive position right from the start.

In *Tilton v. Roemer* (1971), and *Roemer v. Board of Pub. Works* (1973), the Court allowed states to provide money for building construction and for other non-sectarian activities because religious indoctrination was less likely either to be attempted or to be successful, given the nature of both the courses and the less impressionable nature of college students. In a case at the intersection of the establishment and free speech clauses, the Court allowed the speech clause to override separationist concerns. In *Widmar v. Vincent* (1981), the Court refused to allow a state university to deny a religious group use of the university's facilities to meet for religious discussion and prayer. The university grounded its refusal on the establishment clause, but the Court rejected its defense and found that an "equal access" policy was required to avoid discrimination against religious speech, once the university created a public forum; the assistance to religion was deemed only "incidental." And in one of the last Burger Court decisions, the Court unanimously agreed to allow state payment to assist a visually handicapped person who was studying to become a minister (*Witters v. Washington Dept. of Service for the Blind* [1986]).

The Court also dealt with other forms of governmental religious involvement in public schools. In *Wallace v. Jaffree* (1985), the Court struck down an Alabama law that mandated a moment of silence for "meditation or voluntary prayer" because it was clear to seven of the nine justices (the chief justice and Justice Rehnquist dissenting) that the inclusion of "voluntary prayer" in the Alabama legislation was an "'effort to return voluntary prayer' to the schools." And in *Stone v. Graham* (1980), for similar reasons, a five-to-four majority of the Court summarily refused to allow public schools to hang a copy of the Ten Commandments in public school classrooms, issuing a per curiam opinion without oral argument concluding that there was "no secular legislative purpose."

One of the Burger Court's few important free exercise cases also arose in education. In *Wisconsin v. Yoder* (1972), a six-to-one majority concluded that the Old Order Amish, a religious order, could withdraw their children from the public schools after the eighth grade despite the state's compulsory school attendance law. Since the Amish believe that their salvation "requires life in a church community separate and apart from the world and worldly influence," the state's interest in education was subject to strict scrutiny because it impinged on rights protected by the free exercise clause. The state could not meet that test because the Amish alternative of informal education achieved whatever goals the state sought to deliver with its compulsory school attendance.

Because religion has been so intertwined with public life in America, the Burger Court had to struggle with two other issues: religious worship in public bodies and displays of religious symbols on public property. In *Marsh v. Chambers* (1983), a six-to-three majority ignored the *Lemon* test and looked to history and tradition to allow the Nebraska legislature to open each legislative day with a prayer by a Presbyterian minister paid by the state. The following year, in *Lynch v. Donnelly* (1984), a five-to-four majority of the Court allowed Pawtucket, Rhode Island to erect a nativity scene in a local park at Christmas time. The Court called it an "accommodation" to religious belief that did not advance religion but "depict[ed] the pastoral origins of this merely traditional event long recognized as a national holiday." Both opinions for the Court were written by Chief Justice Burger, but the most influential opinion in the two cases was Justice O'Connor's opinion in *Lynch*, in which she reinterpreted the effects prong of the *Lemon* test to focus on whether the government "endorsed" the religion in question. The O'Connor formulation, which was frequently used in subsequent years, reflected a persistent disenchantment with the *Lemon* test. Nevertheless, the test continued to be invoked throughout the Rehnquist Court era, although it was also often ignored and even criticized by many of the justices.

Free Speech: Campaign Finance

Since 1930, when the Supreme Court first struck down a statute for violating the free speech clause of the First Amendment, speech cases have accounted for a substantial portion of the Court's docket. The Burger Court's leading speech cases fall into four categories: electoral campaign financing; commercial speech; offensive speech including obscenity, pornography and vulgarity; and the rights of the press.

Perhaps the most perplexing speech issue to come before the Burger Court was its response to Congress's effort in 1974 to limit electoral campaign contributions and expenditures in the wake of the Watergate scandals. In *Buckley v. Valeo* (1976) (per curiam), the Court ruled that although limitations on both forms of financing would reduce political speech and association, Congress could restrict *contributions* by individuals and groups, including political action committees, in order to avoid both the actuality and appearance of corruption; the Court later made an exception for individual contributions to a public interest group in connection with a proposed ballot measure (*Citizens Against Rent Control v. Berkeley*

[1981]). *Expenditure* limits, however, were struck down, including limits that Congress tried to impose on a candidate's expenditure of personal funds. The Court found that unlike contribution limits, expenditure limits on explicit advocacy for or against a specific candidate—which is how the Court read the statute to avoid finding it unconstitutionally vague—"impose direct and substantial restraints on the quantity of political speech," and were not justifiable; fiscally equalizing the electoral playing field was not an acceptable goal. Fourteen years later, however, the Rehnquist Court allowed Michigan to require the Chamber of Commerce and other business corporations to insist on a segregated fund for expenditures on elections for public office (*Austin v. Michigan Chamber of Commerce* [1990]), although expenditures on referenda and similar issues could not be so limited (*First National Bank v. Belloti* [1978]).

Free Speech: Commercial Speech

Overturning prior law, in 1976 the Court ruled that speech that "does no more than propose a commercial transaction" was entitled to constitutional protection unless it was false or misleading or against public policy (*Va. St. Bd. of Pharmacy v. Va. Citizens Consumer Council, Inc.* [1976]). Restraints on such speech, however, including prior restraints, would not be subject to the most stringent level of judicial scrutiny—strict scrutiny—so long as the restraint advanced a substantial governmental interest and was no more extensive than necessary (*Central Hudson Gas & Electric Co. v. P.S.C. of New York* [1980]). Commercial speech thus received less judicial protection than political, artistic, or other forms of speech, which were normally entitled to strict scrutiny protection. In later years, the Rehnquist Court further refined the *Central Hudson* test.

Free Speech: Obscene, Pornographic, and Vulgar Speech

For over fifteen years, the Warren Court had struggled to define a limited category of speech that would be denied First Amendment protection because it could be categorized as "obscene." The result was confusion. Finally, a newly constituted majority of the Burger Court ruled that expression would be considered "obscene" if "(a) . . . 'the average person, applying contemporary community standards' would find that the work, taken as a whole, appeals to the prurient interest; (b) . . . the work depicts or describes in a patently offensive way, sexual conduct specifically defined by the applicable state law; and (c) . . . the work, taken as a whole lacks serious literary, artistic, political or scientific value" (*Miller v. California* [1973]). Local juries would apply "contemporary community standards" to determine "pruriency" and "patent offensiveness."

Concerned about child abuse, the Court also refused to protect material that put children in sexually explicit settings even if the material would not be considered obscene under *Miller* (*New York v. Ferber* [1982]). And though the Burger Court refused to allow the banning of "indecent" speech, regulating the location of adult movies houses was upheld (*City of Renton v. Playtime Theatres, Inc.* [1986]). Also, the government's power to regulate broadcasting was used to uphold Federal Communications Commission sanctions against a broadcaster for airing indecent speech (*F.C.C. v. Pacifica Foundation* [1978]).

On the other hand, in *Cohen v. California* [1971]), the Court refused to allow California to make it illegal to wear a jacket with the words "Fuck the Draft," underscoring the principle that the state cannot deny protection to speech that is merely offensive, whether morally, aesthetically, or politically.

Free Speech: The Press

One of the Warren Court's landmark decisions was *New York Times Co. v. Sullivan* (1964), in which the Court ruled that the First Amendment required a plaintiff in a libel case to prove that the defendant had defamed him with "actual malice—that is, with knowledge that it [the statement] was false or made with reckless disregard of whether it was false or not." Ten years after the *Sullivan* case, the Court ruled that only "public figure" plaintiffs had to meet this demanding standard in *Gertz v. Robert Welch, Inc.* (1974); the states could define for themselves the standards for suits by private plaintiffs. It remained uncertain when a private citizen who is thrust into public prominence involuntarily would be considered a "public figure." The Court later ruled that if defamatory statements do not involve matters of public concern, but only private matters such as a confidential credit report, they would not be subject to the *Times v. Sullivan* standard (*Dun & Bradstreet, Inc. v. Greenmoss Builders, Inc.* [1985]).

The Court consistently refused to grant the press privileges or protection unavailable to the general public. In 1972, it refused to create a privilege for journalists who were called before a grand jury and ordered to reveal information received confidentially or the source of the information (*Branzburg v. Hayes* [1972]). In libel case litigation (*Herbert v. Lando* [1979]), the Court required the press to open its files for a libel plaintiff suing under the *Sullivan* case, in order to enable the plaintiff to prove actual malice.

The press suffered other defeats at the hands of the Burger Court. In *Zurcher v. Stanford Daily* (1978), the Court denied a college newspaper any special protection against an ex parte warrant of the newsroom. In *Pell v. Procunier* (1974), the Court refused to require a prison administration to allow press interviews with individual inmates, and in 1978, it ruled that both the media and the general public could be denied any access to prisons and most other public institutions (*Houchins v. KQED* [1978]).

The press did gain some significant victories from the Burger Court. The most celebrated victory came in the Pentagon Papers case, or *New York Times Co. v. United States* (1971), in which a bitterly divided six-to-three majority refused to allow the government to enjoin publication of a classified Defense Department study of the origins of the Vietnam War, declaring such an injunction to be an unconstitutional prior restraint. In *Nebraska Press Ass'n v. Stuart* (1976), the Court also found an unlawful prior restraint in a "gag order" against publication of an accused's confession or admissions in a widely publicized murder case. On the other hand, a former government employee was enjoined from publishing information about official activities because he had signed an agreement not to divulge such information without government approval (*Snepp v. United States* [1980]).

Finally, the print press was released from any obligation to allow a target of press criticism a right of reply in *Miami Herald Pub. Co. v. Tornillo* (1974). A year earlier, the Court had also allowed the broadcast networks to refuse to sell air time to the Democratic National Committee and others for political advocacy in *Columbia Broadcasting System v. Democratic Nat'l Committee* (1973), but Congress was allowed to mandate "reasonable access" to the air waves for federal political candidates in *CBS, Inc. v. F.C.C.* (1981).

Prisoners' Rights

The Burger Court's shifting nature was also reflected in its decisions on the rights of prisoners. For decades, the federal courts had refused to exercise any oversight over prison conditions. As part of the increasing concern for social justice in the 1960s, however, the federal courts began to accept prisoner petitions filed under 42 U.S.C. § 1983, the 1871 Civil Rights law. In a summary opinion in 1972 decided without a signed opinion, the unanimous Court made it possible for prisoners to file their own suits, and set a high standard for dismissal of such suits (*Haines v. Kerner* [1972]). The Court followed this up with decisions allowing suits challenging prison conditions to be filed in federal court without first exhausting state judicial and administrative remedies. In short order, the prisoner's right to practice his religion was given protection, mail censorship was limited, arbitrary disciplinary procedures were changed, physical abuse and corporal punishment were condemned, prisoner expression within the institution received some protection, unnecessary visiting restrictions were voided, improvements in medical care were ordered, strip searches were limited, and parole procedures were improved. In many cases, the entire state system was condemned.

In 1974, the tide began to turn. Although prisoners continued to receive some protection, their right to fair procedures in disciplinary hearings was curtailed in *Wolff v. McDounell*. That same year, the Court upheld the authority of states to deny the right to vote to persons convicted of a felony, influencing elections for many years to come in *Richardson v. Ramirez*. In 1979, the rights of pretrial detainees were severely curtailed in *Bell v. Wolfish*. Although it was still possible to bring suits challenging brutal and inhumane conditions, as in *Hutto v. Finney* (1978), by 1986, there was a return to almost total deference to administrative discretion. In later years, the Rehnquist Court would extend such deference to more and more contexts, in the process limiting or overturning Burger Court precedents. Compare, for example, *Lewis v. Casey* (1996) with *Bounds v. Smith* (1978) (prisoners' access to law libraries).

The transition to a more conservative federal judiciary initiated by the Burger Court is now complete. The Rehnquist Court developed and expanded many of the conservative doctrines originated during Chief Justice Burger's tenure, and as this is being written, the Court is again being reshaped along conservative lines. Nevertheless, many of the advances in civil liberties made during Chief Justice Burger's tenure and earlier are still in effect and will probably remain, if only because of the American judiciary's respect for precedent. But predictions about the Supreme Court are notoriously unreliable, and the civil liberties legacy of the Burger Court is unpredictable.

HERMAN SCHWARTZ

References and Further Reading

Barron, Jerome A., and C. Thomas Dienes. *First Amendment Law*. St. Paul, MN: Thomson West, 2000.

Blasi, Vince, ed. *The Burger Court: The Counter-Revolution That Wasn't.* New Haven, CT: Yale University Press, 1983.

Greenhouse, Linda. *Becoming Justice Blackmun.* New York: Henry Holt & Company, 2005.

Jeffries, John. *Justice Lewis F. Powell, Jr.* New York: C. Scribner's Sons; Toronto: Maxwell Macmillan Canada; New York: Maxwell Macmillan International, 1994.

Schwartz, Herman, ed. *The Burger Years.* New York: Viking Press, 1987.

———, ed. *The Rehnquist Court.* New York: Hill & Wang, 2002.

Tribe, Laurence. *American Constitutional Law.* 2d ed. Mineola, NY: Foundation Press, 1988.

Cases and Statutes Cited

Agostini v. Felton, 521 U.S. 203 (1995)

Aguilar v. Felton, 473 U.S. 402 (1984)

Austin v. Michigan Chamber of Commerce, 494 U.S. 652 (1990)

Bell v. Wolfish, 441 U.S. 520 (1979)

Bellotti v. Baird, 443 U.S. 622 (1979)

Bounds v. Smith, 437 U.S. 678 (1978)

Bowers v. Hardwick, 478 U.S. 186 (1986)

Branzburg v. Hayes, 408 U.S. 665 (1972)

Buckley v. Valeo, 424 U.S. 1 (1976)

CBS, Inc. v. F.C.C., 453 U.S. 367 (1981)

Central Hudson Gas and Electric Co. v. P.S.C. of New York, 447 U.S. 557 (1980)

Citizens Against Rent Control v. Berkeley, 454 U.S. 90 (1981)

City of Renton v. Playtime Theatres, Inc., 475 U.S. 41 (1986)

Cohen v. California, 403 U.S. 15 (1971)

Columbia Broadcasting System v. Democratic Nat'l Committee, 412 U.S. 94 (1973)

Committee for Public Education v. Nyquist, 413 U.S. 756 (1973)

Doe v. Bolton, 410 U.S. 179 (1973)

Dun & Bradstreet, Inc. v. Greenmoss Builders, Inc., 472 U.S. 749 (1985)

Eisenstadt v. Baird, 405 U.S. 408 (1972)

Everson v. Board of Education, 330 U.S. 1 (1947)

F.C.C. v. Pacifica Foundation, 438 U.S. 726 (1978)

First National Bank v. Bellotti, 435 U.S. 765 (1978)

Gertz v. Robert Welch, Inc., 418 U.S. 323 (1974)

Griswold v. Connecticut, 381 U.S. 479 (1965)

Haines v. Kerner, 404 U.S. 519 (1972)

Harris v. McRae, 448 U.S. 297 (1980)

Herbert v. Lando, 441 U.S. 153 (1979)

Houchins v. KQED, 438 U.S. 1 (1978)

Hutto v. Finney, 437 U.S. 678 (1978)

Lawrence v. Texas, 539 U.S. 588 (2003)

Lemon v. Kurtzman, 403 U.S. 602 (1971)

Lewis v. Casey, 518 U.S. 343 (1996)

Lynch v. Donnelly, 465 U.S. 668 (1984)

Maher v. Roe, 432 U.S. 464 (1977)

Marsh v. Chambers, 463 U.S. 783 (1983)

Meek v. Pittinger, 421 U.S. 349 (1975)

Miami Herald Pub. Co. v. Tornillo, 418 U.S. 241 (1974)

Miller v. California, 413 U.S. 15 (1973)

Mitchell v. Helms, 530 U.S. 793 (2000)

Mueller v. Allen, 463 U.S. 388 (1983)

Nebraska Press Ass'n v. Stuart, 427 U.S. 539 (1976)

New York v. Ferber, 458 U.S. 747 (1982)

New York Times Co. v. Sullivan, 376 U.S. 254 (1964)

New York Times Co. v. United States, 403 U.S. 713 (1971)

Pell v. Procunier, 417 U.S. 817 (1974)

Planned Parenthood of S.E. Pa. v. Casey, 505 U.S. 833 (1992)

Richardson v. Ramirez, 418 U.S. 24 (1974)

Roe v. Wade, 410 U.S. 113 (1973)

Roemer v. Board of Public Works, 426 U.S. 736 (1973)

Snepp v. United States, 444 U.S. 507 (1980)

Stone v. Graham, 449 U.S. 39 (1980)

Tilton v. Roemer, 403 U.S. 672 (1971)

Va. St. Bd. Of Pharmacy v. Va. Citizens Consumer Council, Inc., 425 U.S. 748 (1976)

Wallace v. Jaffree, 472 U.S. 38 (1985)

Widmar v. Vincent, 454 U.S. 263 (1981)

Wisconsin v. Yoder, 406 U.S. 205 (1972)

Witters v. Washington Dept. of Service for the Blind, 474 U.S. 481 (1986)

Wolff v. McDonnell, 418 U.S. 539 (1974)

Wolman v. Walter, 433 U.S. 229 (1977)

Zurcher v. Stanford Daily, 436 U.S. 547 (1978). 42 U.S.C. § 1983, Civil Rights law of 1871

See also **Abortion; Access to Prisons; Accommodation of Religion; Amish and Religions Liberty; Birth Control; Burger, Warren E.; Campaign Finance Reform, No. 1021; Commercial Speech; Defamation and Free Speech; Equal Protection Clause and Religious Freedom; Establishment Clause Doctrine: Supreme Court Jurisprudence; Establishment of Religion and Free Exercise Clause; Felon Disenfranchisement; Freedom of Speech and Press: Nineteenth Century; Freedom of the Press: Modern Period (1917–Present); Freedom of Speech and Press under Constitution: Early History (1791–1917); Gag Orders in Judicial Proceedings; *Lemon* Test; Miller Test; National Security Prior Restraints; Newsroom Searches; Obscenity; Politics and Money; Prisoners and the Free Exercise Clause Rights; Prisons and Freedom of Speech; Privacy; Public Vulgarity and Free Speech; Rehnquist Court; Rehnquist, William H.; Release Time from Public Schools (For Religious Purposes); Religious Symbols on Public Property; Reporter's Privilege; Right to Reply and Right of the Press; Sodomy Laws; State Aid to Religious Schools; Subpoenas to Reporters; Ten Commandments on Display in Public Buildings; Warren Court; Warren, Earl**

BURGER, WARREN E. (1907–1995)

Chief Justice Warren Earl Burger was the fifteenth chief justice of the U.S. Supreme Court. Appointed in 1969 to the Supreme Court by President Nixon, Burger served for seventeen years until 1986. Born on September 17, 1907, in St. Paul, Minnesota, Burger was the fourth of seven children of Charles Joseph and Katharine Schnittger Burger. Charles Burger was a railroad cargo inspector and traveling salesman, while Katherine Burger (as Warren Burger recalled) ran an "old-fashioned German house" based on "common sense" and respect for traditional values. Burger's paternal grandfather, Joseph Burger, was a Swiss immigrant who joined the Union Army at age fourteen and became a Civil War hero. His maternal parents were immigrants from Germany and Australia.

Because he suffered from polio at age eight, Burger stayed at home for a year. Even then, he was already a fan of the U.S. Constitution and knew he wanted to be a lawyer. Thus, his teacher brought him autobiographies of judges and lawyers. At age nine, Burger began delivering newspapers to help with his family's finances. In high school, Burger did not compile an outstanding academic record, but he was otherwise very active in several extracurricular activities. He was the president of the student council, head of the student court, and editor of the student newspaper. In addition, he participated in several sports, and ended up lettering in football, hockey, swimming, and track. Because of his extensive extracurricular activities, he was awarded a scholarship by Princeton University.

Concluding that the Princeton scholarship was insufficient to meet his financial needs and wanting to help support his family, Burger turned down the offer. He then enrolled in extension classes at the University of Minnesota in 1925, and after two years started attending night classes at the St. Paul College of Law (now the William Mitchell College of Law). He graduated magna cum laude from law school in 1931 and was admitted to the Minnesota Bar the same year. Burger worked as a life insurance salesman while attending college and law school, and served as the student body president. He met his wife, Elvera Stromberg, in college and married her in 1933. They later had two children, Wade and Margaret.

Burger began his legal career as an associate at a law firm in 1931 and became a partner at the firm in 1935. He earned a reputation as a capable lawyer who specialized in corporate, real estate, and probate law. While practicing law, Burger also taught contract law at his alma mater from 1931 to 1953 and was the president of the local junior chamber of commerce in 1935. Unable to sign up for military service during World War II because of a spinal condition, Burger nonetheless served as a member of Minnesota's emergency war labor board from 1942 to 1947. After World War II, he served as a member of the governor's interracial commission from 1948 to 1953. During that period, Burger also became the first president of the St. Paul's Council on Human Relations, wherein his responsibilities included improving the relationship between that city's police and its racial minorities.

A lifelong Republican, Burger played an active part in politics. He was one of the founders of the Minnesota's first Young Republicans organization, and served as floor manager for Harold Stassen's unsuccessful campaigns for the Republican presidential nomination both in 1948 and in 1952. During the 1952 Republican convention when General Eisenhower emerged as the frontrunner, Burger shifted his support to Eisenhower. His support for President Eisenhower led to his appointment in 1953 to head what is now the civil division of the Justice Department. In 1955, President Eisenhower nominated Burger to the U.S. Court of Appeals for the District of Columbia. Although his confirmation stalled in the Senate for several months due to allegations of discrimination charges raised by former Justice Department employees that he had dismissed, Burger was confirmed and seated on the Appeals Court in April 1956. Burger's record on the Appeals Court was largely conservative, especially with respect to criminal cases involving suspects and defendants. Although he served a total of thirteen years on the Appeals Court, he was considered a surprise choice for the Supreme Court.

In 1967, Burger in a speech delivered at Ripon College complained of the "prolonged conflict" characterizing the U.S. system of criminal justice. He noted that the adversary system has become "glorified" to a point whereby defendants are encouraged, even after conviction, to continue their fight with society. President Nixon, who had previously met Burger during the 1948 Republican Convention, must have taken note of that speech when trying to fulfill his own campaign promise to place "political conservatives" and "strict constructionists" on the federal bench. Therefore, on May 21, 1969, President Nixon nominated Burger to fill the seat and position being vacated by Chief Justice Earl Warren on the Supreme Court. Confirmed by the Senate on a seventy-four to three vote on June 9, 1969, Burger was sworn in by his predecessor, Earl Warren, on June 23, 1969. Burger ended up serving seventeen years, one of the longest terms of any Supreme Court chief justices, until September 26, 1986. President Reagan nominated Justice Rehnquist to replace Burger as the nation's sixteenth chief justice.

After his retirement from the Supreme Court, Burger chaired the Commission on the Bicentennial of the United States, a role he took very seriously. Burger was extremely delighted that the 200th birthday of the U.S. Constitution on September 17, 1987, was also his own eightieth birthday. After his wife passed away in 1994, Burger's health rapidly deteriorated and he died of congestive heart failure on June 25, 1995. Chief Justice Burger was laid in state in the Great Hall of the Supreme Court, and buried next to his wife at Arlington National Cemetery on June 29, 1995.

Burger's Judicial Philosophy

Chief Justice Burger proved to be less of a knee-jerk conservative than most hard-line conservatives expected when he was nominated. In fact, the entire Burger Court era did not generate the counter-revolution Warren Court critics were anticipating.

Part of the disappointment felt by hard-line conservatives desiring a different Supreme Court from that of the liberal Warren Court was that they had raised their expectations far too high while forgetting that each justice, including the chief justice, had only one vote.

The Burger Court consisted of five holdovers from the Warren era that served long tenures during the Burger era. Three of these five holdovers—William O. Douglas, William J. Brennan, Jr., and Thurgood Marshall—were regarded as liberal activists, while the other two—Potter Stewart and Byron White—were considered more moderate to conservative justices. In addition to Burger, President Nixon appointed three other justices to the Supreme Court—Harry A. Blackmun, William H. Rehnquist, and Lewis F. Powell. After Nixon, two other justices—John Paul Stevens (appointed by President Ford) and Sandra Day O'Connor (nominated by President Reagan)—joined the Burger Court. During the overall course of the Burger Court, Blackmun and Stevens became part of the liberal bloc, Rehnquist and O'Connor (albeit not always) joined the conservative wing, while Powell generally maintained a centrist position.

Considered as lacking analytical rigor or great eloquence by critics, Burger brought a common-sense approach to his decisions. He tried to strike a balance between liberal excesses and conservative extremes. On most civil rights issues, Burger was a moderate. He believed that school busing should be limited to instances when de jure segregation had actually occurred and not for the purpose of racial balance (*Milliken v. Bradley* [1974]). On affirmative action, Burger maintained that congressionally mandated but not state-enacted preferences could be used to remedy past discrimination (*Fullilove v. Klutznick* [1980], later repealed by *Adarand Constructors v. Pena* [1995] during the Rehnquist era). In *Wisconsin v. Yoder* (1972), writing for the Court, Burger rejected compulsory high school education for the Amish, deeming it a violation of their religious beliefs. But

Burger was protective of the freedom of the press, claiming, for example, that newspapers should not be required to give space to the people they criticize as their right to reply (*Miami Herald Publishing Co. v. Tornillo* [1974]). However, Burger was hostile to other First Amendment issues such as pornography, dirty words, and disruptive speech in schools.

Unlike hard-line conservatives in more recent years, Burger was a "traditional" conservative on many important policy issues. For example, noting that it would only benefit the entire society, he advocated for the rehabilitation of prison inmates by urging job provisions for inmates. In addition, Burger believed in gun control and was a staunch advocate of gun licensing. In a magazine article in 1990 after his Supreme Court years, Burger explained the rationale behind the Second Amendment of the U.S. Constitution as being reflective of the founding fathers' purpose and objectives then, and cautioned against the literal reading of the amendment in today's world.

In the field of criminal justice, Burger acted as predicted. He participated in decisions limiting Warren-era precedents that gave criminal defendants substantial leeway. For example, Burger helped limit the Fourth Amendment exclusionary rule as merely deterring police misconduct rather than a constitutional requirement. He refused to extend the exclusionary rule to grand jury proceedings and "good faith" police seizures of evidence based on invalid warrants. As for *Miranda* warnings, Burger did not have problems with using tainted confessions to impeach a defendant's trial testimony or to obtain other evidence against suspects. He also agreed with the Court's decision not to apply *Miranda* to grand jury proceedings or to instances when police initiate interrogation to avoid an imminent danger to public safety. However, some of Burger's Republican friends were not too happy that he wrote the Court's opinion (albeit with significant assistance from his colleagues) in *United States v. Nixon* (1974) preventing President Nixon from withholding from Congress and the courts materials related to the Watergate affair.

Regardless of what Burger critics thought of his judicial temperament, they uniformly agree that he made a significant and memorable mark on judicial administration in U.S. history. He worked with the American Bar Association on judicial education programs and in creating the Institute of Judicial Administration. He improved the administration of the Supreme Court itself by either creating or adding new administrative positions such as administrative assistant to the chief justice, judicial fellows, public relations professionals, librarians, and clerks. He substantially improved the Court's law library and enhanced its technology. Burger sponsored the National Center for State Courts, championed the creation of the Federal Judicial Center, and encouraged similar organizations to conduct scholarly research on the Court. Burger is celebrated as the chief architect of court mediation, alternative dispute resolution, arbitration, and other alternatives to litigation that are now widely used in U.S. jurisprudence.

Burger Court's Legacy on Civil Liberties

Although the Burger Court left its indelible mark on American civil liberties, it did not produce a seismic change as President Richard Nixon and his political allies would have preferred. Moreover, the Burger Court concentrated on non-economic issues rather than on property rights. Similar to other Supreme Court eras after 1937, the Burger Court did not nullify any economic regulation on substantive due process grounds. However, the Burger Court subjected Bill of Rights issues and other personal non-economic rights matters to strict judicial scrutiny.

On religious liberty, the Burger Court kept and extended many Warren Court precedents outlawing state-sponsored religious exercises in the public schools. Ruling in *Lemon v. Kurtzman* (1971), the Court established a three-pronged test for determining whether laws or government actions affecting religion activities violated the First Amendment establishment clause. Applying the *Lemon* test required that laws affecting religion were to be held constitutional only if they had a secular purpose, had a primary effect that neither advanced nor harmed religion, and did not create an excessive entanglement between church and state. In one particular application of the *Lemon* test, the Burger Court, in a six-to-three majority ruling, invalidated the posting of the Ten Commandments on the walls of classrooms (*Stone v. Graham* [1980]). However, the Burger Court sometimes took on a more expansive view of the First Amendment religion clauses. For example in *Widmar v. Vincent* (1981), the Court, disallowing a state university's concern over violating the establishment clause, concluded that the university could not exclude religious student groups from facilities available to secular student organizations.

On First Amendment free expression and association cases, the Burger Court mostly relied on the Warren era rulings except in certain instances when it clarified the Supreme Court's position on prior restraints on the press. The Burger Court maintained that in order for the government to impose prior restraints on the press, the government must demonstrate a "heavy burden" of justification.

The Burger Court left a strong legacy on equal protection issues. Unlike the unanimity maintained mostly by the Warren era justices on many school desegregation cases, the Burger Court lacked such cohesion. Although the Burger Court unanimously ruled in *Swann v. Charlotte-Mecklenburg Bd. of Education* (1971) that trial judges in desegregation cases had broad remedial powers, Chief Justice Burger elaborated that racial balance was not a constitutional mandate but only a temporary remedy for past de jure segregation. The Burger Court was also split on other major desegregation school cases. For example, in *Milliken v. Bradley* (1974), it was only a five-to-four majority that held that de jure segregation must be distinguished from de facto segregation. The Court's majority was equally adamant that civil rights orders be limited to instances whereby there had been previous intentional discrimination.

On affirmative action cases, the Burger Court did not provide clear guidance. On the one hand, it ruled in *Regents of the University of California v. Bakke* (1978) that states were precluded from imposing racial quotas to correct the effects of past discrimination. On the other hand, the following year the Burger Court decided that under the 1964 Civil Rights Act, Congress did not bar affirmative action quotas voluntarily established by a private company (*United Steelworkers v. Weber* [1979]). In both cases, Burger made clear that he was opposed to affirmative action programs.

SALMON A. SHOMADE

References and Further Reading

Maltz, Earl M. *The Chief Justiceship of Warren Burger, 1969–1986.* Columbia: University of South Carolina, 2000.
Yarborough, Tinsley E. *The Burger Court: Justices, Rulings, and Legacy.* Santa Barbara, CA: ABC-CLIO, 2000.

Cases and Statutes Cited

Adarand Constructors v. Pena, 515 U.S. 200 (1995)
Fullilove v. Klutznick, 448 U.S. 448 (1980)
Lemon v. Kurtzman, 403 U.S. 602 (1971)
Miami Herald Publishing Co. v. Tornillo, 418 U.S. 241 (1974)
Milliken v. Bradley, 418 U.S. 717 (1974)
Regents of the University of California v. Bakke, 438 U.S. 265 (1978)
Stone v. Graham, 449 U.S. 39 (1980)
Swann v. Charlotte-Mecklenburg Bd. of Education, 402 U.S. 1 (1971)
United States v. Nixon, 418 U.S. 683 (1974)

United Steelworkers v. Weber, 443 U.S. 193 (1979)
Widmar v. Vincent, 454 U.S. 263 (1981)
Wisconsin v. Yoder, 406 U.S. 205 (1972)

BURKE, EDMUND (1729–1797)

Edmund Burke, British statesman and political philosopher, and the "father" of modern conservatism, was born in Dublin on January 29, 1729. He was the son of a Protestant lawyer and a Roman Catholic mother. After graduating from Trinity College, Dublin, Burke entered the Middle Temple in London to study law in 1750. He, however, soon abandoned the law for literature. Burke started his political career in 1765 when he became the private secretary for the Marquis of Rockingham. He served in Parliament from 1765 to 1794, almost always in the minority, where he gained fame, power, and influence far beyond most of his compatriots. It is a measure of Burke's genius and force of personality that he managed to achieve political success in a tremendously hierarchical society that viewed the Irish as somewhat less than human and Catholics as little more than idolaters.

Burke's family connections to Catholicism (in addition to having a Catholic mother and sister, he married the daughter of a Catholic doctor) allowed him to witness firsthand the tremendous oppression Catholics labored under in eighteenth-century Britain. This undoubtedly was one of the driving forces of his interest in toleration for minorities, especially in terms of religion.

Until the 1790s, one of Burke's main concerns was liberty. Burke's concept of liberty, however, was not the individualist type celebrated in twenty-first-century America. It was an organic form, closely related to responsibility. For Burke, rights, liberties, and indeed political significance itself, was not found in individuals, but in their collective identities. Humans, according to Burke, were qualified for liberty in proportion to control of their baser instincts, such as selfishness and licentiousness. It was society's task to provide a stabilizing hand when a sense of justice and control were missing in a people. The expansion of liberty should only be done gradually and cautiously, according to Burke.

When Burke entered Parliament, the crisis that would develop into the American Revolution was already at a critical stage. Throughout that crisis, Burke continually attacked the British government's attempt to assert what he considered arbitrary power over the colonists. Through his speeches and writings Burke laid out his case that only by respecting the rights and liberties of the American Colonies could

the British hope to win back their loyalty. He contended that even if the political argument for the arbitrary use of power were strong, prudence and justice would overawe it. For Burke, the revolutionaries were not the Americans, but the British ministry.

Burke's title as the father of modern conservatism is due in large part to his most famous writing—*Reflections on the Revolution in France* (1790). Appalled by the excesses of that revolution, Burke delineated his philosophy on reform and revolution. While accepting the desire (even necessity) for change, he cautioned that any reform was to be approached cautiously and with an eye toward the lessons of history and tradition. By the 1790s, justice and order were the key concepts of government for Burke.

ENOCH W. BAKER

References and Further Reading

Burke, Edmund. *Burke's Political Writings*. Edited by John Buchan. New York: Thomas Nelson and Sons, n.d.
———. *Speeches and Letters on American Affairs*. Edited by Hugh Law. New York: Dutton, 1961.
———. *Reflections on the Revolution in France*. Edited by J. G.A. Pocock. Indianapolis: Hackett Publishing, 1987.
Kirk, Russell. *Edmund Burke: A Genius Reconsidered*. Wilmington, DE: Intercollegiate Studies Institute, 1997.

BURKS v. UNITED STATES, 437 U.S. 1 (1978)

At the robbery trial of David Burks, the defendant presented three unchallenged witnesses testifying that he was insane. In response, the government presented two expert witnesses who did not express definite opinions. The jury nonetheless convicted Burks. He asked for a new trial and argued that the evidence was insufficient to support the guilty verdict. The Sixth Circuit reversed the conviction, agreeing that Tennessee had not fulfilled its burden of proving sanity, but rather than terminating the case it asked the District Court to decide whether a directed acquittal should be entered or a new trial ordered. Burks contended that the double jeopardy clause precluded another trial because the appellate court found the evidence insufficient, which was the equivalent of a judgment of acquittal.

The Supreme Court reversed, remanding Burks for a judgment of acquittal. The Court held that the prosecution could not have another opportunity to convict after it had been given a full and fair opportunity to do so. The Court determined that it made no difference that the determination of evidentiary insufficiency was made by the appellate court because the double jeopardy considerations were identical.

Burks establishes that the double jeopardy clause precludes a second trial once the reviewing court finds the evidence legally insufficient. *Burks* expressly overrules *Bryan v. United States*, *Yates v. United States*, and *Forman v. United States*. Also, any earlier decisions suggesting that moving for a new trial waives one's right to a judgment of acquittal on the basis of evidentiary insufficiency were also overruled.

SARA FAHERTY

Cases and Statutes Cited

Bryan v. United States, 338 U.S. 552 (1950)
Forman v. United States, 361 U.S. 416 (1960)
Yates v. United States, 354 U.S. 298 (1957)

See also **Double Jeopardy (V): Early History, Background, Framing; Proof beyond a Reasonable Doubt**

BURTON, JUSTICE HAROLD (1888–1964)

Harold Hitz Burton, mayor of Cleveland, senator from Ohio and associate justice to the U.S. Supreme Court was born on June 22, 1888, in Jamaica Plain, Massachusetts. After graduating from Bowdoin College, he went on to attend Harvard Law School where he graduated in 1912. After law school, Burton moved to Cleveland, Ohio, where he began his law practice. His law career was interrupted, however, by the outbreak of World War I. Burton served in the army and was wounded in combat for which he received the Purple Heart. After the war, Burton resumed his law practice in Cleveland. In 1935, he ran for and was elected mayor of Cleveland, and served in that capacity until 1940 when he was elected to the U.S. Senate. In 1945, President Truman nominated Burton to the Supreme Court. Burton remained on the Court for thirteen years until his retirement for health reasons in 1958. Justice Burton died on October 28, 1964 from complications due to Parkinson's disease.

While Burton was generally considered a conservative justice who favored a philosophy of judicial restraint, his contributions to civil liberties is best illustrated in his stance on the equal protection of the laws, and nowhere was that more apparent than in his opposition to the doctrine of separate but equal. Writing for the Court in *Henderson v. United States*, Burton found that the Southern Railway Company's practice of limiting black passengers to a small curtained-off section of the dining car, even when open seats were available elsewhere, was a patent violation of Section 3(1) of the Interstate Commerce Act, which made it illegal for a railroad traveling in interstate commerce to subject passengers to "any undue or

unreasonable prejudice or disadvantage." Burton went on to state that equality of treatment was a fundamental right guaranteed to all citizens. Moreover, Burton repeatedly joined in decisions that overturned segregationist laws. In 1948, Burton voted with the majority in *Shelley v. Kraemer*, where the Court found that it was unconstitutional for states to prevent the sale of real property, covered in racially restrictive covenants, to blacks. Then again in 1954, Burton was part of the unanimous decision in *Bolling v. Sharpe*, which found segregated schools in Washington, DC to be an unconstitutional violation of due process protected by the Fifth Amendment. Burton was also part of the unanimous decision in the landmark desegregation case *Brown v. Board of Education*, which was decided on the same day as *Bolling*. Burton was reportedly instrumental in bringing about the unanimous vote. Indeed, in a personal letter written to Chief Justice Earl Warren, Burton reveals his feeling that the *Bolling* and *Brown* cases where probably the most "significant decisions" made during his time on the Court and that it was a honor to have taken part in them. The segregation cases did, as Burton predicted, become two of the most important cases decided during the Warren Court. Accordingly, Burton's support for overturning racial segregation is perhaps his greatest legacy.

MARCEL GREEN

References and Further Reading

Langran, Robert W. "Why are Some Supreme Court Justices Rated as 'Failures'?" *Supreme Court Historical Society 1985 Yearbook*. http://www.supremecourthistory. org/04_library/subs_volumes/04_c19_d.html.
Rudko, Frances Howell. *Truman's Court: A Study in Judicial Restraint*. Westport, CT: Greenwood Press, 1988.

Cases and Statutes Cited

Bolling v. Sharpe, 347 U.S. 497 (1954)
Brown v. Board of Education, 347 U.S. 483 (1954)
Henderson v. United States, 339 U.S. 816 (1950)
Shelley v. Kraemer, 334 U.S. 1 (1948)

BUTLER v. MCKELLAR, 494 U.S. 407 (1990)

When the Supreme Court decides a case in a way that alters the constitutional rights available to a criminal defendant, can prisoners who have already completed their appeals benefit from that case through a petition for a writ of habeas corpus? In *Teague v. Lane* (1989), the Court decided that "new rules" would not be available to habeas petitioners. In *Butler v. McKellar*

(1990), the Court decided, five to four, that if the outcome of a case was "susceptible to debate among reasonable minds," its rule would be deemed new.

Butler had been arrested for assault, about which he declined to speak to the police, invoking his *Miranda* rights. The police then began to ask him about an unrelated rape and murder. The settled law was *Edwards v. Arizona* (1981), prohibiting police from asking a suspect about a criminal charge once the suspect invoked *Miranda. Arizona v. Roberson* (1988), decided after Butler had completed his appeals, extended *Edwards* to questioning about all charges. If *Roberson* were not a new rule, the questioning of Butler was unconstitutional. *Roberson* suggested that it was dictated by *Edwards*, but *Butler* concluded otherwise; lower courts had reached conflicting results before *Roberson* was decided, demonstrating that reasonable minds disagreed. Thus, it was a new rule.

Butler's definition of a new rule was extremely broad; many, if not most, of the cases that the Supreme Court hears involve conflicting decisions among lower courts and would create new rules. However, subsequent new rule cases appeared to cut back on *Butler*.

TUNG YIN

References and Further Reading

Yackle, Larry W. *Reclaiming the Federal Courts.* Cambridge, MA: Harvard University Press, 1994.

Cases and Statutes Cited

Arizona v. Roberson, 486 U.S. 675 (1988)
Edwards v. Arizona, 451 U.S. 477 (1981)
Teague v. Lane, 489 U.S. 288 (1989)

See also Edwards v. Arizona, **451 U.S. 477 (1981); Habeas Corpus: Modern History; Harlan, John Marshall II;** *Miranda v. Arizona*, **384 U.S. 436 (1966); Right to Counsel (VI)**

BUTLER, PIERCE (1866–1939)

Pierce Butler, one of the most conservative justices ever to sit on the U.S. Supreme Court, was born March 17, 1866, in a log cabin on a Minnesota farm. One of six children of Irish immigrant parents, Butler, an ardent patriot and devout Catholic, regarded economic liberty and self-reliance as indispensable components of democracy.

A tireless legal advocate for railroads, who was intolerant of social and political dissent, Butler, as an University of Minnesota regent (1901–1924), spearheaded the removal of professors with unorthodox views. Criticism of his reactionary attitude and perceived corporate bias threatened his 1922 Court nomination.

As a Supreme Court justice, Butler, a rugged individualist, often opposed public control of private economic affairs. Due process, he believed, protected contractual freedom from the unreasonable exercise of state police powers, whose scope he narrowly construed to invalidate industrial regulations in *Weaver v. Palmer Bros. Co.* (1926) and *Burns Baking Co. v. Bryan* (1924). Refusing to balance public and private rights, Butler's *Village of Euclid v. Ambler Realty Co.* (1926) dissent decried zoning ordinances that restricted businesses. Similarly, he invoked economic liberty to invalidate a minimum wage law in *Morehead v. New York ex. rel. Tipaldo* (1936), taxation in *Miller v. Standard Nut Margarine Co.* (1932), and sought to void Social Security in *Steward Machine Co. v. Davis* (1937) (dissent). A vociferous New Deal critic, Butler and three other justices comprised the notorious Four Horsemen, who persisted in interpreting the Constitution inflexibly rather than adapting its limitations to the Depression's changing circumstances.

In contrast, Butler was more deferential toward public restrictions of free speech and citizenship. Rigidly patriotic, Butler was unsympathetic to social agitators. In *United States v. Schwimmer* (1929) and *United States v. MacIntosh* (1931), he upheld governmental authority to reject alien pacifists' citizenship applications, and in *Kessler v. Strecker* (1939) (dissent), Butler thought that the government could deport a former communist. Similarly, his dissents in *Stromberg v. California* (1931) and *Herndon v. Lowry* (1938) demonstrate Butler's willingness to apply criminal syndicalism laws to communists engaged in expressive activity. Concerned about the dissemination of unorthodox and controversial opinions, Butler's dissents in *Near v. Minnesota* (1931) and *Hague v. Committee of Industrial Organizations* (1939) would have permitted public officials to restrict speech as a public nuisance through prior restraint and vague indirect regulations of its content.

Generally solicitous of criminal defendants' procedural rights, Butler criticized federal prohibition officials whose search and seizure efforts violated the Fourth Amendment in *Olmstead v. United States* (1928) (dissent); *United States v. Lefkowitz* (1932), and *Go-Bart Importing v. United States* (1931). Butler also demonstrated a slight civil libertarian bent when he dissented silently from *Buck v. Bell* (1927), which upheld Virginia's sterilization law.

In matters of race, Butler was less vigilant. In *The Alien Land Use Cases* (1923), he sustained laws that restricted Asians from owning land, and sanctioned a poll tax in *Breedlove v. Suttles* (1937) (dissent). Reluctant to expand the scope of due process beyond economic liberty, Butler would have left undisturbed

Texas's all-white primary in *Nixon v. Condon* (1932) (dissent); educational segregation in *Missouri ex. rel. Gaines v. Canada* (1938) (dissent); and the conviction of poor black defendants not afforded effective assistance of counsel in the infamous Scottsboro rape case, *Powell v. Alabama* (dissent).

Pierce Butler, whose social conservatism imbued his constitutional jurisprudence, died November 16, 1939, in Washington, DC.

SAMUEL R. OLKEN

References and Further Reading

Brown, Francis J. *The Social and Economic Philosophy of Pierce Butler*. Washington, D.C.: Catholic University of America Press, 1945.

Danelski, David J. *A Supreme Court Justice Is Appointed*. New York: Random House, 1964.

Olken, Samuel R., *The Business of Expression: Economic Liberty, Political Factions and the Forgotten First Amendment Legacy of Justice George Sutherland*. William & Mary Bill of Rights Journal 10 (Winter 2002): 249–357.

White, G. Edward. *The Constitution and the New Deal*. Cambridge, MA: Harvard University Press, 2000.

Cases and Statutes Cited

The Alien Land Use Cases (1923): *Frick v. Webb*, 263 U.S. 326; *Porterfield v. Webb*, 263 U.S. 225; *Terrace v. Thompson*, 263 U.S. 197; *Webb v. O'Brien*, 263 U.S. 326 (all 1923)

Breedlove v. Suttles, 302 U.S. 277 (1937)

Buck v. Bell, 274 U.S. 200 (1927)

Burns Baking Co. v. Bryan, 264 U.S. 504 (1924)

Euclid v. Ambler Realty Co., 272 U.S. 365 (1926)

Go-Bart Importing v. United States, 282 U.S. 344 (1931)

Hague v. Committee of Industrial Organizations, 307 U.S. 496 (1939)

Herndon v. Lowry, 301 U.S. 444 (1938)

Kessler v. Strecker, 307 U.S. 22 (1939)

Miller v. Standard Nut Margarine Co., 284 U.S. 489 (1932)

Missouri ex. rel. Gaines v. Canada, 305 U.S. 337 (1938)

Morehead v. New York ex. rel. Tipaldo, 298 U.S. 587 (1936)

Near v. Minnesota, 283 U.S. 697 (1931)

Nixon v. Condon, 286 U.S. 73 (1932)

Olmstead v. United States, 277 U.S. 438 (1928)

Powell v. Alabama, 287 U.S. 45 (1932)

Steward Machine Co. v. Davis, 301 U.S. 548 (1937)

Stromberg v. California, 283 U.S. 359 (1931)

United States v. Lefkowitz, 285 U.S. 452 (1932)

United States v. MacIntosh, 283 U.S. 605 (1931)

United States v. Schwimmer, 279 U.S. 644 (1929)

Weaver v. Palmer Bros. Co., 270 U.S. 294 (1926)

BYERS v. EDMONDSON, 712 SO.2D 681 (1999) ("NATURAL BORN KILLERS" CASE)

The judgment rendered concerns the issue of whether the film *Natural Born Killers* is protected speech under the First Amendment, that is, should movie producers, directors, and studios be responsible for encouraging criminal behavior? Attorneys for the producers and director of the movie *Natural Born Killers* petitioned Louisiana's high court to review a lower court ruling that they say is the first of "American court decisions to hold that the creators of a fictional story can be sued for the deviant criminal acts of alleged imitators or copycats." The Louisiana Court of Appeals upheld a District Court summary judgment in favor of the defendants. The Court found that, contrary to plaintiffs' claims, "nothing in [the film] constitutes incitement," and therefore is protected speech.

Patsy Byers, a clerk shot by a young man and woman robbing a convenience store, sued Time Warner, Inc. and Oliver Stone in July 1995, alleging that they were responsible for her paralyzing injuries. Her lawsuit claimed that she was shot because the young couple was enamored with the movie *Natural Born Killers* and its glamorization of violent behavior. According to the attorney for the Byers estate, Time Warner and Oliver Stone should be liable for "intentionally, recklessly, or negligently including in the video subliminal images which either directly advocated violent activity or which would cause viewers to repeatedly view the video and thereby become more susceptible to its advocacy of violent activity."

In May 1998, a Louisiana appeals court reversed the ruling that the trial court should not have dismissed the case and the plaintiffs presented adequate allegations to avoid dismissal on First Amendment grounds. Byers' allegations, which the appeals court said it had to accept as true at the early procedural stage of the lawsuit, are that the movie falls into a category of speech that directly incites and will likely lead to imminent, lawless action, which is unprotected by the First Amendment. In reaching its decision, the Louisiana appeals court relied on *Rice v. Paladin Enterprises, Inc.* (1997), in which the U.S. Court of Appeals for the Fourth Circuit ruled that the First Amendment did not merit wrongful death action against the publishers of an instructional book titled *Hit Man: A Technical Manual for Independent Contractors*.

In their appeal to the Louisiana Supreme Court, attorneys for the defendants noted that "no court in American has ever held a filmaker or film distributor liable for injuries allegedly resulting from imitation of a film." Their argument addressed the issue of whether "the specter of such boundless liability would cause those who create movies, music, books, and other creative works to avoid controversial or provocative subjects."

G. L. TYLER

C

CABLE TELEVISION REGULATION

Cable television regulation began in the late 1940s and 1950s primarily as a local matter. The first cable systems needed easements to construct facilities on public and private land. Local authorities created franchises to provide access to rights of ways, and state regulators addressed questions of access to attach the cable plant to existing utility poles.

Federal regulation first began with questions of whether and how cable operators could retransmit distant and local broadcasters, a controversy that continues 40 years later. Importing major market stations into small communities that might have one TV station, for instance, bringing Denver stations to Casper, Wyoming, made for a good service for customers but created competitive issues for the local station. The Federal Communications Commission (FCC) set limits on the number and kind of stations that could be imported under "ancillary jurisdiction" approved by the U.S. Supreme Court. The Supreme Court also found no copyright liability on the cable operator's part for carrying stations.

Congress began regulating cable, first in 1976 by creating copyright liability for station carriage in tandem with a cable compulsory copyright in those signals, and in 1978 with the first of several laws establishing pole attachment arrangements. In 1984, the first comprehensive federal cable law provided for explicit FCC authority, ground rules for granting and renewing franchises by localities, and public access and leased access channels.

In 1992, because of complaints over high cable rates and access by large-dish satellite competitors to program networks owned by operators, Congress passed the 1992 Act, which led to a complex set of rate regulation of cable rates (generally lifted in the 1996 Telecommunications Act.) The 1992 Act also imposed a requirement that operators generally "must carry" all local TV and alternatively granted TV stations the right to negotiate carriage rights, irrespective of the compulsory copyright created in TV signals in 1976.

The 1996 Telecommunications Act focused on facilities-based competition to incumbent local exchange carriers; cable, as the second wire to residences figured prominently in the debate. Although cable has provided some facilities-based phone competition using its hybrid fiber-coax plant, its primary new offering is cable modem service. Initially considered a cable service, the FCC in 2002 declared cable modem service an "interstate information service," but judicial review may lead to the determination that it is a "telecommunications service."

As cable operators offer modem service along with Voice over Internet Protocol, the laws surrounding its video service may be less significant than its role as an operator of a broadband network. Policies relating to nondiscrimination of applications or attachments to cable's broadband network have engendered considerable policy debates.

Another significant provision of the 1996 Act, Sec. 629, requires the commercial availability of set-top boxes, historically leased by the operator to subscribers both as a marketing matter and a way to control signal theft. Because digital transmissions pose new problems for copyright holders, regulations have also developed on how copying of cable programming may be accomplished along with rules for preventing unauthorized distribution on the Internet.

DANIEL L. BRENNER

CAIN v. KENTUCKY, 387 U.S. 319 (1970)

In a *per curium decision*, based on *Redrup v. New York* (1967), the Supreme Court disposed of *Cain v. Kentucky* and reversed Kentucky's ban of public showings of the film "I, A Woman." Warren Burger, who had been confirmed as Chief Justice in 1969, and Harlan dissented. The Court disposed of two other cases (*Hoyt v. Minnesota* [1970] and *Walker v. Ohio* [1970]) in similar fashion, sparking dissents by Blackmun and Burger, respectively.

Until Burger's appointment, *per curiams* "redrupping" cases followed a fairly standard format with a simple declaration, "The judgment is reversed. *Redrup v. New York*, 386 U.S. 767." Harlan then would provide a dissent that cited his opposition in previous cases that the syllabus would summarize as "Mr. Justice Harlan would affirm the judgment of the state court upon the premises stated in his separate opinion in *Roth v. United States* . . . and his dissenting opinion in *Memoirs v. Massachusetts* . . . ." As the Court's composition shifted and became more conservative, the use of *per curiams* and redrupping attracted new dissenters and declined in frequency.

Burger's appointment meant that Harlan was no longer alone in his dissents to *per curiams* resting on *Redrup's* authority. Both Burger and Harlan thought the Court's majority in *Cain* failed to pay sufficient deference to the states. In *Cain*, they both issued separate dissents. Harlan modified his standard dissent, indicating he thought Ohio's decision presented a "borderline question" but concluded he could not say the state exceeded the "constitutional speed limit" in banning public showings of the film. Burger complained the Court was inflexible and denied the states the opportunity to adopt their own standards or deal with the problem on their own terms.

In *Walker*, Burger cited his dissent in *Cain* but added he found no justification for the Court to assume the role of national, unreviewable board of censorship for the states, "subjectively judging each piece of material brought before it without regard to the findings or conclusions of other courts, state or federal." Blackmun did not participate in *Walker*, but in *Hoyt* he dissented, arguing the Constitution did not

"necessarily prescribe a national and uniform measure" dealing with obscenity, and he was joined by Harlan and Burger.

Burger, Blackmun, and Harlan constituted the core coalition to challenge the majority's use of *per curiams* to overrule state courts that in their eyes conscientiously tried to apply the Supreme Court's standards first laid out in *Roth*.

ROY B. FLEMMING

Cases and Statutes Cited

Cain v. Kentucky, 397 U.S. 319 (1970)
Hoyt v. Minnesota, 399 U.S. 524 (1970)
Redrup v. New York, 386 U.S. 767 (1967)
Walker v. Ohio, 398 U.S. 434 (1970)

CALDER v. BULL, 3 U.S. 386 (1798)

The Connecticut legislature enacted a resolution granting a new hearing in a probate trial. The disappointed heirs challenged the legislative action as a violation of Article 1, Section 10, Clause 1 of the Constitution of the United States, which prohibits any state from passing an "ex post facto" law.

The Supreme Court of the United States unanimously upheld the legislative act, concluding that the ex post facto clause applies only in the criminal context. For example, Connecticut would have been prohibited by the clause from enacting a law establishing criminal sanctions for an activity that was legal at the time it was done. The probating of a will is a civil matter, however, and the federal Constitution's prohibition against ex post facto laws does not cover it.

Calder v. Bull was one of the Supreme Court's first decisions involving limitations on governmental power. It remains a landmark decision for that reason alone. It also remains significant because it was the first case in which members of the Court openly disagreed with one another about how the Constitution should be interpreted. Justice Samuel Chase maintained in his opinion that the meaning of the Constitution—including specific clauses in the Constitution such as the ex post facto clause—cannot be discerned from the text of the Constitution alone. He wrote: "An act of the Legislature (for I cannot call it a law) contrary to the first great principles of the social compact, cannot be considered a rightful exercise of legislative authority . . . . The genius, the nature, and the spirit, of our state governments, amount to a prohibition of such acts of legislation; and the general principles of law and reason forbid them."

Justice James Iredell responded directly to Justice Chase's approach and rejected it. Justice Iredell maintained that the only legitimate form of judicial review is interpretation of the written text of the Constitution. He wrote: "If . . . the legislature of the union, or the legislature of any member of the union, shall pass a law, within the general scope of their constitutional power, the court cannot pronounce it to be void, merely because it is, in their judgment, contrary to the principles of natural justice. The ideas of natural justice are regulated by no fixed standard; the ablest and the purest men have differed upon the subject."

The Chase-Iredell exchange about how to interpret the Constitution has been characterized by scholars as "the opening salvo in a running battle that has never simmered down completely." The specific rule of the case remains good law: the ex post facto clause applies only in the criminal context. One member of the current Court—Clarence Thomas—believes that the clause also applies in the civil context. Consequently, he has suggested that *Calder v. Bull* be overruled: despite the fact that the decision has stood as precedent for 200-plus years.

Before Justice Thomas's concurring opinion in *Eastern Enterprises v. Apfel* (1998), no member of the Supreme Court had called *Calder* into question since William Johnson in the 1829 case of *Satterlee v. Matthewson*. Justice Johnson wrote for himself alone in *Satterlee*, as he did when he first called *Calder* into question in *Ogden v. Saunders* (1827), and Justice Thomas wrote only for himself in *Apfel*. The future of *Calder* seems secure.

SCOTT D. GERBER

Cases and Statutes Cited

Eastern Enterprises v. Apfel, 524 U.S. 498 (1998)
Satterlee v. Matthewson, 27 U.S. (2 Pet.) 380 (1829)

CALERO-TOLEDO v. PEARSON YACHT LEASING CO., 416 U.S. 663 (1974)

Federal and state laws authorize the government to seize and forfeit property that is "tainted" by its connection to specified crimes. In *Calero-Toledo*, the Supreme Court addressed, albeit ambiguously, the question of whether the Constitution's due process clause protects an "innocent owner" from forfeiture when her property was illegally used without her knowledge or consent. Citing a number of precedents, the Court upheld the civil forfeiture of a rented yacht after a marijuana cigarette was discovered onboard, even though the yacht's owner was innocent of wrongdoing and ignorant of the renters' illegal activity.

Justice Brennan's opinion for the Court found forfeiture against the unwitting lessor rational, because it could induce owners to exercise greater care in transferring possession of their property. However, the opinion included dicta implying that the Constitution might mandate a narrower innocent owner defense, protecting owners who are not only unaware of the wrongful activity, but also have done everything "that reasonably could be expected" to prevent it.

On the basis of this language, some lower courts found a limited constitutional defense for owners who are *both* unknowing and non-negligent regarding the illegal use of their property. However, in *Bennis v. Michigan* (1996), the Supreme Court reaffirmed *Caldero-Toledo* with an even broader holding that dropped all reference to any circumstances that might constitutionally protect an unwitting and non-negligent owner. Bennis did not know of, and could not prevent, her husband from using their car for sex with a prostitute, but the Court held five to four that she had no constitutional protection against forfeiture of her interest in the automobile.

Despite the *Calero-Toledo* and *Bennis* cases, innocent owners have alternative remedies. *Statutory* innocent owner defenses have found their way into several forfeiture laws, and the Civil Asset Forfeiture Reform Act of 2000 creates a uniform innocent owner defense applicable to most federal forfeiture procedures. Moreover, federal and most state laws allow for administrative remission or mitigation of unduly severe forfeitures. Finally, the Supreme Court has held that the Eighth Amendment's excessive fines clause applies to forfeitures, and the Court has yet to decide whether subjecting an innocent owner to forfeiture of her property is necessarily excessive.

Caldero-Toledo also found no constitutional violation in the government's denial of notice or a hearing to the owner until after its seizure of the yacht. The Court subsequently modified this holding in *United States v. James Daniel Good Real Property et al.* (1993), finding that a preseizure notice and hearing is required for land, houses, and other real property, because in such cases, advanced notice cannot create a risk that the property will be removed from the jurisdiction.

ERIC D. BLUMENSON

References and Further Reading

Department of Justice. *Asset Forfeiture Law and Practice Manual.* June 1998.
Kessler, Steven L. *Civil and Criminal Forfeiture: Federal and State Practice* §6.01, 1993.
Smith, David B. *Prosecution and Defense of Forfeiture Cases.* Matthew Bender.

Cases and Statutes Cited

Bennis v. Michigan, 516 U.S. 442 (1996)
United States v. James Daniel Good Real Property et al., 510 U.S. 43 (1993)

See also **Civil Asset Forfeiture; Due Process; *United States v. 92 Buena Vista Avenue*, 507 U.S. 111 (1993)**

CALHOUN, JOHN CALDWELL (1882–1850)

John C. Calhoun received an elite education, studying under a prominent reverend tutor, and then graduating from Yale College. After his admission to the South Carolina bar, Calhoun was elected to the South Carolina legislature. He served in the U.S. House of Representatives, then as Secretary of War under James Monroe, the as Vice-President twice, under John Quincy Adams and Andrew Jackson. After resigning his position as Vice-President, he was elected to the U.S. Senate and then served as John Tyler's Secretary of State. At the end of that term, he returned to the Senate, where he served until his retirement. His connection to civil rights centers on two ideas: his belief in states' rights and his defense of slavery.

After the hated Tariff of 1828 (called the Tariff of Abominations in the South) was passed, Calhoun published *The South Carolina Exposition*, which outlined his theory of "state interposition." Also known as Nullification, Calhoun's theory gave individual states the authority to ignore, or nullify, federal law that interfered with any states interests or sovereignty. The South Carolina Legislature eagerly embraced Calhoun's theory and voted to ignore the Tariff, but President Andrew Jackson was outspoken in his intention to enforce the law. Calhoun actually resigned from his position as Vice-President, was immediately elected as U.S. Senator from South Carolina, and began fighting for nullification on the Senate floor. The controversy grew into a crisis as Congress passed the Force Bill, giving Jackson authority to use federal troops to compel South Carolina to enforce the Tariff. Violence was averted only by compromise: Jackson agreed to lower the Tariff, South Carolina rescinded its nullification ordinance, and Calhoun, who wanted South Carolina to remain in the union but insisted on their right to nullify or secede, endorsed the agreement.

Calhoun also consistently defended the institution of slavery. He was a supporter of the "positive good" theory, which described slavery as a beneficial institution. Under positive good rationalization, slavery

civilized blacks. Slaveholders educated, supported, and managed their slaves so that American slaves had reached a level of civilization that no other society of blacks had ever reached before. Thus, slavery allowed both black slaves and white slave owners to thrive. To be sure, the doctrine was not widely accepted outside of the South, but it allowed Calhoun and other slaveholders to justify their institution. In a civil rights irony, Calhoun considered himself a great defender of civil rights because he held property rights sacred. Because slaves were considered property (and neither the Constitution nor the federal government challenged that idea), Calhoun was able to counter abolition movements by citing the Constitution's protections of private property. Finally, as a fierce defender of both South Carolina's and the South's interests, he was concerned about maintaining legislative balance between free and slave states. To that end, he supported the Missouri Compromise, which allowed Missouri into the Union as a slave state while allowing Maine in as a free state.

Calhoun thought of himself as a defender of civil rights; he saw the rights of South Carolina to make laws for its citizens as paramount over the federal government's, and he believed that because southern slaveholders owned slaves, the protection of slavery was simply a matter of protecting property.

JAMES HALABUK, JR.

References and Further Reading

Bartlett, Irving H. *John C. Calhoun: A Biography*. New York: W.W. Norton and Company, 1993.
Thomas, John L., ed. *John C. Calhoun, A Profile*. New York: Hill and Wang, 1968.

CALIFORNIA v. ACEVEDO, 500 U.S. 565 (1991)

The Fourth Amendment's protection against unreasonable searches generally requires law enforcement to obtain a search warrant before initiating a search. In *Carroll v. United States*, the Supreme Court had crafted an exception for moving vehicles, which permitted law enforcement to conduct a warrantless search of an automobile when they had probable cause to believe that contraband was contained somewhere in a vehicle but not when probable cause extended only to a specific container.

Police officers in California observed Charles Acevedo exit the apartment of a man who that morning had picked up a package that they knew contained marijuana. Acevedo placed a brown paper bag, identical in size to one of the marijuana packages, in the trunk of his car and drove off. The officers stopped him, opened the trunk, and discovered marijuana in the bag.

Although the officers only had probable cause to believe that the bag located in the car contained marijuana, rather than the car, the Supreme Court held that the Fourth Amendment did not require the officers to obtain a search warrant before opening the bag. It reasoned that if a warrantless search of a vehicle is permissible, then the Fourth Amendment must also allow a less intrusive search for a closed container based on probable cause. The Court stressed that the search of an automobile based on probable cause to believe that a closed container contains contraband is limited to a search for that object and does not extend to the entire car.

REBECCA L. BARNHART

References and Further Reading

LaFave, Wayne R. *Search and Seizure*, 4th ed. 6 vols. St. Paul: West, 2004.
William E. Ringel, et al. *Searches & Seizures, Arrests and Confessions*, 2nd ed. 3 vols. Deerfield, Ill.: Clark Boardman Callaghan, 1979 [updated three times a year but copyright listed as "1979"].

Cases and Statutes Cited

Carroll v. United States, 267 U.S. 132 (1925)

See also **Automobile Searches;** *Carroll v. United States*, **267 U.S. 132 (1925); Probable Cause; Search (General Definition); Search Warrants**

CALIFORNIA v. GREENWOOD, 486 U.S. 35 (1988)

In *California v. Greenwood*, the police searched a defendant's garbage bags left on the curb. The Supreme Court concluded that the Fourth Amendment did not apply, and thus the police are able to search people's trash with no limitations and without the judicial oversight of a warrant. The Fourth Amendment only applies when a person has an expectation of privacy that society is prepared to recognize as reasonable. The Court reasoned that there was no reasonable expectation in the trash because "[i]t is common knowledge that plastic bags left on or at the side of a public street are readily accessible to animals, children, scavengers, snoops, and other members of the public." The Court also reasoned that the trash was left at the curb "for the express purpose of conveying it to a third party, the trash collector, who might himself have sorted through [the] trash or permitted others, such as the police, to do so."

The Court's reasoning equates privacy with total secrecy. If anything is exposed to others in any way, even if others are unlikely to see it, then according to the Court, there is no reasonable expectation of privacy. According to the dissenting opinion, a study of a person's trash can reveal much about an individual's personality and lifestyle. People often throw out very private items, such as prescription drug bottles, contraceptive devices, old financial documents, personal letters, and so on.

DANIEL J. SOLOVE

References and Further Reading

LaFave, Wayne R., Jerold H. Israel, and Nancy J. King. *Criminal Procedure*. 142–143 (3d ed. 2000).
Solove, Daniel J., *Digital Dossiers and the Dissipation of Fourth Amendment Privacy*, Southern California Law Review 75 (2002): 1083–1168.

See also **Expectation of Privacy; Search (General Definition)**

CALIFORNIA v. LARUE, 409 U.S. 109 (1972)

When a commercial activity requires a license or permit from a government, can a state use this authority to regulate "expression" even if aspects of the conduct do not meet the *Roth* standard of obscenity?

In 1970, the California Department of Alcoholic Beverage Control promulgated rules regulating entertainment in businesses serving alcoholic beverages. On the basis of legislative findings that the "gross sexuality" of topless or bottomless dancing in bars and nightclubs encouraged sexual encounters between the performers and customers, as well as sex crimes and prostitution outside the businesses, California's regulations prohibited live or filmed sexual entertainment that included performances or simulations of specific sexual acts. A three-judge federal district court struck down the regulation as unconstitutional, because some of the proscribed entertainment was not obscene.

This is the Court's first major obscenity decision in which the four Nixon nominees (Burger, Blackmun, Powell, and Rehnquist) participated. In a 6:3 decision reversing the lower court, Rehnquist, writing for the majority with Steward and White joining the four Nixon nominees, does not focus on whether nude dancing could be obscene but rather on its harmful, secondary effects in establishments selling alcoholic beverages and whether state licensing power could regulate nude dancing to minimize its effects. Thus, he did not use the heightened tests usually associated with the "preferred freedoms" of the First Amendment. Instead, he notes the regulations dealt with bars and nightclubs selling liquor, not "a dramatic performance in a theater." He thus uses a rationality test to the department's regulations that are not unreasonable in light of the legislative findings and the questionable effectiveness of other options.

The lynchpin of the *LaRue* decision was Rehnquist's view that the "broad sweep" of the Twenty-first Amendment conferred "something more than the normal state authority" over public health and morals. This amendment gave the states power to regulate the sale of alcohol, authority that, according to Rehnquist, outweighed any First Amendment interest in nude dancing. Brennan, and especially Marshall, attacked Rehnquist's view in their dissents. In subsequent cases dealing with nude dancing and liquor licensing, for example, *New York State Liquor Authority v. Bellanca* (1981) and *City of Newport, Kentucky v. Iacobucci* (1986), both *per curiam* opinions resting on *LaRue*, Stevens, who joined the Court after *LaRue* was handed down, wrote dissenting opinions, launching a campaign challenging Rehnquist's view of the Twenty-first Amendment, which provided a fortuitous way of upholding California's regulations without having to directly address the relationship between nude dancing and the First Amendment.

Finally, in 1996, the Supreme Court in *44 Liquourmart, Inc. v. Rhode Island* (1996) with Stevens writing for the majority disavowed the reasoning in *LaRue* without questioning, however, its holding. According to Stevens, the result in *LaRue* would have been the same if the majority had not relied on the Twenty-first Amendment. States, he argued, with their inherent police powers have ample authority to regulate the sale of alcoholic beverages to avoid "bacchanalian revelries." Equally important, the Twenty-first Amendment, Stevens wrote, does not allow states to "ignore their obligations" under other provisions of the Constitution, nor does it "in any way diminish the force of the supremacy clause."

ROY B. FLEMMING

Cases and Statutes Cited

44 Liquourmart, Inc. v. Rhode Island, 517 U.S. 484 (1996)
California v. LaRue, 409 U.S. 109 (1972)
City of Newport, Kentucky v. Iacobucci 479 U.S. 92 (1986)
New York State Liquor Authority v. Bellanca, 452 U.S. 714 (1981)

CALIFORNIA v. RAMOS, 459 U.S. 1301 (1982)

People who disagree about something can be induced to set aside their disagreement to unite against a common enemy. Prosecutors often use the "common-enemy rule" in death-penalty trials, highlighting the specter of the convicted capital defendant someday getting out of prison to harm the community again. The fear of a predator again walking the streets—the "common enemy" of all the jurors—can be so powerful that jurors will set aside their disagreement over whether to impose life imprisonment or death and rally against the prospect of the defendant's future release.

California v. Ramos presented the Supreme Court with the issue of when a prosecutor may deploy this sort of argument (though neither the Court nor the litigants used the "common-enemy" locution). The capital statute at issue in *Ramos* allowed the jury to consider the fact that a sentence of life imprisonment without the possibility of parole leaves open the *possibility* of future commutation of the sentence by the governor. The defendant argued that this "inject[ed] an unacceptable level of unreliability into the capital sentencing determination" and "deflect[ed] the jury from its constitutionally mandated task of basing the penalty decision on the character of the defendant and the nature of the offense." The Court rejected this challenge to California's allowance of a commutation possibility to be considered in a death-penalty trial. The Court ruled that the possibility of commutation—though remote; indeed, very remote—was relevant to the issue of the defendant's future dangerousness. The Court sidestepped the concern that this remote possibility might warp the jury's decision-making process by emphasizing that the instruction to the jury to consider possible commutation was accurate and the defendant had the opportunity to argue the remoteness of this possibility. Thus, in a broader sense, *California v. Ramos* represents one instance where the Court places enormous—too much?—faith in the adversarial process to reject a constitutional challenge on the basis of the prospect of unreliable capital sentencing. For a contrasting instance where the Court exhibits a profound distrust of the adversarial process, consider its decision in *Roper v. Simmons*, where it constitutionally bans executing juvenile offenders in part because the adversarial process is ill-equipped to decide life or death for juvenile offenders.

DAN WILLIAMS

References and Further Reading

California v. Ramos, 463 U.S. 992 (1983).

Carter, Linda E. and Ellen Kreitzberg, *Understanding Capital Punishment Law*. (2004)

See also Capital Punishment; Capital Punishment and the Equal Protection Clause Cases; Capital Punishment: Due Process Limits; Capital Punishment: History and Politics; Capital Punishment: Eighth Amendment Limits

CALIFORNIA v. TROMBETTA, 467 U.S. 479 (1984)

In *Trombetta*, the Supreme Court held that the Fourteenth Amendment due process clause does not require the government to preserve evidence that could potentially be useful to a criminal defendant.

Trombetta was one of several defendants charged with drunk driving after failing breath tests on California highways. Each defendant unsuccessfully moved to suppress the test results, because the police did not preserve the breath samples so that the defendants could attempt to prove the results were inaccurate. However, the state appellate court ruled that the failure to preserve the breath samples violated the defendants' due process rights.

The U. S. Supreme Court unanimously reversed. The Court explained that although the state has a duty under *Brady v. Maryland* to preserve and disclose exculpatory evidence, that duty does not generally extend to evidence that might or might not be exculpatory. The Court concluded that the destruction of the breath samples did not violate the defendants' rights, because it was very unlikely that retesting of the evidence would have benefited the defendants and because there was no indication that the police had destroyed the samples in a bad faith effort to hamper their defenses.

Trombetta thus made clear that the government is not always required to preserve potentially exculpatory evidence. Four years later, in *Arizona v. Youngblood*, the Court extended *Trombetta* to hold that the police may always destroy potentially exculpatory evidence, including evidence that could conclusively exonerate the defendant, so long as they do not act in bad faith.

DAVID A. MORAN

References and Further Reading

Imwinkelried, Edwin, and Norman Garland. *Exculpatory Evidence*. 2d ed. Michie, 1996.
Stacy, Tom, The *Search for Truth in Constitutional Criminal Procedure*, Columbia Law Review 91 (1991): 1369.
Whitaker, Barbara. "DNA Frees Inmate Years After Justices Rejected Plea." *New York Times*, August 11, 2000.

Cases and Statutes Cited

Arizona v. Youngblood, 488 U.S. 51 (1988)
Brady v. Maryland, 373 U.S. 83 (1963)

See also Arizona v. Youngblood, 488 U.S. 51 (1988); *Brady v. Maryland*, 373 U.S. 83 (1963); Due Process; Fourteenth Amendment

CAMARA v. MUNICIPAL COURT OF THE CITY AND COUNTY OF SAN FRANCISCO, 387 U.S. 523 (1967)

The Fourth Amendment's requirement that the government obtain a warrant before any search or seizure of private property is well established for criminal investigations. Whether a warrant was required when the government conducts a health and safety inspection, an administrative investigation, however, was not established until *Camara v. Municipal Court of the City and County of San Francisco*.

In 1963, a San Francisco public health inspector attempted to search the ground floor of an apartment building after learning that the lessee might be violating the building's occupancy permit. The inspector did not have a warrant, and the lessee refused to consent on three separate occasions. The lessee's refusal to allow the inspection resulted in the lessee's criminal prosecution under San Francisco's housing codes.

The Supreme Court held that administrative health and safety inspections conducted without a search warrant violated the Fourth Amendment. The Court reasoned that a search of private property without proper consent is unreasonable, except in narrowly defined situations, unless it has been authorized by a valid search warrant. Even if the inspections are not conducted to discover criminal activity, administrative inspections made pursuant to fire, health, and housing codes threaten interests of the property owner protected by the Fourth Amendment.

Although the Court held that a warrant is required to conduct administrative searches absent consent, the Court stated that the warrant for such a search need not be based on suspicion that any particular dwelling is in violation of health and safety codes. Rather, it is reasonable for the government to conduct periodic inspections of an entire area to protect the public's health and safety. Moreover, the Court's holding does not prevent prompt inspections of dwellings without a warrant in emergency situations.

KATY H. H. YANG-PAGE

References and Further Reading

Sunby, Scott E., *A Return to Fourth Amendment Basics: Undoing the Mischief of Camara and Terry*, University of Minnesota Law Review 72 (1988): 383–447.

Cases and Statutes Cited

Camara v. Municipal Court of the City and County of San Francisco, 387 U.S. 523 (1967)

See also **Administrative Searches and Seizures; Probable Cause; Search (General Definition); Search Warrants; Warrantless Searches**

CAMERAS IN THE COURTROOM

The phrase "cameras in the courtroom" refers to the presence of news media cameras, both still and television cameras, inside courtrooms recording trial proceedings for the public. Since the early days of the American courts, members of the news media have been present in courtrooms, documenting proceedings for their audience. Before the arrival of cameras, reporters relied on pen and paper and courtroom sketch artists to relay details of trial proceedings to the public. In the television age, the simple installation of a small video camera in an unobtrusive location in a courtroom has allowed a much larger public to view the activities inside a courtroom. Trials are no longer accessible to only those who can fit into often-cramped courtrooms, but thousands, if not millions, turn on a television set to watch a trial. The most famous case in which cameras in the courtroom played a pivotal role was the murder trial of football star O. J. Simpson. Yet the overwhelming presence of the news media and the day-to-day coverage of the trial created a circus-like atmosphere and raised concerns over whether cameras should be permitted to record trial proceedings.

At the heart of the debate over cameras in the courtroom are the two constitutionally guaranteed rights: a defendant's Sixth Amendment right to a fair trial and the news media's First Amendment right of a free press. Those opposed to allowing news media cameras inside courtrooms argue that cameras would cause lawyers to overdramatize their arguments, scare away potential witnesses, and disrupt the solemn conduct of a trial, all of which could be detrimental to the defendant. Proponents of cameras in the courtroom argue that the public should have direct access to how the American judicial system really works. Television, proponents claim, is the best tool for allowing the public into the often shadowy world of the courts without having to attend a trial or having to sit on a jury.

Two cases directly addressing the constitutionality of allowing news media cameras inside courtrooms were brought to the U. S. Supreme Court. The case of *Estes v. Texas* (1964) involved the swindling conviction of Texas businessman Billy Sol Estes. Estes appealed his conviction on the grounds that the presence of the news media cameras infringed on his right to a fair trial. The Court ruled that the defendant's right to a public trial did not mean that the news media had a right to bring in their cameras to record the trial. The Court's decision in *Estes* was amended in the case of *Chandler v. Florida* (1981). The Court examined Florida's rules regarding cameras in the courtroom and concluded that there was not enough evidence to prove that the presence of news media cameras violated the due process of the defendants.

Currently, cameras are not permitted in federal courtrooms, although there have been attempts by the news media to gain access. State courts, however, are more receptive to the idea of cameras in the courtroom, although judges are very cautious in what they will allow the news media to cover.

STEPHANIE HSZIEH

References and Further Reading

Freedman, Warren. *Press and Media Access to the Criminal Courtroom*. New York: Quorum Books, 1988.

Cases and Statutes Cited

Estes v. Texas, 381 U.S. 532 (1964)
Chandler et al v. Florida 449 U.S. 560 (1981)

See also **Estes, Billy Sol; Free Press/Fair Trial**

CAMPAIGN FINANCE REFORM, NO. 1021

A California politician once famously observed: "Money is the Mother's Milk of Politics." For at least a century, the Congress has tried to legislate against this dictum. Since 1907, with the passage of the Tillman Act, which banned corporations from making direct contributions to political parties, Congress has enacted six major laws designed to regulate the use of money in politics. The Federal Corrupt Practices Act of 1925 provided for disclosure of certain federal campaign receipts and expenditures. The Taft–Hartley Act of 1947 subjected labor unions to the kinds of restrictions on campaign giving and spending that covered corporations. Each of these laws was enacted against a background of claimed corruption of the political process by those groups and individuals who wielded financial power.

It was widely believed, however, that these laws were not effective in achieving their objectives of deterring corruption and undue influence. They were narrowed by judicial interpretation and avoided by clever politicians. Indeed, President Lyndon B. Johnson once observed that federal campaign finance law was "more loophole than law."

The fourth major push for reform began building with the high-spending, media-focused presidential campaigns of the 1960s. A well-known book, *The Selling of the President*, fueled fears that politicians were being marketed like toothpaste and that democracy was being sold to the highest bidder. These concerns culminated in the next major piece of campaign finance reform legislation, the Federal Election Campaign Act of 1971. Enacted before Watergate, the Act sought to limit the amount of media advertising that federal candidates could do and vastly expand and improve campaign finance reporting and disclosure to close the loopholes that Lyndon Johnson had noted.

But civil liberties problems soon surfaced as the government tried to use these new provisions against nonpartisan criticism of government officials. If campaign finance laws could be used to prevent the publication of advertisements criticizing the government or subject the speakers to intrusive government regulation, that would raise enormous First Amendment problems of freedom of speech and association. Recognizing these problems, some courts gave a narrow scope to the Federal Election Campaign Act provisions, excluding their application to nonpartisan organizations. (*United States v. National Committee for Impeachment*; *American Civil Liberties Union v. Jennings*).

That sensible resolution of the clash between free speech and campaign finance regulation might have solved the problem had it not been for the Watergate scandals of the early 1970s, partially involving payments for wrongdoing out of President Nixon's reelection campaign funds. Congress was stampeded into enacting the Federal Election Campaign Act Amendments of 1974, a wide-ranging statute that imposed new and Draconian restrictions and penalties on campaign finance activity. This was the fifth major campaign finance enactment of the twentieth century.

It must be remembered, of course, that such activity almost invariably involves the exercise of First Amendment rights: speaking, associating, supporting candidates, electioneering, getting out the vote. Nonetheless, Congress decreed limits on how much any candidate could spend on seeking election, on how much candidates could contribute of their own funds to their own campaigns, how much their supporters could contribute to them, and, most alarmingly, severely limiting (to $1,000 per year) how much *independent* groups and individuals could spend to

speak about candidates during a campaign season. That latter provision effectively made it a crime to run more than a minuscule ad in a newspaper criticizing the President of the United States. The amendments also tightened the disclosure requirements, so that as little as a $15 contribution to any political party—even controversial ones—might be reported to the government. The one positive note was that the new law did provide, for the first time, for public financing of primary and general election campaigns at the Presidential level. Placed in charge of these onerous new speech restrictions was a new federal agency that was under the control and domination of the Congress. Substantial criminal penalties were prescribed for violation of these new campaign finance provisions.

There was an immediate challenge to this far-reaching new law by a coalition of "strange bedfellows," including liberal Senator Eugene McCarthy, conservative Senator James Buckley, the American Conservative Union and the New York Civil Liberties Union (*Buckley v. Valeo*). All these challengers claimed that restrictions on political campaign funding were restrictions on political campaign speech and derogated the First Amendment values of freedom of speech and association. The Court agreed in part. It struck down all limitations on campaign expenditures, reasoning that such restraints cut to the core of First Amendment values while not advancing the valid concerns with political corruption. (The Court also rejected the concept that expenditure limits could be justified on the ground that campaigns had become too "extravagant" or that government could level down the free speech of all citizens.) It also ruled that only those expenditures for activities or advertisements that "expressly advocated" the election or defeat of specified candidates could be subject to any regulation whatsoever. Mere criticism of elected officials, no matter how strong, was immune from regulation.

On the other hand, the Court upheld limitations on contributions to candidates from others (the Court held that candidates could contribute as much as they could to their own campaigns.) The rationale was that large contributions, even though fully disclosed to the public, posed the potential for corruption or the appearance of corruption and could be sharply limited (to $1,000). Likewise, routine disclosure of campaign contributors of as little as $101 could be demanded, though those giving to controversial minor parties might be exempt from such public revelation, a point confirmed in a later case (*Brown v. Socialist Workers '74 Campaign Committee*). The provision of public financing for Presidential candidates was upheld against the challenge that it

CAMPAIGN FINANCE REFORM, NO. 1021

was incestuous for the government to be subsidizing politics and that the particular scheme enacted favored the two major political parties, the Republicans and the Democrats, to the detriment of new, independent, and third parties and their candidates.

Finally, the appointment of the monitoring agency was found to violate separation of powers principles, because the primary designations were made by the Congress, not the President. (A new and properly constituted *Federal Election Commission* was installed shortly thereafter).

For the next twenty-five years, the landmark *Buckley* decision would provide the ground rules for resolving the clash between campaign finance restrictions and First Amendment rights. But two developments of the 1980s and 1990s would set the stage for the sixth major Congressional enactment in this area. They were the raising and spending of "soft money" by political parties for a wide range of electoral activities as long as they did not directly back their chosen candidates and the running of broadcast ads that strongly condemned or praised specific candidates while steering clear of "expressly advocating" any candidate's election or defeat. Many believed that both developments—soft money and issue advocacy—were end runs around the contribution limitations that the Court had consistently upheld, because they involved large contributions from individuals, unions, and corporations, which would be illegal if given directly to candidates themselves or spent for "express advocacy."

These concerns led to the enactment of The Bipartisan Campaign Reform Act of 2002, widely known as the McCain–Feingold law. That act outlawed "soft money" contributions to political parties and broadcast advertising by corporations or unions that even so much as mentioned the name of a federal candidate. Another coalition of candidates and cause organizations challenged these new restrictions as well, led by Republican Senator Mitch McConnell and including groups as diverse as the American Civil Liberties Union, the National Rifle Association, the AFL-CIO, and the Republican National Committee (*McConnell v. Federal Election Commission*). In another landmark ruling, a closely divided Supreme Court upheld this major feature of the law. The Court majority believed that the large soft money contributions to political parties were an effort to skirt the restrictions on contributions to candidates and carried the same potential for corruption or the appearance of corruption. The ban on broadcasting was upheld on the ground that the advertisements were really political, despite the lack of "express advocacy," and could be banned if they were sponsored by corporations or unions or

even nonprofit membership organizations like the ACLU.

Thus, the pendulum has swung back to permit a greater regulation of campaign financing and, therefore, a greater regulation of First Amendment rights.

JOEL M. GORA

References and Further Reading

Association of the Bar of the City of New York. *Dollars and Democracy: A Blueprint for Campaign Finance Reform*, 2000.
Mutch, Robert E. *Campaigns, Congress and the Courts: The Making of Federal Campaign Finance Law*, 1988.
Smith, Bradley A. *Unfree Speech: The Folly of Campaign Finance Reform*, 2000.

Cases and Statutes Cited

Buckley v. Valeo, 424 U.S. 1 (1976)
McConnell v. Federal Election Commission, 124 S. Ct. 619 (2003)

CAMPUS HATE SPEECH CODES

During the 1980s and early 1990s, many colleges and universities responded to incidents of racial and sexual harassment by adopting campus hate speech codes. In 1994, Arati Korwar reported that more than 350 public colleges and universities had adopted some form of a hate speech code. Proponents of the codes contended that their goal, which was to reduce hateful, prejudiced speech, was legitimate, for such speech should receive little or no First Amendment protection. The courts, however, have repeatedly struck down campus hate speech codes on the First Amendment grounds of vagueness, overbreadth, and their tendency to permit content-based discrimination with respect to the topics that may be discussed or the views that may be expressed on campus.

Hate speech codes tend to be enacted in response to pressure from campus groups that become upset about insensitive or offensive student conduct, such as the use of racial epithets, verbally or in writing, or the perpetuation of ethnic and racial stereotypes, often in the context of fraternity functions. Such was the case at the University of Michigan, which adopted a hate speech code after a group of students had become upset over the use of racial epithets on campus, and at the University of Wisconsin, which adopted a hate speech code with a plan called "Design for Diversity" in response to several incidents including two instances of fraternity functions involving racial and ethnic stereotyping.

Using the Supreme Court's "fighting words" doctrine as a springboard, which holds that words that are likely to incite an immediate violent response are not entitled to First Amendment protection, campus hate speech codes have attempted to regulate expressions intended to stigmatize or demean an individual on the basis of the person's race, gender, handicap, religion, national or ethnic origin, age, sexual orientation, marital status, etc. The University of Michigan's policy, for example, prohibited "[a]ny behavior, verbal or physical, that stigmatizes or victimizes an individual on the basis of race, ethnicity, religion, sex, sexual orientation, creed . . . and that . . . [c]reates an intimidating, hostile, or demeaning environment for educational pursuits, employment or participation in University sponsored extra-curricular activities."

When challenged, in *Doe v. University of Michigan* (1989), the court found the University of Michigan's policy to be overbroad, in that it might be applied to restrict speech when the speech in question is merely unseemly or offensive. The court also found the policy to be unconstitutionally vague, because the limits of the scope and reach of the policy were too difficult to discern. In *UWM Post v. Board of Regents of University of Wisconsin System* (1991), the court struck down the University of Wisconsin's quite similar policy on the grounds that the hate speech code permitted the university to engage in content-based discrimination with respect to the types of speech that it would permit on campus, a form of "governmental thought control." These results, combined with the Supreme Court's ruling in *R. A. V. v. City of St. Paul* (1992), which struck down a hate-crime ordinance on First Amendment grounds, created a formidable barrier for hate speech codes that in a succession of later cases involving other universities has not been cleared.

In an effort to address the underlying problems caused by the types of speech in question, such as racial or sexual harassment, without running afoul of First Amendment protections, some colleges and universities have more recently taken the approach recommended by Arthur Coleman and Jonathan Alger in their article, "Beyond Speech Codes: Harmonizing Rights of Free Speech and Freedom from Discrimination on University Campuses." Rather than addressing these underlying problems by prohibiting certain forms of expression, colleges and universities can take the alternative approach of prohibiting the discriminatory harassment itself, even though speech may be involved in the harassing activity. These policies follow the applicable antidiscrimination statutes and standards as closely as possible and avoid any attempt to proscribe particular forms of expression apart from the context of the situation in which such expressions may fit the legal definitions of unlawful harassing activity.

In the higher education context, a violation of Title VI or Title IX occurs if a college or university that receives federal funds fails to provide a nondiscriminatory environment that is conducive to learning. Determining whether a violation has occurred depends on whether the conduct complained of, which may or may not involve speech, is sufficiently "severe, pervasive or persistent" that the victim cannot fully benefit from the educational opportunities provided by the institution. Courts use a "totality of the circumstances" test to assess whether the conduct is sufficiently "severe, pervasive or persistent" standard such that a similarly situated, "reasonable" (not hypersensitive) student would be significantly and adversely impacted in his or her ability to benefit from or participate in educational programs or activities. These protections do not, however, go so far as to entitle a student to complete comfort or agreement with the expressions and opinions encountered in an educational environment. There is a range of conduct that students might find offensive but that is not sufficiently "severe, pervasive or persistent" as to interfere with a "reasonable" student's educational experience.

In creating alternatives to campus hate speech codes, the First Amendment concern to be avoided is that the same words, phrases, or symbols that might be prohibited by a hate speech code could, in an appropriate setting, be important to use to advance the learning process. For example, a hate speech code that prohibits the use of racial epithets may interfere with the study of important literature such as Mark Twain's *Huckleberry Finn,* which uses a particular racial epithet more than 200 times. Study of such literature might even help to address problems of racial bias by making students more aware of the forms and harms of racism if handled with sensitivity and care.

A majority of the Supreme Court recognized in *R. A. V.* that a hostile environment discrimination claim could survive a First Amendment challenge under the standards that the Court set forth in that case. A college or university policy that seeks to prohibit expression animated by racial prejudice or sexist bias as forms of discriminatory harassment will still need to provide enough specific guidance for individuals to be able to understand the types of behavior that are prohibited under the policy to withstand First Amendment–based overbreadth and vagueness challenges.

DAVID T. BALL

221

References and Further Reading

Coleman, Arthur L., and Jonathan R. Alger, *Beyond Speech Codes: Harmonizing Rights of Free Speech and Freedom from Discrimination on University Campuses,* Journal of College and University Law 23 (1996): 91–132.

Korwar, Arati R. *War of Words: Speech Codes at Public Colleges and Universities.* Nashville, TN: Freedom Forum First Amendment Center, 1994.

Shiell, Timothy C. *Campus Hate Speech on Trial.* Lawrence, KS: University Press of Kansas, 2000.

Cases and Statutes Cited

Doe v. University of Michigan, 721 F.Supp. 852 (E.D. Mich. 1989)

R.A.V. v. City of St. Paul, 505 U.S. 377 (1992)

UWM Post v. Board of Regents of University of Wisconsin System, 774 F.Supp. 1163 (E.D. Wis. 1991)

See also **Fighting Words and Free Speech**

CANTWELL v. CONNECTICUT, 310 U.S. 296 (1940)

Jehovah's Witnesses believe proselytizing is an essential part of their faith and, therefore, a religious obligation. As such, they preach on street corners, sell and/or distribute literature about their faith, and often engage in discussions with individuals about what the Witnesses believe. All of these are "activities," and, under the old belief/action dichotomy enunciated by the Court in *Reynolds v. United States* (1879), would not be protected under the First Amendment and could thus be regulated by the states. In a series of cases beginning in the late 1930s, however, the Supreme Court gradually came to the position that the line between belief and action could not always be clearly drawn, especially when certain actions flowed ineluctably from the tenets of the faith.

The Court first brought the First Amendment to bear in *Lowell v. City of Griffin* (1938), when it struck down a municipal ordinance requiring groups to get a permit before handing out pamphlets. That decision, however, had been based on the speech clause; in *Cantwell,* the Court for the first time in the modern era began exploring the meaning of the First Amendment's free exercise clause.

Newton Cantwell had gone door-to-door in overwhelmingly Catholic neighborhoods asking people if they would listen to a recording or receive one of the Witnesses' pamphlets. The materials all included attacks on Catholicism. When the residents objected, police arrested Cantwell, and he was subsequently convicted of failure to secure the necessary permit for door-to-door solicitation from the secretary of public welfare.

The Supreme Court unanimously overturned the conviction, and the majority opinion, by Justice Owen Roberts, is notable for two reasons. First, it relied on the Free Exercise Clause of the First Amendment rather than the Speech Clause. The state had the power to license solicitors, Roberts held, but the arbitrary power lodged in the secretary of public welfare constituted an impermissible form of censorship over religion. The Court would still have trouble deciding whether religious activities came under the protection of the Speech Clause or the Free Exercise Clause (see, for example, Justice Jackson's opinion in *West Virginia Board of Education v. Barnette* [1943]), but in Cantwell at last began to move beyond the simplistic action/belief dichotomy that had been the untouched basis of Free Exercise interpretation since *Reynolds.*

In another important aspect of his opinion, Roberts set out what would become a universal rule of First Amendment jurisprudence, namely, that although a state may regulate the time, place, and manner in which groups hold public meetings or engage in solicitation, it may not ban them altogether or discriminate on the basis of the content of the message.

MELVIN I. UROFSKY

References and Further Reading

Peters, Shawn Francis. *Judging Jehovah's Witnesses: Religious Persecution and the Dawn of the Rights Revolution.* Lawrence, KS: University Press of Kansas, 2000.

Waite, Edward F., The *Debt of Constitutional Law to Jehovah's Witnesses,* Minnesota Law Review 28 (1944): 209.

Cases and Statutes Cited

Reynolds v. United States, 98 U.S. 145 (1879)

Lowell v. City of Griffin, 303 U.S. 444 (1938)

West Virginia Board of Education v. Barnette, 319 U.S. 624 (1943)

CAPITAL PUNISHMENT

Introduction and Early Years

Capital punishment is a punishment option of the federal government in more than two thirds of states in the United States. The method of execution overwhelmingly used is lethal injection, although various states also allow execution by the electric chair, firing squad, gas chamber, and hanging.

Proponents of the death penalty argue that the death penalty serves important functions of deterrence and retribution. Those who argue for abolition of the death penalty, however, argue that the risk of executing the innocent is too great, there is no evidence the death penalty deters crime more than life imprisonment, and complex capital cases are significantly more expensive than life imprisonment cases. Furthermore, abolitionists argue that the death penalty is applied unfairly and arbitrarily to the poor and to people of color. Both sides also make arguments that focus on religious and moral foundations.

Historically and internationally, the death penalty has been used as a punishment for a wide variety of crimes. In North America around 1700, the colonists used the death penalty instead of prison as the main punishment for a range of serious crimes. With the adoption of prison as the normal punishment in the late eighteenth century, the death penalty's use became more limited. Since the late 1970s, capital punishment has only been used in the United States in murder cases.

Although the United States retains capital punishment while much of the world has abandoned the punishment, the United States was initially one of the leaders in the death penalty abolition movement. The Territory of Michigan voted to abolish capital punishment for all crimes except treason in a law that took effect March 1, 1847, more than twenty years before Portugal became the first European country to abolish the death penalty. During the next century, other state legislatures dealt with the issue of whether to abolish capital punishment, but the U. S. Supreme Court only examined the death penalty in a few cases, such as *Wilkerson v. Utah*, where the Court upheld execution by firing squad, and *In re Kemmler*, where the Court upheld execution by electrocution.

Capital Punishment Developments in the Supreme Court

In the 1960s and 1970s, however, the courts began to take a closer look at capital punishment, and organizations like the NAACP Legal Defense and Education Fund organized strategies to attack the punishment on constitutional grounds. In 1971 in *McGautha v. California*, the Supreme Court rejected a constitutional challenge to the procedures used to impose the death penalty.

However, the following year, the Supreme Court held in *Furman v. Georgia* that the death penalty statutes in use at the time violated the Eighth and Fourteenth Amendments of the U.S. Constitution, in effect invalidating the death penalty's use in the United States. There was no clear majority on the rationale for the result in *Furman*, but several Justices reasoned that the procedures used in capital cases at the time gave too much discretion to jurors in deciding whether to impose the death penalty, so that the sentences were arbitrary and often resulted in racial discrimination. Although Justice William J. Brennan, Jr. concluded that the death penalty was degrading to human dignity and Justice Thurgood Marshall also agreed that the death penalty was unconstitutional per se, other Justices' written opinions left open the issue of whether the death penalty violates the constitution in all circumstances.

In 1976, the Court decided several cases that upheld the use of the death penalty and, along with *Furman*, laid the foundation for the modern use of the death penalty in the United States. In *Gregg v. Georgia*, the Court examined new capital punishment statutes that limited the discretion of jurors, and a Plurality held that these statutes did not violate the Eighth and Fourteenth Amendments. The Plurality, in an opinion written by Justice Potter Stewart, concluded that a statute with a list of factors for jurors to consider in sentencing provided "clear and objective standards" and gave adequate guidance to the sentencer. On the same day, the Court upheld other states' guided sentencing statutes in *Jurek v. Texas* and *Proffitt v. Florida*. Subsequent cases, like *Godfrey v. Georgia*, clarified that capital sentencing procedures must provide a way to distinguish the few cases that deserve the death penalty from those cases that do not.

At the same time as *Gregg*, the Court struck down death penalty statutes that automatically imposed the death penalty for certain crimes. In *Woodson v. North Carolina*, the Plurality concluded that in death penalty cases the Eighth Amendment requires consideration of the record and character of the defendant and the circumstances of the crime. Individualized sentencing in capital cases is required, because there is an increased need for reliability because the death penalty is significantly different from all other punishments. The Supreme Court further emphasized the concern about individualized sentencing in *Lockett v. Ohio*, where Ohio's death penalty statute was struck down because it limited a capital jury from being able to consider factors presented to mitigate the sentence.

Thus, two important principles emerge from the Supreme Court's Eighth Amendment capital punishment procedural jurisprudence: (1) sentencing juries must be given clear and objective standards to determine who is eligible for the death penalty and to narrow the group of those executed from the group of all murderers; and (2) the sentencing jury must be allowed to consider mitigating factors that include all aspects of a defendant's character and record, as well as the circumstances of the offense. In 1994, Justice Harry A. Blackmun, who had voted to uphold the death penalty in *Gregg*, argued in dissent in *Callins v. Collins* that these two principles are incompatible and that the death penalty cannot be imposed fairly. Justice Blackmun concluded that "the death penalty experiment has failed" and then dissented from every case affirming a death sentence until retiring later that term.

In 1987 in another significant capital case, *McCleskey v. Kemp*, the Supreme Court considered evidence that the race of the defendant and the victim affects the determination of who receives the death penalty. The Court assumed the evidence was correct, including the statistics that showed that a defendant who kills a white victim is four times more likely to get the death penalty than a defendant who kills a black victim, but held that such racial disparities do not violate the constitution. Justice Lewis F. Powell, who wrote the majority opinion in *McCleskey*, noted after he retired that he regretted upholding the death penalty.

The Modern Death Penalty

Since the 1990s, there has been a growing concern about the use of the death penalty in the United States. In some recent decisions, the Supreme Court has narrowed the use of the death penalty. In the early twenty-first century, the Court reversed prior decisions in two significant cases. In *Atkins v. Virginia*, the Court held that it violates the constitution to execute mentally retarded individuals, and in *Roper v. Simmons* it held that it is unconstitutional to execute juveniles who commit their crimes while younger than eighteen years of age. In both of those cases, the Court reasoned that the Eighth Amendment required it to consider "evolving standards of decency" in American society, including recent political and public opinion changes, resulting in the Court reversing prior decisions.

One reason for the growing concern about the use of the death penalty has been the discovery that since *Furman*, more than 100 prisoners have been exonerated and released from death row. Developments in technology and DNA evidence have contributed to the new discoveries of innocence. Although some members of the Supreme Court stated in *Herrera v. Collins* in 1993 that a claim of innocence might not be the basis of a constitutional claim in itself, concerns about innocence have caused judges, legislators, and jurors to question the value of the death penalty. In 2003, Governor George Ryan of Illinois commuted the sentences of everyone on death row in that state because of recent discoveries of innocent people on death row. In 2000, he had imposed a moratorium on executions in that state for the same reason.

Although Court challenges since *Furman* have been unsuccessful in eliminating the death penalty in the United States, more than half of the countries in the world have abolished the death penalty, at least in practice, and the long-range trend around the world is to abolish the death penalty. For example, since the United States reinstated the death penalty in 1976, more than seventy countries have abolished the death penalty. During that time in the United States, however, there have been close to 1,000 executions and there are more than 3,000 men and women on death rows across the United States. Still, as noted previously, concerns about the use of the death penalty and the unfairness of the system in the United States have continued to grow. The death penalty is used significantly less than it was 100 years ago, leaving the question for the future of whether 100 years from now capital punishment will be used at all.

JEFFREY L. KIRCHMEIER

References and Further Reading

Acker, James, Robert M. Bohm, and Charles S. Lanier, eds. *America's Experiment with Capital Punishment*, 2nd ed. Durham, NC: Carolina Academic Press, 2003.

Death Penalty Information Center web site, http://www.deathpenaltyinfo.org/.

Kirchmeier, Jeffrey L. "Aggravating and Mitigating Factors: The Paradox of Today's Arbitrary and Mandatory Capital Punishment Scheme." *William & Mary Bill of Rights Journal* 6 (1998): 2:345–459.

———, *Another Place Beyond Here: the Death Penalty Moratorium Movement in the United States*, Colorado Law Review 73 (2002): 1:1–116 (article available at http://www.colorado.edu/law/lawreview/issues/summaries/73-1.htm).

Zimring, Franklin E., and Gordon Hawkins. *Capital Punishment and the American Agenda*. New York, NY: Cambridge University Press, 1989.

Cases and Statutes Cited

Atkins v. Virginia, 536 U.S. 304 (2002)
Callins v. Collins, 510 U.S. 1141 (1994)
Furman v. Georgia, 408 U.S. 238 (1972)
Gregg v. Georgia, 428 U.S. 153 (1976)
Herrera v. Collins, 506 U.S. 390 (1993)
In re Kemmler, 136 U.S. 436 (1890)
Jurek v. Texas, 428 U.S. 262 (1976)
Lockett v. Ohio, 438 U.S. 586 (1978)
McCleskey v. Kemp, 481 U.S. 279 (1987)
McGautha v. California, 402 U.S. 183, 196 (1971)
Proffitt v. Florida, 428 U.S. 242 (1976)

Roper v. Simmons, 125 S. Ct. 1183 (2005)
Wilkerson v. Utah, 99 U.S. 130 (1879)
Woodson v. North Carolina, 428 U.S. 280, 305 (1976)

See also **Capital Punishment and the Equal Protection Clause Cases; Capital Punishment and Race Discrimination; Capital Punishment and Resentencing; Capital Punishment and the Right of Appeal; Capital Punishment and Sentencing; Capital Punishment: Proportionality; Capital Punishment Held Not Cruel & Unusual Punishment Under Certain Guidelines; Capital Punishment for Felony Murder; Capital Punishment Reversed; Capital Punishment: 8th Amendment Limits; Capital Punishment: Antiterrorism and Effective Death Penalty Act of 1996; Capital Punishment: Due Process Limits; Capital Punishment: Execution of Innocents; Capital Punishment: History and Politics; Capital Punishment: Lynching; Capital Punishment: Methods of Execution**

CAPITAL PUNISHMENT AND RACE DISCRIMINATION

Race detrimentally affects the administration of capital punishment in the United States. The origins of this situation are found in the former practice of chattel slavery. During this time, people of African descent had a greater risk of being sentenced to death. This risk increased if the victim was Caucasian. For example, slaves was automatically sentenced to death if they were convicted of killing a Caucasian. Conversely, since slaves were not considered human beings, Caucasians could murder blacks with impunity.

After the Civil War, the U. S. Supreme Court ("the Court") held in *Plessy v. Ferguson* that the institutionalized racism doctrine of "separate but equal" did not violate the Equal Protection of Law. The Court's endorsement of this doctrine facilitated the continued viability of these racial disparities in the administration of capital punishment. This was especially evident if a man of African descent was convicted of raping a Caucasian woman. For example, in *Furman v. Georgia,* Justice Marshall notes that between 1930 and 1972, "455 persons, including 48 whites and 405 Negroes, were executed for rape" *Furman v. Georgia*, 408 U.S. 238, 364 and note 151 (Marshall, J. concurring).

These concerns are aggravated by the impact race has on the selection of a capital jury. Since slaves were property, they were not afforded the same criminal procedural rights, including the right to trial by jury, as Caucasians. After slavery's demise, many states enacted laws to continue this exclusionary practice. Consequently, the fate of capital defendants of African descent was historically decided by all white juries. In 1880, the Court held in *Strauder v. West Virginia* that using race to bar someone from serving on a jury violated the Equal Protection of Law. Nonetheless, this admonition was circumvented by prosecutors who exercised their peremptory challenges in a racially discriminatory manner. This was accepted practice until 1965, when the Court decided to prohibit the purposeful racially discriminatory use of peremptory challenges in *Swain v. Alabama.* Defendants alleging a violation had to prove that the prosecutor actually purposefully exercised the peremptory challenge at issue to strike the potential juror because of the juror's race. States were able to continue exercising peremptory challenges in a manner contrary to the Court's rule, because it was difficult for defendants to satisfy this burden of proof.

In the Court's 1972 landmark opinion in *Furman v. Georgia*, several Justices acknowledged that race affects the administration of capital punishment. In 1986, *in Batson v. Kentucky,* the Court attempted to take remedial action by relaxing the burden of proof its earlier decision in *Swain* imposed on a defendant. Accordingly, the Court concluded that the burden of proof could be satisfied if the defendant could establish an inference that the prosecutor exercised a peremptory challenge in a purposefully racially discriminatory manner. The Court permitted the state to refute the inference by articulating a nonpretexual race neutral explanation for the challenge. The next year the Court rendered an opinion in *McCleskey v. Kemp,* a case presenting many of the issues of racial disparity identified and addressed in the Baldus Study. The Baldus Study's findings confirmed the continued presence of the bias historically experienced by people of African descent: The murderers of Caucasians remain more likely to be sentenced to death than those who murdered people of African descent. This was especially the case if the offender was of African descent. Although the Court declined to grant the defendant relief, it did not contradict the validity of the Baldus Study's findings. Subsequent studies examining the interaction between race and the death penalty in other jurisdictions reached conclusions similar to those made in the Baldus Study.

Execution statistics collected from 1976 when the Court's decision in *Gregg v. Georgia* lifted the legal moratorium on the use of the death penalty in the United States reinforce the validity of these findings. Compared with Caucasians, people of African descent comprise a significantly smaller percentage of the population in the United States. In contrast, they are overrepresented on this nation's death rows, because there the number of people of African descent almost equals the number of Caucasians. Two other statistics reveal that the United States's history of racial discrimination continues to adversely affect the administration of capital punishment. First, the overwhelming majority of the victims of the people executed since 1976 were Caucasian. Similarly, the same disparity is found when the number of people of African descent executed for killing Caucasians is compared with the few number of Caucasians executed for killing people of African descent.

ROBERTA M. HARDING

References and Further Reading

Baldus, David C., Charles Pulaski, and George Woodworth, Comparative Review of Death Sentences: An Empirical Study of the Georgia Experience, The Journal of Criminal Law & Criminology 74 (1983): 3:661–753.

Bedau, Hugo Adam, ed. *The Death Penalty in America: Current Controversies.* New York: Oxford University Press, 1997.

Blankenship, Michael B., and Kristie R. Blevins, *Inequalities in Capital Punishment in Tennessee Based on Race: An Analytical Study of Aggravating and Mitigating Factors in Death Penalty Cases,* University of Memphis Law Review 31 (2001): 4:828–859.

Fleury-Steiner, Benjamin. *Jurors' Stories of Death: How America's Death Penalty Invests in Inequality.* Ann Arbor: University of Michigan Press, 2004.

Issac, Unah, and Jack Boger. *Race and the Death Penalty in North Carolina: an Empirical Analysis, 1993–1997.* Raleigh, NC: Common Sense Foundation, 2001.

Lyon, Andrea D., *Naming the Dragon: Litigating Race Issues During a Death Penalty Trial,* DePaul Law Review 53 (2004): 4:1647–1661.

McNally, Kevin, *Race to Execution: Race and the Federal Death Penalty,* DePaul Law Review 53 (2004): 4:1615–1645.

Radelet, Michael L. "Executions of Whites For Crimes Against Blacks: Exceptions to the Rule?" *The Sociological Quarterly* 30, no. 4.(1989): 529–544.

Cases and Statutes Cited

*Batson v. Kentucky,*476 U.S. 79 (1986)
Furman v. Georgia, 408 U.S. 238 (1972)
McCleskey v. Kemp, 481 U.S. 279 (1987)
Plessy v. Ferguson, 163 U.S. 537 (1896)
Strauder v. West Virginia, 100 U.S. 303 (1880)
Swain v. Alabama, 380 U.S. 202 (1965)

See also Brown v. Board of Education, **347 U.S. 483 (1954); Capital Punishment; Capital Punishment and the Equal Protection Clause Cases; Capital Punishment: Lynching;** *Coker v. Georgia,* **433 U.S. 584 (1977); Discriminatory Prosecution;** *Dred Scott v. Sandford,* **60 U.S. 393 (1857); Emancipation Proclamation (1863); Jury Trials and Race;** *Loving v. Virginia,* **388 U.S. 1 (1967); Miscegenation Laws; Race and Criminal Justice; Scottsboro Trials; Segregation; Slavery and Civil Liberties; Thirteenth Amendment**

CAPITAL PUNISHMENT AND RESENTENCING

Sometimes a defendant facing the death penalty once will have to undergo another trial for the same capital offense and face the death penalty again. That sounds odd, in view of the double-jeopardy protection against twice being "put in jeopardy of life or limb" (U.S. Const. Amend. V). In a case in which a defendant has been sentenced to death but achieves a reversal of either the conviction or death sentence, no double-jeopardy concerns arise, because prosecutors as a general rule may retry defendants for the same crime in the aftermath of an appellate reversal. Often, such defendants are relieved to have a second opportunity to avoid a death sentence. Still, there are instances in which a death-sentenced defendant who succeeds in overturning a death verdict will argue that a capital resentencing ought not to be allowed. That occurs when the basis for overturning the death verdict involves a finding, implicit or explicit, that the defendant ought not to have been eligible for the death penalty in the first place.

But what if the defendant received a *life sentence* and later succeeds in overturning the conviction— may the prosecution now retry the defendant and seek a death sentence? Put in stark terms, does a defendant who avoids getting the death sentence in the original trial assume the risk of getting sentenced to death in a second trial, should he succeed in overturning his conviction?

In noncapital cases, prosecutors may retry defendants whose convictions have been reversed and seek the same or tougher sentence as that sought in the original trial. But a capital sentencing process is unlike the conventional sentencing process in that the capital penalty–phase proceeding resembles a trial, with testimony taken and the burden of proof placed on the prosecution to convince the jury to impose death. That fact triggers the Double Jeopardy Clause. In *Bullington v. Missouri,* 451 U.S. 430 (1981), the Supreme Court held that a prosecutor may not seek the death penalty in a retrial against a defendant who has received a life verdict in the original trial. The *Bullington* jury's life verdict, in effect, constituted an "acquittal" vis á vis the death penalty, and that acquittal barred putting the defendant again in jeopardy of losing his life.

Bullington is not as sweeping in its reach as one might think. It is possible that a capital defendant who succeeds in securing a life verdict could be reprosecuted and again face the death penalty. The Supreme Court confronted a not-so-unique situation in *Sattazahn v. Pennsylvania,* 537 U.S. 101 (2003), and authorized a reprosecution for the death penalty on a defendant who had in his original trial secured a life verdict. A jury convicted Sattazahn of capital murder but deadlocked on the issue of whether to impose death (nine voting for life, three for death). Pennsylvania law required the judge to impose a life sentence in the event of a hung jury. Sattazahn successfully appealed his conviction, and on retrial the prosecution sought again to secure a death verdict. The Supreme Court, in a five to four vote, ruled that the Double Jeopardy Clause did not bar putting Sattazahn again in jeopardy of losing his life. Whereas in *Bullington,* the jury rendered a life verdict—thus affirmatively acquitting the defendant of the death penalty—the *Sattazahn* jury's failure to arrive at a verdict meant that there had been no such "acquittal." The dissenters argued that the life sentence, which was mandated by law, terminated the proceedings in defendant's favor, thus barring the renewed attempt to secure a death verdict. But the *Sattazahn* majority construed the Double Jeopardy Clause narrowly, finding that it only applies when there has been an actual jury finding that some element of the prosecution's case had not been proved.

DANIEL R. WILLIAMS

References and Further Reading

Carter, Linda E., and Ellen Kreitzberg. *Understanding Capital Punishment Law*, 2004.

Cases and Statutes Cited

Bullington v. Missouri, 451 U.S. 430 (1981)
Sattazahn v. Pennsylvania, 537 U.S. 101 (2003)

See also **Capital Punishment; Double Jeopardy: Modern History**

CAPITAL PUNISHMENT AND SENTENCING

Currently, forty jurisdictions (thirty-eight states, the federal government, and the military) authorize capital punishment. Although the U. S. Supreme Court has found there to be some constitutional restrictions on the imposition of the death penalty, it has yet to find that the punishment itself is cruel and unusual. In 1972, the Supreme Court effectively overturned all then-existing capital statutes when it held in *Furman v. Georgia* that such statutes must ensure that the death penalty will not be imposed in an "arbitrary and capricious" manner.

In the aftermath of the *Furman* decision, thirty-five states drafted new death penalty statutes. The statutes that the Supreme Court upheld as complying with the

Eighth Amendment included those with the following characteristics: separating the guilt/innocence phase from the sentencing phase of the trial; limiting the types of crimes that would qualify for capital punishment; creating specific aggravating factors, at least one of which must be found to exist before a jury can even consider the death penalty; specialized appellate review of death sentences; requiring that juries weigh aggravating and mitigating factors in determining whether a death sentence is appropriate. The Supreme Court struck down statutes mandating a death sentence for specific crimes, ruling that such statutes violate the Eighth Amendment because they do not allow for an individualized determination of sentence.

Although the specific death penalty sentencing procedures vary by jurisdiction, every state currently has what is referred to as a "bifurcated" trial procedure. In these proceedings, the jury first determines whether the defendant is guilty or not guilty of the offense of capital murder. Then, if a verdict of guilty is returned, the jury determines the defendant's sentence, which, in most jurisdictions, includes a choice between life without the possibility of parole and death. The sentencing phase of a capital trial shares many of the same characteristics as the guilt/innocence phase. For example, double jeopardy provisions have been deemed to apply to a jury "verdict" of life imprisonment, and the defendant is entitled to have a jury determine the existence of aggravating factors. Special rules also apply with respect to selection of jurors for capital cases, a process referred to as "death qualification." This process seeks to eliminate those jurors who would be unable to consider *both* life and death as potential sentences.

Although capital sentencing statutes also vary by jurisdiction, they all essentially involve, in some form, a weighing of mitigating factors against aggravating factors. Generally, if the aggravating factors outweigh the mitigating factors, the jury may return a verdict of death, although it is not always required. Common aggravating factors include the manner in which the killing is committed, any future danger that the defendant may pose, and the status of the victim. Common mitigating circumstances include the age of the defendant at the time the crime was committed, the relative role that the defendant played in the killing, mental health issues suffered by the defendant, lack of prior criminal record, and the defendant's personal background.

JUDITH M. BARGER

References and Further Reading

Carter, Linda E., and Ellen Krietzberg. *Understanding Capital Punishment Law*, LexisNexis Publishing, 2004.

Furman v. Georgia, 408 U.S. 238 (1972)
Gregg v. Georgia, 428 U.S. 153 (1976)
Proffitt v. Florida, 428 U.S. 242 (1976)
Jurek v. Texas, 429 U.S. 262 (1976)

CAPITAL PUNISHMENT AND THE EQUAL PROTECTION CLAUSE CASES

Although the legal institution of slavery was dismantled by the Emancipation Proclamation and the Thirteenth Amendment, discrimination on the basis of race and racially motivated violence continued unabated. That black Americans received a different brand of justice than white Americans was made plain in the passage of Black Codes. These laws explicitly provided for criminal punishments that varied, depending on the race of the victim and the race of the criminal. Crimes involving either white victims or black perpetrators were punished more severely than crimes involving either black victims or white perpetrators.

The Fourteenth Amendment was framed and adopted . . ." to assure to the colored race the enjoyment of all the civil rights that under the law are enjoyed by white persons, and to give to that race the protection of the General Government, in that enjoyment whenever it should be denied by the states" *Strauder v. West Virginia*, 100 U.S. 303, 306 (1986). Among its many other provisions, the Fourteenth Amendment contains the Equal Protection Clause that provides that "[no state shall] deny to any person within its jurisdiction the equal protection of the laws." The principle of equality enshrined in the Equal Protection Clause has famously been described by one Supreme Court Justice as requiring racial neutrality in the application of the laws: "Our Constitution is color-blind, and neither knows nor tolerates classes among citizens." *Plessy v. Ferguson*, 163 U.S. 537, 551 (1896) (Harlan, J., dissenting).

Prosecutors enjoy broad discretion in making critical decisions, such as the determination whether a particular suspect should be formally accused of crime and, if so, what charge or charges should be filed. However, prosecutorial discretion is not completely unfettered. In certain circumstances, the Constitution itself may impose constraints on a prosecutor's power. For example, discriminatory prosecutions are prohibited by the Equal Protection Clause. According to the Supreme Court in *Yick Wo v. Hopkins*, 118 U.S. 356 (1886):

> Though the law itself be fair on its face and impartial in appearance, yet, if it is applied and administered by public authority with an evil eye and an unequal hand, so as practically to make unjust and illegal

discriminations between persons in similar circumstances, material to their rights, the denial of equal justice is still within the prohibition of the Constitution.

Each step in the prosecution of a capital case—arrest, charging, plea bargaining, jury selection, conviction, sentencing, appeal, clemency and execution—is equally subject to the application of inexact standards of decision making. The inevitable result, according to death penalty opponents, is a high risk of arbitrariness in the determination of who is ultimately put to death.

Of course, race is not the only basis on which discriminatory decisions may rest. The American Bar Association has cautioned that prosecutors, in discharging both their investigative and charging functions, "should not invidiously discriminate against or in favor of any person on the basis of race, religion, sex, sexual preference, or ethnicity," whether the person appears as the defendant or as the victim. Standards for Criminal Justice Standard 3-3.1(b) (comment). Thus far, however, the most significant equal protection challenges have been predicated on race discrimination.

Before his execution in Florida's electric chair in 1979, John Spenkelink, a white man condemned to die for the murder of a white man, presented in state and federal court a study purporting to show that the revised Florida death penalty statutes were being applied far more often against killers of whites than against killers of blacks. The following year, two Northeastern University criminologists, William Bowers and Glenn Pierce, published a study of homicide sentencing in Georgia, Florida, and Texas, the three states whose new death penalty statutes were the first to be approved by the Supreme Court after its landmark decision in *Furman v. Georgia*, 408 U.S. 238 (1972).

Bowers and Pierce found that in white victim cases, black defendants in all three states were from four to six times more likely to be sentenced to death than white defendants. In Georgia, black on white killings resulted in death sentences thirty-three times more often than black on black killings. In Florida, a black defendant was thirty-seven times more likely to be sentenced to death if his victim was white than if his victim was black. And in Texas, black killers of white victims were eighty-four times more likely to be sentenced to death than black killers of black victims.

In 1981, John Eldon Smith, a Georgia death row inmate, introduced the Bowers and Pierce study in federal court. The court of appeals rejected the study as too crude to be legally significant, because it failed to take into account dozens of circumstances in each case—other than race—that might have accounted for unequal sentencing patterns.

A far more comprehensive analysis of the impact of race in capital cases was offered on behalf of a different condemned prisoner on Georgia's death row. Warren McCleskey, a black man, was convicted of murder and sentenced to die for his role in the shooting death of white police officer Frank Schlatt during a furniture store robbery.

Iowa law professor David Baldus and a team of researchers examined nearly 2,500 homicide cases that occurred in Georgia between 1973 and 1979. Unlike the less sophisticated study undertaken by professors Bowers and Pierce, Professor Baldus subjected his data to an exhaustive analysis, taking account of 230 variables that could have explained the disparities on nonracial grounds. The Baldus study, like the studies that preceded it, purported to show a disparity in the imposition of the death penalty in Georgia based on the race of the victim and, to a lesser extent, the race of the defendant.

Specifically, the Baldus study showed that for the universe of cases examined, defendants charged with killing white persons received the death penalty in eleven percent of the cases; defendants charged with killing blacks received the death penalty in only one percent of the cases. The death penalty was assessed in twenty-two percent of the cases involving black defendants and white victims; eight percent of the cases involving white defendants and white victims; one percent of the cases involving black defendants and black victims; and three percent of the cases involving white defendants and black victims.

Charging decisions were found to be similarly skewed along racial lines. Prosecutors asked for the death penalty in seventy percent of the cases involving black defendants and white victims; thirty-two percent of the cases involving white defendants and white victims; fifteen percent of the cases involving black defendants and black victims; and nineteen percent of the cases involving white defendants and black victims.

After taking into account nonracial variables, defendants charged with killing whites were found to be 4.3 times as likely to be sentenced to death as defendants charged with killing blacks. Black defendants were 1.1 times as likely to receive as death sentence as other defendants. The troubling conclusion of the Baldus study is that black defendants—such as Warren McCleskey—who kill white victims have the greatest likelihood of receiving the death penalty.

In the Supreme Court, McCleskey argued that the Baldus study demonstrated that the Georgia death penalty system discriminated on the basis of race in violation of the Equal Protection Clause. The Court disagreed five to four. Writing for the majority, Justice Powell noted that a defendant claiming an equal protection violation has the burden to provide "the existence of purposeful discrimination." In addition, the defendant must show that the purposeful discrimination "had a discriminatory effect" on him or her.

McCleskey's sole reliance on the Baldus study and his failure to show how any state actor had acted with discriminatory purpose *in his case* proved fatal to McCleskey's argument and, ultimately, to McCleskey himself. Although the Court has accepted statistics as proof of intent to discriminate in the context of a state's selection of a jury venire and in the context of statutory violations under Title VII of the Civil Rights Act of 1964, the Court refused to find that statistics alone were sufficient to demonstrate that the discretion inherent in the criminal justice system had been abused by racist decision makers.

Nor did the Court find the Baldus study persuasive proof that Georgia violated the Equal Protection Clause by adopting the capital punishment scheme and allowing it to remain in force despite its allegedly discriminatory application. For that claim to prevail, McCleskey would have to show that the Georgia legislature either enacted the statute to further a racially discriminatory purpose or maintained the statute because of the racially disproportionate impact suggested by the Baldus study.

Warren McCleskey died in Georgia's electric chair on September 25, 1991. That same year, retired Justice Lewis Powell, who had authored the majority opinion denying relief to McCleskey was asked by a biographer if he would change any of his votes as a justice if he could. Powell said that he would change his vote in McCleskey's case if he could.

Justice Brennan was one of the four *McCleskey* dissenters. He wrote, "It is tempting to pretend that minorities on death row share a fate in no way connected to our own, that our treatment of them sounds no echoes beyond the chambers in which they die. Such an illusion is ultimately corrosive, for the reverberations of injustice are not so easily confined." *McCleskey v. Kemp*, 481 U.S. 279 (1987) (Brennan, J., dissenting).

The Court's *McCleskey* ruling has been harshly criticized. There are those who have likened the *McCleskey* decision to the Court's discredited opinion in *Plessy v. Ferguson*. According to an editorial that ran in the *Tallahassee Democrat* newspaper:

> It is the same reasoning that enabled the Court in the late 1800s to approve the 'separate-but-equal' doctrine for the nation's schools . . . In *McCleskey* the Court essentially says Blacks must accept a separate-and-unequal system of justice in capital cases.

RANDALL T. COYNE

Cases and Statutes Cited

Furman v. Georgia, 408 U.S. 238 (1972)
McCleskey v. Kemp, 481 U.S. 279 (1987)
Plessy v. Ferguson, 163 U.S. 537, 551 (1896)
Strauder v. West Virginia, 100 U.S. 303, 306 (1986)
Yick Wo v. Hopkins, 118 U.S. 356 (1886)

CAPITAL PUNISHMENT AND THE RIGHT OF APPEAL

Appellate review should ensure that no death sentence is handed down in an arbitrary and capricious manner. When the U.S. Supreme Court voided forty state death penalty statutes in *Furman v. Georgia*, it held that unrestricted jury discretion in imposing a death sentence resulted in arbitrary sentencing. Four years later, in *Gregg v. Georgia,* the U.S. Supreme Court reinstated the death penalty, holding that capital punishment does not violate the Eighth Amendment prohibition against cruel and unusual punishment, provided that a death sentence is not arbitrary and capricious.

After Gregg, all capital crimes are prosecuted in a bifurcated trial, with the guilt–innocence phase conducted separately from the penalty phase. If the jury finds the defendant guilty, the same jury will turn to the question of whether to impose a death sentence. Capital defendants are entitled to meaningful appellate review of both stages of the bifurcated trial.

The Court declared that the sentencing scheme in Gregg was constitutional because the appellate court would review the death sentence in every case to determine whether the jury had imposed death under the influence of passion or prejudice, whether the evidence supported the jury finding of a statutory aggravating circumstance, and whether the death sentence was proportionate to sentences in similar cases. In *Proffitt v. Florida*, handed down the same day as Gregg, the Court endorsed Florida's appellate review process because it guaranteed a review of aggravating circumstances and proportionate sentencing.

Most of the thirty-eight death penalty states provide for automatic appellate review of all death sentences, though in denying cert in *U.S. v. Hammer* the Court implicitly held that a mandatory review is not required by the Constitution. Furthermore, in *Gilmore v. Utah*, the Court found that a defendant could, with full knowledge of his right to seek an appeal, waive that right. In *Sattazahn v. Pennsylvania*, the trial judge imposed a life sentence after a jury hung during the sentencing phase. The defendant appealed, the case was reversed, the defendant was retried, and he received a death sentence at the retrial. On appeal, the Court held that there was no double jeopardy bar to the death sentence on retrial because the life sentence at issue did not amount to an acquittal on the basis of the government's failure to prove one or more aggravating circumstances beyond a reasonable doubt at sentencing during the first trial.

After completing the direct appeals process, capital defendants may exercise their right to file a petition for habeas corpus review. These petitions usually raise new issues that were not expressly part of the trial. Ineffective assistance of counsel, police and prosecutor misconduct, and newly discovered evidence are typical subjects for habeas petitions. The reviewing court must assess whether the alleged error substantially affected the jury in deciding to sentence the defendant to death.

The Federal Death Penalty Act sets out appellate guidelines used in most capital cases. The act requires the appellate court to review the entire record, including the procedures used and evidence admitted during the sentencing and to examine the aggravating and mitigating factors enumerated in the statute. Whereas the appellate court may not reverse for harmless error, it must reverse if it concludes that the jury imposed the death sentence under the influence of passion, prejudice, or any other arbitrary factor.

J. AMY DILLARD

References and Further Reading

Golden, Sara L., *Constitutionality of the Federal Death Penalty Act: Is the Lack of Mandatory Appeal Really Meaningful Appeal?* Temple Law Review (Summer 2001): 429–468.

Cases and Statutes Cited

Gilmore v. Utah, 429 U.S. 1012 (1976)
Gregg v. Georgia, 428 U.S. 153 (1976)
Furman v. Georgia, 409 U.S. 902 (1972)
Proffitt v. Florida, 428 U.S. 242 (1976)
Sattazahn v. Pennsylvania, 537 U.S. 101 (2003)
U.S. v. Hammer, 226 F.3d 229 (3d Cir. 2000)
39 C.J.S. Habeas Corpus § 159

See also **Capital Punishment: Due Process Limits; Habeas Corpus: Modern History**

CAPITAL PUNISHMENT FOR FELONY MURDER

Felony murder must not be confused with murder during the course of a felony. Murder during the course of a felony is an ordinary, intentional murder. When it is committed during the course of certain dangerous felonies, such as robbery, arson, or rape, the felony may be used as an aggravating factor to impose the death penalty.

Felony murder, by contrast, is a legal term of art that means that person can be found guilty of murder, even though he lacks the mental state or *mens rea* ordinarily required for murder, if the killing took place during a felony. Thus, if while robbing a store, the robber's gun goes off accidentally, killing the proprietor, the defendant would lack the *mens rea* for murder, which would be something like malice a forethought or intentional depending on the state. Nevertheless, in many States, he would be guilty of murder anyway, because the killing occurred during the course of a felony. The concept of felony murder has been used to convict people of murder even when their culpability as to death is relatively low, such as where the victim dies of a heart attack during a robbery, where the deceased is a co-felon, shot by the victim of the original crime, and where the victim is shot by a co-felon whom the defendant had no reason to know would be armed.

In *Enmund* v. *Florida*, 458 U.S. 782 (1982), the Supreme Court considered whether a person who aids and abets a felony, but does not commit or have an intention to commit a killing, could be put to death. In a five to four opinion, the Court held that the death penalty in such a case was disproportionate to the crime and therefore violated the Eighth Amendment. The Court did not disapprove of the defendant's conviction for murder, despite the fact that he only served as a driver for the robbery in this case. It was only his death sentence that was struck down. In reaching this conclusion, the Court relied on its 1977 decision in *Coker* v. *Georgia,* 433 U.S. 584, in which it had invalidated, also on proportionality grounds, the death penalty for the crime of raping an adult woman.

The Court limited *Enmund* somewhat in the 1987 case of *Tison* v. *Arizona,* 481 U.S. 137. In *Tison* the death penalty was imposed on two sons whose father had killed a family of four whom the group had abducted at gunpoint during a prison escape. The Court conceded that the sons had neither inflicted the fatal wounds nor intended to kill the victims. Nevertheless, their death sentence was upheld on the ground that they displayed reckless indifference to the deaths: The reckless disregard for human life implicit in knowingly engaging in criminal activities known to carry a grave risk of death represents a highly culpable mental state that is appropriate for capital punishment, held the five to four majority. 481 U.S. at p. 157. This is not surprising considering that reckless indifference to death has traditionally been a mental state sufficient for conviction of murder, regardless of

the felony. Thus, person who shoots randomly into a house and kills someone would be guilty of murder even though he lacked intent to kill. *Tison,* however, limits the death penalty to cases where the defendant not only displays a reckless disregard for life but has also knowingly engaged in criminal activities known to create a grave risk of death. Thus, a participant in a robbery where someone is accidentally killed would not usually be subject to the death penalty.

After *Ring* v. *Arizona,* 536 U.S. 584 (2002), the aggravating factor justifying the death penalty must be found by the jury, beyond a reasonable doubt, not a judge.

Craig M. Bradley

References and Further Reading

Bedau, Hugo, ed. *The Death Penalty in America: Current Controversies,* 1997.
Rosen, Richard, *Felony Murder and the Eighth Amendment Jurisprudence of Death,* B.C. Law Review 31 (1990): 1103–1170.
Roth, Nelson, and Scott Sundby, *The Felony Murder Rule: A Doctrine at the Constitutional Crossroads,* Cornell Law Review 70 (1985): 446–492.

Cases and Statutes Cited

Coker v. Georgia, 433 U.S. 584 (1977)
Enmund v. Florida 458 U.S. 782 (1982)
Ring v. Arizona, 536 U.S. 584 (2002)
Tison v. Arizona, 481 U.S. 137 (1987)

See also **Capital Punishment; Capital Punishment: History and Politics; Capital Punishment: Eighth Amendment Limits**

CAPITAL PUNISHMENT HELD NOT CRUEL AND UNUSUAL PUNISHMENT UNDER CERTAIN GUIDELINES

After its finding the death penalty unconstitutional in *Furman* v. *Georgia,* 408 U.S. 238 (1972), in 1976, the Supreme Court confronted newly enacted death penalty statutes from five states. The cases were *Gregg v. Georgia,* 428 U.S. 153; *Jurek v. Texas,* 428 U.S. 262; *Proffitt v. Florida,* 428 U.S. 242; *Woodson v. North Carolina,* 428 U.S. 280; and *Roberts v. Louisiana,* 428 U.S. 325.

In *Gregg,* rejecting the argument that the death penalty is inherently cruel and unusual punishment, the Court upheld a death sentence for murder, approving the Georgia system of a bifurcated trial in which the guilt and punishment phases are separate, with the jury hearing additional evidence and argument during the punishment phase. The Georgia statute further set out elements of aggravation, one of which must be found beyond a reasonable doubt for death to be imposed, as well as mitigation, that would allow the defendant to avoid the death penalty. Moreover, the Georgia Supreme Court mandatorily reviewed each death sentence to ensure that it was not disproportionate to sentences imposed in similar cases or otherwise on the basis of arbitrary or prejudicial factors.

Again there was no majority opinion, but a joint opinion by Justices Stewart, Stevens, and Powell expressed the plurality view and was agreed with in most respects by an opinion concurring in the judgment by Justice White, joined by Chief Justice Burger and Justice Rehnquist. Justice Blackmun concurred in the judgment as well.

In *Jurek* the same seven Justice majority upheld a similar scheme in Texas, and in *Proffitt* the same Justices upheld a Florida scheme in which the sentence was imposed by a judge. In *Woodson* and *Roberts,* however, a joint opinion by Stewart, Stevens, and Powell, with Justices Brennan and Marshall concurring in the judgment, struck down mandatory death sentences as generally unduly harsh and unworkably rigid (*Woodson,* 428 U.S. at p. 293).

Subsequent to these cases, which reinstated the death penalty and suggested a blueprint for constitutionally acceptable death penalty procedures, the Court has imposed a number of other limitations under the Eighth Amendment. In *Coker v. Georgia,* 433 U.S. 584 (1977) it rejected the death penalty for the rape of an adult woman as disproportionate to the crime, and in *Enmund v. Florida,* 458 U.S. 782 (1982) it held that the death penalty was also disproportionate for one who neither killed nor intended to kill the victim. In *Lockett v. Ohio,* 438 U.S. 586 (1978) it held that the defendant must be allowed to present, as a mitigating factor, any (relevant) aspect of a defendants character or record and any of the circumstances of the offense that he wishes. Id. at p. 604. In *Thompson v. Oklahoma,* 487 U.S. 815 (1988), the Court held that the death penalty could not be applied to a person under the age of sixteen. And in *Atkins v. Virginia,* U.S., 122 S.Ct. 2242 (2002) it likewise exempted the mentally retarded from execution.

CRAIG M. BRADLEY

References and Further Reading

Gross, Samuel L., *The Romance of Revenge: Capital Punishment in America*, Studies in Law, Politics and Society 13 (1993): 71–104.
Model Penal Code and Commentaries. Comment to '210.6. Philadelphia: American Law Institute, 1985.
Radin, Margaret, *The Jurisprudence of Death: Evolving Standards for the Cruel and Unusual Punishment Clause*, U. of Pennsylvania Law Review 126 (1978): 989–1064.

Cases and Statutes Cited

Atkins v. Virginia, U.S., 122 S.Ct. 2242 (2002)
Coker v. Georgia, 433 U.S. 584 (1977)
Enmund v. Florida, 458 U.S. 782 (1982)
Furman v. Georgia, 408 U.S. 238 (1972)
Gregg v. Georgia, 428 U.S. 153 (1976)
Jurek v. Texas, 428 U.S. 262 (1976)
Lockett v. Ohio, 438 U.S. 586 (1978)
Proffitt v. Florida, 428 U.S. 242 (1976)
Roberts v. Louisiana, 428 U.S. 325 (1976)
Thompson v. Oklahoma, 487 U.S. 815 (1988)
Woodson v. North Carolina, 428 U.S. 280 (1976)

See also **Capital Punishment; Capital Punishment: History and Politics; Capital Punishment: Eighth Amendment Limits**

CAPITAL PUNISHMENT REVERSED

In the 1972 case of *Furman v. Georgia,* 408 U.S. 238, the Supreme Court struck down the death penalties of three men. The majority opinion was a brief, unsigned, *per curiam* (for the Court) simply declaring that The Court holds that the imposition and carrying out of the death penalty in these cases constitute cruel and unusual punishment in violation of the Eighth and Fourteenth Amendments. Id. at p. 240. No further elaboration of the Court's reasoning appeared in this opinion.

However, each of the nine Justices wrote a separate opinion explaining the reasons for his agreement (five Justices) or disagreement (four Justices) with the holding. Justice Douglas noted that the death penalty was meted out mostly to the poor young and ignorant, Id. at p. 250, and applied disparately to racial minorities. He concluded that these discretionary (death penalty) statutes are unconstitutional in their operation. They are pregnant with discrimination, and discrimination is an ingredient not compatible with the idea of equal protection of the laws that is implicit in the ban on "cruel and unusual" punishments. Id. at pp. 256–257. He did not consider whether a mandatory death penalty might be constitutional.

Justice Brennan argued that, since the death penalty was being used in only a small percentage of cases in which it was available, and because it was a punishment that did not comport with evolving standards of human dignity, it had become cruel and unusual and therefore was unconstitutional under any circumstances.

Justice Marshall pointed out that the various purposes supposedly served by capital punishment, deterrence, retribution, and so forth, were equally well served by life imprisonment. Id. at p. 359. He further noted that the death penalty had been discriminatorily applied: A total of 3,859 persons have been executed since 1930, of whom 1,751 were white and 2,066 were Negro. Id. at p. 364. He agreed with Brennan that the death penalty should be abolished altogether.

Justice Stewart, like Douglas, did not rule out mandatory death sentences for certain crimes, but as to the cases before the Court he declared, and Justice White agreed:

> These death sentences are cruel and unusual in the same way that being struck by lightening is cruel and unusual. For, of all the people convicted or rapes and murders in 1967 and 1968, many just as reprehensible as these, the petitioners are among a capriciously selected random handful upon whom the sentence of death has in fact been imposed . . . . (T)he Eighth and Fourteenth Amendments cannot tolerate the infliction of a sentence of death under legal systems that permit this unique penalty to be so wantonly and freakishly imposed. Id. at pp. 309–310.

Thus, with no clear majority either declaring the death penalty flatly unconstitutional or explaining under what circumstances it would be acceptable, the states were left in considerable confusion as to how to proceed. By 1976 at least thirty-five states and the federal government had reenacted either mandatory death penalty statutes or statutes containing guidelines by which the penalty could appropriately be imposed. The Court was soon to decide challenges to these enactments. Capital Punishment Held not Cruel and Unusual Punishment Under Certain Circumstances.

CRAIG M. BRADLEY

References and Further Reading

Bedau, Hugo, ed. *The Death Penalty in America: Current Controversies*, 1997.
Kaplan, John, Robert Weisberg, and Guyora Binder. *Capital Murder and the Death Penalty in Criminal Law, Cases and Materials* (4th ed.), 509–564. Gaithersburg, NY: Aspen Law and Business, 2000.
Sellin, Thorsten, ed. *Capital Punishment*, 1967.

Cases and Statutes Cited

Furman v. Georgia, 408 U.S. 238 (1972)

See also **Capital Punishment; Capital Punishment: History and Politics; Capital Punishment: Eighth Amendment Limits**

CAPITAL PUNISHMENT: ANTITERRORISM AND EFFECTIVE DEATH PENALTY ACT OF 1996

When Congress in the mid-1990s began considering reforms of federal post-conviction review, lawmakers faced an ongoing dilemma about the scope of habeas corpus law. That is, should habeas broadly protect constitutional rights of state prisoners through independent federal review, or should habeas be a narrow and extraordinary remedy that does not interfere with comity, finality, and federalism? Congress adopted the latter approach in the Antiterrorism and Effective Death Penalty Act of 1996 (AEDPA), a response to the April 1995 Oklahoma City bombing and one that quickly served as a vehicle for revamping habeas law and, more specifically, for attempting to ensure swifter, more certain imposition of capital punishment.

Particularly during the Warren Court years, habeas corpus was viewed as a means for explicating constitutional norms and broadly protecting individual rights. Critics of this trend argued that the existing system had become too slow, burdensome, and destructive of important state interests in defining and enforcing the criminal law. A variety of reform proposals died in the 1970s, 1980s, and early 1990s. After Republicans gained working control of Congress in 1995, however, and after the Burger and Rehnquist Courts consistently articulated a more restrictive approach to federal habeas review, Congress used the AEDPA to address its disenchantment with habeas jurisprudence. Although the AEDPA applies to capital and noncapital cases, the legislative debate focused on the effect the reforms would have on death penalty cases.

Congressional supporters of the legislation argued that the existing habeas system allowed death row inmates to abuse the process by repeatedly challenging their convictions and death sentences, indefinitely delaying execution of their sentences. Supporters further claimed that, in reviewing state cases, federal courts were improperly substituting their own judgment for that of the state courts. This system was, therefore, bad for federal-state comity, compromised the value of finality, and demeaned federalism, the healthy balance of authority between the state and federal governments. The AEDPA thus requires federal deference in cases involving state prisoners. In those cases, federal courts may grant the writ only if the state court decision involved an unreasonable application of clearly established Supreme Court precedent, or an unreasonable determination of the facts in light of the evidence presented in the state court. Beginning with *(Terry) Williams v. Taylor* (2000), a capital case, the Supreme Court has interpreted these provisions to mean that the state court decision must be objectively unreasonable, not merely incorrect. In addition, the AEDPA provides a presumption of correctness for state court fact-findings, restricts a prisoner's ability to obtain a federal evidentiary hearing, and places severe limits on successive habeas petitions. Finally, the law provides "fast-track" procedures for a limited category of capital cases from qualifying jurisdictions.

The AEDPA was, and remains, controversial. Critics say it improperly hinders the federal judiciary's role as arbiter of federal rights, leaving many constitutional violations unchecked. Still, however, supporters contend the reforms have proven helpful in giving States latitude to administer their penal laws—particularly their systems of capital punishment—with minimal federal judicial interference.

J. RICHARD BROUGHTON

References and Further Reading

Broughton, J. Richard, *Habeas Corpus and the Safeguards of Federalism*, Georgetown Journal of Law & Public Policy 2 (2004): 1:109–168.
Lee, Evan Tsen, *Section 2254(d) of the New Habeas Statute: An (Opinionated) User's Manual*, Vanderbilt Law Review 51 (1998): 1:103–137.
Yackle, Larry W., *A Primer on the New Habeas Corpus Statute*, Buffalo Law Review 44 (1996): 2:381–449.

Cases and Statutes Cited

(Terry) Williams v. Taylor, 529 U.S. 362 (2000)
Antiterrorism and Effective Death Penalty Act of 1996, Pub.L. No. 104-132, 110 Stat. 1217, 1220 (1996), *codified at* 28 U.S.C. §2244 et seq. (2000)

See also **Habeas Corpus: Modern History**

CAPITAL PUNISHMENT: DUE PROCESS LIMITS

The Due Process Clauses in the Fifth and Fourteenth Amendments to the U. S. Constitution have played an important role in efforts to promote fairness in the use of capital punishment. Principles derived from the Eighth Amendment provide the central limitations on the use of the death penalty. However, the Eighth Amendment rules apply in state courts, where most capital prosecutions occur, only because the Supreme Court has deemed them incorporated through the Due Process Clause in the Fourteenth Amendment. Moreover, the Supreme Court has relied on principles of free-standing due process to provide additional special protections in capital cases, and the mandates of due process that apply in all criminal cases also limit capital prosecutions.

From the time of the American founding through the middle of the twentieth century, the notion of *in favorem vitae* ("in favor of life") often moved courts to take extra precautions to promote fairness in capital prosecutions. Concern about the severity of capital punishment manifested itself in many ways by trial judges administering individual capital trials and by appellate courts reviewing capital convictions. Courts frequently interpreted statutes imposing the death penalty literally and strictly so as to avoid their application. Courts also showed special concern for the procedural rights of capital defendants, sometimes justifying this concern openly on the special nature of the death penalty.

In the modern era, the central legal assault on the death penalty has focused on its arbitrary and discriminatory imposition, and the Supreme Court has relied for a remedy on the prohibition against cruel and unusual punishment in the Eighth Amendment, which then applies against the states as a matter of due process. Reform-minded lawyers argued before the Supreme Court in *McGautha v. California*, 402 U.S. 183 (1971), that the then-prevailing practice of submitting the capital sentencing decision to the largely unrestricted discretion of a jury violated principles of free-standing due process. However, the Supreme Court rejected the challenge in an opinion concluding that the articulation of appropriate standards to guide capital sentencers was impossible and that jurors confronted with the capital sentencing decision would generally act appropriately. Nonetheless, the following year, in *Furman v. Georgia*, 408 U.S. 238 (1972), the Court rejected standardless capital sentencing under the Eighth Amendment, concluding that the potential for arbitrariness rendered death sentences imposed under standardless systems cruel and unusual. The Court also later judged revised capital-sentencing statutes under the Eighth Amendment, upholding several that provided for a sentencing hearing with standards while rejecting others that mandated the death penalty on conviction. Most of the modern doctrine regulating capital sentencing proceedings also builds on this Eighth Amendment grounding, with due process operating only as the means of incorporating the rulings against the states.

While relying primarily on the Eighth Amendment to address arbitrariness, the Supreme Court has occasionally turned to general notions of due process to promote other forms of fairness in capital prosecutions. Some of the due process decisions that provide special protection to capital defendants have focused on the provision of notice and an opportunity to be heard at the capital sentencing trial. For example, in *Gardner v. Florida*, 430 U.S. 349 (1977), the Court reversed a death sentence where the sentencing judge had relied in part on a section of a sentencing report that had been kept confidential from the defense. Likewise, in *Lankford v. Idaho*, 500 U.S. 110 (1991), the Court reversed a death sentence where it seemed that the defense had not been adequately notified before the sentencing trial that the death penalty was being considered as a possible punishment.

Decisions that impose special protections in capital cases have also focused on a variety of other issues. For example, in *Green v. Georgia*, 442 U.S. 95 (1979), the Court held that a state could not appropriately object on hearsay grounds to the introduction at a capital sentencing trial of a codefendant's statement that the defendant had not been present when the victim was killed, where the state had previously introduced the same statement against the codefendant to obtain a death sentence at the codefendant's separate trial. Likewise, in *Beck v. Alabama*, 447 U.S. 625 (1980), the Court held that a state could not impose a death sentence when the jury at the guilt-or-innocence trial was not permitted to consider a verdict of guilt of a lesser included noncapital offense, although the evidence would have supported such a verdict. Further, in *Turner v. Murray*, 476 U.S. 28 (1986), the Court held that due process guaranteed a black capital defendant accused of killing a white person the opportunity to question potential sentencing jurors about their racial biases, although the interracial nature of the crime would not alone have triggered such a right in a noncapital case.

Principles of due process that apply in all criminal cases, of course, also protect capital defendants. Long ago, in *Brown v. Mississippi*, 297 U.S. 278 (1936), the Court reversed a capital conviction where the state was allowed to introduce the defendant's "involuntary" confession. Likewise, in *Ake v. Oklahoma*, 470 U.S. 68 (1985), the Supreme Court overturned a capital conviction because the state had denied an indigent defendant the assistance of a court-appointed psychiatrist to help prepare and present his defense at both the guilt-or-innocence and sentencing trials. Also, in *Kyles v. Whitley*, 514 U.S. 419 (1995), the Court set aside a capital conviction where the prosecution had failed to disclose before trial evidence in its possession that was material and favorable to the defense. Furthermore, in *Cooper v. Oklahoma*, 517 U.S. 348 (1996), the Court reversed a capital conviction where the state required the accused to prove his incompetence to stand trial by a standard of proof greater than a preponderance of the evidence. While these kinds of general due process rulings apply in all criminal cases, the Supreme Court has often first announced them in capital prosecutions, which underscores their role in regulating the use of the death penalty.

SCOTT W. HOWE

References and Further Reading

Israel, Jerold H., *Free-Standing Due Process and Criminal Procedure: The Supreme Court's Search for Interpretive Guidelines*, St. Louis University Law Journal 45 (2001): 303–432.

Steiker, Carol S., and Jordan M. Steiker, *Sober Second Thoughts: Reflections on Two Decades of Constitutional Regulation of Capital Punishment*, Harvard Law Review 109 (1995): 355–438.

Thurschwell, Adam. "Federal Courts, the Death Penalty, and the Due Process Clause: The Original Understanding of the "Heightened Reliability" of Capital Trials." *Federal Sentencing Reporter* 14 (2002): 14–36.

Cases and Statutes Cited

Ake v. Oklahoma, 470 U.S. 68 (1985)
Beck v. Alabama, 447 U.S. 625 (1980)
Brown v. Mississippi, 297 U.S. 278 (1936)
Cooper v. Oklahoma, 517 U.S. 348 (1996)
Furman v. Georgia, 408 U.S. 238 (1972) (*per curiam*)
Gardner v. Florida, 430 U.S. 349 (1977)
Green v. Georgia, 442 U.S. 95 (1979)
Kyles v. Whitley, 514 U.S. 419 (1995)
Lankford v. Idaho, 500 U.S. 110 (1991)
McGautha v. California, 402 U.S. 183 (1971)
Turner v. Murray, 476 U.S. 28 (1986)

See also **Capital Punishment: Eighth Amendment Limits;** *McGautha v. California*, **402 U.S. 183 (1971)**

CAPITAL PUNISHMENT: EIGHTH AMENDMENT LIMITS

The U. S. Supreme Court has interpreted the prohibition on "cruel and unusual punishments" in the Eighth Amendment to regulate but not forbid the use of capital punishment. The prohibition applies directly against the federal government and against the states through the Due Process Clause in the Fourteenth Amendment. The prohibition restricts the use of capital punishment in three ways. First, it limits execution methods. Second, it proscribes the death penalty for certain classes of offenders and crimes. Finally, it requires that states take steps to limit arbitrariness in the process for selecting the persons who will receive death sentences.

Limits on Execution Methods

Supreme Court decisions offer only general guidance regarding permissible execution methods. The Court has said little about these questions since *In re Kemmler*, 136 U.S. 436 (1890). Although authorizing electrocution, the *Kemmler* opinion implied that the Eighth Amendment proscribes not only certain barbarous execution methods that were prohibited at the time of the founding but any method that involves the wanton infliction of pain beyond that justified to extinguish life. In the last century, states have used various forms of execution, including hanging, shooting, gassing, electrocution, and lethal injection. All of these methods have usually been upheld by lower courts. In *Louisianna ex rel Francis v. Resweber*, 329 U.S. 459 (1947), the Supreme Court also upheld a second death warrant after the electric charge in a prior electrocution attempt failed to kill the inmate. However, since the 1970s, a few opinions of lower courts or of certain Justices dissenting from a Supreme Court denial of review have concluded that some of the methods, particularly hanging, gassing, and electrocution, are always or at least sometimes cruel and unusual. Disagreement remains over precisely how to analyze such claims. Nonetheless, in the modern era, these questions have eluded resolution by the Supreme Court, in part, because states faced with serious challenges have responded by making lethal injection the sole form of execution or an optional form at the request of the inmate. Although the level of physical pain involved will depend on the chemicals and method used, lethal injection is now generally regarded as the most humane execution method. Indeed, lethal injection became the accepted form of execution by the end of the twentieth century.

Prohibitions on the Use of the Death Penalty

The Supreme Court has derived a "disproportionality" principle from the Eighth Amendment that restricts the use of the death penalty mostly to certain murder cases. The disproportionality notion contemplates that a particular punishment can be excessive in application although it is not proscribed altogether. The Supreme Court first articulated this idea in *Weems v. United States*, 217 U.S. 349 (1910), a noncapital case in which the Justices struck down as excessively harsh for a relatively minor crime a sentence involving twelve years of hard labor and other forfeitures of civil rights. The Supreme Court used the idea in *Coker v. Georgia*, 433 U.S. 584 (1977), to hold

the death penalty categorically impermissible for the rape of an adult woman where no life was taken, and this prohibition has also been applied to other typical, nonhomicidal felonies. The *Coker* conclusion ultimately reflected a value judgment by the Court that the death penalty was too much retribution for Coker's crime, although the Justices also pointed to objective evidence that the death penalty was only rarely imposed in the relevant context. Since *Coker*, the Court has also outlawed the penalty for felony-murder accomplices who are not otherwise highly blameworthy, for the retarded, for previously death-sentenced inmates who are insane, and to those who were juveniles at the time of their crime. The Court has not addressed whether the disproportionality principle forbids the death penalty for treason or similarly serious nonmurder crimes.

Protections against Arbitrariness

The most famous line of Supreme Court cases applying the Eighth Amendment to capital punishment focuses on protections against arbitrariness. These decisions started with *Furman v. Georgia*, 408 U.S. 238 (1972) (*per curiam*), where the Court struck down the then-prevailing approach of submitting the capital sentencing decision to a jury's largely unfettered discretion. After *Furman*, many states quickly passed new death-penalty legislation, and the Supreme Court subsequently concluded that certain procedural protections could satisfy the Eighth Amendment. In a famous quintet of cases decided in 1976, including *Gregg v. Georgia*, 428 U.S. 153 (1976) (plurality opinion), the Supreme Court struck down statutes from North Carolina and Louisiana that mandated the death penalty on conviction, but it upheld statutes from Georgia, Florida, and Texas that provided for a separate sentencing hearing with at least some standards to limit the capital sentencer's discretion.

Two principal doctrines of capital sentencing grow out of the 1976 cases. First, in rejecting the mandatory statutes, the Court concluded that capital defendants are entitled to "individualized consideration" on the sentencing question. The Court distinguished noncapital cases, where mandatory sentencing is permitted, on grounds that the unique severity and finality of the death penalty call for heightened reliability. The Court later amplified on the mandate of individualized consideration in *Lockett v. Ohio*, 438 U.S. 586 (1978) (plurality opinion), holding that a capital sentencer must be free to vote against the death penalty on the basis of any evidence that the offender offers concerning his character, record, or crime.

The Court also stated in the 1976 cases that capital sentencers require guidance but soon modified this idea in *Zant v. Stephens*, 462 U.S. 862 (1983), to require only a narrowing of the death-eligible group. States have met the narrowing mandate by simply requiring the capital sentencer to find the presence of at least one "aggravating" factor from a statutory list before going on to consider mitigating circumstances at a final stage at which its discretion to reject the death penalty is essentially unfettered.

After *Furman*, efforts to attack capital sentences using statistical evidence of arbitrariness have failed. In *McCleskey v. Kemp*, 481 U.S. 279 (1987), the Supreme Court rejected a challenge to Georgia's post-*Furman* capital-selection system that relied on a sophisticated, statistical study finding racial bias. The Court questioned whether the study adequately proved racial bias but concluded, in any event, that compliance with procedural rules satisfied the Eighth Amendment.

SCOTT W. HOWE

References and Further Reading

Denno, Deborah. "Execution and the Forgotten Eighth Amendment" In *America's Experiment With Capital Punishment*, edited by James R. Acker, Robert M. Bohm, and Charles S. Lanier, 547–577. Durham, North Carolina: Carolina Academic Press, 1998.

Howe, Scott W., *The Failed Case for Eighth Amendment Regulation of the Capital Sentencing Trial*, University of Pennsylvania Law Review 146 (1998): 795–863.

Mortenson, Julian Davis, *Earning the Right to be Retributive: Execution Methods, Culpability Theory, and the Cruel and Unusual Punishment Clause*, Iowa Law Review 88 (2003): 1099–1163.

White, Welsh S. *The Death Penalty in the Nineties*. Ann Arbor: University of Michigan Press, 1991.

Cases and Statutes Cited

Coker v. Georgia, 433 U.S. 584 (1977)
Furman v. Georgia, 408 U.S. 238 (1972) (*per curiam*)
In re Kemmler, 136 U.S. 436 (1890)
Lockett v. Ohio, 438 U.S. 586 (1978) (plurality opinion)
Louisianna ex rel Francis v. Resweber, 329 U.S. 459 (1947)
McCleskey v. Kemp, 481 U.S. 279 (1987)
Weems v. United States, 217 U.S. 349 (1910)
Zant v. Stephens, 462 U.S. 862 (1983)

See also **Capital Punishment; Capital Punishment and the Equal Protection Clause Cases; Capital Punishment: Due Process Limits; Capital Punishment: History and Politics; Capital Punishment Reversed; Capital Punishment and Race Discrimination**

CAPITAL PUNISHMENT: EXECUTION OF INNOCENTS

Until recent years, the execution of innocents was mostly an abstract debate. Although abolitionists would point to a handful of cases where innocent individuals allegedly had been put to death, capital punishment supporters dismissed these examples and rejected the notion of wrongful execution as a mere theoretical possibility. Moreover, the U.S. Supreme Court's seminal decision in this area, the 1993 case of *Herrera v. Collins*, held that a free-standing claim of actual innocence was not a basis for federal habeas corpus review in a death penalty case. Throughout most of the modern era of capital punishment, the bulk of discussion involved issues apart from wrongful conviction, such as racial disparities in the death penalty.

Around the time of the *Herrera* decision, a budding innocence movement began to take shape, largely as a result of advances in DNA technology. In 1992, Barry Scheck and Peter Neufeld started the Innocence Project at Cardozo Law School to investigate possible cases of wrongful conviction, and similar programs were initiated across the nation. But it would take a string of events in Illinois to draw public attention to the issue of actual innocence in capital punishment, beginning with a 1998 conference at Northwestern University that brought together scholars, practitioners, and a number of exonerated former death row inmates. Shortly after the conference, Lawrence Marshall and others helped secure the release of Anthony Porter, a wrongfully convicted man who came within two days of execution. In turn, the *Chicago Tribune* published a series of articles describing grave flaws in Illinois's capital punishment system. Since the reinstatement of the death penalty in 1976, the state had executed twelve individuals, whereas thirteen of its death row inmates had been exonerated. In 2000, Illinois Governor George Ryan declared a moratorium on capital punishment on the basis of this information, and three years later Ryan commuted all remaining death sentences.

According to some sources, the modern era of capital punishment has witnessed the release of more than 100 individuals based on evidence of innocence. Leading causes of wrongful conviction include erroneous witness identifications, police or prosecutor misconduct, defective or "junk" science, false confessions, poor legal representation, and dishonest informants. In light of these problems, several states and the federal government have instituted studies of their capital punishment systems, and a number of reforms have been proposed, such as required videotaping of police interrogations and legislation providing post-conviction access to DNA testing. Most recently, the U.S. Supreme Court agreed to hear the case of Paul House, a death row inmate whose case was described by one judge as "a real-life murder mystery, an authentic 'who-done-it' where the wrong man may be executed."

Supporters of capital punishment still contend that no demonstrably innocent individual has been executed in the modern era, that few if any innocents remain or will be placed on death row, and that the minimal risk of wrongful execution is outweighed by the retributive and utilitarian benefits of the death penalty. Nonetheless, the issue of actual innocence has become central to today's debate over capital punishment in America.

ERIK LUNA

References and Further Reading

Armstrong, Ken, and Steve Mills. "The Failure of the Death Penalty in Illinois." *Chicago Tribune* (November 14–18, 1999).

Bedau, Hugo Adam, and Michael L. Radelet, *Miscarriages of Justice in Potentially Capital Cases*, Stanford Law Review 40 (1987): 21–179.

Center on Wrongful Convictions. *Web site available at* http://www.law.northwestern.edu/wrongfulconvictions.

Dwyer, Jim, Peter Neufeld, and Barry Scheck. *Actual Innocence: Five Days to Execution and Other Dispatches from the Wrongly Convicted*. New York: Doubleday, 2000.

Godsey, Mark A., and Thomas Pulley, *The Innocence Revolution and our "Evolving Standards of Decency" in Death Penalty Jurisprudence*, University of Dayton Law Review 29 (2004): 265–292.

Innocence Project. *Web site available at* http://www.innocenceproject.org.

Liebman, James S., *et al.*, *Capital Attrition: Error Rates in Capital Cases, 1973–1995*, Texas Law Review 78 (2000): 1839–1865.

Markman, Stephen J., and Paul G. Cassell, *Protecting the Innocent: A Response to the Bedau-Radelet Study*, Stanford Law Review 41 (1988): 121–160.

Marshall, Lawrence C., *The Innocence Revolution and the Death Penalty*, Ohio State Journal of Criminal Law 1 (2004): 573–584.

Radelet, Michael L., Hugo Adam Bedau, and Constance E. Putnam. *In Spire of Innocence: Erroneous Convictions in Capital Cases*. Boston: Northeastern University Press, 1992.

Rosen, Richard A., *Innocence and Death*, North Carolina Law Review 82 (2003): 61–113.

Symposium: Innocence in Capital Sentencing. *Journal of Criminal Law & Criminology* 95 (2005): 371–636.

Cases and Statutes Cited

Herrera v. Collins, 506 U.S. 390 (1993)

House v. Bell, 386 F.3d 668 (6th Cir. 2004), *cert. granted*, 125 S.Ct. 2991 (U.S. Jun 28, 2005) (No. 04-8990)

Schlup v. Delo, 513 U.S. 298 (1995)

See also **Capital Punishment; DNA and Innocence; Eyewitness Identification; False Confessions;** *Herrera v. Collins*, **506 U.S. 390 (1993); Pardon and Commutation**

CAPITAL PUNISHMENT: HISTORY AND POLITICS

It will be useful to examine this topic by examining six eras of American history.

The Colonial Era

Almost all the American Colonies were established by England, and English penal law was naturally transported across the Atlantic. English law contained many capital offenses, all of which had a Biblical basis, although most also had a pragmatic basis in the protection of person and property. The first of the estimated more than 20,000 executions in American history took place almost as soon as colonization began—in 1608 in Jamestown. Part of the reason for the existence of the death penalty at the outset of colonial history was the absence of any other severe sanction. The idea of prisons for long-term incarceration had not yet been conceived.

Despite the common English influence, there were significant variations among the colonies concerning capital punishment. On one end of the spectrum stood two colonies strongly influenced by Quaker beliefs: West Jersey had no capital offenses, and Pennsylvania levied the ultimate sanction only for murder and treason. On the other end of the spectrum was Virginia, which authorized capital punishment for many of the same crimes (sometimes petty) as in England. And Puritan-influenced colonies like Massachusetts mandated capital punishment for crimes like adultery, sodomy, bestiality, witchcraft, and blasphemy. On average, the colonies each had about ten crimes at any given time for which death was the prescribed sanction, always including murder, and usually including rape, robbery, and arson.

The very early days of colonization manifested a trend that has continued throughout American history: the death penalty was much more prevalent in the South. This was largely due to the influence of slavery. As early as the 1600s southern colonies enacted Slave Codes to suppress any hint of revolt. Those codes prescribed the death penalty for many crimes for slaves that were not so punishable if committed by others.

The first significant abolitionist argument was put forth by Italian lawyer Cesare Beccaria in the 1763 essay *On Crimes and Punishments*. This tract was part of the Enlightenment movement in Europe that was inspired by scientific advances to attempt to supplant traditional Christian dogma with more rationalist discourse. Beccaria argued for extended incarceration with hard labor in lieu of death. The essay was translated into English in 1767 and became influential in America to some of the intellectual elite who were at the forefront of the American Revolution.

From the American Revolution to the Civil War

Among those influenced by Beccaria was Thomas Jefferson, who advocated scaling back severely on the use of capital punishment. Also influenced was Dr. Benjamin Rush, a Philadelphia physician who signed the Declaration of Independence, and who, through a tract written in 1787, became the first vocal abolitionist in the new country. Rush was an advocate for the new penitentiary movement, which aimed to reform criminals in an institutional setting. This movement was a manifestation of the Enlightenment, and its primary spokesperson was English rationalist philosopher Jeremy Bentham, who wrote extensively and in detail about how penitentiaries could secure the greatest happiness for the greatest number in society.

An important gain for abolitionists came in 1794 when Pennsylvania divided murder into two degrees, with only first-degree murder punishable by death. This measure was a compromise between the still-influential Quakers, who would have abolished capital punishment, and retentionist forces. Many other states soon embraced the division of murder into degrees.

By the first decade of the 1800s, the bloom of optimism about penitentiaries had wilted in the light of endemic bad administration and rampant recidivism. Thus, capital punishment continued unabated until the 1840s. Then a tide of abolitionism crested, fueled by religious liberals of Unitarian, Universalist, and Quaker beliefs and rationalist social reformers. This movement was closely affiliated with antislavery activism, since it was clear that capital punishment was inextricably intertwined in the South with the institution of slavery. In 1847, Michigan became the first English-speaking jurisdiction to effectively and permanently (so far) abolish capital punishment, followed by Rhode Island in 1852, and Wisconsin in 1853. However, by the 1850s, social activists began to direct most of their efforts against what they saw as the greatest evil afflicting the country: slavery. Then the Civil War supplanted everything else as a matter of national interest. The movement to abolish the death penalty would not become a major force again until the end of the century.

Two additional important developments occurred in the mid-1800s. First, from colonial days, executions had been carried out in public. But public executions sometimes led to rowdy behavior and even riots. So in 1834, Pennsylvania became the first state to execute a prisoner outside public view. This idea was quickly adopted by most other jurisdictions, although the trend would not completely prevail for a century —the last public execution was conducted in the mid-1930s.

The other important development during this era was according jurors sentencing discretion. Until 1841, juries were not called on to render a sentencing verdict—the mandatory penalty on conviction of a capital offense was death. But in 1841, both Tennessee and Alabama bestowed on the jury the power to choose between a death sentence and an alternative prison sentence. The motivation behind this change is obscure: the best guess is that it was designed to permit jurors to discriminate between black and white defendants. Whatever the reason, this idea was also adopted by many jurisdictions, although mandatory death sentencing for some crimes continued in some states until this practice was struck down by the Supreme Court in 1976.

From the Civil War to World War I

Abolitionist sentiment lay largely dormant as the country struggled through the Civil War and Reconstruction. But around the turn of the century, the movement sprang back to life as part of the Progressive agenda.

By this era, it had become clear that there were two separate streams feeding the abolitionist movement, one religious and the other philosophical. Religiously, the movement was originally supported by "liberal" Christians who valued grace over judgment, and they have continued to be a strong force in the movement to the present. On the other hand, many "conservative" Christians supported capital punishment as legitimated by the Bible and continue that support to the present.

Philosophically, humanists, who believed flourishing of persons was the highest good, objected to the extinguishment of any human life. These reformers, too, have continued to be a strong force in the movement. These abolitionists fall on the "liberal" end of the political spectrum and often believe that life circumstances severely constrain the choices available to those who commit crimes; thus, full-scale responsibility is diluted to the point that these persons cannot deserve a punishment as severe as death. On the other side of the coin, political "conservatives" believe strongly in free will, and thus believe very bad criminals deserve very harsh punishment, which can include the death penalty.

The turn-of-the-century abolitionist movement bore fruit with abolition in nine states between 1907 and 1917. However, the Progressive movement was derailed by World War I, and by 1920 five of the nine states that had abolished the penalty had reinstated it (and two others reinstated it in the 1930s—only in Minnesota and North Dakota has abolition "stuck" until the present).

One important development during this era was the movement to alternatives to hanging as the method of execution. Hanging had proven to be an inexact science that too often resulted in suffering for the condemned, and vicarious suffering for the witnesses. Thus, in 1888, New York became the first jurisdiction to adopt the newly developed electric chair for executions. Fifteen states had followed suit by 1913 and many more by 1950, although hanging and the firing squad persisted in a couple of states.

From World War I to 1957

The abolitionist movement experienced a four-decade period of relative dormancy after World War I. The most likely explanation is that world events—the economic boom of the 1920s, the Great Depression of the 1930s with its concomitant fear of crime, the Second World War and its aftermath, and the Cold War, simply drew attention and energy away from the death penalty issue. With relatively little public attention or protest, more than 5,000 people were executed during this period. (Of course, illegal lynchings, particularly of blacks, accounted for many additional deaths—indeed, it is estimated that in some years illegal lynchings outnumbered legal executions.) The year 1935 constituted the peak year in American history for legal executions, with 199. Still, the execution rate per capita, and per homicide, declined steadily over these four decades.

The search continued for a more humane method of execution. In 1923, Nevada opted for the newly devised gas chamber as a superior alternative to either hanging or electrocution, and thereafter about a dozen other states did likewise.

1957–1976

Beginning in 1957, the moribund abolitionist movement began to gather steam. The abolitionist movement experienced its first lasting successes since North Dakota abolished capital punishment forty-two years earlier: the Territories of Alaska and Hawaii abolished capital punishment shortly before they became states (Delaware abolished in 1958 but reinstated in 1961). Then in 1959, French philosopher Albert Camus wrote an influential polemic against the death penalty, and criminologist Thorsten Sellin published an empirical analysis in which he concluded that the death penalty had no deterrent effect above lengthy imprisonment. In 1960, the execution in California of Caryl Chessman brought the death penalty issue into high focus. Chessman had been sentenced to death for kidnapping but managed by various legal maneuvers to postpone his execution for eleven years, during which time he wrote several best-selling books from death row. Also, the country was experiencing relatively low crime rates. Meanwhile, the pace of executions slowed to a crawl, in large part because appellate review of death penalty cases was becoming relatively routine.

In the mid-1960s, death penalty opponents succeeded in effecting repeal in Iowa and West Virginia. But they also broadened their focus beyond state legislatures, where they had experienced only spotty success, to the courts. In a dissent in *Rudolph v. Alabama* (1963), Supreme Court Justice Arthur Goldberg hinted that more than one Justice was ready to hear arguments against the death penalty on constitutional grounds. In about 1966, the American Civil Liberties Union (ACLU) and the Legal Defense Fund (LDF) of the National Association for the Advancement of Colored People (NAACP) decided to bring court challenges to the death penalty. This coincided with the lowest ebb of American public sentiment in support of the death penalty—a mere forty-two percent in a 1966 Gallup Poll. (Ironically, this turned out to be a brief anomaly—by 1967, as the media was filled with news of a suddenly skyrocketing crime rate, "The Boston Strangler" [Albert DeSalvo] who killed at least thirteen women, and Richard Speck, who murdered eight student nurses in Chicago—death penalty support rose to fifty-three percent and continued climbing another twenty-five percent over the next three decades.)

The LDF decided in 1967 to provide representation to every death-sentenced inmate who had an execution date. This strategy soon tied up virtually every death penalty case that was approaching execution in constitutional challenges. An unofficial death penalty moratorium was affected.

The abolitionists' first major Supreme Court victory came in *Witherspoon v. Illinois* (1968). Professor/litigator Anthony Amsterdam on behalf the LDF convinced the Court that it was unconstitutional to permit the prosecution to strike every potential juror who expressed any scruples against the death penalty.

The retentionists had their day in the sun, though, in a pair of cases, *McGautha v. California* and *Crampton v. Ohio* (1971), in which the Court held that due process did not preclude giving juries unguided discretion to impose the sentence nor did it bar unitary trials in which the issues of guilt and punishment were tried together. Since these were two of the primary abolitionist challenges, the prospect for a major abolitionist victory that would stop capital punishment in its tracks seemed dim.

Yet in the next term, the Court agreed to hear essentially the same challenges but founded on the Cruel and Unusual Punishment Clause of the Eighth Amendment, rather than the Due Process Clause of the Fourteenth Amendment. And in a surprise decision in *Furman v. Georgia* (1972), the Court in a five to four vote held that the death penalty was so unpredictably administered that it violated the Eighth Amendment. The decision had the effect of invalidating the death sentences of every one of the more than 600 prisoners then under death sentences across the country and leaving no state with a constitutional death penalty scheme.

The Court had not held, though, that the death penalty was per se unconstitutional, only that it was not being assessed fairly. This left open the possibility that states could write new legislation that would pass constitutional muster. Many state legislatures hastened to do just that as the opinion polls showed support for capital punishment by far more than half of those polled.

Abolitionists challenged these new statutes, and in 1976 the Court decided that the Georgia statute defining death-eligible crimes via aggravating circumstances and providing for separate guilt/innocence and penalty determinations was constitutional in *Gregg v. Georgia* and so was the Texas statute defining a limited category of death-eligible crimes with a death sentence required if the jury found specified additional facts in *Jurek v. Texas*; but that the North Carolina and Louisiana statutes that made death the mandatory sentence for conviction of certain specified kinds of murder were held unconstitutional in *Woodson v. North Carolina* and *Roberts v. Louisiana*. The Supreme Court was now in the thick of the death penalty battle, where it has remained.

1976 to the Present

The highlights of Supreme Court death penalty jurisprudence after 1976 were that: (1) the death penalty was disproportionate to serious felonies other than murder—*Coker v. Georgia* (1977); (2) defendants must be permitted to present mitigating evidence on any aspect of their character, record, or the circumstances of the offense at the penalty phase—*Lockett v. Ohio* (1978); (3) the common "heinous, atrocious, or cruel" aggravating circumstance was unconstitutionally vague—*Godfrey v. Georgia* (1980); (4) competence of defense counsel was not judged by any higher standard in death penalty cases—*Strickland v. Washington* (1984); (5) even strong statistical evidence was insufficient to prove that the death penalty was administered in a racially biased manner—*McCleskey v. Kemp* (1987); (6) felony murderers who did not personally kill the victim could still be death-eligible if they acted with extreme reckless indifference to human life—*Tison v. Arizona* (1987); (7) that defendants must have been sixteen or older when they committed their crimes to be death-eligible—*Stanford v. Kentucky* (1989); and (8) mentally retarded offenders were not death-eligible—*Atkins v. Virginia* (2002).

Although abolitionists had significant, if mixed, success in the courts, they made little progress in legislatures during this era. Only one state abolished the penalty (Massachusetts), whereas four restored it (Kansas, New York, Oregon, and South Dakota). Furthermore, the federal government vastly expanded the list of federal death offenses, even though the number of federal death penalty cases remained a small slice of the death penalty pie. Public sentiment remained in the range of sixty-five percent to eighty percent support when asked a standard polling question like, "Do you approve of the death penalty for murder?" This figure overstated solid support, though, because when asked an alternative question like, "Do you prefer life without parole instead of the death penalty for murder?" support often slipped by more than twenty percentage points. Nonetheless, politicians during the 1970s through the present sensed that it was the kiss of death to oppose the death penalty, and even many Democrats, like Bill Clinton, gave it lip service.

In the late 1990s, though, the abolitionist forces found a fulcrum that seemed to move public opinion—the possibility of executing innocent persons. This issue came into stark relief in Illinois. There, journalism students showed that several convicts on death row were, in fact, innocent. Indeed, as many convicts had been released from death row for innocence as had been executed since the reinstatement of capital punishment after *Furman*. This prompted Governor George Ryan to impose a moratorium on executions and in 2002 to commute the sentences of all of the more than 160 death-sentenced inmates on the ground that the system under which they were convicted was intolerably riddled with error. The innocence issue, though, had the potential to be a bittersweet one for abolitionists: it seems perhaps more likely to lead to death penalty system reforms than to complete abolition.

During this era, as in all past eras, the death penalty continued to show great variation along regional lines. The vast bulk of executions occurred in the South, with Texas leading the way by a wide margin.

The search for a more humane mode of execution continued during this era. Lethal injection, developed in the 1970s, almost completely displaced other modes of execution.

Executions slowly increased, but court challenges to virtually every death sentence often resulted in reversals. Even for those inmates whose convictions and sentences were upheld, the average time from conviction to execution increased in many states to more than ten years. In the meantime, far more defendants were being sentenced to death than were being executed, so the population of death rows across the country increased to well over 3,000, even as the task of providing legal representation to the condemned became ever more daunting. Still capital punishment seemed firmly entrenched in the United States, particularly in certain regions of the country.

DAVID MCCORD

References and Further Reading

Banner, Stuart. *The Death Penalty: An American History.* Cambridge, MA: Harvard University Press, 2002.

Bedau, Hugo Adam. "Background and Developments" In *The Death Penalty in America: Current Controversies*, edited by Hugo Adam Bedau, 3–25, New York: Oxford University Press, 1997.

Camus, Albert. *Reflections on the Guillotine.* Translated by Richard Howard. Michigan City, IN: Fridtjof-Karla, 1959.

Haines, Herbert H. *Against Capital Punishment: The Anti-Death Penalty Movement in America 1972–1994*, 1996.

Kronenwetter, Michael. *Capital Punishment: A Reference Handbook (2d ed.).* Denver: ABC-CLIO, 2001.

Rush, Benjamin. "An Enquiry into the Effects of Public Punishments Upon Criminals and Upon Society (1787), reprinted in *Capital Punishment in the United States: A Documentary History*, edited by Bryan Vila and Cynthia Morris, 20–23, Westport, CT: Greenwood Press, 1997.

Sellin, Thorsten. *The Death Penalty.* Philadelphia: The American Law Institute, 1959.

Vila, Bryan, and Cynthia Morris, eds. *Capital Punishment in the United States: A Documentary History.* Westport, CT: Greenwood Press, 1997.

Cases and Statutes Cited

Atkins v. Virginia, 536 U.S. 304 (2002)
Coker v. Georgia, 433 U.S. 584 (1977)
Furman v. Georgia, 408 U.S. 238 (1972)
Godfrey v. Georgia, 446 U.S. 420 (1980)
Gregg v. Georgia, 428 U.S. 153 (1976)
Jurek v. Texas, 428 U.S. 153
Lockett v. Ohio, 438 U.S. 586 (1978)
McCleskey v. Kemp, 481 U.S. 279 (1987)
McGautha v. California and *Crampton v. Ohio*, 402 U.S. 183 (1971)
Roberts v. Louisiana, 428 U.S. 325 (1976)
Rudolph v. Alabama, 375 U.S. 889 (1963)
Stanford v. Kentucky, 492 U.S. 361 (1989)
Strickland v. Washington, 466 U.S. 668 (1984)
Tison v. Arizona, 481 U.S. 137 (1987)
Witherspoon v. Illinois, 391 U.S. 510 (1968)
Woodson v. North Carolina, 428 U.S. 280 (1976)

See also **Capital Punishment; Capital Punishment and the Equal Protection Clause Cases; Capital Punishment: Due Process Limits; Capital Punishment: History and Politics; Capital Punishment Reversed; Capital Punishment and Race Discrimination; Capital Punishment: Eighth Amendment Limits**

CAPITAL PUNISHMENT: LYNCHING

Lynching has a long history in the United States, beginning at least around the time of the Revolutionary War. The term "lynching" comes from the practices of Charles Lynch, a Virginia Justice of the Peace who, during the Revolutionary War, helped establish informal courts for the trial and punishment of individuals suspected of engaging in criminal behavior. While lynching originally was associated with imposition of physical punishment for suspected criminal or immoral behavior, since the mid-to-late 1800s, lynching has been understood to mean execution by a group of persons without legal authority for the purpose of punishing a crime or enforcing moral or social standards. Those who engaged in lynching acted outside the legal process to achieve what they claimed was public justice. The so-called "lynch mobs" generally claimed to be acting on behalf of the community, justifying their actions as a necessary means of keeping the peace and promoting moral behavior. It is believed that lynching was committed with the tacit support of the community, and sometimes with the tacit support of the government.

What began as an effort to promote public justice and maintain order eventually became a means of promoting more private goals, such as political and economic gain. For example, vigilante groups formed in the frontier states during the mid 1800s for the avowed purposes of maintaining peace and protecting morals. But these groups eventually engaged in lynching to win political power, as well as the economic benefits that accompany such power. They also used lynching to intimidate or eliminate business competitors.

By the late 1800s, the most common reason for lynching in America was to target and intimidate disfavored racial and ethnic groups. Lynch mobs executed people of many racial and ethnic groups, including African Americans, Native Americans, and Chinese, Japanese, Mexican, and Italian immigrants. Again, political and economic interests played a role, because these lynchings largely were the result of industrial strife and post–Civil War resistance to African-American freedom.

While lynch mobs targeted many racial and ethnic groups, lynching is most commonly associated with the nonlegal execution of African Americans, particularly those living in the South, during and after Reconstruction. Between 1882 and 1968, more than 3,400 African Americans were lynched in the United States. These numbers likely are conservative given that lynchings were not always publicized. Most of the lynchings during the 1882–1968 time period occurred in the South, with Mississippi, Georgia, Texas, Louisiana, and Alabama leading the country in the number of lynchings. Lynching, along with other forms of violence, helped prevent African Americans from fully enjoying economic, social, and political gains after the Civil War.

Lynchings began to decline toward the mid 1900s. By the late 1960s, lynchings had largely subsided, although observers might characterize certain modern-day hate crimes as a type of lynching.

CELESTINE RICHARDS McCONVILLE

References and Further Reading

Dray, Philip. *At the Hands of Persons Unknown, The Lynching of Black America*. New York: Random House, 2002.

DuBois, W. E. B. *Black Reconstruction*, New York: Russell & Russell, 1935.

Ifill, Sherrilyn A., *Creating a Truth and Reconciliation Commission for Lynching*, Law and Inequity: A Journal of Theory and Practice 21 (Summer 2003): 263–311.

Lynching in America: Statistics, Information, Images. http://www.law.umkc.edu/faculty/projects/ftrials/shipp/lynchingyear.html (statistics provided by Tuskegee Institute Archives) (visited January 8, 2004).

NAACP. *Thirty Years of Lynching in the United States: 1889–1918*. New York: Arno Press, 1969.

Steelwater, Eliza. *The Hangman's Knot, Lynching, Legal Execution, and America's Struggle with the Death Penalty*. Boulder, CO: Westview Press, 2003.

Tolnay, Stewart E., and E. M. Beck. *A Festival of Violence*. Urbana: University of Illinois Press, 1995.

See also **Capital Punishment; Capital Punishment and the Equal Protection Clause Cases; Capital Punishment: Due Process Limits; Capital Punishment: History and Politics; Capital Punishment Reversed; Capital Punishment and Race Discrimination; Cross-Burning; *Dred Scott v. Sandford*, 60 U.S. 393 (1857); Due Process; Hate Crimes; Ku Klux Klan; Segregation; Shepard, Matthew**

CAPITAL PUNISHMENT: METHODS OF EXECUTION

Introduction

Jurisdictions with capital punishment use one or more of the following methods to implement the sentence: hanging, firing squad, electrocution, lethal gas, and lethal injection. The Eighth Amendment of the U. S. Constitution bars states from using a method that constitutes Cruel and Unusual Punishment. Lawsuits alleging that the methods violate this federal and state constitutional right have been commenced in both court systems.

Hanging

Hanging has a lengthy history in this country and abroad. It requires attaching one part of a rope to an elevated item, securing the other end of the rope around the person's neck, and suspending the person from the rope. The "short drop" method preceded the "long drop" method. The latter was preferred because the former often resulted in protracted deaths through strangulation. The "long drop" requires constructing a gallows, an edifice with a beam from which the hanging rope is suspended and a floor containing a trap door. A rope treated to eliminate springing is attached to the beam and suspended over the trap door. A noose is created by making a knot in the rope and lubricating it with wax or soap. After ascending the gallows, the condemned's legs are bound and a leather halter is used to secure the arms and hands. Next the person is blindfolded or a hood is placed over his or her head. This is followed by putting the noose around the person's neck and positioning the knot behind the left ear. After the warden signals, the executioner releases the trap door. The weight of the person's body plummeting through the trap door is supposed to cause a rapid fracture and dislocation of the neck, resulting in an instantaneous death. This method's popularity began to wane because of the realization that death often did not occur in this manner. Instead, the person died from strangulation or decapitation. This concern is evidenced by the fact that very few death penalty jurisdictions still authorize using this method and then only if the person selects it or the alternative method is deemed unconstitutional.

Firing Squad

Execution by firing squad also has a lengthy history of being an accepted method of execution. It requires strapping the condemned in a chair that is surrounded by sandbags to absorb the person's blood. Next a target, a white cloth circle, is placed over the person's heart. Then the person is blindfolded or a hood is placed over his or her head. The shooters, positioned behind an enclosure with slots in it exposing the barrels of their rifles, are instructed to shoot at the target. One shooter is not given live ammunition. The firing squad still remains an unpopular method of execution. The few jurisdictions still permitting it also have lethal injection as an alternative method.

Electrocution

Unlike the firing squad, execution by electrocution was once a popular method of execution. Its popularity was partially due to technological advances in the form of the increasing availability of electricity. In 1888, New York became the first death penalty jurisdiction to require that executions be carried out by electrocution rather than by hanging. First, the person is seated in a wooden chair. Leather belts are used to secure the person's chest, groin, legs, and arms. A natural sponge moistened with saline solution is placed on top of the prisoner's shaved head and covered with a metal electrode. Another electrode moistened with conductive jelly is fastened to a shaved area of the prisoner's leg to reduce resistance to the electricity. A hood is usually put over the person's head, and a chin strap secures the head. The electrical current starts flowing through the prisoner's body when the executioner pulls a handle or pushes a button. An

alternating current system is usually used. The initial jolt is around 2,000 volts and lasts for three to five seconds. It is followed by a second reduced charge. If a heartbeat is detected, the cycle recommences and continues until the prisoner is dead. Several jurisdictions still authorize this method, but only one mandates it, and the rest allow the condemned to select another method or make electrocution the default method.

Lethal Gas

Technological advances, this time in the field of chemistry, played a role in the adoption of lethal gas as a method of execution. In 1924, Nevada became the first jurisdiction to eliminate hanging and adopt this method. First, the condemned must be securely strapped to a chair in an airtight chamber. Sulfuric acid is put in a dish under the chair. The executioner moves a lever releasing sodium cyanide pellets into the dish. Mixing these two chemicals produces poisonous hydrogen cyanide gas. The person has been instructed to start inhaling deeply when he or she hears the lever fall. Eventually, the person loses consciousness and dies of hypoxia. Lethal gas never reached the same level of popularity as electrocution, and today very few states authorize its use. All these jurisdictions designate lethal injection as the alternative method.

Lethal Injection

In 1977, Oklahoma became the first death penalty jurisdiction to adopt lethal injection as a method of execution. To carry out an execution this way, the condemned person is strapped to a gurney and then several heart monitors are placed on his or her skin. Two needles, one a back up, are inserted into a vein. Tubes are connected to these needles. These tubes run through a hole in a wall leading to a room adjacent to the execution chamber and, depending on which protocol the jurisdiction uses, are attached to two or three drips that intravenously administer the chemicals. If the three chemical process is used, saline is first injected. Once the warden gives the signal, the curtain preventing the witnesses from seeing the condemned is raised. At this point sodium thiopental, a fast-acting anesthetic, is administered. Pavulon or pancuronium bromide is then injected, paralyzing the person and suppressing the respiratory system. Potassium chloride, the last chemical injected, causes the heart to stop beating. Lethal injection is the most common method of execution in the United States.

ROBERTA M. HARDING

References and Further Reading

Denno, Deborah W., *Is Electrocution an Unconstitutional Method of Execution? The Engineering of Death over the Century*, Wm. & Mary L. Rev. 35 (1994): 2:551–692.
———, *When Legislatures Delegate Death: The Troubling Paradox Behind States Uses of Electrocution and Lethal Injection and What It Says About Us*, Ohio St. L. J. 63 (2002): 1:63–260.
Essig, Mark. *Edison & the Electric Chair: A Story of Light and Death*. New York: Walker & Company, 2003.
Gatrell, V. A. C. *The Hanging Tree: Execution and the English People 1770–1868*. Oxford: Oxford University Press, 1994.
Harding, Roberta M., *The Gallows to the Gurney: Analyzing the Un(Constitutionality) of the Methods of Execution*, Boston Univ. Pub. Int. L. J. 6 (1996): 1:153–178.
Moran, Richard. *Executioner's Current: Thomas Edison, George Westinghouse, and the Invention of the Electric Chair*. New York: Alfred A. Knopf, 2003.

See also **Capital Punishment; Capital Punishment: Eighth Amendment Limits; Cruel and Unusual Punishment (VIII); Cruel and Unusual Punishment Generally; Electric Chair as Cruel and Unusual Punishment**

CAPITAL PUNISHMENT: PROPORTIONALITY

Proportionality in principle justifies, limits, or condemns capital punishment. That deeply held common value—that punishment must not be grossly disproportionate to the crime—dominates U.S. Supreme Court jurisprudence.

When the Court struck down the death penalty (five to four) in *Furman v. Georgia* (1972), Justices Brennan and Marshall held capital punishment per se cruel and unconstitutional. For these and like-minded absolutist opponents, death as punishment is an inhumane, morally disproportionate response to any crime, no matter how heinous. Other death penalty opponents may concede that sadistic mass murdering rapists do deserve to die. "Abstractly," the punishment of death may fit *that* crime. But, they insist, history proves that government can never be trusted to kill proportionately.

In *Furman,* three Justices of the five who concurred found the death penalty only unconstitutional, because it was "freakishly imposed". As then administered, the death penalty was "like being struck by lightning" (Stewart), applied chaotically to a "capriciously selected, random handful"—in no proportion and thus cruel and unusual punishment. Separately concurring in *Furman,* Justice Douglas also condemned the death penalty as unconstitutionally malproportioned, because "disproportionately imposed and carried out on the poor, the Negro, and members of unpopular groups."

After *Furman,* thirty-five states enacted new death penalty statutes. "The punishment must not be grossly out of proportion to the severity of the crime," a plurality warned in *Gregg* in 1976, considering Georgia's new statute. "We cannot say the punishment is invariably disproportionate to the crime," the Court concluded, restoring the death penalty to the United States. "This is an extreme sanction, suitable to the most extreme of crimes."

Was rape, or treason, also a "most extreme" crime? Death was "indeed a disproportionate penalty for the crime of raping an adult woman," Justice White declared for a plurality (*Coker*). Ordinarily, death was a disproportionate penalty for the crime of rape, Justice Powell separately agreed in this case where the rape victim was not otherwise injured. But it "may be that the death penalty is not disproportionate punishment for the crime of aggravated rape." Dissenting Justices in *Coker* also agreed in principle: "I accept that the Eighth Amendment's concept of disproportionality bars the death penalty for minor crimes," Justice Burger, joined by Rehnquist conceded. "But rape is not a minor crime," and death was not necessarily disproportionate for a "chronic rapist" who had been previously convicted of murder and escaped from prison to rape again.

Although the death penalty for child rape and similarly heinous crimes remains an open question, the mantra of modern capital jurisprudence—"death is different"—suggests that Constitutional proportionality inherent in the Eighth Amendment may limit death as punishment only to murder. (See Proportionality in Punishment.)

Five years after *Coker*, the Court in *Enmund*, five to four, held that death was a disproportionate penalty for a getaway car driver who neither intended nor expected his cofelon to shoot and kill their robbery victim. Dissenting in this particular case, Justice O'Connor stated common ground for the Court: "The penalty imposed in a capital case [must] be proportional to the harm caused and the defendant's blameworthiness." How serious the crime, how morally culpable the killer? This depends not only on the harm to the victim, but also on the killer's mental state and motive. In *Tison*, Justice O'Connor, this time in the majority, held that a reckless and depraved indifference to human life without an intent to kill could make death a proportional penalty for a felony murder accomplice.

Harm and blameworthiness—essential components of proportionality—require a particularized consideration of each crime and each criminal. Thus, as constitutional punishment, death must not be grossly disproportionate to the crime, *and* it must not be disproportionate to the criminal's particular culpability, however measured. Capital punishment may neither be applied randomly, nor automatically, for any crime. Thus, the very same day the Court affirmed statutes from Georgia, Florida, and Texas, in *Woodson* and *Roberts*, it struck down North Carolina's and Louisiana's mandatory death penalties.

Since then, in a series of cases, explicitly or implicitly, a substantial majority has insisted that proportionality requires the capital sentencer to consider all relevant mitigating circumstances, not only of the crime, but also the background and character of the criminal (*Lockett* and *Eddings*).

Although proportionality constraints prohibit a state from *mandating* death for all individuals who commit even the most aggravated murder legislatively defined in advance, the Court itself has used proportionality, categorically to *exempt* from a death penalty entire classes of offenses (*Coker*) *and* also offenders. Thus, in 2002, a majority held death per se disproportionate punishment for *any* crime committed by a mentally retarded defendant (*Atkins*). And in 2005, a majority found the death penalty *per se* "disproportionate punishment for offenders under 18." (*Roper*)

Roper intensified controversy over *how to measure* proportionality. Constitutionally disproportionate punishment outlawed by the Eighth Amendment is not static, but must be informed by "the evolving standards of decency of a maturing society." (*Trop*, 1958) All Justices presently agree that "time works changes," that what's 'excessive' "may acquire meaning as public opinion becomes enlightened by a humane justice" (*Weems*, 1910). In determining proportionality *vel non*, the *Roper* majority, along with Justice O'Connor in dissent, would consider the views of the international community, while insisting that in the end the Court determines "moral proportionality" by exercising "our own independent judgment." Justices Scalia and Rehnquist in dissent insisted that Constitutionally mandated "moral proportionality" is an antidemocratic cover, by which individual Justices impose and substitute their subjective personal views for those of legislatures.

While the Court has focused constitutional attention on whether and when death is a too severe response, retributivists insisting on "just deserts" force the opposite proportionality question into the debate:

Is life in prison (with or without parole) a sufficiently unpleasant experience? (See Retribution) A public convinced that prison life is so unbearable that "life is worse than death" may abolish the death penalty, comfortable it has maintained proportionality. An informed public, however, aware that sadists who rape and torture children to death end up watching television and playing volleyball, may insist, that as administered, life without parole destroys the "moral proportionality," which only a death penalty can maintain.

Robert Blecker

Cases and Statutes Cited

Atkins v. Virginia 536 U.S. 304 (2002)
Coker v. Georgia 433 U.S. 584 (1977)
Eddings v. Oklahoma 455 U.S. 104 (1982)
Enmund v. Florida 458 U.S. 782 (1982)
Furman v. Georgia 408 U.S. 238 (1972)
Gregg v. Georgia 428 U.S. 153 (1976)
Lockett v. Ohio 438 U.S. 586 (1978)
Roberts v. Louisiana 428 U.S. 325 (1976)
Roper v. Simmons 125 S.Ct. 1183 (2005)
Tison v. Arizona 481 U.S.137 (1987)

See also **Capital Punishment; Capital Punishment and the Equal Protection Clause Cases; Capital Punishment: Due Process Limits; Capital Punishment: History and Politics; Capital Punishment: Eighth Amendment Limits**

CAPITOL SQUARE REVIEW AND ADVISORY BOARD v. PINETTE, 515 U.S. 753 (1995)

Capitol Square is a 10-acre, state-owned plaza surrounding the statehouse in Columbus, Ohio. For over a century the square had "been used for public speeches, gatherings, and festivals advocating and celebrating a variety of causes, both secular and religious." As authorized by Ohio state statute, the Advisory Board denied a Ku Klux Klan application to place an unattended, unlabeled cross in the square during the Christmas season—while approving other displays, at least one of which was religious. The Klan was then permitted to erect its cross pursuant to a federal court injunction, and the Board appealed, claiming its denial was required by the First Amendment Establishment Clause.

The Supreme Court affirmed the lower courts' action, stating "There is no doubt that compliance with the Establishment Clause is a state interest sufficiently compelling to justify content-based restrictions on [expression]." However, "[r]eligious expression cannot violate the Establishment Clause where it (1) is purely private and (2) occurs in a traditional or designated public forum, publicly announced and open to all on equal terms. Those conditions are satisfied here, and therefore the State may not bar respondents' cross from Capitol Square." The Court declined to deal with the possible political implications of the Klan's racist views because that issue had not been considered in the lower courts.

In addition, there was considerable discussion (and no majority agreement) among the justices on the proper use and application of the so-called endorsement test: whether permission by government for the display on its property of an unlabeled cross sent a message of government promotion of Christianity. Two justices dissented, focusing on the likelihood that the cross sends such a message.

The decision and accompanying disagreements are consistent with the Court's two prior holiday display cases, *County of Allegheny v. American Civil Liberties Union*, 492 U.S. 573 (1989); *Lynch v. Donnelly*, 465 U.S. 668 (1984).

DANIEL G. GIBBENS

Cases and Statutes Cited

Capitol Square Review and Advisory Board v. Pinette, 515 US 753 (1995)
County of Allegheny v. American Civil Liberties Union, 492 U.S. 573 (1989)
Lynch v. Donnelly, 465 U.S. 668 (1984)

CAPTIVE AUDIENCES AND FREE SPEECH

The idea that speech may be curbed to protect the sensibilities of an audience held captive by the speaker is rooted in the notion that governmental power "to shut off discourse solely to protect others from hearing it [is] dependent upon a showing that substantial privacy interests are being invaded in an essentially intolerable manner" *Cohen v. California*, 403 U.S. 15 (1971). This principle is especially applicable to audiences held captive in their own homes. In *Rowan v. United States Post Office Department*, 397 U.S. 728 (1970), the Supreme Court upheld a federal law that permitted mail recipients to require the Post Office not to deliver mailings of "sexually provocative" materials from senders specified by the postal customer. The sanctity of the home is, however, not unlimited. In *Consolidated Edison v. Public Service Commission*, 477 U.S. 530 (1980), the Court struck down a government regulation barring utilities from mailing political matter to their customers along with their bills, and in *Bolger v. Youngs Drug Products Corp.*, 463 U.S. 60 (1983), the Court voided a federal

law banning the mailing of unsolicited advertisements for contraceptives, reasoning that the short "journey from mail box to trash can" was an acceptable burden to preserve free speech. These cases may be reconciled by noting that in *Rowan* the government merely acquiesced to private choice concerning the avoidance of unwanted communications, whereas in *Consolidated Edison* and *Bolger* the government itself decided on the material from which private citizens should be shielded. On that reading, the captive audience doctrine amounts to a privately held veto over speech that intolerably invades substantial privacy interests.

Captive audiences are not confined to the home. In *FCC v. Pacifica Foundation*, 438 U.S. 726 (1978), the Supreme Court upheld discipline of a radio station for broadcasting a vulgar comedy routine during hours that children might be listening. While *Pacifica* involved more factors than a captive audience, both *Lehman v. Shaker Heights*, 418 U.S. 298 (1974), and *Public Utilities Commission v. Pollak*, 343 U.S. 451 (1952), were concerned, respectively, with the captivity of bus passengers subjected to placard advertising and radio programming. Because the passengers had little choice but to listen or watch, Justice Douglas characterized them as captives.

Because the Supreme Court has never fully explained the import of the captive audience principle, its scope remains unclear. For example, may governments require computer and television manufacturers to insert devices that enable users to block certain unwanted programming? The principle reconciling *Consolidated Edison*, *Bolger*, and *Rowan* suggests that governments could do so. What if the blocking technology does not permit unlimited user choice, but merely gives the user a choice among a variety of preselected forms of programming? The same principle suggests that constriction of private choice would be impermissible if mandated by government, but perhaps not if it resulted from only the manufacturers' decisions. In short, there remains uncertainty about what constitutes a captive audience and what governments may do to protect captive audiences from unwanted messages.

CALVIN MASSEY

References and Further Reading

Strauss, Marcy, *Redefining the Captive Audience Doctrine*, Hastings Const. L. Q. 85 (1991): 19.

Cases and Statutes Cited

Bolger v. Youngs Drug Products Corp., 463 U.S. 60 (1983)

Cohen v. California, 403 U.S. 15 (1971)
Consolidated Edison v. Public Service Commission, 477 U.S. 530 (1980)
FCC v. Pacifica Foundation, 438 U.S. 726 (1978)
Lehman v. Shaker Heights, 418 U.S. 298 (1974)
Public Utilities Commission v. Pollak, 343 U.S. 451 (1952)
Rowan v. United States Post Office Department, 397 U.S. 728 (1970)

See also **Bolger v. Youngs Drug Products Corp.,** **463, U.S. 60 (1983); Broadcast Regulation;** *Cohen v.* ***California*, 403 U.S. 15 (1971);** *FCC v. Pacifica* ***Foundation* 438 U.S. 726 (1978);** *Rowan v. United* ***States Post Office Department, No. 399, 397 U.S.** **728 (1970)**

CARDOZO, BENJAMIN (1870–1938)

Benjamin Nathan Cardozo was born into a Sephardic Jewish family in New York City in 1870. Shortly after his birth, his father, Albert Cardozo, was forced to resign his position as a judge on the New York Supreme Court in the wake of charges of corruption. The standard treatments of Benjamin Cardozo's life and career suggest that he spent the better part of his adult life attempting to transcend, consciously or not, the disgrace of his father's professional malfeasance.

As a young teenager, Cardozo was tutored at home by Horatio Alger, Jr. He entered Columbia College at the age of fifteen. On graduation, he matriculated into the Columbia Law School at the age of nineteen, leaving after two years of study but without a law degree. After his departure from law school, Cardozo sat for the New York Bar, and thereafter entered into private practice with his brother, specializing in commercial practice and appellate litigation. Most accounts of Cardozo's work as a lawyer describe him as an extremely able practitioner—a "lawyer's lawyer." After slightly more than two decades of law practice, Cardozo was elected to the New York Supreme Court in 1913 and would take his seat as a justice on the court on January 5, 1914. Five weeks into his first term on the trial court, Cardozo was temporarily designated by Governor Martin Glynn to the court of Appeals (the state's highest court) to help clear a backlog of cases. In 1917, Cardozo was first appointed, and then elected, to a seat on the court of Appeals. It would be through his service on the New York high court that Cardozo would earn his reputation as one of America's most respected jurists. He served on the court of Appeals until 1932, when Cardozo, a Democrat, was appointed to the U. S. Supreme Court by Republican President Herbert Hoover. Cardozo served as an Associate Justice until his death in 1938.

Cardozo has been considered by many to be the quintessential common law jurist, a judicial craftsman respected not only for the quality of his judicial reasoning, but for the quality of his written opinions as well. Fundamental features of the common law define Cardozo's understanding of and approach to the judicial process: sensitivity to the importance of the judicial role in a system of judge-made law; and, the centrality of the judge in the process of legal development, maintaining continuity with the past by respect for the principle of *stare decisis*, while nurturing modest change by keeping the law relevant to changing social circumstances and need. Cardozo accepted the idea that law was not, and should not be, isolated from social life, and that judicial reasoning involved more than the mechanical application of abstract concepts, the relations of which being logically derived. Moreover, he resisted the simplistic notion that the judge is merely an "empty vessel," an unbiased figure through which the law itself might speak. Instead, Cardozo understood the importance of the subjectivity of the judge. The classic exposition of this view came in Cardozo's Storrs Lectures, delivered at Yale Law School and published in 1921 under the title, *The Nature of the Judicial Process*. In one of its most memorable passages, Cardozo observed, There is in each of us a stream of tendency . . .'' which gives coherence and direction to thought and action. Judges cannot escape that current any more than other mortals. All their lives, forces that they do not recognize and cannot name have been tugging at them—inherited instincts, traditional beliefs, acquired convictions; and the resultant is an outlook on life . . . .'' *Roper v. Simmons* 125 S.Ct. 1183 (2005).

In this mental background every problem finds its setting. We may try to see things as objectively as we please. Nonetheless, we can never see them with any eyes except our own.

In other words, we are all—judges included—constituted by the society and culture in which we live; our vision of the world is inevitably a "shaped" vision. To concede, however, that the judicial view is a biased one has obvious implications for the rule of law ideal, if that ideal is understood as government by law and not by persons. Anticipating the possibility of an anxious response to his claims of the inherent subjectivity of the judicial process, Cardozo assured his Yale audience that "[w]e may wonder sometimes how from the play of all these forces of individualism, there can come anything coherent, anything but chaos and the void. Those are the moments in which we exaggerate the elements of difference. In the end there emerges something which has a composite shape and truth and order." Cardozo urged a mature recognition of the fact that judges are inevitably "lawmakers," and of the related point that their lawmaking was based on their ideological orientation. The "business of the judge" is not to "*discover* [my emphasis] the objective truth." Rather, according to Cardozo, the real duty of the judge is to "objectify in law, not my own aspirations and convictions and philosophies, but the aspirations and convictions and philosophies of the men and women of my time." The judge functions, then, as a translator between his or her community and the law, rearticulating the interests and needs of the community into legal form and, in turn, giving voice to the law so that it may continue to speak relevantly and responsively to the community of which it is a part.

Cardozo has generally been characterized as a progressive and innovative jurist. And, his candor about the nature of the judicial process inevitably could be seen to gesture toward later, more radical developments in legal thought, such as Legal Realism. Yet, Cardozo's actual judicial work-product generally appears (or is intended to appear) much more modest in aspiration. For example, in *MacPherson v. Buick Motor Company*, one of the canonical opinions from Cardozo's corpus, he announces an important shift in the law of negligence, yet strives to characterize the decision as one that has simply made more clear an emerging trend in the development of negligence doctrine.

The vast bulk of Cardozo's judicial experience came while serving as an appellate judge on New York's Court of Appeals. Therefore, he rarely dealt with legal issues that today garner so much attention, issues of constitutional law—such issues would come at the very end of his judicial career. However, while on the New York Court of Appeals, he did deal with a number of criminal law/criminal procedure matters. And, although usually thought of as a "liberal" judge, Cardozo's record in this area seems rather more mixed; he often seemed less sympathetic to criminal defendant's rights than one might think a "liberal" judge would be. For example, in *People v. Defore*, Cardozo, writing for the court of Appeals, resisted the adoption of the exclusionary rule in New York and held that evidence obtained through an illegal police search of a criminal suspect's home was, nonetheless, admissible in trial. And, toward the end of his life, while on the U. S. Supreme Court, in his opinion for the Court in *Palko v. Connecticut*, Cardozo rejected the Petitioner's argument that the double jeopardy provision of the Fifth Amendment should be incorporated through the Fourteenth Amendment and applied against the State of Connecticut. The result was to uphold a capital murder conviction obtained in the second trial of the defendant, after the state appealed a second-degree murder conviction from the first trial.

Certainly, there were instances when Cardozo was more receptive to the claims of criminal defendants—for example, joining the decision in *Powell v. Alabama* (otherwise known as one of the "Scottsboro Cases"), which found a constitutional right to counsel in state capital trials. Yet, it was primarily in cases dealing with the freedom of speech that Cardozo's liberal inclinations seemed to be most fully engaged. In *Herndon v. State of Georgia*, Cardozo authored a strongly worded dissent from a decision that rejected, on procedural grounds, the appeal of an African-American communist who had been imprisoned for violating Georgia's anti-nsurrection statute by "inducing others to join in combined resistance to the authority of the state." Here, as elsewhere, Cardozo endorsed Holmes' "clear and present danger" standard as the test to be used in cases involving the incitement of illegal activity, to balance a state's interest in preserving order with an individual's constitutional guarantee of freedom of speech. Indeed, it was in an essay celebrating Holmes' life and career that Cardozo seemed to offer something more than simply an appreciation of Holmes' contribution to the protection of freedom of speech, but a glimpse of his own views as well: "Only in one field is compromise to be excluded, or kept within the narrowest limits. There shall be no compromise of the freedom to think one's thoughts and speak them, except at those extreme borders where thought merges into action. There is to be no compromise here . . . . There is no freedom without choice, and there is no choice without knowledge—or none that is not illusory."

WILLIAM ROSE

References and Further Reading

Cardozo, Benjamin N. *The Nature of the Judicial Process.* New Haven: Yale University Press, 1921/1960.
———, *Mr. Justice Holmes*, Harvard Law Review 44 (1931): 682–692.
Hall, Margaret E. *Selected Writings of Benjamin Nathan Cardozo: The Choice of Tycho Brahe.* New York: Matthew Bender, 1947/1975 reprint.
Kaufman, Andrew L. *Cardozo.* Cambridge: Harvard University Press, 1998.
Polenberg, Richard. *The World of Benjamin Cardozo: Personal Values and the Judicial Process.* Cambridge: Harvard University Press, 1997.
Posner, Richard. *Cardozo: A Study in Reputation.* Chicago: University of Chicago Press, 1990.

Cases and Statutes Cited

Herndon v. State of Georgia, 295 U.S. 441 (1935), Cardozo dissenting

MacPherson v. Buick Motor Company, 217 N.Y. 382 (1916)
Palko v. Connecticut, 302 U.S. 319 (1937)
People v. Defore, 242 N.Y. 13 (1926)
Powell v. Alabama, 287 U.S. 45 (1932)

CAREY v. POPULATION SERVICES INTERNATIONAL, 431 U.S. 678 (1977)

Whether, and to what extent, minors should enjoy the same constitutional rights as adults is one of the most vexing and unsettled questions of constitutional law. In *Carey v. Population Services International*, the Supreme Court considered this question in the context of minors' right to privacy.

In 1976, the Supreme Court decided, in the case of *Planned Parenthood of Central Missouri v. Danforth*, that a state may not impose a blanket requirement that a minor obtain parental consent before getting an abortion. One year later, in *Carey*, the Supreme Court considered a challenge to a New York law regulating access to contraceptives by individuals younger than sixteen.

The law had three provisions. First, it prohibited the distribution of contraceptives to individuals younger than sixteen, except by a physician. Second, it allowed only licensed pharmacists to distribute nonprescription contraceptives to individuals older than sixteen. Finally, the law banned the advertisement or display of contraceptives.

The Supreme Court struck down all three provisions. The Court concluded that the fundamental right of the individual to make decisions about whether to procreate, recognized by the Court in *Griswold v. Connecticut* and *Eisenstadt v. Baird*, was unconstitutionally burdened by the requirement that only licensed pharmacists could distribute condoms. Furthermore, the Supreme Court decided that the prohibition on advertising or displaying contraceptives was an unconstitutional restriction on free speech.

The portion of the Court's decision striking down the prohibition on access to contraceptives by individuals younger than sixteen was joined by only four Justices, however. In that opinion, Justice Brennan rejected the argument that the prohibition could be justified by the state's desire to protect minors' health or morals. Justice Brennan found the state's argument that the law served to deter sexual activity by teenagers to be unworthy of serious consideration, expressing doubts that this method of deterrence would actually work, and further asserting that it was illogical to try to protect teens by making the consequences of their sexual activity more severe and harmful. Justice Brennan noted there was no medical justification for allowing only physicians to distribute nonprescription contraceptives and reaffirmed the vitality of the Supreme Court's earlier decision in *Planned Parenthood of Central Missouri v. Danforth* that the state cannot itself exercise, nor can it give to a third party, an arbitrary veto power over minors' reproductive rights.

Justices White, Powell, and Stevens concurred in Justice Brennan's decision but not his reasoning. Each expressed concern about the breadth of the privacy right recognized by Justice Brennan's opinion and emphasized that states still have broad powers to regulate adolescents' sexual behavior. Nonetheless, all three agreed that the means New York had used to regulate adolescent sexual behavior in this instance were unacceptable.

Thus, in *Carey*, the Court provided an important precedent affirming the right of individuals, including minors, to a realm of sexual and decisional privacy into which the government could not constitutionally intrude; at the same time, however, the Court did not go so far as to recognize an absolute right of sexual autonomy on the part of either minors or adults.

B. JESSIE HILL

References and Further Reading

Cruz, David B., The Sexual Freedom Cases? *Contraception, Abortion, Abstinence, and the Constitution*, Harvard Civil Rights-Civil Liberties Law Review 35 (2000): 2:299–383.
Garrow, David J. *Liberty and Sexuality: The Right to Privacy and the Making of Roe v. Wade*, 600–704, New York: Macmillan, 1994.
Posner, Richard A., *The Uncertain Protection of Privacy by the Supreme Court*, Supreme Court Review (1979): 173.
Tribe, Laurence H. *American Constitutional Law*, 2nd ed., Mineola, NY: Foundation, 1988.

Cases and Statutes Cited

Eisenstadt v. Baird, 405 U.S. 438 (1972)
Griswold v. Connecticut, 381 U.S. 479 (1965)
Planned Parenthood of Central Missouri v. Danforth, 428 U.S. 52 (1976)

See also **Birth Control; Eisenstadt v. Baird, 405 U.S. 438 (1972); Griswold v. Connecticut, 381 U.S. 479 (1965); Planned Parenthood of Missouri v. Danforth, 428 U.S. 52 (1976); Privacy; Right of Privacy; Substantive Due Process**

CAROLENE PRODUCTS v. U.S., 304 U.S. 144 (1938)

This relatively minor case is remembered not for the issue supposedly before the Court, but for a footnote that in the eyes of many scholars launched a constitutional revolution.

The case itself involved a challenge to a federal law that prohibited the interstate shipment of "filled milk," defined in the statute as skim milk "compounded with . . . any fat or oil other than milk fat." The law had clearly been intended to benefit certain parts of the dairy industry, and Carolene Products, convicted of shipping "filled milk," challenged it as exceeding Congress's commerce powers.

Justice Stone practically dismissed this argument out of hand, and in doing so put forward a simple test for weighing the constitutionality of economic regulations. Legislation "affecting ordinary commercial transactions is not to be pronounced unconstitutional unless in the light of the facts made known or generally assumed it is of such a character as to preclude the assumption that it rests upon a rational basis within the knowledge and experience of the legislators." This "rational basis" test became and remains the basic test for economic regulation; it is the least demanding of all constitutional tests, and few laws have ever failed it.

But immediately after the statement of the rational basis test, Stone inserted footnote four. In it he declared:

There may be narrower scope for operation of the presumption of constitutionality when legislation appears on its face to be within a specific prohibition of the Constitution, such as those of the first ten amendments, which are deemed equally specific when held to be embraced within the Fourteenth.

The note went on to say that such legislation would be subject to a "more exacting judicial scrutiny," as could laws aimed at particular religions, the integrity of the political process, or at "discrete and insular minorities."

Although Stone did not himself use the term "strict scrutiny," footnote four led to a new jurisprudence in which economic and other legislation not affecting individual civil rights and liberties would be examined by the courts on a minimal, "rational basis." If the legislature, either Congress or the states, had the general constitutional power—in this instance, to regulate interstate commerce—and had acted with sufficient reason, the courts would not question the wisdom of the policy.

But when it came to individual rights protected by the Constitution, then the courts would apply a much higher standard. The individual would only have to make out a prima facie case that a right had been restricted, and the burden of proof would shift to the state to prove that the limitation of individual liberty resulted from a compelling governmental interest and had been constructed in the least intrusive manner.

In the 1940s, the Court began applying strict scrutiny to laws affecting First Amendment guarantees—especially speech—and statutes affecting race. As a result of footnote four, lower courts began assuming the role of interpreter of property rights vis-à-vis the state, and by applying the rational basis test rarely overturned economic regulation. The Court would rarely grant review in such cases. But in the area of free speech and other constitutionally protected rights—and after 1954 laws classifying people on the basis of race—the Supreme Court became the nation's chief guardian of civil rights and civil liberties.

MELVIN I. UROFSKY

References and Further Reading

Perry, Michael, *Mr. Justice Stone and Footnote 4*, George Mason University Civil Rights Law Journal 35 (1996): 6.
Powell, Lewis F. Jr., *Carolene Products Revisited*, Columbia Law Review 1087 (1982): 82.

CARROLL v. UNITED STATES, 267 U.S. 132 (1925)

The Supreme Court has held that, under the Fourth Amendment to the Constitution, police officers must obtain a warrant to engage in a search or a seizure, unless their activity falls within one of "a few specifically established and well delineated exceptions." One of the most important of these exceptions is the "car search doctrine," often called the "*Carroll* Doctrine," as it was first enunciated in this case.

Carroll was a bootlegging case from Prohibition times. Police officers knew that the "Carroll boys" were bootleggers. They had previously offered to supply undercover agents in Grand Rapids with whiskey. So when officers saw their car by chance, outside Grand Rapids, coming from the direction of Detroit, it was stopped, searched, and sixty-eight bottles of whiskey were found stashed behind the back seat.

Chief Justice Taft, for the majority, was untroubled by the fact that the officers did not have a warrant. Automobiles, unlike "a store, dwelling house, or other structure," are readily mobile, and "it is not practicable to secure a warrant, because the vehicle can be quickly moved out of the locality or jurisdiction in which the warrant must be sought."

That did not mean that officers could lawfully stop every car on the road on the chance that they might find contraband. To undertake a warrantless search and seizure of a car, officers had to possess probable cause.

While the *Carroll* Doctrine still applies, permitting a warrantless search and seizure of a vehicle where officers have probable cause to believe that evidence of crime is present, the Court has subsequently held that it is not justified only by the fact of ready mobility. Instead, the car search exception to the warrant requirement survives today because people have a reduced expectation of privacy in their vehicles due to "pervasive and continuing governmental regulation and controls, including periodic inspection and licensing requirements."

JOHN M. BURKOFF

See also **Automobile Search;** *California v. Acevedo,* **500 U.S. 565 (1991); Probable Cause; Search (General Definition); Warrantless Searches**

CATEGORICAL APPROACH TO FREE SPEECH

The "categorical approach" is a method of judging where decisions are reached through use of a preestablished system of classifications or categories. Judges compare the case before them to cases in the past to determine the category to which the new case belongs. Judges then apply legal rules already developed for that category to resolve the dispute.

In free speech cases, the categorical approach has been the dominant analytical method for many years. Multiple classification schemes have evolved that help courts systematically dissect and compare the complexities of First Amendment free speech disputes. Classification systems are applied to evaluate the nature of the speech being restricted by government, the setting where the speech would occur, and the nature of the speech restriction. Thus, in resolving a free speech case, a judge would determine first whether the speech at issue is "protected" or "unprotected" by the First Amendment. Categories of "unprotected" speech include obscenity, defamation, incitement, and child pornography produced with real children. If the speech were in the "protected" category, the judge would classify the setting of the speech as either some type of "public forum" or else a "non-public forum." The judge would also classify the type of governmental speech restriction as either "content based" or "content neutral." Depending on the outcome of that sequence of categorical moves, the judge would choose which category of "scrutiny" levels to apply to the speech restriction, whether "strict" or "rational basis" or a possible intermediate category.

In First Amendment jurisprudence, the "categorical approach" is usually contrasted with "balancing approaches" and "absolutist approaches."

Balancing approaches involve weighing the competing interests and rights at stake and assessing their relative strengths to decide whether the speaker or the government speech-restriction will prevail. Absolutist approaches take literally the First Amendment's command that "Congress shall make no law abridging the freedom of speech," and only ask whether the restricted speech at issue is genuinely speech rather than conduct.

The categorical approach has been viewed as more speech-protective than balancing approaches, particularly since the U.S. Supreme Court's use of a balancing method to decide a series of McCarthy-era speech cases in favor of government restrictions on speech (*Dennis v. United States* is the prime example). In addition to being seen as more protective generally of free speech rights, the categorical approach is praised by its proponents for being protective of those speech rights most in danger: the rights of unpopular or distasteful speakers. The categorical approach is commended for providing principled, objective guidance to courts, for helping judges take a pro-speech stand against the popular will, and for providing speakers with notice and fair warning about when governments can restrict speech. The categorical approach is also praised for bolstering the images of courts as dispensers of fair and equal treatment and for making judges less vulnerable to charges of legislating from the bench.

Opponents of categorical approaches, however, question the claimed objectivity of free-speech categories. What seem to be fixed, consistent categories can often be manipulated to produce the desired outcome in the case. Thus, liberal judges are more likely to classify as "content-based" laws regulating sexual expression, whereas conservative judges will often classify the same laws as "content-neutral;" conversely, liberal judges are more likely to categorize laws regulating abortion protesters as "content-neutral," whereas conservatives assign them to the "content-based" category of speech restrictions. Critics of the categorical approach charge that it is mere labeling, that it is mechanical and formulaic, and that it is not adaptable to a changing world and new technologies. Critics further complain that categories mask the real but unarticulated assessments of facts and policies that occur whenever judges decide speech cases. To the extent such "silent" covert judging happens, the development of constitutional jurisprudence suffers.

Although balancing approaches have been making a comeback in free-speech cases since the days when they were discredited as too pro-government, the multiple classification schemes that comprise the categorical approach remain the primary means of adjudication of free speech cases for the U.S. Supreme Court and the lower courts. Recent Supreme Court justices who are strong proponents of the categorical approach include Justices Scalia and Kennedy. See Justice Kennedy's defenses of categorical approaches in *Denver Area Educational Telecommunications Consortium* and in *Simon & Schuster*. An example of the Supreme Court using the categorical approach can be seen in Justice Kennedy's opinion for the Court in *Free Speech Coalition*.

The debate between advocates of categorizing and advocates of balancing parallels debates between advocates of "rules" and advocates of "standards."

IRENE SEGAL AYERS

References and Further Reading

Aleinikoff, T. Alexander, *Constitutional Law in the Age of Balancing*, Yale L. J. 943 (1987): 96.

Barron, Jerome A., *The Electronic Media and the Flight from First Amendment Doctrine: Justice Breyer's New Balancing Approach*, U. Mich. J. L. Reform 817 (1998): 31.

Huhn, Wilson R., *Assessing the Constitutionality of Laws that are Both Content-Based and Content-Neutral: The Emerging Constitutional Calculus*, Ind. L. J. 801 (2004): 79.

Scalia, Antonin, *The Rule of Law as a Law of Rules*, U. Chi. L. Rev. 1175 (1989): 56.

Smolla, Rodney A. *Smolla and Nimmer on Freedom of Speech*, vol. 1, 2:55–73. St. Paul, MN: West Group, 2003.

Sullivan, Kathleen M., *Post-Liberal Judging: The Roles of Categorization and Balancing*, U. Colo. L. Rev. 293 (1992): 63.

Cases and Statutes Cited

Ashcroft v. Free Speech Coalition, 535 U.S. 234 (2002)
Dennis v. United States, 341 U.S. 494 (1951)
Denver Area Educational Telecommunications Consortium, Inc. v. Federal Communications Commission, 518 U.S. 727, 780–812 (1996)
Simon & Schuster v. Members of the New York State Crime Victims Board, 502 U.S. 105 (1991)

See also **Absolutism and Free Speech;** *Ashcroft v. Free Speech Coalition*, **535 U.S. 234 (2002); Balancing Approach to Free Speech; Content-Based Regulation of Speech; Content-Neutral Regulation of Speech;** *Dennis v. United States*, **341 U.S. 494 (1951); Intermediate Scrutiny Test in Free Speech Cases; Public Forum Doctrines; Public/Nonpublic Forums Distinction**

CATHOLICS AND RELIGIOUS LIBERTY

The twentieth century witnessed a remarkable realignment of the Roman Catholic Church with the cause of religious liberty. The widespread embrace of individual rights among Western democracies in the eighteenth and nineteenth centuries had been met with skepticism by the Church, which traditionally favored a confessional state and insisted that freedom must rest on truth. This relationship between freedom and truth was understood to require that the state recognize and defend the Church's unique status among religions.

In his 1832 encyclical *Mirari vos*, for example, Pope Gregory XVI lamented the "absurd and erroneous proposition which claims that liberty of conscience must be maintained for everyone." Pope Pius IX, in his 1864 encyclical *Quanta cura*, warned that "if human arguments are always allowed free room for discussion, there will never be wanting men who will dare to resist truth." The encyclical's accompanying Syllabus of Errors listed among "the principal errors of our times" the increasingly popular beliefs that "every man is free to embrace and profess that religion which, guided by the light of reason, he shall consider true," that "it is no longer expedient that the Catholic religion should be held as the only religion of the State, to the exclusion of all other forms of worship," and the broader notion that "[t]he Church ought to be separated from the State, and the State from the Church." These sentiments were prompted, at least in part, by the era's persistent and violent anticlericalism, particularly in Europe; nevertheless, their breadth seemed to sweep in America's more conciliatory experiment in church–state separation.

An Evolving Embrace

The tone and substance of the Vatican's pronouncements on religious liberty had changed dramatically by the mid-twentieth century. The shift was part of a broader reconception of the Church's relationship with the modern world. Modern liberalism's individualist presumptions forced the Church to think more deeply and articulate more carefully the scope and relevance of natural rights. This exercise was not aimed simply at solidifying a defensive posture against individualism; rather, the Church sought to address the more pressing dangers of materialism, fascism, and communism. In other words, the overlap between the Church's world view and modern liberalism became more obvious as other, more foreboding, threats loomed.

First, as market economies spawned great disparities in wealth along with an increased emphasis on material consumption, the Church broadened and deepened its teaching on social justice, effectively linking itself with a broader progressive movement, initially focusing on the economic sphere, especially labor rights, but eventually extending to a variety of issues, including race. These causes facilitated the Church's friendlier stance toward individual rights generally, including religious liberty.

Second, in the wake of World War II, the Church was reminded that liberalism and fascism could not be considered moral equivalents. The Church could not be neutral, at least ideologically, on the contest that left Europe physically and spiritually devastated. More practically, World War II shaped the debate over religious liberty by forcing many European Catholic intellectuals to flee to the United States. A generation of influential thinkers was able to make firsthand comparisons between the American and European approaches to church–state separation. Given their divergent national histories, Americans saw liberalism as grounded in religion, whereas Europeans thought it necessary to escape religion to realize liberalism's promise. As a consequence, religion maintained its public relevance and vitality in the United States; this was not lost on observers.

Third, in the postwar climate, communism emerged as an even more overtly hostile threat, becoming the first political force of global reach founded on atheism. Not only did Western liberalism's emphasis on individual rights offer a preferred aspirational ideal, the rights-based system also offered the only realistic means by which to counter communism's expanding threat.

In addition to these sociopolitical factors, the Church's teaching on religious liberty was influenced by development in its theological stance toward other religions. The twentieth century saw renewed debate regarding the presence of truth and potential for salvation in other faith traditions. In this vein, the Second Vatican Council, in *Gaudium et spes* (1965), asserted the possibility of salvation "not only for Christians, but for all men of good will in whose hearts grace works in an unseen way." The Council also declared, in *Nostra aetate* (1965), that the Church "rejects nothing that is true and holy" in other religions and "regards with sincere reverence those ways of conduct and of life, those precepts and teachings which, though differing in many aspects from the ones she holds and sets forth, nonetheless often reflect a ray of that Truth which enlightens all men." Even more significantly, the Council warned that "[w]e cannot truly call on God, the Father of all, if we refuse to treat in a brotherly way any man, created as he is in the image of God." For purposes of religious liberty, this led to the essential recognition that "[n]o foundation therefore remains for any theory or practice that

leads to discrimination between man and man or people and people, so far as their human dignity and the rights flowing from it are concerned."

The Church's evolving embrace of religious liberty was also shaped by the work of several key Catholic intellectuals. Philosopher Jacques Maritain emphasized natural rights and played a key role in the development of the United Nations Declaration of Human Rights. The theology of Yves Congar, Henri de Lubac, and Karl Rahner displayed an increasing openness to much of modern human experience. Bernard Lonergan sought to reframe the conception of understanding in light of modernity. John Henry Newman made the provocative claim that the experience of the faithful has a role in the development of doctrine. These figures loom large in a story that proceeded, in significant part, as a theory-driven conversation.

But no figure looms as large as that of John Courtney Murray, the American theologian who insisted that state-sponsored religion need not be the Catholic ideal, that separate church and state spheres did not threaten—and indeed could enhance—the vitality of religion in society, and that economic and religious individualism must be distinguished from the political individualism of a rights-based democracy. Reflecting how stark his challenge was, he was forbidden by the Vatican from writing on church–state issues during the mid-1950s. (Indeed, virtually all of these key intellectual figures experienced significant institutional opposition from the Church at some point in their careers.) By the time of the Second Vatican Council (1962–1965), however, Murray managed to play an active role in drafting the key documents on which the Church's support for religious liberty would be based for years to come.

The Second Vatican Council

All of these contributing factors culminated in the Second Vatican Council's Declaration on Religious Freedom, *Dignitatis Humanae* (1965), in which the Church plainly declared that "the human person has a right to religious freedom." The key theoretical development was the Council's recognition of the civil sphere/religious sphere distinction, which facilitated in turn a distinction between moral or religious freedom and civil freedom. The Council stated that "[t]he truth cannot impose itself except by virtue of its own truth," and thus a person's "duty to worship God" demands "immunity from coercion in civil society." This left "untouched," in the Council's estimation, "traditional Catholic doctrine on the moral duty of men and societies toward the true religion and toward the one Church of Christ."

The perceived necessity of articulating a civil freedom of religion emanated from the nature of the human person. As "beings endowed with reason and free will and therefore privileged to bear personal responsibility," the Council explained that the human person must exercise his or her moral obligation to seek and adhere to truth, but that he or she can only do so if immune from external coercion. Thus, religious liberty "has its foundation not in the subjective disposition of the human person, but in his very nature," and immunity from external coercion "continues to exist even in those who do not live up to their obligation of seeking the truth and adhering to it." The dignity of the human person on which the Church's conception of religious liberty is founded is known not only through divine revelation—in particular, the "respect which Christ showed toward the freedom with which man is to fulfill his duty of belief in the word of God"—but also is knowable through the human reason developed over the course of human experience, and so is accessible universally.

The Second Vatican Council denied any suggestion that its declaration amounted to an about-face on religious liberty. While the Council acknowledged that "in the life of the People of God, as it has made its pilgrim way through the vicissitudes of human history, there has at times appeared a way of acting that was hardly in accord with the spirit of the Gospel or even opposed to it," it insisted that "the doctrine of the Church that no one is to be coerced into faith has always stood firm." Subsequently, Pope John Paul II has recognized that the Church's approach to human rights has been dynamic. In 1980, he observed that "[d]uring these last decades the Catholic Church has reflected deeply on the theme of human rights, especially on freedom of conscience and of religion," and that "in so doing, she has been stimulated by the daily life experience of the Church herself and of the faithful of all areas and social groups."

Championing the Cause

In the post–Vatican II era, John Paul II's contributions to the theme of religious liberty stand out, as they reflect his own experience with fascism and communism. His voice deepened the Church's

commitment to the civil sphere/religious sphere distinction, as explored in a 1980 letter:

> On the basis of his personal convictions, man is led to recognize and follow a religious or metaphysical concept involving his entire life with regard to fundamental choices and attitudes. This inner reflection, even if it does not result in an explicit and positive assertion of faith in God, cannot but be respected in the name of the dignity of each one's conscience, whose hidden searching may not be judged by others. Thus, on the one hand, each individual has the right and duty to seek the truth, and, on the other hand, other persons as well as civil society have the corresponding duty to respect the free spiritual development of each person.

Indeed, in John Paul II's estimation, religious liberty is foundational of all other liberties "insofar as it touches the innermost sphere of the spirit." His unwavering commitment to religious liberty became especially noteworthy as he used the Church's moral authority as a leading rallying point of efforts to liberate Soviet bloc countries.

All of this is not to suggest that the Church's vision of religious liberty has simply melded into the vision embodied in mainstream secular liberalism. The Church has long understood religious liberty not just as an individual right, but is a bulwark against state interference with society's religious institutions. And at the individual level, the Church stakes out positions requiring a more robust conception of religious liberty than many modern liberals will grant. For example, the Church expects authentic religious liberty to encompass parents' choice of schooling options for their children. As stated in *Dignitatis Humanae*, the Church expects the government to "acknowledge the right of parents to make a genuinely free choice of schools and of other means of education, and the use of this freedom of choice is not to be made a reason for imposing unjust burdens on parents, whether directly or indirectly." Religious liberty also cannot be equated, in the Church's view, with privatized religion. On this front, the Vatican expressed its concern to the United Nations that "[t]he greater exercise of individual freedoms may result in greater intolerance and greater legal constraints on the public expressions of people's beliefs," and that "what is being challenged, in effect, is the right of religious communities to participate in public, democratic debate in the way that other social forces are allowed to do."

On the core concept of religious liberty, however, civil libertarians have a stalwart ally in the Roman Catholic Church. Moreover, by grounding the case for liberty in the very nature of the human person, the Church's approach may offer a more compelling, less transient justification than the necessarily contingent defense of liberty emerging from the majoritarian and pragmatic foundations used in modern liberal dialogue.

ROBERT K. VISCHER

References and Further Reading

Bruce, Douglass, R., and David Hollenbach, eds. *Catholicism and Liberalism: Contributions to American Public Philosophy*. Cambridge: University Press, 1994.
McGreevey, John T. *Catholicism and American Freedom: A History*. New York: W.W. Norton & Co., 2003.
Murray, John Courtney. *Religious Liberty: Catholic Struggles With Pluralism*. Louisville: Westminster/John Knox Press, 1993.
Steinfels, Margaret O'Brien, ed. *American Catholics and Civil Engagement: A Distinctive Voice*. New York: Rowan & Littlefield, 2004.

CATT, CARRIE CHAPMAN (1859–1947)

In 1859, Carrie Chapman Catt was born Carrie Clinton Lane in Wisconsin. She and her family soon moved to Iowa where she graduated with a bachelor's degree from Iowa State Agricultural College in 1880. During college, she enjoyed public speaking and after reading law for a year after college, she began teaching high school. She then became the school's principal and the superintendent of schools. In 1885, she wed Leo Chapman, the editor of the weekly *Mason City Republican*. She became coeditor of the paper and created a feature known as "Woman's World" to discuss women's rights issues. Due to political problems evolving from accusations made by Leo Chapman in the paper and an eventual lawsuit, the Chapmans sold the paper and left town. Leo looked for work in San Francisco while Carrie stayed with her parents. En route to see Leo, she received word that her husband had died of typhoid fever. Carrie remained in San Francisco for a year, where she worked as a reporter and began lecturing. She then returned to her hometown of Charles City, Iowa, to continue lecturing and working for local newspapers. She also joined the Woman's Christian Temperance Union at this time.

When she attended the Iowa Woman Suffrage Association convention in 1889, the association elected her state lecturer and organizer. At the national suffrage convention in 1890, the two leading woman suffrage organizations reunited as the NAWSA (National American Woman Suffrage Amendment) after a rupture two decades earlier, recognizing both methods of attaining woman suffrage—through state amendments and through a federal constitutional amendment. Also in 1890, Chapman married engineer George Catt. During her first election campaign as a budding feminist politician, Catt went to South Dakota in 1891 to help gain support for a referendum to enfranchise women, and the campaign went disastrously. The following year, the Catts moved to New York. She continued her speaking engagements and became head of the NAWSA's new business committee. Catt wrote detailed instructions on how to start and maintain suffrage clubs, and she significantly helped to both create new and revitalize local clubs. At the 1893 World's Columbian Exposition, Catt began thinking about working with women on an international level. In 1902, she founded the International Woman Suffrage Alliance (IWSA) nearly entirely on her own and despite substantial opposition from her very powerful mentor, Susan B. Anthony. Catt held the presidency of the NAWSA from 1900 to 1904, but resigned her office then due to her husband George's poor health.

Catt continued both her national and international work for women, but her own health was deteriorating. In 1911, in a trip around the world, she announced that the battle for justice must be for the women of the entire world. In 1915, she again became president of the NAWSA and remained its president through the successful passage of the Nineteenth Amendment—which gave women the right to vote—in 1920. Throughout this time period, Catt and the NAWSA supported gaining the vote by constitutional means, whether through individual states or through a federal amendment. States were necessary because they could use their representatives to press for a federal bill, and the federal amendment was essential since it might be nearly impossible to get every individual state to ensure women the franchise.

When the United States declared war on Germany in 1917, the NAWSA decided to stand by the government. Catt would be widely criticized for NAWSA's decision, with pacifists accusing her of selling out to war and antisuffragists criticizing her lack of wartime work. Yet Catt herself had opposed war throughout her life, and in 1915, along with Jane Addams, she helped found the Woman's Peace party. She considered peace to be the greatest objective of any reformer. Catt led a critical suffrage campaign in New York State through the New York Woman Suffrage party that she founded earlier in the decade. Along with New York, six other states passed woman suffrage in 1917. In May 1919, the House ratified the woman suffrage bill, and the Senate followed the following month. After being passed by three quarters of the states, the Nineteenth Amendment passed into law on August 26, 1920.

Once woman suffrage was gained, Catt shifted her emphasis to increasing women's political power. In 1925, Catt organized the first annual Conference on the Cause and Cure of War to promote international solutions to conflict. Throughout her life, Catt led women throughout the world in the quest for suffrage. She died at her home in New York in 1947.

MELISSA OOTEN

References and Further Reading

Catt, Carrie Chapman, and Nettie Rogers Shuler. *Woman Suffrage and Politics: The Inner Story of the Suffrage Movement.* New York: Scribner's, 1926.
Fowler, Robert. *Carrie Catt: Feminist Politician.* Boston: Northeastern University Press, 1986.
Peck, Mary. *Carrie Chapman Catt: A Biography.* New York: The HW Wilson Company, 1944.

See also **Anthony, Susan B.**

CENTRAL HUDSON GAS AND ELECTRIC CORP. v. PUBLIC SERVICE COMMISSION OF NEW YORK, 447 U.S. 557 (1980)

In 1973, when an oil embargo caused fuel shortages, the New York Public Service Commission issued a regulation prohibiting electric companies from advertising to promote electricity use. Central Hudson Gas & Electric, a public utility company, challenged the regulation, arguing that its advertisements were commercial speech protected by the First Amendment.

Before the 1970s, commercial speech was viewed as outside the scope of First Amendment protection. By the mid-1970s, however, the Supreme Court began recognizing some degree of protection for commercial speech, striking down advertising restrictions in *Bigelow* and *Virginia State Board of Pharmacy*.

In *Central Hudson*, the U.S. Supreme Court ruled that the ban on advertisements for electricity violated the First Amendment. In doing so, the Court established a four-part test, balancing government and commercial-speech interests to determine when commercial-speech regulations infringe on free-speech rights. Under this "intermediate scrutiny" test, if the commercial speech is truthful and relates to lawful activity, the regulation must directly advance a substantial government interest and be no more extensive than necessary to serve that interest.

In *Central Hudson*, the Court held that although energy conservation represented a substantial government interest, and the restriction on advertising directly advanced that interest, the restriction was more extensive than necessary, as it banned even advertisements for products and services that use energy efficiently.

Since 1980, the *Central Hudson* test has endured as the standard governing regulation of commercial speech, despite being frequently criticized as too malleable, both by those favoring greater protection for commercial speech and by those favoring more government control over commercial speech. The most vocal critic of the *Central Hudson* test has been U.S. Supreme Court Justice Clarence Thomas, who would deem per se illegitimate any asserted government interest in withholding information from the public to manipulate their choices in the marketplace.

IRENE SEGAL AYERS

References and Further Reading

Blasi, Vincent, *The Pathological Perspective and the First Amendment*, Columbia Law Review 449 (1985): 85:484–89.
Hudson, David L., Jr., *Justice Clarence Thomas: The Emergence of a Commercial-Speech Protector*, Creighton Law Review 485 (2002): 35.
Kozinski, Alex, and Stuart Banner, *Who's Afraid of Commercial Speech?* Virginia Law Review 627 (1990): 76.
Post, Robert, *The Constitutional Status of Commercial Speech*, UCLA Law Review 1 (2000): 48.
Smolla, Rodney A. *Smolla and Nimmer on Freedom of Speech*, vol. 2, 20:1–47, St. Paul, MN: West Group, 2003.
Sullivan, Kathleen, *Cheap Spirits, Cigarettes, and Free Speech: The Implications of* 44 Liquormart, 1996, Supreme Court Review 123 (1996).

Cases and Statutes Cited

Bigelow v. Virginia, 421 U.S. 809 (1975)
Virginia State Board of Pharmacy v. Virginia Citizens Consumer Council, Inc., 425 U.S. 748 (1976)

See also **Balancing Approach to Free Speech; Balancing Test; Commercial Speech; First Amendment Balancing;** *44 Liquormart v. Rhode Island*, **517 U.S. 484 (1996); Freedom of Speech Extended to Corporations; Intermediate Scrutiny Test in Free Speech Cases; Thomas, Clarence;** *Virginia State Board of Pharmacy v. Virginia Citizens Consumer Council, Inc.*, **425 U.S. 748 (1976)**

CENTRAL INTELLIGENCE AGENCY

As a result of the need for intelligence on the Axis Powers during World War II, the Office of Strategic Services (OSS) was created. After the war, policy makers realized the need for foreign intelligence.

Consequently, in 1947 the National Security Act was passed by Congress, creating the Central Intelligence Agency (CIA). The CIA absorbed the duties of the OSS, additionally taking on the responsibility of coordinating, evaluating, and disseminating intelligence from other U.S. agencies and advising both the president and the National Security Council. The CIA was one of the primary agencies on the front lines of the Cold War, often operating clandestinely in enemy territory.

After the 2001 terrorist attacks, political pressure led to the restructuring of the Intelligence Community of the United States. The CIA, once the hub of the community, came under the umbrella of a community-wide Director of National Intelligence (DNI) on February 17, 2005. The CIA still retains the community's most sizable and well-funded Human Intelligence (HUMINT) function, housed within the Directorate of Operations (DO). The DO, often cited as the most controversial and publicized section of the CIA, is only one of four directorates. The Directorate of Intelligence (DI) analyzes and disseminates collected intelligence. The Directorate of Science and Technology assists with technological systems and devices, document creation, disguises, and other technical activities. Finally, the Directorate of Support (DS), formerly the Directorate of Administration, handles finances, logistical support, security and background investigation, and other administrative activities.

The CIA relies heavily on the expertise of undercover foreign operatives even though their use has been controversial even before the CIA was created. As far back as 1876, the Supreme Court heard a case regarding the use of such operatives by the president in which the Court upheld their use. The CIA has often been the subject of criticism and accusations of legal violations because all of their operations are based on secrecy. Even the exact budget of the CIA is kept secret. In a democracy based on openness, this lack of transparency makes some elements of society uncomfortable. Though it could be argued that the secret nature of the organization and its budget are, in fact, the result of democratic governance, wherein the majority of Americans democratically support the decision.

After the creation of the CIA, the agency faced some of its harshest criticism during the Watergate investigation. During this time, President Nixon was accused of attempting to use the CIA to halt an investigation being conducted by the Federal Bureau of Investigations (FBI), which eventually led to accusations of obstruction of justice against President Nixon.

In addition, the CIA has been accused of several violations of civil liberties in foreign countries regarding various assassination plots of foreign leaders. After the CIA failed to recognize the terrorist threat prior to September 11, 2001, the agency has been under a lot of pressure to aggressively locate and stop terrorist organizations. The CIA has been accused of hiding information regarding their knowledge and actions. Often, the CIA has been questioned about their use of torture as an interrogation method, although the CIA has consistently denied that it engages in such violations of law and human rights.

CAROL WALKER

References and Further Reading

Andrew, Christopher. *For the President's Eyes Only*. New York: Harper Collins, 1996.

Breckinridge, Scott D. *The CIA and the U.S. Intelligence System*. Boulder: Westview Press, 1986.

Farren, Mick. *CIA: Secrets of The Company*. Barnes & Noble Books: New York, 2003.

Kessler, Ronald. *The CIA at War: Inside the Secret Campaign Against Terror*, 1st ed. New York: St. Martin's Press, 2003.

Olmsted, Kathryn S. *Challenging the Secret Government: The Post-Watergate Investigations of the CIA and the FBI*. Chapel Hill, NC: University of North Carolina Press, 1996.

Shulsky, Abram, and Gary Schmitt. *Silent Warfare: Understanding the World of Intelligence*. Washington DC: Brassey's Inc., 2002.

CEREMONIAL DEISM

One of the difficult church–state issues is determining when the use of religious language by the government violates the Establishment Clause. During the past quarter century, a few Supreme Court justices have defined certain types of government religious speech as "ceremonial deism"—speech that though religious in nature has a secular purpose and hence is constitutional.

The phrase originates with Eugene Rostow, then Dean of the Yale Law School, who explained in his 1962 Meiklejohn Lecture at Brown University that certain types of religious speech, which he called "ceremonial deism," were "so conventional and uncontroversial as to be constitutional." Although Rostow's speech was unpublished, Harvard law professor Arthur Sutherland discussed Rostow's use of ceremonial deism in an essay in the *Indiana Law Journal* in 1964, which helped to give the concept prominence among jurists and legal scholars.

Twenty years later, in 1984, Justice William Brennan became the first U.S. Supreme Court justice to invoke the phrase ceremonial deism to explain aspects of the Court's Establishment Clause jurisprudence. In his dissenting opinion in *Lynch v. Donnelly* (1984), a case in which the Court considered the constitutionality of a government-supported holiday display that contained religious symbols, Justice Brennan explained that certain types of government religious speech "serve such wholly secular purposes as solemnizing public occasions, or inspiring commitment to meet some national challenge in a manner that simply could not be fully served in our culture if government were limited to purely nonreligious phrases." For Brennan, religious speech such as "the designation of 'in God We Trust' as our national motto, or the references to God contained in the Pledge of Allegiance to the flag can best be understood, in Dean Rostow's apt phrase, as a form of 'ceremonial deism,' protected from Establishment Clause scrutiny chiefly because they have lost through rote repetition any significant religious content." For Justice Brennan, these religious expressions have "an essentially secular meaning."

Five years later, in *County of Allegheny v. ACLU* (1989), another case dealing with the constitutionality of religious symbols in holiday displays, Justice Sandra Day O'Connor also used the phrase ceremonial deism to explain why certain religious speech by government actors does not violate the Establishment Clause: "Practices such as legislative prayer or opening Court sessions with 'God save the United States and this honorable Court' serve the secular purposes of 'solemnizing public occasions' and 'expressing confidence in the future.'" For Justice O'Connor, it was not enough that these forms of religious speech enjoyed long historical practice. Rather, what was crucial was that this use of religious language had a secular purpose, as opposed to a purpose of promoting religion. In that same case, Justice Harry Blackmun also relied on the concept of ceremonial deism for his conclusion that certain forms of governmental religious speech are "not understood as conveying government approval of particular religious beliefs."

More recently, in *Elk Grove Unified School District v. Newdow* (2004), Justice O'Connor again invoked the concept of ceremonial deism when addressing in a concurring opinion the constitutionality of the phrase "under God" in the Pledge of Allegiance recited in public schools. Justice O'Connor described as ceremonial deism that government religious speech about which there is "a shared understanding of its legitimate nonreligious purposes." For O'Connor, four factors were relevant to an assessment of whether religious speech has the requisite "nonreligious purpose" to render it a constitutional expression of ceremonial deism: (1) whether the speech has "been in

place for a significant portion of the Nation's history" and has been "observed by enough persons that it can fairly be called ubiquitous"; (2) whether the speech does not constitute "worship or prayer"; (3) whether there is an absence of reference to a *particular* religion; and (4) whether the speech contains "minimal reference" to religion at all. For Justice O'Connor, the "under God" language in the Pledge of Allegiance satisfied all four factors and hence was constitutional ceremonial deism.

No other justice joined Justice O'Connor's opinion in the *Newdow* case, and no other sitting justice has authored an opinion using the phrase ceremonial deism, but even for those justices who do not expressly rely on the concept of ceremonial deism as part of their Establishment Clause jurisprudence, all of the justices agree that the question whether government speech has a religious or secular purpose is highly relevant to an assessment of the constitutionality of that speech. Many lower courts have used, and continue to use, the concept of ceremonial deism in determining whether government religious speech offends the Establishment Clause.

DAVISON M. DOUGLAS

References and Further Reading

Epstein, Steven B., *Rethinking the Constitutionality of Ceremonial Deism*, Columbia Law Review 96 (1996): 2083–2174.
Sutherland, Arthur, *Book Review (Religion and American Constitutions, by Wilber G. Katz)*, Indiana Law Journal 40 (1964): 83–87.
Warren, Charles Gregory, *No Need to Stand on Ceremony: The Corruptive Influence of Ceremonial Deism and the Need for a Separationist Reconfiguration of the Supreme Court's Establishment Clause Jurisprudence*, Mercer Law Review 54 (2003): 1669–1718.

Cases and Statutes Cited

County of Allegheny v. ACLU, 492 U.S. 573 (1989)
Elk Grove Unified School District v. Newdow, 542 U.S. 1 (2004)
Lynch v. Donnelly, 465 U.S. 668 (1984)

See also **Establishment Clause (I): History, Background, Framing; National Motto "In God We Trust"; O'Connor, Sandra Day; Pledge of Allegiance ("Under God")**

CHAE CHAN PING v. U.S., 130 U.S. 581 (1889) AND CHINESE EXCLUSION ACT

Chinese first emigrated to the United States in large numbers in 1849, when they joined thousands of

Americans and other foreign fortune-seekers in the "gold rush" to the American West. By 1852, there were approximately 25,000 Chinese in California. With the federal government's blessing, more entered in the 1860s, when they provided cheap labor to complete the nation's railroad system. By the time of the 1880 census, 105,465 Chinese were counted in the United States. Concentrated in the West, Chinese made up 8.7 percent of California's population.

As the numbers of Chinese grew and labor needs subsided, the California legislature repeatedly tried to regulate their activities, as did some other Western states. Under California law, Chinese were subject to entry taxes and discriminatory regulation of their businesses, they were not allowed to vote or testify in court, and their children were prohibited from attending school with white children. Most of these state and local statutes were declared invalid by federal courts.

But beginning in the 1870s, California's demand for restrictive legislation began to have a national impact. In an unprecedented series of laws in 1882, 1884, 1888, 1892, 1902, and 1904, Congress enacted the "Chinese exclusion laws," designed to regulate, deter, and ultimately prevent, further Chinese immigration to the United States. The 1882 legislation imposed a ten-year suspension on immigration by Chinese laborers and restricted the ability of Chinese residing in the United States to re-enter after a trip abroad. These restrictions were refined and expanded in subsequent enactments. They quickly had the desired effect; in 1887, Chinese immigration fell to a low of ten admitted Chinese immigrants. However, these laws were not without controversy. With the case of *Chae Chan Ping v. United States*, the Chinese exclusion laws became the first federal immigration laws to be subject to judicial scrutiny.

Chae Chan Ping was a Chinese laborer who entered the United States in 1875. He lived in San Francisco for twelve years until 1887, when he left to visit relatives in China. Before departing, he obtained the "certificate of identity" required by the 1882 and 1884 acts that would permit him to re-enter the United States after his trip.

While Chae Chan Ping was in China, Congress enacted the 1888 Chinese exclusion law, called the Scott Act. Under the act, Congress suspended issuance of identity certificates, and specifically stated that no Chinese who had left the country would be permitted to re-enter, even if they held certificates that had been validly issued before the 1888 Act. Chae Chan Ping was stranded. He attempted to return to the United States less than a week after the 1888 Act came into effect, but he was denied readmission. He sued, claiming that the 1888 Act violated the Constitution and conflicted with treaties between the United States and China that provided for admission of Chinese laborers.

A unanimous Supreme Court upheld the 1888 Act. The Court treated the legislation with extreme deference, invoking the U. S. government's inherent power to control its borders. According to the Court, despite Chae Chan Ping's long-time residence in the United States, his government-issued identity certificate was revocable at any time. Furthermore, the Court opined, if China was concerned about United States' compliance with treaty obligations, it could raise this directly with the political branches. Treaty enforcement was not an issue for judges.

After this decision, Congress further expanded Chinese exclusion laws with the Geary Act in 1892. The 1892 legislation extended suspension of immigration of Chinese laborers for another ten years. It also required that all Chinese laborers living in the United States obtain a certificate of residence from the commission of internal revenue. The certificate would be issued only with the support of an affidavit from a witness (presumably white) who attested to the alien's residence. Without a certificate, the alien would be subject to deportation. Although this statute was challenged on numerous constitutional grounds, it was upheld by the Supreme Court in 1893 in the case of *Fong Yue Ting v. United States* (1893). In 1902, Congress extended the suspension of Chinese immigration once again, this time with no termination date. And in 1904, in the Chinese Exclusion Extension Act, the exclusion provisions were made permanent and extended to citizens of the Philippines.

The Chinese exclusion laws and the cases challenging them have had a lasting impact on immigration law and on the experiences of Chinese in the United States. First, the Chinese exclusion cases established the principle of extreme judicial deference to congressional and executive authority over immigration—a principle that, while often challenged, has never been explicitly revoked. Second, the Chinese exclusion laws set the stage for later race- and ethnicity-based immigration restrictions—for example, the exclusion of Japanese and Koreans in the early 1900s—and even the Japanese internments of the 1940s. With the Chinese exclusion laws, the federal government began regulating who could be an "American," with a significant impact on nonwhite residents and citizens. Third, the implementation of the Chinese exclusion acts served as a model for the identity inspections and documentation requirements that continue to proliferate at the U. S. border. Finally, the Chinese exclusion laws had a significant impact on Chinese families, forcing long (and often permanent) separations. Indeed, the exclusion of Chinese remained part of U. S.

immigration policy until 1943 when, in an act of World War II diplomacy, the laws were repealed by the Magnuson Act and replaced with a strict entry quota for Chinese. Combined with earlier policies such as the Page Act that favored the migration of male laborers, these laws cast a long shadow on the experiences of Chinese Americans.

MARTHA F. DAVIS

References and Further Reading

Chin, Gabriel J. "Chae Chan Ping and Fong Yue Ting: The Origins of Plenary Power." *Immigration Stories 7*, David A. Martin and Peter H. Schuck eds, Foundation Press, 2005.

Gyory, Andrew. *Closing the Gate: Race, Politics and the Chinese Exclusion Act*, Chapel Hill: University of North Carolina Press, 1998.

Hing, Bill Ong. *Making and Remaking Asian America Through Immigration Policy, 1850–1990*. Stanford, CA: Stanford University Press, 1993.

Lee, Erika. *At America's Gates: Chinese Immigration During the Exclusion Era, 1882–1943*. Chapel Hill: University of North Caroline Press, 2003.

McLain, Charles, Jr. *In Search of Equality: The Chinese Struggle against Discrimination in Nineteenth Century America*, Berkeley, CA: University of California Pressb, 1994.

Cases and Statutes Cited

Chinese Exclusion Act, Act of May 6, 1882, c. 126, 22 Stat. 58

Chinese Exclusion Act, Act of July 5, 1884, c. 220, 23 Stat. 117

Chinese Exclusion Act, Act of April 29, 1902, c. 641, 32 Stat. 176

Chinese Exclusion Extension Act, April 27, 1904, c. 1630, 33 Stat. 394

Fong Yue Ting v. United States, 149 U.S. 698 (1893)

Geary Act, Act of May 5, 1892, c. 60, 27 Stat. 25

Magnuson Act (Chinese Exclusion Repeal Act), Act of Dec. 17, 1943, c. 344, 57 Stat. 600

Page Act, Act of March 3, 1875, c. 141, 18 Stat. 477

Scott (Chinese Exclusion) Act, Act of October 1, 1888, c. 1064, 25 Stat. 504

See also **Due Process in Immigration; Noncitizens Civil Liberties; Race and Immigration; Sex and Immigration**

CHAFEE, ZECHARIAH, JR. (1885–1957)

Zechariah Chafee Jr., attorney, professor, legal scholar and well-known champion of civil liberties, was born on December 7, 1885, in Providence, Rhode Island. The son of Zechariah Chafee, Brown University Trustee and president of Builders Iron Foundry, Chafee Jr. attended Brown for his undergraduate degree. Chafee was an excellent student, graduating Phi Beta Kappa in 1907. After graduation, Chafee worked at his father's business for several years. In 1910, after finding the work unsatisfying, Chafee entered Harvard Law School, receiving his law degree in 1913. On graduation, Chafee moved back to Providence to begin his legal career at Tillinghast and Collins. In 1916, Chafee returned to Harvard Law School to take a position as a professor. He would remain at Harvard until his retirement in July 1956. Less then a year after his retirement, Chafee died in Boston, Massachusetts, on February 8, 1957.

Chafee's law school interest in civil liberties crystallized into a focus on the First Amendment as a law professor. Chafee deeply opposed the treatment of anti-war protesters during World War I under the Espionage Act of 1917 and the Sedition Act of 1918, which made it a crime to interfere with the operation of the U.S. military, as well as to speak out against the government or the Constitution. Chafee criticized the statutes as being unconstitutional and laid out his philosophy in a 1919 Harvard Law Review article entitled "Freedom of Speech in Wartime." The article was criticized by a group of Harvard alums that accused Chafee of being a radical and unfit for teaching. They attempted to have Chafee removed from that law school faculty. Although Chafee survived dismissal by a slim one-vote margin, he did not temper his advocacy for the freedom of speech and press. A year later, Chafee published *Freedom of Speech*, which expanded on the views he expressed in the law review article by criticizing current notions of free speech while emphasizing his belief that certain forms of free speech were absolutely essential to a healthy democracy. *Freedom of Speech* would go on the influence First Amendment law for a generation. In 1941, on the eve of the United States' entry into World War II, Chafee republished an updated and revised version of his 1920 book under the new title *Free Speech in the United States*.

In addition to his personal writings, Chafee was an active member in the civil libertarian community. He defended the freedom of speech and civil liberties every chance he could get. In 1920, Chafee, along with future Supreme Court Justice Felix Frankfurter and other prominent attorneys published *To the American People: A Report upon the Illegal Practices of the United States Department of Justice*, which criticized the Justice Department's frequent violations of the Constitution during the Palmer Raids. Chafee also helped to prepare the 1931 *Report on the Lawlessness in Law Enforcement* for the Wickersham Commission, which looked into police misconduct in the administration of justice. Most importantly, however, Chafee had access to or influence on some of the most prominent jurists of the nation including Supreme Court Justices Louis Brandeis, William Cardozo, Hugo Black, and William O. Douglas. Chafee is widely credited with changing Justice Oliver Wendall Holmes' conception of free speech after his opinion in *Schenck v. United States*.

Chafee was not without his critics. In the 1950s during the House Committee on Un-American Activities' (HUAC) investigations of communist plots against the nation, his opponents often described him as a weak-minded liberal who actively aided communists at home and abroad. Moreover, Chafee's legal philosophy has been and continues to be criticized as inaccurate and placing too heavy an emphasis on the World War I Espionage and Sedition Act cases as the beginning of serious judicial consideration of free speech in America.

While Chafee was a noted authority in many areas of law including evidence, copyright law, and civil procedure, for which he drafted the Federal Interpleader Act of 1936, he is best known for his First Amendment analysis. Indeed, Chafee is frequently regarded as the individual most responsible for the modern constitutional interpretation of the freedom of speech.

Chafee's First Amendment theory was based on the idea that free speech served an essential role in a democracy. He believed that the Framers' purpose in passing the First Amendment was to abolish the law of seditious libel, or the defiant criticism of the government, that was commonly used in England. In addition, Chafee believed that the First Amendment not only protected the press from censorship but also allowed the press the ability to have unhindered discussion of public affairs.

Chafee argued that one of the most fundamental responsibilities of a democratic government is to investigate and spread truths that are of universal concern to the population at large. Accordingly, the best means to discover the truth or to learn what problems exist and therefore how to attempt change was to have open and unlimited debate. Chafee thought restrictions on free speech would cause greater damage to a society then any harm that might come as the result of open discussion. Contrary to many of his contemporaries, Chafee believed that open and unlimited discussion was most important during wartime, because it was during war when people are under the most pressure to conform to the majority. During wartime, society had the greatest need to learn both sides of the argument to determine the truth. Under Chafee's analysis, wartime restrictions on speech served only to produce empty, one-sided talk that was useless in determining the truth.

Chafee placed an equally important role for the protection of free speech on the average citizen. He argued that if the community itself didn't stand up for open speech, then laws protecting freedom speech would be ineffective. Chafee believed that community customs against free speech had as destructive an effect on free speech as a restriction by statute.

Chafee believed that two forms of expression existed: expressions of individual interest, where people express themselves on matters that are important to them personally, and expressions of social interest, where people express words that convey ideas that are concerned with essential or socially valuable principles. Chafee wrote that since expressions of social interest focus on the search for truths that will help keep order in society and safeguard morality, they were more important then expressions of individual interest. As a consequence, Chafee argued that expressions of social interest must be afforded the greatest protection from censorship and should only be restricted when it is absolutely certain to incite or cause harm to public safety.

Chafee, however, did not believe that the Framers intended there to be an absolute right to freedom of speech under every circumstance. He thought that obscene, profane, indecent, and defamatory speech should not protected. Chafee argued that these forms of speech were more like acts then words. Moreover, he said that since they offered little if any chance for a counter-argument, they could not convey any socially valuable ideas. Under Chafee's analysis, because of their ability to inflict immediate injury on the listener, incite unlawful acts, or disturb the important societal interests in peace of mind, order, and the training of the young, their expression could be censored, restricted, or punished. For Chafee, however, the scope of what was included in obscene, profane, indecent, and defamatory speech needed to be narrow to protect against the inclusion of unpopular ideas as expressions that cause or incite harm or injury.

Chafee also believed that the freedom of speech, or more specifically, the freedom of debate extended to members of Congress. Indeed, he believed that the right of members to be free to debate was so important to the Framers that they included it in the Constitution under Article 1, Section 6, rather then in the Bill of Rights. He held that there was an intimate connection between the freedom to debate in Congress and the freedom of speech of the private citizen, because the basis for limiting freedom of debate in government was similar to that used to limit freedom of speech in society at large. For Chafee, just as the freedom of speech in society helped in the attainment of truth, freedom of debate in Congress helped to bring about the most efficient management of the government affairs.

Similar to his theories on freedom of speech, Chafee also believed that freedom of debate was not unlimited. He believed that the freedom to debate extended only to what members did as part of the business of Congress. All debate outside of these parameters was open to punishment. The Constitution, however, made clear that only fellow members of Congress had the ability to punish abuses of the freedom of debate. Accordingly, Chafee believed that members had a positive duty to police themselves and ensure that the freedom of debate did not result in slanderous speech against private citizens or interests.

Chafee's arguments for the right of all people to speak their mind without fear of punishment continues to play an important role in American society.

MARCEL GREEN

References and Further Reading

Chafee, Zechariah Jr., *Freedom of Speech in Wartime*, Harvard Law Review 32, (1919): 932.
——. *Free Speech in the United States*. Cambridge, MA: Harvard University Press, 1948.
Smith, Donald L. *Zechariah Chafee, Jr., Defender of Liberty and Law*. Cambridge: Harvard University Press, 1984.

Cases and Statutes Cited

Schenck v. United States, 249 U.S. 47 (1919)

CHAIN GANGS

In the late 1860s, state legislatures authorized judges to sentence offenders to work on chain gangs. Traditionally, these gangs would spend ten to twelve hours a day breaking rocks with sledgehammers while they were bound together at the ankles with heavy chains and shackles. Members of the chain gang were allowed to change their clothes only once a week. They slept chained together and remained chained at all times even when defecating in a bucket—their only toilet.

Prison guards constantly threatened and physically abused chain gang members. Special forms of torture were also used to control the chain gangs. For example, the sweat-box treatment involved locking a prisoner into a wooden box that was too short to stand in but not deep enough to sit in. The prisoner would remain in the box for days while temperatures within the box exceeded 100 degrees.

Because the majority of chain gang members were African-American men, many citizens opposed the existence of chain gangs on the basis of racial discrimination. The brutal and inhumane treatment of chain gang members was also criticized. In addition, organized labor opposed chain gangs because they constituted a form of "slave" labor. As a result of this opposition, chain gangs were eventually eliminated from the United States' landscape sometime around the 1930s.

In 1995, however, chain gangs reappeared in several states including Alabama, Arizona, Florida, Iowa, Kentucky, Oklahoma, Mississippi, Nevada, Tennessee, and Wisconsin. At least five of these states have enacted statutes that require inmates to spend a portion of their sentence working on chain gangs. In the other states, chain gangs participation is permitted but not required.

As a result of the new laws, several inmates have filed lawsuits challenging the use of chain gangs as cruel and unusual punishment in violation of the Eighth Amendment. In *Austin v. James*, a lawsuit filed by the Southern Poverty Law Center (SPLC), the state of Alabama agreed in a settlement to stop chaining inmates together.

The SPLC was also able to secure a finding by the Federal Court that the practice of handcuffing chain gang members to a metal rail (the "hitching post") in the Alabama heat for several hours without water or bathroom breaks was a violation of the Eighth Amendment of the United States Constitution.

Other groups, such as Amnesty International, believe that chain gangs violate international laws such as Article 7 of the International Covenant on Civil and Political Rights and Article 33 of the United Nations Standard Minimum Rules for the Treatment of Prisoners.

JUDITH A. M. SCULLY

References and Further Reading

Oshinsky, David. *Worse than Slavery: Parchman Farm and the Ordeal of Jim Crow Justice*. Free Press Paperbacks, 1996.
Southern Poverty Law Center—*Austin v. James* (Case Number 95 CV 637, U.S.D.C. Alabama 1995) available at http://www.splcenter.org/legal/landmark/prison.jsp.

CHAMBERS v. FLORIDA, 309 U.S. 227 (1940)

Torturing a man to confess a crime is an ancient evil. Subtler pressures can also break a man. Under the Fifth Amendment, *Bram v. United States*, and the Fourteenth Amendment, the Constitution outlaws the use of mental pressure or physical force to get a confession. "And they who have suffered most from secret and dictatorial proceedings have almost always been the poor, the ignorant, the numerically weak, the friendless, and the powerless." Justice Black's steel prose in *Chambers v. Florida* was extolled by Justice Frankfurter as "One of the enduring utterances in the history of the Supreme Court and in the annals of human freedom."

The petitioners were four "ignorant young colored tenant farmers" arrested without a warrant on suspicion of having robbed and murdered an elderly white man. The community was outraged. The sheriff rounded up a group of blacks, locked them in jail, and subjected them to relentless questioning for a week on the fourth floor of the county jail. One was told "if I didn't come across I would never see the sun rise." After a concluding all-night session, Chambers and the other petitioners gave their "sunrise confessions."

Justice Black reversed the Florida Supreme Court and petitioners' death sentences. *Chambers* is half way between Hughes's due process condemnation of coerced confessions in *Brown v. Mississippi* (1936) and Black's later dissent in *Adamson v. California* (1947). Thus in *Chambers* Black speaks of "fundamental standards of procedure in criminal trials" and one of those fundamentals, according to Hugo Black, is the Fifth Amendment's prohibition against self-incrimination. At the time of *Chambers*, the Supreme Court had not yet come around to Justice Black's view; *Twining v. New Jersey* (1908) stood in the way. The "current of opinion" mentioned in a careful footnote in *Chambers* "—that the Fourteenth Amendment was intended to make secure against state invasion all the rights, privileges and immunities protected from federal invasion by the Bill of Rights"—was Hugo Black's own.

Justice Black did something unprecedented in 1968, appearing on national television. With great emotion, Justice Black read from the closing part of his opinion in *Chambers v. Florida*:

Under our constitutional system, courts stand against any winds that blow as havens of refuge for those who might otherwise suffer because they are helpless, weak, outnumbered, or because they are non-conforming victims of prejudice and public excitement. Due process of law, preserved for all by our Constitution, commands that no such practice as that disclosed by this record shall send any accused to his death. No higher duty, no more solemn responsibility rests upon this Court, than that of translating into living law and maintaining this constitutional shield deliberately planned and inscribed for the benefit of every human being subject to our Constitution—of whatever race, creed or persuasion.

"And I think if it's enforced that way, this can be and is bound to be the best Constitution in the world."

PAUL R. BAIER

References and Further Reading

Baier, Paul R. "Introduction to Hugo Black: A Memorial Portrait." *Yearbook Supreme Court Historical Society* (1982): 72–73.
Ball, Howard. *Hugo L. Black: Cold Steel Warrior.* New York and Oxford: Oxford University Press, 1996.
Black, Elizabeth S. "Hugo Black: A Memorial Portrait." *Yearbook Supreme Court Historical Society* (1982): 73–94.
Black, Hugo L., and Elizabeth Black. *Mr. Justice and Mrs. Black.* New York: Random House, 1986.
Frank, John P. *Mr. Justice Black: The Man and His Opinions.* New York: Alfred A. Knopf, 1949.
"*Justice Black and the Bill of Rights,*" Interview by Eric Sevareid and Martin Agronsky, CBS News Special, December 3, 1968 (Burton Benjamin producer), transcript published in *Southwestern University Law Review* 9, no. 4 (1977): 937–951.
Newman, Roger K. *Hugo Black: A Biography.* New York: Pantheon, 1994; Second Edition, New York, Fordham University Press, 1997.

Cases and Statutes Cited

Adamson v. California, 332 U.S. 46 (1947)
Brown v. Mississippi, 297 U.S. 278 (1936)
Bram v. United States, 168 U.S. 532 (1897)
Malloy v. Hogan, 378 U.S. 1 (1964)
Twining v. New Jersey, 211 U.S. 78 (1908)

See also **Bill of Rights: Structure;** *Brown v. Mississippi*, **279 U.S. 278 (1936); Coerced Confessions/Police Interrogation; Due Process; Fourteenth Amendment; Frankfurter, Felix; Hughes Court; Hughes, Charles Evans; Ku Klux Klan; Lincoln, Abraham; Self-incrimination (V): Historical Background; Self-incrimination: Miranda and Evolution**

CHAMBERS v. MISSISSIPPI, 410 U.S. 284 (1973)

Unreasonable application of evidentiary principles against a criminal defendant may violate the U.S. Constitution on any number of grounds, including the Compulsory Process, Due Process, or Confrontation Clauses. *Chambers v. Mississippi*, 410 U.S. 284 (1973), stands for the proposition that the Due Process right to a fair trial is implicated when evidentiary rules deprive a criminal defendant of the right to present evidence critical to his defense.

Chambers involved the shooting of a police officer during a fracas in a Mississippi pool hall. While some evidence pointed to Leon Chambers as the perpetrator, another man—Gable McDonald—later confessed to the crime. McDonald, however, recanted one month after his confession. Unable to inquire fully into the nature of McDonald's confession and recantation on cross-examination at trial due to state evidence rules, Chambers' defense team sought to introduce the testimony of three witnesses to whom McDonald had admitted participation in the shooting. Nevertheless, McDonald's statements to these witnesses were deemed inadmissible hearsay under state law, and Chambers was convicted of murder. In an 8–1 decision, the U. S. Supreme Court reversed Chambers' conviction, finding that state law prevented him from developing his defense and thereby interfered with his Due Process rights.

Although the Supreme Court opinion was crafted narrowly and linked to the facts of the case, *Chambers* has subsequently taken on significance as a landmark case for criminal defendants: a bulwark safeguarding a defendant's right to present exculpatory evidence in his own defense.

DANIEL S. MEDWED

References and Further Reading

Fisher, George. Evidence (2002): 580–586.
Hoeffel, Janet C., *The Sixth Amendment's Lost Clause: Unearthing Compulsory Process*, Wis. L. Rev. (2002): 1275.
Nagareda, Richard A., *Reconceiving the Right to Present Witnesses*, 97 Mich. L. Rev. 1999: 1063.

Cases and Statutes Cited

In re Oliver, 333 U.S. 257 (1948)
Webb v. Texas, 409 U.S. 95 (1972)
Washington v. Texas, 388 U.S. 14 (1967)

See also **Confrontation and Compulsory Process; Defense, Right to Present; Due Process**

CHAMBERS, WHITTAKER (1901–1961)

Whittaker Chambers, born Jay Vivian Chambers in Brooklyn, New York, in 1901, was a central figure in one of the most sensational of the post-1945 Red Scare investigations conducted by the House Un-American Activities Committee (HUAC). Educated at Columbia University in the 1920s and active in college literary and intellectual activities, Chambers became enamored with bolshevism, joining the U.S. Communist Party in 1925. An active member in Communist literary circles, he was recruited for the Communist underground in 1932 where he functioned as a courier, smuggling U.S. government documents to the Soviets. He became disillusioned with communism, however, and broke with the party in the late 1930s.

During his subsequent tenure as an editor for *Time*, Chambers became a more strident anticommunist. He was called before HUAC in 1948 during the Committee's very public investigation into the problem of communists in government. In his testimony, he identified former Communist colleagues, including a bright, well-respected diplomat and civil servant named Alger Hiss, who had traveled at high levels of the Franklin Roosevelt administration. The hearings became a well-publicized standoff between Chambers and Hiss, because Hiss emphatically maintained he had never been a member of the Communist Party. Ultimately, Chambers expanded his allegations to include an accusation that Hiss had also been involved in espionage for the Soviets. Amidst a series of charges and countercharges, as well as a well-publicized face-to-face confrontation with Hiss, Chambers summoned the Committee to his Maryland farm where he very dramatically extracted reels of microfilm from a hollowed out pumpkin, claiming these were classified documents reproduced on Hiss's personal typewriter. Although Hiss continued to maintain his innocence, a subsequent FBI investigation of the documents seemed to validate Chambers's charges. Hiss was ultimately convicted of perjury in 1951. The hearings, however, the first ever televised, contributed greatly to the public fear of the danger of domestic communism and its ability to penetrate American institutions.

Hiss continued to assert his innocence even until his death in 1996. Chambers's allegations, however, have received support in recent years as disclosures in the *VENONA* transcripts of messages sent by Soviet agents in the United States to Moscow during the early 1940s seem to identify Alger Hiss as a Soviet spy.

KAREN BRUNER

References and Further Reading

Haynes, John Earl, and Harvey Klehr. *VENONA: Decoding Soviet Espionage in America*. New Haven: Yale University Press, 1999.
Swan, Patrick A., ed. *Alger Hiss, Whittaker Chambers, and the Schism in the American Soul*. Wilmington, DE: Intercollegiate Studies Institute, 2003.
Tanenhaus, Sam. *Whittaker Chambers*. New York: Random House, 1997.
Weinstein, Allen. *Perjury: The Hiss-Chambers Case*. New York: Knopf, 1978.

See also **Hiss, Alger; House Un-American Activities Committee**

CHANDLER v. FLORIDA, 449 U.S. 560 (1981)

The Supreme Court ruled in *Chandler v. Florida* that the Constitution did not require an absolute ban on cameras in the courtroom, marking a significant change in its thinking on the issue. In 1965 in *Estes v. Texas*, the Court overturned a defendant's conviction based on its finding that the presence of television cameras had violated his right to a fair trial. Television technology was still fairly primitive at the time, however, and the *Estes* Court acknowledged that technological improvements that would make cameras more unobtrusive would require a reexamination of the issue. By the time of *Chandler*, many states had experimented with cameras in the courtroom, and at least ten states allowed them without the consent of the defendant. Florida was one of those states, and in 1981, the Supreme Court reexamined the camera issue when it heard the appeal of two Miami policemen convicted of burglary who claimed that the presence of cameras over their objections had denied them a fair trial. The Supreme Court unanimously disagreed, holding that the presence of television cameras does not inherently violate a criminal defendant's Sixth Amendment rights. While individual defendants retained the ability to show that the presence of cameras had prejudiced their fair trial rights in a specific case, the Court said, an absolute ban on cameras was not justified, given improvements in broadcasting technology. After *Chandler*, restrictions on cameras were eased in most states and today, all fifty states allow still or video camera coverage for some court proceedings.

KATHLEEN K. OLSON

References and Further Reading

Barber, Susanna. *News Cameras in the Courtroom: A Free Press-Fair Trial Debate*. Norwood, NJ: Ablex Publishing, 1987.
Cohn, Marjorie, and David Dow. *Cameras in the Courtroom: Television and the Pursuit of Justice*. Lanham, MD: Rowman & Littlefield, 2002.
Radio-Television News Directors Association & Foundation. "Cameras in the Court: A State-by-State Guide," http://www.rtndf.org/foi/scc.shtml.

Cases and Statutes Cited

Estes v. Texas, 381 U.S. 532 (1965)

See also **Cameras in the Courtroom; First Amendment and PACs**

CHANDLER v. MILLER, 520 U.S. 305 (1997) (CANDIDATES)

In 1990, the Georgia legislature passed a law requiring that each candidate for state office certify that he or she had tested negative for illegal drugs. The statute limited qualification to those who had passed a urinalysis test administered by a state-approved laboratory. The tests sought to identify use of marijuana, cocaine, opiates, amphetamines, and phencyclidines. The statute covered such posts as the governor, the school superintendent, and justices of the state supreme court. Some candidates, including Walker L. Chandler, the Libertarian nominee for Lieutenant Governor, sued the state, arguing that the mandatory drug testing violated the Fourth Amendment.

When the case reached the U. S. Supreme Court, it raised the question of whether the Fourth Amendment allowed states to compel drug tests of candidates absent any showing of individualized suspicion. The Court recognized that the Fourth Amendment, in protecting "the right of the people to be secure in their persons . . . against unreasonable searches and seizures," usually required that searches of a citizen's own body only be permitted when the government had some level of information, such as probable cause, to believe it would find something illegal. The Court had crafted an exception to this general rule to apply only under certain limited circumstances, called "special needs." In these special needs cases, the government pursued information not for criminal prosecution, but for narrow goals beyond those of law enforcement. The Court had previously accepted drug testing as meeting a special need for only certain groups of people, such as student athletes (to protect the educational environment of schools), customs agents (to protect the security of the nation's borders), and railroad employees (to ensure the safety of trains).

To decide whether drug testing of candidates fell within special needs, the Court balanced the competing interests of the public and the individual. In this analysis, special needs were found when the privacy interest implicated by the government search was "minimal" whereas the government interest in the search was "substantial—important enough to override the individual's acknowledged privacy interest." In assessing the citizen's side of the scales, the *Chandler* Court deemed Georgia's testing method to be "relatively noninvasive." The Court, however, was troubled when it focused on the government's side of the equation. Since the state tests could be foiled by abstention before the testing date, Georgia's scheme would be ineffective in identifying illicit drug users. The only purpose remaining in testing candidates was to display the government "commitment to the struggle against drug abuse." Such a "symbolic" need was not enough to be "special," for "diminishing personal privacy for a symbol's sake" did not pass Fourth Amendment muster. The Court therefore held that Georgia's mandatory drug testing of candidates did not "fit within the closely guarded category of constitutionally permissible suspicionless searches."

The long-term impact of *Chandler* remains uncertain. Five years after *Chandler*, the Court reaffirmed drug testing as within special needs in *Board of Education v. Earls*, 536 U.S. 822 (2002). In *Earls*, the Court upheld urinalysis of students participating in extracurricular activities. The language of the *Earls* decision left in doubt whether *Chandler* represented a curtailment of the entire special needs doctrine or merely a refinement in the context of candidates for public office.

GEORGE M. DERY, III

References and Further Reading

Dery III, George M., *Are Politicians More Deserving of Privacy than Schoolchildren? How Chandler v. Miller Exposed the Absurdities of Fourth Amendment "Special Needs" Balancing*, Ariz. L. Rev. 40 (1998): 73.
United States Constitution, Amendment IV.

Cases and Statutes Cited

Board of Education v. Earls, 536 U.S. 822 (2002)
Chandler v. Miller, 520 U.S. 305 (1997)

CHAPLAINS: LEGISLATIVE

The practice of using a chaplain to offer a prayer at the beginning of each legislative session dates back to the first session of the first congress. Since then, state legislatures, the U.S. Congress, and the U.S. Supreme Court have opened sessions with prayers. Some have questioned, however, whether this tradition represents an unlawful entanglement of church and state, violating the Establishment Clause of the Constitution.

The Supreme Court addressed the constitutionality of legislative chaplains in 1983 with *Marsh v. Chambers*, 463 U.S. 783 (1983). Ernest Chambers, a member of the Nebraska legislature, challenged that legislature's practice of opening sessions with a prayer. Chief Justice Burger, writing the opinion for the 6–3 majority, looked at the history of legislative chaplains. He noted that the Continental Congress, whose membership included many framers of the Constitution, used legislative chaplains. Therefore, the Court concluded, the framers themselves did not view legislative chaplains as unconstitutional. Burger

went on to say that the use of legislative chaplains is a "tolerable acknowledgement" of the role of religion in the United States and the beliefs held by many of its citizens. He claimed that the Establishment Clause is not necessarily violated when the actions of the government coincide with religious ends, and that the fact that legislatures have long used without a negative consequence shows that the practice is harmless.

Justice Brennan's lengthy dissent outlined some of the arguments against the constitutionality of legislative chaplains. He first noted that the majority failed to subject the issue to any legal tests.

One issue that the majority did not address was whether the use of legislative chaplains failed the Lemon test. When there is a question of whether a practice violates the Establishment Clause, the Supreme Court generally applies the Lemon test, developed in *Lemon v. Kurtzman*, 403 U.S. 602 (1971). A government action does not violate the Lemon test when (1) the government's action has a legitimate secular purpose; (2) the primary effect of the action is not to either advance or inhibit religion; and (3) the action does not create an "excessive government entanglement" with religion. Brennan noted that a prayer has an inherently religious, rather than secular, purpose. He also notes that the goal of the prayer, to quiet legislators down and put them in a serious frame of mind, could be accomplished in a secular manner, so the use of a religious prayer to that end does not have a secular purpose. He also claimed that the primary effect of the prayer as to "explicitly link religious belief and observance to the power and prestige of the State" and thus to advance religion. He also claimed that by having the government choose a chaplain or chaplains for the invocation, an excessive government entanglement necessarily exists. There is also government entanglement because the issue of legislative chaplains is politically divisive and could cause voters to choose their legislators based on religion. Thus, in Brennan's opinion, the use of legislative chaplains violates all three prongs of the Lemon test, and thus violates the Establishment Clause.

The Lemon test aside, Brennan said that the use of legislative chaplains violates the Establishment Clause. He noted historically that the Establishment Clause has been regarded ensuring a separation of church and state and a neutrality of the government with regard to religion. This practice forces citizens to pay taxes to further Judeo–Christian prayer, when they may or may not believe in such traditions, involves government oversight and regulation of chaplains, and, according to Brennan, trivializes religion "by too close an attachment to the organs of government." The Nebraska legislature was not being neutral toward religion, but was favoring religion over non-religion and Judeo–Christian traditions over others. Similarly, the Nebraska legislature failed to keep the government and religion separate by hiring, employing, and overseeing religious officials performing religious duties. Thus, Brennan stated, the employment of legislative chaplains is unconstitutional.

While it may be true that the framers of the Constitution did not see the use of legislative chaplains as an impermissible establishment of religion, that does not mean the debate ought to end there. There are instances in which we deliberately go against the intent of the framers. Our views on race and gender, for example, have evolved since the passage of the Constitution. Perhaps, even if the framers believed that the Establishment Clause did not apply to legislative chaplains, their employment might be considered no longer appropriate given the ever-increasing religious diversity of our nation.

Thus, despite the holding in *Marsh v. Chambers*, there are still Constitutional issues to examine regarding legislative chaplains.

FATHER ROBERT F. DRINAN, S. J.

Cases and Statutes Cited

Lemon v. Kurtzman, 403 U.S. 602 (1971)
Marsh v. Chambers, 463 U.S. 783 (1983)

CHAPLAINS: MILITARY

Military chaplains originated in biblical times and have long been recognized as an important component of many armed forces. They have served in Western armies since at least the fourth century. From the earliest days of British settlement in the New World, chaplains were employed in American colonial militias. When the Continental Army was formed, chaplains attached to the militia of the thirteen colonies became part of the nation's first army. Military chaplaincy has continued ever since, with its size growing larger in proportion to the increase in the size of the armed forces.

The federal government has viewed chaplains as necessary to the well-being of the military. George Washington, as the first commander-in-chief, felt strongly that they were needed to bolster the morale of his troops. Moreover, before the invasion of predominantly Roman Catholic Canada in September 1775, he ordered his generals "to protect and support the free Exercise of Religion of the Country and the undisturbed Enjoyment of the rights of Conscience in religious Matters."

The military chaplaincy was formally established in July 1775 and is the second oldest branch of the Army, preceded only by the infantry. The Continental Congress passed regulations governing the appointment and salaries of chaplains. The first Articles of War called on soldiers to attend religious services, which were performed twice daily.

Although their noncombatant status was recognized as early as the Council of Regensburg in 742 C. E., in colonial America chaplains fought alongside their comrades—as they did some during the Revolutionary War, the War of 1812, and the Civil War. Others played a more professional role by serving as intelligence gatherers and camp aides. In 1864, an international convention brought about the first treaty that recognized chaplains as noncombatant persons on the battlefield. From that point on, U. S. military chaplains did not fight in armed conflicts.

At first, American chaplains were mostly Protestant ministers, but by the Civil War Catholic priests and Jewish rabbis had also been admitted into the armed forces. Today military chaplains represent more than 200 denominations.

In modern times, the Department of Defense has continued to commission chaplains to accompany United States soldiers at every location they may be serving. Eleven chaplains were killed in World War I. Seventy-seven lost their lives in World War II— during which four became famous when a rabbi, a Catholic priest, and two Protestant ministers offered their life vests to young soldiers as their transport ship was sinking off the North Atlantic coast. The four died as a result of their sacrifice. Eleven chaplains lost their lives in Korea, and thirteen in Vietnam. More than 3,000 Army chaplains were decorated during the twentieth century. More recently, more than 500 chaplains were deployed in Iraq, many of them coming from reserve units.

Today, there are currently some 25,000 American military chaplains, serving primarily in the Army, Navy, and Air Force—on military bases, at front lines, and in medical units. The Chief of Chaplains determines their number and denominations on the basis of current needs of the military population. The Department of Defense recognizes a wide range of religious groups, from traditional faiths such as Christianity, Judaism, and Islam to nontraditional religions such as Wicca.

Chaplains must possess both bachelors and divinity degrees. Like regular military personnel, they are required to meet age and fitness requirements and to engage in military training (although they are exempt from weapons training). They are also subject to military discipline. Although all chaplains have been ordained by their denominational group, because they must be available any place soldiers are deployed, they must also be able to provide religious guidance to persons of other faiths. They are specifically prohibited from converting members of others faiths.

The most difficult responsibility of military chaplains is spiritually and morally to prepare troops to take life and to die, but they also serve as personal counselors. Many are trained in addressing the special concerns of young adults, such as family affairs and substance-abuse issues.

Military chaplains' commissions have come under fire from a Constitutional perspective. Although Congress has been required to provide troops with chaplains in distant parts of the world, their funding has been challenged as a violation of the establishment clause of the First Amendment. Similarly, limitations placed on specific religious observances while in the military have been challenged under the free-exercise clause.

The U. S. Court of Appeals for the Second Circuit addressed the first argument in *Katcoff v. Marsh,* holding that Congress does have the authority to commission chaplains. The court declared that the government's power is derived from Art. I, § 8 of the Constitution, which allows Congress to establish an army for the purpose of "preserving the peace and security, and providing for the defense, of the United States." It viewed the government's goal as one that does not include establishing a religion, but rather "maintain[ing] the efficiency of the Army by improving the morale of our military personnel."

The establishment clause and the statutes creating the military chaplaincy, said the court in *Katcoff,* must be viewed in light of their historical background. Congressional authorization of a military chaplaincy—both before and contemporaneous with the adoption of the First Amendment, and for two centuries thereafter—is "weighty evidence" that the establishment clause was not intended to restrict religious freedom in the military. The purpose of the Constitutional and legislative provisions "is to insure that no religion be sponsored or favored, none commanded, and none inhibited."

Moreover, said the court, the free exercise clause obligates Congress to accommodate the religious practices of military personnel who have been moved to areas outside the United States.

In fact, although free exercise has long been viewed as subordinate to military necessity, chaplains have nevertheless been successful in overcoming various restrictions placed on them by their superiors. For example, the Persian Gulf War presented special dilemmas for Jewish and Christian troops, many of whom found it difficult to practice their religion for fear of offending the predominantly Moslem host countries. Chaplains themselves were ordered to remove religious insignia from their uniforms. Christmas and Passover observances had to be muted or celebrated on ships offshore. By the end of the war, however, chaplains were allowed to wear their insignia and were able to hold both Christian and Jewish services in their encampments and beyond.

KENNETH LASSON

References and Further Reading

10 U.S.C. §§ 3293, 3581 (2000).

Annan, Kent. *Chaplains Who Serve the US Armed Forces,* 6 For God & Country 3 (2002), http://www.pstem.edu/read/inspire/6.3/feature_1/.

Brown, Michael. "Military Chaplains Role in War, History." *Air Combat Command News Service,* April 25, 2003, http://www2.acc.af.mil/accnews/apr03/03147.html.

Department of Defense, Directive 1304.19 §§ 3,5 (Sept. 18, 1993).

Diamond, Mark. *Deployed Chaplains: Faith on the Front Lines, U.S. Military Art Prints,* April 21, 2003, http://www.globalsecurity.org/military/library/2003/04/mil-030421-afpn04.htm.

Drazin, Israel, and Cecil B. Currey. *For God and Country: The History of a Constitutional Challenge to the Army Chaplaincy,* 1995.

Jewish U.S. Marine, http://www.kolot.com/FS1999/rick0004.shtml.

Lasson, Kenneth, *Religious Liberty in the Military: The First Amendment Under 'Friendly Fire,'* Journal of Law & Religion 471 (1992): 9:493.

Malin, Don. *Military Chaplains and Religious Pluralism,* http://www.wfial.org/Articles/Military_chaplains.htm (April 2003).

Odom, Jonathan G., *Beyond Arm Bands and Arms Banned: Chaplains, Armed Conflict, and the Law,* Naval Law Review 1 (2002): 49:5.

Separation: Military Chaplains—Government Chaplains and the Separation of Church and State, http://atheism.about.com/library/FAQs/cs/blcsm_gov_chapmilit.htm.

Sweet, Michael. "Rabbi Brings Torah to Marines in Babylon." *Marine Corps News* June 28, 2003, http://www.usmc.mil/marine.unk/nch2000.nsf/0/DE75471AF9EF7-BE185256D550004E024.

War Over, Some Clergy Still Away on Duty. Christian Century, June 28, 2003, http://www.findarticles.com/cf_dls/m1058/13_120/104681891/print.jhtml. Forty percent of the chaplains in the army were from reserves and sixty percent were from active duty.

Case and Statutes Cited

Katcoff v. Marsh, 755 F.2d 223, 225 (2nd Cir. 1985)

See also **Religious Freedom in the Military**

CHARITABLE CHOICE

Charitable Choice is a set of statutory parameters attached to a social service program with the purpose of making the government more welcoming to all faith-based social service providers. The provision first appeared in the federal comprehensive welfare reform act of 1996. A year later Charitable Choice was extended to welfare-to-work assistance, was next incorporated into the Community Services Block Grant Act of 1998, and finally was made part of the Substance Abuse and Mental Health Services drug treatment programs reauthorized in late 2000. Before the adoption of this provision, it was widely believed that faith-based charities could receive government aid only if the funds were administered by a separately incorporated nonprofit that was secular in its program operations.

When George W. Bush assumed the Presidency in January 2001, he incorporated Charitable Choice as an integral part of a much broader and more ambitious White House Faith-Based & Community Initiatives. By executive order issued December 12, 2002, the President directed that several federal departments ensure nondiscriminatory treatment toward faith-based charities in all the welfare programs they administered.

Charitable Choice interweaves three fundamental principles. First, it imposes on government the duty to refrain from discriminating on the basis of religion with respect to the eligibility of providers seeking to deliver services under one of the government's welfare programs. Rather than examining the nature of the service provider with an eye to excluding those thought overly religious, Charitable Choice requires officials to focus on the nature of the services and the means by which they are provided. The relevant inquiry is not "Who are you?" but "What can you do?" Faith-based providers are not to be preferred, merely allowed to compete on the same basis as all other providers.

Second, the provision imposes on government the duty to refrain from intruding into the religious autonomy of faith-based organizations (FBOs). Charitable Choice extends a guarantee that in religious matters each FBO that competes for funding "shall retain its independence" including "control over the definition, development, practice, and expression of its religious beliefs." Government-funded FBOs continue to be subject to general regulation, of course, and must provide an accounting for public monies received. The guarantee, rather, is that FBOs retain their religious independence from regulations imposed solely as a consequence of receiving the government assistance. There are also specific safeguards from demands to remove religious symbols at an FBO's facility and from regulations requiring FBOs to adjust the makeup of their governing board. A

private right of action vests in FBOs to enforce these guarantees.

Third, Charitable Choice imposes on both government and participating FBOs the duty to refrain from abridging certain religious rights of the ultimate beneficiaries of these welfare programs. When the form of the funding is direct to the social service provider, each beneficiary is empowered with a choice. Beneficiaries who want to receive their services from an FBO may do so—assuming, that is, that an FBO has qualified for a grant. On the other hand, if a beneficiary has religious objections to receiving services from an FBO, then the government is required to provide equivalent alternative services. This is the "choice" in Charitable Choice. When a beneficiary selects an FBO receiving direct funding, the provider cannot discriminate against the beneficiary on the basis of religion.

Charitable Choice is based on an Establishment Clause that accords with the principle of "neutrality." In such a view, when government secures social services without regard to religion, then neither provider nor beneficiary has to alter their religious behavior to do business with the government. Thus the Establishment Clause is understood as minimizing the government's influence over the religious choices made by individuals. Because many beneficiaries freely choose to receive their services from an FBO, it is religion-neutral for the government to provide aid to FBOs on the same basis as other providers. When beneficiaries elect an FBO and receive the secular benefit of the service for which the welfare program is designed, the government is not advancing religion but merely responding to the choices freely made by its citizens. That other voluntarily activities, including religious activities, occur at the FBO is not properly a governmental concern.

Charitable Choice contemplates funding that is structured to be either direct (that is, where the government awards grants to charities who in turn provide services to qualifying beneficiaries) or indirect (that is, where the provider which ultimately receives the government's aid is selected by the beneficiary, such as with vouchers). When the form of the assistance is indirect, the regulations promulgated under Charitable Choice incorporate the Supreme Court's approach to school vouchers and the case of *Zelman v. Simmons-Harris.* Conversely, when the form of the assistance is direct, then the regulations follow the approach upheld in *Mitchell v. Helms.* Consistent with *Mitchell,* the regulations require that no inherently religious activities such as worship or proselytizing take place within the funded program. If any such activities are conducted on a voluntary basis by a participating FBO, then the activities must be separated, by time or location, from the funded program. By following the Court's guidance in *Zelman* and *Mitchell*, the regulations are calculated to rebuff critics who argue that Charitable Choice violates the Establishment Clause.

To reduce regulatory entanglement, Charitable Choice safeguards the freedom of FBOs to employ staff of like-minded faith. The ability to restrict employees and volunteers to those of shared faith is said to be central to maintaining the organization's essential religious character. As Justice William Brennan wrote in his concurring opinion in *Corporation of Presiding Bishop v. Amos*, "Determining that certain activities are in furtherance of an organization's religious mission, and that only those committed to that mission should conduct them, is thus a means by which a religious community defines itself."

The ability of FBOs to consider religion when hiring, a right set out in § 702(a) of Title VII of the Civil Rights Act of 1964, is cross-referenced in Charitable Choice. It was initially assumed that the guarantee of religious "independence" in Charitable Choice overrides conflicting nondiscrimination procurement rules at the state and local level. The latter becomes important if the federal welfare funds involved are administered through the states. That Charitable Choice enables FBOs to compete for funding, whereas retaining the right to staff on a religious basis has become controversial and is largely the reason that attempts to further expand Charitable Choice have stalled in the U. S. Senate. The question of overriding state and local procurement rules is debated in the literature, but as of this writing no court has been asked to pass on the issue.

CARL H. ESBECK

References and Further Reading

Ackerman, David M. *Public Aid to Faith-Based Organizations (Charitable Choice) in the 107th Congress: Background and Selected Legal Issues.* Library of Congress, Congressional Research Service, Report RL31043, August 19, 2003.

Esbeck, Carl H., Stanley W. Carlson-Thies, and Ronald J. Sider. *The Freedom of Faith-Based Organizations to Staff on a Religious Basis.* Wash., DC: Center for Public Justice, 2004, available at <http://www.cpjustice.org/publications/charitable_choice/resources.pdf>.

Laycock, Douglas. *The Constitutional Role of Faith-Based Organizations in Competitions for Federal Social Service Funds.* Testimony Before the House Subcommittee on the Constitution, Committee on the Judiciary, 107th Cong., June 7, 2001, available at <http://www.house.gov/judiciary/72981.pdf>.

Lupu, Ira C., and Robert W. Tuttle. *Government Partnerships with Faith-Based Service Providers: The State of the Law.* Wash., DC: Roundtable on Religion and Social Welfare Policy, December 2002, available at <http://www.religiousandsocialpolicy.org/docs/legal/reports/12-4-2002_state_of_the_law.pdf>.

White House Office of Faith-Based and Community Initiatives. *Protecting the Civil Rights and Religious Liberty of Faith-Based Organizations: Why Religious Hiring Rights Must Be Preserved,* June 23, 2003, available at <http://www.whitehouse.gov/government/fbci/booklet.pdf>.

Cases and Statutes Cited

Corporation of Presiding Bishop v. Amos, 483 U.S. 327 (1987)

Mitchell v. Helms, 530 U.S. 793 (2000) (plurality opinion)

Zelman v. Simmons-Harris, 536 U.S. 639 (2002)

Charitable Choice as applicable to the Temporary Assistance for Needy Families (TANF) Program, 42 U.S.C. § 604a, and regulations thereto, 68 Fed. Reg. 56449 (Sept. 30, 2003), codified at 45 C.F.R. pt. 260

Charitable Choice as applicable to the Community Service Block Grant (CSBG) Act, 42 U.S.C. § 9920, and regulations thereto, 68 Fed. Reg. 56466 (Sept. 30, 2003), codified at 45 C.F.R. pt. 1050

Charitable Choice as applicable to THE Substance Abuse and Mental Health Services Administration (SAMHSA) Drug Treatment Programs, 42 U.S.C. § 300x-65 and 42 U.S.C. § 290kk, and regulations thereto, 68 Fed. Reg. 56429 (Sept. 30, 2003), codified at 42 C.F.R. pts. 54 and 54a

Executive Order 13279, issued December 12, 2002, *Equal Protection of the Laws for Faith-Based and Community Organizations and Permitting Religious Staffing by Faith-Based Federal Contractors*, 67 Fed. Reg. 77141 (Dec. 16, 2002)

The Civil Rights Act of 1964, § 702(a) of Title VII, 42 U.S. C. § 2000e-1(e)

See also **Discrimination by Religious Entities that Receive Government Funds; Establishment Clause Doctrine: Supreme Court Jurisprudence; Title VII and Religious Exemptions**

CHASE COURT (1864–1873)

The Chase Court combined powerful rhetoric in favor of civil liberties with very little protection for civil liberties. The justices in *Ex parte Milligan* (1866) asserted that "the Constitution of the United States is a law for rulers and people, equally in war and peace." Nevertheless, the Chase Court did not challenge any Civil War measure before Appomattox and found procedural reasons to avoid reaching the merits of several important constitutional challenges to Reconstruction measures. The judicial majority in the *Slaughter-House Cases* (1872) asserted that the primary purpose of the constitutional amendments ratified after the Civil War was to secure, "the freedom of the slave race, the security and firm establishment of that freedom, and the protection of the newly-named freemen and citizen from the oppression's of those who have normally exercised on them and dominion over him." Nevertheless, the actual decision the court made sharply limited to protect any rights. In no case did the Chase Court protect the constitutional rights of a person of color. The passivity of the Chase Court in civil rights and the these cases is partly explained in procedural issues that prevented justices from handing down more libertarian rulings. Still, the Chase Court left future libertarians with very quotable phrases, but few workable precedents.

Ex parte Milligan highlights both the passivity and aggressiveness of Chase Court responses to claims of constitutional right. The precise issue in that case was whether President Abraham Lincoln had the legal or constitutional authority to declare martial law and order military trials during the Civil War. When Confederate armies were in the field, both the Taney Chase Courts found various reasons not to adjudicate the constitutionality of those policies. After the shooting was over, a unanimous Chase Court ruled that Lincoln acted unconstitutionally when he tried northern civilians in military courts. Five justices insisted that neither the president nor Congress could declare martial law in localities far from the front lines where ordinary trials had not been disrupted by the war. "Military jurisdiction," Justice David Davis declared, "can never be applied to citizens in states which have upheld the authority of the government, and where the courts are open and the process unobstructed." Four justices, in an opinion written by Chief Justice Salmon Chase, insisted that Congress had broad powers to declare martial law, but that Lampkin Milligan's trial was inconsistent with the rules for trying civilians accused of aiding the Confederacy that Congress had previously set out. The actual result in *Milligan* was relatively uncontroversial, because suspensions of habeas corpus in the north had troubled many Americans during the Civil War and could not be justified after Lee's surrender. The crucial question was whether the justices would use Milligan as a precedent for striking down Northern imposition of martial law in the South after the Civil War.

The first Reconstruction cases heard by the Chase Court suggested that the justices would police civil rights violations in the South as aggressively as the justices policed civil rights violations in the North after the Civil War. In *Cummings v. Missouri* (1866), a five to four judicial majority ruled that states could not require certain state employees is where that they had been loyal to the Union during the Civil War. Such demands, Justice Stephen Field declared, violated both the ex post facto clause and the constitutional prohibition on bills of attainder. A federal law insisting that attorneys practicing in federal courts take a similar oath was declared unconstitutional on the same grounds in *Ex parte Garland* (1866).

Partisan fears or hopes that these cases where the beginning of a full-scale assault on military rule in the Reconstruction South were never realized. The Chase Court was given three opportunities to strike down martial law on the authority of *Ex parte Milligan* but declined to reach the merits of the constitutional issues in each instance. The justices in *Mississippi v. Johnson* (1866) rejected the constitutional attack on martial law by unanimously ruling that federal courts could not issue an injunction to the president that forbade him from executing what state attorneys claimed was an unconstitutional law. The next year, in *Georgia v. Stanton* (1867), the justices unanimously ruled that a state had no standing to challenge a law that state attorneys claimed violated the constitutional rights of state citizens. The justices did, however, initially take jurisdiction to determine whether William McCardle was unconstitutionally imprisoned for publishing anti-Reconstruction editorials in the Vicksburg Times. While oral argument was taking place on the merits, Congress first debated then passed a bill stripping the court of jurisdiction necessary to adjudicate that case. After some debate, the Chase Court majority elected to delay issuing a decision until that bill became law over President Johnson's veto. The justices then ruled that they jurisdiction to decide McCardle's appeal.

These judicial refusals to reach the merits of various constitutional attacks on Reconstruction may have been good faith judging and not a strategic retreat in the face of congressional opposition. The Johnson administration, no friend of martial law in the South, vigorously argued for and supported the result *in Johnson v. Mississippi* and *Stanton v. Georgia*. Most contemporary commentators agree these cases were rightly decided. The judicial decision to delay announcing the result in *Ex parte McCardle* (1868) was consistent with previous Marshall, Taney, and Chase Court practice in cases of no political significance. Almost immediately after denying jurisdiction in *McCardle*, the justices announced they would decide *Ex parte Yerger* (1969), another case raising the constitutionality of martial law in the South. Rather than risk an adverse decision, the Grant administration settled the case.

Chase Court decisions on the rights of former slaves also provided civil libertarians with good language but little law. Justice Miller's majority opinion in *The Slaughter-house Cases* highlighted how the Thirteenth and Fourteenth Amendments were designed to protect the rights of persons of color. Several Chase Court justices while on circuit broadly interpreted this new national commitment to racial equality. Chief Justice

Chase in *In re Turner* (1867) interpreted the Thirteenth Amendment that outlawing certain onerous apprenticeship agreements. Nevertheless, in no case did the Chase Court protect the rights of former slaves, thus failing to establish any precedent that might promote egalitarian rulings in the future.

The Slaughter-house Cases contain the Chase Court's best-known statements on civil rights and liberties. At issue was the constitutionality of a New Orleans law granting a monopoly to certain butchers, butchers who probably bribed the local legislature. Former Justice John Campbell sought to use those cases as a vehicle for making the post–Civil War Constitution an instrument for economic rights rather than for racial equality. In a powerful argument, he asserted that the right to practice common callings was protected by the privileges and immunities clause of the newly minted Fourteenth Amendment and that the denial of such a right was a form of enslavement prohibited by the Thirteenth Amendment. The five to four judicial majority rejected that invitation to expand the post–Civil War Constitution beyond race. Justice Miller asserted that ordinary health regulations were not enslavements and that the privileges and immunities clause protected only such rights of national citizenship as the right to travel to the national capital and the right to be protected when abroad. In his view, a broader interpretation of the Fourteenth Amendment "would constitute this court a perpetual censor upon all legislation of the states." Due process, he continued, had nothing to do with this case and equal protection was largely limited to laws discriminating against persons of color. Four justices dissented. Justice Field insisted that the privileges and immunities clause "refers to the natural and inalienable rights which belong to all citizens." This theme would greatly influence later Supreme Court decisions, but under due process rather than privileges and immunities.

The judicial opinions in *The Slaughter-house Cases* structured the judicial responses to the claim in *Bradwell v. Illinois* (182) that women had a constitutional right to become lawyers. Justice Miller's majority opinion simply repeated his previous claim that no one had a federal constitutional right to practice a common calling. Justice Bradley, who had joined Justice Field's dissent in *Slaughter-House*, insisted that past practice and divine law provided better grounds for rejecting Ms. Bradwell's appeal. "The natural and proper timidity and delicacy which belongs to the female gender," he infamously declared "evidently unfit for many of the occupations of civil life." In Justice Bradley's view, the "paramount destiny and mission of women are to fill the noble and the nine offices of wife and mother. This is

the law of the Creator." Chief Justice Chase, who was dying at the time, dissented without opinion.

This lack of justification may be fitting. The Chase Court is best known for issuing bold statements in favor of protecting rights without actually handing down challenging live violations of rights. The vote that most challenged contemporary understanding of rights, Chief Justice Chase's dissent in *Bradwell*, by comparison, was given without any justification or bold quotation at all.

MARK A. GRABER

References and Further Reading

Hyman, Harold M. *The Reconstruction Justice of Salmon P. Chase: In re Turner and Texas v. White.* Lawrence, KS: University Press of Kansas, 1997.
Kutler, Stanley I. *Judicial Power and Reconstruction Politics.* Chicago: University of Chicago Press, 1968.

Cases and Statutes Cited

Bradwell v. Illinois, 83 U.S. 130 (1872)
Cummings v. Missouri, 71 U.S. 277 (1866)
Ex parte Garland, 71 U.S. 333 (1866)
Ex parte McCardle, 74 U.S. 506 (1868)
Ex parte Milligan, 71 U.S. 2 (1866)
Ex parte Yerger, 75 U.S. 85 (1868)
Georgia v. Stanton, 73 U.S. 50 (1867)
In re Turner, 24 F. Cas. 333 (C.C.D. Maryland, 1867)
Mississippi v. Johnson, 71 U.S. 475 (1866)
Slaughter-House Cases, 83 U.S. 36 (1872)

CHASE, SAMUEL (1744–1811)

Although an ardent patriot, a signer of the Declaration of Independence, and an associate justice of the U. S. Supreme Court who made a significant contribution to nineteenth-century American jurisprudence, Samuel Chase is best known for his interpretation of the Sedition Act of 1798 and his impeachment trial in 1804. Chase was born on April 17, 1744. His mother, Matilda Walker, died at his birth and he was raised by his father, Thomas Chase, an Episcopalian minister renowned for his tenacity, impulsiveness, and tendency to live beyond his means, which led to his imprisonment in 1746 for unpaid debts. The elder Chase passed on these characteristics to his son but also provided him with a sound classical education.

At eighteen, Chase began studying law in the offices of John Hammond and John Hall in Annapolis. Admitted to the bar in 1761, he was appointed prosecutor in the mayor's court, a position that provided him with a meager salary but permitted him to represent clients in civil suits for debt. In

May 1762, he married Ann (Nancy) Baldwin of Anne Arundel County. The couple had seven children, three of whom died in infancy. In 1763, Chase commenced legal practice in Frederick County, Maryland, and became politically active, aligning himself with the country party against the elite-controlled court party. In the following year, he obtained a seat in the assembly. During the Stamp Act crisis, Chase mobilized the "middling sort," participated in the drafting of Maryland's resolutions to the Stamp Act Congress, and helped to organize the Sons of Liberty in Annapolis.

In the early 1770s, Chase assumed a leading role in the movement to lower clerical salaries and tobacco inspection fees, which he regarded as oppressive. He became a member of the nonimportation committee of Annapolis in 1770 and a vigorous supporter of colonial resistance after Britain's imposition of the Intolerable Acts. Selected as a delegate to the First and Second Continental Congresses, Chase embraced the principle of "no taxation without representation," assailed British suppression of colonial trade, and denounced the royal navy's seizure of American ships. He emerged as one of Maryland's leading advocates of Independence, but distanced himself from the colony's radical faction led by John Hall, Matthias Hammond, and Charles Ridgely, whose policies he believed threatened the colony's internal stability and social order. Chase joined Charles Carroll and Benjamin Franklin on the commission sent to Canada to request support for resistance to the imperial authorities.

In the late 1770s, Chase advocated that large states cede their western lands to the union. He also supported the confiscation of British property and the expansion of paper money. His views reflected his speculative interests and difficulty in repaying debts. In 1778, he was accused of having breached public trust by using for speculative purposes confidential information on wheat and flour shortages provided to Congress. Although absolved of these charges, he became the central figure in the infamous flour scandal and was defeated in the 1778 elections for Congress. The scandal plagued him throughout his public life.

Fearing the domination of national affairs by elites, identifying state legislatures as bastions of popular liberties, and regarding the participants in the Constitutional Convention as having exceeded their mandate to amend the Articles of Confederation, Chase initially supported the Antifederalist cause. The adoption of the Bill of Rights, his affinity for English traditions and fear of the radicalism of the French Revolution, and his heightened concern about social unrest after the Whiskey Rebellion and the Fell's Point Riot led to his Federalist conversion.

Presiding over the Court of Oyer and Terminer in Baltimore, Chase sought to distinguish between the freedom and licentiousness of the press in 1794.

Appointed to the Supreme Court in 1796, Chase quickly distinguished himself and contributed to the development of American jurisprudence. In the British debt case, *Ware v. Hylton* (1796), he ruled on the supremacy of national treaties over state law. In *Hylton v. United States* (1796), he recognized the power of the Supreme Court to void congressional legislation deemed to be unconstitutional and declared the federal excise tax on carriages to be a duty. In *United States v. Worrall* (1798), Chase refused arguments to prosecute a crime on the basis of common law, noting that federal courts could not "punish a man for any act, before it is declared by law of the United States to be criminal." In *Calder v. Bull* (1798), he laid foundations for the doctrine of "substantive due process" by acknowledging the importance of fundamental principles not specifically set out in the Constitution.

Chase's interpretation of the Sedition Act of 1798 precipitated strong Republican criticism and culminated in the call for his impeachment in 1804. Alleging irregularities in his handling of John Fries's trial for treason and James Callender's prosecution for seditious libel, as well as judicial indiscretion before a grand jury in Newcastle, Delaware, in 1803 when he denounced President Jefferson's repeal of the Judiciary Act of 1801, John Randolph tabled seven articles of impeachment in the House of Representatives. Although none received the Senate's two-thirds majority required for Chase's removal from the Court, the impeachment trial enshrined him as a symbol of Federalist political partisanship. Samuel Chase died in Baltimore on June 19, 1811.

GORDON S. BARKER

References and Further Reading

Elsmere, Jane Shaffer. *Justice Samuel Chase*. Muncie, IN: Janevar Publishing, 1980.

Haw, James, et al. *Stormy Patriot: The Life of Samuel Chase*. Baltimore: Maryland Historical Society, 1980.

Sharp, James Roger. *American Politics in the Early Republic: The New Nation in Crisis*. New Haven: Yale University Press, 1993.

CHAVEZ, CESAR (1927–1993)

Cesar Chavez, farm worker, civil rights activist, and union leader, was born near Yuma, Arizona, to Librado Chavez and Juana Estrada, who owned a farm and several small businesses. In 1938, the Chavez family lost their property and became migrant farm workers. Chavez's childhood was wrought with racial discrimination and hard work, which severely limited his school attendance.

Chavez enlisted in the U.S. Navy during World War II but returned to migrant farming in 1946. Shortly after, Chavez joined the National Agricultural Workers' Union (NAWU). This started a lifetime dedication to social change and fair treatment for Mexican Americans, particularly migrant farmers. In 1948, Chavez married Helen Fabela and resided in Delano, California, where he was a migrant laborer.

In 1952, Chavez volunteered for the Community Services Organization (CSO) and later became a paid organizer. The CSO, a body devoted to promoting political and civil rights for Mexican Americans, committed itself to the formation of new CSO chapters, voter registration drives, citizenship campaigns, educational improvements, urban developments, and other issues important to improving Mexican Americans' quality of life. Chavez eventually held the position of General Director for the CSO and remained active until 1962, when he left to form a union dedicated to migrant farmers.

Chavez started the National Farm Workers Association (NFWA), which became the United Farm Workers (UFW) in 1973. Inspired by Mahatma Gandhi and Martin Luther King Jr., Chavez became known as a natural leader, dedicated to a militant, yet racially unbiased, nonviolent, grass roots movement. To Chavez, the organization was more than a union; it was a social movement aimed at fixing the restricted civil liberties most members faced. He demonstrated his dedication by fasting and involving union members in masses, boycotts, pilgrimages, and processionals. In doing so, he appealed to the Mexican-American culture of the farm workers. This heritage included Catholicism and a belief in the merits of sacrifice to fight injustice. Chavez also influenced and actively supported the Chicano civil rights movement until some of the reformers advocated violence.

Chavez's union struck numerous times, the first in May 1965. The most notable strike began in September 1965. Another union, the Agricultural Workers Organizing Committee (AWOC) struck and realized it needed the support of the NFWA. Although reluctant, the NFWA leadership voted to strike as well. Eventually, the two unions merged and formed the United Farm Workers Organizing Committee (UFWOC). The strikers used nonviolent tactics such as fasts, pilgrimages, demonstrations, an international grape boycott, and political campaigning amid violence from opposition. In 1970, the five-year long strike ended triumphantly for the union. Most of its demands were met, and many grape growers signed contracts with the strikers.

The UFW had subsequent strikes, but none had the longevity of the Delano grape strike.

Later, California farm workers achieved government-regulated collective bargaining through the instatement of the Agricultural Labor Relations Board. Unfortunately for the UFW, the elections of President Ronald Reagan and California Governor George Deukmejian, both agribusiness allies, slowed union achievements nationwide. Some claimed the UFW had lost its power and criticized Chavez. The reformer and union leader died in his sleep at the age of sixty-six and inadvertently rejuvenated the farm workers' resolve. In 1994, President William Clinton posthumously awarded Chavez the nation's highest civilian honor, the Medal of Freedom.

HEIDI SCOTT GIUSTO

References and Further Reading

Dalton, Frederick John. *The Moral Vision of Cesar Chavez.* Maryknoll, NY: Orbis Books, 2003.

Dunne, John Gregory. *Delano: The Story of the California Grape Strike.* New York: Farrar, Straus & Giroux, 1967.

Etulain, Richard W., ed. *Cesar Chavez: A Brief Biography with Documents.* Boston: Bedford/St. Martins, 2002.

Hammerback, John C., and Richard J. Jensen. *The Rhetorical Career of Cesar Chavez.* College Station: Texas A&M University Press, 1998.

Jensen, Richard J., and John C. Hammerback, eds. *The Words of Cesar Chavez.* College Station: Texas A & M University Press, 2002.

Levy, Jacques E. *Cesar Chavez: Autobiography of La Causa.* New York: W.W. Norton & Company, Inc., 1975.

Taylor, Ronald B. *Chavez and the Farm Workers.* Boston: Beacon Press, 1975.

CHECKPOINTS (ROADBLOCKS)

If police set up a checkpoint (also known as a roadblock) on the highway, requiring all drivers to stop and answer some questions, is that constitutional? The answer is yes if certain conditions are met.

To assess the constitutionality of police conduct, traditional Fourth Amendment analysis provides that the police cannot search a person unless they have both probable cause to believe evidence of crime is located with that person and a warrant authorizing the search. Since the 1960s, however, two lines of cases deviating from this traditional approach have developed to give law enforcement more flexibility. One is stop and frisk law. The other is a series of cases referred to as "special needs" cases. The Fourth Amendment analysis developed in these "special needs" cases governs the constitutionality of highway checkpoints.

The types of cases referred to as "special needs" cases today were originally described as administrative inspection cases. These cases generally involved police activity that focused on goals other than the traditional investigation of crime. Examples include government agents conducting workplace inspections for compliance with occupational health and safety laws and government agents inspecting housing for compliance with local codes. In these cases, police were not required to meet the usual probable cause and warrant requirements. Rather, the Fourth Amendment requirements were relaxed, so that warrants were frequently not required, and the grounds necessary to justify the police conduct were reduced from probable cause to a lesser standard, reasonable suspicion, or eliminated altogether. The Supreme Court defined the reasonableness of government conduct in these cases by using a balancing analysis, balancing the government's need to search against the extent of the invasion to the citizen. One line of cases in this category is the roadblock cases.

The question of whether roadblocks are constitutional was first raised in the mid-1970s in cases where the police stopped cars near the border looking for illegal aliens. After concluding that police could *search* the cars only with probable cause, the Court authorized police to stop the cars and briefly *question* the occupants. If the stops were roving stops, that is, if the police were driving around to select which cars to stop, the police had to justify the stop and questioning by showing reasonable suspicion that led them to that car. This was the holding of *United States v. Brignoni-Ponce*. On the other hand, if the stops were fixed checkpoint stops, police could briefly question car occupants with no grounds whatsoever. The distinction was based on the idea that a fixed checkpoint necessarily limits police discretion, because they cannot pick the cars they stop, they have to take what comes their way. This limit on discretion minimizes the chance of abuse. In contrast, a roving stop allows police to cruise around and select which cars they approach, so in that situation, police have to provide reasons for stopping the cars they did. In combination, these cases indicated that whether grounds were required to stop a car depended to two variables: the intrusiveness of the police activity (search of the car as opposed to brief questioning of the occupants) and the amount of police discretion used (fixed checkpoints as opposed to roving stops).

The law was eventually refined in other types of investigations. When the police in Delaware made roving stops of cars for license and registration checks, and they made the stops randomly—that is, with no grounds to justify why the particular cars were chosen—the Supreme Court in *Delaware v.*

Prouse declared it unconstitutional. But in a significant case decided in 1990, the Supreme Court found it constitutional when Michigan used checkpoint stops to look for persons driving under the influence of alcohol. The Michigan authorities had no grounds for stopping the particular cars, but because their discretion was limited by the fixed character of the checkpoint, the Court approved it. And, the Supreme Court relied on the fact that the purpose of the checkpoint was not so much to investigate crime but to work toward the goal of highway safety. The highway death toll from drunk drivers indicated a special need for police to make the highways safer.

Two more Supreme Court cases complete the law on roadblocks. In 2000, the city of Indianapolis set up fixed checkpoints to briefly question occupants of cars about possession of street drugs. Police articulated no grounds for stopping the cars. In addition, the police had drug-detection dogs present at the roadblock to sniff the cars. The Court held this practice to be unconstitutional on the basis that the primary purpose was to detect evidence of ordinary criminal wrongdoing, so the case fell outside of the special needs category, and the checkpoint stops with no grounds were struck down. Most recently, in 2004, the Court held that a checkpoint set up to question car occupants about a recent hit-and-run case was constitutional. Like the drug checkpoint struck down, the police questioned each car without having any grounds for picking that car. However, the Court determined that asking for information about a recent hit-and-run did qualify as a special need situation, and the checkpoint was not set up merely to do the usual criminal investigation. Thus the checkpoint was constitutional.

In summary, the law today is that under the Fourth Amendment, police can use fixed checkpoints or roadblocks to briefly question occupants of the stopped cars without articulating any individualized reason for stopping that car, if the police purpose is focused on a special need rather than the traditional purpose of detecting evidence of crime. This is significant, because traditional Fourth Amendment law would not allow police to stop or question persons without articulating individualized grounds for selecting that person. However, based on the evolution described previously, the Supreme Court has now authorized police to use roadblocks under the conditions described.

SARAH N. WELLING

Cases and Statutes Cited

Camara v. Municipal Court, 387 U.S. 523 (1967)
City of Indianapolis v. Edmond, 531 U.S. 32 (2001)
Delaware v. Prouse, 440 US. 648 (1979)

Fourth Amendment
Illinois v. Lidster, 540 U.S. 419 (2004)
Marshall v. Barlow's, Inc., 436 U.S. 307 (1978)
Michigan Department of State Police v. Sitz, 496 U.S. 444 (1990)
U.S. v. Brignoni-Ponce, 422 U.S. 873 (1975)

See also Delaware v. Prouse, **440 US. 648 (1979);**
Search (General Definition); Seizures; *United States*
v. Brignoni-Ponce, **422 U.S. 873 (1975)**

CHEMERINSKY, ERWIN (1953–)

Erwin Chemerinsky was born May 14, 1953, in Chicago, Illinois. He grew up on the south side of Chicago in a working class family and was the first member of his family to go to college. He attended Northwestern University and received his Bachelors of Science degree in 1975 with highest distinction. He then earned his Juris Doctorate in 1978, graduating cum laude from Harvard Law School.

After graduating from law school, he began working as an attorney for the U. S. Department of Justice. At the Justice Department, he worked in the Fraud Section of the Civil Division. In 1980, he decided to pursue an academic career and returned to his native Chicago to begin teaching at De Paul University School of Law. Three years later, Professor Chemerinsky began teaching at University of Southern California (USC) Law School, where he continues to teach. He currently is the Sydney M. Irmas Professor of Public Interest Law, Ethics, and Political Science and teaches courses on Constitutional Law and Federal Courts. He has published numerous articles and books including two major treaties on constitutional law and federal jurisdiction.

Professor Chemerinsky has been influential in establishing civil liberties legislation in the state of California. He was instrumental in drafting the California Privacy Protection Act. Moreover, in April 2000, he was selected to investigate civil liberties violations in the Rampart scandal. In this scandal, police officers in the Los Angeles Police Department (LAPD) were accused of making false arrests, framing innocent people, and offering false testimony at trials. Chemerinsky's analysis indicated that civil liberties violations occurred because of flaws and oversights in the police and justice systems. He, therefore, recommended significant changes in both the police and justice systems, which ultimately were instated.

Chemerinsky also has argued a number of civil liberties cases in the federal courts. His most notable work challenged the constitutionality of California's controversial "three strikes" legislation. This legislation requires a person with two prior "serious" or "violent" felony convictions (or "strikes"), who is convicted of a third felony, to be sentenced to twenty-five years to life for the crime. Chemerinsky challenged the constitutionality of this law in *Bray v. Ylst*, arguing the law violated the Constitution's Eighth Amendment prohibition on "cruel and unusual" punishment. The U. S. Court of Appeals agreed. While the *Bray* decision did not invalidate the "three strikes" law generally, it did determine that circumstances exist in which an indeterminate life sentence is "grossly disproportionate" for the crime, and therefore, is unconstitutional.

Professor Chemerinsky continued his challenge of California's "three strikes" law in the U. S. Supreme Court. In *Lockyer v. Andrade*, he argued that, like Bray, Andrade's punishment for petty theft under "three strikes" was unconstitutional. The U.S. Supreme Court, however, ruled that the California Court of Appeals decision, which upheld Andrade's twenty-five year to life sentence, was constitutional. This is because the California court's decision was not contrary to "established federal law."

FRANCENE M. ENGEL

References and Further Reading

Chemerinsky, Erwin. *Federal Jurisdiction*. 4th ed. New York: Aspen Publishers, 2003.
———. *Constitutional Law: Principles and Policies*. 2nd ed. New York: Aspen Law and Business, 2002.
———. *Interpreting the Constitution*. Westport, CT: Praeger, 1987.

Cases and Statutes Cited

Andrade v. Lockyer, 270 F. 3d 743 (2001)
Bray v. Ylst, 283 F. 3d 1019 (2002)
Lockyer v. Andrade, 538 U.S. 63 (2003)

CHESSMAN, CARYL (1921–1960)

Caryl Chessman, born in St. Joseph, Michigan, in 1921, grew up in Glendale, California. During the Depression, Chessman began stealing food to provide for his family. In the late 1930s and early 1940s, Chessman was in and out of jail for auto theft. In January 1948, the state of California charged Caryl Chessman with eighteen counts of robbery, sexual assault, and kidnapping. Two female victims identified Chessman as the "red light bandit," a rapist who used a red light to impersonate police officers. Because Chessman had forcibly removed his victims from their vehicles, he was charged under California's "Little Lindbergh Law" that carried the death penalty. Chessman's capital conviction and unprecedented twelve-year stay on death row fundamentally shaped public opinion and legal precedents on the death penalty nationwide.

At trial Chessman rebuffed the services of a defense attorney and defended himself. Chessman's defense, however, failed for several reasons: He was inexperienced with courtroom procedure, both the judge and prosecuting attorney had strong capital conviction records, and the jury was composed of eleven women and only one man. Death in the gas chamber seemed imminent until the court reporter died two days before Chessman's official sentencing. Sensing an opportunity, Chessman moved for a new trial stating that new trial transcripts would be inaccurate. Although the judge refused his motion, higher court judges repeatedly stayed Chessman's execution citing potential transcription errors.

By early 1952, the California Supreme Court decreed that new trial transcripts were accurate. Chessman's new execution date was set for March 1952; however, over the next eight years, Chessman convinced several California judges, federal judges, and even governor Pat Brown that the new transcripts were flawed. The transcription issue never evaporated, because Chessman took his case to the public in 1954 when he smuggled his autobiography, *Cell 2455 Death Row*, out of San Quentin. Once the book was published, politicians, prison officials, criminologists, and psychiatrists, committed to the ideals of prisoner rehabilitation, claimed that Chessman's literary attainments proved that he had reformed and deserved to live. Chessman continued to demonstrate his rehabilitation by publishing two more books. As public discussion on Chessman's case increased, Americans questioned the efficacy of the death penalty. Many citizens wrote to California Governors Knight and Brown pleading for clemency in Chessman's case. For many, Chessman's legal and public appeals provided proof that the death penalty had no place in modern society.

In the late 1950s, however, increasing crime rates prompted many Americans to conclude that prisoner rehabilitation did not work. American public opinion on capital punishment reversed direction. A 1960 opinion poll indicated a strong approval trend. In 1995, approval of the death penalty reached an unprecedented eighty percent.

In 1962, after exhausting all of his legal and public appeals, Chessman died in the gas chamber. Even though he had lost his personal battle, Chessman ultimately pressed Americans to agree or disagree with the death penalty. Legally speaking, he forced the higher courts to consider new standards of fairness in capital cases.

GARRY D. WICKERD

References and Further Reading

Hamm, Theodore. *Rebel and a Cause: Caryl Chessman and the Politics of the Death Penalty in Postwar California, 1948–1974.* Berkeley: University of California Press, 2001.
Kunstler, William. *Beyond a Reasonable Doubt? The Original Trial of Caryl Chessman.* New York: Morrow Press, 1961.
Parker, Frank J. *Caryl Chessman: The Red Light Bandit.* Nelson Hall, 1975.

See also **Capital Punishment**

CHICAGO SEVEN TRIAL

The 1968 Democratic convention was held in one of the most tumultuous times in recent history. Martin Luther King, Jr., and Bobby Kennedy had been assassinated, racial tensions exploded into riots in cities across the country, and student protests paralyzed college campuses. It felt like the country was coming apart at the seams, and Chicago's law-and-order mayor, Richard Daley, was not about to allow this chaos to engulf his city. The convention turned into a fiasco as police attempted to control massive crowds of civil rights and anti-war protesters who had converged on the convention.

Federal prosecutors indicted eight alleged leaders of the protests for conspiring to violate an anti-riot statute. Defendants included Youth International Party leaders Abbie Hoffman and Jerry Rubin, Students for a Democratic Society national director Rennie Davis, pacifist David Dellinger, and Tom Hayden, the author of the 1962 Port Huron Statement. (The trial of Bobby Seale was severed from the others, resulting in the Chicago Seven.) The strategy of defense lawyers William Kunstler and Leonard Weinglass was to politicize the trial, attempt to win public support, and in effect to continue the protests using the trial as another medium. The trial occasionally degenerated into a circus-like atmosphere, with outbursts from the defendants and repeated citations for contempt of court issued by the presiding judge. Five of the seven defendants were convicted of conspiracy. All of the convictions, along with the contempt citations, were reversed on appeal.

W. BRADLEY WENDEL

References and Further Reading

Lukas, J. Anthony. *The Barnyard Epithet and Other Obscenities: Notes on the Chicago Conspiracy Trial.* New York: Harper & Row, 1970.
Schultz, John. *The Chicago Conspiracy Trial.* New York: Da Capo Press, rev'd ed., 1993.

See also **Kunstler, William M.**

CHICAGO v. MORALES, 527 U.S. 41 (1999)

The City of Chicago passed an ordinance that was aimed at reducing gang presence in Chicago neighborhoods. The ordinance provided that when a police officer saw "a criminal street gang member loitering . . . with one or more persons," the officer "shall order all such persons to disperse." Loitering was defined as remaining in "any one place with no apparent purpose." Anyone failing to obey the dispersal order was subject to arrest.

In *City of Chicago v. Morales*, the Supreme Court found the ordinance facially invalid. The Court reaffirmed its earlier holding of *Kolender v. Lawson*: a penal law is void for vagueness if ordinary people cannot understand what conduct is prohibited, or if it fails to prevent arbitrary and discriminatory enforcement by the police. In *Morales*, the definition of loitering was the principal source of the constitutional problem because it failed to establish minimal guidelines to govern law enforcement. Whether a purpose is "apparent" is an inherently subjective inquiry. Furthermore, too much innocent conduct fell within the ordinance because it did not require a harmful purpose and both gang members and non-gang members could be ordered to disperse.

The ordinance was based on the "broken windows" theory of policing, which posits that officers prevent more serious crime when they eliminate small, visible signs of public disorder. While *Morales* was sympathetic to this approach, the Court was unwilling to uphold an ordinance that effectively allowed police to determine what constituted "disorder" within a particular community.

SARAH E. WALDECK

References and Further Reading

Alschuler, Albert W., and Stephen J Schulhofer, *Antiquated Procedures or Bedrock Rights? A Response to Professors Meares and Kahan,* University of Chicago Legal Forum (1998): 215–244.
Meares, Tracey L., and Dan M. Kahan, *Wages of Antiquated Procedural Thinking: A Critique of Chicago v. Morales,* University of Chicago Legal Forum (1998): 197–214.
Rosenthal, Lawrence, *Policing and Equal Protection,* Yale Law and Policy Review 21 (2003): 53–103.
Strosnider, Kim, *Anti-Gang Ordinances After City of Chicago v. Morales: The Intersection of Race, Vagueness Doctrine, and Equal Protection in the Criminal Law,* American Criminal Law Review 39 (2002): 101–146.
Waldeck, Sarah E., *Cops, Community Policing and the Social Norms Approach to Crime Control: Should One Make Us More Comfortable With the Others?* Georgia Law Review 34 (2000): 1253–1310.

Cases and Statutes Cited

Kolender v. Lawson, 461 U.S. 352 (1983)

See also **Equal Protection of Law (XIV); Gang Ordinances;** *Kolender v. Lawson,* **461 U.S. 352 (1983);** *Papachristou v. City of Jacksonville* **405 U.S. 156 (1972); Vagueness and Overbreadth in Criminal Statutes; Vagueness Doctrine**

CHILD CUSTODY AND ADOPTION

In the area of adoption, the interest that takes center stage is that of the biological parents. As the Supreme Court pointed out in *Troxel v. Granville,* it is well accepted that a biological parent has a fundamental liberty interest in the care, custody, and control of his or her child. Thus, a state generally may not take a child from the custody of his or her biological parent simply because it believes that another parent would do a better job of raising the child. In the case of adoption, this means that prior to handing down an adoption decree, the state must either have the voluntary consent of the parents or the state must have involuntarily terminated the rights of the parents.

One of the most common scenarios in the adoption arena is that of a mother putting her nonmarital child up for adoption, with or without the knowledge and/or consent of the father. Consonant with the constitutional precepts outlined previously, all of the states require that, prior to an adoption, the State must obtain the biological mother's consent and this consent must be informed and free from fraud, coercion, or undue influence. If the consent was not freely given, then the adoption decree is subject to being overturned. In addition, many states allow the mother to revoke her consent within a specified period of time and thus stop the adoption proceeding.

The question of notice to and consent of the biological father for the adoption of a nonmarital child is considerably more complicated. Unlike in the case of a mother, the question of who the father is of a nonmarital child is at times difficult to answer. Given this reality, the states have had to determine how much effort must be expended in giving notice of the adoption proceedings to the putative father(s) and whether the consent of the putative father is necessary. The issue then arises as to whether the resultant state statutory schemes violate the constitutional rights of the putative father.

Prior to 1972, the fathers of nonmarital children were generally afforded little constitutional protection. This changed somewhat in 1972 with *Stanley v. Illinois* where the Supreme Court held that the private interest here, that of a man in the children he has sired and raised, undeniably warrants deference and, absent a powerful countervailing interest, protection. *Stanley v. Illinois,* 405 U.S. at 651.

Because *Stanley* was a custody case, the question remained as to what rights a father had in the adoption arena. The Supreme Court gave partial answers in two cases, *Quilloin v. Walcott* (1978) and *Caban v. Mohammed* (1979). In these cases the Supreme Court found that if a father has established a substantial relationship with his child and has admitted paternity, then he has a constitutional right to consent to or veto an adoption. Thus, in *Quillion* the father was not entitled to veto the adoption even though, in the eleven years of the child's life, he had made some support payments and had visited the child on numerous occasions. He had never had or sought custody and he had not legitimated the child. Conversely, in *Caban* the father was entitled to veto the adoption. He had lived with the mother for five years, during which time the two children were born, he continued to see the children frequently after he and the mother ceased living together, and at one point he had custody of the children.

Caban and *Quilloin* concerned the question of consent. The Supreme Court in *Lehr v. Robertson* addressed the issue of when a putative father is entitled to receive notice of the adoption proceedings. There the Court reiterated that when a putative father has a developed parent–child relationship with his nonmarital child, then his interest in continued contact with the child has substantial constitutional protection. A mere biological link does not merit equal constitutional protection, but it does afford the father the opportunity to form a parent–child relationship. Thus, if there is a biological link, yet the putative father has not developed a parent–child relationship, then the question facing the Court is whether the statutory scheme at issue adequately protected the putative father's opportunity to form such a relationship. In *Lehr* the Court found that New York State's statutory scheme adequately protected the father's opportunity. The statute required that notice of the adoption proceeding be given to seven categories of putative fathers (the categories encompassed situations where the mother and/or the father had somehow acknowledged the father's paternity) and the categories were not likely to omit many responsible fathers. Furthermore, qualification for notice was within the putative father's control. The father in *Lehr* did not register his name with the state and did not fit within the other six categories, thus the state was not required to notify him of the adoption proceedings.

None of the preceding cases addressed the question of what rights a putative father has to veto an adoption when the child is placed for adoption as a newborn and/or the mother hides the child's birth from him. Several state Supreme Court cases have, however, found that a putative father's consent to the adoption may be necessary even if the father does not yet have a parent–child relationship. In such a case, the father's consent is necessary if, once the father learns of the birth of his child, he does all he can to assert his interest in the child and to assume the responsibilities of parenthood. According to these states, this right to veto the adoption can only be overcome if the father is unfit such that the state has the right to terminate his parental rights. It should be noted that these courts, in the process of protecting the right of the natural father, often find themselves in the position of failing to protect the interest of the child in staying with her or his adoptive parents and/or the interest of the adoptive parents in retaining custody of the child.

Other state supreme courts have not, however, afforded putative fathers this same level of protection. For example, in the case of *In re Baby Boy C.,* the D.C. Court of Appeals held that the best interests of the child could trump the father's rights to custody even where the father had grasped his opportunity to form a relationship with the child. Thus, the court granted the adoption without the consent of the father and without a finding that the father was unfit, because granting custody to the father would be detrimental to the child's best interests.

As mentioned earlier, in certain circumstances the state can terminate the parental rights of parents to their child, thus making the child eligible for adoption. However, because, of the nature of the parent's constitutional rights, it is generally held that the state may only terminate the parent's rights if the state can prove that the parent is unfit. Furthermore, the Supreme Court in the *Santosky v. Kramer* case held that the state must prove this lack of fitness with clear and convincing evidence.

As previously noted, traditionally in the area of adoption, the rights of the biological mother of a nonmarital child were often paramount. In the 1970s, the Court began to recognize that the biological father's interest was also worthy of recognition. The question remains, however, regarding the rights of the child and the adoptive parents.

JANET W. STEVERSON

References and Further Reading

Hollinger, Joan Heifetz. "Adoption Law." *The Future of Children*, vol. 3, no. 1, (1993): 43–61.

Kessel v. Leavitt, 204 W.Va. 95, 511 S.E.2d 720 (1988). West Virginia Supreme Court does a very good job of summarizing the current state of the law regarding when the consent of the putative father of a nonmarital child is necessary.

Mnookin, Weisberg. *Child, Family, and State: Problems and Materials on Children and the Law*. 4th Ed. New York: Aspen, 2000.

Cases and Statutes Cited

Caban v. Mohammed, 441 U.S. 380 (1979)

In re Baby Boy C., 630 A.2d 670 (D.C. 1993), cert. denied sub nom. *H.R. v. E.O.*, 513 U.S. 809 (1994)

Lehr v. Robertson, 463 U.S. 248 (1983)

Quilloin v. Walcott, 434 U.S. 246 (1978)

Santosky v. Kramer, 455 U.S. 745 (1982)

Stanley v. Illinois, 405 U.S. 645 (1972)

Troxel v. Granville, 530 U.S. 57 (2000)

CHILD CUSTODY AND FOSTER CARE

In America, the family serves as both the primary vehicle for the care and rearing of children and as a private realm of intimate association and moral autonomy. This tradition of family privacy is rooted in early American common law, inherited in part from England, and in principles of political and personal autonomy on which the United States was founded. Family privacy remains a fundamental principle, but since colonial times and escalating beginning in the Progressive era, the patriarch's power over children has diminished whereas maternal, state, and children's power have increased (Appell 2004; Mason).

Prior to the abolition of slavery, family privacy generally did not extend to slaves, because children born to female slaves legally belonged to the slave master. Indeed, it was not until decades after adoption of the Thirteenth and Fourteenth Amendments that the U. S. Supreme Court began to recognize a zone of family privacy and its attendant parental rights doctrine. The constitutional source of this fundamental family liberty is contested but is found in, or in the penumbra of, constitutional amendments relating to freedom of religion and association, freedom from unreasonable searches and seizures, due process, equal protection, and the natural liberties retained by the people (*Stanley v. Illinois*).

Children and parents share a liberty interest in family integrity and against state intervention (*Santosky v. Kramer*), but children have few liberty interests in opposition to their parents. This imbalance between adult and child rights in the custodial context has become a growing source of controversy since the last half of the twentieth century as children are increasingly viewed as rights-holders, family forms become more fluid, and lawyers and other professionals work directly with, or on behalf of, children (Appell 2004).

Parental Custodial Liberties

The parent–child relationship is so fundamental that the U. S. Supreme Court has extended special protections to parents for custodial decisions regarding child rearing, visitation, health care, education, and religion, for example, *Meyer v. Nebraska*; *Parham v. J.R.*; *Pierce v. Society of Sisters*; *Prince v. Massachusetts*; *Troxel v. Granville*; *Wisconsin v. Yoder*. Parents have a superior right to custody of their children unless the parent is unfit or has abdicated all or part of the parental role (*Stanley v. Illinois*) even when others believe that the child's best interests lay elsewhere (*Santosky v. Kramer*). Furthermore, courts may not base custodial decisions on racial prejudice (*Palmore v. Sidoti*).

States cannot coercively remove a child from parental custody without a hearing (*Stanley v. Illinois*). In termination of parental rights proceedings, parents receive heightened procedural protections not normally available to civil litigants. For example, a court may not terminate parental rights unless the parent has been shown to be unfit or otherwise unable to parent under a heightened standard of proof known as clear and convincing evidence (*Santosky v. Kramer*). Moreover, indigent parents may be entitled to a court-appointed attorney when the termination of parental rights proceedings are complex (*Lassiter v. Dept. Soc. Services*); like criminal defendants, indigent parents are entitled to free transcripts on appeal of termination of parental rights decisions (*M.L.B. v. S.L.J.*).

There are, however, limits to parental freedom to make decisions regarding their children's care and upbringing. These limitations generally arise from other constitutional principles that outweigh parental liberties. Thus parents do not have the right to send their children to a segregated school (*Runyon v. McCrary*) or to abuse or neglect their children (*Stanley v. Illinois*). Moreover, a daughter's reproductive health rights can trump the parent's right to make medical decisions regarding birth control (*Carey v. Pop. Services International*) and abortion (*Bellotti v. Baird*).

State law, within constitutional parameters, normally determines who the mother and father are, and it is those mothers and fathers so defined whose liberties the Supreme Court protects. Generally, the law considers the birth mother and biological or marital father to be parents (*Lehr v. Robertson*; *Michael H. v. Gerald D.*; *Quilloin v. Walcott*). States have, however, recognized custodial rights of stepparents and same sex partners of legal parents by establishing special rules for second-parent adoption and for visitation rights after the adult relationship terminates (Appell 2001).

Foster parents do not have the same liberty interest, if any, in their foster children as parents have in their children (*Smith v. Organization of Foster Families for Equality and Reform*). Similarly, grandparents do not have special liberties regarding their grandchildren on par with the rights of parents (*Troxel v. Granville*), but certain constitutional family privacy protections may be extended to grandparents living with grandchildren (*Moore v. City of East Cleveland*) (plurality).

Children's Custodial Liberties

Children do not have many liberty interests in the custodial context because the Supreme Court views children as always in the custody of another (*Schall v. Martin*). Although children and parents share a liberty interest in their relationship, parents hold most of the rights within that relationship. Thus, although parents have the right to make major decisions about their children's care, education, and custody, children have only limited rights to oppose those decisions.

Children do not have many rights against the state as custodian or protector either. For example, although parents are not entitled to abuse their children, children do not have a right to state protection from that abuse (*DeShaney v. Winnebago County Dept. of Social Services*; *City of Castle Rock v. Gonzalez*). Children also have few liberties when in protective state custody, such as foster care, although presumably they have the right to be free from avoidable harm (*See Reno v. Flores*; *Youngberg v. Romeo*).

Children do, however, have slightly greater liberty interests in other custodial contexts such as school (*Goss v. Lopez*; *New Jersey v. T.L.O.*; *Tinker v. Des-Moines*; *West Virginia Board of Education v. Barnette*)

and the threat of juvenile or penal incarceration (*In re Gault*; *In re Winship*).

Native American Children

Special rules apply to certain custody and foster care proceedings regarding Native American children. These rules both enhance and limit parental and children's liberties and provide special rights for tribes (Indian Child Welfare Act; Appell, 2004).

ANNETTE R. APPEL

References and Further Reading

Appell, Annette R., *Uneasy Tensions Between Children's Rights and Civil Rights*, Nevada Law Journal 5 (2004): 1:141–171.
———, *Virtual Mothers and the Meaning of Parenthood*, University of Michigan Journal of Law Reform 34 (2001): 4:683–790.
Davis, Peggy Cooper. *Neglected Stories: The Constitution and Family Values*, New York: Hill and Wang, 1997.
Guggenheim, Martin. *What's Wrong with Children's Rights*, Cambridge, MA: Harvard University Press, 2005.
Lindsey, Duncan. *The Welfare of Children*, 2nd ed., New York: Oxford University Press, 2004.
Mason, Mary Ann. *From Father's Property to Children's Rights*, New York: Columbia University Press, 1994.
Mnookin, Robert H. *In the Interest of Children: Advocacy, Law Reform, and Public Policy*, New York: W.H. Freeman & Co., 1985.
Woodhouse, Barbara Bennett, *Who Owns the Child?: Meyer and Pierce and the Child as Property*, William & Mary Law Review 33 (1992): 4:995–1122.

Cases and Statutes Cited

Bellotti v. Baird, 443 U.S. 622 (1979)
Carey v. Pop. Services International, 431 US 678 (1977)
City of Castle Rock v. Gonzalez, 125 S. Ct. 2796 (2005)
DeShaney v. Winnebago County, 489 U.S 189 (1989)
Goss v. Lopez, 419 U.S. 565 (1975)
In re Gault, 387 U.S. 1 (1967)
In re Winship, 397 U.S. 358 (1970)
Lassiter v. DSS, 452 U.S. 18 (1981)
Lehr v. Robertson, 463 U.S. 248 (1983
Meyer v. Nebraska, 262 U.S. 390 (1923)
Michael H. v. Gerald D., 491 U.S. 110 (1989)
M.L.B. v. S.L.J, 519 U.S. 102 (1996)
Moore v. City of East Cleveland, 431 U.S. 494 (1977)
New Jersey v. T.L.O., 469 U.S. 325 (1985)
Palmore v. Sidoti, 466 U.S. 429 (1984)
Parham v. J.R., 442 U.S. 584 (1979)
Pierce v. Society of Sisters, 268 U.S. 510 (1925)
Prince v. Massachusetts, 321 US 158 (1944)
Quilloin v. Walcott, 434 U.S. 246 (1978)
Reno v. Flores, 507 U.S. 292 (1993)
Runyon v. McCrary, 427 U.S. 160 (1976)
Santosky v. Kramer, 455 U.S. 745 (1982)

Schall v. Martin, 467 U.S. 253, 268 (1984)
Smith v. Organization of Foster Families for Equality and Reform, 431 U.S. 816 (1977)
Stanley v. Illinois, 405 U.S. 645 (1972)
Tinker v. DesMoines, 393 U.S. 503 (1969)
Troxel v. Granville, 530 U.S. 57 (2000)
West Virginia Board of Education v. Barnette, 319 U.S. 624 (1943)
Wisconsin v. Yoder, 406 U.S. 205 (1972)
Youngberg v. Romeo, 457 U.S. 307 (1982)
Indian Child Welfare Act, 25 USC 1901–1963

See also **Child Custody and Adoption**

CHILD PORNOGRAPHY

In 1982, in *New York v. Ferber*, the Court held that production and dissemination of child pornography—"depictions of sexual activity involving children"—is unprotected by the First Amendment. The Court acknowledged that the Amendment protects nonobscene depictions of sexual activity between adults, but granted states "greater leeway" in regulating child pornography because of its effect on the child performers themselves, without regard for its effect on viewers.

Ferber concluded that states have a compelling interest in "safeguarding the physical and psychological well-being of a minor" and in "prevention of sexual exploitation and abuse of children." The Court also found that "the use of children as subjects of pornographic materials is harmful to the physiological, emotional and mental health of the child" because "the materials produced are a permanent record of the children's participation."

Ferber, decided before the age of computer-generated images, thus took the extraordinary step of removing child pornography from First Amendment protection because of its harmful effects on actual child performers. In dictum, the Court stated that "distribution of descriptions or other depictions of sexual conduct, not otherwise obscene, which do not involve live performance or photographic or other visual reproduction of live performances, retains First Amendment protection." The computer age, however, soon made "virtual" child pornography a pressing national issue. Computers can manipulate, or "morph," an innocent picture of an actual child to create a picture showing the child engaged in sexual activity. An obscene or nonobscene picture of an adult can be transformed into the image of a child. Computer graphics can even generate the realistic image of a nonexistent child.

The federal Child Pornography Prevention Act of 1996 legislated against nonobscene virtual child pornography. The Act reached "any visual depiction, including . . . any . . . computer or computer-generated image[s] or picture[s], whether made or produced by electronic, mechanical or other means . . . where such visual description is, *or appears to be*, of a minor engaging in sexually explicit conduct." (emphasis added). Congress based the 1996 act squarely on virtual child pornography's effect on viewers. The lawmakers found that pedophiles might use virtual images to encourage children to participate in sexual activity and might whet their own sexual appetites with the pornographic images. Congress also found that the existence of computer-generated images could complicate prosecutions of pornographers who do use actual children by making it more difficult to prove that a particular picture used actual children.

In 2002, in *Ashcroft v. Free Speech Coalition*, the Court struck down provisions of the 1996 act relating to materials that appear to depict minors but are produced without using actual children. The plaintiffs did not challenge the provision criminalizing morphing, which (like the materials at issue in *Ferber*) implicates the interests of actual children. *Ashcroft* also left undisturbed the provision criminalizing child pornography using actual children, *Ferber's* target. But *Ashcroft* held that the provisions relating to nonexistent children violated the First Amendment for prohibiting speech that "records no crime and creates no victims by its production." The Court found any causal link between virtual images and actual incidents of child abuse only "contingent and indirect."

The Supreme Court has not decided whether photographs or films of nude or partially nude children, without sexual activity, constitute punishable child pornography or First Amendment-protected expression. *Ferber* stated that "nudity, without more is protected expression," but the statement was dictum because the Court was not reviewing a statute that presented the nudity issue. Most lower courts have regarded photographs and films of nude children, without more, as constitutionally protected expression, but have upheld convictions under statutes that prohibit such depictions made for sexual gratification. As thus limited, the depictions become child pornography proscribable under *Ferber*.

In *Osborne v. Ohio*, the Court upheld a statute that prohibited private possession and viewing of nonobscene child pornography (including private possession and viewing in one's own home), even without proof that the possessor intended to distribute the material. The Court found that because "much of the child pornography market has been driven underground" since *Ferber*, "it is now difficult, if not impossible, to solve the child pornography problem by only attacking production and distribution."

The Child Pornography Prevention Act followed nearly two decades of congressional legislation against child pornography. The Protection of Children Against Sexual Exploitation Act of 1977 added two substantive sections that remain in the federal criminal code. The first section, now 18 U.S.C. § 2251, prohibits the use of children in "sexually explicit" productions and prohibits parents and guardians from allowing such use of their children. The second section, now 18 U.S.C. § 2252, makes it a federal crime to transport, ship, or receive in interstate commerce for the purpose of selling, any "obscene visual or print medium" if its production involved the use of a minor engaging in sexually explicit conduct.

Because the 1977 act required proof that the materials were obscene and that the defendant had a profit motive, the act yielded only a handful of prosecutions in its first five years of operation. Relying on *Ferber*, the Child Protection Act of 1984 prohibited distribution of nonobscene material depicting sexual activity by children and eliminated the "pecuniary profit" element. The 1984 act also legislated against possession by criminalizing the receipt in interstate or foreign commerce of materials showing minors engaged in sexually explicit conduct.

In 1986, Congress prohibited production and use of advertisements for child pornography and created a private civil remedy in favor of persons who suffer personal injury resulting from the production of child pornography. To help effect the proscriptive authority approved in *Ferber*, Congress and a number of states also require photo processors to report customers' sexual depictions of children on film. These statutes typically extend beyond films made by commercial customers, and parents and guardians who do nothing more than film their toddlers on bear skin rugs and the like are sometimes reported. Processors are typically granted immunity from civil or criminal liability arising from filing a required report in good faith.

DOUGLAS E. ABRAMS

References and Further Reading

Abrams, Douglas E., and Sarah H. Ramsey, *Children and the Law—Doctrine, Policy and Practice.* 643–656, 2nd ed., St. Paul, MN: Thomson West, 2003.
Nowak, John E., and Ronald D. Rotunda. *Constitutional Law,* 1395–1396, 7th ed, St. Paul, MN: Thomson West, 2004.

Cases and Statutes Cited

Ashcroft v. Free Speech Coalition, 535 U.S. 234 (2002)
New York v. Ferber, 458 U.S. 747 (1982)
Osborne v. Ohio, 495 U.S. 103 (1990)
18 U.S.C. § 2251

18 U.S.C. § 2252
18 U.S.C. § 2256

*See also Ashcroft v. Free Speech Coalition***, 535 U.S. 234 (2002); Children and the First Amendment; Child Pornography;** *New York v. Ferber***, 458 U.S. 747 (1982);** *Osborne v. Ohio***, 495 U.S. 103 (1990); Unprotected Speech**

CHILDREN AND THE FIRST AMENDMENT

Children hold rights under the First Amendment Speech Clause, but these rights may provide less protection than adults hold. Leading Supreme Court decisions have arisen in the public schools. *Tinker v. Des Moines Independent Community School District* (1969) held that "[s]tudents in school as well as out of school are 'persons' under our Constitution," and do not "shed their constitutional rights to freedom of speech or expression at the schoolhouse gate." *Bethel School District v. Fraser* (1986), however, stated that "the constitutional rights of students in public school are not automatically coextensive with the rights of adults in other settings." *Hazelwood School District v. Kuhlmeier* (1988) stated that students' constitutional rights "must be applied in light of the special characteristics of the school environment."

The Speech Clause may also protect children more than adults. *Ginsberg v. New York* (1968) upheld a statute that prohibited sale to minors of material defined as obscene based on its appeal to children, even where the material would not be obscene for adults. *New York v. Ferber* (1982) held that the Clause does not protect production and dissemination of nonobscene child pornography—"depictions of sexual activity involving children." *Osborne v. Ohio* (1990) held that states may prohibit private possession and viewing of child pornography (even in one's own home), without proof that the possessor intended to distribute the material. *Ashcroft v. Free Speech Coalition* (2002), however, invalidated legislation relating to computer-generated materials that seem to depict minors but are produced without using actual children.

DOUGLAS E. ABRAMS

References and Further Reading

Abrams, Douglas E., and Sarah H. Ramsey. *Children and the Law—Doctrine, Policy and Practice.* 36–52, 643–655, 2nd ed., St. Paul, MN: Thomson West, 2003.
Sullivan, Kathleen M., and Gerald Gunther. *Constitutional Law.* 1114–1120, 1294–1303, 15th ed., New York: Foundation Press, 2004.

Cases and Statutes Cited

Ashcroft v. Free Speech Coalition, 535 U.S. 234 (2002)
Bethel School District v. Fraser, 478 U.S. 675 (1986)
Ginsberg v. New York, 390 U.S. 629 (1968)
Hazelwood School District v. Kuhlmeier, 484 U.S. 260 (1988)
New York v. Ferber, 458 U.S. 747 (1982)
Osborne v. Ohio, 495 U.S. 103 (1990)
Tinker v. Des Moines Independent Community School District, 393 U.S. 503 (1969)

See also **Ashcroft v. Free Speech Coalition, 535 U.S. 234 (2002); Balancing Approach to Free Speech; Child Pornography; Freedom of the Press: Modern Period (1917–Present); Hazelwood School District v. Kuhlmeier, 484 U.S. 260 (1988); In re Gault, 387 U.S. 1 (1967); New York v. Ferber, 458 U.S. 747 (1982); Osborne v. Ohio, 495 U.S. 103 (1990); Prior Restraints; Public Forum Doctrines; Public/Nonpublic Forums Distinction**

CHIMEL v. CALIFORNIA, 395 U.S. 752 (1969)

In *Chimel v. California*, the Supreme Court addressed the permissible scope of a search incident to a lawful arrest under the Fourth Amendment. After the issuance of an arrest warrant for burglary of a coin shop, police officers arrested Chimel in his home. Over his objection, the police conducted a detailed search of Chimel's residence, entering every room, opening drawers, and recovering coins and other suspected stolen items. The trial court found that the search was justified because it was incident to a lawful arrest.

The Supreme Court reversed and found this search unreasonable under the Fourth Amendment, holding that a search incident to arrest is limited to the arrestee's person and the area "within his immediate control." Justice Stewart's majority opinion includes a history of the evolving search incident to arrest doctrine, beginning with its apparent inception in *Weeks v. United States* in 1914. In arriving at the "immediate control" rule, the Court focused on the dual rationale behind allowing police to search in conjunction with an arrest: (1) to ensure officer safety and (2) to prevent the destruction or concealment of evidence. The Court also emphasized the heightened level of intrusion involved in the search of a home.

Justices White and Black dissented, criticizing the "remarkable instability" of this shifting area of law. The dissent argued in favor of the case-by-case "reasonableness" approach previously used by the Court, citing the likelihood of destruction of evidence by a third party while the police obtain a search warrant.

STEPHANIE ROBERTS HARTUNG

References and Further Reading

Katz, Lewis R., *The Automobile Exception Transformed: The Rise of a Public Place Exemption to the Warrant Requirement*, Case W. Res. 36 (1986): 375.
Moskovitz, Myron, *A Rule in Search of a Reason: An Empirical Reexamination of Chimel and Belton*, Wis. L. Rev. 2002 (2002): 657.
Rigg, Robert, *The Objective Mind and "Search Incident to Citation*, B.U. Pub. Int. L.J. 8 (1999): 281.
Salken, Barbara C., *Balancing Exigency and Privacy in Warrantless Searches to Prevent Destruction of Evidence: The Need for a Rule*, Hastings L. J. 39 (1988): 282.

Cases and Statutes Cited

Agnello v. United States, 269 U.S. 20 (1925)
Carroll v. United States, 267 U.S. 132 (1925)
Preston v. United States, 376 U.S. 364 (1964)
Terry v. Ohio, 392 U.S. 1 (1968)
United States v. Lefkowitz, 285 U.S. 452 (1932)
Weeks v. United States, 232 U.S. 383 (1914)

See also **Arrest; Exclusionary Rule; New York v. Belton 453 U.S. 454 (1981); Search (General Definition); Seizures; Warrantless Searches**

CHINESE EXCLUSION ACT

See *Chae Chan Ping v. U.S., 130 U.S. 581 (1889) and Chinese Exclusion Act*

CHRISTIAN COALITION

The Christian Coalition is a Washington, D.C.–based national advocacy group that supports conservative political and religious ideals. The Christian Coalition lobbies Congress, state legislatures, city councils, and school boards on a range of issues, including abortion regulation, religious expression in public schools, social welfare policy, and tax-relief. The Christian Coalition maintains an extensive grassroots network of volunteers and distributes candidate voters' guides prior to elections that describe candidate positions on religious, social, and economic issues. The Coalition maintains its activities concentrate on "traditional family values" and are nonpartisan, but liberal advocacy groups, such as People for the American Way and Americans United for Separation of Church and State, have claimed the Coalition policies and voters' guides favor Republican Party issues and candidates. Despite its disclaimers, the Coalition has become a powerful force in the Republican Party, influencing the latter's position on many social issues.

The Christian Coalition was founded in 1989 by Rev. Marion G. (Pat) Robertson, a television evangelist (host of the "700 Club") and founder of the Christian Broadcasting Network. Robertson created the Christian Coalition after his failed bid for the Republican Party nomination for President in 1988. Early promotional literature stated the group's purpose as to "mobilize and train [theologically conservative] Christians for effective political action." The Coalition's inaugural event was a $500,000 campaign to defund the National Endowment for Humanities. The bulk of Coalition efforts, however, have involved election-related activities such as voter registration, "get-out-the-vote" campaigns, and distributing candidate voters guides. The Coalition experienced initial political success by recruiting unknown conservative candidates for lower level political offices, a strategy described by Coalition Executive Director Ralph Reed as supporting "stealth candidates." By 1995, the Coalition claimed a dominant or substantial role in the Republican parties of thirty-one states. In the 2000 general election, the Coalition distributed 70 million candidate voters' guides, primarily to conservative Christians. The Coalition claimed responsibility for the conservative Republican takeover of Congress in the 1994 election and for securing the election of George W. Bush as President in 2000.

Although the Coalition's agenda concentrated initially on religious and moral issues, Reed expanded the organization's focus to include support for conservative economic policies, health care reform, and increased defense spending. In 1995, the Coalition announced its "Contract with the American Family," which outlined ten legislative or policy goals, including school prayer, regulation of pornography and abortion, the adoption of a flat tax rate, and the abolition of the Department of Education, the National Endowment for the Humanities, and the Corporation for Public Broadcasting. The Republican controlled Congress embraced several of the Coalition's proposals, resulting in legislation authorizing federal funding of religious charities (Charitable Choice) and regulating sexually explicit material on the internet. Criticism of the Coalition's political activity and voters' guides led the Internal Revenue Service to deny the organization's charitable tax-exempt status in 1999. The Coalition reorganized through one of its state affiliates.

An organization related to the Christian Coalition is the *American Center for Law and Justice* (ACLJ). Pat Robertson founded the ACLJ in 1990 as a legal advocacy group "dedicated to defending and advancing religious liberty, the sanctity of human life, and the two-parent, marriage-bound family." Modeled after the American Civil Liberties Union, the ACLJ represents religiously conservative litigants in controversies involving public school student religious activities and abortion clinic protests, among others. Through its general counsel, Jay Sekulow, the ACLJ has argued several leading free speech and religion clause cases before the U.S. Supreme Court, including *Board of Education of Westside Community Schools v. Mergens* (1990), *Lamb's Chapel v. Center Moriches School District* (1993), *Madsen v. Women's Health Center* (1994), and *Santa Fe Independent School District v. Doe* (2000). ACLJ also maintains an active amicus practice before the Supreme Court. ACLJ has been effective in encouraging the Supreme Court to adopt a First Amendment jurisprudence that provides equal access to public facilities and funding for religiously motivated expression and conduct.

STEVEN K. GREEN

References and Further Reading

Boston, Robert. *The Most Dangerous Man in America? Pat Robertson and the Rise of the Christian Coalition.* Amherst, NY: Prometheus Books, 1996.

Brown, Ruth Murry. *For a "Christian America": A History of the Religious Right.* Amherst, NY: Prometheus Books, 2002.

Diamond, Sara. *Roads to Dominion: Right-Wing Movements and Political Power in the United States.* New York: The Guilford Press, 1995.

Green, John C., *et al. Religion and the Culture Wars.* Lanham, Maryland: Rowman & Littlefield Pub., 1996.

Watson, Justin. *The Christian Coalition: Dreams of Restoration, Demands for Recognition.* New York: St. Martin's Press, 1997.

Wilcox, Clyde. *Onward Christian Soldiers? The Religious Right in American Politics.* Boulder, CO: Westview Press, 1996.

Cases and Statutes Cited

Board of Education of Westside Community Schools v. Mergens, 496 U.S. 226 (1990)

Lamb's Chapel v. Center Moriches School District, 508 U.S. 384 (1993)

Madsen v. Women's Health Center, 512 U.S. 753 (1994)

Santa Fe Independent School District v. Doe, 530 U.S. 290 (2000)

CHURCH OF SCIENTOLOGY AND RELIGIOUS LIBERTY

The Church of Scientology is a religious–scientific movement that has been at the center of several legal controversies regarding the government's treatment and regulation of new religious movements.

Since its founding in the early 1950s, the Church has had to struggle for legal recognition as a religion and to counter critics who have claimed the Church's religious and financial practices are a sham. These controversies have engendered a significant amount of litigation in the United States and foreign courts, resulting in mixed successes for the Church. Viewed cumulatively, however, the court decisions reveal the difficulties associated with applying the religious liberty principle to nontraditional religious movements.

The Church of Scientology was founded in the early 1950s by L. Ron Hubbard, best known as a science-fiction writer during the 1930s and 1940s. The religion of Scientology came out of an earlier body of Hubbard's work called Dianetics, which proposes an alternative approach to psychology and psychiatry for treating mental disease and dysfunctioning (See Dianetics: The Modern Science of Mental Health [1950]). The premise of Dianetics is that the human brain has indefinite power but is hampered by painful memories ("engrams") that inhibit its proper functioning and full potential. Through a process called "auditing"—a practice similar to abreation therapy or the uncovering of repressed memories—an individual can restore his or her mind to its full capacity. Hubbard developed a device used in auditing, called an "electropsychometer" ("E-meter")—similar to a skin galvanometer or lie detector—for measuring and treating engrams. After Hubbard adapted his secular theory of Dianetics into the religious philosophy of Scientology, auditing became the latter's central religious practice. Scientology also claims to have elements of spirituality and cosmology, with kinships to Eastern religious traditions, and has developed religious doctrines, rituals, and ceremonies governing matters such as marriage, christenings, and the ordination of clergy.

Legal controversies concerning Scientology have involved whether Scientology is a bona fide religion, thus deserving of First Amendment protections, and whether its practices should be entitled to the same tax privileges as afforded other faiths. The absence of spirituality in Hubbard's earlier science fiction and psychological writings and the parallels in Scientology doctrines led critics to claim that Hubbard created Scientology for financial gain and to retain control over the growing Dianetics movement. In particular, allegations have centered on the Church's graduated fee for auditing sessions, which can run into the thousands of dollars. The Internal Revenue Service initially denied the Church's application for nonprofit tax status, claiming the Church was a commercial operation. In the early 1960s, agents of the Food and Drug Administration conducted a raid on Scientology's Washington, D. C., church to confiscate E-meters, based on government claims the Church was engaged in false and misleading practices through its auditing. In 1969, the U.S. Court of Appeals for the District of Columbia ruled, however, that Scientology is a bona fide religion and the use of the E-meter, being part of a central religious practice, did not constitute false labeling under the federal Food, Drug, and Cosmetic Act. In 1973, the Internal Revenue Service relented by awarding the Church tax-exempt status.

The Church of Scientology's attaining status as a religion has not blunted controversy or litigation. In 1979, Hubbard's wife and several church officials were charged with conspiracy to burglarize federal government offices and steal official documents related to government investigations of Scientology. The Church has also faced civil lawsuits by former members alleging that church officials have engaged in fraud, kidnapping, and severe emotional injury associated with the recruiting and auditing of members.

The most significant legal controversy involved the Internal Revenue Service's refusal to allow individual Scientologists to deduct the costs associated with auditing sessions from their tax liability. In Hernandez v. Commissioner of Internal Revenue (1989), the Supreme Court upheld the IRS determination that auditing fees were not deductible contributions. Although acknowledging Scientology is a recognized church and that auditing is a central religious practice of the religion, the Court agreed with the IRS that the "fixed donation" or fee was not equivalent to a tithe or gift to a church but was payment for a quid pro quo exchange of an identifiable benefit. Furthermore, the Court rejected the Church's claim that this interpretation of the Internal Revenue Code violated the Church's establishment and free exercise clause rights. Distinguishing the auditing fees from pew rents and other religious assessments recognized as deductions, the Court stated that the relevant inquiry is "not whether the payment secures religious benefits or access to religious services, but whether the transaction . . . is structured as a quid pro quo exchange." The Court also found no substantial burden on Scientologists' religious practice arising from the fact that the IRS interpretation imposed a greater financial cost to engage in auditing.

Despite its legal setbacks, Scientology has achieved full legal recognition as a religious denomination in the United States. Scientology has had greater difficulty attaining similar recognition and protection outside the United States, particularly in Germany and Great Britain, where government officials have maintained that Scientology is more a philosophy or commercial enterprise than a religion.

STEVEN K. GREEN

References and Further Reading

Friedman, Jerold A., *Constitutional Issues in Revoking Religious Tax Exemptions: Church of Scientology of California v. Commissioner*, University of Florida Law Review 37 (1985): 565–589.

Horwitz, Paul, *Scientology in Court: A Comparative Analysis and Some Thoughts on Selected Issues in Law and Religion*, DePaul Law Review 47 (1997): 86–154.

Hubbard, L. Ron. *Dianetics: The Modern Science of Mental Health*. New York: Hermitage Press, 1950.

Jentzsch, Herber C. "Scientology: Separating Truth from Fiction." In *New Religious Movements and Religious Liberty in America*, edited by Derek H. Davis and Barry Hankins, 141–161. Waco, TX: J.M. Dawson Institute of Church-State Studies, 2002.

Lamont, Stewart. *Religions Inc.* London: Harrap, 1986.

Melton, J. Gordon. *The Church of Scientology*. Torino, Italy: Signature Books, 2000.

———. "Scientology in Europe: Testing the Faith of a New Religion." In *International Perspectives on Freedom and Equality of Religious Belief*, edited by Derek H. Davis and Gerhard Besier, 57–68. Waco, TX: J.M. Dawson Institute of Church-State Studies, 2002.

Miller, Russell. *Bare-Faced Messiah*. New York: Henry Holt, 1987.

Scientology: Theology and Practice of a Contemporary Religion. Los Angeles: Bridge Publications, 1998.

Cases and Statutes Cited

Christofferson v. Church of Scientology of Portland, 644 P.2d 577 (Or. Ct. App. 1981)

Church of Scientology of California v. Commissioner of Internal Revenue, 823 F.2d 1310 (9th Cir. 1987)

Founding Church of Scientology of Washington, D.C. v. United States, 409 U.S. 1146 (D.C. Cir. 1969)

Hernandez v. Commissioner of Internal Revenue, 490 U.S. 680 (1989)

Van Schaick v. Church of Scientology of California, 535 F. Supp. 1125 (D. Mass. 1982)

Wollersheim v. Church of Scientology, 260 Cal. Rptr. 331 (Cal. Ct. App. 1989)

CHURCH OF THE HOLY TRINITY v. UNITED STATES, 143 U.S. 457 (1892)

Church of the Holy Trinity v. United States shocks supporters of a complete separation of church and state because of Justice David J. Brewer's statement for a unanimous Supreme Court that the United States is a Christian nation. In support of this idea, Brewer even invoked the Establishment of Religion and Free Exercise Clause of the First Amendment that barred Congress from establishing a religion or interfering with the free exercise of religion. *Holy Trinity* reflects the widespread understanding of nineteenth-century Protestant jurists and lay people that the prohibition on an established church in no way undermined the religiosity of the nation itself.

The case began when the Collector of U.S. Customs at the port of New York levied a $1,000 fine against the Church of the Holy Trinity in New York for violating Alien Contract Labor Act of 1885 by hiring the Rev. E. Walpole Warren, an Englishman. The act's broad language made it "unlawful for any person, company, partnership, or corporation . . . to prepay the transportation, or in any way assist or encourage the importation or migration of any alien . . . under contract . . . to perform labor or service of any kind in the United States . . . ." The action against Holy Trinity was taken at the behest John Stewart Kennedy, a wealthy Scottish immigrant, who reasoned that the courts would balk at enforcing the act against a clergyman. Kennedy wanted to bring the act into disrepute and paid the fine and the costs of defense.

Holy Trinity's attorney, Seaman Miller, sought to recover the fine by filing a demurrer raising the question of whether the act applied to a clergyman. Stephen A. Walker, the U. S. District Attorney, did not think much of the drafting skills of the act's writers, but he dutifully argued in 1888 that the law applied. The statute excepted only actors, artists, lecturers, singers, or personal servants. Miller responded that that Congress had targeted cheap, manual labor only. He also invoked briefly the First Amendment's free exercise clause, but this argument was ignored by the circuit court judge. The decision in *United States v. Rector, Etc., of the Church of the Holy Trinity* in 1888 limited the question to whether Congress intended to prohibit the entry of an immigrant who came under contract with a religious society to perform the functions of a minister of the gospel. The judge held that the language of the statute clearly applied, although he believed that no legislative body in this country would have purposefully enacted a law framed so as to cover the case before him.

During Miller's oral argument before the U.S. Supreme Court in January 1892, the justices' questions made clear that they agreed that the only statutory exceptions were actors, lecturers, etc. The assistant attorney general became convinced that his oral argument was unnecessary to success, so merely submitted his brief. He learned the next month that he had lost the case. Justice Brewer insisted that the literal construction of a statute must not result in an absurdity. Congressional debate revealed that the act targeting the immigration of large numbers of laborers willing to work for low pay. Yet Brewer was not done. He then declared that a literal construction was also an absurdity because not legislature, state, or national would act against religion because of the religious character of the American people and their society. Brewer included a list of pronouncements drawn from political and legal documents—including the First Amendment clauses—to prove this. In addition, American laws, customs, and society demonstrated that this is a Christian nation.

Modern liberal church/state scholars have dismissed, too eagerly, the Christian nation statement as mere dictum unnecessary to the reasoning of the decision. In a dissent from *Lynch v. Donnelly* in 1984 where the Court approved of a nativity display on city property, Justice William J. Brennan denounced Brewer for his sectarian arrogance. Today, legal writers are more likely to examine Holy Trinity as part of the debate on the appropriateness of examining legislative history when interpreting statutes. Of course, some were appalled in 1892 by Brewer's statement, but this reaction was not widespread as many Americans shared Brewer's belief in the religious character of their country. In fact, Brewer had made a similar statement for a unanimous Kansas Supreme Court in *Board of Commissioners of Wyndotte Co. v. The First Presbyterian Church of Wyandotte* in 1883. *Holy Trinity* thus exemplifies an evangelical Protestant theory of church-state relations as opposed to a liberal theory.

LINDA PRZYBYSZEWSKI

References and Further Reading

Alien Contract Labor Act, Act of February 26, 1885, 23 Stat. 332.
Hylton, Joseph Gordon, *David Josiah Brewer and the Christian Constitution*, Marquette Law Review 91 (1998): 417–425.
Przybyszewski, Linda. "The Secularization of the Law and the Persistence of Religious Faith: The Case of Justice David J. Brewer." *Journal of American History* 90 (2004).
Vermeule, Adrian, *Legislative History and the Limits of Judicial Competence: the Untold Story of Holy Trinity Church*, Stanford Law Review 50 (1998): 1833–1896.

Cases and Statutes Cited

Board of Commissioners of Wyndotte Co. v. The First Presbyterian Church of Wyandotte, 30. Kan, 620, 637 (1883)
Lynch v. Donnelly, 465 U.S. 668 (1984)
United States v. Rector, Etc., of the Church of the Holy Trinity, C.C. S.D. N.Y. 36 F. 303, 303 (1888)

See also **Establishment of Religion and Free Exercise Clauses;** *Lynch v. Donnelly*, 465 U.S. 668 (1984)

CHURCH OF THE LUKUMI BABALU AYE v. CITY OF HIALEAH, 508 U.S. 520 (1993)

A central theme of the U. S. Constitution, particularly in the balance of powers between the various branches of government and in the federal system itself, is protecting the rights of minorities against the unchecked power of majorities. Alexander Hamilton, writing in *Federalist* 78, saw an independent judiciary as "an essential safeguard against the effects of occasional ill humors in society" and "the injury of the private rights of particular classes of citizens, by unjust and partial laws" (*Federalist* 78).

As unwilling to place fundamental rights at the mercy of democratic but sometimes ephemeral and unjust decisions as under the autocratic whims of a monarch, the Founders sought to further enshrine them in the Constitution itself. The decision of the Supreme Court of the United States in *Church of the Lukumi Babalu Aye* exemplifies the wisdom of amending the Constitution to include a Bill of Rights, particularly the clauses of the First Amendment that promote religious liberty.

The petitioners practiced Santeria ("the way of the saints"), a religion that developed in the crucible of the African slave trade in the New World and fused elements of the Yoruba traditions with those of Roman Catholicism. A central tenet of Santeria involves the invocation of the assistance of orishas (spirits), particularly through the use of animal sacrifice. In 1987 the Church leased land in the City of Hialeah, Florida, and announced plans to build a complex that included a house of worship, school, cultural center, and museum.

The Church's announcement caused an upheaval in the community. The City Council convened an emergency meeting and unanimously passed not only a resolution expressing concern "that certain religions may propose to engage in practices that are inconsistent with public morals, peace or safety," but also a series of ordinances banning certain ritual killings of animals and their use in sacrifices.

The Church responded by suing the City and various officials pursuant to 42 U.S.C. § 1983, claiming that the ordinances violated their rights under the Free Exercise Clause of the Constitution. Federal district and appellate courts upheld the laws, and the Church appealed.

The Supreme Court of the United States held that all of the ordinances were unconstitutional. Writing for a unanimous but conflicted Court, Justice Anthony Kennedy first acknowledged that, under the holding in a 1990 case, *Employment Div'n, Dept. of Human Resources of Ore. v. Smith,* a law that had the incidental effect of burdening a particular religious practice may be constitutional even in the absence of a compelling state interest as long as it was neutral and of general applicability.

The Court found, however, that the City ordinances at issue failed the neutrality test both textually and in their operation. Therefore, the precedent in *Smith* did not apply, and the Court was obliged to evaluate the ordinances under a standard of strict scrutiny, that is, that they had to be justified by a compelling governmental interest and were narrowly tailored to advance that interest.

The Court observed that the legislative history of the ordinances, their wording, and their application all amply demonstrated that their purpose was to suppress animal sacrifice, a central element of Santeria. Because they were overbroad in some respects and underinclusive in others, the Court found that the ordinances constituted a "religious gerrymander ... an impermissible attempt to target petitioners and their religious practices."

For example, the Court found that an ordinance's definition of "sacrifice" was drafted in such a way to permit all forms of killing animals except for religious sacrifice. At the same time, it found that other challenged ordinances were written more broadly than necessary to achieve the City's preferred secular purposes of protecting public health and preventing cruelty to animals. The Court concluded: "The Free Exercise Clause commits government itself to exercise religious tolerance, and upon even slight suspicion that proposals for state intervention stem from animosity to religion or distrust of its practices, all officials must pause to remember their own high duty to the Constitution and to the rights it secures."

In a sense, this case represented little more than an adherence to a line of precedents protecting the rights of religious minorities under both religion clauses of the First Amendment. *See*, for example *Fowler v. Rhode Island* (municipal ordinance violated Free Exercise Clause where interpreted to ban preaching in a public park by Jehovah's Witnesses but permit preaching at Roman Catholic Mass or Protestant service) and *Larson v. Valente* (state law that excepted some, but not all, religious organizations from registration and reporting requirements for charitable solicitations violated Establishment Clause). At the same time, it provided the Court with an opportunity, one particularly evident in the array of concurrences to the Court's judgment, to revisit the decision in *Smith* and to ask whether it may have given the government too much power to inhibit or otherwise burden religious practices.

JOHN S. CELICHOWSKI

References and Further Reading

Goldberg, Steven B. *Seduced by Science: How American Religion Has Lost Its Way*. New York: New York University Press, 2000, 68–83.
Loewy, Arthur H. *Religion and the Constitution: Cases and Materials*. St. Paul, MN: West Group, 1999.
Sullivan, Kathleen. *Constitutional Law* (13th Ed.). Westbury, NY: The Foundation Press, 1997, 1461–1500.

Cases and Statutes Cited

Employment Div'n, Dept. of Human Resources of Ore. v. Smith, 494 U.S. 872 (1990)
Fowler v. Rhode Island, 345 U.S. 67 (1953)
Larson v. Valente, 456 U.S. 228 (1982)

See also **Amish and Religious Liberty; Application of First Amendment to States; Balancing Approach to Free Speech; Bill of Rights: Structure;** *Bob Jones University v. United States,* **461 U.S. 574 (1983);** *Bowen v. Roy,* **476 U.S. 693 (1986);** *Cantwell v. Connecticut,* **310 U.S. 296 (1940); Catholics and Religious Liberty;** *City of Boerne v. Flores,* **521 U.S. 507 (1997); Compelling State Interest; Defining Religion; Employment Division,** *Department of Human Resources v. Smith,* **494 U.S. 872 (1990);** *Engel v. Vitale,* **370 U.S. 421 (1962); English Toleration Act; Equal Protection Clause and Religious Freedom; Equal Protection of Law (XIV); Establishment of Religion and Free Exercise Clauses;** *Everson v. Board of Education,* **330 U.S. 1 (1947); Free Exercise Clause (I): History, Background, Framing; Free Exercise Clause Doctrine: Supreme Court Jurisprudence;** *Goldman v. Weinberger,* **475 U.S. 503 (1986);** *Good News Club v. Milford Central School,* **533 U.S. 98 (2001);** *Hernandez v. Commissioner of Internal Revenue,* **490 U.S. 680 (1989); Jehovah's Witnesses and Religious Liberty; Jews and Religious Liberty; Kennedy, Anthony McLeod;** *Lamb's Chapel v. Center Moriches Union Free School District,* **508 U.S. 384 (1993);** *Lyng v. Northwest Indian Cemetery Protective Association,* **485 U.S. 439 (1988);** *McDaniel v. Paty,* **435 U.S. 618 (1978); Mormons and Religious Liberty; Muslims and Religious Liberty;** *NLRB v. Catholic Bishop of Chicago,* **440 U.S. 490 (1979);** *O'Lone v. Estate of Shabazz,* **482 U.S. 342 (1987);** *Pierce v. Society of Sisters,* **268 U.S. 510 (1925); Prisoners and Free Exercise Clause Rights; Private Religious Speech on Public Property; Quakers and Religious Liberty; Religious Freedom Restoration Act; Religious Land Use and Institutionalized Persons Act;** *Reynolds v. United States,* **98 U.S. 145 (1878); Seventh Day Adventists and Religious Liberty;** *Sherbert v. Verner,* **374 U.S. 398 (1963); State Religious Freedom Statutes; Theories of Civil Liberties;** *United States v. Lee,* **455 U.S. 252 (1982);** *Walz v. Tax Commission of City of New York* **, 397 U.S. 664 (1970);** *Wisconsin v. Yoder,* **406 U.S. 205 (1972)**

CHURCH OF THE NEW SONG AND RELIGIOUS LIBERTY

The Church of the New Song (CNS) is an entity created within the federal correctional system. It has engaged in significant litigation in the federal courts over the past thirty years to gain recognition as a "religion" for purposes of establishing the right of its adherents to practice their religion while incarcerated. Interestingly, the federal courts have split in their response to arguments advanced by CNS. The Eighth Circuit recognized the sect as a religious entity entitled to First Amendment protection in *Remmers v. Brewer*, 494 F.2d 1277 (8th Circuit 1974). In contrast, CNS failed to gain recognition in the Fifth Circuit, which dismissed the CNS appeal from adverse findings by the trial court in *Theriault v. Silber*, 453 F.Supp. 254, 260 (W.D. Tex. 1978), appeal dismissed, 579 F.2d 302 (5th Cir. 1978). The district court concluded:

> The Church of the New Song appears not to be a religion, but rather as a masquerade designed to obtain First Amendment protection for acts which otherwise would be unlawful and/or reasonably disallowed by the various prison authorities but for the attempts which have been and are being made to classify them as 'religious' and, therefore, presumably protected by the First Amendment.

The conflicting findings concerning the legitimacy of CNS's claim to First Amendment protection lie, in part, in the tactics of the entity's founder and leader, Dr. Harry Theriault, a federal inmate with a record of prison escape, violence, and threatened violence. Theriault admittedly created the entity's underlying doctrine, the "Eclatarian faith" while incarcerated and a critical finding of some courts has been that a central tenet of the faith is rebellion against the prison system, judiciary, and government, in general. *Theriault v. Carlson*, 494 F.2d 390, 394 (5th Cir. 1974).

The difficulty in assessing the legitimacy of CNS's claim to constitutional protection is complicated by the recognition of many other nontraditional or non-Western sects whose theological precepts or practices have been accorded protection under the Free Exercise Clause. As the Supreme Court observed in *United States v. Ballard*:

> It embraces the right to maintain theories of life and of death and of the hereafter which are rank heresy to followers of the orthodox faiths. Heresy trials are foreign to our Constitution. Men may believe what they cannot prove. They may not be put to the proof of their religious doctrines or beliefs. Religious experiences that are as real as life to some may be incomprehensible to others. Yet the fact that they may be beyond the ken of mortals does not mean that they can be made suspect before the law. 322 U.S. 78, 87 (1944) (defendant accused of fraud claimed religious leadership of the "I Am" movement).

Federal courts have routinely permitted practitioners of minority sects to assert claims for constitutional protection, typically in actions brought by inmates. *See* for example, *Cruz v. Beto*, 405 U.S. 319, 322 (1972) (Buddhist inmate); *Cooper v. Pate*, 378 U.S. 546 (1964) (Black Muslim inmate); *Teterud v. Gillman*, 385 F.Supp. 153, 160 (S.D. Iowa 1974) (Native American hair length protected against claim of institutional disruption); and *Kennedy v. Meacham*, 540 F.2d 1057 (10th Cir. 1976) (remanding for evidentiary hearing on claims of professed Satanists). The proper resolution of such claims requires conscientious analysis of the purported system of belief and, typically, in the context of inmate litigation, its potential burden or disruption for the institution, as demonstrated by the excellent analysis in *Childs v. Duckworth*, 509 F.Supp. 1254 (D. Ind. 1982). There, the court rejected the claim of a practitioner of the Church of Satan/Fraternity of the Goat that his need to burn incense and candles in his cell was entitled to First Amendment protection.

A similarly thorough analysis was applied by the Iowa court in reviewing the status of CNS as a recognized religion in the Eighth Circuit, with the conclusion being drawn that CNS functioned much as many other religious sects, had a body of beliefs or theology, and did not exist as a sham or to disrupt the institution. *Loney v. Scurr*, 474 F.Supp. 1186, 1193-94 (S.D. Iowa 1979). These findings contrast sharply with those entered by the district court in Texas that contributed to a rather hostile view of the CNS and its founder in the Fifth Circuit, evidenced by its explanation for dismissal of the appeal in *Theriault v. Silber*.

The CNS litigation demonstrates the difficulty in determining when a particular claim of faith is sufficiently well grounded to be accorded protection under the First Amendment. Even when the claim of faith is recognized, that recognition does not necessarily lead to unfettered practice, particular in the context of penal institutions. As the court observed in *Loney v. Scurr*, 474 F.Supp. at 1196: ". . . the free exercise of religion has two aspects the freedom to believe, which is absolute, and the freedom to practice, which is not."

J. THOMAS SULLIVAN

Cases and Statutes Cited

Childs v. Duckworth, 509 F.Supp. 1254 (D. Ind. 1982)
Cooper v. Pate, 378 U.S. 546 (1964) (Black Muslim inmate)
Cruz v. Beto, 405 U.S. 319, 322 (1972)

Kennedy v. Meacham, 540 F.2d 1057 (10th Cir. 1976)
Loney v. Scurr, 474 F.Supp. 1186, 1193-94 (S.D. Iowa 1979)
Remmers v. Brewer, 494 F.2d 1277 (8th Circuit 1974)
Teterud v. Gillman, 385 F.Supp. 153, 160 (S.D. Iowa 1974)
Theriault v. Carlson, 494 F.2d 390, 394 (5th Cir. 1974)
Theriault v. Silber, 453 F.Supp. 254, 260 (W.D. Tex. 1978)
United States v. Ballard

CHURCH PROPERTY AFTER THE AMERICAN REVOLUTION

The American Revolution brought about the dissolution of ties between many religious bodies in America, necessitating separate organizations.

Prior to the American revolution, religious corporations were created either by royal charter or by provincial authority derived from the crown. In this period the Catholic Church was without civil rights in the colonies, and title to its property was held in the name of individuals. With the establishment of the United States, religious orders and organizations began to incorporate: the Augustinian Fathers at Philadelphia in 1796, the Sulpicians at Baltimore in 1805, the Jesuits at Georgetown in 1815, and a few years later the Dominicans by legislative act in Ohio. Also, the Methodists formed in 1784, the Anglicans in 1789, the Baptists in 1784, the Presbyterians in 1785, the Dutch Reformed in 1792, and the Lutherans in 1795.

After the revolution, churches were incorporated ether by special acts of state legislatures or under the provisions of general statutes. The religious corporation in the United States belongs to the class of civil corporations, not for profit, which are organized and controlled according to the principles of common law and equity as administered by the civil courts. The church is a spiritual and ecclesiastical body, and as such does not receive incorporation. It is from the membership of the religious society that the corporation is formed. The general statutes under which religious corporations can now be formed in most of the American states contain provisions authorizing the legislature to alter, amend, or repeal any charter granted. The life of a religious corporation dates in law from its organization, not from the time it began to exercise its corporate powers. But a mere use of corporate powers limited to the maintenance of religious observances is not sufficient to establish a corporation de facto. The primary object of religious incorporation in the United States is the core of real property devoted to the purposes of religion. American courts have consistently recognized that the terms "church" and "incorporated religious society" are not identical. "Church" encompasses objects and purposes that are moral and religious, whereas "church corporation" deals chiefly with care and control of temporalities.

A religious corporation may not engage in business transactions for profit. It may, however, hold revenue-producing property not used by the church, as investment in the form of an endowment. The mortgaging of real property by a religious corporation generally requires the consent of some superior ecclesiastical authority, as well as an order of the court. Because of the objects of religious incorporation is to give a legal person standing in court, such corporations have the right to sue and be sued. It is in civil courts and not in the ecclesiastical courts that the religious corporation has standing. It is from the civil courts that orders or wants will issue, directing or restraining corporate action. Unlike private corporations, the religious corporation can neither merge nor dissolve without the consent of local church body and higher church authorities.

G. L. TYLER

References and Further Reading

Arnold, Jack L. *Church History, American Christianity: 18th Century*.

CICENIA v. LAGAY, 357 U.S. 504 (1958)

Newark police asked Cicenia to report for questioning in a murder case. Cicenia went to the police at 9:00 the next morning. Cicenia's attorney visited the station and asked to see Cicenia throughout the afternoon and evening. Meanwhile, Cicenia was asking to see his lawyer. The two were not permitted to confer until 9:30 PM, when Cicenia had already signed a confession.

The lower courts decided New Jersey's refusal to permit Cicenia counsel during the inquiry did not deprive him of due process.

A five-member majority affirmed, relying on *Crooker v. California*, which allowed police to refuse to honor a general request to consult with a lawyer. The majority acknowledged that, unlike Crooker, Cicenia had already retained a lawyer, but ultimately reached the same conclusion. They admitted a "strong distaste" for New Jersey's tactics, but found no constitutional violation.

The Court acknowledged the right to counsel is critical, but only "one pertinent element in determining from all the circumstances whether a conviction was attended by fundamental unfairness." Because requiring the police to permit accused persons to see an attorney "might impair [their] ability to solve difficult cases," the Court refrained from "laying down any such inflexible rule."

The dissent argued the right to counsel is "fundamental and absolute." Citing *Crooker's* dissent, they lamented, we "regret that we have not taken this case . . . as the occasion to bring our decisions into tune with the constitutional requirement for fair criminal proceedings against the citizen."

Miranda expressly overruled *Cicenia*.

SARA FAHERTY

Cases and Statutes Cited

Crooker v. California, 357 U.S. 433 (1958)
Miranda v. Arizona, 384 US 436 (1966)

See also **Coerced Confession/Police Interrogation**

CINCINNATI v. DISCOVERY NETWORK, INC. 507 U.S. 14 (1993)

The question before the U.S. Supreme Court in *Cincinnati v. Discovery Network* was whether commercial speech should be entitled to the same First Amendment protections as private speech. The defendant was a publishing company that provided educational services to adults in the Cincinnati area and advertised these services in free magazines distributed from newspaper racks on city sidewalks. The city of Cincinnati had granted Discovery Network, Inc. permission to place its distribution racks on public property in 1989, but the following year the city Commissioner of Public Works revoked their permit and a similar permit granted to real estate advertiser Harmon Publishing, claiming that the racks were eyesores and that their placement posed a threat to public safety. The free magazines, the city argued, were "commercial handbills" to which the free press protections of the First Amendment did not apply. The decision affected only sixty-two of the more than 1,500 news racks placed on city property and did not place restrictions on the similar distribution of conventional newspapers.

Discovery Network and Harmon Publishing unsuccessfully challenged the decision in federal court on the grounds that it violated the First Amendment rights of the two companies. The case was appealed to the U.S. Supreme Court, which reversed the federal court's decision by a 6–3 majority on March 24, 1993. The Court held that commercial speech, while enjoying less constitutional protections than noncommercial speech, cannot be restricted without adequate, demonstrable cause. Writing for the majority, Justice John Paul Stevens stated that disseminators of

commercial speech are not entitled to unlimited rights to distribute materials on public property, but that a public entity must be able to justify restricting their activities by demonstrating a "reasonable fit" between the restriction and the stated goals of the restrictions, especially if the restrictions are based in part on the content of the speech. The Court held that the city's decision to ban free magazine racks did not reasonably fit its stated goals of ensuring public safety and aesthetics, as evidenced by the fact that the ban only applied to less that one percent of the city's news racks. These goals, the Court opined, could just as easily be achieved by less restrictive means, such as regulating the size, shape, and appearance of the boxes. Justices William Rhenquist, Byron White, and Clarence Thomas dissented, arguing that commercial speech is subordinate to private speech and thus subject to a greater degree of government regulation.

In reaffirming previous decisions in cases such as *Central Hudson Gas and Electric v. Public Service Commission,* which prohibited government interference in commercial speech without demonstrable cause, the Supreme Court in *Cincinnati v. Discovery Network* clarified, if only partially, the place of commercial speech in American public discourse. The Court's decision validated what at the time was a growing medium for the distribution of free information for commercial purposes by implication extending greater constitutional protections to other media for commercial speech such as telemarketing and infomercials.

MICHAEL H. BURCHETT

References and Further Reading

Belsky, Martin H. *The Rhenquist Court: A Retrospective.* New York: Oxford University Press, 2002.
Cain, Rita Marie, *Call Someone Up and Just Say 'Buy' – Telemarketing and the Regulatory Environment,* American Business Law Journal 31 (February 1994): 4:641–698.
Denniston, Lyle. *"A Major Victory for Commercial Speech."* American Journalism Review 15 (May 1993): 46.
Stewart, David O. "Commercial Break: Supreme Court Bolsters Constitutional Protections for Commercial Speech." *ABA Journal* 79 (June 1993): 42.

Cases and Statutes Cited

Central Hudson Gas and Electric v. Public Service Commission, 447 U.S. 557 (1980)

See also **Bill of Rights: Structure; Content-based Regulation of Speech;** *44 Liquormart v. Rhode Island,* **517 U.S. 484 (1977); Freedom of Speech and Press: Nineteenth Century; Free Speech in Private Corporations; Freedom of Speech Extended to Corporations; Prior Restraints; Public/Nonpublic Forums Distinction**

CITIZENSHIP

Citizenship comprises the legal status conferring full membership in the national political community. In the absence of any other definitive marker of membership, citizenship has been central to the American experience. Citizenship has been an equalizing force among those afforded the status. It has been exclusionary to the extent that race, ideology, and other criteria have been deployed as qualifications.

The two primary routes to citizenship are by birth and by naturalization. The Framers adopted no constitutional provision for citizenship at birth, unable to resolve the citizenship status of blacks. In *Dred Scott v. Sanford*, the Supreme Court held that even free blacks could not qualify as U.S. citizens. The Dred Scott ruling was reversed by the Citizenship Clause of the Fourteenth Amendment, which extends citizenship at birth to all persons born in the territory of the United States and "subject to the jurisdiction thereof." In the Wong Kim Ark decision, the Supreme Court found the clause to apply to the children of Asian parents who were themselves ineligible to naturalize.

Although the Citizenship Clause does not apply to members of Native American tribes and those born in unincorporated territories, most notably Puerto Rico, those groups have been extended birth citizenship by statute. By constitutional practice, territorial birthright citizenship is extended without regard to parental immigration status. Proposed constitutional amendments introduced in the 1990s to deny birthright citizenship to the children of undocumented aliens and temporary immigrants were repulsed. Given the growing population of undocumented aliens in the United States (estimated to be as large as 10 million individuals), the strict rule of territorial birthright citizenship has avoided the difficulties of intergenerational caste.

Citizenship is also extended at birth to the children of U.S. citizens born outside the United States, so long as the citizen parent has resided in the United States prior to the child's birth. Citizenship by descent is extended by statute rather than under the Fourteenth Amendment, as highlighted in *Rogers v. Bellei*. The condition precedent of parental residence limits the possibility of a nonterritorially connected American diaspora.

The Constitution allocates to Congress the power to establish "an Uniform Rule of Naturalization." Eligibility to naturalize was long qualified on the basis of race. The original naturalization statute, enacted in 1790, provided only for the naturalization of "free white persons." Blacks were made eligible to naturalize by statute in 1868. Asian immigrants, however, were long barred from acquiring citizenship. It was not until 1952 that the last race-based criteria for naturalization were repealed.

Racial exclusions aside, conventional wisdom has characterized naturalization requirements as minimal. While this is true in comparative perspective—the thresholds to naturalization have historically been much higher in the European context, for instance—other barriers to naturalization have been and continue to be formidable. From the early twentieth century, naturalization has not been open to those advocating anarchism, communism, and other such doctrines, activity that would otherwise enjoy core First Amendment protection. Naturalization also continues to be statutorily contingent on facility in the English language and a demonstrated understanding of "the fundamentals of the history, and of the principles and form of government, of the United States." Naturalization applicants must pass a test by way of satisfying these requirements. Thousands fail each year, and many others are deterred from applying at all. Naturalization applicants must also pay a nontrivial application fee.

Finally, naturalization has been contingent on a durational residency requirement, first set at two years, briefly raised to fourteen under the Alien and Sedition Acts, reduced to five years in 1802 where it has stood since. Under current law, qualified residency must be as a permanent resident alien. Aliens in other status are thus ineligible to naturalize. Unlike other naturalization requirements, including the oath of naturalization, the durational residency requirement is not waivable.

Whether by birth or naturalization (at least where not procured by fraud), citizenship cannot be terminated without an individual's consent under Supreme Court decisions severely limiting the government's power of expatriation.

As a determinant of constitutional rights, citizenship status has been of declining significance. Some rights have long been extended to aliens, such as the rights of the accused and to equal protection, which the Constitution extends to all "persons." Discrimination against aliens under state law has been restricted to political functions, in the wake of the Court's designation of aliens as a "suspect classification" in *Graham v. Richardson*. Although the federal 1996 welfare reform act deprived noncitizens of important public benefits, many have since been restored. Noncitizens do remain subject to immigration control, including the possibility of removal, and they are also deprived of the franchise, although permanent resident aliens may make campaign contributions. As for the obligations of citizenship, aliens must pay taxes and are subject to conscription. They are exempted only from jury service. Consistent with a constitutional account in which citizenship status is subordinated, Alexander Bickel found "it gratifying that we live under a Constitution to which the concept of citizenship matters very little, that prescribes decencies and wise modalities of government without regard to the concept of citizenship."

As a constitutional value, citizenship may be enjoying a resurgence. Building on Charles Black's interpretation of the Citizenship Clause to include a substantive component in the context of racial equality, scholars have deployed citizenship as the basis for economic, gay, and multicultural rights. Linda Bosniak has argued that the Citizenship Clause is sufficiently expansive to protect the rights of noncitizens. With the Supreme Court's rediscovery in *Saenz v. Roe* of the Privileges and Immunities Clause, which by its terms is citizenship dependent, such theorizing may have jurisprudential consequences. On the other hand, citizenship remains an exclusionary institution insofar as otherwise willing individuals are barred from membership. Although liberal theorists, notably Michael Walzer, argue that justice requires low thresholds to naturalization, most maintain the necessity of residency, language, and other naturalization requirements. The increasing density of transnational interactivity highlights the inherently illiberal aspects of citizenship. Globalization may also challenge the correlation of citizenship status to individual identity, as associational ties fragment and multiply. The increased incidence of dual citizenship and the rise of social movements, on both domestic and global levels, point to the possible dilution of national citizenship as a primary vehicle for community attachment.

PETER J. SPIRO

References and Further Reading

Aleinikoff, T. Alexander. *Semblances of Sovereignty: The Constitution, The State, and American Citizenship.* Cambridge: Harvard University Press, 2002.

Bosniak, Linda, *Constitutional Citizenship Through the Prism of Alienage*, Ohio State Law Journal 63 (2002): 1285.

Black, Charles L., Jr. *Structure and Relationship in Constitutional Law.* Baton Rouge: Louisiana State University Press, 1969.

Eskridge, William N., *The Relationship Between Obligations and Rights of Citizens*, Fordham Law Review 69 (2001): 1721.

Forbath, William E., *Caste, Class, and Equal Citizenship*, Michigan Law Review 98 (1999): 1.

Haney-Lopez, Ian. *White By Law: The Legal Construction of Race.* New York: New York University Press, 1996.

Neuman, Gerald L. *Strangers to the Constitution.* Princeton: Princeton University Press, 1997.

Schachar, Ayelet. "Children of a Lesser State: Sustaining Global Inequality through Citizenship Laws." In *NOMOS XLVI: Child, Family, State*, Iris Marion Young and Stephen J. Macedo, eds. New York: NYU Press, 2003.

Smith, Rogers. *Civic Ideals: Conflicting Visions of Citizenship in U.S. History.* New Haven: Yale University Press, 1997.

Spiro, Peter J., *Questioning Barriers to Naturalization*, Georgetown Immigration Law Journal 13 (1999):479.

Walzer, Michael. *Spheres of Justice.* New York: Basic Books, 1984.

Cases and Statutes Cited

Elk v. Wilkins, 112 U.S. 94 (1884)
Graham v. Richardson, 403 U.S. 365 (1971)
Saenz v. Roe, 526 U.S. 489 (1999)
Scott v. Sanford, 60 U.S. 393 (1857)
Wong Kim Ark v. United States, 169 U.S. 649 (1898)

See also **Aliens, Civil Liberties of; Alien and Sedition Acts (1798); Dual Citizenship; Equal Protection of Law (XIV); Expatriation; State and Federal Regulation of Immigration**

CIVIL ASSET FORFEITURE

Civil asset forfeiture has been part of the federal government's law enforcement arsenal since the founding of the Republic and now exists in all state jurisdictions as well. Civil forfeiture laws establish a legal process by which title to "tainted assets"—including contraband and other assets related to specified criminal activity—is transferred to the government. Although civil forfeiture is generally triggered by criminal conduct, it is accomplished through civil or administrative proceedings and to be distinguished from criminal forfeiture, which can only be imposed after criminal conviction.

Colonial and early federal courts forfeited ships and cargos when used in violation of customs or revenue laws, and subsequent forfeiture laws applied to other categories of contraband and instrumentalities. But modern civil forfeiture laws, initially enacted as part of the War on Drugs in the 1970s, reach much further. Under 21 USC § 881(a) and expansive legislation since, the government is authorized to seize and forfeit drugs; drug manufacturing equipment; cars, houses, and other property used to facilitate drug crimes; and proceeds traceable to drug transactions. Other modern civil forfeiture laws target assets connected to alien smuggling, money laundering, customs offenses, and, under the 2001 Patriot Act, terrorism. State forfeiture laws have also proliferated.

Forfeiture is designed to strip criminals of their undeserved, ill-gotten gains. In theory, forfeitures also can terminate criminal enterprises in a way criminal penalties cannot. Jailing a drug dealer, for example, may simply allow a subordinate to take his place, but seizing the means of production and other capital may shut down a trafficking business for good. In practice, however, forfeiture seems to have done little to incapacitate or deter the multibillion dollar drug trade, because forfeiture losses inflict so small a loss on drug profits.

Whatever their merits as crime-control mechanisms, modern forfeiture laws provide law enforcement with important procedural and financial advantages that, beginning in the mid-1980s, generated greater government reliance on forfeiture and a good deal of concern on the part of legislators, courts, and civil libertarians. Procedurally, a number of benefits accrue to federal and state prosecutors from an ancient legal fiction that dominates all civil forfeiture proceedings: that the *property* is guilty and on trial. This means, first, that forfeiture can be used even when there is insufficient evidence for a criminal case, when the defendant is a fugitive, or even when the defendant has been acquitted. Second, as a "civil action" against the property itself, few constitutional safeguards imposed on criminal prosecutions apply. Courts have found that the claimant has no constitutional presumption of innocence, no right to an appointed attorney, and no right to confront witnesses. The constitution imposes no burden of proof on the government, permitting most states (and the federal government until reform legislation in 2000) to require the claimant to establish the property's "innocence." There is also no constitutional requirement that the property owner be at fault or be prosecuted for the underlying criminal activity. The "disregard for due process" in forfeiture law, as a Second Circuit opinion described it, has deterred property owners from even challenging the government in the vast majority of cases.

However, the government's largely unchecked forfeiture power began to encounter resistance beginning in the 1990s, first from the courts and then from Congress. In 1993, the Supreme Court decided four forfeiture cases against the government. The most significant, *Austin v. United States*, 509 U.S. 602, held that forfeiture constitutes punishment regardless of whether it is labeled civil or criminal and, therefore, is subject to the Eighth Amendment's prohibition on excessive fines. The *Austin* holding should provide recourse for a homeowner whose house is seized because his daughter sold "nickel bags" in her bedroom, for example. Subsequently, a coalition of conservative and liberal lawmakers excised some of the more draconian provisions from most federal forfeiture laws by passing the Civil Asset Forfeiture Reform Act of 2000. This law filled part of the constitutional void by affording a number of due process rights to the

claimant in federal proceedings, including requirements that the government provide adequate notice, prove its case by a preponderance of the evidence, provide counsel to the claimant when the property is his or her primary residence and in limited other circumstances, and temporarily return the property if the claimant would otherwise suffer a substantial hardship. 18 U.S.C. sec. 983. CAFRA also eliminated the short deadline and the ten percent bond federal law had required to challenge a forfeiture, which had effectively denied access to the courts for many claimants. Substantively, CAFRA expanded the number of offenses subject to both civil and criminal forfeiture; unified and refined the defense for innocent owners that had been afforded by earlier federal statutes; and defined the "facilitation" of an offense to require that a "substantial connection" between the asset's use and the criminal conduct (rather than mere incidental involvement, as some courts had permitted). Similar protections do not yet apply in most state proceedings, although CAFRA will likely prompt reform legislation in some states.

Neither CAFRA nor the Supreme Court has addressed another aspect of forfeiture law that is perhaps most responsible for fueling overzealous, sometimes lawless, use of the forfeiture power: since 1984, federal law has authorized law enforcement agencies to retain the drug-related assets they seize for their own use. States have largely followed suit, but even when a state's law earmarks forfeited assets to education or other non-law enforcement purposes, the federal scheme allows a local police force to "federalize" its seizure and receive back eighty percent of the assets for its own budget. Under this arrangement, some local police forces have managed to double or triple their appropriated budgets through forfeitures.

This financial incentive scheme has aroused a number of civil libertarian concerns. First, with facilities, salaries, and positions sometimes dependent on how much money can be generated by their own seizures, police and prosecution agencies may pursue their economic self-interest at the expense of both crime control and due process. This financial incentive may also skew plea bargains in favor of drug kingpins and against "mules" without assets to trade, or, as one federal district court has warned, create "an unduly dangerous propensity to encourage unreasonable searches and detentions." *Buritica v. United States*. Arguably, this prosecutorial conflict of interest is substantial enough to abridge due process under the Supreme Court's dicta in *Marshall v. Jerrico* (1980), although only one lower court decision, in New Jersey, has so held to date. Another concern is that these forfeiture rewards could ultimately produce self-financing, unaccountable law enforcement agencies divorced from legislative oversight. Here too, the issue implicates constitutional protections, and the Supreme Court may one day have to decide whether providing federal executive agencies with the power to finance themselves violates the Appropriations Clause and the separation of powers it was designed to protect. Meanwhile, a few states have passed laws that redirect forfeited funds into education, drug treatment, or other non-law enforcement uses.

ERIC D. BLUMENSON

References and Further Reading

Blumenson and Nilsen, *Policing for Profit: The Drug War's Hidden Economic Agenda*, U. Chi. L. Rev. 35 (1998): 65.

Department of Justice. *Asset Forfeiture Law and Practice Manual*, June, 1998.

General Accounting Office. *Asset Forfeiture: Historical Perspective on Asset Forfeiture Issues*, GAO/T-GGD-96-40, March 19, 1996.

Hyde, Henry. *Forfeiting our Property Rights: Is Your Property Safe From Seizure?*, Washington, DC: Cato Institute, 1995.

Kessler, Steven L. *Civil and Criminal Forfeiture: Federal and State Practice* § 6.01, 1993.

Levy, Leonard. *A License to Steal: The Forfeiture of Property,* Chapel Hill: Univ. of North Carolina Press, 1996.

Smith, David B. *Prosecution and Defense of Forfeiture Cases*, Matthew Bender.

Stahl, Marc B., *Asset Forfeiture, Burdens of Proof and the War on Drugs*, J. Crim. L. & Criminology 274 (1992): 83.

Cases and Statutes Cited

Buritica v. United States, 8 F.Supp.2d 1188 (N. D. Cal., 1998)

Marshall v. Jerrico, 446 U.S. 238, 242 (1980)

State of New Jersey v. One 1990 Ford Thunderbird, No. CUM-L-000720-99 (Cumberland County Sup. Ct., Dec. 11, 2002)

Thompson, Sandra Guerra, *Congressional Reform of Civil Forfeiture: Punishing Criminals Yet Protecting Property Owners*, 14 Fed. Sentencing Reptr. No. 2, pp. 71-75, Sept.-Oct. 2001

See also Calero-Toledo v. Pearson Yacht Leasing Co., **416 U.S. 663 (1974); Due Process;** *United States v. 92 Buena Vista Avenue,* **507 U.S. 111 (1993)**

CIVIL DEATH

While there is disagreement about the origin of "civil death," its definition is undisputed. Civil death ends a person's legal capacity and renders him legally dead. The individual loses his property and can no longer perform any legal functions.

In ancient Athens, an "infamous" offender could be precluded from participating in the functions of citizenship. Through the Roman Empire, civil death was later exported to Germanic tribes and England where the practice came to be known as "outlawry." It developed into a penal sanction referred to as "attainder," which triggered the forfeiture of all civil and property rights. The concept ultimately took hold in the United States, albeit in an attenuated way, even though the Constitution prohibits Corruption of Blood and Bills of Attainder. Civil death applied only to those incarcerated for life or a term of years. Courts held that civil death required a statutory mandate. Until the middle of the twentieth century, consequences of criminal convictions, many of which continued after release from incarceration, included the automatic dissolution of marriage, the denial of licenses, and the inability to enter into contracts or to engage in civil litigation.

By the 1960s, however, civil death had largely disappeared from Europe and North America. Most of the rights of felons were restored, at least on their release from confinement. However, remnants of civil death remain in the United States to this day. Large-scale disenfranchisement after criminal convictions is a consequence of former civil death statutes, as are the denial of the right to hold public office and to serve on a jury.

NORA V. DEMLEITNER

References and Further Reading

Damaska, Mirjan R. "Adverse Legal Consequences of Conviction and Their Removal: A Comparative Study." *J. Crim. L., Criminology & Police Sci.* 59 (1968): 347.

History and Theory of Civil Disabilities, Vand. L. Rev. 23 (1970): 941–1241.

See also **Bill of Attainder; Collateral Consequences; Corruption of Blood**

CIVIL RELIGION

Although the phrase "civil religion" was coined by Jean-Jacques Rousseau, it was the American sociologist Robert Bellah who launched the term into widespread use with his 1967 essay, "Civil Religion in America." The term refers to a coherent body of beliefs that many would argue could give transcendent meaning to a nation's sense of purpose.

Unlike other religious belief systems, which correspond to identifiable religious groups, civil religion is unique in that it does not correspond to any particular religious group or institution in the conventional sense. Rather, civil religion is observed within the public sphere. For example, presidents refer to God during their inaugural addresses, proclaim Thanksgiving Day holidays, and close their speeches with "God Bless America"; Congress has a chaplain; coins bear the nation's motto, "In God We Trust"; and the Supreme Court begins each session with the words, "God save the United States and this honorable Court."

Despite the constitutional separation of church and state in the United States, according to Bellah, Americans like any people inevitably generate for themselves a shared set of beliefs, symbols, and rituals. Together, these may be seen to provide a religious dimension for the whole of America's common life, including the political sphere. There may, however, be situations in which certain manifestations of civil religion, such as the governmental display of a religious symbol, violate the First Amendment's Establishment Clause. While the outcomes of these cases are notoriously difficult to predict, in part because the Supreme Court has not settled on a single test to be applied in all such cases, the Court has on several occasions expressed concern that governmental expression of civil religion may create the perception that government endorses or disapproves of individual religious choices; for example, *County of Allegheny v. ACLU* (1989) (display of crèche in public building unconstitutional); *McCreary County v. ACLU* (2005) (O'Connor, J., concurring) (display of Ten Commandments on county courthouse walls unconstitutional).

American civil religion displays certain Christian influences, but this does not mean that it is itself a form of Christianity. To illustrate, American civil religion includes a wide variety of references to God, whereas references to Christ and other sectarian beliefs are extremely rare. This, according to Bellah, is because there is a clear division of function between conventional religion, to which the spheres of personal piety and voluntary social action are allocated, and civil religion, which lies within the realm of a nation's public self-understanding.

The genesis of American civil religion lies in the Puritan leader John Winthrop's 1630 sermon, "A Model of Christian Charity," which set the purpose of the Massachusetts Bay Colony according to a God-given standard: "Thus stands the cause between God and us. We are entered into covenant with Him for this work. We have taken out a commission . . . . For we must consider that we that we shall be as a city upon a hill. The eyes of all people are upon us." Winthrop and the Puritan founders of the Massachusetts Bay Colony believed that they had a duty to God to create a community that all could respect and admire. In keeping with the Puritans' understanding that

political communities were to be held to divine standards, from the colonial period through the years of the early Republic days of thanksgiving were proclaimed not only to express gratitude to God but also to call for the nation to engage in a collective act of soul-searching—rigorous inquiry into whether the nation was fulfilling the expectations that God was understood to have established for it.

Although in its original form civil religion was understood to offer a critical vantage point on the nation's conduct, civil religion can be used, as Bellah concedes, to fuse God, country, and flag into a form of nation worship that would permit no place for dissent or for questioning the acts of those in positions of political leadership. Civil religion's original emphasis, however, entailed the sense that national goals and accomplishments should be measured according to transcendent standards, rather than the self-justifying assumption that God is always on the side of one's own nation or that out of respect for God all persons should support their country, right or wrong.

To those who have criticized civil religion as the shallow worship of the "American Way of Life," Bellah counters that American civil religion contains profound religious insights that compare favorably to those of the more conventional forms of religion. Civil religion "is a genuine apprehension of universal and transcendent religious reality . . . as revealed through the experience of the American people," Bellah claims. To make his point, Bellah comments that he is "not at all convinced that the leaders of the churches have consistently represented a higher level of religious insight than the spokesmen of the civil religion." The theologian Reinhold Niebuhr contends, "Lincoln's religious convictions were superior in depth and purity to those, not only of the political leaders of his day, but of the religious leaders of the era."

A brief description of Lincoln's Gettysburg Address can serve to illustrate how civil religion can function within the nation's public discourse. On that occasion, Lincoln sought to inspire a nation overwhelmed by the horrible loss of life to rededicate themselves to the Union's cause. On one level, Lincoln began a ceremony to dedicate a battlefield cemetery was "altogether fitting and proper." "In a larger sense," however, according to Lincoln, "we can not dedicate—we can not consecrate—we can not hallow—this ground. The brave men, living and dead, who struggled here, have consecrated it, far above our poor power to add or detract." Those who had come to dedicate the cemetery could only, from Lincoln's perspective, truly dedicate *themselves,* by devoting themselves to the cause for which so many Union soldiers had died: "that this nation, under God, shall have a new birth of freedom—and that government of the people, by the people, for the people, shall not perish from the earth." Though it may be said that Lincoln here was using civil religion simply to advance the nation's interests, many have concluded with Bellah that civil religion, as practiced by Lincoln and others, is significant to the extent that it offers a deeper perspective, beyond the mere worship of a nation's way of life, or the advancement of national self-interest, which might otherwise be absent from American public discourse.

References and Further Reading

Bellah, Robert N. *Broken Covenant: American Civil Religion in Time of Trial*. Chicago: University of Chicago Press, 1992.
———. "Civil Religion in America." In *Beyond Belief: Essays on Religion in a Post-Traditional World*, 168—189. New York: Harper & Row, 1970.
Lincoln, Abraham. "Address Delivered at the Dedication of the Cemetery at Gettysburg" (1863). In *The American Intellectual Tradition: A Sourcebook, 1630—1865*, vol. 1, edited by David A. Hollinger and Charles Capper, 527. Fourth edition. New York: Oxford University Press, 2001.
Marty, Martin E. *A Nation of Behavers*. Chicago: University of Chicago Press, 1976.
Niebuhr, Reinhold. "The Religion of Abraham Lincoln." In *Lincoln and the Gettysburg Address*, edited by Allan Nevins, 39. Urbana, IL: University of Illinois Press, 1964.
Winthrop, John. "A Modell of Christian Charity" (1630). In *The American Intellectual Tradition: A Sourcebook, 1630-1865*, vol. 1, edited by David A. Hollinger and Charles Capper, 7—15. Fourth edition. New York: Oxford University Press, 2001.

Cases and Statutes Cited

County of Allegheny v. ACLU, 492 U.S. 573 (1989)
McCreary County v. American Civil Liberties Union, U.S. 125 S.Ct. 2722 (2005)

CIVIL RIGHTS ACT OF 1866

The Civil Rights Act of 1866 became law on April 9, 1866, by a two-thirds majority overriding President Andrew Johnson's veto. The first aim of the Act was to provide federal protection to emancipated African Americans, giving practical effect to the Thirteenth Amendment. It was the first in a series of Reconstruction-era Civil Rights Acts.

An immediate concern of the Thirty-Ninth Congress was to invalidate the Black Codes emerging from southern legislatures after the Civil War. Promulgated first in 1865, these laws limited the civil rights of freedmen to own real and personal property, to freely seek employment or redress in the courts on terms equal to whites, and established harsher criminal penalties for blacks than for whites, among other depredations.

Although early Black Codes were invalidated by the Act, oppressive elements of them were renewed and survived the Act, such as vagrancy laws that put blacks without employment in jeopardy of being jailed, fined, or forced into compulsory labor. Together with terrorizing effects of the Ku Klux Klan and similar organizations, the purposes of the Act were substantially undermined.

Sections 1 and 2 of the Act have proved most important in the history of civil rights. Section 1 declared all persons born in the United States, excepting Indians not taxed, as citizens of the United States, contrary to the decision of *Dred Scott v. Sandford*. It granted to all citizens the right "to make and enforce contracts, to sue, be parties, and give evidence, to inherit, purchase, lease, sell, hold, and convey real and personal property, and to full and equal benefit of all laws and proceedings for the security of person and property, as is enjoyed by white citizens." Section 2 provided a criminal penalty for persons who, under color of state law, deprived any citizen of the rights granted on account of race. This was a significant expansion of basic rights and liberties to former slaves. While not specifically protecting freedom of expression, the law was designed to guarantee minimum due process protections for former slaves, and many of the law-makers believed this would help protect their rights to speech, petition, and assembly. The act would also lead to the Fourteenth Amendment, which ultimately made most of the Bill of Rights applicable to the states.

James Wilson sponsored the Act in the House of Representatives; Lyman Trumbull in the Senate. The latter captured its spirit with the statement that "any statute which is not equal to all, and which deprives any citizen of civil rights which are secured to other citizens, is an unjust encroachment upon his liberty; and is, in fact, a badge of servitude which, by the Constitution, is prohibited."

Whether the Act was within the Constitutional authority of the federal government, however, was a controversial point in Congress. Representative John Bingham, a framer of the Fourteenth Amendment, strongly supported the aims of the Act but believed it beyond constitutional authority. This cloud was a substantial motivation for the ratification of the Amendment, which eliminated any uncertainty.

The Act was reenacted in full by the Enforcement Act of 1870. Sections 1 and 2 of the Act are perpetuated in 42 U.S.C. §§ 1981-82, which is the form in which it has remained relevant to modern controversies.

Jones v. Alfred H. Mayer Co., decided by the Court in 1968, addressed a complaint by Jones and his wife that a housing developer refused to sell them a residence on account of their race. The Court held on the basis of its reading of the legislative history of the Civil Rights Act of 1866 that 42 U.S.C. § 1982 prohibited "*all* racial discrimination, private as well as public, in the sale or rental of property, and that the statute, thus construed, is a valid exercise of the power of Congress to enforce the Thirteenth Amendment."

A dissent took strong objection to the majority's account of the legislative history, declaring it "ill considered and ill-advised" to apply the Act to private discrimination, rather than solely to state action. It had been clear to the Court in 1883 in the *Civil Rights Cases*, for instance, that the Act "was intended to counteract State laws and proceedings, and customs having the force of law" and not the actions of individuals without color of state law. The *Civil Rights Cases* invalidated the Civil Rights Act of 1875, however, and as to the 1866 Act its discussion was dicta.

The majority interpretation was extended to section 42 U.S.C. § 1981 in *Runyon v. McCrary*, which held that the Civil Rights Act of 1866, as codified the United States Code, prohibits racial discrimination generally in the making and enforcement of private contracts.

Regardless of the merits of dissenting opinions, the principle that the 1866 Civil Rights Act prohibits private racial discrimination was expressly reaffirmed in *Patterson v. McClean Credit Union*, after the Court invited arguments to reconsider the issue and has not since been in jeopardy of reversal.

LAWRENCE G. SALZMAN

References and Further Reading

Bernstein, David E. Only *One Place of Redress: African Americans, Labor Regulations and the Courts from Reconstruction to the New Deal*. Duke University Press, 2001.

Bickel, Alexander M., *The Original Understanding and the Segregation Decision*, Harvard L. Rev. 1 (1955): 69.

Fairman, Charles. 7 *History of the Supreme Court of the United States: Reconstruction and Reunion 1864–1868*, 1207–1300, MacMillan Co., 1971.

Foner, Eric. *Reconstruction: America's Unfinished Revolution 1863–1877*. New York: Harper & Row, 1988.

Cases and Statutes Cited

Civil Rights Act of 1875, 18 Stat. 335 (1875)

Civil Rights Cases, 109 U.S. 3 (1883)
Dred Scott v. Sandford, 60 U.S. (19 How.) 393 (1856)
Enforcement Act of 1870, 16 Stat. 141 (1870)
42 U.S.C. §§ 1981–82
Jones et ux. v. Alfred H. Mayer Co., et al., 392 U.S. 409 (1968)
Patterson v. McClean Credit Union, 491 U.S. 164 (1989)
Runyon v. McCrary, 427 U.S. 160 (1976)

See also **Bingham, John Armor; Civil Rights Act of 1875;** *Civil Rights Cases*, **109 U.S. 3 (1883);** *Dred Scott v. Sandford*, **60 U.S. 393 (1857); Fourteenth Amendment; Ku Klux Klan; Slavery and Civil Liberties; Thirteenth Amendment; Vagrancy Laws**

CIVIL RIGHTS ACT OF 1875

One of the major and last pieces of civil rights legislation passed during the era of Reconstruction, the Civil Rights Act of 1875 sought to ensure that all citizens, regardless of race, were protected against discriminatory acts in both public and private venues.

Passed during a lame-duck session of a Republican-controlled Congress, the act sought to ensure the freedom of access to the "full and equal enjoyment of the accommodations, advantages, facilities, and privileges" of many public venues, including inns, hotels, railroad cars, theaters, and other "places of public amusement" regardless of race. The act was passed under the authority of both the Thirteenth and Fourteenth Amendments to the U.S. Constitution. Lead by Republican U.S. Senator Charles Sumner, the act's intent was the ensure that freedoms and rights were guaranteed to blacks and that private individuals could not discriminate based on race. If an individual violated the act, they were subject to fines of no less than $500 or thirty days in prison.

The act was rarely enforced, however, and in 1883, the U.S. Supreme Court struck down the law as unconstitutional (the *Civil Rights Cases*, 109 U.S. 3). The Court's majority held that Congress had overstepped its authority to regulate private behavior. It would be eighty-two years before Congress passed another act dealing with civil rights, following the imposition of state-sanctioned segregation and Jim Crow laws, most notably in the South.

J. MICHAEL BITZER

References and Further Reading

Foner, Eric. 2002. *Reconstruction: America's Unfinished Revolution, 1863–1877*. New York: HarperCollins.

Cases and Statutes Cited

Civil Rights Cases, 109 U.S. 3 (1883)

CIVIL RIGHTS ACT OF 1964

With the twentieth century civil rights movement well underway, Congress passed one of the two major acts focused on prohibiting and providing remedies for discrimination against blacks. The 1964 Civil Rights Act, along with the Voting Rights Act of 1965, is a comprehensive piece of legislation designed to attack racial segregation, as well as discrimination based on gender, in public accommodations, employment, and by any private individual or organization that receives federal funding.

The 1964 act came after the passage of the 1957 and 1960 civil rights acts, which sought to protect voting and provide federal protection to ensure voting by blacks. However, racial discrimination in voting and other facets of American society, particularly in the South, prompted President John F. Kennedy to push for a civil rights act. However, it was after Kennedy's assassination that the bill gained major moment in Congress, due in large part to President Lyndon B. Johnson's call for equal rights for all Americans, regardless of race.

The first section of the act focused on voting and barred discriminatory techniques to voter registration; however, the use of such discrimination techniques as the literacy test, which were used to deny voting privileges to blacks and poor whites, would be dealt with major reforms protecting the right to vote would come a year later with the Voting Rights Act. The second section (Title II) prohibits discrimination in any public accommodations (inns, hotels, restaurants, and theaters for example), even though they may be privately owned. This section was based on the power of Congress to regulate interstate commerce and was subsequently upheld (unlike the Civil Rights Act of 1875) by the U.S. Supreme Court in *Heart of Atlanta Motel v. United States* and *Katzenbach v. McClung*. Title III of the act promoted the concept of desegregation of public schools, begun with the 1954 and 1955 U.S. Supreme Court decisions in *Brown v. Board of Education*. Title VI prohibits discrimination to any public or private organization that receives federal funding. Finally, Title VII outlaws discrimination based on race, national origin, gender, or religion in employment practices. This section was upheld as constitutional in the 1971 case of *Griggs v. Duke Power Co.*, which also held that the act prohibited both intentional discriminatory practices and those practices that had a "disparate impact" on minorities. In addition, the U.S. Supreme Court ruled that Title VII sanctioned the use of hiring and promotion practices to counter historical discrimination in employment. This has lead to the controversy of affirmative action as a policy to alleviate past discrimination in present-day situations. Finally, by outlawing discrimination based on gender, the Civil Rights Act extends beyond racial discrimination also to areas of "sexual harassment."

In conjunction with the Voting Rights Act of 1965, the Civil Rights Act of 1964 has provided the impetus for major societal changes in regard to all kinds of discrimination and to protect and ensure civil liberties for all Americans.

J. MICHAEL BITZER

References and Further Reading

Graham, Hugh Davis. *The Civil Rights Era: Origins and Development of National Policy 1960–1972*. New York: Oxford University Press, 1990.

Klarman, Michael J. *From Jim Crow to Civil Rights: the Supreme Court and the Struggle for Civil Rights*. New York: Oxford University Press. 2004.

Kotz, Nick. *Judgment Days: Lyndon Baines Johnson, Martin Luther King, Jr., and the Laws that Changed America*. New York: Houghton-Mifflin, 2005.

Lawson, Stephen F. *Black Ballots: Voting Rights in the South, 1944-1969*. New York: Columbia University Press, 1976.

Mann, Robert. *The Walls of Jericho: Lyndon Johnson, Hubert Humphrey, Richard Russell and the Struggle for Civil Rights*. New York: Harcourt Brace, 1996.

Cases and Statutes Cited

Brown v. Board of Education of Topeka, KS, 347 U.S. 483 (1954)

Griggs v. Duke Power Co., 401 U.S. 424 (1971)

Heart of Atlanta Motel v. United States, 379 U.S. 241 (1964)

Katzenbach v. McClung, 379 U.S. 294 (1964)

CIVIL RIGHTS CASES, 109 U.S. 3 (1883)

A U.S. Supreme Court case striking down as unconstitutional the last of the Reconstruction-era acts designed to protect against discrimination based on race, the Civil Rights Act of 1875 sought to outlaw racial discrimination on both public and private acts.

The decision focused on five different instances in which whites denied blacks admission to various venues like inns, theaters, and a railroad car. Through a narrow interpretation of the Thirteenth and Fourteenth Amendments to the U.S. Constitution, an eight-justice majority found that Congress overstepped its constitutional authority in passing the 1875 act. In their attempt to bar discrimination in public accommodations, Congress used the Civil War amendments to affect both public and private acts of inequality based on race. However, the justices interpreted the amendments narrowly as prohibitions against state governments, and not against private individuals who operated public inns, hotels, and other public accommodations. The act of refusing individuals the right to stay at a private inn, due to a person's race, did not amount to "a badge or incident of slavery," Justice Bradley wrote, echoing a legal theme that would serve as the foundation for Jim Crow laws in a segregated South.

In his dissent, Justice John Marshall Harlan, a Southerner and former slaveholder, attacked the narrow interpretation of the Civil War amendments and instead argued that Congress had the broad power to protect the rights of blacks against all "badges of slavery." This case, along with *Plessy v. Ferguson*, effectively removed the federal government from civil rights enforcement for more than eighty years, allowing states to impose segregation and Jim Crow laws that discriminated on the basis of race.

J. MICHAEL BITZER

References and Future Reading

Klarman, Michael J. *From Jim Crow to Civil Rights: the Supreme Court and the Struggle for Civil Rights.* New York: Oxford University Press, 2004.

Cases and Statutes Cited

Plessy v. Ferguson, 163 U.S. 537 (1896)

See also **Equal Protection of Law (XIV)**

CIVIL RIGHTS LAWS AND FREEDOM OF SPEECH

The goal of civil rights is to achieve equality, itself definable in various ways, in place of discrimination. Free speech can powerfully advance that goal, and hence is often linked historically with it. Yet free speech can also mean the expression of ideas or attitudes that are at odds with civil rights, and hence there are times when the two are in conflict or at least in tension with one another.

The civil rights movement, and civil rights laws in the United States, center first and foremost on the idea of racial equality, especially in opposition to the pervasive discrimination that was long directed against Black Americans. Free speech, and freedoms of association and assembly which have close practical links to free speech, in turn have a long and positive association with the cause of civil rights, dating back to the movement for the abolition of slavery before the American Civil War. Freedom of speech was uncertain at best for many opponents of slavery. The abolitionist editor Elijah Lovejoy

was shot dead and his press destroyed by a mob in Alton, Illinois, in 1837. Southern opponents of slavery, like Angelina and Sarah Grimké of South Carolina, fled or were driven out of the South. Southern postmasters would not deliver anti-slavery literature, and Congress for some years during the 1830s and 1840s even adopted a "gag rule" against anti-slavery petitions.

For a century after the Civil War, segregation and discrimination ("Jim Crow") made for a racial caste system in the American South. Protest against Jim Crow was often perilous, just as protest against slavery had been. In the 1890s the offices of several black newspapers were destroyed by mobs, including—after it printed an editorial against lynching—the offices of the Memphis, Tennessee, "Free Speech." Throughout the South, there were many decades of violence, both official and unofficial, against opponents of segregation. As protest against Jim Crow gathered force in the 1950s and early 1960s, civil rights rallies and marches were broken up by force. Civil rights demonstrators, including Dr Martin Luther King, were arrested, and there were notorious incidents of police dogs and fire hoses being turned on marchers. Three civil rights workers were murdered in Mississippi in 1964 with the apparent connivance of the police, and churches where civil rights meetings took place were attacked, including the Baptist church in Birmingham, Alabama, where four children were killed by a bomb in 1963.

With advocacy of civil rights under threat, civil rights and free speech became intertwined as causes: support for the one seemed easily interchangeable with support for the other. Constitutional law reflected this. In the 1950s and 1960s, the U.S. Supreme Court quashed disorderly conduct convictions of civil rights marchers, for example, and struck down parade permit laws as applied against civil rights demonstrations. The hostility of Southern officials, courts, and juries against civil rights advocates provoked a series of Supreme Court decisions safeguarding free speech and freedom of association, in some cases perhaps extending those concepts further than they might have been extended were it not for the struggle over civil rights. Thus, in *NAACP v. Alabama*, when the state of Alabama sought the local membership lists of a national civil rights organization in the course of a civil lawsuit, the Supreme Court held that freedom of association, with its "close nexus" to freedom of speech, precluded the disclosure, despite otherwise liberal "discovery" rules in litigation, since rank-and-file members would be open to local reprisals if their identity were revealed. In *NAACP v. Claiborne Hardware*, the Supreme Court also upheld, on free speech grounds, a business boycott organized by civil rights groups in Mississippi, although in addition to peaceful picketing and urgings to support the boycott, there had admittedly been threatening speeches and publications by the organizers against those in the local Black community who failed to observe the boycott. And the law of libel took a new constitutional direction in *New York Times v. Sullivan*, when an Alabama police commissioner sued the *New York Times* and was awarded $1.25 million in damages by a local jury over an advertisement criticizing law enforcement for a "reign of terror" against peaceful civil rights groups in the South. The Supreme Court not only quashed the verdict, it laid down very narrow conditions under which a "public figure" could successfully sue for libel, so that statements that would readily be deemed libelous in many other countries and, at common law, are now immune from lawsuits in the United States. It is at least imaginable that these cases, with their liberal view of what should be protected as free speech and freedom of association—even at the expense of other values or interests—might have been decided differently had they not arisen in the civil rights context.

By the mid-1960s, the social and legal revolution associated with the civil rights movement brought an end to the old regime of racial segregation and discrimination in the South. With the end of Jim Crow, the climate of threat and violence against opponents of segregation, once so pervasive in the South, also came to an end. Campaigns for civil rights certainly continued, aimed at achieving racial justice, defined in various ways. The success of the civil rights movement in the South also inspired others to frame their causes in civil rights terms: ethnic advocates, feminists, sexual minorities, and many others put their claims in this framework. These civil rights advocates, like advocates of any cause, have an obvious interest in freedom of speech and of assembly and association. In this sense, there continues to be important common ground between civil rights and free speech. But with the disappearance of the sort of hostility to free speech that typified the Jim Crow South, various tensions between civil rights and free speech have also come to the surface.

The tension was implicit, in a sense, even in landmark legislation like the Civil Rights Act of 1964. By forbidding employment discrimination, for example, the law inevitably diminished freedom of association for employers who wished to discriminate. It also amounted to a direct ban on certain sorts of "speech," such as "Whites only" or "No Irish need apply" in employment advertisements. It can plausibly be said that freedom of association is always subject to a variety of limitations, especially in economic life,

and that discriminatory want ads are "verbal acts" and hence should not be protected as free speech. In any event, the national interest in banning discrimination was great. Yet the fact remains that prohibiting discrimination does affect freedom of association; as for "verbal acts," the distinction between "expressive speech" and "verbal acts" is a notoriously slippery one. Even here, then, there was some inevitable tradeoff, however fully justified the Civil Rights Act was.

In the decades that followed, a variety of civil rights laws, regulations, and policies have been directed at least in part at the expression of insulting or otherwise unwelcome attitudes or opinions, revealing more sharply and perhaps more troubling how civil rights and free speech interests can sometimes diverge.

Hate Speech

Criminal penalties for racial insults, and commonly for sexual or religious insults as well, have been adopted in several states. The courts have generally struck down these laws on free speech grounds, although in *R.A.V. v. City of St Paul*, four Justices of the Supreme Court indicated that they would uphold such laws if they were restricted to "fighting words" and did not seek to punish a broader range of insults such as those which (merely) "arouse anger" or "resentment."

Hate Crimes

The federal sentencing guidelines, and many state laws, punish various crimes—such as assault and vandalism—more severely if the crime was committed because of the race, ethnicity, gender, or sexual orientation of the victim. Unlike "hate speech" laws, the Supreme Court has upheld "hate crime" legislation, on the theory that punishment often takes motive into account; that the culprit has been convicted of a crime, not an opinion; and that the law may consider "bias" crimes to be especially dangerous to society, by terrorizing particular groups for example, and hence may punish the crimes more severely. From a free speech point of view, the trouble is that the extra punishment is for the culprit's attitude or opinion, not for the crime itself. In that sense, "hate crimes" smack of the old criminal syndicalism laws, which punished ordinary crimes more severely if they were committed with socialist or anarchist motivations.

Speech Codes

Many colleges and universities, public and private, have adopted "speech codes," which, typically, prohibit speech that "stigmatizes" anyone on the basis of race, ethnicity, gender, sexuality, or on any number of other bases. Supporters urge that these codes are necessary to ensure that members of groups who might otherwise be stigmatized should feel welcome on campus. Critics say that these codes contribute to enforcing a climate of political conformity on campus, since any expression of unwelcome intellectual or political views can easily be alleged to stigmatize one or another group. When adopted by public institutions, the courts have mostly struck down these codes as content based, vague, and likely to chill free expression. The state of California, by statute, also forbids private colleges to impose limits on free speech that would be unconstitutional on a public campus. But many private colleges and universities elsewhere maintain such speech codes.

Harassment in the Workplace

Federal and state employment discrimination laws have been interpreted to forbid speech in the workplace that creates a "hostile environment" on the basis of race, gender, ethnicity, or various other characteristics. Speech by employers or fellow employees that might be deemed harassment, if "pervasive" enough, can range from racial or ethnic slurs and sexual propositions to religious proselytizing, posting sexually suggestive pictures (including reproductions of works of art), and statements about political or social questions felt to be offensive. If an employee is harassed by fellow employees, it can be the basis for a discrimination suit against the employer. Hence employers have a strong incentive to forbid any workplace speech that could arouse complaint; and an employer might not give much weight to free speech concerns where it is a question of controlling the speech of employees, not the employer's own speech. The tension between civil rights and free speech interests may be particularly stark here, because there is surely a danger to the effectiveness of equal employment laws if employees can be driven from their jobs by systematic verbal abuse. Yet most people spend a large part of their waking lives at work. Employers,

pressured by federal and state civil rights enforcement agencies, and under threat of civil lawsuits, may seek to avoid harassment claims by closely policing what employees say, what topics they discuss, what views they express, and how they express them: even during mealtimes and work breaks, and with little regard for the chill on free expression.

Freedom of Association

Speech and advocacy by an organized group will usually get a better hearing than speech from an isolated individual: hence the obvious link between freedom of association and freedom of speech. But a group promoting a particular cause may "speak" with more unity and more effectiveness if membership is restricted to those likely to support the cause. To what extent can such groups lawfully discriminate in their membership? For example, may an organization promoting the advancement of an ethnic group restrict itself to members of that ethnicity? In 1984, the Supreme Court in *Roberts v. U.S. Jaycees* held that Minnesota civil rights laws could require the Jaycees to admit women as members, although the Jaycees' stated purpose was "promoting the interests of young men." In 2000, in *Boy Scouts of America v. Dale*, the Supreme Court apparently reversed itself by deciding, on free speech grounds, that the Boy Scouts could exclude adult gay volunteers, despite a New Jersey law forbidding discrimination against gays, because opposition to homosexual activity was one of the principles advocated by the Scouts. In recent decades, civil rights advocates have mostly favored a narrow right of "expressive association" and a robust enforcement of nondiscrimination laws, even as against noncommercial groups, and especially—as with the Jaycees and the Scouts—where advocacy is not the main or the only purpose of the group.

Feminism and Pornography

Many feminist activists and academics support bans on pornography, and a few cities and towns have enacted such bans on the theory that pornography is degrading to women and hence is discriminatory. Pornography in this context is typically defined as "sexually explicit subordination of women," whether in words or pictures. This definition is much broader than the constitutional definition of obscenity: its ban would extend to works that have literary or artistic value, for example. Even some proponents of such laws are troubled when the law is enforced against homosexual or avant-garde literature, as has happened in Canada and other jurisdictions with feminist-inspired bans. Proponents of banning pornography do not deny the conflict with free speech: some deny that free speech is very valuable, but most urge that feminist civil rights concerns should weigh more heavily because pornography is "low value" speech. But celebrated twentieth-century campaigns against censorship involved works like James Joyce's *Ulysses*, which had been banned as pornographic, and which might well fall under the feminist ordinances as well. When cities and towns in recent years passed "civil rights" laws against nonobscene pornography—and when Congress enacted restrictions on internet pornography—the courts struck down these laws on free speech grounds. Feminists and their supporters continue to debate, however, whether pornography should be banned and, if so, with what limits and definitions.

Inasmuch as civil rights are about equality, there is always a potential for conflict with free speech, especially when civil rights are thought to be threatened by inimical attitudes, insults, or ideas. Yet if the equality sought by civil rights is an equality of rights, few if any political rights are more fundamental than freedom of speech. Both as a matter of prudence and of principle, therefore, civil rights advocates might do well to respect and to defend free speech. It would be difficult to achieve civil rights, or any social change, without freedom to speak, to persuade, and to organize. And erosions of free speech compromise the goal of civil rights by eroding one of the fundamental rights which it is, or ought to be, the very purpose of civil rights to guarantee, equally, to all.

MAIMON SCHWARZSCHILD

References and Further Reading

Bernstein, David E. *You Can't Say That! The Growing Threat to Civil Liberties from Antidiscrimination Laws*. Washington DC: Cato Institute, 2003.
Miller, William Lee. *Arguing About Slavery*. New York: Alfred A. Knopf, 1996.
Rauch, Jonathan. *Kindly Inquisitors: The New Attacks on Free Thought*. Chicago: University of Chicago Press, 1993.
Schauer, Frederick. *Free Speech: A Philosophical Inquiry*. Cambridge: Cambridge University Press, 1982.
Strossen, Nadine. *Defending Pornography: Free Speech, Sex, and the Fight for Women's Rights*. New York: Scribner, 1995.

Cases and Statutes Cited

Boy Scouts of America v. Dale, 530 U.S. 640 (2000)
NAACP v. Alabama, 357 U.S. 449 (1958)
NAACP v. Claiborne Hardware, 458 U.S. 886 (1982)
New York Times v. Sullivan, 376 U.S. 254 (1964)
R.A.V. v. City of St Paul, 505 U.S. 377 (1992)
Roberts v. United States Jaycees, 468 U.S. 609 (1984)
Civil Rights Act of 1964, Public Law 82-352 (78 Stat. 241)

CIVILIAN COMPLAINT REVIEW BOARDS

A civilian review board is a group of citizens who are given responsibility for investigating or reviewing complaints of misconduct by police officers. These groups are responsible for holding police officers accountable to the public.

In most instances civilian review board members are appointed by local government officials. The boards are established through municipal ordinances, state statutes, orders from municipal mayors, popular vote, or less often, by request from police chiefs. Each board is unique in terms of the amount of investigatory power it possesses. Some boards are given the power to subpoena witnesses, to discipline officers, and to access police files. Some of these boards also have the power to conduct evidentiary hearings and investigate allegations of racial profiling. Most civilian review boards, however, do not have investigation powers, and they are restricted to reviewing the internal police investigation. These boards do not have any power to discipline police officers, and they merely make recommendations to police administrators who have the power to reject these recommendations without consequence. In some jurisdictions boards are composed entirely of citizens, whereas others have both police and citizen members.

Many police officers oppose the formulation of civilian review boards, because they believe they are capable of policing themselves. Police officers also oppose civilian review, because they fear that their authority will be reduced, and they believe that they need a veil of secrecy to effectively operate. In addition, many police officers believe that civilians generally lack an understanding of the pressures of law enforcement and should, therefore, not be empowered to second guess the actions of police officers.

Thirty of the fifty largest communities, as well as many smaller cities in the United States, have instituted civilian review boards.

JUDITH A. M. SCULLY

References and Further Reading

Best Practices in Police Accountability. A web site dedicated to information and resources on civilian review, www.policeaccountability.org.

Civilian Review Sample Model. Available at www.aclufl.org/ take_action/download_resources/civilian_review.model. cfm.

Shielded from Justice: Police Brutality and Accountability in the United States, a Human Rights Watch Report (1998) available at http://hrw.org/reports98/police/ uspo92.htm.

CLARK, RAMSEY (1927–)

One of the most controversial figures in the field of civil liberties litigation, Ramsey Clark is many things to many people. Perhaps to everyone he is a test case for the fundamental principle of the adversary system of justice that all defendants, regardless of the charge lodged against them and no matter how odious their conduct may have been, are innocent until proven guilty and entitled to a zealous defense at law. As familiar as the principle has become, in the annals of American legal history and culture, as well as on prime-time evening television programs, like *Law & Order*, it has surely been honored more in the breach than in the observance.

William Ramsey Clark, born in Dallas, Texas, in 1927, is the son of U.S. Supreme Court Justice Tom Clark. After serving in the U.S. Marine Corps and graduating from the University of Texas, Clark received a law degree from the University of Chicago and was admitted to the Texas bar in 1951. Clark was a member of the Clark, Reed, and Clark law firm from 1951 to 1961 and was an Assistant Attorney General, then Deputy Attorney General in the Kennedy and Johnson Administrations, 1961 to 1966. In March of 1967, when Tom Clark stepped down from his position on the U.S. Supreme Court, President Lyndon Johnson named Clark's son, Ramsey, Attorney General of the United States.

Contemporary critics of Clark from the left of the American political spectrum look back on his two years as Attorney General as a time when the radical lawyer showed his true colors. He admired J. Edgar Hoover, they allege, instructed the F. B. I. to look for conspiratorial designs in the 1967 race riots in Watts and Newark, and in 1968 was still a sufficient supporter of the Vietnam War to be willing to prosecute Dr. Benjamin Spock and Yale's Rev. William Sloan Coffin, Jr., for conspiring to promote illegal resistance to the draft. But Clark's prosecution of the case may not have reflected his deepest political values and commitments. After all, the attorney for Coffin, Hale and Door's James St. Clair, later represented a cornered President Richard Nixon and was himself criticized by Yale's chaplain for being, in the draft resistance litigation, "all case and no cause." The Boston Globe heralded St. Clair for "accepting clients from across the ideological spectrum." If Clark's legal career is assessed as a whole, the same could easily be said of him, and in praise rather than criticism, so long as one buys into the central claims of an adversary legal process.

At the same time, some of Clark's supporters point out that he supervised U.S. Marshals when they were sent to Oxford, Mississippi, ensuring the enrollment of James Meredith at the University, helped write and secure passage of the Voting Rights Act of 1965 and the Civil Rights Act of 1968, and famously sought to block J. Edgar Hoover's wiretaps of the Rev. Dr. Martin Luther King, Jr. Assuming one regards the civil rights movement of the 1960s as part of the legacy of progressive politics, it is hard to understand *Salon* writer Ian Williams claim that Clark's "long march leftward only began afterward," after, that is, Clark's tenure as Attorney General.

Generally omitted from Clark balance sheets drawn up by friends, as well as enemies, would be an entry for one of his most interesting confrontations as Attorney General—with none other than the infamous Howard Hughes. As part of an elaborate scheme to take over the gaming industry in Las Vegas, Hughes had presented his chief aid, Robert Maheu, with a blueprint for further acquisition of land, hotels, casinos, and so forth. After closing its casino and operating the Bonanza exclusively as a hotel, thus obviating the need to secure a gaming license, Hughes would then purchase the Silver Slipper and the Stardust, all the while retaining an option to buy the Silver Nugget. With public support from Las Vegas newspaperman and power broker, H. M. 'Hank' Greenspun, Hughes and Maheu were confident they could win gambling licenses from Nevada authorities for the Stardust and Silver Slipper. But Hughes' scheme went awry when U.S. Justice Department lawyers intervened and threatened to initiate antitrust litigation against Hughes if he persisted in his plan to buy the Stardust.

While an assistant attorney general in charge of the Justice Department's Criminal Division sent Clark a memo stating that Hughes would drive undesirable elements out of Las Vegas and suggested that F.B.I. Director Hoover looked favorably on Hughes' expansion in Nevada, the Antitrust Division would not budge and their boss, Attorney General Clark, backed them up. Maheu then appealed to Nevada's two U.S. Senators and then-Governor Laxalt who promptly wrote Clark a letter warning of "permanent damage" to Nevada's economy if Hughes' acquisition plans were frustrated. But it was "to no avail," according to Hughes biographers Donald L. Barlett and James B. Steele. Ramsey Clark, they report, "stood firm. When Hughes realized that the federal government fully intended to sue him, he caved in and withdrew his offer for the Stardust." Barlett and Steele go so far as to assert that this "was one of the very few times in a career distinguished by harmonious relations with government agencies that Howard Hughes had been thwarted." Things would soon change, they observe wryly, with the inauguration of President Richard Nixon.

With the Republicans back in power, Clark joined the antiwar movement and would make a controversial visit to North Vietnam in 1972. Two years later, he ran unsuccessfully as the Democratic Party's candidate for the U.S. Senate from New York (losing out to antiwar Republican, Jacob Javits) and has subsequently devoted himself to providing legal advice to a wide range of public figures and organizations. His clients have included David Koresh of the ill-starred Branch Davidian Church; Native-American political activist and federal penitentiary resident, Leonard Peltier; right-wing conspiracy theorist and demagogue, Lyndon LaRouche; a leader of the Rwandan genocide; former Yugoslavian President Slobodan Milosevic; the Palestine Liberation Organization; Father Philip Berrigan and the Harrisburg Six (prosecuted for allegedly planning to kidnap Henry Kissinger and try him for war crimes); Sheik Omar Abd El-Rahman, the "Blind" Sheik, convicted of participating in the first World Trade Center bombing; and Lori Berenson, an American woman jailed in Peru for alleged contacts with the Tupac Amaru radical movement.

It would be interesting to compare the hostility with which Ramsey Clark's representation of unpopular clients has occasionally been greeted with that directed, for example, toward Harvard professor, Alan Dershowitz, for his representation of O. J. Simpson, Leona Helmsley, and Klaus von Bulow; or William Kunstler, whose clients included H. Rap Brown, Angela Davis, El Sayyid Nosair, and Malcolm X. Indeed, with respect to the American Indian Movement and Islamic fundamentalists accused of terrorism in the U.S., Kunstler and Clark shared some of the same clients. Kunstler, it will be recalled, "was respected for his belief in justice and his commitment to the rights of the defendant," as ABC's Peter Jennings put it in his on-air report of Kunstler's death; the courageous defender of the "underdog" had even been granted a starring role in one episode of *Law & Order*, with a script written virtually to marquee Kunstler's view of the Constitution. Perhaps unlike Kunstler, however, Ramsey Clark's politics, his choice of clients, something, seem to have placed him beyond the pale for many commentators on the legal scene.

In one of the sharpest interrogations of Clark's conduct, Ian Williams argues that in 1998, "Clark attended a human rights conference in Baghdad, Iraq, where in his keynote speech he pointed out how 'the governments of the rich nations' . . . dominated the wording of the Universal Declaration of Human Rights, which showed 'little concern for economic, social, and cultural rights.'" Williams may feel he has thus demonstrated with this example the hypocritical relationship between Clark and his presumed "Kunstleresque" stature as a defender of individual rights and civil liberties. But unless Clark is dishonest for saying what he said where he said it, then it is a statement with which it is hard to disagree.

First, consider Harold Laski's observation that the gap between liberalism's promises and performance has always been wide. *Any* hopeful promises "governments of the rich nations" have made to the rest of the countries of the world have rarely been kept; certainly not kept in a way that would change significantly the quality of life for the world's poor. From promises of safety against tyrannical regimes and marauding armies, guarantees against the ravages of hunger and disease, to promises of debt reduction or curtailment of agricultural subsidies to developed economies, the rich nations have generally turned a blind eye to the human catastrophe endured day in and day out by the wretched of the earth.

Second, one need only recall Anatole France's famous aphorism about the law, which in its majesty, prohibits the rich as well as the poor from sleeping beneath the bridges of Paris. Human rights proclaimed by middle class revolution and Western cultural tradition are often of little use to the great mass of people living on earth today, and this sad irony has become so well worn that by now it seems almost pointless to repeat it. That Ramsey Clark is willing to do so, in Baghdad or anywhere else, seems less evidence of devious character or fatal inconsistency than an almost Pollyannaish willingness to maintain faith in the prospect of real social change. How can anyone have confidence in the future, with so little accomplished, these many years after France's skewering of a purely formal equality before the law? In Dickens' *Hard Times*, a working class schoolgirl is asked if she is not pleased to be living in such a thriving and prosperous state as Britain. Her instructor is horrified when she responds she would have to know, first, who had got the money and whether or not any of it was hers. Again, Dickens was writing in the middle of the nineteenth century. Comments along these same lines by Ramsey Clark are long overdue, and criticizing him for making them in Baghdad is as silly as castigating Bill Clinton, not for having protested the Vietnam but for having done so at Oxford.

No criticism of Ramsey Clark is heard more frequently than that he does not simply provide legal representation for his clients but, goes further, and offers support for their politics and apologies for their alleged misdeeds. He cannot seem to separate out the legal value of zealous advocacy, central to the system, from the dangerous assault on liberal values many of his clients perpetrate, on the very margins or fringes of the system. Nevertheless, in the summer of 2005, Clark was the target of a very different kind of attack. The Associated Press reported that "Saddam Hussein's chief lawyer quit the Iraqi dictator's Jordan-based legal team" because "some of the team's American members were trying to control the defense and tone down his criticism of the U.S. presence in Iraq." The attorney specifically rejected Ramsey Clark's defense strategy, saying that Clark "had often asked me to refrain from criticizing the American occupation of Iraq and the U.S.-backed Iraqi government." No one would claim that Ramsey Clark "is all case and no cause." But, perhaps Clark simply appreciates that different degrees of identification with clients can be appropriate depending upon the circumstances of individual cases. Unlike his politics, Clark, like most lawyers, is unlikely to share his defense strategy with reporters.

Ariah Naier, once the leader and, arguably, moral conscience of the American Civil Liberties Union, defended the constitutional rights of bedraggled remnants of wartime fascism and obnoxious new Nazi skin heads who demonstrated publicly in Skokie, Illinois, despite the offense thus given to many in the Chicago Jewish community, including some survivors of the Holocaust and many more relatives of those who did not survive. What could protecting the rights of thugs whose hatred for rights is notorious have to do with civil liberty? Naier was often asked this question by deeply perplexed supporters of his values and his organization. It is a hard question, appropriately directed at Ariah Naier and his comrades in the cause of civil liberty, as well as at Ramsey Clark and his colleagues in the legal profession. When prominent Massachusetts attorney John Adams was asked to provide legal representation for soldiers who fired on unruly citizen-rebels in what was called the "Boston Massacre," Adams did not hesitate. What, he wondered, could be more important to the citizen of a democracy than the right to a lawyer? For better or for worse, Ramsey Clark continues to answer that question in ways not very different from early American patriot John Adams of Boston.

ANTHONY CHASE

References and Further Reading

Barlett, Donald L., and Steele, James B. *Empire: The Life, Legend, and Madness of Howard Hughes.* New York: W.W. Norton, 1979.
"Top Hussein Lawyer Quits, Chides U.S." *USA Today,* July 7, 2005.
Williams, Ian. "Ramsey Clark: The War Criminal's Best Friend" (*Salon.com*, June 21, 1999).

CLARK, TOM CAMPBELL (1899–1977)

Tom C. Clark was one of the more controversial justices of the twentieth century Supreme Court. His 18 years on the Court were filled with controversies and shifts among the justices as they decided issues. Clark himself took the unusual step of resigning from the Court in 1967. He did this to avoid any question of conflict of interest when his son, Ramsey Clark, took the position of U.S. Attorney General. Knowing that Ramsey himself or his subordinates would argue cases before the Court that could be interpreted as at least a violation of propriety in court, led the father to resign.

Tom Clark was born in Dallas, Texas, on September 23, 1899. Having been born and raised in a family of lawyers, Clark followed in the family profession, graduated from the University of Texas law school in 1922. After some years of practice in the family firm and a stint as a district attorney of Dallas, Clark moved to Washington, D. C., where he worked for the government during World War II.

Clark's support in 1944 of Harry S. Truman's bid for Franklin D. Roosevelt's vice-president at the Democratic Party convention led Truman when president to nominate Clark as Attorney General.

An opening on the Supreme Court followed four years later. Some amount of controversy followed Clark's nomination by President Truman; nevertheless, the vote in the Senate was seventy-three to eight in favor of Clark taking the vacancy on the Court.

As Attorney General, Clark had to deal with the growing Red Scare that gripped the nation after the breakdown of the alliance that had won World War II. On the international scene, the concept of a Cold War dominated that breakdown. At home, the Red Scare had significant political overtones for the Truman administration as the accusation of being "soft on communism" was leveled against the Democratic administration.

Clark was at the center of the maelstrom surrounding the Red Scare; even in Clark's own administration of the justice department, there was pressure on him to take action against communists, their party, and those accused of being disloyal, if not guilty of, espionage. The main call for action was from J. Edgar Hoover, Director of the FBI who, although ostensibly subordinate to Clark nevertheless, put pressure on the Justice Department in his crusade to destroy the Communist Party and all those he believed were the enemies of this nation. Behind Senator Joseph McCarthy (Rep. Wisc.) was Hoover. During the years 1950 to 1954, Hoover supplied McCarthy and the House Un-American Activities Committee (HUAC) with information surreptitiously given to these fellow crusaders. Hoover also placed FBI men on the staffs of McCarthy and HUAC.

In an attempt to counterattack charges of "soft on communism" and recover from the losses in the 1946 election, in 1947 Clark following Truman's Executive Order 9335, created the nation's first peacetime loyalty program.

The next year, 1948, Clark issued a list of 123 allegedly subversive organizations. It was compiled for use of the Federal Loyalty Review Board. Again, the purpose was to demonstrate how vigorous Truman was in exposing true "subversives." In fact, however, the list was used by many individuals, as well as public loyalty boards. The "list" was used to discredit anyone who might, for any reason, have joined any of these organizations.

The creation and use of this "subversive list" was more than a political tool. It indicated just how far the nation and its leaders would go to show vigor in searching for Reds under the beds; the result was crippling to the civil rights of all citizens.

In 1951, the Supreme Court found the Clark listing process unconstitutional. It was the only major victory won by those opposing the Red Scare until 1957. Justice Clark did not take part in the decision, since he had partaken in the creation of the loyalty system and was responsible for the "subversive organizations list."

To some extent, Clark typified a type of New Dealer: one who would give the widest latitude possible to Congress and the executive branch on economic issues but was very narrow on civil rights. The terrible Great Depression seems to have sent the message that only the widest interpretation of the law would restore the economy. The civil rights of individuals and groups were of less consequence and required less concern or protection. Had Clark been able to vote to support the "subversive organization list" in 1951, there is little doubt he would have voted to sustain the loyalty program.

Another case that Clark was not able to participate in was the appeal of the eleven (the twelfth was too ill to be tried) national leaders of the Communist Party, in *Dennis v. United States*, 341 U.S. 643 (1961). The government prosecutors did not need his vote to confirm the guilt of the communists (six to affirm; two

against; Clark not participating). This time and for some years thereafter, the government's prosecutions of communists and others trapped in the Red Scare resulted, almost invariably, in confirmation of guilt by the Supreme Court.

A change of the Supreme Court's makeup began in 1953, following the death of Chief Justice Frederick M. Vinson; Earl Warren was appointed Chief Judge; John M. Harlan II and William J. Brennan, Jr., were appointed as associate justices. The result was a new majority ready to recognize the importance of the First Amendment and place curbs on the use of the Red Scare to justify guilty verdicts. The holdouts from joining this new majority (now dissenters) included Justice Clark.

With these changes in the makeup of the Supreme court, the Justice Department, Hoover, and his FBI lost the ability to punish citizens with jail and fines because of what they believed, what organizations they belonged to, and even what they read. Beyond the change in personnel, the change in the Court can be attributed to not only the changed makeup in the Court but also to the dissipation of the Red Scare throughout the nation.

Two developments signify the importance of what was happening: the 1954 televised Army–McCarthy Hearings and the 1957 decision by the Supreme Court in the *Yates v. United States*, 354 U.S. 298 (1957). Justice Clark led the battle to sustain the guilt of the Yates defendants, but he failed to convince his brethren. The defendants were all from the California branch of the Communist Party. Following the track laid out in the prosecution of the Dennis case defendants, all nineteen of them were found guilty, fined, and were to serve prison terms. In Yates, the new Court majority stated that only when the government could show that any defendant did some act or took some action (beyond believing) could a citizen be found guilty of the Smith Act. More was required to meet the higher standard imposed by the Court majority.

In 1949, when Clark joined the Court, it seems that Chief Justice Vinson was the colleague whose views Clark followed. This changed, however, as the years passed; the influence of Chief Justice Warren can be seen, particularly in 1954, when Warren led the battle for attacking the race issue (*Brown v. Board of Education*, 347 U.S. 483 [1954]). Clark joined with the other eight justices in the unanimous decision.

During his mature years on the bench, Clark wrote many excellent and important decisions. A review of his participation confirms that Clark, particularly in those later years on the Court, was with the majority in most decisions; one list of majority vs. minority positions taken by Clark counts forty-six majority listing and only sixteen minority positions by him.

He also moved from being the leading dissenter on First Amendment issues during the period 1955 and forward to a more flexible view of such issues. He was not implacable; he moved from majority to minorities as he felt the case deserved.

Clark is perhaps best known as the author of the Court's controversial decision on *Mapp v. Ohio*, 367 U.S. 643 (1961). In this decision, the Court held that in state criminal trials, the use of evidence obtained in violation of the Fourth Amendment must be excluded. The roots of Mapp took hold, albeit in the face of a continuing controversy, down to this day.

Two areas where Clark wrote for a majority reflected his abiding interest in religious issues that came before the Court, as Mapp showed his strong interest in criminal law. In *Abington School District v. Schemmpp*, 374 U.S. 203 (1963), the Court banned the recitation of bible reading in public school classrooms. In the 1965 case of *U.S. v. Seeger*, 380 U.S. 163 (1965), Clark again used his formidable writing skills to obtain a majority opinion that broadened that right of a citizen called to army service, to ask for conscientious objector status on the grounds of what that person's religion stated about killing and war.

To study the Supreme Court career of Tom C. Clark is to open a significant window on the difficult years that followed World War II. In the latter years, he was still the major voice in opposing any weakening of the government's use of the courts to attack those he thought posed a threat to the country's security. Justice Clark also demonstrated his independence as a justice who could move between minority and majority sides, particularly where issues of criminal conduct and religious issues were before the Court.

ARTHUR J. SABIN

References and Further Reading

Ferrell, Robert H. *Harry S. Truman: A Life*. Columbia: University of Missouri Press, 1994.

Friedman, Leon, and Fred L. Israel. *The Justices of the United States Supreme Court 1789–1969 Their Lives and Major Opinions: Volume IV*. New York: Chelsea House Publishers, 1969.

Hall, Kermit L. *The Oxford Companion to the Supreme Court of the United States*. New York: Oxford University Press, 1992.

Klingman, William K. *Encyclopedia of the McCarthy Era*. New York: Facts on File, Inc., 1969.

Marcus, Maeva. *Truman and the Steel Seizure Case: The Limits of Presidential Power*. New York: Columbia University Press, 1977.

McCoy, Donald R. *The Presidency of Harry S. Truman*. Lawrence: University of Kansas, 1984.

Sabin, Arthur J. *In Calmer Times: The Supreme Court and Red Monday*. Philadelphia: University of Pennsylvania Press, 1999.

CLASSIFIED INFORMATION

Classified information is information held by executive agencies of government that only persons with special permission ("clearance") are allowed to see. While the term "classified" is of fairly recent origin, executive efforts to withhold information from the general public, the press, Congress, and the courts go back to the earliest days of the Republic.

The constitutional basis, if any, for such efforts has been equally long disputed. Accountability of government to the people is a fundamental principle, and secrecy inherently compromises it, since one cannot judge or modify policies one does not know of. The Constitution addresses government control of information in several different provisions. One is the requirement that the President *shall*–not may–inform Congress from time to time of the state of the union.

The only provision aimed explicitly at secrecy is Article I, section 5, which provides that "Each House shall keep a Journal of its Proceedings, and from time to time publish the same, excepting such Parts as may *in their Judgment* require Secrecy (emphasis added)." Obviously, this is not a grant of power to the executive branch.

The separation of powers system entails numerous types of interbranch communication. Practices dating back to Washington's presidency include congressional requests for information from the President or his department heads and presidential transmittals that asked Congress to keep certain information confidential. Over time, the President realized that the two Houses would not invariably abide by his requests and that individual members might sometimes leak information on their own. This led to the confrontation over Jay's Treaty, in which Washington refused outright to honor a call for papers by the House of Representatives. This episode is sometimes invoked as precedent for "executive privilege" to withhold information. Yet, in actuality, the House adopted resolutions of protest, declaring the President's act unconstitutional.

Similar conflicts would recur from time to time, with varying results depending on the political situation. Appeals for secrecy were often effectively pressed when national defense and foreign policy concerns were at stake, but Congress never formally relinquished its role as "grand inquest of the nation."

A formalized system for protecting these types of information awaited America's rise to great power status and the coinciding expansion of the executive bureaucracy, both of which massively increased the quantity of potentially sensitive official documents. Today's classification system originated in 1951, when President Truman, without a legislative mandate, issued an executive order authorizing officials in both military and civilian agencies to designate information as "confidential," "secret," or "top secret." Over time additional, even more restrictive, designations have evolved. The power to classify is wielded by thousands of officials in many different agencies. The criteria are rather permissive: classification is permitted if release "could reasonably be expected to cause damage to the national security." Because control of information confers power, both high-level policy makers and ordinary officials have incentives to err on the side of secrecy. Currently, the government produces millions of classified documents each year.

Details of the guidelines have been repeatedly revised, but the constant is that classification limits access to those cleared by the executive branch, after careful background checks, to receive a specific category of information. Most members of Congress, the judiciary, the media, and the public are excluded, and disclosure to such persons or possession by them could perhaps be criminally prosecuted. Since provisions for automatic declassification after a period of years have not been effectively implemented, the system obstructs historical research, as well as debate on current policy issues.

The courts have had very limited involvement with the growth, administration, and regulation of the secrecy system. Since 1967, anyone may file a request for any identifiable document under the Freedom of Information Act, but there is an exception for information that is properly classified. Under a 1974 amendment, such a request may lead to court review of whether the document can safely be declassified, in whole or in part. This procedure is protracted and costly and is, of course, unavailable where the very existence of the information is unknown.

A few cases seem to acknowledge a power of the President, whether "inherent" or arguably implied by legislation, to withhold information sought by parties in litigation. Courts have sometimes been reluctant even to examine the requested documents to balance the requesting party's need against the alleged need for secrecy. The executive action complained of is then unreviewable. See *Totten v. United States*, 92 U.S. 105 (1876), *United States v. Curtiss-Wright Corp.*, 299 U.S. 304 (1936), *Chicago and Southern Airlines v. Waterman Steamship Corp.*, 333 U.S. 103 (1948), *Knauff v. Shaughnessy*, 338 U.S. 537 (1950), *United States v. Reynolds*, 345 U.S. 1 (1953), *Haig v. Agee*, 453 U.S. 280 (1981), *Department of the Navy v. Egan*, 484 U.S. 518 (1988).

The Court has also upheld the oaths of secrecy required of certain officials given access to classified information and enforced them with life-long

prepublication clearance requirements and confiscation of profits–even where no classified information was disclosed. *Snepp v. United States*, 444 U.S. 507 (1980).

On the other hand, in *New York Times Co. v. United States*, 403 U.S. 713 (1971), the Court declined to enjoin publication of the Pentagon Papers, despite an insistent claim of danger to national security. In *United States v. Nixon*, 418 U.S. 683 (1974), the President was ordered to surrender his Oval Office tapes to the Special Prosecutor. Nixon had considered invoking national security in this case but for some reason did not do so, relying instead on a distinct privilege for confidential advice.

In sum, the courts are scarcely an effective check on executive secrecy in the domain of national security information. Since Congress and the media have usually shown an equal timidity, it seems that the needed institutional check does not exist. The implications for civil liberties are potentially grave: first, the rights to speak, publish, and participate in debate are hampered by withholding of crucial information. Second, individuals may be subject to loss of employment, denial of redress for damages, revocation of passports, deportation (for aliens), even (for "unlawful combatants") indefinite detention, based on classified information they are not allowed to see.

DANIEL N. HOFFMAN

References and Further Reading

Hoffman, Daniel N. *Governmental Secrecy and the Founding Fathers: A Study in Constitutional Controls.* Westport, CT: Greenwood Press, 1981.

Cases and Statutes Cited

Chicago and Southern Airlines v. Waterman Steamship Corp., 333 U.S. 103 (1948)
Department of the Navy v. Egan, 484 U.S. 518 (1988)
Haig v. Agee, 453 U.S. 280 (1981)
Knauff v. Shaughnessy, 338 U.S. 537 (1950)
New York Times Co. v. United States, 403 U.S. 713 (1971)
Snepp v. United States, 444 U.S. 507 (1980)
Totten v. United States, 92 U.S. 105 (1876)
United States v. Curtiss-Wright Corp., 299 U.S. 304 (1936)
United States v. Nixon, 418 U.S. 683 (1974)
United States v. Reynolds, 345 U.S. 1 (1953)

CLEAR AND PRESENT DANGER TEST

The phrase "clear and present danger," as a criterion for determining when the government can constitutionally punish individuals for their speech, appeared for the first time in the opinion for the U.S. Supreme

Court by Justice Oliver Wendell Holmes, Jr., in the case of *Schenck v. United States* (1919). In *Schenck* and two companion cases, the Court considered the constitutionality of convictions obtained under the federal Espionage Act against various pamphleteers and public speakers for speaking out against World War I and thus allegedly impeding military recruitment. In upholding their convictions, Holmes wrote:

> The most stringent protection of free speech would not protect a man in falsely shouting fire in a theatre and causing a panic . . . . The question in every case is whether the words used are used in such circumstances and are of such a nature as to create a clear and present danger that they will bring about the substantive evils that Congress has a right to prevent. It is a question of proximity and degree.

The "clear and present danger" concept eschewed consideration of the speaker's "bad" intentions or motivations and focused on the likelihood that an utterance would have consequences dangerous to the country, such as interference with military recruitment. This disinclination to probe into a speaker's private beliefs or intentions was, in a general sense, protective of civil liberty. But it also seemed to authorize criminal punishment for speech even when the speaker had little control over, or even knowledge of, its consequences. Moreover, these "consequences" of a speech or pamphlet were little more than speculations made by courts and prosecutors, who in times of war were unlikely to err on the side of the speaker.

That Holmes had applied the clear and present danger test to *uphold* convictions in *Schenck* and its companion cases convinced contemporary liberals that the test offered little protection for unpopular speech. But Professor Zechariah Chafee of Harvard Law School argued in the *New Republic* that Holmes's "clear and present danger" phrase was actually libertarian in spirit, because it established that the government must meet a high standard before it could punish speech consistently with the First Amendment. Both Chafee and U.S. District Court Judge Learned Hand, who had suggested a more speech-protective "incitement to violence" First Amendment test in a 1917 case, communicated with Holmes after the *Schenck* decision in a tactful effort to move Holmes toward a greater appreciation of the free speech values at stake.

These efforts proved partly successful when, only a few months after *Schenck*, Holmes dissented in *United States v. Abrams*. In *Abrams*, the Court upheld the convictions of several anarchists for distributing literature condemning the U.S. government's postwar military policy in the Soviet Union. Holmes (joined by Justice Louis D. Brandeis) now condemned any

government "attempts to check the expression of opinions that we loathe and believe to be fraught with death, unless they so imminently threaten immediate interference with the lawful and pressing purposes of the law that an immediate check is required to save the country." His dissent became a rallying point for supporters of free speech and remains one of the most stirring statements in the free speech literature.

During the 1920s, the Court upheld a number of state-court convictions for subversive advocacy, always over a dissent by Holmes and/or Brandeis. In the best-known of these cases, *Whitney v. California* (1927), Brandeis wrote a separate opinion in which he sought to put more "teeth" into the "clear and present danger" formula: "[N]o danger flowing from speech can be deemed clear and present, unless the incidence of the evil apprehended is so imminent that it may befall before there is opportunity for full discussion . . . [and] even imminent danger cannot justify resort to prohibition of these functions essential to effective democracy, unless the evil apprehended is relatively serious." Like Holmes's dissent in *Abrams*, Brandeis's *Whitney* opinion inspired civil libertarians. But it was not until the late 1930s and 1940s that a more liberal Court gradually transformed the free speech opinions of Holmes and Brandeis from lonely dissents into the law of the Constitution.

By 1937, a majority of the Court had seized hold of the "clear and present danger" test and adopted the libertarian gloss Brandeis had placed on it in his separate opinion in *Whitney*. Over the next few years the Court expanded the test's application to circumstances far removed from the "seditious speech" situation for which it had been devised; it used the test to reverse convictions under state law for house-to-house soliciting, for picketing, and for criminal contempt in publicly criticizing a judge during a pending case. Some, notably Justice Felix Frankfurter, deprecated this unsystematic application of the "clear and present danger" test, arguing that the Court was using it as a substitute for discriminating, case-by-case analysis of free speech problems.

The Court's hospitality to civil liberties arguments diminished in the years after World War II. The clear and present danger test, as a meaningful protection of free speech, disintegrated in the *Dennis* case (1951), in which the Court upheld the convictions of American Communist Party leaders under the Smith Act, which prohibited the organizing of a group for the purpose of teaching the advisability of violently overthrowing the government. Several justices suggested that the assumptions underlying the "clear and present danger" concept were poorly adapted to a new and dangerous world. Courts could not engage in nice calculations of how clear, present, or grave a danger must be before the government could act to preempt the subversive activities of secret organizations presumably under the direction of a foreign dictator. In *Dennis* and ensuing cases, the Court largely disclaimed the authority to second-guess the legislative and executive branches in their determinations that those with radical political views or affiliations were subject to a variety of criminal and civil disabilities.

The Court returned to a more speech-protective jurisprudence in the 1960s, especially after political protest became associated more with the civil rights movement than with left-wing radicalism. Ironically, the Court gave perhaps its final nod to the clear and present danger test in 1969, when it specifically overruled *Whitney* while overturning the convictions of Ku Klux Klan members under an Ohio criminal syndicalism statute for organizing a rally. The "clear and present danger" test has long since departed the legal scene, partly because the problem of seditious speech that gave birth to it is no longer at the center of the First Amendment docket. But with the War on Terrorism and legislation like the Patriot Act, this situation may soon change.

CLYDE SPILLENGER

References and Further Reading

Gunther, Gerald, *Learned Hand and the Origins of Modern First Amendment Doctrine: Some Fragments of History*, Stanford Law Review 27 (February 1975), 719–773.
Kalven, Harry. *A Worthy Tradition: Freedom of Speech in America.* New York: Harper & Row, 1988.
Rabban, David M. *Free Speech in Its Forgotten Years.* Cambridge University Press, 1997.
Stone, Geoffrey. *Perilous Times: Free Speech in Wartime from the Sedition Act of 1798 to the War on Terrorism.* New York: W.W. Norton, 2004.

Cases and Statutes Cited

Abrams v. United States, 250 U.S. 616 (1919)
Brandenburg v. Ohio, 395 U.S. 444 (1969)
Dennis v. United States, 341 U.S. 494 (1951)
Schenck v. United States, 249 U.S. 47 (1919)
Whitney v. California, 274 U.S. 357 (1927)

CLONING

The right to reproduce is generally deemed to be a fundamental right in American law. Reproductive cloning is an extension of that right. The scientific and then legal construct of reproductive cloning will be explored. (Therapeutic cloning is no different from any other medical treatment and is dealt with elsewhere.)

Cloning: The Scientific Background

Cloning, until now the subject of the fictional analysis of the type found in the novel *The Boys from Brazil* (1976), has become a medical reality with the recent cloning of a sheep, a horse, a cat, and a dog. Indeed, there is no doubt that in a very short number of years, it will be medically possible to clone human beings, and there is already extensive discussion about whether such conduct should be permissible.

To discuss cloning, one must understand exactly what cloning is. Every human being currently in the world is the product of a genetic mixture: One's father provides half of one's nucleic genetic material, and one's mother contributes the other half; this genetic material is united in the process that we call fertilization, which normally happens after intercourse but can also happen in a petri dish after in vitro fertilization (IVF). A child bears a genetic similarity to his mother and father but cannot be genetically identical to either one of them, because each has only contributed half of their genetic materials. Every person has, along with his or her nucleic DNA, mitochondrial DNA that is not located in the nucleus of the cell but in the cytoplasm. This mitochondrial DNA is inherited solely from one's mother through the egg that she provides and is identical to hers; mitochondrial DNA creates certain proteins needed to function (particularly for respiration—energy metabolism on the cellular level). A father contributes no mitochondrial DNA to his children. As noted in an editorial in *Nature*, a woman with a mitochondrial disease might be able to produce children free of the disease by having the nucleus of her egg implanted in a donor's oocyte, thus providing the same chromosomal genetic code, but with disease-free mitochondrial DNA.

Siblings who are not identical twins share some of the genetic materials of their parents; however, since each sperm and each egg take a different (sub)set of material from the parents, each sibling has a unique genetic makeup based on a combination of portions of their parents' genes different from that found in their siblings. Identical twins, though, are the product of a single fertilized egg of a unique genetic makeup that splits in half after fertilization, leaving two fully formed zygotes that develop into two fully formed—but genetically identical—siblings. (Both the nucleic and the non-nucleic DNA are the same.) These two children share an absolutely identical genetic makeup and until recently represented the only case in which two people could have an identical genetic makeup.

In the current state of cloning technology, genetic material is isolated from cells taken from a donor. This genetic material is then introduced into the nucleus of an egg/ovum whose own nucleic genetic material has been destroyed, so as to produce an egg/ovum that contains a full set of genetic material identical to the nucleic genetic material of the donor. If the genetic material is taken from one person, and the egg is taken from another, the non-nucleic genetic material of the clone will be that of the egg donor, and not the gene donor, whereas the nucleic genetic material will be from the gene donor. A woman could avoid this "problem" and produce a "full clone" by using her own genetic material and one of her own eggs/ova in the cloning process; that clone will have the exact same DNA makeup as its clonor.

Through stimulation, the egg/ovum with transplanted nucleic genetic material is induced to behave like a fertilized egg, and it then starts the process of cellular division and development as if it is a newly fertilized diploid with genetic materials from a mother and a father. It divides and reproduces, and when implanted into the uterus of a gestational mother, the zygote will grow and develop into a fully formed fetus that will eventually be born from the uterus of its gestational mother. In the current state of technology, all fertilized eggs—including cloned ones—are implanted in a uterus and are carried to term like all normal pregnancies.

The child who is born from this gestational mother is genetically identical to the donor(s) of the genetic material and bears no genetic relationship to the gestational mother. It is not a combination of the genetic material of two people (the mother and father). It is, instead, genetically identical to the one who donated the DNA (or perhaps the two women who donated the nuclear DNA and mitochondrial DNA). It is as if, on a genetic level, this person produced an identical twin, many years after the first person was born. It is impossible to genetically distinguish cells of the clone from cells of the clonor, because their genetic makeup remains absolutely identical. Indeed, there is no reason why this process could not be done from the cells of a person who is deceased.

American Law

To date, there is no case law addressing cloning and no statutes prohibiting cloning. As a general proposition, the guiding principles found in American law governing assisted reproduction are predicated on two concepts: The first is that reproduction is a protected right in American Law, and the second is the desire of American law to assign "parenthood"—both maternal and paternal identity—to the individuals who are expected to function *in loco parentis* of

the child when it is born. Thus, contractual regulation of the terms of surrogacy is permitted so as to ensure that the one who "wants" the child is the parent. Sperm donors can "waive" their paternal rights, and adoption can end the parental rights of natural parents. Generally speaking, unlike the common law tradition, modern American law views status issues (such as parenthood) as something that law *determines*, rather than something that law *discovers*. Law can change the natural order of relationships in this view.

Cloning will undoubtedly be yet another such area. While there is a popular sentiment and considerable scholarship to categorically prohibit such activity, one suspects that, in reality, there is no likelihood that human cloning will be banned in all fifty states. Statutes will be passed that regulate cloning and regulate the "market" to ensure that the wishes of the parties—as to status, paternity, and a host of other issues—are met. Indeed, one can already see such a consensus developing. Professor Laurence Tribe, a well-known constitutional law scholar, endorsed the free market approach to cloning. A recent New York Times article accurately captures the spirit of modern medical ethics in America in the reproductive area by noting:

> In the hubbub that ensued [after the first sheep, 'Dolly' was cloned], scientist after scientist and ethicist after ethicist declared that Dolly should not conjure up fears of a Brave New World. There would be no interest in using the technology to clone people, they said. They are already being proved wrong. There has been an enormous change in attitudes in just a few months; scientists have become sanguine about the notion of cloning and, in particular, cloning a human being . . . . The fact is that, in America, cloning may be bad but telling people how they should reproduce is worse . . . .

In America, freedom to choose one's own reproductive method, and market forces that make such choices profitable, will determine who the parent is and what the law should permit. America is not ruled by ethics. It is ruled by law. While there well might be restrictions on embryo research, legal restrictions on reproductive cloning are fraught with constitutional issues, because they impact on the basic right to reproduce.

MICHAEL J. BROYDE

References and Further Reading

Amer, Mona S., *Breaking the Mold: Human Embryo Cloning and its Implications for a Right to Individuality*, UCLA L. Rev. 1659 (1996): 43.

Broyde, Michael, *Cloning People: A Jewish View*, Connecticut Law Review 30 (1998): 2503–2535.

Katz, Sanford N., *Re-writing the Adoption Story*, Fam. Advoc. 5 (1982): 9.

Kolata, Gina. "Human Cloning: Yesterday's Never Is Today's Why Not?" *N.Y. Times*, Dec. 2, 1997.

Stumpf, Andrea, *Redefining Mother: A Legal Matrix for New Reproductive Technologies*, Yale L. J . 96 (1986): 187.

The Science of Cloning: Sheep: see I. Wilmut *et al.* "Viable Offspring Derived from Fetal and Adult Mammalian Cells." (Letters) 385 *Nature* (27 February 1997) at page 810; Horse: see Cesare Galli et al. "Pregnancy: A Cloned Horse Born to its Dam Twin." (Brief Communications) 424 *Nature* (07 August 2003) at page 635; Cat: see Taeyoung Shin et al. "A Cat Cloned by Nuclear Transplantation." (Brief Communications) 415 *Nature* (21 February 2002) at page 859; Dog: see Byeong Chun Lee et al. "Dogs Cloned from Adult Somatic Cells." (Brief communications) 436 *Nature* (04 August 2005), at page 641.

Tribe, Laurence. "Second Thoughts on Cloning." *N.Y. Times*, Dec. 5, 1997.

Cases and Statutes Cited

Johnson v. Calvert, 851 P.2d 776 (Cal. 1993)
Zablocki v. Redhail, 434 U.S. 374 (1978)

See also **Reproductive Freedom**

COERCED CONFESSIONS/POLICE INTERROGATIONS

Confessions are deemed the "gold standard" that assure convictions. The majority of confessions are garnered through an interrogation process. Detainees rarely spontaneously confess. Promises, inducements, and sometimes coercion are used by law enforcement officers to obtain confessions. For confessions to withstand legal scrutiny, they must be trustworthy and free and voluntary in nature. However, trustworthiness was the lynchpin for determining whether a confession would be excluded. In the first reported case challenging a coerced confession, *Commonwealth v. Dillon*, the court's major concern was not the fact that the twelve-year-old defendant was deprived of food or clothing for three days but that he voluntarily made his confession. At the time of *Commonwealth v. Dillon* (1792), no constitutional basis existed to challenge a coerced confession. The Thirteenth, Fourteenth, and Fifteenth Amendments would give the federal government greater power to review state actions.

Law enforcement has developed sophisticated methods of interrogation that disarm or put at ease detainees. Different levels of coercion exist to induce detainees to confess. The law does allow for coercive tactics but draws the line at such tactics as physical and psychological torture. The 1930s saw the development of the modern doctrine of coerced confessions. *Brown v. Mississippi* was the seminal case that raised the question of coerced confessions to a constitutional level. The U.S. Supreme Court determined that law enforcement would not be able to use torture as a coercive tactic to garner confessions.

Three black men—Henry Shield, Yank Ellington and case namesake Ed Brown—were accused of the murder of a white farmer, Raymond Stewart. A white mob seized Ellington from his home and hung him by a rope from a tree. Despite being nearly lynched twice by the mob, Ellington continued to protest his innocence. The mob eventually released him and allowed Ellington to return to his home. Kemper County sheriff deputies decided to arrest Ellington and administered a beating to him until he finally confessed to the murder. The sheriff deputies later arrested Brown and Shields and proceeded to torture them. They were bent over chairs and beaten with buckled leather straps until their backs were cut to pieces. The whipping continued until they confessed. A grand jury indicted Brown, Ellington, and Shields the next day for murder.

Defense attorneys for Brown, Ellington, and Shields did not challenge the admissibility of their confessions. The trial court found the "free and voluntary" confessions admissible. The Mississippi jury convicted Brown, Ellington, and Shields of murder, and the court sentenced them to die. The Mississippi Supreme Court upheld the convictions. The court set an execution date for Brown, Ellington, and Shields. However, the United States Supreme Court agreed to review the case.

The Brown defense team raised the then novel argument that the convictions should be overturned due to the violation of the Fifth Amendment right against self-incrimination. The tortured confessions of Brown, Ellington, and Shields were not "free and voluntary."

The Supreme Court in the era of *Brown v. Mississippi* did not recognize self-incrimination as a constitutional issue. The Fifth Amendment of the U.S. Constitution says no one "shall be compelled in any criminal case to be a witness against himself." The language is directed at the use of the legal process to compel testimony in a criminal trial. The Kemper County deputies did not compel Brown, Ellington, or Shields to testify against themselves in the courtroom. They tortured the defendants in the station house. Prior to *Brown v. Mississippi*, the Supreme Court found on numerous occasions that individual state courts were not subject to the Fifth Amendment.

The Bill of Rights directed what the federal government could do to its citizens, not to state courts. Defense counsel for Brown, Ellington, and Shields had to use a new constitutional standard to get the Supreme Court to review the case.

The Fourteenth Amendment Due Process Clause prevents states from depriving ". . . any person of life, liberty or property without due process of the law." Defense counsel for Brown, Ellington, and Shields asserted that the actions of torturing the defendants to garner confessions violated their due process rights. The Supreme Court was generally reluctant to intervene into state actions. However, the Court acknowledged that the state of Mississippi had gone too far. Justice Hughes in writing the opinion remarked, "The state is free to regulate the procedure of its courts in accordance with its own conceptions of policy, unless in so doing it offends some principle of justice so rooted in the traditions and conscience of our people as to be ranked as fundamental." Mississippi was free to govern as it chose but it could not violate the basic principle of justice in doing so. The Court stated, "the freedom of the state in establishing its policy is the freedom of constitutional government and is limited by the requirement of due process of law."

Justice Hughes found that the constitution prohibited coercive tactics in obtaining confessions. "Coercing the supposed state's criminals into confessions and using such confessions so coerced from them against them in trials has been the curse of all countries . . . . the Constitution recognized the evils that lay behind these practices and prohibited them in this country." The trial court knew Brown, Ellington, and Shields confessed after being tortured yet declined to act. The Mississippi Supreme Court declined to address the due process violations when Brown, Ellington, and Shields appealed their convictions. The Supreme Court had to enforce constitutional rights the state of Mississippi refused to do. The Supreme Court unanimously overturned the convictions and developed a new doctrine that would allow federal review of state actions in criminal cases if constitutional violations existed.

Coercion after Brown

Subsequent to the Brown ruling, trial judges had to apply not only state laws for admissibility of confessions but also had to adhere to a new federal due process standard. The South became the predominant source for coerced confessions. The tactics used by southern law enforcement officers became typified by the use of torture of numerous blacks until they induced confessions.

In *Chambers v. Florida*, the Supreme Court held that confessions could be coerced psychologically as well as physically. The robbery and murder of an elderly white man prompted Florida law enforcement to detain twenty-five to forty black men without a warrant for a week. After interrogators used sleep deprivation and hunger as manipulation tools, four detainees confessed.

Texas Rangers took an illiterate plantation worker into the woods for a week and beat him until he confessed to a rape. At trial, the defendant steadfastly refused to admit that he confessed. The trial court convicted the plantation worker and sentenced him to death. In *White v. Texas*, the issue was the singular coerced confession but the state of Texas proffered a novel argument before the Supreme Court. Texas argued that since the defendant denied ever making or signing the confession, White should be denied the right to argue the state of Texas violated his due process rights. The Court rejected the argument and overturned White's conviction. The Court found that since the state insisted on publishing the confession to the jury, the confession was subject to constitutional review.

The Supreme Court struck down convictions in a series of southern cases that each had the theme of a tortured confession. In *Ward v. Texas*, Justice Byrnes stated,

> This Court has set aside convictions based upon confessions extorted from ignorant persons who have been subjected to persistent and protracted questioning, or who have been threatened with mob violence, or who have been unlawfully held incommunicado without advice of friends or counsel, or who have been taken at night to lonely and isolated places for questioning. Any one of these grounds would be sufficient cause for reversal. All of them are to be found in this case.

The Court set due process standards that states continued to flout. In *McNabb v. United States*, the Court reversed the homicide convictions of two brothers with fourth grade educations from an isolated rural area who confessed after two continuous days of interrogation. The holding spawned what came to be known as the McNabb Rule. Police were to show "with reasonable promptness" some legal cause for holding persons. The Court would not allow convictions to stand where the police failed to promptly allow defendants a preliminary hearing. The Court did not, however, apply a per se blanket exclusion rule to coerced confessions.

The Court extended the McNabb Rule in *Mallory v. United States*. Washington D.C. police arrested a nineteen-year-old black janitor for the rape of a white woman. Mallory was not told of his right to counsel or to a preliminary examination before a magistrate, nor was he warned he could be silent and that any statement made by him could be used against him. The police interrogated him for several hours, and he then confessed. The police used a court stenographer to record the confession and the deputy coroner to certify that no evidence of physical or psychological coercion existed. Mallory went before court the next day. Mallory's trial was delayed a year to determine whether he was competent to stand trial. The trial proceeded with the strongest evidence being Mallory's confession. Mallory was found guilty. The court sentenced Mallory to death for rape. The Supreme Court reversed the conviction and found the confession inadmissible. The Court held that the D.C. violated federal law that required Mallory be brought before a magistrate "without unnecessary delay."

The McNabb-Mallory Rule put law enforcement on notice that a statement obtained from a defendant during a period of unnecessary delay in having a probable cause determination should be excluded. Federal law dictates that law enforcement delays in taking a defendant before a judicial officer greater than six hours makes any confession gotten inadmissible.

In *Lisenba v. California*, the Court acknowledged the police illegally detained the defendant for a two-week period before he confessed to murdering his wife, yet the court found Lisenba to be an intelligent man who minimized his own culpability. The Court gave inconsistent holdings. Just two years after Lisenba, the Court reversed a conviction based on a confession garnered from thirty-six hours in detention. In *Ashcraft v. Tennessee*, the Court began to liken the standards for confessions induced from long detentions to those held up to the constitutional scrutiny of a confession used in a public trial. The Court used the same rationale in *Watts v. Indiana*. Police interrogations began to be held to strict courtroom standards.

In *Malinski v. New York*, a police officer killing led to overzealous police interrogation tactics. New York police had no suspects in the killing of Officer Leon Fox. Malinski and his brother-in-law, Spielfogel, ran a "protection raceket" and promised each other if one became imprisoned, the other was to care for his family. Spielfogel went to prison, but Malinski breached his end of the agreement. Spielfogel became upset and had contact with the police. The police picked up Malinski but did not bring him to a police station. The police brought Malinski to a Brooklyn hotel and had him strip naked for three hours. They continuously questioned Malinski in the nude and dressed only in a blanket and socks. Spielfogel was

brought to the hotel and left alone with Malinski. He confessed soon thereafter. The police drove Malinski to scenes of the crime where he again confessed. Malinski stayed at the hotel three more days before being brought before a magistrate. Malinski signed a written confession while in custody. Malinski confessed a total of four times. Malinski was tried and convicted of Fox's murder.

Malinski challenged the admission of the first oral confession. The trial judge found the confession specious but he allowed it for issues of voluntariness of the written confession. However, the trial judge instructed the jury to disregard the statement unless it was voluntarily given beyond a reasonable doubt. While the judge instructed the jury to potentially disregard the confession, the prosecutor made several references during the trial to the oral confession. The Supreme Court found that one coerced confession corrupted the use of the other three and reversed Malinski's conviction.

The due process doctrine for coerced confessions reached its zenith.

Due Process Limitations

The Supreme Court began to refine the due process doctrine. In *Stein v. State*, the New York police arrested the codefendants, Cooper and Stein, and interrogated them for robbery and murder. Four defendants were arrested in total. The police initially detained Cooper's father to persuade him to confess. Cooper refused. The Parole Department detained Cooper's brother and threatened his freedom. In total, the police interrogated Cooper for more than thirty-six hours. He eventually confessed. The police confined Stein in the basement of an army barracks. An army officer initially interrogated Stein. Over the course of twenty-four hours, police interrogated Stein, and he eventually confessed after being told about the Cooper confession.

Cooper and Stein had bruises and injuries at their arraignment, but their defense counsel did not raise the issue at trial. However, defense counsel did challenge the use of the confessions. One of the codefendants, Dorfman, testified against Cooper and Stein at trial. The trial court also admitted their confessions, and Cooper and Stein were convicted. Cooper and Stein appealed to the Supreme Court. They claimed the police use of physical and psychological coercion induced them to confess.

The Supreme Court examined the trial court and was critical of the claims of Cooper and Stein. They chose not to testify, and the Court theorized that was due to their prior records. The Court found it could not state what prompted the jury to find the defendants guilty. Was it the coerced confessions or was it the testimony and other State evidence? The Court refused to attempt to second-guess the jury. The Court had to examine whether the confessions were obtained in violation of Cooper and Stein's due process rights.

The Court examined the intelligence and character of Cooper and Stein. Justice Jackson stated, "these men were not young, soft, ignorant or timid . . . they were not inexperienced in the ways of crime or its detection, nor were they dumb as to their rights." Justice Jackson also noted the fact that Cooper negotiated the terms under which he would confess undermined his argument of coercion.

The Court set new standards with Stein. Due process rights would not attach to cases in which the doctrine was meant to protect the innocent not be used as a loophole to protect the guilty. Station house confessions would not be held to the same standard as courtroom testimony. On a case-by-case basis, the personality of the accused would be examined along with other relevant circumstances. The admission of confessions would be examined by the totality of the circumstances.

The Warren Court

President Dwight Eisenhower nominated former California Governor Earl Warren Chief Justice to the U.S. Supreme Court in 1953. Justice Warren created a revolution in criminal law and criminal procedure that culminated in *Miranda v. Arizona*. The Warren Court reviewed cases with greater scrutiny and held law enforcement accountable by reversing several convictions on technical grounds. Confessions became a central component.

Justice Warren began carve out fundamental rights for defendants and challenge conventional law enforcement procedures. In *Gideon v. Wainright*, Florida state court charged Gideon with breaking and entering a poolroom with intent to commit a felony under Florida law. Appearing in court without funds and without a lawyer, Gideon asked the court to appoint him counsel. The court refused, and Gideon represented himself. The jury found him guilty and he received a five-year prison sentence. Justice Black succinctly stated, "The right of one charged with crime to counsel may not be deemed fundamental and essential to fair trials in some countries, but it is in ours."

The Court began to give a nuanced definition of what it meant to have counsel. A Mexican immigrant and murder suspect continued to request his attorney while being interrogated, but the police refused his request. The Supreme Court held that once a suspect becomes the target of an investigation and was not warned about his constitutional rights, he is entitled to representation under the Sixth and Fourteenth Amendments. *Escobedo v. Illinois* gave suspects the right to counsel during the interrogation phase. The Court began to grant constitutional guarantees at the critical interrogation phase for defendants.

What prompted the Court was the police interrogation of Ernesto Miranda. He was a Mexican immigrant of limited intelligence who confessed to a kidnapping and rape after a two-hour detention. While the police detained and interrogated Miranda, they never informed him of his right to counsel or of his Fifth Amendment right against self-incrimination. The trial court convicted Miranda and sentenced him to sixty years in prison. The Arizona Supreme Court affirmed the conviction. Miranda appealed to the Supreme Court.

The Supreme Court gave defendants the most clearly detailed and defined rights and created a firestorm in the law enforcement community that still reverberates. *Miranda v. Arizona* was the first of four combined cases appealed before the Supreme Court to clarify issues of the right of defendants while in custody and under interrogation. Justice Warren held the prosecution may not use statements, whether exculpatory or inculpatory, stemming from custodial interrogation of the defendant unless it demonstrates the use of procedural safeguards effective to secure the privilege against self-incrimination. Justice Warren's opinion became the verbatim Miranda Warnings that are so well known today: (1) an individual held for interrogation must be clearly informed that he has the right to consult with a lawyer and to have the lawyer with him during interrogation; (2) an individual indicates that he wishes the assistance of counsel before any interrogation occurs, the authorities cannot rationally ignore or deny his request on the basis that the individual does not have or cannot afford a retained attorney; and (3) it is necessary to warn him not only that he has the right to consult with an attorney, but also that if he is indigent a lawyer will be appointed to represent him.

Law enforcement feared that Miranda warnings would have a chilling effect on their interrogation procedures. Justice Warren acknowledges that fear in the Miranda opinion:

> In dealing with statements obtained through interrogation, we do not purport to find all confessions

inadmissible. Confessions remain a proper element in law enforcement. Any statement given freely and voluntarily without any compelling influences is, of course, admissible in evidence. The fundamental import of the privilege while an individual is in custody is not whether he is allowed to talk to the police without the benefit of warnings and counsel, but whether he can be interrogated. There is no requirement that police stop a person who enters a police station and states that he wishes to confess to a crime, or a person who calls the police to offer a confession or any other statement he desires to make. Volunteered statements of any kind are not barred by the Fifth Amendment and their admissibility is not affected by our holding today.

Justice Warren makes it clear that interrogations are still allowed to be a key investigation strategy. However, the Court demanded higher standards from law enforcement in the interrogation room.

Permissible Coercion

The legal prerequisite for a confession is voluntariness, but to some degree coercion is used in police interrogations. As the Supreme Court stated in *Oregon v. Mathiason*, "Any interview of one suspected of crime by a police officer will have coercive aspects to it, simply by virtue of the fact that the police officer is part of the law enforcement system which may ultimately cause the suspect to be charged with a crime." No legal test exists that will provide complete freedom from a suspect's perceived coercion during the course of a police interrogation. To prohibit coercion would mean prohibiting all police interrogations—something society would not contemplate.

Although judges determine whether a confession is admissible, some state legislatures have attempted to establish their own tests. Most of the tests proved to be unsatisfactory, and some have only confused the issue. New York was the exception in drafting legislation that clearly defined a confession "involuntarily made":

(a) By any person by the use or threatened use of physical force upon the defendant or another person, or by means of any other improper conduct or undue pressure which impaired the defendant's physical or mental condition to the extent of undermining his ability to make a choice whether or not to make a statement; or

(b) By a public servant engaged in law enforcement activity or by a person acting under his direction or in cooperation with him;

(c) By means of any promise or statement of fact, which promise or statement creates a substantial risk that the defendant might falsely incriminate himself; or

(d) In violation of such rights as the defendant may derive from the constitution of this state or the United States.

Courts quickly resolve cases in which the issue on confession voluntariness hinges on the infliction of direct physical harm on the suspect. Confessions that involve such occurrences are patently rejected. The general rationale for the blanket exclusion centers on the realization that an innocent person may confess, and admission of such a confession would be an affront to the integrity of the judicial system.

Ambiguity does exist with confessions obtained through indirect coercion such as a lengthy interrogation by two or more interrogators or the deprivation of food, water, sleep, or toilet facilities. Many variables are present regarding the suspect's tolerability or sensitivity to what occurred and to the degree and extent of the deprivations. The Supreme Court found any interrogation inherently coercive, but as in *Oregon v. Mathiason* (where the defendant was free to leave after confessing) the coercive effects did not rise to a due process violation.

The presence of multiple interrogators during a lengthy interrogation time period is one of the most blatant uses of indirect force. For the prosecution to prove their case, they must present as witnesses all officers involved in the interrogation process. The Illinois Supreme Court ruled in *People v. Ardenarczyk* that when a defendant in criminal prosecution objects to confession as being result of threats and violence, the burden is on the people to show that confession was made voluntarily, and evidence must show all circumstances under which confession was made. Courts have also held that the number of interrogators and the length of interrogation do not automatically render a confession inadmissible.

The threat factor of coercion does invalidate confessions. When an interrogator led a suspect to believe that unless he confessed he would face great bodily harm or death, the court in *People v. Flores* found coercion. A mother being threatened with the loss of her children invalidated the confession in *Lynum v. Illinois*.

Threatening behavior in an interrogation is distinguished from outright threats. An interrogator is allowed to question roughly, to question suspects assuming guilt, express impatience with a potentially lying suspect, or bluff a suspect into believing that evidence was secured to ensure a conviction. The "good cop – bad cop" interrogation scenario is allowed as long as the "bad cop" does not taint the interrogation with force or the threat of force. The comments must be limited to derogatory remarks and expressions of impatience.

The semantics of an interrogator's phraseology can be perceived as coercive. The interrogator's use of the word "better" in trying to persuade a suspect to confess can be construed as coercive if it is interpreted as "you had better confess" versus "it would be better for you to confess." In *Edwards v. State*, the court found a confession inadmissible based on the coercive effects of a letter. Just before the defendant confessed, a police officer urged the defendant to tell the truth and showed the defendant a letter supposedly written to the officer by an inmate of the state penitentiary (which contained statements amounting to a recommendation that it was better for a person accused of a crime to do what officers told him to do what the police officers urged). The confession, supported by the letter, constituted an inducement to the defendant and made the confession inadmissible in the murder prosecution.

Promises

When an interrogator uses language that leads a detainee to believe that confessing could lead to leniency, the confession becomes questionable. The mere promise of a lighter sentence does not vitiate a confession. A promise of leniency that may induce a false confession is what courts abhor.

Exhorting a detainee to tell the truth is permissible, because it is considered free from inducing false confessions. However, when an interrogator attempts to make specific promises, courts consider such language coercive. In *Hillard v. State*, the interrogating officer promised Hillard that he would "go to bat" for him. The court found that such a promise was an inducement that provoked an involuntary confession. An interrogator may report that a detainee has been cooperative as long as there is no specific promise of a lesser sentence. Detainees are without counsel during interrogations, and such promises or plea bargains are the purview of attorneys.

An interrogator can make limited promises such as keeping incriminating statements from family members, reduced bail recommendations, or assisting with psychiatric treatment after incarceration. A more explicit promise such as putting a homosexual detainee in the "gay cell" was found in *State v. Greene* to invalidate the confession.

Trickery and Deceit

The Supreme Court has given leeway to interrogators to use trickery and deceit during the interrogation process. In *Frazier v. Cupp*, the Court upheld the conviction of Frazier—dismissing his argument that his confession was involuntary and induced by the deceit of his interrogator. Oregon law enforcement officers detained Frazier as a murder suspect along with his cousin Rawls. An officer deliberately lied to Frazier and told him that Rawls confessed. Frazier then confessed. On appeal, Frazier claimed coercion. Justice Marshall rejected Frazier's claim and found he was a man of normal intelligence who knowingly waived his right to silence. Justice Marshall surmised that under the totality of the circumstance, none of Frazier's constitutional rights were violated.

Interrogators are given latitude by the courts to use aggressive and deceitful tactics in questioning detainees. Interrogators can lie about having positive fingerprint identification placing a detainee at a crime scene. One suspect can be pitted against another in seeking to obtain a confession. Even lying about victims is not considered sacrosanct. Interrogators have condemned and maligned victims hoping the suspects would confess. One officer blatantly told a murder suspect that the victim was still alive. However, in the Illinois Supreme Court a detective crossed the line when he lied to a suspect by falsely claiming that they obtained his fingerprints from the burgled residence and that the victim positively identified him. The court found that in determining whether a confession was voluntarily made, the defendant's confession was made freely, voluntarily, and without compulsion or inducement of any sort.

Present Day: Harmless Error

The Supreme Court began a retreat from the Warren Court's judicial activism. The case that signaled the greatest retreat was *Fulminate v. Arizona* (1991). The Supreme Court overruled prior cases and found coerced confessions could be deemed harmless error. Harmless error means that coerced confessions could be used in a trial if the prosecutor can prove beyond a reasonable doubt that the coercive actions did not violate due process rights.

Oreste Fulminate was in an Arizona detention center for a gun violation when another inmate befriended him. The inmate, Anothy Sarivola, began to question Fulminate about the murder of his stepdaughter. Sarivola worked for Arizona law enforcement and was given the specific task of befriending Fulimante hoping he would confess to Sarivola. Fulminate began to get threats from other detainees. Sarivola promised to protect Fulminate if he told Sarivola the truth about the murder. Fulminate admitted to the charge. Fulminate was released from prison and later confessed to Sarivola's fiancé.

The State of Arizona prosecuted Fulminate for murder. During the trial, Fulminate attempted to have the confessions deemed inadmissible. The trial court disagreed. The confessions were admitted into evidence, and the court found Fulminate guilty and sentenced him to death. Fulminate appealed his conviction claiming violations of the Fifth and Fourteenth amendments.

Fulminate's appellate history became complicated. The Arizona Supreme Court disagreed with Fulminate's initial appeal but allowed the case to be heard again. On rehearing, the court did reverse Fulminate's conviction. The Supreme Court decided to hear the case. The Supreme Court broke from the history of prior cases that held there is no such thing as a coerced confession being harmless error. Many in the criminal justice system feared that the Supreme Court would begin to retreat on the well-established doctrine of coerced confessions.

The Future

In the post September 11th world, the U.S. government has used unprecedented power in its war against terrorism. The government has the power to suspend the civil liberties of its citizens by incurring the enemy combatant status. Once the status is invoked, the person is placed outside the purview of American law and jurisprudence. An enemy combatant is not allowed to have regular contact with an attorney, has no judicial review, and may be detained indefinitely. The unchecked power that is granted to federal law enforcement without review could lead to circumstance similar to *Brown v. Mississippi*.

Enemy combatants are not entitled to general court trials. Military tribunals are established to try cases due to national security issues. The tribunal does not have a court of higher review. Once the tribunal decides the case, the defendants have no appellate rights. Coercive tactics can arise in cases where there exists no governing body to review federal agents' actions. Coercive tactics include physical and psychological interrogations techniques that render detainees/enemy combatants with no legal recourse. Legal challenges to the enemy combatant status are underway that present fundamental constitutional questions to the Supreme Court: (1) do they have a right to remain silent; (2) can they be compelled to be a witness against themselves; (3) can a "free and voluntary" confession be given or used in court when

a detainee has been deprived of his fundamental constitutional rights?

GENEVA BROWN

References and Further Reading

Nasheri, Hedieh, and Victor J. DeMarco, *True Confessions?: A Critique of* Arizona v. Fulminate, Am. J. Crim. L. 273, 21.
Raddack, Jesselyn, *United States Citizens Detained As Enemy Combatants: The Right to Counsel as a Matter of Ethics*, William and Mary Bill of Rights Journal 12 (2003): 221.

Cases and Statutes Cited

Brown v. Mississippi, 279 U.S. 278 (1936)
Chambers v. Florida, 309 U.S. 227 (1940)
Frazier v. Cupp
Fulminate v. Arizona
Malinski v. New York
Miranda v. Arizona, 384 U.S. 436 (1966)
Ward v. Texas
Padilla ex rel. *Newman v. Bush*, 233 F. Supp. 2d 564, 599 (S.D.N.Y. 2002)
Supreme Court Historical Society
www.supremecourthistory.org/02_history/subs_timeline/images_chiefs/014.html
Title 18 of the United States Code Section 3501(c)

See also **Due Process; Race and Criminal Justice**

COHEN v. CALIFORNIA, 403 U.S. 15 (1971)

In 1968, Paul Cohen peaceably entered the Los Angeles County Courthouse wearing a jacket visibly bearing the words "Fuck the Draft," deliberately denouncing American involvement in Vietnam. He was convicted and sentenced to thirty days in jail under California Penal Code §415 that prohibited conduct that "maliciously or willfully disturbs the peace." The California Court of Appeal upheld the conviction, ruling Cohen's attire had "a tendency to provoke others" to violence or to disrupt the peace.

U.S. Supreme Court Justice John Marshall Harlan II ruled that because Cohen's conviction relied on the offending words, his actions amounted to speech—not conduct—and were, therefore, protected under the First and Fourteenth Amendments. The rest of the opinion addressed state limits in restricting speech. Noting that Cohen neither showed intent to incite actual draft resistance, nor aimed any fighting words at bystanders, nor was there was a crowd "standing ready to strike out" against his words, Harlan maintained the government had no authority to censor speech for fear that violence or disruption could break out. He reminded the bench that the right to free expression was "powerful medicine" in a diverse population, because it cultivates "a more capable citizenry and more perfect polity"—products especially important to a nation divided by war. Nor was Harlan persuaded that "Fuck" was a particularly inflammatory word requiring government regulation. He warned against sanitizing free speech without clear standards for measuring appropriateness because "one man's vulgarity is another's lyric." Furthermore, such cleansing could cripple the emotive function of communication; often "grammatically palatable" words fail to express the emotions and ideas underlying expressive speech adequately. Harlan also rejected the state's claim that Cohen's jacket was especially egregious in the "decorous atmosphere" of the courthouse, because the penal code did not put Californians on notice that certain words or conduct were impermissible in specified circumstances. The speech also did not fall within the state's police powers to prohibit obscenity where there was no intent to stimulate an erotic response from the people in the courthouse. Finally, Cohen's words did not engage California's authority to protect privacy and shield people from vulgarities, because those in the courthouse were neither captive nor powerless to avoid his jacket—they could simply look away. In a five to four split, Harlan reversed Cohen's conviction.

Cohen is frequently cited in free speech cases, especially if matters of taste, audience captivity, or the suppression of ideas are at issue. Its legacy in First Amendment litigation, however, is cloudy because it is rarely central to Supreme Court rationale. The Court often sidesteps the ruling by distinguishing it as peculiar to the California courthouse circumstances. On its face, *Cohen* places most profanity under First Amendment protections by separating it from obscenity considerations. The opinion also invalidates state laws prohibiting all profanity in public, unless they define factors such as audience or location. In all, it seems that Harlan rescued profanity's emotive function from state efforts to restrict expression to preserve social and moral order.

DOMINIC DEBRINCAT

References and Further Reading

Cohen, William, *A Look Back at Cohen v. California*, UCLA Law Review 34 (1987): 1575–1614.
Krotoszynski, Ronald J., Jr., Cohen v. California: *"Inconsequential" Cases and Larger Principles*, Texas Law Review 74 (1996): 1251–1256.

Cases and Statutes Cited

California Penal Code §415

See also **Application of First Amendment to States; Fighting Words and Free Speech; Freedom of Speech: Modern Period (1917–Present); Harlan, John Marshall II; Obscenity; Police Power of the State; Public Vulgarity and Free Speech; Speech and its Relation to Violence**

COHEN v. COWLES MEDIA COMPANY, 501 U.S. 663 (1991)

Journalists often promise confidentiality to news sources; in *Cohen v. Cowles Media Co.*, the U.S. Supreme Court ruled the First Amendment does not protect journalists who break promises of confidentiality.

Dan Cohen, a spokesperson for a 1982 gubernatorial candidate in Minnesota, offered reporters documents damaging to an opposing candidate. Reporters for two newspapers agreed to protect Cohen's identity, but their editors decided to publish Cohen's name to show that one candidate's campaign was leaking damaging information about an opponent on the eve of the election. After publication of these stories, Cohen lost his job and sued the newspapers. A jury awarded Cohen damages; the Minnesota Supreme Court set the jury verdict aside, ruling that enforcing promises between reporters and sources would chill debate about political campaigns.

By a five to four vote, the U.S. Supreme Court overruled the state supreme court and held that promissory estoppel, a legal doctrine protecting people who rely on promises, could be applied to the press. Drawing on a well-established line of cases, the Court emphasized that the press has no special immunity from laws that apply to everyone. Reporters cannot break into a home to gather news, nor can reporters break promises to sources with impunity. The Court rejected claims that promissory estoppel would harm freedom of the press, stating that the law "simply requires those who make promises to keep them."

Cohen reiterates the doctrine that enforcement of generally applicable laws against the press is "constitutionally insignificant" and does not trigger heightened judicial review.

WILLIAM E. LEE

References and Further Reading

Easton, Eric B., *Two Wrongs Mock a Right: Overcoming the Cohen Maledicta That Bar First Amendment Protection for News-gathering*, Ohio State Law Journal 58 (1997): 1135–1216.

Richards, Jeffrey A., *Note: Confidentially Speaking: Protecting the Press from Liability for Broken Confidentiality Promises*, Washington Law Review 67 (1992): 501–519.

Rothenberg, Eliot C. *The Taming of the Press: Cohen v. Cowles Media Company.* Westport, CT: Praeger, 1999.

See also Branzburg v. Hayes, **408 U.S. 665 (1972);** **Journalism and Sources; Subpoenas to Reporters**

COHN, ROY (1927–1986)

Roy M. Cohn, a young ambitious attorney, gained fame in the 1950s for the intense pursuit of communist sympathizers during his tenure as chief counsel for Senator Joseph McCarthy's (R-WI) Subcommittee on Investigations of the Government Operations Committee. Cohn was born in 1927 in New York City, the son of Al Cohn, a New York State judge and Democratic Party functionary and Dora Cohn, the daughter of a wealthy banker.

Cohn's legal career became linked very early to anticommunism. A graduate of Columbia College and Columbia Law School, Cohn was admitted to the New York bar in 1948 and immediately became an assistant U.S. attorney in New York City. In this capacity he participated in the Smith Act prosecution of the eleven top Communist party leaders in the country of that same year and also played an active part in the espionage prosecution of Julius and Ethel Rosenberg in 1951. In 1952 Cohn landed in Washington, D. C. as special assistant to U.S. Attorney General James McGranery. Cohn's first assignment was running a grand jury searching out communist sympathizers on the U.S. staff at the United Nations Secretariat. He soon went on to prosecute Johns Hopkins professor Owen Lattimore for perjury. Lattimore, a sometime State Department advisor on China, had been on the board of the left wing journal *Amerasia,* in the office of which federal agents had found stolen classified State Department documents in 1945. Senator Joseph McCarthy had denounced Lattimore in 1951 as the top Soviet espionage agent in the United States. The charges were eventually dismissed, but Cohn's role as prosecutor and the efforts of several right wing admirers brought Cohn to the attention of McCarthy, who selected the young attorney to be chief counsel of his investigating subcommittee in 1953.

Intelligent, although intense and often abrasive, Cohn became McCarthy's most trusted aide. Cohn drew headlines almost immediately on his appointment when he and his young millionaire friend,

G. David Shine, took off on a well-publicized trip through Europe checking for pro-Communist literature in U.S. Information Agency libraries overseas. The boondoggle highlighted the arrogant naiveté of the two young men who spent much time enjoying, at State Department expense, the food and lodgings of the continent. Their crusade also brought the frenzied removal of hundreds of books from the American embassy libraries including works of Mark Twain, Dashiell Hammett, and Langston Hughes.

Cohn's fortunes, however, became inextricably linked with McCarthy's during the Army–McCarthy hearings of 1954. In fact, it was Cohn's actions in seeking favorable treatment by the military for his friend, Shine, which instigated those proceedings and set in motion the events that resulted in McCarthy's downfall. When McCarthy leveled charges against the U.S. Army of harboring and even promoting communists and called General Ralph Zwicker "not fit to wear the uniform." the Army retaliated with its own charges, producing a chronology of Cohn's efforts to keep Shine, who had just been drafted, out of the Army. The chronology also documented subsequent demands from Cohn that resulted in preferential treatment for Army Private Shine, including suspension of rigorous training activities and extraordinarily frequent weekend passes. The televised hearings regarding the charges and countercharges gave audience to McCarthy's brutish behavior, ultimately producing the Senator's humiliation at the hands of Army counsel Robert Welsh and Cohn's eventual resignation.

Not one to creep quietly away into the night, Roy Cohn returned to New York and private practice, embarking on what would become a controversial legal career. Until his death, Cohn represented dozens of high-profile clients, including several Mafia bosses, gaining a reputation as a skillful powerbroker. He hobnobbed with the rich and famous at New York's celebrity gathering spots and was well connected to the media. He encountered his own legal difficulties during the 1960s and 1970s when he was tried, although never convicted, of bribery and fraud, as well as jury tampering. His refusal to pay income taxes brought prosecution for tax evasion.

Cohn's high-energy lifestyle included the company of numbers of young men, and it was widely assumed that Cohn was homosexual. He never acknowledged it, however, nor his did he admit to his subsequent infection with AIDS. He died of the disease in 1986.

KAREN BRUNER

References and Further Reading

Oshinsky, David. *A Conspiracy So Immense: The World of Joe McCarthy.* New York: The Free Press, 1983.

Reeves, Thomas C. *The Life and Times of Joe McCarthy.* New York: Stein and Day, Publishers, 1982.
von Hoffman, Nicholas. *Citizen Cohn.* New York: Double-day and Co., 1988.

See also **Communist Party**

COKER v. GEORGIA, 433 U.S. 584 (1977)

Rape was punishable by death in many ancient and medieval cultures, as well as in colonial and modern American criminal law. But shortly after it revived state death penalty schemes in *Gregg v. Georgia* (1976), the U.S. Supreme Court was asked to determine whether the Eighth Amendment's ban on cruel and unusual punishments prohibited the death penalty for rape.

In 1974, Ehrlich Anthony Coker escaped from a Georgia prison and entered the home of Allen and Elnita Carver. Coker bound Mr. Carver, then raped Mrs. Carver at knifepoint before kidnapping her. The Carvers survived the attack. Coker was sentenced to death under Georgia law for the rape.

Justice Byron White's plurality opinion for the Supreme Court reversed the sentence, finding the death penalty disproportionate to the crime of raping an adult woman. The plurality first looked to objective factors, citing the rarity of both capital rape statutes in modern America and of jury-imposed death sentences for rape in those few jurisdictions that authorized it. In addition, the plurality concluded that rape did not compare with murder in terms of moral depravity or injury to the victim. Justice Lewis Powell wrote an important separate concurrence arguing that some rapes could be so brutal as to warrant capital punishment, but that Coker's crime did not involve serious or lasting injury.

Coker remains controversial and potentially far-reaching. Notably, the Court left open the possibility that capital punishment for many non-homicide crimes—including child rape, aggravated kidnapping, treason, and espionage—might be unconstitutional.

J. RICHARD BROUGHTON

References and Further Reading

Bedau, Hugo Adam, ed. *The Death Penalty in America.* New York: Oxford University Press. 1997.

Cases and Statutes Cited

Gregg v. Georgia, 428 U.S. 153 (1976)
Coker v. Georgia, 433 U.S. 584 (1977)

See also **Capital Punishment;** *Furman v. Georgia*, **408 U.S. 238 (1972);** *Gregg v. Georgia*, **428 U.S. 153 (1976); Rape: Naming Victim**

COLAUTTI v. FRANKLIN, 439 U.S. 379 (1979)

In the wake of the Supreme Court's recognition in *Roe v. Wade* that the constitutional right to privacy included the right to choose an abortion, the states, no longer able to outlaw abortion, made several attempts to regulate it. In *Colautti v. Franklin*, the Supreme Court considered the constitutionality of a Pennsylvania law providing that physicians performing abortions must attempt to preserve the life and health of an aborted fetus that is viable or may be viable. Without deciding whether a more clearly drafted law requiring such a standard of care would be constitutional, the Court struck the law as unconstitutionally vague.

The Pennsylvania law stated that a physician performing an abortion involving a fetus that is viable or may be viable must exercise the same care to preserve the life and health of the fetus as if the physician intended the fetus to be born alive and to use the abortion method most likely to preserve the life and health of the fetus, so long as another method was not necessary to preserve the life and health of the mother.

The Supreme Court decided the law was void for vagueness. Specifically, the Court held that it was unclear what was meant by the phrase "may be viable" and how this was different from the phrase "is viable." It was unclear whether the phrase "may be viable" referred to a point in time prior to actual viability. If the statute was an attempt by the state to define viability differently from how it had been defined in *Roe v. Wade*, the Court explained, it would be unconstitutional. Drawing on its decision in *Doe v. Bolton*, the Supreme Court emphasized that the physician must be given broad discretion to determine viability, defined as the point at which, in the physician's reasonable medical judgment, the fetus had a reasonable likelihood of survival outside the womb.

An additional reason for the statute's vagueness was that it held the physician criminally liable regardless of fault or intent. The Court noted that criminal statutes that do not require intent on the part of the wrongdoer are often constitutionally problematic, since they have a tendency to create a trap for the unwary individual who may be acting in good faith.

Finally, the law was vague, because it did not make clear whether the woman's health and life must always take precedence over the fetus's health and life, or whether the law required the physician in some circumstances to sacrifice the woman's health for the fetus's survival. Seven years later, in *Thornburgh v. American College of Obstetricians and Gynecologists*, the Supreme Court decided that a state may not force a tradeoff between a woman's health and that of her fetus; the woman's health and life must always be paramount.

Colautti is primarily a case about abortion regulation and about unconstitutional vagueness. *Colautti*'s statement that the physician must be given wide discretion to determine important issues such as viability, however, may have been undermined by the Supreme Court's subsequent, less deferential approach in *Webster v. Reproductive Health Services* and *Planned Parenthood v. Casey*.

B. JESSIE HILL

References and Further Reading

Daly, Erin, *Reconsidering Abortion Law: Liberty, Equality, and the New Rhetoric of* Planned Parenthood v. Casey, American University Law Review 45 (1995): 1:77–150.

Garrow, David J. *Liberty and Sexuality: The Right to Privacy and the Making of Roe v. Wade*, 600–704, New York: Macmillan, 1994.

Tribe, Laurence H. *American Constitutional Law*, 2nd ed., Mineola, NY: Foundation, 1988.

Cases and Statutes Cited

Doe v. Bolton, 410 U.S. 179 (1973)
Roe v. Wade, 410 U.S. 113 (1973)
Planned Parenthood v. Casey, 505 U.S. 833 (1992)
Thornburgh v. American College of Obstetricians and Gynecologists, 476 U.S. 747 (1986)
Webster v. Reproductive Health Services, 492 U.S. 490 (1989)

See also **Abortion;** *Doe v. Bolton*, **410 U.S. 179 (1973); Privacy;** *Planned Parenthood v. Casey*, **112 S.Ct. 2791 (1992); Right of Privacy;** *Roe v. Wade*, **410 U.S. 113 (1973); Substantive Due Process;** *Thornburgh v. American College of Obstetricians and Gynecologists*, **476 U.S. 747 (1986); Vagueness Doctrine; Void for Vagueness**

COLEMAN v. THOMPSON, 501 U.S. 722 (1991)

In 1982, a Virginia jury found Roger Coleman guilty of the rape and murder of his sister-in-law. The trial judge sentenced Coleman to death. During his subsequent efforts to persuade Virginia's courts to overturn his conviction, Coleman narrowly missed the deadline for filing an appeal with the Virginia Supreme Court—the papers arrived at the courthouse one day late. Because Coleman had violated the state's procedural rules, the Virginia Supreme Court ordered Coleman's appeal dismissed.

Coleman then filed a habeas corpus lawsuit in federal court, arguing that Virginia officials had violated his constitutional rights. By this time, the case was beginning to draw national attention, because Coleman's attorneys were amassing evidence that indicated, in their judgment, that Coleman was innocent. When Coleman's case reached the U.S. Supreme Court, however, the Court refused to consider Coleman's legal claims. Overruling the Warren Court's ruling in *Fay v. Noia* (1963), and building on rulings by the Burger Court in *Francis v. Henderson* (1976) and *Wainwright v. Sykes* (1977), the Rehnquist Court held that, ordinarily, a federal court must dismiss a state prisoner's habeas lawsuit if that prisoner previously failed to follow all of the state's procedural rules. Because Coleman had failed to meet one of Virginia's filing deadlines, the Court dismissed his federal lawsuit. Coleman was executed on May 20, 1992, only days after appearing on the cover of *Time* magazine under the headline "This Man Might Be Innocent." The legal rule announced in *Coleman v. Thompson* remains the rule today.

TODD E. PETTYS

References and Further Reading

Hertz, Randy, and James S. Liebman. *Federal Habeas Corpus Practice and Procedure*. Charlottesville: LexisNexis, 4th ed., 2001.

Tucker, John C. *May God Have Mercy: A True Story of Crime and Punishment*. New York: Dell Publishing, 1997.

Cases and Statutes Cited

Fay v. Noia, 372 U.S. 391 (1963)
Francis v. Henderson, 425 U.S. 536 (1976)
Wainwright v. Sykes, 433 U.S. 72 (1977)

See also **Capital Punishment; Capital Punishment: Execution of Innocents; Habeas Corpus: Modern History**

COLLATERAL CONSEQUENCES

Collateral consequences, often also called collateral sanctions, civil disabilities, or civil penalties, are the indirect legal effects of a criminal conviction. In contrast to the penalties imposed at trial, such as incarceration, probation, or a fine, they flow either automatically from the fact of a criminal conviction or may be administratively imposed on conviction. They may be based on state or federal law. Collateral consequences differ from private discrimination based on a criminal conviction, because they result from state action.

The distinction between collateral sanctions and primary penalties remains ambiguous. Courts generally consider all indirect sanctions— those not imposed directly by the court even though they result from a subsequent state action—collateral, and therefore not punishment. Constitutional protections otherwise extended to criminal offenders at sentencing, such as the Ex Post Facto Clause, do not apply to indirect sanctions. The accused usually has no right to be informed about collateral sanctions at the plea colloquy.

Some jurisdictions have established rules requiring courts to inform criminal defendants of potential immigration consequences. Lack of such information has led to the reversal of convictions. Courts have required such advance information only for a few other drastic collateral sanctions, such as civil commitment for sex offenders.

Criminal defendants are rarely informed of the panoply of collateral consequences that may befall them, largely because none of the players in the criminal justice system have easy access to such information. Collateral sanctions may be grouped into three categories: restrictions on an ex-offenders' participation in the political life (among them disenfranchisement, ban on holding public office, exclusion from serving on a jury; deportation); limitations on employment opportunities (among them a host of licensing restrictions, denial of gun licenses, restrictions on participation in government programs, suspension of driver's license); limitations on governmental benefits (among them denials of public housing and food stamps; denial of student loans). While some collateral sanctions are based on a direct connection between the criminal conduct and the collateral sanction— pedophiles are barred from employment in schools or day-care centers—many others lack such a connection. The former serve an incapacitative function; the latter remain largely unjustified.

Because of their scope, collateral consequences frequently hinder the rehabilitation or re-entry of ex-offenders. They limit their ability to obtain employment and to obtain transitionary housing and welfare benefits. Violations of collateral sanctions lead to criminal sanctions, many with substantial penalties attached. Collateral penalties also have a dilatory impact on the ex-offenders' families, especially their children and their communities.

While collateral sanctions have long existed in U.S. law, they have dramatically expanded in number and scope during the 1980s and 1990s. Automatic sanctions have impacted drug and sex offenders most dramatically, in many cases without a specific link between the crime of conviction and the collateral sanction.

Ex-offenders may encounter substantial difficulties in removing collateral sanctions. Some states provide relief that is awarded almost automatically and leads to the full restoration of rights; others require gubernatorial pardons to allow ex-offenders to regain at least some rights.

NORA V. DEMLEITNER

References and Further Reading

ABA Standards for Criminal Justice. 3rd Ed. Collateral Sanctions and Discretionary Disqualification of Convicted Persons, 2004.

Chin, Gabriel J. and Richard W. Holmes, Jr., *Effective Assistance of Counsel and the Consequences of Guilty Pleas*, Cornell L. Rev. 697 (2002): 87.

Demleitner, Nora V., *Preventing Internal Exile: The Need for Restrictions on Collateral Sentencing Consequences*, Stan. L. & Pol'y Rev. 153 (1999): 11.

———, *'Collateral Damage': No Re-entry for Drug Offenders*, Vill. L. Rev. 1027 (2002): 47.

Mauer, Marc, and Meda Chesney-Linds, eds. *Invisible Punishment: The Collateral Consequences of Mass Imprisonment*. The New Press, 2002.

Mele, Christopher, and Teresa A. Miller, eds. *Civil Penalties, Social Consequences*. Routledge, 2005.

Office of the Pardon Attorney. U.S. Dep't of Justice, Federal Statutes Imposing Collateral Consequences Upon Conviction.

Petersilia, Joan. *When Prisoners Come Home: Parole and Prisoner Reentry*, 2003.

See also **Civil Death; Corruption of Blood; Criminalization of Civil Wrongs; Sentencing Guidelines**

COLONIAL CHARTERS AND CODES

The early colonial charters, compacts, patents, agreements, and codes were generally not very sympathetic to civil liberties, because they would be understood today. Neither the Virginia Company Charter of 1606 nor the Massachusetts Bay Charter of 1629 contained anything that would have protected civil liberties. The 1609 Charter of Virginia empowered the Virginia Company to "ordain, and establish all Manner of Orders, Laws, Directions, Instructions, Forms and Ceremonies of Government and Magistracy, fit and necessary for and concerning the Government of the said Colony and Plantation; And the same, at all Times hereafter, to abrogate, revoke, or change, not only within the Precincts of the said Colony, but also upon the Seas, in going and coming to and from the said Colony, as they in their good Discretion, shall think to be fittest for the Good of the Adventurers and inhabitants there." Another section of the

Charter required that laws Virginia's "Statutes, Ordinances and Proceedings as near as conveniently may be, be agreeable to the Laws, Statutes, Government, and Policy of this our Realm of England." But the two provisions and the rest of the charter allowed for arbitrary and harsh rule that denied basic liberties to most settlers in the colony. This second Virginia charter made it clear that religious dissent would not be tolerated. The charter declared that the Company would not allow settlers who accepted "the Superstitions of the Church of Rome," and further provided that on one could enter the colony who had not "taken the Oath of Supremacy."

The Maryland charter of 1632 merely proclaimed that the law of England would be the basis of the laws of the colonies. The charter allowed the proprietor to impose martial law to suppress rebellions or sedition. While founded as a haven for English Catholics, the Maryland charter authorized religious worship according to the "Eclesiastical laws of our Kingdom of England." Thus, the Maryland settlers did not get any new rights of expression or protection from the sometimes arbitrary criminal justice of England and were perhaps subject to even harsher and more arbitrary law. Even the Pennsylvania charter of 1781 contained nothing at all that connected to civil liberties. The settlers of New Hampshire, for example, agreed in 1639 to the following declaration when creating a government: "We his loyal Subjects Brethern of the Church in Exeter situate and lying upon the River Pascataqua with other Inhabitants there, considering with ourselves the holy Will of God and o'er own Necessity that we should not live without wholesome Lawes and Civil Government among us of which we are altogether destitute; in the name of Christ and in the sight of God combine ourselves together to erect and set up among us such Government as shall be to our best discerning agreeable to the Will of God professing ourselves Subjects to our Sovereign Lord King Charles according to the Libertyes of our English Colony of Massachusetts, and binding of ourselves solemnly by the Grace and Help of Christ and in His Name and fear to submit ourselves to such Godly and Christian Lawes as are established in the realm of England to our best Knowledge, and to all other such Lawes which shall upon good grounds be made and enacted among us according to God that we may live quietly and peaceably together in all godliness and honesty." Similarly, when the colonies in Massachusetts and Connecticut joined together in 1639 under "The Articles of Confederation of the United Colonies of New England," they provided no protection for due process, freedom of expression, or religious liberty. The document proclaimed that one of the purposes of settlement was to "advance the Kingdom of our Lord Jesus Christ and to enjoy the liberties of the Gospel in purity with peace," but this did not imply that all people—even all Christians—would have religious freedom in these colonies.

By the end of the Seventeenth Century the newer colonies began with a greater sense of civil liberties. The Carolina charter of 1663 noted that "it may happen that some of the people and inhabitants of the said province, cannot in their private opinions, conform to the publick exercise of religion, according to the liturgy, form and ceremonies of the church of England, or take and subscribe the oaths and articles, made and established in that behalf." Taking this into consideration, the charter allowed the proprietors to give "indulgencies and dispensations" to such persons. This was a major step toward religious toleration. This move toward greater protections for liberty in the charters can be seen most clearly in Rhode Island. The "Patent for Providence Plantations," granted by Parliament in 1643, contained no protections of civil liberties or religious freedom, even though the founder of the colony, Roger Williams, established Rhode Island as a haven for people of all faiths. However, the Rhode Island charter of 1663 was even more expansive in its support for religious liberty, providing that "noe person within the sayd colonye, at any tyme hereafter, shall bee any wise molested, punished, disquieted, or called in question, for any differences in opinione in matters of religion, and doe not actually disturb the civill peace of our sayd colony; but that all and everye person and persons may, from tyme to tyme, and at all tymes hereafter, freelye and fullye have and enjoye his and theire owne judgments and consciences, in matters of religious concernments, throughout the tract of lance hereafter mentioned; they behaving themselves peaceablie and quietlie, and not useing this libertie to lycentiousnesse and profanenesse, nor to the civill injurye or outward disturbeance of others; any lawe, statute, or clause, therein contayned, or to bee contayned, usage or custome of this realme, to the contrary hereof, in any wise, notwithstanding." The 1691 Massachusetts allowed "liberty of Conscience allowed in the Worshipp of God to all Christians (Except Papists)," which was an improvement over the earlier regime in Massachusetts, which had been hostile to all non-Puritans, but was hardly civil libertarian.

This notion appeared more emphatically in the two charters granted to settlers in 1701 by William Penn: the Delaware Charter of 1701 and the Pennsylvania Charter of 1701. These are among the earliest formal documents in American history to use the term "civil liberties" as it is understood today. These charters did not come from the King or Parliament. Instead they were granted to the settlers of both places by William Penn, who was the proprietor of Pennsylvania, which until 1701 included present-day Delaware. Penn's charters noted that: "no People can be truly happy, though under the greatest Enjoyment of Civil Liberties, if abridged of the Freedom of their Consciences, as to their Religious Profession and Worship." Thus, the charter provided that "no Person or Persons, inhabiting In this Province or Territories, who shall confess and acknowledge One almighty God, the Creator, Upholder and Ruler of the World; and professes him or themselves obliged to live quietly under the Civil Government, shall be in any Case molested or prejudiced, in his or their Person or Estate, because of his or their conscientious Persuasion or Practice, nor be compelled to frequent or maintain any religious Worship, Place or Ministry, contrary to his or their Mind, or to do or suffer any other Act or Thing, contrary to their religious Persuasion." This was an enormously expansive grant of religious toleration, although the charter did not grant full religious freedom to all people. The next clause provided that "all Persons who also profess to believe in Jesus Christ, the Saviour of the World, shall be capable (notwithstanding their other Persuasions and Practices in Point of Conscience and Religion) to serve this Government in any Capacity, both legislatively and executively." This provision allowed all Christians to hold office, which made Pennsylvania and Delaware far more progressive than Britain, even if it was protective of liberty by modern standards.

In a subsequent part of the charter, Penn provided that "the First Article of this Charter relating to Liberty of Conscience, and every Part and Clause therein, according to the true Intent and Meaning thereof, shall be kept and remain, without any Alteration, inviolably for ever."

In criminal law the Pennsylvania and Delaware charter contained a major recognition of the rights of the accused that was unknown in England. Penn provided that "all Criminals shall have the same Privileges of Witnesses and Council as their Prosecutors." This simple statement would later lead to the confrontation clause and assistance of counsel clause in the Sixth Amendment. The charter also abolished the English practice of denying inheritance to the heirs of anyone who committed suicide. This provision reflected Penn's generally humane view of law while it also protected property.

The last charter of the colonial period, granted to Georgia, in 1732 adopted the general support for Protestant religious freedom and anti-Catholicism. The charter provided that:

And for the greater ease and encouragement of our loving subjects and such others as shall come to inhabit in our said colony, we do by these presents, for us, our heirs and successors, grant, establish and ordain, that forever hereafter, there shall be a liberty of conscience allowed in the worship of God, to all persons inhabiting, or which shall inhabit or be resident within our said provinces and that all such persons, except papists, shall have a free exercise of their religion, so they be contented with the quiet and peaceable enjoyment of the same, not giving offence or scandal to the government.

In general, the colonial charters did little to expand existing English liberty, except in the area of religious toleration, where a few colonies, like Rhode Island, Pennsylvania, and Delaware, set a new standard for religious liberty. Granted by the King or Parliament, the charters reflected the need of the mother country to govern the colonies. There was little idealism in these charters and thus few innovations in civil liberties. The great exception was the two charters granted by William Penn.

PAUL FINKELMAN

References and Further Reading

Thorpe, Francis N. *The Federal and State Constitutions Colonial Charters, and Other Organic Laws of the States, Territories, and Colonies Now or Heretofore Forming the United States of America.* Washington, DC: Government Printing Office, 1909.

COLORADO REPUBLICAN FEDERAL CAMPAIGN COMMITTEE v. FEDERAL ELECTION COMMISSION, 518 U.S. 604 (1996)

Should political parties on their own be able to spend unlimited amounts of money on behalf of their candidates? The Supreme Court stated yes, upholding on First Amendment free speech grounds the right of political parties to make independent expenditures.

In *Buckley v. Valeo*, the Supreme Court upheld the constitutionality of limits on political contributions to candidates and political parties, even though money spent implicated free speech–like issues. In *Buckley* the Court also stated that money spent by third-party groups independently of campaigns was protected by the First Amendment and could not be limited, but that money spent in coordination with a candidate would be counted against the latter's contribution limits. However, unresolved was whether money spent independently by political parties on behalf of candidates could be limited? This was the subject of Colorado Republican Federal Campaign Committee.

In this case the Colorado Republican Party spent money to attack Tim Wirth, the likely Democratic Party U.S. Senate candidate in 1986. At the time of the ads, the Republicans did not have a candidate. The issue in the case was whether the ads were coordinated and subject to limits, or an independent expenditure, free from limits.

In a divided seven to two opinion, Justice Breyer wrote the plurality opinion ruling that these contributions were independent expenditures. The First Amendment protects the right of political parties to make them without limit on behalf of candidates, so long as spending is not coordinated with candidates. The Court reached this conclusion by simply drawing on its arguments in *Buckley* that independent expenditures are protected by the First Amendment, whether made by political parties or other entities.

DAVID SCHULTZ

References and Further Reading

Hasen, Richard L. *The Supreme Court and Election Law.* New York: New York University Press, 2003.

Cases and Statutes Cited

Buckley v. Valeo, 424 U.S. 1 (1976)

See also **First Amendment and PACs; Campaign Finance Reform**

COLORADO v. CONNELLY, 479 U.S. 157 (1986)

In *Colorado v. Connelly*, the Supreme Court explicitly held that police coercion was an indispensable element to a finding that a confession was "involuntary" under the Due Process Clause. The Court further held that the government need only establish wavier of *Miranda* rights under a preponderance of the evidence standard.

Defendant Connelly had approached a police officer and, without prompting, confessed to murdering someone. After receiving *Miranda* rights, the defendant elaborated on his confession, stating that he had killed a particular young woman in November of 1982. Police records confirmed that the body of an unidentified woman had been found several months later. The defendant then directed police officers to the crime scene.

The following day, while meeting with the public defender's office, the defendant became confused and disoriented, stating that "voices" had driven him to confess. At a suppression hearing, a psychiatrist testified that the defendant was suffering from "command hallucinations" that interfered with his ability to make free choices. The state courts suppressed defendant's statements on the basis that they were involuntary.

The Court reversed in an opinion authored by Chief Justice Rehnquist, holding that there could be no due process violation without some element of police overreaching. Because the police had nothing to cause the defendant's confession, his statements should have been admitted. Justices Brennan and Marshall dissented, finding that the majority opinion denied the defendant the right to make an important choice with a "sane mind."

M. K. B. DARMER

References and Further Reading

Benner, Laurence A., *Requiem for Miranda The Rehnquist Court's Voluntariness Doctrine in Historical Perspective,* Washington University Law Quarterly 67 (1989): 59.
Darmer, M. K. B., *Beyond Bin Laden and Lindh: Confessions Law in an Age of Terrorism*, Cornell Journal of Law and Public Policy 12 (2003): 319–364.
Dix, George E., *Federal Constituional Confession Law: The 1986 and 1987 Supreme Court Terms*, Texas Law Review 67 (1988): 231; 244–246, 276.

Cases and Statutes Cited

Miranda v. Arizona, 384 U.S. 436 (1966)

See also **Coerced Confessions/Police Interrogations;** *Miranda* **Warning**

COMMERCIAL SPEECH

Commercial speech is a subset of speech that is protected by the First Amendment. Its status as protected speech is of relatively recent vintage. It was only in 1976 that the Supreme Court announced that "commercial speech" was entitled to some, limited First Amendment protection in *Virginia Pharmacy v. Virginia Citizens' Council.* Prior to that case most observers thought commercial speech clearly unprotected on the basis of the Court's decision in 1942 in *Valentine v. Chrestensen.* There the Court had thought it self-evident that the First Amendment offered no "restraint [analogous to that imposed on political speech] on government as respects purely commercial advertising." Almost a decade later, in 1951, the Court had again rebuffed the First Amendment argument of a door-to-door magazine salesman in *Breard v. Alexandria.*

So *Virginia Pharmacy* represented a new turn in the Court's treatment of commercial speech. Nevertheless, *Virginia Pharmacy* did not clearly define what constituted "commercial speech." One definition proposed in the case was that commercial speech was speech that "does no more than propose a commercial transaction." However, this does not do much more to define the boundaries than the term "commercial speech itself." And although the Court in *Virginia Pharmacy* used the terms "commercial advertising" and "commercial speech" interchangeably, it was not clear it meant to suggest that "commercial speech" and "commercial advertising" were synonymous, and thus that the boundaries of the new doctrine would be confined to advertising. Subsequent decisions of the Court have suggested that the two terms are not synonymous and that the category of commercial speech is broader than simply advertising. Nevertheless, as several commentators have noted, the definition of commercial speech remains unclear, and the ambiguities in the Court's decisions in this area have laid the foundation for future struggles over the boundaries of protection for this type of speech.

The turn to protection for commercial speech, although somewhat abrupt from the perspective of the Court's decisions, was nevertheless presaged in the academic literature. Despite the brevity of the Court's dismissal of the notion of protection for commercial speech in *Valentine v. Chrestensen* in 1942, the social and economic conditions that would later generate arguments for the protection of commercial speech were well under way in the 1940s. Advertising and public relations were twentieth century outgrowths of the industrial revolution, and the accompanying technological developments that enhanced the speed of communications allowed for the mass production of an ever-larger proliferation of products—many of which were relatively indistinguishable from one another. The competition for custom led manufacturers to rely on increasingly large-scale advertising and promotional efforts—from package design, print ads and billboards, to radio and then television ads and sponsorship of particular shows. As the twentieth century progressed, the role advertising played in generating and maintaining sales seemed, to many observers, as crucial as the manufacturing process itself, despite always having somewhat mixed empirical support for the cause-and-effect relationship between advertising and sales. Lagging behind somewhat, but developing along similar lines, was the public relations business and the practice of promoting a product or service by issuing press releases and trying to get the media to report on it. By the late twentieth century this practice had become well established, threatening in some ways to swamp traditional advertising, because the advantage of the public relations approach is that if the media picks up information from a press release and reports on it, the item has

greater credibility than an ad and at less cost since there is no charge for news coverage.

Parallel to these developments in the markets were other social developments—an increased focus on civil rights for women, blacks, and other historically disadvantaged groups, an increased degree of respectability for protest and dissent, perhaps growing out of the antiwar movement and protest against the war in Vietnam, loosening of restrictions on women's reproductive choices to turn over more control to the individual and increased visibility for certain types of nonconformity and what might be viewed as a return to the relatively greater sexual permissiveness of the 1930s and 1940s. All these changes, and perhaps many others, involved an increased focus on the individual as rights holder. During this same period, roughly after the trajectory of the industrial revolution was a shift in the theory of the corporation away from the charter and the contractarian theories to an entity theory that proposed that a corporation was a "person" for purposes of the law. These various developments converged in the 1970s and played a part in the development of what became known as the commercial speech doctrine.

The first hint of new attitude on the part of the Court came in *New York Times v. Sullivan* in 1964. Although the case is often not thought of as a commercial speech case, it, like *Chrestensen*, involved an ad. But this time it was the civil rights struggle and defamation law that stood in the spotlight. *Sullivan* involved an ad paid for by various supporters of Dr. Martin Luther King who sought donations from the public to raise money for Dr. King's defense. The ad described clashes between police and civil rights marchers and specific instances of violence that had been perpetrated by, or ignored by, law enforcement. Sullivan, a police commissioner, although unnamed in the text of the ad, felt sufficiently implicated in what he deemed were illegal police practices that he alleged he had been libeled because the ad contained some inaccuracies. The question presented was whether the First Amendment protected defendants' from liability, for their statements and the publisher for running the ad, despite those inaccuracies.

The Court concluded that it did even though the vehicle for their statements was a paid advertisement and even though the publisher published the ad in exchange for money. The Court asserted that neither of these facts necessarily disqualified the speech from First Amendment protection. The Court distinguished *Chrestensen* as dealing with "purely commercial advertising." In contrast, in the *Sullivan* case the Court found that the speech in question was the sort of key political speech that the First Amendment was intended to protect. Nevertheless, since a broader ruling might have swept away defamation law altogether, the Court held that absent evidence of malice speech about public figures on matters of public concern was fully protected.

A few years later, in 1973, this observation, that merely appearing in an ad does not make something "commercial," was repeated in *Pittsburgh Press v. Human Relations Commission*. There the Court upheld a cease and desist order to a newspaper requiring it to stop the practice of listing the help wanted ads by gender, a practice that was arguably rendered illegal by Title VII. But it still did not announce a fully articulated theory of what constituted "commercial speech" and what level of protection such speech should receive. Only two years later another case came before the Court that again arguably involved commercial speech but that also implicated other protected rights. The case, *Bigelow v. Virginia*, involved the criminal prosecution of a newspaper publisher for printing ads announcing the availability of abortions in New York, under a statute criminalizing the sale or circulation of material encouraging abortions. Because the statute itself was clearly unconstitutional with respect to noncommercial expression, particularly in light of the Court's decision in *Roe v. Wade*, it was unclear whether the fact that the expression took the form of an ad was of any significance. Arguably, it might have been had the Court been operating under the old *Chrestensen* schema. But *Sullivan* and *Pittsburgh Press* seemed to point in the other direction and, indeed, the Court felt constrained to add that it was not the case that if speech was related to commerce it was of no value to "the marketplace of ideas."

Finally, in 1976, the Court rendered a decision in a case that squarely presented a question that seemed to involve purely commercial speech without any of the overtones of civil rights issues intertwined in the previous cases. In *Virginia Board of Pharmacy v. Virginia Citizens' Consumer Council*, a consumer group challenged the State's prohibition on the advertising of drug prices. Virginia asserted that the ban on the advertising of price information was intended to promote professionalism by deterring a decline into a price war by pharmacists, a result that was liable to undercut the quality of their services. The Court did not find this argument convincing and concluded that there was no legitimate state interest in keeping consumers ignorant of truthful information. Any other conclusion, the Court held, would be unduly paternalistic where consumers' interest in the information was keen and relevant to their decision-making process.

Despite the protection afforded commercial speech in this case, the Court held protected the publishing of price information on the grounds of the listeners'

right to receive the information rather than on any notion of the speakers right to speak. Moreover, the Court did not elevate the protection announced in this new doctrine to the level of the full protection afforded political speech. Commercial speech would only be protected, the Court held, to the extent that it was truthful and not misleading or illegal and where the regulation in question was not supported by a legitimate public interest by legislation reasonably calculated to address that interest. Protection of the public's right to receive information did not, the Court felt, prevent the government from seeing that the information stream ran "cleanly."

At last a doctrine had been announced. And a definition of sorts had even emerged. In *Virginia Pharmacy* the Court referred to speech that "does no more than propose a commercial transaction." And at first, even to the Court to the extent that in later parts of the opinion it seemed to use the terms "commercial speech" and "commercial advertising" interchangeably, this definition seemed to mean "advertising"— want ads, print ads, television ads, but apparently the term seemed sufficiently self-explanatory that no other definitional clarification was offered. However, the test for the assessment of governmental regulation was further refined in *Central Hudson Gas & Electric Service v. Public Service Commission*. In *Central Hudson* the Court announced the four-part test that, despite some criticisms, has survived up to the present day as the test for commercial speech.

According to the Court in *Central Hudson*, for commercial speech to be protected it must first be (1) truthful and involve a legal activity. If the speech in question meets that prong, it is entitled to intermediate scrutiny. So for governmental regulation of such speech to be acceptable it must (2) reflect a substantial governmental interest (3), and actually advance that substantial interest but do so (4) in a way that is no more extensive than necessary to advance the government's legitimate interest. These last two portions of the test are often referred to as testing "the fit" between the interest to be protected or advanced and the implementing regulation.

While initially the Court seemed to address the "fit" question with a fair amount of deference to governmental judgments in cases such as *Posadas de Puerto Rico Associates v. Tourism Co. of Puerto Rico* and *Board of Trustees v. Fox*, in recent years the Court has become increasingly more inclined to strictly construe the test against the government and to strike down governmental restrictions where it finds the "fit" is not very tight. Examples of this trend are *City of Cincinnati v. Discovery Network, Inc.* and *Edenfield v. Fane*. Indeed, as Professor David Vladeck noted in a law review article in 2003, "The Court has not upheld a single restraint [against commercial speech] in the past decade."

What has occurred in the past decade is ever-greater pressure to consider the definition of commercial speech and what is or is not included in its ambit. As noted previously, initially it seemed that "commercial speech" was coextensive with "commercial advertising." But subsequent cases made clear that this could not be the case. In *Bolger v. Youngs Drugs* the Court confronted the attempt to prevent the distribution of informational pamphlets about condoms. The bulk of the text was informative only, but the brochure included product identification and thus presented a case of "mixed" speech. The Court concluded that the pamphlet could not be suppressed simply because it contained some elements that were commercial. In deciding whether speech was commercial, the Court proposed that a fact-intensive review of the context was required, and it found three elements of particular relevance: (1) the use of the advertising form, (2) a reference to a specific product, and (3) an underlying economic motive on the part of the speaker. The presence of all three characteristics was a strong indication that the speech in question was "commercial." But even with all three factors present, as they were in *Bolger*, this did not preclude protection for the speech. Any regulation of such speech would still need to meet the requirements of the *Central Hudson* test.

Such discussions have only raised more questions rather than settling them. And as marketing forms have proliferated, the variety of ways in which commercial expression occurs, many of which seem far away from directly "propos[ing]" a commercial transaction, the doctrine seems to cover less and less. Does corporate image advertising, that is, advertising intended to address the corporation's image, as, for example, in Wal-Mart's ads addressing its labor practices or BP's advertising regarding its environmental practices, count as "commercial speech" since they don't explicitly propose a commercial transaction. Indeed, much traditional advertising does not propose a commercial transaction either, at least not directly. Do the marketing practices of pharmaceutical representatives to doctors on, for example, off-label uses of drugs, count as commercial speech, despite occurring outside of the media? What about speech by nonprofit corporations operated as research or public relations arms of for-profit corporations? Can their speech be designated as "commercial" because of the connection with a for-profit enterprise? Does format matter? If something appears in the form of a press release, does this necessarily mean it is not commercial speech? And if it is not commercial, does that mean it is fully protected? These and many other questions with very important ramifications for marketing practices, as well as social and governmental regulatory power, remain unanswered.

Moreover, the very first prong of the *Central Hudson* test, the requirement that the speech be truthful and not misleading and involve a legal activity has revealed more ambiguity over time than appeared at first blush. Of course the first prong is one that in other First Amendment contexts would be seen as problematic, since typically the argument in favor of protection of a multiplicity of opinions is that it is only through airing all sides of a debate that truth is best arrived at. Nevertheless, because *Virginia Pharmacy* and many of the subsequent cases involved concrete information that was verifiable, in that case prices, the problems raised by the first prong have not been deeply probed. Some of the other cases that fall into this category are *Rubin v. Coors Brewing Co.* (alcohol content on labels) and *44 Liquormart v. Rhode Island* (price). When the ad deals less with concrete information and more with just product visuals or announcements, the Court has, to date, shown little willingness to engage in a more nuanced parsing of what constitutes "misleading," such as where cigarette advertising makes smoking look glamorous or life enhancing. There is some argument that to the extent that smoking raises serious health risks such advertising is misleading.

However, far from indicating a greater willingness to regulate commercial speech in the absence of a specific claim, the weight of opinion seems to be inclining for greater protection for commercial speech. Indeed, some commentators have urged that the ambiguities in the commercial speech doctrine and the uncertainties of the boundaries be clarified by elevating commercial speech to the same status as political speech. In fact, the extent that promotion of consumption arguably also promotes a particular social and political agenda, an argument exists that commercial speech is political.

No case underscored the weight of this trend more clearly than the 2003 case of *Nike v. Kasky*. The *Nike* case involved a claim by a California activist, Kasky, that Nike's public statements and public relations campaign aimed at defending its labor practices in response to criticism of those practices, contained numerous false statements that amounted to false advertising, unfair competition, and fraud and deceit. Kasky was suing under a provision of California law that allowed any citizen, acting as a "private attorney general," to bring such claims on behalf of the citizens of the state. Nike responded to the complaint with a demurrer, claiming that all of its statements were completely protected by the First Amendment. Despite Kasky's claim that these statements were motivated by the desire to promote sales and boost the company's image and thus were "commercial" in nature, Nike maintained that its statements were offered in self-defense and represented a contribution to the debate on globalization. Such statements were, it claimed, fully protected and thus the First Amendment represented a complete bar to Kaksy's lawsuit.

The California trial and appellate courts agreed with Nike and dismissed the case with prejudice. A divided California Supreme Court disagreed and reversed, finding that at least some of the statements could constitute commercial speech and thus remanding the case back to the trial court for further proceedings. Nike petitioned the Supreme Court for review, and it was granted. Although both sides had several *amici* filing briefs in support of their position, Nike had the bulk of them, including one from the AFL-CIO, which, while explicitly disclaiming support for either party, nevertheless supported Nike's claim that its speech was not commercial. News media coverage also was, by and large, supporting Nike.

In the end, the Court decided that review had been improvidently granted, because reversal of a motion to dismiss did not represent a sufficiently final judgment to confer jurisdiction on the Court. Still, the concurring and dissenting opinions written in connection with the dismissal suggested that a majority of the Court found Nike's claim to protection compelling. This in turn suggests that a major overhaul of the commercial speech doctrine may occur if another case comes before the Court soon. And although the *Nike* can be seen as a harbinger of greater protection for commercial speech, a case presenting significantly different facts might shift the momentum, since it was clear from the briefs submitted in support of Kaksy by several states and by members of Congress, that significant expansion of the protection for commercial speech might imperil other governmental regulatory efforts that the Court may not have considered—for example, in the areas of corporate governance such as Sarbanes-Oxley, or with respect to the regulation of the sale of pharmaceuticals. At present, all definitional questions remain unanswered, and with the recent change in the makeup of the Court, the Court's future direction may be relatively difficult to predict. Still, the commercial speech area promises to be one of the most interesting, active, and far-reaching areas of the Court's Constitutional jurisprudence to come.

TAMARA R. PIETY

References and Further Reading

Baker, C. Edwin. *Human Liberty and Freedom of Speech*. Oxford University Press, 1989.

Chemerinsky, Erwin, and Catherine Fisk, *What is Commercial Speech? The Issue not Decided in* Nike v. Kasky, Case Wes. Res. L. Rev. 1143 (2004): 54.

Collins, Ronald K. L., and David M. Skover. *The Death of Discourse*. Westview Press, 1996.

Greenwood, Daniel J.H., *Essential Speech: Why Corporate Speech is Not Free*, Iowa L. Rev. 995 (1998): 83.

Horwitz, Morton J. *The Transformation of American Law: 1870–1960*. Oxford University Press, 1992.

Kosinski, Alex, and Stuart Banner, *The Anti-History and the Pre-History of Commercial Speech*, Tex. L. Rev. 627 (1990): 71.

Langvardt, Arlen W., and Eric L. Richards, *The Death of Posadas and the Birth of Change in Commercial Speech Doctrine*, Am. Bus. L. J. 483 (1997): 34.

Morrison, Alan B., *How We Got the Commercial Speech Doctrine: An Originalist's Recollections*, Case Wes. Res. L. Rev. 1189 (2003): 54.

Neuborne, Burt, *A Rationale for Protecting and Regulating Commercial Speech*, Brook. L. Rev. 437 (1980): 46.

Redish, Martin H., *The First Amendment in the Marketplace: Commercial Speech and the Value of Free Expression*, Geo. Wash. L. Rev. 429 (1971): 39.

Schauer, Frederick F., *Commercial Speech and the Architecture of the First Amendment*, U. Cinn. L. Rev. 1181 (1988): 56.

Shiner, Roger A. *Freedom of Commercial Expression*. Oxford University Press, 2003.

Vladeck, David C., *Lesson From a Story Untold: Nike v. Kasky Reconsidered*, Case Wes. Res. L. Rev. 1049 (2003): 54.

Cases and Statutes Cited

44 Liquormart, Inc. v. Rhode Island, 517 U.S. 484 (1996)

Bigelow v. Virginia, 421 U.S. 809 (1975)

Board of Trustees v. Fox, 492 U.S. 469 (1989)

Bolger v. Youngs Drug Prods. Corp., 463 U.S. 60 (1983)

Breard v. Alexandria, 341 U.S. 622 (1951)

Central Hudson Gas & Electric Corp. v. Public Serv. Comm'n of New York, 447 U.S. 557 (1980)

Lorillard Tobacco Co. v. Reilly, 533 U.S. 525 (2001)

New York Times v. Sullivan, 376 U.S. 254 (1964)

Nike v. Kasky, 539 U.S. 654 (2003)

Posadas de Puerto Rico Assoc. v. Tourism Co. of Puerto Rico, 478 U.S. 328 (1986)

Rubin v. Coors Brewing Co., 514 U.S. 476 (1995)

Virginia State Bd. of Pharmacy v. Virginia Citizens Consumer Council, 425 U.S. 748 (1976)

Valentine v. Chrestensen, 316 U.S. 52 (1942)

See also **First Amendment and PACs**

COMMITTEE FOR PUBLIC EDUCATION AND RELIGIOUS LIBERTY v. NYQUIST, 413 U.S. 756 (1973)

One of the more controversial issues confronting the U.S. Supreme Court in the church–state area has been the question of the constitutionality of government aid to religious schools. The Court's jurisprudence in this area has ebbed and flowed during the past half century. During the early 1970s, the Court was particularly skeptical of such financial assistance, consistently rejecting government efforts to provide aid to private sectarian schools. One of the more important of the Court's decisions during that time period was *Committee for Public Education and Religious Liberty v. Nyquist* in which the Court declared unconstitutional a New York statute that provided for (1) "maintenance and repair" grants to private schools serving children from low-income families, (2) tuition reimbursement grants for low-income parents whose children attended private schools, and (3) tax relief (in the form of a tax deduction) for parents whose children attended private schools but who did not qualify for a tuition reimbursement grant. The Court, with Justice Lewis Powell writing for a six to three majority, concluded that all aspects of the New York statute had the primary effect of advancing religion in violation of the Establishment Clause. The importance of the *Nyquist* decision lies particularly in the Court's ruling on the tuition grants and tax deduction provisions that benefitted parents directly and religious schools only indirectly.

During the early 1970s, private schools educated a significant portion of New York's schoolchildren— approximately twenty percent. The New York state legislature expressed concern that the "fiscal crisis in nonpublic education . . . has caused a diminution of proper maintenance and repair programs, threatening the health, welfare and safety of nonpublic school children" in low-income urban schools. The legislature thus established the maintenance and repair grant program to "ensure the health, welfare and safety" of children attending such schools. The legislature also worried that any "precipitous decline in the number of nonpublic school pupils would cause a massive increase in public school enrollment and costs" and would "aggravate an already serious fiscal crisis in public education." Accordingly, it enacted the tuition grant and tax benefit programs to relieve private school parents of some of the costs of their children's education. In so doing, the legislature observed that a "healthy competitive and diverse alternative to public education is not only desirable but indeed vital to a state and nation that have continually reaffirmed the value of individual differences."

Although the legislation encompassed both religious and nonreligious private schools, eighty-five percent of the nonpublic schoolchildren in New York attended a church-affiliated school. Moreover, virtually all of the schools eligible for the maintenance and repair grants were operated by the Catholic Church. A private organization, known as the Committee

for Public Education and Religious Liberty, challenged all aspects of the New York statute as violative of the Establishment Clause. The Supreme Court concluded that to pass constitutional muster, "the law in question must first reflect a clearly secular legislative purpose, second, must have a primary effect that neither advances nor inhibits religion, and, third, must avoid excessive entanglement with religion."

The Court concluded that the New York law had a secular purpose but that all aspects of the program had the primary effect of advancing religion. With respect to the maintenance and repair grants, the Court noted that the program did not limit the grants to the "upkeep of facilities used exclusively for secular purposes," and hence the monies could be used to support directly the religious mission of the school. With respect to the tuition reimbursement grants, the Court noted that "there can be no question that these grants could not, consistently with the Establishment Clause, be given directly to sectarian schools." The Court then concluded that the fact that the tuition reimbursement monies were given to the parents, rather than directly to the school, was not constitutionally significant—either way, "the effect of the aid is unmistakably to provide desired financial support for nonpublic, sectarian institutions." Finally, the Court concluded that the tax deductions had the same impermissible effect, even though the tax benefits accrued directly to the parents, not the religious schools.

Three justices—Warren Burger, William Rehnquist, and Byron White—dissented on the tuition reimbursement and tax deduction aspect of the state's plan (they joined the majority with respect to the repair and maintenance grants). In dissenting, they relied on the Court's recent decision in *Walz v. Tax Commission* (1970) in which the Court had upheld property tax exemptions for religious institutions noting that "the grant of a tax exemption is not sponsorship since the government does not transfer part of its revenue to churches but simply abstains from demanding that the church support the state . . . . There is no genuine nexus between tax exemption and establishment of religion." The majority had distinguished *Walz* in part by arguing that exempting religious property from the taxing power of the state was different from providing a tuition grant or tax deduction to private citizens who choose a private sectarian school for their children's education. The dissenters rejected that distinction.

The Court would revisit *Nyquist* almost thirty years later in *Zelman v. Simmons-Harris* (2002), a case in which the Court considered the constitutionality of the government providing vouchers to parents for use at public or private schools (including private sectarian schools). The *Nyquist* decision posed a constitutional problem for the voucher plan. The Court distinguished *Nyquist* in part on the grounds that the voucher program in *Zelman* encompassed both public and private schools, whereas the tax benefits at issue in *Nyquist* benefitted only private school parents. Under the Court's more recent doctrine, tax benefits, so long as they are neutral with respect to all schools (religious and nonreligious, public and private), are likely constitutional.

DAVISON M. DOUGLAS

References and Further Reading

Lawrence, Rebecca, *Comment. The Future of School Vouchers in Light of the Past Chaos of the Establishment Clause Jurisprudence*, University of Miami Law Review 55 (2001): 419–452.

Note, *State Aid to Private Schools: Reinforcing the Wall of Supervision*, Albany Law Review 38 (1974): 611–631.

Zelinsky, Edward, *Are Tax 'Benefits' Constitutionally Equivalent to Direct Expenditures?* Harvard Law Review 112 (1998): 379–433.

Cases and Statutes Cited

Walz v. Tax Commission, 397 U.S. 664 (1970)
Zelman v. Simmons-Harris, 536 U.S. 639 (2002)

See also **State Aid to Religious Schools**

COMMITTEE FOR PUBLIC EDUCATION AND RELIGIOUS LIBERTY v. REGAN, 444 U.S. 646 (1980)

During the 1970s and early 1980s, the U.S. Supreme Court considered a large number of constitutional challenges to various forms of government aid to religious schools. In each of these cases, plaintiffs argued that the aid in question violated the Establishment Clause of the Constitution. In *Committee for Public Education and Religious Liberty v. Regan* (1980), the Court considered the constitutionality of a New York statute that authorized the use of public funds to reimburse both secular and religious private schools for costs incurred in "the administration, grading, and . . . reporting of the results of [state-prepared and state-mandated] tests and examinations." The legislation was part of a state effort to make sure that private schools maintained minimal secular educational standards—an important goal given the significant percentage of the state's children who attended private schools. In a five-to-four decision, the Court sustained the constitutionality of the law.

Seven years earlier, the Supreme Court in *Levitt v. Committee for Public Education* (1973) struck down

an earlier version of the New York law that provided reimbursement for tests prepared by private school teachers, noting that it was impossible to determine whether such tests involved religious instruction. The Court concluded that "the State is constitutionally compelled to assure that the state-supported activity is not being used for religious indoctrination" and that the New York law failed to provide that assurance. In response, the New York legislature amended its statute to provide reimbursement only for the personnel costs incurred in grading and reporting the results of tests prepared by the *state*. The amended statute also imposed tight controls to make sure that state reimbursements did not exceed the value of the actual grading services provided by the private school teachers.

In assessing the constitutionality of the amended New York law, the Court applied the familiar "Lemon" test (from the Court's 1971 decision in *Lemon v. Kurtzman*) pursuant to which a law is constitutional "if it has a secular legislative purpose, if its principal or primary effect neither advances nor inhibits religion, and if it does not foster an excessive government entanglement with religion." The Court, with Justice Byron White writing, concluded that the amended law satisfied that test: "grading the secular tests furnished by the State . . . is a function that has a secular purpose and primarily a secular effect" since both the purpose and effect of the tests was to ensure that schoolchildren are being provided "an adequate secular education." Moreover, the amended New York law also provided for "ample safeguards against excessive or misdirected reimbursement," a feature absent from the original statute. In upholding the constitutionality of the New York statute, the Court relied on *Wolman v. Walter* (1977), a case in which the Court had upheld an Ohio statute whereby the state provided, among other things, state-prepared standardized tests and grading services to children attending sectarian schools.

Four justices—Harry Blackmun, William Brennan, Thurgood Marshall, and John Stevens—dissented. They emphasized that in *Wolman*, the statutory scheme "did not involve direct cash assistance" to any private school. In fact, the Ohio law at issue in *Wolman* involved only the provision of state-prepared tests to children attending sectarian schools, which were then graded by an independent commercial service, whereas the New York law reimbursed private schools for the cost of grading the tests and reporting the scores. For the dissenters, secular aid, like a standardized test, could be provided to children attending religious schools so long as no cash payments were made to the schools. The majority had found that feature constitutionally insignificant: "[The dissenters] insist on drawing a constitutional distinction between paying the nonpublic school to do the grading and paying . . . some independent service to perform that task, even though the grading function is the same regardless of who performs it . . . . In either event, the nonpublic school is being relieved of the cost of grading state-required, state-furnished examinations . . . . None of our cases require us to invalidate these reimbursements simply because they involve payments in cash."

By upholding the payment of monies to sectarian schools, the Court made a slight move in the direction of permitting greater government aid to religious schools—signaling the direction the Court would take over the course of the next quarter century.

DAVISON M. DOUGLAS

References and Further Reading

Avitabile, Alex S., *Comment. P.E.A.R.L. v. Regan: Permitting Direct State Aid to Parochial Schools,* Brooklyn Law Review 47 (1981): 469–515.
Pryor, Elizabeth Scott, *Comment. Permissible State Aid to Parochial Schools: A Plea for Neutrality,* Emory Law Journal 33 (1984): 487.

Cases and Statutes Cited

Lemon v. Kurtzman, 403 U.S. 602 (1971)
Levitt v. Committee for Public Education, 413 U.S. 472 (1973)
Wolman v. Walter, 433 U.S. 229 (1977)

See also **State Aid to Religious Schools**

COMMON LAW OR STATUTE

Common law is law that evolves over time based on custom, practice, and precedent from judicial decisions—it often is called judge-made law—and is found in cases and opinions. Statutory law, by comparison, represents law created by legislative bodies at the federal, state, and local level, ranging from the U.S. Congress to city councils and is found in compilations called codes, such as the U.S. Code embodying federal laws, or ordinances.

Although constitutional law is a primary source of civil liberties, both common law and statutory law directly affect and, sometimes, embody civil liberties. For instance, the common law developed and recognized a right to privacy long before the U.S. Supreme Court discovered a constitutional right to privacy in *Griswold v. Connecticut* (1965). Sometimes, however, the common law conflicts with civil liberties. For example, the common law of defamation that protects individuals' reputations restricts the civil liberty of

free speech embodied in the First Amendment. In that area, the Supreme Court was forced in *New York Times v. Sullivan* (1964) to adopt the actual malice standard to balance the common law's protection of reputation with the U.S. Constitution's protection of free expression.

Like the common law, statutory law can have both positive and negative effects on civil liberties. For instance, federal statutes have been enacted to protect voting rights and to prevent discrimination. Conversely, recently enacted federal statutes like the USA Patriot Act and the Homeland Security Act restrict the liberties of speech and privacy.

CLAY CALVERT

References and Further Reading

Holmes, Jr., Oliver Wendell. *The Common Law.* Boston: Little, Brown, & Co., 1881.

Cases and Statutes Cited

Griswold v. Connecticut, 381 U.S. 479 (1965)
Homeland Security Act, Public Law No. 107-296
New York Times v. Sullivan, 376 U.S. 254 (1964)
USA Patriot Act, Public Law No. 107-56

See also **Balancing Approach to Free Speech; Defamation and Free Speech; Freedom of Speech: Modern Period (1917–Present)**

COMMUNICATIONS DECENCY ACT (1996)

The Communications Decency Act (CDA) of 1996, an amendment to the Telecommunications Reform Act of 1996, aimed to protect children by regulating the content of the Internet. The legislation, introduced by Senator James Exon (D-Nebraska), could theoretically have led to the fining and imprisonment of anyone who used an offensive word in an electronic communication. It had the potential to smother both free expression and the infant Internet. The Supreme Court ruled this effort at censorship to be unconstitutionally broad in June 1997.

The CDA formed part of an effort to update laws relating to the telecommunications industry in light of dramatic technological advancements. While the other parts of the telecommunications bill removed barriers that restricted the growth of media business, Congress also decided to regulate the content of the material distributed by these companies. Previous communications law banned the deliberate telephone transmission of obscene material. The new CDA covered all methods of telecommunication. In addition, existing federal laws against importing obscene material or transporting such material across state lines for sale or distribution were now applicable to computer-transmitted materials.

The CDA prohibited the display of sexual and excretory material deemed "patently offensive" in "a manner available to a person under 18 years of age." It targeted both text and images in public areas of the Internet. In a revision of the CDA by the House, the indecency provision of the amendment was changed to update the 1873 Comstock Act. This amendment, introduced by longtime abortion opponent Representative Henry Hyde (R-Illinois), banned electronic dissemination of information "designed, adapted, or intended for producing abortion or for any indecent or immoral use or any . . . notice of any kind giving information, directly or indirectly, where, how, or of whom, or by what means any such mentioned article, matter, or things may be obtained or made . . . ." Violation of the CDA brought a penalty of up to two years in prison and a maximum fine of $250,000. The Senate approved the Telecommunications Reform Act by a vote of ninety-one to five with the House supporting it by a vote of 414 to sixteen. President Bill Clinton signed the bill into law on February 8, 1996.

Part of the problem with the legislation lay with Congress's lack of knowledge about electronic communication. Senator Patrick Leahy, an opponent of the CDA, estimated that only six other senators had used the Internet. Unfamiliar with the technology, they did not understand how the Internet worked. They apparently thought that it was like cable television, with channels that could easily be regulated. Senators were also unaware that much of the available pornography came from foreign sources that would not be affected by American laws.

The new law met with immediate opposition. The online community condemned the CDA as state-sanctioned censorship. The American Civil Liberties Union, along with twenty-five anticensorship organizations, filed a lawsuit against the Justice Department challenging the constitutionality of the law on the day that it went into effect. On February 26, 1996, a coalition of thirty-five groups, including the American Library Association, the Recording Industry Association of America, the National Writers Union, and commercial online providers America Online, CompuServe, Microsoft, and Prodigy, filed a second lawsuit against the CDA. Lawyers for the opponents of the CDA argued both that the law banned certain speech that was suitable for adults and that such a ban would be unenforceable. It would not be possible for online service providers to verify the identity and age of each person browsing the Internet.

On June 12, 1996, the U.S. District Court in Philadelphia imposed a preliminary injunction against enforcement of the CDA. The judges ruled that the CDA violated First Amendment guarantees of free speech and Fifth Amendment protections against vaguely defined criminal conduct. The judges stated that the government had provided no compelling reason to restrict speech. The availability of software that enabled parents to regulate the Internet use of their children led the judges to further conclude that the government had not met its obligation to use the least restrictive means to regulate speech.

The Justice Department, under Attorney General Janet Reno, appealed the decision. The Supreme Court ruled on June 26, 1997, in *Reno v. American Civil Liberties Union*, that the CDA was unconstitutional, because it was so broad that it would have banned material about breast cancer and AIDS awareness, as well as such art as Michelanglo's nude *David*. Seven justices supported the decision, with Justices Sandra Day O'Connor and William Rehnquist agreeing in part and dissenting in part. Congress has made subsequent efforts to restrict Internet content, but no bill was made into law.

CARYN E. NEUMANN

References and Further Reading

Drucker, Susan J., and Gary Gumpert, eds. *Real law @ Virtual Space: Communication Regulation in Cyberspace.* Cresskill, NJ: Hampton Press, 2005.
Godwin, Mike. *Cyber Rights: Defending Free Speech in the Digital Age.* Boston: MIT Press, 2003.

Cases and Statutes Cited

Telecommunications Act of 1996, Pub. LA. No. 104-104, 110 Stat. 56 (1996)

See also **Abortion; American Civil Liberties Union; Comstock, Anthony; Obscenity;** *Reno v. ACLU*, **521 U.S. 844 (1997)**

COMMUNISM AND THE COLD WAR

Formed in 1919, the Communist Party of the United States (CPUSA) grew to approximately 60,000 members during The Great Depression as it worked to eliminate poverty, racial inequality, and exploitation of workers. However, during the escalating Cold War of the late 1940s and 1950s, membership plummeted as many Americans took CPUSA members to be spying for the Soviet Union and, more generally, undermining American institutions and government. This perception became especially widespread after the victory of the Communists in the Chinese civil war and the Soviet Union's development of nuclear weapons, both in 1949. Private organizations and branches of the state and national governments expelled, investigated, and punished CPUSA members, suspected members, individual Communists, and fellow travelers. Many of these undertakings rode roughshod over Communists' civil liberties, but individuals and organizations defended their actions by underscoring the security concerns of the Cold War.

The most important private organizations to strike out against Communists were universities, labor unions, and the movie industry. Many universities dismissed faculty members, librarians, and research scientists because of real or merely suspected Communist sympathies. In the union movement the Congress of Industrial Organizations (CIO) had during the 1930s and 1940s come to include Communist-led unions, but in 1949 the CIO leadership expelled the electrical workers' union for supposed Communist leanings. Nine other leftist unions were subsequently expelled, and when the CIO merged with the American Federation of Labor (AFL) in 1955, the new AFL-CIO was avowedly anti-Communist. In Hollywood, after the House Committee on Un-American Activities (HUAC) investigated Communist infiltration of the movie industry, the industry began blacklisting Communists and suspected Communists, thereby ruining the careers of dozens of writers, actors, and technicians and indirectly reducing the social commentary included in movie fare.

Most large cities and states also contributed to the persecution of Communists during the Cold War. Southern cities were especially aggressive in attempting to drive out Communists, even though fewer Communists lived in the South than in any other region. Birmingham, Alabama, for example, passed an ordinance imposing a fine and six-month jail sentence for each day a Communist remained in Birmingham. Thirteen states had legislative committees or commissions comparable to HUAC. In 1953, Massachusetts' Special Commission to Study and Investigate Communism and Subversive Activities and Related Matters in the Commonwealth questioned eighty-five individuals regarding the CPUSA membership. Boston newspapers published their names and addresses, and many lost jobs and friends as a result. Many states enacted laws requiring state employees to sign loyalty oaths. Some states required members of the CPUSA and other Communist organizations to register, and a few states banned membership in organizations thought to be subversive. These laws' obviously impaired Communists' freedoms of speech, assembly, and association.

The most powerful threats to civil liberties came on the federal level, and all three branches of the federal government attempted to restrict and root out Communists. Congress passed the Smith Act (1940), which made advocating the overthrow of the U.S. government or belonging to an organization that did so a criminal offense; the Taft–Hartley Act (1947), which required union leaders to sign affidavits swearing they were not Communists; and the McCarren Act (1950), which required the CPUSA, members of CPUSA, and members of Communist front organizations to register with the federal government. Congress used HUAC and other committees in both the Senate and the House to investigate supposed Communists and Communist activities. Joseph McCarthy, a Senator from Wisconsin, was the most rabid of the red-baiters, and the term "McCarthyism" came to be used for assigning guilt by association, tarnishing reputations by innuendo, and manipulating public opinion. Congressional investigations by McCarthy and others discouraged Communists from exercising their rights to say and publish what they wished and from belonging to clubs, groups, and organizations of their choosing.

The executive branch did not stand in the way of this legislation but rather in some instances attempted an anti-Communist one-upmanship. President Harry S. Truman, for example, in 1947, established the Federal Loyalty Program by executive order. The Program led to the reprimand and termination of federal employees with Communist ties. J. Edgar Hoover's Federal Bureau of Investigation was an eager tracker of Communists, and attorneys in the Justice Department of course prosecuted supposed offenders under the new federal statutes and other existing laws. The most important prosecution was that of Eugene Dennis, General Secretary of the CPUSA, and ten other CPUSA leaders for violation of the Smith Act. The trial took place in 1949 in the federal courthouse in New York City's Foley Square and devolved into a government expose of the CPUSA. In the midst of Cold War hysteria it seemed not to matter that many of the broadsides and pamphlets the prosecution used as evidence were published before the enactment of the Smith Act.

When statutes and prosecutions were challenged in appeals to the Supreme Court, the nation's highest tribunal also proved susceptible to political paranoia. In *American Communications Association v. Dowds* (1950) the Court refused to toss out a federal law requiring union leaders to disavow the CPUSA. The Court also upheld the Smith Act conviction of CPUSA officials in *Dennis v. United States* (1951), rejecting in the process the argument that the law violated the First Amendment's guarantee of freedom of speech. A strong connection existed between the

Soviet Union and the CPUSA, the Court said, and Congress had the duty and power to prevent the CPUSA from advancing the Soviet Union's interest in the overthrow of the United States. The Smith Act did not impede free discussion but rather guarded against the advocacy of violence. Indeed, the Court maintained, the CPUSA's expressed intent to overthrow the United States presented a clear and present danger to the government.

Only in the 1960s did the government begin to acknowledge forcefully the rights and liberties of Communists. In 1964, for example, the Supreme Court ruled in *Aptheker v. Secretary of State*, that the revocation of Communist Party officials' passports under the Subversive Activities Control Act unconstitutionally denied the plaintiff's liberty to travel. More generally, the intolerance and stigmatizing that had so marked the late 1940s and 1950s abated. Even though the Vietnam War was fought in the 1960s and early 1970s in part to stop the successive fall of Southeast Asian governments to Communists, few blamed the unsuccessful war effort on domestic Communists. At the peak of the Cold War, by contrast, a fear was present in many circles of the Communists in our midst. Communists and suspected Communists saw their civil liberties ignored and were harmed in other ways as well. Intolerance and witch-hunting were part of American life, and the national mood was often repressed, suspicious, and paranoid.

DAVID RAY PAPKE

References and Further Reading

Belknap, Michael R. *Cold War Political Justice: The Smith Act, the Communist Party, and American Civil Liberties.* Westport: Greenwood Press, 1977.
Caute, David. *The Great Fear: The Anti-Communist Purge under Truman and Eisenhower.* New York: Simon & Schuster, 1978.
Haynes, John Earl. *Red Scare or Red Menace? American Communism and Anticommunism in the Cold War Era.* Chicago: Ivan R. Dee, 1996.
Kutler, Stanley I. *The American Inquisition: Justice and Injustice in the Cold War.* New York: Hill & Wang, 1982.
Selcraig, James Truett. *The Red Scare in the Midwest, 1945–1955.* Ann Arbor: UMI Research Press, 1982.
Steinberg, Peter L. *The Great "Red Menace": United States Prosecution of American Communists, 1947–1952.* Westport: Greenwood Press, 1984.

Cases and Statutes Cited

Aptheker v. Secretary of State, 378 U.S. 500 (1964)
American Communications Association v. Dowds, 339 U.S. 382 (1950)
Dennis v. United States, 341 U.S. 494 (1951)

See also **Blacklisting; Communist Party; Due Process; Extremist Groups and Civil Liberties; Hiss, Alger; McCarthy, Joseph; Rosenberg, Julius and Ethel; State Constitutions and Civil Liberties; Vinson Court; Warren Court**

COMMUNIST PARTY

One of the most significant developments during the First World War in 1917 was the overthrow of the despotic government controlled by Nicholas II, Czar of all of the Russians, on March 12, 1917.

On November 7, 1917, another revolution took place in Russia, this time led and controlled by the Bolshevi (Russian for "majority"). Like the leadership in the first revolution, they were influenced by the writings of Karl Marx. But the Bolshevi took Marx further under the leadership of V. I. Lenin, who called for a sudden and violent revolution, aimed at the creation of the "dictatorship of the proletariat."

The success of the communists led by Lenin preached a system of collective ownership of property. Given these goals (which would destroy capitalism) and the Soviet exit from World War I, it is understandable that nations coming out of the devastating war would see a significant threat to their political and economic way of life in the Russian Revolution of November 1917.

Indeed, within a matter of two years, Communist parties were organized throughout Western and Southern Europe and in Latin America. The Communist Party of the United States (CPUSA) was organized in 1919.

This nation and the world were rocked to the core by the devastating Great Depression of the 1930s. The Great Depression opened up the "Great Opportunity" for the Communist Party.

The Party worked mainly through unions (especially the Congress of Industrial Organizations—the C.I.O.) as the spearhead of its drive against capitalism, racism, and exploitation of the working class. Regardless of the terrible deprivations suffered by millions during the Great Depression, there was a deep-rooted antagonism against radicals and their solutions; the hope engendered by Franklin D. Roosevelt leading the nation in the "war" against the Great Depression showed the willingness to wait and give the economy a chance to recover. The "jump start" came in the form of World War II (1939–1945) in Europe and then in America. The Communist Party supported the war once Russia was attacked by Nazi Germany in June 1941; until then, the Party called for isolation from another capitalist war.

Through the 1930s, the CPUSA claimed the hearts and minds of a number of persons (including intellectuals, stage and movie stars) who approved of the announced program of the Party.

With the end of World War II, the alliance that won the war began to break apart. Instead of alliance, the world was introduced to the concept of a Cold War between the United States and its allies and Russia with Joseph Stalin as its communist leader. The domestic result of the Cold War between these countries was a Red Scare in the United States—a fear of communists, their Party, and those who followed in the path of their beliefs.

The Red Scare came as a result of a push to demonize all who were in the Party and those who agreed with the party line. The main figure was J. Edgar Hoover, Director of the Federal Bureau of Investigation (FBI). His aim was to destroy the Communist Party and all those who followed the Party program. He viewed the Party as a cancer on the nation's body. Hoover carried on his anticommunist crusade, even during those years when, with great energy, the CPUSA supported the war.

Using materials such as CPUSA internal meeting minutes, the FBI gathered information in clear violation of the Fourth Amendment. Illegal wiretaps, surreptitiously obtained letters, breaking into Party offices (Black Bag jobs), and a number of other quite illegal methods were used. Ultimately a criminal suit was filed against twelve national Party leaders.

The case, *Dennis v. United States*, 341 U.S. 497 (1951), was designed to break the back of the CPUSA and it did effectively do so, sending all defendants to jail, including all attorneys representing the defendants. All of the defendants were charged with violation of the Smith Act (1940), which made it a federal offense to advocate the forceful overthrow of the government. The times dictated the guilty verdicts for these defendants and for a parade of secondary CP functionaries.

At its height of membership during the 1930s, there were probably 80,000 CPUSA card-carrying members. By the end of the Dennis case (and those that followed), there were probably only 15,000–20,000 left.

Reeling from serious body blows in the American court system, from a Red Scare mentality that looked for "Reds under the beds," and the belief that all major problems in the nation and in the world were the result of the Communist Party and their followers, further reduced the number of members.

Even the charged attitude of the Supreme Court expressed in four cases decided in 1957 came too little

and too late to pump blood into the dying veins of the CPUSA.

The Communist Party was never outlawed as such, but that made no pragmatic difference. Some will argue that the Party killed itself with its slavish attachment to the Soviet Communist Party line. In all, it was a terrible time for liberalism, Communism, the CPUSA, and for the American justice system. It was also a time of harm to the body of civil, political, and economic freedoms in our nation.

ARTHUR J. SABIN

References and Further Reading

Buhle, Mari Jo, et al., eds. *Encyclopedia of the American Left*. New York and London: Garland Publishing, Inc., 1980.

Clifford, Clark, and Richard Holbrooke. *Counsel to the President: a Memoir*, New York: Random House, 1991.

Howe, Irving, and Lewis Closer. *The American Communist Party a Critical History*. New York: Fredrick A. Praeger, 1962.

Klingaman, William K. *Encyclopedia of the McCarthy Era*. New York: Facts on File, Inc., 1996.

Sabin, Arthur J. *In Calmer Times: The Supreme Court and Red Monday*. Philadelphia: University of Pennsylvania Press, 1999.

Schrecker, Ellen. "McCarthyism and the Decline of American Communism, 1945–1960" In Michael E. Brown, et al., eds. *New Studies in the Politics and Culture of U.S. Communism*, 123–140. New York: Monthly Review Press, 1993.

———. *Many are the Crimes: McCarthyism in America*, New York: Little, Brown, and Company, 1998.

COMPANY TOWNS AND FREEDOM OF SPEECH

With industrial development in the United States in the first half of the twentieth century, some companies found that it was more practical to provide housing for employees near the factory, mine, etc. They would buy a substantial amount of land, build homes, pave roads, and lay sewers. The resulting "company town" was like any other town in almost every respect, except that title rested in the companies' private hands. As large percentages of workers in many industries lived in company towns, the question arose as to whether individual liberties were protected.

In 1946, the Supreme Court held that on such land, while held in private hands, individuals still maintained constitutional rights. In *Marsh v. Alabama* the Court overturned the trespassing conviction of a Jehovah's Witness who had attempted to distribute literature in the company town Chickasaw, Alabama. The Court wrote, "The more an owner, for his advantage, opens up his property for use by the public in general, the more do his rights become circumscribed by the rights of those who use it." Chickasaw had been sufficiently opened to the public to mandate that First Amendment activity be allowed. The function to which the property was placed was tantamount, not where title to the land rested.

Company towns faded away, but the basic conflict did not. Analysis of individual rights on private property remains influenced by *Marsh*, such as in modern shopping centers, with proponents of greater individual liberties seeking protection under *Marsh* but private property owners often resisting.

MARK C. ALEXANDER

Cases and Statutes Cited

Marsh v. Alabama, 326 U.S. 501 (1946)

COMPELLING STATE INTEREST

Judicial review of government restrictions of individual rights takes different forms depending on the nature of the right and the infringement. The most stringent form, "strict scrutiny," requires that the restriction be necessary to serve a compelling state interest.

The modern Supreme Court demands a compelling state interest in essentially two circumstances. First, some (although not all) infringements on fundamental rights receive strict scrutiny. Fundamental rights include textually specified rights such as the protections of speech and religion found in the Bill of Rights, and also some unenumerated rights, such as the right to travel interstate or the right of access to the courts. Second, discrimination either with respect to a fundamental right or on the basis of a "suspect classification" will receive strict scrutiny under Equal Protection doctrine. Suspect classifications include race, national origin, religion, and alienage.

In essence, the demand for a compelling state interest is the codification of a balancing test that weighs the governmental regulatory interest against the individual's liberty. The specific demand for a "compelling" interest dates back to Justice Felix Frankfurter's 1957 concurring opinion in *Sweezy v. New Hampshire* and was adopted by the Court one year later in *NAACP v. Alabama*.

While there has been much debate over how and whether the Court should go about identifying unenumerated fundamental rights, the process of deeming an interest compelling has received much less attention. The Court has never clearly explained how it assesses the importance of an interest, and relatively few scholars have addressed the subject.

KERMIT ROOSEVELT, III

References and Further Reading

Gottlieb, Stephen, *Compelling Governmental Interests: An Essential but Unanalyzed Term in Constitutional Adjudication*, B.U. L. Rev. 68 (1988): 917.
Symposium, *Conference on Compelling Governmental Interests: The Mystery of Constitutional Analysis*, Alb. L. Rev. 55 (1992): 535.

Cases and Statutes Cited

Sweezy v. New Hampshire, 354 U.S. 234, 265 (1957)
NAACP v. Alabama, 357 U.S. 449, 463 (1958)

See also Balancing Test

COMPULSORY VACCINATION

The question of whether or not one can be forced to submit to a medical vaccination against a contagious disease pits the police power of the states found in Amendment X against the rights of the individual to due process in Amendment XIV. The police power is generally understood to include the requisite powers to secure the health, safety, and general welfare of the population. The question of compulsory vaccination reached the U.S. Supreme Court in the 1905 case of *Jacobson v. Massachusetts*. Because of the potential for deadly outbreaks of smallpox, the State of Massachusetts enacted a law that permitted cities to require residents to be vaccinated against the disease and provided for a fine of five dollars for failure to obtain the vaccination. Jacobson argued that he could not be compelled to submit to vaccination, because it would violate his constitutional rights under the Preamble and Amendment XIV. The requirement was, he asserted, unreasonable, arbitrary, and oppressive and interfered with his right to care for his own body and his own health. The Supreme Court quickly dismissed the allegation that the Preamble to the Constitution was the "source of any substantive power," but considered the question of whether the Massachusetts law violated the due process clause of Amendment XIV. Justice Harlan, writing for the majority, noted that many restraints are placed on an individual's liberties, but that these are necessary to protect the health of the larger community; a person or minority of people cannot dominate the greater good. The state could constitutionally require individuals to be vaccinated.

MARY L. VOLCANSEK

Cases and Statutes Cited

Jacobson v. Massachusetts, 197 U.S. 11 (1905)

COMSTOCK, ANTHONY (1844–1915)

Vice crusader Anthony Comstock was born in Connecticut in 1844. His father was Thomas Anthony Comstock, a farmer and sawmill owner, and his mother was Polly Lockwood. Comstock's mother died when he was ten, and he attended public schools in his youth in New Canaan and New Britain. During the Civil War, he served in the Union army for two years. After the war, he held a variety of jobs across New England and the South before settling in New York City. In 1871, he married Margaret Hamilton, and after their only child died in infancy, they adopted a daughter.

Comstock was deeply impressed, and even obsessed, with the disparities he saw between the moral "values" he believed most Americans possessed and the behavior that the government, meant to "protect" the people, would tolerate. Particularly concerned by growing urban centers that seemed large, impersonal, amoral, and indifferent to the "innocents" moving into them, Comstock set out to change governmental response to such immorality. Comstock won the support of influential persons who helped him organize a special committee of the Young Men's Christian Association to conduct a war on vice and, in essence, entrap criminals. When some YMCA members balked at such action, Comstock and friends formed the autonomous committee known as the New York Society for the Suppression of Vice. For the rest of his life, Comstock would serve as the society's secretary and principal agent with his friends providing him money, respectability, and influence. In 1873, together they persuaded Congress to strengthen the law against sending obscene material through the U.S. mail. Congress appointed Comstock as special agent of the U.S. Post Office with broad responsibilities for prosecuting the law's violators. Comstock held this position until his death.

In 1880, Comstock published a memoir of his ten-year crusade against vice entitled *Frauds Exposed; or, How the People are Deceived and Robbed, and Youth Corrupted, being a Full Disclosure of Various Schemes Operated through the Mails, and Unearthed by the Author.* In the book, he attacked lotteries, bogus banks, jewelry frauds, real estate scams, and false plans for medical aid to the poor. In all his work, Comstock consistently upheld his often-deviant means of entrapping violators, making strong-armed arrests, and his merciless persecution of violators in the courts. Some findings suggest that Comstock enjoyed somewhat widespread support. A special committee of the New York legislature not only absolved him of wrongdoing but also concluded that his work was vital and essential to the community's safety and decency, despite a petition circulating at the time signed by fifty thousand citizens calling for the repeal of all Comstock laws.

Later in his life, Comstock became obsessed with what he thought was a rising tide of obscenity. He managed to remove tons of pamphlets and paraphernalia from the U.S. mails pertaining to birth control and abortion. He prosecuted abortionist and contraceptionist Ann Trow Lohman (also known as Madame Restell) and rejoiced when she chose suicide over facing trial. Comstock also prosecuted Victoria Woodhull and her sister Tennessee Claflin for publishing an account in their newsletter *Weekly* of Henry Ward Beecher's extramarital affairs. Comstock also increasingly prosecuted artists and critics. In 1887, he raided a reproduction of French paintings, including many nudes, at Knoedler's Gallery in New York City. In response, the Society of American Artists condemned Comstock's interference. Comstock countered by publishing a pamphlet, *Morals vs. Art,* in which he delineated that morality overrode all other considerations, and art was only desirable if it promoted, or at least did not counter, morality.

Comstock also attacked books, including the popular turn-of-the-century dime novels that he believed led youths down a path of crime and asserted that even many literary classics should only be read by mature scholars. He also protested against exotic dancers, plays, and many other public amusements that he felt corrupted morality. Aware that his crusades actually drew much more attention to these "immoral" acts than would have otherwise with no such publicity, Comstock seemed to care little, deriving satisfaction from the many convictions he won, fines collected, and in general, vice suppressed. Comstock continued his crusade for moral absolutism until his death, influencing the federal government and many states to pass more stringent antiobscenity laws. He helped form other vice societies such as the New England Watch and Ward Society, and the Society for the Suppression of Vice remained in existence long after his death. He died in New Jersey in 1915.

MELISSA OOTEN

References and Further Reading

Beisel, Nicola Kay. *Imperiled Innocents: Anthony Comstock and Family Reproduction in Victorian America.* Princeton, NJ: Princeton University Press, 1997.
Broun, Heywood. *Anthony Comstock, Roundsman of the Lord.* Literary Guild of America, 1927.
Pivar, David. *Purity Crusade: Sexual Morality and Social Control, 1868–1900.* Westport, Conn.: Greenwood Press, 1973.

See also **Obscenity**

CONCEPT OF "CHRISTIAN NATION" IN AMERICAN JURISPRUDENCE

For much of American history, the U.S. Supreme Court and various state courts have characterized the United States as a "Christian nation." In recent years, however, courts have generally stopped making such references, and some justices and judges have expressly sought to distance themselves from these earlier proclamations.

During the nineteenth century, the Supreme Court issued several opinions in which it referred to the United States as a Christian nation. In *Vidal v. Girard's Executors* (1844), for example, a case involving a challenge to a will on the grounds that it devised property for a purpose "hostile to the Christian religion," the Court rejected the will challenge but did characterize the United States as a "Christian country." Similarly, in two slave trade cases, the Court characterized the United States as one of the "Christian nations" of the world: *The Antelope* (1825); *The Kate* (1864). Confronted with the question of the scope of American consulate jurisdiction, the Court in a few cases resolved the issue by distinguishing between the "Christian countries" and non-Christian countries of the world: *In re Ross* (1891); *Dainese v. Hale* (1875). Similarly, the Court repeatedly legitimated broad Congressional control over the property rights of Indian tribes, noting that Congress would be constrained by "such considerations of justice as would control a Christian people in their treatment of an ignorant and dependent race": *Beecher v. Wetherby* (1877). In the late nineteenth century, the Court decided a number of cases adverse to the interests of the Mormon religion, relying on the fact that certain Mormon practices such as polygamy were contrary to the "spirit of Christianity" and to the "laws of all civilized and Christian countries." See, for example, *The Late Corporation of the Church of Jesus Christ of Latter-Day Saints v. United States* (1890); *Davis v. Beason* (1890).

The Supreme Court's most forthright claim that the United States is a Christian nation, however, came in Justice David Brewer's opinion in *Church of the Holy Trinity v. United States* (1892). In that opinion, Brewer set forth a lengthy argument for his claim that the United States is a religious, and specifically Christian, nation in the context of analyzing the intent of Congress in enacting a particular statute. Justice Brewer quoted several colonial charters, state constitutions, and state supreme court decisions that referred to the central importance of Christian belief in the life of the American people; cited the practice of various legislative bodies of beginning their sessions with prayer; and noted the large number of churches

and Christian charitable organizations that exist in every community in the country as evidence that the United States is a Christian nation. In 1905, Justice Brewer expanded on his *Holy Trinity* decision in a series of lectures at Haverford College entitled "The United States is a Christian Nation," which were subsequently published as a book by the same title. Justice Brewer's contemporaries made similar observations about the American polity. For example, British observer Lord Bryce commented in his 1888 two-volume study of the United States, *The American Commonwealth*, that "Christianity is in fact understood to be, though not the legally established religion, yet the national religion."

During the nineteenth century, a few state supreme courts also asserted that Christianity was part of the common law of the United States. The Pennsylvania Supreme Court, for example, claimed that "Christianity . . . is, and always has been, a part of the common law of Pennsylvania": *Updegraph v. Commonwealth* (1824). The Ohio Supreme Court disagreed: The assertion that "'Christianity is a part of the common law of this country,' lying behind and above its constitutions . . . can hardly be serious . . . . The only foundation . . . for the proposition, that Christianity is part of the law of this country is the fact that it is a Christian country, and that its constitutions and laws are made by a Christian people": *Board of Education of Cincinnati v. Minor* (1872).

During the twentieth century, the Supreme Court stopped characterizing the United States as a Christian nation. In *United States v. Macintosh* (1931), the Court rejected an application for citizenship on the grounds that the applicant, claiming religious objections, had refused to pledge his unconditional support for this nation's future war efforts. Justice George Sutherland, writing for a narrow majority, noted that "[w]e are a Christian people . . . acknowledging with reverence the duty of obedience to the will of God," and that obedience to the nation's military endeavors was "not inconsistent with the will of God." The *Macintosh* decision was the last time that the Supreme Court expressly characterized the United States as a Christian nation, although in 1952, in *Zorach v. Clauson*, Justice William Douglas did write for the Court that "[w]e are a religious people whose institutions presuppose a Supreme Being."

Even after the Supreme Court stopped referring the United States as a Christian nation, some state court judges continued to do so. The Mississippi Supreme Court announced in 1950 that "[o]ur great country is denominated a Christian nation": *Paramount-Richards Theatres v. City of Hattiesburg* (1950). The Oklahoma Supreme Court claimed in

1959: "[I]t is well settled and understood that ours is a Christian Nation, holding the Almighty God in dutiful reverence": *Oklahoma v. Williamson* (1959). In 1998, Alabama state judge Roy Moore defended the display of the Ten Commandments in his courtroom on the grounds that the U.S. Supreme Court in *Holy Trinity* had recognized that "the United States is a Christian Nation": *In re State of Alabama ex rel. James v. ACLU of Alabama* (1998).

But in recent years, some Supreme Court justices and lower federal court judges have attempted to distance the courts from its "Christian nation" heritage. In *Lynch v. Donnelly* (1984), for example, Justice William Brennan criticized the Court's decision upholding a governmental display of a creche as "a long step backwards to the days when Justice Brewer could arrogantly declare for the Court that 'this is a Christian nation.'" Similarly, writing for the U.S. Court of Appeals for the Sixth Circuit, Judge Avern Cohn noted in 2000: "We have come a long way from when it was acceptable that . . . a member of Congress could introduce a bill [in 1880] saying, 'Whereas, The people of the United States are a Christian people, and firmly believe in God, the Father Almighty, Maker of heaven and earth; and in Jesus Christ His only Son, our Lord . . .', . . . or that the Supreme Court of Oklahoma could say: 'it is well settled and understood that ours is a Christian Nation, holding the Almighty God in dutiful reverence'": *American Civil Liberties Union v. Capital Square Review and Advisory Board* (2000).

DAVISON M. DOUGLAS

References and Further Reading

Brewer, David. *The United States a Christian Nation*. Philadelphia: J.C. Winston Co., 1905.

Bryce, James Bryce. *The American Commonwealth*. 3 volumes. New York: Macmillan & Co., 1888.

Green, Steven K., *Justice David Josiah Brewer and the 'Christian Nation' Maxim*, Albany Law Review 63 (1999): 427–476.

Hylton, J. Gordon, *David Josiah Brewer and the Christian Constitution*, Marquette Law Review 81 (1998): 417–425.

Cases and Statutes Cited

American Civil Liberties Union v. Capital Square Review and Advisory Board, 210 F.3d 703 (6th Cir. 2000)

The Antelope, 23 U.S. 66 (1825)

Beecher v. Wetherby, 95 U.S. 517 (1877)

Board of Education of Cincinnati v. Minor, 23 Ohio St. 211 (1872)

Church of the Holy Trinity v. United States, 143 U.S. 457 (1892)

Dainese v. Hale, 91 U.S. 13 (1875)

Davis v. Beason, 133 U.S. 333 (1890)

In re Ross, 140 U.S. 453 (1891)

In re State of Alabama ex rel. James v. ACLU of Alabama, 711 So.2d 952 (Ala. 1998)

The Kate, 69 U.S. 350 (1864)

Late Corporation of the Church of Jesus Christ of Latter Day Saints v. United States, 136 U.S. 1 (1890)

Lynch v. Donnelly, 465 U.S. 668 (1984)

Oklahoma v. Williamson, 1959 Ok 207 (1959)

Paramount-Richards Theatres v. City of Hattiesburg, 210 Miss. 271 (1950)

United States v. Macintosh, 283 U.S. 605 (1931)

Updegraph v. Commonwealth, 11 Serg. & Rawle 394 (Pa. 1824)

Vidal v. Girard's Executors, 43 U.S. 127 (1844)

Zorach v. Clauson, 343 U.S. 306 (1952)

See also **Douglas, William Orville**

CONFRONTATION AND COMPULSORY PROCESS

Constitutional Bases

Adopted in 1791, the Sixth Amendment of the U.S. Constitution guarantees the defendant in a criminal trial the right "to be confronted with the witnesses against him," and "to have compulsory process for obtaining witnesses in his favor."

The confrontation clause is designed to ensure the truthfulness of witness testimony against a defendant in a criminal trial. It accomplishes this by forcing the prosecution's witnesses to testify in front of the party on trial and by allowing the defendant's counsel to challenge the credibility and reliability of the witness's testimony through cross-examination.

Also, rules of evidence such as Rule 801—the Hearsay Rule—of the Federal Rules of Evidence, stems from the Sixth Amendment right to confrontation and precludes the prosecution in a criminal trial from using as evidence statements made by witnesses not actually present at trial. The U.S. Supreme Court has carved out a number of exceptions to this rule, including instances where the prosecution is able to show a good-faith, but unsuccessful, effort in getting a witness to testify. For exceptions, see Federal Rules of Evidence 801(d)(E) through 804.

The compulsory process clause provides a defendant the court's subpoena power to compel witnesses to testify. To exercise this right, a defendant must demonstrate that the witness's testimony would be relevant, suitable, and favorable to him or her.

The confrontation and compulsory process clauses have grown in scope through a number of key U.S. Supreme Court cases.

Confrontation Clause

In drafting the Sixth Amendment, the Framers intended to incorporate the common law right to confrontation to prevent in the United States the type of abuses suffered by the likes of Sir Walter Raleigh in his trial in England. See, *United States v. Inadi*, 475 U.S. 387, 411 (1986). When John Adams was a defense attorney in a criminal case he said— "[e]xaminations of witnesses upon Interrogatories, are only by the Civil Law. Interrogatories are unknown at common Law, and Englishmen and common Lawyers have an aversion to them if not an Abhorrence of them": 2 Legal Papers of John Adams 207 (Wroth and Zobel eds., 1965).

The U.S. Supreme Court has found violations of the Confrontation Clause when the prosecution introduced at trial statements from accomplices and witness that were not subject to cross-examination. See, *Lilly v. Virginia*, 527 U.S. 116 (1999) (custodial confession of accomplice); *Idaho v. Wright*, 497 U.S. 805 (1990) (statements by victim to doctor made with participation of police investigating defendant); *Lee v. Illinois*, 476 U.S. 530 (1986) (accomplice's custodial confession); *Berger v. California*, 393 U.S. 314 (1969) (*per curiam*) (testimony from preliminary hearing); *Brookhart v. Janis*, 384 U.S. 1 (1966) (confession of accomplice taken during interrogation); and *Pointer v. Texas*, 380 U.S. 400 (1965) (testimony at preliminary hearing).

In the well-known case of *Bruton v. United States*, 391 U.S. 123 (1968), the Court held that in a joint trial the Confrontation Clause prohibits the admission of the codefendant who does not testify when the confession also incriminates the defendant. See also *Roberts v. Russell*, 392 U.S. 293 (1968) (per curiam); *Cruz v. New York*, 481 U.S. 186 (1987); and, *Gray v. Maryland*, 523 U.S. 185 (1998). But, the Court has also allowed the use of prior testimony from a witness against the accused because the witness was subject to cross-examination during the prior testimony. See *Ohio v. Roberts*, 448 U.S. 56 (1980), one of the most significant cases in confrontation jurisprudence. And, in *Bourjaily v. United States*, 483 U.S. 171 (1987), the Court allowed co-conspirator's statement to another co-conspirator); *United States v. Inadi*, 475 U.S. 387 (1986) (same); *Dutton v. Evans*, 400 U.S. 74 (1970) (same).

In the recent confrontation landmark case of *Crawford v. Washington*, 541 U.S. 36 (2004), the Court reaffirmed a principle in one of its line of cases that the Sixth Amendment right to confrontation precludes the admission of "testimonial" hearsay unless the witness is unavailable and there was a prior opportunity for full cross-examination. This controversial decision has been viewed as a double-edged sword by commentators. See *Crawford v. Washington*: A Critique. Miguel A. Mendez; Stanford Law Review, Vol. 57, 2004.

Compulsory Process

In *Washington v. Texas* (388 U.S. 14 (1967)), the Court found that through the Fourteenth Amendment, the Sixth Amendment compulsory process clause extends to criminal trials in state courts. It further held that principals, accomplices, and accessories to a crime might be introduced as witnesses for co-defendants to the same crime(s). In *Washington* the Court stated of this concept:

> The right to offer the testimony of witnesses, and to compel their attendance, if necessary, is in plain terms the right to present a defense, the right to present the defendant's version of the facts as well as the prosecution's to the jury so it may decide where the truth lies. Just as an accused has the right to confront the prosecution's witnesses for the purpose of challenging their testimony, he has the right to present his own witnesses to establish a defense. This right is a fundamental element of due process of law . . . .

Washington at 19-23. This right is not absolute. The compulsory process right is not absolute, and a court may refuse to allow a defense witness to testify where defense counsel did not identify the desired witness to gain a tactical advantage. See *Taylor v. Illinois*, 484 U.S. 400 (1988). See also *United States v. Wallace*, 32 F.3d 921 (5th Cir. 1994).

The compulsory process clause has also been the subject of debate in two notorious cases involving the U.S. President—*Clinton v. Jones*, 520 U.S. 681 (1997) and *United States v. Nixon*, 418 U.S. 683 (1974).

EZEKIEL E. CORTEZ

References and Further Reading

Amar, Akhil Reed. *The Constitution and Criminal Procedure*. 129–131 & n.194, 1997.
Berger, Margaret A., *The Deconstitutionalization of the Confrontation Clause: A Proposal for a Prosecutorial Restraint Model*, Minn. L. Rev. 76 (1992): 559.
Dickinson, Joshua C., *The Confrontation Clause and the Hearsay Rule: The Current State of a Failed Marriage in Need of a Quick Divorce*, Creighton L. Rev. 33 (2000): 763.
Friedman, Richard D., *Confrontation: The Search for Basic Principles*, Geo. L. Rev. 86 (1998): 1011.
"The Voice Of Adjudication": The Sixth Amendment Right To Compulsory Process Fifty Years After *United States*

Ex Rel. Touhy v. Ragen, Milton Hirsh, *Florida State University Law Review* Vol. 30:81.

See also **Confrontation Clause; Defense, Right to Present**

CONFRONTATION CLAUSE

The Confrontation Clause of the Sixth Amendment to the U.S. Constitution declares, "In all criminal proceedings, the defendant shall enjoy the right . . . to be confronted with the witnesses against him." The Clause protects a criminal defendant's presumptive guarantee of an opportunity for effective *face-to-face* cross-examination of his accusers. The Clause is thus implicated in a child abuse case in which the child testifies in a separate room visible to the defendant only by closed circuit television or in admitting the child's hearsay statements even when he or she has never testified under oath.

The Clause cannot be understood in isolation but rather must be seen as complementing other Sixth Amendment rights, such as those to a public trial by jury with the effective assistance of counsel. Together, these rights make "crucial workings of the government visible and keep . . . the overwhelming prosecutorial powers of the government in check." Public cross-examination in a public trial helps to ensure that any effort by the prosecution to shape tainted evidence in secret or by improper methods faces public scrutiny.

The confrontation concept has ancient roots, particularly in English trials challenging civil-law–like trials by affidavit. During the American Revolutionary period, the right became associated with the struggle to enhance citizen power against the state, and its absence from the original, unamended constitution was one of the reasons cited by Anti-Federalists for their opposition to ratification of that document. Many historians thus see the direct purpose of the Clause as restraining government power.

The U.S. Supreme Court has apparently come to agree. Recently it replaced the *Ohio v. Roberts* test for admitting hearsay, which required proof of reliability by means of "particularized guarantees of trustworthiness" or a showing that a hearsay exception was "firmly rooted" in American history. This nearly toothless test was overruled in *Crawford v. United States,* which held that "testimonial" hearsay statements may not be used at trial unless the declarant is then unavailable and the accused had a prior opportunity for cross-examining the witness. The Court was vague about its definition of "testimonial," but it clearly requires government involvement in creating evidence or the witness's expectation of such involvement. Although commentators generally agree that the *Crawford* test will do a better job than *Roberts* in restraining the state and is more consistent with the Clause's history, some authors worry that *Crawford* will make it harder for the criminal justice system to protect vulnerable populations. In particular, in child abuse, elder abuse, and battered women cases, victims are often afraid, and unwilling to testify. Other commentators worry instead that *Crawford* does not go far enough, the opportunity for "effective" cross-examination being meaningless unless supplemented by broad defense rights to pretrial discovery so that defense counsel has the informational tools with which to wage war with Leviathan.

ANDREW E. TASLITZ

References and Further Reading

Amar, Akhil Reed. *The Constitution and Criminal Procedure.* 125–131 1997.
Berger, Margaret, *The Deconstitutionalization of the Confrontation Clause: A Proposal for a Prosecutorial Restraint Model,* Minn. L. Rev. 76 (1992): 557.
Douglass, John G., *Beyond Admissibility: Real Confrontation, Virtual Cross-Examination, and the Right to Confront Hearsay,* Geo. Wash. L. Rev. 67 (1999): 191.
Mosteller, Robert M., *Crawford v. Washington: Encouraging and Ensuring the Confrontation of Witnesses,* Richmond L. Rev. 39 (2005): 511.
Raeder, Myrna, *Domestic Violence, Child Abuse, and Trustworthiness Exceptions After Crawford,* Crim. J. 20 (2005): 24.
Symposium Issue, *Crawford and Hearsay: One Year Later,* Crim. J. 20 (2005): 1–80.
Taslitz, Andrew E., *What Remains of Reliability and Freestanding Due Process After Crawford v. Washington,* Crim. J. 20 (2005): 39.

See also **Confrontation and Compulsory Process; Defense, Right to Present**

CONGRESSIONAL PROTECTION OF PRIVACY

Congress has often lagged behind other institutions in the protection of individual privacy. State laws often provide greater privacy protections than their federal counterparts, and courts and legal commentators have often presaged Congressional action. Despite its general laggardness, however, Congress' forays into privacy law are numerous and varied. When Congress does act, it often seems torn between competing values: individual freedom vs. national security, or individual privacy vs. free-market principles. As a result, Congressional protection of privacy often falls far short of what privacy advocates would urge and, in most cases, below that of even state legislative efforts.

The earliest federal efforts to protect privacy centered on the Census of the Population and the Census of Manufactures. The nineteenth and early twentieth centuries saw various Congressional attempts to assure citizens that any information gathered under the Censuses would be held in strictest confidence. Congress passed laws criminalizing the disclosure of any nonstatistical data gathered by the Censuses.

Other than the Census, however, Congress was slow to act to protect information privacy concerns. While state courts and legislators were busy developing various legal remedies to protect individual privacy, Congress was silent. It was not until various high-profile controversies, including Watergate and revelations of FBI profiling of civil rights activists, that Congress began to act. A number of important privacy-related hearings were held by Congress in the 1960s and, as a result, a consensus began to emerge that some federal laws were required to protect individual privacy and curb government excesses.

Although most privacy advocates urged Congress to pass a comprehensive privacy law, governing all data collection, compilation, and dissemination practice in the public and private sectors, Congress chose to pass narrower laws that generally left the free-market unregulated. The Privacy Act (1974) did apply to all information held by the federal government and included a number of important rights for citizens such as the right to be notified of information uses, the right to access government files, and the power to have errors corrected. Despite the Privacy Act's broad protections, it did not apply to the private sector.

Private sector regulation was limited to specific areas where the data in question were believed to be highly sensitive. As a result, Congress in the 1970s did pass a number of laws to protect credit information, Fair Credit Reporting Act (1970), financial privacy, Right to Financial Privacy Act (1978), and education records: Family Education Rights and Privacy Act (1974). A number of laws were also passed to limit the federal government's power to engage in surveillance of citizens, Wiretap Statute (1968, 1970), Foreign Intelligence Surveillance Act (1978), and to, later, to protect electronic and digital communications and information: Electronic Communications Privacy Act (1986), Computer Fraud and Abuse Act (1984). These acts, amended from time to time, reveal Congress' general intent to leave the private sector generally free from privacy regulation while protecting those areas deemed most dangerous and sensitive.

This piecemeal approach continued throughout the 1980s and to the present. Over the last few decades, Congress has passed laws to protect video rental information, Video Privacy Protection Act (1998); drivers' license information, Drivers Privacy Protection Act (1996); data related to television and telephone habits, Cable Privacy Protection Act (1984), Telephone Consumer Protection Act (1991), strengthened financial privacy, Gramm-Leach-Bliley (1999); and passed strong medical data privacy legislation, *HIPAA* (1996).

The last decade has witnessed strong pressure on Congress to pass new laws protecting online privacy and, in the aftermath of 9/11, to pass laws that balance privacy and security interests. Passage of the USA PATRIOT Act (2001) reworked many prior privacy rules and granted the federal government increased antiterrorism powers to investigate and use data previously held confidential under various laws and regulations. As technologies and new national security threats emerge, Congress will be asked to review its current approaches. Numerous privacy advocates continue to call for more comprehensive privacy legislation that would regulate all private and public sector data collection. Although Congress has seldom been visionary in its privacy laws, there is no doubt that this is an issue that will increasingly form part of its agenda.

DOUGLAS J. SYLVESTER

References and Further Reading

Burnham, David A. *The Rise of the Computer State*. New York: Random House, 1983.

Cate, Fred H., *et al.*, *Financial Privacy, Consumer Prosperity, and the Public Good*. Washington, DC: Brookings Institution Press, 2003.

Hisson, Richard T. *Privacy in a Public Society: Human Rights in Conflict*. New York: Oxford University Press, 1987.

Packard, Vance O. *The Naked Society*. New York: Pocket Books, 1964.

Sylvester, Douglas J., and Sharon M. Lohr, *The Security of Our Secrets: A History Of Privacy And Confidentiality In Law And Statistical Practice*, Denver University Law Review, vol. 83, no. 1 (2005).

Warren, Stephen A., and Louis Brandeis, *The Right to Privacy*, Harvard Law Review, vol. 4. no. 1 (1890): 193–220.

Westin, Alan F. *Privacy and Freedom*. New York: Atheneum, 1967.

Cases and Statutes Cited

Cable Privacy Protection Act of Oct. 30, 1984, 98 Stat. 2794

Computer Fraud and Abuse Act of Oct. 12, 1984, Pub.L. 98-473, 98 Stat. 2190

Fair and Accurate Credit Transaction Act of Dec. 4, 2003, 111 Stat. 1952

Fair Credit Reporting Act of Oct. 26, 1970, c. 41, 84 Stat. 1127

Foreign Intelligence Surveillance Act of 1978, Pub. L. No. 95-511, 92 Stat. 1783

Health Insurance Portability and Accountability Act of Aug. 21, 1996 ("HIPAA"), 110 Stat. 2023

Right to Financial Privacy Act of Nov. 10, 1978, P.L. No. 95-630, 92 Stat. 3697

Telephone Consumer Protection Act of 1991, 105 Stat. 2394

The Driver's Privacy Protection Act of Sept. 13, 1994, 108 Stat. 2099

The Electronic Communications Privacy Act of 1986 ("ECPA"), 100 Stat. 1848

The Family Educational Rights and Privacy Act, Pub. L. No. 93-380, 88 Stat. 571

The Financial Modernization Act of Nov. 12, 1999 ("Gramm-Leach-Bliley Act"), 113 Stat. 1445

The Privacy Act of 1974, Pub. L. No. 93-579, 88 Stat. 1896

Title III of the Omnibus Crime Control and Safe Streets Act of 1968 ("Wiretap Statute"), 82 Stat. 211

Uniting and Strengthening America by Providing Appropriate Tools Required to Intercept and Obstruct Terrorism ("USA PATRIOT Act"), Act of Oct. 26, 2001, PL 107-56, 115 Stat. 272

Video Privacy Protection Act, Act of Oct.21, 1998, P.L. No. 100-618, 102 Stat. 3195

See also **Anonymity in Online Communications; Cable Television Regulation; Electronic Surveillance, Technological Monitoring, and Dog Sniffs; Fair Credit Reporting Act, 84 Stat. 1127 (1970); Freedom of Information Act (1966); National Security; 9/11 and the War on Terrorism; Nixon, Richard Milhous; Omnibus Crime Control and the Safe Streets Act of 1968 (92 Stat. 3795); Privacy; Privacy, Theories of; State Constitution, Privacy Provisions; Terrorism and Civil Liberties; Video Privacy Protection Act (1980); Wiretapping Laws**

CONNALLY v. GEORGIA, 429 U.S. 245 (1977)

After a search of John Connally's house, marijuana was seized based on a search warrant issued by a local justice of the peace. Connally was then indicted, tried, and convicted in the Superior Court of Georgia in Walker County for possession of marijuana in violation of the Georgia Controlled Substances Act.

Connally appealed his conviction to the Supreme Court of Georgia, and later to the U.S. Supreme Court, on the basis that the justice of the peace who issued the warrant was not a neutral party because he had an interest in issuing the warrant. Georgia Code allowed a justice of the peace to charge $5 for issuing a warrant. If no warrant was issued, they could receive no fee. The fee was given to the county, which then paid the fee to the issuing justice.

The Supreme Court held that the Georgia statute was not valid because of its linkage of receiving compensation for warrants granted. The decision relied on the precedent set in *Tumey v. Ohio*, which held that an officer of the court could not issue a warrant when he or she had direct gain in the manner. The justice of the peace stood to benefit financially by issuing a warrant, which, therefore, might cloud his judgment when

deciding whether to issue or deny the warrant. The issuance of this search warrant was found to be in violation of the protections provided by the Fourth and Fourteenth Amendments of the U.S. Constitution.

CAROL WALKER

References and Further Reading

LaFave, Wayne R. *Search and Seizure: A Treatise on the Fourth Amendment*, 4th ed. St. Paul, Minn.: West, 2004.

Maltz, Earl. *The Fourteenth Amendment and the Law of the Constitution*. Durham, NC: Carolina Academic Press, 2003.

Wilson, Bradford P. *Enforcing the Fourth Amendment: A Jurisprudential History*. New York: Garland Press, 1986.

Cases and Statutes Cited

Tumey v. Ohio, 273 U.S. 510 (1927)

See also **Due Process; Impartial Decisionmaker**

CONNOR, EUGENE "BULL" (1897–1973)

Eugene "Bull" Connor, born in Selma, Alabama, in 1897 was commissioner of public safety in Birmingham during civil rights crusades of the 1950s and 1960s. His confrontation with Martin Luther King, Jr., in 1963 brought him notoriety as the ugly face of southern racism.

In his six terms as chief law officer in Birmingham between 1937 and 1953 and 1957 and 1963, Connor's reputation and political support thrived on his staunch enforcement of racial segregation. His leadership of the public safety department was based on racism and cronyism. After a sexual scandal forced him out of office in 1953, he fought his way back to power four years later with appeals to white fears of racial integration. His strong support of segregation, however, set him on a collision course with the increasingly assertive civil rights movement.

The nation had its first glimpse of Bull Connor's tactics in the spring of 1961, when Freedom Riders set off on an interstate bus journey through the South to publicize the persistence of segregated bus terminals. After violent collisions with whites in Rock Hill, South Carolina, and Anniston, Alabama, riders were greeted at the Birmingham bus station by Ku Klux Klan thugs who beat the protesters as they exited from the bus. The absence of any police protection for the riders occurred as a result of an arrangement between Connor and the Klan to allow Klansmen fifteen minutes to work on the passengers.

Two years later, in May 1963, Connor's reputation as an ugly, stubborn racist was reinforced when the commissioner was confronted by Reverend Martin

Luther King, Jr.'s civil rights crusade. Birmingham, which King had characterized as the most segregated city in the South, was riven by racial tensions. White businessmen had been economically damaged by months of black boycotts of the segregated downtown stores that had only white restrooms. Connor's vigorous enforcement of the city's segregation ordinances had eventually driven many of Birmingham's business leaders to introduce a city government reform plan that would eliminate Connor's office. Meanwhile, for months King and the Southern Christian Leadership Conference had been staging demonstrations against the city's segregated facilities. The civil rights marches, however, by May, had been attracting diminishing participation, even after King himself went to jail for defying an injunction not to march. King decided to boost the flagging support for his crusade by sending hundreds of children out into the streets day after day. After mass arrests had filled city jails, Connor ordered the use of high-pressure fire hoses and police dogs to turn back the demonstrators. The televised brutal confrontation between defenseless black children, snarling dogs, and apparently heartless police brought the obscenity of southern racism directly into the living rooms of Northern whites. King's strategy did, in fact, energize Northern liberals, as well as the Kennedy administration, leading to the passage of the Civil Rights Act of 1964 that would finally outlaw segregation in public facilities. In Birmingham, the resulting economic consequences of racial disorder propelled white business owners in the city to more actively negotiate with civil rights leaders over accommodating black demands. Connor, himself, was forced out of office finally at the end of the May 1963 as the result of the structural reform of Birmingham's city government. He ended his public career, safely shelved by the white business community, as president of the Alabama Public Services Commission until his retirement in 1972.

Bull Connor became the symbol of the intransigent Southern racism of the civil rights era. Ironically, however, it was Connor's obstinate defense of segregation in Birmingham that ultimately was the catalyst for its demise. Speaking about his effect on the administration's civil rights bill of 1963, President John F. Kennedy observed that Connor had done as much for civil rights as had Abraham Lincoln.

KAREN BRUNER

References and Further Reading

Branch, Taylor. *Parting of the Waters: American in the King Years: 1954–1963*. New York: Simon and Schuster, 1988.
Nunnelly, William A. *Bull Connor*. Tuscaloosa, AL: University of Alabama Press, 1991.

CONSCIENTIOUS OBJECTION, THE FREE EXERCISE CLAUSE

The first amendment to the U.S. Constitution provides "Congress shall make no law respecting an establishment of religion, or prohibiting the free exercise thereof; or abridging the freedom of speech, or of the press; or the right of the people peaceably to assemble, and to petition the government for a redress of grievances." The restraint on prohibitions of the free exercise of religion has significant implications for conscientious objectors to government regulation including military conscription.

Conscientious objectors are those who are unable to comply with a regulation because of a sincerely held conviction. The objector may seek to be exempt from an affirmative regulation requiring behavior, such as a military draft, or a prohibitory regulation preventing certain behavior such as the wearing of religious garb.

The free exercise clause protects some religiously motivated objections, although other law may accommodate additional types of objections. In military conscription cases, for example, current law recognizes objections based on religious belief, as well as on dictates of conscience equivalent to a sincerely held religious belief. Although a statute regulates the exemption of conscientious objectors from military conscription, the free exercise clause apparently motivated the legislature to enact the series of statutes, and it continues to guide the Court in its interpretation of the statute. The statute, 50 USC 456(j), states that "Nothing contained in this title shall be construed to require any person to be subject to combatant training and service in the armed forces of the United States who, by reason of religious training and belief, is conscientiously opposed to war in any form." It continues to distinguish "religious training and belief" from a "merely personal moral code." This statute expanded earlier exemption statutes that required membership in religious institutions. The current statute allows those unaffiliated with a religious institution to claim conscientious objector status. It recognizes objection to all wars but not to specific wars. This provision of the statute has been upheld but not extended by the U.S. Supreme Court. See *Gillette v United States*, 401 U.S. 437, 1971.

Conscientious objector cases often turn on an objection to regulations supporting war, but they may also be about the right to an exemption from regulation to permit an exercise of religion such as the wearing of religious clothing, the ritual use of regulated drugs, marriage practices such as polygamy, or the taking of oaths. The clause also has implications for a wide range of military-related issues from forced conscription to mandatory participation in other programs such as high school ROTC programs and even unemployment law.

Early cases involving the free exercise clause distinguished between belief and conduct, so that while belief was unfettered, conduct could be regulated. See *Reynolds v U.S.*, 98 U.S. 145 (1879). A long line of Mormon and Seventh Day Adventist cases expanded and contracted the scope of the protection before *Sherbert v Verner* 374 US 398 (1963) adopted the requirement of a "compelling state interest" to justify burdening the free exercise of religion. *Gillette* (401 U.S. 437) used this compelling interest test to deny CO status to a draft registrant who objected to the Vietnam War but not to wars of national defense. Justice Douglas dissented that "conscience and belief were the main ingredients of First Amendment rights of free speech and religion" and "that the statute as written was constitutionally infirm under the First Amendment." Douglas's view that "if exemption was afforded to persons holding religious or conscientious scruples against all wars, so must it be afforded to those with religious or conscientious objection to participation in particular wars." The majority rejected this argument, deciding that the government interest in a fair exemption system outweighed the right of conscience.

Conscientious objection cases require statutory construction of 50 USC 456 to measure it against Constitutional requirements of the establishment, free exercise, and even due process clauses. Exemptions for conscientious objectors have been used since early colonial days. In *U.S. v Macintosh*, 283 U.S. 605,633 (1931), Chief Justice Hughes noted that such exemptions are "indicative of the actual operation of the principles of the Constitution." Modern cases extended the religious belief requirement to beliefs that fill the same function as religious beliefs, although the Justices often split on the rationale for such an exemption. In *United States v. Seeger*, 380 U.S. 163 (1965), the Court extended the statutory exemption to a nontheist whose conscience did not permit participation in war but who did not identify his belief as religious in nature (the 1948 statute, Provision 6(j) of the Universal Military Training and Service Act of 1948, required that the objection be based on a belief in a Supreme Being). The Court held that a belief occupying the place of religion would suffice. The *Seeger* analysis centered on the Establishment Clause's prohibition on establishing a particular religion, but Justice Douglas noted in a concurrence that the free exercise and equal protection clauses prohibit preferring one religion over another.

Welsh v. United States, 398 U.S. 333 (1970), followed *Seeger*, and the plurality opinion revealed the complexity of the Court's analysis of exemption cases. Welsh reversed the conviction of Elliott Welsh II who had a deeply held conviction to war as unethical and immoral, although he did not identify this as religious nor profess belief in a Supreme Being. The majority evaluated the intensity and sincerity of the belief. Justice Harlan's concurrence rejected the majority's reliance on intensity as a valid test of compliance with the statute. He noted that the statute violated the establishment clause and that the language of the statute "cannot be construed . . . to exempt from military service all individuals who in good faith oppose all war . . ." (See *Welsh* at 348–354). Rather, the exemption should be reconciled with the establishment clause by specifically including "those like the petitioner who have been unconstitutionally excluded from its coverage" (*Welsh* at 367).

The *Welsh* dissent, however, noted the close relationship of the establishment and free exercise clauses. While Congress intended to exclude purely moral objections, "Congress may have granted the exemption because otherwise religious objectors would be forced into conduct that their religions forbid and because in the view of Congress to deny the exemption would violate the free exercise clause or at least raise grave problems in this respect" (*Welsh* at 369).

The free exercise clause has been applied to conscientious objection to a spectrum of military involvement. From cases requiring saluting the flag, the training to or bearing of arms, taking of an oath to bear arms, or a range of other activities linked to military service and goals, government regulations have been challenged by those who argue that their religious beliefs require accommodation. These cases evidence the same shift as in free exercise cases generally from the *Reynolds* standard to the *Sherbert* "compelling interest" test. See, for example, *Gillette v U.S.*, 401 US 437 (1971), upholding the "substantial" government interest in conscription over the individual's free exercise of religion; and *Spence v Bailey*, 465 F 2d 797 (6th cir. 1972), stating that religious objections to mandatory participation in a high school ROTC program would not unduly burden officials. In cases involving military regulation of noncivilians, review has generally been more deferential than for regulation of civilians. See, for example, *Goldman v Weinberger*, 475 US 503 (1986) allowing the military to prohibit wearing of a yarmulke, although Congress later legislated to allow religious apparel while in uniform (Pub. L. 100-180, Sec 508(a)(2), 101 Stat. 1086 (1987); 10 USC Sec 774.

Modern cases involving religious objection to military conscription continue to follow the requirements summarized in *Clay v. United States*, 403 U.S. 698, 705(1971) for the implementation of the Military Selective Service Act Section 6(j): that the objection be to war in any form, that the objection be based on religious training or belief or the equivalent, and that the belief be sincere. Clay involved Cassius Clay, aka Muhammed Ali, who objected to war not declared by Allah. Because the Justice Department did not clearly state which of the three tests formed the basis for its decision, the Supreme Court reversed the conviction without reaching the selective opposition to war issue.

JEAN BINKOVITZ

CONSPIRACY

The common law definition of conspiracy is an agreement between two or more individuals to commit an unlawful act, such as murder, or to commit a lawful act by unlawful means, such as artificially increasing the price of goods through collusion. In jurisdictions that follow the common-law definition, the term "unlawful" includes, but is not limited to, acts and means that are criminal; acts and means that are "prejudicial to the public, oppressive of individuals, or done for a malicious purpose" also suffice. Some jurisdictions, however, statutorily limit conspiracy to agreements to commit a criminal offense.

Conspiracy has been a crime since the reign of Edward I in the late thirteenth century. The early common law defined conspiracy narrowly; the crime encompassed only conspiracies to obstruct justice, normally through false accusation of criminal conduct, and required the wrongly accused individual be indicted and then acquitted of the crime. The first major expansion of conspiracy came in the 1611 decision *Poulterer's Case*, where the Court of Star Chamber held that a conspiracy was punishable even if it was unsuccessful. Not surprisingly, the decision led to a dramatic increase in conspiracy prosecutions, and by the end of the seventeenth century conspiring to commit any criminal offense was punishable. Finally, by the mid-nineteenth century, conspiracy had adopted its current common-law form, punishing conspiracies to commit lawful acts by legal means, as well as conspiracies to commit unlawful acts.

As with all crimes, conspiracy is defined by the combination of a certain act and a certain mental state. The act requirement of conspiracy is unique, in that the requirement is satisfied by the defendant's decision to enter into the conspiracy. The testimony of one of the conspirators is the ideal method for proving the agreement but is not required given the secretive nature of conspiracies. Indeed, the prosecution does not have to show that the conspirators actually exchanged words explicitly communicating agreement. A "tacit understanding" is sufficient, and that understanding can be inferred circumstantially from the coordinated actions of the conspirators themselves.

The mental requirement is more complex, because the crime of conspiracy actually requires two mental states: an intent to enter into the conspiratorial agreement and an intent to commit the unlawful act that is the object of the agreement. The intent to enter into the agreement is rarely contested, because the prosecution will not charge a defendant with conspiracy without evidence of the agreement. Whether the defendant intended to commit the unlawful act is thus the critical issue in most conspiracy prosecutions.

At common law, a conspiracy was punishable even if the conspirators had done nothing in furtherance of the conspiracy beyond the agreement itself. In the absence of a statute providing otherwise, this is still the rule. The federal conspiracy statute and many state conspiracy statutes, however, require proof that one of the conspirators committed an "overt act" in furtherance of the conspiracy. The purpose of the overt-act requirement is to ensure that the conspiracy was underway, not "a project still resting solely in the minds of the conspirators." Virtually any act will satisfy the overt-act requirement, legal as well as illegal.

A conspiracy and its unlawful object, where criminal, are separate and distinct offenses. As a result, a defendant can be convicted of both conspiracy and the underlying crime and can be convicted of conspiracy even when the underlying crime is not prosecuted or results in an acquittal. When convicted of both, the sentences can be added on to each other, and there is no requirement that the sentence for the conspiracy be shorter than the sentence for the underlying crime.

There are two basic rationales for the crime of conspiracy. First, by criminalizing the conspiratorial agreement itself, conspiracy permits law enforcement to authorities to intervene against criminally minded individuals before they carry out the more harmful underlying crime. Second, conspiracy as a freestanding crime protects the public from the heightened dangers of concerted criminal activity. A criminal plan carried out by a group is far more likely to succeed than one carried out by an individual and is capable of causing far greater harm. Moreover, the existence of a conspiratorial group always has the potential to branch out into new and different kinds of crimes.

The crime of conspiracy has always been controversial. To begin with, the crime gives the prosecution substantive and procedural advantages unparalleled elsewhere in the criminal law—advantages that led Judge Learned Hand to famously describe conspiracy as "the darling of the modern prosecutor's nursery." One such advantage is simply the crime's inherent vagueness, both in terms of its applicability to non-criminal objectives and its definition of the required mental state. Such vagueness makes a conspiracy charge particularly difficult to defend.

A critical procedural advantage for the prosecution is what's known as the "co-conspirator hearsay exception," which permits any incriminating statement made by a conspirator during and in furtherance of the conspiracy to be used against all of his co-conspirators. In fact, a conspirator's incriminating statement can even be used against a co-conspirator who joined the conspiracy *after* the statement was made.

The most problematic advantage, however, is the prosecution's ability to try all of the members of a conspiracy jointly. Such joint trials dramatically increase the possibility of guilt by association, where an innocent defendant is convicted either because jurors are unable to keep the evidence against the different defendants separate or simply because they assume that if one defendant is guilty, all of them must be.

These advantages help explain why prosecutors have often misused the crime of conspiracy for political purposes. Efforts to organize labor unions were consistently prosecuted as criminal conspiracies in the nineteenth century. And conspiracy prosecutions were effective tools for silencing the protected speech of peace and anti-war activists during World War I and of communists and alleged communists during the McCarthy Era.

KEVIN JON HELLER

References and Further Reading

LaFave, Wayne R. *Substantive Criminal Law 2*. Ch. 12. St. Paul: West Publishing, 1986.
Sayre, Francis B., *Criminal Conspiracy*, Harvard Law Review 35 (1922): 2:393–427.

Cases and Statutes Cited

Harrison v. United States, 7 F.2d 259 (2d Cir. 1925)
Poulterer's Case, 77 Eng. Rep. 813 (1611)

See also **Dennis v. United States, 341 U.S. 494 (1951); Schenck v. United States, 249 U.S. 47 (1919)**

CONSTITUTION OF 1787

The U.S. Constitution of 1787 did not contain a bill of rights, because the overwhelming majority of the delegates did not believe that one was necessary. They were creating a government of limited powers and did not think that these powers included the right to generally regulate civil liberties. Thus, the Framers did not include any general protections for freedom of religion, speech, the press, or assembly, because they quite frankly did not believe Congress could ever legislate on such matters. They did anticipate a federal criminal law, but not one at the convention believed it was necessary to guard against warrantless searches or prosecution without grand jury indictments because the Framers simply could not imagine that any representative government could act in such a manner. In opposing the addition of a bill of rights, Roger Sherman of Connecticut explained that the national legislature could "be safely trusted" to protect liberty. [2 Farrrand 588–589] Similarly, he argued that no special protection freedom of the press was necessary because "the power of Congress does not extend to the Press." [2 Farrand 617–618] A majority of the convention agreed with Sherman both times. Sherman may have been wrong about this, but it's position was not taken out of hostility to civil liberties. The Framers were naïve in this regard, but not tyrannical.

While generally not protecting civil liberties, the Constitution contains a number of clauses that are protective of civil liberties. There are also provisions that could threaten civil liberties, especially in the absence of a bill of rights.

Protections of Civil Liberties in the Constitution

While not generally protecting freedom of speech, the "Speech and Debate Clause" of Article I, Sec. 6, Par. 1, does protect the freedom of members of the House and Senate to speak freely and openly when debating issues in Congress. This was a critical provision in the development of open government and representative government. At the same time, however, this clause has allowed demagogues, like Senator Joseph McCarthy, to destroy the reputations of innocent Americans without fear or interference from the courts.

Article I, Sec. 8 provided for the granting of copyrights to authors. This is generally seen as an important stimulus for the growth of literature and publishing in America. The protection of copyright is seen as essential to a free press to the extent that authors and publishers need economic and legal protection for their work.

Article I, Sec. 9, Par. 2 allows for the suspension of habeas corpus only under very limited circumstances: when there has been an invasion or rebellion *and* the public safety requires it. This clause prevents arbitrary suspensions. Indeed, the only sustained suspension took place during and after the Civil War, when there were true rebellions in the nation. During World War II habeas was suspended in Hawaii, which was a war zone. The Japanese Internment was technically not a suspension of habeas, although it unfortunately had a similar affect for Japanese Americans. The strict requirement for habeas suspension contrasts with the easier methods by act of Parliament in Britain.

Tied to the habeas clause is the prohibition on ex post facto laws and bills of attainder. These clauses were important additions to the Constitution that limited the ability of the government to punish people for their political acts and viewpoints. Article 1, Sec. 10, Par. 1 also prohibited the state from passing such laws. The Constitution did not, however, prohibit the states from suspending habeas corpus in situations other than rebellion or invasion. This meant that if martial law had to be declared in the event of a natural or man-made disaster, it would be done at the local or state level.

Two clauses dealing with religion are perhaps the most important protections for civil liberties in the original Constitution. Article II, Sec. 1, Par. 7 and Art. VI, Sec. 1, Par. 3 both provide that in taking the oath of office state and federal officials "shall be bound by Oath or Affirmation" to support the Constitution. By adding the term "or Affirmation," the framers opened office holding to Quakers and members of other pietistic faiths who refused to take "oaths." In addition, by not including an oath to "God" or an oath on a Bible, the Framers placed no religious impediments to officeholders such as existed in England, where members of Parliament had to swear an oath on the Protestant, King James Bible. More importantly, the same clause of Art. VI also declared that "no religious Test shall ever be required as Qualification to any Office or public Trust under the United States." At the time eleven of the thirteen states had some form of religious test for office holding, as did every nation in Europe. The United States thus became the first nation in the world to allow people of any religion, or no religion at all, to hold office. Significantly, Jews had already held some offices in the new nation, including one who was an officer on George Washington's personal staff during the Revolution. The Constitution reaffirmed that in this nation anyone, of any religion, could hold office.

The other major protections for civil liberties were in Article III of the Constitution. Section 2, Par. 2 of that Article provided that all prosecutions under federal law would be by jury, and the trials would have to take place in the state where the alleged crime was committed. This would prevent the government from moving defendants far from their homes and witnesses, as England had done before the Revolution. Section 3, Paragraph 1 of this Article set out a high standard for treason: that it could consist only of "levying War" against the United States or "adhering to their enemies, giving them Aid and Comfort," and that no conviction could take place without two witnesses to the same "overt act" or a confession in "open court." England allowed prosecutions for constructive treason—that is for statements, or even cartoons or drawings—that could be construed as treasonous. No overt act was necessary for the crime, and two witnesses to the same act were not necessary for conviction. Paragraph three of this section of the Constitution also prohibited the government from punishing the descendants or heirs of those convicted of treason, which had been done in England.

Threats to Civil Liberties

Although creating a government with limited powers, the Constitution was open-ended on many issues. Article I, Sec. 8 allowed Congress to regulate interstate trade. Even if Congress could not abridge freedom of the press, it might prevent political literature from being sent across state lines if the content was deemed unacceptable to a political majority. This would also be accomplished by denying the use of the mail to certain categories of publications. Starting the 1870s with the Comstock Act, Congress prohibited "obscene materials" from the mail. For more than fifty years this included any material that women could have used to learn about birth control. Authorities prosecuted and jailed the founder of family planning in America, Margaret Sanger, under this statute. During World War I, the post office prohibited papers critical of war policies from being circulated through the mail. In the 1960s, the Congress tried to use the commerce clause to prevent antiwar activists from crossing state lines, although this law, known as the H. Rap Brown law (after a black activist), was struck down as violating the First Amendment.

The power to regulate naturalization (Art. I, Sec. 8, Part. 4) has also been used to threaten civil liberties. Aliens have been deported, or threatened with deportation, for exercising free speech rights. Also, immigration laws, which are tied to naturalization, have been used to discriminate against people on the basis of political ideology and ethnicity. Sometimes this has been used to protect the nation from those who might harm the country (fascists, communists, terrorists), but it has also been used merely to weed those with unpopular ideas, such as pacifists or advocates of polygamy, that did not pose any security threat to the nation.

The fugitive slave clause (Art. IV, Sec. 2, Par. 3) provided that runaway slaves would be "delivered up" on the claim of the owner, without any due process requirements. This would lead to kidnappings and the removal of people who had claims to freedom. At the time this clause was barely debated, but it had great potential, which was played out in the first six decades of the nineteenth century to deny fundamental rights to African Americans.

Provisions That Both Protect and Threaten Civil Liberties

A number of provisions can both threaten or protect civil liberties, depending how they are implemented. For example Article I, Sec. 8, Par. 15 allows for the use of the militia to suppress insurrections, whereas Article IV, Sec. 4 allows the use of the army to protect the states from rebellions and insurrections. These clauses have been used to suppress those who would violate the civil liberties of others—such as the use of the army to suppress the Ku Klux Klan after the Civil War or the use of the Army and the state national guards (the militia) to help integrate public schools and state universities in the South in the 1950s and 1960s. But, this clause was also used to suppress labor strikes, where workers were seeking high wages or better working conditions, but not threatening violence.

Article I, Sec. 9 prevented Congress from ending the African slave trade for twenty years. On the other hand, when the twenty years were up, Congress was able to end the trade. To the extent that enslavement is the most outrageous denial of civil liberty, this clause can be seen as cutting in both directions on civil liberties.

The most significant clauses that could have threatened, or protected, civil liberties were tied to those places—such as the territories and the national capital—where Congress had the exclusive right to legislate. The Framers argued that a Bill of Rights was unnecessary for the Constitution because the states, not Congress, would pass most general laws. The regulation of the press, for example, would be left to state law under the constitution. However, in the territories and the planned federal district—what became Washington, D.C.—the Congress would function as a state legislature. Thus, without a bill of rights the Congress would be able to deny or protect fundamental liberties without any constitutional guidance or limitation.

Conclusion

In the end, the Constitution did not greatly threaten civil liberties, because it created a government of limited powers. However, the potential for great harm to fundamental liberties could be found throughout the Constitution. With no bill of rights the Congress might find it necessary to suppress free speech or freedom of the press in times of war. The government might find it "necessary and proper" to favor one faith or one general religious ideology to accomplish some policy goal. The government might decide that a treaty required the suppression of some liberty at home to achieve a foreign policy goal. The Framers did not see these potential dangers—or did not believe them realistic, and thus did not think the Constitution needed a bill of rights. The First Congress, using the power to amend the Constitution, would remedy the lack of a bill of rights.

PAUL FINKELMAN

References and Further Reading

Borden, Morton. *Jews, Turks, and Infidels*. Chapel Hill: University of North Carolina Press, 1984.

Farrand, Max, ed. *The Records of the Federal Convention of 1787*. 4 vols. New Haven: Yale University Press, 1966.

Finkelman, Paul, *James Madison and the Bill of Rights: A Reluctant Paternity*, Supreme Court Review 1990 (1991): 301–347.

Levy, Leonard W. *Origins of the Bill of Rights*. New Haven: Yale University Press, 1999.

Urofsky, Melvin I., and Paul Finkelman. *A March of Liberty: A Constitutional History of the United States*. 2 vols. New York: Oxford University Press, 2002.

CONSTITUTION OVERSEAS

The Constitution for the United States contains four provisions that can provide some basis for extending the jurisdiction of the Constitution beyond territorial borders:

1. The power of Congress to declare war and issue letters of marque and reprisal.
2. The power of Congress to punish as crimes "piracy and felonies on the high seas" and "offenses against the laws of nations."
3. The power of Congress to fund and regulate military forces everywhere.
4. The commander-in-chief power of the President to command those forces.

With those exceptions, the jurisdiction of the Constitution and statutes and official acts under its authority were originally considered limited to the territory of the nation. This included the territory of states, nonstate territories, and was extended, by the law of nations, to coastal waters, naval vessels flying the U.S. flag, and the grounds of U.S. diplomatic facilities abroad.

By international status of forces agreements, such jurisdiction has been partially extended to the grounds of U.S. military bases abroad. It has long been accepted that U.S. law governs U.S. military personnel anywhere they operate, and by extension, certain civilian contractors under the terms of their contracts.

Although it has been generally accepted that U.S. officials have no authority to officially act on foreign citizens on the territories of their own nations, there has been a movement, beginning in the twentieth century, to extend extraterritorial jurisdiction to civilian U.S. citizens abroad, to foreign nationals charged with "crimes against humanity," and to "enemy combatants" against U.S. forces of any nationality.

The first criminal prosecutions for "crimes against humanity" were in the Nuremberg Trials of German nationals after World War II. The alleged authority for such criminal prosecutions was the unconditional surrender of Germany, which was deemed to have conferred plenary power to the victorious Allies to exercise sovereignty over German territory and its citizens. However, the U.S. Constitution delegates no such power to its officials in such circumstances, even if the surrender could be considered some kind of "treaty," which it was not, since it was not presented to the Senate for ratification as a treaty. The President as commander-in-chief has authority to command U.S. military forces but no power to command civilians of foreign nations no longer in a state of war against us.

In *Reid v. Covert*, 354 U.S. 1 (1957) the U.S. Supreme Court reversed a conviction of a civilian resident on a U.S. military abroad and issued a clear statement of its findings:

1. When the United States acts against its citizens abroad, it can do so only in accordance with all the limitations imposed by the Constitution, including Art. III, 2, and the Fifth and Sixth Amendments . . . .
2. Insofar as Art. 2 (11) of the Uniform Code of Military Justice provides for the military trial of civilian dependents accompanying the armed forces in foreign countries, it cannot be sustained as legislation which is 'necessary and proper' to carry out obligations of the United States under international agreements made with those countries; since no agreement with a foreign nation can confer on Congress or any other branch of the Government power which is free from the restraints of the Constitution . . . .
3. The power of Congress under Art. I, 8, cl. 14, of the Constitution, "To make Rules for the Government and Regulation of the land and naval Forces," taken in conjunction with the Necessary and Proper Clause, does not extend to civilians—even though they may be dependents living with servicemen on a military base . . . .
4. Under our Constitution, courts of law alone are given power to try civilians for their offenses against the United States . . . .

On the other hand, in *United States v. Verdugo-Urquidez*, 494 U.S. 259 (1990), the U.S. Supreme court sustained a conviction of a foreign national convicted on the basis of evidence obtained in Mexico without a search warrant, finding that:

The Fourth Amendment does not apply to the search and seizure by United States agents of property owned by a nonresident alien and located in a foreign country.

Extension of criminal jurisdiction to civilian contractors associated with the Department of Defense was legislated in the 2000 Military Extraterritorial Jurisdiction Act. Congress knew that it is nearly impossible to charge civilians under the Uniform Code of Military Justice, even if they work alongside active-duty service members. However, since the Constitution only extends to military personnel, this raises a question of whether the contracts of such civilians make them members of the armed forces subject to the jurisdiction of either U.S. military or civil courts. If not, the only authority would seem to be to prosecute them as "pirates" for warlike acts committed without state authority.

U.S. courts have also thus far sustained assertions of authority to tax U.S. citizens on their earnings from sources not only within U.S. territory, but from foreign sources, and not only while residing on U.S. territory, but while domiciled abroad. Since the U.S. Constitution delegates coercive authority only over "persons" and not "citizens," this would constitute either the extension of U.S. legal jurisdiction to personal jurisdiction over U.S. citizens everywhere, even if they are not contractually part of U.S. military forces, or a conflict with equal protection, which requires equal treatment of persons, not just citizens. U.S. statute does extend voting rights to expatriates in congressional and presidential elections (although the U.S. Constitution delegates power to Congress only to regulate congressional elections), which would avoid violating the principle of "no taxation without representation" but presents an issue of "jurisdiction creep" that has not been adequately tested.

The military actions in Afghanistan and Iraq, and detentions of persons suspected of "terrorism," has raised several constitutional issues. Many of them center around the availability of due process protection for prisoners held at the Guantanamo Bay base on the island of Cuba. This base is held by the United States under the terms of a simple lease that does not contain a cession of legal jurisdiction over the land leased to the United States. However, such jurisdiction is also not exercised by Cuba. This has created a kind of legal "no-man's-land," where U.S. officials have sought to hold detainees as a way to avoid the supervision of any but military tribunals.

On Nov. 8, 2004, Federal District Judge James Robertson ruled that the Bush administration had not followed a lawful procedure in declaring Salim Ahmed Hamdan, held at Guantanamo, an "enemy combatant" who was not entitled to protections and privileges under the Geneva Convention. The "combatant status review tribunals"—used by the Pentagon to decide whether to hold detainees—are not a "competent" court to make such a determination, Robertson said. And the military commission process, which prosecutes detainees using secret evidence and unnamed witnesses, "could not be countenanced in any American court," the judge ruled.

The U.S. Supreme Court held in *Rasul v. Bush*, 542 U.S. 466 (2004), that non-U.S. citizen prisoners at Guantanamo may file habeas corpus petitions challenging their imprisonment, as well as claims under federal law concerning the conditions of their confinement. Legislation was introduced in Congress to remove such jurisdiction from the federal courts, but the constitutionality of such legislation is itself in doubt.

JON ROLAND

References and Further Reading

de Vattel, Emmerich. *The Law of Nations.*(1758) Joseph Chitty, ed. Philadelphia: Johnson, 1883. http://www.constitution.org/vattel/vattel.htm.

Du Ponceau, Peter Stephen. *A Dissertation on the Nature and Extent of the Jurisdiction of the Courts of the United States.* Philadelphia: Small, 1824. http://www.constitution.org/cmt/psdp/juris.htm.

Grotius, Hugo. *The Law of War and Peace.* (1625). http://www.constitution.org/gro/djbp.htm.

Stimson, Edward S. *Conflict of Criminal Laws.* Chicago: Foundation Press, 1936. http://www.constitution.org/cmt/stimson/con_crim.htm.

CONSTITUTIONAL AMENDMENT PERMITTING SCHOOL PRAYER

The appropriate role of religion in public schooling has long been controversial. At the time of the nation's founding, few people believed that education could be divorced from religion; religious instruction was viewed as being indispensable for the inculcation of virtue and morality in children. The founders of the nineteenth century common school movement believed, however, that important religious values could be isolated from specific dogmas and tenets that separated denominations and could be taught in a manner acceptable to children of all faiths. The leaders of the common schools—Horace Mann being the most notable figure—were all Protestants, so the "nonsectarian" instruction—teacher-led prayer and readings from the King James version of the Bible—had a distinctly Protestant tone. Early opposition to school prayer and Bible reading came from Catholics, Jews, and a handful of freethinkers, but their attacks on the religious exercises led only to intransigence among education leaders and occasional violence between Protestant nativists and Catholic immigrants. Over time, particularly in cities with large immigrant populations, public schools began to moderate or even dispense with organized religious exercises.

The first attempt to preserve the practices of prayer and Bible reading through a constitutional amendment occurred in the ill-fated Blaine Amendment of 1876. Although the primary focus of the Blaine Amendment was to prevent the payment of public funds to parochial schools, the proposal also contained a provision authorizing school boards to retain school prayer and Bible readings. That latter provision was included in reaction to an 1872 decision by the Ohio Supreme Court affirming the Cincinnati school board's ban on school prayer and Bible reading (*Minor v. Board of Education*). In 1888, again in response to concerns of Protestant leaders that public schools were dispensing with the religious exercises, Congress held hearings on a constitutional amendment proposed by Senator Henry W. Blair that would have prohibited the removal of prayer and Bible reading. The proposal died in committee.

During the late-nineteenth and early-twentieth centuries, a handful of state courts struck down devotional school prayer and Bible reading as violative of state constitutional provisions (Wisconsin 1890, Nebraska 1903, Illinois 1910); however, the majority of challenges to such practices failed, with state courts finding the practices constitutional.

The late-nineteenth and early-twentieth century challenges to prayer and Bible reading were based on state constitutional provisions, coming before the incorporation of the First Amendment's Establishment Clause in 1947. In 1948, the U.S. Supreme Court struck down a practice of allowing school children to be released from class for religious instruction by non-school personnel (*McCollum v. Board of Education*). Four years later, however, the high court stepped back from its controversial decision and upheld "release time" for religious instruction, provided it occurred off school premises (*Zorach v. Clauson*).

Based on the long-standing practice of religious exercises in public schools, therefore, the Supreme Court's 1962 and 1963 decisions holding prayer and Bible reading to be a violation of the Establishment Clause were extremely controversial. Several members of Congress, led by Representative Frank Becker (R-NY), proposed constitutional amendments to preserve school prayer and Bible reading. Congress held hearings on the "Becker Amendment" in 1964, and initially the measure seemed destined for passage. Only a highly organized effort by mainstream Protestant and Jewish groups, led by the National Council of Churches, defeated the proposed amendment in committee. Subsequent proposed amendments by Senator Everett Dirksen (R-IL) in 1966 and Representative Chambers Wylie (R-OH) in 1970 also died in committee.

Time failed to moderate opposition to the Court's school prayer decisions among religious conservatives. During the late 1970s, a resurgent Religious Right, led by evangelicals Jerry Falwell of the Moral Majority and Pat Robertson of the Christian Broadcasting Network, put a school prayer amendment at the top of their agenda along with an amendment to reverse the Court's 1973 abortion decision (*Roe v. Wade*). Candidate Ronald Reagan expressed sympathy with a prayer amendment and, after his election as President, Reagan issued a call in 1982 for an amendment: "Nothing in this Constitution shall be construed to prohibit individual or group prayer in public schools or other public institutions. No person shall be required by the United States or any State to participate in prayer." Initially, passage of the "Reagan Amendment" seemed assured. However, moderate Republican Senator Mark Hatfield (R-OR), supported by mainstream religious groups such as the

Baptist Joint Committee on Public Affairs, proposed a compromise statute, the Equal Access Act, which authorized student religious club meetings in public secondary schools. After moderate evangelical groups including the Christian Legal Society and the National Association of Evangelicals signaled their support, Congress enacted the Equal Access Act instead of the Reagan Amendment.

Despite the resolution of the Equal Access Act, agitation for a constitutional amendment to protect prayer and Bible reading has resurfaced occasionally, particularly after controversial court decisions. In 1992 and 2000, the Supreme Court struck down prayers at public school graduation ceremonies and athletic events, respectively (*Lee v. Weisman*; *Santa Fe Independent School District v. Doe*). Those holdings, and similar holdings by lower courts, elicited proposed constitutional amendments in Congress by Representatives Henry Hyde (R-IL) and Ernest Istook (R-OK), including one to strip the federal courts of jurisdiction to hear school prayer controversies. To date all such proposals have failed.

STEVEN K. GREEN

References and Further Reading

Alley. Robert S. *Without a Prayer: Religious Expression in Public Schools*. Amherst, NY: Prometheus Books, 1996.
DelFattore, Joan. *The Fourth R: Conflicts Over Religion in America's Public Schools*. New Haven: Yale University Press, 2004.
Green, Steven K. "Evangelicals and the Becker Amendment: A Lesson in Church-State Moderation." *Journal of Church and State* 33 (1991): 541–567.
Ravitch, Frank S. *School Prayer and Discrimination*. Boston: Northeastern University Press, 1999.
Stokes, Anson Phelps, and Leo Pfeffer. *Church and State in the United States*. New York: Harper and Row, Pub., 1964.

Cases and Statutes Cited

Engel v. Vitale, 370 U.S. 421 (1962)
Lee v. Weisman, 505 U.S. 577 (1992)
McCollum v. Board of Education, 333 U.S. 203 (1948)
Minor v. Board of Education, 23 Ohio St. 211 (1872)
Santa Fe Independent School District v. Doe, 530 U.S. 290 (2000)
School District of Abington Township, 374 U.S. 203 (1963)
Zorach v. Clauson, 343 U.S. 306 (1952)

CONSTITUTIONAL CONVENTION OF 1787

The delegates to the Constitutional Convention of 1787 (known as the Framers) were initially concerned with creating a stronger, centralized government that would allow for regulation of trade and commerce, provide for a stronger national defense, and reduce tensions and jealousies between the states. The Framers were also concerned about a fair allocation of power in national Congress and the necessity of having a government that could collect taxes and function. The leading Framers decried what the called the "imbecility" of the government under the Articles of Confederation, which was unable to accomplish very much. The Framers believed they were creating a government of relatively limited power, which could only legislate in those areas that were enumerated through specific grants of power to Congress.

Given their vision of a limited government, the Framers were relatively unconcerned about "civil liberties" under the new regime. They believed that the regulation of most behavior would be at the state level, and thus they did not see civil liberties as a particularly important concern for the national government. Most of the Framers did not believe that Congress had the power to regulate freedom of the press or create a state religion, and, therefore, they saw no reason to discuss such powers in the Convention or provide for their protection in the Constitution. Furthermore, most of the Framers could not conceive of a representative government trampling on the fundamental liberties of the people. In their view, kings, princes, and dictators threatened the liberties of the people; legislatures chosen by the people could not do so.

There was, of course, an internal logic to this argument. In England the people had forced the king to grant them rights. King John I signed the Magna Carta at sword point, surrounded by knights and other great men of the realm who demanded he guarantee them certain rights. Over the next four centuries all Englishmen came to believe that they were entitled to some of these rights. In the seventeenth century Englishmen demanded more rights and wrested them from the King in the Civil War, the Glorious Revolution, and through acts of Parliament. The English Bill of Rights was a statute passed by Parliament as part of the Revolution. This history led some Framers to believe that the United States did not need a "bill of rights," because there was no monarch from which to wrest these rights. On the contrary, they argued that a bill of rights was unnecessary in a government of limited powers in which the people would be sovereign. In a debating congressional power over the army and the militias, James Madison asserted the widely held belief that "the greatest danger to liberty is from large standing armies, it is best to prevent them by an effectual provision for a good Militia." [2 Farrand 338] This argument led to a number of provisions

that kept the military under strict civilian control. It would eventually lead to the Second Amendment, guaranteeing that Congress lacked the power to abolish the state militias ("A well regulated Militia, being necessary to the security of a free State . . ."), but did have the power to regulate them and set rules for government them.

These many understandings about the origin of liberties and the threats to them led the Framers to ignore civil liberties issues until the very end of the Convention. The delegates debated the nature of government from the end of May until the end of July without discussing issues that are today considered fundamental aspects of civil liberties. Some protections of civil liberties were taken for granted. In an early debate, for example, James Madison cited "the diversity of religious Sects" to support the idea of checks and balances [1 Farrand 108]. Madison assumed these sects would have the liberty to practice their faiths as they wished. There was no sense in this, or any other debate, that the constitution had to protect religious freedom. Madison and others assumed that Congress would have no power to regulate religious practice and that the states would have to allow religious liberty because of the growing diversity of the nation. In the early debates in the Convention, Madison noted that "religion itself may become a motive to persecution & oppression," but he argued that large electoral districts, not a bill of rights, would protect against this [1 Farrand 135].

When the draft constitution was first presented, in early August, it contained a few provisions that protected civil liberties. It guaranteed the right to trial by jury for federal criminal offense and guaranteed that the trial would take place in the state where the alleged crime was committed. This would emerge in the final Constitution in Article III, Sec. 2, par. 3. The draft Constitution also defined treason as only "levying war against the United States," thus eliminating constructive treason or other definitions of treason based on speech or belief.

On August 18, both Madison and Charles Pinckney proposed adding what became the copyright clause of Article I, Sec. 8 of the Constitution. This clause would serve authors and publishers and was key to the development of a free press, although it was seen at the time as more of a protection of economic interests than of civil liberties.

On August 20, almost three months after the beginning of the Convention, a delegate made the first proposals for specific protections of civil liberties. Charles Pinckney of South Carolina proposed a series of additions to the draft constitution. Some of these eventually became part of the original constitution, including the clause limiting the suspension of the writ of habeas corpus, the prohibition of religious tests for office holding, and the prohibition on simultaneous multiple office holding. The first two would be keys to protecting civil liberties in the new nation. The third helped prevent the concentration of power in the hands of a few officials. Pinckney also proposed an explicit clause declaring that "the military shall always be subordinate to the Civil power." The final Constitution would not have such specific provision, but the spirit of this proposal is clearly evident in the clauses that give Congress authority to make all rules for the military and to appropriate money for the military, while making the president, a civilian, the Commander-in-Chief of the Army and Navy. Finally, Pinckney proposed a clause that would later be incorporated into the Bill of Rights. One was a statement that "The Liberty of the Press shall be inviolably preserved." The second would form the first clause of what became the Third Amendment: "No soldier shall be quartered in any House in time of peace without the consent of the owner." Indeed, while the order would be changed slightly, these eighteen words would form the first eighteen words of what became the Third Amendment [2 Farrand 341-42].

In retrospect, it seems astounding that no one at the Convention suggested any of these provisions during the first three months of debate. The best explanation for this is that no one thought such protections of liberty were necessary until after the Constitution took shape, and the framers understood the extent of power the new national government would have. It may seem ironic to modern Americans that the first person to make these proposals was Pinckney, who is most remembered as the most articulate and vociferous defender of slavery and the African slave trade at the convention and the man who, along with Pierce Butler, proposed the fugitive slave clause. However, this connection between civil liberties and slavery should be not seen as ironic. Masters of slaves, like Pinckney, were fully aware of their own civil liberties, and the need to preserve them, even as they denied more fundamental liberties to their slaves.

On the same day Pinckney proposed these additions, George Mason offered a clause that was distinctly hostile to civil liberties. Mason proposed that Congress have the power "to enact sumptuary laws." Such clause would have allowed Congress to regulate how people dressed, limiting certain kinds of clothing to people certain social classes. Governor Morris, one of the richest men at the Convention and one of the largest landholders in the nation, argued that such laws "tended to create a landed Nobility." Indeed, such a provision would have given Congress the power to establish social classes and regulate personal expression. Mason argued that such laws were

necessary to make sure all citizens maintained "manners." The Convention wisely voted this proposal down [2 Farrand 344]. Mason would later be remembered for his strident demands for a bill of rights and his refusal to sign the Constitution, because it lacked one. Yet, here he wanted to create a class-based society that would have denied to some people the fundamental right to choose how to dress themselves. Later that day Mason also opposed only allowing the United States to punish treason, arguing that the national government would have only a "qualified sovereignty" [2 Farrand 347]. Such an analysis had strong implications for civil liberties, because it would allow the state to define treason more broadly than merely "making war" on the nation. This would allow the states to use treason to suppress nonviolent opposition to state policies and, as such, suppress civil liberties.

On August 22, the Convention accepted a proposal by Elbridge Gerry and James McHenry to prohibit ex post facto laws and bills of attainder. No one at the Convention opposed a prohibition on bills of attainder that should be banned, but the ex post facto provisions roused the ire of a number of attorneys in the Convention, including Oliver Ellsworth and James Wilson, both of whom would serve on the Supreme Court. They argued that a ban on ex post facto laws was unnecessary, because, as Ellsworth put it, everyone knew that such laws "were void of themselves." Wilson argued that such a clause would insult the Convention by leading people to believe that the delegates were "ignorant of the first principles of legislation." In response to these arguments, Daniel Carroll of Maryland pointed out that the states has passed and enforced ex post facto laws, despite the universal belief they were unconstitutional. Wilson jumped on this argument to make a point held by many at the Convention—that a bill of rights or any constitutional provision on civil liberties was useless, because such constitutional prohibitions were unenforceable. Wilson noted that a number of states had passed ex post facto laws despite state constitutional prohibitions. Hugh Williamson agreed with Wilson, noting that in his home state of North Carolina the legislature had ignored the state constitution and passed such laws. Nevertheless, he believed a constitutional prohibition had much value "because the Judge can take hold of it." In other words, Williamson argued that judicial review would allow courts to strike down laws that violated the Constitution. After a bit more debate, the Convention adopted the provision banning ex post facto laws, just as it had banned bills of attainder [2 Farrand 375-76].

In the weeks that followed, the Convention finished debating and refining the articles dealing with the legislative, executive, and judicial branches. These debates and votes considered various clauses touching on civil liberties, such as jury trials for accused criminals and the civilian control of the military. The Convention also adopted the slave trade provision of Article I, Sec. 9, which allowed the African slave trade to remain open until at least 1808. This was not a civil liberties issue per se, but it clearly affected the civil liberties of approximately 100,000 Africans who were imported into the country, mostly between 1800 and 1808. The Convention also adopted the Fugitive Slave Clause or Article IV, Sec. 2, Par. 3. No one at the Convention articulated any fear that this clause would jeopardize civil liberties, either of blacks or their white allies. From the 1830s to the Civil War, the implementation of this clause would deprive numerous people—free blacks, fugitive slaves, and white abolitionists—of their civil liberties. But this potential problem was not obvious to anyone at the Convention.

On August 30, with the heated debate over the African slave trade behind them, the Convention returned to finalizing the document. The delegates agreed, without debate, to add the words "or affirmation" to the clause on the presidential oath and later did the same for all other required oaths. This allowed Quakers and others who were opposed to taking oaths, to hold office under the new Constitution. This can be seen as the first constitutionally sanctioned accommodation to religion under the Constitution. Charles Pinckney once again proposed that there be no religious tests for office holding. Roger Sherman thought this was unnecessary because "the prevailing liberality" was "a sufficient security ag[ain]st. such tests" [2 Farrand 468]. The Convention wisely rejected Sherman's protest and unanimously accepted Pinckney's proposal. The Convention then spend spent nearly two weeks revising the rest of the Constitution and debating the powers of the president and how it would be both elected and removed from office. The delegates were worried about presidential power and the tyranny of the executive. The debates obviously had implications for civil liberties, which could easily be destroyed by a president turned dictator. But there was not explicit discussion of civil liberties. On September 10, the Convention turned the draft Constitution over to a Committee of Style, which came back on the 12th with what was more or less the final version of the Constitution.

At this point, after almost three and half months of debate, a few delegates suddenly noticed that the Constitution did not have a bill of rights. Hugh Williamson noted that the Constitution did not have a provision to protect the right of a jury trial in civil cases. Nathaniel Gorham asserted that it "was not possible to discriminate equity cases from those in which juries are proper" and thus "this issue should be left to the legislature." Elbridge Gerry, who a week later would refuse to sign the Constitution, argued that juries were necessary "to guard ag[ain]st corrupt judges" [2 Farrand 587]. George Mason, who would also refuse to sign the Constitution, said that a statement of the general principle of having juries, where appropriate, could resolve this issue.

But, the lack of a protection of civil juries was not the real problem. Mason asserted, for the first time in the Convention, that "He wished the plan had been prefaced with a Bill of Rights, & would second a Motion if made for the purpose–It would give great quiet to the people; and with the aid of the State declarations, a bill might be prepared in a few hours." Elbridge Gerry, then proposed a bill of rights. Roger Sherman of Connecticut replied that the state bills of rights were not repealed by the Constitution and would be sufficient to protect the liberties of the people. He also argued that the national legislature "may be safely trusted" to protect liberty. Mason answered that the laws of the United States would be "paramount to the State Bills of Rights," implying that liberties protected by states could be trumped by federal law or even by the federal courts. The state delegations then voted unanimously to reject the call for the addition of a Bill of Rights. Mason and Gerry doubtless supported the measure in their delegations, but no delegation supported them [2 Farrand 588-89].

The next day (September 13) Mason once again asked for a clause allowing Congress to pass sumptuary laws. The convention agreed to send this to a committee, but it never emerged from the committee. On the 14th the disgruntled Mason tried to remove the ban on "ex post facto" laws, arguing that the phrase was unclear. The Convention voted this down. The Convention then rejected a motion to add a clause "that the liberty of the Press should be inviolably observed." Roger Sherman argued it was unnecessary because "the power of Congress does not extend to the Press." Four states, Massachusetts, Maryland, Virginia, and South Carolina, supported this provision, but the rest did not [2 Farrand 617-18].

This was the last debate over a bill of rights. The next day George Mason announced he would not sign the Constitution. His speech, which was later published, was a wholesale denunciation of the Constitution and reflected his deep dissatisfaction with a stronger national government. He began the speech with a statement about the lack of a bill of rights:

There is no Declaration of Rights, and the laws of the general government being paramount to the laws and constitution of the several States, the Declaration of Rights in the separate States are no security. Nor are the people secured even in the enjoyment of the benefit of the common law (which stands here upon no other foundation than its having been adopted by the respective acts forming the constitutions of the several States).

However, nowhere else in the speech did he complain about the lack of protection for civil liberties. He complained about the continuation of the African Slave Trade, which would lower the value his own state's excess slaves, but he also complained that the regulation of trade in general would hurt the South. While not focusing on any specific civil liberties that were not protected, Mason did, however, attack the Constitution for prohibiting ex post facto laws, which most civil libertarians consider one of the great protections of liberty in the Constitution.

Mason's last speech, as well as the brief debate in September over a protection of a free press, helps explain why the Framers did not include a bill of rights in the Constitution. Most of the delegates agreed with Roger Sherman that a bill of rights was unnecessary, because they believed that Congress lacked the power to regulate religion or the press or any other fundamental liberties. Mason, who is often credited with pushing for the Bill of Rights after the Constitution was ratified, seems to have raised the issue mostly to express his general displeasure over the Constitution. It is extremely doubtful that Mason or Gerry would have signed the document, even if "the plan had been prefaced with a Bill of Rights," as he "wished." The fact that he waited until the last week of the Convention to raise this issue suggests that the Bill of Rights and civil liberties in general was not a high priority for him. Pinckney, who happily signed the Constitution, thought that the Framers should explicitly protect the "liberty of the Press," and four delegations agreed with him. However, the rest of the Convention did not, accepting Sherman's position that it was unnecessary. The majority of the Framers also must have understood that if they protected the press, they would have to protect every other civil liberty. Otherwise opponents of the Constitution would accuse them of planning to subvert all other liberties. Thus, the Framers rejected the demand for a bill of rights as unnecessary. The lack of a bill of rights would become an issue in the debate over ratification, but probably they Framers were wiser for refusing to be trapped into a debate of that issue at the Convention.

PAUL FINKELMAN

References and Further Reading

Farrand, Max, ed. *The Records of the Federal Convention of 1787*. 4 vols. New Haven: Yale University Press, 1966.

Finkelman, Paul, *James Madison and the Bill of Rights: A Reluctant Paternity*, Supreme Court Review 1990 (1991): 301–347.

Levy, Leonard W. *Origins of the Bill of Rights*. New Haven: Yale University Press, 1999.

Urofsky, Melvin I., and Paul Finkelman. *A March of Liberty: A Constitutional History of the United States*. 2 vols. New York: Oxford University Press, 2002.

CONTENT-BASED REGULATION OF SPEECH

One of the most important principles of First Amendment jurisprudence states that the government may not regulate speech solely on the basis of its content. Public debate would be distorted, and individual autonomy impaired, if the government were allowed to pick and choose certain ideas, viewpoints, or types of information to suppress. A law is content based if it limits or restricts speech that concerns an entire topic ("subject matter discrimination") or that expresses a particular stance or ideology ("viewpoint discrimination"). The Supreme Court generally invalidates content-based speech regulations unless the government can meet an exacting standard of justification known as "strict scrutiny" analysis.

The content distinction is a relatively recent development in First Amendment law. The Court first established its importance in *Police Department of Chicago v. Mosely* (1972). In that case, postal worker Earl Mosely challenged a Chicago ordinance that prohibited all picketing outside schools except for "peaceful picketing of any school involved in a labor dispute." Mosely had for several months picketed a high school that he believed engaged in racial discrimination. The Court struck down the ordinance because it applied selectively, depending on what message picketers carried on their signs. Writing for the Court, Justice Marshall explained that "above all else, the First Amendment means that government has no power to restrict expression because of its message, its ideas, its subject matter, or its viewpoint."

Pursuant to strict scrutiny analysis, content regulations of speech are unconstitutional unless they are (1) justified by a compelling state interest; and (2) narrowly drawn to achieve that interest with the minimum abridgement of free expression. The compelling-interest prong of the test ensures that speech cannot be restricted just because the majority finds it offensive. For example, in *Texas v. Johnson* (1989), the Court invalidated the conviction of a protestor who burned an American flag at the Republican National Convention. Although Texas claimed that its flag desecration statute served to prevent breaches of the peace and encourage respect for the flag, the Court found these arguments unconvincing. Rather, the Court concluded that the statute's real purpose was to eliminate political protests considered by many to be insulting and unpatriotic. In his opinion for the Court, Justice Brennan noted that "the bedrock principle underlying the First Amendment . . . is that the Government may not prohibit the expression of an idea simply because society finds the idea itself offensive or disagreeable."

Even where a compelling justification exists, a content-based speech regulation will not meet the requirements of strict scrutiny if it is overbroad and limits too much speech. In *Simon & Schuster v. Members of the New York State Crime Victims Board* (1991), the Supreme Court unanimously declared New York's "Son of Sam Law" unconstitutional as penalizing expression based on its content. The law provided that all profits made by criminals who wrote about their illegal activities were to be redistributed to crime victims, whereas criminals who wrote about other topics could keep their earnings. Although the Court agreed that the state had a compelling interest in preventing criminals from capitalizing on their crimes, it held that the New York statute was not sufficiently narrow in scope. Had the law been in effect at the time, the Court noted that it would have placed a financial disincentive on valuable works of literature by authors such as Malcolm X, Thoreau, Martin Luther King, Jr., and even Saint Augustine.

Although the Court generally treats content discrimination with disfavor, the justices do not always agree about what constitutes content-based regulation. In *Hill v. Colorado* (2000), for instance, six of the nine justices upheld a Colorado statute that made it a crime to approach within eight feet of another person outside a medical facility without consent "for the purpose of passing a leaflet or handbill to, displaying a sign to, or engaging in oral protest, education, or counseling with such other person." The majority concluded that the statute was neither content nor viewpoint based because it applied equally to "all 'protest,' to all 'counseling,' and to all demonstrators whether or not the demonstration concerns abortion, and whether they oppose or support the woman who has made the abortion decision." Content-neutral speech restrictions are subject to a less-demanding level of judicial scrutiny; therefore, the Court was able to uphold the statute as a valid time, place, and manner regulation. Dissenting, Justice Scalia argued that the abortion clinic no-approach buffer zone was "obviously and undeniably content-based"

because its intent and practical effect was to limit the speech of abortion opponents.

One of the paradoxes in First Amendment jurisprudence is that despite both the obvious importance of the content distinction and the Court's absolutist-sounding rhetoric in cases such as *Mosely*, the Constitution does not always prohibit content-based regulations of speech. The Court has identified certain categories of expression that are unprotected (such as libel, obscenity, or fighting words) or entitled only to limited protection (such as commercial speech) under the First Amendment. These speech categories, which undeniably are defined by their content, are exceptions to the rule that all content-based regulations are presumptively unconstitutional. Rather, in these areas, the Court has determined that a compelling interest already exists for treating the entire category of speech as outside the boundaries of First Amendment protection.

Yet even within these unprotected categories of speech, the government does not have free rein to regulate expression based on content. In *R.A.V. v City of St. Paul*, the Court overturned a city ordinance that prohibited hate speech based on race, color, religion, or gender, but not political affiliation or sexual orientation. In his opinion for the Court, Justice Scalia explained that although the state could outlaw all fighting words, the city's partial ban impermissibly discriminated within that speech category on the basis of content. The government may not make content distinctions even within these lower classes of speech solely because of official disapproval of the ideas expressed. "Thus," Justice Scalia wrote, "the government may proscribe libel; but it may not make the further content discrimination of proscribing only libel critical of the government."

NICOLE B. CÁSAREZ

References and Further Reading

Chemerinsky, Erwin, *Content Neutrality as a Central Problem of Freedom of Expression: Problems in the Supreme Court's Application*, S. Cal. L. Rev. 74 (2000): 49–64.
Farber, Daniel A. *The First Amendment*, 2nd ed. New York: Foundation Press, 2003.
Redish, Martin H., *The Content Distinction in First Amendment Analysis*, Stan. L. Rev. 34 (1981): 113151.
Stone, Geoffrey R., *Content Regulation and the First Amendment*, Wm. & Mary L. Rev. 25 (1983):189–252.

Cases and Statutes Cited

Hill v. Colorado, 530 U.S. 703 (2000)
Police Department of Chicago v. Mosely, 408 U.S. 92 (1972)
R.A.V. v. City of St. Paul, 505 U.S. 377 (1992)

Simon & Schuster v. New York State Crime Victims Board,
502 U.S. 105 (1991)
Texas v. Johnson, 491 U.S. 397 (1989)

See also **Anti-Abortion Protest and Freedom of Speech; Categorical Approach to Free Speech; Content-Neutral Regulation of Speech; Flag Burning; Time, Place & Manner Rule; Viewpoint Discrimination in Free Speech Cases**

CONTENT-NEUTRAL REGULATION OF SPEECH

While phrased in absolute terms, the free speech clause has been interpreted to require a greater level of justification for government regulation of the content of speech and a lesser degree of justification for speech regulations that apply without regard to the content of speech. When governments impose the latter form of speech regulations, they are called content-neutral regulations of speech. The essential distinction between content-based regulation of speech and content-neutral speech regulations is that the former regulates on the basis of *what* is said, whereas the latter regulates on the basis of either *how*, *when*, or *where* the speech is uttered, or is only an incidental restriction on speech that has as its purpose the regulation of some conduct that is not related to speech. Some facially content-neutral laws are treated as content based if their application hinges on what the speaker says (for example, a law against disturbing the peace is treated as content based when it is applied because of what the speaker says). Some content-based laws are treated as content neutral if their purpose is to address the "secondary effects" of that speech, effects that are not produced by what is said but are merely adventitious by-products of the regulated speech. Content-neutral regulations of speech can be subdivided into three main types: restrictions on the time, place, or manner of speech; restrictions on conduct that have only an incidental and unintended effect on expression that is part of the regulated conduct; and restrictions intended to control the "secondary effects" of regulated speech.

Time, Place, or Manner Regulations

In general, governments may regulate the time, place, or manner of speech, so long as the restrictions on speech "are justified without reference to the content of the regulated speech, . . . are narrowly tailored to serve a significant governmental interest, and . . . leave open ample alternative channels for communication of the information" *Clark v. Community for Creative Non-Violence,* 468 U.S. 288, 293 (1984). This rule was articulated as early in 1949, in *Kovacs v. Cooper,* 336 U.S. 77 (1949), in which the Supreme Court upheld a ban on "loud and raucous" sound trucks. In *Ward v. Rock Against Racism,* 491 U.S. 781 (1989), the Court clarified its requirement that content-neutral time, place, or manner regulations be "narrowly tailored to serve a significant governmental interest" by noting that such regulations "need not be the least restrictive or least intrusive means of doing so . . . . So long as the means chosen are not substantially broader than necessary to achieve the government's interest, [a] regulation will not be invalid simply because a court concludes that the government's interest could be adequately served by some less-speech-restrictive alternative." In recent years the Supreme Court has stressed the importance of leaving open "ample alternative channels of communication." In *Ladue v. Gilleo,* 512 U.S. 43 (1994), for example, the Court struck down a municipal ordinance banning almost all signs displayed on or in residences. The majority noted that the city had "almost completely foreclosed a venerable means of communication that is both unique and important" and opined that the danger posed to free speech by bans of an entire medium of communication is that "such measures can suppress too much speech."

The line between content-based and content-neutral regulations was blurred in *Hill v. Colorado,* 530 U.S. 703 (2000), in which the Court upheld a ban on approaching a person in close proximity to a medical facility to "engage in oral protest, education, or counseling" without the other person's consent. The majority thought the ban was content neutral because it applied to any such speech, not just abortion protests. The dissenters claimed that the ban was content based because it was triggered by what the speaker says.

Regulations of Symbolic Conduct or Symbolic Speech

Government regulation of conduct does not generally implicate the free speech guarantee, but because some conduct does communicate ideas, the Supreme Court has crafted a test to determine when it is permissible for governments to regulate conduct when such regulation also restricts the symbolic speech imbedded in the regulated conduct. In *United States v. O'Brien,* 391 U.S. 367 (1968), the Supreme Court upheld a ban on the knowing destruction or mutilation of a military draft registration certificate, as applied to David O'Brien, who publicly burned his draft card as part of a demonstration against the Vietnam War. The Court assumed that O'Brien's action was sufficiently communicative to invoke the free speech clause but concluded that the government's ban on destruction or mutilation of a draft card was valid because it was "within the constitutional power of the Government" (considered apart from the free speech issue); furthered "an important or substantial governmental interest" (facilitating the military draft); the governmental interest was "unrelated to the suppression of free expression;" and the "incidental restriction on [free speech was] no greater than is essential to the furtherance of [the governmental] interest." Although *O'Brien* created the test for symbolic speech or conduct, the case was much criticized as an erroneous application of the principle, especially because there was evidence in the legislative record that the statute was enacted to punish this particularly inflammatory mode of protesting the Vietnam War.

The heightened level of scrutiny demanded by *O'Brien* only applies when the regulation impinges on "conduct with a significant expressive element" or "where a statute based on a nonexpressive activity has the inevitable effect of singling those out engaged in expressive activity" *Arcara v. Cloud Books*, 478 U.S. 697 (1986). In general, conduct "possesses sufficient communicative elements to bring the First Amendment into play" when the actor intends "to convey a particularized message" and there is a great likelihood "that the message would be understood by those who viewed it" *Texas v. Johnson*, 491 U.S. 397 (1989).

A series of flag-burning and flag desecration cases have cemented the principle that, under the *O'Brien* test, the government's asserted interest must not only be real but unrelated to the suppression of ideas. In *Spence v. Washington*, 418 U.S. 405 (1974), and in *Smith v. Goguen*, 415 U.S. 566 (1974), the Court found that the government's interest in promoting respect for the American flag was related to the suppression of ideas. In *Spence* the Court overturned a conviction for taping a peace sign to a flag, and in *Smith* the Court struck down a conviction for sewing a flag to the seat of one's pants. This came to a head in *Texas v. Johnson*, in which the Court overturned Johnson's conviction for "desecration of a venerated object," conduct that consisted of burning the American flag. A year later, in *United States v. Eichman*, 496 U.S. 310 (1990), the Supreme Court also voided the federal Flag Protection Act of 1989. Because the flag is an unalloyed symbol of the nation, its use—whether it ranges from display to destruction—inevitably involves communication of some idea, be it respect

or contempt for America. Thus, the Court saw the governmental interest in proscribing destruction of the flag to be inherently related to the suppression of the idea of contempt for America and the flag for which it stands. Of course, the principle applies more broadly than just to flag burning. In *Schacht v. United States*, 398 U.S. 58 (1970), the Supreme Court invalidated the application of a federal law forbidding the wearing of an American military uniform without authorization to an actor performing in a dramatic protest of the Vietnam War, because another federal law permitted the wearing of American military uniforms in theatrical productions so long as "the portrayal does not tend to discredit" the military. The interplay of the two statutes provided proof that the government's interest in limiting the wearing of military uniforms in dramas was related to the suppression of ideas.

The flag-burning cases produced calls for a constitutional amendment to permit punishment of flag burners. Although some of those proposals have received the requisite majority in the House of Representatives, none have been approved by the Senate.

While many of the cases dealing with symbolic speech have involved the politically charged issue of flag desecration, the most recent applications have involved more prosaic and salacious matters. In each of *Barnes v. Glen Theatre, Inc.*, 501 U.S. 560 (1991) and *City of Erie v. Pap's A.M.*, 529 U.S. 277 (2000), the Supreme Court upheld state laws banning public nudity, as applied to nude dancing. The Court conceded that there was some protected expression in nude dancing but thought that the government's interest in prohibiting such conduct was sufficiently unrelated to the suppression of the erotic ideas inherent in nude dancing to warrant application of the *O'Brien* test. Moreover, because the ordinance at issue in *Erie* permitted dancers to perform wearing only "pasties" and G-strings, the inhibition on the expressive element of the dancers' performance was as minimal as the required garments.

The Secondary Effects Doctrine

The third type of content-neutral regulations are those that address the so-called secondary effects doctrine. The essence of this doctrine is that content-based regulations of speech that are intended to regulate conduct that is closely associated with the regulated speech but that is not produced by the content of the speech are treated as if they are content neutral, and thus valid if they are narrowly tailored to serve a significant government interest and leave open ample alternative channels of communication. This is, of course, a legal fiction, but one that the Supreme Court has created to deal almost exclusively with the collateral effects of pornographic, but not obscene, speech. In *Young v. American Mini Theatres*, 427 U.S. 50 (1976), the Court upheld a Detroit zoning law that required purveyors of pornographic materials to disperse throughout the city. The purpose of the law was to ameliorate the problems of public drunkenness, drug dealing, theft, and other criminal behavior that is closely associated spatially with concentrations of smut houses, but which is not produced by the consumption of smut. The plurality opinion in *Young* made much of the fact that pornographic expression is of lesser value than other speech. This doctrine was extended in *Renton v. Playtime Theatres, Inc.*, 475 U.S. 41 (1986), in which the Court upheld a municipal zoning ordinance that required movie theaters exhibiting pornographic films to locate in a limited portion of the community. The doctrine was extended even further in *City of Erie v. Pap's A.M.*, in which the Court applied the secondary effects doctrine to conclude that Erie's substantial governmental interest in prohibiting nude dancing was to alleviate the secondary effects of such tawdry expression and that this interest was unrelated to the suppression of ideas.

Not every effect of regulated speech is a secondary effect. When the behavior that the government seeks to control by regulating speech is the natural, foreseeable reaction of listeners' reaction to the speech, such effects are not treated as secondary effects. The District of Columbia enacted a law barring the display within 500 feet of an embassy any sign that might bring the foreign government into "public odium [or] disrepute." D. C. defended the law as intended to address the secondary effects of demonstrations against foreign governments: an increased risk of public disorder and crime. The Supreme Court rejected that argument in *Boos v. Barry*, 485 U.S. 312 (1988): "Listeners' reactions to speech are [not] 'secondary effects.'" Because the law focused "on the direct impact of speech on its audience," the law was regarded as content based and thus subject to the strict scrutiny test in free speech cases.

Content-neutral regulations are subject to a lesser degree of scrutiny than content-based regulations, because there seems to be less danger that the government is attempting to skew the nature of public discourse. Moreover, content-neutral regulations are far more likely to have some plausible noncensorial reason for their enactment. But because content-neutral regulations have the potential to foreclose all speech, or all of a given type of speech, by drawing the scope of the regulation broadly the Supreme Court has insisted on the intermediate level of scrutiny embodied

by the combination of the time, place, or manner and the *O'Brien* tests.

CALVIN MASSEY

References and Further Reading

Kagan, Elena, *Private Speech, Public Purpose: The Role of Governmental Motive in First Amendment Doctrine*, U. Chi. L. Rev. 415 (1996): 63:446–463.
Stone, Geoffrey, *Content-Neutral Restrictions*, U. Chi. L. Rev. 54 (1987): 46.
———, *Content Regulation and the First Amendment*, William & Mary L. Rev. 189, (1983): 25:207–217.

Cases and Statutes Cited

Arcara v. Cloud Books, 478 U.S. 697 (1986)
Barnes v. Glen Theatre, Inc., 501 U.S. 560 (1991)
Boos v. Barry, 485 U.S. 312 (1988)
City of Erie v. Pap's A.M., 529 U.S. 277 (2000)
Clark v. Community for Creative Non-Violence, 468 U.S. 288, 293 (1984)
Hill v. Colorado, 530 U.S. 703 (2000)
Kovacs v. Cooper, 336 U.S. 77 (1949)
Ladue v. Gilleo, 512 U.S. 43 (1994)
Renton v. Playtime Theatres, Inc., 475 U.S. 41 (1986)
Schacht v. United States, 398 U.S. 58 (1970)
Smith v. Goguen, 415 U.S. 566 (1974)
Spence v. Washington, 418 U.S. 405 (1974)
Texas v. Johnson, 491 U.S. 397 (1989)
United States v. Eichman, 496 U.S. 310 (1990)
United States v. O'Brien, 391 U.S. 367 (1968)
Ward v. Rock Against Racism, 491 U.S. 781 (1989)
Young v. American Mini Theatres, 427 U.S. 50 (1976)

See also **Abortion Protest Cases; Anti-Abortion Protest and Freedom of Speech,** *City of Erie v. Pap's A.M.,* **529 U.S. 277 (2000); Content-Based Regulation of Speech, Draft Card Burning; Flag Burning; Freedom of Speech and Press: Nineteenth Century; Freedom of Speech: Modern Period (1917–Present); Intermediate Scrutiny Test in Free Speech Cases; O'Brien Content-Neutral Free Speech Test; O'Brien Formula;** *Renton v. Playtime Theatres, Inc.,* **475 U.S. 41 (1986); Secondary Effects Doctrine; Speech versus Conduct Distinction; Symbolic Speech; Theories of Free Speech Protection; Two-Tiered Theory of Free Speech;** *United States v. O'Brien,* **391 U.S. 367 (1968);** *Young v. American Mini Theaters, Inc.,* **427 U.S. 50 (1976)**

COOLIDGE v. NEW HAMPSHIRE, 403 U.S. 443 (1971)

In *Coolidge v. New Hampshire*, the Supreme Court addressed the question of which state officials may validly issue search warrants.

In 1964, a fourteen-year-old girl was murdered in Manchester, New Hampshire. A subsequent investigation led the police to suspect Edward H. Coolidge,

Jr., of the crime. The police presented their evidence to the State Attorney General who supervised the investigation and who would later serve as chief prosecutor at Coolidge's trial. Acting in his capacity as a justice of the peace under New Hampshire law, the Attorney General issued a search warrant for Coolidge's car. The police impounded the car, vacuumed its carpet, and discovered evidence linking Coolidge to the murder. State courts rejected Coolidge's claim that the search violated the Fourth and Fourteenth Amendments.

In an opinion written by Justice Potter Stewart, the Supreme Court held that the Constitution prohibits the issuance of a warrant except where probable cause has been found by a "neutral and detached magistrate" who independently assessed the evidence collected by the police. In *Coolidge*, the chief investigator/prosecutor in this case was not sufficiently "neutral and detached." Only a plurality of the Court, however, found that the search did not fall under any of the exceptions to the warrant requirement and that the evidence against Coolidge should have been suppressed.

Coolidge affirms the principle that the Fourth Amendment serves as a check on the power of police to search and seize property without a prior, independent assessment by a neutral state official.

LARRY CUNNINGHAM

References and Further Reading

LaFave, Wayne R. "The 'Neutral and Detached Magistrate' Requirement." Sec. 4.2 of *Search and Seizure: A Treatise on the Fourth Amendment*. Vol. 2. 4th ed. St. Paul: Thomson/West, 2004.

See also **Probable Cause; Search (General Definition); Search Warrants; Stewart, Potter; Warrant Clause; Warrantless Searches**

COPYRIGHT LAW AND FREE EXERCISE

The First Amendment forbids Congress from making any law prohibiting the free exercise of religion. The federal copyright statute grants copyright holders a court-enforced power to prevent third parties from using religious texts. Nevertheless, copyright is unlikely to violate the Free Exercise Clause. In 1990, the Supreme Court held that the Free Exercise Clause does not require the government to grant religious exemptions to neutral laws of general applicability, *Employment Division v. Smith*. Since copyright doctrine makes no distinctions based on the content of works or the religious status of their authors, copyright is a neutral law of general applicability.

Courts could accommodate the needs of persons wishing to use copyright-protected material for religious purposes without permission by using several different copyright doctrines. Courts could refuse copyright to works allegedly dictated to humans by divine beings on the ground that copyright requires a human author. Courts could find that seemingly infringing uses are allowed as "fair use." Fair use allows some actions that otherwise would be copyright infringement after balancing the purpose and nature of the use (including whether it is commercial or nonprofit), the nature of the copyrighted work, the amount used, and the economic burden on the copyright holder, Title 17 United States Code, Section 107. One could argue that religious worship is a socially valuable nonprofit use under the first factor. Courts could narrow the copyright protection of the religious work through the "idea/expression dichotomy." Copyright only protects the way an idea or fact is expressed, but not the idea or fact, Title 17 United States Code, Section 102(b). If only a few ways of expressing something are possible, the expression and content are said to merge, allowing no copyright protection. One could argue that religious practice requires access to the exact words of a divine message; no paraphrase is equivalent. Even if the court decides that copyright has been infringed, it could accommodate religiously motivated infringement by granting only money damages instead of ordering the use stopped.

The courts generally have been unsympathetic to these arguments. For example, a believer was held to infringe the copyrights of the Urantia Foundation when she made numerous electronic copies of the Urantia Book for free distribution to other potential believers. The court was not swayed by the claimed celestial authorship of the scripture, insisting that the human "intermediaries" were "authors" for purposes of the copyright statute, *Urantia Foundation v. Maaherra*. In *Urantia*, religious practice was not greatly affected, because the copied work was available to anyone at a reasonable price from the copyright holder. Copyright has been enforced even when the copyright holder may have intended to prevent any use of the religious book. The World Wide Church of God (WWCG) holds copyright in Pastor General Herbert W. Armstrong's *Mystery of the Ages* (MOA). After distributing more than nine million free copies of MOA, the WWCG decided to halt distribution because of doctrinal changes. WWCG was out of print for at least ten years. Two former WWCG ministers started a separate church dedicated to the original teachings of MOA; all members were required to read MOA to be considered for baptism. The separatist ministers were held to have infringed WWCG's copyright when they began printing and distributing new copies of MOA without permission. The court did not find relevant that the new church was more dedicated to the teachings of MOA's author than was the MOA-suppressing copyright holder. The court gave great weight to WWCG's claim that it intended to publish an annotated version of MOA sometime in the future. The separatist ministers were ordered to cease publication and distribution of MOA, *Worldwide Church of God v. Philadelphia Church of God.*

Many intellectual property cases involve the Church of Scientology's attempts to keep secret various church materials disseminated by disaffected former scientologists. The Free Exercise Clause has been of scant help to either side in these cases. Seemingly to prevent Establishment Clause issues, the courts generally apply standard copyright doctrine without taking religious motivations into account. Two Establishment Clause issues loom in such copyright disputes. First, copyright is usually considered a type of personal property. Allowing copyright infringement for religious use would constitute limiting one person's property rights to accommodate another person's religious belief. This might violate the Establishment Clause by showing favoritism toward one religious sect. Second, deciding which of competing sects is more in line with the beliefs of the spiritual work's author might violate the Establishment Clause by entangling the court in issues of religious doctrine.

The copyright statute includes one specific exemption for religious worship. According to section 110(3) of title 17 of the United States Code, copyright is not infringed by "performance of a nondramatic literary or musical work or of a dramatico-musical work of a religious nature, or display of a work, in the course of services at a place of worship or other religious assembly." In other words, if church members have a legally obtained copy of a hymnbook or scripture, they can sing or read the words aloud during worship services without obtaining a license from the copyright holder. A license would otherwise be necessary, because a copyright holder has the exclusive right not only to make and distribute copies of his work but also to allow the work to be performed publicly. This statutory exemption has not been discussed by any court opinions, but Professor Cotter argues that it violates the Establishment Clause by favoring religion over secularism.

In addition, a court could hold that otherwise infringing activity must be allowed because of the Religious Freedom Restoration Act (RFRA), which protects religious practices from substantial burdens created by laws of general applicability unless the law is the least restrictive means of furthering a compelling government interest. Congress enacted the RFRA in reaction to *Employment Division v. Smith.* No court has accepted the argument that copyright enforcement is a substantial burden for purposes of RFRA, not even the *Worldwide Church* case discussed previously. In 1997, the Supreme Court held the RFRA to be unconstitutional as applied to state statutes, *City of Boerne v. Flores.* Copyright is a federal statute, so it is not touched by *Boerne.*

MALLA POLLACK

References and Further Reading

Cotter, Thomas F., *Guttenberg's Legacy: Copyright, Censorship, and Religious Pluralism*, California Law Review 91 (2003): 232.

Cases and Statutes Cited

City of Boerne v. Flores, 521 U.S. 507 (1997)
Employment Division, Department of Human Resources v. Smith, 494 U.S. 872 (1990)
Urantia Foundation v. Maaherra, 114 F.3d 955 (9th Cir. 1997)
Worldwide Church of God v. Philadelphia Church of God, Inc., 227 F.3d 1110 (9th Cir. 2000)

See also **Church of Scientology and Religious Liberty; City of Boerne v. Flores, 521 U.S. 507 (1997); Employment Division, Department of Human Resources v. Smith, 494 U.S. 872 (1990); Establishment Clause: Theories of Interpretation; Establishment of Religion and Free Exercise Clauses; Religious Freedom Restoration Act**

CORPORATION OF THE PRESIDING BISHOP OF THE CHURCH OF JESUS CHRIST OF LATTER-DAY SAINTS v. AMOS, 483 U.S. 327 (1987)

The Supreme Court in *Corporation of Presiding Bishop of the Church of Jesus Chris of Latter-Day Saints v. Amos* (1987) addressed the important issue of whether statutory exceptions to otherwise generally applicable laws are constitutionally permissible as an accommodation to religious freedom. The nine to zero decision in the case became more important after the Supreme Court's holding in *Employment Division, Department of Human Resources of Oregon v. Smith* (1990) that religious exemptions to generally applicable laws are not constitutionally required. Indeed, Justice Scalia in *Smith* specifically stated that issues of religious freedom are most appropriately within the purview of the political process, a constitutional possibility that *Amos* allows but *Smith* explains is not required.

The specific issue in *Presiding Bishop* was whether a religious organization exemption from Title VII of the Civil Rights Act of 1964 violates the Establishment Clause. The claimant, Mayson, worked at the

Deseret Gymnasium in Salt Lake City, Utah, a non-profit public facility owned and operated by the Church of Jesus Christ of Latter-Day Saints. The church discharged him in 1981 because he failed to qualify for a "temple recommend," a religious worthiness standard for church members. Following his discharge for religious reasons, he brought a civil rights class action against the church, under Section 703 of Title VII, for discriminating in employment on the basis of religion. The church defended on the basis of Section 702, which exempts religious organizations from the proscription against religious discrimination. At trial Mayson successfully argued that the exemption provided in Section 702 violates the Establishment Clause, because it has the primary effect of advancing religion, contrary to the *Lemon* test.

Justice White, writing for the Court, reversed the district court's judgment, holding that the state may accommodate religion by statutory exemptions without violating the establishment Clause. Despite variant explanations of why statutory exemptions may be constitutionally permissible, no justice dissented from the Court's essential holding that the establishment clause does not prohibit the state from ever accommodating religious freedom through statutory exemptions.

Justice White's majority opinion held that to avoid conflicting with the establishment clause, any religious exemption must pass the three-pronged *Lemon* test, a test Section 702 clearly passed. Under *Lemon's* secular purpose test, the 702 exemption served "a permissible legislative purpose to alleviate significant governmental interference with the ability of religious organizations to define and carry out their religious missions." In response to Mayson's argument that it was difficult to imagine how working in a gym would affect a religious organization's "religious activities," the Court concluded that narrowly defining a religious institution's "religious activities" would unduly burden the religious organization's ability to define and carry out its religious mission.

With regard to the *Lemon* issue of secular effect, the Court held that this test is violated only where "the *government itself* has advanced religion through its activities and influence." In *Presiding Bishop* Congress had not advanced religion by the exemption, but simply had permitted the religious institution to advance its own religious purposes. Because Congress's incidental advancement of the religious institution could not reasonably be attributable to the government, the exemption did not trigger a Lemon violation of an impermissible religious effect. With regard to *Lemon*'s entanglement prong, the Court held that deferring to the religious institution for the determination of what constituted a "religious

activity" diminished any likelihood of entanglement. Indeed, how could any court effectively trump a religious institution's evaluation of what constitutes "religious activity" without seriously violating the proscription against entanglement?

Justice Brennan, with whom Justice Marshall joined, agreed that the legislature might have a constitutional secular purpose of deferring as a matter of religious freedom to the religious community's sense of their religious mission. Justice Brennan acknowledged that the "authority to engage in this process of self-definition inevitably involves what we normally regard as infringement on free exercise rights, since a religious organization is able to condition employment in certain activities on subscription to particular religious tenets." However, Justice Brennan conceded that "[w]e are willing to countenance the imposition of such a condition because we deem it vital that, if certain activities constitute part of a religious community's practice, then a religious organization should be able to require that only members of its community perform those activities."

Justice O'Connor, in a concurring opinion, suggested that the religious accommodation could also be justified on the basis of her endorsement test alternative to the *Lemon* analysis. She reasoned that while any religious exemption may conflict with the *Lemon* proscription against any legislative purpose beneficial to religion, some exemptions might be justifiable as a matter of respect to the free exercise of religion. The question should not be whether the exemption is beneficial to religion but rather whether the accommodation provides "unjustifiable awards of assistance to religious organizations." To resolve this issue, Justice O'Connor suggested that the test ought to ask "whether government's purpose is to endorse religion and whether the statute actually conveys a message of endorsement." To ascertain whether the statute conveys a message of endorsement, the relevant issue is how it would be perceived by an objective observer who is acquainted with the text, the legislative history, and the implementation of the statute. As applied to the facts, Justice O'Connor concluded that "[b]ecause there is a probability that a nonprofit activity of a religious organization will itself be involved in the organization's mission, in my view the objective observer should perceive the Government action as an accommodation of the exercise of religion rather than as a Government endorsement of religion."

Amos has since been cited repeatedly for two line-drawing propositions for statutory exemptions that are beneficial to religious communities: (1) that the state may accommodate religious freedom through the political process, unless (2) that "accommodation" crosses the establishment line by endorsing religion to the objective observer. Without the principle of religious accommodationism announced in *Amos*, Justice Scalia's relegation of religious freedom to the political processes in *Smith* would leave precious little for the free exercise of religion other than the equal protection mandate acknowledged in *Church of the Lukumi Bablu Aye v. City of Hialeah* that the state not actively target religion.

RICHARD COLLIN MANGRUM

Cases and Statutes Cited

Corporation of the Presiding Bishop of the Church of Jesus Christ of Latter-Day Saints v. Amos, 483 U.S. 327 (1987)
Church of the Lukumi Babalu Aye v. City of Hialeah, 508 U.S. 520 (1993)
Employment Division, Department of Human Resources of Oregon v. Smith, 494 U.S. 872 (1990)
Lemon v. Kurtzman, 403 U.S. 602 (1971)

CORRIGAN v. BUCKLEY, 271 U.S. 323 (1926)

In *Corrigan v. Buckley*, the U.S. Supreme Court unanimously rejected a legal challenge to racially restrictive covenants and thereby made a significant contribution to the upsurge in residential segregation that took place in America's cities during the first half of the twentieth century.

In 1917, in *Buchanan v. Warley*, the Court found that municipal ordinances requiring residential segregation violated the fourteenth amendment, relying in significant measure on the fact that it was the *government* that had mandated the segregation. In response to that decision, in cities across the country, residents entered into private contracts whereby they agreed not to sell or rent their homes to blacks (or members of other minority groups), thereby accomplishing the same goal that the drafters of the municipal ordinances had sought to achieve.

The *Corrigan* case involved a racially restrictive covenant in the District of Columbia. In 1921, several residents of the District had entered into a covenant pursuant to which they promised to never sell their home to "any person of the negro race or blood." The next year, Irene Corrigan, one of the white residents who had signed the covenant, contracted to sell her home to a Negro, Helen Curtis. Another white homeowner, John Buckley, sued to block the sale of the home on the grounds that it violated the restrictive covenant. After a lower court granted relief to the plaintiff and the Court of Appeals for the District of Columbia affirmed, the defendants appealed to the Supreme Court. The defendants argued that the covenant itself (not its judicial enforcement) violated several provisions of the U.S. Constitution, including the Fifth, Thirteenth, and Fourteenth Amendments. At this time, the Supreme Court's jurisdiction over cases from the District of Columbia was limited to matters raising "substantial" federal claims. The Court determined that the appellants had presented no such claims and hence dismissed the appeal "for want of jurisdiction." In reaching that conclusion, the Court concluded that both the Fifth and Fourteenth Amendments limited only the action of the government, not private parties, and that the Thirteenth Amendment, which prohibited slavery and involuntary servitude, had no application to the sale of real estate. Although the defendants had not challenged the constitutionality of the judicial enforcement of the covenant at any point in the litigation, they did raise the enforcement issue in their arguments to the Supreme Court. The Court noted that this issue was not properly before it, but nevertheless observed—in dicta—that this argument was also "lacking in substance." Although the Court did not clearly resolve the question whether judicial enforcement of racially restrictive covenants was constitutional, a difficult one since such enforcement arguably implicated state action, after the *Corrigan* decision, state courts across the nation cited *Corrigan* for the view that the judicial enforcement of such covenants did not violate the Constitution.

The *Corrigan* case legitimized racially restrictive covenants and gave encouragement to white property owners to use such covenants to retain the racial integrity of residential neighborhoods. Their use was extensive and contributed to the solidification of the black ghetto in many northern cities. For example, by the 1940s, eighty-five percent of the housing in Detroit and eighty percent of the housing in Chicago was encumbered by a racially restrictive covenant.

Finally, in 1948, the U.S. Supreme Court in *Shelley v. Kraemer* (1948) declared that judicial enforcement of racially restrictive covenants did violate the Fourteenth Amendment. But the legacy of several decades of enforcement of these covenants meant that residential segregation was well entrenched in most major American cities, a pattern that has never been undone.

DAVISON M. DOUGLAS

References and Further Reading

Massey, Douglas S., and Nancy A. Denton. *American Apartheid: Segregation and the Making of the Underclass.* Cambridge: Harvard University Press, 1993.
McGovney, D. O., *Racial Residential Segregation by State Court Enforcement of Restrictive Agreements, Covenants or Conditions in Deeds is Unconstitutional*, California Law Review 33 (1945): 5–39.
Vose, Clement E. *Caucasians Only: The Supreme Court, the NAACP, and the Restrictive Covenant Cases.* Berkeley: University of California Press, 1959.

Cases and Statutes Cited

Buchanan v. Warley, 245 U.S. 60 (1917)
Shelley v. Kraemer, 334 U.S. 1 (1948)

See also **Fourteenth Amendment; State Action Doctrine**

CORRUPTION OF BLOOD

The doctrine of corruption of blood mandated that when a person committed a criminal or treasonous act, he and his entire family became outlaws. As a consequence, the offender forfeited all of his property, real and personal. In addition, the offender could no longer transfer his property, either during his lifetime or on death. The property itself fell to the crown.

Blackstone indicates in his commentaries that the Normans introduced corruption of blood into English law on their conquest of the Isles. After 1066, civil disabilities were imposed through "attainder," a procedure that declared a criminal convicted of treason or a felony "attained." Attainder immediately led to corruption of blood, forfeiture and loss of all civil rights. This denial of all rights became referred to as "civil death."

By the late eighteenth century, the penalty had come under attack in England as unduly harsh and lacking in use, as rehabilitative principles began their ascent during the Age of Enlightenment. During this time, the English parliament created felonies without corruption of blood as penalty. It ultimately abolished corruption of blood in 1870.

The U.S. Constitution rejected the penalty in the Corruption of Blood Clause of Article III. It limits forfeiture for treason to the traitor's lifetime and indicates its hostility to the punishment also in the Bill of Attainder Clause. These are among the substantive values, as Alexander Hamilton noted, included in the Constitution itself. Why the founding fathers rejected corruption of blood remains unclear, but they seem to have been concerned about creating familial, rather than individual, punishment. The decisions in *Wallach v. Riswick* and Justice Miller's dissent in *Ex parte Garland* both point in this direction. After the constitutional prohibitions, the federal government passed complementary legislation that remained on the books until the 1980s.

Several state constitutions also contain corruption of blood clauses. However, despite federal and state prohibitions, the problems created by corruption of blood continued because of civil death provisions that prohibited inmates, and especially lifers, from entering into contracts and from inheriting property. Therefore, their rights to grant property to their children was limited, albeit they were not restricted from bequeathing property they held at the time of conviction to their children. Modern forfeiture statutes also raise some of the same problems inherent in the corruption of blood penalty.

Despite the attempt to protect children from the sins of their parents, in many other situations, the law penalizes children for choices their parents made. This held particularly true for children born out of wedlock but continues to other groups of children, such as the noncitizen children of undocumented immigrants who may be barred from access to certain public goods. Moreover, the prohibition on corruption of blood does not entail prohibition on other consequences of a criminal offense, many of which also impact the offender's family. Among them are the denial of welfare benefits to the offender, restrictions on access to one's children because of incarceration, and inability to provide appropriately for one's family because of statutory limitations on employment.

Nora V. Demleitner

References and Further Reading

U.S. Const. art. I, 9. cl. 3, art. I, 10, cl. 1; art. III, 3, cl. 2.
William Blackstone, Commentaries.
History and Theory of Civil Disabilities, Vand. L. Rev. 23 (1970): 941.
Stier, Max, *Note, Corruption of Blood and Equal Protection: Why the Sins of the Parents Should Not Matter*, Stan. L. Rev. 44 (1992): 727.

Cases and Statutes Cited

Ex parte Garland, 71 U.S. (4 Wall) 333 (1866)
Wallach v. Van Riswick, 92 U.S. 202 (1875)

See also **Bill of Attainder; Civil Death; Collateral Consequences**

COUNSELMAN v. HITCHCOCK, 142 U.S. 547 (1892)

This case concerns the breadth of the protection against self-incrimination under the Fifth Amendment. The defendant, Counselman, invoked his Fifth Amendment privileges in refusing to answer specific questions from a federal grand jury. Because of the existence of a federal statue granting immunity from prosecution on the basis of evidence the witness had provided during a criminal proceeding, Counselman was charged with contempt. He filed a petition for a writ of habeas corpus, arguing that he could legitimately invoke the Fifth Amendment, because its protection was broader than that offered by the statute.

The case went on appeal to the U.S. Supreme Court, where it was heard in December 1891 and decided in January 1892, with Justice Samuel Blatchford writing for a unanimous Court. The Court agreed with Counselman's contention, saying that the protection provided by the federal law was limited by the fact that, while the evidence obtained through his testimony could not be used against him in a federal proceeding, it could be used as a basis for obtaining information that might be used in another case against him. The Court thus acknowledged the limited protection offered by the federal statute. Congress subsequently revised the law, prohibiting the prosecution of a witness granted immunity for his involvement in the matter about which he testified.

In a period when relatively little attention was being paid to the scope of civil liberties protection offered by the federal Bill of Rights, the ruling in this case was significant because the Court, given the opportunity, was willing to acknowledge the broad scope of the guarantees against self-incrimination offered by the Fifth Amendment.

REBECCA S. SHOEMAKER

References and Further Reading

Constitutional Rights at the Junction: The Emergence of the Privilege against Self-Incrimination and the Interstate Commerce Act, Virginia Law Review, 81 (1995): 7:1989–2042.
Levy, Leonard. *Origins of the Fifth Amendment; the Right against Self-incrimination* New York: Oxford University Press, 1968.

See also **Coerced Confessions/Police Interrogations; Self-incrimination (v): Historical Background**

COUNTY AND CITY SEALS WITH RELIGIOUS CONTENT

One issue that frequently generates controversy in the United States is whether the use of religious symbols or language on government property constitutes an establishment of religion in violation of the Establishment Clause. One example of the use of religious symbols or language on government property is the use of religious language or imagery on the official seals of cities and counties. On a number of occasions, plaintiffs have challenged the constitutionality of such usages. The U.S. Supreme Court has never considered such a case, but a few lower courts have done so. These courts have tended to focus on whether the use of the religious imagery or language has a primary effect of advancing religion or would be reasonably viewed as constituting an endorsement of religion. If so, then the seal violates the Establishment Clause.

Most courts that have occasion to consider such a case have held that religious content on a city or county seal violates the Establishment Clause. In 1985, the U.S. Court of Appeals for the Tenth Circuit sitting en banc considered the constitutionality of a Bernalillo County, New Mexico, seal that contained the Spanish motto "Con Esta Vencemos," which means "With This We Conquer," arched over a gold Latin cross. The district court had found that the seal's religious imagery had only historical, not religious, significance, because it denoted the role of the Catholic Church in the settlement of the American Southwest. The Tenth Circuit disagreed, holding that the seal had "the primary effect of advancing religion" and so violated the Establishment Clause. By way of example, the court noted that those persons who encounter a police officer with the county seal emblazoned on his car could reasonably assume that the "officers were Christian police, and that the organization they represented identified itself with a Christian God" *Friedman v. Board of County Commissioners* (1985). Thereafter, the county removed the religious language and replaced the Latin cross with an ancient Native American sun symbol.

In 1989, the Tenth Circuit again considered the constitutionality of a government seal—one for the city of St. George, Utah—that included a depiction of the city's Mormon temple. The district court found on a summary judgment motion that the illustration of the temple did not have the primary effect of endorsing the Mormon Church, but the Tenth Circuit reversed, holding that there was an issue of fact as to whether the depiction constituted a governmental endorsement of religion and remanded for a trial: *Foremaster v. City of St. George* (1989).

In 1991, the U.S. Court of Appeals for the Seventh Circuit found that two Illinois city seals—the first of which contained a Latin cross along with various secular symbols and the second of which also contained a Latin cross along with the words "God Reigns"—violated the Establishment Clause, because they constituted an endorsement of the Christian religion: *Harris v. City of Zion* (1991); *Kuhn v. City of Rolling Meadows* (1991).

In 1995, the Tenth Circuit again considered the constitutionality of a city seal—for Edmond, Oklahoma—that contained four quadrants, one of which depicted a Latin cross. The court rejected the city's argument that the seal reflected "the unique history and heritage of Edmond" and concluded that the use of the cross on the seal violated the Establishment Clause: *Robinson v. City of Edmond* (1995).

In 1998, a federal district court found that a city seal for Stow, Ohio, containing, along with other secular symbols, a Latin cross superimposed on an open book, had the primary effect of advancing Christianity and thus violated the Establishment Clause" *ACLU v. City of Stow* (1998). The following year, in 1999, a federal district court found that a city seal in Republic, Missouri, that contained a symbolic representation of a fish—a Christian symbol—along with other secular images violated the Establishment Clause: *Webb v. City of Republic* (1999).

One court, however, has sustained the constitutionality of a city seal containing religious content. In 1991, the U.S. Court of Appeals for the Fifth Circuit found that the seal of the city of Austin, Texas, that incorporated the family coat of arms of Stephen F. Austin for whom the city was named did not violate the Establishment Clause even though the coat of arms included a Latin cross: *Murray v. City of Austin* (1991).

On at least one occasion, the use of a county name itself has been challenged as violating the Establishment Clause. In 1994, the U.S. Court of Appeals for the Ninth Circuit considered a constitutional challenge to use of the word "Sacramento" on the Sacramento county seal because the English word, "sacrament," is a term associated with Christianity. The district court dismissed the lawsuit on standing grounds and the Ninth Circuit affirmed: *O'Leary v. County of Sacramento* (1994).

DAVISON M. DOUGLAS

References and Further Reading

Curtis, Ralph, *Religious Symbols on Municipal Seals and Logos*, Journal of Contemporary Law 19 (1993): 287–300.

Hill, David S., *City of Edmond v. Robinson: The Coercion-Standing Test—A New Approach to Religious Symbols Under the Establishment Clause?* Utah Law Review 2000 (2000): 643–669.

McCabe, Kevin J., *Note: Toward a Consensus on Religious Images in Civic Seals Under the Establishment Clause: American Civil Liberties Union v. City of Stow*, Villanova Law Review 46 (2001): 585–611.

Cases and Statutes Cited

ACLU v. City of Stow, 29 F. Supp. 2d 845 (N.D. Ohio 1998)

Foremaster v. City of St. George, 882 F.2d 1485 (10th Cir. 1989)

Friedman v. Board of County Commissioners, 781 F.2d 777 (10th Cir. 1985)

Harris v. City of Zion, 927 F.2d 1401 (7th Cir. 1991)

Kuhn v. City of Rolling Meadows, 927 F.2d 1401 (7th Cir. 1991)

Murray v. City of Austin, 947 F. 2d 147 (5th Cir. 1991)

O'Leary v. County of Sacramento, 19 F.3d 1440 (9th Cir. 1994) (unpublished)

Robinson v. City of Edmond, 68 F.3d 1226 (10th Cir. 1995)

Webb v. City of Republic, 55 F. Supp. 2d 994 (W.D. Mo.1999)

See also **Establishment Clause (I): History, Background, Framing**

COVINGTON, HAYDEN (1911–1980)

Hayden Covington, a graduate of the San Antonio Bar Association School of Law (later St. Mary's University School of Law), ranks among the most overworked and underappreciated attorneys in American history. During the middle part of the twentieth century, he handled as many as fifty major cases every year involving the civil liberties of Jehovah's Witnesses, who faced an unparalleled wave of religious persecution because of their uncommon beliefs and sometimes peculiar behavior. His indefatigable work helped usher in a new era in American constitutional law, the "rights revolution" that reached its apogee under the Warren Court of the 1960s.

Unleashed in a courtroom, Covington could be a whirlwind. A brief magazine profile published in 1943, marveling at his athletic delivery of oral arguments, compared him to a cyclone. After watching the frenetic Witness attorney argue several cases in the early 1940s, a Supreme Court clerk cracked that while Covington might not have talked a greater length longer than other attorneys appearing before the nation's highest bench, he undoubtedly performed more calisthenics. Covington's loud attire also was conspicuous: he argued one important case while sporting a vibrant green suit and a red plaid tie.

But while Covington's demeanor in the courtroom was easy to mock, his record was one that any lawyer would envy. Between 1938 and 1955, he prevailed in more than two dozen cases heard by the U.S. Supreme Court, a record that prompted more than one sympathetic observer to compare him to the likes of Thurgood Marshall. Such landmark cases as *Minersville School District v. Gobitis*, 310 U.S. 586 (1940), *Cantwell v. Connecticut*, 310 U.S. 296 (1940), and *West Virginia v. Barnette*, 319 U.S. 624 (1942) bore his unmistakable imprimatur. His work in these cases and myriad others prompted one national magazine to call him an extraordinary precedent-breaker. Indeed, Covington was nothing short of relentless in asking the high court to scrap ossified judicial precedents and broaden judicial protections for civil liberties.

Asked to explain why he and his fellow Witnesses defended their civil liberties so zealously in the courts, Covington said that they were simply devout

Christians following a precedent established in the Scriptures by the likes of the apostle Paul. The Witnesses were like the earliest Christians, Covington suggested, because they used the courts not only to secure their own freedoms but also to help ensure religious liberty for all Christians.

Covington's star faded in the 1960s and 1970s. He clashed with the leaders of his faith and was at one point "disfellowshipped" (effectively excommunicated). Until his death in 1980, he also was dogged by rumors that he suffered from a drinking problem. But even as he floundered, Covington managed to briefly return to prominence as an attorney in the late 1960s by helping the boxer Muhammad Ali contest his military draft classification in court.

SHAWN FRANCIS PETERS

References and Further Reading

Ali, Muhammad. *The Greatest: My Own Story*. New York: Random House, 1975.

Newton, Merlin Owen. *Armed with the Constitution: Jehovah's Witnesses in Alabama and the U.S. Supreme Court*. Tuscaloosa, AL: University of Alabama Press, 1995.

Penton, M. James. *Apocalypse Delayed: The Story of Jehovah's Witnesses*, 2nd ed. Toronto: University of Toronto Press, 1997.

Peters, Shawn Francis. *Judging Jehovah's Witnesses: Religious Persecution and the Dawn of the Rights Revolution*. Lawrence, KS: University Press of Kansas, 2000.

Cases and Statutes Cited

Cantwell v. Connecticut, 310 U.S. 296 (1940)
Minersville School District v. Gobitis, 310 U.S. 586 (1940)
West Virginia v. Barnette, 319 U.S. 624 (1943)

COX v. LOUISIANA, 379 U.S. 536 (1965)

The First Amendment rights to freedom of speech and assembly have long been used as tools to spur political reform in our country. In December of 1961, a few years before President Lyndon B. Johnson signed the 1964 Civil Rights Act, Reverend Elton Cox led approximately 2000 African-American students in a civil rights march in Baton Rouge, Louisiana, to protest the recent arrest of students picketing racially segregated establishments. It began at the old State Capitol building and was to proceed to the courthouse where the picketers were being held.

Cox refused to disband the group when contacted by authorities. Near the courthouse, Cox explained the march to the police chief, who gave directions to stay on the sidewalk across the street and to refrain from interfering with traffic. The marchers followed the instructions. When Cox encouraged marchers to demand service at segregated diners, there was muttering and grumbling from a group of several hundred white onlookers. The local sheriff then stated that the protestors were now violating the law and ordered them to disband. Police began grabbing some students. Within moments, the police used tear gas on the demonstrators.

The next day, the police arrested Cox for disturbing the peace and for obstructing public passages (the sidewalk across the street from the courthouse) and other offenses. Cox was convicted. The Louisiana Supreme Court upheld his convictions. The Supreme Court granted *certiorari* to determine whether these convictions infringed on Cox's First Amendment rights to freedom of speech and assembly.

The Supreme Court reversed the convictions. The conduct of the marchers, which included singing, clapping, and cheering, did not exceed the sort of activities expected at a peaceful assembly and did not establish a breach of the peace. The Supreme Court cited cases like *Edwards v. South Carolina*, which protected similar First Amendment conduct and held that the breach of the peace statute, as interpreted by the Louisiana Supreme Court, was unconstitutionally overbroad. As for the argument that encouraging demonstrators to demand service at segregated lunch counters could result in violence, the Court noted that the free speech and free assembly rights could not be denied based on hostility to the assertion or exercise of such rights. The Supreme Court explained that the function of free speech is to invite dissent, induce unrest, or stir people to anger.

When considering the statute that prohibited the obstruction of public passages, the Supreme Court distinguished between communicating ideas through conduct from communicating ideas through "pure speech" and rejected the claim that communicative conduct was afforded the same protections as pure speech. Although Cox's conduct violated the statute, the statute violated the First Amendment, because it granted local authorities unfettered discretion to restrict speech and assembly by deciding which views would be permitted. The Supreme Court overturned this conviction as well. *Cox v. Louisiana* was one of several important cases for the Civil Rights movement. It also helped protect the rights of freedom of speech and assembly from impermissible restrictions by local authorities exercising unfettered statutory discretion.

VINCENT L. RABAGO

References and Further Reading

Kalven, Harry, *The Concept of the Public Forum: Cox v. Louisiana*, SUP. CT. REV. 1 (1965)

Police Dep't v. Mosley, 408 U.S. 92, 96, 99 & n.6 (1972)
(speech in public forums).
Tribe, Laurence. American Constitutional Law, § 12-24, at
986, 2d ed., Mineola, NY: Foundation, 1988.

Cases and Statutes Cited

Edwards v. South Carolina, 372 U.S. 229 (1963)
Civil Rights Act of 1964

See also **Civil Rights Act of 1964; Civil Rights Laws
and Freedom of Speech; Demonstrations and Sit-ins;
First Amendment and PACs; Speech Tests; Freedom of
Assembly; Freedom of Assembly Infringed; Freedom of
Speech and Public Property; Incitement to Violence
and Free Speech; Johnson, Lyndon Baines; Public
Forum Doctrines**

COX v. NEW HAMPSHIRE, 312 U.S. 569 (1941)

A group of Jehovah's Witnesses was convicted in
New Hampshire of violating a state statute that prohibited public processions without a permit. The religious group had staged an unauthorized march in
downtown Manchester to advertise their religious
and political beliefs. After their arrest, the group
sued the state for violating their Fourteenth Amendment rights to freedom of speech, press, worship, and
assembly. The Supreme Court unanimously rejected
their claims, arguing that the licensing laws served a
limited and practical purpose of promoting social
order and did not violate their civil liberties. The
courts emphasized that the marchers were convicted
for breaking the licensing statute, not for distributing
information, holding public meetings, or expressing
religious beliefs. Moreover, the group could have
advertised its beliefs without breaking the law by
getting a permit for an organized march. Also, there
was no indication that the licensing laws were
applied in a discriminatory manner to censor the
Jehovah's Witnesses or any other group, so the constitutional challenge was inapplicable. The Court
shows here that the expression of civil liberties can
be reasonably restrained, through the government's
traditional regulation of the use of streets, in the
interest of social order. The case is one of many
cases where the Court has held that nondiscriminatory restrictions on time, place, and manner of speech
are reasonable for a public forum. The case is distinguished from those in which the challenged laws
explicitly or more severely restrict freedom of speech
and assembly, where such laws have been declared
unconstitutional.

DAVID D. BURNETT

References and Further Reading

Baker, C. E., *Unreasoned Reasonableness: Mandatory Pa-
rade Permits and Time, Place, and Manner Regulations,*
Northwestern Law Review 78 (1983): 937–1024.
Goldberger, D., *A Reconsideration of* Cox v. New Hamp-
shire: *Can Demonstrators Be Required to Pay the Costs of
Using America's Public Forums?* Texas Law Review 62
(1983): 403–451.
Paying for Free Speech: The Continuing Validity of Cox v.
New Hampshire, Washington University Law Quarterly
64 (1986): 985–995.

Cases and Statutes Cited

Cox v. New Hampshire, 312 U.S. 569 (1941); *Lovell v.
Griffin*, 303 U.S. 444 (1938)

See also **Accommodation of Religion; Balancing Ap-
proach to Free Speech; Content-Based Regulation of
Speech; Content-Neutral Regulation of Speech; Equal
Protection Clause and Religious Freedom; Establish-
ment of Religion and Free Exercise Clauses; Fourteenth
Amendment; Freedom of Speech and Press: Nineteenth
Century; Jehovah's Witnesses and Religious Liberty;
Private Religious Speech on Public Property; Religion
in "Public Square" Debate; Religious Symbols on Public
Property; Zoning and Religious Entities; Zoning Laws
and Freedom of Speech**

COY v. IOWA, 487 U.S. 1012 (1988)

An individual charged with sexually assaulting two
young girls was convicted after a jury trial in which a
screen placed between him and the girls blocked him
from their sight when they testified. In authorizing use
of the screen, the trial judge relied on a state statute
intended to make child-victims feel less uneasy in
giving their testimony.

In *Coy v. Iowa*, the U.S. Supreme Court held that
the Sixth Amendment right of a criminal defendant
"to be confronted with the witnesses against him"
guarantees a face-to-face encounter between a witness
and the accused. It reasoned that such an encounter is
essential to fairness and to the perception of fairness,
in part, because "[i]it is always more difficult to tell a
lie about a person 'to his face' than 'behind his
back.'" The Court also held that the screen violated
the accused's confrontation right. Without deciding
whether any exceptions exist to the requirement of a
face-to-face encounter, it concluded that, because the
trial judge did not find that the complaining witnesses
needed special protection, use of the screen in this
case could not fit within any conceivable exception.
Two Justices who concurred in the six-member majority opinion, however, believed that the right to a

face-to-face encounter is "not absolute" and that use of certain procedural devices designed to protect a child witness from the trauma of testifying in court may sometimes be permissible—a view the Court subsequently adopted in *Maryland v. Craig.*

DAVID S. RUDSTEIN

References and Further Reading

Brustein, Sharon Parker, Coy v. Iowa: *Should Children Be Heard and Not Seen?* University of Pittsburgh Law Review 50 (1989): 4:1187–1208.

Hasselbach, W. Andrew, *Placing a Child Victim of Sexual Abuse Behind a Screen During Courtroom Testimony as Violation of Sixth Amendment Confrontation Clause:* Coy v. Iowa, University of Cincinnati Law Review 57 (1989): 4:1537–1566.

LaFave, Wayne R., Jerold H. Israel, and Nancy J. King. *Criminal Procedure*, 1110–1111, 4th ed., St. Paul: Thompson-West, 2004.

Cases and Statutes Cited

Maryland v. Craig, 497 U.S. 836 (1990)

See also **Confrontation Clause; Incorporation Doctrine; Maryland v. Craig, 497 U.S. 836 (1990)**

CRANE v. JOHNSON, 242 U.S. 339 (1917)

This case stems from a statute California enacted to regulate the field of medicine. The statute created a board of medical examiners to prescribe a specific course of study, administer an examination, and issue licenses for those practicing medicine. The statute defined "medicine" broadly to encompass traditional medicine, such as surgery and prescription drugs, and nontraditional medicine, such as chiropractics and faith-based healing. Drugless practitioners who healed with prayer were exempt from the statutory requirements, whereas other nontraditional practitioners were not.

For the past seven years, the plaintiff in this case practiced nontraditional, faith-based medicine in Los Angeles, California. His practice used faith, hope, mental suggestion, and mental adaptation. The plaintiff challenged the enforcement of the statute against him on the basis of its distinction between drugless practitioners and prayer healers. He claimed that the state was incompetent to make such a distinction. He also alleged that the statute violated the Equal Protection Clause of the Fourteenth Amendment, because the classification among drugless practitioners did not relate to a legitimate purpose.

The Court held that the statute was enforceable. The distinction between drugless practitioners and

prayer practitioners was rooted in a legitimate basis and was therefore not arbitrary. According to the Court, the basis of the state's distinction came from the fact that the state considered the plaintiff's medical practice to be that of drugless medicine. His medical practice required skills that could be enhanced through practice and specialized knowledge. Alternately, the Court considered the practice of prayer-based medicine to be akin to the practice of religion, an area that could not be constitutionally regulated by the state.

The precedent established in this case has since permeated the regulation of alternative medicine throughout the country. States are now creating more stringent standards for nontraditional medical practitioners. They are mandating these practitioners to attain state certifications prior to claiming to practice medicine, and they are becoming stricter in their enforcement of noncompliance with these statutory requirements.

ALISON P. RIVCHUN

References and Further Reading

Cohen, Michael H., *Healing at the Borderland of Medicine and Religion: Regulating Potential Abuse of Authority by Spiritual Healers*, Journal of Law and Religion 18 (2002-2003): 373–426.

Kallmyer, J. Brad, *A Chimera In Every Sense: Standard of Care for Physicians Practicing Complementary and Alternative Medicine*, Indiana Health Law Review 2 (2005): 225–265.

Noah, Lars, *Ambivalent Commitments to Federalism in Controlling the Practice of Medicine*, Kansas Law Review 53 (2004): 149–193.

Silverman, Ross D., *Regulating Medical Practice in the Cyber Age: Issues and Challenges for State Medical Boards*, American Journal of Law and Medicine 26 (2000): 255–276.

Smalley, Ruth Ellen, *Will a Lawsuit a Day Keep the Cyberdocs Away? Modern Theories of Malpractice as Applied to Cybermedicine*, Richmond Journal of Law and Technology 7 (Winter 2001): 29–56.

Cases and Statutes Cited

Truax v. Raich, 239 US 33 (1915)
West's Ann. Cal. Bus. & Prof. Code § 2100

CRANE v. KENTUCKY, 476 U.S. 683 (1986)

In *Crane v. Kentucky,* 476 U.S. 683 (1986) the Supreme Court held that the defendant's Fourteenth and Sixth Amendment rights to a fair trial were violated when the trial judge excluded testimony regarding the physical and psychological circumstances of a confession, based on the fact that a pretrial hearing had already been held on the issue of voluntariness of the confession.

Crane, at the age of sixteen, was questioned about the murder of a convenience store clerk and began voluntarily confessing to numerous past crimes and, after being moved to a formal interrogation facility, eventually confessed to the murder in question. The police had no physical evidence against Crane, only the confession. Crane sought to suppress his confession at trial, but the judge ruled the voluntariness issue had been addressed and could not be relitigated before a jury.

The Supreme Court had previously held in *Sims v. Georgia*, 385 U.S. 538 and *Jackson v. Denno*, 378 U.S. 368, that the circumstances surrounding the taking of a confession are "relevant to two separate inquiries, one legal and one factual." How a confession is derived, such as the issue of voluntariness, is a matter of legality and was appropriately addressed during the pretrial hearing. In *Crane*, the Supreme Court held that the issue of the physical and psychological circumstances under which a confession was derived is relevant to the factual issue of innocence or guilt and must be allowed as a defense at trial in the presence of a jury.

JEANNINE M. EIBAND

Cases and Statutes Cited

Jackson v. Denno, 378 U.S. 368
Sims v. Georgia, 385 U.S. 538

See also **Coerced Confessions/Police Interrogations; Defense, Right to Present**

CREATIONISM AND INTELLIGENT DESIGN

Background

Writing in the 1830s, Alexis de Tocqueville identified the place of religion in society as one of the major differences between the United States and Europe. The continuing truth of this observation can be seen in the prevalence of belief in creationism: Americans are more skeptical about evolutionary thinking than any other developed nation. Survey data consistently report that approximately forty-five percent of Americans believe in the literal truth of Genesis and approximately forty percent believe that God guides evolutionary developments. These proportions have, if anything,

tended to rise in recent years. Only approximately ten percent accept the Darwinian orthodoxy of natural selection as a result of random mutations that generate reproductive advantage. The proportions in Europe are almost exactly reversed, with subscribers to the Genesis story being virtually undetectable in most national surveys. Even religiously conservative countries like Poland show majority acceptance of the Darwinian account, not least because this has been the official position of the Roman Catholic church since the issue of the encyclical, *Humani Generis,* in 1950.

It is, then, hardly surprising that the teaching of science in high schools has become a major source of social conflict in the United States almost from the point at which evolution ceased to be a topic confined largely to specialists and was established as a central theme of modern biology. The belated synthesis of Darwin's theories of how a process of natural selection might work and of Mendel's observations on the inheritance of specific characteristics within species, during the first decade of the twentieth century, entered high school curriculum after World War I and almost immediately came into collision with the faith beliefs of large numbers of ordinary Americans, particularly, but not exclusively, in the South and Midwest. In contrast to Europe, the public provision of education is a highly devolved matter in the United States, with relatively little federal involvement and even states having limited central authority over local school boards. At the same time, the First Amendment erects a strong barrier to any arm of the American state acting in any way that may seem to endorse any religious belief or, indeed, belief in preference to nonbelief. This immediately creates a tension between the desire of local communities to prescribe a public school curriculum that reflects their faith beliefs and the Constitutional objection to the promotion of religion by public bodies.

Early Challenges

The publication of high school biology textbooks, from 1919 onwards, that included coverage of evolution provoked a backlash from fundamentalist religious leaders, including campaigns for state legislation to ban the teaching of this subject. Tennessee was the first state to legislate, in 1925, but community leaders in Rhea County linked up with the ACLU to fight a test case against this law. Local science teacher John Scopes volunteered to be prosecuted. Although the evolutionists are usually thought to have won a moral victory in the "Scopes Trial" (*Tennessee v Scopes*, 1925), the defendant was convicted and fined. The State Supreme Court reversed the verdict on technical grounds but recommended that the state attorney general should not pursue the matter further. The Tennessee statute was not repealed until 1967. In the absence of a Constitutional test, similar laws were passed in Mississippi (1926) and Arkansas (1928), and publishers voluntarily omitted the topic of evolution from most 1930s high school biology textbooks. Each state and community reached its own accommodation between biblical literalism and evolutionary thought until the perceived challenge of Soviet technology in the late 1950s provoked national elites to press for the modernization of science education, overriding local objections as their counterparts in Europe had long since done.

This generated the First Amendment challenge, which Scopes had failed to accomplish, to the 1928 Arkansas statute. On the recommendation of its biology teachers, the Little Rock School Board adopted a high school textbook for the 1965–1966 session that included a chapter on evolution. One teacher, Susan Epperson, asked the courts to declare that the statute was invalid and that she would not be committing a criminal offense by teaching from the prescribed text Although her claim was initially upheld, on a combination of Fourteenth and First Amendment grounds, as a violation of her rights to freedom of speech, it was overturned on appeal. The State Supreme Court held that the 1928 act was a valid direction by the state government about the actions of its employees in their official capacity. The case was further appealed to the U.S. Supreme Court, in *Epperson v Arkansas* (1968), which found for Epperson. There is a certain mythology about this: Mr Justice Fortas took a strong First Amendment approach, whereas his colleagues simply thought that the state law was too vague to be constitutional on Fourteenth Amendment grounds. In the longer term, however, Fortas's analysis has prevailed.

In effect, Fortas anticipated the *Lemon* analysis of the First Amendment, formulated three years later, which set a three-part test for the constitutionality of statutes bearing on religious issues: they must have a secular purpose; their principal effect must neither advance nor inhibit religion; they must not foster "an excessive government entanglement with religion." In looking to the "secular purpose" element, the Supreme Court has not confined itself to looking exclusively at evidence of legislators' intent but also at the activities of groups lobbying in support of statutes.

The Supreme Court decision in *Epperson* blocked the possibility of legally prohibiting the teaching of evolution in public schools. However, this remained as offensive as ever to large and influential faith communities, who sought to dilute its impact by two new strategies. One was to require classroom teachers to give "equal treatment" to Biblical and Darwinian accounts of the origin and development of species. Creationism was relabelled as "creation science" and presented as an alternative scientific account. The other was to require that students be cautioned about the status of the Darwinian account, either by having teachers read a prescribed statement or by placing stickers on biology textbooks warning that elements of the content were controversial.

The first of these was evaluated by the Supreme Court in *Edwards v Aguillard* (1987). With Justice Scalia dissenting, the Court held that the statute's stated secular purpose, of protecting the rights of teachers to talk about creationism, was a sham: the legislature's disavowal of religious purpose was undermined by the evidence of active lobbying by faith groups. However, the most important element of the decision was its declaration that creationism—or creation science—was inherently religious in its nature. It could not be subject to normal academic tests of its validity, it was historically permeated by religious entanglements, and, at its heart, it requires belief in a supreme being as creator. Any doctrine that requires a prior faith belief is inherently religious, whether or not the word "God" is actually spoken in the classroom and cannot be promoted in the public school curriculum.

The Supreme Court has not ruled directly on the issue of stickers or disclaimers, although three justices (Scalia, Rehnquist, and Thomas) indicated their willingness to hear the issue when an application for *certiorari* was refused in *Freiler v Tangipahoa* (1999).

The Tangipahoa Parish Board of Education in Louisiana had adopted a resolution in 1994 disavowing evolution and requiring teachers to read a disclaimer. A group of parents appealed against this to the district court, which found in their favor, a decision affirmed by the Fifth Circuit, following *Lemon* and, ultimately, *Epperson*. The sticker issue has not been definitively adjudicated, although a case arising from a sticker introduced in 2002 by the School Board in Cobb County, Georgia, was still before the federal courts in 2005. This does, however, seem likely to face the same hurdles unless a change in the balance of the Supreme Court leads to a fundamental restatement of the established interpretation of the First Amendment.

Intelligent Design Creationism

After *Epperson* and *Edwards,* it became clear that creationists would need a new strategy if they were to be able to sustain their challenge to the entrenchment of scientific materialism in public school curricula. Intelligent Design Creationism (IDC) is the result. Its promoters seem to have observed that two propositions associated with the post-*Epperson* developments in creation science, namely that competing views on any issue deserve equal treatment and that free speech by those who disagree with orthodoxies, should be protected and are capable of generating widespread support beyond fundamentalists because of their resonance with general American values. Provided that the explicitly religious elements of creationism could be eliminated, accounts of the origin and development of species that imply the intervention of a creator might be introduced into the high school curriculum with a sufficient measure of support from nonbelievers to render First Amendment challenges more difficult to sustain. IDC is the result.

IDC abandons the Biblical literalism of previous generations in favor of an approach first formulated by the Reverend William Paley (1743–1805), an important eighteenth century theologian and philosopher. Paley's *Natural Theology* (published 1802) was the dominant intellectual statement against which Darwin's generation reacted. Paley argued that, were we to find a watch lying on the ground, we would necessarily infer that its parts had been framed and put together for a purpose. This evidence of design would, in turn, imply the existence of a designer. In a similar way, Paley argues that the intricacy and complexity of the universe, as exemplified in structures like the human eye, implies the existence of a Design and a Designer. Although contemporaries like David Hume (1711–1776), in his discussion of miracles, attacked this line of argument, it remained influential well into the nineteenth century, and elements can still be seen in the mainstream Christian acceptance of "theistic evolution." However, whereas IDC stresses the constant engagement of the Designer, theistic evolutionists like the Reverend John Polkinghorne (b.1930), a former professor of mathematical physics at Cambridge and an influential theologian, tend to think more in terms of a Cosmic Planner, who may have supplied the raw material of the universe and its basic physical laws but who now, at most, supplies an occasional nudge to the system, deep in the uncertainties of the quantum world.

IDC is the core of what its advocates describe as the "Wedge Strategy" devised during the 1990s by a group of writers associated with the Discovery Institute's Center for Science and Culture in Seattle. Whereas all modern science rests broadly on the principle of naturalism—that events can only be explained by natural and hence observable causes—the Wedge movement seeks to insert a space for "supernaturalism."

that some, if not all, events in the world have a supernatural cause that is inaccessible to observation and objective verification. IDC, however, seeks to avoid specifying the source of that supernatural cause to evade the First Amendment proscriptions. In theory, the Designer could be an alien being from another galaxy or a time-traveling cell biologist. In practice, though, IDC advocates identify the Designer with the Christian God. Nevertheless, IDC is set out as an alternative scientific program with its own alternative school texts like *Pandas and People* (1989).

By redefining science in a way that leaves space for the supernatural and by suppressing the explicitly religious elements of the argument from design, IDC advocates hoped to take their approach outside the scope of *Epperson* and *Edwards*, relying on commonly held notions of "fair play" to mobilize support for their attempt to drive their wedge into the high school curriculum.

This strategy was tested and found wanting by the district court in Pennsylvania in the fall of 2005. On October 18, 2004, the Dover Area School Board resolved that high school students should be made aware of problems with Darwin's theory of evolution and of the possibility for other theories "including but not limited to intelligent design." The Board determined that, from January 2005, teachers would be required to read a disclaimer that asserted compliance with state policy on the science curriculum, and the standardized tests through which this would be assessed, but drew attention to the alternative offered by IDC and referred students to the *Pandas and People* text. A group of parents, teachers, and former School Board members brought an action, *Kitzmiller v Dover Area School District,* seeking to have this declared unconstitutional. After a six-week trial, the judge, known as something of a conservative, handed down a lengthy and stinging judgment declaring the Board's actions to be in breach of the First Amendment and severely censuring the conduct of a number of Board members, officers, and their advisers. The judge closely follows precedent to determine whether the Board's actions would constitute a message of official "endorsement or disapproval" of religion to an objective student or adult in the school district.

In summary, the judge holds that an objective observer would know that IDC and references to "gaps" or "problems" in evolutionary theory are creationist strategies for weakening education about evolution. He outlined a wealth of statements by leading IDC advocates asserting the identification of the Designer with the Christian God. The supernatural elements of IDC make it inherently religious. The judge goes on to discuss whether students would see the disclaimer as an official endorsement of religion. He holds that the phrasing, effectively saying "the State of Pennsylvania requires us to teach you evolution but we don't really believe it and think you should study this inherently religious account instead," constitute a message of religious endorsement comparable to that struck down in *Freiler*. Turning to the understanding of the Board's action in the wider community, he notes the evidence of newsletters and public meetings that present IDC in religious terms and from correspondence and articles in the local press that show it was perceived as such by local residents. Again, he holds that there has been a clear endorsement of religion by a public body. This leads to an unequivocal finding against the School Board on First Amendment grounds, coupled with strong criticism of the conduct of members in office and of their behavior, including frequent evasion and outright lying, in court.

However, the judge also discusses a number of the other issues raised in the case, in the hope, he declares, of avoiding "the obvious waste of judicial and other resources" that would be incurred in further trials. In particular, he directly evaluates the question of whether IDC *is* science, as distinct from his evaluation of whether it is an expression of religious belief. This has a wider importance, because an alternative IDC strategy has been to seek to have school boards or other public bodies redefine what counts as science to encompass IDC. The State Board of Education in Kansas, for example, has been in turmoil over this issue since 1999. In *Kitzmiller*, the judge finds that IDC fails the test on three grounds: that it invokes and permits supernatural causation; that its argument of "irreducible complexity," that some biological phenomena are too complex to have arisen by the chance processes of evolution, is flawed and illogical; and that its negative attacks on evolution have been successfully refuted. Its only textbook contains outdated concepts and badly flawed science. IDC is, in the end, a theological position, which has no place in a science curriculum.

Kitzmiller is, of course, at best a limited precedent in one federal district. The judgment is unlikely to be reviewed by higher courts, since control of the Dover School Board changed in November 2005 elections, just as the trial was ending. However, it is hard to see how the judge's analysis can be faulted or how First Amendment obstacles to IDC can be overcome, unless there is a major reassessment of *Lemon* by the Supreme Court. Evolution's place in lawful high school science curricula would seem to be secure from challenge unless IDC supporters can produce convincing empirical evidence to support their claims to have presented an alternative.

One last argument, which was not discussed in *Kitzmiller,* may be worth mentioning, namely, whether a requirement to teach evolution in high schools violates teachers' free speech rights under the First Amendment. There are a number of cases on this that make it clear that the rights of teachers are abridged during the school day, whether they are actually teaching or not. In the course of their employment, teachers' speech is official speech on behalf of their employers and subject to whatever restrictions apply to those employers. As public employees, then, teachers cannot lawfully speak in ways that violate the *Lemon* test by appearing to endorse or promote religious belief or nonbelief. This prohibition can extend into their private time if there is a danger that they might be identified as representatives of that public body. For example, a teacher may not organize, out of school hours, a religious society meeting in premises rented from their own school but can do this on the premises of another school where there is no risk of confusion about their status as a private individual. A requirement to teach evolution as part of a standard science curriculum is a lawful exercise of the employer's rights, and termination of a contract for teaching any version of creationism in science curriculum time is a lawful exercise of the employer's responsibility not to breach their First Amendment obligations. This does not, of course, prevent the examination of IDC within a religious studies curriculum, any more than it prevents examining the Book of Genesis as part of a comparative study of the creation myths told by various faith communities.

Conclusion

Given the financial resources available to the conservative Christian interests that have sustained creationism in various guises for almost a century, and the evidence of the scale of creationist belief in the contemporary United States, it is unlikely that the legal setback in Dover will end the confrontation between some forms of religious belief and the scientific community in the American courts. However, it does seem that a more ingenious intellectual strategy than IDC will need to be devised to overcome the established interpretation of the First Amendment, unless this is revised by the Supreme Court.

ROBERT DINGWALL

References and Further Reading

Brauer, Matthew J., Barbara Forrest, and Steven G. Gey, *Is it Science yet? Intelligent Design Creationism and the*

Constitution, Washington University Law Quarterly 83 (2005): 1:1–149.

Coleman, Simon, and Leslie Carlin, eds. *The Cultures of Creationism: Anti-Evolutionism in English-Speaking Countries* Aldershot: Ashgate.

Manson, Neil A., ed. *God and Design: The Teleological Argument and Modern Science*, London: Routledge, 2003.

Pennock, Robert T., ed., *Intelligent Design Creationism and Its Critics: Philosophical, Theological and Scientific Perspectives*, Cambridge, MA, MIT Press, 2001.

Reule, Deborah A., *The New Face of Creationism: The Establishment Clause and the Latest Efforts to Suppress Evolution in Public Schools*, Vanderbilt Law Review 54, (2001): 2555–2610.

Russo, Charles J., *Evolution v Creation Science in the US: Can the Courts Divine a Solution?* Education Law Journal 3, September (2002): 152.

Cases and Statutes Cited

Edwards v Aguillard, 482 U.S. 578 (1987)

Epperson v. Arkansas, 393 U.S. 97 (1968)

Freiler v Tangipahoa Parish Bd. of Educ., 385 F.3d 337 (5th Cir. 1999)

Kitzmiller et al. v Dover Area School District et al. (2005) (accessed at http://www.aclupa.org/downloads/Dec20opinion.pdf)

Lemon v Kurtzman 403 U.S. 602 (1971)

State of Tennessee v John Thomas Scopes (1925) (accessed at http://www.law.umkc.edu/faculty/projects/ftrials/scopes/scopes.htm)

John Thomas Scopes v. The State of Tennessee, 154 Tenn. (1 Smith) 105 (1927), 289 S.W. 363

Tangipahoa Parish Bd. of Educ.v. Freiler, 530 U.S. 1251 (2000)

See also **Edwards v. Aguillard, 482 U.S. 578 (1987); Epperson v. Arkansas, 393 U.S. 97 (1968); Fortas, Abe; Fourteenth Amendment; Lemon Test; Rehnquist, William H.; Scalia, Antonin; Thomas, Clarence**

CRIMINAL CONSPIRACY

Conspiracy is a crime that requires (1) an intent to commit a crime, (2) an agreement between two or more persons to commit that crime, and (3) an overt act by one of them in furtherance of the agreement. For example, conspiracy is met when three persons agree to commit a bank robbery and one of the persons gets the bank's blue prints to plan the robbery.

One purpose for the crime of conspiracy is that it allows police to intervene before the crime that is the object of the conspiracy occurs. In our example, police can intervene and arrest the defendant for conspiracy without waiting for the bank robbery. Here conspiracy allows official intervention before the commission of the (harmful) substantive crime that is the goal of the conspiracy.

Now assume that our conspirators go ahead and commit the bank robbery. In some jurisdictions, the defendants can still be charged with conspiracy. In this situation the crime is justified because collective action presents a greater risk to society than individual action and so warrants additional punishment. Collective action is more dangerous because it makes success of the crime more likely.

Prosecutors like to charge conspiracy because it gives them several advantages. Recognizing this, in 1925 in *Harrison v. U.S.*, Judge Learned Hand famously called conspiracy "that darling of the modern prosecutor's nursery." Because of these advantages and some vagueness in the definition of the crime, it is controversial.

SARAH N. WELLING

References and Further Reading

Brickey, Kathleen F. *Corporate Criminal Liability: A Treatise on the Criminal Liability of Corporations, Their Officers, and Agents* §§ 6:01-6:28 (2d ed. 1992).

Johnson, Phillip, *The Unnecessary Crime of Conspiracy*, Cal. L. Rev. 61 (1973): 1137.

LaFave, Wayne R. *Criminal Law* §§ 12.1–12.4, 4th ed., 2003.

Marcus, Paul, *Conspiracy: The Criminal Agreement in Theory and in Practice*, Geo. L. J. 65 (1977): 925.

Cases and Statutes Cited

Harrison v. United States, 7 F.2d 259, 263 (2d Cir. 1925)

See also **Chicago Seven Trial**

CRIMINAL LAW/CIVIL LIBERTIES AND NONCITIZENS IN THE UNITED STATES

The Fourth, Fifth, and Sixth Amendments to the U.S. Constitution ensure that defendants enjoy traditional due process rights in all domestic criminal law proceedings. Like their U.S. citizen counterparts, noncitizens are afforded basic rights to notice of the charges filed, to a lawyer to represent them, and to a speedy and public trial. The U.S. Supreme Court, however, has simultaneously recognized limits on certain noncitizens' ability to invoke the Fourth Amendment's protection against unreasonable governmental searches and seizures. Designed to deter unlawful governmental conduct, the Fourth Amendment ensures that law enforcement conduct proper investigations of alleged criminal conduct, otherwise risking that the evidence they obtain may be thrown out of court or that they may be subject to civil suit. That the Fourth Amendment's scope may be limited when the suspect in a criminal investigation is a noncitizen raises concerns especially when certain immigration law violations trigger criminal sanctions—for instance, in cases of reentering the United States surreptitiously or smuggling noncitizens across the border.

Three limits on the Fourth Amendment's applicability to noncitizens are worth noting. First, the government is permitted a wide berth in conducting investigative stops during roving patrols of the U.S. interior adjacent to the border in its search for undocumented migrants. While the Supreme Court held unconstitutional a roving patrol investigative stop made without either a warrant or probable cause in *Almeida-Sanchez v. United States*, two years later in *United States v. Brignoni-Ponce*, the Court held that during such operations, agents did not have to comply with the regular "probable cause" standard to justify an immigration stop leading to the discovery of an undocumented person; satisfying "reasonable suspicion" is sufficient and that may be based on a variety of factors including a suspect's apparent Mexican ancestry.

Second, the government is held to a higher "probable cause" Fourth Amendment standard when it conducts searches at fixed immigration checkpoints than when it engages in roving border patrols; it need not, however, comply with this higher standard when simply stopping vehicles and questioning their occupants. In *United States v. Ortiz*, the Court held that government officers must have probable cause before they may search private vehicles at fixed checkpoints removed from the border. In *United States v. Martinez-Fuerte*, however, the Court allowed the government to stop vehicles to question their occupants about their immigration status at fixed checkpoints, reasoning that this was less of an intrusion than a full search.

Finally, when the government obtains evidence from abroad pursuant to an illegal search, it may use that evidence at the stateside criminal trial of a noncitizen defendant. In *United States v. Verdugo-Urquidez*, the Supreme Court refused to bar evidence illegally seized abroad for use in a domestic drug trial of a noncitizen. The Court reasoned that because the noncitizen defendant had insufficient connections with the United States, he was not part of "the People" the Fourth Amendment was intended to protect.

VICTOR C. ROMERO

References and Further Reading

Johnson, Kevin R., *The Case Against Race Profiling in Immigration Enforcement*, Washington University Law Quarterly 78 (2000): 675–736.
LaFave, Wayne R. et al. *Criminal Procedure, Third Edition.* St. Paul: West Group, 2000.
Neuman, Gerald L. *Strangers to the Constitution: Immigrants, Borders, and Fundamental Law.* Princeton: Princeton University Press, 1996.
Romero, Victor C., *The Domestic Fourth Amendment Rights of Undocumented Immigrants: On Guitterez and the Tort Law-Immigration Law Parallel*, Harvard Civil Rights-Civil Liberties Law Review 35 (2000): 57–101.

Cases and Statutes Cited

Almeida-Sanchez v. United States, 413 U.S. 266 (1973)
United States v. Brignoni-Ponce, 422 U.S. 873 (1975)
United States v. Ortiz, 422 U.S. 891 (1975)
United States v. Martinez-Fuerte, 428 U.S. 543 (1976)
United States v. Verdugo-Urquidez, 494 U.S. 259 (1990)

See also **Aliens, Civil Liberties of; Equal Protection of Law (XIV); Race and Criminal Justice**

CRIMINAL SYNDICATION ACT
See Anti-Anarchy and Anti-Syndicalism Acts

CRIMINALIZATION OF CIVIL WRONGS

Traditionally there was a clear line between civil and criminal law. The civil law, for example, contracts, property, and torts, sought to balance private rights and to restore wronged parties to their rightful positions. The criminal law, on the other hand, was primarily a way for society in general to express its outrage at harmful conduct: it was a way to enforce deeply held norms. Thus, the traditional so-called common law crimes included homicide, rape, arson, and theft. Thus, the law properly recognizing the difference between bad conduct, for example, breach of contract, and conduct that would be criminal, for example, rape.

While the theories underlying the need for criminal and civil law overlapped somewhat, in practice there were clear legal differences. One, for example, could be held civilly liable for negligent conduct (or for the conduct of subordinates). But to be held criminally liable, one had to act deliberately, recklessly, or wantonly. There were good reasons for the difference. Whereas one held civilly liable would lose money, a person found criminally liable would lose his freedom and civil rights. Colloquially, there is a difference between the shame of being sued and the shame of having a criminal record. Moreover, almost everyone in a civilized society knows that murder is wrong. But civil issues such as whether property has been adversely possessed, or whether a prescriptive easement exists, are usually more complex. The demarcation between civil and criminal misconduct ensured that those who harmed the rights of others would pay for the harm caused but that they would not have the force of the criminal law brought down on them. Today that has changed: the line is blurred.

State and local governments enact myriad and sometimes Byzantine civil regulations covering everything from how a multinational corporation may issue stock to whether a small landowner can build on his property. Unfortunately, from a civil liberties perspective, these regulations increasingly carry with them criminal penalties. As Professor Gainer noted in *Federal Criminal Code: Past and Present*, there are tens of thousands of pages of regulatory violations that carry with them criminal penalties. Moreover, as an ABA report noted: "So large is the present body of federal criminal law that there is no conveniently accessible, complete list of federal crimes." In other words, the breach of a regulation that one is ignorant of can carry with it criminal penalties. Worse, if one wanted to ensure he did not violate any criminal laws, he or she wouldn't be able to reference a list.

Still worse is that the Environmental Protection Agency doesn't adequately understand what regulatory violations carry with them criminal penalties. The line between criminal and civil wrongs moves each time a new director of the EPA is appointed.

James DeLong best summed up the problem in *Go Directly to Jail: The Criminalization of Almost Everything*: "The criminalization of highly complex and often conflicting [civil] regulations with virtually no requirement of intent" means that "even the well educated and well informed cannot be sure what the law is and what they must do to comply with it."

MICHAEL C. CERNOVICH

References and Further Reading

ABA Report. *The Report of the ABA Task Force on the Federalization of Criminal Law*. Washington: ABA, 1998.

Baker, John S., Jr. *Measuring the Explosive Growth of Federal Crime Legislation*. Washington: The Federalist Society for Law and Public Policy, 2004.

Gainer, Ronald L., *Federal Criminal Code: Past and Present, Buff*, Crim. L. Rev. 46 (1988): 2.

Healy, Gene, ed. *Go Directly to Jail: The Criminalization of Almost Everything*. Washington: Cato, 2004.

Lynch, Timothy. *Polluting Our Principles, Cato Institute Policy Analysis No. 223* (April 10, 1995).

Meese, Edwin III, *Big Brother on the Beat: The Expanding Federalization of Crime*, Texas Review of Law and Politics 1 (Spring 1997): 1.

See also **Federalization of Criminal Law**

CROMWELL, OLIVER (1599–1658)

Oliver Cromwell, soldier and statesman, Lord Protector of England in the 1650s, was born in 1599, into a lower middle class family. For the first forty years of his life he was a farmer (1599–1640), followed by twelve years as a member of Parliament and a senior military officer (1640–1652), and then five years as Lord Protector of England (1653–1658).

Cromwell believed in Providence and the role of God in bringing about a holy Commonwealth. As God's instrument to lead his people, his providentialism led him to reject forms of church government, institutions, and rituals. His religion was biblical and Christocentric. He supported unity among various religious groups of the godly nation and hoped that it would lead to increased liberty of conscience. His hope for toleration for various denominations did not succeed because of controversies among the various protestant sects, whereas his later parliaments also refused to provide for full liberty of conscience. John Morrill concludes that "Cromwell's achievements as a soldier are great but unfashionable; as religious libertarian great but easily mis-stated; as a statesman inevitably stunted." (Morrill, "Cromwell, Oliver." Oxford DNB. p. 352).

His support for religious liberty did not extend after his death, for more than a generation the Church of England reestablished itself in England until 1689, when a Toleration Act, rather than comprehension, passed Parliament and created an "established" rather than a "national" state church and gave dissenters, under some state restrictions, the ability to practice their religion.

JOEL FISHMAN

References and Further Reading

Cromwell, Oliver. *The Writings and Speeches of Oliver Cromwell*. With an Introduction, Notes and a Sketch of his Life by Wilbur Cortez Abbott, with the assistance of Catherine D. Crane. Published: Cambridge, Harvard Univ. Press, 1937–1947. 4 v.

Morrill, John. "Cromwell, Oliver." *Oxford Dictionary of National Biography*. Vol. 14. 328–353. Oxford: Oxford University Press, 2004.

———, ed. *Oliver Cromwell and the English Revolution*. London: Longman, 1990.

Roots, Ivan, ed. *Cromwell, A Profile*. New York, Hill and Wang, 1973.

CROSS BURNING

Perhaps no symbol in American history carries with it the strong sense of infamy and controversy as the burning cross. Justice Thomas, dissenting in a 2003 U.S. Supreme Court opinion, penned, "Cross burning has almost invariably meant lawlessness and understandably instills in its victims well-grounded fear of physical violence." Whether or not a burning cross conveys a message seems settled, especially against the backdrop of the Ku Klux Klan and the

African-American struggle during Reconstruction and the Civil Rights Movement.

What has been, and continues to be, debated is whether a state should be free to proscribe and criminalize the act of burning a cross?

The U.S. Supreme Court's 2003 ruling in *Virginia v. Black* provides an exhaustive overview of both the expressive elements of burning a cross and the constitutional constraints that exist that limit the manner in which a state can criminalize the act of burning a cross.

In *Virginia v. Black*, the U.S. Supreme Court held that Virginia could criminalize the burning of a cross provided that it was done "with the intent of intimidating any person or group or persons." The Court found that cross burning was a particularly virulent type of intimidation. The Court relied on previous First Amendment precedent and exceptions related to "true threats" and "fighting words" that may be regulated in a manner consistent with the Constitution.

Although the Court held that the act of burning a cross for the purposes of intimidation could be criminalized without offending the First Amendment of the Constitution (made applicable to the states by the Fourteenth Amendment), the Court further held that there are instances where crosses are burned without any intention to intimidate. For example, Justice White, concurring in *R.A.V. v. St. Paul*, (1992) stated, "[b]urning a cross at a politically rally would almost certainly be protected expression."

Whenever expressive conduct such as a burning cross is intertwined with such strong historical underpinnings, a short review of the symbol's place in American culture becomes relevant.

Cross burning was used as early as the fourteenth century as a means for Scottish tribes to signal one another. Sir Walter Scott used the burning cross to symbolize both a summons and a call to arms. The integration of the burning cross into American subculture began in the spring of 1866 in Pulaski, Tennessee. The Ku Klux Klan (hereinafter "Klan"), an organization that originated as a social club, transformed into a group that resisted Reconstruction efforts and fought to exclude freed blacks from the political process. The Klan's victims included not only African Americans but also northern whites known as "carpetbaggers" and southern whites who disagreed with the Klan's policies or methods. Justice Thomas, concurring in *Capitol Square Review and Advisory Board v. Pinette* (1995), reminded us that the Klan not only disfavored individuals on racial and geographical bounds but also on religious and political grounds, hating Jews, Catholics, and Communists alongside "Yankees" and blacks. The Klan, which had generally died out in the late 1870s, was "reborn" around 1915. The "second" Klan's first initiation ceremony, on Stone Mountain, Georgia (near Atlanta), used a 40-foot burning cross.

Throughout the life of the "second" Klan, cross burnings were used as a tool to intimidate and threaten imminent violence against individuals and groups the Klan disfavored. The burning cross was not only an outward symbol to send a message to others but also served as a symbol to identify and express shared ideology and purpose among Klan members.

The Commonwealth of Virginia, in its Petitioner's Brief in the *Virginia v. Black* case, summed up the common perception of cross burning's expressive effect: "A white, conservative, middle-class Protestant, waking up at night to find a burning cross outside his home will reasonably understand that someone is threatening him. His reaction is likely to be very different than if he were to find, say, a burning circle or square. In the latter case, he may call the fire department. In the former, he will probably call the police."

MARC M. HARROLD

References and Further Reading

Brannon, Chris L., *Note, Constitutional Law—Hate Speech—First Amendment Permits Ban on Cross Burning When Done with the Intent to Intimidate*, Miss. L. J. 73 (Fall 2003): 323.
Gey, Steven G., *A Few Questions About Cross Burning, Intimidation, and Free Speech*, Notre Dame L. Rev. 80 (2005): 1287.

Cases and Statutes Cited

Virginia v. Black, 538 U.S. 343 (2002)
Capitol Square Review and Advisory Bd v. Pinette, 515 U.S. 753 (1995)
R.A.V. v. St. Paul, 505 U.S. 377 (1992)

CRUEL AND UNUSUAL PUNISHMENT (VIII)

The Eighth Amendment forbids the infliction of cruel and unusual punishments. This constitutional prohibition is itself unusual, because in using the intrinsically subjective terms "cruel" and "unusual," it necessarily calls for the use of judgment. Determining the meaning of the Eighth Amendment, then, first requires ascertaining on whose judgment the clause hinges.

The judgment as to what is cruel and unusual, and therefore what is unconstitutional, cannot be that of Congress or the president, because the Bill of Rights was enacted to curtail the power of the federal government. The Eighth Amendment, like most of the Bill of Rights, applies to state governments through the incorporation doctrine, and as such, it cannot be left to the judgment of the states to determine the contours of the cruel and unusual punishment clause. The Constitution is also meant to protect vulnerable minorities from the tyranny of majority whim; such protection would be meaningless if the interpretation of what is cruel and unusual was determined by the views of a majority of the people. Since *Marbury v. Madison*, it has been the recognized province of the federal judiciary to interpret the Constitution; however, the Supreme Court has repeatedly stated that the cruel and unusual punishment clause cannot merely reflect the subjective views of what the Supreme Court Justices find repugnant.

The paradox of whose view of acceptable punishments should shape the cruel and unusual punishment clause has been resolved by adopting an ad hoc collection of doctrines drawing from various sources of authority. Deference is generally given to state governments to define appropriate punishments for given crimes. However, state and federal governments are subject to three core restrictions. First, punishments cannot be arbitrary, capricious, or barbaric. Second, at least in some circumstances, punishments can be overruled for being disproportionate to a defendant's culpability. Third, punishments must not be contrary to a national consensus as to evolving standards of decency. The first two restrictions have largely being developed with reference to judicial views of acceptability of certain punishments: a punishment is overruled if the Justices consider it disproportionate or arbitrary. The third restriction is facilitated by judicial aggregation of state legislation, and to a lesser extent jury determinations: the less often a punishment is available or imposed in a state jurisdiction, the more likely the Supreme Court is to rule that it is contrary to a national consensus and thus unconstitutional.

The foregoing description overstates the clarity of Eighth Amendment jurisprudence. In recent years, some Supreme Court Justices have challenged the appropriateness of a proportionality requirement; in its defense, other Justices have argued that the proportionality requirement and the national consensus test are in fact one doctrine. There is also strong Supreme Court division over the application of the evolving consensus doctrine. It is also unclear whether "cruel" and "unusual" constitute separate prohibitions or whether "cruel and unusual" is one proscription. Each of these ambiguities contributes to an enormous jurisprudential uncertainty surrounding the cruel and unusual punishment clause.

In addition, the death penalty has been treated differently from all other punishments, resulting not just in special rules for capital punishment but a schism in the overall approach of the Supreme Court to capital and noncapital forms of punishment. Arguably, the Supreme Court has largely abdicated its role in determining the bounds of nondeath penalty punishments, while simultaneously adding so many limits to the application of the death penalty as to be gradually rendering it, although constitutional in theory, unconstitutional in practice.

Despite the confusion surrounding Eighth Amendment jurisprudence, it is possible to identify four types of challenge that could be made to the constitutionality of a given criminal sentence. Constitutional challenges can be made as to: first, the type of punishment inflicted; second, the process followed in imposing the punishment; third, the category of crime to which a punishment may attach; and fourth, the categories of defendant against whom a punishment can be imposed. However, because of the "death is different" jurisprudence, the rules of each of these four types of challenge are bifurcated according to whether the punishment is death or some other sentence.

Types of Punishment

Supreme Court precedent as to which types of punishment are constitutional has taken two forms: specific sanctions or prohibitions of particular types of punishment, and general doctrine promulgating guidelines as to when punishments can ever be appropriate.

Of the specific rulings, the most contested concerns the constitutionality of the death penalty. As is discussed in the subsequent subsections, the death penalty has been highly restricted as to when and to whom it can apply, but imposition of the death penalty per se was upheld under the Federal Constitution in *Gregg v. Georgia*.

Generally, the Supreme Court has refrained from ruling on whether particular forms of capital punishment are unconstitutional. Four types of capital punishment have been sanctioned to the extent that the Supreme Court has refused to prohibit them when the issue came before it. In *Wilkinson v. Utah*, death by shooting was authorized; in *Gomez v. U.S.*, use of the gas chamber was allowed; in *Glass v. Louisiana*, use of the electric chair was permitted; and in *Campbell v. Wood*, death by hanging was tolerated. However, the latter three cases contained only cursory consideration of the type of punishment by the majority, but strong dissents on point.

Historically, a variety of forms of corporal punishment were occasionally used in the colonies, including lashing, branding, and even ear-cropping and tongue-cutting. Various forms of physical humiliation, such as stocks and the Scarlet letter, were more commonly used. Two key cases have held nondeath penalty punishments unconstitutional. *Weems v. U.S.* held that a lengthy punishment including hard labor in stocks, combined with the loss of basic rights, including over property and voting, was excessive for the crime of falsifying records. *Trop v. Dulles* held that denationalization for military desertion was cruel and unusual.

The Supreme Court has gone back and forth as to whether these cases constituted a general requirement of proportionality in nondeath penalty sentences. In *Rummel v. Estelle*, the court considered that there is no proportionality test: the punishment in *Weems* was excessive because of the *combination* ofx punishments. But in *Harmelin v. Michigan*, Justice Kennedy's concurrence suggested a grossly disproportionate test exists, and this has since been adopted by the Supreme Court in *Lockyer v. Andrade*, although the court stressed it was only applicable in extreme and rare cases. Of particular note, exceptionally long punishments, including multiple life sentences, can be imposed even for relatively minor offences if defendants have prior felony convictions.

The use of corporal punishment and more torturous forms of capital punishment have been discontinued, but most of this change has not come through judicial decisions, but rather through social change and legislative rejection. Although the Supreme Court has disallowed few types of punishment, it has constitutionally enshrined societal rejection of the application of the death penalty to certain types of crime and categories of defendant, as well as closely monitoring the process by which the death penalty is imposed.

Proper Procedure in Death Penalty Legislation

Unlike the high level of deference given to the states in imposing noncapital punishments, the Supreme Court has actively developed detailed procedural requirements that must be satisfied for death penalty legislation to withstand scrutiny. Death penalty jurisprudence is divided into two eras: "pre-Furman" and "post-Furman." In 1972, in *Furman v. Georgia*, the Supreme Court ruled that the death penalty as it was then implemented was unconstitutional because of its discretionary nature and its indeterminate and haphazard application, which rendered it arbitrary, and thus cruel and unusual.

A national four-year hiatus on capital punishment followed *Furman*, but in that period thirty-five states and Congress reinstated the death penalty in new statutes that attempted to meet the Supreme Court's procedural requirements. The Supreme Court again addressed the constitutionality of the death penalty in 1976 in *Gregg v. Georgia*. The Georgia Act at issue in the case provided a list of aggravating and mitigating circumstances that could be found by a jury or a judge, in a trial with separate stages for guilt and sentencing determinations, and provided for the possibility of higher court review. These clear processes satisfied the Court, although Justices Brennan and Marshall vigorously dissented, arguing that the death penalty is per se unconstitutional.

Since 1976, imposition of the death penalty has been permissible; however, the Court has continued to add procedural hurdles to the process. *Woodson v. North Carolina* held that the death penalty cannot be a mandatory punishment for a crime. *Lockett v. Ohio* held that a sentencer must consider a range of mitigating factors, including the defendant's age, character, and record, and the circumstances of the offence. *Beck v. Alabama* held that the jury must have the option of considering a verdict of a lesser, non-capital offense. Most of these developments have been prodefendant, although not all: for instance, *Payne v. Tennessee* ruled that it is now permissible to have victim impact statements given during the sentencing phase.

In addition to these specific procedural restrictions, the death penalty can only be imposed in ways that are proportionate and conform to recognized societal evolving standards of decency. These two requirements have provided the basis for restrictions on when and to whom the death penalty can apply.

Categories of Crime

Historically, the death penalty could be applied as punishment for a variety of crimes. It had previously been upheld as fit punishment for murder, rape, attempted rape, arson, assault, kidnapping, and robbery. However, starting in 1977 in *Coker v. Georgia*, the Supreme Court began applying the evolving standards of decency doctrine, which it developed in *Trop v. Dulles*, to death penalty jurisprudence. Noting that eighteen states had made rape a capital punishment prior to the *Furman* ruling, the Court emphasized that only three states had reinstituted the death penalty for rape by 1977, and two of those states only imposed the death penalty when the victim was a child. On this basis, as well as an assessment of proportionality that showed that the punishment was excessive, the Court ruled that imposing the death penalty for rape of an adult woman is unconstitutional.

In that case, Chief Justice Burger in dissent and Justice Powell in concurrence strongly criticized the majority holding on a number of fronts. First, since the death penalty moratorium had only been lifted the previous year in *Gregg*, it could not safely be concluded that legislatures had time to express their community standards in new legislation. Second, Coker was a recidivist rapist and murderer who had escaped from prison, then committed armed robbery, theft, kidnapping, and rape. Even if society considers the death penalty for rape generally disproportionate, it may not do so for a repeat felon for whom no other punishment would be effective: a recidivist serving a life sentence who would otherwise be in no way deterred from committing further rapes when he escapes again, or even within prison. Third, the majority based its finding on indications that society found the death penalty unacceptable when imposed for rape without aggravating brutality, but it was not clear that society found the death penalty disproportionate for all rapes. As such, the ruling was unnecessarily broad.

This division on the Court, between Justices willing to make broad findings of community consensus against imposition of the death penalty for a variety of crimes and those seeking stronger evidence of a clearer and more specific national consensus before constitutionally enshrining it, continues today. Nevertheless, the evolving standards doctrine has been used to rule the death penalty inapplicable for felony-murder without intent to kill in *Enmund v. Florida*, and for "ordinary" murder in *Godfrey v. Georgia*. Today, the death penalty can only be applied for murder with aggravating circumstances.

The only significant restriction on the categories of crime for which noncapital punishments can be imposed is that sentences cannot be imposed for a person's status of being. This includes, for example, being a drug addict or an alcoholic, or suffering from a disease. It is unconstitutional to punish someone for who they are rather than for an act that they have committed.

Categories of Defendants

The evolving standards doctrine and the proportionality test have both been used in similar fashion to restrict the application of the death penalty to certain categories of defendants. *Ford v. Wainwright*xx prohibited execution of offenders who are insane at the time of the proposed execution. *Atkins v. Virginia* proscribed execution of the mentally retarded. This case reversed the 1989 ruling in *Penry v. Lynaugh*, on the basis that an additional sixteen states had discontinued the practice since then, when only two states had exempted the mentally retarded. In 1981, *Stanford v. Kentucky* held that execution of minors was not cruel and unusual, but in 1988, *Thompson v. Oklahoma* held that execution of those sixteen and younger was unconstitutional, and in 2005 in *Roper v. Simmons*, the Supreme Court held that execution of anyone younger than eighteen is cruel and unusual.

Each of these decisions rested to a large extent on the fact that trends in state legislation were in the direction of the relevant limit on the death penalty in each case. However, it is unclear how many states are required to make the change before the Court will recognize an evolving national consensus. In addition, the Court is divided as to whether it only counts states that prohibit execution of the class of defendant or whether the Court also counts states that do not have the death penalty at all in their tally of states that consider execution of the given class of defendant cruel and unusual.

Two other doctrines on which these cases rested remain equally unsettled: First, the majorities in *Atkins* and *Roper* each also relied on notions of culpability and proportionality, arguing that juveniles, like the mentally retarded, are incapable of adequately controlling their impulses or comprehending the criminal process and thus are less responsible and less able to mount an effective defense. But Chief Justice Rehnquist and Justices Scalia and Thomas rejected the applicability of these doctrines, arguing evolving standards should be the only basis of challenging the death penalty. Second, in the *Roper* case, Justice Kennedy's Opinion of the Court also gave consideration to the views of the international community. Although these views were considered only persuasive, and not authoritative, this move was enormously controversial, with elected representatives going so far as to propose impeaching judges who cite such evidence in future cases.

Conclusion

There are many areas of debate and doctrinal uncertainty in death penalty jurisprudence; nevertheless, the Supreme Court is continuing to develop numerous restrictions on the application of the death penalty, without fully resolving these ambiguities. In contrast, Eighth Amendment jurisprudence relating to noncapital offenses is marked by Supreme Court inaction. Given the result in *Lockyer*, when the Supreme Court upheld multiple life sentences for minor offences under the "three strikes" law, it seems unlikely that this strongly deferential approach will change in the near future. As such, we can expect to see an increased cabining of cruel and unusual punishment jurisprudence to an almost exclusive focus on limiting the circumstances in which capital punishment can be imposed.

TONJA JACOBI

References and Further Reading

Berkson, Larry Charles. *The Concept of Cruel and Unusual Punishment*, 1975.

Coyne, Randall, and Lyn Entzeroth. *Capital Punishment and the Judicial Process*, 1994.

Foley, Michael A. *Arbitrary and Capricious: the Supreme Court, the Constitution, and the Death Penalty*, 2003.

Hoffman, Joseph L. "The 'Cruel and Unusual Punishment' Clause: a Limit on the Power to Punish or Constitutional Rhetoric?" In Bodehamer, David J., and James W. Ely, Jr. eds, *The Bill Of Rights in Modern America*, 1993.

Cases and Statutes Cited

Atkins v. Virginia 536 U.S. 304 (U.S. 2002)
Beck v. Alabama 447 U.S. 625 (U.S. 1980)
Campbell v. Wood, 511 U.S. 1119 (U.S. 1994)
Coker v. Georgia, 433 U.S. 584 (U.S. 1977)
Enmund v. Florida, 458 U.S. 782 (U.S. 1982)
Ford v. Wainwright, 477 U.S. 399 (U.S. 1986)
Furman v. Georgia, 408 U.S. 238 (U.S. 1972)
Glass v. Louisiana, 471 U.S. 1080 (U.S. 1985)
Godfrey v. Georgia, 446 U.S. 420 (U.S. 1980)
Gomez v. United States District Court, 503 U.S. 653 (U.S. 1992)
Gregg v. Georgia, 428 U.S. 153 (U.S. 1976)
Harmelin v. Michigan, 501 U.S. 957 (U.S. 1991)
Lockett v. Ohio, 438 U.S. 586 (U.S. 1978)
Lockyer v. Andrade, 538 U.S. 63 (U.S. 2003)
Marbury v. Madison, 5 U.S. 137 (1803)
Payne v. Tennessee, 501 U.S. 808 (U.S. 1991)
Penry v. Lynaugh, 492 U.S. 302 (U.S. 1989)
Roper v. Simmons, 125 S. Ct. 1183 (U.S. 2005)
Rummel v. Estelle, 445 U.S. 263 (U.S. 1980)
Stanford v. Kentucky, 492 U.S. 361 (U.S. 1981)
Thompson v. Oklahoma, 487 U.S. 815 (U.S. 1988)
Trop v. Dulles, 356 U.S. 86 (U.S. 1958)
Weems v. U.S., 217 U.S. 349 (1910)
Wilkerson v. Utah, 99 U.S. 130 (1879)
Woodson v. North Carolina, 428 U.S. 280 (U.S. 1976)

CRUEL AND UNUSUAL PUNISHMENT GENERALLY

The Eighth Amendment to the U.S. Constitution provides that "Excessive bail shall not be required, nor excessive fines imposed, nor cruel and unusual punishments inflicted." The U.S. Supreme Court has worked for the past century to define the phrase "cruel and unusual punishments." At its inception, the phrase was meant to place some restriction on the types of punishments permitted in the context of criminal offenses, specifically prohibiting tortuous and barbaric punishments. However, over the years it has been interpreted to apply not only to the methods of punishment permitted, but also to the proportionality and implementation of punishments.

History of Cruel and Unusual Punishment Clause

The first prohibition against tortuous and barbarous punishments was written into American law in 1641 in a document entitled "Body of Liberties," which was enacted in the Colony of Massachusetts. Nearly fifty years later, the phrase "cruel and unusual punishments" appeared in the English Declaration of Rights of 1688, ratified by William and Mary. The clause was later incorporated verbatim into the Virginia Declaration of Rights of 1776 and in substantially similar form in the Eighth Amendment to the U.S. Constitution in 1791.

When the Cruel and Unusual Punishments clause of the Eighth Amendment was adopted, its full meaning was unclear. However, state and federal courts alike originally interpreted the Clause to prohibit certain methods of punishment that were deemed to be tortuous or barbaric. In 1892, the U.S. Supreme Court first indicated that the Clause might be construed not only as a barrier to certain tortuous or barbaric punishments but also to punishments that were excessive under the circumstances. In 1910, a slim majority of the Supreme Court held that that the Cruel and Unusual Punishments clause should be expanded to include disproportionate punishments. The defendant in the case at issue was convicted under a statute that required a sentence of fifteen years at hard labor for anyone convicted of making a false entry in a government payroll book. Although the punishment was not cruel and unusual per se, it violated the Eighth Amendment in that case because it was grossly disproportionate to the crime of forging public records.

There were no other significant applications of the Clause until 1958, when the Supreme Court decided *Trop v. Dulles*. At issue in that case was whether expatriation was a cruel and unusual punishment for the crime of military desertion. The Supreme Court found that the extreme punishment of expatriation, which involves the "total destruction of the individual's status in organized society," constituted cruel and unusual punishment. In *Trop v. Dulles,* the court first developed the concept of "evolving standards of decency." Under this theory, the Eighth Amendment is deemed to draw its meaning from "the evolving standards of decency that mark the progress of a maturing society." Four years later, the Supreme Court held in another landmark case that it is cruel and unusual to make drug addiction a criminal offense.

The next significant Supreme Court decision regarding the Cruel and Unusual Punishments clause occurred in 1972, when the court declared that all existing capital punishment statutes violated the Eighth Amendment. Although the court did not hold that the death penalty was cruel and unusual per se, it declared that the imposition of the death penalty through the existing statutes violated the Eighth Amendment because death sentences were being imposed in an "arbitrary and capricious" manner. In 1976, the Supreme Court reviewed newly drafted death penalty statutes from Georgia, Florida, and Texas and upheld the statutes against Eighth Amendment challenges, because the statutes provided juries with sufficient guidance in the decision-making process and permitted individualized sentencing for each defendant. Since 1976, a majority of the Supreme Court has upheld the death penalty against per se Eighth Amendment challenges but has declared that the application of the death penalty is cruel and unusual in cases involving the rape of an adult woman, insane defendants, mentally retarded defendants, and defendants who were younger than eighteen at the time the crime was committed.

Although death penalty cases make up the majority of Cruel and Unusual Punishment claims, the Supreme Court has also applied the Clause to prison conditions and treatment of prisoners and to repeat offender statutes, often referred to as "three strikes" laws.

Evolving Standards of Decency

As early as 1910, the Supreme Court recognized the progressive nature of the Eighth Amendment when it indicated that the Amendment "may acquire meaning as public opinion becomes enlightened by a humane justice." In 1958, the Supreme Court affirmatively held that the interpretation of what constitutes "cruel and unusual" punishment changes over time, because it is judged by the "evolving standards of decency that mark the progress of a maturing society."

The Supreme Court has indicated that the determination of current societal standards of decency should be guided by objective factors to the maximum extent possible. In the context of death penalty claims, such factors include state and federal legislation, jury

verdicts, and national and international views. Although there is much disagreement regarding the role that international views should play in a constitutional analysis, some of the Supreme Court justices have indicated that international opinion, although in no way binding on the Court, should be considered in some manner as part of a societal standard of decency analysis.

In addition to the objective factors, the Court also applies its own judgment to determine whether a particular punishment contributes to an accepted sentencing goal or whether it is nothing more than the needless imposition of pain and suffering. In the context of capital cases, the Court determines whether the punishment of death effectively contributes to either deterrence or retribution.

The Cruel and Unusual Punishments clause is unique in that it has been interpreted to change over time, unlike other Constitutional provisions. As society develops and matures over time, it is certain to maintain its pivotal role in the evolution of the American criminal justice system.

JUDITH M. BARGER

References and Further Reading

Bukowski, Jeffrey D., *The Eighth Amendment and Original Intent: Applying the Prohibition Against Cruel and Unusual Punishments to Prison Deprivation Cases is Not Beyond the Bounds of History and Precedent*, Dick. L. Rev. 99 (1994): 419.
Furman v. Georgia, 408 U.S. 238 (1972).
Granucci, Anthony F., *Nor Cruel and Unusual Punishments Inflicted:" The Original Meaning*, Cal. L. Rev. 57 (1969): 839.
Gregg v. Georgia, 428 U.S. 153 (1976).
Jurek v. Texas, 429 U.S. 262 (1976).
Proffitt v. Florida, 428 U.S. 242 (1976).
Trop v. Dulles, 356 U.S. 86 (1958).
Varland, Brian W., *Marking the Progress of a Maturing Society: Reconsidering the Constitutionality of Death Penalty Application in Light of Evolving Standards of Decency*, Hamline L. Rev. 28 (2005): 311.
Weems v. United States, 217 U.S. 349 (1910).

See also **Capital Punishment and Sentencing;** *Trop v. Dulles*, **356 U.S. 86 (1958)**

CRUZAN v. MISSOURI, 497 U.S. 261 (1990)

Nancy Cruzan is the first case in which the Supreme Court of the United States (the Court) had to decide on the issue of "right to die" under the U.S. Constitution. In a five to four decision, the Court struggled to balance individual rights with state interests.

In January 1983, Nancy Cruzan lost control of her car in a serious accident. Her breathing and heartbeat were recovered; however, she remained in a coma for approximately three weeks before she progressed to an unconscious state. Surgeons implanted a gastrostomy feeding and hydration tube to ease feeding, but subsequent rehabilitative efforts failed to recover her from the so-called persistent vegetative state, in which she "exhibits motor reflexes but evinces no indications of significant cognitive function." Seeing no chance of regaining her mental faculties, Cruzan's parents asked a court authorization to terminate the artificial nutrition and hydration. Recognizing her medical condition, the trial court believed that Nancy Cruzan had a fundamental right under both Missouri and U.S. Constitutions to "refuse or direct the withdrawal of 'death prolonging procedures.'" The trial court also found reliable Cruzan's conversation with a housemate friend, in which Nancy Cruzan expressed her unwillingness to continue her life if she could not "live at least halfway normally." The Missouri Supreme Court reversed and refused to read the State Constitution so broadly to support a person's right to terminate medical treatment in every circumstances. Rather, the Missouri Supreme Court found the roommate's story unreliable and held that there was not "clear and convincing" evidence to support the termination.

In a close call, the Court affirmed the State Supreme Court's decision. First, reviewing relevant state cases, the Court found that the common-law doctrine of informed consent is always viewed as encompassing a competent individual's right to refuse medical treatment. However, reluctant to establish such a doctrine under the Constitution, the Court simply "assumed" that the U.S. Constitution would grant a similar right to a competent person. Second, the Court refused to extend such a right to incompetent persons and held that states may adopt certain procedural requirements to safeguard relevant state interests. In the present case, after a balance, the Court validated Missouri's claimed interest in "the protection and preservation of human life" and approved Missouri's imposition of heightened evidentiary requirements (that is, the incompetent's wish to withdraw treatment must be proved by "clear and convincing" evidence) against potential abuses that might result harsh erroneous decisions. Justice O'Connor filed a separate concurring opinion and clarified her belief that a right to refuse unwanted medical treatment might be inferred from the Constitution. In another concurring opinion, Justice Scalia traced the traditional opposition of suicide by states and struggled with the distinction between action (for example, suicide) and inaction (right to refuse treatment). Rather, Justice Scalia believed that this is not a proper issue for the Constitution. Justices Brennan, Marshall, and Blackmun dissented. They argued that Nancy Cruzan "has a fundamental right to be free of unwanted artificial nutrition and hydration," and her incompetent condition does not deprive her of such a right. The state's general interest in the preservation of life cannot subdue Nancy Cruzan's particularized interest, and the procedural obstacles placed by the Missouri Supreme Court imposed an impermissible burden on Nancy Cruzan's right. Compared with the majority, the dissenters would clearly assign more weight to evidence provided by family members and friends in determining Cruzan's personal wishes. Justice Stevens filed a separate dissenting opinion and argued that the State Supreme Court's decision totally ignored Nancy Cruzan's best interests. Rather, the state should have given appropriate respect to her best interests when it evaluated evidence based on the "clear and convincing" standard.

Six months after the Court's ruling, Nancy Cruzan died after her family and friends presented new evidence and the judge ruled that there was clear evidence to show her wishes. The significance of *Nancy Cruzan* lies in the fact that the Court recognized a competent patient's right to terminate medical treatment, although states may impose necessary protection procedures to incompetent patients. However, the Court refused to go one-step further to honor active euthanasia or physician-assisted suicide (see *Washington v. Glucksberg*, 521 U.S. 702 (1997); *Vacco v. Quill*, 521 U.S. 793 (1997)), leaving the line between active and inactive euthanasia arguable. *Nancy Cruzan* and later relevant cases showed a continuous weighing by the courts the value of life against the value of death and what is the meaning of diminished human lives to the incompetent patients.

BIN LIANG

References and Further Reading

Angell, Marcia. "The Supreme Court and Physician-Assisted Suicide—The Ultimate Right." *The New England Journal of Medicine* 336 (1997): 50–53.

Annas, George J., *The "Right to Die" in America: Sloganeering from Quinlan and Cruzan to Quill and Kevorkian*, Duquesne University Law Review 34 (1996): 875–897.

Baggett, Sandy D., *In Search of a Right to Die: Preventing Government Infliction of Pain*, University of Tennessee Law Review 65 (1997): 245–292.

Bopp, James Jr., and Daniel Avila, *The Due Process "Right to Life" in Cruzan and its Impact on "Right-to-Die" Law*, University of Pittsburgh Law Review 53 (1991): 193–233.

——, *Perspectives on Cruzan: The Siren's Lure of Invented Consent: A Critique of Autonomy-Based Surrogate Decisionmaking for Legally-Incapacitated Older Persons*, Hastings Law Journal 42 (1991): 779–815.

Martyn, Susan R., and Henry J. Bourguignon, *Perspective on Cruzan: Coming to Terms with Death: The Cruzan Case*, Hastings Law Journal 42 (1991): 817–858.

Robertson, John A., *Cruzan and The Constitutional Status of Nontreatment Decisions for Incompetent Patients*, University of Georgia Law Review 25 (1991): 1139–1203.

Ronzetti, T. A. Tucker, *Constituting Family and Death Through the Struggle with State Power: Cruzan v. Director, Missouri Department of Health*, University of Miami Law Review 46 (1991): 149–204.

Cases and Statutes Cited

Vacco v. Quill, 521 U.S. 793 (1997)
Washington v. Glucksberg, 521 U.S. 702 (1997)

CUBAN INTERDICTION

Interdiction of vessels at sea to deter migration dates back to the early days of the Republic, when interdiction was used to interfere with the forced migration of slaves. Similarly, persons fleeing war, persecution, or economic and political upheaval have been arriving at American shores since at least 1793, when waves of white refugees poured into U.S. ports fleeing a slave insurrection in Santo Domingo. That insurrection led to the establishment of Haiti in 1801. Those refugees, however, were welcome on U.S. shores, particularly in the slave-owning South.

It was not until the 1980s, however, that the United States began to aggressively use interdiction in the open seas to prevent migration. The catalyst for the change in federal policy seems to have been the Mariel Boatlift in 1980 during which approximately 124,000 Cuban migrants entered the United States. Marielitos, as these refugees came to be known, were detained, in some cases, indefinitely, in others, until a family or individual could be found to serve as a sponsor. The Mariel crisis and an influx of Haitians fleeing economic and political repression in Haiti led President Reagan to issue Executive Order 12324 on September 23, 1981, which ordered the Coast Guard to interdict vessels carrying undocumented aliens and return them to their point of origin. The order, thus, required interdiction, screening of migrants aboard vessels to determine whether they qualified as refugees under American and international law, and return of those who did not.

Interdiction became a favored practice to deter undocumented migration, as federal constitutional and immigration law became more protective of migrants in the United States. Once on shore, statutory and constitutional protections provide some degree of process to undocumented immigrants; interdiction at sea allowed the government to deter migrants from entering the United States without having to extend any due process or statutory protections to those seeking refuge in the United States. Although President Reagan's order preserved some degree of screening on board vessels, the policy changed in the wake of the overthrow of Haitian president Jean Aristide in 1991, when a new influx of Haitians were received on U.S. shores. In 1992, President Bush issued Executive Order 12807 directing the Coast Guard to interdict undocumented migrants at sea and repatriate them. President Bush's order terminated screening of migrants to determine whether they were entitled to refugee status. This order was challenged and upheld by the U. S. Supreme Court in *Sale v. Haitian Centers Council, Inc.*

Few Cuban migrants, however, were interdicted at sea until the 1990s; interdiction to deter migration was directed primarily at Haitians. Beginning in 1991, however, when Castro again signaled a willingness to allow Cubans to leave Cuba without interference from the Cuban government, the rate of Cuban interdictions increased, peaking dramatically in 1994, when 37,191 Cubans were interdicted at sea. Most of these Cubans were detained in Guantanamo, as were their Haitian counterparts. After litigation and public criticism of the practice, most Guantanamo Cuban detainees were released to a sponsor in the United States or returned to Cuba pursuant to an agreement worked out between the Cuban and U.S. governments.

Today, the U.S. Coast Guard continues to use interdiction of undocumented migrants at sea to quickly return them to their country of origin and to avoid what the Coast Guard refers to as "the costly processes required if they successfully enter the U.S." The largest group of migrants to be interdicted in fiscal year 2005 continue to be persons from the Caribbean, with the largest number to come from the Dominican Republic (3,520), followed by Cubans (2,532), and Haitians (1,850). Since 1982, a total of 57,800 Cubans have been interdicted at sea.

M. Isabel Medina

References and Further Reading

Hamm, Mark S. *The Abandoned Ones: The Imprisonment and Uprising of the Mariel Boat People*. Boston: Northeastern University Press, 1995.

Palmer, Capt. Gary W., USCG, *Guarding the Coast: Alien Migrant Interdiction Operations at Sea*, Connecticut Law Review 29 (1997): 1565–1615.

Rivera, Mario A. *Decision and Structure: U.S. Refugee Policy in the Mariel Crisis*. Lanham, MD: University Press of America, 1991.

Rosenberg, Lori D., *International Association of Refugee Law Judges Conference: The Courts and Interception: The United States Interdiction Experience and Its Impact on Refugees and Asylum Seekers*, Georgetown Immigration Law Journal 17 (2003): 199.

U.S. Coast Guard. *"Alien Migrant Interdiction-Overview"* http://www.uscg.mil/hq/g-o/g-opl/AMIO/AMIO.htm (2005).

U.S. Coast Guard, *"History of the U.S. Coast Guard in Illegal Immigration (1794–1971)"* http://www.uscg.mil/hq/g-o/g-opl/AMIO/amiohist.htm (2005).

Cases, Statutes, and Executive Orders Cited

Sale v. Haitian Centers Council, Inc., 509 U.S. 155 (1993)

Cuban American Bar Association, Inc. v. Christopher, 43 F. 3d 1412 (11th Cir. 1995)

Haitian Refugee Center, Inc. v. Christopher, 43 F. 3d 1431 (11th Cir. 1995)

Cuban Refugee Adjustment Act, Pub. L. No. 89-732, 80 Stat. 1161 (1966)

Executive Order 12324, 46 Fed. Reg. 48,109 (1981)

Executive Order 12807, 57 Fed. Reg. 23,133 (1992)

Presidential Proclamation No. 4865, 46 Fed. Reg. 48,108 (1981)

CULTURAL DEFENSE

Strictly speaking, there is no such thing as a "cultural defense." Instead, the term refers to all of the ways in which a defendant can use evidence of his cultural background—the "shared organization of ideas that includes the intellectual, moral, and aesthetic standards" prevalent in his community of origin—to argue that his conduct was either not criminal, should be excused, or should be punished less severely.

Courts have traditionally been hostile to cultural defenses, viewing them as incompatible with the Rule of Law, the idea that "to apply a law justly to different cases is simply to take seriously the assertion that what is to be applied in different cases is the same general rule." More recently, however, three different kinds of cultural defenses have begun to gain a degree of judicial acceptance.

First, courts have allowed defendants to use cultural evidence to show that they lacked the mental state required by a particular crime. An example is *People v. Moua*, in which a young Hmong man was accused of raping and kidnapping a young Hmong woman. Prior to trial, the defendant introduced evidence that abducting and having intercourse with an unmarried woman against her will, and despite her protests, was an expected part of the Hmong's "marriage by capture" tradition. The court dismissed the charges on the ground that the defendant lacked the specific intent required by rape and kidnapping.

Second, courts have allowed defendants to use cultural evidence to establish criminal defenses such as provocation, self-defense, duress, and necessity. In *People v. Croy*, for example, a jury acquitted a Native American man accused of murdering a police officer after a historian testified that, in light of the U.S. government's repeated persecution of the defendant's tribe, the defendant could have reasonably believed he was acting in self-defense.

Third, courts have allowed defendants to use cultural evidence as a mitigating factor during sentencing. Such evidence is particularly common in child-abuse cases, where the defendant argues that he should be given a lenient sentence because he was simply disciplining his child in accord with his cultural traditions. For example, a Mexican woman was sentenced to probation for beating her son with a spoon and biting him after she introduced evidence that such punishment was standard discipline in Mexico.

There are two basic rationales for recognizing cultural defenses. To begin with, such recognition promotes individualized justice, the idea that the defendant's punishment should match his personal culpability. An individual who commits a criminal act either because his cultural values required him to do so or because he did not know the act was illegal in the United States is not as personally culpable as someone who commits the same criminal act freely and with knowledge of its illegality.

Recognizing cultural defenses also promotes cultural pluralism. By judging individuals according to the standards and values of their native cultures, cultural defenses help preserve those cultures, maintain a culturally diverse society, and ensure that minority groups are not penalized simply for being different.

KEVIN JON HELLER

References and Further Reading

Levine, Kay L., *Negotiating the Boundaries of Crime and Culture: A Sociolegal Perspective on Cultural Defense Strategies*, Law and Social Inquiry 28 (2003): 1:39–86.

Note: *The Cultural Defense in Criminal Law*, Harvard Law Review 99 (1986): 6:1293–1311.

Renteln, Alison Dundes. *The Cultural Defense.* New York: Oxford University Press, 2004.

Cases and Statutes Cited

People v. Moua, No. 315972-0 (Cal. Super. Ct. Fresno County Feb. 7, 1985)

People v. Croy, 710 P.2d 392 (Cal. 1985)

CUMMINGS v. STATE OF MISSOURI, 71 U.S. 277 (1866)

See Test Oath Cases

D

DANDRIDGE v. WILLIAMS, 397 U.S. 471 (1971)

The federal welfare program called Aid to Families with Dependent Children (AFDC), enacted as part of the Social Security Act of 1935, was repealed in 1996. Under AFDC, states calculated a standard of need for each family, then allocated welfare grants based on that standard. Generally, the standard of need increased with each additional person in the household. However, some states, like Maryland, imposed an upper limit on the amount of money a family might receive.

Several families affected by Maryland's policy sued the state under the Equal Protection Clause, arguing that the maximum grant irrationally discriminated against children in large families. The Supreme Court upheld the policy in a five-to-three decision. Applying the minimum level of constitutional scrutiny, the Court held that the policy was rational. The Court credited Maryland's argument that it maintained financial equity between welfare recipients and the working poor and created an incentive for members of large families to seek employment.

Dandridge was one of a series of cases initiated in the late 1960s and early 1970s to test the constitutionality of state welfare policies. Many of these cases were successful, and some poverty rights activists believed that the Supreme Court would eventually establish a constitutional right to welfare. *Dandridge*, however, signaled that the Court was prepared to approach state welfare policies with greater deference. In the wake of 1996 welfare reform, lower courts have cited *Dandridge* to uphold state policies that deny benefit increases when a child is born to a family on welfare, thus permitting states to use financial disincentives to deter poor women from having a child while receiving government benefits.

MARTHA F. DAVIS

References and Further Reading

Davis, Martha. *Brutal Need: Lawyers and the Welfare Rights Movement, 1960–1973*. New Haven, CT: Yale University Press, 1993.
Krislov, Samuel, *The OEO Lawyers Fail to Constitutionalize a Right to Welfare: A Study of the Uses and Limits of Judicial Process*, Minnesota Law Review 58 (1973): 211–245.
Lawrence, Susan E. *The Poor in Court: The Legal Services Program and Supreme Court Decision Making*. Princeton, NJ: Princeton University Press, 1990.
Sparer, Edward. "The Right to Welfare." In *The Rights of Americans: What They Are—What They Should Be*, Norman Dorsen, ed. New York: Pantheon Books, 1971, 65–93.

Cases and Statutes Cited

Social Security Act of 1935, Pub. L. No. 74-271, 49 Stat. 620

See also **Equal Protection of Law (XIV); Fourteenth Amendment;** *Goldberg v. Kelly***, 397 U.S. 254 (1970);** *Wyman v. James***, 400 U.S. 309 (1971)**

DARROW, CLARENCE (1857–1938)

The most celebrated criminal defense lawyer of the twentieth century, Clarence Seward Darrow achieved near legendary status in a series of highly publicized cases in which he championed individual rights and progressive political causes. He was born in Kinsman, in rural northeastern Ohio. His father, a seminary graduate who became a freethinker, worked as a furniture maker and undertaker. His mother, whom Darrow called his greatest influence, died when he was fifteen. His parents instilled a lifelong reverence for books, which expressed itself in later literary efforts at fiction and criticism, culminating in a masterful autobiography, *The Story of My Life* (1932).

Darrow attended preparatory school for one year (1873) at Allegheny College. Though an indifferent student and contemptuous of formal education, he taught school for three years in Ohio while he read law. He studied law for one year at the University of Michigan (1877–1878) and apprenticed with a lawyer in Youngstown, Ohio, where he was admitted to the Ohio bar.

Darrow practiced law and participated in Democratic Party activities in rural northern Ohio. He moved to Chicago in 1887 where he sought out the patronage of Judge John Peter Altgeld, who arranged Darrow's appointment as legal counsel for the city of Chicago. In 1891, Darrow joined the law department of the Chicago and Northwestern Railway. He also advised Altgeld during his successful campaign for governor in 1892.

Darrow's sympathy for poor people and victims of injustice led him to join numerous reform clubs. A lifelong opponent of capital punishment, he encouraged Governor Altgeld to pardon the surviving anarchists convicted of the terrorist bombing during the Chicago Haymarket riot. He also intervened after Chicago's popular mayor was assassinated, challenging the killer's competence in an unsuccessful effort to prevent his execution.

Sympathizing with labor and disapproving of the industrialists' influence over political power, Darrow resigned in 1894 as counsel for the railroad in order to represent Eugene Debs, the militant president of the American Railway Union. Prior to New Deal legislation, employers enlisted the aid of law enforcement to crush unions by charging organizers with criminal conspiracy. This crime broadly prohibited two or more persons from agreeing to do anything unlawful, and pro-owner prosecutors reasoned that labor's goal was the unlawful injuring of employers' economic interests.

Darrow rose to prominence representing union leaders in criminal cases. His vigorous defense of Debs at his criminal conspiracy trial is credited with causing the railroad to influence the government to drop the case. (This did not prevent Debs from being convicted of contempt for violating a federal injunction.) In 1898, Darrow defended Thomas I. Kidd, general secretary of the Amalgamated Woodworkers' International Union, who was tried for criminal conspiracy in Oshkosh, Wisconsin. Darrow's jury argument lasted two days. Drawing on sources from the Bible to Victor Hugo, Darrow lionized Kidd as a "great soul" devoted to "humanity's holy cause" and accused the prosecutors and industrialists of being the true conspirators for their effort to prevent freedom of association for the sake of property rights. The jury found Kidd not guilty. In 1903, Darrow added to his reputation as a labor lawyer, representing the United Mine Workers in arbitration proceedings in Pennsylvania, where he won the workers wage increases and back pay.

In 1908, Darrow defended radical union leader William D. ("Big Bill") Haywood in Iowa, where he was tried for the murder of former governor Frank Steuenberg. Darrow persuaded the jury to reject the testimony of the state's main witness, a confessed killer, and the jury acquitted Haywood.

In 1911 union leaders persuaded Darrow to represent the McNamara brothers, union activists charged with the terrorist bombing of the *Los Angeles Times* building that claimed twenty-one victims. Darrow eventually pled his clients guilty, avoiding death sentences for them, but in doing so he permanently alienated organized labor. In this highly charged atmosphere, Darrow was accused of attempting to bribe two jurors. He was obliged to remain in Los Angeles for two years and faced two separate trials. The first trial provided the occasion for one of his greatest speeches, and the jury acquitted him. In the second trial, the jury could agree neither to convict nor acquit. Though the case was eventually dropped, his reputation suffered.

Darrow returned to Chicago, economically and emotionally depleted, where he rebuilt his practice, specializing in criminal cases. He returned to civic prominence as a pro-war spokesman during the Great War and as an opponent of the League of Nations after the war.

Darrow distinguished himself from most populists and progressives by his outspoken support for African-American rights. In the 1890s, he promoted the creation of Chicago's first interracial hospital. In 1910, he defended interracial marriage in an address to a precursor of the NAACP. His biographer Kevin Tierney records that Darrow gave more time and money to African-American causes than any other white person of the day.

In 1925, Darrow defended eleven members of the Sweet family and their friends, who had been charged with conspiracy to commit murder. The death occurred when Dr. Ossian Sweet, an African American, moved into a white neighborhood of Detroit and a mob attacked his home. When Sweet and other occupants defended themselves, a bystander was shot and killed. Darrow's forceful confrontation of race hatred and energetic assertion of the right to self defense resulted in a hung jury. A few months later, the state retried one of Sweet's brothers. Darrow won an outright acquittal, and the remaining charges were dropped.

Darrow's two most publicized cases occurred during the 1920s. In 1924, he defended Leopold and Loeb, two young college graduates who murdered a teenage neighbor. Public sentiment strongly favored executing the killers, who came from wealthy Jewish families and whose motive was intellectual thrill-seeking. Darrow entered pleas of guilty and devoted himself to the improbable goal of saving his clients from hanging. His argument remains one of the most forceful pleas against capital punishment, and it convinced the sentencing judge to impose life prison terms. The crime inspired numerous books, plays, and films, and Darrow's defense established him as a national spokesperson against capital punishment.

In the summer of 1925, Darrow appeared for the defense in the Scopes "monkey trial" in Dayton, Tennessee, where a schoolteacher was charged with violating a state statute banning the teaching of evolution. William Jennings Bryan, populist orator and former Democratic presidential candidate who had campaigned for the legislation, agreed to serve as special prosecutor. Scopes was convicted as expected, though his judgment was later reversed because the judge rather than jury fixed the fine. The national news media closely covered Darrow's defense of science and his ridicule of religious ignorance. The case helped marginalize the antievolution crusade as a rural movement and identified science with tolerance and religion with censorship. Darrow dramatized the conflict by calling Bryan as an expert witness on Christianity and questioning him about Biblical passages that seemingly required interpretation. The case was popularized for later generations by the film *Inherit the Wind* (1960).

Darrow's career vindicated the importance of defense lawyers in protecting groups and individuals from efforts to control unpopular thought and behavior by criminal law enforcement. He was by temperament an agnostic who questioned the reality of freedom of will and an individualist who asserted his right to drink during Prohibition. He insisted on the value of privacy, protesting, "Wouldn't it be better that every rogue and rascal in the world should go unpunished than to say that detectives could put a Dictograph into your parlor, your dining room, in your bedroom, and destroy that privacy which alone makes life worth living?"

While he recognized the need for collective action to achieve social reform, Darrow's skepticism left him equally suspicious of moral absolutes and of popular opinion. This explains how his populist convictions could coexist with hostility to expansive government power, accounting for paradoxes such as his support for Democratic candidates and opposition to New Deal programs. He flirted with electoral politics only twice, running unsuccessfully for Congress in 1896 as a Democrat and successfully for the Illinois legislature in 1902 as an Independent. He held appointed positions, including chair of the National Recovery Review Board in 1934.

A humanist who viewed all humans as flawed, Darrow's strategy, which succeeded even when his clients were guilty of wrongdoing, was to fight to establish a broader vision of a controversy in which his clients' conduct did not deserve condemnation. In an age when judicial construction of the Bill of Rights provided fewer protections, he employed common-law doctrines like the presumption of innocence and right to self-defense to protect unpopular clients against the totalitarian tendencies he feared were inherent in the modern state.

Darrow married Jessie Ohl in 1880, and the couple moved to Andover, Ohio. The couple's only child, Paul Edward Darrow, was born in 1883. The Darrows were divorced in 1897. In 1903, Darrow married Ruby Hamerstrom, a journalist with whom he had no children.

MICHAEL H. HOFFHEIMER

References and Further Reading

Boyle, Kevin. *Arc of Justice: A Saga of Race, Civil Rights, and Murder in the Jazz Age.* New York: H. Holt, 2004.

Cowan, Geoffrey. The People v. Clarence Darrow: *The Bribery Trial of America's Greatest Lawyer.* New York: Times Books, 1993.

Darrow, Clarence. *Resist Not Evil.* Chicago: C. H. Kerr, 1903.

———. *Farmington.* New York: Charles Scribner's Sons, 1932.

———. *Attorney for the Damned: Clarence Darrow in the Courtroom,* Arthur Weinberg, ed. Chicago: University of Chicago Press, 1957.

———. *Crime: Its Causes and Treatment.* Montclair, N.J.: Patterson Smith, 1972.

———. *The Story of My Life.* New York: Da Capo Press, 1996.

Higdon, Hal. *Leopold and Loeb: The Crime of the Century.* Urbana: University of Illinois Press, 1999.

Larson, Edward J. *Summer for the Gods: The Scopes Trial and America's Continuing Debate Over Science and Religion.* New York: Basic Books, 1997.

Sayer, James Edward. *Clarence Darrow: Public Advocate.* Monograph series no. 2. Dayton, OH: Wright State University, 1978.

Stone, Irving. *Clarence Darrow for the Defense.* Garden City, NY: Doubleday, Doran and Company, 1941.

Tierney, Kevin. *Darrow: A Biography.* New York: Thomas Y. Crowell Publishers, 1979.

Vine, Phyllis. *One Man's Castle: Clarence Darrow in Defense of the American Dream.* New York: Amistad, 2004.

See also **Capital Punishment; Prohibition; Scopes Trial**

DAVIS v. ALASKA, 415 U.S. 308 (1974)

In *Davis*, the Supreme Court established that the Sixth Amendment Confrontation Clause generally guarantees criminal defendants the right to relevant cross-examination of prosecution witnesses about their criminal records.

Davis was tried for burglarizing a bar and stealing the safe. The prosecution's star witness was a teenager, Green, who testified that he saw Davis standing on the road near where the empty safe was later found. Since Green had recently been adjudicated as a juvenile delinquent for two burglaries, Davis's attorney wanted to question Green about his juvenile record to show that Green was eager to identify Davis in order to deflect suspicion from himself. However, the state courts barred Davis from revealing Green's prior record because juvenile adjudications were confidential under state law.

Davis appealed to the U.S. Supreme Court, which reversed by a vote of seven to two. The Court stressed that criminal defendants have the right to conduct probing cross-examinations of their accusers in order to discredit them. Since witnesses have traditionally been discredited by their criminal histories, the Court concluded that Davis should have been allowed to reveal Green's criminal history and that his Confrontation Clause right to do so trumped the state's interest in keeping juvenile records confidential. Since *Davis*, the Court has occasionally struck down other limits on cross-examination, such as the ruling in *Olden v. Kentucky*, 488 U.S. 227 (1988), barring a rape defendant from revealing the complainant's sexual relationship with another key witness, while emphasizing that judges still retain discretion to protect witnesses from unnecessary harassment.

DAVID A. MORAN

References and Further Reading

Jonakait, Randolph N., *Restoring the Confrontation Clause to the Sixth Amendment*, UCLA Law Review 35 (1988): 557.

Cases and Statutes Cited

Olden v. Kentucky, 488 U.S. 227 (1988)

See also **Confrontation Clause; Defense, Right to Present**

DAVIS v. BEASON, 133 U.S. 333 (1890)

Davis v. Beason (1890) was an appeal to the U.S. Supreme Court of a conviction for unlawfully attempting to register to vote in violation of an Idaho statute that denied the franchise to would-be voters who practiced polygamy, belonged to an organization that practiced polygamy or taught, advised, counseled, or encouraged polygamy. The statute also required that applicants swear an oath to that effect.

The Utah statute was created in a nationwide atmosphere of anti-Mormon sentiment and must be viewed in the context of the federal acts of Congress aimed at the Church of Jesus Christ of Latter-day Saints (Mormons). From 1852, when Brigham Young made public a church practice that had gone on underground for at least two decades, to at least 1890, when the church officially banned the practice, the public practice of polygamy was the touchstone that ignited popular sentiment against the young church.

Samuel Davis and other Mormons registered to vote in Utah and, in so doing, as required by the Utah statute, took an oath stating that they were not polygamists and did not belong to any organization that taught or encouraged polygamy. Thus, because they belonged to the Mormon Church that practiced and encouraged polygamy, they had committed perjury and violated the statute. Davis argued that the statute under which he was convicted violated the Free Exercise Clause of the First Amendment.

The case was short on constitutional analysis, relied heavily upon the first Mormon case of two years prior, *Reynolds v. United States*, 98 U.S. 145 (1878), and was transparent in its condemnation of Mormon beliefs, "To call [the Mormons'] advocacy [of polygamy] a tenet of religion is to offend the common sense of mankind."

As it had done in *Reynolds*, the Court first distinguished Mormonism from true religion, describing it as a "cultus or form of worship of a particular sect." The Court stated that the First Amendment religious freedoms were enacted as a response to the "oppressive measures" enacted by the dominant religions in European countries, but were never intended to protect acts "inimical to the peace, good order, and morals of a society."

What if certain sects had advocated promiscuity, suttee (the Hindu practice of a wife throwing herself upon her deceased husband's funeral pyre), or human sacrifice, the Court asked. "Suppose one believed that human sacrifices were a necessary part of religious worship, would it be seriously contended that the civil government under which he lived could not interfere to prevent a sacrifice?"

The Court concluded with a note that at least thirteen state constitutions expressly excluded "acts of licentiousness" from free exercise protection, including those of California, Colorado, Connecticut, Florida, Georgia, Illinois, Maryland, Minnesota, Mississippi, Missouri, Nevada, New York, and South Carolina.

The case was the third in a series of defeats for the polygamous Mormon Church, following *Reynolds v. United States* (1878) and *Murphy v. Ramsey*, 114 U.S. 15, 45 (1885). It hit the church particularly hard because, in upholding the state law, the Court made it impossible for Mormons to vote in local elections and greatly diminished the local political clout that Mormons had previously been able to wield due to their geographic concentration. However, the final and most serious blow to Mormon polygamy was to come five years later in *Late Corp. of the Church of Jesus Christ of Latter-day Saints v. United States*.

KEITH E. SEALING

References and Further Reading

Ostling, Richard, and Joan Ostling. *Mormon America: The Power and the Promise.* New York: Harper, 1999.
Sealing, Keith, *Polygamists out of the Closet: Statutory and State Constitutional Prohibitions Against Polygamy Are Unconstitutional Under the Free Exercise Clause*, Ga. St. U. L. Rev. 17 (2001): 691.
Van Wagoner, Richard. *Mormon Polygamy: A History.* Gaithersburg, MD: Signature Books, 1989.

See also Reynolds v. United States, 98 U.S. 145 (1878)

DAWSON, JOSEPH MARTIN (1879–1973)

Joseph Martin Dawson, ordained Baptist minister and advocate of religious liberty and church–state separation, was cofounder of Americans United for the Separation of Church and State, for which he served as first acting director and executive secretary (1947–1948). The first full-time executive director of the Baptist Joint Committee on Public Affairs (1946–1953), Dawson left an indelible mark on Baptist social thought, linking it for decades with a brand of church–state separationism that shaped a generation of American jurists, including Justice Hugo Black.

Born in 1879 near Waxahachie, Texas, Dawson was a natural leader with a passion for writing and preaching, which served him well throughout his career as a champion of religious liberty. A graduate of Baylor University (1904 valedictorian), Dawson was founding editor of the school's student paper, *The Lariat.* During and after college, Dawson served as pastor at several Texas churches, including a thirty-one-year stint (1915–1946) at the First Baptist Church of Waco.

Under the influence of the writings of Walter Rauschenbusch, Dawson incorporated elements of the "social gospel" in his sermons and publications. An opponent of racial prejudice, Dawson once publicly condemned the Ku Klux Klan from the pulpit of the First Baptist Church to an audience consisting almost entirely of Klan members.

Dawson opposed government funding of religious institutions, including hospitals and schools, as well as the use of public schools to teach religious doctrine. As Dawson writes in *Journal of Church and State*, "What the Constitution of the United States forbids and what the constitutions of all the states forbid . . . is the making of any law or the action of any government authority in pursuance of any law that involves the interlocking of the official functions of the state (or any of its agencies) with the official functions of any church." This view, according to Dawson, is consistent with military chaplaincy and clergy offering invocations at legislative sessions because, in both cases the government is not making an agreement or contract with a religious organization, but rather, with "an individual qualified to perform the services asked for." Ironically, many contemporary separationists disagree.

In 1951, Dawson was instrumental in helping to convince President Harry S. Truman not to assign a U.S. ambassador to the Vatican. Dawson found common cause with nativists and secularists in their suspicion of the influence of Roman Catholic immigrants on American public life. But what some considered a legitimate concern to preserve American democracy, others saw as religious bigotry. Writes Dawson in *Separate Church and State Now*: "The Catholics . . . would abolish our public school system which is our greatest single factor in national unity and would substitute their old-world, medieval parochial schools, with their alien culture." This sentiment, however, was widely helped by pre-Vatican II American Protestants, including conservatives, liberals, and moderates.

In 1957, Baylor honored its distinguished alumnus and former trustee by founding the J. M. Dawson Institute of Church–State Studies, which began publishing the *Journal of Church and State* in 1959.

FRANCIS J. BECKWITH

References and Further Reading

Dawson, Joseph Martin. *Christ and Social Change*. Philadelphia: The Judson Press, 1937.
———. *Separate Church and State Now*. New York: R. R. Smith, 1948.
———. *America's Way in Church, State, and Society*. New York: Macmillan, 1953.
———. *Baptists and the American Republic*. Nashville, TN: Broadman Press, 1956.
———. "The Meaning of Separation of Church and State in the First Amendment." *Journal of Church and State* 1 (1959):37–42.
———. *A Thousand Months to Remember: An Autobiography*. Waco, TX: Baylor University Press, 1964.
Dunn, James. "The Ethical Thought of Joseph Martin Dawson." Th.D. diss., Southwestern Baptist Theological Seminary, 1966.
Hamburger, Philip. *Separation of Church and State*. Cambridge, MA: Harvard University Press, 2002.
Reynolds, J. A. "Dawson, Joseph Martin." In *The Handbook of Texas Online*, http://www.tsha.utexas.edu/handbook/online/articles/print/DD/fda52.html.
Summerlin, Travis L. "Church–State Relations in the Thought of Joseph Martin Dawson." Ph.D. diss., Baylor University, 1984.

See also **Americans United for Separation of Church and State; Baptists in Early America; Catholics and Religious Liberty; Wall of Separation**

DAYS OF RELIGIOUS OBSERVANCE AS NATIONAL OR STATE HOLIDAYS

One question that has arisen on several occasions is whether the government can establish a day of religious observance as an official state or national holiday consistent with the Establishment Clause of the First Amendment. Some observers argue that to do so constitutes an unconstitutional establishment of the religion whose special day has been designated an official holiday. Courts have considered claims that declaring Good Friday or Christmas Day an official holiday is an unconstitutional establishment of religion. The courts are divided on the issue as it pertains to Good Friday, generally sustaining the constitutionality of the holiday if a secular purpose exists. By the same token, courts have uniformly concluded that declaring Christmas Day a government holiday poses no constitutional problem because of the secular nature of the day.

In 1995, the U.S. Court of Appeals for the Seventh Circuit held that an Illinois state law maintaining Good Friday as a holiday on which schools must be closed violated the Establishment Clause (*Metzl v. Leininger*, 57 F. 3d 618, 7th Cir., 1995). The court noted that Good Friday is the *only* religious holiday on which schools must be closed in Illinois (schools are not required to close, for example, on Jewish

holidays). Because Illinois law already permitted students to miss school on religious holidays, the court concluded that the special accommodation for Good Friday served no secular purpose and thus violated the Establishment Clause. The court did note in dicta, however, that if the state had defended the holiday on the grounds that the schools would otherwise experience a high degree of absenteeism on that day, the case might have been decided differently.

A few other courts have also found that making Good Friday a state holiday violates the Establishment Clause when the purpose appears to be to promote Christian worship. For example, a federal district court in Wisconsin in *Freedom From Religion Foundation v. Thompson*, 920 F. Supp. 969 (W.D. Wisc., 1996), held that a Wisconsin statute providing that "[o]n Good Friday the period from 11:00 A.M. to 3:00 P.M. shall uniformly be observed [as a state holiday] for the purpose of worship" violated the Establishment Clause. Similarly, a California state appellate court held unconstitutional a California governor's order that state offices be closed from noon until 3:00 P.M. on Good Friday—the three most sacred hours of that religious holiday (*Mandel v. Hodges*, 127 Cal. Rptr. 244, 1976).

But other courts have rejected claims that establishing Good Friday as a state holiday violates the Establishment Clause when the decision is motivated by secular reasons. For example, the U.S. Court of Appeals for the Sixth Circuit upheld the constitutionality of a Kentucky statute making Good Friday a state holiday on the grounds that the legislature acted in order to provide a holiday on the third busiest travel day of the year (*Granzeier v. Middleton*, 173 F. 3d 568, 6th Cir., 1999). Similarly, the U.S. Court of Appeals for the Fourth Circuit upheld a Maryland statute making Good Friday and the Monday after Easter Sunday school holidays on the grounds that the schools would otherwise have a high rate of absenteeism on those days (*Koenick v. Felton*, 190 F. 3d 259, 4th Cir., 1999). The U.S. Court of Appeals for the Seventh Circuit upheld an Indiana law giving state employees a holiday on Good Friday when the state presented evidence that the purpose was to create a holiday during a time period when there would otherwise be four months without one (*Bridenbaugh v. O'Bannon*, 185 F.3d 796, 7th Cir., 1999).

Yet another circuit court, the U.S. Court of Appeals for the Ninth Circuit, found that a Hawaii statute declaring Good Friday a state holiday did not violate the Establishment Clause since, in the court's view, Good Friday in Hawaii had become the first day of an annual three-day spring weekend devoted to shopping and recreational pursuits and that the establishment of that day as a holiday merely accommodated those secular activities (*Cammack v. Waihee*, 932 F.2d 765, 9th Cir., 1991). Finally, a federal district court in Ohio rejected a claim that giving municipal workers a holiday on Good Friday violated the Establishment Clause since the purpose of the holiday was to satisfy union demands, not to advance the religion of Christianity (*Franks v. City of Niles*, 29 Fair Empl. Prac. Cas. (BNA) 1114, N.D. Ohio, 1982).

On the other hand, courts are uniform in their conclusion that declaring Christmas Day a state holiday does not violate the Establishment Clause. Even the Seventh Circuit judges in *Metzl v. Leininger* (1995), who found the Illinois law making Good Friday a state holiday to violate the Establishment Clause, conceded that designating Christmas Day (and Thanksgiving Day) a state holiday did not offend the Constitution: "Some holidays that are religious, even sectarian, in origin, such as Christmas and Thanksgiving, have so far lost their religious connotation in the eyes of the general public . . . [that they] have only a trivial effect in promoting religion" (*Metzl v. Leininger*, 1995). Similarly, a federal district court judge in Ohio rejected a challenge to Christmas Day as a government holiday on the grounds that the day had become a secular holiday (*Ganulin v. United States*, 71 F. Supp. 2d 824, S.D. Ohio, 1999). Four justices of the U.S. Supreme Court in *Lynch v. Donnelly*, 465 U.S. 668 (1984), agreed that making Christmas Day a state holiday did not violate the Establishment Clause:

> When government decides to recognize Christmas Day as a public holiday, it does no more than accommodate the calendar of public activities to the plain fact that many Americans will expect to spend time visiting with their families, attending religious ceremonies, and perhaps enjoying some respite from preholiday activities. The Free Exercise Clause, of course, does not necessarily compel the government to provide this accommodation, but neither is the Establishment Clause offended by such a step.

State statutes that prohibit the sale of intoxicating liquors on designated religious holidays have received limited judicial scrutiny. But in 1981, the Connecticut Supreme Court declared a state statute unconstitutional that prohibited the sale of alcohol on Good Friday, holding that such law constituted an establishment of the Christian religion (*Griswold Inn v. State*, 183 Conn. 552, 1981).

DAVISON M. DOUGLAS

References and Further Reading

Brookman, Justin, *The Constitutionality of the Good Friday Holiday*, N.Y.U. L. Rev. 73 (1998): 193.

Hartenstein, John M., *A Christmas Issue: Christian Holiday Celebration in the Public Elementary Schools is an Establishment of Religion*, Cal. L. Rev. 80 (1992): 981.
Kleinfelder, Megan E., *Good Friday, Just Another Spring Holiday?* U. Cinn. L. Rev. 69 (2000): 329.

Cases and Statutes Cited

Bridenbaugh v. O'Bannon, 185 F.3d 796 (7th Cir. 1999)
Cammack v. Waihee, 932 F.2d 765 (9th Cir. 1991)
Franks v. City of Niles, 29 Fair Empl. Prac. Cas. (BNA) 1114 (N.D. Ohio 1982)
Freedom From Religion Foundation v. Thompson, 920 F. Supp. 969 (W.D. Wisc. 1996)
Ganulin v. United States, 71 F. Supp. 2d 824 (S.D. Ohio 1999)
Granzeier v. Middleton, 173 F. 3d 568 (6th Cir. 1999)
Griswold Inn v. State, 183 Conn. 552 (1981)
Koenick v. Felton, 190 F. 3d 259 (4th Cir. 1999)
Lynch v. Donnelly, 465 U.S. 668 (1984)
Mandel v. Hodges, 127 Cal. Rptr. 244 (1976)
Metzl v. Leininger, 57 F. 3d 618 (7th Cir. 1995)

See also **Establishment Claus (I): History, Background, Framing; Sunday Closing Cases and Laws**

DEATH PENALTY
See Capital Punishment

DEBS, EUGENE V. (1855–1926)

Eugene Debs was one of the most important figures in American labor history. He is most often remembered for being a proponent of socialism, but long before his time as the leader of the Socialist Party in the United States, Debs worked as a crusader for American workers. He was born to Alsatian immigrants and grew up in Terre Haute, Indiana. Debs left school at the age of fourteen to work for an Indiana railroad. As a young railway worker, he learned to appreciate the hardships that laborers endured on their jobs, leading him to pursue an active voice for workers' rights at a very young age.

Most of Debs's early labor activity involved the railroad. He quickly gained recognition through his involvement with the Terre Haute lodge of the Brotherhood of Locomotive Firemen and was elected the organization's secretary in 1875. Rising quickly through the ranks, he was recognized as the national secretary of the brotherhood by 1881. Initially, Debs held conservative views when it came to labor questions. For example, he argued against his group participating in the national railroad strikes of 1877.

It was at this time that Debs also gained an interest in participating in government. He first entered political service by running for city clerk of Terre Haute in

1879, and by 1885 he had enough support to win a seat in the Indiana State Assembly. Debs drew support from workers and business leaders in his hometown.

One of the qualities that allowed Eugene Debs to remain at the forefront of labor organization in the United States was his ability to change his ideals over time. When he first became involved in labor, he believed that small craft unions were more important than national organizations such as the Knights of Labor. For example, Debs refused to allow his members to participate in 1885 strikes against railroads brought by the Knights of Labor. Within a few years, however, Debs changed his views after seeing the inability of small labor organizations to deal with business managers effectively. Debs also began to speak out against the powers of corporate leaders in the United States, claiming that corporations hindered the majority of Americans from receiving a fair wage. By 1893, Debs had resigned as secretary of the Brotherhood of Locomotive Firemen and he began to organize a new labor organization, the American Railway Union (ARU).

Debs formed the American Railway Union in a politically charged atmosphere. Many members of the ARU came from the disgruntled ranks of the Pullman Palace Car Company. George Pullman angered labor leaders by his treatment of those that worked for his company. Pullman lowered wages, laid off workers, and raised prices at his company stores; his employees had no say in the matter. Pullman refused to listen to Debs's pleas for arbitration, so Debs led the American Railway Union into action. In June 1894, the union refused to handle Pullman cars and soon tied up most of the railroad traffic in the Midwest.

In response, the railroads brought in strikebreakers and developed a scheme to involve the federal government in the strike. Railroad leaders ordered the strikebreakers to attach Pullman cars to mail cars so that interfering with delivery of the mail would bring in the government. The U.S. attorney general as well as President Grover Cleveland used the power of the federal government to bring injunctions against labor leaders and enforce the timely delivery of the mails. The federal courts also brought cases against many of the labor activists, including Debs. On July 13, 1894, a federal district court sentenced Debs to six months in jail for violating a federal injunction. The sentence was upheld by the Supreme Court in the case of *in re Debs* (1895), in which the court claimed the sentence was just in protecting the interests of national sovereignty, where the government had the duty to protect interstate commerce and the delivery of the mails.

While in prison, Debs studied socialism and believed it could save the American worker. By 1897, he was putting together a socialist movement in the United States. Debs found success by building a coalition that embraced all viewpoints in the socialist sphere, ranging from moderate reformers to loyal Marxists. He soon organized the Social Democratic Party, mainly from holdovers from the American Railway Union. Debs ran for President in 1900 and received over four thousand votes. From this modest beginning, Debs became the leading spokesman for the Socialist Party in the United States. By the election of 1912, in a four-way race for the presidency with Woodrow Wilson, Theodore Roosevelt, and William Howard Taft, Debs received 6 percent of the vote, or almost nine hundred thousand votes.

Even though he never achieved the presidency, Debs tirelessly campaigned for workers' rights. He traveled the country participating in strikes and defending workers in industrial disputes. Debs also reached out to workers through print media when he became the associate editor of the Socialist publication, *Appeal to Reason*, in 1907.

Perhaps the greatest example of Debs's fiery rhetoric was leveled at the U.S. government for its participation in World War I. Debs declared that he was against all wars except for the one that would result in a worldwide socialist revolution. He urged American men not to serve in the military and spoke out against the war all over the country. For his remarks, Debs was prosecuted under the Alien and Sedition Act passed during the Wilson administration. He was eventually arrested and given a twenty-year prison sentence for encouraging resistance to the draft; he served three years in a federal prison in Atlanta, Georgia. While a prisoner in Atlanta, Debs made his final run for the presidency in 1920, polling over a million votes. On Christmas Day, 1921, the Republican president, Warren G. Harding, commuted Debs's sentence to time served and he was released. Debs spent the final years of his life in Terre Haute trying to recover his health from the time he spent in prison. He is remembered for tirelessly promoting the rights of all people and pushing for government reforms.

CHRISTOPHER R. TINGLE

References and Further Reading

Currie, Harold W. *Eugene V. Debs.* Boston: Twayne Publishers, 1976.
Salvatore, Nick. *Eugene V. Debs: Citizen and Socialist.* Urbana: the University of Illinois Press, 1982.

DEBS v. UNITED STATES, 249 U.S. 211 (1919)

In *Debs v. United States*, the Supreme Court, in a unanimous opinion written by Justice Holmes, upheld the conviction of Eugene V. Debs, the American socialist, who was convicted of violating the Espionage Act of 1917, a statute that Congress enacted two months after the United States entered World War I. The Espionage Act made it unlawful to cause or attempt to cause insubordination or to obstruct recruitment for the armed forces. Debs had given two speeches opposing the war effort and the draft.

In affirming his conviction, the Court relied on the so-called "clear and present danger test," which Justice Holmes had first articulated in the case of *Schenck v. United States*, 249 U.S. 47 (1919), another Espionage Act case decided during the same term in which the Court decided *Debs*. Although the First Amendment protects freedom of speech, the clear and present danger test allows speech to be punished "if the words used are used in such circumstances and are of such a nature as to create a clear and present danger that they will bring about the substantive evils that Congress has a right to prevent" (*Schenck*, 249 U.S. at 52).

The clear and present danger test rests on the idea that certain speech is fairly viewed as an *act*, and the government has the power to prohibit certain acts. On the authority of this test, Congress enacted the Smith Act in 1940, which prohibited advocating force to overthrow the U.S. government. The statute was used to punish political dissenters, principally communists, during World War II in the early 1940s and during the "red scare" in the late 1940s and 1950s.

Eventually, the clear and present danger test was replaced by the so-called incitement test, first articulated in *Brandenburg v. Ohio*, 395 U.S. 444 (1969). Under the incitement test, the government may punish only speech that is an incitement to imminent lawless action.

DAVID R. DOW

Cases and Statutes Cited

Brandenburg v. Ohio, 395 U.S. 444 (1969)
Schenck v. United States, 249 U.S. 47 (1919)

DEBTOR'S PRISONS

Debtor's prisons existed in America from colonial days until the 1833 federal law abolishing the confinement of debtors. Federal debtor's prisons may have been abolished in 1833, but they persisted in the states. Persons owing money to the local, state, or national government or to private citizens could be incarcerated to force the indebted to pay what they owed to the debtors. The majority of the inmates in debtor's prisons owed money to private individuals. Their incarceration served as a persuasive method of collecting debt and as an incentive to others to settle debts. The prisoners lived in the debtor's prisons and paid for their room, board, and meals from the "goalers" or "jailers." The term "goal" applied to both prisons pronounced as "jail," a term used in modern times. These prisons were separate from prisons housing those convicted of crimes.

Many debtor's prisons grew overcrowded, and disease ran rampant in these unsanitary prisons. Many prisoners could not pay back their debts and relied on friends and relatives to pay what they owed in order to be freed from jail. The practice of using debtor's prisons stopped as governments and people sought to use other methods of debt collection, such as property confiscation, without resorting to prisons. In modern America, people are still put into prison for nonpayment of alimony, various instances of fraud, refusal to pay child support, and other monetary violations. The debt owed in these cases is substantially higher than that owed by those jailed in colonial years. The system of debtor's prisons is gone, but the law continues utilizing incarceration as a form of persuasion for debt collection.

JASON M. SOKIERA

References and Further Reading

Holton, Woody. *Forced Founders: Indians, Debtors, Slaves, and the Making of the American Revolution.* Chapel Hill: University of North Carolina Press, 1999.
Rhode, Steve. "The History of Credit and Debt," http://www.myvesta.org/history/history_debtorprison.htm, (2003).

DECLARATION OF INDEPENDENCE

The Declaration of Independence stands as a rejection of British tyranny as well as the emboldened embrace of a republican form of democracy that has, albeit imperfectly, stood the test of time in America. The Declaration of Independence draws from and expanded upon a notion of natural rights—the principle that government's role in relation to its people is to provide for the protection of certain key rights that derive from nature and are therefore inalienable and fundamental. After brief introductory remarks regarding the need for independence, the often quoted second paragraph begins: "We hold these truths to be self evident, that all men are created equal, that they are endowed by their Creator with certain unalienable Rights, that among these are Life, Liberty and the pursuit of Happiness." It continues by describing the role of government in a republican democracy so as to secure these rights and describes the foundation for government as not being divined from the heavens (as in the British system), but from the people.

It is no surprise that Jefferson then outlined the many colonial grievances against British rule, including taxation without representation, since the notion of a people-based democratic rule constituted an overwhelming rejection of the tyrannical rule of unchecked power over the citizenry the colonists had suffered at the hands of the English. The Declaration of Independence persists as an outline of American popular governance. Since government derives its sovereignty from the people via the polls, it is thus subject to ongoing revision through the casting of ballots by the electorate. Next, the government cannot infringe on certain core "unalienable rights" of the people, such as the right to due process of liberty or the protection against governmental takings of property without just compensation. There is also a lasting irony in the notion that while the founding fathers rejected the subservience of British rule, they at the same time struggled with the enslavement of African Americans on their own shores. Slavery in America defied some of the principles of freedom for all, a notion that embodied the words of American independence.

JAMES F. VAN ORDEN

References and Further Reading

Becker, Carl. *The Declaration of Independence.* New York: Harcourt Brace, 1922.

DEFAMATION AND FREE SPEECH

To be defamed is to be falsely described. To bear false witness against someone has been prohibited since biblical times. That prohibition can be found in Exodus, the second book of the Bible. Later, Iago in Shakespeare's *Othello* said, "Good name in man and woman, dear my lord, is the immediate jewel of their souls: Who steals my purse steels trash . . . But he that filches from me my good name robs me of that which not enriches him, and makes me poor indeed." In modern times, in the United States, states seek to protect their citizens from harm caused by statements that steal one's good name by letting their citizens recover damages by means of tort law. A tort is a civil wrong that allows someone who is wronged to

bring a lawsuit to recover compensation for harm caused by the wrong. The tort of defamation enables someone whose good name has been stolen—who has been defamed—to bring a lawsuit to seek monetary compensation for damage to reputation and for emotional distress.

Because defamation is a tort, it is developed by states, not the federal government, through their judicial decisions or legislative enactments. Because there are fifty states, as well as the District of Columbia and U.S. territories, each of which formulates its own tort law, defamation law can vary from state to state.

General Principles of Defamation

Despite variations among states as to the scope of defamation law, defamation has some consistent principles. Defamation is speech: libel is written, slander is oral. For a statement to be defamatory, generally it must be about an individual, it must be published, and it must tend to injure that individual's reputation in the community. Publication does not necessarily mean printed and distributed, although that is a familiar method of publication. A statement can also be published if it is overheard by someone other than the person defamed. The definition of community may also be debated. One can ask whether a statement is defamatory if its injury comes from what a small group of people will think of the person defamed, or whether the opprobrium must come from a larger population. If a plaintiff proves that he or she has been defamed, the next step is to seek compensation.

Tort actions protect citizens from harm by compensating them for that harm. Besides benefiting the plaintiff, compensation for harm can also deter a tortfeasor from committing further harm. The availability of compensatory damages can deter others as well. In addition to awarding compensatory damages, juries may also award punitive damages against a tortfeasor, another deterrent. One purpose of the availability of damages in defamation law, therefore, is to deter harmful speech.

While speech can cause harm, speech is also protected from governmental infringement by the First Amendment to the Constitution. Thus arises a conflict between a state's use of its judicial system to protect its citizens from harmful speech and society's goal of encouraging robust debate free from state interference. Beginning in 1964 with New York Times *v.* Sullivan, 367 U.S., 254 (1964), the Supreme Court of the United States decided a number of cases to balance those competing interests.

New York Times v. Sullivan—Actual Malice Standard for Public Figures

In 1960, the *New York Times* published an advertisement signed by the "Committee to Defend Martin Luther King and the Struggle for Freedom in the South." The advertisement said that "thousands of Southern Negro students are engaged in widespread nonviolent demonstrations in positive affirmation of the right to live in human dignity as guaranteed by the U.S. Constitution and the Bill of Rights." It accused the police in Montgomery, Alabama, of terrorizing those students. L.B. Sullivan was the elected city commissioner who supervised the police. Because some of the statements in the advertisement were incorrect, he sued the *New York Times* for defamation and recovered $500,000. In reversing that recovery, the Supreme Court said erroneous statement is inevitable in free debate and held that in order to protect debate, the First Amendment required a federal rule that prohibits a public official from recovering damages for a defamatory falsehood unless he proves that the statement was made with "actual malice," that is, with knowledge that it was false or with reckless disregard of whether it was false or not. This statement has become the widely quoted standard for determining when a public officer may recover damages for defamation.

In 1967, the Supreme Court applied this actual malice standard to actions brought against public figures. The result of this standard is that a plaintiff's claim for defamation will be dismissed, and therefore will not go to trial, unless the plaintiff has evidence that would prove that the defamer acted with malice as defined by the Supreme Court. If a plaintiff does present evidence at trial, he or she can only recover damages if the jury believes the evidence about malice. Proving malice is a high hurdle for a public official or a public figure to overcome. Because of this, if an official or public figure loses a defamation case, the loss does not necessarily mean that the challenged statements are true, only that the publisher did not act with malice.

Negligence Standard for Private Individuals

In 1974, the Supreme Court decided *Gertz v. Robert Welch, Inc.*, 418 U.S., 323 (1974). That defamation case was brought by Elmer Gertz, a lawyer who was neither a public official nor a public figure. He had represented the family of a man who was killed by a policeman. The policeman had been convicted of the man's murder, and the family was suing him for damages. Robert Welch, Inc. published a magazine that warned of a conspiracy to discredit local police so that they would be replaced by people who would support a communist dictatorship. The magazine published a story that falsely accused Gertz of being a communist and of helping to frame the policeman. The jury awarded Gertz $50,000, but the verdict was overruled by the judge because Gertz had not proved that the magazine editor had acted with malice when he published the author's story. Gertz, therefore, recovered nothing.

In *Gertz*, because the plaintiff was a private individual, the Supreme Court rebalanced a state's interest in protecting reputations with the Constitutional interest in protecting speech. The Court sent the case back to the trial court to apply a standard different from the *New York Times* malice standard. The new standard articulated in *Gertz* that is applicable to private individuals differs from the standard of *Sullivan* in two ways. First, a private plaintiff can bring suit by showing that the defendant acted with some fault, even if the fault does not amount to malice. If the plaintiff cannot prove malice, however, the manner in which a plaintiff can prove damages is limited. Unlike in *Sullivan*, in which no justice dissented, in *Gertz* the justices split, five votes to four. Two of the dissenters would have reinstated the jury's verdict and allowed state law to govern. In contrast, the other two would not have permitted liability on a showing of mere negligence.

Negligence

The standard that the Court articulated in *Gertz* was that a private individual did not need to prove malice, but could recover for defamation by proving that the defendant was merely negligent. The Court explained that a different standard is necessary for private plaintiffs because they do not have the same access to the media to deliver their messages as public officials and public figures have. The Court did not give states free rein to determine how to apply defamation law to private individuals, however. The Court held that the First Amendment limited damages for these plaintiffs to recovery of actual damages, but not the usual presumed damages often awarded in defamation cases. The significance of this ruling requires an understanding of the unusual remedial structure of defamation law.

Damages for Defamation

In most tort actions a plaintiff must present evidence of harm before a jury can award damages to compensate the harm. In defamation *per se* actions, however, traditionally a jury could award presumed damages to the plaintiff. Defamation is per se when the defamatory statement is particularly injurious, such as an accusation of the commission of a crime. For defamation per se, a jury could assess damages, not based on evidence of actual injury to the plaintiff but rather based on the seriousness of the defamatory statement. A jury could presume from the egregiousness of the statement that it must have caused damage. From that presumption the jury could award whatever amount it determines to be appropriate. In that case the plaintiff is not required to produce any evidence that the statement actually harmed his or her reputation or caused emotional distress.

Not all defamatory statements would entitle a plaintiff to presumed damages. If the statement is not defamatory on its face, it will be labeled *per quod*. Often such statements are defamatory only because those who hear them know the context. In many states that lesser libel or slander may not be actionable unless the plaintiff can prove that the statement caused special damages, which are measurable economic losses such as lost wages. Without proof of economic injury, a plaintiff cannot bring suit, cannot prove that the statement is defamatory, and cannot recover for harm to reputation or emotional distress. In this way defamation law eliminates cases deemed less important, with importance measured by whether or not the plaintiff was injured financially. This approach devalues the impact of mental anguish but is consistent with other traditional areas of tort law, which do not recognize mental anguish as a compensable harm. Consistent with that approach, some states require a plaintiff to prove that his or her reputation was damaged by the defamation before permitting recovery for emotional distress.

In *Gertz*, the Court held that without proof of malice, a plaintiff could not recover traditional presumed damages because the largely uncontrolled discretion of juries to award damages where there is no loss unnecessarily compounds the potential of any system of liability for defamatory falsehood to inhibit the vigorous exercise of First Amendment freedoms. Elimination of presumed damages for negligent, but not malicious, defamation means that a private plaintiff must prove actual harm to reputation or prove emotional distress.

The Supreme Court was explicit, however, that after proving loss, whether economic, reputational, or emotional, a plaintiff could recover both special damages: those out-of-pocket economic losses as well as damages for harm to reputation and for humiliation and mental anguish. The Court did not set the constitutional bar for recovery so that damages would be recoverable only if the defamatory statement caused economic injury. While state law cannot permit greater recovery for defamation than allowed under the First Amendment, states may permit less. Thus, some states may retain the traditional rule that to recover anything for certain types of defamatory statements, a plaintiff must prove economic injury (special damages).

Truth

Another legal presumption that the Supreme Court invalidated as interfering with vigorous debate was the traditional presumption that a defamatory statement is false; truth is a defense that, if proved, would enable a defendant to avoid liability. In *Philadelphia Newspapers, Inc. v. Hepps*, 475 U.S. 767 (1986), the Supreme Court held that when a plaintiff sues a media defendant for defamation, if the statement involves a matter of public concern the plaintiff must bear the burden of proving that the statement is false. Allocation of burden of proof is a procedural matter that becomes important when evidence is inconclusive—when neither party can prove the truth or falsity of a statement. When that evidence is inconclusive, the party who needs to prove something (who has the burden of proof) will lose. The Supreme Court said that requiring a media defendant to prove the truth of a matter of public concern deters such speech because of the fear that liability will unjustifiably result. As in *Gertz*, the justices in *Hepps* split five votes to four. The four dissenters stated that requiring a private person to prove that a defamatory statement is false gives a character assassin an absolute license to defame by means of statements that can be neither verified nor disproved.

Private Plaintiffs and Matters of Private Concern

In 1985, a little over twenty years after having decided *Sullivan*, the Supreme Court ruled that state defamation law may apply without constitutional restrictions in suits that do not involve matters of public concern. The case, *Dun & Bradstreet, Inc. v. Greenmoss Builders*, 472 U.S. 749 (1985), involved an incorrect statement in a credit report about a private company. The report was sent to five subscribers, with the caveat that the subscribers were not to reveal the information. Greenmoss Builders brought suit in defamation, and the jury awarded it $50,000 in presumed or compensatory damages and $300,000 in punitive damages. The jury did not find malice as defined by *Sullivan*. This raised the question of whether the standard of *Gertz* for recovery of damages should apply, which would allow recovery only for proven damages.

In *Greenmoss*, none of the opinions written by the justices had more than four votes. A majority of justices agreed on the result of the case, but not the reasoning. Four of the justices distinguished *Greenmoss* from *Gertz* on the ground that the statements in *Greenmoss* were not matters of public concern. Those justices reasoned that speech that is not of public concern has reduced constitutional value and its protection is outweighed by the state's interest in protecting a person's good name—a basic concept of the essential dignity and worth of every human that is at the root of any decent system of ordered liberty. Two justices who concurred in the result would overrule *Gertz* to allow the states more freedom to apply their defamation laws to protect private individuals.

One of those justices, Justice White, questioned the wisdom of the *Sullivan* case, with which he joined in 1964. In retrospect, he would recommend limiting damages in cases involving public matters in a *Gertz*-like manner rather than require a showing of malice before an action may be brought. According to Justice White, the malice standard has created two evils: first that the stream of information about public officials and public affairs is polluted by false information, and second that the defeated plaintiff may be destroyed by falsehoods that might have been avoided with a reasonable effort to investigate the facts. Four justices in *Greenmoss* dissented on the ground that even speech about economic matters such as credit reports implicates matters of public concern. Those four would have retained the rules articulated in *Gertz* for *Greenmoss*, limiting recovery to proven damages and not permitting recovery of presumed or punitive damages.

CANDACE SAARI KOVACIC-FLEISCHER

References and Further Reading

Bollinger, Lee C., and Geoffrey R. Stone, eds. *Eternally Vigilant: Free Speech in the Modern Era*. Chicago: Chicago University Press, 2002.

Smolla, Rodney A. *Law of Defamation*, 2nd ed., Eagen, Minn.: Thomson West, last update 2005.

Sullivan, Kathleen M., and Gerald Gunther. *Sullivan and Gunther's First Amendment Law*, 2nd ed. University Casebook Series, St. Paul, Minn.: Thomson West Press, 2003.

DEFENSE OF MARRIAGE ACT

On September 21, 1996, the Defense of Marriage Act was signed into law. It was developed in response to the possibility and fear that same-sex marriage might soon become legal, at least in Hawaii. In the House Committee on the Judiciary's Report on the Defense of Marriage Act, the committee referred to the Hawaii case as an orchestrated legal assault being waged against traditional heterosexual marriage by gay rights groups and lawyers. In *Baehr v. Lewin*, 852 P.2d 44 (1993), individuals whose applications for marriage were denied solely on the ground that they were of the same sex filed a complaint alleging that the denial of licenses violated their right to privacy and equal protection as guaranteed by the Hawaii Constitution. The First Circuit Court, City and County of Honolulu, granted the defendant's motion for judgment on the pleadings, and the plaintiffs appealed.

The Hawaii Supreme Court held that pursuant to the Hawaiian Constitution, the applicant couples did not have a fundamental constitutional right to same-sex marriage arising out of the right to privacy or otherwise. Moreover, the court held that pursuant to the Hawaiian Constitution, sex was a suspect classification for purposes of equal protection analysis and was subject to the strict scrutiny test. Therefore, the statute in question was presumed to be unconstitutional unless on remand the defendant Lewin surpassed the requirements set forth under the strict scrutiny test.

The Defense of Marriage Act has two primary purposes. The first is to defend the institution of traditional heterosexual marriage. The second is to protect the right of the states to formulate and determine their own public policy in regards to the implications that might result in the recognition by one state of the right for homosexual couples to acquire marriage licenses.

The act, which allows other states to disregard completely an otherwise valid same-sex marriage, has two distinct parts. Section 2, entitled "Powers Reserved to the States," amends 28 U.S.C. 1738 by adding a new section, 1738C to provide that:

> No State, territory, or possession of the United States, or Indian tribe shall be required to give effect to any public act, record, or judicial proceeding of any other State, territory, possession or tribe respecting a relationship between persons of the same sex that is treated as a marriage under the laws of such other State, territory, possession or tribe, or a right or claim arising from such relationship.

The committee would emphasize the narrowness of this provision in that it merely provides that, in the event that Hawaii or some other state permits same-sex couples to marry, other states will not be obligated or required, by operation of the Full Faith and Credit Clause of the U.S. Constitution, to recognize that marriage, or any right or claim arising from it. Section 2 therefore is concerned exclusively with the potential interstate implications that might result from a decision by one state to issue marriage licenses to same-sex couples. Proponents of interstate recognition of same-sex marriage assert that the language of the Full Faith and Credit Clause of the U.S. Constitution requires states to give full faith and credit to such marriages performed in other states.

Section 3 defines marriage for federal purposes by providing that:

> In determining the meaning of any Act of Congress, or any ruling, regulation, or interpretation of the various administrative bureaus and agencies of the United States, the word "marriage" means only a legal union between one man and one woman as husband and wife, the word spouse refers only to a person of the opposite sex who is a husband or a wife.

There is nothing novel about the definitions contained in Section 3. The definition of marriage is derived from *The State of Washington, Singer v. Hara*, 522 P.2d 1187, 1191-92 (Wash. App. 1974); that definition—a legal union of one man and one woman as husband and wife—has found its way into the standard law dictionary. It is fully consistent with the Supreme Court's reference, over one hundred years ago, to the union for life of one man and one woman in the holy estate of matrimony. The definition of spouse obviously derives from and is consistent with this definition of marriage.

The most important aspect of this provision is that it applies to federal law only. It does not, therefore, have any effect on the manner in which any state might choose to define the words "marriage" and "spouse." The determination of who may marry in the United States is uniquely a function of state law. The general rule for determining the validity of a marriage is *lex celebrationis*—that is, a marriage is valid if it is valid according to the law of the place where it was celebrated.

The legal and social implications of the Defense of Marriage Act will have a profound impact in the arena of civil rights. By passing this act, Congress is not only condoning discrimination against same-sex couples but is also perpetuating it. Specifically precluding same-sex couples from marrying perpetuates discrimination against same-sex couples, just as miscegenation laws perpetuated racial discrimination. The consequences include denying these couples the rights and benefits of marriage such as inheritance

rights, as well as making the children of such marriages illegitimate if these families were to cross state lines.

Such rights and benefits are by no means nominal. Legal as well as economic benefits extended to spouses include property rights, tax breaks, veterans' and social security benefits, testamentary benefits, recovery for loss of consortium, employment benefits, lower insurance premiums, spousal testimonial privileges, financial support upon separation, and status of next of kin to make medical decisions or burial arrangements. Furthermore, laws that make class-based distinctions, whether based upon race, gender, sexual orientation, or religion, proclaim to the world that the targeted group is different and should be treated as such.

MARIANGELA VALLE–PETERS

References and Further Reading

Ryan, Brett P., *Love and Let Love: Same Sex Marriage, Past, Present, and Future and the Constitutionality of DOMA*, U. Haw. L. Rev. 22 (2000): 185.
Paige, Rebecca S., *Wagging the Dog—If the State of Hawaii Accepts Same-Sex Marriage Will Other States Have to? An Examination of Conflict of Laws and Escape Devices*, Am. U. L. Rev. 47 (1997): 165.
Treuthart, Mary Patricia, *Adopting a More Realistic Definition of "Family,"* Gonz. L. Rev. 26 (1991): 91.
Eskridge William N. Jr., *A History of Same-Sex Marriage*, Va. L. Rev. 79 (1993): 1419.

Cases and Statutes Cited

Murphy v. Ramsey, 114 U.S. 15, 45 (1885)
28 U.S.C. §1738(c)
1 U.S.C. §7
H.R. Rep. 104-664, 1996 U.S.C.C.A.N 2905 (1996)
U.S. Const. art. IV, §1 (Full Faith and Credit Clause)

See also **Same-Sex Marriage Legalization**

DEFENSE, RIGHT TO PRESENT

The Constitution guarantees a criminal defendant the right to present a complete defense to the charges against him or her. The right to present a defense is not explicitly stated in the Constitution, and the Supreme Court did not speak of a general right of criminal defendants to present evidence until the twentieth century. Indeed, many American jurisdictions placed severe restrictions on the ability of defendants to present evidence in their defense until relatively recent times. For example, many jurisdictions in the nineteenth century flatly precluded criminal defendants from testifying in their own behalf because it was thought that they were likely to perjure themselves. It was not until the Supreme Court's 1960 decision in *Ferguson v. Georgia*, 365 U.S. 570 (1961), that all such bans were finally declared unconstitutional.

By the middle of the twentieth century, however, the Supreme Court had begun to recognize a general right to present a defense and, over the next several decades, the Court found the right to be implied by several different constitutional provisions. In 1948, in *In re Oliver*, 233 U.S. 257 (1948), the Supreme Court declared that the Due Process Clause provides a criminal defendant "an opportunity to be heard in his defense," including the right "to offer testimony." In *Taylor v. Illinois*, 484 U.S. 400 (1988), the Court held that the Sixth Amendment Compulsory Process Clause guarantees defendants the right not only to subpoena favorable witnesses but also to present their testimony. Finally, in *Rock v. Arkansas*, 483 U.S. 44 (1987), the Court recognized that the Fifth Amendment Self-Incrimination Clause, as well as the Compulsory Process and Due Process Clauses, implies that a criminal defendant has the right to present his or her testimony as part of the defense case.

Litigation over the right to present a defense usually arises when a jurisdiction's evidentiary rules preclude criminal defendants from presenting certain types of evidence in their defense. Since the right to present a defense is of constitutional magnitude, the Supreme Court has held that rules of evidence and criminal procedure must occasionally yield to a defendant's need to introduce evidence in his or her favor.

Therefore, the Court concluded in *Chambers v. Mississippi*, 410 U.S. 284 (1973), that the defendant's due process right to present a defense outweighed a state rule against hearsay evidence that had been invoked to exclude testimony that another man had confessed to the crime for which the defendant was on trial. Similarly, the Court declared in *Washington v. Texas*, 388 U.S. 14 (1967), that the defendant's Compulsory Process Clause right to obtain witnesses in his favor trumped a state rule barring the defendant from presenting the testimony of his or her alleged accomplices and codefendants. In *Cool v. United States*, 409 U.S. 100 (1972), the Court ruled that a judge unconstitutionally burdened the defendant's Compulsory Process Clause right to call a codefendant who testified in her favor by instructing the jury that it should be exceptionally cautious in accepting the codefendant's testimony. The Court held in *Rock* that a state rule barring a witness whose testimony had been hypnotically refreshed had to yield to the defendant's constitutional right to testify in her defense.

However, the right to present a defense is not absolute, and the Supreme Court has upheld several types of limitations on the right. First, the exclusion of defense evidence may be justified by society's interest in conducting orderly trials. Thus, defense evidence may be excluded if the defendant fails to abide by the rules of pretrial discovery or is attempting to surprise the prosecutor unfairly. Therefore, in *Williams v. Florida*, 399 U.S. 78 (1970), the Court upheld state laws requiring defendants to give pretrial notice of their intent to present certain defenses, such as alibi and insanity, or face exclusion of evidence relating to those defenses; the Court has also upheld exclusion as a sanction for other types of discovery violations. In *Taylor*, for example, the Court affirmed a judge's ruling excluding the testimony of a defense witness as a sanction against defense counsel who had failed to disclose his plan to call the witness until the trial was underway.

Second, a defendant's right to present a defense may yield to local rules designed to improve the reliability of the trial process. Therefore, in *United States v. Scheffer*, 523 U.S. 303 (1998), the Supreme Court upheld a military justice rule that precluded the defendant from presenting polygraph evidence in his favor. The Court explained that "state and federal rulemakers have broad latitude under the Constitution to establish rules excluding evidence from criminal trials. Such rules do not abridge an accused's right to present a defense so long as they are not 'arbitrary' or 'disproportionate' to the purposes they are designed to serve."

Third, the Supreme Court has curtailed the right to present a defense by limiting the right to the introduction of evidence in support of the defense. The Court held in *Gilmore v. Taylor*, 508 U.S. 333 (1993), that the right to present a defense does not, therefore, include the right to have the judge deliver instructions to the jury in support of the defense.

Fourth, a jurisdiction may entirely eliminate the right to present a particular defense entirely by changing the law so as to eliminate the defense. For example, the Supreme Court in *Montana v. Egelhoff*, 518 U.S. 37 (1996), upheld a state law prohibiting defendants from proving that they lack the mental state necessary to be guilty of a crime by introducing evidence of their voluntary intoxication. The Court in *Egelhoff* viewed the prohibition on defense evidence of voluntary intoxication as permissible because states have traditionally been accorded the freedom to define crimes and the available defenses to those crimes.

Even with these limitations, criminal defendants still enjoy a core constitutional right to present relevant and reliable evidence in support of their defenses. Subject to reasonable rules designed to assure a fair and orderly trial, a defendant must be permitted to present favorable witnesses and evidence. The right to present a defense thus protects defendants from those local authorities who may otherwise be all too willing to tilt the scales of justice in favor of the prosecutor.

DAVID A. MORAN

References and Further Reading

Stacy, Tom, *The Search for Truth in Constitutional Criminal Procedure*, Columbia Law Review 91 (1991): 1369.
Westen, Peter, *The Compulsory Process Clause*, Michigan Law Review 73 (1974): 71.

Cases and Statutes Cited

Chambers v. Mississippi, 410 U.S. 284 (1973)
Cool v. United States, 409 U.S. 100 (1972)
Ferguson v. Georgia, 365 U.S. 570 (1961)
Gilmore v. Taylor, 508 U.S. 333 (1993)
In re Oliver, 233 U.S. 257 (1948)
Montana v. Egelhoff, 518 U.S. 37 (1996)
Rock v. Arkansas, 483 U.S. 44 (1987)
Taylor v. Illinois, 484 U.S. 400 (1988)
United States v. Scheffer, 523 U.S. 303 (1998)
Washington v. Texas, 388 U.S. 14 (1967)
Williams v. Florida, 399 U.S. 78 (1970)

See also **Chambers v. Mississippi, 410 U.S. 284 (1973); Due Process; Rock v. Arkansas, 483 U.S. 44 (1987); Self-Incrimination (V): Historical Background; *Taylor v. Illinois*, 484 U.S. 400 (1988); *Washington v. Texas*, 388 U.S. 14 (1967)**

DEFIANCE OF THE COURT'S BAN ON SCHOOL PRAYER

For much of the twentieth century, religion was an important part of the curriculum in many K–12 public schools. In the early 1960s, however, the Supreme Court held that prayer and Bible reading were unconstitutional in those schools. In *Engel v. Vitale*, 370 U.S. 421 (1962), the Court held that a short nondenominational prayer composed by the New York Board of Regents and recommended by it for daily use in the public schools violated the Establishment Clause of the First Amendment. The Court reasoned that "in this country it is no part of the business of government to compose official prayers for any group of the American people to recite as a part of a religious program carried on by government." The following year, in *Abington School District v. Schempp*, 374 U.S. 203 (1963), the Court held that it was unconstitutional for school boards to require the reading of Bible passages or the recitation of the Lord's Prayer in public schools. The Court declared: "In the relationship

between man and religion, the state is firmly committed to a position of neutrality." In both cases the Court forcefully asserted that the separation of church and state was best for government and for religion.

Among religious leaders, conservative Christian evangelicals and Roman Catholics were the primary opponents of the decisions. The vast majority of Protestant leaders and organizations approved of *Engel* and *Schempp*. Indeed, after *Engel*, thirty-one Protestant leaders published a manifesto asserting that the Court's ruling protected "the integrity of the religious conscience and the proper function of religious and governmental institutions." Jewish leaders, moved in part by a concern about their minority status in an overwhelmingly Christian nation, concurred in supporting public secularism.

Despite the opinions of many religious leaders, the majority of Americans disagreed with the Court. Indeed, the school prayer and Bible reading decisions were met with strong opposition and noncompliance from the public. The Supreme Court received five thousand letters denouncing *Engel*, and a Gallup Poll showed that 80 percent of Americans favored prayer in the public schools. Critics accused the Court of secularizing the United States and promoting communist atheism. Disturbed by the intensity of the public response to *Engel*, Justice Clark took the unusual step of denouncing press coverage of the case in an American Bar Association speech.

Engel and *Schempp* were openly defied in the South, where public officials encouraged the resistance, and in the Midwest. There was a greater degree of compliance with the decisions in the rest of the country. When school boards continued classroom religious practices in northern states, states attorneys general ordered them to stop doing so. Despite the resistance, *Engel* and *Schempp* worked changes in classroom practices. One national survey showed that the percentage of classrooms in which prayers were recited declined from 60 percent before 1962 to 28 percent in the 1964–1965 school year; the percentage in which Bible reading was taking place declined from 48 to 22 percent.

Congress also responded strongly to the Court's decisions. Within days of the *Engel* decision, senators introduced five proposed constitutional amendments to overturn it, and the House received twenty-nine proposals to revoke the Court's ruling. By 1975, 215 such amendments had been introduced in Congress. While none of those proposed amendments was successful (they were opposed by the majority of Protestant religious leaders and the Catholic Church eventually adopted a neutral stance), the proponents of school prayer did get Congress to enact the 1984 Equal Access Act. The act, which the Court upheld in

Board of Education v. Mergens, 496 U.S. 226, 247 (1990), provides that K–12 public schools must treat student religious groups who wish to use meeting rooms equally with nonreligious groups.

Those concerned about the diminishing role of religion in the United States have also tried to work around the *Engel* and *Schempp* decisions. More than twenty years after those decisions, twenty-five states permitted or required that a moment of silence be observed in public school classrooms. In *Wallace v. Jaffree*, 472 U.S. 38 (1985), the Supreme Court held that one such statute, a 1981 Alabama statute authorizing a period of silence "for meditation or voluntary prayer," violated the Establishment Clause because it had no secular legislative purpose and was a poorly disguised effort to return prayer to public schools. More recently, the Court has sustained Establishment Clause challenges to prayers at public school graduations (*Lee v. Weisman*, 505 U.S. 577, 1992) and at high school football games (*Santa Fe Independent School District v. Doe*, 530 U.S. 290, 2000). In both cases the Court held that government may not coerce anyone to support or participate in a religious exercise. Notwithstanding the Court's consistent position banning prayer and Bible reading in public schools, noncompliance continues to be a problem.

DENISE C. MORGAN

References and Further Reading

Alley, Robert S. *School Prayer: The Court, the Congress, and the First Amendment*. Buffalo, NY: Prometheus Books, 1994.
Dent, George W., Jr., *Religious Children, Secular Schools*, Southern California Law Review 61 (1988): 4:864–942.
Jeffries, John C., Jr., and Ryan, James E., *A Political History of the Establishment Clause*, Michigan Law Review 100 (2001): 2:279–370.

DEFINING RELIGION

The First Amendment prohibits laws "respecting an establishment of religion" or "prohibiting the free exercise thereof." Three terms are crucial to determining the meaning of the religion clauses of the First Amendment: "establishment of religion," "free exercise," and "religion." Much of the debate over the meaning of the religion clauses concerns the first two terms, but the meaning of the third term is equally important and in many respects even more difficult to resolve. Defining religion is crucial because the First Amendment prohibits the government from "establishing" a set of beliefs and practices only if those beliefs and practices fall within the category of "religion." Likewise, the government's general authority

to regulate behavior is much more constrained if that behavior can be characterized as "religious."

The task of defining "religion" as that term is used in the First Amendment religion clauses is complicated by the fact that the courts often seem to apply one definition of religion to problems arising under the Establishment Clause and a different definition to problems arising under the Free Exercise Clause. This task will become more difficult as the country becomes religiously more diverse. An increasing number of citizens belong to nontraditional faiths, and their beliefs will not always fit easily within the framework of Western religion with which the courts are most familiar.

Traditional Definitions of Religion

Until the middle of the twentieth century, the task of defining constitutionally protected religion was viewed by the Supreme Court as a relatively simple one. During the nineteenth century the constitutional significance of religion was often viewed as coextensive with the dominance of the Christian faith. In Justice Joseph Story's 1851 *Commentaries on the Constitution*, for example, he wrote that the "real object of the [First Amendment] was, not to countenance, much less to advance, Mahometanism, or Judaism, or infidelity, by prostrating Christianity; but to exclude all rivalry among Christian sects, and to prevent any national ecclesiastical establishment." Although the Supreme Court never took quite such a narrowly focused view of the subject, until well into the twentieth century the Court continued to define religion in a way that coincided with Christianity and other Western religions. In *United States v. Mcintosh*, 283 U.S. 605 (1931), Chief Justice Charles Evans Hughes described religion in the most traditional manner possible: "The essence of religion is belief in a relation to God involving duties superior to those arising from any human relation."

Broadening the Definition of Religion: The Conscientious Objector Cases

A series of cases involving conscientious objectors to the draft during the Vietnam War caused the Court to move beyond the traditional definition of religion in First Amendment cases. These cases involved a provision of the military conscription laws that exempted from military service individuals who were conscientiously opposed to participation in war in any form because of their "religious training and belief." The statute defined "religious training and belief" in the traditional way as "an individual's belief in a relation to a Supreme Being involving duties superior to those arising from any human relation, but [not including] essentially political, sociological, or philosophical views or a merely personal moral code." If the Court had adhered to the literal meaning of this provision, it would have been faced with a statute that would deny conscientious objector status to many different groups of believers, agnostics, and atheists whose views on religion did not fit the traditional model.

In contrast to the narrow precision of its previous opinions on the subject, the Court took a more ecumenical and open-ended approach to the definition of religion in its conscientious objector cases. The Court started by asserting that "in no field of human endeavor has the tool of language proved so inadequate in the communication of ideas as it has in dealing with the fundamental questions of man's predicament in life, in death or in final judgment and retribution." The Court then attributed to Congress the intent to include within its conscientious objector provision "the ever-broadening understanding of the modern religious community."

The Court thus interpreted the statutory term "religious" by reference to the broad ideas of modern theologians such as Paul Tillich. At one point the Court noted that, in developing its standard, it was reminded of Tillich's notion that God is "the source of your being, of your ultimate concern, of what you take seriously without any reservation." The Court derived the basic holding of the case from this concept of an "ultimate concern." According to the Court, the statutory term "religious training and belief" applied to anyone who expressed a "sincere and meaningful belief which occupies in the life of its possessor a place parallel to that filled by the God of those admittedly qualifying for the exemption." The Court then used this definition to extend conscientious objector status to several individuals whose religious views were abstract and theologically unspecific. In a later decision the Court would extend its broad approach to the concept of religion to cover applicants whose views bordered on atheism.

Bifurcating the Definition of Religion

Despite the fact that the Court's conscientious objector decisions technically only involved a matter of statutory interpretation, the decisions had clear constitutional overtones. Indeed, Justice Harlan noted

that the Court's rather tortured interpretation of the statute was necessary because "limiting this draft exemption to those opposed to war in general because of theistic beliefs runs afoul of the religious clauses of the First Amendment." Thus, the Court's broad interpretation of religion became the touchstone of the Court's modern Free Exercise Clause decisions. Under these decisions, the Court extended constitutional protection to members of nontraditional religious groups, such as the Native American Church, as well as individuals whose religious beliefs were derived solely from their individual religious introspection, rather than from a specific organized faith.

The Court has not, however, applied this same expansive view of religion to its interpretations of the Establishment Clause. At first glance, this seems inconsistent with the constitutional text, which mentions the word religion only once and seems to imply that the term should be defined identically with regard to both clauses. The problem with this interpretation is that it would create serious difficulties for any modern government. Everything that modern government does in some way exerts an impact on what some people "take seriously without reservation." If this expansive definition were used consistently in all First Amendment contexts, virtually everything the government does would potentially be activity "respecting an establishment of religion."

In response to this problem, some constitutional theorists have suggested bifurcating the First Amendment definition of religion. Under this scheme, the courts would use a broad definition of religion in enforcing the Free Exercise Clause (to provide the broadest possible protection of individual liberty) and a narrow definition in enforcing the Establishment Clause (to give government the broadest possible authority in the areas of education and social services). One such suggestion is Laurence Tribe's early recommendation that the Free Exercise Clause should protect all "arguably religious" activities and that the Establishment Clause should permit government to engage in any "arguably nonreligious" action.

This suggestion generated its own negative response. There are two main criticisms of the argument for a bifurcated definition of religion. The first is that this argument conflicts with the unitary implications of the constitutional text. The second is that a bifurcated definition would create three different tiers of religion, each of which would receive different constitutional treatment. Under such a system, a traditional form of religious belief would be unquestionably religious and therefore actions motivated by this belief would receive free exercise protection, but the religion would be prohibited from receiving direct government support or endorsement. Conversely, secular beliefs that are unquestionably nonreligious would receive no free-exercise protection, but would not be barred under the Establishment Clause from receiving direct government support or endorsement. Any category of beliefs and actions that included some religious elements along with some secular elements, however, would receive favorable treatment under both constitutional provisions because such beliefs would be arguably religious and arguably nonreligious.

Modern Definitions for Establishment Clause Cases

For whatever reason, the Supreme Court has never adopted a bifurcated definition of religion. It has also, however, never defined religion in the Establishment Clause context. In *Edwards v. Aguillard*, 482 U.S. 578 (1987), a case involving state-mandated teaching of creationism, the Court emphasized that "concepts concerning God or a supreme being of some sort are manifestly religious"; however, the Court has never stated whether any other indicia of religion are necessary or sufficient to trigger the application of the Establishment Clause. The lower courts have occasionally mentioned other factors that contribute to a finding that a particular set of beliefs is religious. In one prominent case, Judge Arlen Adams mentions three factors: whether the beliefs concern fundamental problems of human existence; whether the beliefs purport to provide a comprehensive belief system; and whether the beliefs include the formal indicia of religion, such as an administrative structure, rituals, clergy, liturgies, and holidays.

The Supreme Court has embraced no single test that will definitively determine in every case whether an Establishment Clause case implicates "religion." Conversely, the test for religion announced by the Court in the conscientious objector cases is so broad that the Free Exercise Clause is potentially implicated in a variety of different contexts. In the end, the courts seem to have settled on an instrumental as well as intuitive definition of religion. The definition applied in the Establishment Clause context is narrow enough to permit the government to do its modern job of providing social services and operating public schools that teach a broad range of subjects (including controversial topics such as morality and evolution). Conversely, the definition of religion applied in the free-exercise context is expansive enough to avoid having any citizen suffer at the hands of the government solely because that person's unpopular religious beliefs offend the political and religious majority.

STEVEN G. GEY

References and Further Reading

Choper, Jesse H., *Defining "Religion" in the First Amendment*, U. Ill. L. Rev. 579 (1982).
Feofanov, Dmitry N., *Defining Religion: An Immodest Proposal*, Hofstra L. Rev. 23 (1994): 309.
Freeman, George, *The Misguided Search for the Constitutional Definition of "Religion,"* Ga. L. J. 71 (1983): 1519.
Greenawalt, Kent, *Religion as a Concept in Constitutional Law*, Calif. L. Rev. 72 (1984): 753.
Note, Toward a Constitutional Definition of Religion, Harv. L. Rev. 91 (1978): 1056.

Cases and Statutes Cited

United States v. Macintosh, 283 U.S. 605 (1931)
United States v. Seeger, 380 U.S. 163 (1965)

See also **Accommodation of Religion; Atheism; Ceremonial Deism; Concept of "Christian Nation" in American Jurisprudence; Free Exercise Clause (I): History, Background, Framing; Religion in "Public Square" Debate; Selective Draft Law Cases (1918), Selective Service Act of 1917**

DEJONGE v. OREGON, 299 U.S. 353 (1937)

In 1934, about three hundred people attended a meeting organized by the Communist Party in Portland, Oregon, to support a maritime workers' strike. Fewer than 15 percent of them were Communist Party members. Speaker Dirk DeJonge, a party member, spoke against police shootings of strikers and raids on party headquarters and workers' halls. He encouraged attendees to buy party literature, join the party, and gather people to attend another Communist Party meeting the following night.

Police raided the orderly meeting, confiscated party literature, and arrested DeJonge and three other meeting organizers. DeJonge was charged, convicted, and sentenced to seven years in prison under the Oregon criminal syndicalism statute for helping conduct a Communist Party meeting. Criminal syndicalism laws prohibit advocating or organizing a group to use unlawful means to overthrow business owners or government. The prosecution did not claim that DeJonge advocated illegal acts, but did present Communist Party literature from other sources that suggested the party supported such advocacy.

The Supreme Court struck down the conviction as a violation of the essence of constitutionally guaranteed personal liberty. The Court ruled unanimously that government may not proscribe "the holding of meetings for peaceable political action." The First Amendment, as applied through the Due Process Clause of the Fourteenth Amendment, prohibits

411

states from regulating free speech or assembly that does not incite violence or crime. In 1969, in *Brandenburg v. Ohio*, 395 U.S. 444 (1969), the Court said states may forbid only advocacy of criminal acts that is directed toward and likely to produce imminent illegal action.

SUSAN DENTE ROSS

References and Further Reading

Blasi, Vincent, *The Pathological Perspective and the First Amendment*, Colum. L. Rev. 85 (1985): 449.
Parrish, Michael E., *New Deal Symposium: The Great Depression, the New Deal, and the American Legal Order*, 59 Wash. L. Rev. 723 (1984).
U.S. Constitution. Amendments One, Fourteen.

Cases and Statutes Cited

Brandenburg v. Ohio, 395 U.S. 444 (1969)

DELAWARE v. PROUSE, 440 U.S. 648 (1979)

The Supreme Court in this case made it clear that police officers may not ordinarily stop a person's car without probable cause or reasonable suspicion of criminal activity. The car in *Delaware v. Prouse* was stopped by a police officer who had not observed any suspicious activity at all. He claimed to have made the stop randomly, just to make a spot check to see if the driver possessed his license and registration.

Upon approaching the stopped car, the officer smelled marijuana and, ultimately, he found some inside. The Court held that the marijuana should be suppressed because the officer had no right under the Fourth Amendment to the Constitution to stop the car, given the driver's reasonable expectation of privacy.

Justice White reasoned for the majority that permitting such suspicionless spot checks would only contribute marginally, if at all, to the goal of highway safety. Since the Court could not "conceive of any legitimate basis upon which a patrolman could decide that stopping a particular driver for a spot check would be more productive than stopping any other driver," approving such stops would have created a "grave danger" of abuse of discretion. "This kind of standardless and unconstrained discretion," Justice White concluded, "is the evil the Court has discerned when . . . it has insisted that the discretion of the official in the field be circumscribed."

Subsequent Supreme Court decisions have permitted police to operate suspicionless, drunk-driving roadblocks when they take great care to avoid this sort of "standardless and unconstrained discretion" in the selection of cars to be stopped. But, the core of the *Prouse* decision remains vital and has been applied in other settings as well—for example, when a city sought to stop cars simply to see whether occupants possessed drugs.

JOHN M. BURKOFF

See also **Automobile Searches;** *California v. Acevedo,* **500 U.S. 565 (1991);** *Carroll v. United States,* **267 U.S. 132 (1925); Checkpoints (roadblocks); Probable Cause; Search (General Definition); Seizures**

DEMONSTRATIONS AND SIT-INS

Demonstrations and sit-ins served as powerful tools in the struggle for equality in the civil rights movement and other civil liberty struggles. Both forms of protest adhere to the principles of nonviolence endorsed by such figures as Mahatma Ghandi in India and Dr. Martin Luther King, Jr. in the United States.

The most famous example of a sit-in occurred in 1960 in Greensboro, North Carolina. In February 1960, four African-American students from Greensboro A&T sat at a Woolworth's lunch counter. The lunch counter was not integrated and the four men were refused service. This began a three-month-long struggle to integrate the lunch counter. Each day, more African-American students and supporters sat down at the counter and were refused service. They withstood verbal and physical abuse, threats, and jail time and persevered in their efforts. The lunch counter eventually integrated and the sit-in first begun in Greensboro spread throughout the South as increasing numbers of civil rights groups adopted the sit-in strategy. Despite the abuse, at no time did the students and supporters of the Greensboro sit-in resort to violence.

Demonstrations have taken place for centuries and usually serve as public forums to protest injustice and wrongs perceived by the people. In the modern era, demonstrations serve as important ways in which to get a particular viewpoint or message spread to others. Demonstrations are often used for political reasons, with various groups attempting to get their messages heard. The civil rights movement used demonstrations effectively to gain media attention on their struggle and turn America against prejudice and bigotry.

JASON M. SOKIERA

References and Further Reading

Bermanzohn, Sally Avery. *Through Survivors' Eyes: From the Sixties to the Greensboro Massacre.* Nashville, Tenn.: Vanderbilt University Press, 2003.

Hairston, Otis L., Jr. *Greensboro North Carolina* (Black America Series). Mount Pleasant, S.C.: Arcadia Publishing, 2003.

DENATURALIZATION

As discussed earlier, U.S. citizenship may be acquired at birth or through the statutory process of naturalization. A U.S. citizen may lose citizenship in two ways. Loss of citizenship can occur when or if the citizen voluntarily relinquishes it through an act of expatriation. A person may also lose citizenship through the process of denaturalization or revocation of citizenship. Denaturalization may occur when an individual has failed to comply with all of the prerequisites for naturalization and, as a result, naturalization was improperly granted.

The general statutory requirements for naturalization require that an individual be eighteen years of age and a lawful permanent resident; meet the applicable continuous residence and physical presence requirements; demonstrate good moral character, attachment to the principles of the Constitution, and a favorable disposition to the good order and happiness of the United States; demonstrate understanding of English and U.S. government and history; and be not otherwise barred from naturalization. There are some exceptions to these general requirements identified in the statute and discussed generally elsewhere. Revocation of naturalization can occur if lawful permanent residence was improperly granted since one of the statutory grounds for naturalization requires that the individual possess the status of a lawful permanent resident.

The Immigration and Nationality Act identifies the grounds for denaturalization and the process for revocation of citizenship. Revocation of naturalization will occur if a person illegally procured citizenship or citizenship was obtained by concealment of a material fact or willful misrepresentation. The government bears the burden of proof and must establish by clear and convincing evidence that naturalization was improperly granted based on one of these grounds.

Revocation can only occur if the government can establish that the naturalized citizen intentionally concealed a material fact or intentionally made a material misrepresentation. The government must further prove that the naturalization was granted based on the material misrepresentation or concealment. Examples of material facts that can result in denaturalization if intentionally made include such facts as the length and location of residence in the United States, marital or family status, occupation, name or other facts of identity, and past criminal record.

Naturalization may be illegally procured if an individual failed to satisfy one of the statutory requirements for naturalization. As noted earlier, this ground for denaturalization can reach a naturalized citizen's initial status as a lawful permanent resident and any prior immigration status in the United States as a noncitizen. There is some overlap between this ground for denaturalization and the intentional material misrepresentation or concealment ground; however, they are separately identified in the statute and viewed as separate grounds.

Denaturalization can occur at any time if naturalization was improperly granted based on misrepresentation or concealment, or if naturalization was illegally procured. The denaturalization process generally occurs through a judicial proceeding instituted by a U.S. attorney in a U.S. district court. The civil suit to revoke citizenship is filed in the judicial district where the naturalized citizen resides. A suit may only be filed if there is good cause indicating that there are grounds for denaturalization. The government will only prevail in the denaturalization lawsuit if it can present clear and convincing evidence of one of the two grounds for denaturalization. This significant burden on the government is designed to protect the status of citizenship.

ENID TRUCIOS-HAYNES

References and Further Reading

Gallagher, Anna Marie. *Immigration Law Service*, 2nd ed. St. Paul, Minn.: West Publishing, 2004, Chapter 14.
Immigration and Nationality Act §312(a), 8 U.S.C. § 1423(a).
Immigration and Nationality Act §313, 8 U.S.C. § 1424.
Immigration and Nationality Act §316 (a), (b), 8 U.S.C. § 1427(a), (b).
Immigration and Nationality Act §318, 8 U.S.C. § 1429.
Immigration and Nationality Act § 329(a), (b), 8 U.S.C. § 1440(a), (b).
Immigration and Nationality Act §340(h), 8 U.S.C. § 1451(h).
Immigration and Nationality Act § 349(a), 8 U.S.C. § 1481(a).
Kungys v. U.S., 485 U.S. 759 (1988).
Kurzban, Ira J. *Immigration Law Sourcebook*, 9th ed. Washington, D.C.: American Immigrant Lawyers Association, 2004.
Legomsky, Stephen. *Immigration and Refugee Law*, 4th ed. Foundation Press, 2005, 1312.
Mailman, Gordon, and Yale–Loehr. *Immigration Law and Procedure*. New York: Matthew Bender, § 100.02 [1][a].
Rosenberg v. U.S., 60 F. 2d 475 (3d Cir. 1932).
Schneiderman v. United States, 320 U.S. 118 (1943).
U.S. v. Costello, 275 F. 2d 355 (2d Cir. 1960).
U.S. v. D'Agostino, 338 F. 2d 490 (2d Cir. 1964).
U.S. v. DeLucia, 256 F. 2d 487 (7th Cir. 1958).
U.S. v. Rossi, 319 F. 2d 701 (2d Cir. 1963).

DENNIS v. UNITED STATES,
341 U.S. 494 (1951)

In *Dennis v. United States*, the U.S. Supreme Court upheld the conviction of eleven national leaders of the Communist Party (CPUSA) under the Smith Act (Alien Registration Act) of 1940 for conspiring to organize the CPUSA to "teach and advocate the overthrow and destruction of the Government of the United States by force and violence." *Dennis* was the leading precedent upholding cold war prosecution of communists and others suspected of leftist sympathies during the 1950s.

The Truman administration, led by Attorney General Tom Clark, sought Smith act indictments against the CPUSA leadership in 1948 to fend off Republican criticism that Democrats were lax in ferreting communists out of positions of influence in American life, and also as a way of indirectly promoting Truman's aggressive and expensive policy of containment of the Soviet Union. The trial before U.S. District Court Judge Harold Medina in New York City was a raucous affair that resulted in convictions of all the defendants, followed by contempt citations of their attorneys. The U.S. Supreme Court upheld those contempt convictions when they were appealed (*Sacher v. United States*, 343 U.S. 1, 1952; *In re Isserman*, 345 U.S. 286, 1953). These convictions and subsequent disbarment of some of counsel had a chilling effect on the availability of legal representation for radicals during the cold war.

On appeal of the Smith Act convictions, Chief Judge Learned Hand wrote for the court of appeals panel, affirming the convictions on the basis of a reworked clear-and-present-danger test: "whether the gravity of the 'evil,' discounted by its improbability, justifies such invasion of free speech as is necessary to avoid the danger." In the case of communists, Hand thought the answer to be clearly in the affirmative because he considered communism to be a mortal menace to American freedom. Under the Hand formula, if the apprehended evil is great enough, its likelihood can be remote and still provide a basis for government censure.

On appeal to the Supreme Court, the justices affirmed by a vote of six to two. (Justice Tom Clark recused himself because of his earlier participation in the case as attorney general.) Chief Justice Fred Vinson wrote the plurality opinion, in which only three other members of the Court joined. (This opinion, despite lacking majority status, is accepted as *the* opinion for the Court and will be treated as such here.)

Like Judge Hand, Justice Vinson subscribed wholeheartedly to the then prevalent belief that the CPUSA was "a highly organized conspiracy, with rigidly disciplined members" committed to "overthrow of the Government by force and violence." In this view, the CPUSA had a unique constitutional status, placing it and its members at least partially outside the protections that the First Amendment afforded other political movements.

With those assumptions constituting the foundation of his opinion, the Chief Justice then went on to endorse Judge Hand's sliding-scale calculus. He applied it in such a way as to permit the federal government to suppress what he called "advocacy" as well as "incitement." In doing so, he forced free-speech doctrine, and the clear-and-present-danger test in particular, back into its World War I era formulation, which considered a mere bad tendency as within government's power to crush. Vinson also adopted Justice Felix Frankfurter's balancing approach (as opposed to Justice Hugo Black's absolutism), weighing national security against individual liberty to communicate. Security easily won. The Vinson opinion permitted government to go beyond its unquestioned power to suppress actual evils like insurrection and incitement to punish communicative activities that had previously enjoyed some degree of First Amendment protection: advocacy, organizing, and belonging to political groups.

Yet, despite the speech-suppressive result of his holding, *in dicta* Justice Vinson inconsistently endorsed Justice Oliver Wendell Holmes's dissent in *Gitlow v. New York*, 268 U.S. 652 (1925), and Justice Louis D. Brandeis's concurrence in *Whitney v. California* (1927), both of which repudiated bad-tendency readings and provided a wide latitude for political speech. Such incompatibilities in Justice Vinson's opinion help account for its short-lived actual influence.

Because Vinson's opinion was only a plurality, the concurrences assumed greater than usual significance. Frankfurter construed away the clear-and-present-danger test altogether. This required considerable intellectual contortion on his part since he had previously identified himself with Justices Holmes and Brandeis, whose views would have condemned the *Dennis* result and its doctrine. He dismissed the Holmes/Brandeis vision as "a sonorous formula," as "dogmas too inflexible" to be applied in the real world, and as merely "attractive but imprecise words." As a substitute for clear and present danger, now drained of all meaning, Frankfurter substituted balancing, which had the double vice of enhancing judicial power while invariably privileging government authority over freedom of speech.

Justice Robert H. Jackson's concurrence went even further than Justices Vinson's and Frankfurter's in embracing an apocalyptic vision of Communism. From that metajudicial assumption, he derived an unlimited power of government to suppress speech. In his view, communists could claim no effective constitutional protection for their activities.

Justices Black and William O. Douglas dissented, Black expressing the "hope . . . that in calmer times, when present pressures, passions and fears subside," a later Court would "restore the First Amendment liberties to the high preferred place" they had previously occupied.

Justice Black's hope was realized seventeen years later in *Brandenburg v. Ohio*, 395 U.S. 444 (1968), which did in fact reinstate the Holmes/Brandeis reading of clear and present danger to canonical status. Since then political discourse has enjoyed nearly absolute immunity from government suppression. But in the interim, *Dennis* plowed wide inroads into First Amendment liberties, depriving not only communists but also much of the American Left of freedoms to speak, publish, organize, and agitate enjoyed by all other Americans. It was the major constitutional bulwark of the cold war.

Moreover, though *Dennis* has been ignored by judges and condemned by academics and civil libertarians since 1968, it has never been overruled. It remains valid precedent, at least technically, available to authorize suppression of the speech, press, and assembly liberties of some feared, loathed, and/or radical group in the future.

WILLIAM M. WIECEK

References and Further Reading

Belknap, Michal R. *Cold War Political Justice: The Smith Act, the Communist Party, and American Civil Liberties.* Westport, CT: Greenwood Press, 1977.
Kutler, Stanley I. *The American Inquisition: Justice and Injustice in the Cold War.* New York: Hill and Wang, 1982.
Murphy, Paul L. *The Constitution in Crisis Times, 1918–1969.* New York: Harper & Row, 1972.
Urofsky, Melvin I. *Division and Discord: The Supreme Court Under Stone and Vinson, 1941–1953.* Columbia: University of South Carolina Press, 1997.
Wiecek, William M., *The Legal Foundations of Domestic Anticommunism: The Background of* Dennis v. U.S., Supreme Court Review (2001): 375–434.

Cases and Statutes Cited

Brandenburg v. Ohio, 395 U.S. 444 (1969)
In re Isserman, 345 U.S. 286 (1953)
Sacher v. United States, 343 U.S. 1 (1952)

DEPARTMENT OF HOMELAND SECURITY

The Department of Homeland Security (DHS) was created on November 25, 2002, by the Homeland Security Act. In the wake of the attacks of September 11, 2001, President Bush established the Office of Homeland Security by executive order. Following congressional calls for the reorganization and refocusing of government agencies to bolster national security, the Office of Homeland Security was supplanted by a full-scale department to be headed by a new secretary of homeland security. After much wrangling between the president and Congress over the scope and the extent of legislative oversight of the new entity, DHS came into being in the largest government reorganization since the 1940s. It subsumed twenty-two existing federal agencies consisting of approximately 180 thousand federal employees, and represents the third largest government department.

The Department of Homeland Security's mandate is to reduce America's vulnerability to terrorism, prevent terrorist attacks inside the country, and manage recovery efforts in the event of such an attack. Agencies such as the Immigration and Naturalization Service, the Secret Service, the Federal Emergency Management Administration, the Customs Service, and others were placed under the department's authority. Former Pennsylvania Governor Tom Ridge was named as the first secretary of homeland security.

A primary aim of the Homeland Security Act is to assist with the collection, analysis, and sharing of intelligence information relating to security threats to the homeland and to enabling DHS to be proactive in forestalling attacks. However, threats to national security inevitably create tensions with the constitutional liberties and freedoms Americans have long cherished. The breadth and nature of DHS's mandate have generated significant criticism from civil libertarians who argue that the legislation undermines privacy rights and government openness by restricting public access to government information while lowering barriers to the monitoring and interception of electronic communications.

The Freedom of Information Act (FOIA) of 1966 provides a right to the public to have access to information regarding government activities to prevent "wrongdoing" by the federal government; however, section 214 of the Homeland Security Act provides blanket authorization for DHS to withhold certain information relating to national security-related "critical infrastructure" if provided voluntarily by private companies. While supporters contend that such a provision is critical to encouraging the sharing of critical information with the government, critics note that information voluntarily provided to DHS by a nuclear power company related to a nuclear spill could not be shared with other government regulatory agencies or the general public. Section 214, it is contended, significantly undermines the purpose of FOIA.

Section 225 expands the government's ability to monitor electronic communications absent a judicial warrant. One provision within this section expands the scope of cases in which Internet service providers (ISPs) are shielded from liability for turning over private communications to the government. Although prior statutes went further to protect the privacy of ISP subscribers from unreasonable searches and seizures in line with the Fourth Amendment, the new law lowers the standard necessary to permit disclosure of private Internet communications. The section also expands the government's ability to install monitoring devices temporarily without a warrant on certain electronic devices in an "emergency situation" or on computers deemed "protected," which Courts have understood to mean those involved in or affecting interstate or foreign commerce or communication. Although the standard of a "reasonable expectation of privacy" that has governed consideration of Fourth Amendment searches and seizures is in a state of flux and may well have shrunk in this new world of Internet connectivity, section 225 certainly narrows the scope of privacy rights over certain electronic communications.

The Homeland Security Act has also been criticized for eroding individual rights by authorizing the president to suspend collective bargaining rights for DHS employees if he or she deems that union activities are having a "substantial adverse impact" on homeland security. The act also limits liability, even in cases of negligence, for makers of critical vaccines against smallpox or anthrax with whom the department has contracted.

Sensitive to the civil liberties implications of the legislation, section 705 of the law created a position for the officer for civil rights and civil liberties while section 222 creates a privacy officer. The former is tasked with conducting investigations on allegations of civil rights abuses in DHS and providing advice to the secretary of homeland security as to matters concerning civil liberties. The officer, for example, has established a training program for DHS employees called Civil Liberties University. The privacy officer is similarly responsible for advising the secretary and for reporting on the privacy implications of DHS activities and new technologies.

Although DHS includes some administrative structures to review the privacy and civil rights effects of the Homeland Security Act, this has not prevented groups such as the American Civil Liberties Union from initiating litigation concerning border security practices or the sharing of airline passenger screening procedures. The focus on homeland security appears unlikely to recede in importance in the near future, so pressures on civil liberties will no doubt endure.

ANDREW FINKELMAN

References and Further Reading

Jones, Karen E., *Comment and Casenote: The Effect of the Homeland Security Action on Online Privacy and the Freedom of Information Act*, University of Cincinnati Law Review 72: 787.
Thessin, Jonathan, *Recent Developments: Department of Homeland Security*, Harvard Journal on Legislation 40 (2003): 513.

See also **Electronic Surveillance, Technological Monitoring, and Dog Sniffs; 9/11 and the War on Terrorism; Patriot Act; Wiretapping Laws**

DERSHOWITZ, ALAN (1938–)

Alan Dershowitz, professor of law at Harvard University, is a prolific writer, social activist, and legal commentator who has been described by *Newsweek* as "the nation's most peripatetic civil liberties lawyer and one of its most distinguished defenders of individual rights."

Early in his career Dershowitz clerked for Supreme Court Justice Arthur Goldberg. At the time of his teaching appointment at the age of 28, he was the youngest tenured faculty member ever at Harvard Law School. Dershowitz, who specialized in appellate work, has since been involved in a number high-profile criminal defense cases, including the trial of Claus Von Bülow, and served as an advisor to O. J. Simpson's defense team. Acknowledging that his philosophy as a civil-liberties lawyer is to "challenge the government at every turn," Dershowitz has campaigned for Jews in the former Soviet Union and has taken on less highly publicized cases involving issues of individual rights, many of them on a pro bono basis.

Dershowitz articulated his concept of civil rights, which he views as deriving from past human experiences with injustice rather than from God or natural law, in a 2002 book entitled *Shouting Fire: Civil Liberties in a Turbulent Age*. He has been at the forefront of a discussion, provoked by the events of September 11, concerning the legality and propriety of the use of torture in exceptional circumstances. Addressing the hypothetical "ticking bomb scenario" in which torture is contemplated as a means of last resort to extract information needed to forestall a massive terrorist attack and save lives, Dershowitz's proposal to regulate torture through a "warrant" system has sparked debate among civil-rights lawyers and academics. The concept of a torture warrant system—a delicate balance of conflicting rights that ensures judicial oversight and government accountability at the cost of establishing a damaging legitimizing precedent for torture—represents a salient new component in Deshowitz's concept of civil liberties.

ANDREW FINKELMAN

References and Further Reading

Dershowitz, Alan. *Shouting Fire: Civil Liberties in a Turbulent Age.* Boston: Little, Brown, 2002.
Williams, Marjorie, and Ruth Marcus. 1991. Courting fame, fanning flames: lawyer Alan Dershowitz, from rogues to riches. *The Washington Post,* February 10, F1.

DESIGNATED PUBLIC FORUMS

First Amendment law concerning government regulation of the freedom of speech tends to develop in strands. One such strand is forum analysis, which concerns the constitutional limitations on government control of speech and expression on government property.

The Supreme Court's forum analysis includes three types of forums. The traditional public forum includes public streets, sidewalks, and parks, all places historically reserved for expressive activities. The designated public forum is any other government property intentionally held open for expressive activities. The nonpublic forum comprises all of the remaining government property, such as jails and military bases. The forum label dictates the analysis the court will apply.

The Supreme Court uses essentially the same test for traditional and designated public forums. The test has several requirements. First, the government generally cannot enact content based regulations that discriminate against a particular message (*Widmar v. Vincent*, 454 U.S. 263, 1981). Second, the government can enact content-neutral time, place, and manner regulations, but only if the regulations are reasonable (*Perry Education Ass'n v. Perry Local Educators' Ass'n,* 372 U.S. 229, 1963). Reasonable regulations are defined by the Supreme Court as those that are narrowly tailored to serve a substantial government interest and leave open ample alternative channels of communication (see, for example, *Ward v. Rock Against Racism*, 491 U.S. 781, 1989).

It is important to emphasize that heavy use does not dictate whether a designated public forum is created. Instead, the government's intent is critical. Thus, airports generally are not designated public forums but rather nonpublic forums, because they are places where people congregate to travel, not to speak (see, for example, *International Society for Krishna Consciousness, Inc. v. Lee,* 502 U.S. 1022, 1992). Similarly, a public school during school hours is a nonpublic forum and not a designated public forum because it is dedicated to teaching and learning, not to freedom of expression (see, for example, *Bethel School District No. 403 v. Fraser,* 478 U.S. 675, 1986).

On the other hand, public schools opened to the community for the after-hours exchanges of communication can become designated public forums. If a public school becomes a designated public forum after hours, school officials are prevented from excluding certain groups because of their message (see, for example, *Good News Club v. Milford Central School,* 553 U.S. 98, 2001). (The exclusion of a religious group from after-hours discussions of character and morals while allowing all other nonreligious groups to do so is impermissible content based discrimination.)

S. FRIEDLAND

Cases and Statutes Cited

Bethel School District No. 403 v. Fraser, 478 U.S. 675 (1986)
Good News Club v. Milford Central School, 553 U.S. 98 (2001)
International Society for Krishna Consciousness, Inc. v. Lee, 502 U.S. 1022 (1992)
Perry Education Association v. Perry Local Educators' Association, 372 U.S. 229 (1963)
Ward v. Rock Against Racism, 491 U.S. 781 (1989)
Widmar v. Vincent, 454 U.S. 263 (1981)

DEWITT, GENERAL JOHN (1880–1962)

John DeWitt, the army general in charge of Japanese American relocation in World War II, was born in 1880 at Fort Sidney, Nebraska, and reared on army posts. Eager to join the Spanish–American War of 1898, DeWitt left Princeton University in his sophomore year. The conflict left a lasting impact on DeWitt, and instead of returning to Princeton, he decided to join the regular army. His responsibilities in the military included work as a supply officer, desk duty, and Philippines tours of service before serving in France during World War I as director of supply and transportation for the First Army Corps. Dewitt served in the War Department from 1919 to 1930 in positions that included chief of the storage and issue branch, acting assistant chief of staff, and assistant commandant of the General Staff College. In 1930, he became quartermaster general and in 1937 was named commandant of the Army War College. Two years later, DeWitt became commander of the West Coast Fourth Army and the Ninth Corps Area.

General DeWitt's appointment as commander on the West Coast and the 1941 Pearl Harbor attack by the Japanese Imperial Navy would be important factors resulting in the internment of Japanese Americans in prison camps. Prior to the Pearl Harbor attack, DeWitt had a history of racist behavior toward African Americans and Asians during his career in the then segregated army; he preferred that they serve in the more dangerous and combat-focused infantry units. Fueled by his disdain for minorities and by widespread fear of more attacks by the Japanese military, DeWitt put in place a plan to restrict the rights of Japanese Americans.

Although unsubstantiated by the other federal agencies, DeWitt made claims to government officials against Japanese and Japanese Americans that they were enemy aliens with no loyalty to the United States, had committed acts of espionage, and therefore had to be detained. As a result of public hysteria on the West Coast, President Franklin D. Roosevelt signed Executive Order 9066 on February 12, 1942, making it legal for the United States to confine Japanese Americans to internment camps in the western United States. General DeWitt directed the operation to round up approximately one hundred twenty thousand Japanese and Japanese Americans into internment camps.

Nearly fifty years after the internment of Japanese Americans, the U.S. government acknowledged that their internment had been a mistake derived from fear and prejudice. The Justice Department made the decision no longer to defend internment and Congress enacted a bill of redress for internment camp survivors in which President Reagan included an apology.

DeWitt's career in the U.S. Army spanned almost fifty years. He retired in 1947 with the Distinguished Service Medal at the rank of lieutenant general. Seven years after his retirement, Congress promoted DeWitt to full general. He died in 1962 of a heart attack.

BA-SHEN WELCH

References and Further Reading

Daniels, Roger. *Concentration Camps: North American Japanese in the United States and Canada During World War II*. Malabar, FL: Robert E. Krieger Publishing Company, Inc., 1981.

Irons, Peter. *Justice at War: The Story of the Japanese American Internment Cases*. New York: Oxford University Press, 1983.

United States Army Quartermaster Museum. Major General John L. DeWitt 28th quartermaster general February 1930–February 1934 (online). Fort Lee: USA Quartermaster Center (retrieved 2 July 2003). Available from http://www.qmfound.com/MG_John_DeWitt.htm.

DIAL-A-PORN

Dial-a-porn services provide prerecorded, sexually explicit messages via telephone. In 1983, following concerns that young people were being harmed by exposure to offensive and damaging messages that were easily accessible, Congress amended the Communications Act of 1934. Section 223(b) prohibited obscene or indecent telephone communications to any person under eighteen years of age or to any other person without that person's consent.

Critics of the legislation claimed that it was unconstitutional content based regulation of free speech. After the Second Circuit ruled that indecency is not a separate category of speech, Congress amended section 223(b) to prohibit all indecent and obscene commercial telephone communications directed to any person, regardless of age.

In *Sable Communications v. FCC*, 492 U.S. 115 (1989), the Supreme Court upheld Congress's total ban on obscene transmissions. Since obscenity is not protected by the First Amendment, Congress may regulate the dissemination of obscene materials, so long as it has a legitimate governmental interest in such regulation. It struck down, however, the total ban on indecent communications, which may be regulated only when a compelling governmental interest exists, and then only by the least restrictive means available. Although the Court held that the welfare of minors is a compelling governmental interest, a total ban on indecent communication was not the least restrictive means to further that interest.

In response, Congress enacted the Helms amendment, prohibiting any indecent commercial telephone communication available to minors, but allowing a waiver for adults agreeing to abide by a "presubscription" procedure. The Second Circuit has since upheld the amendment.

DEBORAH ZALESNE

References and Further Reading

Burrington, William W., and Thaddeus J. Burns, "*Hung Up on the Pay-Per-Call Industry? Current Federal Legislative* and Regulatory Developments," Seton Hall Legis. Journal 17 (1993): 359, 365.

Cases and Statutes Cited

Carlin Communications v. FCC, 837 F.2d 546, 560 (2d Cir. 1988)
Dial Information Services Corp. v. Thornburgh, 938 F.2d 1535 (2d Cir. 1991), cert. denied, 112 S.Ct. 966 (1992)
Sable Communications v. FCC, 492 U.S. 115 (1989)
Communications Act of 1934, 47 U.S.C. § 223(b) (1983)
Communications Act of 1934, 47 U.S.C. § 223(b) (1990) (Helms amendment)

DICKERSON v. UNITED STATES, 530 U.S. 428 (2000)

Prior to the leading case of Miranda v. Arizona, 384 U.S. 436, decided in 1966, the U.S. Supreme Court used the standard of "voluntariness" in determining the admissibility of a confession. The Miranda decision replaced this standard in most cases with a prescribed set of warnings that must be given prior to custodial interrogation. Failure to give the warnings would render a confession inadmissible, even if it were given voluntarily.

In the midst of the widespread criticism that Miranda generated, Congress enacted 18 U.S.C. section 3501, which purported to overturn Miranda insofar as it applied in federal criminal cases. Under the statute, which was totally ignored for thirty years, the failure to give the warnings did not prevent a confession from being admitted as long as it was voluntary.

In Dickerson v. United States the trial court granted Dickerson's motion to suppress a statement he made to the F.B.I. on the ground that the Miranda warnings had not been given. The Fourth Circuit Court of Appeals reversed, holding that under section 3501 the confession was voluntary and therefore admissible. In reversing the court of appeals, the U.S. Supreme Court held that the rule in Miranda was based on the Constitution and, as such, could not be overruled by an act of Congress. The Court refused to overrule Miranda on its own, finding that it has become part of routine police procedures and that subsequent cases have reaffirmed Miranda's core ruling while reducing its negative impact on legitimate police practices.

STEVEN B. DOW

References and Further Reading

Dripps, Donald A., Constitutional Theory for Criminal Procedure: Dickerson, Miranda, and the Continuing Quest for Broad-but-Shallow, William & Mary Law Review 43 (2001): 1–77.

LaFave, Wayne R., Jerold H. Israel, and Nancy J. King. Criminal Procedure, 4th ed. St. Paul, MN: Thomson/West, 2004.
Prebble, Amanda L., Manipulated by Miranda: A Critical Analysis of Bright Lines and Voluntary Confessions Under United States v. Dickerson, University of Cincinnati Law Review 68 (2000): 555–588.

Cases and Statutes Cited

Miranda v. Arizona, 384 U.S. 436 (1966)
18 U.S.C. section 3501 (1994)

See also Coerced Confessions/Police Interrogation; Miranda Warning

DIES, MARTIN (1900–1972)

Martin Dies, born in Colorado, Texas, in 1900, served in the House of Representatives from 1931 to 1944, where he gained notoriety as the first chairman of the House Un-American Activities Committee. A protégée of Speaker of the House John Nance Garner, Dies was initially an early supporter of President Franklin Roosevelt's New Deal. He ultimately became disillusioned with the program, however, and in 1938 he introduced a resolution to create a special committee to "investigate subversive and un-American propaganda" with which he hoped to attack the New Deal.

Between 1938 and 1944, during his tenure as chairman of the HUAC, Dies used the committee's wide-ranging mandate to hunt for communists, generating much publicity from the unsupported charges of Communist and Nazi subversion that emanated from HUAC hearings. Dies's tactics became the model for the later subversion investigations of the post-1945 "red scare."

The committee fed on names. Witnesses before the committee were asked to identify those they suspected of being communist. They were permitted to ramble and indulge in blind accusations with little guidance from the chairman or committee members. Membership records of alleged communist organizations were released publicly without substantiation. Hearings before HUAC were rarely impartial and reflected Dies's political persuasion. After 1939, consulting seldom, if at all, with other committee members, Dies turned HUAC hearings into a one-man road show that often gave right-wing extremists an arena to cast suspicion on liberal organizations and individuals.

Although Dies left the House in 1944, the committee was reauthorized in 1945, becoming the most notorious of the McCarthy era investigating committees. Dies re-entered Congress in 1953, but by this time his reputation had been eclipsed by that of Joseph

McCarthy. Dies was not appointed to HUAC. He left Congress in 1959, but continued his devotion to the anticommunist cause as a dedicated member of the John Birch society. He died in 1972.

KAREN BRUNER

References and Further Reading

Goodman, Walter. *The Committee: The Extraordinary Career of the House Committee on Un-American Activities.* New York: Farrar, Straus and Giroux, 1968.

Ogden, August Raymond. *The Dies Committee: A Study of the Special House Committee for the Investigation of Un-American Activities.* Washington, DC: Catholic University Press, 1945.

See also **House Un-American Activities Committee; John Birch Society; McCarthy, Joseph; New Deal; Roosevelt, Franklin Delano**

DISCIPLINING LAWYERS FOR SPEAKING ABOUT PENDING CASES

Lawyers sometimes believe that it is important to influence public opinion as part of the representation of a client. Perhaps the aim is to present a favorable case to potential jurors, or perhaps the client is a public figure whose reputation may be affected by the outcome of the proceedings. In any event, when lawyers discuss a pending case at a news conference or make statements to reporters, these extrajudicial comments may have a negative impact on the fairness of the trial process. Courts and bar associations therefore seek to limit speech concerning pending cases. These limitations pose a conflict between two constitutional rights: the First Amendment press-freedom guarantee and the litigants' right to a fair trial, protected by the Sixth Amendment.

The Supreme Court has tried to balance these rights. After a mid-century trial accompanied by a media frenzy, the Court granted a writ of habeas corpus sought by a doctor who had allegedly killed his wife, on the grounds that the publicity prevented him from receiving a fair trial (*Sheppard v. Maxwell*, 384 U.S. 333, 1969). In the wake of the *Sheppard* case, many states adopted rules to limit extrajudicial statements by lawyers. The Court considered a First Amendment challenge to one of these rules and concluded in a divided decision that many existing rules were unconstitutionally vague (*Gentile v. State Bar of Nevada*, 501 U.S. 1030, 1991). The rule in effect in most jurisdictions now prohibits a lawyer from making an extrajudicial statement that will have a "substantial likelihood of materially prejudicing an adjudicative proceeding."

W. BRADLEY WENDEL

References and Further Reading

Cole, Kevin, and Fred Zacharias, People v. Simpson: *The Agony of Victory and the Ethics of Lawyer Speech*, Southern California Law Review 69 (1996): 1627–1678.

Cases and Statutes Cited

Gentile v. State Bar of Nevada, 501 U.S. 1030 (1991)
Sheppard v. Maxwell, 384 U.S. 333 (1969)
ABA Model Rules of Professional Conduct, Rule 3.6 (2002)

See also **Cameras in the Courtroom; Due Process; Gag Orders in Judicial Proceedings; *Gentile v. State Bar of Nevada*, 501 U.S. 1030 (1991); Right of Access to Criminal Trials; Rights of the Accused**

DISCIPLINING PUBLIC EMPLOYEES FOR EXPRESSIVE ACTIVITY

A public employee's right to free speech under the First Amendment is not unlimited and employers have the right to discipline employees for expressive activity under certain circumstances (*Pickering v. Board of Education*, 391 U.S. 563, 1968). The employer has an interest in ensuring that its employees do not undermine its operations or interfere with accomplishment of its objectives. At the same time, employees do not give up their constitutional rights when they accept government employment. Indeed, government employees may play a particularly important role in enlightening the public about governmental operations by contributing to public debate and alerting the public about potential wrongdoing. Thus, the courts have developed a test for determining when public employers can discipline their employees for expressive activity.

The threshold requirement for protected speech is that it must relate to a matter of public concern. If speech relates to an employee's private grievance, discipline based on the speech does not implicate the First Amendment. (For further information, see Matters of Public Concern Standard in Free Speech Cases.) In addition, even if the speech addresses matters of public concern, when the employee's speech rights are outweighed by the disruption that the speech causes to the operations of government, the employer can discipline the employee for speech. The more central the speech is to matters of concern to the public, the more disruptive to government operations it must be in order to justify discipline. The impact of the speech on discipline, working relationships, work performance, and government operations is a significant consideration in weighing the government's interests

(*Rankin v. McPherson*, 483 U.S. 378, 1987). In the 2005 term (*Garcetti v. Ceballos*, 361 F.3d. 1168, 9th Cir. 2004, cert. granted, 125 S. Ct. 1395, 2005), the Supreme Court had to decide whether an employee who brings to light suspected wrongdoing in speech required by job duties is protected from discipline, thus further refining the balancing test.

In some cases, the government disputes that discipline was motivated by the employee's protected speech, asserting a lawful basis for the discipline. To prevail on a constitutional claim, the employee must prove that the protected speech was a motivating factor in the employer's decision to discipline (*Mt. Healthy City School District Board of Education v. Doyle*, 429 U.S. 274, 1977). The employee must show that the person who made the decision was aware of the speech. In addition, proof of actual motivation is necessary; this can involve evidence such as the timing of the discipline in relation to the speech, employer unhappiness with the speech, or the pretextual nature of the employer's asserted reason for the discipline. If the employee proves that the speech motivated the employer, the employer can avoid liability by showing that it would have disciplined the employee for legitimate reasons even if the employee had not engaged in the protected speech. When there is disagreement about what the employee actually said, the employer may rely on what it reasonably and in good faith believes was said in deciding whether to discipline the employee (*Waters v. Churchill*, 511 U.S. 661, 1994). To ensure that it acts reasonably, the wise employer will investigate prior to discipline when employee statements may have First Amendment protection.

ANN C. HODGES

References and Further Reading

Deskbook Encyclopedia of Public Employment Law, Malvern, PA: Center for Education and Employment Law, 2005.

Hudson, David L., Jr. *Balancing Act: Public Employees and Free Speech*, First Amendment Center, 2002.

Smolla, Rodney A. *Smolla and Nimmer on Freedom of Speech*, vol. 2, Eagan, MN: Thomson/West, 2005.

Cases and Statutes Cited

Garcetti v. Ceballos, 361 F.3d. 1168 (9th Cir. 2004), *cert. granted*, 125 S. Ct. 1395 (2005)

Mt. Healthy City School District Board of Education v. Doyle, 429 U.S. 274 (1977)

Pickering v. Board of Education, 391 U.S. 563 (1968)

Rankin v. McPherson, 483 U.S. 378 (1987)

Waters v. Churchill, 511 U.S. 661 (1994)

See also **Matters of Public Concern Standard in Free Speech Cases; Mt. Healthy City School District Board of Education v. Doyle, 429 U.S. 274 (1977); Pickering v. Board of Education, 391 U.S. 563 (1968); Rankin v. McPherson, 483 U.S. 378 (1987); Speech of Government Employees**

DISCOVERY MATERIALS IN COURT PROCEEDINGS

In civil as well as criminal court proceedings, discovery serves as a tool whereby all parties to an action can discover, before a trial on the matter's merits, precisely what evidence will be offered at the trial. The discovery process provides each party to an action the opportunity to examine the evidence that will be used against them as well as to find or discover the evidence to be used in their favor. The rules of procedure place few limits on the kinds of evidence subject to discovery, whereas the rules of evidence place significant limits on the admissibility of discovered evidence at trial. For example, a deposition transcript may be used, in whole or in part, but only pursuant to the applicable rules of evidence governing admissibility and the applicable rules of procedure that set out particular conditions precedent to their use.

Because the facts conceded in a party's responses to requests for admission are not subject to dispute at trial, these responses are commonly used for document authentication, for impeachment purposes, or as proof of the existence or nonexistence of an element of a claim. Physical examinations can be used to prove the extent of a party's injuries. Expert witnesses may be called to give their conclusions or opinions regarding information, likely obtained through discovery, provided to them before trial. In court proceedings, discovery is an equalizer, arming all parties to an action access to the same information before it is presented to the trier of fact.

KATHRYN H. CHRISTOPHER

References and Further Reading

Federal Rules of Civil Procedure. St. Paul, MN: Thompson/West, 2005.

Federal Rules of Criminal Procedure. St. Paul, MN: Thompson/West, 2005.

Federal Rules of Evidence. St. Paul, MN: Thompson/West, 2005.

Friedenthal, Jack H., Mary Kay Kane, and Arthur R. Miller. *Civil Procedure*, 4th ed. St. Paul, MN: Thompson/West, 2005.

Giannelli, Paul C. *Understanding Evidence*. New York: Matthew Bender & Company, Inc., 2003.

Imwinkelried, Edward J. *Evidentiary Foundations*, 5th ed. New York: Matthew Bender & Company, Inc., 2002.

Park, Roger C., David P. Leonard, and Steven H. Goldberg. *Evidence Law: A Student's Guide to the Law of Evidence as Applied in American Trials*. St. Paul, MN: West Group, 1998.

Shreve, Gene R., and Peter Raven–Hansen. *Understanding Civil Procedure*, 3rd ed. New York: Matthew Bender & Company, Inc., 2002.

DISCRIMINATION BY RELIGIOUS ENTITIES THAT RECEIVE GOVERNMENT FUNDS

Religious entities currently receive government funds in a variety of ways and for a variety of purposes. Increasingly, the government is turning to nongovernmental entities—including religious and secular nonprofit organizations—to provide the sorts of services that the government used to provide directly. As a result, religious groups presently receive funds from state and federal governments to provide all kinds of social services, from elementary education to drug rehabilitation. In fact, under the federal programs begun in 1996 known generally as "charitable choice," religious groups have the right to participate in various funding opportunities on the same terms as secular organizations.

This raises a number of political and constitutional issues. First is the straightforward issue of whether such funding is constitutionally permissible. Much of the Supreme Court's Establishment Clause jurisprudence over the last fifty years has centered on whether (and to what extent) religious entities can receive government funds. Yet, its decisions in cases like *Mitchell v. Helms*, 530 U.S. 793 (2000), and *Zelman v. Simmons–Harris*, 536 U.S. 639 (2002), seem to suggest that as long as religious groups are not privileged over competing secular groups, they can constitutionally receive government funds to do social-service work.

Aside from the issue of funding is another difficult one, which is just as contentious and even more complicated. This issue is one of discrimination. It is widely accepted that the government cannot discriminate on the basis of religion when hiring employees. The Constitution's Equal Protection and Free Exercise Clauses require this. Yet, it is just as widely accepted that religious groups should have the right to so discriminate. This, too, is seen as a matter of free exercise. Accordingly, religious organizations are exempt from the Title VII statute, which generally forbids businesses from discriminating against employees on the basis of religion. Charitable choice thus creates a problem by crossing up these two competing intuitions. What should happen when religious groups receive government funds in programs like charitable choice? Should they continue to enjoy the right to select staff along religious lines? Should they, like governmental actors, be barred from engaging in this sort of discrimination?

This question is one on which people vehemently disagree. Both sides have good points to make. On one hand, allowing religious organizations to keep their Title VII exemption is, in a sense, to allow government-funded discrimination. It means that workers in publicly funded positions (performing what had until recently been government work) can be terminated solely because of their religious beliefs. While it may be fine for religious groups to prefer coreligionists in their own affairs, surely the government—under the Equal Protection and Establishment Clauses—must ensure that when it acts, all of its citizens are treated equally. Moreover, given that religious groups are the only groups that have the right to staff religiously, they are being unfairly privileged over secular organizations, perhaps in violation of the Establishment Clause.

Yet, those who defend religious staffing in charitable choice have their arguments as well. They point to the fact that religious staffing has always been a prerogative of religious organizations, and for good reason. In a diverse country, religious staffing is what enables a group to maintain a religious identity; it is part and parcel of their right under the Free Exercise Clause to practice their religion. Without a right to hire along religious lines, a Jewish social-justice organization might well become Jewish in name only. To tell a religious group that it can have government funds only if it gives up its right to staff religiously, supporters argue, would be essentially to bribe them out of their religious identity—a quintessential violation of the unconstitutional-conditions doctrine.

How this debate will be resolved is far from clear. As for current practice, the law is mixed. Title VII exempts religious groups without regard to whether they are receiving government funds. As a result, the general rule is that religious organizations can discriminate along religious lines. Yet there are exceptions to this rule. In some programs (like the AmeriCorps VISTA program, for example), special federal contracting rules require all parties contracting with the government (including religious ones) to pledge that they will not discriminate on the basis of religion. States and cities sometimes have quite similar rules for their contracting partners. In such cases, the default rule is reversed and religious organizations must give up their religious staffing rights to receive government funds. There is no doubt, however, that this issue is of increasing importance in the charitable-choice debate. Indeed, battles over this discrimination issue have been a central impediment to legislative proposals to expand charitable choice, principally because those working against charitable choice have made it the fulcrum of their attack. How the foregoing issues will play out in the Congress and the courts is perhaps impossible to predict.

As a concluding note, it is important to keep in mind that this discussion has only been concerned with discriminations on the basis of religion. Title VI of the *Civil Rights Act* of 1964 prohibits all organizations that receive federal funds, religious and secular alike, from discriminating in employment on the basis of race, color, or national origin. (As those defending religious staffing like to note, Title VI does not list religion as a protected characteristic.) No federal law currently prohibits employment discrimination on the basis of sexual orientation, so religious and secular organizations are entitled to discriminate on that basis with the use of federal funds. Lastly, it is worth noting that, while they protect the right of religious groups to discriminate on the basis of religion in hiring, charitable-choice provisions do not permit religious groups to discriminate among *beneficiaries* on the basis of religion. Under current federal law, that sort of religious discrimination is flatly condemned, although some worry that it may exist in practice.

CHRISTOPHER C. LUND

References and Further Reading

Esbeck, Carl H., Stanley W. Carlson–Thies, and Ronald J. Sider. *The Freedom of Faith-Based Organizations to Staff on a Religious Basis.* Washington, DC: Center for Public Justice, 2004.
Green, Steven K., *Religious Discrimination, Public Finding, and Constitutional Values*, Hastings Constitutional Law Quarterly 30 (2003): 1:1–55.
Laycock, Douglas, *The Underlying Unity of Separation and Neutrality*, Emory Law Journal 46 (1997): 1:43–74.
Lund, Christopher C., *Of Government Funding, Religious Institutions, and Neutrality*, Tulsa Law Review 40 (2004): 2:321–342.
Lupu, Ira C., and Robert W. Tuttle. *Government Relationships With Faith-Based Providers: The State of the Law.* Albany, NY: Roundtable on Religion and Social Welfare Policy, 2002.
Saperstein, David, *Public Accountability and Faith-Based Organizations: A Problem Best Avoided*, Harvard Law Review 116 (2003): 6:1353–1396.

Cases and Statutes Cited

Mitchell v. Helms, 530 U.S. 793 (2000)
Zelman v. Simmons–Harris, 536 U.S. 639 (2002)
42 U.S.C. § 2000e (Title VII)
42 U.S.C. § 604a (Charitable Choice)

See also **Accommodation of Religion; Charitable Choice; Equal Protection Clause and Religious Freedom; Establishment Clause Doctrine: Supreme Court Jurisprudence; Establishment of Religion and Free Exercise Clause; Free Exercise Clause Doctrine: Supreme Court Jurisprudence; *Mitchell v. Helms*, 463 U.S. 793 (2000); Religion in "Public Square" Debate; Religious Freedom Restoration Act; School Vouchers; State Action Doctrine; State Aid to Religious Schools; State Regulation of Religious Schools; Tax Exemptions for Religious Groups and Clergy; Title VII and Religious Exemptions; Unconstitutional Conditions; *Zelman v. Simmons–Harris*, 536 U.S. 639 (2002)**

DISCRIMINATORY PROSECUTION

In deciding whom to prosecute, prosecutors may not deliberately use impermissible arbitrary criteria, such as race, religion, national origin, or the exercise of protected statutory or constitutional rights. This discriminatory prosecution violates the defendant's equal protection rights under the Fourteenth Amendment or as incorporated through the Due Process Clause of the Fifth Amendment if the case is federal. A finding of discriminatory prosecution generally justifies a dismissal of the indictment or conviction unless the state can establish a compelling justification for its selectivity. A discriminatory prosecution claim does not serve as a defense on the merits to the underlying charge; it is simply a constitutional defect in the prosecution rather than a determination of a defendant's innocence or guilt.

Just as the legislative branch is prevented from enacting laws that deny equal protection, so too is the executive branch restrained from enforcing laws in a way that denies equal protection. As the Supreme Court in *Yick Wo v. Hopkins*, 118 U.S. 356 (1886), explained well over a century ago in reference to an administrative agency's actions, "[t]hough the law itself be fair on its face, and impartial in appearance, yet if it is applied and administered by public authority with an evil eye and an unequal hand, so as practically to make unjust and illegal discriminations between persons in similar circumstances, material to their rights, the denial of equal justice is still within the prohibition of the Constitution."

While the foregoing is relatively uncontroversial, the more debatable issue is what elements a defendant must prove to prevail in a claim of discriminatory prosecution and how a defendant can obtain such evidence. Allegations of discriminatory prosecution are very difficult to prove. Courts almost invariably reject defendants' claims.

Discriminatory prosecution claims are judged according to ordinary equal protection standards. In *Wayte v. United States*, 470 U.S. 598 (1985), the Court stated that the defendant must show that the prosecutor's charging decision "had a discriminatory effect and that it was motivated by a discriminatory purpose." Courts have required a burden of proof ranging from a reasonable inference of impermissible discrimination to convincing evidence.

Proof of a discriminatory effect, also referred to as a disparate impact, requires showing that similarly situated people, in an identifiable group other than the defendant's, were not but could have been prosecuted. Obtaining such evidence may be very difficult, especially if the similarly situated people's offenses have not come to the attention of the police, perhaps because they focused their efforts on one group rather than another. Even if a discriminatory effect can be shown, this does not show that the prosecutor purposefully caused or intended such an effect. Defendants must instead produce evidence that they have been intentionally and purposefully singled out for prosecution on the basis of arbitrary or invidious criteria. Put differently, a defendant must show that the prosecutor chose to prosecute because of, rather than in spite of, the defendant's membership in an identifiable group.

Just as it is difficult to prove discriminatory prosecution, it is also difficult for a defendant to obtain discovery of evidence from the prosecution to establish the claim. In *United States v. Armstrong*, 517 U.S. 456 (1996), defendants moved for discovery on their claim that federal "crack" cocaine laws were selectively enforced against blacks. The Supreme Court held that in order to obtain discovery regarding the state's charging practices, a defendant must establish a "colorable basis" for discriminatory effect and discriminatory purpose. To demonstrate discriminatory effect, the defendant must make a "credible showing" that the state could have, but failed, to prosecute similarly situated people of a different race. A defendant cannot simply point at the race of those prosecuted and presume that people of all races commit all types of crimes. A colorable basis refers to evidence tending to show the existence of discriminatory effect and intent. This showing appears to be less onerous than a prima facie case but more difficult than a nonfrivolous showing.

The Supreme Court in *Armstrong* reasoned that restricting a defendant's access to discovery would be a significant barrier to the litigation of insubstantial claims. Requiring a credible showing would serve to balance a state's interest in vigorous law enforcement and a defendant's interest in avoiding selective prosecution. Many legal commentators, however, argue that the defendant's burden is too onerous, primarily because the facts that might show discriminatory prosecution, especially those that might show discriminatory intent, are often exclusively in the prosecutor's possession.

Nonetheless, courts have sound reasons for their highly deferential approach to prosecutors' charging decisions. Because of concerns about separation of powers, courts are reluctant to intrude on a province constitutionally assigned to the executive branch. In addition, prosecutors have special expertise that courts institutionally do not have in assessing the severity of a crime, the probability of a conviction, public opinion, or the deployment of scarce prosecutorial resources. Courts also fear that subjecting a prosecutor's motives and decision-making to outside scrutiny might chill law enforcement, or that a less restrictive approach to discriminatory prosecution claims would unleash an unmanageable number of such claims, resulting in additional long delays and costs in the criminal justice system. Finally, there is the underlying presumption that a prosecutor properly discharges his or her official duties in good faith.

On the other hand, this restrictive approach may eliminate legitimate claims. It may be very difficult for a defendant to prove racial and other forms of discrimination since discrimination is much more subtle than in the past and may even be unconscious. Some empirical studies purport to show that minorities with prior criminal records and convicted of drug offenses who refuse to plead guilty or who are associated with white victims are charged and punished more severely than comparable nonminorities. In addition, if the criminal justice system is perceived as unfair or racist because the courts fail to recognize discriminatory prosecution, then communities may cooperate less with the police, resulting in less effective law enforcement. Because there is rarely a judicial remedy for discriminatory prosecution claims, it remains true that the primary check against prosecutorial abuse is political.

ANTONY PAGE

References and Further Reading

Davis, Angela J., *Prosecution and Race: The Power and Privilege of Discretion*, Fordham Law Review 67 (1998): 13–67.

McAdams, Richard H., *Race and Selective Prosecution: Discovering the Pitfalls of Armstrong*, Chicago Kent Law Review 73 (1998): 605–667.

Poulin, Anne B., *Prosecutorial Discretion and Selective Prosecution: Enforcing Protection After* United States v. Armstrong, American Criminal Law Review 34 (Spring 1997): 1071–1125.

Cases and Statutes Cited

McCleskey v. Kemp, 481 U.S. 2779 (1987)
Oyler v. Boles, 368 U.S. 448 (1962)
United States v. Armstrong, 517 U.S. 456 (1996)

Wayte v. U.S., 470 U.S. 598 (1985)
Yick Wo v. Hopkins, 118 U.S. 356 (1886)

See also **Equal Protection of Law (XIV); Race and Criminal Justice**

DISESTABLISHMENT OF STATE CHURCHES IN THE LATE EIGHTEENTH CENTURY AND EARLY NINETEENTH CENTURY

It is one of the ironies of our constitutional history that at the time the U.S. Constitution was adopted, including its requirement that the newly created federal government refrain from establishing religion, churches established by state law not only were permitted by state constitutions of the time, but also were common (Tarr, 1989). Establishment was accomplished via measures that imposed taxes on citizens to support the officially recognized church, attendance requirements, and religious oaths (McLoughlin, 1971, pp. 767–797; 849–850; 1183). In the years following the ratification of the Constitution, however, a movement to disestablish state churches made rapid progress. The principal driving force behind the drive to disestablish state churches in the late eighteenth and early nineteenth centuries was opposition to paying taxes to support a church other than the one that an individual attended. In addition, the movement's supporters also wished to prevent the civil government from coming between individuals and God and to be free to worship without interference (Tarr, p. 82; Adams and Emmerich, 1989).

State Establishment of Religion

During the time of the nation's founding, states imposed taxes and assessments to pay pastors and religious teachers. In Virginia, the *Bill for Establishing a Provision for Teachers of the Christian Religion*, introduced in 1784, would have continued the pre-Revolution practice of using general taxes to support the state's church (Tarr, 1989, 81–82). Vermont's legislature passed a law in 1783 that established its system of religious taxation (McLoughlin, 1971, 797–798). There, each town by majority vote established a denomination as the town's church, which would then be supported by local taxes (McLoughlin, 798). Citizens who did not want to pay a tax to that church could, through a system of certificates, become exempt from that tax.

Connecticut and Massachusetts also levied taxes for the support of churches and religious schools in the late 1700s, and both provided for some exemptions (McLoughlin, 922–925; 1162; 1205). New Hampshire went further. Its religious taxes were written into its first constitution (McLoughlin, 844–845), under which each town established its religion and assessed taxes on its inhabitants to support the schools and ministries. Unlike other states, however, New Hampshire did not provide for any exemptions for dissenters.

States also used religious oaths to establish a state church. Early constitutions, such as those of New Jersey, Georgia, South Carolina, and New Hampshire, required anyone seeking public office to profess a belief in Christianity and Protestantism (Adams and Emmerich, 1989, 1576). North Carolina and Pennsylvania required citizens to take strict belief oaths before holding public office, and Delaware required "all officeholders to profess belief in the Trinity and the divine inspiration of the Bible" (Adams and Emmerich, pp. 1576–1577). Vermont's 1777 constitution included a loyalty oath, as did Massachusetts' original constitution (McLoughlin, 1971, pp. 797; 1184).

The Disestablishment Movement

The fight over religious taxes sparked the disestablishment movement, and eliminating taxes was the crucial act of disestablishment in many states. The Virginia proposal to use tax revenues to support Christian teachers was so unpopular that, after its defeat, the victors were able to pass Thomas Jefferson's *Bill for Establishing Religious Freedom*, which included the provision that "no man shall be compelled to frequent or *support* any religious worship, place or ministry whatsoever" (Padover, 1943). As early as 1783, Connecticut's legislature began passing laws exempting people from religious taxation (McLoughlin, 1971, 922–923). After support for state churches declined, however, the legislature tightened the exemption requirements in 1790 (McLoughlin, p. 926). These renewed religious requirements—the combination of paying taxes or having to show church membership and attendance—once again fueled opposition. A year later, the strict requirements were repealed, effectively disestablishing the state church in Connecticut (McLoughlin, pp. 937–938).

Massachusetts and New Hampshire took longer to repeal their religious taxes. As late as 1803, New Hampshire courts refused to grant exemptions to dissenters from religious taxes (McLoughlin, 1971, 863–870, citing *Muzzy v. Wilkins*, 1803). Eventually, forcing citizens to pay taxes to religious denominations to which they did not belong led to passage of New Hampshire's Toleration Act of 1819, which ended religious taxation (McLoughlin, pp. 895; 898–902). The end of religious taxes in Massachusetts was finalized in 1833 (McLoughlin, p. 1259) through enactment of the eleventh amendment to the state constitution (McLoughlin, pp. 1205–1206; 1253–1260).

The U.S. Constitution eliminated religious tests for holding federal office (U.S. Const., Art. VI, Cl. 3: "[N]o religious Test shall ever be required as a qualification to any Office or public Trust under the United States."), and states eventually followed the federal lead (Adams and Emmerich, 1989, 1578). The increased role in public affairs by various sects and the growth of religious pluralism led to the elimination of religious tests (Adams and Emmerich, p. 1578–1579; McLoughlin, 1971). "[B]y 1793 Delaware, South Carolina, Georgia, and Vermont had completely removed religious tests from their constitutions" (McLoughlin). The voters of Massachusetts supported abolishing the oath requirement for public office, although this did not occur until 1920 (McLoughlin, pp. 1184–1185). In fact, some religious oath provisions remained in place until 1961, when they were finally struck down when the Supreme Court overturned a Maryland law requiring officeholders to declare their belief in God (see *Torasco v. Watkins*, 367 U.S. 488, 1961).

SAMUEL A. MARCOSSON

References and Further Reading

Adams, Arlin M., and Charles J. Emmerich, *A Heritage of Religious Liberty*, U. Pa. L. Rev. 137 (1989): 1559, 1621–1622.

Borden, Morton. *Jews, Turks, and Infidels*. Chapel Hill: University of North Carolina Press, 1984.

McLoughlin, William G. *New England Dissent 1603–1833*. Cambridge, Mass.: Harvard University Press, 1971.

Padover, Saul K., ed. *The Complete Jefferson: Containing His Major Writings, Published and Unpublished, Except His Letters*. Reprint Services Corp., 1943, 946–947.

Tarr, G. Alan, *Church and State in the States*, Wash. L. Rev. 64 (1989): 73.

DIVERSITY IMMIGRATION PROGRAM

Source and Purpose

Immigration is the act of moving to or settling in another country or region, temporarily or permanently. The Diversity Immigration Program, also popularly known as the "DV lottery program," is a congressionally mandated immigrant visa program administered on an annual basis by the Department of State under the authority of section 203(c) of the Immigration and Nationality Act (INA). More specifically, as amended, section 203 of the act creates a new class of immigrants known as "diversity immigrants." Since 1990, the act makes available 55,000 permanent resident visas annually to persons from countries with low rates of migration to the United States. To qualify, DV visa applicants must comply with simple, but strict, eligibility standards, which require first being chosen by a computer-generated random lottery. The act provides that visas are made available to six geographic regions; however, a greater number of visas go to regions and countries with lower rates of immigration to the United States and no visas go to citizens of countries who have sent more than fifty thousand immigrants to the United States in the past five years. It also limits the number of visas a country may receive to no more than 7 percent in any given year.

History and Events That Led to the DV Program

In its effort to diversify, the legislative history of the Diversity Visa Program is remarkably distinct from previous immigration laws such as the Quota and National Origin Acts of 1921, 1924, and by extension 1952; these overtly discriminated on the basis of national origin in the issuance of immigrant visas to aliens seeking entry to the United States. In 1965, Congress imposed a general prohibition against these forms of discrimination by establishing a seven-category preference system. The passage of the Immigration Act of 1990 was a major overhaul of the 1965 Immigration Nationality Act and therefore consistent with its goals. While It creates new categories of immigrants, it furthers the widely held view of America as a country of immigrants. To be sure, the 1990 act can be traced from a 1981 report issued by a congressional Select Commission on Immigration and Refugee Policy. In that report, the commission recommended three goals upon which Congress could fashion U.S. immigration policy: (1) family reunification; (2) economic growth balanced with the view of protecting the U.S. labor market; and (3) cultural diversity consistent with national unity. These goals served as the basis of the 1990 act; the third served as the foundation for the Diversity Visa Program.

Goals and Actions

Critics decry the 1990 act as simply another bad legislative scheme designed to lure cheap foreign labor. However, advocates and especially President George H. W. Bush sold the 1990 statute as a blend of tradition of family reunification and increased immigration of skilled individuals to meet U.S. economic needs of the 1990s. The act also made several policy changes that are worth noting in contrast to the 1965 statute. For example, the annual allocation of numerically restricted visas was set at two hundred seventy thousand under the 1965 act, but the 1990 law established a flexible worldwide cap based on family, employment, and "diversity" by increasing the total eligible immigration under the new flexible cap. It also provided for unrestricted immigration of certain immediate relatives of U.S. citizens and residents while placing emphasis on employment considerations.

The old preferences for occupation, especially the so-called third and fifth of the 1965 act, placed similar emphasis on employment and immediate families. The new law provides more latitude and flexibility. While it provides for diversity immigrants, it explicitly excludes natives of countries that are oversubscribed. It also requires that prospective immigrants establish that they have at least a high school education or its equivalent with at least two years of work experience in an occupation requiring at least two years of training or experience.

Summarily, the 1990 act increased the total immigration under the overall flexible cap of 675 thousand immigrants beginning in fiscal year 1995, which was preceded by the 700 thousand levels during the years 1992 through 1994. In all, the 675 thousand level consists of 480 thousand family-sponsored individuals, 140 thousand employment-related immigrants, and fifty-five thousand "diversity" immigrants to whom visas are randomly assigned to facilitate the selection of persons from previously underrepresented countries. While the diversity immigration lottery program so far accounts for little more than one-third of the ten-year cumulative increase in permanent immigration, it appears to have had the effect of boosting the employment-related immigration category that was a major objective of the new law. However, critics remain unimpressed and argue that immigration from other parts of the world, such as Africa, is still disproportionately underrepresented under current immigration law.

Impact on Rights and Civil Liberties

An important aspect of the Immigration Act of 1990 is that it repealed the prohibition on politics and policy as grounds for denial of visas to the United States. Specifically, the act revised all grounds for exclusion and deportation by significantly rewriting the political and ideological grounds for exclusion. It ended the ban on communist nonimmigrant visa applicants in effect since 1952 and authorized the attorney general of the United States to revise and establish new nonimmigrant admission categories. The act also authorized the attorney general to grant temporary protected status to undocumented nationals of designated countries subject to armed conflict and natural disasters.

It also created a new subcategory for religious persons seeking immigrant visas under a "special immigrant admission" category. Prior to the 1990 act, religious workers were simply not categorized at all; the new designation limited the number of persons to whom visas are granted under this category. Critics charge that limiting the number of religious workers amounts to the denial of free exercise of religion, but this view has yet to face judicial scrutiny. The act also established a short-term amnesty program to grant legal residence to up to 165 thousand spouses and minor children of immigrants who were granted amnesty under the Immigration Reform and Control Act of 1986 (IRCA).

Summary

From numerical restriction to worldwide flexible cap, the overall impact of the U.S. immigration policy of diversity immigration under the 1990 immigration act has been a marked improvement over previous legislation. Focusing on legal immigration by enabling family-based immigration, the act appears to have had the effect of boosting employment-related immigration—one of its major objectives, as well as increased diversity-based immigration. Certainly, opening new immigration possibilities for immigrants from parts of the world previously underrepresented, oppressed, or fleeing from oppression to be part of the American experience of freedom is central to a new immigration policy. The debate over illegal immigration and perhaps the legalization of those already in the country continues as evidenced by recent congressional debates.

MARC GEORGES PUFONG

References and Further Reading

Bush, George H. W. *Statement on Signing the Immigration Act of 1990*, November 29, 1990. (S. 358, approved November 29, Public Law No. 101-649). http://bushlibrary.tamu.edu/research/papers/1990/90112910.html.

Immigration and Nationality Act Amendment of 1965, Pub. L. No. 89-236, 79 Stat. 911 (codified as amended in scattered sections of 8 U.S.C.).

Immigration Act of November 29, 1990 (104 Statutes at Large 4978).

Pub. L. No. 101-649, §§ 131-162, 104 Stat. 4997-5012 (codified at 8 U.S.C.A. § 1153(c) (2000)).

Select Commission to Study and Evaluate . . . Existing Laws, Policies, and Procedures Governing the Admission of Immigrants and Refugees to the United States. Pub. L. No. 95-412, 92 Stat. 907 (1978).

Select Committee on Immigration and Refugee Policy, 97th Cong., 1st Session, U.S. Immigration Policy and the National Interest XI (Joint Committee, 1981).

Subcommittee on Immigration, Refugee and International Law, House Committee on the Judiciary, 101st Cong, 2nd Session, *Family Unity and Employment Opportunity Immigration Act of 1990* (Amendment in the Nature of a Substitute to the Comm. Print, May 7, 1990).

DNA AND INNOCENCE

DNA—the common abbreviation for deoxyribonucleic acid—is the genetic substance that determines the characteristics of all living things. DNA consists of two long, interlocking molecular chains. The links of these chains are called bases and a portion of these bases is unique to each human being. Only identical twins share the exact same sequence of DNA bases. Consequently, DNA bases hold the key to distinguishing biologically between one human being and another.

At crime scenes, DNA samples can be collected from blood, hair, skin, saliva, and/or semen. These samples can then be compared to the DNA profiles of suspects in the case. In addition, as a result of the federal government establishing an index system called CODIS (Combined DNA Index System), samples of DNA gathered at crime scenes can be compared to DNA profiles stored in state data banks. In the United States, all fifty states have enacted laws to provide for the collection and retention of DNA samples of all individuals convicted of murder and/or sex offenses. Forty-seven states require all violent offenders to submit DNA samples and thirty states actually require "all felons" to provide DNA samples to be stored in CODIS. Currently, CODIS contains information from over six hundred fifty thousand convicts.

Although CODIS was instituted in 1994, DNA evidence has been extremely useful in helping to identify, apprehend, and convict some of the most violent criminals in sexual assault and homicide cases since the mid-1980s. When properly collected, tested, and preserved, DNA provides an accurate means of identifying and eventually convicting individuals who left DNA at the scene of a crime.

However, DNA can also be and has been a viable tool for exonerating the innocent. Every year since 1989, the FBI has reported that, in 25 percent of the sexual assault cases that they handled, the primary suspects were excluded by forensic DNA testing. To date, there have been at least 150 cases in which DNA technology has been used to eliminate suspects who were charged with serious crimes that they did not commit or to exculpate individuals who were wrongfully convicted.

Approximately fifty nonprofit legal clinics in the United States now utilize DNA technology to help establish the innocence of their clients. Many of these clinics, referred to as "innocence projects," are housed at universities where students of law, journalism, and/or forensics work together under the supervision of attorneys to establish evidence that will exonerate wrongfully convicted individuals.

These innocence projects make use of state statutes that allow defendants to access DNA testing in order to prove their innocence. Thirty-eight states have now enacted postconviction state statutes related to DNA testing. Most state statutes, however, are limited in scope. For example, in many jurisdictions, DNA testing is limited to defendants who have claimed innocence at trial. Consequently, defendants who plead guilty in state courts are prohibited from accessing DNA testing. Thirty-three states also deny access to DNA testing if the defendant fails to request testing within six months of being found guilty.

Like state prisoners, federal prisoners are also allowed access to DNA testing if they assert their innocence. Under the Innocence Protection Act (which took effect on October 30, 2004), a federal criminal defendant may obtain DNA testing by filing a motion on or before October 2009 or within three years of being convicted.

In addition to establishing rules and procedures to govern DNA testing of federal prisoners, the Innocence Protection Act also provides funding to state governments to review systematically all death penalty cases in which DNA testing may be appropriate. The law does not, however, compel states to develop postconviction DNA testing and procedures equal to the federal guidelines. Consequently, many state criminal defendants can and will be denied access to DNA testing.

One of the simplest ways in which defendants are denied access to DNA testing is when prosecutors and state officials, under political pressure to reduce crime, destroy physical evidence as soon as the appeals process is exhausted. In destroying the evidence, these officials destroy the possibility of a defendant's access to DNA testing. More stringent state laws governing the retention of physical evidence in criminal cases could help resolve this problem and thereby guarantee greater access to justice for the wrongfully accused and convicted. Technology is always advancing, so often physical evidence can be subjected to new DNA tests that had not previously existed. This new technology could be the key to freedom for some individuals. But without the physical evidence to test, no such hope of freedom exists.

In the event that exculpatory DNA evidence is obtained, a new trial will generally be granted. In some instances, however, exculpatory DNA has not resulted in the granting of a new trial. For example, when Joseph O'Dell presented a Virginia court with exculpatory DNA evidence, the court indicated that the evidence did not matter and O'Dell was subsequently executed. Unfortunately, courts in other jurisdictions have also concluded that newly discovered exculpatory DNA evidence does not necessarily mandate a new trial. Thus, although DNA testing has the potential to exonerate the innocent, it is not always procedurally embraced by the justice system.

In other instances, the potential of DNA to exonerate the innocent is mismanaged as a result of poor testing procedures. For example, the Pennsylvania State Crime Lab discovered that one of its scientists had performed shoddy DNA testing. They were consequently forced to schedule the retesting of 615 cases. The New Jersey State Crime Lab discovered that its scientists had failed to control for contamination of DNA samples and they subsequently reopened 102 cases for retesting. Similarly, the manager of the DNA Unit at the Oklahoma City Police Department Crime Lab was fired because of flawed analysis. It was disclosed that none of the scientists who worked in the DNA section of the Houston Police Department Crime Lab was qualified by education or training to do his or her job. As a result of this discovery, evidence in 378 cases had to be redone.

In 2005, another DNA scandal was brought in to public light. It was revealed that a Virginia State Crime Lab senior analyst responsible for conducting DNA tests in capital cases had made significant mistakes in DNA testing. As a result of this, 160 cases had to be re-examined. The mistakes committed by this analyst came to light after it was discovered that a DNA test that clearly supported the innocence claims of Earl Washington, Jr., a death row inmate, had been ignored. According to an audit report of the Virginia State Crime Lab, not only did the laboratory's leading DNA analyst generate erroneous test results in a capital case, but also the laboratory's system of retesting samples to catch these errors completely failed. The external audit of the Virginia State Crime Lab (allegedly the best DNA lab in the country) provided proof that crime labs should not be allowed to police themselves. Considering the professional relationship between crime labs and police departments, it is not surprising that a pro-prosecution bias sometimes exists and blinds individuals to the reality of exculpatory DNA evidence. If, however, DNA testing is to be used in the pursuit of justice, expert oversight of state police crime labs may be necessary to address this problem.

Despite the challenges that DNA testing presents, it is clear that DNA has the potential to provide reliable evidence of guilt as well as innocence. If the United States, as a society, is to realize this potential fully, management of and access to DNA testing must be improved and eventually perfected.

JUDITH A. M. SCULLY

References and Further Reading

Bureau of Justice Statistics, U.S. Department of Justice. *Survey of DNA Crime Laboratories*, 2001.
"The Case for Innocence." *Frontline*, www.pbs.org, aired January, 2000; updated October 2000.
"Convicted by Juries, Exonerated by Science: Case Studies in the Use of DNA Evidence to Establish Innocence After Trial," The National Institute of Justice Research Report, 1996. www.ncjrs.org/pdffiles/dnaevid.pdf.
Edds, Margaret. *An Expendable Man: The Near Execution of Earl Washington Jr.* New York: New York University Press, 2004.
Evans, Colin. *The Casebook of Forensic Detection.* New York: John Wiley, 1996.
Kurtis, Bill. *The Death Penalty on Trial: Crisis in American Justice.* Public Affairs Publisher, 2004.
National Commission on the Future of DNA Evidence, www.ojp.usdoj.gov/nij/topics/forensics/dna/commission/.
National Institute of Justice. "Postconviction DNA Testing: Recommendations for Handling Requests." September 1999, available at ncjrs.org/pdffiles1/nij/177626.pdf.
Scheck, Barry, and Peter Neufeld. "DNA and Innocence Scholarship." In *Wrongly Convicted: Perspectives on Failed Justice*, Saundra D. Westervelt and John Humphrey, eds. New Brunswick, NJ: Rutgers University Press, 2001.
Scheck, Barry, Peter Neufeld, and Jim Dwyer. *Actual Innocence.* New York: Random House, 2000.
Swedlow, Kathy, *Don't Believe Everything You Read: A Review of Modern Post Conviction DNA Testing Statutes*, Cal. W. L. Rev. 38 (Spring 2002): 355.
Urs, Lori. "*Commonwealth v. Joseph O'Dell*: Truth and Justice or Confuse the Courts? The DNA Controversy." *New England Journal on Criminal and Civil Confinement* (Winter 1999): 25.
Wambaugh, Joseph. *The Blooding.* New York: Bantam, 1989.

DNA TESTING

Deoxyribonucleic acid, or DNA, is the genetic information contained within the nucleus of cells. It is found in all living cells in the body and determines how the body grows and develops; it is essentially a recipe book for life. DNA controls inherited characteristics, such as the color of one's eyes and hair. DNA is made up of many millions of pieces of discrete information and their exact combination in any person is unique except for identical twins, who share the same DNA. DNA testing, sometimes called DNA profiling or fingerprinting, does not examine a person's entire DNA; instead, it focuses on a few highly variable components of the genetic code. This means that a DNA test gives a probability that two samples with the same genetic components come from the same person, a related person, or an unrelated person.

The techniques behind DNA testing were first developed in the United Kingdom by Sir Alec Jeffreys at the University of Leicester in 1984. Professor Jeffreys was a microbiologist studying inherited genetic variations between people. While he was examining the human myoglobin gene, he noticed what he called a "minisatellite"—a small sequence of DNA that was repeated many times and was theoretically open to a number of slight variations due to mutation and replication. By using these minisatellites as landmarks, Jeffreys was able to find and analyze systematically the differences in people's DNA.

Collection of DNA Evidence

DNA evidence can be recovered from a wide variety of cells and is very easily left behind at a crime scene. It can be recovered from buccal cells found in saliva, from semen, blood, or even from hair follicles. DNA can also be preserved for a long time, and some tests have been performed on remains that are hundreds of years old. The collection of DNA for testing can be a painless and comparatively nonintrusive process using a mouth swab or a hair, but most states in the USA require a blood sample to be drawn.

DNA Testing in the Courtroom

The world's first use of DNA testing in court was in a British immigration case in 1985 to determine the identity of a young boy. The boy in question had been born in the United Kingdom and was the son of British citizens of Ghanaian extraction. He traveled to Ghana and, upon his return, his passport

was rejected as a possible forgery. The courts had to determine whether he was the boy in the passport or some other relative from Ghana. The family's lawyer asked Jeffreys for help and he was able to develop a genetic "fingerprint" that proved the boy was who his family said he was. Testing is frequently used in this way to determine paternity in cases where that is disputed.

The world's first application of DNA profiling in a criminal case also took place in the United Kingdom, in 1986. In that case two young girls had been raped and murdered three years apart, but the cases were similar enough that police suspected that they were victims of the same man. The police arrested someone who confessed to the second murder, but not the first, and asked Jeffreys to compare forensic evidence gathered from the two cases with those of the man in custody. The DNA profile showed that the same man was responsible for both murders, but that the man who had confessed was not that person. The police collected DNA samples from over five thousand local men and ultimately used the DNA evidence in the successful prosecution of the murderer, who tried to avoid detection by sending a friend to give a DNA sample in his place. DNA profiling first appeared in a courtroom in the United States in *State of Florida v. Tommy Lee Andrews*, 533 So. 2d 841 (Fla. Dist Ct. App 1988), and helped to convict Andrews of rape.

DNA Dragnets

As its name suggests, a DNA dragnet involves requesting a DNA sample from a large number of people in the hopes of obtaining a sample that matches one recovered from a crime scene. If the sample does not match, the police can eliminate that person from their inquiries, though police can become suspicious if a person refuses to give a sample. There is usually some attempt to target a particular subsection of the public—for example, local males within a particular age range and/or of a particular race—but this still encompasses a great many people.

In the United States a DNA dragnet can be particularly controversial because it is generally held that the Fourth Amendment protects one from "mass suspicionless searches" (*Veronia School Dist. v. Acton*, 94-590, 515 U.S. 646, 1995). Moreover, the idea that refusing to give a DNA sample might make the police more suspicious seems to defeat the spirit of the law's presumption of innocence. Problems can also arise depending upon the manner of the police in collecting samples. There have been a number of instances in the

United States where DNA dragnets have been used, and people have subsequently complained that the police pressured them into giving samples and did not make it seem like a voluntary process. These problems have been exacerbated in cases in which a racial group was the target of a dragnet, leading to charges of racism in the execution of the dragnet.

Perhaps the greatest potential concern with DNA dragnets relates to the police use of the sample. Will it be compared only to the sample from the crime that sparked the dragnet or will it also be compared against samples recovered from other, unrelated crime scenes? Once the sample shows that the person is not connected to this crime, will the sample be destroyed or saved for future use and entered into the DNA database? Most jurisdictions now guarantee that a sample given in a dragnet will be returned or destroyed, along with any record of the DNA profile after it has been compared to the evidence and found not to be a match.

DNA Databases

Police forces rapidly understood the potential for DNA testing to be a powerful tool for law enforcement. As the techniques to analyze DNA became more sophisticated, faster, and cheaper, the possibility of creating a DNA database modeled after long established fingerprint databases grew to a reality. DNA samples recovered from a crime scene could be compared against a permanent record of known DNA samples. This created the possibility of suspects being positively identified many years after the offense took place, thus helping to solve so-called cold cases. A standardized repository for DNA evidence would also allow police in different jurisdictions to link crimes committed by the same person. The United Kingdom became the first country in the world to create a national DNA database in 1995. In the United States the Federal Bureau of Investigation's National DNA Index System became operational in 1998.

Collecting Samples for the DNA Database

Most jurisdictions now have laws mandating DNA testing and entry into a DNA database. Some limit this to those convicted of crimes such as murder and rape, but the trend has been to expand the range of offenses covered to all felonies, with the aim of constructing a database containing DNA samples from all the "active criminals" within that jurisdiction. Some protest against this as a violation of privacy, but the generally accepted position is that, when one commits a crime, one loses some rights and the collection of DNA from convicted criminals to construct a database is now almost universally accepted.

One problem common during the initial stages of setting up a DNA database and requiring DNA samples to be given was whether such measures could be applied retroactively. Should those already convicted and serving time in prison be required to give samples? Should those released on parole be required to give a DNA sample? While there is still no definitive pronouncement on these matters in the United States, the consensus is that DNA samples can be taken from prisoners, even if their offenses took place before the enabling legislation, and from those convicted afterwards. It can also be a condition of parole to provide a DNA sample, though opinion is divided on the question of whether those already given parole could be forced to give samples if that was not a requirement of their parole, and some jurisdictions have allowed this.

Problems with DNA Databases

Unlike fingerprints, DNA samples contain information that reveals something about the private life of the subject. This raises extra concerns regarding how this information is used.

DNA samples can reveal whether the person has genetic disorders or propensities towards medical conditions that have not yet manifested. This could place the state in a position in which it knows more about the health of the subject than the subject does. Subjects could even find out information about their health from the state that they would rather not have known. This also raises concerns about access to this information, particularly by private companies providing services such as insurance.

One of the biggest differences between the information in fingerprints and DNA tests is whose privacy interests are at stake. Fingerprints are thought to be unique, unrelated to other physical characteristics, and devoid of familial connection. DNA, on the other hand, can be very similar between blood relations. Criminals forfeit some of their privacy when they are convicted of a crime and must submit fingerprints and DNA samples to aid future identification. Their family members have not been convicted of anything, but the state will gain substantial information about them through the sample. In 2004, the United Kingdom saw the world's first conviction based upon familial DNA in the National DNA Database. Evidence recovered from the scene was almost identical to a sample in the database and police traced the family tree until they found the person responsible. As DNA databases grow in size, such convictions will become more likely in the future, leading some to question whether it is ethical to store and trace DNA information in this way.

Cross-Jurisdictional Issues for DNA Databases

There are concerns about who can have access to a DNA database, especially across jurisdictional boundaries and when one jurisdiction has different standards for collecting and maintaining evidence. For example, one jurisdiction might require samples taken from someone arrested but not convicted of a crime to be destroyed, but another might retain that sample. As the technical sophistication of databases increases and information is shared more across jurisdictions, the problems of differing sensitivities to the privacy considerations will come to the fore, as will the ethical use of information from one jurisdiction that would have been destroyed or never collected in another.

Implications of the Use of DNA Testing

As DNA testing is becoming more sophisticated and the relationship between genes is better understood, the range of information one can glean from a DNA is growing. DNA can provide information on gender, race, and eye color that could be used in conjunction with traditional policing techniques to link a particular person with a DNA sample. This raises the possibility of increasingly sophisticated DNA "photofits" of the person being sought.

While the extent to which our genetic makeup determines us as individuals is unknown, there is the suggestion that one day everything from eyesight to left handedness to sexual orientation could be revealed by DNA testing. The sheer range and wealth of information might force a re-examination of the ways with which DNA testing is dealt.

The potential to use DNA evidence to link people conclusively to crimes committed decades earlier can have a far reaching impact on the calculus to determine the statute of limitations on crimes, especially of a sexual nature. This capacity has led to pressure to extend the timeframe to prosecute in the knowledge

that, while witnesses' memories may deteriorate over time, forensic evidence, if properly tested and stored, can provide reliable evidence for many years to come.

DNA and Innocence

DNA can also be and has been used to show that through a miscarriage of justice, an innocent person has been convicted of an offense. This is troubling for any justice system and all the more so when the person was convicted of a capital crime. The availability of DNA evidence has prompted changes to allow new appeals based on DNA evidence.

GAVIN J. REDDICK

References and Further Reading

Laurie, Graeme. *Genetic Privacy: A Challenge to Medico-Legal Norms.* New York: Cambridge University Press, 2002.
Lazer, David. *DNA and the Criminal Justice System: The Technology of Justice.* Boston: MIT Press, 2004.
National Conference of State Legislatures. "DNA and Crime," http://www.ncsl.org/programs/health/genetics/dna.htm.
National Criminal Justice Reference Service. "What Every Law Enforcement Officer Should Know About DNA Evidence," http://www.ncjrs.org/nij/DNAbro/intro.html.
Rothstein, Mark A., ed. *Genetic Secrets: Protecting Privacy and Confidentiality in the Genetic Era.* New Haven, CT: Yale University Press, 1999.
Tutton, Richard, and Oonagh Corrigan, eds. *Genetic Databases: Socio-ethical Issues in the Collection and Use of DNA.* New York: Routledge, 2004.

Cases and Statutes Cited

State v Andrews, 533 So. 2d 841 (Fla. Dist Ct. App 1988)
Vernonia Sch. Dist. 47J v. Acton, (94-590), 515 U.S. 646 (1995)

See also **Capital Punishment and Right of Appeal; Cloning; Duty to Obey Court Orders; Right of Privacy; Search (General Definition); Search Warrants; State Constitution, Privacy Provisions**

DOE v. BOLTON, 410 U.S. 179 (1973)

In the 1960s, there was a marked change in attitude among physicians and attorneys toward abortion, which since the late nineteenth century had been a crime in most states except when performed to save the life of the mother. The American Medical Association and the American Bar Association advocated a more liberal approach to the interests of women in terminating unwanted pregnancies. In 1962, the American Law Institute (ALI) included a more tolerant abortion statute in its Model Penal Code. Approximately one-fourth of the states, including Georgia, enacted new abortion laws modeled after the ALI draft. In *Doe v. Bolton*, the Supreme Court ruled that the relatively enlightened Georgia abortion law was inconsistent with a woman's right to end her pregnancy as delineated in the companion case decided the same day—*Roe v. Wade*, 410 U.S. 113 (1973).

Mary Doe, an indigent married Georgia citizen, was denied an abortion after eight weeks of pregnancy for failure to meet any of the conditions in the 1968 Georgia abortion statute. Georgia law prohibited abortion except when continued pregnancy would endanger a pregnant woman's life or injure her health, the fetus would likely be born with a serious defect, or the pregnancy resulted from rape. The law also limited the availability of abortion to Georgia residents and required that abortions be performed in hospitals accredited by the Joint Commission on the Accreditation of Hospitals (JCAH) and be approved by the hospital's abortion committee. The law also demanded that two other physicians concur in the attending physician's judgment that abortion is advisable.

The Supreme Court, in a seven-to-two decision, ruled in favor of the plaintiff, citing its holding in *Roe* that personal liberty as protected by the Due Process Clause of the Fourteenth Amendment includes the decision to terminate a pregnancy. The Court made clear that abortion was a medical procedure to be undertaken at the discretion of the attending physician. The state cannot prevent even late-term abortions if the physician judges that the abortion is necessary to protect the female patient's physical or mental health. In *Doe* the Court interpreted the concept of mental health broadly, allowing the physician to weigh physical, emotional, psychological, familial, and age factors—all of which are relevant to the patient's well-being.

The limitation of abortion to the three conditions specified in the Georgia law violates the rule announced in *Roe* that, during the first trimester, the state cannot place any restraints on a woman's right to terminate her pregnancy for whatever reason. The Court found each of the procedural requirements unduly burdensome as well. The state cannot require that abortions be performed in a hospital, that abortions be approved by a hospital committee, or that two additional physicians concur in the abortion decision. These limitations interfere with the attending physician's exercise of his or her professional judgment. The Court struck down the residency requirement on the grounds that the Privileges and Immunities Clause of Article IV, section 2, protects persons who enter a state seeking medical services, including abortion.

The broad definition of health in *Doe* ensured that pregnant women would be able to exercise their constitutional right to abortion throughout each of the three trimesters of pregnancy with minimal interference from the state.

KENNETH M. HOLLAND

References and Further Reading

Curriden, Mark. "*Doe v. Bolton*: Mary Doe Has a Change of Heart, Pickets Abortion Clinics." *ABA Journal* 75 (1989): 26–27.
Glidewell, Gail, *"Partial Birth" Abortion and The Health Exception: Protecting Maternal Health or Risking Abortion on Demand?* Fordham Urban Law Journal 28 (2001): 1089–1150.
Jipping, Thomas J., *Informed Consent to Abortion: A Refinement*, Case Western Reserve Law Review 38 (1988): 329–386.
Sargent, John D., *Analysis of the United States Supreme Court Decisions Regarding Abortions:* Roe v. Wade, *No. 70-18, and* Doe v. Bolton, *No. 70-40, decided January 22, 1973*. Washington, DC: Congressional Research Service, Library of Congress, 1973.

Cases and Statutes Cited

Roe v. Wade, 410 U.S. 113 (1973)

See also **Abortion; Privileges and Immunities (XIV); *Roe v. Wade*, 410 U.S. 113 (1973)**

DOMESTIC VIOLENCE

Domestic violence is abusive behavior within an individual in an intimate relationship or within family bonds. It includes wife-beating and, more generally, abuse of an intimate partner, whether married or not, and regardless of sexual orientation, child abuse, sibling abuse, and elder abuse. Nonetheless, when discussed, it most often refers to the violence used to control a wife or girlfriend, perhaps because, statistically, abuse of women by their male partners is the most reported and prevalent of family violence. Notwithstanding this understanding, intimate abuse is one of the most underreported crimes in society. Most statutes that address domestic violence include any single act of physical violence. However, most activists and theorists refer to a pattern of abusive conduct by an intimate designed to control his partner. Some scholars estimate that upwards of 50 percent of all women will be victims of battering during their lifetimes.

Control of an intimate is essential in defining the nature of domestic abuse. It is not uncommon for the batterer to blame his victim for his violence. Some of the most dangerous times for a victim of abuse are when she decides to leave her abuser and during pregnancy. During these times, the abuser loses some, if not all, control over the abused and attempts to regain control through force.

History

In early American history, following English common law and ecclesiastical tenets, women were afforded very few rights. Unmarried women were considered to be under the control of their fathers until marriage. Upon marriage, however, women were subject to the marital unity under the doctrine of coverture, which meant that a wife had no legal identity outside her husband. Some of the effects of these rules included women's inability to contract or to own property. The legal doctrine of chastisement had the greatest significance to the perpetuation and sanction of physical violence against women. Sir Henry Blackstone, in discussing the rights and responsibilities of husbands vis-a-vis their wives, said of English common law:

> The husband also (by the old law) might give his wife moderate correction. For, as he is to answer for her misbehaviour, the law thought it reasonable to intrust him with this power of restraining her, by domestic chastisement, in the same moderation that a man is allowed to correct his servants or children.

During the mid-nineteenth century, married women's property acts, granting women the right to own property, were instituted across the United States and roughly accompanied the abandonment of coverture and the repudiation of chastisement. These changes in status, primarily for white women, came at approximately the same time as change in other forms of social status, namely, slavery. In fact, there is evidence that the emancipation of black slaves assisted in the formal repudiation of chastisement. One of the first cases to renounce chastisement, *Fulgham v. State*, 46 Ala. 143 (1871), was as much about ensuring that a male emancipated slave did not feel equal to white males as it was about denouncing physical violence against wives. After citing Judge Blackstone for the proposition that "the authority . . . to chastise" was asserted primarily, if not exclusively, by "the lower rank of the people," the court in *Fulgham* said:

> A rod which may be drawn through the wedding ring is not now deemed necessary to teach the wife her duty and subjection to the husband. The husband is therefore not justified or allowed by law to use such a weapon, or any other, for her moderate correction. The wife is not to be considered as the husband's slave.

Thus, the complexities of societal violence confronted by those in poverty and by people of color became part of the landscape that permitted the political abandonment of wife-beating. Stereotypes of poverty and race, while fueling change for some women, continue even today to impede protection or redress for others.

Repudiation of chastisement altered social condoning of spousal violence in form, but not in substance. That is, after the abandonment of chastisement, courts continued to enforce male privilege of control in the home, even to the extent of tacit acceptance of violent conduct, through deference to family privacy. This deference reinforced norms of violence in the home through the guise of nonintervention by the state.

Modern History

The beginnings of the modern-day battered woman's movement in the mid-1970s are generally attributed to the feminist antirape movement of the 1960s and its existing organizational and political structures. Early strategies of the battered women's movement avoided legal remedies and redress by formal institutions. The law and these institutions were viewed as patriarchal and accommodating to the social structures that permitted intimate violence. Instead, activists established shelters as a means for protection and escape from the abusive relationship and engaged in public awareness campaigns.

In addition to nonlegal means for protection, the movement later began to use the justice system. The focus was to find means of reform that would eliminate, rather than perpetuate, violence in the home. Part of the strategy was to challenge notions of family privacy that denied protection from marital violence.

Activism in domestic violence led to the development of the battered woman syndrome as a judicially recognized description of victim's responses in abusive relationships. Recognition of this syndrome allows an expert to explain to a jury the mental state of a reasonable person in the defendant's situation. This kind of testimony is often necessary to support a defense of self in the context of a murder prosecution.

Recent efforts to reform the legal system and its ability to address domestic violence include no-drop prosecution rules, mandatory arrest, and inclusion in hate crime legislation. Some of these efforts are controversial and are as yet not fully tested for efficacy. Activists' reform efforts, within and outside the legal system, will continue as long as violence within the home exists as a social problem.

Other recent efforts for reform include those within the federal system such as the Violence Against Women Act of 1994, Pub. L. No. 103-322, §§ 40001-40703, 108 Stat. 1902. This legislation includes funding for shelters, encouraging arrest and prosecution, and incentives for prevention through education and support programs. Unfortunately, in *United States v. Morrison*, 529 U.S. 598 (2000), the Supreme Court significantly undercut the ability of this legislation to redefine intimate violence as a public problem rather than merely a matter of private concern. It held that Congress exceeded its authority under the Commerce Clause and section five of the Fourteenth Amendment by creating in the act a federal civil remedy for persons victimized by gender-motivated violence. The Violence Against Women: Civil Rights for Women Act, 42 U.SC.S. § 13981 (2000), was promulgated to allow for a private right of action within the constitutional limits addressed by *Morrison*.

Resistance by activists to using the legal system for redress was not entirely unfounded. Current areas of concern involve ways in which the legal system is turned against battered women. This includes dependency or failure to protect actions by child welfare authorities against the battered woman for conduct by an abusive partner. When child protection may be the ultimate objective, removing a child from a non-abusing parent may nonetheless be detrimental to the child and may punish an individual for conduct not within her control.

Custody matters in family court are also problematic in abusive situations. Abusers often use children as leverage in maintaining control over their partners. Many judges disregard evidence of spousal abuse in considering the best interests of the child. This approach does not take into account the impact on the child in witnessing abuse of one parent by the other. Joint custody arrangements are routinely imposed, allowing the abuser access to his partner through the child and continuation of physical and emotional abuse. This result is gradually lessening as legislatures and judges include abusive behavior as a factor in the best interests analysis.

ZANITA E. FENTON

References and Further Reading

Blackstone, William. *Commentaries*. 444–445.
Dobash, R. Emerson, and Russell Dobash. *Violence Against Wives: A Case Against the Patriarchy*. New York: Free Press, 1979.
Gordon, Linda. *Heroes of Their Own Lives: the Politics and History of Family Violence, Boston 1880–1960*. New York: Viking Press, 1988.
Schechter, Susan. *Women and Male Violence: The Visions and Struggles of the Battered Women's Movement*. Cambridge, Mass.: South End Press, 1982.
Siegel, Reva B., *The Rule of Love: Wife Beating as Prerogative and Privacy*, Yale L. J. 105 (1996): 2117.

Cases and Statutes Cited

Bradley v. State, 1 Miss. 156 (Miss.1824)
Fulgham v. State, 46 Ala. 143 (1871)
State v. Kelly, 97 N.J. 178, 478 A.2d 364 (N.J. 1984)
United States v. Morrison, 529 U.S. 598 (2000)
Wanrow v. State, 88 Wash.2d 221, 559 P.2d 548 (Wash.1977)

See also **Equal Protection of Law (XIV); Marital Rape; Rape: Naming Victim; Sex and Criminal Justice**

DON'T ASK, DON'T TELL

"Don't ask, don't tell" is a shorthand description for policies regulating who can serve in the U.S. armed forces. These policies generally restrict the admission and service of homosexuals in the military. While some form of restriction on military service by these individuals is as old as the nation, today's more restrictive military policies were first adopted during World War II.

The current military policies were enacted into statutory law in 1993. These provisions were implemented as provisions of the National Defense Authorization Act of fiscal year 1994, public law 103-160, and have been codified at 10 U.S.C. sec. 654. This legislation was a reaction to promises made by then presidential candidate Bill Clinton during the 1992 presidential campaign. Clinton had suggested that he would, after taking office, issue an Executive Order that would override the policies of the Department of Defense limiting the service of homosexuals in the military. The candidate's proposal was, at least in part, offered in recognition of the brutal murder that same year of a Navy enlisted man.

Development of a New Policy

The issue of the service of homosexuals in the military received substantial attention during 1993. The first part of the debate came with a report from the General Accounting Office, Congress's primary investigative and accountability agency, with a survey of the military policies and practices of twenty-five other nations.

On July 19, 1993, President Clinton announced a new policy on homosexuals in the military. This new policy consisted of several essential elements: those in the military would be judged on their performance and not their sexual orientation; the practice of not asking or inquiring about sexual orientation during the enlistment procedure would continue; an open statement made by a service member that he or she is a homosexual would create a rebuttable presumption that the individual intends to engage in prohibited conduct; and the provisions of the Uniform Code of Military Justice would be enforced in an even manner regardless of the service member's sexual orientation. The new policy was substantially based on sexual orientation. Yet, the term was not expressly defined.

The new policy announced by the Clinton administration was initially intended to be a "don't ask, don't tell, don't pursue" measure. But the President did not include "don't pursue" in his announcement. The secretary of defense added to the uncertainty about the announced policy when he testified before Congress that individual service members could publicly acknowledge their homosexuality without risking a military criminal investigation, but the individual statements might still be credible grounds for a military criminal investigation.

Many believe that the ambiguities in the newly announced administration policy encouraged Congress to act by including a provision in the 1994 National Defense Authorization Act. This measure was signed into law by the President on November 30, 1993. Section 571 of the public law, now codified at 10 U.S.C. sec. 654, describes homosexuality in the military as an "unacceptable risk to the high standards of morale, good order and discipline, and unit cohesion that are the essence of military capability." The law also codified the grounds on which a service member might be discharged.

On December 22, 1993, the Secretary of Defense announced regulations to implement the provisions of the new statute. These new regulations attempted to balance the statutory prohibition on the service in the armed forces by homosexuals and President Clinton's previously expressed desires. The new regulations provided that no one would be asked questions about his or her sexual orientation upon entering the armed forces. However, homosexual conduct could be grounds for rejecting a military enlistment, appointment, or induction.

In the years following the implementation of the "don't ask, don't tell" policies, records kept by the Department of Defense show that the number of discharges for homosexuality has increased. Data from the Servicemembers Legal Defense Network (SLDN) show that 617 service members were discharged during fiscal year 1994, with the number of discharges rising to 1,273 in 2001. The number of discharges has declined in the following years to 653 in 2004.

The Court's Consideration of Homosexuality in the Military

There have been numerous court challenges to the "don't ask, don't tell" policy since 1993. Most federal district and appeals courts have affirmed the regulations and their application as a necessary part of the military's needs for discipline and good order. However, two U.S. Supreme Court decisions have led to questions about the policy's continued validity.

The U.S. Supreme Court in its 1986 decision in *Bowers v. Hardwick*, 478 U.S. 186 (1986), held that there is no fundamental right to engage in consensual homosexual sodomy. Other federal courts followed this precedent in affirming the discharge of service members for overt homosexual activities. Most of these appellate decisions found that there was a rational relationship between the military's needs for unit cohesion and discipline and the policies adopted restricting homosexuals from serving in the military.

However, in 2003, the Supreme Court in *Lawrence v. Texas*, 539 U.S. 558 (2003), found a Texas statute that prohibited sexual acts between same-sex couples unconstitutional. In this opinion, the Court focused on the liberty interests protected by the Due Process Clause of the Fourteenth Amendment of the Constitution. The *Lawrence* decision holds that this liberty interest in privacy even protects a right for adults to engage in consensual and legal homosexual conduct.

While neither Supreme Court decision directly challenged the military's policies governing the service of homosexuals in the military, the *Lawrence* decision poses a problem for the armed forces. Article 125 of the Uniform Code of Military Justice defines sodomy as a court martial event for which criminal punishment may be imposed. That provision is now called into question by this most recent decision.

An indirect challenge to the "don't ask, don't tell" policies was before the U.S. Supreme Court during its 2005 term. This appeal challenged the right of the federal government to deny federal funds to institutions barring military recruiters from their campuses because of the military's policies regarding the service of homosexuals. A decision is expected in 2006.

JERRY E. STEPHENS

References and Further Reading

Balkin, Jack, and Geoffrey Bateman, eds. *Don't Ask, Don't Tell: Debating the Gay Ban in the Military*. Boulder, CO: Lynne Rienner Publishers, 2003.
Eskridge, William N. *Gaylaw: Challenging the Apartheid of the Closet*. Cambridge, MA: Harvard University Press, 1999.

Cases and Statutes Cited

Bowers v. Hardwick, 478 U.S. 186 (1986)
Lawrence v. Texas, 539 U.S. 558 (2003)
National Defense Authorization Act for Fiscal Year 1994,
  Public Law 103-160, sec. 571, codified at 10 U.S.C.
  sec. 654

DOUBLE JEOPARDY (V): EARLY HISTORY, BACKGROUND, FRAMING

Origins of the Guarantee

The Double Jeopardy Clause of the Fifth Amendment protects a person from being placed twice in jeopardy for the "same offense." While the exact origins of this guarantee against double jeopardy are not known, there can be no doubt that it possesses a long history. Ancient Jewish law contained references to principles encompassed by double jeopardy law; early Greek and early Roman law provided some form of protection against double jeopardy; and a prohibition against double jeopardy, emanating from a reading given to a verse in the Old Testament by Saint Jerome in 391, entered canon law as early as 847.

English Common Law

By the second half of the eighteenth century, the protection against double jeopardy was firmly established in English common law through the pleas of *autrefoits acquit* (a former acquittal), *autrefoits convict* (a former conviction), and pardon. Indeed, in his *Commentaries*, published between 1765 and 1769, William Blackstone, perhaps the most influential writer on the common law, stated that the principle that "no man is to be brought into jeopardy of his life, more than once for the same offense," upon which the pleas are based, constitutes a "universal maxim of the common law."

Various theories have been offered to explain the introduction of the double jeopardy principle into the common law. One theory postulates that it came from the Continent through canon law or through Roman law. Another theory suggests that the twelfth-century power struggle between Thomas à Becket, Archbishop of Canterbury, and King Henry II, which ended in Henry's retreating from his claim that the royal courts could punish clerics after they were convicted of a crime and stripped of their clerical status in

an ecclesiastical court, led to the introduction of the principle. Still another theory claims that the protection against double jeopardy merely evolved over hundreds of years from Anglo–Saxon criminal procedure.

The scope of the common law's protection against double jeopardy in the hundred years following the Norman Conquest in 1066 cannot be ascertained. The available evidence suggests that the earliest rulers paid little heed to questions of double jeopardy. For example, the Charter of Liberties issued by Henry I in 1101 did not contain a protection against double jeopardy, and in 1163, Henry II claimed he could try a cleric for murdering a knight despite the cleric's acquittal of that offense in an ecclesiastical court.

Some cases decided at the beginning of the thirteenth century apparently recognized some protection against double jeopardy, but Magna Carta, which was originally issued by King John in 1215, contained no protection against double jeopardy. It is clear, however, that by the middle of the century the principle against double jeopardy had entered the common law. Nevertheless, its subsequent development and emergence into modern double jeopardy law was slow, perhaps because the power to prosecute for offenses had not yet coalesced in the state. At least since the Norman Conquest, criminal prosecutions could be brought not only by the king, but also by a private person in an action against another individual demanding punishment for the particular wrong the person suffered rather than for the offense against the public. By its very nature, the protection against double jeopardy constitutes a limitation upon the power of the state to prosecute and punish an individual, so the state's gathering of the power to prosecute individuals is a prerequisite to a true double jeopardy situation.

Modern double jeopardy law began to emerge in England in the last half of the seventeenth century. By that time prosecutions by the king had begun replacing private prosecutions as the preferred method of prosecution. In addition, Edward Coke's *Institutes* had been published posthumously in 1641 and 1644. Coke detailed the pleas of *autrefoits acquit*, *autrefoits convict*, and pardon and described the basis for double jeopardy, clarifying the concept and emphasizing its importance. Moreover, during the late 1600s, English courts began dealing with a variety of double jeopardy issues, expanding the protection against double jeopardy considerably. Among other things, the Court of King's Bench held that a prosecutor could not seek a new trial following an acquittal (*The King v. Read*) and that an acquittal in another country barred a subsequent prosecution for the same offense in England (*Rex v. Hutchinson*). It also prohibited the practice frequently engaged in by trial judges of discharging the jury when an acquittal appeared imminent in order to afford the prosecutor the opportunity to bring a stronger case in a new trial (*The King v. Perkins*).

Double Jeopardy Protection in America before the Adoption of the Fifth Amendment

While double jeopardy law continued developing in England during the seventeenth century, it began to take root in the North American colonies. The first colonial enactment containing an express guarantee against double jeopardy appeared in 1641 when the Massachusetts Bay Colony enacted a detailed charter of liberties that served as the model for other colonies and constituted a forerunner of the federal Bill of Rights. The Massachusetts Body of Liberties of 1641 guaranteed that "[n]o man shall be twise sentenced by Civill Justice for one and the same Crime, offense, or Trespasse."

Shortly thereafter, Connecticut, in its Code of 1652, adopted a provision against double jeopardy that it took from the Body of Liberties. In addition, the Fundamental Constitutions of Carolina, a document drafted by John Locke but never adopted, included a clause stating that "[n]o cause shall be twice tried in any one court, upon any reason or pretence whatsoever."

After the Revolutionary War, the former colonies formed the United States of America under the *Articles of Confederation*. The articles, however, contained neither a Bill of Rights nor an express protection against double jeopardy. Most state constitutions at that time also did not contain an express guarantee against double jeopardy. The first state constitution to incorporate a protection against double jeopardy was the New Hampshire Constitution of 1784. It provided that "[n]o subject shall be liable to be tried, after an acquittal, for the same crime or offense." In 1790, Pennsylvania ratified a new constitution containing a clause providing that "[n]o person shall, for the same offense, be twice put in jeopardy of life or limb."

Courts in several of the colonies and, after independence, the states recognized a prohibition against double jeopardy through decisional law. For example, courts in Virginia and New York acknowledged the English common law pleas of a former conviction and a former acquittal. Courts in Connecticut (*Hannaball v. Spalding*, 1 Root 86, Conn. Super. Ct., 1783; *Coit v. Geer*, 1 Kirby 269, Conn. Super. Ct., 1787) and

Pennsylvania (*Respublica v. Shaffer*, 1 Dall. 236, Pa. Ct. Oyer and Terminer, 1788) also recognized a protection against double jeopardy.

The Adoption of the Fifth Amendment Guarantee against Double Jeopardy

As originally adopted, the U.S. Constitution did not contain a bill of rights. Its failure to do so caused great concern among the country's populace and many of its leaders, including Thomas Jefferson. When the First Congress convened in 1789, Representative James Madison sought to rectify this omission by introducing a series of proposed amendments, including all those that ultimately became the Bill of Rights. One of Madison's proposed amendments provided that "[n]o person shall be subject, except in cases of impeachment, to more than one punishment or one trial for the same offense." A select committee of the House of Representatives redrafted the proposal to read: "No person shall be subject, [except] in case of impeachment, to more than one trial or one punishment for the same offense."

During the debates on this proposal in the House, several representatives opposed the provision because they believed its language prohibiting more than one trial for the same offense contradicted established law and would, for instance, prevent a convicted individual from obtaining a new trial if prejudicial error infected the individual's initial trial. One representative, arguing that the objective of a guarantee against double jeopardy is to preclude multiple punishments for a single offense, sought to amend the proposal by striking the words "one trial or," but his proposed amendment was soundly defeated. An attempt to amend the proposal by inserting the words "by any law of the United States" after the words "same offense" also failed. The House subsequently adopted the proposed amendment concerning double jeopardy as submitted by the select committee and sent it and other proposed amendments to the Senate for its concurrence.

The Senate rewrote the proposed amendment on double jeopardy by substituting the phrase "be twice put in jeopardy of life or limb by any public prosecution" for the words "except in case of impeachment, to more than one trial or punishment." It later deleted the words "by any public prosecution" and, after joining the provision with several others, approved it in its current form. The House agreed to the Senate's version, and Congress submitted it to the states (along with other proposed amendments) for ratification.

The states ratified the double jeopardy provision (as well as nearly all the other proposed amendments) in 1791, making it part of the Fifth Amendment.

DAVID S. RUDSTEIN

References and Further Reading

Cogan, Neil H., ed. *The Complete Bill of Rights: The Drafts, Debates, Sources, and Origins*. New York: Oxford University Press, 1997, 297–314.

Friedland, Martin L. *Double Jeopardy*. Oxford, England: Clarendon Press, 1969, 1–16.

Hunter, Jill. "The Development of the Rule Against Double Jeopardy." *Journal of Legal History* 5(1) (1984):3–19.

Rudstein, David S. *Double Jeopardy: A Reference Guide to the United States Constitution*. Westport, Conn.: Praeger, 2004, 1–15.

Sigler, Jay A. *Double Jeopardy: The Development of a Legal and Social Policy*. Ithaca, NY: Cornell University Press, 1969, 1–37.

Cases and Statutes Cited

Coit v. Geer, 1 Kirby 269 (Conn. Super. Ct. 1787)

Hannaball v. Spalding, 1 Root 86 (Conn. Super. Ct. 1783)

The King v. Perkins, Holt. K.B. 403, 90 Eng. Rep. 1122 (1698)

The King v. Read, 1 Lev. 9, 83 Eng. Rep. 271 (1660)

Respublica v. Shaffer, 1 Dall. 236 (Pa. Ct. Oyer and Terminer 1788)

Rex v. Hutchinson, 3 Keble 785, 84 Eng. Rep. 1011 (1677) (discussed in *Beak v. Thyrwhit*, 3 Mod. 194, 87 Eng. Rep. 124 (K.B. 1688))

See also **Bill of Rights: Structure; Bills of Rights in Early State Constitutions; Colonial Charters and Codes; Constitutional Convention of 1787; Double Jeopardy: Modern History; Madison, James; Magna Carta; Massachusetts Body of Liberties of 1641; New Hampshire Constitution of 1784; Ratification Debate, Civil Liberties in; State Constitutions and Civil Liberties**

DOUBLE JEOPARDY: MODERN HISTORY

> Nor shall any person be subject for the same offense to be twice put in jeopardy of life or limb (U.S. Constitution, Amendment Five).

Twenty simple words contained in the Fifth Amendment to the U.S. Constitution protect individuals against being subjected to double jeopardy for any crime. While the phrase "double jeopardy" is commonly understood to prohibit multiple prosecutions and multiple punishments for the same criminal offense, the parameters of the Fifth Amendment promise are often difficult to distill and appreciate.

History provides only slight guidance to the contours of this protection. Instead, at least in the United States, the double jeopardy doctrine has been amplified, if not solidified, by judicial interpretations of these often quoted twenty simple words.

History

Double jeopardy is neither a new nor uniquely American concept. Rather, the principle of double jeopardy dates back to the early Roman period and has a historical pedigree spanning well over one thousand years. In fact, there are primitive notions of double jeopardy appearing in the Bible. In the book of Nahum, we are assured in one translation that "he will not take vengeance twice on his foes" and, in an alternate translation, "affliction will not rise up a second time." While jurists and scholars debate the origins of double jeopardy, traces of the doctrine can be readily distilled from English common law. The doctrine does not, however, appear in the Magna Carta.

The first known codified reference to double jeopardy was set forth in the *Digest of Justinian*. Therein, the pronouncement was made that "the governor should not permit the same person to be again accused of a crime of which he had been acquitted." The concept continued to change and improve through many kings and queens in England. Thereafter, the writings of Lord Coke and William Blackstone were commingled to provide us with the modern day concept of double jeopardy. Lord Coke is credited with carving out the three categories to which double jeopardy historically applied: *autrefois acquit, autrefois convict,* and former pardon. Blackstone further advanced the doctrine by pronouncing that "the plea of *autrefois aquit*, or a formal acquittal, is grounded on the universal maxim . . . that no man is to be brought into jeopardy of his life more than once for the same offense."

A main distinction between historical doctrine and modern double jeopardy provisions is that the former only applied to capital crimes. In modern times, double jeopardy is not limited only to crimes affecting "life or limb" but, rather, applies to all criminal prosecutions and punishments in which an individual is at risk of multiple attacks on his or her liberty.

Colonial Massachusetts gave birth to the modern American approach to double jeopardy in its Body of Liberties published in 1641. As one author noted, "[t]his document bears a close resemblance to the Bill of Rights later to become a stock feature of American constitutions, state and federal." Similar to prior pronouncements, the Body of Liberties provided that "no man shall be twice sentenced by civil justice for one and the same crime, offense, or trespass."

Over one hundred years later, in 1784, New Hampshire became the first state to protect against double jeopardy in its Bill of Rights, proclaiming that "no subject shall be liable to be tried, after an acquittal, for the same crime or offense." James Madison's proffering at the Constitutional Convention five years later was strikingly similar to the previous colonial offerings declaring that "no personal shall be subject, except in case of impeachment, to more than one trial, or one punishment for the same offense." Yet, it was not until 1790 in the Pennsylvania Declaration of Rights that a phrase resembling our modern phraseology appeared. The Pennsylvania Declaration of Rights succinctly stated that "no person shall, for the same offense, be twice put in jeopardy of life or limb." From these ideals sprang the modern protection contained in twenty simple words.

International Application

In modern times, remnants of double jeopardy exist in many countries, including Australia, Canada, the United Kingdom, parts of Asia, and the United States. In fact, protection against double jeopardy is now provided for in the International Covenant on Civil and Political Rights and the European Union Constitution and numerous documents governing international criminal tribunals, including the International Criminal Tribunal for Yugoslavia, the International Criminal Tribunal for Rwanda, and the nascent International Criminal Court.

There are significant differences, however, between the English and American perspective of precisely when "jeopardy" attaches. The English rule, which retains the common-law approach, limits application of double jeopardy to instances in which a defendant has been acquitted or convicted. In other words, the English rule requires a full, completed trial. In contrast, the American rule attaches jeopardy as soon as the jury is sworn, in a jury trial, or when the prosecution offers its first piece of evidence in a trial before the court. Thus, the concept of jeopardy attaches much earlier in the American legal system than in its English counterpart.

Despite the apparent staying power of the general double jeopardy concept, England recently diluted its double jeopardy protection with parliamentary passage of the Criminal Justice Act 2003. England's departure from the stricter version existing in the United States permits a subsequent prosecution following acquittal for certain offenses, such as murder, rape, kidnapping and manslaughter, when new and compelling evidence arises. Additionally, individuals acquitted prior to 2003 may nonetheless be subject to prosecution retroactively under the act. The revised English approach was motivated by notorious trials in which individuals adjudged not guilty later confessed to committing the crimes for which they were accused. Societal tolerance for such perceived travesties of justice waned and the English legislators responded to victims' rights groups in altering their previously steadfast approach to double jeopardy.

American Application

While numerous countries maintain variations of double jeopardy, the American approach remains one of the more potent provisions. Enshrined in the Constitution, the proscription against double jeopardy cannot be undermined by the kind of legislative pronouncement that occurred in England and appears to be under way in Australia. Furthermore, unlike Korea, where the prosecution can appeal a defendant's acquittal, only in the rarest instances may the state or federal government appeal a criminal judgment.

The American interpretation, however, has not always provided criminal defendants a formidable defense. For nearly two hundred years, the Fifth Amendment's double jeopardy protection was limited solely to actions by the federal government and its subdivisions. Not until the Supreme Court's 1969 decision in *Benton v. Maryland*, 395 U.S. 784 (1969), did the Double Jeopardy Clause extend equally to state governments. *Benton* considered the Fifth Amendment promise against multiple prosecutions and multiple punishments to "represent a fundamental ideal in our constitutional heritage" and, accordingly, held double jeopardy to be applicable to the states through incorporation of the Fourteenth Amendment. Having so found, the Supreme Court decision in *Benton* mandates that double jeopardy determinations now be governed by federal standards rather than state nuances.

Nonetheless, states retain certain flexibility under double jeopardy due to the dual sovereignty doctrine. In 1922, the Supreme Court explicitly recognized the power of distinct sovereigns to prosecute an individual for criminal conduct falling within the jurisdiction of both in *United States v. Lanza*, 260 U.S. 377 (1922). Thereafter, in 1985, the Court further expanded the dual sovereignty doctrine to permit separate prosecutions by distinct state sovereigns in *Heath v. Alabama*, 474 U.S. 82 (1985). By holding that each state has independent power to determine an individual's guilt or innocence under the state's criminal code for all conduct occurring within that state, the Supreme Court permitted a subsequent prosecution of Heath for murder, which resulted in a much harsher sentence than had been received in the other state prosecution. The Supreme Court held that separate, independent sovereigns possess the right to try a criminal defendant for conduct occurring within their separate borders. The conduct, constituting independent criminal acts in each state, is not protected by double jeopardy because the conduct offends both sovereigns equally.

The dual sovereignty doctrine was extended recently to embrace dual prosecution by the federal government and tribal courts on Indian reservations in *United States v. Lara*, 541 U.S. 193 (2004). Thus, although the Fifth Amendment protects against multiple prosecutions by the same sovereign—or subdivisions thereof—double jeopardy poses no bar to separate prosecutions by independent sovereigns.

Two of the more renowned instances of separate prosecutions by independent sovereigns include the Rodney King case defendants' subsequent federal trials following state acquittals and Terry Nichols's subsequent state capital trial following a federal trial resulting in a life sentence.

Finally, double jeopardy does not affect the ability of a private individual to sue civilly for conduct that may be prohibited by criminal and civil law. The paradigm example continues to be the O. J. Simpson case, in which Simpson was subsequently sued civilly for wrongful death following his acquittal for murder.

Multiple Prosecutions

In its most literal sense, the Double Jeopardy Clause protects against multiple prosecutions after an individual has been acquitted. Double jeopardy ensures that the prosecution will put forth its strongest case first and allow a jury, rightly or wrongly, to assess the defendant's guilt.

In the United States, jeopardy attaches once the jury is sworn or once the prosecution introduces evidence in a trial before the court. Once jeopardy attaches, courts and prosecutors are prevented from retrying an individual for the same offense unless: (1) the jury is unable to return a verdict, or (2) a mistrial is granted and there is a manifest necessity to retry the defendant in the interest of justice. This second category presumes the absence of prosecutorial or judicial misconduct in securing the mistrial.

Finally, although the ability of the government to appeal criminal convictions is extremely limited, a defendant's successful appeal will not bar his or her reprosecution on double jeopardy grounds as voluntary appeal operates as a wavier to reprosecution.

The double jeopardy limitation of the same offense does not preclude multiple counts emanating from a single criminal episode and does not prohibit multiple prosecutions for separate crimes against separate individuals, even when there was but a single criminal act, such as two murders during a single robbery. Rather, the "same offense" test as set forth in *Blockburger v. United States*, 284 U.S. 299 (1932), to "determine whether there are two offenses or only one is whether each provision requires proof of an additional fact which the other does not." A good example of the *Blockburger* test in application is the Supreme Court's decision in *Brown v. Ohio*, 432 U.S. 161 (1977), where the Court determined that an attempted second prosecution for stealing an automobile was barred by double jeopardy when the defendant had previously been convicted of operating the same vehicle without the owner's consent. Finding that the misdemeanor count of joyriding was a lesser-included offense of auto theft, the Court held that the defendant had been twice put in jeopardy for the same offense and reversed the subsequent prosecution.

As a reminder that double jeopardy operates as a limitation on courts and prosecutors, the *Brown* Court struck down the state court's interpretation of double jeopardy, stating that the "Double Jeopardy Clause is not such a fragile guarantee that prosecutors can avoid its limitations by the simple expedient of dividing a single crime into a series of temporal or spatial units."

Likewise, the Supreme Court found in *Ashe v. Swenson*, 397 U.S. 436, that the doctrine of collateral estoppel is embodied by the Double Jeopardy Clause. In *Ashe*, the defendant had been accused of participating in the robbery of six men at a poker game. Prosecutors decided to try the defendant for only one of the robberies first. At this trial, the main issue was identity and the jury returned a verdict of not guilty due to insufficient evidence. During the subsequent trial, defendant raised the defense of double jeopardy when the state presented a much stronger argument regarding identification. The Court had no difficulty finding this second attempted trial to be barred by double jeopardy through the application of collateral estoppel (the issue of identity having been resolved in the first trial), remarking that "for whatever else that constitutional guarantee may embrace, it surely protects a man who has been acquitted from having to 'run the gauntlet' a second time."

Multiple Punishments

A person may not be punished twice for the same offense. The difficulty often arises in defining punishment. For instance, individuals that appeal their criminal conviction may be reprosecuted and repunished and this does not violate double jeopardy. However, someone who has been convicted of a lesser included offense may not be retried or later punished for the greater crime, even following a successful appeal. This is because failure to convict on the greater offense retains the initial jeopardy and subsequent efforts to resurrect the previously faced, though defeated, charge are barred.

Similarly, once an individual has successfully avoided the death penalty in the initial proceeding, a successful appeal of the case will not permit retrial where the defendant is again subjected to possible capital punishment. Instead, an individual that was spared the death penalty is presumed to have had jurors find in his or her favor on the capital issues and can only be reprosecuted with a potential prison term. Other than death penalty cases, there is no limit on resentencing following a proper retrial.

Another important question under the multiple punishment doctrine is whether civil fines, forfeitures, and administrative proceedings qualify as "punishment." The general rule is that matters that are remedial in nature and not intended as punishment do not equate to punishment. Loss of driving license following a charge of driving while intoxicated is the prime example of an administrative sanction that is not considered as punishment for double jeopardy purposes.

The more controversial issue is whether a civil forfeiture of a home, car, or simply monetary funds qualifies as "punishment" under double jeopardy. The general answer following the Supreme Court's decision in *United States v. Ursery*, 518 U.S. 267 (1996), is that civil forfeitures do not constitute punishment under double jeopardy. Despite the fact that civil forfeitures may contain punitive elements, the *Ursery* Court found sufficient nonpunitive elements involved to permit application of civil forfeiture and criminal sanction in the same proceeding without violating double jeopardy. While civil forfeitures may be immune from claims of double jeopardy, such fines and forfeitures may nonetheless be subject to review under the Eight Amendment proscription against cruel and unusual punishment.

MARY M. PENROSE

References and Further Reading

Sigler, Jay A. "A History of Double Jeopardy." *American Journal of Legal History* 7 (1963):285.

Cases and Statutes Cited

Ashe v. Swenson, 397 U.S. 436
Benton v. Maryland, 395 U.S. 784 (1969)
Blockburger v. United States, 284 U.S. 299 (1932)
Brown v. Ohio, 432 U.S. 161 (1977)
Heath v. Alabama, 474 U.S. 82 (1985)
United States v. Lanza, 260 U.S. 377 (1922)
United States v. Lara, 541 U.S. 193 (2004)
United States v. Ursery, 518 U.S. 267 (1996)

DOUGLAS v. CALIFORNIA, 372 U.S. 353 (1963)

In *Douglas v. California*, 372 U.S. 353 (1963), decided the same day as *Gideon v. Wainwright*, 372 U.S. 335 (1961), the Supreme Court held that the right to the assistance of counsel at state expense applied to defendants on a first level of appeal, extending *Gideon* to the first stage of appeal. In *Douglas*, two defendants were charged with thirteen felonies and both were represented by a single public defender. Both of the defendants were convicted after trial and both appealed. The defendants requested counsel be appointed for them on appeal and the court refused to grant their request, even though neither of them could afford to pay a lawyer.

Under California statutory law, a rule of criminal procedures requires state appellate courts upon the request for a lawyer to review the record independently to see whether counsel would be helpful. If the court concludes that counsel would be helpful, counsel should be appointed. The California appellate court stated it had gone through the record and reached the conclusion that "no good whatever could be served by the appointment of counsel." It then upheld the defendants' convictions and held that the court had properly refused to give them counsel at state expense.

The U.S. Supreme Court reversed the defendants' convictions. It disagreed with the California appellate court and found that the California procedure allowing the state court to decide whether counsel was necessary to be unconstitutional. The Court held that the procedure violated the Equal Protection Clause of the Fourteenth Amendment because "the type of an appeal a person is afforded . . . hinges upon whether or not he can pay for the assistance of counsel." If a defendant can pay, explained the Court, the appeals court will consider his appeal in full, which includes written briefs and oral argument by counsel. If he cannot, the court is allowed to prejudge the merits before it even decides whether a lawyer should be appointed. According to the Court, "the indigent, where the record is unclear or the errors are hidden, has only the right to a meaningless ritual, while the rich man has a meaningful appeal."

In so holding the Court made clear that it was not deciding whether a lawyer would have to be appointed for a poor person at any higher level of appeal beyond the first-level appeal after a conviction in a criminal case.

Justice Clark dissented. He began by noting that "the overwhelming percentage of appeals by indigents are frivolous and that California has adopted a procedure that saves it the unnecessary expense of the 'useless gesture' of providing counsel in such cases." The justice would have held that this procedure did not violate Due Process or Equal Protection. In support of his conclusion, Justice Clark pointed to the U.S. Supreme Court's procedure for dealing with petitions for review by unrepresented poor people: in the prior term of the Court, it had decided over 1200 such applications without appointing any lawyers or requiring a full record. California, he noted, furnishes a complete record to every poor person and, if counsel is requested, (1) appoints counsel; or (2) makes an investigation of the record to determine whether counsel would be advantageous. As Justice Clark concluded, "People who live in glass houses had best not throw stones."

Justice Harlan, joined by Justice Stewart, separately dissented. Justice Harlan did not believe that Equal Protection was relevant and would have held that due process did not require the appointment of a lawyer on a first appeal. First, Justice Harlan explained that the states are free to pass a statute "of general applicability that may affect the poor more harshly than it does the rich," but that the Equal Protection clause does not require the states to "lift the handicaps flowing from differences in economic circumstances." Second, as for due process, Justice Harlan was not willing to find that a defendant would be deprived of adequate appellate review without a lawyer. Justice Harlan did not believe that the state's rule was "so arbitrary or unreasonable" to render it unconstitutional.

LISSA GRIFFIN

Cases and Statutes Cited

Douglas v. California, 372 U.S. 353 (1963)

See also **Betts v. Brady, 316 U.S. 455 (1942); Due Process;** *Gideon v. Wainwright*, **372 U.S. 335 (1963);** *Powell v. Alabama*, **287 U.S. 45 (1932); Right to Counsel;** *Ross v. Moffitt*, **417 U.S. 600 (1974)**

DOUGLAS, WILLIAM ORVILLE (1898–1980)

William O. Douglas served longer on the U.S. Supreme Court than any other justice, and his thirty-six-year tenure spanned major transformations in mid-twentieth-century American society. After a brief stint as a lawyer in a large New York law firm, Douglas turned to teaching, first at Columbia and then at the Yale Law School, where he became one of the leaders of the legal realism school. During the New Deal he came to Washington first as a commissioner and than as chair of the Securities Exchange Commission. He also became a poker buddy of Franklin Roosevelt, who named him to the Court to succeed Louis D. Brandeis in February 1939.

Justice Douglas's judicial opinions do not fit within any particular school of legal doctrine, although he is associated with the legal realists and considered an activist and a liberal jurist. In fact, he resisted the concept of legal doctrine and rejected any set of propositions from which resolutions of legal controversies could be deduced. Instead, he believed that his job as a justice was to make decisions about specific sets of facts in their particular social, economic, and political contexts. As situations changed, his decisions changed. Initially, he did not appear to be any sort of champion of civil liberties; by the time he retired, he was hailed as one of the staunchest defenders of individual liberties ever to sit on the Court.

Justice Douglas brought to the Court a distinctive approach to law and judging and insisted on an empirical approach to legal problems in the light of actual social, political, economic, and psychological realities. For the legal realists, concentration on doctrine and precedents masked the vital actuality of present circumstances. Although Justice Douglas sometimes referred approvingly to "sociological jurisprudence," he avoided describing himself as a legal realist or as a functionalist. He was far too independently minded to associate with anything that sounded like orthodoxy.

Having rejected legal doctrine as a basis for judicial decision making, the justice gradually developed a distinctive judicial style. In simplest terms, he considered his job to decide cases. Justice Douglas believed he was responsible for making his own decision in each case that came before the Court and said that he agreed with Thomas Jefferson that each judge should give his individual opinion in every case. Explaining decisions was of secondary importance to deciding cases. Justice Douglas generally avoided established legal doctrine. He said he was opposed to *stare decisis*, the judicial practice of deciding cases based on precedent, because present controversies should be decided on their own terms, rather than by applying past cases. Particularly in constitutional cases, the justice thought *stare decisis* was an excuse for not making hard choices about how to apply constitutional values to new circumstances. He often said that he would rather create a precedent than find one.

The Douglas approach to judicial decision-making has been often criticized as result oriented: first deciding the result he wanted to reach and then building an argument for the correctness of that outcome. Critics also have disparaged some of his judicial opinions as careless, slapdash polemics. Justice Douglas was generally unperturbed by criticisms that he was result oriented or intellectually untidy. For him, life, including law, was just like that. Judicial opinions should provide solutions to real-life problems, not academic dissertations about legal doctrine. Sometimes he gave no reasons at all. Since deciding the case was the point of judging, and supporting reasons were far less important, it is not surprising that he did not often invest a lot of time developing the latter.

Justice Douglas had an uncanny ability to understand what was at issue in complicated cases and to envision new ways of looking at them. A typical Douglas opinion is filled with facts and may even have an appendix or two to provide even more background for his view of the case. He would first focus on the facts at issue and then find a key, pivotal issue at the heart of the legal controversy. In the latter part of his judicial career, he grasped cases especially quickly because he believed that legal controversies, like much of human behavior, fall into cyclical patterns, recurring every decade or so.

The justice's opinion for the Court in *Griswold v. Connecticut*, 381 U.S. 479 (1965), which recognized a penumbral right of privacy in the Constitution, provides a typical as well as famous example of his characteristic approach to judicial decision-making. In *Griswold*, the Court held unconstitutional a Connecticut criminal statute prohibiting the use and distribution of contraceptives. Justice Douglas saw the heart of the case as marital privacy: "Would we allow the police to search the sacred precincts of marital bedrooms for telltale signs of the use of contraceptives?" he asked, and then answered: "The very idea is repulsive to the notions of privacy surrounding the marriage relationship." The justice's opinion found that the penumbras of various constitutional guarantees establish a "right of privacy older than the Bill of Rights," which protects marriage as "a coming together for better or for worse, hopefully enduring, and intimate to the degree of being sacred." His insight into what was really at stake in *Griswold* retains remarkable vitality.

According to Justice Douglas, the Constitution not only established the Supreme Court's political role, but also provided a set of general principles that the Court was to apply. These constitutional principles provided a philosophy which must be interpreted and applied by judges in light of their lives and experiences. For the justice, such a dynamic approach to constitutional interpretation was not at all incompatible with strict construction. Justice Douglas considered himself a strict constructionist, like Hugo Black, because he believed strict construction meant not subtracting from or making exceptions to constitutional freedoms. He also considered himself a strict incorporationist because he believed that all of the rights contained in the Bill of Rights were incorporated into the Fourteenth Amendment's due process guarantee against state and local action that deprives individuals of liberty.

Among the more interesting examples of Justice Douglas's adjustment of constitutional guarantees to contemporary circumstances was his 1946 opinion in *United States v. Causby*, 328 U.S. 256 (1946). The case was brought by a North Carolina chicken farmer whose property served as a glide path for military aircraft using an adjacent airport during World War II. The farmer sought compensation under the Takings Clause of the Fifth Amendment because the overflights made his property less valuable. Justice Douglas's opinion recognized two important realities. First, modern air transport requires use of the air space above private property as part of the public domain, where airplanes can fly without restriction by those who own the land below. At the same time, the farmer's particular circumstances involved frequent low-level takeoffs and landings. That particular pattern of overflights, so low that they frightened the farmer's chickens literally to death, was a government use of the farmer's land. Since this government use made the farmer's land less valuable, the farmer was entitled to recover just compensation for his loss.

For Justice Douglas, applying constitutional guarantees that the government will not take property without paying just compensation required focusing on what was really at stake: the devaluation of the chicken farmer's land by the government's overflights. In a sense, the decision is result oriented: big government should bear the financial loss rather than the small farmer. But the opinion's apt focus on the particular circumstances of the case also exemplifies the justice's characteristic ability to apply the Constitution to new circumstances and technologies.

Change was at once inevitable and beneficial in his view. Unconstrained by commitment to doctrinal consistency, Douglas was notably uninhibited about changing his mind. There are many instances of cases in which he simply admitted that an earlier decision or view was wrong. In the l940s, the Supreme Court decided a series of cases that involved the constitutionality of compelling school children to salute the American flag. In *Minersville School District v. Gobitis*, 310 U.S. 586 (1940), Justice Douglas first voted with the majority of the Court that Jehovah's Witnesses children could be compelled to salute the flag, even though doing so violated their religious beliefs. Three years later, in *Board of Education v. Barnette*, 319 U.S. 624 (1943), he changed his mind and joined Justice Black in a concurring opinion that argued that forced expression contrary to an individual's religious principles violates the First Amendment.

In 1952, Justice Douglas forthrightly declared that he had changed his views with regard to the constitutionality of electronic surveillance. Dissenting in *On Lee v. United States*, a case involving a narcotics agent carrying a hidden microphone, he simply confessed that his earlier tolerance of electronic surveillance in *Goldman v. United States* (1942) had been mistaken. "I now more fully appreciate the vice of the practices spawned by . . . *Goldman*. Reflection on them has brought new insight to me. I now feel that I was wrong in the *Goldman* case" (in not voting to overrule *Olmstead v. United States*, 277 US 438, 1928, which had found wiretapping to be constitutional).

In addition to cases in which Justice Douglas changed his mind and said so, his flexible approach in deciding particular cases greatly annoyed some of his judicial colleagues, especially Felix Frankfurter. The Japanese exclusion cases and the Rosenberg espionage case are two prominent examples. In these cases, which involved highly charged political controversies, the justice did not see himself or his decisions as inconsistent. In his view, he simply responded to the particular circumstances of various aspects of the cases to help resolve difficult tensions among strongly held values and interests.

The three Japanese exclusion cases, *Hirabayashi v. United States*, 320 U.S. 81 (1943), *Korematsu v. United States*, 323 U.S. 214 (1944), and *Ex parte Endo* (1944), contested the legality of military orders that imposed curfews, relocation, and detention of Japanese on the West Coast after the attack on Pearl Harbor. Justice Douglas filed a concurring opinion in *Hirabayashi* that upheld the legality of a curfew order against persons of Japanese ancestry. He voted with the majority in *Korematsu*, in which the Supreme Court upheld an order excluding persons of Japanese ancestry from military areas of the West Coast and providing for their relocation and detention. Although the justice opposed racial and ethnic

discrimination and said so repeatedly in his opinions, he thought that the wartime circumstances presented by the *Korematsu* and *Hirabayashi* cases involved a genuine national emergency sufficiently grave to warrant interference with individual civil rights.

Justice Douglas's sense that the nation was in imminent danger was probably particularly acute because, during this time, he was a frequent visitor at the White House, where the fear of Japanese invasion of the West Coast must have been palpable. However, his opinion for the Court in *Ex parte Endo* focused on the conceded fact that Mitsuye Endo was a loyal American citizen who posed no danger to the war effort or national security. Justice Douglas's context-bound realist view saw that the government's exclusion of Endo was unjustified and therefore unconstitutional.

Much of William O. Douglas's judicial philosophy focused on the importance of individual freedom and equality. In his 1958 book, *Right of the People*, he declared, "Our Society is built upon the premise that it exists only to aid the fullest individual achievement of which each of its members is capable. Our starting point has always been the individual, not the state."

The justice's concerns about individual freedom were mostly focused on threatened government oppression, although he sometimes also expressed misgivings about domination of independent entrepreneurs by what he called the unelected "industrial oligarchy." Early in his judicial career he was sometimes willing to subordinate individual rights to broader government interests. For example, in the emergency circumstances of World War II, Justice Douglas thought it constitutionally acceptable to sacrifice the rights of individuals of Japanese ancestry in the interests of national security.

In the early 1950s, he became increasingly concerned about the dangers posed by government regimentation of individual freedom. He came to believe that one of the most important purposes of the Constitution was to restrain government. Dissenting in *Laird v. Tatum* (1972), he declared, "The Constitution was designed to keep government off the backs of the people. The Bill of Rights was added to keep the precincts of belief and expression, of the press, of political and social activities free from surveillance." In Justice Douglas's view, "The aim [of the Bill of Rights] was to allow men to be free and independent and to assert their rights against government."

Justice Douglas provided the most comprehensive discussion of his views regarding individual freedoms guaranteed by the Constitution in connection with the 1973 abortion cases, *Doe v. Bolton*, 410 U.S. 179 (1973), and *Roe v. Wade*, 410 U.S. 93 (1973), in which the Supreme Court invalidated Georgia and Texas abortion statutes on privacy grounds. In his concurring opinion in *Bolton*, he described what he called "a reasoning" about individual rights, which are guaranteed by the Bill of Rights and are included within the right to liberty protected against state government interference under the Fourteenth Amendment to the Constitution. Douglas suggested three concentric circles of individual rights:

"First is the autonomous control over the development and expression of one's intellect, interests, tastes, and personality." The justice saw these rights, including freedom of conscience and free exercise of religion, as aspects of freedom of thought and conscience that were absolutely protected under the First Amendment without any exceptions or qualifications. In this absolutely protected area, he also placed the right to remain silent under the Fifth Amendment.

"Second is freedom of choice in the basic decisions of one's life respecting marriage, divorce, procreation, contraception, and the education and upbringing of children." These fundamental rights, including the right of privacy involved in *Griswold* and the abortion cases, were outside the absolute protection of the First Amendment and were therefore subject to some reasonable control by the regulatory power of government. Nevertheless, any regulation had to be narrowly drawn and supported by a compelling state interest.

"Third is the freedom to care for one's health and person, freedom from bodily restraint or compulsion, freedom to walk, stroll, or loaf." These rights protected individuals as they interacted with others out in the world where the individual, although not exactly immune from government regulation, nevertheless retained certain rights to be let alone by the government, even in relatively public circumstances."

The particular individual freedom with which Justice Douglas is most closely associated is the right of privacy. He derived many of his views about protecting individual privacy against government interference from his predecessor on the Court, Louis D. Brandeis. But he nearly always referred to a right "of" privacy, rather than Justice Brandeis's right "to" privacy. Moreover, Justice Douglas's right of privacy was solely focused on governmental threats to privacy. He rejected imposing damage liability for invasions of privacy by the news media, which Brandeis had suggested many years earlier. For example, dissenting in *Public Utilities Commission v. Pollak* (1952), the justice argued that when the government forced a "captive audience" of riders on the publicly licensed street cars in the District of Columbia to listen to radio broadcasts, such action infringed on the privacy rights of individuals to be let alone by the government.

After repeatedly calling for recognition of a constitutional right of privacy in a series of dissenting opinions, Justice Douglas eventually persuaded a majority of the Court to adopt his views about privacy in *Griswold*. In that case, he characterized the right of privacy as based on "several fundamental constitutional guarantees" of individual freedom, including the First Amendment right of association, the Third Amendment's prohibition of quartering soldiers, the Fourth Amendment's prohibition of unreasonable searches and seizures, and the Fifth Amendment's prohibition of compelled self-incrimination. His opinion for the Court found the right of privacy in the penumbras of these constitutional guarantees. In Justice Douglas's view, "Specific guarantees of the Bill of Rights have penumbras, formed by emanations from those guarantees that help give them life and substance. Various guarantees create zones of privacy."

For Justice Douglas, the right of privacy was part of the meaning of the Constitution, even though the word "privacy" does not appear in the text. One had only to open one's eyes and one's mind to see it. He believed that the right of privacy is consistent with strict construction of the Constitution because it is part of what the Bill of Rights means. Since he also believed that all of the guarantees of individual freedom in the Bill of Rights are included as aspects of the liberty protected against state action under the due process clause of the Fourteenth Amendment, states such as Connecticut were constrained to respect the right of privacy along with the rest of the Bill of Rights. The justice did not believe that the right of privacy was the same thing as substantive due process, which he rejected as simply fastening extra-constitutional personal views and economic preferences of particular justices on the Constitution. The right of privacy was, for him, part and parcel of the Constitution.

Justice Douglas came to agree with Justice Black that First Amendment guarantees of freedom of expression and religion permit no governmental regulation of any kind with regard to speech, press, religion, conscience, or association. In the appeal of the conviction of the Communist Party leaders (*Dennis v. United States*, 341 U.S. 494, 1951), Justice Douglas entered a short but extremely effective dissent that tore apart the weak reasoning of Chief Justice Vinson's majority opinion upholding the convictions. He searched the record to find evidence—any evidence—that the defendants had done anything else than talk and could find no proof that that had committed a single act of any sort, even conspiracy to act. Although vilified at the time for his defense of free speech even for communists, Justice Douglas's dissent has become one of the great markers in free speech jurisprudence. Thomas Emerson noted an essential ingredient in his thought: a "remarkable ability to grasp the realities of the system of free expression." For Justice Douglas, free speech could only be understood in the larger context of facts. The power of his dissent lies in his reliance on the facts of the case.

Justice Douglas dissented in obscenity cases such as *Roth v. United States*, 354 U.S. 476 (1957), in which he stated, "The First Amendment, its prohibition in terms absolute, was designed to preclude courts as well as legislatures from weighing the values of speech against silence. The First Amendment puts free speech in the preferred position." Even though the justice was a victim of obnoxious press accounts of his personal life, he believed that awarding damages for defamation or invasion of privacy was unconstitutional because it involved penalizing the media for disseminating information. For example, he concurred in rejecting the invasion of privacy action in *Time v. Hill*, 385 U.S. 374 (1957), which involved a sensationalized magazine account of a family's experience as hostages of escaped criminals. He was concerned that the possibility of having to pay damages might discourage publication.

Because he believed in the intrinsic worth of each individual, Justice Douglas consistently favored equality of opportunity. A case involving a special admissions program for minority applicants to the University of Washington Law School (*DeFunis v. Odegaard*, 1974) presented a particularly difficult equal protection question. The majority found the case moot because the nonminority plaintiff was in his last semester of law school and would graduate no matter what the Court decided. Justice Douglas thought the Court should decide the case.

Repeatedly insisting on racial neutrality and decrying racial, religious, and ethnic quotas, the justice took a hard look at law school admissions practices. After carefully considering the circumstances, he concluded that the law school's special admissions process was constitutional because, in his view, it was designed to individualize and to equalize the treatment of applicants from minority backgrounds. "I think a separate classification of these applicants is warranted, lest race be a subtle force in eliminating minority members because of cultural differences," he wrote. At the same time, he also insisted that "there is no constitutional right for any race to be preferred." For Justice Douglas, equal protection, like many constitutional values, involved a complex balancing of the realities of the situation. Individualized treatment in this instance satisfied his understanding of the spirit of equal protection.

The justice's concerns about individual equality are also reflected in his application of equal protection guarantees to strictly scrutinize legislative classifications that affect fundamental rights. Among the most interesting examples of this approach to equal protection guarantees was his inventive 1942 opinion for the court in *Skinner v. Oklahoma*. His opinion describes Oklahoma's Habitual Criminal Sterilization Act at issue in the case as "legislation which involves one of the basic civil rights of man. Marriage and procreation are fundamental to the very existence and survival of the race. There is no redemption for the individual whom the law touches . . . . He is forever deprived of a basic liberty."

Therefore, the opinion concludes, the Court should apply "strict scrutiny of the classification" that differentiated between those convicted of grand larceny and others convicted of such similar property crimes as embezzlement. Careful scrutiny was required "lest unwittingly, or otherwise, invidious discriminations are made against groups or types of individuals in violation of the constitutional guaranty of just and equal laws." Since Oklahoma provided no reasons why it needed to sterilize people who had been three times convicted of grand larceny, but not people who had been three times convicted of embezzlement, the statute was unconstitutional. "The equal protection clause would indeed be a formula of empty words if such conspicuously artificial lines could be drawn," when such fundamental individual rights as the right to have children is at stake. Justice Douglas later applied this strict scrutiny approach in invalidating Virginia's $1.50 annual poll tax as a condition for voting in state elections in *Harper v. Virginia State Board of Elections* (1966). His idea that legislative classifications that affect fundamental individual rights must be strictly scrutinized by the courts has proved to be powerful as well as enduring.

William O. Douglas's judicial work was as eclectic as it was prolific. People tend to agree strongly or equally strongly to disagree with his independent-minded judicial philosophy, much as they intensely liked or disliked the blunt-spoken and impatient man. Some of his judicial opinions have a remarkable resonance and eloquence. Some are political tracts. Still others appear to have been carelessly thrown together. Through it all, Justice Douglas had an insight into the American spirit, an ability to articulate constitutional values, and a power to provoke thought and argument that few Supreme Court justices have equaled.

MELVIN I. UROFSKY

References and Further Reading

Ball, Howard, and Philip J. Cooper. *Of Power and Right: Hugo Black, William O. Douglas and America's Constitutional Revolution.* New York: Oxford University Press, 1992.

Belknap, Michal R. *Cold War Political Justice: The Smith Act, the Communist Party, and American Civil Liberties.* Westport, CT: Greenwood Press, 1977.

Douglas, William O. *Go East, Young Man: The Early Years.* New York: Random House, 1974.

———. *The Court Years: The Autobiography of William O. Douglas.* New York: Random House, 1980.

Emerson, Thomas, *Mr. Justice Douglas' Contribution to the Law: The First Amendment*, Columbia Law Review 74 (1974): 354.

Murphy, Bruce Allen. *Wild Bill: The Legend and Life of William O. Douglas.* New York: Random House, 2003.

Simon, James. *Independent Journey.* New York: Harper & Row, 1980.

Urofsky, Melvin, *William O. Douglas as a Common Law Judge*, Duke Law Journal 41 (1991): 133.

Wasby, Stephen L., ed., *"He Shall Not Pass This Way Again." The Legacy of Justice William O. Douglas.* Pittsburgh: University of Pittsburgh Press, 1990.

White, G. Edward. "The Anti-Judge: William O. Douglas and the Ambiguities of Individuality." In *The American Judicial Tradition*, New York: Oxford University Press, 1988.

DOUGLASS, FREDERICK (1818–1895)

Born Frederick Augustus Washington Bailey, Frederick Douglass liberated himself from his Baltimore owner's possession at the age of twenty. Beaten and exploited by a series of plantation owners, Douglass nonetheless taught himself to read and write. He found relative safety in New Bedford, Massachusetts, calling himself Douglass and securing work as a manual laborer. He subscribed to William Lloyd Garrison's *The Liberator*, an abolitionist paper, and within a few months he became a full-time lecturer for the Massachusetts Anti-Slavery Society. Traveling with Garrison and other abolitionists, Douglass developed a reputation as a powerful, passionate speaker, and his greatest asset was his ability to speak firsthand of the horrors of slavery.

As Douglass spoke about his enslavement, he was forced to be vague about his circumstance. As an escaped slave, Douglass could be recaptured and sent back to his master. He was encouraged to write his story and, by the summer of 1845, had published *The Narrative of the Life of Frederick Douglass.* The book was an immediate success, but Douglass had included enough information to identify his former master, so friends implored him to go to Europe. Douglass spent most of the next two years touring the British Isles, returning to find that supporters had raised enough money to purchase his freedom.

Returning home committed to continuing his abolitionist activity, Douglass decided to create his own paper. Advised by his friend William Lloyd Garrison that an abolitionist paper written by a black man would not succeed financially, Douglass nonetheless pressed forward. An argument over the issue ended the friendship between the two men, and Douglass moved to Rochester, New York, and began publishing the *North Star.* Unwilling to take direction from Garrison or any other white abolitionist and believing that blacks should be more prominent in abolitionist activities, Douglass began to believe that emancipation could be achieved through political means. To that end, much of the *North Star*'s message was directed toward free blacks, calling for their self-improvement and cooperation.

Openly supportive of other reform movements, such as temperance and women's rights, Douglass also attracted attention from more militant reformers. John Brown tried to recruit him for his assault on Harper's Ferry, but Douglass refused.

After President Lincoln's assassination, Andrew Johnson offered the position of head of the Freedman's Bureau, which Douglass declined. Douglass supported Ulysses S. Grant in his run for the 1868 presidency, then turned his attention to other political matters. He worked for the passage of the Fifteenth Amendment, which guaranteed blacks the right to vote, then was appointed president of the Freedman's Savings and Trust Company. Three years later Douglass received another political appointment, this time as the U.S. Marshal for Washington, D.C. He served in that and other political positions until his retirement.

Thousands of schoolchildren read Douglass's autobiography in English and history classes. Few other examples tell as profound a story as Douglass's writing. Born a slave, self-educated and self-liberated, Douglass had only just begun his real life's work when he wrote his autobiography. The real success came years later: political activist and ideological crusader, Douglass embraced not only the cause of abolitionism, but also feminism and temperance.

JAMES HALABUK, JR.

References and Further Reading

Douglass, Frederick. *Narrative of the Life of Frederick Douglass, An American Slave, Written by Himself.* Boston: Bedford Books, 1993.

Quarles, Benjamin. *Frederick Douglass.* New York: Da Capo Press, 1948.

DRAFT CARD BURNING

Several years before mass demonstrations protesting America's involvement in the Vietnam War became commonplace in the 1970s, David Paul O'Brien, along with three others, stood on the steps of the South Boston, Massachusetts, courthouse and, in front of a crowd of people, burned his selective service registration certificate, better known as a draft card. It was March 31, 1966, and O'Brien's protest provoked the crowd to attack him and his companions. Among the onlookers were several FBI agents; after ushering O'Brien inside the courthouse, they arrested him for violation of Title 50 of the *United States Code*, section 462(b), prohibiting the willful and knowing mutilation or destruction of a registration certificate. Throughout the course of the litigation, O'Brien claimed that his conviction was barred by the First Amendment. At trial, he admitted that he knowingly destroyed his draft card, but took the position that his conduct was intended to be public affirmation of his disapproval of the draft and the war, and the lawful exercise of free speech.

O'Brien was convicted in the District Court for the District of Massachusetts. On appeal, the First Circuit held that the statute criminalizing the mutilation of the draft card was an unconstitutional infringement on the defendant's rights of free speech. It did, however, affirm his conviction based upon a regulation that required persons to carry their registration cards with them at all times, a crime with which he had not been charged or convicted.

O'Brien and the United States appealed. The Supreme Court granted certiorari and, in what might be considered a landmark case, held that the question of whether "expressive conduct" or "symbolic speech"—that is, activity containing speech and nonspeech elements—is protected by the First Amendment will be governed by a four-prong test. The so-called "*O'Brien* test" is generally acknowledged to be less exacting than strict scrutiny and is sometimes referred to as "intermediate scrutiny":

> [A] government regulation is sufficiently justified if it is within the constitutional power of the Government; if it furthers an important or substantial governmental interest; if the governmental interest is unrelated to the suppression of free expression; and if the incidental restriction on alleged First Amendment freedoms is no greater than is essential to the furtherance of that interest (*United States v. O'Brien*, 391 U.S. 367, 377, 1968).

Writing for the Court, Chief Justice Earl Warren refused to concede that O'Brien's conduct was actually intended to send a message; however, he proceeded to apply the test to the facts of that case. After first acknowledging that Congress's power to raise and support armies and to make all laws necessary and proper to achieve that end is extremely broad, the Court proceeded to announce four purposes of the selective service registration card and the restrictions relating to prohibition against mutilation, none of which was aimed at expression.

First, the Court said, the certificate was proof that the holder has registered for the draft. In a time of national crisis, possession of the registration card (which, along with the certification card that also had to be kept on one's person, contained all relevant information concerning the holder's draft status) facilitated "immediate induction, no matter how distant in our mobile society [the registrant] may be from his local board." Second, the cards together facilitated communication with the local draft boards. Boards could respond to requests for information more easily if the person requesting the information had all this information on hand at all times. Third, carrying both cards was a reminder to the holder that he had to inform the local draft board of any changes in the information, such as his residential address. Finally, the prohibition against mutilation assisted the government in achieving the permissible purpose of prohibiting alteration of the cards for a deceptive reason.

The Court then disposed of O'Brien's argument that these interests were already furthered by the requirement that the cards be kept on one's person because the two statutes protect overlapping but different governmental interests. The Court noted that the antidestruction provisions would apply to a person's mutilating a third party's certificate, but the possession requirements applied only to the owner of the certificates. The Court dealt with the fourth prong—the narrowness of the regulation—merely by concluding that it could perceive no alternative that would more narrowly achieve the government interests at stake.

Finally, the Court addressed O'Brien's contention that the statute was passed with the intent of curtailing speech, an argument that had factual support. O'Brien relied on statements made by three congressmen that the statute was enacted to stop dissidents from burning the cards in protest of the war in Viet Nam. The majority summarily disposed of the arguments by reaffirming long-standing Supreme Court jurisprudence that legislative purpose is difficult to ascertain and is not a legitimate basis for declaring a facially constitutional statute unconstitutional. Besides, the Court said, hearings before the Senate and House Armed Services Committees spoke not only to the "defiant" destruction of the cards, but also to the necessity of maintaining them to ensure the smooth functioning of the selective service system, a goal unrelated to expression.

Justice Harlan issued a brief concurrence to make explicit his belief that the *O'Brien* test would not "foreclose consideration" under the First Amendment of claims based upon regulations at issue that passed that test, but had the effect of preventing entirely communication of the speaker's views. O'Brien, he said, had other ways of making his position heard.

Justice Douglas dissented. Congress, he said, had no authority to conscript persons in the absence of a declaration of war; therefore, the statutes at issue were beyond Congress's power. The justice would have addressed that issue, not raised by O'Brien, but raised apparently by a number of cases in which the Supreme Court had refused to grant certiorari.

The *O'Brien* case is frequently referred to as the "leading case" in First Amendment jurisprudence when courts are called upon to evaluate so-called "content-neutral" statutes—that is, statutes not aimed at the message being expressed. The Supreme Court has directly relied on *O'Brien* in deciding a number of First Amendment cases since 1968. Twice, the Supreme Court has applied the O'Brien test to ordinances regulating public nudity. In *Barnes v. Glen Theaters*, 501 U.S. 560 (1991), and *City of Erie v. Pap's A.M.*, 529 U.S. 57 (2000), first a plurality then a majority of the Court applied *O'Brien* and held that public nudity statutes (which prohibited nude dancing and required dancers to wear pasties and g-strings) were constitutional, even though they imposed an incidental burden on expression, because a government clearly has the authority to regulate societal order and morality and, in these cases, it did so in a manner unrelated to expression. The requirement that dancers wear pasties and a g-string was a "de minimus" interference with the dancers' abilities to send the erotic message.

Two years earlier, the Court considered applying *O'Brien* to one of the numerous flag-burning statutes that have come before the Court. In *Texas v. Johnson*, 491 U.S. 397 (1989), the Court rejected applying the more lenient standard because Texas could not posit a purpose to the statute prohibiting mutilation of the flag that was unrelated to speech; therefore, the "more exacting" strict scrutiny standard applied. The Court did, however, reconfirm that not all conduct with a communicative element will be suitable for the *O'Brien* approach. Not only must the intent to communicate a message be present, but there must be a great likelihood that observers would understand the message sought to be communicated.

Although the genesis of the *O'Brien* test was a case involving what is called "symbolic speech" or "expressive conduct" (in which the effect on speech is only "incidental"), the standard has been applied to factual situations bearing little resemblance to those of the original case, though not without criticism. In *Turner Broadcasting v. F.C.C.*, 520 U.S. 180 (1997), the Supreme Court held the "must carry" provisions of the FCC were content-neutral regulations that "advance[d] important governmental interests unrelated to the suppression of free speech and [did] not burden substantially more speech than necessary to further those interests," citing *O'Brien*.

Following the lead of the Supreme Court, lower courts have frequently used *O'Brien* interchangeably with the "time place and manner" test generally applicable to any content-neutral statute or regulation, whether its effect on speech is incidental or not. *O'Brien*'s "balancing approach" has also been said to have spawned the standard currently used by the Supreme Court to evaluate laws and regulations that affect commercial speech, causing some confusion among courts and frequent disapproval from constitutional scholars.

CONSTANCE L. RUDNICK

References and Further Reading

Chemerinsky, Erwin. *Constitutional Law Principles and Policies*, 2nd ed. New York: Aspen, 2002, 1026–1032.

Emerson, Thomas. *The System of Freedom of Expression*. New York, Vintage, 1970, 80–87.

Hall, Kermit, ed. *The Oxford Companion to the Supreme Court of the United States*. New York: Oxford Press, 1992, 597–599; 602.

Mallamud, Jonathan, *Judicial Intrusion Into Cable Television Regulation: The Misuse of* O'Brien *in Reviewing Compulsory Carriage Rules*, Vill. L. Rev. 34 (August 1989): 467.

Martin, Melanie Ann, 1992 *Note Constitutional Law—Non-Traditional Forms of Expression Get No Protection: An Analysis of Nude Dancing Under* Barnes v. Glen Theatre, Inc., 27 Wake Forest L. Rev. 1061 (Winter 1992).

Seid, Richard A., *A Requiem for* O'Brien: *On the Nature of Symbolic Speech*, Cumb. L. Rev. 23 (1992/1993): 563.

Werhan, Keith, *The* O'Brie*ning of Free Speech Methodology*, Ariz. St. L. J. 19 (Winter 1987): 635.

Zick, Timothy, *Cross Burning, Cockfighting, and Symbolic Meaning: Toward a First Amendment Ethnography*, Wm. & Mary L. Rev. 45 (April 2004): 2261.

Cases and Statutes Cited

Barnes v. Glen Theaters, 501 U.S. 560 (1991)
City of Erie v. Pap's A.M., 529 U.S. 57 (2000)
Texas v. Johnson, 491 U.S. 397 (1989)
Turner Broadcasting v. F.C.C., 520 U.S. 180 (1997)
United States v. O'Brien, 391 U.S. 367, 377 (1968)

DRED SCOTT v. SANDFORD,
60 U.S. 393 (1857)

The *Dred Scott v. Sandford* case served as a catalyst for providing blacks civil rights and civil liberties under the U.S. Constitution. Specifically, the case helped put an end to slavery in the United States and granted blacks citizenship, due process rights, equality under the law, and voting rights. Ironically, though, this expansion of rights and liberties to blacks did *not* come about from the ruling in this case. Rather, the expansion of rights and liberties came about from the country's struggle to overturn the Supreme Court's ruling in *Dred Scott v. Sandford*.

Dred Scott was born in Virginia in 1799. He was a slave of the Peter Blow family. In 1830, the Blows moved to St. Louis, Missouri. Two years later, Peter Blow died, and Scott was sold to Dr. John Emerson, an army surgeon who traveled across the country. Scott accompanied Dr. Emerson on his travels, which included traveling to the free territories of Illinois, Wisconsin, and upper Louisiana from 1833 to 1843. While in the Wisconsin territory, Scott met and married Harriet Robinson, who also was a slave. As a result of the marriage, Harriet's ownership was transferred to Emerson. Dred and Harriet had two children. In 1843, Dr. Emerson died, and Emerson's widow, Eliza Sandford, then began hiring out the Scott family to work for others.

In 1846, Dred and Harriet Scott asked the courts to recognize them as free people, since they had traveled with their master, Dr. John Emerson, to the free territories of Illinois, Wisconsin, and upper Louisiana from 1833 to 1843. The Scotts believed that under the precedent to *Rachel v. Walker*, 4 Missouri Rep. 350 (1836), they should be granted their freedom, since this Missouri court ruling declared that slaves were entitled to freedom in a slave state if they at one time had residency in a free state. The *Rachel v. Walker* case, along with other Missouri precedents, established the legal principle in Missouri of "once free, always free." This was a straightforward case that should have led to the Scotts' freedom based on the *Rachel* precedent; however, problems of hearsay led to a mistrial in 1847. Dred Scott pursued his case for freedom once again in 1850 and his case encountered multiple appeals, all the way up to the U.S. Supreme Court.

By the time Dred Scott's case was appealed to the U.S. Supreme Court, Mrs. Emerson's brother, John Sandford, had assumed responsibility for Dr. Emerson's estate, and thus Scott's suit was filed against Sandford. Sandford questioned whether Scott had the right to sue in a federal court. Specifically, Sandford questioned whether blacks could be citizens of the United States. Likewise, Sandford's attorney challenged the constitutionality of the Missouri Compromise of 1820, asserting that Congress did not have the authority to ban slavery in the territories.

In a seven-to-two ruling, Chief Justice Roger Taney ruled that blacks were not citizens of the United States. To defend this position, Taney pointed out that this ruling was consistent with the intentions of the men who founded the United States. Taney argued that the language of the Declaration of Independence as well as the history of the times indicated that the country's founders did not intend for slaves or their descendents to be citizens of the United States. In fact, even if a former slave received his or her freedom, Taney explained that the founding fathers never intended for blacks to be considered citizens.

Moreover, Taney emphasized that this view against citizenship for blacks remained the predominant public opinion during the writing and ratification of the Constitution. This idea, he argued, could be witnessed in the Constitution. In Article I, section 9, the Constitution granted the states the right to import slaves until 1808. Additionally, Article IV, section 2 required the states to return escaped slaves to their owners. Chief Justice Taney argued that these two portions of the Constitution indicated that the framers of the document did not view members of the black race as citizens of the government.

In short, Taney ruled that blacks lacked civil rights and civil liberties. More specifically, the Supreme Court ruled that blacks, freedmen as well as slaves, were not "citizens" within the meaning of the Constitution. Thus, while it was possible for blacks to be citizens of an individual state, the Constitution precluded blacks from being citizens of the United States. As a result, this meant that Scott did not have the right to sue in federal courts, and that he and other blacks were considered "property" under the Constitution. Furthermore, Taney ruled that Scott was still a slave and was not a free man based on the fact that he traveled to free territories in the United States. Finally, Taney went on to declare the Missouri Compromise unconstitutional.

Although the Supreme Court's ruling did not grant Dred Scott his freedom, he and the rest of his family did receive their freedom later that year. Peter Blow's sons, who helped pay Scott's legal fees, had promised to purchase the Scott family and set them free if they lost their case in the U.S. Supreme Court. In 1857, Mrs. Emerson sold the Scotts back to the Blow family, who subsequently set Dred and Harriet free. Nine months after receiving his freedom, Dred Scott died of tuberculosis.

The Supreme Court ruling in this case exerted an impact on blacks beyond Dred Scott himself. Reaction to the *Dred Scott* ruling was mixed and did not settle the controversial slavery issue for the United States. Rather, the Court's decision only furthered the country's division over the slavery issue, which ultimately led to the Civil War. The other two branches of government eventually responded with attempts to overcome the issues surrounding slavery. In 1862, Congress passed the Act of June 19, 1862, which prohibited slavery and involuntary servitude in any of the territories of the United States. That same year, Congress also passed legislation prohibiting slavery in the District of Columbia and repealed the Fugitive Slave Act. Likewise, in 1863, President Lincoln issued the Emancipation Proclamation, which announced that slaves who lived in rebellion states would be free once these states were under the control of the Union army.

Despite these efforts of the legislative and executive branches to eradicate the effects of the *Dred Scott* case, these efforts were inconsistent with the original Constitution. Consequently, the document had to be amended to overcome the problems of slavery and to promote the civil rights and civil liberties of blacks.

With the end of the Civil War, three Reconstruction amendments were written and ratified to overcome the *Dred Scott* ruling. Specifically, these amendments recognized and promoted civil rights and civil liberties for blacks. In 1865, slavery and involuntary servitude were abolished with the ratification of the Thirteenth Amendment. Likewise, in 1868, the Fourteenth Amendment recognized all persons born or naturalized in the United States as "citizens." This amendment specifically overturned *Dred Scott*'s ruling that blacks were not U.S. citizens. Moreover, the Fourteenth Amendment prohibited the states from denying blacks, as well as all other citizens, "equal protection" of the laws and "due process of law." Finally, in 1870, the Fifteenth Amendment extended voting rights to black males. Thus, although the case of *Dred Scott v. Sandford* is notorious for its denial of rights and liberties to blacks, the three constitutional amendments that overturned this ruling have been instrumental in protecting civil rights and civil liberties of all American citizens.

FRANCENE M. ENGEL

References and Further Reading

Ehrlich, Walter. *They Have No Rights: Dred Scott's Struggle for Freedom*. Westport, CT: Greenwood Press, 1979.

Fehrenbacher, Don Edward. *Slavery, Law and Politics: The Dred Scott Case in Historical Perspective*. New York: Oxford University Press, 1981.

Finkelman, Paul. Dred Scott v. Sandford: *A Brief History With Documents*. Boston: Bedford Books, 1997.

Herda, D. J. *The Dred Scott Case: Slavery and Citizenship*. Hillside, NJ: Enslow Publishers, 1994.

Cases and Statutes Cited

Rachel v. Walker, 4 Missouri Rep. 350 (1836)

DRUG TESTING

President Reagan announced the War on Drugs in a televised speech in 1982. Shortly thereafter, federal agencies began to drug test their employees randomly, particularly those involved in law enforcement and those in safety-sensitive positions. The Supreme Court's first foray into defining the contours of the constitutionality of drug testing of federal government employees came in the companion cases *Skinner v. Railway Labor Executives' Association*, 489 U.S. 602 (1989), and *National Treasury Employees Union v. Von Raab*, 489 U.S. 656 (1989).

Skinner involved the drug testing of federal railway employees who had been involved in serious train accidents. In upholding the drug testing regulations, the Court relied on the "special needs" exception to the Fourth Amendment as articulated in *Griffin v. Wisconsin*, 483 U.S. 868 (1987). The Court also noted that the Federal Railway Administration had made a finding that there was a high rate of alcoholism and drug abuse among railway workers. Finally, the Court held that public safety was a concern that outweighed the privacy interests of the railway workers, focusing on the fact that trains were dangerous instruments when in the hands of inebriated workers.

Von Raab, decided on the same day, upheld the drug testing regulations of the Commission of Customs. The regulations provided for random, suspicionless drug testing of all customs officers because they carried weapons and many of them engaged in drug interdiction activities. The Court accepted the government's argument that there was a serious crisis brewing in law enforcement due to drug abuse and held that the government had a compelling interest in randomly testing its customs officers, emphasizing the "extraordinary" dangers of drug interdiction.

Following these two cases, the D.C. circuit adopted a "nexus" test in *Harmon v. Thornburgh*, 878 F.2d 484 (D.C. Cir. 1989), requiring the government to prove a direct nexus between the employee's position and the possible safety repercussions that could result from drug or alcohol abuse. This nexus test tends to invalidate most drug testing schemes of federal government workers unless the government can prove that a very serious safety issue exists. A few states, such as Alaska and Massachusetts, have declared all random, suspicionless drug testing to be in violation of state constitutions.

Later, the Supreme Court heard two cases relating to random, suspicionless testing of public high school students: *Veronia School District 47J v. Acton*, 515 U.S. 646 (1995), and *Board of Education of Independent School District of Pottawatomie County v. Earls*, 536 U.S. 822 (2002). In *Veronia*, the Court upheld the random, suspicionless drug testing of high school athletes, holding the deterrence of student drug use to be at least as important as the schemes in *Skinner* and *Von Raab*, particularly since high school athletes faced potential physical injury during sports activities. The Court also noted that children entrusted to the care of public schools had lesser expectations of privacy than adults, a holding the Court relied on in *Earls* as well. There, the Court upheld the random, suspicionless drug testing of public high school students who participated in any extracurricular activity, even those that would pose no danger to the children, such as choir.

The Court's lone invalidation of a drug testing scheme occurred in *Chandler v. Miller*, 520 U.S. 305 (1997). There, the Court invalidated Georgia's requirement that all candidates for state office must submit to a drug test. Georgia made no showing of any concrete threat that would serve to show a special need for the test. Also, the Court noted that the test would not serve to deter illicit drug use because the test was not a secret and drug abusers could abstain for a sufficient time period before the test.

Public opinion about drug testing shifted dramatically after President Reagan's drug war declaration in 1982. Private employers and landlords began drug testing employees and tenants. State and federal public housing authorities began to require tenants to consent to drug tests as a condition of residence. Many state government and private employers require a pre-employment drug screen as a condition of employment. Federal and state agencies sometimes require organizations that receive grants to adopt drug testing policies. Finally, and perhaps most pervasively, individuals convicted of crimes and placed on probation or released on parole are usually subjected to random drug tests as a condition of their release from detention.

Scholars disagree as to the efficacy and constitutionality of drug testing. The magnitude of false positives and negatives detracts from the usefulness of drug testing as a deterrent to drug abuse. Anecdotal evidence suggests that, for example, marijuana users switched to cocaine when their employers began random drug testing because traces of cocaine use leave the body much more quickly. Moreover, an entire industry of manufacturing chemicals that disguise drug abuse has arisen. Recent scientific evidence suggests that expert testimony in criminal cases about the accuracy of drug tests is deeply flawed.

MATTHEW L. M. FLETCHER

References and Further Reading

American Civil Liberties Union. "Drug Testing: A Bad Investment," http://www.aclu.org/Files/Files.cfm?ID=9998&c=184 (1999).

Charles, Guy-Uriel, *Fourth Amendment Accommodations: (Un)Compelling Public Needs, Balancing Acts, and the Fiction of Consent*, Michigan Journal of Race and Law 2 (1997): 1:461–512.

Lang, David, *Get Clean or Get Out: Landlords Drug-Testing Tenants*, Washington University Journal of Law and Policy 2 (2000): 459–487.

Zeese, Kevin B. *Drug Testing Legal Manual and Practice Aids*, 2nd ed. Deerfield, IL: Clark, Boardman, Callahan, 2000.

Cases and Statutes Cited

Anchorage Police Department Employees Association v. Municipality of Anchorage, 24 P.3d 547 (Alaska 2001)

Board of Education of Independent School District of Pottawatomie County v. Earls, 536 U.S. 822 (2002)

Chandler v. Miller, 520 U.S. 305 (1997)

Griffin v. Wisconsin, 483 U.S. 868 (1987)

Guiney v. Police Commission of Boston, 582 N.E.2d 523 (Mass. 1991)

Harmon v. Thornburgh, 878 F.2d 484 (D.C. Cir. 1989)

National Treasury Employees Union v. Von Raab, 489 U.S. 656 (1989)

Skinner v. Railway Labor Executives' Association, 489 U.S. 602 (1989)

Veronia School District 47J v. Acton, 515 U.S. 646 (1995)

See also ***Chandler v. Miller*, 520 U.S. 305 (1997) (candidates); *Griffin v. Wisconsin*, 483 U.S. 868 (1987); *National Treasury Employee Union v. Von Raab*, 489 U.S. 656 (1989); *Skinner v. Railway Labor Executives' Association*, 489 U.S. 602 (1989); *Veronia School District 47J v. Acton*, 515 U.S. 646 (1995); War on Drugs**

DRUGS, RELIGION, AND LAW

Law on many levels regulates access to drugs, complicating any incorporation of an interdicted substance within religious ceremonies. Arguments to obtain that liberty implicate issues on at least three levels. Drug restrictions exist on federal and state levels, and thus the religiously motivated drug users must confront the impediments at both levels.

Previously, an obvious source of support would have been the free exercise clause of the Constitution's First Amendment. As explained later, after the ruling in *Employment Div., Dept. of Human Resources of Oregon v. Smith (II)*, 494 U.S. 872 (1990), that line of reasoning today offers little solace. The best option remains explicit legislative exemptions for the religious use of drugs, specifically (for example, the American Indian Religious Freedom Act) or through the judicial interpretation of more general statutes that command respect for religious practices.

Free Exercise Protections of Religious Practices

Religious liberty in the United States has never been absolute, despite its place as a preferred liberty in law and in the national imagination. The limited scope of the protection of religion was driven home during the anti-Mormon hysteria of the late nineteenth century and the line of polygamy cases that began with *Reynolds v. U.S.*, 98 U.S. 145 (1878). *Reynolds* announced a belief/action dichotomy, holding that the former was absolutely protected, but the latter was not. The government remained "free to reach" actions "in violation of social duties or subversive of good order," regardless of any religious command.

Thereafter, it would become a matter of dispute about which religious practices the state needed to allow, by refraining from passing some laws altogether or by granting exemptions from general laws that would otherwise conflict with religious beliefs and practices. Cases would address whether the state's justification for any imposed burden need be only rational, or compelling, for interfering with this First Amendment right.

On no topic has this context been more enduring than the use of drugs within religious ritual. Although the conflict could arise, at least in theory, over any controlled substance, sustained litigation has primarily targeted peyote and marijuana.

The Peyote Cases

Peyote use is regulated by federal and state governments, requiring the religiously motivated person wishing to ingest peyote to seek exemption from both. One such group that occasionally incorporates peyote use into its ritual practices is the Native American Church (NAC). Although peyote is a controlled substance under federal law, since 1971 the Church

has been granted an exemption (21 C.F.R. 1307.31). Lingering issues concern peyote use by persons who are not members of the NAC and peyote use that is illegal under state laws that do not grant an exemption similar to the federal regulations. For example, in *Peyote Way Church of God, Inc., v. Thornburgh*, 922 F.2d 1210 (5th Cir., 1991), it was unsuccessfully argued that limiting the peyote exemption to only one religion violated the Establishment Clause. Courts have also been unwilling to allow peyote use by NAC members who are not Native Americans (*U.S. v. Warner*, 595 F.Supp. 595, D.C.N.D., 1984).

Although some states had offered religious exemptions for peyote use—most notably in *People v. Woody*, 394 P.2d 813 (Cal. 1964)—many did not. The illegality of religious peyote in Oregon occasioned the litigation of *Employment Div. v. Smith (II)*, which held that the free exercise clause alone does not require exemption from a generally applicable law, including those proscribing a certain class of drugs. As part of the reaction against this drastic curtailment of religious freedom, Congress enacted Public Law 103-344 (108 Stat. 3125, October 6, 1994), which amended the American Indian Religious Freedom Act to grant a religious exemption for peyote at state and federal levels. Significantly, this new exemption is not limited only to the Native American Church, but extends to peyote use "by an Indian for bona fide traditional ceremonial purposes in connection with the practice of a traditional Indian religion."

Nonpeyote Cases

On the surface, marijuana might appear to offer many of the same features as peyote: traditional use of a proscribed substance by an identifiable religious and ethnic minority, Rastafarians. Thus far that analogy has not succeeded. *State v. McBride*, 955 P.2d 133 (Kan. 1998), ruled that Rastafarians are not "similarly situated" to Native Americans because: "(1) Peyote is consumed by the NAC members only at specific and infrequent religious ceremonies, whereas Rastafarians may consume marijuana in any quantity at any time; (2) peyote generally is not abused at the same rate as marijuana; and (3) the Kansas and federal NAC exemptions were passed under the ambit of the federal trust responsibility, which seeks to preserve the cultural and political integrity of Native American tribes."

The third prong particularly, should it continue to be relevant, would permanently prevent the peyote exemption from serving as a precedent for the creation of a religious exemption of any other controlled substances. Other religious groups less favorably situated have also failed in their claims for religious marijuana use, including Hindus (*Leary v. U.S.*, 383 F.2d 851, 5th Cir., 1967), Black Muslims (*U.S. v. Spears*, 443 F.2d 895, 5th Cir., 1971), and members of the Ethiopian Zion Copic Church (*Olsen v. Drug Enforcement Admin.*, 878 F.2d 1458, D.C.C., 1989).

As an alternative to explaining why drug-ingestion rituals fall outside the protections of the Free Exercise Clause, courts have occasionally attempted to circumvent the religious liberty claim altogether by denying that the practice at issue qualifies as "religious" in the constitutional context. For example, in *U.S. v. Koch*, 288 F.Supp. 439 (D.C.D.C. 1968), the federal district court denied the use of LSD (lysergic acid diethylamide) by the Neo-American Church in part because the organization failed to satisfy the judges that it was a genuine religion. Yet, even when that hurdle is surmounted, if it can be shown that other adherents freely practice the religion without resort to the illegal drug, the ritual may fail to qualify as "intrinsic" to the faith, minimizing the burden imposed by a ban on its use.

Conclusions

The lessons from this thick body of jurisprudence are fairly straightforward. At the federal level, the likelihood of winning a free exercise claim to use a controlled substance in religious rituals is minute. This tactic rarely succeeded in the best-case scenario—peyote use by Native Americans—and was categorically rejected by the U.S. Supreme Court. While the special relationship between Native Americans and the federal government secured for them a legislative exemption, no other group can count on similar largesse.

In contexts in which a balancing test will still be applied, the state's interest in controlling access to mind-altering substances can be expected to continue to be deemed compelling. This interest will trump any burden on the religious practice inflicted by an inability to perform its sacred rituals.

Nonetheless, this area of the law continually evolves, as religious organizations initiate further suits in hopes of securing a right to worship in their chosen manner. Most recently, the Supreme Court has agreed to hear *Gonzales v. Centro Espirita Beneficiente Uniao do Vegetal*, 389 F.3d 973 (10th Cir. 2004), cert. granted Apr. 18, 2005, to decide whether the Religious Freedom Restoration Act of 1993 should allow the church access to hoasca, an hallucinogenic tea. As one line of argument is closed, new ones may be asserted, such as Renteln's (2004)

argument that criminalizing substances unfamiliar to our culture under an unproven presumption that they are necessarily harmful can violate the right to culture recognized in international law. These efforts represent an ongoing effort to forge a balance between the well-intentioned secular needs of society and the religious spirit of its multicultural citizens.

JAMES M. DONOVAN

References and Further Reading

Epps, Garrett. *To an Unknown God: Religious Freedom on Trial*. New York: St. Martin's Press, 2001.
Long, Carolyn N. *Religious Freedom and Indian Rights*. Lawrence: University Press of Kansas, 2000.
Renteln, Alison Dundes. *The Cultural Defense*. New York: Oxford University Press, 2004.

Cases and Statutes Cited

Employment Div., Dept. of Human Resources of Oregon v. Smith (II), 494 U.S. 872 (1990)
Gonzales v. Centro Espirita Beneficiente Uniao do Vegetal, 389 F.3d 973 (10th Cir. 2004)
Leary v. U.S., 383 F.2d 851 (5th Cir. 1967)
Olsen v. Drug Enforcement Admin., 878 F.2d 1458 (D.C.C. 1989)
People v. Woody, 394 P.2d 813 (Cal. 1964)
Peyote Way Church of God, Inc., v. Thornburgh, 922 F.2d 1210 (5th Cir. 1991)
Reynolds v. U.S., 98 U.S. 145 (1878)
State v. McBride, 955 P.2d 133 (Kan. 1998)
U.S. v. Spears, 443 F.2d 895 (5th Cir. 1971)
U.S. v. Warner, 595 F.Supp. 595 (D.C.N.D. 1984)
American Indian Religious Freedom Act, P.L. 95-341 (92 Stat. 469, Aug. 11, 1978)
American Indian Religious Freedom Act Amendments of 1994, P.L. 103-344 (108 Stat. 3125, Oct. 6, 1994)
Religious Freedom Restoration Act, P.L. 103-141 (107 Stat 1488, Nov. 16, 1993)
Special Exempt Persons: Native American Church, 21 C.F.R. 1307.31

See also **Accommodation of Religion; Exemptions for Religion Contained in Regulatory Statutes; Free Exercise Clause Doctrine: Supreme Court Jurisprudence; Free Exercise Clause (I): History, Background Framing; Native Americans and Religious Liberty; War on Drugs**

DUAL CITIZENSHIP

Long disfavored though never formally unlawful, dual citizenship is now completely tolerated under U.S. law and practice. Many nineteenth-century immigrants to the United States technically held the status of dual nationals because their countries of origin refused to recognize the transfer of allegiance to their new homeland. However, active dual citizenship was policed by expatriation measures providing for the termination of U.S. citizenship upon undertaking certain activities as a national of another state, including voting in foreign elections, serving in foreign armed forces, or holding office in a foreign state. Mere residence in a foreign country of alternate nationality or the use of a foreign passport could result in the termination of U.S. citizenship.

Dual citizenship was also the target of harsh moral condemnation. It was often compared to bigamy; Theodore Roosevelt described it as a "self-evident absurdity." In the early and middle twentieth century, the incidence of dual nationality declined as countries of origin came more commonly to terminate original citizenship upon naturalization in the United States.

The Supreme Court's 1968 decision in *Afroyim v. Rusk* found the termination of citizenship unconstitutional when it was not intended by the individual. Although *Afroyim* and subsequent cases do not protect the status of dual citizenship as such, current practice allows the retention of U.S. citizenship upon naturalization in another country in all cases. At the same time, the laws of other countries are more liberally permitting the retention of citizenship upon naturalization in the United States; many naturalizing Americans today (including those from Mexico) are routinely retaining their citizenship of origin. In the face of greater global mobility, more individuals are born with multiple citizenship to parents of different nationality. As evidenced by the 1997 European Convention on Nationality and its increasing tolerance in the practice of nation-states, there is evidence that dual citizenship may come to be conceived of as an associational human right under international law.

PETER J. SPIRO

References and Further Reading

Hansen, Randall, and Patrick, Weil, eds. *Dual Nationality, Social Rights and Federal Citizenship in the U.S. and Europe*. New York: Berghahn Books, 2002.

Martin, David A., and Kay Hailbronner, eds. *Rights and Duties of Dual Nationals: Evolution and Prospects*. The Hague: Kluwer Law International, 2003.

Schuck, Peter H. "Plural Citizenships." In *Immigration and Citizenship in the 21st Century*, Noah M. J. Pickus, ed. Lanham, MD: Rowman & Littlefield Publishers, 1998, 149–192.

Spiro, Peter J., *Dual Nationality and the Meaning of Citizenship*, Emory Law Journal 46 (1997): 1412.

See also **Citizenship**

DUE PROCESS

The term "due process" appears in the U.S. Constitution in the Fifth and Fourteenth Amendments, but it is not defined there. It is one of those fundamental legal concepts that arises from Anglo–American legal tradition, and we need to look to history for the meaning. The key word is "due," meaning fair or that to which one has a right, as in the phrase, "Give him his due." But historical precedent does not leave the definition of fairness entirely to some natural sense of justice or allow us to be satisfied that process is "due" if it is merely uniform and equally applied. Implicit in the concept is a minimum standard of protection of rights that might be achieved by different procedures, but is unlikely to be protected unless certain procedures are strictly enforced to some minimum degree.

In the amendments, the phrase is qualified by the phrase "of law," and legal scholars and judges have equated "due process of law" with the phrase "by the law of the land," suggesting that it could be defined by positive law, such as a statute, or by natural law, common law, or traditional judgments of equity. The phrase "by the law of the land" was first established in 1215 in Magna Carta: "No freemen shall be taken or imprisoned or disseised or exiled or in any way destroyed, nor will we go upon him nor send upon him, except by the lawful judgment of his peers or by the law of the land."

This was rendered into statute in 1354: "No man of what state or condition he be, shall be put out of his lands or tenements nor taken, nor disinherited, nor put to death, without he be brought to answer by due process of law." This was further affirmed in 1628 in the Petition of Right: ". . . no freeman may be taken or imprisoned or be disseized of his freehold or liberties, or his free customs, or be outlawed or exiled, or in any manner destroyed, but by the lawful judgment of his peers, or by the law of the land."

The equivalence of the phrases "due process of law" and "law of the land" was asserted by Coke in his *Second Institutes*, in which he specified that "law" meant "the common law" or "by the indictment or presentment of good and lawful men . . . or by writ original of the Common Law."

The phrase appears again in 1647 in the *Heads of the Proposals Offered by the Army:*

That the right and liberty of the Commons of England may be cleared and vindicated as to a due exemption from any judgment, trial or other proceeding against them by the House of Peers, without the concurring judgment of the House of Commons: as also from any other judgment, sentence or proceeding against them, other than by their equals, or according to the law of the land.

The phrase later appeared in 1776 in the Virginia Declaration of Rights: ". . . that no man be deprived of his liberty, except by the law of the land or the judgment of his peers."

These usages suggest that "law of the land" is distinguished from jury verdicts. However, in the Fifth and Fourteenth Amendments it is apparent that "law of the land" and "judgment of his peers" have been combined in the phrase "due process." Thus, we can conclude that jury verdicts and, for that matter, the indictments or presentments of grand juries are subsumed in the broader concept of "due process."

Due process can be legislative or administrative, as well as judicial, because legislative and executive branch officials may conduct proceedings that have a judicial aspect, which may ultimately affect individual rights, but the focus here will be on judicial proceedings, since most dispositions of individual rights eventually involve the judiciary.

In general, due process is bounded to a finite period of time, with a beginning and an end, and may be classified into types and divided into phases. The two most common types are the *inquisitorial,* to acquire information and reach a finding, and the *dispositive,* to decide the assignment and operation of rights, powers, and duties. Inquisitorial proceedings, sometimes called "ex parte," generally involve only one side of an issue, whereas dispositive proceedings are generally adversarial, allowing contenders to argue their side of the case. Original parties may be joined by intervenors, who enter the case as additional parties, or by *amici curiae*, who offer commentary and perhaps evidence not offered by the parties, but in the public interest.

A hearing on a petition for a search, seizure, arrest, or execution of judgment is inquisitorial, as is a grand jury proceeding, a legislative issuance of a declaration of war or letters of marque and reprisal, or investigatory hearings of legislative committees. It is a violation of due process to conduct only an inquisitorial proceeding when a dispositive proceeding is required or to proceed with a dispositive proceeding if an inquisitorial proceeding is required to precede and authorize it.

Most of judicial due process is centered on one or more courts, which are a specialized form of deliberative assembly with specific powers to make certain kinds of decisions in certain ways. A court proceeding may be called a hearing or a trial. It is composed of various officers with specialized duties. Presiding over the proceedings is the bench, which may consist of one or more officials, often called "judges" in Anglo American courts and "presidents" or other titles in the courts of some other countries. Other officers of the court include the bar, consisting of the attorneys for the parties, and witnesses, jurors, bailiffs,

recorders, clerks, and perhaps others. Even the audience may be officers if sworn to perform certain duties during the proceedings, such as witnessing them.

A trial jury is a specialized form of subassembly within the larger court, with its officer, the foreman, and procedures for reaching a verdict. A grand jury, however, is an inquisitorial assembly with the power to subpoena witnesses, interrogate them under oath, and report their findings. They also have the special power to authorize a criminal prosecution and appoint or ratify the appointment of the prosecutor, who will usually appear before it as a complainant and present his evidence.

Dispositive due process generally begins with some kind of due notice, usually called a petition or complaint, served on the defendant or respondent. It may enter an inquisitorial phase (sometimes called discovery), proceed through a series of fair hearings leading to a finding (often called a verdict), and then to an order of the court, called a sentence in a criminal proceeding. This order may consist of a disablement, or restriction, of the exercise of a right of a party called the defendant or respondent, a deprivation of a right disabled, and a warrant to some agent to execute the deprivation. That or another court may exercise continuing oversight on the execution until it is completed, which terminates the due process.

Due process proceedings may be criminal, leading to a punitive deprivation of life, liberty, or property, or civil, leading to a nonpunitive deprivation of any of those rights. The level of protection of defendants or respondents is higher in criminal than in civil proceedings Beginning with the opinion in *Dred Scott*, courts began to make the distinction between *procedural* and *substantive* due process. While courts have not consistently defined the distinction, the notion of substantive due process generally speaks to the question of *how much* protection, as distinct from *how to* provide that protection.

Although not usually discussed in such terms, the distinction can be seen by examining the requirements for jury verdicts to authorize the court to grant the petition of the plaintiff or prosecutor. It is procedural that the verdict be rendered by a jury and not the bench, but substantive that the jury be of a certain size (twelve in criminal cases) and that its verdict be a supermajority of the jurors, in civil cases, or unanimous, in criminal cases. It also enters as rules of evidence, "preponderance" in civil cases and "beyond a reasonable doubt" in criminal cases, or "probable cause" to authorize a search warrant.

Contrary to the Declaration of Independence that "life, liberty, and the pursuit of happiness" are "unalienable" rights, the exercise of all rights, except due process rights, may be disabled and deprived by some kind of due process, even if the rights are not removed. Therefore, the right to due process is the most fundamental for the exercise of rights. The problem remains, then, of determining the minimum levels of substantive protection and how much variation of procedural due process is consistent with maintaining that substantive level. This is not defined with sufficient specificity in constitutions, and while court precedents may define it in many ways, those precedents may collide with statutes that represent the findings of the legislative branch or the constitutions of states, provisions of which may be challenged in federal courts.

The question sometimes arises whether a person has a positive right to petition and get a fair hearing (called "oyer" in old English usage) and a just decision (called "terminer" in old English usage). The answer is that the right to petition is only the right not to be punished for petitioning and, while there is a right to terminer if a court of competent jurisdiction accepts a petition and grants oyer, there is no right to oyer, except for prerogative writs (see the following). This does not affect whether one has a justiciable right, only whether he or she will get the support of the court in enforcing his right. A court is a public service and the expenditure of a scarce resource, to which no one can have a justiciable or constitutional right to a sufficient allocation. All one can have is a right to a fair opportunity for oyer and terminer under the principle of equal protection, lacking which a person must enforce his or her rights by extrajudicial means.

The main purpose of public courts is not to protect everyone's rights, but rather to avoid the conflict, and perhaps violence, that can arise from extrajudicial enforcement. The public policy of almost every country is to demand that everyone defer extrajudicial enforcement of their rights if that can lead to conflict and seek the support of a court, if the courts are open, whose judgments can then inform the public which side of a dispute to join in supporting. When the court and public join in helping people enforce their rights, it is less likely that the party judged to be in the wrong will resist. It should always be kept in mind, however, that, ultimately, courts have no power to command that is not based on public consent and support from one judgment to the next. They do not have armies, and if officials and civilians ignored their orders, the rule of law would collapse.

This leads to an important element of due process called "presumption," to which the parties to various kinds of disputes have certain rights. The most fundamental of these is the right to a presumption of nonauthority, which is most clearly represented in the Ninth Amendment to the U.S. Constitution. It is the basis for the presumption in favor of the defendant, putting the burden of proof on the plaintiff or prosecutor. It is also the basis for the right of private prosecution of a public right and to have oyer and terminer on petitions for the common-law prerogative writs, such as *quo warranto, habeas corpus, mandamus, prohibito, procedendo,* and *certiorari.* The court has a duty to hear cases concerning these writs before other cases, and the public has a duty to consider issuing by default if the respondent and court, having been duly noticed, fail to respond or to hold oyer and terminer, respectively.

The key element of notice can take many forms. A filing with a court is a notice to the court and, while some courts have arrogated a power to refuse to accept certain filings, this is no more proper than it would be for a witness to refuse to accept a subpoena or for a citizen to refuse to accept a summons to appear for jury duty; he is considered noticed when it is presented to him, whether he accepts it or not. The defendant in a case is deemed noticed by a summons to appear and answer the petition of the plaintiff or prosecutor, and if he ignores it, he is subject to penalties or a default judgment. A criminal arrest is a kind of notice to appear for arraignment and may or may not be custodial—that is, be combined with detention. On a petition for a prerogative writ, notice is to a public or private official to prove his authority to perform or not perform certain acts or, as with a *quo warranto,* to act or continue holding an office.

A public notice is one posted at one or more public places or in a publication of record. It is used for such purposes as to call for a public assembly or election or for a militia muster; to announce a public sale, perhaps on a foreclosure or to satisfy a judgment; or as a way to reach a public or private party whose identity or whereabouts are unknown, such as the owner of unclaimed property or property on which taxes are overdue.

The substantive component of notice is that the respondent must have sufficient time to respond and prepare to respond. For example, the traditional and usually statutory periods for responding to a petition for a prerogative writ were three to twenty days, depending on the distance of the respondent from the court, and usually twenty days for public notices. If the respondent needs more time to prepare a response, he or she may petition the court for additional time, called a continuance, but granting a continuance is generally at the discretion of the court.

There are a number of open issues involving due process. For example, during the period just before and after the founding of the United States, the standard of due process was to argue all issues of law in the presence of the jury, especially in criminal cases.

It was understood that although the primary role of the jury was to bring a verdict on the facts, in bringing a general verdict of guilty or not guilty, they necessarily had to review the decisions of the bench and could only do so if they heard all the legal argument that led to such decisions. However, beginning in the second third of the nineteenth century, first in England and then in the United States, courts began to demand that legal argument be made in written pleadings, mostly presented to the bench prior to convening the jury, and decided in chambers or out of the hearing of the jury.

This process has been called "Mansfieldization" by some, after Lord Mansfield, an English jurist of the late eighteenth century, who led the courts toward this practice. He was opposed by Lord Camden, whose views on the role of the jury in reviewing the legal argument were more popular with English Whigs and with the founders of the United States. Today, the bench will hold a party or his attorney in contempt or initiate disbarment of a lawyer if he mentions the law in the presence of the jury, other than perhaps in the course of raising an objection. The evidence of history strongly supports the position that this practice is a violation of the due process rights of defendants.

Another controversy concerns the practice of holding persons as material witnesses or for contempt of court at the sole discretion of a judge, for long periods of time, without access to counsel. If they were charged with a crime, these individuals would have to be released for lack of access to counsel, lack of speedy trial, lack of compulsion of witnesses, or other due process violations. There is no express provision of the U.S. Constitution that authorizes criminal prosecution for contempt of court. The power is asserted by judges as an inherent power of courts. They also assert the power to make their own rules of judicial procedure, even contrary to legislative statutes, and to control who may be admitted to the practice of law in their courts by a customary practice of admitting lawyers to the bar and disbarring them or prosecuting laypersons for the unauthorized practice of law.

An ongoing controversy concerns the traditional doctrine or practice of *stare decisis*, which means "let the decision stand." There is an ancient doctrine of law to decide like cases alike, sometimes called the First Law, and the constitutional requirements for equal protection and due process would seem to incorporate it. Certainly, court precedents that preceded the adoption of the written U.S. Constitution and were well known to the founders are historical evidence of what the founders meant when they used similar language in the Constitution. The requirement

for finality of due process also supports the related doctrine of *res judicata* that things decided in a case do not have to be decided again, unless error or abuse can be shown. It is also reasonable to use court decisions in exemplary cases to clarify ambiguities in written constitutions or statutes and sharpen the boundaries of interpretation.

The problem arises when past decisions or opinions involving similar issues are treated as *binding* rather than as merely *persuasive* in deciding other cases. Court decisions and opinions can progressively depart from original understanding until decisions that rely more on precedents than on original text, structure, or historical evidence can depart from the meaning of the enactments in important ways. A judicial process that never returns to original text, structure, and history to re-examine precedent and correct departures or does so only at the top level of the U.S. Supreme Court (which has recently been accepting only about eighty of the eight thousand cases submitted to it each year) cannot be considered constitutional due process. Lower courts can try to distinguish issues in their cases from past precedents to return to original understanding, but this is too often an exercise in legal sophistry that builds a body of precedents that can support almost any decision at all. It leaves too much to the discretion of the bench, thereby subverting the rule of law.

The Fourteenth Amendment expanded the field of controversy over due process. In extending the jurisdiction of federal courts of general jurisdiction to cases between a citizen and his state over infringement of rights recognized for citizens of the United States, it presented the problem that such rights, or "immunities," could not be defined merely as the complement of delegated powers. The essential idea of the Ninth and Tenth Amendments is that public action that Congress is not authorized to disable or restrict is a right and any declaration of a right is a restriction on delegated powers. Thus, deciding immunity when there is only one sovereign is logically straightforward, in principle.

But states are also sovereigns with their own constitutions that delegate other powers not delegated to U.S. officials by the U.S. Constitution. Powers not delegated to state officials by state constitutions define immunities under the state constitution or statutes, but that still leaves a zone of potential contention where powers are delegated by a state constitution that intrudes into the immunities defined by nondelegation of powers by the U.S. Constitution. Most of this zone of contention arises from the "police powers" provisions of state constitutions to authorize legislation of the health, safety, order, or morals of the public. There is no such broad provision in the U.S. Constitution. The vagueness of state police powers could be interpreted to authorize infringement of almost any federal immunity. This has left the federal courts to adopt standards of review and rational basis tests and a distinction between "fundamental" and "nonfundamental" rights. Only the first of these is protected from state action. This has led the U.S. Supreme Court to authorize state departures from the standards of federal due process in what is called "selective incorporation" of federal immunities.

JON ROLAND

References and Further Reading

Coke, Sir Edward. *Institutes of the Laws of England, Part II.* London: 1641. http://www.constitution.org/coke/coke2nd.htm.
Haines, Charles Grove. *The Revival of Natural Law Concepts.* London: Oxford University Press, 1930, Chaps. 5, 6. http://www.constitution.org/haines/haines_005.htm.
Magna Carta, Art. 39. See also Art. 55. http://www.constitution.org/eng/magnacar.htm.
Matthews v. Eldridge, 424 U.S. 319 (1976). Often cited as defining sufficient condition of a due process claim, it is sometimes mistakenly taken as a necessary condition to limit standing to those who have suffered actual injury, contrary to the historic right to prosecute public rights privately. http://laws.findlaw.com/us/424/319.html.
Petition of Right, 1628. Art. 3. http://www.constitution.org/eng/petright.htm.
Roland, Jon. "Presumption of Nonauthority and Unenumerated Rights," http://www.constitution.org/9ll/schol/pnur.htm.
Winter, Steven L., *The Metaphor of Standing and the Problem of Self-Governance.* 40 Stan. L. Rev. 1371 (July 1988). http://www.constitution.org/duepr/standing/winter_standing.htm.
Wood, Horace G. *A Treatise on the Legal Remedies of Mandamus and Prohibition,* Habeas Corpus, Certiorari, *and* Quo Warranto. Albany: Little, 1896, section on quo warranto. http://www.constitution.org/cmt/woodhg/wood-hc.htm.

See also **Incorporation Doctrine**

DUE PROCESS IN IMMIGRATION

"Whatever the procedure authorized by Congress is, it is due process as far as an alien denied entry is concerned" (*United States ex rel. Knauff v. Shaughnessy,* 338 U.S. 537, 544, 1950). On the other hand, all "persons within the United States," citizens and noncitizens alike, are entitled to the procedural protections of the Due Process Clauses of the Constitution (*Zadvydas v. Davis,* 533 U.S. 678, 693, 2001). To determine the due process rights of noncitizens, it is therefore critical to determine who is "within the United States." To understand the due process rights of noncitizens more completely, it is also important to distinguish briefly between the substantive constitutional rights of aliens (or the lack thereof) and their procedural rights.

Procedural versus Substantive Rights

From the earliest days of federal regulation of immigration beginning in the latter half of the nineteenth century, the Supreme Court has deferred to Congress's substantive policy choices. Pursuant to the Court created "plenary power" doctrine, Congress can fashion substantive immigration law and policy virtually free from what we might call domestic constitutional norms. For instance, Congress has used race and ideology as criteria for who can enter and remain in the United States (for example, *Chae Chan Ping v. United States* [*The Chinese Exclusion Case*], 130 U.S. 581, 1889; *Kleindienst v. Mandel,* 408 U.S. 753, 1972).

In contrast, the Court has been less deferential to the political branches' procedural treatment of noncitizens in the United States. Neither the federal nor the state governments can criminally punish a noncitizen without affording the noncitizen the same trial rights due a citizen (*Wong Wing v. United States,* 162 U.S. 228, 1896). Noncitizens are also entitled to due process protections before they can be deported. In *Yamataya v. Fisher* (*The Japanese Immigrant Case*), 189 U.S. 86, 101 (1903), the Court established that a noncitizen was entitled "all opportunity to be heard upon questions involving his right to be and remain in the United States. No such arbitrary power can exist where the principles involved in due process of law are recognized." Noncitizens considered not within the United States, however, receive no constitutional due process protection.

Who Is "Within the United States"?

Only noncitizens who are within the United States are entitled to the Constitution's guarantee of due process. This presents no problems for the hundreds of millions of persons with no connection or desire to interact with the United States. But, the lack of procedural guarantees can create a myriad of problems for those wishing to come to the United States and those physically within the borders but not considered "within the United States."

Noncitizens who apply for visas and/or who present themselves at the border seeking entry are entitled only to those procedural protections provided by Congress or the executive branch. For those whose ties to the United States are attenuated, the lack of due process guarantees results, at most, in inconvenience. As the ties grow stronger, the lack of protection can be devastating. For example, *United States ex rel. Knauff v. Shaughnessy*, 338 U.S. 537 (1950), involved a "war bride" attempting to come to the United States to live with her U.S. citizen husband. She was excluded from the United States as an alleged threat to national security. The Supreme Court upheld the decision not to give her a hearing, deferring to the attorney general's conclusion that giving her a hearing would compromise national security.

Significant ties to the United States and inability to travel to another country can exacerbate the harshness of the rule that only noncitizens "within" the United States are entitled to the Constitution's due-process protections. The plight of Ignatz Mezei amply illustrates the stakes. Mezei had lived a life of "unrelieved insignificance" with his family in Buffalo, New York, for a quarter of a century when he left on an extended journey to visit his ailing mother behind what was then emerging as the Iron Curtain. Upon his attempted return to the United States, he was excluded in the interest of national security and, like Ellen Knauff, he was denied a hearing and a chance to confront his accusers. Since no other country would take him, he was confined indefinitely on Ellis Island. Since he had not been admitted into the United States, he was entitled to none of the Constitution's procedural protections (see *Shaugnessy v. United States ex rel. Mezei*, 345 U.S., 206, 1953).

Noncitizens, like Mezei, who are at the border (including those arriving to interior airports), although physically present on U.S. soil, have not passed through an immigration checkpoint and therefore have not been admitted to the United States and are not entitled to due process. For humanitarian reasons, the United States may allow an otherwise excludable alien to visit the United States. Instead of admitting the alien into the country, the United States grants the alien "parole," which allows the government to maintain the legal fiction that the noncitizen is not within the United States and therefore is not entitled to due-process protections.

To ameliorate the harshness of a strict territorial demarcation, the Court, in *Landon v. Plasencia*, 459 U.S. 21 (1982), concluded that a permanent resident alien returning to the United States after a brief sojourn abroad had not cut her ties to the United States so severely as to be entitled to no due-process protection.

The Process Due

For those noncitizens entitled to the Constitution's due-process protection, the further question is what process is due. To determine whether the government's action comports with constitutional minima, the Court balances the individual's interest at stake against the interest of the government in using its current procedures. The risk that the government's current procedures could wrongfully deprive the individual of that interest coupled with the anticipated value of different or additional procedures provides the fulcrum upon which these competing interests are balanced (*Mathews v. Eldridge*, 424 U.S. 219, 334-335, 1976).

MICHAEL A. SCAPERLANDA

References and Further Reading

Aleinikoff, Alex, *Due Process and "Community Ties": A Response to Martin*, University of Pittsburgh Law Review 44 (1983): 237–260.

Chin, Gabriel, Victor Romero, and Michael Scaperlanda, eds. *Immigration and the Constitution*, vol. 3, *Shark Infested Waters: Procedural Due Process in Constitutional Immigration Law*. New York: Garland, 2000.

Cole, David, *In Aid of Removal: Due Process Limits on Immigration Detention*, Emory Law Journal 51 (2002): 1003–1039.

Martin, David, *Due Process and Membership in the National Political Community: Political Asylum and Beyond*, University of Pittsburgh Law Review 44 (1983): 165–235.

Motomura, Hiroshi, *The Curious Evolution of Immigration Law: Procedural Surrogates for Substantive Constitutional Rights*, Columbia Law Review 92 (1992): 1625–1704.

Nafziger, *Review of Visa Denials by Consular Officials*, Washington University Law Review 66 (1991): 1–105.

Saito, Natsu, *The Enduring Effect of the Chinese Exclusion Cases: The "Plenary Power" Justification for On-Going Abuses of Human Rights*, Asian Law Journal 10 (2003): 13–36.

Scaperlanda, Michael, *Polishing the Tarnished Golden Door*, Wisconsin Law Review 1993 (1993): 965–1032.

———, *Are We That Far Gone? Due Process and Secret Deportation Proceedings*, Stanford Law and Policy Review 7 (1996): 23–30.

———, *Partial Membership: Aliens and the Constitutional Community*, Iowa Law Review 81 (1996): 707–773.

Weisselberg, Charles, *The Exclusion and Detention of Aliens: Lessons From the Lives of Ellen Knauff and Ignatz Mezei*, University of Pennsylvania Law Review 143 (1995): 933–1034.

Cases and Statutes Cited

Chae Chan Ping v. United States (The Chinese Exclusion Case), 130 U.S. 581 (1889)

Demore v. Kim, 123 S.Ct. 1708 (2003)

Kleindienst v. Mandel, 408 U.S. 753 (1972)

Landon v. Plasencia, 459 U.S. 21 (1982)

Mathews v. Eldridge, 424 U.S. 219 (1976)

Shaugnessy v. United States ex rel. Mezei, 345 U.S. 206 (1953)

United States ex rel. Knauff v. Shaughnessy, 338 U.S. 537 (1950)

Wong Wing v. United States, 162 U.S. 228 (1896)

Yamataya v. Fisher (The Japanese Immigrant Case), 189 U. S. 86 (1903)

Zadvydas v. Davis, 533 U.S. 678 (2001)

See also **Bill of Rights: Structure;** *Chae Chan Ping v. U.S.*, **130 U.S. 581 (1889) and Chinese Exclusion Act; Citizenship; Aliens, Civil Liberties of; Criminal Law/ Civil Liberties and Noncitizens in the United States; Due Process; Due Process of Law (V and XIV); Indefinite Detention;** *Kleindienst v. Mandel*, **408 U.S. 753 (1972); 9/11 and the War on Terrorism; Noncitizens, Civil Liberties; Plenary Power Doctrine**

DUE PROCESS OF LAW (FIFTH AND FOURTEENTH)

The Fifth Amendment of the U.S. Constitution contains a clause that prohibits the national government from depriving a person of "life, liberty, or property, without due process of law." The Fourteenth Amendment has a similarly worded clause that applies to state governments. Other than applying to different levels of government, the two clauses have the same basic meaning.

In its most general sense, due process of law is another term for rule of law, the principle that government cannot act against persons unless it has a legal basis for doing so. This principle does not preclude most government takings of life, liberty, and property, but only those that are arbitrary or capricious in nature. More specifically, due process of law requires that in order to deprive a person of life, liberty, or property, the government must notify the person that it wants to do just that and then must, in a fair hearing, convince an impartial judge or court that the person has violated some previously enacted, but valid, law.

In this general sense, due process of law has an ancient lineage. As early as 1215, it was guaranteed by the Magna Carta, one of several documents that now make up the English Constitution. Therein, the king of England promised that "[n]o freeman shall be arrested, or imprisoned, or disseized, or outlawed, or exiled, or in any way molested; nor will we proceed against him, unless by the lawful judgment of his peers or by the law of the land." The principle of due process of law was reaffirmed in the Petition of Right (1628), for it said that English freemen could "be imprisoned or detained only by the law of the land, or by due process of law, and not by the king's special command without any charge." It was also at the heart of John Locke's *Second Treatise of Government* (1690), which significantly influenced the thinking of those who established the American political system. Before the Constitution was ratified, most state constitutions had a due process clause.

Although the general meaning of the two due-process clauses is clear, exactly what kinds of government actions violate the clauses is not clear. In its first case interpreting the due-process clause of the Fifth Amendment, the Supreme Court said, "The Constitution contains no description of those processes which it was intended to allow or forbid. It does not even declare what principles are to be applied to ascertain whether it be due process" (*Murray's Lessee v. Hoboken Land and Improvement Company*, 18 How., 59 U.S., 272, 1856). Consequently, the Court has had to spell out exactly what due process of law means, and in doing so, it has significantly expanded its power of judicial review and generated considerable controversy.

The Court's decisions interpreting the clauses fall into two categories: (1) those dealing with *procedural* due process (whether the application or enforcement of a law violated due process) and (2) those dealing with *substantive* due process (whether a law itself violated due process).

Procedural Due Process

Issues involving procedural due process usually arise in criminal cases in which the Court must decide whether a person's conviction of a crime resulted from a fair judicial proceeding. As for what counts as a fair proceeding, until approximately the 1960s, the Court's answer depended on which of the two due-process clauses it was interpreting. The Court has said relatively little about the procedural due process guaranteed by the Fifth Amendment, mainly because there are other provisions in the Bill of Rights that guarantee, as against the federal government, specific aspects of procedural due process. Quite different has been the Court's interpretation of the Due Process Clause of the Fourteenth Amendment. Because it was the only constitutional provision the Court could use to guarantee procedural due process in state criminal proceedings, the Court has written much about its meaning.

At first, however, the Court interpreted that clause rather narrowly. For example, it said that the clause does not require states to use a grand jury as the way to indict persons of capital crimes (*Hurtado v. California*, 110 U.S. 516, 1884) or prohibit them from requiring persons accused of crimes to answer questions at their trials (*Twining v. New Jersey*, 211 U.S. 78, 1908). In the latter case, however, the Court said:

> It is possible that some of the personal rights safeguarded by the first eight Amendments against national action may also be safeguarded against state action, . . . If this is so, it is not because those rights are enumerated in the first eight Amendments, but because they are of such a nature that they are included in the conception of due process of law.

By the 1920s, the Court began using the Due Process Clause of the Fourteenth Amendment to overturn convictions that it felt had not been fairly obtained. For example, in *Moore v. Dempsey*, 261 U.S. 86 (1923), it overturned the convictions of five black men for murder because their trial was so influenced by a racially prejudiced mob that the Court held that it was a travesty. Most importantly, in *Brown v. Mississippi*, 297 U.S. 278 (1936), the Court unanimously held that states could not use coerced confessions to convict persons of crimes.

Decisions like these, however, were usually the result of the Court's examining fully and carefully the record of what occurred before and during a trial. Even in the famous case of *Powell v. Alabama*, 287 U.S. 45 (1932), in which the Court overturned the convictions of nine black teenagers for raping two white girls (on the grounds that they were denied aid of counsel), it did not hold that in all criminal or even felony trials the Due Process Clause requires that the accused be afforded effective counsel. Rather, the Court justified its decision on the basis of the circumstances of the case and the characteristics of the defendants. Not surprisingly, five years later, in *Palko v. Connecticut*, 302 U.S. 319 (1937), the Court refused to hold that a right against double jeopardy is part of procedural due process guaranteed by the Fourteenth Amendment. It did so on the grounds that specific procedural rights mentioned in the Bill of Rights, like the right against double jeopardy, are not "fundamental" rights "implicit in the concept of ordered liberty."

In the mid-twentieth century, however, the Court changed its mind on this issue. It decided that most of the rights of the accused guaranteed in the Bill of Rights were included within the procedural due process guaranteed by the Fourteenth Amendment. It held in 1949 that unreasonable searches and seizures like those prohibited by the Fourth Amendment cannot be conducted by state officials without violating due process of law (*Wolf v. Colorado*, 338 U.S. 25, 1949) and, in 1961, that evidence obtained through such unconstitutional searches and seizures cannot be used in state courts against persons accused of a crime (*Mapp v. Ohio*, 367 U.S. 643, 1961).

After that, the Court held that due process of law means that persons accused of serious crimes not only have a right to counsel, but also must be provided with a lawyer by the state if they do not have the means to pay for one (*Gideon v. Wainwright*, 372 U.S. 335, 1963); that persons tried in state courts cannot be forced to answer questions or testify in their defense (*Malloy v. Hogan*, 378 U.S. 1, 1964); and that defendants in state courts must be given the opportunity to confront and cross-examine witnesses against them (*Pointer v. Texas*, 380 U.S. 400, 1965). *Klopfer v. North Carolina*, 386 U.S. 213 (1967), required states to provide speedy trials to persons accused of crimes; *Duncan v. Louisiana*, 391 U.S. 145 (1968), said that persons accused of serious crimes have a right to be tried by juries in state courts; and *Benton v. Maryland*, 395 U.S. 784 (1969), held that states cannot try persons more than once for the same crime.

Since the 1960s, although the Supreme Court has elaborated on the meaning of the specific rights mentioned in the preceding paragraph, it has not created any additional procedural due-process rights. It could still do this, however. Moreover, the Court can always declare any deprivation of life, liberty, and property to be a violation of procedural due process if it believes that all the facts in a case show that the deprivation was the product of an unfair procedure.

Finally, the Court has held that procedural due process (a fair hearing of some sort) must also be afforded in various kinds of noncriminal (for example, civil, administrative, juvenile) proceedings that could lead to the loss of a person's liberty or property. What exactly is required in such proceedings? The Court has said that a variety of processes and hearings, depending on the situation, can work to ensure due process of law and legislatures have a role to play in determining what is required (*Bell v. Burson*, 402 U.S. 535, 1971), but that "the hearing must provide a real test" (*Fuentes v. Shevin*, 407 U.S. 67, 1972).

Substantive Due Process

The constitutional law of substantive due process is quite different from and more controversial than that of procedural due process. Here the basic issue is whether a law, as distinguished from its application or enforcement, is inconsistent with due process of law. When the Supreme Court first addressed the meaning of the Due Process Clause of the Fifth

Amendment, it said, "The article is a restraint on the legislative as well as on the executive and judicial powers of the government . . ." (*Murray's Lessee v. Hoboken Land and Improvement Company*, 1856). Later, the Court said, "It is not every act, legislative in form, that is law. Law is something more than mere will exerted as an act of power" (*Hurtado v. California*, 1884).

Laws can violate the principle of due process of law in four ways. First, they can do so if they require judges or law enforcement officials to use a procedure inconsistent with procedural due process. The Court has thus said, "It is manifest that it was not left to the legislative power to enact any process which might be devised" (*Murray's Lessee v. Hoboken Land and Improvement Company*, 1856). An example of a law that authorized a procedure inconsistent with due process of law was the one struck down in *Chicago, Milwaukee and St. Paul Ry. Co. v. Minnesota*, 134 U.S. 118 (1890), which gave a regulatory commission the power to set the rates for railroads without holding hearings and allowing the railroads to present evidence.

Second, a law violates due process if it is arbitrary or inherently unfair. The emphasis here is not on a law's effect—the liberty or property that it takes, prohibits, or regulates—but on its nature as law. Even if the liberty or property it takes is very minor, a law can still violate due process if it does not possess the requisite character of law. On this point, the Court has said, "It [a law] must be not a special rule for a particular person or a particular case," but a "*general* law" . . . Arbitrary power . . . is not law, whether manifested as the decree of a personal monarch or of an impersonal multitude" (*Hurtado v. California*, 1884).

How might a law, regardless of its effects on liberty or property, be unfair or arbitrary? Two examples of such a law are bills of attainder and ex post facto laws, both of which are explicitly prohibited in Article One, sections 9 and 10, of the Constitution. Bills of attainder are unfair because they inflict punishment on specified persons even though a court of law has not found them guilty of violating any existing laws, and ex post facto laws are equally unfair because they apply retroactively and thereby punish persons for doing something that was not illegal when they did it. Very similar to these kinds of laws are "acts of confiscation," "acts directly transferring one man's estate to another," and legislative acts deciding specific cases that should have been decided by courts or reversing decisions already made by courts (*Hurtado v. California*, 1884).

Another kind of law that the Supreme Court considers to be arbitrary, regardless of what it regulates or prohibits, is one that has no "rational basis"—that is, that serves no public purpose or interest. When a law deprives persons of their life, liberty, or property for no apparent reason relating to the common good, the Court is likely to assume that it is the result of a legislature's incompetence or animosity toward those harmed by the law.

Third, a law violates due process if it is "so vague that men of common intelligence must necessarily guess at its meaning and differ as to its application . . ." (*Connally v. General Construction Co.*, 269 U.S. 385, 1926). On the other hand, because of the inherent imprecision of language and the need for government to do its business without having to be perfect, the Court has also said that "no more than a reasonable degree of certainty can be demanded" (*Boyce Motor Lines Inc. v. United States*, 342 U.S. 337, 1952).

Fourth, even if a law is not inherently arbitrary, unfair, or unclear, it may still violate due process of law if it deprives persons of an especially important private interest (liberty or property). As early as 1875, the Court used the term "fundamental rights" to refer to the especially important private interests protected by the due process clauses (*United States v. Cruikshank*, 92 U.S. 542, 1975). What rights are fundamental? The Court's answer to this question has evolved over time. Traditionally, the "liberty" that could not be taken without due process of law was that of freedom from physical restraint or imprisonment, but now the word refers to a range of behaviors that the Court believes deserve special protection from legislation.

Whatever these fundamental rights are, however, they are not absolute; they can be abridged by the government if it can make a strong enough case for doing so. This means that in cases involving government regulation of fundamental rights, the Court must utilize some kind of criterion or "test" to determine whether the government's reasons for the regulation are strong enough to justify the regulation. There are, moreover, different tests for different kinds of fundamental rights and they, like the rights, have changed over time. This fourth component of substantive due process has been, by far, the most significant part of the Court's interpretation of the two due process clauses, and its development has been long, complicated, and very controversial.

The idea of substantive due process seems to have arisen first in 1856 in the Court of Appeals of New York, which in *Wynehamer v. People*, 13 N.Y. 378 (1856), declared a New York law prohibiting the possession of liquor to be in violation of that state's due-process clause. One year later, in the infamous case of *Dred Scott v. Sandford*, 19 How. (60 U.S.) 393 (1857), the U.S. Supreme Court used the Due Process

Clause of the Fifth Amendment to strike down the portion of the Missouri Compromise that excluded slavery from certain U.S. territories. It held that "[a]n act of Congress which deprives a citizen of the United States of his liberty or property, merely because he came himself or brought his property into a particular Territory of the United States, and who had committed no offense against the laws, could hardly be dignified with the name of due process of law." Then, in *Hepburn v. Griswold*, 8 Wallace 608 (1870), the Court implied that a federal law that authorized the national government to issue paper money that was not redeemable in hard currency but was legal tender for payment of all debts deprived creditors of their property without due process of law guaranteed by the Fifth Amendment. In record time, however, the Court reversed itself and upheld the law in *Second Legal Tender Cases*, 12 Wallace 457 (1871).

In the meantime, in 1868, the Fourteenth Amendment was added to the Constitution. In addition to prohibiting states from abridging "the privileges or immunities of citizens of the United States" and denying "to any person . . . the equal protection of the laws," it prohibited them from depriving "any person of life, liberty, or property, without due process of the laws."

In the *Slaughterhouse Cases*, 16 Wall. (83 U.S.) 36 (1873), the Court was asked to hold that all three of these provisions were violated by a Louisiana law that, for public health reasons, gave one company a monopoly on the slaughtering of animals in the New Orleans area. The plaintiffs who challenged the law were the slaughterers who had been put out of business. Their attorney argued that they had a natural right to practice their trade and that the three provisions were intended to protect that right as well as individual freedom and free enterprise in general. He also argued that the due process clause guaranteed more than procedural due process. Although the Court upheld the law, the idea of substantive due process was given credibility, not only by the plaintiffs' attorney but also by one of the four dissenters, Justice Joseph Bradley, who wrote, "[A] law which prohibits a large class of citizens from adopting a lawful employment, or from following a lawful employment previously adopted, does deprive them of liberty as well as property, without due process of law."

Not surprisingly, therefore, in spite of the *Slaughterhouse Cases* decision, attorneys for businesses, corporations, and others whose property rights were threatened by legislation continued to press the Supreme Court to interpret both due process clauses as guaranteeing substantive, and not merely procedural, due process.

Although during the 1870s and 1880s, the Court resisted using the due process clause to strike down laws, its dicta in several cases and a growing number of dissenting opinions indicated that it was becoming more sympathetic to the idea of substantive due process. Noteworthy is what the Court said in *Mugler v. Kansas*, 123 U.S. 623 (1887): "The courts are not bound by mere forms. They are at liberty—indeed are under a solemn duty—to look at the *substance* of things, whenever they enter upon the inquiry whether the legislature has transcended the limits of its authority."

The breakthrough came in the 1890s. First, the Court struck down rates established for railroads by different state regulatory commissions as "unreasonable" and thus as deprivations of property without due process of law. Then, in *Allgeyer v. Louisiana*, 165 U.S. 578 (1897), which nullified a Louisiana law that banned businesses in that state from buying insurance from companies not licensed to do business in that state, the Court enunciated freedom of contract as a fundamental right protected by the due process clause of the Fourteenth Amendment. In essence, this right meant that individuals and businesses could enter into contracts without the state's dictating the parties to or terms of the contracts.

After *Allgeyer*, the Court used the Due Process Clause of the Fourteenth Amendment and the doctrine of liberty of contract to overturn state laws that limited the number of hours that bakers could work (*Lochner v. New York*, 198 U.S. 45, 1905); outlawed yellow-dog contracts (promises by workers not to join labor unions) (*Coppage v. Kansas*, 236 U.S. 1, 1915); forbade courts to issue injunctions against picketing (*Truax v. Corrigan*, 257 U.S. 312, 1921); created a special court to handle labor disputes (*Wolf Packing Co. v. Court of Industrial Relations*, 262 U.S. 522, 1923); and set minimum wages for employees (*Morehead v. Tipaldo*, 298 U.S. 587, 1936). The Court also used the Due Process Clause of the Fifth Amendment to nullify federal laws that banned yellow-dog contracts (*Adair v. United States*, 208 U.S. 161, 1908) and set minimum wages for female employees in the District of Columbia (*Adkins v. Children's Hospital*, 261 U.S. 525, 1923).

During this same period, the Court actually upheld many more laws challenged as violations of due process of law than it overturned. What was the difference between the laws upheld and those not upheld? According to the Court, the laws that were nullified were "unreasonable"—in purpose, in the means for achieving that purpose, or in the degree of restraint imposed upon liberty or property. Sometimes the Court contended that a law was "arbitrary," by which it usually meant that the restrictions it imposed were more severe than its benefits to the public. Both tests were very vague, and their use allowed the Court to make decisions of the sort traditionally reserved to legislatures, thereby greatly enhancing its power of judicial review.

When the Court first began using substantive due process to nullify laws, the rights that it protected were primarily property rights, such as freedom to choose and practice an occupation and freedom of contract. However, it soon occurred to some justices and lawyers that if the due process clauses could be used to protect property rights, they could and should also be used to protect other "fundamental rights." For example, in dissenting opinions, Justices Harlan and Marshall contended that the rights to free speech and press, the "right to enjoy one's religious belief, unmolested by any human power," and the "right to impart and receive instruction" were protected by the due process of law (*Patterson v. Colorado*, 205 U.S. 454, 1907; *Berea College v. Kentucky*, 211 U.S. 548, 1908). Other justices made similar statements.

Not surprisingly, therefore, in *Meyer v. Nebraska*, 262 U.S. 390 (1923), which nullified a Nebraska law forbidding the teaching in schools of any language other than English, the Court said that the liberty protected by the due process clause includes not only "freedom from bodily restraint" and economic rights, but also the right "to acquire useful knowledge, to marry, establish a home and bring up children, to worship God according to the dictates of his own conscience, and generally to enjoy those privileges long recognized at common law as essential to the orderly pursuit of happiness by free men." Two years later, on the grounds that the right of parents to direct the education of their children was a fundamental right protected by due process of law, it overturned an Oregon law that made private schools illegal (*Pierce v. Society of Sisters*, 268 U.S. 510, 1925). Then, just one week later, in *New York v. Gitlow*, 268 U.S. 652 (1925), the Court said that "freedom of speech and of the press . . . are among the fundamental personal rights and 'liberties' protected by the due process clause of the Fourteenth Amendment . . ."

Other substantive rights guaranteed in the First Amendment were gradually added to the list of rights protected by the Due Process Clause of the Fourteenth Amendment—freedom of assembly in 1937, *De Jonge v. Oregon*, 299 U.S. 353 (1937), free exercise of religion in 1940 (*Cantwell v. Connecticut*, 310 U.S. 296, 1940) and in 1947 the ban on laws respecting an establishment of religion (*Everson v. Board of Education*, 330 U.S. 1, 1947).

Some scholars and Supreme Court justices use the phrase "selective incorporation of the Bill of Rights into the due process clause of the Fourteenth Amendment" to describe the process whereby First Amendment rights and certain procedural rights (discussed in "Procedural Due Process" in this entry) guaranteed in the Bill of Rights were included within the meaning of the Due Process Clause of the Fourteenth Amendment and thus protected from state laws and actions. The "incorporation" is said to be "selective" because it happened gradually and because the Court has never held that due process of law includes all the rights guaranteed in the Bill of Rights. (For example, the right to be indicted by a grand jury has never been incorporated.)

Ironically, not long after the Court decided that certain nonproperty rights were among the fundamental rights protected from legislation by due process of law, it changed its mind about the importance of property or economic rights. In several decisions in the 1930s, the Court upheld state and federal laws that had been passed to deal with the economic problems caused by the Great Depression but had been challenged on the grounds that they violated liberty of contract and related property rights. The Court upheld the laws and, in *United States v. Carolene Products Co.*, 304 U.S. 144 (1938), explicitly stated that economic regulations would be upheld in the face of due process challenges provided they had a "rational basis"—a test that most laws could easily pass. In contrast, it said that laws that abridge other fundamental rights, especially those specifically mentioned in the Bill of Rights, and that are challenged as violations of due process of law would be subjected to a much higher level of scrutiny. This difference in treatment of economic and noneconomic rights is often referred to as the "double standard."

Once the Court decided to use substantive due process to protect noneconomic rights, it did not stop with those explicitly mentioned in the Constitution. In *Griswold v. Connecticut*, 381 U.S. 479 (1965), it held that a right to privacy was a fundamental right protected by due process of law, which, it later held, included within it the right of a pregnant women to abort a fetus prior to its viability (*Roe v. Wade*, 410 U.S. 93, 1973). The Court has said that substantive due process also protects the right of extended family members to live together (*Moore v. City of East Cleveland*, 431 U.S. 494, 1977); the right of a competent person to refuse unwanted medical treatment (*Cruzan v. Missouri*, 497 U.S. 261, 1990); and the right of parents alone (and not others) to rear their children (*Troxel v. Granville*, 530 U.S. 57, 2000). In *Lawrence v. Texas*, 539 U.S. 558 (2003), the Court held that the liberty protected by due process includes the liberty of consenting adults, including those of the same sex, to engage in whatever private sexual conduct they choose.

Many of these decisions were justified on the basis of the Ninth Amendment, which says, "The enumeration in the Constitution, of certain rights, shall not be construed to deny or disparage others retained by the people." During the period in which it decided to protect the previously mentioned rights, however, the Court also declined to use substantive due process to protect a range of other behaviors or "rights" because it did not feel they were fundamental.

Perhaps the Court's most extreme expansion of substantive due process occurred in 1954, the year it used the Equal Protection Clause of the Fourteenth Amendment to nullify state laws requiring that public schools be racially segregated. Because there is no equal protection clause that applies to the federal government, in *Bolling v. Sharpe*, 347 U.S. 497 (1954), it used the Due Process Clause of the Fifth Amendment to prohibit segregated public schools in the District of Columbia. The Court thereby essentially equated the equal protection and due process clauses of the Constitution, and it now uses the Due Process Clause of the Fifth Amendment to nullify any congressional law that, if passed by a state, would violate the equal protection clause of the Fourteenth Amendment.

In summary, the scope of the due process of law guaranteed by the Fifth and Fourteenth Amendments is quite large and expanding. It prohibits laws from being enforced or applied in a way that violates the specific rights of the accused listed in the Bill of Rights or that violates the general principle of fairness. It also prohibits laws that are unfair, unclear, or restrictive of First Amendment freedoms and other substantive rights that the Court has deemed or may yet deem to be fundamental. Although the Court has been fairly restrained about increasing the rights it considers fundamental, in the future that could change.

ELLIS M. WEST

References and Further Reading

Barnett, Randy, ed. *The Rights Retained by the People: The History and Meaning of the Ninth Amendment*. Fairfax, VA: George Mason University Press, 1989.

Bodenhamer, David. *Fair Trial: Rights of the Accused in American History*. New York: Oxford University Press, 1992.

Cortner, Richard C. *The Supreme Court and the Second Bill of Rights: The Fourteenth Amendment and the Nationalization of Civil Liberties*. Madison: University of Wisconsin Press, 1981.

Ely, James W. *The Guardian of Every Other Right: A Constitutional History of Property Rights*. New York: Oxford University Press, 1992.

Garrow, David J. *Liberty & Sexuality: The Right to Privacy and the Making of* Roe v. Wade. New York: MacMillan, 1994.

Hamilton, Walton H. "The Path of Due Process of Law." *Ethics* 48 (April 1938):269–296.

Keynes, Edward. *Liberty, Property, and Privacy: Toward a Jurisprudence of Substantive Due Process*. University Park: Pennsylvania State University Press, 1996.

Levy, Leonard W. *Origins of the Fifth Amendment*. New York: Oxford University Press, 1968.

Orth, John V. *Due Process of Law: A Brief History*, Lawrence: University Press of Kansas, 2003.

Paul, Ellen F., and Howard Dickman. *Liberty, Property, and the Future of Constitutional Development*. Albany: State University of New York Press, 1990.

Seigan, Bernard. *Economic Liberties and the Constitution*. Chicago: University of Chicago Press, 1980.

Warren, Charles, *The New "Liberty" Under the Fourteenth Amendment*, Harvard Law Review 39 (1926): 431–465.

Cases and Statutes Cited

Adair v. United States, 208 U.S. 161 (1908)

Adkins v. Children's Hospital, 261 U.S. 525 (1923)

Allgeyer v. Louisiana, 165 U.S. 578 (1897)

Bell v. Burson, 402 U.S. 535 (1971)

Benton v. Maryland, 395 U.S. 784 (1969)

Berea College v. Kentucky, 211 U.S. 548 (1908)

Bolling v. Sharpe, 347 U.S. 497 (1954)

Boyce Motor Lines Inc. v. United States, 342 U.S. 337 (1952)

Brown v. Mississippi, 297 U.S. 278 (1936)

Cantwell v. Connecticut, 310 U.S. 296 (1940)

Chicago Milwaukee and St. Paul Ry. Co. v. Minnesota, 134 U.S. 118 (1890)

Connally v. General Construction Co., 269 U.S. 385 (1926)

Coppage v. Kansas, 236 U.S. 1 (1915)

Cruzan v. Missouri Department of Health, 497 U.S. 261 (1990)

De Jonge v. Oregon, 299 U.S. 353 (1937)

Dred Scott v. Sandford, 19 How. (60 U.S.) 393 (1857)

Duncan v. Louisiana, 391 U.S. 145 (1968)

Everson v. Board of Education, 330 U.S. 1 (1947)

Fuentes v. Shevin, 407 U.S. 67 (1972)

Gideon v. Wainwright, 372 U.S. 335 (1961)

Griswold v. Connecticut, 381 U.S. 479 (1965)

Hepburn v. Griswold, 8 Wallace 608 (1870)

Hurtado v. California, 110 U.S. 516 (1884)

Klopfer v. North Carolina, 386 U.S. 213 (1967)

Lawrence v. Texas, 539 U.S. 558 (2003)

Lochner v. New York, 198 U.S. 45 (1905)

Malloy v. Hogan, 378 U.S. 1 (1964)

Mapp v. Ohio, 367 U.S. 643 (1961)

Meyer v. Nebraska, 262 U.S. 390 (1923)

Moore v. City of East Cleveland, 431 U.S. 494 (1977)

Moore v. Dempsey, 261 U.S. 86 (1923)

Morehead v. Tipaldo, 298 U.S. 587 (1936)

Mugler v. Kansas, 123 U.S. 623 (1887)

Murray's Lessee v. Hoboken Land and Improvement Company, 18 How. (59 U.S.) 272 (1856)

New York v. Gitlow, 268 U.S. 652 (1925)

Palko v. Connecticut, 302 U.S. 319 (1937)

Patterson v. Colorado, 205 U.S. 454 (1907)

Pierce v. Society of Sisters, 268 U.S. 510 (1925)

Pointer v. Texas, 380 U.S. 400 (1965)

Powell v. Alabama, 287 U.S. 45 (1932)

Roe v. Wade, 410 U.S. 93 (1973)

Second Legal Tender Cases, 12 Wallace 457 (1871)

Slaughterhouse Cases, 16 Wall. (83 U.S.) 36 (1873)

Troxel v. Granville, 530 U.S. 57 (2000)
Truax v. Corrigan, 257 U.S. 312 (1921)
Twining v. New Jersey, 211 U.S. 78 (1908)
United States v. Carolene Products Co., 304 U.S. 144 (1938)
United States v. Cruikshank, 92 U.S. 542 (1975)
Wolf v. Colorado, 338 U.S. 25 (1949)
Wolf Packing Co. v. Court of Industrial Relations, 262 U.S. 522 (1923)
Wynehamer v. People, 13 N.Y. 378 (1856)

See also **Application of First Amendment to States; Capital Punishment: Due Process Limits; Due Process in Immigration; Economic Rights in the Constitution; Incorporation Doctrine; Incorporation Doctrine and Free Speech; Privileges and Immunities (XIV); Retained Rights (Ninth Amendment); Vagueness and Overbreadth in Criminal Statutes; Vagueness Doctrine**

DUNCAN v. LOUISIANA, 391 U.S. 145 (1968)

Duncan v. Louisiana was argued January 17, 1968, and decided May 20, 1968, by a vote of seven to two. Justice White delivered the opinion for the Court, with Justices Harlan and Stewart dissenting. The Court held that the defendant, accused under Louisiana law of simple battery, a misdemeanor punishable by a maximum of two years' imprisonment and a $300 fine, was entitled under the Sixth and Fourteenth Amendments to a jury trial, even though Duncan was sentenced to sixty days in jail and a $150 fine. The decision reaffirmed the right to a jury trial in criminal cases as a fundamental right even if the offense is petty.

In the lower courts, Duncan was tried and convicted of simple battery. The State of Louisiana argued, successfully, that a jury trial was only required in cases in which capital punishment and hard labor may be imposed. Justice White reversed the Louisiana Supreme Court by arguing that fundamental issues of liberty were at stake and cited *Powell v. Alabama*, 287 U.S. 45 (1932) for his rationale.

In *Duncan*, Justice White summarized the history and importance of trial by jury, dating back to the Magna Carta. Fearful of possible judicial bias in cases, the justice explained why trial by jury remains an important fixture in the U.S. legal system:

> The guarantees of jury trial in the Federal and State Constitutions reflect a profound judgment about the way in which law should be enforced and justice administered. A right to jury trial is granted to criminal defendants in order to prevent oppression by the Government . . . If the defendant preferred the common-sense judgment of a jury to the more tutored but perhaps less sympathetic reaction of the single judge, he was to have it (pp. 155–156).

Justice Harlan, whom Justice Stewart joined, dissented. His dissent centered around the notion of states' rights. Justice Harlan argued that a state has historically held the responsibility for "operating the machinery of criminal justice within its borders."

AARON R. S. LORENZ

DUSKY v. U.S., 362 U.S. 402 (1960)

To satisfy any theory of punishment, a criminal defendant must be competent to stand trial. In making this determination, the trial court in *Dusky* tested whether the defendant was oriented to time and place and had some recollection of the events. On appeal, defense counsel argued that Dusky was not competent to stand trial under 18 U.S.C. § 4244 because he was not able to assist properly in his defense.

The U.S. Supreme Court reversed the trial court's holding and redefined the test for competency to stand trial. According to *Dusky*, trial courts must determine whether the defendant has a present rational and factual understanding of the proceedings against him and whether he has the present ability to assist counsel with a reasonable degree of rational understanding. The Court remanded the case for another determination of the defendant's present competency to stand trial in accordance with the articulated standard.

In recent years, the Court has continued to assess the standard for competency to stand trial. As explained in *Godinez v. Moran*, 509 U.S. 398 (1993), the *Dusky* standard represents the constitutional minimum for testing a defendant's competency to stand trial, enter a guilty plea, or waive his right to counsel. In *Ford v. Wainwright*, 477 U.S. 399 (1986), the Court addressed a similar question and held that a capital defendant must be competent for execution and must understand that he is being executed and why. To maintain integrity in the criminal justice system, courts must assess a defendant's competency at all critical stages of the proceedings.

J. AMY DILLARD

References and Further Reading

Bonnie, Richard J., *The Competency of Criminal Defendants*: Beyond Dusky *and* Drope, U. Miami Law Review 47 (1993): 539–601.

Cases and Statutes Cited

Dusky v. U.S., 362 U.S. 402 (1960)
Ford v. Wainwright, 477 U.S. 399 (1986)
Godinez v. Moran, 509 U.S. 398 (1993)

See also **Insanity Defense; Mentally Ill**

DUTY TO OBEY COURT ORDERS

Relatively unyielding is the rule that a party must do what is required of him by the court order that resolves his case. (For example, an injunction might require a defendant never to take specified action.) In this, the rule differs from the much more complex and malleable rules (*stare decisis* and collateral estoppel) concerning the consequences for later cases of an earlier court decision's fact finding and legal reasoning.

Compliance with court orders is essential to our conception of the "rule of law." President Nixon's grudging acquiescence to the Watergate subpoenas makes clear that the rule of compliance binds the government as well as ordinary persons. Basic order depends on government and citizens alike abiding by official adjudications until they are dislodged by a higher court. Consequently, as the Supreme Court made clear in *United States v. United Mine Workers*, 330 U.S. 258, 293-94 (1947), courts usually require compliance even with erroneous court orders until they are overturned on appeal. Even if the order is invalidated, the appellate court will regard it, in effect, as valid for the period before it was overturned.

In *Walker v. Birmingham*, 388 U.S. 307, 318-20 (1967), the Supreme Court suggests in dicta that an erroneous court order enjoining constitutionally protected activity might be disobeyed if it is determined on appeal that (1) the order was legally wrong; (2) prompt attempts had been made to appeal; and (3) rights would have been lost by obeying the order pending relief on appeal. For example, if someone is ordered not to speak concerning politics until after the next election and no appeal is available very soon, then it is a reasonable gamble that he may disobey the order until the appeal can be decided. However, he takes the risk, among others, that the appellate courts will find (1) that the original order complied with the constitution or (2) that he had avenues of meaningfully swifter review. If either is found and he has disobeyed the order, then he is likely to be in contempt. It is also possible that an order resulting from certain court proceedings regarded as shams or as completely lawless need not be followed.

Action against those not complying with a court order takes a variety of forms including (1) contempt proceedings, resulting in fines or terms of confinement or (2) executive seizure of property necessary to satisfy the order. A court order also exerts great force outside the issuing court. The federal constitutional text, federal statutes, and related federal common law require that state and federal courts honor and enforce each other's judgments.

GORDON G. YOUNG

References and Further Reading

Palmer, J., *Note: Collateral Bar and Contempt: Challenging a Court Order After Disobeying It*, Cornell L. Rev. 88 (2002): 215.

Cases and Statutes Cited

United States v. United Mine Workers, 330 U.S. 258, 293-94 (1947)
Walker v. Birmingham, 388 U.S. 307, 318-20 (1967)

DWI

State laws forbid driving while intoxicated, or DWI. The offense is also referred to in some jurisdictions as DUI (driving under the influence), OWI (operating while intoxicated), or OUI (operating under the influence). The enforcement of these laws involves searches and seizures subject to the Fourth Amendment.

The two types of DWI offenses are driving while impaired and driving while alcohol or drugs are present in the body. Driving while impaired requires proof that drugs or alcohol affected the operator's physical or mental functions. Although no particular level of alcohol or drugs is proscribed, test results showing alcohol content in the body are evidence of impairment.

In contrast, driving while drugs or alcohol are in the body does not require proof of impairment. Instead, these laws require only that a forbidden level of alcohol be found in the body, as measured by breath, blood, or urine. Statutes often presume driving under the influence from 0.08 percent alcohol content in the blood. The 0.08 standard is a reduction from the formerly prevailing standard of 0.10. The lower standard exemplifies increasingly strict DWI statutes, which also have imposed greater punishments as social tolerance of drunk driving has decreased.

Fourth Amendment issues arise in DWI enforcement at two phases of DUI investigation: (1) the initial police–citizen encounter and (2) the detection of alcohol content in the suspect's body.

The police–citizen encounter typically begins with a stop of a vehicle. Such a stop is a "seizure" under the Fourth Amendment. The Fourth Amendment permits police to stop a vehicle to detect drunk driving under three circumstances. First, police can stop the vehicle to investigate for drunk driving if they have reasonable suspicion to believe that the offense is being committed, as the U.S. Supreme Court held in *Michigan v. Long*, 463 U.S. 1032 (1983). This is the same legal basis used in *Terry v. Ohio*, 392 U.S. 1 (1968), to permit stopping a pedestrian.

Second, as the Supreme Court held in *Whren v. United States*, 517 U.S. 806 (1996), police can stop a vehicle for a traffic violation. Police can use the time spent in citing the motorist to look for indications of other crimes, including drunk driving. If reasonable suspicion of DWI arises, the officer may detain the driver further to investigate.

Third, police can establish checkpoints to find drunk drivers. Checkpoints are allowed but must be fixed—roving patrols are not allowed—and must be of limited duration and nondiscriminatory in determining which motorists are stopped.

The Fourth Amendment also protects citizens from searches in the form of compulsory drug or alcohol tests, as the Court held in *Schmerber v. California*, 384 U.S. 757 (1966). *Schmerber* said that although police generally must obtain warrants, they can obtain blood without a warrant if they have probable cause, their method of obtaining the sample is reasonable, and a warrant cannot be secured before the alcohol in the body will dissipate.

The driver is required by most state laws to consent to these tests and provide samples of breath or blood. The theory of "implied consent" is that the state driving laws can condition the privilege of driving upon consent to such a test. In some states, the driver's license of a motorist who refuses the test is subject to suspension or revocation. A more recent trend, adopted earlier in countries such as Canada and Australia, is to make refusal to submit to the test a crime.

JEFFERSON L. LANKFORD

Cases and Statutes Cited

Michigan v. Long, 463 U.S. 1032 (1983)
Schmerber v. California, 384 U.S. 757 (1966)
Terry v. Ohio, 392 U.S. 1 (1968)
Whren v. United States, 517 U.S. 806 (1996)

See also **Checkpoints (roadblocks); Drug Testing; Exemplars; Probable Cause;** *Skinner v. Railway Labor Executives, Association*, **489 U.S. 602 (1989); Stop and Frisk**

DWORKIN, ANDREA (1946–2005)

With the 1979 publication of her book, *Pornography: Men Possessing Women*, Andrea Dworkin established herself as a feminist poised on the procensorship camp of the pornography debates, alongside theorists such as Catharine MacKinnon. In *Pornography*, Dworkin argued that the major theme of pornography as a genre is male power. She postulated that pornography does not fall under the protection of the First Amendment's Free Speech Clause because that amendment only protects those who can exercise the rights it protects. She argued that pornography trades in a class of people who have been systematically denied the rights protected by the First Amendment, so pornography should not receive First Amendment protection.

Along with Catharine MacKinnon, Dworkin coauthored an antipornography ordinance first introduced in Minneapolis in 1983. Dworkin and MacKinnon based the ordinance on their definition of pornography as a discriminatory practice based on sex. They included speech and action under their ordinance, arguing that speech and action work together to form a discriminatory system of sexual exploitation based upon sex-based powerlessness, which generates sex-based abuse. They also argued that photographic porn should be indisputably classified as action since they believed it only receives classification as speech because the women in pornographic photography have been depicted as objects or as commodities by the pornography. Thus, the speech belongs to those people who control the consumption of the images—the pornographers—and not the women featured in the pictures.

In the ordinance, Dworkin and MacKinnon constructed pornography as a human rights violation against women; they posited that men learn to sexually abuse women through pornography because pornography creates, in their words, a physiologically real conviction in men that women want to be abused. They argued that their antipornography ordinance articulated, for the first time, how pornography uses and affects women by recognizing an "energetic" agent of male domination over women. The First Amendment, they argued, cannot protect pornography because it would then be protecting exploitation since, by their definition, pornography functions as sexual exploitation that produces sexual abuse and discrimination. Through the Indianapolis ordinance (which was ultimately declared unconstitutional), Dworkin and MacKinnon postulated that porn in any form constituted an act inescapably linked to the general disempowerment of women. Pornography thus shows the "truth" of women's enslavement to men.

In a 1985 case, *American Booksellers Association, Inc., et al v. William H. Hudnut II*, 84-3147 (1985), a unanimous federal appeals court upheld the district court finding that the ordinance functioned too broadly and violated the First Amendment.

Dworkin wrote several other books, including *Intercourse* (published in 1987), in which she maintained that, according to men, the inferiority of women originates in sex, where women are inherently unequal;

since men have the "right" to exploit women in sex, then they have the right to possess women in other realms as well. Marriage, according to Dworkin, perpetuated an institution of inequality because of what women must do to attract husbands. She continued to work, write, and lecture on topics concerning women's rights and sexuality until her death in 2005.

MELISSA OOTEN

References and Further Reading

Dworkin, Andrea. *Pornography: Men Possessing Women.* New York: Perigee, 1979.
———. *Intercourse.* New York: The Free Press, 1987.
———. *Letters from a War Zone: Writings, 1976–1989.* New York: E. P. Dutton, 1989.
———. *Heartbreak: The Political Memoir of a Feminist Militant.* New York: Basic Books, 2002.
Dworkin, Andrea, and Catharine MacKinnon. *Pornography and Civil Rights: A New Day for Women's Equality.* Minneapolis, MN: Organizing Against Pornography, 1988.
———, eds. *In Harm's Way: The Pornography Civil Rights Hearings.* Cambridge, MA: Harvard University Press, 1997.
Soble, Alan. *Pornography, Sex, and Feminism.* Amherst, NY: Prometheus, 2002.

Cases and Statutes Cited

American Booksellers Association, Inc., et al v. William H. Hudnut II, 84-3147 (1985)

See also **MacKinnon, Catharine; Strossen, Nadine**

E

ECONOMIC REGULATION

The Framers of the Constitution who met in Philadelphia in 1787 were all or nearly all well-off property owners. One of their major concerns was the need to protect property owners in the unprecedented experiment in democracy that they were proposing. A major defect of democracy, they feared, was that debtors, always greatly outnumbering creditors, would be able to pass laws relieving themselves of their debt obligations. Probably the most important of the very few restrictions placed on the states in the original Constitution, therefore, was a provision prohibiting the states from passing any law "impairing the Obligation of Contracts," the principal purpose of which was to prevent debtor relief legislation. Further, James Madison, the principal author of the Constitution, in preparing a first draft of a bill of rights from suggestions made by many of the ratifying states, decided on his own to add a provision that private property may not be "taken for public use without just compensation."

In the last third of the nineteenth century following the Civil War, the nation experienced, in the near-total absence of government regulation, the greatest growth of industrial development and wealth in history. Alleged abuses of economic power by railroads and other large business entities led to demands for national economic regulation. The Interstate Commerce Commission was created in 1887 to regulate the railroads, and the Sherman Antitrust Act was adopted in 1890 to protect free market competition from business combines. Similar developments took place at the state level with the adoption of various price and wage controls and other economic and business regulations.

Attorneys for railroads, grain elevators, and other businesses subjected to economic regulation repeatedly besieged the Supreme Court to hold such regulations unconstitutional under the Due Process Clauses of the Fourteenth Amendment, applicable to the states, and the Fifth Amendment, applicable to the federal government. The clauses, providing that no person shall be deprived of "life, liberty, or property without due process of law," were understood to impose only a requirement of fair legal procedures. The attorneys argued that the Court should interpret the clauses as also placing a restriction on the substance of law, permitting the justices to declare unconstitutional any law they considered "unreasonable." After first dismissing this argument as based on "some strange misconception of the scope" of the Due Process Clause, the Court finally succumbed at the end of the nineteenth century, creating the oxymoronic doctrine of "substantive due process."

The Court thereafter and through the first third of the twentieth century invalidated more than 180 business or economic regulations as violating the "liberty of contract" that the Court read into the Due Process Clause or as simply "unreasonable" (most challenged regulations, however, were upheld). This period in the Court's history became known as the *Lochner* era, epitomized by the Court's 1905 decision in *Lochner v. New York*, holding unconstitutional a New York law that limited the working hours of bakers to sixty hours a week. The Court held that this restriction on liberty of contract between bakers and employers was not necessary to protect the health of bakers, and that it was not a legitimate use of state power to seek to improve the condition of the working class.

During the same period, the Court invalidated two federal anti–child labor laws as beyond the power of Congress to regulate interstate commerce and to tax. It then stopped the carrying out of President Franklin Roosevelt's New Deal during his first term (1933–1936) by invalidating a series of attempts to regulate the national economy as beyond Congress's commerce power and as a violation of substantive due process.

Two important five-to-four decisions in 1934, however, pointed in a different direction. In *Nebbia v. New York*, the Court upheld price controls on the dairy industry, making clear that such controls were no longer generally impermissible. Even more remarkably, in *Home Building & Loan Ass'n v. Blaisdell*, the Court upheld a Minnesota mortgage moratorium law that prevented unpaid creditors from foreclosing on property, precisely the type of debtor relief measure that the Contracts Clause was meant to prohibit. The effect of the decision was virtually to read the clause out of the Constitution as a limitation on state economic regulation. The clause enjoyed a surprising partial revival in the late 1970s when two state laws were found to be in violation, but later decisions indicate that the revival is over.

The era of judicial concern with economic regulation came to a sudden and apparently complete end in 1937, often referred to as the year of the "constitutional revolution." Overwhelmingly reelected in 1936, President Roosevelt undertook to keep the Court from continuing to frustrate his New Deal by proposing what became known, derisively, as his "Court-packing" plan. If justices over seventy years of age failed to retire, the plan would have permitted the appointment of additional justices up to a total of fifteen. While the plan, which aroused intense opposition, was pending in Congress, the Court, almost entirely due to a change in the position of a single justice, Owen Roberts, handed down two opinions that seemed to reverse the position it had taken on federal and state economic regulation just the year before.

In *NLRB v. Jones & Laughlin Steel Corp.* (1937), the Court upheld application of the National Labor Relations Act, prohibiting the firing of union organizers, to a steel mill as a valid exercise of Congress's power to regulate interstate commerce. In *West Coast Hotel Co. v. Parrish* (1937), the Court upheld a state minimum wage law after invalidating a similar law the year before. Whether or not the pending plan was

the cause, the Court made what was called "the switch in time that saved nine." The plan was then defeated, but President Roosevelt was able to claim that although he lost the battle, he had won the war. *Jones & Laughlin* and companion cases initiated the Court's withdrawal from attempts to limit Congress's regulation of economic and business affairs by means of the commerce power, and *West Coast Hotel* signaled the end of the Court's invalidation of state regulations of business or economic affairs on the basis of substantive due process.

The Fifth Amendment's prohibition of the taking of private property for public use without just compensation, originally applicable only to the national government, was held in the late 1900s to be, in effect, applicable to the states as well through the Fourteenth Amendment. The Court has read the "public use" requirement very broadly so as to impose no real limit on the taking of property by eminent domain. It is clear that just compensation is required when government takes possession of or asserts title to property. In *Pennsylvania Coal Co. v. Mahon* (1922), the Court held that compensation may also be required when a regulation of the use of property reduces its value even when the government does not take possession.

The Court has not, however, been able to state a rule as to what constitutes such a "regulatory taking," and none was again found until several regulatory taking claims were upheld in a series of five-to-four decisions beginning in 1987. The five more conservative justices attempted to breathe new life into the Taking Clause by holding that even a temporary restriction on the use of property could constitute a taking requiring compensation, that a regulation that deprives property of "all economically beneficial or productive use" constitutes a taking per se (automatically), and that a property owner could base a taking claim even on restrictions that were on the property before he bought it. Finally, the Court held that when government requires a permit for a certain use of property (for example, to build a house), any conditions attached to a grant of the permit must be related to the reason for requiring a permit.

Much of the increased protection apparently given property owners by these decisions was undone, however, by the Court's decision in *Tahoe-Sierra Preservation Council, Inc. v. Tahoe Regional Planning Agency* (2002) denying a regulatory taking claim. The Court very much limited, if it did not effectively overrule, both its earlier temporary regulatory taking decision, and its per se rule by holding that a regulation that prohibited all productive use of property for (at least) thirty-two months did not constitute a taking per se because the property retained value because productive use will be possible when and if the restriction is removed.

In sum, Congress's virtually unlimited power to regulate economic and business affairs under the Commerce Clause, the demise of the doctrine of economic substantive due process, the virtual elimination of the Contract Clause, and the very limited application of the Taking Clause mean that there are now very few constitutional restrictions on either national or state regulation of economic and business affairs.

LINO GRAGLIA

References and Further Reading

Ackerman, Bruce. *Private Property and the Constitution.* New Haven, CT: Yale University Press, 1977.

Alsop, Joseph, and Turner Catledge. *168 Days.* New York: Doubleday Doran, 1938.

Corwin, Edward. *Liberty Against Government.* Baton Rouge: Louisiana State University Press, 1948.

Epstein, Richard. *Takings: Private Property and Eminent Domain.* Cambridge, MA: Harvard University Press, 1985.

Rossiter, C., ed. *The Federalist Papers, No. 10 (Madison).* New York: Penguin Books, 1961.

McClosky, Robert. *The American Supreme Court.* Chicago: University of Chicago Press, 1960.

Novak, John, and Ronald O. Rotunda. *Constitutional Law.* 7th ed. St. Paul, MN: Thomson West, 2004.

Twiss, Benjamin. *Lawyers and the Constitution: How Laissez Faire Came to the Supreme Court.* New Haven, CT: Princeton University Press, 1942.

Wright, Benjamin F. *The Growth of American Constitutional Law.* Boston and New York: Houghton Mifflin, 1942.

Cases and Statutes Cited

Home Building & Loan Ass'n v. Blaisdell, 290 U.S. 398 (1934)

Lochner v. New York, 198 U.S. 45 (1905)

Nebbia v. New York, 291 N.Y. 502 (1934)

NLRB v. Jones & Laughlin, 301 U.S. 57 (1937)

Pennsylvania Coal Co. v. Mahon, 260 U.S. 393 (1922)

Tahoe-Sierra Preservation Council v. Tahoe Regional Planning Agency, 535 U.S. 302 (2002)

West Coast Hotel Co. v. Parrish, 300 U.S. 379 (1937)

U.S. Const. art. I, sec. 10; Fifth and Fourteenth Amendments

ECONOMIC RIGHTS IN THE CONSTITUTION

Protection of the rights of property owners has long been a vital function of the Anglo-American legal system. In particular, the English constitutional tradition stressed individual property rights as an important bulwark of freedom from arbitrary government. The Magna Carta (1215) contained a number of provisions that safeguarded property ownership. Foremost among these was the provision that "no freeman shall be taken, imprisoned, disseised . . . except by the lawful judgment of his peers and by the law of the land." With this language, the Magna Carta sought to secure owners against deprivation of their liberty or property without due process of law.

The property-conscious tenets of English constitutionalism were powerfully reinforced by the political theorist John Locke. He maintained in his famous *Second Treatise on Government* (1689) that private property existed under natural law before the creation of political authority, and that one of the principal functions of government was to protect property. Locke rejected the view that property could be created only by government. In Locke's thought, property ownership was closely connected with the preservation of liberty. Property was seen as giving people basic security and was therefore a necessary predicate to the enjoyment of other individual liberties. William Blackstone, in his influential *Commentaries on the Laws of England* (1765–1769), also attached great significance to the protection of property. He classed the free use and disposal of property as an "absolute right, inherent in every Englishman." Blackstone stressed the high regard of law for private property and the exclusive dominion of owners, but he noted that the use of property was subject to control by law. In particular, he insisted that English common law mandated the payment of compensation to persons whose property was taken for public use.

Revolutionary Era

By the time of the American Revolution the right to property was central to legal and political thought. Property was viewed as the linchpin upon which other rights rested. Indeed, the American colonists repeatedly invoked safeguards of property rights in their struggle with England. Economic issues, such as taxation without representation and restrictions on colonial trade, were crucial in shaping the drive for independence. The colonists therefore manifested a deep concern for property rights as part of their effort to devise constitutional restraints on governmental power.

Not surprisingly, the initial state constitutions contained a number of provisions to protect the rights of property owners. Several state constitutions asserted that the right to acquire and possess property was a natural right. Some states sought to promote free trade and the incentive to accumulate property by prohibiting grants of monopoly. Echoing the Magna Carta, a number of constitutions also declared that no person could be "deprived of his life, liberty, or property but by the law of the land." In addition, several states incorporated into their constitutions the common law principle that compensation should be paid when private property was taken for public use. Similarly, the Northwest Ordinance of 1787 included language protective of property ownership and contractual arrangements. Besides law of the land and Takings Clauses, the ordinance stated that no law should "interfere with or affect private contracts." These property guarantees were forerunners of provisions in the federal Constitution and Bill of Rights.

Notwithstanding the professed devotion to the security of property, the actual behavior of Americans during the Revolutionary era resulted in widespread despoliation of property rights. State legislators enacted bills of attainder declaring named Loyalists to be guilty of treason and confiscating their property without a judicial trial. Similarly, states, most notably Virginia, placed legal obstacles to the recovery of private debts owed to British merchants. Moreover, in the aftermath of the break with England, state lawmakers frequently interfered in debtor–creditor relations with a variety of measures designed to assist debtors. A particular sticking point was the issuance of depreciated paper currency, a move seen by merchants and creditors as amounting to confiscation of their economic interests. The seizure of Loyalist property and the repudiation of debts did not bode well for the security of economic rights in the new republic. As a result, many political leaders became convinced that the states could not adequately protect property ownership.

Constitution and Bill of Rights

Heirs to the English constitutional tradition linking tradition and liberty, the Framers of the Constitution in 1787 were anxious to secure property rights and halt the abuses that characterized the Revolutionary era. They also understood the advantages of private property as the basis for a strong national economy. Envisioning a unified commercial nation, the Framers recognized that uncertain ownership and contractual rights discouraged investment and inhibited economic growth. Many provisions of the Constitution therefore relate to economic interests. The Contract Clause bars states from enacting any law "impairing the obligation of contracts." Moreover, the states were prohibited from enacting bills of attainder and from making anything other than gold or silver coin legal tender for the payment of debts. The Constitution curtailed the power of Congress to levy "direct" taxes by requiring that such levies be apportioned

among the states according to population. Congress was authorized to regulate interstate and foreign commerce, thus encouraging the growth of a national market for goods. Mindful of the emerging importance of intellectual property, the framers gave Congress the power to award copyrights and patents to authors and inventors. It should further be noted that several provisions in the Constitution were concerned with the protection of property in slaves.

The high priority assigned by the Framers to property rights was further evidenced in the *Federalist Papers*. In *Federalist 54*, for instance, James Madison asserted that "government is instituted no less for the protection of the property, than of the persons of individuals." In addition to the specific provisions relating to economic interests, the Framers anticipated that the structural arrangements of the new federal government, with its system of checks and balances between branches of government, would foster a political climate in which property rights would be secure.

The Constitution as originally drafted did not include a Bill of Rights to guarantee individual liberty. The Framers felt that a Bill of Rights was unnecessary because they proposed to create a national government of limited powers. The absence of a Bill of Rights, however, proved to be one of the major obstacles in winning ratification of the new Constitution by the states. Accordingly, the proponents of the Constitution informally agreed to adopt a bill of rights in order to secure ratification. James Madison took the lead in drafting this bill of rights. For the most part he drew upon traditional guarantees already recognized in state bills of rights or English common law. Madison had long been an advocate for private property rights, and he included important protections for property ownership in the proposed bill of rights. The Fifth Amendment provides in part that no person shall be "deprived of life, liberty, or property, without due process of law; nor shall a private property be taken for public use, without just compensation." It is revealing that Madison placed this language in the same amendment with procedural safeguards governing criminal trials. This step emphasized the close association of property rights with personal liberty in his mind.

Madison amplified his thinking about property rights in a 1792 essay published shortly after ratification of the Bill of Rights. Madison broadly defined property as including more than physical objects. Madison treated important individual liberties, such as freedom of expression and religious conscience, as forms of property. He cautioned against either direct or indirect violations of property rights by governmental action. Indeed, Madison may well have been seeking to buttress support for civil liberties by associating them with the strong protections afforded private property. The essay suggests that Madison himself would lean toward a muscular reading of the property clauses in the Constitution.

The inclusion of specific constitutional guarantees of property in the federal Constitution led to similar moves by the states. Many states adopted clauses from the Constitution and Bill of Rights when they fashioned their own fundamental laws. State constitutions generally included a Contract Clause, protected persons against deprivation of property without due process, and required that just compensation be paid when property was taken by the state for public use. These state developments reinforced the high standing of property and contractual rights in the constitutional culture. Moreover, it bears emphasis that the Bill of Rights was initially understood as restraining just the federal government. Only the Contract Clause applied to the states and provided a basis for federal court oversight of state legislation interfering with economic rights. It followed that property owners looked primarily to state constitutions as safeguards of their rights. Even where state constitutions did not contain specific property guarantees, state courts tended to treat the rights set forth in the federal Bill of Rights as articulating fundamental constitutional principles. In *Gardner v. Village of Newburgh* (1816), for instance, the distinguished jurist James Kent ruled that, even in the absence of an express state constitutional provision, owners of land were entitled as a matter of natural equity to compensation when their property was taken for public use.

From the outset of the new republic, federal courts made clear their willingness to curtail state infringement of property and contractual rights. In the important case of *Vanhorne's Lessee v. Dorrance* (1795), Justice William Patterson, who had been an active member of the Constitutional Convention, characterized the pivotal role of private property in Lockean terms. Declaring that "the right of acquiring and possessing property, and having it protected, is one of the natural, inherent and inalienable rights of man," he added, "the preservation of property . . . is a primary object of the social compact." As this suggests, the right to acquire and use property was seen by the framers as a bedrock principle of social order, a right that was crucial for the enjoyment of individual liberty and economic growth.

Nineteenth Century

The interdependence of economic rights and political freedom was a major principle of American constitutionalism throughout the nineteenth century. In *Wilkinson v. Leland* (1829), for instance, Justice Joseph Story expressed this view in striking language: "That government can scarcely be deemed to be free, where the rights of property are left solely dependent upon the will of a legislative body, without any restraint. The fundamental maxims of a free government seem to require, that the rights of personal liberty and private property should be held sacred."

To vindicate this vision of the importance of economic rights, the Supreme Court under Chief Justice John Marshall developed a broad reading of the Contract Clause. In essence, the Court concluded that the Contract Clause covered both private bargains and agreements to which states were parties, such as land sales and grants of corporate charters. In revealing language, Marshall in *Fletcher v. Peck* (1810) characterized the various constitutional restraints on state legislative power, including the Contract Clause, as a "bill of rights for the people of each state." In the *Dartmouth College Case* (1819), the Contract Clause was invoked to guarantee the contractual nature of state-granted charters of incorporation from abridgement. Although the Contract Clause decisions of the Marshall Court upset local interests and states rights theorists, there was little criticism directed against the Court's defense of private property and contractual arrangements. In fact, the Marshall Court was expressing a widely shared constitutional norm. Not only did Marshall and his colleagues give vitality to the property-conscious value to the framers, but they did much to set the parameters of American constitutionalism for more than a century.

Marshall's successor as chief justice, Roger B. Taney, was more inclined to uphold state regulatory authority, but he also did much to protect property rights and facilitate economic growth. In cases such as *Bronson v. Kinzie* (1843), the Court under Taney applied the Contract Clause to uphold private credit arrangements against state legislative interference. This line of decisions reflected the high standing of contracts in the legal culture of the nineteenth century as a vehicle by which individuals participated in the expanding market economy.

At the state level courts began to treat the due process norm as protecting economic rights. In the landmark case of *Wynehamer v. People* (1856), for example, the New York Court of Appeals ruled that a prohibition statute constituted a deprivation of property without due process when applied to liquor already owned when the measure took effect. By the eve of the Civil War a number of state courts had fashioned substantive guarantees of property from the due process concept. This principle found expression in the maxim that laws which took property from

A and transferred it to B amounted to a deprivation of property without due process.

The centrality of property to the constitutional order did not rule out any role for public controls. States possessed a general legislative authority, known as the police power, to enact laws protecting public health, safety, and morals. Yet such regulations restricted the rights of owners to utilize their property. Moreover, both the federal and state governments could exercise the power of eminent domain to take private property for public use. State governments aggressively employed eminent domain to acquire property to promote transportation projects, and delegated the power to canal and railroad companies. Of course, property owners were entitled to just compensation when their property was taken.

The bedrock status of property rights in the constitutional order was dramatically illustrated during the Civil War. Although property in slaves was destroyed by the Thirteenth Amendment, Congress refused to adopt a sweeping confiscation policy calculated to seize all the property of persons supporting the Confederacy. Reluctant to disturb the property rights of individuals, even those in rebellion, Congress in 1862 passed a weak measure that authorized confiscation only after condemnation proceedings before a court. The presidential administration of Abraham Lincoln showed no enthusiasm for confiscation and did little to enforce the act. In marked contrast to the experience of the Revolutionary era, the Civil War debates over confiscation served to underscore the sanctity of private property, and to stigmatize confiscation as an illegitimate exercise of governmental power.

Property rights and private economic ordering continued to occupy a key position in constitutional doctrine throughout the late nineteenth century. For example, the Civil Rights Act of 1866 enumerated the right to make contracts and acquire property as among the liberties guaranteed to freed persons. Moreover, the Supreme Court invoked the Contract Clause in numerous cases to prevent municipalities from repudiating their bonded debt, thus protecting investment capital.

Supporters of economic rights, however, increasingly shifted their focus to the Due Process Clause of the Fourteenth Amendment. A central constitutional question was the extent to which this amendment, ratified in 1868, imposed new limits on state authority. Thomas M. Cooley, an influential treatise writer, asserted that the Due Process Clause was a substantive as well as a procedural restraint on state legislative power. He paved the way for a muscular interpretation of the Fourteenth Amendment. Initially, however, the Supreme Court was reluctant to see the Fourteenth Amendment as establishing a basis for federal court review of state law. In the *Slaughterhouse Cases* (1873), the justices adopted a narrow reading of that amendment. Similarly, the Supreme Court in *Munn v. Illinois* (1877) affirmed state regulatory power, rejecting a due process challenge to state laws that regulated the prices charged by railroads and allied industries.

Yet by the 1880s the Court was increasingly receptive to arguments that the Due Process Clause of the Fourteenth Amendment protected fundamental individual rights, such as the ownership and use of private property, from unwarranted encroachment by state government. In essence, federal judges did not accept legislative exercises of the police power at face value. Rather, they assessed legislative controls on economic activity against a reasonableness standard, invalidating those deemed arbitrary or beyond the legitimate scope of government. It bears emphasis that most state laws, and especially those protecting health and safety or fostering public morals, passed constitutional muster.

Still, the due process norm afforded considerable protection for economic rights. In *Allgeyer v. Louisiana* (1897), the Supreme Court held that the Due Process Clause guaranteed the liberty to make contracts. Freedom to enter contracts was treated as the constitutional baseline. States had to justify laws that limited contractual freedom, a requirement that set the stage for conflict between individual economic freedom and social legislation. Further, the Court ruled in *Chicago, Burlington & Quincy Railroad v. Chicago* (1897) that the just compensation principle concerning taking of property was applicable to the states as an element of due process in the Fourteenth Amendment. In effect, the just compensation rule became the first provision of the Bill of Rights to be "incorporated" into the Fourteenth Amendment Due Process Clause. In a closely related development, the Court determined that the governmental taking of property from one person for the private use of another constituted a deprivation of property in violation of due process.

The Supreme Court looked with particular skepticism on laws that appeared to redistribute property to achieve greater economic equality. To compel the redistribution of private property was viewed as threatening the very individual autonomy that respect for property promised to safeguard from governmental encroachment. This rejection of redistributive claims found expression in a series of cases which held that regulated industries, such as railroads, were constitutionally entitled to a reasonable return upon their investment. In other words, states could not impose confiscatory rates that would impair the value of property. Even more dramatic were the decisions in

Pollock v. Farmers' Loan & Trust Company (1895), invalidating the 1894 income tax as an unconstitutional direct tax. This levy, which affected only a small number of upper-income taxpayers, breached the widely accepted norm enjoining equality of rights and duties. *Pollock* represented the culmination of longstanding constitutional principles that restricted the power of government to redistribute wealth.

Twentieth Century

The traditional place of property rights in American constitutionalism was challenged in the early twentieth century. Concerned about a variety of problems arising from urbanization and industrialization, the Progressive movement urged a more active role for federal and state governments in redressing the economic and social imbalances associated with the new industrial society. Progressives called for the imposition of workplace safety standards, minimum wage laws, and limits on the hours of work, measures that curtailed contractual freedom. They also successfully pushed for adoption in 1913 of the Sixteenth Amendment, which authorized Congress to tax incomes, effectively overturning the *Pollock* decisions and opening the door to redistributionist use of the taxing power. At the same time, theorists began to reconceptualize property ownership as a set of social relationships rather than as dominion over an object. Property was analyzed in terms of being a cluster or bundle of rights, an approach that emphasized the contingent and changing nature of ownership. By suggesting that property did not imply any fixed set of rights, this theory sought to undermine the constitutional position of property and make room for greater governmental regulation of economic behavior.

The response of the Supreme Court to these novel political and intellectual currents was mixed. The majority of the justices remained suspicious of laws that altered free-market ordering or infringed on property rights. In the landmark case of *Lochner v. New York* (1905), for example, the Court struck down a statute limiting the hours of work in bakeries as violative of the liberty of contract protected by the Fourteenth Amendment. Similarly, the Court invoked the Due Process Clause to invalidate minimum wage laws for women. Judicial solicitude for the rights of property owners resulted in a significant victory for civil rights. In *Buchanan v. Warley* (1917), the Supreme Court voided a city ordinance mandating racial segregation in residential areas as a deprivation of property without due process. More commonly, the Court relied on due process review to eliminate entry barriers that

impeded competing enterprise. Thus, in *New State Ice Co. v. Liebmann* (1932), the Court declared unconstitutional a state licensing law that had the practical effect of fostering a monopoly in established ice companies by excluding competitors. Suggesting the link between economic liberty and other rights, the Court equated the right of free speech with entrepreneurial freedom.

In addition to relying on the Due Process Clause, the Supreme Court strengthened the protection afforded property owners under the Fifth Amendment Takings Clause. Speaking for the Court, Justice Oliver Wendell Holmes, Jr. in *Pennsylvania Coal Co. v. Mahon* (1922) ruled that a regulation of the use of property could be so severe as to amount to a taking of property which required compensation. Although agreeing that property could be controlled to some extent, he cautioned that "if regulation goes too far it will be recognized as a taking."

Yet the Court was prepared to accommodate much of the economic regulation associated with the Progressive movement. The justices sustained in *Muller v. Oregon* (1908) a state law restricting the working hours for women in factories and laundries. They likewise approved workers' compensation laws that mandated payment to employees injured in industrial accidents without regard to fault. Moreover, the Court in *Village of Euclid v. Ambler Realty Company* (1926) upheld the validity of comprehensive zoning laws to control land use patterns against due process objections.

The Great Depression and the election of Franklin D. Roosevelt as president in 1932 were watershed events in American history. Roosevelt's New Deal program was premised on the belief that government should intervene in the economy and actively promote social welfare. This political philosophy was sharply at odds with traditional constitutional doctrines stressing a limited role for government and a high regard for private property. Not surprisingly, the Supreme Court was initially hostile to much of the New Deal's regulatory program. Following a lacerating struggle, however, the Court in 1937 began to uphold New Deal legislation and largely abandoned its longstanding commitment to economic rights. Freedom of contract was stripped of its constitutional base. A major component of New Deal constitutionalism was a dichotomy between property rights and other personal liberties. In *United States v. Carolene Products Co.* (1938), the Court indicated that in due process cases it would afford a higher level of judicial scrutiny for a preferred category of personal rights, such as free speech and religious freedom, than for property rights. Such a distinction was contrary to the belief of the Framers that protection of property was essential for political liberty, but this constitutional double standard soon became the reigning paradigm. For decades thereafter economic rights were of scant concern to judges or scholars, and they downplayed the historical importance of property as a bulwark of individual autonomy.

Obituaries for property rights, however, proved to be premature. Starting in the 1980s, jurists and scholars rediscovered the constitutional dimensions of property rights. A series of Supreme Court decisions have revitalized the regulatory doctrine and helped to restore property rights to the forefront of academic debate. Wealth redistribution, which has rarely aroused sustained interest, was replaced by tax-cutting initiatives. International developments also contributed to the resurgence of interest in economic rights. With the collapse of communist regimes throughout the world, new governments have looked to the restoration of private property as a route to economic growth and political freedom.

The historic link between economic rights and the preservation of individual liberty retains considerable vitality even in an age with far-reaching economic regulations. Private property tends to diffuse power and resources throughout society, and thus shield all personal liberties by limiting a concentration of power in governmental hands. Other important rights, such as free speech and voting, would be unlikely to check governmental abuses without secure property rights to encourage political independence. With citizens under the economic thumb of the government, the exercise of personal and political freedom is illusory. Indeed it is difficult to find examples of free societies that do not respect private property.

JAMES W. ELY, JR.

References and Further Reading

Alexander, Gregory S. *Commodity & Propriety: Competing Visions of Property in American Legal Thought, 1776–1970.* Chicago: University of Chicago Press, 1997.

Benedict, Michael Les, *Laissez-Faire and Liberty: A Re-Evaluation of the Meaning and Origins of Laissez-Faire Constitutionalism,* Law and History Review 3 (1985): 243–331.

Bruchey, Stuart, *The Impact of Concern for the Security of Property Rights on the Legal System of the Early American Republic,* Wisconsin Law Review (1980): 1135–58.

Ely, James W., Jr. *The Guardian of Every Other Right: A Constitutional History of Property Rights.* 2nd ed. New York: Oxford University Press, 1998.

———, *The Marshall Court and Property Rights: A Reappraisal,* John Marshall Law Review 33 (2000): 1023–61.

Horwitz, Morton J. *The Transformation of American Law, 1870—1960.* New York: Oxford University Press, 1992.

Nedelsky, Jennifer. *Private Property and the Limits of American Constitutionalism: The Madisonian Framework and Its Legacy.* Chicago: University of Chicago Press, 1990.

Pipes, Richard. *Property and Freedom.* New York: Alfred A. Knopf, 1999.

Rose, Carol M., *Property as the Keystone Right?* Notre Dame Law Review 71 (1996): 329–66.

Scheiber, Harry N., ed. *The State and Freedom of Contract.* Stanford, CA: Stanford University Press, 1998.

Cases and Statutes Cited

Allgeyer v. Louisiana, 165 U.S. 578 (1897)

Bronson v. Kinzie, 42 U.S. 311 (1843)

Buchanan v. Warley, 245 U.S. 60 (1917)

Chicago, Burlington & Quincy Railroad v. Chicago, 166 U.S. 226 (1897)

Fletcher v. Peck, 10 U.S. 87 (1810)

Gardner v. Village of Newburgh, 12 Johns. Ch. 162 (N.Y. 1816)

Lochner v. New York, 198 U.S. 45 (1905)

Muller v. Oregon, 208 U.S. 412 (1908)

Munn v. Illinois, 94 U.S. 113 (1877)

New State Ice Co. v. Liebmann, 285 U.S. 262 (1932)

Pennsylvania Coal v. Mahon, 260 U.S. 393 (1922)

Pollock v. Farmers' Loan & Trust Company, 157 U.S. 429 (1895), 158 U.S. 601 (1895)

Slaughterhouse Cases, 83 U.S. 36 (1873)

Trustees of Dartmouth College v. Woodward, 17 U.S. 518 (1819)

United States v. Carolene Products Co., 304 U.S. 144 (1938)

Vanhorne's Lessee v. Dorrance, 2 Dallas 304 (1795)

Village of Euclid v. Amber Realty Company, 272 U.S. 365 (1926)

Wilkinson v. Leland, 27 U.S. 627 (1829)

Wynehamer v. People, 13 N.Y. 378 (1856)

EDWARDS v. AGUILLARD, 482 U.S. 578 (1987)

This case is part of the ongoing cultural struggle over teaching evolution in public schools that began with the 1925 Scopes trial. The issue previously had come before the U.S. Supreme Court in *Epperson v. Arkansas* (1968), and continues to be a point of controversy in American life.

In *Edwards v. Aguillard*, the Court dealt with a 1981 Louisiana statute that prohibited "the teaching of the theory of evolution in public schools unless accompanied by instruction in 'creation science.'" Although no school was obligated to teach creation science or evolution, if one was taught, the other had to be taught as well. In a seven-to-two decision, the Court held that the statute violated the Establishment Clause.

The Court assessed the statute under the first prong of the three-prong test *Lemon* test: "[T]he statute must have a secular legislative purpose." It evaluated several secular purposes claimed by Louisiana, concluding that none were convincing. It is rare that a court finds a statute in violation of *Lemon*'s first prong. For virtually all statutes that have failed the second prong, a statute's "principal or primary effect must be one that neither advances nor inhibits religion."

The Court first evaluated the state's claim that the statute was intended to protect academic freedom. After agreeing with the Fifth Circuit Court of Appeals that "the Act was not designed to further" academic freedom, the Court rejected the state's claim in oral argument that the legislature intended to protect academic freedom by requiring a fair and balanced and more comprehensive science curriculum even though it "may not [have] use[d] the terms 'academic freedom' in the correct legal sense." But even if that were true, the Court argued, the statute's construction was not tailored to accomplish this goal, since the statute in fact limited the curriculum and a teacher's academic freedom by forbidding instruction in evolution unless creation science was offered. Citing the statute's legislative history, including public comments by the statute's sponsor that he would have preferred that neither creationism nor evolution be taught, the Court concluded that the secular purpose claimed by the state was a sham.

The Court, agreeing with the Fifth Circuit, held that the statute's requirements—including the production of curriculum guides only for creationism, prohibition of discrimination only against creationists, and acquiring of resources and advice only from creation scientists—had the "purpose of discrediting 'evolution by counterbalancing its teaching at every turn with the teaching of creationism . . . .'" Thus, the statute did not advance fairness, as the state argued.

The Court also held that the statute's purpose was to advance a particular religious viewpoint, the Genesis account of creation. The Court looked at the "historic and contemporaneous link between the teachings of certain religious denominations and the teaching of evolution." According to the Court, the legislative history "reveals that the term 'creation science,' as contemplated by the legislature that adopted this Act, embodies the religious belief that a supernatural creator was responsible for the creation of humankind." Also, the statute and its sponsor targeted one theory, evolution, which some citizens, including the statute's sponsor, believe is hostile to their religious faith. But the Constitution "'forbids alike the preference of a religious doctrine or the prohibition of a theory which is deemed antagonistic to a particular dogma.'"

Edwards is an important case because it contains a standard that courts may use to assess a statute that requires a public school science curriculum on the topic of origins: (1) the statute's historical continuity with the creation/evolution battles throughout the twentieth century; (2) how closely the curricular content required by the statute parallels the creation story in Genesis, and/or whether the curricular content prohibited or regulated by the statute is treated as such because it is inconsistent with the creation story in Genesis; (3) the motives of those who support the statute in the legislature; and (4) whether the statute is a legitimate means to achieve appropriate state ends.

The only dissenting opinion was penned by Justice Antonin Scalia (joined by Chief Justice William Rehnquist). Among Scalia's many comments is his criticism of the Court's "religious motive test" to determine a statute's purpose. He argues that legislative motive, even if it is religious, is not the same as the actual purpose of the statute, which may be secular. Scalia also points out that legislators may support the same legislation for a variety of motives, and that "political activism by the religiously motivated is part of our heritage," which includes feeding the hungry and sheltering the homeless.

Because the Court stated that its opinion did "not imply that the legislature could never require that scientific critiques of prevailing scientific theories be taught," *Edwards* does not exclude the teaching of scientific views that are critical of evolution but that are not based exclusively on the authority of religious writings.

FRANCIS J. BECKWITH

References and Further Reading

Beckwith, Francis J. *Law, Darwinism & Public Education: The Establishment Clause and the Challenge of Intelligent Design.* Lanham, MD: Rowman & Littlefield, 2003.

Campbell, John A., and Stephen C. Meyer, eds. *Darwinism, Design, and Public Education.* East Lansing, MI: Michigan State University Press, 2003.

Carter, Stephen L., *Evolutionism, Creationism, and Teaching Religion as a Hobby,* Duke Law Journal 1987 (1987): 977.

Darwin, Charles. *On the Origin of Species.* Facsimile of the 1st edition (1859), with introd. by Ernst Mayr. Cambridge, MA: Harvard University Press, 1964.

Dembski, William A., and Michael Ruse, eds. *Debating Design: From Darwin to DNA.* New York: Cambridge University Press, 2004.

Greenawalt, Kent, *Establishing Religious Ideas: Evolution, Creationism, and Intelligent Design,* Notre Dame Journal of Law, Ethics & Public Policy 17 (2003): 2:321–97.

Johnson, Phillip E. *Darwin on Trial.* Chicago: Regnery Gateway, 1991.

Miller, Kenneth R. *Finding Darwin's God: A Scientist's Search for Common Ground Between God and Evolution.* New York: Cliff Street Books, 1999.

Numbers, Ronald. *Darwinism in America.* Cambridge, MA: Harvard University Press, 1998.

Pennock, Robert T., ed. *Intelligent Design Creationism and Its Critics: Philosophical, Theological, and Scientific Perspectives.* Cambridge, MA: MIT Press, 2001.

Ruse, Michael. *The Evolution Wars: A Guide to the Debates.* Santa Barbara, CA: ABC-CLIO, 2000.

EDWARDS v. AGUILLARD, 482 U.S. 578 (1987)

Cases and Statutes Cited

Balanced Treatment for Creation-Science and Evolution-Science in Public School Instruction. *La. Rev. Stat. Ann.* sec. 17:286.1–17:286.7 (West 1982)
Epperson v. Arkansas, 393 U.S. 97 (1968)
Lemon v. Kurtzman, 403 U.S. 602, 613 (1971)

See also **Epperson v. Arkansas, 393 U.S. 97 (1968); Lemon Test; Scopes Trial; Teaching "Creation Science" in Public Schools; Teaching Evolution in Public Schools**

EDWARDS v. ARIZONA, 451 U.S. 477 (1981)

In *Edwards*, the police arrested and questioned the defendant after advising him of his *Miranda* rights. He initially consented to questioning but later asked for an attorney. Questioning stopped at that time. The next day, police questioned him against his will, without counsel present. He answered freely and later confessed after the police played him the taped statement of an alleged accomplice. At trial, he challenged the confession, but the judge admitted it because it was voluntarily given.

In a nine-to-zero reversal, the Supreme Court analyzed its *Miranda v. Arizona* (1966) and *Schneckloth v. Bustamonte* (1973) holdings, and determined that the Constitution affords special protection to the right to counsel that cannot be protected by a merely voluntary waiver. It held that a confession can only be admitted when the suspect both voluntarily *and* knowingly relinquishes his Fifth Amendment right to counsel. The Court went further to protect the right, holding that once it has been invoked, a valid waiver must contain more than responses to police-initiated questioning. However, the Court noted that if the defendant initiates a subsequent conversation, he could be deemed to have waived his right.

Chief Justice Burger concurred in the judgment but voiced concern over the majority's expansive holding. A second concurrence faulted the majority's reliance on "initiation" as part of the waiver analysis. Subsequent cases interpreted *Edwards* broadly, leading the Court, in *Minnick v. Mississippi* (1990), to announce a bright-line rule that once a suspect invokes the right to counsel, he cannot be reinterrogated without counsel present.

SARA E. LINDENBAUM

References and Further Reading

Shapiro, Eugene L., *Thinking the Unthinkable: Recasting the Presumption of* Edwards v. Arizona, Oklahoma Law Review 53 (2000): 1:11–34.

Tomkovicz, James J., *Standards for Invocation and Waiver of Counsel in Confession Contexts*, Iowa Law Review 71 (1986): 4:975–1061.

Cases and Statutes Cited

Minnick v. Mississippi, 498 U.S. 146 (1990)
Miranda v. Arizona, 384 U.S. 436 (1966)
Schneckloth v. Bustamonte, 412 U.S. 218 (1973)

See also **Miranda Warning; Rights of the Accused; Right to Counsel**

EDWARDS v. CALIFORNIA, 314 U.S. 160 (1941)

When Californian Fred Edwards drove his destitute brother-in-law from Texas into California in 1939, Edwards violated a California statute criminalizing transportation of indigents into California. State and local governments had long restricted the movement of the poor because poverty had historically been considered a "moral pestilence." During the Great Depression many poor citizens fled the South and Southwest for more prosperous states such as California, only to be greeted with hostile poor laws and with California's claim that exclusion was a valid use of its police powers.

In *Edwards v. California*, the Supreme Court unanimously struck down the California statute as unconstitutional, clearly establishing a right to travel across state borders. A majority of the Court argued that California's attempt to isolate itself from the national problems of poverty and labor migration violated the Commerce Clause, which prohibited states from restricting the movement of people and property across state lines. The Court also expressed its support for New Deal antipoverty programs and its rejection of the idea that poverty automatically presumed immorality.

Four justices concurred in the result but argued that by using the Commerce Clause, the Court in effect equated poor citizens with cattle and fruit. These justices instead relied on the constitutional clauses protecting the privileges and immunities of citizenship. However, the Court had just two years earlier rejected the use of the Privileges or Immunities Clause of the Fourteenth Amendment to limit federal legislative powers, and the majority in *Edwards* did not want to revisit that issue.

JAMES W. FOX, JR.

References and Further Reading

Katz, Michael B. *In the Shadow of the Poorhouse: A Social History of Welfare in America*. New York: Basic Books, 1986.

Patterson, James T. *America's Struggle Against Poverty in the Twentieth Century*. Cambridge, MA: Harvard University Press, 2000.

Tribe, Laurence H. *American Constitutional Law*. Mineola, NY: Foundation, 1988.

See also **Right to Travel**

EDWARDS v. SOUTH CAROLINA, 372 U.S. 229 (1963)

This case was decided by the Supreme Court in 1963. It was one of numerous cases involving civil rights demonstrations to come before the Court. *Edwards* decided several important issues that facilitated the ability of groups to make these protests. It involved a demonstration by 187 black high school and college students. They marched to the South Carolina State House grounds in groups of about fifteen, then walked single file or two abreast in an orderly way on the sidewalks around the grounds, carrying signs protesting segregation. As the demonstration continued, about 355 onlookers, mostly hostile to the demonstrators, congregated on the grounds. These spectators impeded the traffic flow around the State House. The response of law enforcement officials was to order the student demonstrators to disperse. When they failed to do so, they were arrested, charged, and convicted for a breach of the peace.

The Court held that state government ground such as the State House grounds were quintessential public fora where First Amendment activities were entitled to the greatest protection. The Court also held that these rights were to be protected against a hostile audience. This ensured the "heckler's veto" could not justify stifling the demonstrators. That holding established a wide range of protection for nonviolent protests. The Court said "the Fourteenth Amendment does not permit a State to make criminal the peaceful expression of unpopular views." The Court found that state and local governments could not use their breach of the peace statutes to arrest or imprison peaceful demonstrators.

PATRICK FLYNN

References and Further Reading

Weaver, Russell L., and Arthur D. Hellman *The First Amendment: Cases, Materials and Problems*. Charlottesville, Va.: LexisNexis, 2002.

Friedman, Leon, and Richard Mark Gergel. "Matthew J. Perry's Contribution to the Development of Constitutional Law." In *Matthew J. Perry: The Man, His Times, and His Legacy*, edited by W. Lewis Burke and Belinda Gergel, 105–10. Columbia: University of South Carolina Press, 2004.

EISENSTADT v. BAIRD, 405 U.S. 438 (1972)

Appellee Baird delivered a lecture on contraception to a group of college students in which he displayed contraceptive materials and then gave one of the students a package of contraceptive foam in violation of a Massachusetts law. The law at issue criminalized the distribution of contraceptives. Yet, the statute provided, in part, that a "registered physician may administer to or prescribe for any married person drugs or articles intended for the prevention of pregnancy or conception" (*Eisenstadt v. Baird* [1972]). Appellee, having been charged with violation of the Massachusetts law, challenged its constitutionality in a writ of habeas corpus upon his conviction.

The question presented was whether there was some ground of difference between married and unmarried persons that rationally explained their different treatment under the law. The Supreme Court invalidated the statute on equal protection grounds. It held that the statute, viewed as a prohibition on contraception, per se, violated the rights of single persons under the Equal Protection Clause of the Fourteenth Amendment. As the Court indicated, the legislative intent of the statute, as explained by the state courts, was unclear. One state court found that the prohibition was directly related to the state's goal of "preventing the distribution of articles designed to prevent conception which may have undesirable, if not dangerous, physical consequences" (*Commonwealth v. Baird* [1969]). Another Massachusetts court, however, found that "a second and more compelling ground for upholding the statute" was to protect morals through "regulating the sexual lives of single persons" (*Sturges v. Attorney General* [1970]. The state further argued to the Supreme Court that the purpose of the statute was to promote marital fidelity.

The Supreme Court rejected all of these purported goals of the statute at issue. As written, in making contraceptives available to married persons without regard to their intended use, the statute did nothing to prohibit the illicit sexual activities of married persons. With regard to the purported goal of discouraging premarital sexual intercourse, the effect of the statute would be to make the birth of an unwanted child the punishment for fornication. Clearly, such an outcome would be at odds with the proffered objective. Finally, with regard to the purported goal of protecting individuals from dangerous consequences, the statute forbade physicians from distributing contraceptives even when needed to protect the patient's health.

Writing for four members of the Court, Brennan explained that although the Court has recognized that the Fourteenth Amendment does not prohibit states from treating different classes of persons in different ways, the Equal Protection Clause does prohibit the state from doing so arbitrarily. A classification must be reasonable and must rest on some grounds having a fair and substantial relation to the object of the legislation. Similarly situated persons must be treated alike. As discussed above, in this case, the evils that the statute purported to address applied equally to both married and unmarried persons. Therefore, the discrimination against unmarried persons was found to be invidious. Although *Griswold v. Connecticut* found a right to privacy only in the marital relationship, a married couple is an association of two people each with a separate intellectual and emotional make-up (striking down a law that forbade the use of contraceptives by married persons). The right to privacy, thus, is a right of the *individual* "to be free from unwarranted governmental intrusion into matters so fundamentally affecting a person as the decision whether to bear or beget a child" (*Eisenstadt*).

Although decided on equal protection grounds, the Court's language was consistent with the noneconomic substantive due process cases of 1920s and 1960s. *Eisenstadt* continues to be cited in most cases addressing abortion and an individual's right to privacy. Indeed, the right to privacy found in *Griswold* and *Eisenstadt* paved the way for *Roe v. Wade* (1973); *City of Akron v. Akron Ctr. for Reproductive Health* (1983) (relying in part on *Eisenstadt* in invalidating ordinance requiring all second trimester abortions to be done in a hospital). Most recently, the Supreme Court relied on *Eisenstadt* in striking down a state law criminalizing sodomy, stating, "the right to make certain decisions regarding sexual conduct extends beyond the marital relationship" (*Lawrence v. Texas* S.Ct. [2003]).

EMILY R. FROIMSON

Cases and Statutes Cited

City of Akron v. Akron Ctr. for Reproductive Health, 462 U.S. 416 (1983)
Commonwealth v. Baird, 355 Mass. 746, 247 N.E.2d 574 (1969)
Eisenstadt v. Baird, 405 U.S. 438 (1972)
Griswold v. Connecticut, 381 U.S. 479 (1965)
Lawrence v. Texas, 123 S.Ct. 2472, 2477 (2003)
Roe v. Wade, 410 U.S. 113 (1973)
Sturges v. Attorney General, 358 Mass. 37, 260 N.E.2d 687 (1970)

ELDRED v. ASHCROFT, 537
U.S. 186 (2001)

The U.S. Constitution has a special provision allowing Congress to enact copyright and patent statutes. Article one, section eight, clause eight reads: "The Congress shall have the power . . . . [t]o promote the Progress of Science and the useful Arts, by securing for limited Times to Authors and Inventors the exclusive Right to their respective Writings and Discoveries" (Copyright Clause). According to the Supreme Court, the Copyright Clause grants Congress a limited power; the clause provides an incentive for creative persons, but its main purpose is to benefit the public (*Feist Publications, Inc. v. Rural Telephone Service Co., Inc.* [1991]).

Copyright protection has changed greatly during the history of the United States. The first Congress passed the first Copyright Act in 1790. That statute allowed fourteen years of protection with the option of renewing protection for another fourteen years. The act only protected books, charts, and maps from persons producing close copies. Over time Congress has expanded copyright protection in many ways, including by covering many different types of works (such as songs and movies), protecting them from more types of competition (such as translations, sequels, and public performances), giving authors the entire term without needing to request renewal, and extending the length of protection. In 1998, Congress passed the Copyright Term Extension Act (CTEA), which changed the copyright term for most works from fifty years after the author died to seventy years after the author died. The extension covered not only works created after the CTEA, but those already in existence (referred to as "retrospective extension"). The CTEA was nicknamed the "Mickey Mouse Act" because it prevented Walt Disney's famous cartoon from losing copyright protection. Like Disney, many of the other businesses that lobbied Congress to pass the CTEA had already successful works about to lose copyright protection.

Many businesses and nonprofit organizations specialize in distributing works that are no longer under copyright protection. Several of them sued, claiming that retrospective extension is beyond Congress's power under the Copyright Clause and violates the First Amendment. In *Eldred*, the Supreme Court rejected both of these claims.

Discussing the Copyright Clause, the Supreme Court declared that "a page of history is worth a volume of logic." The CTEA is constitutional because earlier statutes had included retrospective extensions.

Second, the Court rejected arguments about the purpose of the Copyright Clause. Economists had demonstrated that the change in term length had no appreciable value to an author deciding whether to write a new work or to a publisher deciding whether to print a new work. Opponents of the act argued that the Copyright Clause's sole purpose was to provide an incentive for the creation of new works; the act failed to provide such an incentive, and therefore, was beyond Congress's power. Additionally, during the long period when copyright protection had included an optional renewal term, most authors had not filed for renewal. The dearth of renewals demonstrates that most works quickly stop producing money for their authors and publishers. However, many works are "orphans," that is, their authors and publishers are not exploiting them, but members of the public cannot use them either, because they cannot locate these authors and publishers to obtain copyright permission. Extending the copyright term increases the number of orphan works and the number of years that these orphan works are used by no one. In sum, opponents of the CTEA argued that it placed much too high a burden on public use of works in comparison to the incentives provided to authors and publishers.

The Supreme Court refused to conduct its own balance of the CTEA's burdens and benefits. Instead, the Court deferred to Congress's judgment about needed incentives; it also approved Congress's decision to base policy on all of the creation of new works, incentives for distributing old works, and international harmonization of copyright law.

Regarding the First Amendment challenge, the Court called copyright "the engine of free expression." Additionally, the Court felt that works under copyright protection did not present First Amendment problems for two reasons. First, certain publicly beneficial uses (such as criticism and parody) are allowed without authors' permission (called "fair use"). Second, copyright only protects expression (the way the author explains his point); it does not prevent others from reusing facts or ideas.

Eldred demonstrates Supreme Court deference to Congress. However, the limit of the Court's deference is not clear because the suit only involved retrospective extension.

MALLA POLLACK

References and Further Reading

Yu, Peter K., ed. *Extending Mickey's Life:* Eldred v. Ashcroft *and the Copyright Term Extension Debate.* Cambridge, Mass.: Kluwer Law International, 2005.

Lessig, Lawrence. *Free Culture: How Big Media Uses Technology and the Law to Lock Down Culture and Control Creativity.* New York: Penguin Press, 2004.

Loyola of Los Angeles Law Review. "*Eldred v. Ashcroft*: Intellectual Property, Congressional Power and the Constitution." *Loyola of Los Angeles Law Review* 36, no. 1 (2002). Symposium issue. http://llr.lls.edu/volumes/v36-issue1/.

Cases and Statutes Cited

Feist Publications, Inc. v. Rural Telephone Service Co., Inc., 499 U.S. 340 (1991)

See also **Content-Neutral Regulation of Speech; Fair Use Doctrine and First Amendment; Intellectual Property and the First Amendment; Satire and Parody and the First Amendment**

ELECTRIC CHAIR AS CRUEL AND UNUSUAL PUNISHMENT

On August 6, 1890, William Kemmler became the first person to be executed via electric chair. He was also the first person to argue that this method of execution was a violation of the Eighth Amendment of the U.S. Constitution (*In re Kemmler* [1890]).

Kemmler's execution, like several other executions by electric chair, has been described as a gruesome event. In most electrocutions, the prisoner is strapped into a chair with leather belts across the chest, thighs, legs, and arms. Two copper electrodes are then attached—one to the leg and the other to a helmet. A leather mask or black cloth is placed over the prisoner's face. The executioner then presses a button to deliver the first shock of between 1,700 and 2,400 volts. This lasts somewhere between thirty seconds and one minute. Smoke usually comes out of the prisoner's leg and head. A doctor then examines the individual, who if not dead is given another jolt of electricity. A third and fourth are given if necessary. In at least one instance, the death of Ethel Rosenberg, five jolts of electricity were needed. In some instances, the process can last between six and nineteen minutes.

After electrocution the body temperature rises to about 138°F. The fluids inside the body "boil" the internal organs. Justice William Brennan of the U.S. Supreme Court stated in his dissent to the denial of certiorari in *Glass v. Louisiana* (1985), that during an electric chair death

the prisoner's eyeballs sometimes pop out and rest on his cheeks. He often defecates, urinates, and vomits blood and drool. The body turns bright red as its temperature rises, and the prisoner's flesh swells and his skin stretches to the point of breaking. Sometimes the prisoner catches on fire, particularly if he perspires excessively. Witnesses hear a loud and sustained sound like bacon frying, and the sickly sweet smell of burning flesh permeates the [death] chamber.

Despite the fact that this description of death by electric chair sounds cruel, the U.S. Supreme Court has never determined that this method of execution is "cruel and unusual" in violation of the Eighth Amendment of the U.S. Constitution.

In order for a punishment to violate the Eighth Amendment, it must be both cruel and unusual. According to the U.S. Supreme Court, punishment that involves torture or unnecessary pain is cruel. However, the fact that a punishment is cruel alone does not make it unconstitutional. It must also be "unusual," which has been defined by the Court in terms of consistency. This means that a punishment is unconstitutional only if it is not applied consistently to all like crimes. The underlying notion is that individuals will not be subjected to arbitrary, humiliating, or whimsical punishment outside the normal course of the law.

Lower courts have also examined the issue of whether the electric chair constitutes a form of cruel and unusual punishment under state constitutions. In these cases, the analysis is dominated by the length of time that it takes for the prisoner to die and the pain involved in the execution. For example, the Supreme Court of Florida accepted evidence of "instantaneous unconsciousness" and therefore no "unnecessary and wanton pain" when it upheld electrocution as a method of execution (*Provenzano v. Moore* [1999]). On the other hand, Georgia's highest court held that use of the electric chair was cruel and unusual punishment because electrocution "inflicts purposeless physical violence and needless mutilation that makes no measurable contribution to accepted goals of punishment." The Court also held "that death by electrocution, with its specter of excruciating pain and its certainty of cooked brains and blistered bodies, violates the prohibition against cruel and unusual punishment" (*Dawson v. State* [Ga. 2001]).

At one time in history, electrocution was used in twenty-six states as the preferred form of execution. Since 1924, however, there has been a clear movement away from this method of execution.

In 2005, death by electrocution is mandatory in only one state—Nebraska. However, in *Palmer v. Clarke* (2003), Judge Bataillon questioned the legitimacy of this form of execution by noting in dicta that the Court would find, in accordance with "evolving standards of decency," that execution by electrocution is both cruel and unusual particularly since there is no evidence that electrocution is either quick or painless.

In addition to Nebraska, nine other states explicitly authorize electrocution as a form of execution—Alabama, Arkansas, Florida, Illinois, Kentucky, Oklahoma, South Carolina, Tennessee, and Virginia.

From 1890 until 2005, more than 4,460 people have been sentenced to death by electrocution in the United States. We remain the only nation in the world that continues to allow this form of execution.

JUDITH A. M. SCULLY

References and Further Reading

Banner, Stuart. *Death Penalty: An American History*. Cambridge, MA: Harvard University Press, 2003.
Capital Defense Weekly. *The Shocking Truth About Death in the Electric Chair*. N.d. http://members.aol.com/karlkeys/chair.htm.
Harding, Roberta M., *The Gallows to the Gurney: Analyzing the (Un)constitutionality of the Methods of Execution*, Boston University Public Interest Law Journal 6 (1996): 153.

Cases and Statutes Cited

Dawson v. State, 554 S.E.2d 137 (Ga. 2001)
Glass v. Louisiana, 471 U.S. 1080 (1985)
In re Kemmler, 136 U.S. 436 (1890)
Palmer v. Clarke, 293 F.Supp. 2d 1011 (D. Nebraska 2003)
Provenzano v. Moore, 744 So.2d 413 (1999)

ELECTRONIC SURVEILLANCE, TECHNOLOGY MONITORING, AND DOG SNIFFS

The fundamental question for examining any possible civil liberties violations for electronic surveillance, technology monitoring, and dog sniffs is whether a prohibited search occurred under the Fourth Amendment. A prohibited search occurs when a person has a subjective expectation of privacy that society will objectively recognize and that expectation of privacy is violated. The analysis is on the person because as the U.S. Supreme Court stated in *United States v. Katz*, "the Fourth Amendment protects people not places." The first part of the analysis is whether the person has exhibited a subjective expectation of privacy by looking at the location and what acts were taken to protect privacy. The analysis concludes with whether society will recognize that expectation as objectively reasonable. Accordingly, the use of electronic surveillance, technology monitoring, and dog sniffs hinges on whether there was an expectation of privacy for the person, object, or place being searched and that search violated an expectation of privacy. This civil liberty interest against unreasonable searches is protected by the exclusionary rule, which prohibits the use of evidence obtained in violation of the Fourth Amendment. However, if the government obtains a valid probable cause warrant, then the searches would not fall under the Fourth Amendment prohibition.

Electronic Surveillance

Electronic surveillance by the government is regulated by the Electronic Communications Privacy Act (ECPA) and the Fourth Amendment. The ECPA is a broad statute that regulates government regarding the interception and attempted interception of wire, oral, or electronic communications, access to electronic communication service, and remote computing services, and pen register surveillance. The Fourth Amendment restrictions are whether the person has a subjective expectation of privacy that society is objectively willing to recognize. However, the Foreign Intelligence Surveillance Act (FISA) has exceptions to the surveillance requirements under the ECPA for national security matters.

The ECPA has three main sections that cover what the government can and cannot do with regard to obtaining electronic communications, information stored on computers, and pen register surveillance. The ECPA also covers actions by individuals and nongovernmental entities and has civil and criminal penalties for unlawful access. However, for civil liberties purposes, only government restrictions are covered below.

The first section covering the interception of wire, oral, and electronic communication sets forth the rules that the government must abide by making the application for an interception and the restrictions on the use of the information that is obtained. This section was originally introduced as Title III of the Omnibus Crime Control and Safe Streets Act of 1968 (also known as Title III). This section covers the actual content of wire and electronic communication, and the ECPA sets forth the metes and bounds of when and how the interception can occur. The ECPA restricts the use of the information intercepted when the interception does not comply with requirements of the ECPA.

The second section covers the processes for the government to obtain access to electronic communication services and remote computing services and the information contained by the services. Because different types of information are deemed to have varying privacy interests, the ECPA has five mechanisms from which the government can obtain information from the services. These five mechanisms include subpoenas, subpoenas with notice, court order, court order with notice, and a search warrant, which are tailored in light of the privacy interests of the information being requested. Even if the information regulated under this section is obtained without complying with the requirements of the ECPA, the ECPA does not explicitly restrict the use of this information as evidence. However, the information could be restricted under the exclusionary rule if it is obtained in violation of the Fourth Amendment.

The third section covers processes for the government to conduct pen register surveillance and the information obtained therein (also known as the "pen/trap statute"). This section covers the address and other noncontent information for wire and electronic communication. Information obtained outside of the requirements of the ECPA is not explicitly disallowed as evidence unless the method of obtaining the information violates the Fourth Amendment and is thus excluded under the exclusionary rule.

The first question for electronic surveillance that does not fall under the ECPA is whether the surveillance is a search. If the surveillance is not a search, then there cannot be a Fourth Amendment violation for the surveillance. The surveillance is a search under the Fourth Amendment when the person has a subjective expectation of privacy that society will objectively recognize and that privacy is violated by the search. Generally any information that a person puts out into public view falls outside of the purview of the expectation of privacy that society will objectively recognize.

For example, the use of a pen register to record phone numbers dialed from a telephone is not a search. Even if a person thinks that the phone numbers dialed are private, that expectation is not reasonable because the telephone company routinely monitors and records the numbers dialed for troubleshooting and billing purposes. Accordingly, since a reasonable person knows that the numbers dialed are turned over to the telephone company, then there is no reasonable expectation of privacy for the dialed numbers and therefore no search has occurred when the government obtains those numbers. This lack of privacy would most likely be extended to other address types of information such as email addresses and website addresses in which the traffic has been exposed to third parties but not necessarily the content of the traffic. However, as noted above pen register surveillance is now regulated by the ECPA but a person still has a lowered expectation of privacy when information is turned over to a third party.

The lack of privacy for the information turned over to third parties extends to most types of information that are obtained by electronic surveillance that third parties would have or which do not fall under the ECPA. There is a lowered expectation of privacy when the communication is knowingly exposed to a third party. For example, when an undercover agent or informant has a microphone from which a conversation is recorded, there is no reasonable expectation of privacy because the conversation has been exposed to the third party. In these situations, no search has occurred because the people have exposed their conversations to the person who has the microphone.

Other situations where the objective expectation of privacy is too minimal to be considered a search under the Fourth Amendment include ham radio communication and citizen's band radio. However, a person having a conversation over a cordless phone would in general have a reasonable expectation of privacy that society would recognize because although it is conceivable that the conversation could be overheard, it is reasonable for a person to expect that the conversation is private. This expectation of privacy extends to a person having a conversation in a phone booth, a hotel room, and other locations when the person has taken the steps to exclude others from the conversation, and society recognizes those exclusionary steps as objectively reasonable. Accordingly, the key factor in the determination is not simply whether the communication can be intercepted but whether it is reasonable for the communication to be intercepted by another.

Thus, if the electronic surveillance falls under the ECPA, then the government has to abide by the restrictions in the ECPA. However, even if the government does not abide by the restrictions in the ECPA, it does not necessarily violate the person's Fourth Amendment rights. Generally, electronic surveillance is not a search under the Fourth Amendment unless the person has a subjective expectation of privacy that society is objectively willing to recognize and that expectation of privacy is violated. However, when the government has a warrant issued with probable cause, then the government can in general conduct the search by the means specified in the warrant.

Technology Monitoring

The issue of whether technology monitoring by the government is a search hinges on whether the monitoring invades on a person's subjective expectation of privacy that society objectively recognizes. If there is no invasion of privacy, then no search under the Fourth Amendment has occurred. However, technology that provides information about a physically protected area that could not be searched without a warrant constitutes an unreasonable search when the technology is not in general public use. Where the government is using technology that is not in general public use such as thermal imaging devices, then the government must obtain a search warrant to utilize the technology.

In general, when a person knowingly exposes his or her activity to the public or third parties, then that activity can be monitored by the government through public or third party means. For example, the government can use global positioning system (GPS) or radio beacons attached to the exterior of a car to track the location of packages or containers that a person receives from a third party or common carrier. The tracking beacon is simply a way for the government to monitor the location of the package that the government could otherwise do by visual tracking methods. The tracking beacon is just an extension of the allowable methods by which a person can be tracked.

Technology monitoring also includes closed caption television monitoring (CCTV), audio monitoring, and infrared monitoring. CCTV monitoring is widespread in various countries throughout the world in airports, trains, subways, on public streets, police stations, and other public places. Generally, these types of surveillance that occur in public places are not searches because people are knowingly exposing their activities to the public view. However, technology monitoring using CCTV, audio monitoring, and infrared monitoring that occur outside of public view such as in a person's private home without a valid search warrant would violate a person's reasonable expectation of privacy. However, if the person invites a third party into the home, then the monitoring that the third party brings into the home is reasonable because the person invited the third party into the home and exposed the internal workings of the home to the third party. Accordingly, CCTV, audio, and infrared monitoring have to work within the same confines as other types of technology monitoring in that they violate a person's Fourth Amendment rights when the person has a reasonable expectation of privacy that society objectively recognizes.

The government can also monitor an employee's activity with the employer's consent when the employee has no reasonable expectation of privacy regarding whether the employer can monitor work activities. However, to dispel any expectation of privacy, the employer should disclose to the employee that the employer can and will monitor the employee's activities. This monitoring can also extend to government employees as long as the employees are aware that their expectation of privacy is lowered because the government is monitoring. The issue of whether the monitoring is a search hinges on whether the employee is aware of the monitoring and thus has a lowered expectation of privacy in regards to the activity or location being monitored.

Accordingly, the issue of whether technology monitoring is a search under the Fourth Amendment hinges on whether the person being monitored has a subjective expectation of privacy that society objectively recognizes. In general, people in a public place have a limited expectation of privacy unless they have taken the steps necessary to shield their activities from public view. In addition, the monitoring must not intrude into places that are protected places such as the interior of a person's home without a search warrant that was issued with probable cause. Thus, the government can use different methods of technology monitoring without a warrant as long as the means do not intrude on a person's reasonable expectation of privacy that society objectively recognizes and as long as the technology means does not intrude on a protected area with technology that is not commonly available by the public.

Dog Sniff

Dog or canine sniffs do not in general compromise any legitimate expectation of privacy as long as the dog and the officer are legally allowed to be where the sniff occurs. The key issue for any Fourth Amendment violations involving a dog sniff is whether the dog is in a place that it can legally be since a dog sniff itself does not intrude on areas that are hidden from public view. A person does not have a reasonable expectation of privacy in an odor radiating from an object because the odor has been put into the public view by its release from the object. Additionally, dog sniffs do not show the interior of protected areas but simply indicate the presence or absence of contraband items. Accordingly, as long as the dog is in a location that it can legally be then the sniff is not a search under the Fourth Amendment. However, if the dog and the handler are not in a location where they legally can be, then the dog sniff is a search under the Fourth Amendment because the presence of the dog and its handler is itself a search.

Even if the dog sniff is not a search, the seizure that leads to the dog sniff may become unreasonable under the Fourth Amendment if the person or items have been unlawfully detained by the police. The seizure of an automobile at a checkpoint does not turn the subsequent sniff by the dog into a search as long as the stop is lawful in nature and is not extended beyond what is reasonable. The reasonableness question for detaining people or items hinges on whether under the Fourth Amendment the government has reasonable suspicion for detaining the people or items for the dog sniff and has specific and articulable facts for the suspicion. In addition, the government must work diligently to obtain a trained dog for the

sniff when people or items are seized under reasonable suspicion. However, when the people have placed themselves or items into the public view and the odor is radiating to the public place, then no reasonable suspicion is needed because the dog sniff of the radiating smell is not a search and the person or items have not been seized. The government can utilize a dog sniff for checked luggage on planes, trains, and busses, shipped packages, storage lockers, trailers, and cars, as long as the items have not been seized or the seizure of those items is reasonable.

In general, a dog sniff on items in public view is not a search. However, the sniff can become an unreasonable search under the Fourth Amendment if the person or items to be sniffed are detained beyond a reasonable time or without reasonable suspicion. Accordingly, a dog sniff is not a search under the Fourth Amendment because the privacy interest of odor radiating from a person or item is not a reasonable privacy interest protected by the Fourth Amendment.

LINDA F. HARRISON

References and Further Reading

Ball, Kirstie, and Frank Webster, eds. *Intensification of Surveillance: Crime, Terrorism and Warfare in the Information Age.* London: Pluto Press, 2003.

Bloom, Robert M. Searches, *Seizures, and Warrants: A Reference Guide to the United States Constitution.* Westport, CT: Praeger Publishers, 2003.

City of Indianapolis v. Edmond, 531 U.S. 32 (2000).

Hall, John Wesley. *Search and Seizure.* Charlotteville, VA: Lexis Law Publishing, 2000.

LaFave, Wayne R. *Search and Seizure: A Treatise on the Fourth Amendment.* St. Paul, MN: Thomson West, 2004.

Newburn, Tim, and Stephanie Hayman. *Policing, Surveillance and Social Control: CCTV and Police Monitoring of Suspects.* Devon, UK: Willan Publishing, 2001.

Schneier, Bruce, and David Banisar, eds. *The Electronic Privacy Papers: Documents on the Battle for Privacy in the Age of Surveillance.* New York: John Wiley & Sons, 1997.

Sharpe, Sybil. *Search and Surveillance.* Aldershot, England: Ashgate Publishing, 2000.

USA Patriot Act of 2001, 115 Stat. 272.

U.S. Department of Justice, Computer Crime and Intellectual Property Section. "Searching and Seizing Computer and Obtaining Electronic Evidence in Criminal Investigations." July 2002. http://www.usdoj.gov/criminal/cybercrime/s&smanual2002.pdf.

Cases and Statutes Cited

Electronic Communications Privacy Act (ECPA) of 1986, 100 Stat. 1848

Foreign Intelligence Surveillance Act (FISA) of 1978, 92 Stat. 1783

Illinois v. Caballes, 125 S.Ct. 834 (2005)

Katz v. United States, 389 U.S. 347 (1967)

Kyllo v. United States, 533 U.S. 27 (2001)

Mapp v. Ohio, 367 U.S. 643 (1961)
O'Conner v. Ortega, 480 U.S. 709 (1987)
Silverman v. United States, 365 U.S. 505 (1961)
Smith v. Maryland, 442 U.S. 735 (1979)
United States v. Byrd, 31 F.3d 1329 (5th Cir. 1994)
United States v. Dixon, 51 F.3d 1376 (8th Cir. 1995)
United States v. Gonzalez, 328 F.3d 543 (9th Cir. 2003)
United States v. Hernandez, 313 F.3d 1206 (9th Cir. 2002)
United States v. Johnson, 990 F.2d 1129 (9th Cir. 1993)
United States v. Karo, 468 U.S. 705 (1984)
United States v. Knotts, 460 U.S. 276 (1983)
United States v. Matlock, 415 U.S. 164 (1974)
United States v. McIver, 186 F.3d 1119 (9th Cir. 1999)
United States v. Michael, 645 F.2d 252 (5th Cir. 1981)
United States v. Place, 462 U.S. 696 (1983)
United States v. Rose, 669 F.2d 23 (1st Cir. 1982)
United States v. Shovea, 580 F.2d 1382 (10th Cir. 1978)
United States v. Simons, 206 F.3d 392 (4th Cir. 2000)
United States v. Sukiz-Grado, 22 F.3d 1006 (10th Cir. 1994)
United States v. Smith, 978 F.2d 171 (5th Cir. 1992)
United States v. Sundby, 186 F.3d 873 (8th Cir. 1999)
United States v. Ward, 144 F.3d 1024 (7th Cir. 1998)
United States v. White, 42 F.3d 457 (8th Cir. 1994)
U.S. Constitution, Fourth Amendment

See also **Administrative Searches and Seizures; Airport Searches; Anonymity in Online Communication; Automobile Searches; Checkpoints (roadblocks); Invasion of Privacy and Free Speech; 9/11 and the War on Terrorism; Plain View; War on Drugs; Warrantless Searches; Wiretapping Laws**

ELK GROVE UNIFIED SCHOOL DISTRICT v. NEWDOW, 542 U.S. 1 (2004)

In *Elk Grove Unified School District v. Newdow*, the Supreme Court declined to resolve the constitutionality of the inclusion of the words "under God" in the Pledge of Allegiance when recited in public schools. Instead, the Court found that the plaintiff in the case lacked standing to sue and thereby reversed a controversial decision by the U.S. Court of Appeals for the Ninth Circuit that had found the "under God" language in the Pledge when recited by public schoolchildren violative of the Establishment Clause.

A California school district required each elementary school class in the district to recite the Pledge of Allegiance every day. The father of a schoolchild objected, claiming that the inclusion of the words "under God" in the Pledge constituted religious indoctrination in violation of the Religion Clauses of the First Amendment (even though his daughter was not compelled to participate in the recitation). The U.S. Court of Appeals for the Ninth Circuit found that the recitation violated the Establishment Clause. This decision sparked a national controversy, and the U.S. Congress promptly passed a resolution—unanimously

in the Senate and with only five nay votes in the House—condemning that decision.

The Supreme Court accepted review and held that the father, who was a noncustodial parent of the schoolchild, lacked standing to bring the action. The Court emphasized that the father's standing derived entirely from his relationship with his daughter, and that their interests were not parallel and were potentially in conflict. Since the father lacked standing, the Court dismissed the case, thereby reversing the decision of the Ninth Circuit.

Three justices, however, dissented from the majority's discussion of standing. These justices, all of whom wrote separate opinions, would have reached the merits of the case and found that the school recitation of the Pledge with the "under God" language *did not* offend the Establishment Clause. (A fourth justice, Antonin Scalia, recused himself from consideration of the case because of prior public comments critical of the Ninth Circuit's ruling.)

In his separate opinion, Chief Justice William Rehnquist concluded that the recitation of the Pledge did not violate the Establishment Clause:

> I do not believe that the phrase 'under God' in the Pledge converts its recital into a 'religious exercise' . . . . Instead, it is a declaration of belief in allegiance and loyalty to the United States flag and the Republic that it represents. The phrase 'under God' is in no sense a prayer, nor an endorsement of any religion . . . . Reciting the Pledge, or listening to others recite it, is a patriotic exercise, not a religious one; participants promise fidelity to our flag and our Nation, not to any particular God, faith, or church.

Justice Sandra Day O'Connor, in her opinion, argued that the recitation of the Pledge did not violate the "endorsement test." For Justice O'Connor, quoting her earlier concurring opinion in *Lynch v. Donnelly* (1984), endorsement "sends a message to nonadherents that they are outsiders, not full members of the political community, and an accompanying message to adherents that they are insiders, favored members of the political community." Justice O'Connor concluded that recitation of the Pledge sent no such message. Justice O'Connor concluded that the "under God" language in the Pledge constituted an expression of "ceremonial deism" which did not offend the Establishment Clause.

Finally, Justice Clarence Thomas concluded that the recitation of the Pledge *did* violate the Establishment Clause as interpreted by the Court because it "coerced" young children "to declare a belief" that this is "one Nation under God." Hence, for Justice Thomas, "as a matter of our precedent, the Pledge policy is unconstitutional." But, Justice Thomas went further, arguing that almost all of the Court's prior Establishment Clause cases were wrongly decided because, in his view, the Establishment Clause does not apply to the states. Justice Thomas recognized that the Court in prior cases had "incorporated" the Establishment Clause through the Fourteenth Amendment to apply to the states, but he concluded that that incorporation was inappropriate as a matter of history. Because, in Justice Thomas's view, the Establishment Clause does not apply to the states, the recitation of the Pledge by a local California school district was not unconstitutional.

In light of the resolution of the *Elk Grove* case on standing grounds, the constitutionality of recitations of the Pledge in public schools remains uncertain.

DAVISON M. DOUGLAS

References and Further Reading

Collins, Todd, *Lost in the Forest of the Establishment Clause:* Elk Grove v. Newdow, Campbell Law Review 27 (2004): 1–38.
Gey, Steven, *'Under God,' The Pledge of Allegiance, and Other Constitutional Trivia*, North Carolina Law Review 81 (2003): 1865–925.
Hancock, Kevin P., *Comment: Closing the Endorsement Test Escape-Hatch in the Pledge of Allegiance Debate*, Seton Hall Law Review 35 (2005): 739–88.

Cases and Statutes Cited

Lynch v. Donnelly, 465 U.S. 668 (1984)

See also **Ceremonial Deism; Establishment Clause (I): History, Background, Framing; Pledge of Allegiance ("Under God")**

ELLSWORTH COURT (1796–1800)

The "Ellsworth Court" is the title attributed to the Supreme Court during the tenure of Oliver Ellsworth as chief justice of the United States, from March 1796 to December 1800. Ellsworth, of Connecticut, was the de facto leader of the Federalist faction in Congress prior to his appointment. In addition, Ellsworth had been instrumental in the passage of the Judiciary Act of 1789 that established the basic structure of the federal judiciary. Ellsworth was the third chief justice of the United States, attaining the office after John Rutledge failed to achieve confirmation after becoming chief justice by recess appointment.

Prominent associate justices to serve during Ellsworth's time as chief justice include William Cushing, Samuel Chase, James Iredell, William Paterson, Bushrod Washington, and James Wilson. Justice Alfred Moore also served briefly during this period, resigning due to ill health and dissatisfaction with his duties. As with the Jay Court, each of these jurists was selected by President George Washington and was considered sympathetic to Federalist principles. The Ellsworth Court met twice annually in Philadelphia, which was then the temporary national capital.

Unlike the contemporary Supreme Court, the Ellsworth Court consisted of only six justices. The composition of the Supreme Court during Ellsworth's tenure was geographically balanced with members drawn from each region of the United States. This was the norm for the early Supreme Court, as it facilitated "circuit riding" duties and stifled disputes among sectional interests.

Circuit riding was a hallmark of the Supreme Court in its first century, requiring justices to hold court alongside district judges twice each year in a judicial circuit assigned to them. Justices rode circuit each year following the February and August terms of the Supreme Court. Many justices found circuit riding objectionable as it required extensive travel for weeks or months at a time. Although this aspect of the justices' duties provoked discontent, their repeated appeals to Congress yielded little relief.

Although it remained relatively small, the workload of the Supreme Court under Ellsworth's leadership was greater than during the tenures of John Jay and John Rutledge (1789–1795). The institution's docket during Ellsworth's tenure was generally dominated by admiralty and diversity cases, many of which resulted from contemporaneous American treaty obligations. The years 1796 and 1797 in particular saw escalation in the Supreme Court's workload, with more than fifty cases considered in 1796 and nearly thirty in 1797. Along with maritime and economic disputes, the justices faced some controversies with ramifications for American civil liberties. The most significant of these concerned seditious libel and the legitimacy of criminal prosecutions under federal common law.

Federal indictments for sedition and acts of rebellion had occurred as early as 1792, but these issues became particularly important during Ellsworth's tenure. Domestic furor over Jay's Treaty (1795–1796) and strained relations with France created a volatile political climate. Following the scandalous XYZ Affair, the federal government prepared for war with France and sought to discourage domestic dissent. This contributed to the passage of the Sedition Act (1798). This statute clearly stipulated that sedition was a criminal act, as it had been considered by jurists previously on the basis of common law. This proved controversial, with some legislators asserting that the act merely codified existing common law, and others believing it to be an infringement of Americans' civil liberties guaranteed by the Constitution.

The Supreme Court justices enforced the Sedition Act in the circuit courts, with Chief Justice Ellsworth advocating the position that the act was in agreement with constitutional principles and the common law. The other justices were sympathetic with this position and enforced the Sedition Act, sometimes vigorously. Both ordinary citizens and members of the press were prosecuted under the Act, most often for criticism of President John Adams and the Federalists in Congress. The Sedition Act came to be viewed as a tool of the Federalists to thwart dissent and became a contentious issue in the election of 1800. Both the Sedition Act and the notion of federal common-law crimes were attacked by Thomas Jefferson and the Democratic-Republicans. The Supreme Court never addressed the Sedition Act directly, as it expired in 1801 and was not renewed by the Democratic-Republicans after their electoral victory in 1800.

Interestingly, the Ellsworth Court preceded the Supreme Court's 1803 decision in *Marbury v. Madison* (1803), but its justices apparently agreed on the legitimacy of judicial review. The justices clearly considered the constitutionality of a federal tax in *Hylton v. United States* (1796), although they did not strike down the relevant statute. In addition, the Court's decision in *Ware v. Hylton* (1796) provided perhaps the Supreme Court's earliest expression of the supremacy of federal law. While *Ware* dealt specifically with a conflict between a Virginia statute and a federal treaty with Britain, the invocation of the Supremacy Clause was an important declaration of the precedence of federal over state laws.

A notable institutional development during this period was the decline of *in seriatim* opinions under Ellsworth's leadership. Unlike his predecessors as chief justice, Ellsworth employed the prestige of his position to craft a single majority opinion. While in contrast to English tradition, this custom had been followed on the Connecticut court on which Ellsworth had previously served. While the practice of justices publishing *in seriatim* opinions did not diminish completely until the tenure of Chief Justice John Marshall (1801–1835), the Ellsworth Court issued consolidated majority opinions in every case in which the chief justice participated.

Chief Justice Ellsworth retained his position until December 1800, when he resigned after four and a half years of judicial service. Prior to his resignation, Ellsworth had been appointed as minister to France in 1799–1800 and was instrumental in the effort to thwart a naval war with America's former ally. While serving abroad Ellsworth's health declined considerably, and it is believed to have contributed substantially to his decision to step down. Ellsworth was succeeded as chief justice by John Marshall of Virginia, whose own contributions to the legal and political development of the Supreme Court would be immense.

RICHARD L. VINING

References and Further Reading

Casto, William R. *The Supreme Court in the Early Republic: The Chief Justiceships of John Jay and Oliver Ellsworth.* Columbia: University of South Carolina Press, 1995.

Gerber, Scott D., ed. *Seriatim: The Supreme Court Before John Marshall.* New York: New York University Press, 1998.

Goebel, Julius Jr. *History of the Supreme Court of the United States. Volume I: Antecedents and Beginnings to 1801.* New York: Macmillan Company, 1971.

Cases and Statutes Cited

Hylton v. United States, 3 Dall. 171 (1796)

Judiciary Act of 1789, Act of September 24, 1789, 1 Stat. 73

Marbury v. Madison, 5 U.S. 137 (1803)

Sedition Act of 1798, Act of July 14, 1798, 1 Stat. 596

Ware v. Hylton, 3 Dall. 199 (1796)

See also **Alien and Sedition Acts (1798);** *Calder v. Bull,* **3 U.S. 386 (1798); Chase, Samuel; Common Law or Statute; Freedom of Speech and Press under the Constitution: Early History (1791–1917); Jefferson, Thomas; Judicial Review; Marshall, John; National Security and Freedom of Speech; Natural Law, 18th Century Understanding; Seditious Libel**

ELROD v. BURNS, 427 U.S. 347 (1976)

Cook County, Illinois was notorious for patronage. The Democratic Party hired supporters for city and county jobs and required them to work on behalf of its political candidates. When Richard Elrod was elected Cook County sheriff in 1970, he promptly fired several Republican employees of the office. Those fired brought suit under the First Amendment, alleging that they were discharged because they were not Democrats.

The Supreme Court agreed, relying upon its decisions in loyalty oath cases, such as *Keyishian v. Board of Regents* (1967), which held that conditioning a public job upon political belief was unconstitutional. Firing an employee based on political belief or association amounted to coercion of the individual's freedom of association and could deter others who would like to apply for city jobs from the free exercise of speech and association.

The defendants argued that political patronage was necessary to ensure efficient and loyal employees and to maintain a strong democratic political party system. Applying the high level of review required when government action affects First Amendment rights, the Court rejected this argument. These interests could be served by politically based dismissals of policymaking employees only (defined in *Branti v. Finkel* [1980] as those where "party affiliation is an appropriate requirement for the effective performance of the public office involved").

Elrod prohibited political firing, but left political hiring an open question. This was held unconstitutional in *Rutan v. Republican Party of Illinois* (1990). *Elrod* also invited lawsuits about the reasons employees had been fired and whether they were policymakers and thus exempt from *Elrod*'s prohibition.

CYNTHIA GRANT BOWMAN

References and Further Reading

Allswang, John M. *Bosses, Machines and Urban Voters.* Rev. ed. Baltimore: Johns Hopkins University Press, 1986.
Bowman, Cynthia Grant, *'We Don't Want Anybody Sent': The Death of Patronage Hiring in Chicago*, Northwestern University Law Review 86 (1991): 1:57–95.

Cases and Statutes Cited

Branti v. Finkel, 445 U.S. 507 (1980)
Keyishian v. Board of Regents, 385 U.S. 589 (1967)
Rutan v. Republican Party of Illinois, 497 U.S. 62 (1990)

See also **Branti v. Finkel, 445 U.S. 507 (1980); Political Patronage and the First Amendment; Rutan v. Republican Party of Illinois, 497 U.S. 62 (1990); Unconstitutional Conditions**

EMANCIPATION PROCLAMATION (1863)

On January 1, 1863 President Abraham Lincoln issued the Emancipation Proclamation, which declared that slaves living in most of the Confederate states were forever free. The Proclamation was certainly one of the most important advances in civil liberties, because it provided for freeing from slavery millions of African Americans. At the same time, from the perspective of slave owners, the proclamation was a huge violation of civil liberties because it took their "property" away from them without any compensation. From the perspective of constitutional law, the Proclamation was extremely problematic. The Constitution prohibited the government from taking private property without compensation. Furthermore, the Constitution protected slavery a variety of ways and

the Supreme Court, in *Dred Scott v. Sandford* (1857), had held that slavery was a privileged form of property deserving of special constitutional protection. Finally, it was not at all clear that under the Constitution the president ever had power to unilaterally act in such a way as to deprive citizens of their property.

President Lincoln understood all of these issues, and thus he drafted the Proclamation carefully. He excluded from the Proclamation those portions of the Confederacy, such as New Orleans and parts of Virginia, which were under the control of the United States. In the rest of Confederacy, Lincoln acted in his capacity as commander-in-chief of the Army to emancipate all slave on the grounds they constituted a military asset to those states in rebellion.

By proceeding in this manner, Lincoln avoided a number of constitutional pitfalls. Since he acted as commander-in-chief, he presumably did not need any authorization from Congress. Clearly Lincoln could order the Army to destroy or confiscate the property of Confederates in order to suppress the rebellion. Freeing the slaves was simply another form of destroying property that those in rebellion were using to make war on the United States. Lincoln could plausibly argue that the Constitution was in force where the Confederate government operated. Thus, by limiting the Proclamation to those regions of the United States that were under the control of the Confederates, Lincoln could argue that emancipation was not a "taking of private property" as contemplated in the Fifth Amendment, because the Constitution was not in force in the Confederacy. Alternatively, he could argue that the writ of habeas corpus had been suspended in all of those states in rebellion, and thus the military could seize property (and emancipate slaves) as needed to suppress the rebellion.

Each of these theories was sufficient to justify freeing the slaves of rebel masters while the war was in progress, but it was not clear what would happen to the emancipated slaves when the war ended. Lincoln had some reason to believe that the Supreme Court might overturn the Proclamation, or enforce a judgment against the United States for taking private property without just compensation in violation of the Fifth Amendment. This was especially plausible because the Supreme Court was still dominated by pro-slavery justices, and continued to be until led by Chief Justice Roger B. Taney, the author of the *Dred Scott* decision. Thus, Lincoln was delighted when Congress passed the Thirteenth Amendment and sent it on to the states for ratification. Once ratified, this Amendment freed all remaining slaves in the nation and prevented any former masters from making any claims on the U.S. government for the value of their emancipated slaves.

The Emancipation Proclamation was the most significant antislavery action by the U.S. government until the adoption of the Thirteenth Amendment. The Proclamation freed millions of slaves. That freedom, however, would only be secured as the U.S. Army moved deeper in the South, crushing the rebellion. However, after January 1, 1863, the nature of the Civil War was permanently altered. It was still a war to preserve and restore the Union. But, after that date it was also a war to extend the most fundamental civil liberty—freedom to millions of African Americans who were held in slavery. After Lincoln issued the Proclamation, the U.S. Army became the greatest army of liberation the world had ever known, bringing liberty everywhere it went.

PAUL FINKELMAN

References and Further Reading

Franklin, John Hope. *The Emancipation Proclamation.* Garden City, NY: Doubleday, 1963.
McPherson, James. *Battle Cry of Freedom.* New York: Oxford University Press, 1988.

Cases and Statutes Cited

Dred Scott v. John F.A. Sandford, 60 U.S. (19 How.) 393 (1857)

EMERGENCY, CIVIL LIBERTIES IN

Discussions of civil liberties in emergency are plagued by the recurrent problem of defining the kind of situation designated by the term "emergency." According to German jurist Carl Schmitt, sometimes thought of as the theorist of the Third Reich, the "exception"— closely related to the emergency—can only be declared, not defined; hence, "Sovereign is he who decides on the exception." Justice Stone, concurring in *Duncan v. Kahanamoku* (1946), a case involving martial law, described "the power which resides in the executive branch of the government to preserve order and insure the public safety in times of emergency, when other branches of the government are unable to function, or their functioning would itself threaten the public safety." As he explained, "[t]he Executive has broad discretion in determining when the public emergency is such as to give rise to the necessity of martial law, and in adapting it to the need." While the emergency may coincide with war, it need not do so. Likewise, although foreign relations may be implicated, the emergency may possess a largely domestic compass, as in the case of civil unrest. It may, indeed, be in the nature of the emergency to defy definition except in contradistinction to a "normal" state of affairs. And, in general, in an emergency, the survival of the nation is thought to be at stake. In this respect, the emergency stands in the lineage of the "raison d'etat," or "reason of state," which designates, according to one formulation, "the doctrine that whatever is required to insure the survival of the state must be done by the individuals responsible for it, no matter how repugnant such an act may be to them in their private capacity as decent and moral men." Initially derived from Italian political theory, this concept found expression in the Anglo-American context in John Locke's discussion of prerogative in the *Second Treatise of Government*. Although economic emergencies have sometimes swept the United States—most notably during the Great Depression—the most prevalent associations with emergency involve the imminent threat of violence.

The main questions that arise in considering emergency situations involve who identifies or constructs the existence of an emergency, and by what means; the scope of extraordinary powers sought to resolve the declared emergency; and the emergency's duration. As Schmitt's and Justice Stone's comments suggest, the executive has traditionally taken charge of designating emergency situations. Some constitutions, like that of Poland, contain explicit provisions concerning emergencies and specify the mechanism by which an emergency is to be announced; that is not the case in the United States. The most relevant constitutional clauses include those articulating Congress's power to declare war and to call forth the militia (art. I, sec. 8, cls. 11 and 14), and the provision for suspension of the writ of habeas corpus (art. I, sec. 9, cls. 2). Despite the congressional nature of these related powers, the president has, in emergency situations, often issued an executive order concerning the emergency or simply taken what he asserts is necessary action. In the attempt to reduce the likelihood of executive overreaching during and through times of emergency, the constitutions of many other countries, such as Estonia, have granted legislatures a greater role in declaring and limiting the duration of emergencies. Some have argued that this strategy is currently being or should be employed in the United States as well. A proposal put forth by Professor Bruce Ackerman would involve a "supermajoritarian escalator," under which the president would be given "the power to act unilaterally only for the briefest period—long enough for the legislature to convene and consider the matter, but no longer," and subsequent action would have to be approved by ever-increasing supermajorities in Congress. Professors John Ferejohn and Pasquale Pasquino assert that a similar reliance on legislative action to delegate emergency powers to the executive has been on the rise internationally, and that a "new model of emergency powers . . . has evolved over the past half century, at least for the advanced or stable democracies."

A related concern implicates the scope of the emergency powers exercised, and who is authorized to employ them. To the extent that the president acts in an emergency, he may do so either pursuant to a statute or through authority derived directly from particular provisions of Article II of the Constitution. In *Youngstown Sheet & Tube Co. v. Sawyer* (1952), involving President Truman's seizure of the steel mills "to avert a national catastrophe which would inevitably result from a stoppage of steel production" when a strike was threatened during the Korean War, Justice Jackson's concurrence articulated three categories of presidential action and described the relative legitimacy of each. According to Jackson's typology, "[w]hen the President acts pursuant to an express or implied authorization of Congress, his authority is at its maximum," while "in absence of either a congressional grant or denial of authority," a "zone of twilight" exists where the president may have concurrent authority with Congress, and, finally, the president's "power is at its lowest ebb" when he "takes measures incompatible with the expressed or implied will of Congress." After the events of September 11, 2001, the government has, however, insisted in several instances that Article II of the Constitution grants the president a more extensive overarching power than its individual clauses alone provide. For example, in the case of Yaser Esam Hamdi, a U.S. citizen captured during hostilities in Afghanistan and subsequently held in a naval brig in South Carolina, the government claimed that "the Executive possesses plenary authority to detain [citizens considered "enemy combatants"] pursuant to Article II of the Constitution" (*Hamdi v. Rumsfeld* [2004]). The extent to which the president can exercise power independent of congressional authorization during times of emergency thus remains subject to dispute. Granting the president greater capacity in emergencies could have an adverse impact on civil liberties because it would diminish the check on executive aggrandizement provided by the constitutional separation of powers.

Tactics employed to deal with the emergency may also directly infringe upon civil liberties through three mechanisms, or a combination of them: legislation granting the government greater powers of surveillance or limiting the freedom of association, executive action contravening or exceeding the scope of statutes designed to protect certain rights, or reduction in the compass of those liberties that are constitutionally based. Historically, noncitizens have been subject to the most dramatic restrictions on their civil liberties, as David Cole has demonstrated in *Enemy Aliens*, and, with the increasingly international reach of the United States, those located outside the country have suffered more extreme forms of rights deprivation. The judiciary has tended to acquiesce in the political branches' violation of civil liberties during emergency, either by refraining from vindicating individuals' rights until after a particular crisis has ended, as in the post–Civil War case *Ex parte Milligan* (1866), or by upholding the government's actions on the grounds of necessity, as in the World War II case *Korematsu v. United States* (1944). Which alternative is worse has been the subject of some dispute. Whereas some commentators—such as Kathleen M. Sullivan—insist that constitutional norms should remain the same during times of emergency, others—such as Mark Tushnet and Oren Gross—maintain that accommodation is the right approach, whether achieved by the Supreme Court's recognition of a difference between normal and emergency situations or by allowing public officials to take extralegal measures in moments of crisis that the public may or may not subsequently ratify. A recent empirical study by Lee et al. has concluded counterintuitively that emergency does affect judicial decision making, but only with respect to non-war cases.

The right of habeas corpus is the only one that the Constitution explicitly contemplates suspending under certain circumstances. Because of the placement of the Suspension Clause amid the limitations upon Congress's powers in Article I, scholars and judges have concluded that the legislature alone has the capacity to restrict availability of the writ. The executive branch has not, however, accepted this judgment without resistance. In 1861, towards the beginning of the Civil War, President Lincoln proclaimed a suspension of the writ in certain areas; although Chief Justice Taney, riding circuit, vehemently rejected the constitutionality of this purported suspension, in the 1861 case *Ex parte Merryman*, the Supreme Court itself never adjudicated the question. Congress subsequently granted the president authority to suspend habeas corpus "during the Rebellion"—an authority that Lincoln rapidly and comprehensively implemented—but simultaneously provided for judicial review of detentions (An Act Relating to Habeas Corpus). More recently, under President George W. Bush, the government contended that the writ was not available to "enemy combatants" or to those detained outside the territorial limits of the United States. The Supreme Court's opinions in *Rasul v. Bush* (2004) and *Hamdi v. Rumsfeld* confirmed respectively, however, that at least a partial right of habeas corpus remained for individuals held at the military base in Guantanamo Bay, Cuba, and that, in general, "a citizen-detainee seeking to challenge his classification as an enemy combatant must receive notice of the factual basis for his classification, and a fair opportunity to rebut the Government's factual assertions before a neutral decisionmaker."

Internment has also been employed in a manner comparable to executive branch detention. Subsequent to the bombing of Pearl Harbor, President Franklin Delano Roosevelt issued Executive Order 9066, which excluded Japanese Americans, including citizens, from certain areas of the West Coast, on the grounds of military necessity; Congress soon criminalized failure to obey this directive. Fred Korematsu, a Japanese American, was convicted of violating the order. In its decision on his appeal, the Supreme Court insisted that racial classifications should be subject to strict scrutiny—but that the exclusion of Japanese Americans under emergency circumstances satisfied this searching review. In doing so, Justice Black deferred to the judgment of the "war-making branches" that "exclusion of the whole group was . . . a military imperative" (*Korematsu v. United States*). Although recognized as one of the most reviled cases that the Supreme Court has ever decided, *Korematsu* remains good law. At the same time, however, the Court in *Ex parte Endo* (1944), in language reminiscent of the technique of constitutional avoidance, construed the War Relocation Authority's continued detention of loyal Japanese Americans—as opposed to their exclusion from particular areas—as exceeding its delegated capacity; the decision effectively coincided with the end of the relocation camps.

The government has infringed on civil liberties in times of emergency in ways short of detention or internment as well. During World War I and the subsequent red scare, as well as the cold war, among other periods of conflict, First Amendment freedoms of speech and association were statutorily curtailed, with the Supreme Court's partial acquiescence. Commentators have likewise argued that the Fourth Amendment's prohibition against unlawful searches and seizures has been relaxed during times of emergency. The most notable recent examples include the expansion of various forms of surveillance under the USA Patriot Act, passed just days after the attacks of September 11, 2001, as well as President Bush's secret program for collecting data on telephone calls routed through the United States.

Finally, measures taken during emergency have often curtailed the cluster of rights surrounding the trial of an accused individual. During both the Civil War and World War II, the executive established military commissions and tried various individuals under these tribunals, thus circumventing a number of due process guarantees, including that of trial by jury. In ruling on the constitutionality of these commissions, the Supreme Court held that, although the government cannot subject civilians to trial by military tribunal when the courts are actually open (*Ex parte Milligan*), it may so prosecute allegedly unlawful combatants, whether citizens or not (*Ex parte Quirin* [1942]). The "war on terrorism" has sparked renewed debate about the constitutionality, advisability, and legality under international law of trial by military commission. While the Bush administration initially promoted the notion of trying al-Qaeda operatives and other suspected terrorists by military tribunal, it soon resorted to a strategy of indefinite detention at Guantánamo Bay and elsewhere. Language from the plurality's opinion in *Hamdi* suggested that the government might meet the due process standards for establishing that an individual should be identified as an "enemy combatant" "by an appropriately authorized and constituted military tribunal." The *Hamdan v. Rumsfeld* (2005) case—granted certiorari during the October 2005 term—likewise concerns the validity under domestic and international law of a trial by military commission. The Supreme Court has, however, declined to answer the question of whether the government can, consistent with the public's First Amendment right of access to certain types of judicial proceedings, close so-called "special interest" deportation hearings (*North Jersey Media Group v. Ashcroft* [2003]).

Finally, the duration of emergency—or even of war—may have implications for its effect on civil liberties as well. To avoid the situation of permanent or semipermanent emergency—such as occurred in South Africa under apartheid—many countries' constitutions prescribe temporal limitations upon declared emergencies. The current "war on terrorism" does not, however, possess a well-defined endpoint. Nor is it likely under the Court's current construction of political question doctrine that the question of the termination of this—or any war—would be subject to judicial review (*Baker v. Carr* [1962]).

BERNADETTE MEYLER

References and Further Reading

Ackerman, Bruce, *The Emergency Constitution*, Yale Law Journal 113 (2004): 5:1029–1092.

Amar, Akhil Reed, and Vikram David Amar, *The New Regulation Allowing Federal Agents to Monitor Attorney–Client Conversations: Why It Threatens Fourth Amendment Values*, Connecticut Law Review 34 (2002): 4L1163–1167.

Cole, David. *Enemy Aliens*. New York: New Press, 2003.

———., *The New McCarthyism: Repeating History in the War on Terrorism*, Harvard Civil Rights-Civil Liberties Law Review 38 (2003): 1:1–30.

Dauber, Michele Landis, *The Sympathetic State*, Law and History Review 23. (2005): 2:387–442.

Detroit Free Press v. Ashcroft, 303 F.3d 681 (6th Cir. 2002).

Ellmann, Stephen. *In a Time of Trouble: Law and Liberty in South Africa's State of Emergency*. Oxford: Oxford University Press, 1992.

Epstein, Lee, Daniel E. Ho, Gary King, and Jeffrey A. Segal, *The Supreme Court During Crisis: How War Affects Only Non-War Cases*, New York University Law Review 80. (2005): 1:1–116.

Ferejohn, John, and Pasquino, Pasquale, *The Law of the Exception: A Typology of Emergency Powers*, International Journal of Constitutional Law 2 (2004): 2:210–239.

Friedrich, Carl J. *Constitutional Reason of State: The Survival of the Constitutional Order*. Providence, RI: Brown University Press, 1957.

Gross, Oren, *Chaos and Rules: Should Responses to Violent Crises Always Be Constitutional?* Yale Law Journal 112 (2003): 5:1011–1034.

Gudridge, Patrick O., *Remember Endo?* Harvard Law Review 116 (2003): 7:1933–1970.

Home Bldg. & Loan Assn. v. Blaisdell, 290 U.S. 398 (1934).

Koh, Harold Hongju, *The Case Against Military Commissions*, American Journal of International Law 96 (2002): 2:337–344.

Lichtblau, Eric. "Officials Want to Expand Review of Domestic Spying." *New York Times*, December 25, 2005.

Locke, John. *Two Treatises of Government*. Edited by Peter Laslett. Cambridge: Cambridge University Press, 1988.

Mark Tushnet, *Defending Korematsu? Reflections on Civil Liberties in Wartime*, Wisconsin Law Review 2003 (2003): 273–307.

Mayer, Jane. "Outsourcing Torture: The Secret History of America's 'Extraordinary Rendition' Program." *New Yorker*, February 14 and 21, 2005.

Posner, Eric A., and Vermeule, Adrian, *Accommodating Emergencies*, Stanford Law Review 56 (2003): 3:605–44.

Reed, Christopher. "Are American Liberties At Risk?" *Harvard Magazine*, January–February 2002: 100–1 (summarizing Kathleen M. Sullivan's Tanner Lecture on "War, Peace, and Civil Liberties").

Rehnquist, William H. *All the Laws but One: Civil Liberties in Wartime*. New York: Vintage Books, 2000.

Rostow, Eugene, *The Japanese American Cases—A Disaster*, Yale Law Journal 54 (1945): 3:489–533.

Rotenberg, Marc, *Privacy and Secrecy After September 11*, Minnesota Law Review 86 (2002): 6:1115–1136.

Schmitt, Carl. *Political Theology: Four Chapters on the Concept of Sovereignty*. Trans. George Schwab. Cambridge, MA: MIT Press, 1985.

Stone, Geoffrey R. *Perilous Times: Free Speech in Wartime from the Sedition Act of 1798 to the War on Terrorism*. New York: W.W. Norton & Co., 2004.

Tribe, Lawrence H., and Gudridge, Patrick O., *The Anti-Emergency Constitution*, Yale Law Journal 113 (2004): 8:1801–1870.

Wedgwood, Ruth, *Al Qaeda, Terrorism, and Military Commissions*, American Journal of International Law 96 (2002): 2:328–337.

Whitehead, John W., and Aden, Steven H., *Forfeiting 'Enduring Freedom' for 'Homeland Security': A Constitutional Analysis of the USA PATRIOT Act and the Justice Department's Anti-Terrorism Initiatives*, American University Law Review 51 (2002): 6:1081–1133.

Cases and Statutes Cited

Albanian Constitution of 1998, Article 173

"An Act Relating to Habeas Corpus," 12 Stat. at Large, 755 (1863)

Baker v. Carr, 369 U.S. 186, 213 (1962)

Constitution of Poland of 1997, Article 228

Duncan v. Kahanamoku, 327 U.S. 304 (1946)

Estonian Constitution of 1992, Articles 65, 129

Ex parte Endo, 323 U.S. 283, 287 (1944)

Executive Order Concerning the Detention, Treatment, and Trial of Certain Non-Citizens in the War Against Terrorism, 66 *Federal Register* 57 (November 13, 2001): 833

Hamdan v. Rumsfeld, 415 F.3d 33 (D.C. Cir. 2005), *cert. granted* 126 S.Ct. 622 (November 7, 2005)

Hamdi v. Rumsfeld, 542 U.S. 507 (2004)

Korematsu v. United States, 323 U.S. 214, 215–16 (1944)

Ex parte Merryman, 17 F. Cas. 144 (1861)

Ex parte Milligan, 71 U.S. 2 (1866)

North Jersey Media Group v. Ashcroft, 308 F.3d 198 (3d Cir. 2002), *cert. denied* 538 U.S. 1056 (May 27, 2003)

Ex parte Quirin, 317 U.S. 1 (1942)

Rasul v. Bush, 542 U.S. 466 (2004)

USA Patriot Act of 2001, Pub. L. No. 107-56, 115 Stat. 272 (2001)

Youngstown Sheet & Tube Co. v. Sawyer, 343 U.S. 579 (1952)

EMERSON, THOMAS IRWIN (1907–1991)

Thomas Irwin Emerson was a noted legal scholar and civil rights and civil liberties advocate. Born in Passaic, New Jersey, he graduated Phi Beta Kappa from Yale College (1928), attended Yale Law School and was editor-in-chief of the *Yale Law Journal*. While at the law school he studied under, among others, Robert Maynard Hutchins, and was a friend and classmate of William O. Douglas. He received his law degree in 1931.

A few years after graduating from law school, Emerson worked at the National Recovery Administration, on the National Labor Relations Board, and in the Attorney General's Office. During World War II, he then served as general counsel for the Office of Economic Stabilization and for the Office of War Mobilization and Reconversion. In 1948 he ran for governor of Connecticut as the People's Party candidate, and in 1950–1951 was the president of the National Lawyers Guild.

Emerson served on the Yale law faculty from 1946 to 1976; in 1955 he was named the Lines Professor of Law. He authored or edited four books and numerous articles, including an autobiographical work entitled, *Young Lawyer for the New Deal: An Insider's Memoir of the Roosevelt Years* (1991).

Civil Rights

As a young lawyer Emerson was employed at Engelhard, Pollak, Pitcher and Stern. Working with Walter Pollak—one of the lead lawyers who argued *Gitlow v. New York* (1925) and *Whitney v. California* (1927)—Emerson was on the legal team that successfully appealed the convictions of the Scottsboro Boys. In that case eight black teenagers were sentenced to death for the alleged rapes of two white women. Emerson and his colleagues challenged the convictions on Fourteenth Amendment grounds, arguing that due process required the appointment of counsel by state courts for indigent defendants in capital cases. The Court in *Powell v. Alabama* (1932) agreed by a seven-to-two margin, thereby launching a new era in civil rights law.

Early in January of 1950, Emerson filed an important *amicus* brief—joined by Dean Erwin Griswold of Harvard and Professor John P. Frank of Yale, among others—in *Sweatt v. Painter* (1950) on behalf of 188 law professors. The brief defended the claim of Heman Marion Sweatt that he had been denied equal protection under the Fourteenth Amendment when the University of Texas Law School refused to admit him on the basis of race; instead it referred him to a newly created state law school for blacks. The brief also challenged the viability of *Plessy v. Ferguson* (1896) and argued that inequality was inherent in segregation. The Court, in a nine-to-zero decision, held that the separate systems of education were not equal and sustained Sweatt's claim, thus mandating his admission to the University of Texas Law School. Both the brief and the holding helped to set the stage for the Court's ruling in *Brown v. Board of Education* (1954).

Emerson co-edited (initially with David Haber and then with Haber and Norman Dorsen, et al.) *Political and Civil Rights in the United States* (1967–1979), the first casebook of its kind and a voluminous treatment of the subject that included the reproduction of many original documents.

Freedom of Expression

Throughout his life Thomas Emerson was a staunch defender of freedom of expression. As early as 1948 he co-authored (with David Helfeld) a scholarly 143-page article entitled "Loyalty Among Government Employees," in which he argued that government loyalty programs were repressive and violated the First Amendment. Two years later Emerson openly condemned the University of California regents for firing 157 university employees suspected of being communists or communist sympathizers. During a "Bill of Rights Conference" in New York (July 17, 1949) Emerson, an active member of the American Civil Liberties Union's (ACLU) Free Speech Committee, strongly defended a resolution calling for restoring civil liberties for members of the Socialist Workers Party who had been caught up in government loyalty sweeps. Morris Ernst, a noted ACLU lawyer, and others took a different view and defeated the resolution.

In 1957, Professor Emerson successfully represented Paul Sweezy, a university teacher, in the Supreme Court case involving legislative inquiries concerning his ties to the Progressive Party and about a lecture he gave on socialism. The petitioner, who declined to respond to such inquiries, prevailed on due process grounds (*Sweezy v. New Hampshire* [1957]).

Emerson's most enduring contribution to First Amendment law was his widely respected book, *The System of Freedom of Expression* (1970), which grew out of an earlier work entitled *Toward a General Theory of the First Amendment* (1966), which in part was based on a 1963 article published in the *Yale Law Journal*. Tracking in format the presentation offered by Zechariah Chafee in *Free Speech in the United States* (1941), Emerson's 750-page tome offered a comprehensive survey and analysis of nineteen broadly defined areas of free speech law.

In *The System of Freedom of Expression*, Emerson argued that the "system of freedom of expression in a democratic society rests upon four main premises:" (1) "freedom of expression is essential as a means of assuring individual self-fulfillment," (2) "freedom of expression is an essential process for advancing knowledge and discovering truth," (3) "freedom of expression is essential for participation in decision making by all members of society," and (4) "freedom of expression is a method of achieving a more adaptable and hence a more stable community, of maintaining the precarious balance between healthy cleavage and necessary consensus." Hence, for Emerson, First Amendment freedom was "essential to all other freedoms." It was, he stressed, "a good in itself, or at least an essential element in a good society."

While not entirely subscribing to either the Black or Douglas "absolutist" approaches to the First Amendment, Emerson was highly critical of the Supreme Court's ad hoc balancing and clear-and-present-danger tests. His presumptively protective theory of expression was based, in meaningful part, on the "distinction between 'expression' and 'action' and the difference in degree of social control allowed over each." Thus, the more expression was actually "linked to action" or the more it had the "same immediate impact as action," the more it became a candidate for government regulation. Absent such direct consequences linked to harmful actions, Emerson's theory would protect expression.

One of his later writings on the First Amendment was his 1983 article "Freedom of the Press under the Burger Court." He wrote, "The Burger Court has taken a 'crabbed view' of the First Amendment and has exhibited a 'disturbing insensitivity' to the role of the press. In doing so, it has significantly reduced the protections afforded the press by the First Amendment." The Burger Court's press rulings—reflected in cases such as *Gertz v. Robert Welch, Inc.* (1974, libel) and *Branzburg v. Hayes* (1972, reporter's privilege)—he concluded, "bode ill for the future."

Right to Privacy

Emerson's greatest achievement as a lawyer was his victory in *Griswold v. Connecticut* (1965), a case he argued in the Supreme Court. Emerson represented the petitioners, Estelle Griswold and Dr. Thomas Buxton, who had been prosecuted under a state law that banned the use and distribution of contraceptives, even to married couples. The Court ruled seven-to-two in favor of the petitioners. In an opinion by Justice Douglas, it was declared that the Connecticut statute violated the right of marital privacy deemed within the penumbra of specific guarantees of the Bill of Rights and hence protected under the Fourteenth Amendment. The ruling thus foreshadowed the holding in *Roe v. Wade* (1973), the landmark abortion case.

Women and Equality

Eleven months before the equal rights amendment's (ERA) final approval by Congress, Emerson coauthored "The Equal Rights Amendment: A Constitutional Basis for Equal Rights for Women." The 113-page article (in support of the ERA) offered an authoritative analysis of the probable impact of the proposed amendment. Several years later, in November 1977, Emerson testified before a subcommittee of the House Judiciary Committee concerning the ERA. Taking issue with his Yale Law School colleague

Charles L. Black, Emerson argued that Congress could constitutionally extend the ratification period of the proposed amendment by a simple majority vote rather than by a two-thirds vote of each house. Agreeing with Emerson, in 1978 Congress by a 233-to-189 vote extended the ratification period by five years, though to no avail.

During that period, Emerson also wrote the foreword to *Sexual Harassment of Working Women* (1979) by Catharine A. MacKinnon, a friend and former student. "Sexual harassment," he began, "has been one of the most pervasive but carefully ignored features of our national life." Emerson's concern about this problem reflected his parallel concerns about "real" equality:

> MacKinnon undertakes to give a new dimension to the Equal Protection Clause.... [She] argues that the focus in equal protection law should not be on the 'differences,' or whether the differences are 'arbitrary' rather than 'rational,' but upon the basic issue of inequality. In other words, the courts should consider whether the treatment by the law results in systematic 'disadvantagement' because of group status .... Such an approach deserves serious consideration.

That consideration, however, did not prevent him from taking exception to Professor MacKinnon's claim that there should be civil law remedies for women who suffered harm from the alleged effects of pornography. Writing in the *Yale Law and Policy Review* (1984), Emerson declared: "My claim arises not from Professor MacKinnon's statement of the problem but from her proposals for a solution." While he granted that "pornography plays a major part in establishing and maintaining male supremacy," he also believed that if MacKinnon's proposals were tested against First Amendment law, "there is no way her solution of the pornography problem can be sustained." He concluded on an emphatic note: "Any attempt to deal with the problem of pornography through government suppression would involve a dangerous evisceration of the First Amendment."

RONALD K. L. COLLINS

References and Further Reading

Chafee, Zechariah Jr. *Free Speech in the United States.* Cambridge, MA: Harvard University Press, 1941.
Dorsen, Norman, *Thomas Irwin Emerson,* Yale Law Journal 85 (1976): 463.
Emerson, Thomas Irwin., *Loyalty Among Government Employees,* Yale Law Journal 58 (1948): 1.
———. *Toward a General Theory of the First Amendment.* New York: Random House, 1966.
———. *The System of Freedom of Expression.* New York: Random House, 1970.

———. "Freedom of the Press under the Burger Court." In *The Burger Court*, edited by Vince Blasi. New Haven, CT: Yale University Press, 1983.

———, *Pornography and the First Amendment: A Reply to Professor MacKinnon*, Yale Law and Policy Review 3 (1984): 130–143.

———. *Young Lawyer for the New Deal: An Insider's Memoir of the Roosevelt Years*. Savage, MD: Rowman and Littlefield, 1991.

———., *The Writings of Thomas Irwin Emerson*, Yale Law Journal 101 (1991): 327.

Emerson, Thomas I., Barbara Brown, Gail Frank, and Ann Freedman, *The Equal Rights Amendment: A Constitutional Basis for Equal Rights for Women*, Yale Law Journal 80 (1971): 871.

Emerson, Thomas I., David Haber, Norman Dorsen, eds. *Political and Civil Rights in the United States*. 1st–4th eds. 2 vols. Boston: Little, Brown, 1967–1979.

MacKinnon, Catharine A, with Thomas I. Emerson. *Sexual Harassment of Working Women*. New Haven, CT: Yale University Press, 1979.

Yale Law Library. *Thomas Irwin Emerson: 1907–1991*. Memorial Booklet. New Haven, CT: Yale Law Library, 1991.

Cases and Statutes Cited

Branzburg v. Hayes, 408 U.S. 665 (1972)
Brown v. Board of Education of Topeka, Kansas, 347 U.S. 483 (1954)
Gertz v. Robert Welch Inc., 418 U.S. 323 (1974)
Gitlow v. New York, 268 U.S. 652 (1925)
Griswold v. Connecticut, 381 U.S. 479 (1965)
Plessy v. Ferguson, 163 U.S. 537 (1896)
Powell v. Alabama, 287 U.S. 45 (1932)
Roe v. Wade, 410 U.S. 113 (1973)
Sweatt v. Painter, 339 U.S. 629 (1950)
Sweezy v. New Hampshire, 354 U.S. 234 (1957)
Whitney v. California, 274 U.S. 357 (1927)

EMPLOYMENT DIVISION, DEPARTMENT OF HUMAN RESOURCES v. SMITH, 494 U.S. 872 (1990)

This is currently the leading case on the scope of the First Amendment's prohibition against laws that "prohibit the free exercise" of religion. The case attracted little notice during its prolonged consideration by the Court. However, in its opinion, the Court's majority announced an entirely new doctrine of free exercise, reinterpreting or discarding much seemingly settled doctrine and sharply limiting the effect of the Free Exercise Clause. In *Smith,* the Court held that "neutral, generally applicable laws" do not violate the clause even when they limit or entirely prohibit the practice of minority religions. The clause, the Court said, is violated only when government intentionally targets religious practice. The result has since been subject to withering academic and public criticism, all the more intense because the Court gave no hint to the parties or the public that it was considering abandoning precedent and fashioning a new rule. *Smith* remains controversial today, and has inspired no fewer than three federal statutes designed to overturn its result in whole or part.

The case arose in 1984, when a private, government-funded alcohol and drug abuse treatment agency in Roseburg, Oregon, fired two of its employees, Alfred Leo Smith, Jr. and Galen W. Black, because they had participated in the tipi ceremony of the Native American Church and had consumed peyote as part of the ceremony. The Native American Church, a loose federation of congregations and church bodies, is the main representative in the United States of peyotism, the religious worship of the hallucinogenic peyote cactus. Indian lore and anthropological records suggest that people in the New World have been making ceremonial use of peyote for well over 10,000 years. In the nineteenth century, peyotism assumed its present shape in the United States, and during the late twentieth century public health specialists studying native people began to suggest that the ritual and peyote itself were useful methods of treating alcoholism and drug addiction, at least among indigenous populations. It was this possibility that led Galen Black, a white man and a recovering alcoholic, to participate in a tipi ceremony in late 1983. When his employers found out that he had consumed peyote at the ceremony, they dismissed him, suggesting that the use of peyote constituted "drug abuse" and "relapse" into substance abuse. Al Smith, a Klamath Indian with many years of experience with the church, then also consumed peyote to protest against what he saw as disrespect for Native-American traditions. The agency fired him as well, and the Employment Division of the State Department of Human Resources denied both men unemployment compensation, alleging that they had been dismissed for work-related "misconduct."

The two men brought separate lawsuits against the division in the Oregon State courts, and in 1986 the Oregon Supreme Court held that the denial of unemployment compensation violated the Free Exercise Clause. The state court relied on a precedent called *Sherbert v. Verner* (1963), in which the Court had ordered the State of South Carolina to pay unemployment compensation to a Seventh-Day Adventist who refused a job because it required Saturday work, forbidden by her faith. The Oregon Court reasoned that the two cases were equivalent, even though Oregon law technically forbade the use of peyote by anyone, even for religious reasons.

The U.S. Supreme Court granted certiorari, vacated the state court opinion, and remanded the case (*Employment Division v. Smith* [1988], *Smith I*). The

Court majority ordered the state court to determine whether religious use of peyote violated state law. If so, the majority suggested, this fact might distinguish the case from *Sherbert*. On remand, however, the state court simply stated that Oregon law did not appear to provide a religious exemption to the prohibition on peyote. Citing its own rule against advisory opinions, it declined to consider whether the state law violated the Oregon Constitution. Instead, it reaffirmed its holding that *Sherbert* required payment to Smith and Black as a matter of *federal* constitutional law. Once again, the state petitioned the Supreme Court for certiorari, which was granted in 1989. Representatives of the Native American Church, fearing the effects of a loss, attempted to negotiate a settlement. Oregon agreed, provided that Smith and Black would return the compensation they had received. Smith refused, and the case went forward.

Smith II was briefed and argued by both parties and all amici as a case about the proper application of *Sherbert*. In that case, the Court had suggested that state laws that "burden[ed]" religious practice could pass First Amendment muster only if they furthered a "compelling state interest." The State of Oregon argued that its public policy of refusing any exemptions to its drug laws was a "compelling interest"; Smith and Black argued that, because the state had not actually prosecuted Smith and Black, the only "state interest" present in this case was the state's desire to conserve funds in its unemployment compensation fund—an interest the *Sherbert* Court had already rejected as less than "compelling."

When the Court announced its opinion in *Smith II*, shock waves traveled around the religious community. Without giving any hint to anyone that it was considering doing so, the Court had decided, in an opinion by Justice Antonin Scalia, to scrap the *Sherbert* rule and replace it with a new rule, hitherto unknown, that was significantly less protective of religious minorities who found themselves in conflict with majority beliefs. Unless such a minority plaintiff could show that the law burdening her belief had been passed with the purpose or intention of discriminating on religious grounds, the Free Exercise Clause would provide no protection at all. "Neutral, generally applicable laws" that unintentionally gutted minority religions were not subject to any heightened scrutiny by the Court. Minorities facing such "incidental" burdens were directed to seek exemptions from the political process rather than from courts. In order to reach this result, Justice Scalia reinterpreted much of the Court's prior free exercise jurisprudence as dealing with "hybrid cases," involving two or more provisions of the Bill of Rights, rather than free exercise alone. He also relied heavily upon the Court's decision in *Minersville School District v. Gobitis* (1940), one of the Court's more reviled precedents—and one that had been overturned by *West Virginia Board of Education v. Barnette* (1943), only three years after it was decided. Justice Scalia further explained that the growing religious diversity of the American people meant that "we cannot afford the luxury of deeming *presumptively invalid*, as applied to the religious objector, every regulation of conduct that does not protect an interest of the highest order."

Religious groups across the political and theological spectrum mobilized in opposition to the decision. In 1993, Congress passed the Religious Freedom Restoration Act (RFRA), which directed the courts to apply the *Sherbert* test to any state or federal law or regulation that burdened a religious practice. (Although seeking to reverse the doctrine of *Smith*, the religious coalition deliberately excluded peyotists and cooperated in the creation of legislative history suggesting that a prohibition of peyotism might pass the "compelling interest" test.) In passing RFRA, Congress relied on the enforcement clause in section 5 of the Fourteenth Amendment. In 1997, the Supreme Court, in *City of Boerne, Texas v. Flores* (1997), held that RFRA, as applied to states, exceeded Congress's power under section 5. In response, Congress in 2000 enacted the Religious Land Use and Institutionalized Persons Act, which made use of the commerce and spending powers to impose the "compelling interest" test on state actions that burdened religious organizations or persons in zoning and prison-discipline cases. To date, the new act has been upheld by the federal courts of appeals.

Meanwhile, the Native American Church, with the assistance of Sen. Daniel Inouye, persuaded Congress in 1994 to pass the American Indian Religious Freedom Act Amendments (AIRFAA). AIRFAA prohibits the federal or state governments from outlawing the use of peyote by Native Americans as part of a traditional native religion, or from denying native peyotists state benefits because of their religious use of peyote.

The *Smith* rule, however, remains the Court's statement of the constitutional scope of the Free Exercise Clause. Justice David Souter, who joined the Court after its decision in *Smith*, has criticized the rule as leaving free exercise doctrine "in tension with itself," and Justice O'Connor, who concurred in the result in *Smith* but defended the *Sherbert* rule, has also called for *Smith* to be overruled.

GARRETT EPPS

Cases and Statutes Cited

American Indian Religious Freedom Act Amendments, 1994, 42 U.S.C. sec. 1996a

City of Boerne, Texas v. Flores, 521 U.S. 507 (1997)
Employment Division v. Smith, 485 U.S. 660 (1988) (*Smith I*)
Minersville School District v. Gobitis, 310 U. S. 586 (1940)
Religious Freedom Restoration Act, 42 U.S.C. sec. 2000bb
Religious Land Use and Institutionalized Persons Act, 42 U.S.C. sec. 2000cc et seq
Sherbert v. Verner, 374 U.S. 398 (1963)
West Virginia Board of Education v. Barnette, 319 U.S. 624 (1943)

ENGEL v. VITALE, 370 U.S. 421 (1962)

One of the most controversial issues involving the Establishment Clause of the First Amendment is the constitutionality of prayer in public schools. Public school prayer had been a common feature in government-operated schools throughout the nineteenth century and the first half of the twentieth century, but in 1962 the Court found the practice unconstitutional in *Engel v. Vitale*.

In *Engel*, the Court considered the constitutionality of the following prayer which the state of New York required to be said aloud in every public school classroom each day: "Almighty God, we acknowledge our dependence upon Thee, and we beg Thy blessings upon us, our parents, our teachers and our Country." A group of parents brought suit, alleging that the recitation of this official prayer in the public schools was contrary to their beliefs and religious practices and violated the Establishment Clause of the First Amendment.

Although New York intended the prayer to be nonsectarian and observance on the part of students to be voluntary (no student was compelled to say the prayer), the Court, with Justice Hugo Black writing, held that the state-mandated prayer offended the Establishment Clause. The Court determined that the Establishment Clause barred more than simply the preference of one religion over another; it also required that the government remain neutral between religion and nonreligion. The Court found it irrelevant that objecting students were permitted to leave the classroom during the recitation of the prayer:

> The Establishment Clause . . . does not depend upon any showing of direct governmental compulsion and is violated by the enactment of laws which establish an official religion whether those laws operate directly to coerce non-observing individuals or not . . . . When the power, prestige and financial support of government is placed behind a particular religious belief, the indirect coercive pressure upon religious minorities to conform to the prevailing officially approved religion is plain.

The Court made an appeal to history to justify its position:

The history of governmentally established religion, both in England and in this country, showed that whenever government had allied itself with one particular form of religion, the inevitable result had been that it had incurred the hatred, disrespect and even contempt of those who held contrary beliefs.

In a separate concurrence, Justice William Douglas conceded that a "religion is not established in the usual sense merely by letting those who choose to do so to say the prayer that the public school teacher leads." But Douglas was troubled by the fact that New York had financed a religious exercise and had thereby inserted "a divisive influence into our communities." To Douglas, "the First Amendment leaves the Government in a position not of hostility to religion but of neutrality . . . . The philosophy is that if government interferes in matters spiritual, it will be a divisive force."

Justice Potter Stewart was the lone dissenter in *Engel* (Justices Frankfurter and White did not participate in the decision). Stewart concluded that by requiring the recitation of the prayer, New York had not "established an 'official religion' in violation of the Constitution." Rather, argued Stewart, New York had merely recognized

> the deeply entrenched and highly cherished spiritual traditions of our Nation—traditions which come down to us from those who almost two hundred years ago avowed their 'firm Reliance on the Protection of divine Providence' [quoting the Declaration of Independence] when they proclaimed the freedom and independence of this brave new world.

The Court's decision in *Engel* decision produced widespread opposition in the United States. Justice Tom Clark, who joined the majority in *Engel*, took the unusual step of defending the decision in a public speech in which he emphasized the narrowness of the Court's holding. In response to *Engel*, many efforts were launched in Congress to secure a constitutional amendment that would permit school prayer. Although enjoying broad support, all of these efforts failed. Since *Engel*, the Court has not departed from its view that public school prayer, composed by the state and led by school officials, is unconstitutional. The following year, in *Abington School District v. Schempp* (1963), the Court expanded on the *Engel* holding by finding state-endorsed prayer also unconstitutional; *Schempp* involved the recitation of the Lord's Prayer in the public schools. Subsequent legal debates have centered on the constitutionality of moments of silence or prayer by private persons in public schools. In every such case, the Supreme Court has found the public school prayer in question unconstitutional. But even today, *Engel* remains contentious for many Americans and is properly described as one of the most controversial Supreme Court decisions of the twentieth century.

DAVISON M. DOUGLAS

References and Further Reading

Stone, Geoffrey R., *In Opposition to the School Prayer Amendment*, University of Chicago Law Review 50 (1983): 823–848.
Sutherland, Arthur E. Jr., *Establishment According to Engel*, Harvard Law Review 76 (1962): 25–62.

Cases and Statutes Cited

Abington School District v. Schempp, 374 U.S. 203 (1963)

See also **Establishment Clause Doctrine: Supreme Court Jurisprudence; Prayer in Public Schools**

ENGLISH BILL OF RIGHTS, 1689

The Bill of Rights was the most important document of the Glorious Revolution, and constituted the core of the Revolution settlement. Among the primary causes of the revolution was conflict over whether James II possessed "dispensing power," or prerogative to absolve a person from the duty to obey a particular law, and if he could thereby exercise the legislative power without consent of Parliament. After James II fled to France, William of Orange convened a convention Parliament to reestablish the government. A committee designed to resolve the issue of succession drew up a Declaration of Rights, which was to comprise the bulk of the Bill of Rights (the exclusion of Roman Catholics and spouses of Roman Catholics from the throne was included in the bill but not the declaration). However, the declaration needed the committee's approval, the support of a majority of both houses of Parliament and the acquiescence of William: bargains and compromises had to be struck, among them that James could not be accused of violating a contract, and that the monarch could exercise dispensing power only with consent of Parliament. The Bill of Rights was enacted on December 16, 1689; in 1701, the Act of Settlement, an "Act for the further limitation of the Crown, and better securing the rights and liberties of the subject," further strengthened Parliament against the monarchy. Beyond clarifying monarchical authority and situating legislative power with the king and both houses of Parliament, the Bill of Rights included among its provisions that "raising or keeping a standing army" in peacetime required parliamentary consent; that Protestant subjects "may have arms for their defense

suitable to the conditions and as allowed by law;" that "excessive bail ought not to be required, nor excessive fines imposed, nor cruel and unusual punishments inflicted;" that parliamentary debate ought to be free; and that the subjects possessed the right to petition the king and the right of jury trials.

Although the English Bill of Rights certainly was part of the Framers' intellectual background, scholars disagree about its significance: whereas some have highlighted the similarities between the two bills of rights, others have held that the English experience was obviously not taken by the Americans to be authoritative. Nevertheless, comparing the two texts helps to illuminate some of the American framers' choices both to reflect and to deviate from this earlier document. Two recent controversies in American constitutional interpretation have focused attention on the proper understanding and the degree of influence of the English Bill of Rights on the American Constitution.

Remarkably, at least since *Weems v. United States* (1910), some of the most salient Eighth Amendment cases have focused at least in part on the question of whether the English Bill of Rights granted a right to proportionate punishment. The opinions in *Furman v. Georgia* (1972), in particular, debate the influence of the tenth section of the English Bill of Rights at substantial length; notably, Justice Thurgood Marshall's concurrence featured a noteworthy discussion of the origins of the provision. Justice Lewis Powell's dissent in *Rummel v. Estelle* (1980) suggested that English constitutional law was deeply concerned about disproportionality, and argued that this held enduring importance for Eighth Amendment jurisprudence even in noncapital cases. Further, Powell's majority opinion in *Solem v. Helm* (1983) located a right to proportionate punishment in the English Bill of Rights. However, Justice Potter Stewart argued that the Framers focused on prohibiting torture rather than proportionality in his opinion in *Gregg v. Georgia* (1976), as did Burger in his dissent to *Solem v. Helm* (1983). This view was echoed in *Harmelin v. Michigan* (1991), in which Justice Antonin Scalia argued that the "cruel and unusual punishments" provision was not intended to forbid disproportionate sanctions.

Historical investigations of the English Bill of Rights have also shaped recent Second Amendment jurisprudence. Historian Joyce Lee Malcolm has recently argued that the seventh article of the English Bill of Rights granted Protestants an individual right to bear arms, and that the Framers had this provision in mind when they drafted the Second Amendment. Both Scalia (in *Matter of Interpretation*) and Judge Samuel Cummings, in *United States v. Emerson* (1999), have cited Malcolm's work in this context.

Although some prominent historians have challenged Malcolm's understanding of the English Bill of Rights, as well as the claim that the seventh article influenced the Framers, the debate has generated fresh interest in the legacy of the English Bill of Rights for American constitutionalism.

MELISSA SCHWARTZBERG

References and Further Reading

Granucci, Anthony, 'Nor Cruel and Unusual Punishments Inflicted': The Original Meaning, California Law Review 57 (1969): 839.

Maitland, F.W. Constitutional History of England. Delanco, NJ: Legal Classics Library, 2000.

Malcolm, Joyce Lee. To Keep and Bear Arms: The Origin of an Anglo-American Right. Cambridge, MA: Harvard University Press, 1994.

Scalia, Antonin. A Matter of Interpretation: Federal Courts and the Law. Princeton, NJ: Princeton University Press, 1997.

Schwoerer, Lois, Symposium on the Second Amendment: Fresh Looks: To Hold and Bear Arms: The English Perspective, Chicago-Kent Law Review 76 (2000): 26.

Weston, Corinne Comstock, and Janelle Renfrow Greenberg. Subjects and Sovereigns: The Grand Controversy over Legal Sovereignty in Stuart England. Cambridge: Cambridge University Press, 1981.

Cases and Statutes Cited

An Act Declaring the Rights and Liberties of the Subject and Settling the Succession of the Crown. (English Bill of Rights, 1689). 1 Gul. & Mar., sess. 2, c. 2. In Act for the Further Limitation of the Crown, and Better Securing the Rights and Liberties of the Subject (Act of Settlement, 1701). 12 Gul. III, c. 2. In Andrew Browning, ed., English Historical Documents, 1660–1714. New York: Oxford University Press, 1953

Browning, Andrew, ed., English Historical Documents, 1660–1714. New York: Oxford University Press, 1953. http://www.yale.edu/lawweb/avalon/england.htm

Furman v. Georgia, 408 U.S. 238 (1972)

Gregg v. Georgia, 428 U.S. 153 (1976)

Harmelin v. Michigan, 501 U.S. 957 (1991)

Rummel v. Estelle, 445 U.S. 263 (1980)

Solem v. Helm, 463 U.S. 277 (1983)

United States v. Emerson, 46 F Supp. 598 (N.D. Tex. 1999)

Weems v. United States, 217 U.S. 349 (1910)

See also **Bill of Rights: Structure; Cruel and Unusual Punishment (VIII); English Tradition of Civil Liberties; Right to Bear Arms (II)**

ENGLISH TOLERATION ACT

A 1689 Act of Parliament granted increased religious freedom for Protestants whose beliefs or practices did not conform (hence, nonconformists) to the national Church of England. The act allowed dissenters separate places of worship, as well as their own preachers and teachers.

Of the many issues taken up by the Convention Parliament at the height of the Glorious Revolution in January 1689, none proved more difficult than settlement in the church. Although historians disagree regarding the depth of political division within English society at the end of the seventeenth century, few doubt the magnitude of religious tensions throughout the Stuart period. Indeed, religious loyalties shaped the political affiliations that caused the Glorious Revolution. Just as England wrestled over royal prerogative and Parliamentary rule, Tories versus Whigs, so too was the nation having to choose between the established church and nonconforming Protestantism, Anglicans versus Dissenters. Dissent had escalated during previous periods of toleration in a way that generated grave concern among Anglicans (a term describing members of the Church of England that really only entered common usage in the nineteenth century). Furthermore, religious fervor was easily politicized, rendering dissent against the church equivalent to dissent against the state. It was no small coincidence that Tories favored royal prerogative to the same degree that Whigs feared arbitrary rule, nor that the former tended to be Anglicans while the latter accepted dissent. A significant distrust of centralized power united politics and religion.

The rash of Protestant sectarianism that fomented during Cromwell's Commonwealth in the 1650s (for instance, Baptists, Presbyterians, Congregationalists, and Quakers) gave way to the post-Restoration discord among three main camps: separatists who dissented against, and desired toleration from, the established church; hard-line Anglicans who refused to concede anything to anyone; and Presbyterians who were open to compromise, namely a settlement with Anglicans that did not include toleration for separatists. Despite the fact that Protestant Dissenters constituted less than 6 percent of the total English population, their influence was disproportionately large. Parliament was pressured to consider three statutory alternatives relating to the Church of England: abolition of the sacramental oath required of office holders (mandated by the Test and Corporation Acts of 1661 and 1673); the incorporation of moderate dissenters (known as "comprehension"); and complete freedom of worship, including even the more radical dissenters (toleration). These proposals represented increasing levels of challenge to Anglican supremacy; each threatened the status quo.

In 3,100 words and nineteen paragraphs, the act did not repeal any laws relating to religion per se, nor did it exempt anyone from the obligation to tithe for the established church. On the other hand, certain dissenting practices would henceforth be tolerated, but only for "certified" Protestants willing to sign loyalty oaths. The act makes repeated mention of these professions of loyalty, demonstrating the insecurity still prevalent within both the political realm and the Church of England. Future tolerance was predicated upon an oath "to be true and faithful to King William and queen Mary and . . . abhor, detest, and renounce . . . any authority of the see of Rome." Although comprehension never passed and toleration did not extend to non-Christians, Quakers, or Catholics, Parliament granted nonconforming Protestants outside the Church of England the freedom to worship in their own meetinghouses under their own leaders.

The Toleration Act gained royal assent in May 1689, thus becoming one of the most important elements of the Revolution settlement. Through the act, Parliament demonstrated that it had statutory authority stretching beyond royal prerogative; it also put an end to Anglican hegemony as it liberalized religious practice. In the first year after passage of the act, hundreds of non-Anglican places of worship were licensed; two decades later, parishes of the Church of England outnumbered other Protestant meeting places by fewer than four to one.

R. OWEN WILLIAMS

References and Further Reading

Harris, Tim. *Politics under the Later Stuarts, 1660–1715.* London: Longman Group, 1993.
Hoppit, Julian. *A Land of Liberty? England 1689–1727.* Oxford: Oxford University Press, 2000.

ENGLISH TRADITION OF CIVIL LIBERTIES

The Bill of Rights in the U.S. Constitution, which has been critical in defining the civil liberties enjoyed by Americans, reflects the influence of political struggles that occurred in seventeenth-century England. Indeed, the roots of American liberty lie in the constitutional conflicts that pitted Parliament against the English monarch and defenders of England's "ancient liberties" against attempts by the Stuart kings to exercise unlimited executive power. The gradual resolution of this conflict, often referred to as the English Revolution, established a tradition of constitutionally limited government based on custom, the common law, and a series of momentous written declarations, including the Petition of Right (1628), the Agreement of the People (1647), and the Bill of Rights (1689), each of which will be discussed below.

In the Middle Ages, liberty was understood to consist of exclusive privileges and immunities claimed by corporate bodies such as guilds or the clergy, rather than rights that were universal because they belonged to all members of society. Such liberty could be claimed by individuals only as members of those organizations. Thus, freedom was more a matter of social status than a quality inherent in individuals per se, and was exclusive rather than inclusive because it depended on the possession of property or special status in society. However, the events of the English Revolution—which began to germinate early in the reign of Charles I (1625–1649), deepened during the period of the personal rule (when Charles ruled for eleven years without calling a single Parliament), exploded into Civil War during the 1640s, and was finally concluded in the Glorious Rebellion of 1689—led the English to rethink and expand their understanding of the meaning of liberty. Although these struggles produced a less expansive understanding of civil liberties than Americans were to embrace at the writing of their constitution a century later, they did lay a foundation on which the American understanding of civil liberty could evolve.

Freedom in the English Revolution

As the term is being used in this article, the English Revolution was a long, drawn-out affair, provoked by the efforts of the Stuart monarchs to impose absolute rule. Based on their belief that all political authority flowed from the Crown, the Stuarts conducted themselves in ways that deeply offended members of Parliament. The Stuart doctrine of "royal absolutism," which was defended in well-known works of the period, such as Sir Robert Filmer's *Patriarcha*, theorized that all privileges enjoyed by Parliament were grants from the king rather than inherent rights. Armed with this theory, the early Stuart monarchs, James I (1603–1625) and his son, Charles I, frequently exercised governing powers without the cooperation or consent of Parliament. This assertion of royal power led Parliament to engage in an equally vigorous search to define its own privileges. What was Parliament's legitimate role in government? In the search for answers to this question, Parliament pushed forward a discussion not only of its own liberties but indeed a nearly century-long debate over the rights of the English people. In their absolutist zeal, the Stuarts tried to restrict Parliament's role when it was sitting and often resorted to ruling without Parliament altogether. This policy reached its zenith in 1629 when Charles I initiated eleven years of rule without calling

Parliament into session. This period, known as the "personal rule" period, led to civil war in the 1640s. The Civil War (1642–1649), which ended with the execution of Charles I, brought into focus the civil liberty issues that would be a continuing source of tension until they were resolved in the Glorious Rebellion (1689).

What were those issues? Perhaps the most fundamental issue dividing king and Parliament was the issue of taxation. The Stuarts sought to use the prerogative power to impose taxes without parliamentary approval. This policy led to notoriously unpopular forms of royal revenue such as "forced loans," which were based on a theory of the king's right to seize his subjects' property for public purposes at his discretion. Members of Parliament spoke out strongly against this breach of their property rights. To blunt such criticism, the Stuarts resorted to arresting individual members of Parliament (MPs), which was seen as an attack on the MPs' right of free speech. They also utilized the Star Chamber, a juryless court whose members served at the pleasure of the king, to send offending MPs to prison or impose severe penalties on them for acts of political opposition. To quell spreading protests against this abuse of power, the monarchy imposed heavy censorship on an emerging opposition press. All published materials were subject to strict censorship by the Archbishop of Canterbury, and severe punishments, including mutilations and death sentences, could be imposed for violators.

Direct censorship of the press was reinforced by the doctrine of seditious libel, which treated criticisms of the government or individual office holders as a crime because it was thought to undermine respect for public authority. The Star Chamber helped to establish this doctrine in the 1606 case *De Libellis Famosis*, but it was subsequently incorporated into the common law and the English government continued to draw upon it to punish dissent long after abolition of the Star Chamber in 1641. Following the Glorious Rebellion, Parliament would finally end formal press censorship in 1695, but the law of seditious libel persisted and served as a tool to restrain criticism of the government. Libel cases were to be heard by juries after adoption of Fox's Libel Act of 1692, but in eighteenth-century England and colonial America alike, juries typically upheld government prosecutions for seditious libel.

In sum, during the reign of the early Stuart monarchs a momentous struggle developed over the competing claims of royal prerogative and parliamentary privilege. This struggle put issues of basic rights of property, free speech and press, and trial by jury on the agenda of English national politics.

Seventeenth-Century Milestones in the Development of English Liberties

One of the most important milestones in the evolution of English liberty was the Petition of Right put forward by Parliament and signed in 1628 by King Charles I. The petition sought to formalize Parliament's claim that the king could not impose taxes without its consent. Under the leadership of Sir Edward Coke, the era's most distinguished jurist and defender of the common law, Parliament asserted that its role in raising taxes could be traced back to the Magna Carta and was an inviolable element of the "ancient constitution." The first step toward the petition was a "protestation" by Parliament in 1621, which asserted MPs' right of free speech. King James famously repudiated this claim by tearing out the page where it appeared in the *Commons Journal*, and Sir Edward Coke was sent to prison for eight months for his advocacy of the right. Because both James and Charles ignored the protestation, Parliament resorted to the Petition of Right. The petition asserted that citizens could not be forced to loan money to the king or be imprisoned for not doing so, thereby highlighting the importance of the right of habeas corpus as an essential protection of the individual against the arbitrary exercise of power. Parliament enacted the Petition of Right as a statute in order that it would be treated as law by the king, but to no avail. When Charles I dismissed the 1628 Parliament and entered on the personal rule period, he proceeded to violate freely the principles articulated in the petition. Even though the Petition of Right did not succeed in limiting absolutist power in the short run, however, it affirmed principles of constitutional liberty that would remain on the political agenda until they eventually were enshrined in law and practice.

The personal rule foundered in the late 1630s due to the king's inability to raise sufficient revenue without Parliament's collaboration. Charles's need for money led to the famous Long Parliament, which convened in November 1640. Determined to restore constitutional rule and protect parliamentary liberties, MPs passed the Triennial Act, which called for regular sittings of Parliament. They abolished the Star Chamber and other prerogative courts, thereby laying a foundation for a more independent judiciary. In declaring forced loans illegal, they affirmed the sanctity of property rights. But the Long Parliament was unable to reconcile with King Charles, and England plunged into civil war in 1642, a war that finally ended with the king's execution for treason in January 1649. During the Civil War, the discussion of English liberties spread beyond the traditional political elite and produced a second milestone in English thinking about civil liberty.

The decisive factor in Parliament's victory in the Civil War, Oliver Cromwell's New Model Army, facilitated the rise of the Levellers, a popular movement for the extension of civil liberties. The Levellers put forward ideas that became staples of the written constitutions and bills of rights that were adopted in America. Reformers who lacked the status of gentlemen, the Levellers professed to speak for the common people of England. They opposed not only the tyranny of the king but also the potential for tyranny by Parliament. The Levellers made common cause with the Agitators (regimental leaders in the New Model Army who shared their views) to put forward claims for the individual rights that belonged equally to all Englishmen. These ideas were innovative and anticipated the modern conception of rights because they were based on the presumption of human rationality rather than on precedent. In this respect, they anticipated the famous doctrines of John Locke's *Two Treatises of Government*, which was published four decades later.

Leveller ideas were advanced in an Agreement of the People, which has been regarded as the first written constitution in modern history. It proposed limiting both royal and parliamentary power through a written charter that would derive its authority directly from the people. The Levellers contended that Parliament should not exercise a judicial function, thereby contributing to the notion of separation of powers that subsequently figured so prominently in the American conception of limited government. They attacked the use of bills of attainder, which were used by Parliament as well as the king to punish individuals legislatively. They expressed a demand for freedom of speech, not just for MPs but for all Englishmen. In an age when persons were drawn and quartered or even hanged for dissident religious views, they advocated freedom of conscience in matters of religion and for general suffrage of all men, a goal that was not to be fulfilled in English history for two more centuries. In essence, the Levellers contended that Parliament was the trustee of the people, which implied that its authority was limited by inherent rights that were beyond the reach of government. Although Leveller aspirations were far ahead of their times, some of their goals were achieved in a more modest, but nonetheless decisive fashion during the Glorious Rebellion in 1689, which produced the historic Bill of Rights.

Although Charles I was executed in 1649 and the monarchy abolished temporarily, experiments with republican government during the 1650s failed, and when the English monarchy was restored in 1660 the limits of royal power were still unresolved. During the reign of Charles II, this question again became politically explosive over the prospect that his successor, James II (1685–1688), might restore a Catholic dynasty to the English throne. To enforce his pro-Catholic policies, James (a professing Catholic) turned to the prerogative power just as his father, Charles I, had done. He dissolved Parliament and threatened his dissenting subjects with a standing army. This turn back toward absolutism led a rebellious Parliament to invite the Protestant Dutch prince, William of Orange, and his wife Mary (daughter of James II) to accept the Crown of England under conditions specified by Parliament. When Prince William's army forced James's abdication, the Glorious Rebellion finally defeated the absolutist tendencies of the English monarchs and brought the king under the law. The Rebellion's most famous achievement, the Bill of Rights adopted in December 1689, was a third milestone in the development of English liberty.

The English Bill of Rights does not contain guarantees of free speech rights for individuals. Such guarantees first appeared a century later in the setting of the American and French revolutions. It did, however, guarantee the right of free speech to MPs during parliamentary debates. What had been considered at the beginning of the century a privilege granted by the king now became a right that the king could not deny. In this sense, the Bill of Rights vindicated the claim made by Sir Edward Coke some sixty years earlier that the liberty of the English people depended on the liberty of Parliament. On that basis, the high priority given to parliamentary rights made sense. Leaders of the Glorious Rebellion did not consider that Parliament itself could threaten the civil liberties of the citizens. Later generations seem to have agreed. The English people accepted the doctrine of parliamentary sovereignty established by the Glorious Rebellion, and Britain did not develop a system of separate powers with checks and balances, or a system of judicial review. In this latter regard, however, the Glorious Rebellion did open the way to a more independent judiciary by limiting the Crown's power to appoint and dismiss judges at will. The 1701 Act of Settlement consolidated the principle of judicial independence by providing for lifetime appointment of judges. The Bill of Rights also stipulated that any attempt to impose taxes without the authorization of Parliament was illegal. Subsequently, no English monarch has attempted to override this provision, and in the eighteenth century legislative supremacy in this matter became accepted practice in the colonial assemblies in America.

During the Civil War, English parliamentarians had come to appreciate the importance of a right to bear arms and the danger of standing armies, a danger that the excesses of James II had reinforced. Hence, the Bill of Rights specifies that all Protestant Englishmen could retain arms for their own defense, as provided by law. However, we should note that the Bill of Rights actually preserved discrimination against Roman Catholics and it explicitly prohibited any Roman Catholic from occupying the English throne. In this respect it fell well short of the aspirations for religious freedom and tolerance advocated by the Levellers forty years earlier. Englishmen had also developed a strong aversion to the forced quartering of soldiers, which they saw as an invasion of their liberty. Thus, the Bill of Rights includes a prohibition against a standing army in peacetime, except by consent of Parliament.

Finally, although the Bill of Rights was not written from the point of view of individual rights of citizens, it did provide certain critical legal protections to persons accused of crimes. Let us bear in mind that it was a common practice of Stuart monarchs to imprison their subjects without trial or bail and to use courts such as the Star Chamber to inflict cruel punishments on political adversaries. With these abuses in mind, the authors of the English Bill of Rights included provisions that anticipated the concern in the American Bill of Rights with due process of law. These provisions included a prohibition against excessive bail, the repudiation of cruel and unusual punishment, and the right to a jury trial.

Civil Liberties in Colonial America

It is somewhat paradoxical that, despite their attacks on civil liberties in England, the Stuart monarchs adopted more forward-looking policies in the American colonies, especially with regard to religious freedom. Because most colonial charters were nondiscriminatory, religious freedom was encouraged in early seventeenth-century America, even as religious conflict was tearing England apart. Maryland's Toleration Act of 1649 was more generous with religious liberty than England's Bill of Rights. Meanwhile, during the reign of Charles II, the grant of religious freedom was written into the charters of Rhode Island, the Carolinas, and Pennsylvania.

More generally, the American colonists were strongly influenced by the English Bill of Rights to regard themselves as living under a constitutional system that limited government's power over the individual. American lawyers were familiar with Edward Coke's *Commentaries on the Common Law*, from which they derived the notion that Parliament itself was under the law. The colonists strongly believed that they enjoyed the rights granted to all English citizens. Consider the following illustrations. The Massachusetts Body of Liberties (1641) included the right of free speech and assembly, the right to bail, legal counsel, and trial by jury, and prohibited excessive bail and cruel punishment. In Pennsylvania, the Frame of Government (1682) enshrined these same rights and offered detailed procedural guarantees for the criminally accused. On the eve of the American Revolution, the Virginia Constitution of 1776 opened with a declaration of rights that presaged the national bill of rights and anticipated the famous due process rights contained in the Fourth through Eighth Amendments to the U.S. Constitution. In short, the Americans, more vigorously than their English brethren, embraced the Leveller legacy that civil liberty depends on restraining the power of government and enshrining the protection of individual rights in a written constitution.

MICHAEL DODSON

References and Further Reading

Barth, Alan. "The Heritage of Civil Liberties." In *The Rights of Free Men*, edited by James E. Clayton, 110–24. New York: Alfred E. Knopf, 1984.

Davies, Stevie. *A Century of Troubles: England 1600–1700*. London: Pan Macmillan, 2001.

Hexter, J.H., ed. *Parliament and Liberty: From the Reign of Elizabeth to the English Civil War*. Stanford, CA: Stanford University Press, 1992.

Jones, James R., ed. *Liberty Secured? British Freedom Before and After 1689*. Stanford, CA: Stanford University Press, 1992.

Kelly, Alfred H., ed. *Foundations of Freedom in the American Constitution*. New York: Harper and Brothers, Publishers, 1954.

Levy, Leonard W. *Origins of the Bill of Rights*. New Haven, CT: Yale University Press, 1999.

Schwartz, Bernard. *The Great Rights of Mankind: A History of the American Bill of Rights*. New York: Oxford University Press, 1977.

Schwoerer, Lois G. "The English Bill of Rights, 1689: A Perspective on Liberty." In *Three Beginnings: Revolution, Rights and the Liberal State*, edited by Stephen F. Englehart and John Allphin Moore Jr., 93–114. New York: Peter Lang, 1994.

Smith, David L. *The Stuart Parliaments, 1603–1689*. London: Arnold, 1999.

Wolfe, Don M. *Leveller Manifestoes in the Puritan Revolution*. New York: Humanities Press, 1967.

Wormuth, Francis D. *The Origins of Modern Constitutionalism*. New York: Harper and Brothers, 1949.

Zaret, David. "Tradition, Human Rights, and the English Revolution." In *Human Rights and Revolutions*, edited by Jeffrey N. Wasserstrom, Lynn Hunt, and Marilyn B. Young, 43–58. Lanham, MD: Rowman and Littlefield Publishers, Inc., 2000.

ENTRAPMENT AND "STINGS"

Entrapment is a defense to criminal charges based on the idea that the defendant was induced to commit the crime by government agents. The defense is often raised in drug crimes, child pornography crimes, bribery, and prostitution. These "victimless crimes" are often prosecuted based on undercover investigations, which are colloquially known as stings.

Entrapment is an affirmative defense, meaning the defendant admits that he committed the crime but seeks to avoid punishment by explaining the conduct. In effect, the defendant is saying, "Yes, I committed the crime, but you should not punish me because the government made me do it."

The entrapment defense is hard to define because government encouragement to commit a crime is not per se impermissible; merely setting a trap to ensnare a criminal is not entrapment. The courts often say that a line must be drawn between the trap for the unwary innocent and the trap for the unwary criminal. A court must evaluate where that line is to be drawn based on the facts of each case by focusing on the individual defendant's predisposition and police conduct.

Two basic theories for the entrapment defense have evolved, and jurisdictions in the United States are about evenly split on which is best. One approach focuses on the defendant and asks whether the defendant is worthy of punishing. The theory is that persons should not be held liable for acts they would not have committed without encouragement from a government agent. This approach focuses on the actual mental state of individual defendant, and is often called the subjective approach. Judge Learned Hand described the rationale in *United States v. Becker* (1933) as "a spontaneous moral revulsion against using the powers of government to beguile innocent, though ductile, persons into lapses which they might otherwise resist." This is the approach used in the federal courts.

The Supreme Court recently clarified this subjective approach to the defense in *Jacobson v. United States* (1992). *Jacobson* was a child pornography case wherein the defendant received repeated invitations and inquiries from several fictitious organizations. He was also invited to place orders with several businesses. Many of the communications from the bogus organizations referred to freedom of speech and censorship. The Court held that Jacobson's conviction for receiving child pornography could not stand because the government had not shown that "Jacobson was predisposed, independent of the Government's acts and beyond a reasonable doubt, to violate the law by receiving child pornography

through the mails." By the time he committed the offense, in other words, Jacobson had already been exposed to so much inducement by the government that he had become predisposed to commit it, but only because of the government's inducement. Thus, the government must prove that a defendant was predisposed to commit the offense, and was so predisposed before any government action to induce the commission of the offense.

The second approach to the defense is based on using the defense as a tool to regulate police conduct. If the defendant has a defense to crimes committed when police are heavily involved, the prosecution will be worthless, so the defense will extinguish any incentive the police have to set up abusive stings. This approach focuses on the police conduct without regard to the mental state of the particular defendant being prosecuted. This definition of entrapment is often referred to as objective because it focuses on police conduct without regard to the particular defendant's mental state. This is the approach used in a majority of state courts.

These somewhat conflicting rationales have translated into two definitions of the entrapment defense. For jurisdictions focusing on the defendant's mental state, the government can overcome the defense by showing that the particular defendant was predisposed to commit the offense. If the defendant was predisposed to commit the offense, it does not matter what the government agents did, as the defense is unavailable. For jurisdictions focusing on police conduct, the defense is established if the conduct of the government agents is so intrusive that an ordinary law-abiding person would have been enticed to commit the offense. If this is so, the police went too far and need to be deterred from such investigations. For example, in one case a friend (actually an undercover police officer) approached the defendant and begged her to buy her food stamps because she needed money to buy Christmas presents for her children; when the defendant was prosecuted for trafficking in food stamps, she claimed entrapment.

An important difference between the objective approach focusing on police conduct and the subjective approach focusing on the defendant's mental state is that predisposition of the defendant is irrelevant under the objective approach, while under the subjective approach, it is the key element. This means that in jurisdictions adopting the subjective approach, the government can introduce at trial evidence of the defendant's bad conduct as proof of predisposition. This bad conduct, normally excluded from trial as irrelevant under the rules of evidence, is rendered admissible under the subjective definition of the defense.

This evidentiary impact of the subjective approach is a drawback for defendants.

One question frequently raised by the defense is whether a defendant may be targeted for investigation in the absence of any suspicion. In other words, must the government justify why the defendant was chosen as the target for a sting? The Supreme Court has never directly addressed the question of whether the government must demonstrate some level of suspicion before targeting a defendant. Generally the lower appellate courts have concluded that no suspicion is required.

A defendant cannot use the defense of entrapment when a private agent induces commission of the offense.

SARAH N. WELLING

References and Further Reading

Bennett, Warren, *From Sorrells to Jacobson: Reflections on Six Decades of Entrapment Law, and Related Defenses in Federal Court*, Wake Forest Law Review 27 (1992): 829.

Marcus, Paul. *The Entrapment Defense.* 2nd ed. Charlottesville, VA: Michie Butterworth, 1995.

Paton, Scott C., *The Government Made Me Do It: A Proposed Approach to Entrapment Under* Jacobson v. United States, Cornell Law Review 79 (1994): 995.

Seidman, Louis M., *The Supreme Court, Entrapment, and Our Criminal Justice Dilemma*, Supreme Court Review 1981 (1981): 111.

Cases and Statutes Cited

United States v. Becker, 62 F.2d 1007, 1009 (2d Cir. 1933)
Jacobson v. United States, 503 U.S. 540 (1992)

See also **Child Pornography; Due Process; Entrapment by Estoppel**

ENTRAPMENT BY ESTOPPEL

In the American criminal justice system, individuals are held to the principle that "ignorance of the law is no excuse." Essentially, this rule means that an accused may not escape criminal liability by alleging that he was unaware that his conduct was illegal. All people are presumed to know the law, and to act in accordance with it. However, courts have recognized a narrow exception to this rule where an accused relies on information from an official state actor and acts in accordance with that information. This exception is referred to as "entrapment by estoppel," "reasonable reliance," or "good faith reliance on a state actor's advice."

The U.S. Supreme Court discussed the constitutional aspect of the defense in *Raley v. Ohio* (1959) and *Cox v. Louisiana* (1965). In these decisions, the Court recognized that individuals should not be prosecuted for engaging in conduct specifically authorized through government advice. Prior to these decisions, state courts had considered the issue with varying results, weighing the need for bright-line rules on the one hand, against the potential for government misconduct and the conviction of individuals with little or no moral culpability on the other. In 1962, the American Law Institute included a codified form of entrapment by estoppel in the Model Penal Code, a version of which many states subsequently adopted.

The specific elements of the defense of entrapment by estoppel may vary slightly by jurisdiction; however, to rely on the defense, an accused must essentially show that (1) the legality of the conduct was officially authorized by a government agent, (2) the accused relied on this acknowledgement, (3) the reliance was reasonable, and (4) given the reliance, prosecution would be unfair. "Official" authorization can be found in statutes, judicial decisions, or interpretations offered by relevant government actors in an official capacity. Under no circumstances are individuals permitted to rely on their own interpretation of a law as a defense, no matter how reasonable that interpretation may be. This principle was noted in *People v. Marrero* (1987), in which a New York court upheld a conviction even though half of the judges who considered the issue agreed with the defendant's interpretation of the law in question. Additionally, as the court found in *Miller v. Commonwealth* (1997), the government agent must be one who is charged with the interpretation, administration, or enforcement of the law at issue.

There are several justifications for the defense of entrapment by estoppel. First and foremost, the defense recognizes that it is fundamentally unfair to convict an individual for conduct that is authorized by the government, even if that authorization later turns out to be erroneous. Second, individuals who act in compliance with the government's interpretation of a law, even if that interpretation is erroneous, lack the moral culpability necessary to justify a criminal conviction. Finally, holding individuals criminally liable for complying with the government's interpretation of a law may have the effect of inhibiting otherwise lawful behavior and undermining society's confidence in the government.

JUDITH M. BARGER

References and Further Reading

Cohen, Mark S., *Entrapment by Estoppel*, Colorado Lawyer 31 (February 2002): 45–48.

Dressler, Joshua. "When Mistake of Law Is a Defense: Exceptions to the General Rule." In *Understanding*

Criminal Law, 168—177. 3rd ed. New York: Lexis Publishing, 2001.

Parry, John T., *Culpability, Mistake, and Official Interpretations of Law*, American Journal of Criminal Law 25 (1997): 1–78.

Pasano, Michael S., Walther J. Tache, and Thierry Oliver Desmet. "Using the Defense of Entrapment by Estoppel." *Champion*, May 26, 2002, 20–4.

Cases and Statutes Cited

Cox v. Louisiana, 379 U.S. 559 (1965)
Miller v. Commonwealth, 492 S.E.2d. 482 (Va. 1997)
People v. Marrero, 597 N.E.2d 1068 (N.Y. 1987)
Raley v. Ohio, 360 U.S. 423 (1959)

See also Due Process; Entrapment by Estoppel; *Raley v. Ohio,* 360 U.S. 423 (1959)

EPPERSON v. ARKANSAS,
393 U.S. 97 (1968)

The legal conflict over the teaching of Darwinism in public schools began with the 1925 Scopes trial. But it was not until 1968 that the U.S. Supreme Court, in *Epperson v. Arkansas*, struck down as unconstitutional an antievolution statute similar to the one upheld in both Scopes and the Tennessee Supreme Court (*Scopes v. State* [1927]).

This case concerns the constitutionality of a 1929 Arkansas statute that prohibited the teaching of evolution—in either textbooks or by classroom instructors—in all state-supported educational institutions, including universities, colleges, and public schools. The statute defined evolution as "the theory or doctrine that mankind ascended or descended from a lower order of animals."

In the beginning of the 1965 school year, Susan Epperson, a tenth-grade biology teacher in Little Rock, was provided with a new textbook from which she was to instruct her students. Unlike the one she had used the previous school year, this textbook "contained a chapter setting forth 'the theory about the origin . . . of man from a lower form of animal.'" This put Epperson in a quandary: if she uses the state-required textbook, she violates the state's law and subjects herself to criminal prosecution and termination. Joined by other parties, Epperson filed a suit in Chancery Court. That court held that the statute violated Epperson's First Amendment freedom of speech and thought. The court also prohibited the state from terminating Epperson based on any alleged violation of the statute. The Arkansas Supreme Court reversed on appeal.

The Supreme Court held that the statute was unconstitutional because it violated both the Free Exercise and Establishment Clauses of the First Amendment. The Court concluded that the statute proscribed evolution solely because it is inconsistent with the creation story in the Book of Genesis. The court cited two reasons for this conclusion: (1) "no suggestion has been made that Arkansas' law may be justified by considerations of state policy other than the religious view of some of its citizens," and (2) "fundamentalist sectarian conviction was and is the law's reason for existence." The second reason was supported by the historical origin of the Arkansas statute and its connection to the Tennessee statute adjudicated in Scopes. Thus, the statute had *no secular purpose.*

The Court did not base its holding, as the Chancery Court did, on the teacher's right to freedom of speech, but rather, on the principle that "government . . . must be neutral in matters of religious theory, doctrine, and practice." Arkansas' statute was not religiously neutral, for it did not prohibit from its academic institutions all discussion of human origins, but rather, singled out one view to prohibit, evolution, because of its apparent conflict with a religious belief.

Epperson's importance lies in its establishing the principle of "religious neutrality" as central to public school curricula, especially in the sciences. That principle, however, cuts both ways, for it means that scientific criticisms of evolution that may be consistent with certain religious beliefs may pass constitutional muster. For such views typically appeal to public reasons—empirical facts and widely held conceptual notions—that do not contain religious texts or dogmas.

FRANCIS J. BECKWITH

References and Further Reading

Beckwith, Francis J. *Law, Darwinism & Public Education: The Establishment Clause and the Challenge of Intelligent Design.* Lanham, MD: Rowman & Littlefield, 2003.

Campbell, John A., and Stephen C. Meyer, eds. *Darwinism, Design, and Public Education.* East Lansing: Michigan State University Press, 2003.

Carter, Stephen L., *Evolutionism, Creationism, and Teaching Religion as a Hobby*, Duke Law Journal 1987 (1987): 977.

Darwin, Charles. *On the Origin of Species.* Facsimile of the 1st edition (1859), with introd. by Ernst Mayr. Cambridge, MA: Harvard University Press, 1964.

Dembski, William A., and Michael Ruse, eds. *Debating Design: From Darwin to DNA.* New York: Cambridge University Press, 2004.

Greenawalt, Kent, *Establishing Religious Ideas: Evolution, Creationism, and Intelligent Design*, Notre Dame Journal of Law, Ethics & Public Policy 17 (2003): 2:321–397.

Johnson, Phillip E. *Darwin on Trial.* Chicago: Regnery Gateway, 1991.

Miller, Kenneth R. *Finding Darwin's God: A Scientist's Search for Common Ground Between God and Evolution.* New York: Cliff Street Books, 1999.

Numbers, Ronald. *Darwinism in America.* Cambridge, MA: Harvard University Press, 1998.

Pennock, Robert T., ed. *Intelligent Design Creationism and Its Critics: Philosophical, Theological, and Scientific Perspectives.* Cambridge, MA: MIT Press, 2001.

Ruse, Michael. *The Evolution Wars: A Guide to the Debates.* Santa Barbara, CA: ABC-CLIO, 2000.

Cases and Statutes Cited

Arkansas (Anti-Evolution) Statute. Initiated Act No. 1, Ark. Acts 1929; Ark. Stat. Ann. ss 80–1627, 80–1628 (1960 Repl. Vol.)
Arkansas v. Epperson, 242 Ark. 922, 416 S.W. 2d 322 (1967)
Scopes v. State, 154 Tenn. 105 (1927)

See also **Edwards v. Aguillard, 482 U.S. 578 (1987); Scopes Trial; Teaching "Creation Science" in Public Schools; Teaching Evolution in Public Schools**

EQUAL ACCESS ACT

The Equal Access Act (EAA), enacted with broad bipartisan support by Congress in 1984, prohibits public school districts receiving federal financial assistance from discriminating among noncurriculum-related student groups who want to use school premises. Once schools have created a limited open forum within the definition of EAA, those schools cannot deny student access to school premises on the basis of "religious, political, philosophical, or other speech content." An immediate effect of EAA was that student religious groups, previously denied use of school facilities in such federal circuit court of appeal cases as *Brandon v. Board of Education* (1980) and *Lubbock Civil Liberties Union v. Lubbock Independent School District* (1982) because of concern about advancing or sponsoring religion in violation of the Establishment Clause, now had a federal statutory right to meet on the same terms as other noncurriculum-related student groups. The language and purpose of the EAA was influenced by a Supreme Court decision, *Widmar v. Vincent* (1981), where the Court held with reference to a public university that, once it had opened its facilities to use of a wide range of student groups, it had created a limited public forum and was prohibited under the free speech clause from denying the use of its facilities to student religious groups. In enacting EAA, Congress deliberately selected the term, "limited open forum," so as not to confuse rights granted under EAA with those granted, as in *Widmar*, under the free speech clause's limited public forum. A limited open forum exists whenever one or more noncurriculum-related student groups meets on school premises during noninstructional time. While EAA does not define what constitutes noncurriculum-related student groups, the Supreme Court, in upholding the constitutionality of EAA against an Establishment Clause challenge in *Board of Education of the Westside Community Schools v. Mergens* (1990), provided a useful analytical framework for determining the curricular relatedness of student groups. The EAA defines noninstructional time as that which is "set aside by the school before actual classroom instruction begins or after actual classroom instruction ends." In order to assure that students have a fair opportunity to conduct meetings under a school's limited open forum, meetings must be voluntary and student-initiated; cannot be government sponsored; can be attended by government employees only in a nonparticipatory capacity; cannot materially or substantially interfere with the educational activities of the school; and cannot be directed, conducted, or regularly attended by nonschool persons. In clarifying the statute's prohibition on government-sponsored meetings, EAA defines "sponsorship" as "promoting, leading, or participating in a meeting," but expressly excludes from sponsorship "the assignment of a teacher, administrator, or other school employee to a meeting for custodial purposes." Congress in enacting EAA provided assurance to public schools that the statute was not intended to "limit the authority of the school, its agents or employees, to maintain order and discipline on school premises, to protect the well-being of students and faculty, and to assure that attendance of students at meetings is voluntary." However, Congress also placed broad limitations on every level of government and its subdivisions, including school districts, to prohibit them from: influencing the content of prayer or religious activities, requiring that any person participate in prayer or religious activities, expending more than incidental funds to provide space for student meetings, compelling school agents or employees to attend meetings where the content of speech at a meeting would be contrary to a person's beliefs, sanctioning meetings otherwise unlawful, limiting the rights of groups not of a specified size, and abridging the constitutional rights of any person. The EAA allows for private enforcement of the statute by students who claim that they have been denied equal access rights, but the statute expressly prohibits the federal government from denying or withholding federal financial assistance to any school.

The Equal Access Act has been extended to a wider range of student groups than religious clubs, such as gay/straight clubs. Protection under EAA's limited open forum may overlap with free speech's limited public forum which means that students denied access to school premises could have both statutory and constitutional claims.

RALPH D. MAWDSLEY

References and Further Reading

Equal Access Act, 20 U.S.C. sec. 4071–4074 (1984).
Establishment Clause, U.S. Const., First Amendment.
Free Speech Clause, U.S. Const., First Amendment.
Mawdsley, Ralph, *The Equal Access Act and Public Schools: What Are the Legal Issues Related to Recognizing Gay Student Groups?* Brigham Young University Education and Law Journal 2001 (2001): 1:1–33.

Cases and Statutes Cited

Board of Education of the Westside Community Schools v. Mergens, 496 U.S. 226 (1990)
Brandon v. Board of Education of Guilderland Central School District, 635 F.2d 971 (2d Cir. 1980)
Lubbock Civil Liberties Union v. Lubbock Independent School District, 669 F.2d 1038 (5th Cir. 1982)
Widmar v. Vincent, 454 U.S. 283 (1981)

EQUAL PROTECTION CLAUSE AND RELIGIOUS FREEDOM

The Equal Protection Clause of the Fourteenth Amendment to the U.S. Constitution serves to ensure that all persons are afforded equal treatment by the government, including governmental treatment of religious groups. Through the Fourteenth Amendment, the Religion Clauses of the First Amendment were first incorporated against the states in 1947 through *Everson v. Board of Education*. More recently, the courts have tended to ground treatment of religious groups in the First Amendment instead of an equal protection clause analysis grounded in the Fourteenth.

Ordinarily, equal protection acts to protect members of minority groups, in general, from unfair treatment in a majoritarian system. An equal protection analysis is triggered when the government treats similarly situated individuals dissimilarly or when government action affects an individual's fundamental rights under the Constitution. Classifications based on a "suspect class" (for example, race) are subjected to "strict scrutiny." That is, in order for the government action to survive, the government must have a "compelling state interest," and the governmental action must be "narrowly tailored" to accomplish that interest. The courts consider certain characteristics that strongly correlate with suspect classes: historical subjugation, political powerlessness, distinct attributes, and immutability, all of which are prevalent

in minority religious groups. When the equal protection inherent in the Religion Clauses is imported, the requirements of the Free Exercise Clause can conflict with a stigma-based equal protection. The government may not endorse one religion over another.

In the area of free speech and equal protection, religious groups are protected in their speech and press activities at the same level as other groups and individuals. However, the Religion Clauses do not provide greater protection to the religious groups in proselytizing. As a result, the Free Exercise Clause does not provide rights unavailable to other groups under the free speech clause where expression is concerned.

Also, in public education religious groups are afforded a right similar to any other group to gather under either a free exercise or free speech analysis. In application, however, certain minority religious groups, particularly disfavored groups such as Wiccan or Satanist groups may face hurdles in gaining the constitutional rights that apply.

One of the major factors that differentiate religion, specifically religious practice from other suspect classifications, is the belief structure inherent in religion. A constitutional doctrine that bends to every belief (and claimed belief) may place religious doctrine ahead of the legal mandate of neutral laws. In *Employment Division v. Smith* (1990), the Supreme Court diminished the scrutiny required by the equal protection aspect of the Religion Clauses as applied to neutral laws of general applicability.

Despite the lower level of scrutiny afforded to religious groups in the face of neutral laws, laws that treat religious groups less favorably than cultural, educational, and civic groups may be struck down. For example, in *Fairfax Covenant Church v. Fairfax County School Board* (1994), the U.S. Court of Appeals for the Fourth Circuit struck down a law setting rental rates of school facilities higher for churches than other nonprofit organizations.

MICHAEL KOBY

Cases and Statutes Cited

Employment Division v. Smith, 494 U.S. 872 (1990)
Everson v. Board of Education, 330 U.S. 1 (1947)
Fairfax Covenant Church v. Fairfax County School Board, 17 F.3d 703 (4th Cir. 1994)

EQUAL PROTECTION OF LAW (XIV)

Oliver Wendell Holmes, Jr.'s famous quip that equal protection is "the usual last resort of constitutional arguments" would today be accepted more as a positive than a negative commendation. Given the importance of equality in today's America, many are surprised to discover that neither the original Constitution nor the Bill of Rights contains a reference to equality. Neither the founders nor the members of the First Congress chose to borrow at all from Thomas Jefferson's memorable proclamation in the Declaration of Independence "that all Men are created equal."

The Civil War, what some scholars have termed America's true revolutionary experience, changed that. Significantly, Abraham Lincoln in his Gettysburg Address marked the founding of "a new nation, conceived in Liberty, and dedicated to the proposition that all men are created equal" to 1776 and not to the Constitution of 1787. Within a month of Lincoln's speech, Congress came to grips with the issue of framing an amendment abolishing slavery. One version, put forth by Senator Charles Sumner would have provided that "all persons are equal before the law, so that no other person can hold another as a slave." Sumner, however, was rebuffed; opponents of his formula wanted no part of language "copied from the French Revolution," preferring "the good old Anglo-Saxon language employed by our fathers in the [Northwest O]rdinance of 1787."

No such objection was raised to the inclusion in the first section of the proposed Fourteenth Amendment that "[n]o State shall . . . deny to any person within its jurisdiction the equal protection of the laws." Today, equality is universally embraced as a value of American society, but different people have vastly different ideas of what it means and what the Fourteenth Amendment's guarantee of equal protection requires.

The Fourteenth Amendment: Framing and Early History

The language of the Fourteenth Amendment clearly reflected earlier language from the Civil Rights Act of 1866. Indeed, many who voted for the Fourteenth Amendment felt that it was necessary in order to constitutionalize the 1866 legislation that hitherto rested solely on Congress's power to enforce the Thirteenth Amendment. Among other things, the Civil Rights Act provided that

all persons born in the United States . . . citizens of the United States . . . that] such citizens, of every race and color . . . shall have the . . . equal benefit of all laws and proceedings for the security of person and property, as is enjoyed by white citizens, and shall be subject to like punishment, pains, and penalties, and to none other, any

law, statute, ordinance, regulation, or custom, to the contrary notwithstanding.

Unfortunately, the Thirty-ninth Congress's debates offer little help as to exactly what equal protection meant. The general consensus among scholars is that in addition to putting the 1866 Act on firmer constitutional ground, it was intended to ensure that, were the Democrats to regain power, they would have to amend the Constitution to undo the protections for the freedmen. This said, the most prominent historian of the Fourteenth Amendment, Charles Fairman, summed up the problem facing later generations seeking to plumb the depths of meaning of the equal protection clause by observing that "in the main the [authors of the Freedom Amendments] did not discern the obduracy of problems lying on the shady side of victory." Americans of the twenty-first century continue to be divided and uncertain as to what equal protection means.

Unlike the Bill of Rights, which waited until the twentieth century for judicial interpretation, the Fourteenth Amendment and in particular the first section were interpreted a scant five years after ratification, or as Justice Samuel F. Miller wrote in the opinion of the Court in *The Slaughterhouse Cases* (1873), "in the light . . . of events, almost too recent to be called history, but which are familiar to us all . . . ." Speaking for a five-member majority, Miller dismissed the butchers' claims that by granting the Crescent City Slaughter-House Company a monopoly the Louisiana legislature had deprived them of the equal protection of the laws.

[N]o one can fail to be impressed with the one pervading purpose found in them all [that is, The Freedom Amendments], lying at the foundation of each, and without which none of them would have even be suggested; we mean the freedom of the slave race, the security and firm establishment of that freedom, and the protection of the newly-made freedman and citizen from the oppressions of those who had formerly exercised unlimited dominion over him.

Specifically addressing the meaning of equal protection, Miller concluded simply that it was

[t]he existence of laws . . . which discriminated with gross injustice and hardship against [African Americans] as a class, was the evil to be remedied . . . . It is so clearly a provision for that race and that emergency, that a strong case would be necessary for its application to any other.

The Court continued in a similar vein in *Strauder v. West Virginia* (1880), striking down a statute barring African Americans from jury service. In that opinion, though, Justice William Strong allowed that the guarantees of equal protection extended beyond the former slaves, protecting both "white men" and "naturalized Celtic Irishmen."

Subsequent decisions, most notably those in *The Civil Rights Cases* (1883) and *Plessy v. Ferguson* (1896), made Miller's and Strong's language ring hallow. In the former case, the Court held that prosecutions under the Civil Rights Act of 1875 of private individuals for discriminating against blacks went beyond the powers of Congress. In *Plessy*, Justice Henry Brown found that state-mandated segregation on railroad cars was reasonable, in contrast to hypothetical "laws requiring colored people to walk upon one side of the street, and white people upon the other." Brown's distinction built on Justice Stanley Matthews' earlier opinion in the case of *Yick Wo v. Hopkins* (1886). There Matthews had used the equal protection clause to protect the Chinese operators of laundries in San Francisco from the discriminatory application of a facially neutral ordinance designed to reduce dangers from fire. According to Matthews, "No reason for [its current enforcement] is shown, and the conclusion cannot be resisted, that no reason exists except hostility to the race and nationality to which [Yick Wo] belong[s] . . . ."

Using this standard, the Court upheld various measures enacted to impose segregation under the banner of "separate but equal," actions that would undo all the advances that the former slaves had gained during Reconstruction. For its part, the equal protection clause was used sporadically to allow the Court an additional check on state economic legislation with which it disagreed, although in this area the Due Process Clause played a much more important role. Other than these exceptions, the equal protection clause slipped into the same degree of irrelevance to which the Court in *The Slaughterhouse Cases* had relegated the Fourteenth Amendment's "privileges and immunities" clause.

The Demise of the Old Court and the Rise of the New Court

Matters stood pretty much unchanged until the 1930s. Then, the struggle between the Court and the New Deal, culminating in the so-called "switch in time that saved nine," produced a Court that adopted a very different role than any of its predecessors. Although Congress had rejected President Franklin Roosevelt's effort to appoint additional judges and thus secure a majority of justices willing to uphold challenged New Deal legislation, the Court in 1937 appeared to give way, first upholding a state minimum wage law and

later, the constitutionality of the National Labor Relations Board. Commentators, accordingly, generally refer to Roosevelt as having lost the battle over expanding the size of the Court, but winning the war to save the New Deal.

For the Court, this was a time of adjustment from the "Old Court's" concern with property to the "New Court" and its protection of civil rights and liberties. In 1938, in an otherwise unremarkable case, Justice Harlan Fiske Stone traced the basic outlines of this new role. Frequently dubbed a "double standard," the famous footnote four of *United States v. Carolene Products* (1938) set forth a highly deferential standard for legislation dealing with economic matters. In contrast, a far more rigorous test was established for legislation that dealt with noneconomic individual rights.

> [A] narrower scope for operation of the presumption of constitutionality [is appropriate for] legislation [that] appears on its face to be within a specific prohibition of the Constitution, such as the first ten amendments . . ., or which restricts those political processes which can ordinarily be expected to bring about repeal of undesirable legislation, [or] review of statutes directed at particular religions . . . or national, . . . or racial minorities . . . [or] prejudice against discrete and insular minorities . . . .

The NAACP and the Challenge to "Separate But Equal"

The Court's changed attitude was not lost on Court watchers and, in particular, on those who sought to fight Jim Crow laws. In 1939, the National Association for the Advancement of Colored People (NAACP) took steps to strengthen its already nineyear-old legal attack on segregation by establishing the Legal Defense Fund with future Supreme Court Justice Thurgood Marshall as its first head. A year earlier, the NAACP had scored a major victory against segregation before the Supreme Court in the case of *Missouri ex rel. Gaines v. Canada* (1938). Missouri had a policy providing for payment of tuition of African-American law school applicants attending an out-of-state law school. It eventually agreed to start an all-black law school in Missouri. Neither was enough to satisfy Chief Justice Charles Evans Hughes who spoke for a six-to-two Court in finding that Missouri had failed to provide a "legal education substantially equal to those which the State there offered for persons of the white race."

World War II brought other changes to American society that raised further questions about segregation.

The war effort required a total mobilization of the population, and one consequence was that jobs formerly monopolized by white men were now open to blacks and to women. This development attracted a growing stream of southern blacks moving to northern cities where they were able to vote and gain some share of political power. The racist ideology preached by Hitler and the discovery of the horrors of the Holocaust raised further discomfiting questions about America's own policies on race. The gradual breakup of the European colonial empires and the contest for the hearts and minds of these new nations with the Soviet Union gave a new urgency to re-examining the prewar racial status quo.

With the end of the war, the NAACP renewed its attack on educational segregation. In the wake of *Gaines*, some southern states had expanded educational opportunities for blacks, albeit on a segregated basis. South Carolina's new governor, former associate justice James Byrnes returned from Washington to warn South Carolinians that Washington, and in particular the Supreme Court, was likely to demand more equality as the price the South must pay for maintaining "separate but equal."

Two victories soon validated the NAACP's 1930 decision to attack segregation in education. Even before these, however, the Vinson Court signaled a significant change in its 1948 decision in *Shelley v. Kraemer.*

The White Court had previously struck down an effort to enforce residential segregation in *Buchanan v. Warley* (1917) on grounds typical of the "Old Court," that is, the fact that Kentucky's restriction interfered with an individual's liberty of contract. Restrictive covenants posed quite a different issue. These were conditions placed in deeds to property limiting the right of the property owner to either to rent or sell the property to persons of certain ethnic or racial backgrounds. They had been upheld in *Corrigan v. Buckley* (1926) in a unanimous decision by a Court that included Holmes, Louis Brandeis, and Stone. As had been true in *The Civil Rights Cases*, the Court found no state action and therefore no equal protection violation. In contrast, in *Shelley*, Chief Justice Fred Vinson for a unanimous Court—three justices not participating—now found judicial enforcement of covenants to be "state action."

The 1950 education decisions were also unanimous. *Sweatt v. Painter* and *McLaurin v. Oklahoma* caused the Court to consider whether separate could ever be equal. In *Sweatt*, Texas, after much litigation, had finally established a law school for blacks. Again Chief Justice Vinson spoke for the Court. He accepted Thurgood Marshall's argument that there was no way that this newly established law school could ever be the equal of the existing white law school. Vinson noted that even if the facilities were equal, the education could not be. By the state's excluding

> members of the racial groups which number 85 percent of the population . . . and include most of the lawyers . . . with whom petitioner will inevitably be dealing . . . we cannot conclude that the education offered . . . is substantially equal to that which he would receive if admitted to the University of Texas Law School.

In *McLaurin,* Oklahoma had admitted a veteran African-American teacher into the university's graduate program in education. Instead of establishing a separate doctoral program at an existing black-only state school, it proceeded to require McLaurin to sit behind a cordon in class that separated him from his fellow classmates and to sit at tables in both the library and cafeteria labeled as reserved for "colored." Although Vinson's opinion in *McLaurin* was brief, it may have presaged more than *Sweatt* what the Court would write in the 1954 decision of *Brown v. Board of Education.* By so separating him from his fellow graduate students, Oklahoma had denied McLaurin "his personal and present rights to equal protection of the laws . . . . [He] must received the same treatment . . . as students of other races." By denying this, Oklahoma adversely affects McLaurin's education and the education of his future students. "Their own education will necessarily suffer to the extent that his training is unequal to that of his classmates. State-imposed restrictions which produce such inequalities cannot be sustained."

Buoyed by these victories, Marshall and his team at the Legal Defense Fund prepared to make their long-planned frontal attack on public education at the elementary and secondary levels. Their decision to concentrate on graduate and professional education had been a tactical one. They realized that since this involved fewer students, it was likely to produce less of a backlash than an attack on public schools. They also thought that by challenging separate but equal at law schools, they would have a more sympathetic hearing from the justices.

Still they realized that the Court of the 1950s was itself an institution that might be hesitant to wade into this highly explosive area. The Court's prestige had not fully recovered from the scars suffered in its battle with Roosevelt. The Court was also more conservative. The Truman appointees had tilted the Court away from the very liberal tint it had taken on in the 1940s. This combination had created a Court that largely embraced the judicial role known as self-restraint, a notion that Holmes had championed and which had been enthusiastically embraced by Justice Felix Frankfurter. According to C. Herman Pritchett, the Vinson Court took "[t]he strong legislature–weak judiciary formula which Holmes developed for the . . . purpose of controlling judicial review over state economic legislation," and extended it to legislation that touched directly upon guarantees of individual liberties found in the Constitution.

Despite these concerns, the NAACP undertook to mount a series of challenges to public school segregation. Five state cases were combined in what has come to be known as *Brown v. Board of Education* (1954), arguably the Court's most important decision of the twentieth century. Each had been carefully selected to force the Court finally to address squarely whether "separate but equal" was still good law. First argued in 1952, the Court took the unusual step of ordering a second set of arguments set for October 1953. Clearly, the justices realized the political implications of a decision setting aside a precedent that not only had survived since 1896 but had been repeatedly invoked by the Supreme Court, a fact that South Carolina's attorney, John W. Davis, vigorously reminded the Court. Before the second round of argument, Chief Justice Vinson died and President Dwight D. Eisenhower nominated California Governor Earl Warren to succeed him. Although scholars disagree as to how the Court would have voted in 1953, they seem universally to credit Warren with ensuring that the Court would speak with one voice in *Brown*. The Warren opinion seems to have been as much directed at the general public than to academics or lawyers. One of the chief justice's biographers noted that more than any thing else, Warren was guided by a desire for fairness, and if anything was not fair it was segregation.

After reviewing the Court's previous rulings on educational segregation, Warren proceeded to address the particular issues in elementary and secondary education.

> To separate them from others of similar age and qualifications solely because of their race generates a feeling of inferiority as to their status in the community that may affect their hearts and minds in a way unlikely ever to be undone . . . . We concluded that in the field of public education the doctrine of "separate but equal" has no place. Separate educational facilities are inherently unequal.

Current Controversies

The unanimity that Warren had worked to achieve in *Brown* was maintained throughout his tenure (1953–1968) despite little support from the political branches of government and dogged opposition by public officials form the old Confederacy. Warren's

successor, Warren Earl Burger, was not so successful in this regard. Although he held the Court together in the first of the busing cases, *Swann v. Charlotte-Mecklenburg School District* (1971), the unanimity ended two years later in another busing case, *Keyes v. School District No. 1, Denver* (1973) from which Justice William Rehnquist dissented, and further deteriorated in *Milliken v. Bradley* (1974) with the issue of de jure versus de facto segregation producing a five-to-four split, a margin that would be repeated frequently in subsequent cases involving race.

The issue of affirmative action, although not provoking the violence that frequently surrounded busing, has proven to be more enduring. In early opinions, the Burger Court adopted the "disparate impact" theory, and held that job qualifications must be closely related to job performance. Affirmative action in education proved more troublesome. By a vote of five to four, the Court found the quota adopted by a California medical school violated the Civil Rights Act of 1964, but a different five-member majority found that the equal protection clause did not preclude a school from considering race as one factor in admissions. Subsequent decisions of the Burger and Rehnquist Courts appeared to undermine the finding of *Regents of the University of California v. Bakke* (1978). Despite concerns that the transformation of the Court effected by the appointees of Presidents Reagan and Bush would result in a holding that racial preferences could be used only when there was evidence of past discrimination, another five-to-four Court in 2003 upheld the use of race as one factor in making decisions. Justice Sandra Day O'Connor's opinion in *Grutter v. Bollinger* (2003) in fact put Justice Lewis Powell's opinion in *Bakke* on much firmer precedential ground than it had ever enjoyed previously. (Powell's *Bakke* opinion had been only a judgment of the Court; the core of his decision was not fully accepted by any of the eight other justices.)

O'Connor found that "the Law School's use of race [was] justified by a compelling state interest," the school's and society's interest in having diversity in education and in the legal community. "Strict scrutiny" meant for O'Connor that racial "classifications are constitutional only if they are narrowly tailored to further compelling state interests . . . ."

Suspect Categories and Fundamental Rights

Early opinions, such as *The Slaughterhouse Cases* and *Strauder*, had emphasized that the equal protection clause was designed for "the newly emancipated negroes." Paragraph three of *Carolene Products*'s footnote four returned to this theme and provided a basis upon which the concept of "suspect categories" developed and the requirement that such classifications be subjected to "strict scrutiny," serve a "compelling state interest," and be "narrowly tailored" to the achievement of that interest.

Footnote four's promise in this regard was first realized in the 1940s. Justice William O. Douglas used "strict scrutiny" to strike down an Oklahoma law that required the sterilization of a three-time offender in *Skinner v. Oklahoma* (1942). Ironically, however, the emergence of the idea of race as a modern-day "suspect category" surfaced first in what is generally labeled the infamous case of *Korematsu v. United States* (1944). An executive order signed by President Franklin Roosevelt gave the military power to designate military zones "from which any and all persons" might be excluded. General John DeWitt carried the order out on the West Coast. When queried why Italian and German aliens were not included, he replied "a Jap is a Jap," and this was "a war of the white race against the yellow race." Justice Hugo Lafayette Black sustained Korematsu's conviction for not reporting for evacuation, while at the same time holding that

> all legal restrictions which curtail the civil rights of a single racial group are immediately suspect. That is not to say that all such restrictions are unconstitutional. It is to say that courts must subject them to the most rigid scrutiny.

None of the early education cases made mention of suspect categories or strict scrutiny, but in finally addressing the sensitive subject of state antimiscegenation statutes (*Loving v. Virginia* [1967]), the Warren Court invoked strict scrutiny to strike down a statute that punished blacks and whites equally.

The requirement that legislation challenged under the equal protection clause be reasonable or rational, the standard used in *Yick Wo* and *Plessy*, was now reserved only for situations that did not involve fundamental rights or suspect categories, the "New Court" applying it, for example, to economic classifications. These received deferential scrutiny; it was sufficient that government was able to establish a legitimate goal for its legislation and to demonstrate that the means employed had a rational relationship to the goal.

In addition to race and ethnicity, the late Warren Court appeared interested in expanding the number of suspect categories adding illegitimacy. The Burger Court seemed to add alienage. Subsequently, however the Burger Court cut back on both.

More significant during the Warren Court was the use of "strict scrutiny" in reviewing equal protection claims that involved rights identified as fundamental, such as the rights to vote in *Reynolds v. Sims* (1964), and *Harper v. Virginia State Board of Elections* (1966), and access to courts in *Douglas v. California* (1963).

The Burger Court signaled in *San Antonio Independent School District v. Rodriguez* (1973) a reluctance to expand neither fundamental rights nor suspect categories. By a five-to-four vote, it rejected the claim that poverty constituted a "suspect class," and education, a "fundamental right."

Equal Protection and Gender

In contrast to its general reluctance and that of the succeeding Rehnquist Court to expand on either concept, the Burger Court began a judicial revolution affecting gender-based classifications. Although the Court in *Reed v. Reed* (1971) claimed that it was simply determining whether the differential treatment prescribed by the challenged Idaho statute was reasonable, two years later a four-member bloc sought to elevate gender to suspect status in *Frontiero v. Richardson* (1973). Justice William Brennan, who had argued in *Frontiero* that gender should be treated as a suspect category, subsequently fashioned what has been referred to as an intermediate test between suspect and nonsuspect classes or rationality with bite. According to Brennan in *Craig v. Boren* (1976), "classifications based on gender must serve important governmental objectives and must be substantially related to achievement of those objectives." With the appointments of Justices Sandra Day O'Connor and Ruth Bader Ginsburg and, despite the failure of the equal rights amendment to win ratification, the Court has moved ever closer to placing gender on the same level as race. Justice Ginsburg's opinion in the 1996 case of *United States v. Virginia* (1996) called for "skeptical scrutiny of official action denying rights or opportunities based on sex," while at the same time conceding that "[t]he heightened review standard our precedent establishes does not make sex a proscribed classification." Unanswered is whether under "skeptical scrutiny" any classification based on gender would survive that would not survive under "strict scrutiny."

Equal protection, despite Holmes's observation, is surely no longer a forgotten section of the Constitution.

FRANCIS GRAHAM LEE

References and Further Reading

Abraham, Henry J. "Some Post-*Bakke*-and-*Weber* Reflections on 'Reverse Discrimination.'" In *Taking the Constitution Seriously: Essays on the Constitution and Constitutional Law*, edited by Gary L. McDowell. Dubuque, IA: Kendall-Hunt, 1981.

Cottrol, Robert J., Raymond T. Diamond, and Leland B. Ware. Brown v. Board of Education: *Caste, Culture, and the Constitution*. Lawrence: University Press of Kansas, 2003.

Fairman, Charles. *Reconstruction and Reunion, 1864–88, Part One*. New York: Macmillan, 1971.

Graglio, Lino A. *Disaster by Decree: The Supreme Court Decisions on Race and the Schools*. Ithaca, NY: Cornell University Press, 1976.

Kelly, Alfred H., Winfred A. Harbison, and Herman Belz. *The American Constitution: Its Origin and Development*. Vol. 2, 7th ed. New York: W.W. Norton, 1991.

Klarman, Michael J. *From Jim Crow to Civil Rights: The Supreme Court and the Struggle for Racial Equality*. New York: Oxford University Press, 2004.

Kluger, Richard. *Simple Justice: The History of* Brown v. Board of Education *and America's Struggle for Equality*. New York: Alfred A. Knopf, 1975.

Lee, Francis Graham. *Equal Protection: Rights and Liberties under the Law*. Santa Barbara, CA: ABC-CLIO, 2003.

Myrdal, Gunnar. *An American Dilemma: The Negro Problem and Modern Democracy*. New York: Harper, 1944.

Patterson, James T. Brown v. Board of Education: *A Civil Rights Milestone and Its Troubled Legacy*. New York: Oxford University Press, 2001.

Pritchett, C. Herman. *Civil Liberties and the Vinson Court*. Chicago: University of Chicago Press, 1954.

Reams, Bernard D. Jr., and Paul E. Wilson. *Segregation and the Fourteenth Amendment in the States*. Buffalo, NY: William S. Hein, 1975.

Wilkinson, J. Harvie. *From* Brown *to* Bakke: *The Supreme Court and School Integration, 1954–1978*. New York: Oxford University Press, 1979.

Cases and Statutes Cited

Brown v. Board of Education of Topeka, Kansas, 347 U.S. 483 (1954)
Buchanan v. Warley, 245 U.S. 60 (1917)
The Civil Rights Cases, 109 U.S. 3 (1883)
Corrigan v. Buckley, 271 U.S. 323 (1926)
Craig v. Boren, 429 U.S. 190 (1976)
Douglas v. California, 372 U.S. 353 (1963)
Frontiero v. Richardson, 411 U.S. 677 (1973)
Grutter v. Bollinger, 539 U.S. 306 (2003)
Harper v. Virginia Board of Elections, 383 U.S. 663 (1966)
Keyes v. School District No. I, Denver, 413 U.S. 189 (1973)
Korematsu v. United States, 323 U.S. 214 (1944)
Loving v. Virginia, 388 U.S. 1 (1967)
McLaurin v. Oklahoma State Regents, 339 U.S. 637 (1950)
Milliken v. Bradley, 418 U.S. 717 (1974)
Missouri ex rel. Gaines v. Canada, 305 U.S. 337 (1938)
Plessy v. Ferguson, 163 U.S. 537 (1896)
Reed v. Reed, 404 U.S. 71 (1971)
Regents of the University of California v. Bakke, 438 U.S. 265 (1978)
Reynolds v. Sims, 377 U.S. 533 (1964)
Shelley v. Kraemer, 334 U.S. 1 (1948)
San Antonio Independent School District v. Rodriguez, 411 U.S. 1 (1973)
Skinner v. Oklahoma, 316 U.S. 535 (1942)
The Slaughterhouse Cases, 83 U.S. 36 (1873)
Strauder v. West Virginia, 100 U.S. 303 (1880)
Swann v. Charlotte-Mecklenburg Board of Education, 402 U.S. 1 (1971)
Sweatt v. Painter, 339 U.S. 629 (1950)
United States v. Carolene Products, 304 U.S. 144 (1938)
United States v. Virginia, 518 U.S. 515 (1996)
Yick Wo v. Hopkins, 118 U.S. 356 (1886)

EQUAL RIGHTS AMENDMENT

The equal rights amendment (ERA) is best known as a proposed amendment to the U.S. Constitution, almost ratified in the 1970s, that would have specifically barred government-sanctioned discrimination on the basis of gender. However, the 1970s ERA was the second version of this amendment. An earlier, potentially broader version had been proposed by suffragists shortly after women were granted the right to vote in 1920. Further, many states have incorporated their own versions of an ERA into their state constitutions. These state-level ERAs provide a window into the impact that a federal ERA might have had on women's legal status in the United States.

The Legal and Historic Context of the ERA

The original U.S. Constitution was written at a time when only white men were deemed to be public citizens with the right to vote, hold property, and hold office. Because of this common understanding, there was little need to specifically address gender in a public, political document such as the Constitution. Except for the generic use of male pronouns, the language of the Constitution is gender-neutral, and might be taken to apply to both men and women. But there is virtually nothing in the historical record to indicate that the founders of the Republic considered, or intended to address, women's status.

Instead, for much of U.S. history, the Constitution was deemed to apply to men alone. Upper-middle-class women began to mobilize for greater legal equality in the early nineteenth century. In 1848, abolitionists Lucretia Mott and Elizabeth Cady Stanton convened a women's convention in Seneca Falls, New York. The 1848 Declaration of Sentiments adopted by the convention was one of the first public demands for women's legal equality. Deliberately paraphrasing the Declaration of Independence, the Declaration of Sentiments' second paragraph begins: "We hold these truths to be self-evident: that all men and women are created equal." After the Civil War, leading women's rights activists Susan B. Anthony and Sojourner Truth fought in vain to have women included in the new constitutional amendments giving rights to former slaves. Instead, the Equal Protection Clause of the Fourteenth Amendment to the U.S. Constitution is a model of terse drafting, providing simply that a state shall not "deny to any person within its jurisdiction the equal protection of the laws." Without independent personhood, women, white or black, were not protected by this clause. Similarly, the Fifteenth Amendment, ratified in 1870, granted freed male slaves—but not women, white or black—the right to vote.

Decades of marches, litigation, civil disobedience, and activism followed, and women finally gained the right to vote—and constitutional recognition—with the passage of the Nineteenth Amendment in 1920. By that time, suffragists were already planning the next phase of their campaign for women's legal equality. Voting aside, many laws and informal practices perpetuated men's privileged status and relegated women to second-class citizenship. In 1923, while in Seneca Falls for the seventy-fifth anniversary of the 1848 Women's Rights Convention, Alice Paul, the head of the National Women's Party and a leading suffragist, introduced a new constitutional ERA. The proposed ERA read in its entirety: "Men and women shall have equal rights throughout the United States and in every place subject to its jurisdiction. Congress shall have power to enforce this article by appropriate legislation."

Alice Paul and other activists in the National Women's Party worked tirelessly in support of the amendment, but progress was slow. Among other things, labor leaders were concerned that women's equality would eliminate protective labor laws that treated men and women differently. Significant women's groups, such as the League of Women Voters, the Consumers' League, and the YWCA, also opposed the amendment strategy, believing that preserving special treatment for women was preferable to blanket equality. Many other women's groups remained on the sidelines. Despite the efforts by the National Women's Party, the amendment campaign made little progress through the 1920s and 1930s. By 1937, the only major women's group to endorse the ERA was the National Federation of Business and Professional Women's Clubs. Hoping to breathe new life into the campaign by narrowing its scope and focusing more directly on governmental (as opposed to private) discrimination, in 1943, Paul rewrote the ERA to track the language of the post–Civil War constitutional amendments. The substantive

provision stated: "Equality of rights under the law shall not be denied or abridged by the United States or by any state on account of sex."

Although the ERA was introduced in every subsequent session of Congress, there was still no favorable congressional action. In 1946, it was passed out of committee and narrowly defeated by the full Senate; in 1950 and 1953, the Senate passed the ERA, but with a rider that nullified important aspects of the amendment. Finally, in the 1960s, the newly re-energized women's rights movement, led by the National Organization for Women, broke the logjam. Women's equality became politically acceptable. Organized labor groups like the National Education Association and the United Auto Workers called for the ERA's ratification. The League of Women Voters reversed their longstanding position and endorsed the amendment. The 1943 version of the ERA passed the U.S. Senate and the House of Representatives by the requisite two-thirds majority, and on March 22, 1972, it was sent to the states for ratification. At the time, Congress placed a seven-year time limit on the ratification process.

In the first year, the ERA received twenty-two of the thirty-eight state ratifications needed. But as ERA opposition forces rallied, the pace of ratification slowed. Twelve more states had ratified the amendment by 1976. In 1977, Indiana became the thirty-fifth and final state to ratify the ERA. As the 1979 ratification deadline approached, at the behest of women's rights leaders, Congress granted an extension until June 30, 1982.

However, political momentum was turning against the ERA. Phyllis Schlafly, founder of the National Committee to Stop ERA, became a prominent spokesperson against ratification. Schlafly and other ERA opponents tailored their messages to women who might be persuaded to oppose equal rights. They argued that that the ERA would eliminate women's privacy rights, requiring co-ed bathrooms and physical education classes, and that women would be sent into combat alongside men. Further, they claimed, a federal ERA would create a constitutional right to abortion. In 1980, the Republican Party removed support of the ERA from its platform and Ronald Reagan, an active opponent of the ERA, was elected president. Despite massive mobilization by pro-ERA activists, there were no more ratification votes, and the effort to amend the Constitution by the 1982 deadline fell three states short.

The ERA has been reintroduced in every session of Congress since that time. Passage of the reintroduced ERA would again require a vote of two-thirds of each house of Congress and ratification by thirty-eight states. Under an alternative strategy advanced by some activists, Congress could repeal the 1982 time limit on ERA ratification, opening up the possibility of final ratification sometime in the future if three additional states approve.

The ERA's Impact

Because the ERA was never ratified, the U.S. Supreme Court has not been directly called upon to construe it. However, the Supreme Court's decisions in the area of women's equality have played a role in the ERA debate. In particular, because the Court has construed women's equal protection rights in areas that would have been addressed by the ERA, some argue that regardless of whether the ERA was legally significant in an earlier time, it is now no longer necessary. On the other hand, because existing Supreme Court jurisprudence on women's equality has developed on a case-by-case basis, it leaves gaps that would arguably be filled by a more comprehensive constitutional amendment.

Until 1971, the U.S. Supreme Court had never struck down a state or federal law on the basis of its discrimination against women. This fact gave considerable impetus to the ERA movement, since it appeared that existing constitutional doctrine might not be capable of addressing women's equality. However, in 1971, the Court in *Reed v. Reed* struck down an Idaho law that barred women from administering estates in probate court. And in 1973, in *Frontiero v. Richardson*, the Court struck down the federal law providing gender-based benefits to military dependents. The federal ERA specifically figured in the latter case. The Court's opinion, written by Justice William Brennan, held that the statutory scheme was unconstitutional and applied the highest level of skepticism, that is, strict scrutiny, in evaluating the gender-based classifications. Strict scrutiny had previously been reserved for race-based classifications. However, only four justices joined that opinion. A fifth justice concluded that the statute was illegal even without any special scrutiny. And three other justices, led by Justice Lewis Powell, concluded that while the statute was illegal, it was inappropriate to decide the particular level of scrutiny to be applied to sex-based classifications while the ERA—then before the states—was pending ratification.

Although ERA ratification remained open until 1982, the standard of scrutiny to be applied to sex-based classifications was settled earlier, in 1976. In *Craig v. Boren*, a case concerning sex-based laws regulating underage drinking, the Court finally adopted an intermediate scrutiny standard, lower than that applied in cases of race discrimination. Under the intermediate standard, a sex-based classification must be substantially related to an important governmental purpose.

In subsequent cases, the Supreme Court has found that a number of sex-based laws can meet this intermediate standard, including selective service laws, and laws delineating rights of mothers and fathers of out-of-wedlock children. Many other laws and practices, however, have been struck down as unconstitutional, including unequal single-sex schools, sex-based peremptory challenges to jurors, and sex-based allocation of government benefits. These decisions of the Supreme Court and lower courts have done much to undermine the perceived urgency of ratifying the ERA. Similarly, statutes like Title IX of the Education Amendments of 1972 have provided redress for much of the educational discrimination that once faced women and girls. In short, the purposes that the ERA was intended to address when it was introduced in 1943 have been to some extent superseded by developments dictated by the courts and Congress.

The legislative history of the ERA, however, suggests that a constitutional ERA would have required more than the spotty intermediate scrutiny standard developed by the courts. An authoritative source for this interpretation is a 1970 *Yale Law Journal* article that comprehensively reviews the potential applications of the ERA. The article, which is cited in the *Congressional Record* on the ERA debate, interprets the ERA to require the highest level of scrutiny, and surveys labor legislation, domestic relations law, criminal law, and equality in the military. Under its analysis, the ERA would not have permitted separate but equal facilities for women except in those areas where privacy involving personal bodily functions dictated separation of the sexes. Further, the Yale authors conclude that the ERA would have required a restructuring of the military to involve women equally in the draft and in all aspects of military activity.

State ERAs

Although the federal ERA ultimately failed, a number of state constitutions contain their own separate ERAs. Some of these equality provisions, like those in Wyoming and Utah, were part of the original state constitutions. Others, like those in Massachusetts and Illinois, were enacted at the time the federal ERA effort was at its height. In all, eighteen state constitutions have some version of a constitutional sex-based equality provision. State courts cases construing these provisions provide instructive examples of the national impact that might have been felt from a federal ERA had it been tested and applied in the courts.

First, while the 1943 version of the federal ERA, tracking earlier constitutional amendments, has been construed to apply only to governmental action, some state ERAs have been applied more broadly. For example, some Pennsylvania state courts have indicated that the state's ERA is not limited to governmental activities but extends protections from sex discrimination to every sphere of state life.

Second, as predicted by the Yale authors, many of these state ERAs have been construed to include exceptions for personal privacy and biological functions unique to one sex. Thus, an ERA state may still provide single-sex bathrooms in its government buildings, and may extend pregnancy-related benefits (as opposed to parental benefits) only to women. However, some states have taken a broad view of what is biologically "unique" about the sexes. For example, under one Texas court's construction, a state may have a law criminalizing women's exposure of their chests while not imposing such requirements on men.

Third, some state ERAs have been construed to permit affirmative action and to go beyond preferences to uphold rigid, sex-based quotas. For example, a Washington State rule that required parity on political committees was upheld under that state's ERA.

Fourth, in several states, abortion funding restrictions have been struck down as violating state ERAs. New Mexico is an example. Applying the state's ERA, the New Mexico Supreme Court examined whether any similar funding restrictions had been imposed on men needing medical procedures. Finding none, the court concluded that the policy singling out a procedure needed only by women reflected a gender bias that was illegal under the ERA.

Finally, it is important to note that not all state ERAs have been construed so aggressively. The state ERA of Virginia, for example, has been held to require no more than the scrutiny accorded under the federal constitution, that is, intermediate scrutiny. Because of this, the Virginia ERA has little independent force.

Contemporary ERAs

Times have changed since 1943. The constitutional backdrop for the ERA debate is considerably more complex. In the intervening years, social movements have strengthened and waned. National politics have shifted to the right. Many women's rights activists are working to promote U.S. participation in global women's rights efforts, including urging the federal government to ratify the International Convention on the Elimination of All Forms of Discrimination Against Women. But despite these developments, many members of the women's movement, particularly organizations such as the National Organization for Women and the Feminist Majority Foundation, continue to work to promote a constitutional equality amendment for women. Toward that goal, in 1995, the National NOW Conference adopted a working draft of a new constitutional equality amendment.

Reflecting the influence of more contemporary approaches to constitutional drafting, the proposed amendment is significantly longer and more detailed than prior ERA proposals. For example, it specifically addresses the standard of scrutiny to be applied ("the highest"), rather than leave that issue to be resolved by the courts. Further, the amendment goes beyond sex discrimination to provide for equal rights without regard to "sex, race, sexual orientation, marital status, ethnicity, national origin, color or indigence." It also specifically permits affirmative action. Interestingly, however, NOW's proposed constitutional equality amendment comes full circle, rejecting a focus on governmental action and returning in its opening paragraph to the broad, original language proposed by Alice Paul in 1923: "Women and men shall have equal rights throughout the United States and in every place subject to its jurisdiction."

MARTHA F. DAVIS

References and Further Reading

Archer v. Mayes, 213 Va. 633 (1973).

Berry, Mary Frances. *Why ERA Failed*. Bloomington: Indiana University Press, 1986.

Brown, Barbara, Thomas I. Emerson, Gail Falk, and Ann E. Freedman, *The Equal Rights Amendment: A Constitutional Basis for Equal Rights of Women*, Yale Law Journal 80 (1971): 5:871–985.

Friesen, Jennifer. *State Constitutional Law: Litigating Individual Rights, Claims and Defenses*. Charlottesville, VA: Lexis Publishing, 2000.

Mansbridge, Jane J. *Why We Lost the ERA*. Chicago: University of Chicago Press, 1986.

Marchioro v. Chaney, 585 P.2d. 487 (Wash.), aff'd on other grounds, 442 U.S. 191 (1979).

McBride-Stetson, Dorothy. *Women's Rights in the U.S.A: Policy Debates and Gender Roles*. 3rd ed. New York: Routledge, 2004.

MJR's Fare of Dallas v. City of Dallas, 792 S.W.2d 569 (Tex. Ct. App. 1990).

National Organization for Women. *NOW and Economic Equity*. http://www.now.org/issues/economic/cea.html.

New Mexico Right to Choose/NARAL v. Johnson, 975 P.2d 841 (Becker, N.M. 1998).

Susan D. *The Origins of the Equal Rights Amendment: American Feminism Between the Wars*. Westport, CT: Greenwood Press, 1981.

Cases and Statutes Cited

Convention on the Elimination of All Forms of Discrimination Against Women, adopted December 18, 1979, art. 6, 1249 U.N.T.S. 13, 17
Craig v. Boren, 429 U.S. 190 (1976)
Frontiero v. Richardson, 411 U.S. 677 (1973)
Reed v. Reed, 404 U.S. 71 (1971)
Title VII of the Civil Rights Act of 1964, 42 U.S.C. sec. 2000e, et seq
Title IX of the Education Amendments of 1972, 20 U.S.C. sec. 1681–1688

See also **Anthony, Susan B.; Equal Protection of Law (XIV); Ginsburg, Ruth Bader; National Organization for Women; Schlafly, Phyllis Stewart; Stanton, Elizabeth Cady; State Constitutional Distinctions**

CITY OF ERIE v. PAP'S A.M., 529 U.S. 277 (2000)

An Erie, Pennsylvania, law outlawed the act of appearing in public, either knowingly or intentionally, in a "state of nudity." Respondent Pap's A.M. (a Pennsylvania corporation) ran "Kandyland," a strip club that featured totally nude female erotic dancers. In order to comply with the law, the dancers at Kandyland had to wear, at a minimum, "pasties" and a "G-string."

Pap's filed suit seeking declaratory relief and a permanent injunction against the enforcement of the ordinance. The Court of Common Pleas struck the ordinance down as unconstitutional. The Commonwealth Court reversed. The Pennsylvania Supreme Court reversed this ruling and held that the ordinance violated Pap's freedom of expression under the First and Fourteenth Amendments to the U.S. Constitution.

The Pennsylvania Supreme Court followed the U.S. Supreme Court's ruling in *Barnes v. Glen Theatre, Inc.* (1991) and held that nude dancing is expressive conduct entitled to some level of First Amendment protection. The Pennsylvania Supreme Court found that the ordinance was not content-neutral and therefore applied strict-scrutiny review.

The U.S. Supreme Court, in *Pap's*, held that the ordinance should be analyzed under the framework set forth by the Court in *United States v. O'Brien* (1961). The Court held that the ordinance at issue satisfied *O'Brien*'s four-factor test and was therefore constitutionally valid. The Court held that the ordinance was within Erie's power to protect public health and safety, it furthered an important governmental interest related to the "secondary effects" of nude dancing, it was unrelated to the suppression of free expression, and the restriction was no greater than is essential to the furtherance of the government interest.

MARC M. HARROLD

References and Further Reading

Harrold, Marc M., *Stripping Away at the First Amendment: The Increasingly Paternal Voice of Our Living Constitution*, University of Memphis Law Review 32 (Winter 2002): 403.
Leahy, Christopher Thomas, *The First Amendment Gone Awry: City of Erie v. Pap's A.M., Ailing Analytical Structures, and the Suppression of Protected Expression*, University of Pennsylvania Law Review 150 (2002): 1021–1078.

Cases and Statutes Cited

Barnes v. Glen Theatre, Inc., 501 U.S. 560 (1991)
United States v. O'Brien, 391 U.S. 367 (1968)

ERZNOZNIK v. CITY OF JACKSONVILLE, 422 U.S. 205 (1975)

A Jacksonville, Florida, ordinance prohibited drive-in theaters (and only drive-in theaters) from exhibiting any films that contained nudity visible from a public street or place. Erznoznik, manager of a drive-in theater, was charged with showing an R-rated film, *Class of '74*, which ran afoul this law. The theater's screen was visible from the street and a church parking lot. Florida's courts upheld the ordinance after Erznoznik challenged its constitutionality. Although the film was not declared obscene, this case is one of several related to the Court's emerging secondary-effects doctrine dealing with nudity.

Jacksonville argued that it could protect its children and citizens against unwilling exposure to offensive material. At oral argument, the city added that the ordinance prevented displays of nudity which might affect traffic safety. In a six-to-three decision, the Supreme Court struck down the ordinance as both overbroad and not content-neutral. Powell, writing for the majority, was joined by Brennan, Douglas, Stewart, Marshall, and Blackmun. Burger, joined by Rehnquist, dissented as did White. The conference vote had been deadlocked at four to four because Douglas was in the hospital. At conference, Powell and Stewart voted to uphold the ordinance but later switched their votes; White, it appears, changed his vote after Powell circulated his opinion.

The ordinance, according to Powell, "sweepingly forbids display of all films containing any uncovered buttocks or breasts, irrespective of context or pervasiveness." As examples, he mentions a "baby's buttocks, the nude body of a war victim . . . newsreel scenes of the opening of an art exhibit." The problem thus arises that when a government, acting as a censor, decides to "shield the public from some kinds of speech on the ground that they are more offensive than others, the First Amendment strictly limits its power." Moreover, the ordinance "discriminates among movies solely on the basis of content . . . however innocent or educational" the nudity might be in the films; the ordinance was not content-neutral, as films without nudity could be just as distracting or disturbing for people in nearby areas or driving motor vehicles.

White's brief dissent objects to Powell's conclusion in Part IIA of his opinion, where Powell writes, "Thus, we conclude that the limited privacy interests of persons on the public streets cannot justify [Jacksonville's] censorship of otherwise protected speech on the basis of its content." White states this "broadside" goes too far if it means expressive nudity on public streets or in other public places cannot be banned because of the limited privacy rights of other persons in those places who may "merely look the other way." White, however, agrees that the ordinance is fatally overbroad, and if the majority had limited itself to this conclusion he may not have dissented.

Roy B. Flemming

References and Further Reading

Dickson, Del. *The Supreme Court in Conference (1940–1985)*. New York: Oxford University Press, 2001.
Woodward, Bob, and Scott Armstrong. *The Brethren*. New York: Simon and Schuster, 1979.

ESCOBEDO v. ILLINOIS, 378 U.S. 478 (1964)

Danny Escobedo was arrested by police and told that another suspect, Benedict DiGerlando, had named him as the person that fired the fatal shot that killed Escobedo's brother-in-law Manuel. Escobedo, refusing to admit his involvement, asked to see his lawyer. At about the same time, Escobedo's lawyer arrived and asked to speak to his client. Both Escobedo and his lawyer were denied their requests. After some time, the police officers told Escobedo that if he would testify against DiGerlando they would set him free. Without access to his lawyer and without being informed of his right to remain silent, Escobedo made statements against DiGerlando that incriminated himself. These statements were later used to help convict Escobedo of murder.

The Supreme Court of Illinois affirmed the conviction, holding that the statements were admissible because they were made voluntarily even though without the assistance of counsel. The U.S. Supreme Court reversed. The Court found that statements shall be inadmissible when the circumstances of an investigation are such that (1) the person under investigation becomes the target of the investigation, (2) he is not informed of his right to remain silent, (3) he has asked for but been denied access to counsel, and (4) he makes statements that will be prejudicial later at trial. The Court's opinion severely restricted how police obtain confessions by making it clear that the right to counsel extends beyond the formal institution of proceedings to include pre-indictment examinations. The opinion would lead to the landmark *Miranda v. Arizona* decision.

Marcel Green

References and Further Reading

Israel, Jerold H., Yale Kamisar, and Wayne R. LaFave. *Criminal Procedure and the Constitution*. St.Paul, MN: West, 2005.

Cases and Statutes Cited

Miranda v. Arizona, 384 U.S. 436 (1966)

See also **Coerced Confessions/Police Interrogations; *Miranda* Warning; Right to Counsel**

ESTABLISHMENT CLAUSE (I): HISTORY, BACKGROUND, FRAMING

Since the Establishment Clause is located at the beginning of the First Amendment, it is referred to at times as our "first freedom": "Congress shall make no law respecting an establishment of religion . . . ." This article will provide a general guide to understanding the Establishment Clause by describing the historical context of its framing, the process by which it was drafted, and the history of its interpretation and application.

Historical Background

In medieval Europe, after the fall of the Roman Empire and the failure of the attempt to replace it with a Christian empire, political power was fragmented. The bond of a common religion was the only bond that united Western Christian society. In this context, as difficult as it is to imagine today, religious persecution seemed to be not only unavoidable, but necessary. It was taken for granted that rulers had both the right and a duty to punish religious error. With the coming of the Reformation in the sixteenth century, Protestants and Catholics disagreed vehemently about the true content of Christian doctrine, but both groups assumed that a ruler's power would continue to be used to root out and eradicate the errors of those who disagreed with the prevailing side. Reformation-era civil authorities were expected to use their power to enforce religious uniformity.

Accordingly, when the New England colonies were founded by the Puritans, a group known for its commitment to the "New Reformation" project of purifying the Church of England, New England's colonial legislatures, courts, and magistrates involved themselves in supporting the Puritan faith and suppressing any dissenters. Any who refused to comply were free to leave, in the eyes of the Puritan leadership. Any who would not leave were to be punished, in an effort to force the dissenters to abandon their ways and return to living in conformity with Puritan beliefs and expectations.

The most significant early challenge to religious conformity in New England arose when certain colonists who had come to believe that infant baptism could not be biblically justified would either turn their backs or walk out of church to avoid participating in the baptism of children. These early Puritan dissenters, who came to be known as "Baptists," were then hailed into court, where they were warned or fined. Those who refused to pay their fines were imprisoned, and the most defiant were whipped.

Meanwhile, in 1636, after being banished from the Massachusetts Bay Colony for his own disagreements with Puritan authorities, Roger Williams had founded the new colony of Providence Plantations, just to the south, where Baptists were free to worship as they pleased. The Puritans' efforts to suppress those Baptists who remained in Massachusetts continued, unsuccessfully, until 1679. That year, a letter came from King Charles II in which he expressed his support for "freedom and liberty of conscience" for all non-Catholic Christians. Puritan authorities responded by halting the practice of imposing criminal punishments on those who refused to conform to Puritan beliefs and practices.

Although Puritan authorities no longer attempted to enforce religious conformity by persecuting dissenters as criminals, they did continue to attempt to promote the Puritan (or, as it came to be known, Congregational) religion in various ways. Massachusetts authorities subjected Baptists and other dissenters to a compulsory religious taxation system that was designed to fund Congregational churches in every settlement. The authorities also required that only the preachers and churches that they had approved could engage in religious activity. This effectively barred non-Puritan worship in Massachusetts until William and Mary issued Massachusetts a new charter in 1691 that granted religious freedom to all Protestants. As for the religious tax, those who refused to pay could be imprisoned, and their property seized and sold at auction to pay the bill. The prosecution of those who refused to pay the tax continued until the early 1700s, when a series of laws was passed to exempt dissenters from this religious tax. The courts interpreted these exemption laws very narrowly, however, with the result that dissenters were still often subjected to imprisonment and the seizure and sale of their property thereafter.

By the outbreak of the Revolution, Puritanism's hold on religion in New England had loosened to the point that each locality was permitted to choose (by majority vote) which church to establish. The will of the majority in a given locality determined which church (usually but not always a Congregational church) would receive the religious taxes collected there. It would not be until 1782 that the Baptists succeeded in having this system declared to be a violation of the Massachusetts Constitution.

Elsewhere, not all colonies had formally established a single church as the official religion. In Pennsylvania, Delaware, New Jersey, Rhode Island, and most of New York, no one church was officially established. There were, however, laws requiring religious tests for office; blasphemy laws; and other forms of legal support for the Christian faith. Most of these were still in place through the period that the Constitution was ratified and the First Amendment adopted.

In five Southern colonies, however, from Maryland through Georgia, plus the four counties of metropolitan New York, the Church of England had become the established church. Maryland had originally been founded as a haven for Catholics fleeing persecution in England, but the Glorious Revolution of 1688, which brought about the replacement of Catholic King James II with the Protestants William and Mary, sparked a wave of anti-Catholicism in Maryland that led to the establishment of the Church of England there. Throughout these Southern colonies, laws were enacted to require attendance at Anglican services, to provide financial support for Anglican clergy, to control the clergy selection process, to dictate religious doctrine, to give certain civil powers to church officials, and to penalize participation in non-Anglican worship.

By the mid-1700s, the influx into Virginia of dissenting missionaries who had been inspired by the evangelistic fervor of the Great Awakening had led to the creation of a system that permitted non-Anglicans to worship freely if they were to obtain one of a limited number of licenses. Initially, Presbyterians, Baptists, and other dissenters complied with this system. In the mid-1760s, however, a new type of Baptists, known as Separate-Baptists (ex-New England Congregationalists who had split from their former churches in rigid adherence to the Baptist position on infant baptism) began sending missionaries to Virginia. The Separate-Baptists refused to comply with Virginia's licensure laws on the grounds that civil governments had no authority to license preachers, for God alone governs the church. From 1768 to 1775, Virginia authorities jailed about forty Separate-Baptists for preaching without a license.

In 1774, after a young James Madison witnessed the jailing of some of these Separate-Baptist preachers, he wrote to a friend that he could no longer countenance the "diabolical, hell-conceived" religious persecution in his home state. By 1776, Madison had succeeded in persuading Virginia's Revolutionary Convention to adopt the Virginia Declaration of Rights, which guaranteed for all the right to "the free exercise of religion." In that same year, Virginia's legislature suspended the collection of the compulsory taxes that had been supporting the Church of England, and in 1779 these taxes were repealed. Free exercise protections were not extended, however, to Anglican clergy, who when they were ordained in England were required to take an oath of allegiance to the Crown. The Anglican clergy who refused to violate their oaths were mobbed, beaten, and driven from their pulpits.

In 1785, Patrick Henry championed a bill that would have established Christianity as the state religion of Virginia and imposed a tax that could be directed to the Christian denomination of one's choice (or in the alternative to support public education), but a powerful coalition of dissenters and disestablishment statesmen, led by Madison and Thomas Jefferson, was able to defeat the bill. The next year, the Virginia Statute of Religious Freedom, authored by Jefferson, was enacted. It prohibited any form of compulsory support of religion and guaranteed the rights of all to worship freely.

At the outbreak of the Revolution, nine of the thirteen colonies still had established churches. Only Virginia had, by the time of the adoption of the Establishment Clause, squarely considered and rejected the establishment of religion. Massachusetts, in the course of adopting its new Constitution in 1780, had actually strengthened its system of localized establishments, and every state but Virginia restricted

the right to hold office on religious grounds. Five of these states limited public office to Protestants.

The ratification of the U.S. Constitution of 1787 put an end to religious tests for office holding. Article six provides that "no religious test shall ever be required as a Qualification to any Office or public Trust under the United States." This, the only explicit religious liberty in the Constitution, was controversial due to the risk that it would allow Catholics (who it was feared might persecute Protestants if they were ever to attain a political majority) or non-Christians to hold office.

Drafting

In the years after independence, leading up to the enactment of the First Amendment, many leaders became convinced that the public spiritedness of the Revolutionary era was waning. Some attributed this decline to the collapse of the established church, especially in the South. Virginia had lost half of its clergy during the Revolution, and Connecticut, one-third. In response to this concern, movements arose in nearly every state to institute or strengthen broadly inclusive religious establishments. Civic leaders looked to religion to provide an appreciation of the importance of the common good, which was seen as crucial to the success of the republican form of government.

The countervailing force was concern for religious liberty, which Madison had used as a campaign issue in defeating James Monroe for election from their Virginia district to the first U.S. House of Representatives. Virginia's Baptists had helped Madison to get elected, and when he succeeded, they did not hesitate to remind him of their interest in religious liberty.

Upon arrival, Madison was the spokesperson for religious freedom in the first session of Congress, the session that would begin by considering more than two hundred state-sponsored proposals for amending the new Constitution. Out of these, Madison culled nineteen, and added one of his own. Initially, he planned to work these amendments into the body of the existing Constitution, rather than append them to it in the form of a bill of rights.

With respect to religious freedom, Madison began by proposing his own idea, that the states be prohibited in Article I, section 10, from violating "the equal rights of conscience." With respect to the federal government, Madison proposed that to Article I, section 9, be added: "The civil rights of none shall be abridged on account of religious belief or worship, nor shall any national religion be established, nor shall the full and equal rights of conscience be in any manner, or under any pretext infringed."

When a House committee took up Madison's proposals, some representatives were concerned that the anti-Establishment provision in the clause pertaining to the federal government might be interpreted to preclude the courts from protecting the legal rights of clergy. Others worried that the reference to "national religion" conflicted with the structure of the federal system. To avoid these problems, the prohibition against the establishment of a national religion, in the passive voice, was replaced by the subject "Congress," in the active voice. This clarified that the provision was intended, at the time that the First Amendment was drafted, to limit the powers of the federal legislature only. (Only much later would the U.S. Supreme Court interpret the effect of the Fourteenth Amendment in terms of making the First Amendment apply to the states.) The version that then passed the House read as follows: "Congress shall make no law establishing religion, or to prevent the free exercise thereof, or to infringe the rights of conscience."

The Senate did not support Madison's idea about prohibiting the states from violating equal rights of conscience, which effectively ended the First Congress's consideration of that possibility. In considering the House's proposal pertaining to the federal government, the Senate countered that Congress should be barred from establishing "articles of faith or a mode of worship," rather than "religion" in a more general sense, apparently in an attempt to permit financial support for religion but not the endorsement of doctrine or practice. The Senate also dropped the House proposal's final phrase, about noninfringement of the rights of conscience, presumably because the retained free exercise protection was seen as inclusive of the rights of conscience.

In conference, the House and the Senate finally agreed upon the final version of the Religion Clauses of the First Amendment that Congress passed in 1789 and the states ratified in 1791: "Congress shall make no law respecting an establishment of religion, or prohibiting the free exercise thereof." Two key changes had been made. First, whereas the House had urged that Congress should be barred from making laws "establishing religion," and the Senate, from "establishing articles of faith or a mode of worship," the conference committee proposed that Congress should be prohibited from making laws "respecting an establishment of religion." Financial support for religion in those states that continued to support churches with taxes would not be disturbed, nor would any other aspect of the existing state religious establishments. Congress could pass no law

"respecting an establishment of religion," whether at the federal or state level, whether the purpose of such a law would be to create or to dismantle it. Second, once the Senate's references to "articles of faith" and "a mode of worship" were replaced simply with "religion," the Senate's ban on Congress "prohibiting the free exercise of religion" could be shortened to "prohibiting the free exercise thereof," which avoided a second reference to the term "religion," and thus any possibility that the second reference to religion could be interpreted as having a different meaning than the first.

By the end of the drafting process, the First Congress had developed a proposal to protect religious freedom that contained two complementary halves: the Establishment Clause, which seeks to prevent the imposition *of* religion by the government, and the Free Exercise Clause, which seeks to prevent governmental imposition *on* religion. Or as John Witte describes it in *Religion and the American Constitutional Experiment*, the Establishment Clause prohibits the government from *pre*scribing religion, and the Free Exercise Clause prohibits the government from *pro*scribing religion.

One of the primary current debates about the Establishment Clause focuses on whether it was drafted to prohibit any government support for religion, including support offered on a nonpreferential, inclusive basis, or whether it merely intended to prohibit government support for religion offered on a selective, or preferential, basis. Douglas Laycock, among others, who argue that the drafters of the Establishment Clause intended to prohibit not only governmental preference for one religion over others but also governmental aid to all religions even-handedly, point to the fact that the Senate considered but ultimately rejected four different drafts of the Establishment Clause that would have easily lent themselves to the latter interpretation. Still others, such as Michael Malbin, contend that the drafters intended to permit even-handed, nonpreferential government support for all religion by agreeing to prohibit any law respecting "*an* establishment of religion," because hypothetically they might instead have chosen "*the* establishment of religion." Their choice of "an" establishment of religion, Malbin maintains, suggests that the drafters intended to bar only selective governmental support for religion, whereas a reference to "the" establishment of religion would have reflected the intent to ban inclusive, even-handed governmental support.

This debate has even split the Supreme Court, as is evident in the opposing views expressed by Justice Souter, for a five-justice majority, taking the position that the drafters intended for the Establishment Clause to prohibit even-handed support for religion in general, and Justice Scalia, on behalf of four justices in dissent, taking the position that they did not so intend, in *McCreary County v. American Civil Liberties Union* (2005). Noah Feldman concludes that the answer to this question "seems shrouded in uncertainty," due in large part to the lack of any consensus at the time regarding whether even-handed governmental support for religion violated basic principles of religious freedom. What *was* clear to the Framers was that governmental support for selected religious groups and not others *did* violate the principles that they were attempting to enshrine in the Establishment Clause.

Interpretation and Application

Prior to 1940, the courts interpreted the Religion Clauses of the First Amendment to apply only to Congress, and most questions of religious liberty were left to the states to resolve under their own constitutions. By and large during the early years of the republic, state and local governments did not disturb mainstream Christian activities, but the efforts of evangelical Catholics, Baptists, and Methodists were hampered in New England; abuses against Unitarians, Adventists, and Christian Scientists were ignored in the middle colonies; and Catholics, conservative Episcopalians, and evangelical Protestants were presented with obstacles in the South. In most areas, apart from the largest eastern cities, the religious rights of Jews, Muslims, Native Americans, and enslaved African Americans were not respected. During this period, state and local governments promoted a "public" or civil religion that was generally Christian in character by using religious symbols and ceremonies, subsidizing religious programs, providing special legal protections to certain religious groups, promoting the teaching of basic Christian values, and prohibiting certain conduct on explicitly religious grounds.

Religious groups that could not fit comfortably within the religiously homogenous climate of the early republic were expected to leave, with the frontier providing a "release valve" for religious nonconformists like Mormons, Catholics, Baptists, and Methodists. In the mid- to late nineteenth century, however, the traditional Protestant homogeneity of the East was disrupted by influxes of Methodists, Baptists, and Roman Catholics along with scores of newly formed religious groups such as Disciples, Jehovah's Witnesses, Pentecostals, Unitarians, and Universalists. These diverse groups challenged state and local policies that promoted traditional Protestantism, with the Baptists and Methodists calling for genuine separation of church and state. State and local governments responded by seeking out ways to hamper the efforts of the new groups, such as by denying charters to Catholic schools and preaching permits to Jehovah's Witnesses. In the face of such overt discrimination, these dissenting groups turned to the federal courts for relief.

In the landmark cases of *Cantwell v. Connecticut* (1940) and *Everson v. Board of Education* (1947), the U.S. Supreme Court determined for the first time that the Religion Clauses of the First Amendment applied equally to local, state, and federal government. The *Everson* Court's ruling sent the message that state and local support for the beliefs and activities of dominant religious groups would now be open to challenge.

In the wake of the *Everson* decision, hundreds of Establishment Clause cases poured into the lower courts. Nearly three-quarters of those that reached the Supreme Court represented challenges to prevailing patterns of state and local support for religious education. As summarized by John Witte in "From Establishment to Freedom of Public Religion," this series of Supreme Court Establishment Clause rulings banned religion from the public schools, whether in the form of prayers, moments of silence, the reading of scripture, the storage of religious books, the teaching of doctrine, the display of symbols, or the use of religious services or facilities. These rulings also banned public support for religious schools, whether in the form of salaries, services, reimbursements for administering required examinations, loans of state-required educational resources or counseling services, or tax deductions or credits for tuition costs.

By 1971, the Court had formulated a three-part Establishment Clause test to guide its decision making. As set forth in *Lemon v. Kurtzman*, any government action challenged under the Establishment Clause needs to satisfy three criteria. It must (1) have a secular purpose, (2) not have a primary effect that either advances or inhibits religion, and (3) not foster any excessive entanglement between government and religion. If the government's action fails to meet any of these three criteria, under the *Lemon* test the Establishment Clause has been violated and the government must discontinue the offending activity.

Some members of the Supreme Court have come to question the adequacy of the *Lemon* test for resolving Establishment Clause disputes. In the 1984 case of *Lynch v. Donnelly*, Justice O'Connor offered a distinctive perspective in a concurring opinion that emphasized the impression that an ordinary citizen would have regarding the activity in question. Her perspective, now known as the "endorsement test," asks whether a reasonable observer would view the government's action as either official endorsement or disapproval of religion. Her concern was that governmental endorsement of religion might give some members of the community whose beliefs have been officially recognized the impression that they have some special civil status, or conversely, the impression that they lack such status if their beliefs have not been sanctioned. Justice O'Connor consistently applied the endorsement test to Establishment Clause cases that she helped to decide, but it has never been embraced by a majority of the justices as a replacement for the *Lemon* test.

Five years after *Lynch*, in the 1989 case of *County of Allegheny v. ACLU*, Justice Kennedy unveiled another challenge to the *Lemon* test, the "coercion test." Justice Kennedy's concern was that the Court's contemporary Establishment Clause jurisprudence tends to manifest a certain degree of hostility toward religion, in contrast to the pattern of positive interaction between government and religion that can be observed through the course of U.S. history. To avoid undue governmental hostility toward religion, Justice Kennedy would give government a fair degree of latitude in accommodating and acknowledging religion, so long as government has not coerced someone to support or participate in religion. Justice Kennedy has continued to apply his coercion test to Establishment Clause cases, but (as with the endorsement test) the coercion test has not been embraced by a majority of justices as a replacement for the *Lemon* test.

Given the multiplicity of competing tests, every Establishment Clause case that reaches the Supreme Court presents an opportunity for the Court to set *Lemon* aside in favor of another test. Much speculation attends every Establishment Clause decision, as Supreme Court observers await a clarification of Establishment Clause jurisprudence.

When the manner in which the Court has resolved Establishment Clause cases is carefully analyzed, however, it becomes clear that the Court has never confined itself to any of these three competing Establishment Clause tests in resolving these cases. Rather, the Court has consistently, although not systematically, applied a series of questions to scrutinize the government's conduct for Establishment Clause violations. The following paragraphs present these questions in their logical sequence, although any given Supreme Court ruling might not treat all of them, and might not do so in the same order.

The threshold Establishment Clause issue is whether a constitutionally significant governmental imposition of religion has taken place. Without such a finding, the Court need not proceed to consider the challenge any further. In considering this issue, the Court has found that not all governmental impositions

of religion are constitutionally significant: the burden that allowing parents to deduct the cost of parochial education from their taxable income imposes on all other taxpayers was found to be too attenuated to be constitutionally significant in *Mueller v. Allen* (1983). Nor is the expression of religion by nongovernmental actors an Establishment Clause violation: the temporary placement of crosses by the Ku Klux Klan on the grounds of Ohio's state capitol was an instance of private, not governmental, action and thus no Establishment Clause violation in *Capital Square Review and Advisory Board v. Pinette* (1995).

If a constitutionally significant governmental imposition of religion is found, the issue becomes whether there is a legitimate governmental purpose behind the action in question. If there is not, then government must discontinue engaging in the challenged activity. In *Mueller*, for example, it was legitimate for the government to grant parents of parochial school children a tax deduction to defray the parents' educational expenses, to promote the health of private schools, and to support quality education. On the other hand, a requirement that an official prayer be read at the start of every public school day for the sake of the "moral and spiritual training" of the students was found not to have a legitimate Establishment Clause purpose in *Engel v. Vitale* (1962).

If the government is able to assert with some degree of persuasiveness that a legitimate purpose lies behind its action, the issue becomes whether the case in question arises in the special context in which there is a significant risk of governmental entanglement in the operational autonomy of religious institutions. This, the third prong of the *Lemon* test, justifies governmental refusal to get involved in the operation of religious institutions, for example, by exempting them from certain types of taxes to avoid the necessity of scrutinizing their internal financial records, as in *Walz v. Tax Commission* (1970), or due to the monitoring that would be necessary to prevent publicly funded special education teachers from teaching religion in parochial schools, as in *Lemon*.

Provided a case involving a constitutionally significant governmental imposition of religion and a legitimate governmental purpose does not stand to entangle government in the operational autonomy of religious institutions, a series of four questions can be employed to scrutinize the nature of the relationship between the imposition of religion and the governmental interest that has been asserted to legitimate the action. In this kind of case, if the answer to any of these four questions is "yes," an Establishment Clause violation has occurred.

First, the Court can ask whether there is a clear indication that the governmental purpose that has been asserted is actually a pretext to mask other, illegitimate governmental motives. In *Wallace v. Jaffree* (1985), for example, Alabama's provision for a moment of silence for "meditation or voluntary prayer" in the public schools, when a previous version of the statute in question had authorized only a moment for "meditation," revealed the inappropriately religious motives behind the statutory change.

Second, the Court can inquire as to whether there is a lack of solid evidence regarding the existence of the problem that the government claims it is trying to solve. In *Everson,* in which public funding of transportation to parochial schools was challenged, the Court determined that the evidence showed that there are no alternatives to public school transportation systems that are equally safe for the children. In *Texas Monthly v. Bullock* (1989), by contrast, the Court found that the evidence did not support the government's claim that it was necessary to exempt religious publications from a sales tax to avoid violating religious beliefs or inhibiting religious activity.

Third, the Court can consider whether there are adequate alternative means that would enable the government to achieve its purposes without implicating Establishment Clause concerns. To illustrate, in *Everson,* the Court found that there are no alternatives to publicly funded school transportation systems that are equally safe for children. In *Abington Township School District v. Schempp* (1963), by contrast, Justice Brennan's concurring opinion emphasized that students can be taught morality just as effectively by studying the speeches of great Americans as they could by studying the Bible.

Fourth, the Court can ask whether the government has delegated one of its core functions to a group chosen according to a religious criterion. To illustrate, in *Larkin v. Grendel's Den* (1982), the Court disallowed a statute that granted veto power over applications for liquor licenses to churches within 500 feet of an applicant's premises. Similarly, in *Kiryas Joel Village School District v. Grumet* (1994), the Court ruled that the creation of a special school district to serve a village inhabited solely by members of a particular Jewish sect violated the Establishment Clause.

As the foregoing discussion reveals, the court has consistently employed a series of several different questions when resolving Establishment Clause cases that are not all reflected in the three-prong *Lemon* test, nor in the even more narrowly focused "endorsement" or "coercion" tests. These latter two tests focus mainly on the first threshold question that the Court has tended to ask in analyzing Establishment Clause cases: whether a constitutionally significant governmental imposition of religion has taken place. They do not incorporate the other areas of inquiry to which the Court has attended in resolving the Establishment Clause cases that have come before it. Adoption of either one of these tests, therefore, would compress the Court's Establishment Clause analysis, limiting it to resolving these cases on the basis primarily of what has historically amounted to a threshold determination about whether a constitutionally significant governmental imposition of religion has taken place.

Since it is notoriously difficult to define "religion," and since constitutional theorists continue to dispute whether the word "religion" as used in the Establishment Clause prohibits governmental support for religion in any form, as opposed to support for a particular religion or a subset of religious groups, exclusive reliance by the Court on the "endorsement" or "coercion" tests would leave the Court to use imprecise, disputed concepts in resolving Establishment Clause cases without the benefit of asking some of the key questions that it has used to resolve such cases in the past. The result would be that the outcome of cases would be even less predictable than it has already become, as cases are resolved based solely on whether the government has or has not done something that is "religious" in nature, and if so whether it has done something that is *inappropriately* "religious" or not.

DAVID T. BALL

References and Further Reading

Cobb, Sanford H. *The Rise of Religious Liberty in America: A History*. New York: Macmillan, 1902.

Feldman, Noah, *The Intellectual Origins of the Establishment Clause,* New York University Law Review 77 (2002): 346–428.

Laycock, Douglas, *'Nonpreferential' Aid to Religion: A False Claim about Original Intent,* William and Mary Law Review 27 (1986): 875–923.

Levy, Leonard W. *The Establishment Clause: Religion and the First Amendment.* New York: Macmillan, 1986.

Madison, James. Letter to William Bradford, January 27, 1774. Quoted in Sanford H. Cobb, *The Rise of Religious Liberty in America: A History.* New York: Macmillan, 1902.

Malbin, Michael J. *Religion and Politics: The Intentions of the Authors of the First Amendment.* Washington, D.C.: American Enterprise Institute for Public Policy Research, 1978.

McConnell, Michael W., *Establishment and Disestablishment at the Founding, Part I: Establishment of Religion,* William and Mary Law Review 44 (2003): 2105–2208.

McLoughlin, William G. *New England Dissent, 1630–1833: The Baptists and the Separation of Church and State.* 2 vols. Cambridge, MA: Harvard University Press, 1971.

Noonan, John T., Jr. *The Lustre of Our Country: The American Experience of Religious Freedom.* Berkeley: University of California Press, 1998.

Reynolds, Noel B., and W. Cole Durham, Jr., eds. *Religious Liberty in Western Thought.* Atlanta, GA: Scholars Press, 1996.

Witte, John Jr., *From Establishment to Freedom of Public Religion*, Capital University Law Review 32 (2004): 499–518.

——. *Religion and the American Constitutional Experiment: Essential Rights and Liberties*. Boulder, CO: Westview Press, 2000.

Cases and Statutes Cited

Abington Township School District v. Schempp, 374 U.S. 203 (1963)

Cantwell v. Connecticut, 310 U.S. 296 (1940)

Capital Square Review and Advisory Board v. Pinette, 515 U.S. 753 (1995)

County of Allegheny v. ACLU, 492 U.S. 573 (1989)

Engel v. Vitale, 370 U.S. 421 (1962)

Everson v. Board of Education, 330 U.S. 1 (1947)

Kiryas Joel Village School District v. Grumet, 512 U.S. 687 (1994)

Larkin v. Grendel's Den, 459 U.S. 116 (1982)

Lemon v. Kurtzman, 403 U.S. 601 (1971)

Lynch v. Donnelly, 465 U.S. 668 (1984)

McCreary County v. American Civil Liberties Union, 125 S.Ct. 2722 (2005)

Mueller v. Allen, 463 U.S. 388 (1983)

Texas Monthly v. Bullock, 489 U.S. 1 (1989)

Wallace v. Jaffree, 472 U.S. 38 (1985)

Walz v. Tax Commission, 397 U.S. 664 (1970)

See also **Baptists in Early America**

ESTABLISHMENT CLAUSE DOCTRINE: SUPREME COURT JURISPRUDENCE

The First Amendment to the U.S. Constitution provides that "Congress shall make no law respecting an establishment of religion, or prohibiting the free exercise thereof." This single, integrated statement limits the power of the federal government in religious life. But it contains two distinct principles—free exercise and nonestablishment—that the courts have often treated separately. The Free Exercise Clause prohibits governmental interference with the religious practice of private individuals and groups; as such it resembles other personal liberties in the Constitution such as freedom of speech. But the second component, the Establishment Clause, is unusual among constitutional limitations. Government typically may promote or embrace particular ideas as long as it leaves people free to dissent, but the Establishment Clause prohibits government from promoting religious doctrines in certain ways, and from creating certain relationships with religious institutions. These mandates may be crucial to both religious freedom and social peace. But because they restrict government more than with respect to nonreligious ideas, the Establishment Clause has been especially difficult and controversial

to interpret in the circumstances of modern, pervasive government. Just what promotion of and involvement with religion are prohibited?

Background and Adoption

The "establishment[s] of religion" familiar to the founders had three main features, present in varying degrees in the Church of England and in the colonial establishments (Anglicanism in the South, Puritan Congregationalism in New England). One feature was governmental *coercion* to support the favored church: mandatory membership, mandatory financial contributions, and even prohibitions on practicing other faiths and preaching their doctrines. Prohibitions on dissenting faiths largely disappeared by the time of the founding, with the rise of the "free exercise" ideal; but requirements of financial support for religion continued. A second feature was government *regulation* of the established church, including selection of clergy and oversight of doctrine and liturgy (for example, Parliament approved the successive Books of Common Prayer). The third feature was *symbolic recognition* of the favored faith, through official ceremonies and titles. The monarch headed the Church of England, bishops held seats in the House of Lords, and state ceremonies incorporated the established faith.

The practice of establishment rested on both theological and political rationales: protecting the true faith, maintaining social unity, and promoting ideals that would make citizens virtuous. Likewise, the rise of disestablishment in the colonies and the early American republic rested on both theological and political arguments. Certain Christian leaders from Roger Williams through founding-era Baptists argued that the union of religion and government would interfere with the individual's free response to God and would corrupt (in Williams's words) the "garden" of the church with the "wilderness" of the world. Meanwhile, Enlightenment figures such as Thomas Jefferson and James Madison attacked establishments on the ground that they threatened social peace and minority rights—"destroy[ing]," in Madison's words, "moderation and harmony . . . amongst [society's] several sects," and "degrad[ing] from the equal rank of Citizens all those whose opinions in Religion do not bend to those of the Legislative authority."

The latter quotes come from Madison's "Memorial and Remonstrance" against a 1785 proposal in Virginia to renew tax assessments in support of clergy. Madison masterfully combined political arguments with theological (for example, that "ecclesiastical establishments" have undermined "the purity and efficacy" of religion). Disestablishment in America, unlike its counterpart in France, was generally not hostile to religion, and indeed took much of its inspiration from Baptists and other dissenting Protestant groups. Most Americans continued to believe that religion was essential to civic virtue (an "indispensable suppor[t]" for "political prosperity," in George Washington's words). They simply concluded, in increasing numbers, that governmental promotion of religion would weaken, rather than strengthen, it in its social role.

By the late 1780s, these arguments had led to the elimination of taxes for clergy support in the majority of states. Virginia, the most notable case, rejected even a liberalized proposal that would have allowed a citizen to direct to which sect his payment would go. But the pattern was not uniform: clergy taxes remained in three New England states well after the adoption of the Constitution (the last system, in Massachusetts, was repealed in 1833). Like the defeated Virginia proposal, these taxes permitted dissenters to support their own clergy or opt out altogether: yet even these nonpreferential systems were typically referred to as "establishments."

Thus, when the First Amendment was ratified in 1791, states remained divided over the basic principle of disestablishment (in contrast, all had some commitment to basic free exercise for dissenters). But this division did not matter, for the amendment's purpose was to restrain the new federal government from interfering in religious matters; the Bill of Rights left untouched the states' powers over religion. The brevity of congressional debates over the religion provision reflects that the founders were not thinking about the many questions that might arise if state governments were limited from interacting with religion. Despite this brevity, the First Amendment prohibition on laws "respecting an establishment of religion" has some clear meanings. As noted above, a tax to support religion almost certainly qualified as an establishment even when it was nonpreferential among denominations or faiths; this proposition is confirmed by the fact that the Senate rejected several proposals to prohibit establishment of "one religious sect or society" and instead ultimately approved the broader ban on "an establishment of religion." Moreover, given the Framers' agreement on the inviolability of religious conscience, they almost certainly rejected federal power to coerce anyone to practice religion.

A far more complicated historical question, however, concerns noncoercive acknowledgements of religion: official prayers, religious proclamations, and religious symbolic displays. Such practices can implicate several concerns underlying disestablishment—diluting the religious message to a politically acceptable content, alienating citizens who dissent from it—and some in the founding generation criticized the practices in the name of a stricter separation of church and state. President Jefferson refused to follow his predecessors in issuing Thanksgiving proclamations, and Madison in a series of letters and memoranda in the 1820s and 1830s attacked such proclamations as well as congressional prayers. Yet the practices were commonplace in the early republic: the First Congress initiated daily prayers, and the congressional chaplaincy and Washington began the nearly unbroken practice of presidential Thanksgiving proclamations. Just how ecumenical such expressions were required to be is also ambiguous. Although most of them referred in general terms to God or the "Supreme Being," many people in the founding generation would likely have agreed with the narrower position of Joseph Story (in 1835) that the First Amendment was intended "not to countenance, much less to advance Mahometanism, or Judaism, . . . but to exclude all rivalry among Christian sects."

As the nineteenth century progressed, formal disestablishment mixed even more with government promotion of a generalized Protestantism, producing what historians have called a "de facto establishment." A series of revivals driven by evangelicals, especially Methodists and Baptists, made Americans much more thoroughly and explicitly religious, and this widespread faith pervaded public discourse. Much of this expression occurred within state governments, but it nonetheless reflected Americans' understanding of the disestablishment ideal. A different controversy arose in the mid-1800s when Catholics departed the new, Protestant-dominated public school system and sought equal funding for their own schools. Most states banned such support in their own constitutions—a move that has been controversial ever since—thus extending the founding-era ban on specifically religious taxes to prohibit even general tax support for education from including religiously affiliated schools.

State Establishments, Federalism, and Incorporation

As enacted, the First Amendment, like the rest of the Bill of Rights, bound only the federal government. But the Supreme Court has held, of course, that the adoption of the Fourteenth Amendment in 1868 made most of the Bill of Rights applicable to state and local government actions. The incorporation of the Establishment Clause was declared in *Everson v. Board of Education* (1947). Although several commentators have argued that the Fourteenth Amendment was not intended to incorporate the Bill of Rights, the Court continues to adhere emphatically to incorporation (see, for instance, *Wallace v. Jaffree* [1985]).

Special challenges have been raised to the incorporation of the Establishment Clause. The clause, it is asserted, was meant not just to prohibit establishment of a national church, but as much to prohibit federal interference with the state establishments still existing in 1791. This interpretation could explain the peculiar phrasing "no law respecting an establishment." In Justice Thomas's words, "the Establishment Clause is best understood as a federalism provision—it protects state establishments from federal interference but does not protect any individual right," which in turn "make[s] incorporation of the Clause [to limit state governments] difficult to understand" (*Elk Grove Unified School Dist. v. Newdow* [2004] [concurring in the judgment]). Thomas would incorporate, at most, the aspects of non-Establishment that protect individuals from direct coercion. But no other justice has joined him; the Court implicitly follows Justice Brennan's argument that a fully incorporated Establishment Clause makes sense "as a co-guarantor, with the Free Exercise Clause, of religious liberty" for individuals against all levels of government (*Abington School Dist. v. Schempp* [1963] [concurring opinion].

Modern Interpretation: The *Lemon* Test and Church–State Separation

The modern Court's Establishment Clause interpretations reflect a fundamental tension. As American society has become more religiously diverse—with Christians joined by substantial numbers of Jews, Muslims, and Eastern-religion adherents as well as atheists and believers in generalized spirituality—any religious involvement by government appears more partial to one group of citizens and thus threatens some of the general harms of establishment: division among faiths and alienation of dissenters. At the same time, given the pervasive activity of the modern welfare state, to keep government wholly separate from religion can discriminate against religious citizens and artificially restrict religion's role in public life.

The tension appeared in the very first modern Establishment Clause case, *Everson* (1947), where a local government reimbursed parents' costs for sending their children to parochial schools on public buses. The majority opinion by Justice Hugo Black began by

emphasizing a strict "wall of separation between Church and state" (quoting Thomas Jefferson) that prohibited "any tax in any amount . . . to support any religious activities." Next, however, the opinion argued that the First Amendment prohibited excluding individuals, "because of their faith, or lack of it, from receiving the benefits of public welfare legislation," and it ended up narrowly approving the reimbursements. Strict church–state separation conflicted with and gave way to the equal participation of religion in the widespread programs of the welfare state.

In *Lemon v. Kurtzman* (1971), however, the Court formulated a general Establishment Clause test that, as applied, elevated strong church–state separation over equal religious participation. *Lemon* required that a law (1) have a secular legislative purpose, (2) have a primary effect that neither advanced nor inhibited religion, and (3) not create an excessive entanglement between church and state. Under this framework, the Court in the 1970s and early 1980s struck down several programs of government aid to religious education through a "Catch 22": if the statute allowed aid to benefit religious teaching in church-related schools, it violated the "primary effect" prong, but if it imposed restrictions on religious uses, policing those restrictions created "excessive entanglement." The no-advancement and no-entanglement prongs both required separation from the religious school.

The *Lemon* test, or nascent versions of it, also invalidated religious exercises and symbols in public schools: classroom prayers (*Engel v. Vitale* [1962]), classroom Bible readings (*Schempp*), postings of the Ten Commandments (*Stone v. Graham* [1980]), and classroom "moments of silence" (*Jaffree*). These decisions found it insufficient for Establishment Clause purposes that the exercises were formally voluntary and were general enough in content to encompass many different faiths. The clause, the Court said, reflected the broader "belief that a union of government and religion tends to destroy government and to degrade religion" (*Engel*). Thus, the government should not promote religion even in noncoercive or denominationally neutral ways; government must be neutral toward religion altogether.

Although official religious practices in public schools could be invalidated based on their religious "effects," in several cases (*Stone*, *Jaffree*) the Court struck them down under the first *Lemon* prong for lack of a "secular purpose." To invalidate a law solely because of an impermissible legislative intent, without regard to a forbidden effect, is an unusual principle in constitutional law, and reflects a prophylactic approach: the Court seeks to keep the government from even trying to involve itself in religious matters.

These decisions also led some observers to suggest that government might violate the Establishment Clause if it relied too heavily on religious doctrines as the basis even for legislation on facially nonreligious matters such as abortion or other issues of sexuality. See, for instance, *Webster v. Reproductive Health Services* (1989) (Stevens J., dissenting) (arguing that abortion law based on declaration that life begins at conception "serves no identifiable secular purpose"). The Warren Court invalidated an Arkansas law forbidding the teaching of evolution in public schools—a remnant of the Scopes-era fundamentalist movement—on the ground that the law could not "be justified by considerations of state policy other than the religious views of some of its citizens" (*Epperson v. Arkansas* [1968]. Since then, however, the Court has generally affirmed the legitimate role of religious activism in politics, noting that "[a]dherents of individual faiths and individual churches frequently take strong positions on public issues" and have the right to do so "as much as secular bodies" (*Walz v. Tax Commission* [1970]). In the same vein, the fact that denials of government funding for abortions "coincide with the religious tenets of the Roman Catholic Church does not, without more, contravene the Establishment Clause" (*Harris v. McRae* [1980]).

Lemon's Decline and Less Separationist Alternatives

The *Lemon* test came under substantial attack from some justices and commentators. Some found the test too indeterminate, especially in the various rulings on when a law's "primary effect" was to advance religion or promote a secular goal such as education. But other objections ran deeper.

Some critics objected to the requirement that government not advance any religious proposition. They argued that the demand of neutrality was contradicted by the long historical tradition of government endorsements of religion: legislative prayers, presidential proclamations, symbolic displays, official mottoes, and statements such as "in God we trust" on coins and "under God" in the Pledge of Allegiance. As Justice Kennedy claimed, "A test for implementing the protections of the Establishment Clause that, if applied with consistency, would invalidate longstanding traditions cannot be a proper reading of the Clause" (*County of Allegheny v. American Civil Liberties Union* [1989] [concurring in part and dissenting in part]). Indeed, some critics observed, landmark founding-era documents themselves argued for religious liberty on religious grounds—"Almighty God hath

created the mind free," began Jefferson's bill establishing religious freedom in Virginia—and thus, paradoxically, might have been ruled invalid under the neutrality or no-advancement tests. Some critics argued that because many religious ideas concern matters of morality and justice, government cannot be neutral toward them but must embrace or reject them as it does secular ideas.

Critics of "neutrality" tended to train their attack on the decisions invalidating government-sponsored religious ceremonies or symbols. The Court turned to a historical approach in *Marsh v. Chambers* (1983), upholding the practice of legislative prayer on the basis that it had been instituted by the First Congress—three days before adoption of the Religion Clauses—and the delegates could not have "intended the Establishment Clause to forbid what they had just declared acceptable." Relying solely on this history, the Court did not apply *Lemon* or any other analytical test. It used history not to develop a general legal principle reflecting the clause's original meaning, but simply to validate the specific practice in question. Accordingly, it was unclear if or how *Marsh* would apply to any other issue, and the Court has never followed the *Marsh* approach again.

Then-Associate Justice Rehnquist offered an alternative principle to *Lemon*: the Establishment Clause was intended only "to prevent the establishment of a national religion or the governmental preference of one religious sect over another. (*Jaffree* [Rehnquist, J., dissenting]). He relied on quotes from the congressional debates on the First Amendment, as well as on many founding-era official statements endorsing religion in generalized form. But no one else on the modern Court ever limited the Establishment Clause solely to forbidding preferences between sects. As Professor Douglas Laycock pointed out, the first Congress's rejection of drafts that would have prohibited only preferences for one sect further undermines the no-preferences position as a general Establishment Clause rule. Recently, however, Justice Scalia has urged the more limited position that the government must be neutral toward religion in financial aid cases, but may favor religion in noncoercive acknowledgments as long as they are nonpreferential among monotheistic faiths (*McCreary County v. American Civil Liberties Union* [2005] [dissenting opinion]).

Indeed, the more persistent alternative to *Lemon* is the no-coercion test: government may promote or acknowledge religion (perhaps only in generalized form) but may not coerce anyone to profess or participate in religion. The test fits much of the historical record, for most official acknowledgments of religion appear in noncoercive settings: nonbinding proclamations, or displays on government property. But proponents of the neutrality approach answer that limiting the Establishment Clause's reach to coercive practices would make it redundant with the Free Exercise Clause, which (arguably) prohibits coercion to practice religion as well as not practice religion. In addition, they argue, noncoercive acknowledgments still threaten the harms at which the Establishment Clause was aimed—social division, alienation of dissenting citizens, corruption of religious integrity—especially in a society as pluralistic in religious views as America.

After several years of raising doubts about *Lemon*, the Court relied on the non-coercion test in *Lee v. Weisman* (1992), striking down officially sponsored prayers at public school graduation ceremonies. But *Weisman* specifically declined to overrule *Lemon*, and it referred to noncoercion as only the undisputed "minimum" guarantee of the Establishment Clause. Moreover, proponents of the test divided over its meaning, with Justice Kennedy's majority opinion finding "subtle" peer pressure on dissenting students to participate in the prayer, while Justice Scalia's dissent insisted that only coercion "by force of law and threat of penalty" was unconstitutional. Thus, the no-coercion test remained doubtful in both its status and its scope as of early 2006.

The other chief criticism of the *Lemon* test was that despite its invocation of "neutrality," it actually produced hostility and discrimination against religious ideas and religiously motivated citizens. This objection primarily targeted the decisions on financial aid, which disqualified religious schools from the tax-financed support available to public and secular private schools. Those rulings treated public education was "neutral" because it explicitly advanced neither religious nor antireligious views. But critics argued that education limited to secular viewpoints competes with education based on religious viewpoints, and therefore providing equal aid to religious schools coincides more with Establishment Clause values of neutrality and individual choice in religious matters. These arguments, unlike the criticisms of the school prayer decisions, eventually made substantial headway on the Court.

Recent Case Law: Equal Access for Religion, But No Government Endorsement

The Rehnquist Court (1986 to 2005) retreated from strong church–state separationism in its Establishment Clause rulings, but only in part.

The major shift came in financial aid cases, where the Court more and more allowed religious institutions to participate on equal terms with nonreligious institutions. The "equal access" principle developed with respect to the less controversial issue of whether religious groups could meet voluntarily on public school grounds on the same terms as other student groups. Beginning with *Widmar v. Vincent* (1981), involving evangelical students at a public university, the Court held that permitting religious meetings along with other meetings did not violate the Establishment Clause and indeed, in several cases, was required by the Free Speech Clause principle of viewpoint neutrality. See also, for example, *Board of Education v. Mergens* (1990) (high school groups); and *Good News Club v. Milford Central School* (2001) (elementary school students).

Soon after *Widmar*, financial aid cases were reconceptualized as involving equal access for religion to government funding. *Mueller v. Allen* (1983) upheld a state tax deduction for tuition and other educational expenses of families, even though the vast majority of deductions went for religious schooling and the tuition benefit was not limited to the secular aspects of such schooling. Under a strict application of the *Lemon* approach, these features would have doomed the program. But the Court, while still using *Lemon*'s phrases, emphasized different features: The deduction's terms were neutral and thus created no incentive for parents to choose religious schools over public or secular private schools. The emphasis on neutral terms and individual choice continued in *Witters v. Dept. of Services* (1986), which allowed a blind student to use generally available state rehabilitation funds to study for the ministry at an evangelical Bible college. Under the program, the aid flowed to religious teaching "only as a result of the genuinely independent and private choices of aid recipients," much like a state employee "donat[ing] all or part of [his] paycheck to a religious institution."

The "private choice" approach culminated in *Zelman v. Simmons-Harris* (2002), which upheld the inclusion of religious schools in a program of vouchers for students in Cleveland's failing public schools. Like the tax deductions and rehabilitation funds, the voucher's terms were neutral and left the family the choice of the school at which to use it. The Court also found that "genuine secular alternatives" existed—charter and magnet public schools, secular private schools—so that children would not be pushed into religious education to escape poor public schools. *Zelman* set forth a permissive blueprint for aid, and by treating public schools as simply one "secular alternative" to religious education, it rejected *Lemon*'s premise that they were a neutral baseline.

But *Zelman* has not entirely displaced the separationist, *Lemon*-oriented approach. In *Locke v. Davey* (2004), the Court held that although a state program of college scholarships could include students studying theology in preparation for the ministry, the Free Exercise Clause did not require their inclusion. The majority gave the state discretion because it found "strong Establishment Clause interests" in denying public funding for clergy training, interests grounded in history as far back as Madison's "Memorial and Remonstrance" and the rejection of taxes to support teachers of Christianity. Although *Davey's* application beyond clergy training is uncertain, the decision limits the argument that religion must be allowed equal participation in private-choice programs.

Moreover, when an aid program falls outside the rubric of "private choice," the Court has continued a *Lemon*-like approach. In *Mitchell v. Helms* (2000), a splintered Court upheld a federal law providing computers and other instructional equipment and materials to public and private, including religious, schools. Justices O'Connor and Breyer, the decisive votes, upheld the program only because it included safeguards to prevent "diversion" of materials to religious uses. They argued that direct aid to religious schools fell closer to the core prohibitions of the Establishment Clause than did aid to individuals who could use it at religious schools. This distinction—if it survives changes in the Court's makeup—significantly affects funding not only of education but of social services, where aid often flows through direct government contracts with providers.

In contrast to its increasing approval of aid to private religious activities, the Rehnquist Court reaffirmed the decisions prohibiting government's own religious activity. The Court refused to limit the Establishment Clause to cases of coercion against individuals, instead gravitating toward a test championed by Justice O'Connor: government should not act with the purpose or effect of endorsing (or disapproving of) religion or any religious view. Endorsement of a religious view, she argued, "sends a message to nonadherents that they are outsiders, not full members of the political community," and a message to adherents that they are favored "insiders" (*Lynch v. Donnelly* [1984] [concurring]). The no-endorsement test gathered a majority in *County of Allegheny v. ACLU* (1989), which invalidated a county courthouse's stand-alone display of a nativity scene (distinguishing the *Lynch* case, which had upheld a municipal nativity display accompanied by numerous secular Christmas symbols).

The endorsement test paralleled *Lemon* in looking beyond coercion to more subtle effects such as government messages concerning the status of citizens.

Accordingly, critics found the approach too subjective and complained that government disagrees on issues with dissenters every day without thereby consigning them to general second-class status. The "outsider" argument thus requires another step showing why disagreements on religious issues are of special concern. That step might be that religious debates are irrelevant to government policy, so the public divisions they create are unnecessary; that religious divisions are especially heated and irreconcilable; or that religious identity is more central to persons than are particular political views, and thus the alienation produced by government favoritism is deeper. But all of these propositions are debatable, some of them extremely so.

The Court recently reaffirmed its restrictions on even noncoercive government symbolism, by invalidating a display of the Ten Commandments in a county courthouse (*McCreary County*). Although the display also included historic secular documents of law and government, the majority interpreted it in the light of immediate previous displays that had been solely religious in nature, as well as numerous religious statements from county officials. The decision thus reaffirmed *Lemon's* "secular purpose" prong, indeed arguably stiffening it by requiring that the secular motive not just exist but be "primary."

Even approaches based on separationism and neutrality, however, can be expected to permit some religious statements and displays by government—although it is not always clear how to explain this logically. Religious elements may appear in a broader display that overall does not endorse religion: a crèche with secular Christmas symbols as was upheld in *Lynch v. Donnelly*, or a Ten Commandments plaque as one of an assortment of monuments on public grounds representing various historic events and ideas as was upheld in *Van Orden v. Perry* (2005). Moreover, individual justices who vote to invalidate some government symbols or statements have justified others—"In God we trust" on coins, "under God" in the Pledge of Allegiance—as examples of "ceremonial deism," a category of short, highly generalized religious references, often with a long-standing history, that impose on no one's liberty and may indeed have developed largely ceremonial rather than specifically religious meanings. See, for instance, *Newdow* (O'Connor, J., concurring).

To approve religious references only by stripping them of their religious meaning surely calls to mind the founding-era concern that official establishments undermine the purity and vigor of religion. It is also doubtful that some of these references, such as "under God" in the Pledge, have lost religious import. Justice Breyer was likely more honest when he explained his decisive vote to uphold the Decalogue display in

Van Orden: striking down all official religious symbols, especially longstanding ones, would be more divisive than are the symbols themselves. But Breyer provided no clear line for whether a display was permitted or forbidden; the jurisprudence in this area remains uncertain.

The recent cases reveal a shift in answers to the question posed at the outset of this entry: beyond protecting individuals from being coerced to engage in religion, what limits does the Establishment Clause impose on government? In the nineteenth and early twentieth centuries, the majority generally understood disestablishment to prevent tax-financed support for religious schools, but to permit governmental expression endorsing a generalized Christianity. At the dawn of the twenty-first century, the Supreme Court case law has moved in the opposite direction: greater latitude for religious schools and social services to receive aid on equal terms with nonreligious institutions, but significant limits on official endorsement even of familiar symbols like the Ten Commandments. The shift has several causes. The welfare state's widespread spending on social programs makes the denial of aid to religious providers appear less as nonentanglement and more as discrimination. And while increasing religious pluralism in America makes any explicit religious statement by government look more and more partial, financial aid can be defined in secular terms and in theory can be available to a wide range of religious groups. The pervasive modern state has reduced the viability of strict separationism as an ideal, and the competing ideals of equality, neutrality, and individual choice are more hospitable to aid programs than to explicit government endorsement of any religious view.

The Establishment Clause and Religious Institutional Autonomy

Finally, one potential implication of the Establishment Clause remains relatively unexplored by the Court: the use of the clause as a shield to protect religious institutions from government interference, at least in core or inherently religious matters such as doctrine, liturgy, and the selection of clergy. Establishments typically involved government oversight of such religious matters—albeit in the name of preserving the favored faith—and a prime purpose of disestablishment was to separate the structures of church and state to ensure the autonomy of religious life. The Establishment Clause may play an increased role in protecting religious institutional autonomy as Free Exercise Clause protections have declined with the Court's holding (*Employment Division v. Smith* [1990]) that religiously motivated conduct generally has no constitutional claim to exemption from "neutral law[s] of general applicability."

A few Court decisions have sounded the theme of Establishment Clause immunity from regulation. Most explicitly, the Court invalidated financial aid to religious schools on the ground that the regulation accompanying aid produces "excessive entanglement" (*Lemon*) and "the spectre of government secularization of a creed" (*Aguilar v. Felton* [1985]). Ironically, such rulings used the school's autonomy as a ground to strike down aid that the school wished to receive. "Pure" protections of religious institutional autonomy, by contrast, have invoked the Religion Clauses in general, a rationale consistent with, but not explicitly mentioning, the Establishment Clause. Under a century-long series of decisions involving property disputes between church factions, civil courts deciding such cases must sometimes defer to the resolution of the matter by the highest authority within the church (*Watson v. Jones* [1872], *Serbian E. Orthodox Diocese v. Milivojevich* [1976]. Although states may often apply "neutral principles" of property or trust law to such disputes, they must defer to the internal church authority whenever the controversy requires interpretation of religious concepts or involves "religious authority or dogma" (*Jones v. Wolf* [1979], *Milivojevich*, *Smith*). Applying these principles, lower courts have barred suits by clergy against churches for employment discrimination, suits against clergy and churches for "malpractice" in religious counseling, and—in some cases—suits against churches for negligent hiring or supervision of clergy who commit torts. Whether these decisions extend to nonclergy positions in religious institutions is uncertain at best, although the Supreme Court in *NLRB v. Catholic Bishop* (1979) held that application of collective bargaining laws to teachers in parochial schools would raise serious constitutional questions concerning church–state entanglement. Institutional autonomy from regulation remains among the least explored implications of the Establishment Clause.

THOMAS C. BERG

References and Further Reading

Conkle, Daniel O., *Toward a General Theory of the Establishment Clause*, Northwestern University Law Review 82 (1988): 1113–1194.

Esbeck, Carl H., *Dissent and Disestablishment: The Church–State Settlement in the Early Republic*, Brigham Young University Law Review 2004 (2004): 4:1385–592.

Laycock, Douglas, *'Nonpreferential' Aid to Religion: A False Claim About Original Intent*, William and Mary Law Review 27 (1986): 875–921.

Lupu, Ira C., *Government Messages and Government Money:* Santa Fe, Mitchell v. Helms, *and the Arc of the Establishment Clause,* William and Mary Law Review 42 (2001): 771–822.

McConnell, Michael W., *Coercion: The Lost Element of Establishment,* William and Mary Law Review 27 (1986): 933–941.

McConnell, Michael W., John H. Garvey, and Thomas C. Berg. *Religion and the Constitution.* Boulder, CO: Aspen Publishers, 2002.

Smith, Steven D., *The Rise and Fall of Religious Freedom in Constitutional Discourse,* University of Pennsylvania Law Review 140 (1991): 149–239.

Sullivan, Kathleen M., *Religion and Liberal Democracy,* University of Chicago Law Review 59 (1992): 195–223.

Cases and Statutes Cited

Abington School Dist. v. Schempp, 374 U.S. 203 (1963)

Aguilar v. Felton, 473 U.S. 402 (1985)

Board of Education v. Mergens, 496 U.S. 226 (1990)

County of Allegheny v. American Civil Liberties Union, 492 U.S. 573 (1989)

Elk Grove Unified School District v. Newdow, 542 U.S. 1 (2004)

Employment Division v. Smith, 494 U.S. 872 (1990)

Engel v. Vitale, 370 U.S. 421 (1962)

Epperson v. Arkansas, 393 U.S. 97 (1968)

Everson v. Board of Education, 330 U.S. 1 (1947)

Good News Club v. Milford Central School, 533 U.S. 98 (2001)

Harris v. McRae, 448 U.S. 297 (1980)

Jones v. Wolf, 443 U.S. 595 (1979)

Lee v. Weisman, 505 U.S. 577 (1992)

Lemon v. Kurtzman, 403 U.S. 602 (1971)

Locke v. Davey, 540 U.S. 712 (2004)

Lynch v. Donnelly, 465 U.S. 668 (1984)

Marsh v. Chambers, 463 U.S. 783 (1983)

McCreary County v. American Civil Liberties Union, 125 S. Ct. 2722 (2005)

Mitchell v. Helms, 530 U.S. 793 (2000)

Mueller v. Allen, 463 U.S. 388 (1983)

NLRB v. Catholic Bishop, 440 U.S. 490 (1979)

Serbian E. Orthodox Diocese v. Milivojevich, 426 U.S. 696 (1976)

Stone v. Graham, 449 U.S. 39 (1980)

Van Orden v. Perry, 125 S.Ct. 2854 (2005)

Wallace v. Jaffree, 472 U.S. 38 (1985)

Walz v. Tax Commission, 397 U.S. 664 (1970)

Watson v. Jones, 13 Wall. 679, 722–724 (1872)

Webster v. Reproductive Health Services, 492 U.S. 490 (1989)

Widmar v. Vincent, 454 U.S. 263 (1981)

Witters v. Dept. of Services, 474 U.S. 481 (1986)

Zelman v. Simmons-Harris, 536 U.S. 639 (2002)

ESTABLISHMENT CLAUSE: THEORIES OF INTERPRETATION

The Establishment Clause of the First Amendment to the Constitution provides that "Congress shall make no law respecting an establishment of religion . . . ."

The aim of the Establishment Clause is to keep the government neutral in matters of religion (*Epperson v. Arkansas* [1968], *McCreary County v. ACLU* [2005]). The Supreme Court has used a number of different approaches to determine whether a government action has departed from the neutrality principle and unconstitutionally established religion.

The Court has most often used the *Lemon* test, a three-prong test announced in *Lemon v. Kurtzman* (1971). More recently, however, Justice Sandra Day O'Connor has moved the Court towards more frequent use of the "endorsement test." See, for instance, *Lynch v. Donnelly* (1983) (O'Connor, J., concurring), *County of Allegheny v. ACLU* (1989) (O'Connor, J., concurring), and *Santa Fe Ind. Sch. Dist. v. Doe* (2000). Still another test that has gained some currency on the Court is the "coercion test" articulated by Justice Anthony Kennedy. See *Allegheny* (Kennedy, J., dissenting in part). In light of the Court's turbulent approach in this area, as well as changes in the Court's membership, it is reasonable to characterize the Establishment Clause as an area in transition.

The *Lemon* Test

When applying the *Lemon* test, courts will find no establishment of religion if the government action (1) has a secular legislative purpose, (2) does not have the effect of advancing or prohibiting religion, and (3) does "not foster 'an excessive entanglement with religion'" (*Lemon* [internal citations omitted]).

First, the challenged law or action must have a legitimate secular purpose. In *Stone v. Graham* (1980) (*per curiam*), for example, the Supreme Court struck down a state law requiring that the Ten Commandments be hung on the walls of Kentucky classrooms. The Court looked beyond the secular purpose proffered by the legislature and found that the "preeminent purpose for posting the Ten Commandments on schoolroom walls is plainly religious in nature." Similarly, in *Wallace v. Jaffree* (1985), the Court found an unconstitutional purpose behind a law whose sponsor had confirmed that it was "an 'effort to return voluntary prayer' to the public schools." More recently, in *McCreary County v. ACLU* (2005), the Court found that a Ten Commandments display in a courthouse violated the Establishment Clause. Critical to the Court's decision was that the initial display included only the Ten Commandments and a subsequent display, erected after the first was challenged, included religious excerpts from historical documents. The Court found the purpose behind the display was to "favor religion." As the Court noted in

McCreary, "the principle of neutrality has provided a good sense of direction: the government may not favor one religion over another, or religion over irreligion."

The second prong of the *Lemon* test looks at whether the effect of the challenged government action is the establishment of religion. In *Lynch*, the Court upheld a crèche surrounded by other secular Christmas symbols, including a Santa Claus house, reindeer, and a Christmas tree, because the display's effect was not to establish religion over nonreligion or endorse one particular sect over another. Similarly, in *Allegheny*, the Court approved a holiday display that included a menorah, a Christmas tree, and a plaque explaining a secular connection. The inclusion of the secular elements with the religious ones meant that the display did not have the effect of establishing religion. However, the Court held unconstitutional a separate display, consisting solely of a crèche sitting on another piece of government property. By displaying the crèche on its own, without the surrounding secular items, the county sent "an unmistakable message that it supports and promotes the Christian praise to God that is the crèche's religious message." Similarly, student-led prayer before high school football games had the unconstitutional effect of endorsing religion in *Santa Fe*. There, the Court found that forcing students to make religion a factor in deciding whether to attend the games had the "effect of coercing those present to participate in an act of religious worship."

The entanglement prong of the *Lemon* test is focused primarily on government spending that supports religion and the resulting government intrusion into religious organizations. In *Lemon* itself, the policies of two states to spend tax dollars to support religious schools were found unconstitutional because of excessive entanglement. To determine if the entanglement between government and religion is excessive, the Court looks at "the character and purposes of the institutions that are benefited, the nature of the aid that the State provides, and the resulting relationship between the government and the religious authority." Because of the intrusive government oversight necessary to administer financial aid, the Court in *Lemon* found excessive entanglement in the states' laws. A similar monetary and oversight analysis for the entanglement prong was applied to a Texas sales tax exemption for religious publications in *Texas Monthly v. Bullock* (1989). The statute required that applicants for the exemption prove to government officials that their "message or activity is consistent with 'the teaching of the faith.'" This entanglement could also lead to the perception that government has approved some religions and disapproved others (*Bullock* quoting

United States v. Lee [1982] [Stevens, J., concurring]). Where government action, especially concerning money, could result in intrusive oversight of religion, the Court has found excessive entanglement and an Establishment Clause violation.

The Endorsement Test

The endorsement test grew out of the effects and purpose prongs of the *Lemon* test. In *Lynch*, Justice O'Connor suggested that the Court should focus its attention not on generalized inquiries into the purpose and effect of the challenged government action, but instead should ask whether the action was taken with the purpose, or had the effect, of endorsing religion (*Lynch* [O'Connor, J., concurring]). She also suggested analyzing government action from the standpoint of the "reasonable observer," asking whether that observer would believe her standing in the political community was based on adherence or nonadherence to that message. In *Lynch* itself, the surrounding secular symbols neutralized the religious nature of the crèche, ensuring that a reasonable observer would not feel the government was endorsing the crèche's religious message. However, in *Allegheny*, there were no secular symbols surrounding the crèche, which to Justice O'Connor conveyed "a message to nonadherents of Christianity that they are not full members of the political community, and a corresponding message to Christians that they are favored members of the political community." This religious symbol in a government building had the "the unconstitutional effect of conveying a government endorsement of Christianity."

Justice O'Connor's theory of endorsement animates the majority opinions in *Wallace, Allegheny,* and *Santa Fe*. In *Wallace*, the majority framed the analysis of the purpose prong as "whether the government intends to convey a message of endorsement or disapproval of religion." In *Allegheny*, the majority noted the recent trend in Court decisions of paying "close attention to whether the challenged governmental practice either has the purpose or effect of 'endorsing' religion." Finally, in *Santa Fe*, the Court deemed school-sponsored religious speech "impermissible because it sends the ancillary message to members of the audience who are nonadherants 'that they are outsiders, not full members of the political community, and an accompanying message to adherants that they are insiders, favored members of the political community'" (*Santa Fe* citing *Lynch*). While the Court still applies the *Lemon* framework in these cases, its analysis of the effects and purpose prong has been transformed by Justice O'Connor's endorsement test. In most cases, the previously generalized inquiry into purpose and effect has been narrowed into a search for one particular purpose (to endorse) and one specific effect (endorsement).

The Coercion Test

Justice Kennedy has proposed a coercion test for Establishment Clause cases, and Justice Thomas has recently incorporated this idea into his own opinions (*Allegheny* [Kennedy, J., dissenting], *Van Orden v. Perry* [2005] [Thomas, J., concurring]). Justice Kennedy suggested in *Allegheny* that actions should be invalidated only when they "further the interests of religion through the coercive power of government." He suggested that coercion, rather than "infringement on religious liberty by passive or symbolic accommodation" is the evil that the Establishment Clause is designed to guard against. Justice Kennedy incorporated the coercion analysis in his opinion for the majority in *Lee v. Weisman* (1992). There, a public school graduation prayer led by a rabbi was found to violate the Establishment Clause. Kennedy held that "at a minimum, the Constitution guarantees that government may not coerce anyone to support or participate in religion or its exercise, or otherwise act in a way which 'establishes a [state] religion or religious faith, or tends to do so'" (internal citations omitted). Because children were coerced to either participate in or protest a religious exercise, the school violated the Establishment Clause in *Lee*.

Justice Thomas has recently begun to advocate use of the coercion test as well. He argued in *Van Orden* that the original constitutional meaning of establishment was coercion. "The Framers understood an establishment 'necessarily [to] involve actual legal coercion'" (*Van Orden* [Thomas, J., concurring] quoting *Elk Grove Unified Sch. Dist. v. Newdow* [2004] [Thomas, J., concurring in the judgment]). Justice Thomas had argued in *Newdow* that "'government practices that have nothing to do with creating or maintaining . . . coercive state establishments' simply do not 'implicate the possible liberty interest of being free from coercive state establishments'" (*Van Orden* quoting *Newdow* [Thomas, J., concurring]). While Justice Kennedy was the first member of the contemporary Court to propose use of the coercion test, he has not suggested that it be adopted to represent the full scope of the Establishment Clause's reach. As his opinion in *Lee* intimated, he sees refraining from coercion as the "minimum" that is required of

government. Justice Thomas, on the other hand, has opined that *only* coercive governmental measures can violate the Establishment Clause.

In light of these crosscurrents in the Court's Establishment Clause jurisprudence, it is difficult to predict with any confidence which approach (if any) will come to dominate the Court's analysis in the future. Because of her centrality in the development and application of the endorsement test, Justice O'Connor's departure from the Court heightens this uncertainty. There are few, if any, signs of the emergence on the Court of a consistent, clear majority in favor of a single approach to deciding Establishment Clause cases.

SAMUEL A. MARCOSSON

References and Further Reading

Levy, Leonard W. *The Establishment Clause: Religion and the First Amendment*. Chapel Hill: University of North Carolina Press, 1994.
McConnell, Michael W., *Religious Freedom at a Crossroads*, University of Chicago Law Review 59 (1992): 1:115–194.
Shiffrin, Steven H., *The Pluralistic Foundations of the Religion Clauses*, Cornell Law Review 90 (2004): 1:9–95.

Cases and Statutes Cited

County of Allegheny v. ACLU, 492 U.S. 573 (1989)
Elk Grove Unified School District v. Newdow, 542 U.S. 1 (2004)
Epperson v. Arkansas, 393 U.S. 97 (1968)
Lee v. Weisman, 505 U.S. 577 (1992)
Lemon v. Kurtzman, 403 U.S. 602, 613 (1971)
Lynch v. Donnelly, 465 U.S. 668 (1984)
McCreary County v. American Civil Liberties Union, 125 S. Ct. 2722 (2005)
Santa Fe Ind. Sch. Dist. v. Doe, 530 U.S. 290 (2000)
Stone v. Graham, 449 U.S. 39 (1980)
Texas Monthly v. Bullock, 489 U.S. 1 (1989)
U.S. v. Lee, 455 U.S. 252, 262 (1982)
Van Orden v. Perry, 125 S.Ct. 2854 (2005)
Wallace v. Jaffree, 472 U.S. 38 (1985)

ESTABLISHMENT OF RELIGION AND FREE EXERCISE CLAUSES

The First Amendment of the U.S. Constitution begins as follows: "Congress shall make no law respecting an establishment of religion, or prohibiting the free exercise thereof." The first clause is commonly called the Establishment Clause, and the second the Free Exercise Clause. Together they are commonly called the Religion Clauses. Their meaning, however, is a matter of considerable debate.

Do the Clauses Have Different Meanings?

The first issue is whether the two clauses have different meanings or are two different ways of making the same point. Scholars who say the latter contend that the clauses together were intended to prevent Congress from directly addressing and legislating on the subject of religion or any religious issue. They take this position, first, because during the ratification of the Constitution several of its defenders stated that it was not intended to grant Congress any power over religion. For example, at the Virginia Ratifying Convention, James Madison said, "There is not the shadow of right in the general government to intermeddle with religion. Its least interference with it would be a most flagrant usurpation." Second, they note that the Constitution's opponents, unconvinced by Madison's and similar assurances, insisted that an amendment be added to the Constitution to make it abundantly clear that Congress has no jurisdiction over religion. Finally, both the First Amendment's initial words, "Congress shall make no law . . . .," and the fact that Madison originally intended for it to become part of Article I, section 9, of the Constitution, which lists restraints on the powers granted Congress in section 8, imply that the Religion Clauses were meant to deny Congress any jurisdiction over religion.

Those scholars who interpret the Religion Clauses as a single provision meant to prevent the national government from legislating on the subject of religion are, however, divided over why early Americans wanted such a provision. Some scholars contend that the Religion Clauses were intended to protect states' rights. They note that many of the Constitution's opponents feared that the new national government it created would be so powerful as to significantly weaken, if not destroy, the state governments. They also note that the states traditionally had the power to legislate on the subject of religion. The Religion Clauses, they reason, were intended to protect this power of the states by denying it to the national government.

Other scholars say that the reason the Religion Clauses gave jurisdiction over religion to the states was because the nation was so divided over the issue of church–state relations that the framers of the Religion Clauses could not possibly have agreed on what policy toward religion the national government should have. Rather than proposing a policy that would have been controversial and divisive, they drafted the Religion Clauses simply as a way of saying that the issue should be left up to the individual states to resolve. In either case, whether to protect states' rights or to avoid dealing with an issue "too hot to handle," the Religion Clauses have no substantive meaning, that is, they express no position on what the proper relationship between religion and government should be. Rather, they uphold the principle of federalism.

Another, larger group of scholars, while agreeing that the Religion Clauses were meant to deprive the national government of jurisdiction over religion, contend that they did so primarily, if not entirely, for substantive reasons. They point out that most early Americans thought that whenever *any* government legislates on the subject of religion it poses a threat to religious freedom and to the integrity of religion itself, and often leads to conflict among different religions and to political instability. They also note that according to the contract theory of government, originally propounded by John Locke and widely accepted by early Americans, liberty of conscience is an inalienable right—one that persons can never and have never ceded to any government's control.

In contrast to the preceding interpretations of the Religion Clauses, the Supreme Court and some scholars have said that the Establishment and Free Exercise Clauses have different meanings and were not intended to deprive the government of all jurisdiction over religion. Essentially the Court has said that the Free Exercise Clause prohibits the government from *harming or disfavoring* religion in general, any particular religion, or any person or group because of her/his/its religion, and the Establishment Clause prohibits it from *aiding or favoring* the same. It has also said that for the Free Exercise Clause, but not the Establishment Clause, to be violated, coercion must be present or threatened.

If the Clauses Have Different Meanings, Can They Be Reconciled?

The Court's interpretation of the Religion Clauses has proven to be problematic, because it makes it difficult for courts to apply them in cases without creating conflict between the clauses. Is it possible for the government to avoid harming religion without aiding it, and vice versa? The answer depends on the kind of harm or aid that is prohibited—direct and intentional or indirect and unintentional. If it is the former, then conflict between the two clauses can be avoided, for there is no reason why the government's not directly and intentionally harming religion means that it is necessarily aiding religion, and vice versa. According to this interpretation, what the two clauses require is government *neutrality* toward all religions and between religion and nonreligion, and this can be achieved if the government avoids directly legislating either for or against religion, any particular religion, or any person or group because of his/her/its religion.

On the other hand, if the Court were to hold that the Religion Clauses prohibit harm and aid that is indirect and unintentional as well as direct and intentional, then it becomes difficult if not impossible to reconcile the two clauses. For example, if the Free Exercise Clause is interpreted as prohibiting *all* government-imposed restraints or burdens on religion so that persons or groups do not have to obey valid, secular, generally applicable laws, provided they have a sincere religious reason for not doing so, then it can be argued that the government is favoring or giving special treatment to religious persons and groups, because nonreligious ones are not entitled to such exemptions. At times, however, this is how the Court has interpreted the Free Exercise Clause (see *Sherbert v. Verner* [1963] and *Wisconsin v. Yoder* [1971]). Similarly, if the Establishment Clause is interpreted as prohibiting *all* government aid to religion so that educational and welfare-type programs that are primarily secular in nature but sponsored and operated by religious organizations are precluded from receiving government funding, then it can be argued that the government is disfavoring or discriminating against religious organizations, because nonreligious organizations are allowed to receive the government funding. At times, however, this is how the Court has interpreted the Establishment Clause (see *Lemon v. Kurtzman* [1971] and *Aguilar v. Felton* [1985]).

Since approximately 1990, primarily to avoid interpreting the Religion Clauses in a way that would cause them to conflict with each other, the Court has adopted neutrality as the guiding principle to be followed when it decides cases arising under the Religion Clauses. In effect, it has said that it is only direct, intentional harm or aid that is prohibited by the free exercise and Establishment Clauses, respectively. In *Employment Division, Dept. of Human Resources v. Smith* (1990), therefore, the Court held that the Free Exercise Clause does not guarantee a right to religion-based exemptions from valid, secular, generally applicable laws that only indirectly and unintentionally harm the exercise of religion, and in *Agostini v. Felton* (1997) and *Zelman v. Simmons-Harris* (2002), the Court upheld government funds going to parochial schools because the aid to religion was indirect and secondary.

Some scholars have criticized the Court's move to neutrality as the unifying principle of the Religion Clauses. Those who believe that the Free Exercise Clause guarantees a right to religion-based exemptions from valid, secular laws contend that the basic

principle underlying and unifying both Religion Clauses is not neutrality but religious *freedom*. They argue that even indirect and unintentional government regulations of or burdens on the exercise of religion should be disallowed except in those cases when the government can provide "compelling" reasons for them. On the other hand, those who believe that the Establishment Clause prohibits even indirect and unintentional aid to religion contend that the basic principle underlying and unifying both Religion Clauses is *separation* of government and religion. They argue that government funding of church-run secular programs inevitably involves government control over and entanglement in religion.

The Court, however, is not likely to adopt either the *freedom* or *separation* interpretation of the Religion Clauses, even though theoretically either one could work to unify the clauses. The main problem with both is that as a practical matter there cannot be either complete religious freedom or complete separation of government and religion, and yet there is no workable test for determining where to "draw the line," that is, when to compromise either freedom or separation. In contrast, *neutrality*, which prohibits only direct, intentional harm or aid to religion, is relatively easy to apply and, thus, seems likely to remain as the dominant principle for reconciling the Religion Clauses.

ELLIS M. WEST

References and Further Reading

Amar, Akhil R. *The Bill of Rights: Creation and Reconstruction.* New Haven, CT: Yale University Press, 1998.

Conkle, Daniel O., *The Path of American Religious Liberty: From the Original Theology to Formal Neutrality and an Uncertain Future*, Indiana Law Journal 75 (Winter 2000): 1–36.

Kurland, Philip B. *Religion and the Law: Of Church and State and the Supreme Court.* Chicago: Aldine, 1962.

Laycock, Douglas, *Formal, Substantive, and Disaggregated Neutrality Toward Religion*, DePaul Law Review 39 (1990): 993–1018.

Sherry, Suzanna, *Lee v. Weisman: Paradox Redux*, Supreme Court Review 1992 (1993): 123–153.

Smith, Steven D., *The Rise and Fall of Religious Freedom in Constitutional Discourse*, University of Pennsylvania Law Review 140 (1991): 149–240.

———. *Foreordained Failure: The Quest for a Constitutional Principle of Religious Freedom.* New York: Oxford University Press, 1995.

Cases and Statutes Cited

Agostini v. Felton, 521 U.S. 203 (1997)

Aguilar v. Felton, 473 U.S. 402 (1985)

Employment Division, Dept. of Human Resources v. Smith, 494 U.S. 872 (1990)

Lemon v. Kurtzman, 403 U.S. 602 (1971)
Sherbert v. Verner, 374 U.S. 398 (1963)
Wisconsin v. Yoder, 406 U.S. 205 (1972)
Zelman v. Simmons-Harris, 536 U.S. 639 (2002)

See also Establishment Clause (I): History, Background, Framing; Establishment Clause Doctrine: Supreme Court Jurisprudence; Free Exercise Clause (I): History, Background, Framing; Free Exercise Clause Doctrine: Supreme Court Jurisprudence

ESTATE OF THORNTON v. CALDOR, 472 U.S. 703 (1985)

Estate of Thornton v. Caldor is an important case because it limited the ability of states to require private employers to accommodate the religious beliefs of employees. In Estate of Thornton, the U.S. Supreme Court struck down a Connecticut statute that required private employers to allow employees to take their Sabbath day off regardless of which day that was. Some scholars consider Estate of Thornton to be part of a "one-two punch" impacting those whose religious beliefs or practices require them to refrain from work on the Sabbath. The first "punch" came in the early 1960s when the Supreme Court upheld "Sunday closing laws" against challenges under the Establishment Clause (McGowan v. Maryland [1961]), and under the Free Exercise Clause (Braunfeld v. Brown [1961]. These laws required businesses to close on Sunday, even though this could have a profound impact on religious minorities such as Jews and Seventh Day Adventists, who would also have to close their stores on Saturday, thus effectively closing those businesses for the entire weekend. In fact, the Connecticut law in question was part of its "Sunday closing law," and was an attempt to accommodate those who would be forced to work on their Sabbath. The Connecticut Supreme Court struck down the general Sunday closing provisions of the law under the Connecticut Constitution, but the provision requiring employers to allow employees to take their Sabbath day off was not challenged in that case.

In an opinion by Chief Justice Burger, the Court applied the Lemon test and held that the Connecticut law violated the Establishment Clause. The Lemon test requires that a law have a secular purpose, a primary effect that neither advances or inhibits religion, and that the law not excessively entangle government and religion. The Court held the Connecticut law violated this test because the statute's primary effect was to advance a "particular religious practice." The Court pointed out that the law gave employees the absolute power to designate their Sabbath day, and to take off on that day if required by

religious concerns. The Court also noted that the law had no exceptions based on employer necessity. Therefore, employees could not be penalized for taking their Sabbath day off even if doing so caused the employer significant economic harm, forced the employer to close down its business, or forced other workers, including those with greater seniority under a valid seniority system, to cover for employees who took their Sabbath day off. Moreover, only those who asserted religious reasons for taking the day off were protected under the law. Thus, other employees with a valid reason for taking the day off would not receive similar consideration under the law.

Many who have criticized this decision have done so because when combined with the "Sunday closing law" cases Estate of Thornton could lead to a regime where the dominant faith's Sabbath is accommodated and arguably preferred by government, while government is prevented from requiring private entities to accommodate those who are negatively effected by the government preference. After Estate of Thornton, states cannot protect employees who are religiously compelled to take their Sabbath day off by requiring employers to allow them to do so. The critics suggest that in light of the "Sunday closing cases" this result favors mainstream Christianity.

FRANK S. RAVITCH

Cases and Statutes Cited

Braunfeld v. Brown, 366 U.S. 599 (1961)
Lemon v. Kurtzman, 403 U.S. 602 (1971)
McGowan v. Maryland, 366 U.S. 420 (1961)

ESTELLE v. SMITH, 451 U.S. 454 (1980)

In this case, the defendant was charged with capital murder stemming from his participation in an armed robbery. The trial judge ordered a psychiatric exam to determine whether Estelle was competent to stand trial. After the defendant was tried and convicted, the doctor who conducted the pretrial examination testified for the state at the sentencing hearing on the issue of whether Estelle would be a future danger to society. Pursuant to Texas law, the jury answered the "future dangerousness" question and two other required questions in the affirmative, and the judge imposed the mandatory death penalty. The U.S. Supreme Court reversed. Justice Burger, writing an opinion in that all justices joined or concurred, held that the admission of the doctor's testimony violated Estelle's Fifth Amendment privilege against compelled self-incrimination. The defendant was not advised prior to the psychiatric examination that he had a right to remain silent, and that any statement he made could be used against him at a capital sentencing proceeding, as required by the famous case *Miranda v. Arizona* (1966). Moreover, Estelle was denied his Sixth Amendment right, as defense counsel was not notified that the competency examination would encompass the issue of future dangerousness, and the defendant had no opportunity to consult with his counsel in deciding whether to submit to the examination.

In the years since *Estelle* was rendered, it has been narrowed by two subsequent Supreme Court decisions. In *Penry v. Johnson* (2001), the Court held that where a defendant chooses to offer expert testimony regarding his mental condition at trial or sentencing, earlier unwarned and uncounseled statements made to a psychiatrist may be used against him. In *Allen v. Illinois* (1986), the Court held five to four that use of psychiatric examinations in proceedings to commit individuals found to be "sexually dangerous persons" is not prohibited by the Fifth Amendment, as the proceedings are civil not criminal.

SUSAN R. KLEIN

References and Further Reading

Comment, *The Right to Counsel During Court-Ordered Psychiatric Examinations of Criminal Defendants*, Villanova University Law Review 26 (1980): 135.
Cochran, Gregory R., *Is the Shrink's Role Shrinking? The Ambiguity of Federal Rule of Criminal Procedure 12.2 Concerning Government Psychiatric Testimony in Negativing Cases*, University of Pennsylvania Law Review 147 (1999): 1403.
Wright, Charles. *Federal Practice and Procedure*. 3rd ed. St. Paul, MN: West Group, 1999, and 2003 pocket part.

Cases and Statutes Cited

Allen v. Illinois, 478 U.S. 364 (1986)
Miranda v. Arizona, 384 U.S. 436 (1966)
Penry v. Johnson, 532 U.S. 782 (2001)

See also **Capital Punishment; Capital Punishment and the Equal Protection Clause Cases; Capital Punishment: Due Process Limits; Capital Punishment: History and Politics; Capital Punishment Reversed; Capital Punishment and Race; Self-Incrimination (V): Historical Background**

ESTELLE v. WILLIAMS, 425 U.S. 501 (1975)

Williams reinforced the concept that defendants must make timely objections; otherwise, any constitutional violations would be deemed harmless error. Williams was held in custody pending trial. On the day of trial, Williams asked for and was denied by the jail, his civilian clothes. Consequently, Williams was tried and convicted in clothes that were distinctly marked as prison clothes. Williams did not make an objection to wearing these clothes.

The Court (six to two) found that Williams's wearing prison clothes at trial was harmless error because he did not make a timely objection. The Court held that it would violate the Fourteenth Amendment if an accused were compelled to trial in prison clothes because the jurors could be biased against him. However, the accused must make an objection in a timely manner so that the trial judge may rule on the issue. In the instant case, it was the trial judge's practice to allow the accused to wear his civilian clothes. Because Williams had no defense to present at trial and the defense counsel referenced his prison attire at trial, it appeared that Williams wore his jailhouse clothes only to elicit jury sympathy. There was nothing in the record to show that Williams was forced to stand trial in these clothes or that there was any reason to excuse the defense from raising an objection.

Justices Marshall and Brennan dissented on the grounds that Williams's due process rights were not waived when he did not knowingly consent to being tried in his prison clothes.

AUDREY I-WEI HUANG

References and Further Reading

Chapman v. California, 386 U.S. 18 (1967).
Fischer, Paul A. Annotation: Propriety and Prejudicial Effect of Compelling Accused to Wear Prison Clothing at Jury Trial—Federal Cases. *American Law Reports, Federal Series* 26 (2005): 535.
Hernandez v. Beto, 443 F. 2d 634 (Fifth Cir.), cert. denied, 404 U.S. 897 (1971).
Illinois v. Allen, 397 U.S. 337 (1970).
Turner v. Louisiana, 379 U.S. 466 (1965).

See also **Harmless Error; Substantive Due Process**

ESTES, BILLIE SOL (1925–)

Billie Sol Estes, the subject of media-tainted trial, was born in the Panhandle of Texas in 1925 and reared in Abilene. He moved to Pecos in 1951 with the hopes of starting an agricultural business. By 1960, Estes had built a fortune through land and business purchases. To help amass his fortune Estes would befriend prominent politicians, most notably then-Senate majority leader, Lyndon Johnson of Texas, who would later become vice president and president of the United

States. He would also befriend Johnson's presidential running mate, John F. Kennedy.

In 1961, Estes's cotton holdings became the subject of a Department of Agriculture investigation. In 1962, the *Pecos Independent and Enterprise* began publishing a series of stories detailing Estes's fraudulent business practices, which led to an indictment charging that he had created a multimillion-dollar scheme that illegally manipulated government cotton allotments. The indictment and pretrial maneuvers that followed garnered tremendous media attention due to the fact that Estes was a well-known Texas businessman who had close connections with prominent politicians; his pretrial hearing was carried live on television and radio.

During the trial under the rules of the Texas courts, cameras and still photographers were allowed in the courtroom to record the Estes trial, in which he was convicted of fraud for swindling hundreds of farmers. Estes sued the State of Texas, claiming that he did not receive a fair trial as a result of the publicity associated with his pretrial and trial.

The Supreme Court overturned his conviction in *Estes v. Texas* (1965) citing Estes's rights to due process were violated due to excessive publicity, and ruling that Estes should have a new trial. He was retried without cameras in the courtroom and convicted again of fraud and sentenced to prison. Sixteen years later the Court would overturn its *Estes* decision in *Chandler v. Florida* (1981).

BA-SHEN WELCH

References and Further Reading

Moore, Roy L. *Mass Communication Law and Ethics*. 2d ed. Mahwah, NJ: Lawrence Erlbaum Associates, 1999.
Pecos Enterprise. *Bill Sol's Back in Town*. Pecos Enterprise Archives. http://www.pecos.net/news/arch2002/012302p.html.

Cases and Statutes Cited

Estes v. Texas, 381 U.S. 532 (1965)
Chandler v. Florida, 449 U.S. 560 (1981)

EUGENIC STERILIZATION

The latter half of the nineteenth century witnessed great scientific advances in a number of fields, including biology. Charles Darwin's *On the Origins of the Species by Means of Natural Selection* and Gregor Mendel's experiments shed light on the hereditary transmission of characteristics, prompting consideration of how to use this knowledge to aid humanity.

In 1883, the English scientist Sir Francis Galton was the first to coin the phrase "eugenics," which means "good in birth" in Greek. Eugenics was concerned with applying principles of animal husbandry to humans, encouraging positive genetic traits and eliminating negative genetic traits by controlling who could breed and pass on their genes.

The scientific approach to human breeding found particular resonance in the Progressive movement in the United States. That movement was concerned with improving the conditions of the worst-off in society. Eugenics offered the promise that through the application of scientific principles, future generations of such unfortunates could avoid being born, improving the lot of all society. The rudimentary understanding of genetics at the time conceptualized such ills as pauperism, criminality, insanity, immorality, and low intelligence as negative hereditary characteristics that could be "bred out" of the bloodline. Progressive eugenicists sought to ensure that those possessing these characteristics would decline as a proportion of the population by encouraging or mandating the sterilization of people who displayed those characteristics.

While the ideas behind eugenics found favor across the world, the United States led the way in their practical application with Indiana becoming the first state to pass a law enabling the sterilization of persons for eugenic purposes in 1907. A further twenty-two states passed similar laws by 1926, and by 1940, thirty states had passed eugenic sterilization laws, with California and Virginia being particularly strong proponents. Most states provided for involuntary eugenic sterilization, whereby the state could forcibly sterilize a person found to be unfit to have children, because such offspring would be a similar burden on society.

The Supreme Court ruled involuntary eugenic sterilization laws constitutional in the case of *Buck v. Bell* (1927). The eight-to-one decision was announced with an opinion by Oliver Wendell Holmes declaring, "It is better for all the world, if instead of waiting to execute degenerate offspring for crime, or to let them starve for their imbecility, society can prevent those who are manifestly unfit from continuing their kind . . . . Three generations of imbeciles are enough." In *Skinner v. Oklahoma* (1942), the Supreme Court limited the use of involuntary eugenic sterilization for habitual criminals.

For a number of years eugenics was widely accepted; it was taught in many of the nation's colleges, eugenicists took part in state fairs across the nation and a number of famous people supported eugenics, including Presidents Theodore Roosevelt and Calvin Coolidge; John Maynard Keynes, the noted economist; and Margaret Sanger, the founder of Planned Parenthood. The popularity of eugenics declined in the late 1930s, but involuntary eugenic sterilizations continued in the United States until 1979, by which time over 60,000 Americans had been sterilized.

The concern for the gene pool in the United States that was expressed through eugenic sterilization laws can also be seen in its miscegenation laws and the curtailment of immigration from Southern and Eastern Europe (whose immigrants were seen as particularly degenerate and a threat to future generations of Americans) in the Immigration Act of 1924.

The American eugenic sterilization laws formed the basis for similar laws across the world, starting in the Swiss canton of Vaud in 1928. Denmark, Sweden, Finland, Belgium, Austria, Norway, and Germany were among those countries to embrace eugenic sterilization laws a way of dealing with hereditary defects and controlling the growth of ethnic minorities. Despite the United Kingdom's early association with the eugenics movement, political opposition prevented the adoption of eugenic sterilization laws.

Eugenic sterilization was carried out most vigorously in Nazi Germany. Adolf Hitler cited the United States and its laws aimed at genetic purity as an example for the world in his book *Mein Kampf*, and there was much interaction between eugenicists in the United States and Germany until the late 1930s. Nazi Germany sterilized hundreds of thousands of people between 1933 and 1945. Between 1939 and 1941, the logic of eugenic sterilization was carried to its conclusion and over 70,000 people deemed to be a burden on the state were forcibly euthanized.

Despite the association of eugenics and eugenic sterilization with the Nazi regime, the United States and much of Northern Europe continued to carry out eugenic sterilizations for the remainder of the twentieth century, although many countries repealed these laws by the 1980s and 1990s. Japan did not begin its program of eugenic sterilization until after World War II, starting in 1948 and continuing until 1996.

State-mandated eugenic sterilization is no longer a current concern in the field of American civil rights and civil liberties. Many states have apologized for their prior actions and a return to eugenic sterilization programs seems unlikely. Instead, the concern is more focused on similar results being achieved through coercion.

One fear is that advances in DNA testing raise the possibility that genetic defects could be accurately identified and that information used to affect decisions about reproduction to ensure "designer babies." Fetuses possessing unfavorable genetic material could be aborted, or in vitro fertilization techniques used to ensure that only children with the couple's favored genetic characteristics are born.

State coercion is seen as a bigger concern for the reproductive freedom of individuals. Some have called for the state to restrict access to welfare payments for those unwilling to be sterilized or have other long-term birth control procedures such as implants. Others see the existence of federally funded voluntary sterilizations as promoting a program of eugenic sterilization. These sterilizations, in addition to those provided by a number of charities, are performed on the poor with disproportionately large numbers from ethnic minorities. The argument is that by funding sterilization instead of other means of birth control the state encourages individuals to undergo sterilization simply because they cannot afford other options.

GAVIN J. REDDICK

References and Further Reading

Kevles, Daniel J. *In the Name of Eugenics: Genetics and the Uses of Human Heredity*. Cambridge, MA: Harvard University Press, 1998.

Klein, Wendy. *Building a Better Race: Gender, Sexuality, and Eugenics from the Turn of the Century to the Baby Boom*. Berkeley: University of California Press, 2001.

Sofair, Andre N., and Lauris C. Kaldjian. "Eugenic Sterilization and a Qualified Nazi Analogy: The United States and Germany, 1930–1945." *Annals of Internal Medicine* 132 (2000): 312–9.

Cases and Statutes Cited

Buck v. Bell, 274 U.S. 200 (1927)
Skinner v. Oklahoma, 316 U.S. 535 (1942)

EUTHANASIA

Euthanasia is ending a life before its natural end, motivated by a concern for the welfare of the killed person. It is this motivation that distinguishes euthanasia from simple homicide or suicide and it is sometimes called "mercy killing" for this reason.

Voluntary Euthanasia versus Involuntary Euthanasia

In cases of voluntary euthanasia, the persons killed made requests for their lives to be ended prematurely, often in cases of terminal illness. In cases of involuntary euthanasia, the persons killed expressed no such desire, and may have even expressed an opinion to the contrary. This may seem incongruous with the idea of euthanasia being motivated out of a concern for the welfare of the person, but in such cases the persons may be considered incapable of fully understanding their own best interests. The most extreme examples of involuntary euthanasia occurred in Nazi Germany when thousands of disabled people were killed by the state, although these killings were also motivated by the prevailing theory of eugenics.

Choosing to End One's Life

Ancient civilizations differed in their approaches towards people choosing to end their own life; some viewed it as taboo, others saw ending one's life to retain dignity as laudable. The Western tradition was most heavily influenced by Judeo-Christian views that suicide was against God's will, and these views were incorporated into laws. The American colonies followed the English tradition of viewing suicide as a crime, a position that continued until changes in the latter part of the twentieth century to encourage attempted suicides to seek medical attention.

For many theorists the right to privacy places some aspects of life beyond state regulation. These claims of privacy are most compelling when they concern intimate aspects of one's life and the control of one's own body (*Griswold v. Connecticut* [1965] and *Roe v. Wade* [1973]). Some extend this reasoning and argue that individuals should be able to decide when they want to end their lives by doing harm to that body; they argue that there is a right to die. Under this theory, laws preventing one from ending one's own life are unwarranted intrusions into a person's autonomy.

The Role of Medical Professionals in Euthanasia

Those seeking their own death may want assistance, either because their medical condition renders them incapable of taking their own life, or because they want to make sure that any attempt is both successful and as painless as possible. Medical professionals are uniquely placed in that they have both extensive contact with seriously ill people and the ability to hasten their death through refraining from treating them, or administering drugs to ensure a painless death. However, requests to assist a patient seeking death conflict with the Hippocratic oath sworn by all doctors to "neither prescribe nor administer a lethal dose of medicine to any patient even if asked nor counsel any such thing."

Active versus Passive Euthanasia

Active euthanasia entails an intervention to bring about the death of the subject, frequently a lethal dose of medication; a doctor who assists in this violates the Hippocratic oath and such conduct is illegal in the United States. The 1980s and 1990s saw a determined effort by some states, particularly in the West, to make euthanasia easier, and in 1994 Oregon legalized physician-assisted suicide by referendum. However, due to court challenges it was not implemented until after a second referendum in 1997. The highest-profile euthanasia advocate was Dr. Jack Kevorkian, who assisted in many deaths and was later imprisoned in 1999. The U.S. Supreme Court ruled that the Due Process Clause of the Fourteenth Amendment does not confer a right to physician-assisted suicide (*Washington v. Glucksberg* [1997]).

Internationally, there are only a few countries that explicitly permit physician-assisted suicide. Switzerland legalized euthanasia in 1947, but it was the legalization of physician-assisted suicide in the Netherlands (2000) and Belgium (2002) that reignited the international debate on euthanasia.

Passive euthanasia entails failing to take action that would otherwise save the life of the subject. There is considerable debate as to what falls within the scope of the passive category from complying with a "do not resuscitate" order, not providing life-saving medication, or even withholding food and water. It is considered to be legally, medically, and ethically sound to refrain from life-giving treatment if the patient so desires. In the United States, a person can refuse medical treatment, and actions that violate this constitute an assault, forming the legal and ethical justification for allowing passive euthanasia. The Supreme Court has ruled that the Due Process Clause does not extend this right to relatives of a patient incapable of making his or her wishes known (*Cruzan v. Missouri* [1990]). This has contributed to the rise of so called "living wills," documents drawn up in advance specifying under what conditions medical treatment should be withheld.

The active/passive distinction in euthanasia is considered to be extremely important from the standpoint of the Supreme Court and medical ethicists, although others maintain that this is a false distinction and that both are morally equivalent actions taken with the understanding that a hastened death will be the result. In addition, many question allowing someone to choose a potentially slow and painful death through refusing medical treatment, but denying them the chance to die quickly and relatively painlessly with medical assistance. The consequences of this distinction are felt most by people who, because of their condition, are incapable of quickly ending their own life, although the Supreme Court refused an Equal Protection Clause challenge to this distinction in *Vacco v. Quill* (1997).

Euthanasia is an extremely controversial topic in an aging society with the medical capacity to prolong life to an extent far greater than previously possible. Advocates cite the importance of allowing people to die with dignity, rather than to live on in pain, and to allow them to make their own decisions to end their own lives as peacefully and painlessly as possible. Those opposed to euthanasia are concerned that this would lead to the deaths of those who do not want to die, either through social pressure to cease being a burden on their families and request euthanasia, or the well-meaning but misguided carrying out involuntary euthanasia. As medical technology advances, the importance of this issue will increase, although the chances of resolution seem remote.

GAVIN J. REDDICK

References and Further Reading

Dworkin, Ronald. *Life's Dominion: An Argument about Abortion, Euthanasia, and Individual Freedom.* New York: Vintage, 1994.
Kevorkian, Jack. *Prescription Medicide: The Goodness of Planned Death.* Amherst, N.Y.: Prometheus Books, 1993.
Minois, George. *History of Suicide: Voluntary Death in Western Culture.* Baltimore: Johns Hopkins University Press, 2001.
Moreno, Jonathan, ed. *Arguing Euthanasia: The Controversy over Mercy Killing, Assisted Suicide, and the "Right to Die".* New York: Touchstone, 1995.
Neeley, G. Steven. *The Constitutional Right to Suicide: A Legal and Philosophical Examination.* New York: Peter Lang, 1994.
Quill, Timothy E. *Death and Dignity: Making Choices and Taking Charge.* New York: W.W. Norton & Company, 1994.

Cases and Statutes Cited

Cruzan v. Director, Missouri Dept. of Health, 497 U.S. 261 (1990)
Griswold v. Connecticut, 381 U.S. 479 (1965)
Roe v. Wade, 410 U.S. 113 (1973)
Vacco v. Quill, 521 U.S. 793 (1997)
Washington v. Glucksberg, 521 U.S. 702 (1997)

See also **Ballot Initiatives; Kevorkian, Jack; Oregon's Death with Dignity Act (1994); Penumbras; Privacy; Privacy, Theories of; Reproductive Freedom; Substantive Due Process; Theories of Civil Liberties**

EVERS, MEDGAR WILEY (1925–1963)

An African-American civil rights activist who fought racial violence in Mississippi, worked to secure voting rights, and coordinated movements leading to desegregation of state educational institutions and public accommodations, Medgar Wiley Evers was born in 1925 in Decatur, Mississippi.

During World War II, Evers served in the Army in England and France where he experienced nonsegregated institutions and formed friendships with whites. Upon returning to Mississippi, he challenged the Jim Crow voting system in 1946 by registering to vote, but he was prevented from voting. He completed high school and graduated in 1950 from Alcorn College, where he played an active role in student organizations and athletics.

Evers promoted the National Association for the Advancement of Colored People (NAACP) while working for an African-American insurance company. In 1954, he applied to the University of Mississippi law school. When his application was denied, he moved to Jackson to become the first Mississippi field secretary for the NAACP, the only full-time civil rights advocate in the state.

During the 1950s he investigated racial violence against African Americans, helping bring national attention to the murders of George Lee and Lamar Smith and to the attempted murder of Gus Courts— all shot for attempting to vote or actually voting. He helped investigate the murder of fourteen-year-old Emmett Till. He continued to investigate crimes and police brutality against African Americans in the 1960s. Aaron Henry summarized, "In most of these cases, we were not able to get punishment for guilty parties, but at least we got them into court and into the spotlight of public attention."

In the face of massive state resistance to *Brown v. Board of Education*, Evers encouraged action pressing for the integration of local schools, supported litigation that desegregated the University of Mississippi in 1962, and cooperated with Justice Department lawsuits that challenged state practices which denied voting rights to African Americans. He encouraged boycotts, demonstrations, and other activities aimed at desegregating public facilities.

Evers was convicted of criminal contempt for his criticism of the unjust conviction of Clyde Kennard. The reversal of Evers's conviction by the state supreme court in *Evers v. State* (Miss. 1961) signaled a modest but significant retreat from judicial suppression of political speech. This case illustrates the important connection between the protection of civil liberties and the struggle for black civil rights in the 1950s and 1960s.

In 1963, Evers was murdered by a white supremacist. Despite overwhelming evidence, two all-white juries failed to convict, seemingly confirming the view that no white man could be convicted of killing an African American in Mississippi. Evers's death galvanized public opinion, demonstrated the need for federal enforcement of civil rights, and motivated the adoption of new federal civil rights laws.

In 1994, Evers's killer was retried and finally convicted of murder. The result symbolized the change in attitudes towards racial violence, proved the value of criminal justice in promoting racial reconciliation, and inspired the reopening other cold cases from the civil rights era.

Evers married Myrlie Beasley in 1951 and had three children with her. After his death, she became a prominent spokesperson for civil rights, serving as chair and interim president of the NAACP.

MICHAEL H. HOFFHEIMER

References and Further Reading

Bailey, Ronald. *Remembering Medgar Evers*. Oxford, MS: Heritage Publications, 1988.

Brown, Jennie. *Medgar Evers*. Los Angeles: Melrose Square, 1994.

DeLaughter, Bobby. *Never Too Late: A Prosecutor's Story of Justice in the Medgar Evers Case*. New York: Scribner, 2001.

Evers, Medgar Wiley. *The Autobiography of Medgar Evers: A Hero's Life and Legacy Revealed Through His Writings, Letters, and Speeches*. Edited by Myrlie Evers-Williams and Manning Marable. New York: Harper Collins, 2005.

Evers, Myrlie B. *For Us the Living*. Jackson: University Press of Mississippi, 1996.

Henry, Aaron, with Constance Curry. *Aaron Henry: The Fire Ever Burning*. Jackson: University Press of Mississippi, 2000.

Nossiter, Adam. *Of Long Memory: Mississippi and the Murder of Medgar Evers*. Reading, MA: Addison-Wesley, 1994.

Voller, Maryanne. *Ghosts of Mississippi: The Murder of Medgar Evers, The Trials of Byron de la Beckwith, and the Haunting of the New South*. Boston: Little, Brown, 1995.

Cases and Statutes Cited

Brown v. Board of Education of Topeka, Kansas, 347 U.S. 483 (1954)

Evers v. State, 131 So. 2d 653 (Miss. 1961)

See also **National Association for the Advancement of Colored People (NAACP); Voting Rights (Compound)**

EVERSON v. BOARD OF EDUCATION, 330 U.S. 1 (1947)

This landmark Supreme Court decision is important for two reasons. One, it held for the first time that the Establishment Clause of the First Amendment ("Congress shall make no law respecting an establishment of religion . . . .") is incorporated into the Due Process Clause of the Fourteenth Amendment ("[N]or shall any State deprive any person of life, liberty, or property, without due process of law . . . .") and, thus, applies to state governments as well as the federal government. Two, the Court's *Everson* opinion was the first to give an extensive, if not authoritative, interpretation of the Establishment Clause.

Facts, Issues, and Holdings

In 1941, New Jersey passed a statute authorizing local school districts to provide transportation to children going to either public or private schools. In turn, the Township of Ewing began reimbursing parents for money they spent on the public transportation of their children to either public or private schools. In Ewing, however, the only children who did not go to public schools went to Catholic schools, which taught them not only secular subjects, but the tenets and practices of Catholicism. A district taxpayer challenged the constitutionality of the state law on the grounds that it violated the Due Process Clause of the Fourteenth Amendment in two ways. First, the law authorized the taking of private property and spending it for a private, not public, purpose. Second, the law was one "respecting an establishment of religion," which, because it was prohibited by the First Amendment, was also prohibited by the Fourteenth Amendment. By a five-to-four vote, the Court upheld the law.

Justice Hugo Black wrote the opinion for the majority. He rather easily disposed of the first argument that the law had a private rather than a public purpose. He said that the law's purpose was to protect the safety of the children by enabling them to "ride in public busses to and from schools rather than run the risk of traffic and other hazards incident to walking or 'hitchhiking.'" It did not matter, he said, that the public money went to individuals as reimbursement for what they had already spent. Subsidies and loans to private individuals and businesses that serve to promote a public good "have been commonplace practices in our state and national history."

As for whether the Establishment Clause applied to state and local governments via the Fourteenth Amendment, Black simply assumed that it did. All that he did to justify his assumption was cite a brief passage from *Murdock v. Pennsylvania* (1943) that said the Fourteenth Amendment had made the First Amendment "applicable to the states."

More troublesome for Black was the issue of what the Establishment Clause prohibited. Although he quickly asserted that the Establishment Clause prohibited government from funding "any or all religions," he noted that it was difficult to distinguish "between tax legislation which provides funds for the welfare of the general public and that which is designed to support institutions which teach religion." Black even suggested that in deciding cases like this the Court had no margin for error—that the First Amendment required it, in effect, to walk a tightrope. Although the Establishment Clause does not allow tax funds to go to institutions that teach religious doctrines, the Free Exercise Clause, he said, disallows government's excluding any persons, "because of their faith, or lack of it, from receiving the benefits of public welfare legislation."

The main issue, therefore, was how to categorize the law. Was it a general welfare provision or a law that supported the teaching of religion? The Court majority concluded it was the former. Although Black conceded that the state's providing free school transportation indirectly aided the church schools (and thus the teaching of religion), by causing some children, who otherwise would not do have done so, to attend those schools, he said the same could be said of the state's providing police protection to children going to and from schools. Obviously, he said, the state was not required to remove general government services, such as police and fire protection, from church schools. Black concluded: "The State contributes no money to the schools. It does not support them. Its legislation . . . does no more than provide a general program to help parents get their children, regardless of their religion, safely and expeditiously to and from accredited schools."

Justice Black's History and Interpretation of the Establishment Clause

If Black had said only what was summarized above, the *Everson* decision might have caused hardly a ripple, but he did not. He felt obliged to give a definitive interpretation of the Establishment Clause. In an often-quoted passage, he said:

> The "establishment of religion" clause of the First Amendment means at least this: Neither a state nor the Federal Government can set up a church. Neither can

pass laws which aid one religion, aid all religions, or prefer one religion over another. Neither can force nor influence a person to go to or to remain away from church against his will or force him to profess a belief or disbelief in any religion. No person can be punished for entertaining or professing religious beliefs or disbeliefs, for church attendance or nonattendance. No tax in any amount, large or small, can be levied to support any religious activities or institutions, whatever they may be called, or whatever form they may adopt to teach or practice religion. Neither a state nor the Federal Government can, openly or secretly, participate in the affairs of any religious organizations or groups and *vice versa*. In the words of Jefferson, the clause against establishment of religion by law was intended to erect "a wall of separation between Church and State."

To justify this interpretation of the Establishment Clause, Black presented a lengthy account of its origin. He relied primarily on James Madison's "Memorial and Remonstrance" and Thomas Jefferson's "Virginia Statute of Religious Liberty," both of which were opposed to a bill in Virginia that would have taxed persons for the purpose of supporting all Christian clergy. More specifically, Black wrote that

> the provisions of the First Amendment, in the drafting and adoption of which Madison and Jefferson played such leading roles, had the same objective and were intended to provide the same protection against government intrusion on religious liberty as the Virginia [Jefferson's] statute.

Black, however, did not stop here. Aware that his "wall of separation" interpretation of the Establishment Clause was difficult to reconcile with the actual holding of the Court, he enunciated another "purpose of the First Amendment." It "requires the state to be a neutral in its relations with groups of religious believers and nonbelievers; it does not require the state to be their adversary. State power is no more to be used so as to handicap religions, than it is to favor them." Ultimately, then, Black justified the *Everson* decision on the grounds of neutrality, not separation.

Black's opinion has been widely and sharply criticized by both scholars and justices on the Court. At the time, the dissenting opinions, written by Justices Robert Jackson and Wiley Rutledge, who wanted the law nullified, complained that the Court's decision was simply inconsistent with Black's interpretation of the Establishment Clause, especially with his assertion that "[n]o tax in any amount, large or small, can be levied to support any religious activities or institutions, whatever they may be called, or whatever form they may adopt to teach or practice religion." They insisted that the New Jersey law breached the "wall of separation between Church and State."

Since then, Black's opinion has been criticized for other reasons: for simply assuming that the Establishment Clause, even though it guarantees no "liberty" and may have been intended to protect state establishments of religion, was incorporated into the Due Process Clause of the Fourteenth Amendment; for interpreting the Establishment Clause so broadly as to make the Free Exercise Clause superfluous; for saying that the clause prohibits not just aid to one religion, but aid to all religions; for saying that the clause prohibits religious organizations from "participating" in the affairs of government; for asserting without any evidence that it was the views of Virginians, especially Madison and Jefferson, that are reflected in the Religion Clauses; and for failing to present evidence from the drafting of the clauses by the First Congress.

Perhaps above all else, Black's opinion can be criticized for spawning what most scholars consider to be a series of confusing and inconsistent Court decisions based on the Religion Clauses of the First Amendment. By being indecisive and saying that the Religion Clauses require both *separation* of government and religion, *and* government *neutrality* between religion and nonreligion, Black gave the justices of the Court two different principles that for decades competed for dominance. In some decisions, separation prevailed; in others neutrality did. Eventually, however, the Court rejected the principle of separation in favor of the principle of neutrality.

ELLIS M. WEST

References and Further Reading

Formicola, Jo R., and Hubert Morken, eds. *Everson Revisited: Religion, Education, and the Law at the Crossroads.* Lanham, MD: Rowman & Littlefield, 1997.

Kauper, Paul G., Everson v. Board of Education: *A Product of the Judicial Will*, Arizona Law Review 15 (1973): 307–326.

Murray, John Courtney, *Law or Prepossessions?* Law and Contemporary Problems 14 (1949): 23–43.

Sorauf, Frank J. *The Wall of Separation.* Princeton, NJ: Princeton University Press, 1976.

Cases and Statutes Cited

Murdock v. Pennsylvania, 319 U.S. 105 (1943)
Virginia Statute for Religious Freedom (1786), *Statutes at Large* 12 (1823): 84

See also **Application of First Amendment to States; Establishment Clause Doctrine: Supreme Court Jurisprudence; Establishment of Religion and Free Exercise Clauses; History and Its Role in Supreme Court Decision Making on Religion; Incorporation Doctrine; State Aid to Religious Schools**

EX PARTE MILLIGAN, 71 U.S. 2 (1866)

The *Milligan* opinion, issued just after the Civil War ended, held that Lambdin Milligan's trial by military commission was unconstitutional. Vehemently denounced by Republicans who viewed it as a threat to military reconstruction in the South, and somewhat limited by its own facts and by subsequent cases, the opinion still stands as one of the Supreme Court's most important decisions on civil liberties and the limits of military authority over civilians.

Milligan, a lawyer practicing in southern Indiana, was an outspoken critic of both President Lincoln and Indiana's Republican Governor Oliver P. Morton. A Democrat who unsuccessfully sought his party's nomination for governor in 1860, Milligan opposed the war and infringements of civil liberties by state and federal officials. After 1862, Democrats controlled both houses of the Indiana legislature. State politics became extremely partisan as the 1864 presidential and gubernatorial elections drew near, and Democrats and Republicans alike formed secret societies to support their parties. Milligan's association with one such society, the Sons of Liberty, led to his subsequent arrest and trial by military commission.

The Sons of Liberty, founded in part to get out the vote for Democratic candidates, also made initial plans to free thousands of Confederate soldiers held in Illinois and other states; the group may have also accepted money from Confederate agents in Canada. In August 1864, federal officials arrested Milligan and a handful of others, charging them with conspiracy, affording aid and comfort to the enemy, and other offenses. The Indianapolis military trials lasted from September to December 1864, partially amid the electoral campaign. The commission found Milligan guilty and sentenced him to death. The precise extent of Milligan's involvement in the Sons of Liberty remains unclear.

Milligan and two others filed writs of habeas corpus with the federal court in Indianapolis, which certified the legal issues in the case to the Supreme Court. Milligan argued in part that military commissions had no power to try civilians like himself where the regular courts were open and functioning. The military trial meant that Milligan did not receive many constitutional protections afforded defendants tried by civilian courts, including the right to a jury of residents of Indiana and the right to be tried only for conduct that Congress had criminalized by law.

All nine justices agreed that the military commission that tried Milligan was unlawful, but they were deeply divided in their reasoning. The majority opinion, authored by Justice Davis, a longtime friend and political ally of Lincoln, reasoned broadly that neither Congress nor the president could authorize military trials of civilians, except in the actual theater of war where the regular courts were not functioning.

Chief Justice Chase, writing for the four-person concurrence, reasoned that Congress had not authorized the trial of Milligan; indeed, the Habeas Corpus Act of 1863 required that prisoners like Milligan had to be indicted by a grand jury or released. A grand jury had met just prior to Milligan's arrest, but had failed to indict him. This settled the matter for Chase, who thought the majority erred by considering whether Congress would have the power to authorize military commissions if it attempted to do so. Chase also believed that the majority erred in how it answered this hypothetical question: he reasoned that Congress would have the power to establish such commissions.

Justice Davis's famous opinion for the Court includes sweeping and often-cited language about the limits of government power during war. The opinion, however, met with immediate and vitriolic criticism from Republicans who charged that the Court's reasoning would have lost the war for the Union and that Congress's efforts at military reconstruction in the South would be fatally undermined. In 1868, the Court appeared ready to consider the constitutionality of military commissions authorized by reconstruction legislation in *Ex parte McCardle*. Congress, however, revoked the appellate jurisdiction of the Supreme Court over this and similar habeas appeals, and the Court honored the revocation.

Twentieth-century commentators sometimes applauded Milligan as a vitally important civil liberties opinion. Others argued that it has had little practical effect, noting that the Court issued it only after Confederate troops had surrendered and the war was over. An American citizen tried by a military commission during World War II relied in part on *Milligan* to support his petition for a writ of habeas corpus. The Court rejected the petition and distinguished *Milligan* on the grounds that the World War II defendant had actually joined the Nazis, while Milligan was not part of the enemy armed forces and was not subject to the laws of war. The president's detention of "enemy combatants" in the United States following the September 11, 2001 terrorist attacks has once again raised fundamental questions about civil liberties and military authority, and has focused new attention on *Milligan*.

INGRID BRUNK WUERTH

References and Further Reading

Fairman, Charles. *History of the Supreme Court of the United States: Reconstruction and Reunion: 1864–1888.* Vol. VI, Part I. New York: Macmillian Company, 1971.

Klement, Frank L. "The Indianapolis Treason Trials and *Ex parte Milligan.*" In *American Political Trials*, edited by Michal R. Belknap. Westport, Conn.: Greenwood Press, 1981.

Rehnquist, William H. *All the Laws but One.* New York: Alfred A. Knopf, 1998.

Warren, Charles. *The Supreme Court in United States History.* Vol. 3, 1856–1918. Boston: Little, Brown, and Co., 1923.

Cases and Statutes Cited

Ex parte McCardle, 74 U.S. 506 (1869)

See also **Military Tribunals; 9/11 and the War on Terrorism**

EX PARTE VALLANDIGHAM, 28 F.CAS. 874 (1863)

This case deals with the conflict between free expression and military necessity during the course of war. It represents the struggle between free speech rights and the imperiled security of the Union.

On September 24, 1862, President Lincoln issued a proclamation suspending the writ of habeas corpus and declaring martial law. In March 1863, President Lincoln appointed General Ambrose Burnside to the post of Union commander of the Department of Ohio. Thereafter, General Burnside issued General Order No. 38, which announced that "[i]t must be distinctly understood that treason, expressed or implied, will not be tolerated in this department." General Burnside's issuance of General Order No. 38 resulted in what turned out to be the Civil War's most celebrated arrest and prosecution for disloyal speech.

In May 1863, Clement Vallandigham addressed a large meeting of citizens where he described the war as "wicked, cruel, and unnecessary;" characterized General Order No. 38 as a "base usurpation of arbitrary authority;" and contended that "the sooner the people informed the minions of the usurped power, that they will not submit to such restrictions upon their liberties, the better."

Based on the speech, Vallandigham was arrested and brought before a five-member military commission and charged with "[p]ublicly expressing in violation of General order No. 38 . . . sympathy for those in arms against the government of the United States, and declaring disloyal sentiments and opinions with the object and purpose of weakening the power of the government in its efforts to suppress an unlawful rebellion."

After a two-day trial, at which Vallandigham refused to plead because he contended that the tribunal had no lawful authority over a civilian, the commission found Vallandigham guilty as charged and sentenced him to confinement "in some fortress of the United States, . . . there to be kept during the war." President Lincoln commuted the sentence a few days later, and Vallandigham was banished from military lines.

Vallandigham filed a petition for writ of habeas corpus arguing that his constitutional rights had been violated, including his right to due process of law, the right to be tried on the indictment of a grand jury, the right to a public trial by an impartial jury, the right to confront witnesses against him, and the right to have compulsory process for witnesses in his behalf. Judge Humphrey H. Leavitt denied Vallandigham's petition, basing his decision on moral grounds rather than precedent.

Judge Leavitt explained that

[t]he court cannot shut its eyes to the grave fact that war exists, involving the most eminent public danger, and threatening the subversion in destruction of the constitution itself. In my judgment, when the life of the republic is in peril, he misstates his duty and obligation as a patriot who is not willing to concede to the constitution such a capacity of adaptation to circumstances as may be necessary to meet a great emergency, and save the nation from hopeless ruin. Self-preservation is a paramount law.

Addressing the specific circumstances of this case, Judge Leavitt observed that "[a]rtful men, disguising their latent treason under hollow pretensions of devotion to the Union," have been "striving to disseminate their pestilent heresies among the masses of the people." Judge Leavitt found that General Burnside was reasonable in perceiving "the dangerous consequences of these disloyal efforts" and in resolving, "if possible, to suppress them," because the "evil was one of alarming magnitude." Judge Leavitt concluded by stating that those who criticized the government in time of crisis "must learn that they cannot stab its vitals with impunity."

Ex parte Vallandigham raised basic civil libratory issues—the power of the military to try civilians and imprison or otherwise punish people for antiwar speech. Lest we not forget, without free speech, we would not have democracy.

PATRICK H. HAGGERTY

References and Further Reading

Curtis, Michael Kent. *Free Speech, "The People's Darling Privilege": Struggles for Freedom of Expression in American History.* Durham, NC: Duke University Press, 2000.
Klement, Frank L. *The Limits of Dissent: Clement L. Vallandigham & The Civil War.* Lexington: University of Kentucky Press, 1970.
Rehnquist, William H. *All the Laws But One: Civil Liberties in Wartime.* New York: Alfred A. Knopf, 1998.
Vallandigham, James L. *A Life of Clement L. Vallandigham.* Baltimore: Turnbull Bros., 1872.

EX POST FACTO CLAUSE

Ex post facto laws are laws which apply to an event which occurred in the past. They are a form of retroactive legislation. Most are enacted as an attempt by a legislature to identify specifically one person or group of persons who are to be punished by the legislation. The U.S. Constitution prohibits such retroactive legislation in Article I, section 9, clause 3. While this is a constitutional provision that only applies to the federal government, a parallel provision in Article I, section 10, clause 1, applies to the states.

The twin constitutional provisions prohibiting ex post facto laws were limited in their application by the U.S. Supreme Court in the 1798 decision of *Calder v. Bull* (1798). The Court held that legislatures can not pass a law subjecting someone to a fine or period of imprisonment for an act that was not unlawful when it was done. This meant that the ex post facto provisions in the U.S. Constitution would apply only to penal and criminal statutes. In addition to limiting the application of the ex post facto provisions, Justice Samuel Chase suggested strongly that many types of retroactive legislation are generally unjust and as a general rule should be avoided.

In his opinion, Justice Chase wrote the authoritative formulation of the kinds of retroactive legislation that would fall within the Constitution's prohibition of ex post facto legislation:

1st. Every law that makes an action done before the passing of the law, and which was innocent when done, criminal; and punishes such action. 2d. Every law that aggravates a crime, or makes it greater than it was, when committed. 3d. Every law that changes the punishment, and inflicts a greater punishment, than the law annexed to the crime, when committed. 4th Every law that alters the legal rules of evidence, and receives less, or different testimony, than the law required at the time of the commission of the offence, in order to convict the offender.

The Supreme Court's decision in *Calder v. Bull* reflected the ideas of many of this nation's founders. Alexander Hamilton had written, for example, in *The Federalist Papers* Number 84 of a strong opposition to " [t]he creation of crimes after the commission of the fact, or, in other words, the subjecting of men to punishment for things which, when they were done, were breaches of no law . . ."

The essential character of all ex post facto legislation is its retroactive application. But within the meaning of the prohibition as defined in *Calder v. Bull*, not all retroactive legislation is barred by the Constitution's dual provisions. For example, laws that require the deportation of certain aliens for past conduct have been held as not penalizing a person for his or her past conduct. One such case is *Marcello v. Bonds* (1955) where an order deporting a resident alien was affirmed by the Supreme Court because of an earlier drug conviction. Other laws, such as those challenged in *Kansas v. Hendricks* (1997), which have changed the length or nature of the incarceration for certain convicted sexual offenders have been held to be civil in nature. Thus, the additional commitment to a mental health facility because the offender was determined to be a danger to self or to others has been upheld.

A provision enacted by the California legislature, which extended the statute of limitations for a crime beyond the one-year period for prosecution following the commitment of the crime, was found in *Stogner v. California* (2003) to violate the ex post facto barrier when the purpose was to revive a previously time-barred prosecution. The allegations in the *Stogner* prosecution were that the alleged sexual offenses had occurred more than twenty years prior to the revision of California's three-year statute of limitations. This distinction between civil and penal laws was also made in the decision in *Smith v. Doe* (2003) in the same U.S. Supreme Court term upholding the application of provisions of Alaska's "Megan's Law," which required convicted sex offenders to register with local police departments. The Supreme Court noted that the legislature intended to create a civil regulatory scheme and one that was not clearly punitive in nature.

Three considerations usually underlie any evaluation of enacted ex post facto laws. First, ex post facto laws are generally believed to violate the Constitution's separation of powers. The Constitution assigns to the executive and judicial branches the responsibility for handing out punishment against individuals found to have committed crimes. The legislative branch, by contrast, is expected to make laws of general application. Second, ex post facto laws may violate First Amendment principles if the intended punishment is seen to have a chilling effect on otherwise constitutionally protected speech or actions. And, third, ex post facto laws are generally unfair in that they fail to provide adequate notice to individuals that their actions may have criminal consequences.

JERRY E. STEPHENS

References and Further Reading

Congressional Research Service. *The Constitution of the United States of America: Analysis and Interpretation.* Washington, D.C.: U.S. Government Printing Office, 2004.

Monk, Linda R. *The Words We Live By: Your Annotated Guide to the Constitution.* New York: Hyperion, 2003.

Rotunda, Ronald D., and John E. Nowak. *Treatise on Constitutional Law: Substance and Procedure.* 3rd ed. St. Paul, MN: West Group, 1999.

Cases and Statutes Cited

Calder v. Bull, 3 U.S. (3 Dall.) 386 (1798)
Kansas v. Hendricks, 521 U.S. 346 (1997)
Marcello v. Bonds, 349 U.S. 302 (1955)
Smith v. Doe, 538 U.S. 84 (2003)
Stogner v. California, 539 U.S. 607 (2003)

EXCLUSIONARY RULE

The exclusionary rule forbids the introduction of certain evidence in court, in an attempt to ensure that the state and federal governments do not violate individuals' constitutional rights. The rule applies to criminal trials and as a general matter forbids the use of evidence that was obtained as a result of a violation of the Fourth or Fifth Amendments in the government's case-in-chief, that is, in the part of the trial where the government presents its evidence of the defendant's guilt. Accordingly, if the police, on a wild hunch, break down a person's front door and discover drugs in the house, the drugs may not be used to convict the homeowner of drug possession.

There are several exceptions to this rule, however, which will be discussed in more detail below. The rule does not apply to civil proceedings and does not apply to pretrial or sentencing hearings in a criminal prosecution. Even at trial, if the defendant testifies falsely, the government can rebut the defendant's testimony by using the illegally obtained evidence. Furthermore, if the police obtain a warrant that is defective in some way, so that the resulting search is unconstitutional, the evidence found may still be admitted at trial in the prosecution's case-in-chief if the police were acting in reasonable good faith on the warrant.

The exclusionary rule ordinarily applies to ban the government from using not only the evidence that is found during an unconstitutional search, but also that evidence that is found *because of* that search. So, a search that turns up a lead to further evidence will result in suppressing both the lead and the additional evidence. But not all evidence that is found as a result of the unconstitutional action will be excluded. If the connection between the illegality and the evidence is too attenuated, or if the police would have found the evidence by legal means, then the exclusionary rule does not apply. Lastly, the exclusionary rule is an available remedy only for the individual whose person or property was searched or seized. If a search of a person turns up evidence of his friend's crime, the friend will usually be unable to have that evidence suppressed.

Arguments for and against the Exclusionary Rule

The Supreme Court has held since *Weeks v. United States* (1914) that the exclusionary rule bars the use in federal trials of evidence that was obtained by violating the Fourth Amendment, which prohibits "unreasonable searches and seizures." It was not until *Mapp v. Ohio* (1961), however, that the Supreme Court required states to use the exclusionary rule as well. The rule was originally based on two considerations. First, the Court wanted to deter police from violating the Constitution. If any evidence illegally seized by the police could not be used in the defendant's trial, then (the theory went) there would be no reason to commit the violation in the first place. Second, the Court thought it was wrong to involve the judicial process in the constitutional violation. That is, even though the judiciary did not commit the unreasonable search, the Court thought it improper that the Court take part in the constitutional violation by using its fruits. In later years this second justification has fallen out of favor and the courts now exclusively rely on the deterrence rationale, as the Supreme Court itself pointed out in *Stone v. Powell* (1976) and *United States v. Janis* (1976).

The rule remains controversial today because its effect is to make it more difficult to convict guilty criminal defendants. In the example in the first paragraph, there is no doubt that the homeowner whose house was unconstitutionally searched by police was guilty of drug possession. Justice Benjamin Cardozo, who was then a judge on the New York Court of Appeals, most famously stated the disadvantage of the exclusionary rule: "The criminal is to go free because the constable has blundered" (*People v. Defore* [1926]). Moreover, the exclusionary rule does nothing to compensate innocent persons for violations of their Fourth Amendment rights. An illegal search that turns up no evidence will never be subject to the exclusionary rule because there will be no trial, yet the rights of that innocent person were violated just as much as were the rights of the manifestly guilty person for whom the exclusionary rule is a

get-out-of-jail-free card. Nevertheless, to the extent the exclusionary rule deters unlawful police conduct, there will be fewer violations of the Fourth Amendment rights of the innocent and the guilty, so perhaps the rights of the law-abiding are served in some way by the application of the rule to the nonlaw-abiding.

There are considerable instances when the rule does not deter police conduct. This can happen for several reasons. First, the officers may not know that their conduct violates the Constitution. They may think they are following the Fourth Amendment, but a judge may later disagree. In that instance, the exclusionary rule—like any penalty—will not deter a violation, for the officer will not know that he is subjecting himself to the penalty. Second, if the person whose property is searched is not prosecuted (or if the case is plea bargained), then the exclusionary rule never comes into play. The exclusionary rule then does nothing to protect the rights of persons who will not be prosecuted. As a result, whatever deterrent effect the exclusionary rule has is lessened because a certain portion of unconstitutional searches will not result in exclusion. Third, officers may not be deterred from committing violations if the exclusionary rule is applied months or years after the unconstitutional search, and the passage of time makes it hard for the officer to learn from his error, if he is ever told of the exclusion at all. Fourth, an officer bent on violating the Fourth Amendment may be able to lie in court and avoid the exclusionary rule that way, lessening the deterrent value of the rule.

On the other hand, police departments have become more conscious of the Fourth Amendment in the years since *Mapp*, and officers whose searches cannot yield convictions eventually feel some heat from the officials whom the voters expect to put criminals behind bars. Even as to the first objection—that officers cannot reasonably be expected to know the details of Fourth Amendment doctrine—there is vast disagreement. Several states have concluded that the exclusionary rule does deter officers, and if it causes officers to be cautious even when they are approaching the constitutional line, so much the better.

The Good Faith Exception

The Supreme Court has decided, however, that the police act "reasonably," and therefore there is no need to exclude evidence if the police were acting reasonably in good faith reliance on a warrant—even if that warrant is later determined to be invalid (*United States v. Leon* [1984]). If, for example, the police lack probable cause to obtain a search warrant, but they apply for the warrant anyway and a judge issues one, evidence found in that search will be admissible if the officers' reliance on the warrant was reasonable and in good faith. The Court has decided that police cannot be expected to second-guess judges, and if a judge finds that there is probable cause, the police should not be expected to doubt that determination.

There are, however, some important limitations on the use of the good faith exception. If the judge signs the warrant because he is deceived by the police, then the police are not acting in good faith and the exception does not apply. Also, if probable cause is so lacking, or if the warrant wholly fails to specify the place to be searched or the items to be seized such that no reasonable officer would believe that the warrant is valid, the exception will not apply.

Leon's good faith exception is merely one instance where illegally obtained evidence is admitted in court despite the exclusionary rule. Perhaps most significant, the exclusionary rule does not apply in civil cases, and even in criminal cases the rule applies only to trials. Accordingly, illegally obtained evidence may be introduced before grand juries or at sentencing hearings. The Supreme Court has explained that the exclusionary rule is most likely to achieve its deterrent objective in criminal trials (as the government is often tempted to violate the Fourth Amendment in the investigation of crimes), and that accordingly the rule need not be extended to cover other proceedings. Nevertheless, as critics have pointed out, if the integrity of the courts is thought to be undermined by the use of illegally obtained evidence (as *Weeks* maintained), the admission of such evidence in civil and criminal trials would equally undercut that interest.

Habeas Corpus

Habeas corpus proceedings—which are technically civil but often involve federal court review of state court criminal prosecutions—are somewhat more complicated. A defendant convicted in state court can bring an action for a writ of habeas corpus in federal court, which would require the state to justify its continued imprisonment of the criminal defendant. Ordinarily, if the federal court finds that the state conviction was obtained through a violation of the Constitution—for example, because the state failed to respect the defendant's request for a jury trial—the federal court would require the state to conduct a new trial or release the prisoner. Under *Stone v. Powell*, however, the result is different when the prisoner objects to his conviction based on a violation of the Fourth Amendment exclusionary rule.

Suppose that a state tries a defendant for murder, and a key piece of evidence is the defendant's knife stained with the victim's blood. The police obtained that knife, however, by violating the Fourth Amendment—perhaps because they unreasonably failed to obtain a search warrant. *Mapp* makes the exclusionary rule applicable to the initial state trial. The state courts, however, believe that no warrant was necessary, so they allow the knife into evidence. After the defendant is convicted, he petitions for a writ of habeas corpus, claiming that his constitutional rights were violated. Even if the federal court hearing his claim agrees that the police violated the Constitution, the defendant will not receive a new trial. *Stone v. Powell* concluded that the deterrent effect on the police of applying the exclusionary rule to habeas corpus proceedings simply does not justify the costs of setting convicted, guilty criminals free.

Even this rule, however, has limits. If the state gave the defendant no chance at the original trial to argue that his Fourth Amendment rights were violated, then he would be able to argue the violation on habeas review. And—although the Supreme Court has not yet decided this question—if the state court decision admitting the evidence was clearly and obviously wrong, the federal court might conclude that in effect the defendant was not given "an opportunity for a full and fair litigation of [his] Fourth Amendment claim," requiring a new trial. As a general matter, however, a prisoner will not receive habeas relief if a state court wrongly admits unconstitutionally obtained evidence at his trial.

The Impeachment Exception

Furthermore, the exclusionary rule applies only to the prosecution's case-in-chief—that part of a criminal trial where the government sets forth its proof of the defendant's guilt. If the defendant takes the witness stand to testify, however, the prosecution can use unconstitutionally obtained evidence to "impeach" the defendant, that is, to demonstrate that the defendant's statements are untrue. The Court has reasoned that defendants should not be able to use the exclusionary rule to enable them to commit perjury (*United States v. Havens* [1980]). This impeachment exception, however, applies only when the defendant himself takes the stand. The Supreme Court held in *James v. Illinois* (1990) that the prosecutor may not use unconstitutionally obtained evidence to impeach the testimony of other defense witnesses.

Fruit of the Poisonous Tree

The exclusionary rule typically extends not only to the evidence found during an unconstitutional search, but also to evidence that is discovered because of the illegal search. Thus, if the police enter a house unconstitutionally and find drugs and a letter indicating where other drugs could be found, both the letter and the drugs at that house would be excluded because they were found during an unconstitutional search. But what if the police then go to the place referenced in the letter and find the other stash of drugs? Are those drugs admissible? The general answer is no, because those drugs are "fruit of the poisonous tree," that is, they were found as the result of unconstitutional police action, and they too must be excluded.

Like all the other aspects of the exclusionary rule, however, this one has exceptions. First, if the police discover the evidence illegally but then their investigation takes them to the same evidence without violating the Constitution, they have established an "independent source" for the evidence—independent, that is, from the constitutional violation—and the evidence will be admitted (*Murray v. United States* [1988]). Second, if the police discover evidence unconstitutionally but can demonstrate that they *would have* discovered the same evidence had no constitutional violation occurred, the evidence will be admitted under the "inevitable discovery" exception (*Nix v. Williams* [1984]). Third, if the unconstitutional police action is so removed from the acquisition of the evidence that "the deterrent effect of the exclusionary rule no longer justifies its cost," the attenuation doctrine serves to admit the evidence (*Wong Sun v. United States* [1963]). It is unclear when exactly a court will determine that there has been sufficient attenuation, but relevant factors include the amount of time elapsed between the unconstitutional action and the discovery of the evidence, and how flagrant the violation of the Constitution was. Additionally, if the suspect provided the evidence in a display of his own free will, or if the evidence consisted of another person's testimony, a court is likely to find that the evidence was attenuated from the violation.

Although both the direct evidence traceable to a constitutional violation and the indirect "fruits" of that violation are ordinarily inadmissible in a trial of the person whose rights were violated, the exclusionary rule does not apply where the defendant is someone *other* than the person who was subject to an unconstitutional search or seizure. So, suppose the police unconstitutionally break in to *A*'s apartment, where they find drugs and a letter from *B* to *A* proposing a drug transaction. At trial, *A* will have the letter and the drugs suppressed because of the constitutional violation. *B*, however, will not be able to contest the admission of the evidence against him, because *his* rights were not violated; the police broke into *A*'s apartment and invaded *A*'s privacy, not *B*'s.

The Fifth Amendment Exclusionary Rule

Although most observers are familiar with the exclusionary rule's applicability to Fourth Amendment violations, the rule applies also to violations of the compulsory Self-Incrimination Clause of the Fifth Amendment. In fact, while the text of the Fourth Amendment makes no explicit mention of exclusion, the Fifth Amendment contains an exclusionary rule that does not require judicial construction. That amendment provides that "[n]o person . . . shall be compelled in any criminal case to be a witness against himself." Accordingly, where a court, the police, or another agency of government compels a statement by a criminal defendant—where the statement is made involuntarily because of the threat of criminal sanctions or physical harm, for example—that statement may not be admitted at the defendant's trial for any purpose. The amendment presupposes that coerced statements are inherently unreliable, and therefore it would harm the truth-seeking process of trials for such evidence to be admitted.

More controversial has been the Supreme Court's decision in *Miranda v. Arizona* (1966), in which compulsion would be *presumed* if the defendant were subjected to custodial interrogation and he were not provided the now-famous *Miranda* warnings. Under *Miranda*, then, *voluntary* statements are subject to the exclusionary rule. Because such voluntary statements *are* reliable, however, the Supreme Court has held that they will be excluded only from the prosecution's case-in-chief. In other words, when the prosecution puts forward its evidence that the defendant committed a crime, that evidence cannot include the un-*Mirandized* statement. If the defendant takes the stand and testifies in his own defense, however, and makes statements contradicting the excluded statement, then the prosecution can make use of the un-*Mirandized* statement. The Supreme Court has held that excluding evidence from the prosecution's case-in-chief is necessary to ensure that the police will not violate *Miranda*, but the Court is unwilling to apply the exclusionary rule to allow the defendant to lie on the stand, when the lie could be exposed by using the un-*Mirandized* statement.

A further controversy centers on the application of the exclusionary rule to evidence obtained as the result of a *Miranda* violation. Suppose a suspect is interrogated without *Miranda* warnings and makes a voluntary confession to a murder, in which he discloses the location of the murder weapon. The police then give the suspect the *Miranda* warnings and ask the suspect to repeat the confession, which he does. The first confession is excluded from the prosecution's case-in-chief.

The protections in the Bill of Rights are written in lofty terms, guaranteeing freedoms and invoking ideals that continue to inspire us. The exclusionary rule is both an attempt to realize those ideals and to take account of the practical necessities of investigating, prosecuting, and punishing crime. As a result, the doctrine is a hodgepodge of conflicting decisions and will remain so as long as the country continues to debate the price that it is willing to pay to protect its civil liberties.

MICHAEL DIMINO

References and Further Reading

Amar, Akhil Reed. *The Constitution and Criminal Procedure: First Principles*. New Haven, CT: Yale University Press, 1997.

Amsterdam, Anthony G., *Perspectives on the Fourth Amendment*, Minnesota Law Review 58 (1974): 3:409–39.

Dressler, Joshua *Understanding Criminal Procedure*. 3d ed. Newark, NJ: Matthew Bender & Co., 2002.

Hall, John Wesley, Jr. *Search and Seizure*. Vol. 1, 3d ed. Charlottesville, VA: LEXIS Law Publishing, 2000.

Kamisar, Yale, *In Defense of the Search and Seizure Exclusionary Rule*, Harvard Journal of Law and Public Policy 26 (2003): 1:119–40.

LaFave, Wayne R. *Search and Seizure: A Treatise on the Fourth Amendment*. Vol. 1, 4th ed. St. Paul, MN: Thomson West, 2004.

Stuntz, William J., *The Virtues and Vices of the Exclusionary Rule*, Harvard Journal of Law and Public Policy 20 (1997): 2:443–55.

Whitebread, Charles H., and Christopher Slobogin. *Criminal Procedure: An Analysis of Cases and Concepts*. 4th ed. New York: Foundation Press, 2000.

Cases and Statutes Cited

James v. Illinois, 493 U.S. 307 (1990)
Mapp v. Ohio, 367 U.S. 643 (1961)
Miranda v. Arizona, 384 U.S. 436 (1966)
Murray v. United States, 487 U.S. 533 (1988)
Nix v. Williams, 467 U.S. 431 (1984)
People v. Defore, 150 N.E. 585, 587 (N.Y. 1926)
Stone v. Powell, 428 U.S. 465, 485 (1976)
United States v. Havens, 446 U.S. 620 (1980)
United States v. Janis, 428 U.S. 433, 446 (1976)
United States v. Leon, 468 U.S. 897 (1984)
Weeks v. United States, 232 U.S. 383 (1914)
Wong Sun v. United States, 371 U.S. 471 (1963)

See also **Bivens v. Six Unknown Named Agents of Federal Bureau of Narcotics, 403 U.S. 388 (1971); Search (General Definition); Seizure**

EXEMPLARS

The Fifth Amendment provides that "no person . . . shall be compelled in any criminal case to be a witness against himself." This restriction on government power, commonly known as the privilege against self-incrimination, is designed to protect individual autonomy by forcing the government to obtain evidence against a defendant through its own labors, rather than by "the cruel, simple expedient of compelling it from his own mouth."

The classic example of the privilege against self-incrimination is the right to remain silent when questioned by government officials, established in the seminal case *Miranda v. Arizona* (1966). Questions about the scope of the privilege also commonly arise, however, when the prosecution attempts to compel a defendant to produce a sample of his handwriting, fingerprints, or similar kind of physical evidence. Such examples are collectively known as exemplars.

With few exceptions, courts have rejected claims that the compelled production of exemplars violates the privilege against self-incrimination. The privilege extends only to "testimonial" evidence—evidence that in some sense discloses the contents of the defendant's mind—and the Supreme Court has consistently held that exemplars are not testimonial. The classic case in this regard is *Schmerber v. California* (1966), where the Court noted that the incriminating potential of a blood test results from chemical analysis, not from any testimony or otherwise communicative act on the part of the defendant.

Courts have permitted the compelled production of a wide variety of exemplars on the ground that they were nontestimonial and thus not protected by the privilege against self-incrimination, including examples of the defendant's blood, fingerprints, footprints, DNA, handwriting, voice, urine, and breath.

Courts have also held that compelling a defendant to exhibit his body to an eyewitness in a manner that promotes identification is nontestimonial. Thus, defendants have been required to shave their beards and have their hair trimmed, reveal their teeth and tattoos, wear clothes and masks allegedly worn by the perpetrator, and re-enact the physical actions involved in a crime.

In addition to privilege challenges, defendants have also argued that the compelled production of exemplars violates the Fifth Amendment's guarantee of due process and the Fourth Amendment's right to be free from unreasonable searches and seizures. Fourth Amendment challenges involving external physical features such as voice or hair regularly fail, on the ground that defendants have no reasonable expectation of privacy in those characteristics, because they are normally exposed to others in everyday life. Courts have held, however, that probable cause is required to compel the production of more physically intrusive exemplars such as blood or x-rays.

Due process challenges, although generally rejected, have occasionally succeeded when a voice exemplar or crime re-enaction was so suggestive of the defendant's guilt that it effectively undermined the defendant's presumption of innocence. It is impermissible, for example, to require a defendant to "put on a ski mask, wave a toy gun, and shout 'give me your money or I'm going to blow you up.'"

KEVIN JON HELLER

References and Further Reading

Connor, Michael A., *The Constitutional Framework Limiting Compelled Voice Exemplars: Exploration of the Current Constitutional Boundaries of Governmental Power over a Criminal Defendant*, San Diego Law Review 33 (1996): 1:349–83.
Levy, Leonard W. *Origins of the Fifth Amendment: The Right Against Self-Incrimination*. New York: Oxford University Press, 1968.
United States v. Olvera, 30 F.3d 1195 (1994).

Cases and Statutes Cited

Miranda v. Arizona, 384 U.S. 436 (1966)
Schmerber v. California, 384 U.S. 757 (1966)

See also **Due Process;** *Miranda v. Arizona*, **384 U.S. 436 (1966);** *Schmerber v. California*, **384 U.S. 757 (1966)**

EXEMPTIONS FOR RELIGION CONTAINED IN REGULATORY STATUTES

Discussions of the relation of religion and secular law of the United States often center on constitutional controversies arising out of the Free Exercise and Establishment Clauses of the First Amendment. That narrow focus, however, overlooks the practical and conceptual importance of the thousands of ways in which subconstitutional sources of law such as statutes and common law rules also play a defining role in mapping out the boundaries of civil and religious authority. This entry discusses, in particular, the many federal and state statutes that explicitly provide religious institutions and religiously motivated individuals with exemptions from otherwise applicable secular law. Such statutes seek, variously, to accommodate religious conscience, recognize the relevance of religious norms, minimize intrusion into religious life, acknowledge religious diversity, adjust regulatory regimes to take religious facts into account, or simply oblige religious interest groups. Exemption statutes have been criticized on various grounds, and sometimes pose particular difficulties, although courts have generally indicated that they are not unconstitutional simply for setting out distinctive legal treatment for religion and religious persons. In any event, their existence and variety are vital features of the legal landscape of religion in the United States whose practical significance and larger normative meaning need to be appreciated and understood.

This entry does not attempt an exhaustive account of statutory exemptions. It does try to provide a framework for considering a range of examples, and to suggest how such provisions illuminate the law's effort to understand and accommodate the normative force of religious life.

Statutory religion-based exemptions can be categorized in a variety of ways. Some create specific exemptions; others create general regimes of exemption. Some accommodate minority religious beliefs; others protect religious self-governance. Some demonstrate a willingness to put aside state interests; others further state interests in the face of the fact of religious diversity.

The oldest and most common form of statutory religion-based exemptions are specific exceptions from otherwise applicable legal norms. As Michael McConnell pointed out in an important study, several of the original American colonies exempted members of certain dissenting faiths from oath requirements, military conscription, and—ironically—assessments to support an established church. Since those early years, as religious diversity in the United States has exploded, and as the degree and scope of governmental regulation have grown even more dramatically, the number of exemption statutes and the range of issues they cover, have grown proportionately. A merely illustrative sampling of such provisions might include, for example, statutes exempting persons with contrary religious beliefs from immunization requirements, exemptions from certain drug laws and certain forms of alcohol regulation, exemption from autopsy requirements, qualified exemptions for Christian Scientists to employ spiritual healers rather than doctors under certain circumstances, qualified exemption of persons whose religions forbid acquiring insurance from the rule requiring automobile owners to obtain liability insurance, exemptions for persons who religion forbids the taking of photographs from the requirement that they have a photograph on their driver's license, a federal statute allowing military personnel in uniform to wear items of religious apparel under certain conditions, qualified exemptions from certain mandatory autopsy requirements, exemptions of religiously motivated students from certain parts of an otherwise required public school curriculum, exemptions of certain religious believers (such as the Amish) from certain otherwise mandatory provisions of the building codes, and qualified exemptions of certain religious employers from otherwise applicable requirements that their prescription benefit plans cover contraceptives.

All the statutes just listed detail accommodations for religion in particular contexts. A very different category of more recent statutes dating from the 1990s, such as the federal Religious Freedom Restoration Act (RFRA) and similar legislation in at least eleven states, set out instead a general, abstract, standard for drawing the boundaries between secular and religious authority across the whole legal domain. These statutes have a distinct quasiconstitutional coloration, and their history is intertwined with the modern development of the constitutional law of religion.

For many years, the courts have grappled with the question of whether the constitutional protection of free exercise includes any sort of fundamental right to be exempt from laws that directly conflict with religious norms. In *Reynolds v. United States*, its 1879 decision upholding laws against polygamy, the Supreme Court answered "no." Beginning in 1963, however, with *Sherbert v. Verner*, the Supreme Court held in a line of cases that the Free Exercise Clause guaranteed religious believers a prima facie right to be exempt from laws that directly conflicted with the demands of their faith unless the government could demonstrate that its law was the least restrictive means to further a compelling state interest. Then, in 1990, in *Employment Division v. Smith*, the Court all but overruled this line of cases. It held, subject to some important qualifications, that the Free Exercise Clause could not be used to challenge laws that were otherwise "neutral" and "generally applicable." RFRA and its state counterparts sought, in effect, to reinstate the *Sherbert* test as a statutory rather than constitutional entitlement. In *City of Boerne v. Flores* (1997), the Supreme Court struck down, as beyond the Congress's powers under section five of the Fourteenth Amendment, the federal RFRA's application to state laws. But the statute remains applicable to federal laws, and the State RFRA's remain in force as well.

Like most analytic divides, the distinction between specific and general exemption statutes is often a matter of degree. Thus, for example, some exemption statutes are so detailed as to actually name the religions to which they apply, although most do not. Meanwhile, in the wake of *Flores*, Congress enacted the Religious Land Use and Institutionalized Persons Act (RLUIPA), which mandated a compelling interest test in two specified albeit still broad categories of state laws, subject to a set of jurisdictional predicates that had been absent in the original RFRA. RLUIPA, which might be described as situated somewhere between the "specific" and "general" paradigms of exemption statutes, survived at least one Establishment Clause challenge in *Cutter v. Wilkinson* (2005).

The statutes discussed so far—whether at the specific or general end of the spectrum—still have in common the goal of accommodating the demands of religious norms that happen to come into conflict with the demands of certain secular laws. Such exemptions, by their terms, only apply to persons, usually in minority faith traditions, for whom such a conflict exists. A whole other category of exemption statutes has a quite different goal: to minimize, more broadly, the intrusion of the state into the self-government of religious communities. These institutional autonomy statutes stand out from other exemption statutes in at least two respects. To begin with, they generally protect churches and other religious institutions rather than individuals. More important, they generally apply with equal force to *all* religious communities, and do not depend on the existence of a particular conflict between secular law and religious belief. Examples of such institutional autonomy provisions include: exemptions of certain religious organizations from the reach of certain civil rights laws, whether or not the discrimination at issue is religiously motivated; exemption of churches from certain of the reporting and oversight provisions in the Internal Revenue Code and certain state statutes; and special provisions for churches in state charitable corporation laws.

Again, the distinction outlined here often blurs at the edges. For example, the statutory clergy–penitent privilege as enacted in the various states applies across the board, both to faith traditions that include something like a "seal of confession" and to those that do not. In a sense, then, the imperative to protect the distinctive religious practice of certain faiths has expanded, by analogy, to establish a principle protecting against undue intrusion into the religious communications of all faiths. Nevertheless, the conscientious element has not disappeared entirely: in some states, the question of whether the "penitent" can waive the privilege turns on whether revealing the confidence would violate the tenets of the clergyman's faith.

A final, more subtle, way of categorizing exemption statutes goes to the relation between the exemption and the underlying legal norm to which the exemption applies. In many cases, exemptions clearly reflect a willingness to compromise or limit the reach of an underlying legal norm, and to do so in favor of religious rights. In other cases, though, the relation between the exemption and the underlying norm is more complicated. For example, many state marriage statutes, while ordinarily requiring marriages to be solemnized by a single, licensed celebrant, make an exception for marriages conducted in faith traditions such as the Society of Friends (Quakers) in whose marriage rituals there is no such officiant. Such provisions, however, do not really compromise the state's policy that marriages be entered into with some formality and deliberation, but instead effectuate that policy in the face of the diverse ways in which religious communities organize their formal and deliberative rituals.

The most interesting cases, of course, are those in which it is not entirely apparent how an exemption relates conceptually to the underlying legal norm. For example, the federal Humane Slaughter Act purports on its face to spell out two equivalent and equally acceptable modes of animal slaughter, either by rendering the animal unconscious before killing it, or "by slaughtering in accordance with the ritual requirements of the Jewish faith or any other religious faith that prescribes a method of slaughter whereby the animal suffers loss of consciousness by anemia of the brain . . . ." This textual equivalence reflects the fact that Jewish and similar methods of slaughter were themselves designed to be humane. A puzzle remains, however, why, if the two methods are truly equivalent, permission for the second would be limited to the "ritual" context.

The number, breadth, and variety of religious exemptions contained in federal and state statutes suggests some important conclusions about the place of religion in the American legal imagination. Over the years, some commentators have suggested that the Religion Clauses of the First Amendment bar any or at least most classifications based on religion. Indeed, there is a strain of discomfort with apparent religious discrimination that goes back to colonial times and continues in the Supreme Court's emphasis on the principle of "neutrality" in both its Free Exercise and Establishment Clause cases. In a small number of cases, lower courts have held exemption statutes unconstitutional when they are drafted so as to protect only certain named religions or only "recognized religions." More famously, the Supreme Court, in its conscientious exemption decisions in the 1960s, stretched the language of the law to encompass persons whose beliefs played a role in their lives functionally equivalent to that of religion, and suggested that a more literal reading would pose problems under the Establishment Clause. Nevertheless, beyond these few counter-instances, statutory religion-based exemptions have generally been upheld, and the

Supreme Court has made clear, in cases such as *Corporation of the Presiding Bishop of the Church of Jesus Christ of Latter-Day Saints v. Amos* (1987) and *Cutter v. Wilkinson*, and even in its decision in *Employment Division v. Smith*, that legislatures are entitled to go beyond formal equality and neutrality to take into account the distinctive normative dilemmas facing adherents of certain faiths and the unique character of religion and religious communities more generally.

Beyond the concern for equality and neutrality, however, lies a deeper jurisprudential puzzle. In *Reynolds v. United States*, the Court held not only that the Free Exercise Clause did not protect religious polygamists from the enforcement of antibigamy statutes, but that recognizing such a right would "in effect . . . permit every citizen to become a law unto himself." Some 110 years later, in *Smith*, the Court quoted this language approvingly and went on to state that recognizing a right to religion-based exemptions in the Free Exercise Clause would create a "constitutional anomaly." These statements suggest that a general doctrine of constitutionally required religion-based exemptions, particularly those that depend on the religious beliefs of specific claimants, would not only be wrong in the Court's view, but would violate the rule of law itself. The puzzle, of course, is why exemptions violate the rule of law if required by courts as a constitutional right, but not if enacted by legislatures as a statutory entitlement. The tension here might reflect problems with the Court's Free Exercise doctrine. It might also, however, suggest a particular legislative capacity, not only to respect religious conscience but to recognize, in an almost political sense, the diversity and juridical dignity of nonstate normative perspectives.

To underscore this point, consider one last example: the New Jersey Declaration of Death Act requires that individuals be declared dead if they have "sustained irreversible cessation of all functions of the entire brain," but makes an exception for persons whose religious beliefs would require the more traditional cardiorespiratory definition of death. The question arises whose rights this provision is protecting. In a sense, it cannot be the individual in question, since the state would otherwise consider him or her dead. Nor is it even the person's next of kin, since it is his or her religious views and not theirs that are dispositive. The answer might be that the state is deferring, not so much to the rights of an individual, but to the legitimacy of a normative system alongside its own.

PERRY DANE

References and Further Reading

Dane, Perry, *'Omalous' Autonomy*, Brigham Young University Law Review 2004 (2004): 5:1715.

Kurland, Philip B. *Religion and the Law: Of Church and State and the Supreme Court.* Chicago: Aldine, 1962.

Lupu, Ira C., *Reconstructing the Establishment Clause: The Case Against Discretionary Accommodation of Religion,* University of Pennsylvania Law Review 140 (1991): 555, 580–609.

McConnell, Michael W., *The Origins and Historical Understanding of Free Exercise of Religion,* Harvard Law Review 103 (1990): 1409–1517.

Newsom, Michael deHaven, *Some Kind of Religious Freedom: National Prohibition and the Volstead Act's Exemption for the Religious Use of Wine,* Brooklyn Law Review 70 (2005): 739.

Cases and Statutes Cited

City of Boerne v. Flores, 521 U.S. 507 (1997)

Corporation of the Presiding Bishop of the Church of Jesus Christ of Latter-day Saints v. Amos, 483 U.S. 327, 340 (1987)

Cutter v. Wilkinson, 125 S.Ct. 2113 (2005)

Employment Division, Dept. of Human Resources v. Smith, 494 U.S. 872 (1990)

Humane Slaughter Act, 7 U.S.C. 1901–1906

New Jersey Declaration of Death Act, N.J. Stat. sec. 26:6A-5 (2006)

Religious Freedom Restoration Act, 42 U.S.C. 2000bb to 2000bb-4

Religious Land Use and Institutionalized Persons Act, 42 U.S.C. 2000cc to 2000cc-5

Reynolds v. United States, 98 U.S. 145, 167 (1879)

Sherbert v. Verner, 374 U.S. 398 (1963)

See also **Establishment of Religion and Free Exercise Clauses;** *Employment Division, Department of Human Resources v. Smith,* **494 U.S. 872 (1990); Establishment Clause Doctrine: Supreme Court Jurisprudence; Free Exercise Clause Doctrine: Supreme Court Jurisprudence; Religious Freedom in the Military; Religious Freedom Restoration Act; Religious Land Use and Institutionalized Persons Act of 2000**

EXPATRIATION

Expatriation is the voluntary relinquishment of nationality and allegiance. In this context, nationality is more or less synonymous with citizenship, and allegiance means the multifaceted bond joining citizen and state. Not surprisingly for a country born in rebellion, the United States has always recognized a right of allegiance transfer on the part of those becoming Americans. However, it was not until after passage of the Fourteenth Amendment that Congress first acknowledged the right of Americans to forsake U.S. citizenship.

Thereafter, the critical question became whether the government might unilaterally strip nationality, as a punishment or otherwise. Beginning with the act of March 3, 1865, Congress asserted authority to treat certain actions (desertion and draft evasion) as evidence of an American's intent to abandon U.S. allegiance. In the Expatriation Act of 1907, Congress made loss of American nationality the automatic consequence of either naturalization elsewhere or a pledge of foreign allegiance. In the same statute, Congress declared that whenever a naturalized American returned to his or her homeland and resided there for two years it proved an intent to abandon U.S. nationality, and that any American woman forfeited her nationality by marrying a foreigner. Shortly thereafter, a native Californian who had married a British subject permanently residing in California was refused registration as a California voter on the grounds that she was no longer a U.S. citizen. Her appeal of that judgment failed when the U.S. Supreme Court in *Mackenzie v. Hare* (1915) accepted that Congress could make marriage to a foreigner an irrefutable presumption of the bride's expatriating intent. Congress repealed the provision for denationalization by marriage in 1922, but in the Nationality Act of 1940, added to the list of acts evidencing expatriation voting in a foreign election, service in the armed forces or government of a foreign power, and treason against the United States. Then, in the Expatriation Act of 1954, Congress added attempting by force to overthrow the government of the United States, advocating such an attempt, and participating in a seditious conspiracy. Four years later, in *Perez v. Brownell* (1958), the Supreme Court upheld the denationalization of a native Texan who had admitted sojourning in Mexico to avoid military service, and, while there, voting in political elections. That he denied any intention of renouncing his American nationality was immaterial. By the mid-twentieth century, therefore, Congress was confident that the Constitution allowed it to unilaterally denationalize, and the Supreme Court agreed.

But the Court soon changed its mind, declaring in *Trop v. Dulles* (1958) that, even if Congress had the power to denationalize, it could not do so as a sanction for wartime desertion without violating the Eighth Amendment's prohibition of cruel and unusual punishments. A decade later, in *Afroyim v. Rusk* (1967), the Court held unconstitutional the government's refusal to renew a naturalized American's U.S. passport because he had voted in an Israeli election. Overruling *Perez,* the Court struck down the relevant section of the Nationality Act on the grounds that for all those "born or naturalized in the United States," nationality is conferred by the Constitution itself and cannot be revoked by ordinary legislation. In 1980, the Court ruled in *Vance v. Terrazas* (1980) that, to establish expatriation, the government had to prove by a preponderance of the evidence that an American specifically intended to forsake U.S. nationality. Under the Constitution today, therefore, expatriation is the only lawful form of denationalization, and an American's intention in this regard cannot be established simply by the drawing by Congress of an inference from an act, however incompatible Congress might find that act with continued allegiance.

Only those born in the United States and those, who having first immigrated to the United States have completed the process of naturalization, are citizens in the constitutional sense of *Afroyim* and *Terranzas*. Children born abroad to American citizens, for example, enjoy American nationality not as a constitutional right but as the consequence of an act of Congress. Whether such "statutory" Americans are also constitutionally protected from involuntary denationalization remains an open question.

JOHN PAUL JONES

References and Further Reading

Aleinikoff, T. Alexander, *Theories of Loss of Citizenship*, University of Michigan Law Review 84 (1986): 1471.

Boudin, Leonard B., *Involuntary Loss of American Nationality*, Harvard Law Review 73 (1960): 1510.

Gordon, Charles, *The Citizen and the State: Power of Congress to Expatriate American Citizens*, Georgetown Law Journal 53 (1965): 315.

Jones, J.P., *Limiting Congressional Denationalization after Afroyim*, University of San Diego Law Review 17 (1979): 121.

Roche, John. P., *The Loss of American Citizenship—The Development of Statutory Expatriation*, University of Pennsylvania Law Review 99 (1950): 25.

U.S. Department of Justice, Office of Legal Counsel. *Survey of the Law of Expatriation* (June 12, 2002). http://www.usdoj.gov/olc/expatriation.htm.

Cases and Statutes Cited

Afroyim v. Rusk, 387 U.S. 253 (1967)
Mackenzie v. Hare, 239 U.S. 299 (1915)
Perez v. Brownell, 356 U.S. 44 (1958)
Trop v. Dulles, 356 U.S. 66 (1958)
Vance v. Terranzas, 444 U.S. 252 (1980)

See also Citizenship

EXTRADITION

Extradition is the process through which an individual held by one country is transferred to another country to face criminal prosecution or serve a criminal sentence. In the United States, extradition is possible only pursuant to a valid extradition treaty; in the absence of such a treaty, the government has neither the right to demand extradition of an individual from a country nor the right or obligation to extradite an individual to that country. The United States has valid extradition treaties with most countries; notable exceptions include Afghanistan, Russia, Saudi Arabia, and China.

There are two substantive requirements for extradition. First, the offense for which extradition is requested must be an extraditable offense under the relevant treaty. Most extradition treaties include an exhaustive list of extraditable offenses. Others provide that all offenses of a certain severity—those that qualify as felonies, for example—are extraditable.

Second, the offense for which extradition is sought must be criminal under the laws of both the United States and the other country. This "dual criminality" requirement is designed to ensure that extradition is granted only for offenses that are considered serious by both countries.

Even if these requirements are met, there are a number of exceptions to extradition. The most controversial is what is known as the "political offense" exception, which prohibits the United States and its extradition partners from extraditing individuals whose offenses were either directed specifically at the government, such as treason and espionage, or involved a common crime like murder that was "so connected with a political act that the entire offense is regarded as political." Courts have used the political offense exception, for example, to refuse to extradite members of the Irish Republican Army (IRA) to the United Kingdom.

The nature of the applicable punishment can also serve as a ground for denying extradition. A number of treaties preclude extradition for offenses for which the requesting country can impose the death penalty. Such a provision permitted France to refuse to extradite Ira Einhorn, the "Unicorn Killer," to the United States until U.S. authorities promised not to execute him if convicted. (He was finally extradited to the United States in July 2001 to face trial for a 1977 murder.)

Individuals in the United States for whom extradition is sought are entitled to a hearing before a neutral magistrate. The magistrate's only responsibility, however, is to determine whether the charged offense is extraditable under the relevant treaty and, if it is, whether there is probable cause to believe the individual committed the offense. The extradition hearing is not a full trial; the normal rules of evidence do not apply, and the individual does not have an absolute right to confront the witnesses against him, call his own witnesses, or even introduce evidence that contradicts the prosecution's evidence. Moreover, the magistrate cannot take into account the treatment that the individual will receive in the requesting country.

If the magistrate determines that the individual is extraditable, the secretary of state retains the authority to deny extradition, and can deny extradition on humanitarian grounds. If the magistrate determines that the individual is not extraditable, however, the secretary cannot reverse the magistrate's decision.

KEVIN JON HELLER

References and Further Reading

Bassiouini, M. Cherif. *International Extradition: United States Law and Practice.* New York: Oceana Publications, 2002.

Bush, Jonathan A., *How Did We Get Here? Foreign Abduction After* Alvarez-Machain, *Stanford Law Review* 45 (1993): 3:939–83.

EXTREMIST GROUPS AND CIVIL LIBERTIES

The people of this nation have a great deal to be proud of and to celebrate. At holiday celebrations, the media is ready with hyperbolic words that praise this nation. And why not? The spectacular rise from a barely occupied wilderness to the most powerful nation on Earth in a remarkably short period of time is amazing and worthy of praise.

This was to be a nation built on the labor of many races and a variety of religions; a county that can build anything and everything; who believed in capitalism and not in kings; a nation that votes and accepts change through elections. All of these qualities and more are part of the American national heritage. Less known and not celebrated is this fact: since the formation of colonies, this nation has demonstrated a streak of intolerance, xenophobia, and violence that continues to this time. It can be argued that at every stage of American development, one finds examples of extremist groups in operation.

An example can be seen in religious groups or splinter groups who demonstrate fanaticism. During the 176 years of colonial status, there were instances of violence and extreme measures taken in most colonies against Catholics, Jews, Quakers, and within competing Protestant sects. Before 1692, there were forty-four witchcraft trials and during 1692, there were three hangings in Massachusetts alone. As the fanaticism died down, some 150 prisoners accused of witchcraft were released by the end of the year. One difference between European witchcraft and colonial practices was that in Europe, those found guilty of alleged heresy were burned at the stake, while colonials found guilty of being witches or possessed of the devil, were hung.

Examples of religious intolerance during the colonial period included the banishment of Roger Williams because he rejected the right of civil authorities to legislate in matters of conscience. He and his followers had to flee the Massachusetts Colony or risk persecution. From the Salem witch trials through Mormon battles to exist in a hostile religious climate, one finds terror and violence used against various religious groups.

Beyond extremist groups that took violent action against small, generally vulnerable religious persons and groups, there were extremist groups who persecuted people because of their race. The history of the Ku Klux Klan after the Civil War demonstrates the use of murder, lynching, torture, and other extreme measures to prevent black people from exercising their newly found freedoms.

Even the passage into constitutional law of three amendments initially aimed at empowering blacks could not stop the overwhelming power of extremist groups in the South from having their way. The Thirteenth, Fourteenth, and Fifteenth Amendments to the Constitution (as well as additional specific laws) did not stop extremist groups from using terror and acts of violence against blacks, Asians, and Native Americans.

Another manifestation of extremists was the vigilante movement that appeared mainly in the last decades of the nineteenth century and into the early twentieth century. They claimed that the regular justice system was not working to their liking (too slow, too sympathetic to defendants). This led various extremist groups of vigilantes to hold their own "courts" and mete out punishments (including death) to those caught in their net.

In all of these instances of extremist acts, there is a continuing question that seems to be insoluble: what should a nation, through its representatives, its executive, and its system of law do when confronted by one or more organizations that reject the sovereignty of the nation over them? The challenge thrown up by extremists groups is to assert that the national government had failed to adequately act to protect its citizens. Note that this was before September 11, 2001. The obverse can also be seen in hate groups that refuse to admit that the government has any right to control their lives, tax them, or educate them. Frequently the message was bundled with one of racial hatred and religious violence. It was and still is a classic case of safety versus freedom. How much freedom are we (as a nation) willing to give up for safety?

This nation, as is true of many others in the early twenty-first century, has to cope with a new enemy: terrorists. These terrorists come from extremist groups that differ from the long line of earlier extremists in that they seek to win their goals through fear—paralyzing fear of violence emanating from religious, political, and cultural extremists willing to *destroy themselves* in order to destroy the lives of masses of people and public institutions. They are religious, political, and cultural fanatics beyond anything this and other nations have seen in modern times. They pose a continuing threat to the relatively open boundaries of Western democracies, and they are able to hide behind the existence of their fellow countrymen, who while they may have no involvement in these extremist plans with deadly aims, carry the color of skin and difference in religion as makers of a potential enemy. To date, there have been few instances of actively branding the innocent as an answer to how to identify the truly radical and dangerous. The question is how long will this be the case?

Because so much has changed since September 11, 2001, the need to confront how the nation and its leadership should deal with extremists is crucial.

The existence of extremist groups currently demands that our nation continually evaluate how we should react to these killers and terrorists. Are these murderers entitled to enter the American justice system? Should they be given the protection of the rights under First Amendment and other amendments? All of these issues present the ultimate issue of how we preserve our freedoms at the same time as we effectively protect our citizens and the safety of our national infrastructure.

One clue as to how to deal with extremists is to study the history of extremists in this country. In that history we note that in the twentieth century, extremists organized around leaders who preached hatred of minorities and encouraged the formation of militia-type members. They claimed that their enemy (among others) was the federal government, considered to be under "Zionist control." One response of these hate groups included moving to relatively open and empty territory, such as in Montana and Utah, where they could practice their beliefs and claim their right to challenge the right of any government over them. The 1980s and 1990s were times of concern in law enforcement circles that extremist groups also targeted violence against law officers and judges.

Three major incidents occurred that explain changes in extremist groups compared to before 9/11/01: the Ruby Ridge shootout, the Waco standoff, and the Oklahoma City bombing of a federal building in 1995; 168 people were killed in the Oklahoma bombing.

September 11 overwhelmed all instances of domestic violence until that time except the earlier bombing of the Twin Towers in 1993, which introduced foreign terrorists. Three thousand people were killed as a result of the Twin Towers attack in Manhattan. This crime was committed by Muslim extremist groups. This terrible event created a demarcation point in what has turned out to be a war against extremist groups by the government. Military action in Afghanistan and Iraq followed. What was announced as a war to overthrow the dictatorship became a terrorist plan of destruction against the U.S. presence in Iraq and Afghanistan.

Compare 9/11/01 to what happened in Ruby Ridge, Utah. In brief, a warrant had been issued to be served by the U.S. Marshals Service upon a resident in this area. Armed with what have been called illegal "shoot-to-kill" orders, a firefight took place as the occupants attempted to resist the service of the federal warrant, leaving two dead. Although the ties of those involved to radical causes and groups was less than clearly established, the killings became the rallying cry for extremists who, for religious, political, or racial hate reasons used what happened as proof that the federal government was out to destroy their extremist group.

Three years after Ruby Ridge, in 1995, two American citizens, Timothy McVeigh and Terry Nichols, plotted the destruction of the Alfred R. Murrah federal building as revenge for the events of Waco; the plot climaxed in an act of terror on the second anniversary of Waco. Both McVeigh and Nichols were followers of extremist groups. Until 9/11/01, the McVeigh and Nichols action was the deadliest attack on American soil. McVeigh believed that his act of destruction of lives and property would be the opening call for all rightwing extremist organizations to rise up in revolution against the national government.

Preceding McVeigh were other "lone-wolf" actors including William Krar, a white supremacist who was arrested having in his possession enough sodium cyanide to kill 6,000 people. Another was Eric Rudolph, a domestic terrorist who killed people in an abortion clinic and at the 1996 summer Olympics.

One of the results of the Oklahoma bombing was actually a decline in domestic terrorists, "lone wolves," or extremist organizations. But those who study these movements warned what while the number of those involved in rightwing (as well as leftwing extremist groups) have diminished, the hard-core believers are still there. They point to neo-Nazis, white supremacists, and Christian identity groups that are still functioning. They advise that while the number of militia groups has dropped from 900 (prior to Oklahoma bombing) to 150, homegrown haters and hate groups are still there—and dangerous.

Since 9/11/01, we are a different nation. To gain an appreciation of this assertion, consider the following.

The presence of extremists in groups and in "lone-wolf" attacks has been a part of American culture since colonial days. There has been an apparent relationship between the openness of American society and the extremes of totalitarian extremism. The use of violence by extremists is a method of taking control into one's own hands, and has been directed to the production of fear: Where will they strike next?

The nineteenth and twentieth centuries contained many forms of extremism. Until 9/11/01, these forms of extremism have come from white, Protestant individuals and groups and were intended to implant fear into minority groups—or as a control device to keep blacks and other racial or religious minorities from asserting their constitutional rights.

The national government has from time to time used extremist tactics to attack those who were considered dangerous. Examples are the destruction of the Industrial Workers of the World (Wobblies); the use of troops to break strikes; and the first red scare (1918–1920) and the second (1946–1957) that played on the paranoia regarding communists or leftists as dangerous to the existence of the country.

Extremism is found in the left as well as the right in the political spectrum. John Brown fits into the category of leading extremists. Certain groups of environmentalists and animal rights groups can be seen as current extremists of the left.

The planning to destroy large numbers of people and a country's economy takes advantage of the openness of borders as well as public transportation. Most of the planning can take place thousands of miles away from the targets.

The ability to kill people and harm a nation's infrastructure with little chance to catch or to stop the terrorist act is a reality because members of the extremist group frequently intend to kill themselves as a sacrifice to the "cause."

Until 9/11/01, most people in the United States neither understood nor cared about the Muslim religion. Certain Muslim extremists hate Western nations and particularly the United States, believing that this nation has and will continue to corrupt and weaken their culture. They also believe that the aim of the United States and their allies is to conquer Muslim nations for their oil.

Not one nation openly supports the Muslim fanatics; instead, bands of these fighters "float" from one nation to another. They seem to have an endless number of men, women, and children ready to sacrifice their lives for their religious cause. This is a technique that the United States and its allies have not seen prior to 9/11/01.

Brutalities such as beheading are used against anyone they consider an enemy, and at times for no valid reason but to promote fear in countries where such behavior is neither understood nor acceptable. Some countries have already bent to the will of fanatic groups to avoid the relentless war being waged, thus rejecting American leadership in the war against fanatics.

In the words of Benjamin Franklin, "They that give up essential liberty in order to obtain a little temporary safety deserve neither liberty nor safety." This statement may no longer be entirely valid. Certainly it is subject to challenge: a little "temporary safety" in the sense Franklin made this statement is no longer possible in today's world. Oceans, mountain ranges, densely populated cities and industrial areas, as well as buildings of every kind have proven to be no barrier to terrorists.

There has been (thus far) an absence of suicides in domestic extremist groups but there seems to be no feasible way of providing the safety that Franklin addressed, especially if airlines, ships, trains, shopping malls, among many other possibilities, may become effective targets for suicidal terrorists. The slide down the slippery slope of restricting liberties seems to afford at least the appearance of "doing something" to respond effectively to the threat posed by these extremists.

The red scares that followed World Wars I and II yielded legislation aimed at ensuring the loyalty of its citizens. Action was taken against those whose beliefs were not orthodox. Aliens were shipped out of the country. Criminal legal procedures were taken against alleged subversives.

With the collapse of Soviet Russia, the cold war seemed to yield a period of peaceful times; 9/11/01 shattered that peace. Terrorists were actually trained in this country to fly large aircraft, and turned that skill into opportunities for death and destruction.

Looking back at the red scare years, there was not a single instance of any communist having a cache of arms, military training, bombing, or attempt to use suicide terrorists on targets. What they were most guilty of was their beliefs. On the other hand, such rightwing groups as the National Alliance, Aryan Nations, and Creativity Movement were frequently trained in armed conduct. They gathered weapons with the goal of creating some sort of revolution. They carried out armed actions; between 1995 and 2005, fifteen law enforcement officers were killed by these antigovernment fanatic groups. Still, however, there was no realistic chance that they would even successfully mount an attempt to kill masses of people or disrupt the nation. When threats became possible, they came from *outside the nation.*

The response of the administration that came in the wake of the successful killing of some 3,000 people as well as destroying the Twin Towers, was to rush through Congress with little or no dissent, a law commonly called the USA Patriotic Act. The basic idea was to give law enforcement agencies powerful tools with which to respond to the terrorist act of 9/11/01, and to stop further acts of violence against this nation.

As the act rushed through Congress, there was little thought given to the civil rights issues involved, although there was a section of the law that expressed the sense that all Americans, including Arab Americans, must be protected.

The heart of the act was to direct and authorize actions against those who might attempt attacks on Americans and the American infrastructure. To a significant extent, the Patriot Act set aside restrictions as to what the federal government could do that the government could not do since 1976. The Federal Bureau of Investigation (FBI) has used bugging devices, letter opening, invasion of offices and homes, infiltration of domestic organizations, and many other illegal or extralegal acts. Hoover died in 1972 and there followed a wide-ranging congressional committee whose work revealed abuse of power by Hoover and his FBI. These restrictions, coming out of a congressional committee's work, allowed the government to once again use these powers and techniques. Additionally, this means that the FBI can monitor groups and public meetings, and the Internet. The FBI could even send undercover agents to suspected houses of worship.

As of this writing, the effectiveness of those operating under the umbrella of the Patriot Act remains to be seen. That the act (most of it permanent as of early 2006) raises important issues of infringement of civil rights seems evident. Secret trials, hidden detainees, torture, and profiling are intended to break the will of those who seek to sway history through terror. In the case of aliens alleged to be terrorists, it appears that no concern for their civil rights limits our government. Intrusions and detentions are the price these people pay as the nation continually seeks out its enemies. Only time will answer the question of whether the nation has gone too far to ensure its safety against extremists. Perhaps the times have been so catastrophic in scope that the Patriot Act as well as other measures will justify the curtailment of civil rights and liberties. The march of history will eventually answer.

ARTHUR J. SABIN

EYEWITNESS IDENTIFICATION

Police investigation often entails interviewing those who were eyewitnesses to an offense, attaining a description of the culprit, and then later presenting a suspect or suspects to the eyewitness in a lineup or other identification procedure. Lineups, also known as identification parades in Britain, involve a corporeal identification procedure where persons appear before the witness. In a lineup, the witness reviews those who have been assembled and determines whether the culprit is among them. In a photo spread, a noncorporeal identification procedure, an array of photos is placed before the witness. In a show-up identification procedure, which may be corporeal or noncorporeal, the witness is presented with a single individual rather than several, and thus has no others to select from or compare. During a lineup or show-up, persons may be asked to move about or speak so that the eyewitness may use memory of action or speech as well as appearance to make an identification.

Many social scientists and judges believe that erroneous identification testimony is one of the leading causes of wrongful convictions. All eyewitness identification procedures are tests of recognition memory, seeking a match between the memory of the perpetrator and the person presented. Eyewitness identification actually engages three tasks: perception of the original perpetrator, storage in memory, and retrieval from memory. Psychologists studying the fallibility of each task have made suggestions to improve the reliability of eyewitness identification. Error may arise when the witness selects an individual who is the best match, even if that match is not perfect. A sequential lineup presenting one person at a time and attaining a yes or no decision for each minimizes the likelihood of such comparative or relative judgments, and is recommended by the American Psychology/Law Society (AP/LS). Informing the eyewitness that the perpetrator may not be present further reduces comparative judgment. As police conducting the identification procedure may communicate their own view that they have apprehended the right person and pressure the witness, the AP/LS also recommends a double-blind procedure where those administering the procedure are not aware which person is the suspect.

Since 1967, the Supreme Court has overseen procedures in an effort to reduce unreliability and the likelihood of convicting the innocent. Motions to suppress or exclude possibly mistaken eyewitness identification testimony rely on varying constitutional arguments. If an illegal detention or arrest violating the defendant's Fourth Amendment prohibition against unreasonable seizure preceded the identification procedure, testimony regarding the out-of-court procedure will be excluded as a fruit of the poisonous tree, and possibly also the in-court identification (*United States v. Crews* [1980]). Lineup participants who are ordered to repeat the words used by the culprit during the crime are not denied their Fifth Amendment privilege against self-incrimination as this is not a testimonial communication (*United States v. Wade* [1967]). However, the Sixth Amendment right to assistance of counsel does attach when a defendant appears in a lineup after the criminal prosecution has begun, and denial of counsel will require exclusion of some identification testimony (*Wade*). When suggestive procedures of any type create a substantial likelihood of misidentification, due process will require exclusion of all identification testimony from the witness (*Manson v. Brathwaite* [1977]).

MARGERY M. KOOSED

References and Further Reading

Borchard, E.M. *Convicting the Innocent: Sixty-Five Actual Errors of Criminal Justice*. New Haven, CT: Yale University Press, 1932.

Gross, Samuel H., *Loss of Innocence: Eyewitness Identification and Proof of Guilt*, Journal of Legal Studies 16 (1987): 395–493.

Judges, Donald P., *Two Cheers for the Department of Justice's Eyewitness Evidence: A Guide for Law Enforcement*, Arkansas Law Review 53 (2000): 231–297.

Koosed, Margery M., *The Proposed Innocence Protection Act Won't—Unless It Also Curbs Mistaken Eyewitness Identifications*, Ohio State Law Journal 63 (2002): 263–314.

Rattner, Arye, *Convicted but Innocent: Wrongful Convictions and the Criminal Justice System*, Law and Human Behavior 12 (1988): 283–93.

U.S. Department of Justice. *Eyewitness Evidence: A Guide for Law Enforcement* (1999). http://www.ncjrs.org/txtfiles1/nij/178240.txt.

Wells, Gary L., Mark Small, Steven Penrod, Roy S. Mulpass, Solomon M. Fulero, and C.A.E. Brimacombe, *Eyewitness Identification Procedures: Recommendations for Lineups and Photospreads*, Law and Human Behavior 22 (1998): 603–647.

Cases and Statutes Cited

Manson v. Brathwaite, 430 U.S. 98 (1977)
United States v. Crews, 445 U.S. 463 (1980)
United States v. Wade, 388 U.S. 218 (1967)

See also **Due Process; Lineups; Right to Counsel**

FAIR CREDIT REPORTING ACT, 84 STAT. 1127 (1970)

The collection, compilation, and dissemination of consumer credit information in reports ("consumer reports") is not a recent development. The first credit reporting agency (CRA), Retail Credit Company, began compiling consumer reports as early as 1899. Today, the consumer credit reporting industry is dominated by three major companies, Experian, Equifax (the descendant of Retail Credit Company), and Trans Union. Together, these three CRAs hold records on more than 200 million consumers and provide crucial economic information to lenders, retailers, and employers in millions of transactions every day. Indeed, it is difficult, if not impossible, to imagine our economy without them or the thousands of others.

Despite the obvious importance and value of CRAs, they also have the potential to affect the privacy and livelihood of millions of Americans. Over time, poor collection and dissemination practices by CRAs resulted in real dangers to individual privacy. By the 1960s, consumer reports not only tracked credit history but many also included personal information, including sexual orientation, drinking habits, and even cleanliness. Compounding these problems were the lax disclosure practices many CRAs used—making consumer reports available to almost anyone willing to pay a fee. In addition, many of these consumer reports were highly inaccurate—containing obsolete, incomplete, or even fraudulent data. Finally, CRAs policies made it virtually impossible for consumer to see or correct their own consumer reports.

Out of this mess Congress passed the Fair Credit Reporting Act (FCRA) of 1970. Congress' intent in passing FCRA was to address the most important problems associated with CRAs' past practices. In particular, FCRA addressed the two major areas of abuse: (1) dissemination of consumer reports to unauthorized parties and (2) creation of inaccurate, false, incomplete, or obsolete consumer reports. In addressing these problems, FCRA created a complex regulatory framework that imposes obligations on CRAs and provides rights and remedies to consumers. This important legislation, therefore, represents the first attempt by Congress to protect individual privacy from the intrusive and, at times, abusive practices of private industry.

FCRA created a very broad definition of CRA, encompassing any entity that regularly prepares and disseminates consumer reports. As a result, bill collection agencies, cable companies, banks, and even universities have been held to be CRAs. Congress also insisted on a broad definition of consumer report—defining it to include any report that "touches" on an individual's creditworthiness, credit standing, credit capacity, character, general reputation, personal characteristics, or modes of living.

Under FCRA, CRAs are required to enact "reasonable procedures to assure maximum possible accuracy" in consumer report information. Among the steps CRAs must take are: (1) removing inaccurate or obsolete data on notice or discovery; (2) informing consumers of adverse actions taken as a result of a consumer report; (3) allowing consumers to challenge the accuracy, currency, or completeness of information contained in consumer reports; and (4) removing or changing challenged data that cannot be confirmed within a reasonable period of time. Finally, CRAs are prohibited from disclosing consumer reports for anything other than a "permissible purpose." Permissible purposes include, among others, requests for reports to employers (with consent), as part of an application for credit, or to allow financial institutions to review the creditworthiness of current customers.

CRAs are also required to make consumer reports available to consumers for review and correction. Prior to 2003, the provision of reports was only required in two circumstances: (1) on request and for a fee or (2) when an adverse action has been taken based on the report. In 2003, Congress amended FCRA with passage of the Fair and Accurate Credit Transactions Act (FACTA). Among the many changes made to FCRA, this latest amendment now requires all the three major CRAs to provide a copy of a consumer's report, without fee, once a year on request.

Unlike many privacy and consumer protection laws, FCRA authorizes private lawsuits. Injured consumers may sue for economic and punitive damages. Criminal prosecutions may be brought against both CRAs and those who fraudulently obtain consumer reports. These robust remedial provisions have led many individuals to sue CRAs and users of consumer reports for damages caused by inaccurate information and unauthorized disclosures. In addition, the Federal Trade Commission has been active in enforcing FCRA's provisions—mostly recently obtaining a $2.5 million settlement from the major CRAs based on their sale of consumer reports to advertisers and marketers (*Trans Union v. FTC* [2001]).

In the decades since its passage, FCRA has required various amendments to capture the current practices and capabilities of CRAs. The most fundamental change in consumer reports has been the creation of "credit scores." Credit scores (using proprietary formulas created by CRAs) have become more important for assessing the creditworthiness of consumers than the consumer reports on which they are based. Yet FCRA, in its original formulation, does not govern credit scores. In 2003, Congress amended FCRA to require disclosure of credit scores, including explanations of their use, for a fee. As consumer reports become increasingly important in a credit-rich and electronic market, we may assume that FCRA will be amended again. Indeed, FCRA has recently been amended by the USA Patriot Act to give law enforcement greater access to credit and financial information.

DOUGLAS J. SYLVESTER

References and Further Reading

Cate, Fred H., *et al. Financial Privacy, Consumer Prosperity, and the Public Good.* Washington D.C.: Brookings Institution Press, 2003.
FTC Commentary on FCRA, 16 C.F.R. Part 600.
Maurer, Virginia G., *Common Law Defamation and the Fair Credit Reporting Act.* Georgetown Law Journal 72 (1983): 95–134.
Smith, H. J. *Managing Privacy: Information Technology and Corporate America.* Chapel Hill: University of North Carolina Press, 1994.
Westin, Alan F. *Privacy and Freedom.* New York: Atheneum, 1967.

Cases and Statutes Cited

Fair and Accurate Credit Transaction Act of Dec. 4, 2003, 111 Stat. 1952
Fair Credit Reporting Act of Oct. 26, 1970, c. 41, 84 Stat. 1127
Trans Union v. FTC, 245 F.3d 809 (D.C. Cir. 2001), *cert. denied*, 536 U.S. 915 (2002)
Uniting and Strengthening America by Providing Appropriate Tools Required to Intercept and Obstruct Terrorism ("USA PATRIOT Act"), Act of Oct. 26, 2001, 115 Stat. 272

See also **Congressional Protection of Privacy; 9/11 and the War on Terrorism; Privacy; Terrorism and Civil Liberties**

FAIR LABOR STANDARDS ACT AND RELIGION

Religious institutions usually are subject to laws of general applicability. A particularly contentious situation involves the interplay between one such generally applicable law, the federal Fair Labor Standards Act, providing minimum wage and overtime premium pay to employees, and religiously affiliated institutions operating as employers of largely secular enterprises. The government and/or the employees contend that the employees are entitled to the FLSA rights and protections. Meanwhile, the religiously affiliated employer contends that the workers are volunteers, or, because the enterprise is related to the social justice ministry of the religion, its employment practices are exempt from the FLSA by First Amendment separation of church and state and free exercise principles.

The landmark United States Supreme Court decision governing these disputes is *Tony and Susan Alamo Found. v. Secretary of Labor.*

In *Tony and Susan Alamo Found*, the Supreme Court unanimously affirmed the decision of the Eighth Circuit that the Fair Labor Standards Act, the federal minimum wage law, protected persons used in the commercial enterprises of religious foundations.

This particular application of federal wage law did not violate the free exercise rights of the employees and did not constitute excessive entanglements of the government with the religious foundation. Because the Foundation had thoroughly involved itself in operating business commercial enterprises, it had effectively deprived itself of the mantle of religious exemption and immunity from compliance as an employer with the federal minimum wage law.

The Alamo Foundation was a nonprofit religious organization. Its proclaimed mission was Christian evangelism and active corporal works of mercy to disadvantaged persons. The Foundation derived its income from operating a variety of commercial businesses, including service stations, retail clothing and grocery outlets, hog farms, roofing and electrical construction companies, a record-keeping company, a motel, and companies engaged in the production and distribution of candy. These businesses were staffed largely by the Foundation's unpaid associates. They received clothing, room, and board but no cash wages in return for their services.

Other than its peculiar nonwage practices, for all practical purposes the Foundation was substantially equivalent, in its day-to-day operations, with other secular employers. The fact that the workers of the religious foundation considered themselves charitable volunteers serving their religion, and not employees within the meaning of the FLSA, was not determinative.

The Court deemphasized the free exercise elements of the case and, instead, highlighted the federal wage law issues because of the pervasive commercial nature of the Foundation's various business enterprises.

The free exercise clause of the First Amendment does not require an exemption from a governmental program unless, at a minimum, inclusion in the program actually burdens the freedom to exercise religious rights. Application of the FLSA to the foundation workers who were engaged in commercial ventures did not violate the workers' free exercise rights under the First Amendment, because they remained free to donate their FLSA-mandated wages back to the Alamo Foundation.

Religious organizations do not have carte blanche to exploit persons employed in their commercial ventures. Free exercise claims by those persons, disavowing their labor law and employment rights, are properly unavailing. The Court implicitly recognized the potential coercive influence of religious institutions on their employees, pressuring the workers to assert positions contrary to their legal rights.

Since the Court's Alamo decision in 1985, several federal circuit courts of appeals have issued decisions in full accord with the Alamo precedent.

In *Reich v. Shiloh True Light Church of Christ*, the court determined that children younger than the age of sixteen employed in the commercial enterprises of a religious institution as part of their religious belief that they should receive vocational training are covered employees under the FLSA. Church youth participated in the Shiloh Vocational Training Program, through which they performed various construction projects. In turn, customers paid the Church for the services performed. Children younger than the age of sixteen did not receive wages for their work. Instead, they received lump sum payments that the Church characterized as gifts. In these situations where free labor is for the supposed benefit of the worker, the general test applied by the courts is whether the employer or the employee is the primary beneficiary of the free labor. Because the Church was the primary beneficiary of the labor, the children were in fact employees and thus entitled to the protections of the FLSA.

Applicability of the FLSA often arises in religiously affiliated schools. *Dole v. Shenandoah Baptist Church* involved application of the FLSA to lay faculty at the Roanoke Valley Christian Schools operated by the Shenandoah Baptist Church. The Church asserted that application of the FLSA would violate both the free exercise and establishment clauses of the First Amendment. The court disagreed, holding that the FLSA applies to church run schools that are enterprises within the meaning of the FLSA. Any minimal free exercise burden was justified by the compelling government interest in enforcing the minimum wage and equal pay provisions of the FLSA. Likewise, in *DeArment v. Harvey*, a church-operated a private religious school was subject to the FLSA. The school used a unique learning technique composed of a self-study program for the students. A supervisor and class monitor assisted the students in their studies. The students themselves were responsible for independent learning, whereas the supervisors graded papers, answered students' questions, conducted prayer services, and counseled students. Both the supervisor and the class monitors were required to be born again Christians, and these employees considered their work an integral component of their personal ministry. However, despite the contention that their employment was part of their religious ideology, the Court applied *Shenandoah*, holding that the FLSA applied to both the class monitors and supervisors. The ministerial exemption of the FLSA is narrowly limited in its application. Clearly, this exception includes ordained clergy, as well as employees essential to carry out particular religious rituals.

In light of the narrow applicability of the ministerial exception, religious organizations engaged in commercial enterprises will usually be deemed employers of employees subject to the FLSA.

DAVID L. GREGORY

References and Further Reading

Gregory, David L., *The First Amendment Religion Clauses and Labor and Employment Law in the Supreme Court, 1984 Term*, New York Law School Law Review 31 (1986): 1.

Miller, Scott D., *Revitalizing the FLSA*, Hofstra Labor and Employment Law Journal 19 (2001): 1.

Rowan, Regan C., *Solving the Bluish Collar Problem: An Analysis of the DOL's Modernization of the Exemptions to the Fair Labor Standards Act*, U. Pennsylvania Journal of Labor and Employment Law 7 (2004): 119.

Cases and Statutes Cited

DeArment v. Harvey, 932 F.2d 721 (8th Cir. 1991)
Dole v. Shenandoah Baptist Church, 899 F.2d 1389 (4th Cir.) cert denied, 498 U.S. 846 (1990)
Fair Labor Standards Act, 29 USC 201 et. seq.
The First Amendment of the United States Constitution
Reich v. Shiloh True Light Church of Christ, 85 F.2d 6161 (4th Cir. 1996)
Tony and Susan Alamo Foundation v. Secretary of Labor, 105 S. Ct. 1953 (1985)

See also **Exemptions for Religion Contained in Regulatory Statutes;** *Tony and Susan Alamo Foundation v. Secretary of Labor***, 471 U.S. 290 (1985)**

FAIR USE DOCTRINE AND FIRST AMENDMENT

A certain tension exists between copyright law and first amendment values. Copyright law has a particularly broad sweep today. It extends to books, creative literature, visual art, photographs, videos, sound recordings, and computer programs. Copyright protection also extends to the "derivative" forms of this work, including translations, performances, and digital reproductions. Even noncommercial use of copyrighted work can be illegal, as when copyrighted music is downloaded on one's home computer.

Conventional wisdom has it that copyright law resolves any first amendment concerns by recognizing two limitations. First, the Copyright Act denies protection to "ideas," "concepts," facts, or "principles" per se and instead protects only their "expression." Second, potential infringers are permitted to make "fair use" of copyrighted material. Because of these two limitations, the first amendment seldom plays a role in suits for copyright infringement. As Justice Ruth Ginsburg has written, existing copyright law contains "built-in free speech safeguards."

The fair use doctrine has been recognized by courts for more than 160 years, although it was not codified by Congress until 1976. The Copyright Act currently permits the fair use of copyrighted work "for purposes such as criticism, comment, news reporting, teaching. . .scholarship, or research." When determining whether a defendant has engaged in fair use of copyrighted work, courts consider four statutory factors. They consider (1) the purpose and character of the defendant's use, including whether the use is commercial or nonprofit; (2) the nature of the copyrighted work; (3) the amount of copyrighted work that has been used; and (4) the effect of the defendant's use on the existing or potential market value of the work. The Supreme Court has emphasized that all these factors are to be weighed together and that no bright-line test exists for achieving this "sensitive balancing of interests."

In recent years, the Court has shown greatest solicitude for "transformative" use of copyrighted work when applying the fair use doctrine. The transformation standard focuses on the extent to which the alleged infringer "adds something new, with a further purpose or different character, altering the first with new expression, meaning, or message." This transformative use of copyrighted material, although not necessary to a fair use defense, lies "at the heart of the fair use doctrine's guarantee of breathing space within the confines of copyright." When the alleged infringer "transforms" copyrighted work, even the infringer's commercial exploitation of the transformed product is unlikely to negate the fair use defense. For example, in *Campbell v. Acuff-Rose Music, Inc.*, the Court found that the rap group "2 Live Crew" had engaged in protected fair use when it parodied the classic Roy Orbison song, "Oh, Pretty Woman" and profited by both recording and performing its parody.

Current law thus achieves a compromise between copyright and First Amendment values. Whether it is a sound compromise is a matter of debate. Professor Rebecca Tushnet, writing in the *Yale Law Journal*, has recently argued that the fair use doctrine protects only one version of first amendment values—a version that esteems the alleged infringer's transformative expression—while ignoring a version that recognizes the value of nontransformative uses like copying. In particular, the fair use doctrine's emphasis on transformative expression is said to ignore the interest of the public audience in gaining greater access to valued expression. It remains to be seen whether alternative versions of a compromise between copyright and first amendment values, like Tushnet's, will ultimately gain traction in Congress or the courts.

MICHAEL S. FINCH

References and Further Reading

Boorstyn, Neil. *Boorstyn on Copyright*. 2nd Ed., Vol. 1, 12-4–12-38. 2000.
Goldstein, Paul. *Copyright*. 2nd Ed., Vol. 2, 10:1–10:71. Supp., 2005.
Leval, Pierre N., *Toward a Fair Use Standard*, Harvard Law Review 103 (1990): 1105.
Tushnet, Rebecca, *Copy This Essay: How Fair Use Doctrine Harms Free Speech and How Copying Serves It*, Yale Law Journal 114 (2004): 535.

Cases and Statutes Cited

Campbell v. Acuff-Rose Music, Inc., 510 U.S. 569 (1994)
Eldred v. Ashcroft, 537 U.S. 186 (2003)
Copyright Act of 1976, 17 U.S.C. §§ 102, 107

FAIRNESS DOCTRINE

The fairness doctrine was developed by the Federal Communications Commission (FCC) to ensure fairness and balance in broadcasters' coverage of controversial public issues. Because radio and television broadcasters enjoy a governmental license to use part of the "scarce" broadcast spectrum, they must act in the public interest. The fairness doctrine is one means by which the FCC attempted historically to serve the public interest. The fairness doctrine existed in some form from 1949 until the late 1980s, when it was repealed by the FCC. It had greatest influence between 1962 and 1976.

The fairness doctrine took specific form in rules such as the "personal attack" rule and the "political editorializing" rules that were challenged in *Red Lion Broadcasting Co. v. Federal Communications Commission*. Under the personal-attack rule, when a person involved in an issue of public interest was attacked during a broadcast, the station was obligated to give him an opportunity to respond. Under the political-editorializing rule, when a political candidate was endorsed in an editorial, his opponent had the right to respond.

In *Red Lion,* the Supreme Court upheld these rules and the fairness doctrine. The Court rejected claims (1) that the FCC lacked statutory authority to implement the fairness doctrine, and (2) that the doctrine infringed broadcaster's first amendment rights. Responding to the first amendment challenge, the Court observed:

> Because of the scarcity of radio frequencies, the Government is permitted to put restraints on licensees in favor of others whose views should be expressed on this unique medium. But the people as a whole retain their interest in free speech by radio and their collective right to have the medium function consistently with the

ends and purposes of the First Amendment. It is the right of the viewers and listeners, not the right of the broadcasters, which is paramount.

This view of government's need to regulate broadcast fairness because of medium scarcity has not weathered well over time. In 1985, the FCC released a report concluding that the fairness doctrine did not promote the public interest, that it "chilled" broadcast speech, and that it was effectively obsolescent. Since then, attempts to reinstate some form of the fairness doctrine have failed politically, with greatest opposition coming from members of the Republican Party.

MICHAEL FINCH

References and Further Reading

Krattenmaker, Thomas, and Lucas Powe, *The Fairness Doctrine Today: A Constitutional Curiosity and an Impossible Dream*, Duke Law Journal 1985 (1982): 151.
Logan, Charles, Jr., *Getting Beyond Scarcity: A New Paradigm for Assessing the Constitutionality of Broadcast Regulation*, California Law Review 85 (1997): 1687.

Cases and Statutes Cited

Communications Act of 1934, *as amended* 47 U.S.C. § 301 *et seq.*
Red Lion Broadcasting Co. v. Federal Communications Commission, 395 U.S. 367 (1969)

FALSE CONFESSIONS

One of the most compelling forms of evidence in a criminal trial is a confession of the crime by the accused. This evidence is so compelling because most people believe it highly unlikely that someone would confess to a crime they did not commit, especially a serious crime. Although intuitively appealing, this common belief has been disproved by many recent studies. Not only do individuals falsely confess, they sometimes do so without outside justification—such as the desire to protect someone else—and they confess to very serious crimes, including capital murder. In fact, false confessions are one of the three most commonly cited factors in death penalty cases that have been reversed or resulted in an executive pardon due to the defendant's actual innocence.

There are many reasons why an individual might falsely confess. Some individuals falsely confess due to outside justifications such as protecting another individual. However, mentally coercive police interrogation techniques are the more common cause of false confessions in cases that have been overturned. Although these techniques are designed to elicit genuine confessions, they also risk encouraging false confessions, especially when dealing with juveniles or mentally challenged suspects. Typical techniques include isolating the suspect from others and encouraging a confession through the use of deception and mental coercion. In response to these interrogation techniques, some individuals actually come to believe that they committed the crime. Others succumb to the pressure of the interrogation and falsely confess due to a highly suggestive or compliant mental state. Although the mentally retarded and individuals with subaverage intelligence are most at risk for falsely confessing, most individuals who have been proven to have falsely confessed are of average intelligence.

Most of the false conviction studies that have been conducted have focused mainly or exclusively on individuals who have falsely confessed to murder and been sentenced to death. Some of these individuals have come within minutes of execution before receiving reprieves that eventually led to their exoneration. As a result of these and other jurisdictional studies, a handful of states—including Alaska, Illinois, Minnesota, and Wisconsin—have instituted legislative or judicial requirements that police interrogation sessions be videotaped as a prerequisite to admission of statements at trial. Some jurisdictions apply the requirement only to juvenile cases or interrogation of murder suspects, but others apply it to all criminal cases, and some police departments require videotaping as a matter in internal policy. Although not generally required, the most effective use of videotaping is to record the entire interrogation along with the statement itself. This technique provides an objective and complete record for courts and attorneys to review to determine the reliability of statements.

False confessions have many negative effects—most notably on the wrongfully convicted defendant—but also on the victims of the crime and society, who are still vulnerable to the commission of further criminal acts by the actual perpetrator, and the criminal justice system itself, which relics on the faith of the people for its effectiveness.

JUDITH M. BARGER

References and Further Reading

Drizin, Steven A., and Richard A. Leo, *The Problem of False Confessions in the Post-DNA World*, North Carolina Law Review 82 (2004): 891.

Gross, Samuel R., *et al.*, *Exonerations in the United States, 1989 through 2003*, Journal of Criminal Law and Criminology 95 (2005): 523.

White, Welsh, *False Confessions and the Constitution: Safeguards Against Untrustworthy Confessions*, Harvard C.R.-C.L. Law Review 32 (1997): 105.

Wisconsin v. Jerrell, 699 N.W.2d 110 (2005).

Cases and Statutes Cited

Minnesota v. Scales, 518 N.W.2d 587 (1994)
Stephan v. Alaska, 711 P.2d 1156 (1985)

FALSE LIGHT INVASION OF PRIVACY

The tort of false light invasion of privacy has been recognized in the majority of American states and codified in Section 652E of *The Second Restatement of Torts*. It protects the interest of individuals in not being placed before the public in an embarrassing, humiliating, or otherwise objectionable false light. Whether this interest is properly characterized as a dignitary or a reputational interest is a matter of dispute among courts and commentators.

Although the false light tort closely resembles and substantially overlaps with the tort of defamation, its scope differs. Whereas defamation is limited to derogatory statements that significantly impair a person's community standing or associational opportunities, even a non-disparaging statement is actionable as an invasion of privacy if the false light is of a kind that would be—as the *Restatement* puts it—"highly offensive to a reasonable person." Thus, there can be liability even if the false light is laudatory, as when a star athlete who served honorably but uneventfully in the military is falsely depicted as a war hero, or when a hostage victim is falsely described as bravely resisting her brutal captors.

The First Amendment limits the availability of false light actions, but the precise nature of this limitation is uncertain. In 1967, in *Time, Inc. v. Hill,* the U.S. Supreme Court held that the rule of *New York Times v. Sullivan*—which requires public official plaintiffs in defamation cases to prove that the defamatory falsehood was published "with knowledge that it was false or with reckless disregard of whether it was false or not"—applies as well in false light cases. However, it is uncertain whether the holding of *Hill* survives the Court's subsequent ruling in *Gertz v. Robert Welch, Inc.* that private figure defamation plaintiffs need only prove negligence. This issue was left unresolved in *Cantrell v. Forest City Publishing Co.,* the Supreme Court's only other false light decision. Some lower courts continue to adhere to *Hill,* whereas others permit private figure false light plaintiffs to recover on a showing of negligence.

Early predictions that the false light tort would ultimately supplant the older tort of defamation have not been fulfilled. Some courts, including the highest courts of several states, have rejected the tort altogether, whereas a number of others have limited its scope in various ways. Academic commentary on the tort has been predominantly critical, with some writers urging its outright abolition and others recommending that it be confined to nondefamatory falsehoods. Chief among the reasons for judicial and academic resistance is the danger, which is exacerbated by the tort's uncertain boundaries, of a chilling effect on constitutionally protected speech. There is also concern that the false light tort adds unnecessary complexity to defamation litigation, that it may enable plaintiffs to circumvent various speech-protective rules that have traditionally restricted recovery for defamation, and that the harm caused by a nondefamatory falsehood is seldom serious enough to warrant legal remedy.

MICHAEL MADOW

References and Further Reading

Keeton, W. Page, *et al. Prosser and Keeton on the Law of Torts*. St. Paul, MN: West Publishing, 1984.
Prosser, William L., *Privacy*, California Law Review 48 (1960): 3:383–423.
Schwartz, Gary T., *Explaining and Justifying a Limited Tort of False Light Invasion of Privacy*, Case Western Reserve Law Review 41, No. 3 (1991): 885–919.
Warren, Samuel D., and Brandeis, Louis D., *The Right to Privacy*, Harvard Law Review 4 (1890): 5:193–220.
Zimmerman, Diane L., *False Light Invasion of Privacy: The Light That Failed*, New York University Law Review 64 (1989): 2:364–453.

Cases and Statutes Cited

Cantrell v. Forest City Publishing Co., 419 U.S. 245 (1974)
Gertz v. Robert Welch, Inc., 418 U.S. 323 (1974)
New York Times Co. v. Sullivan, 376 U.S. 254 (1964)
Time, Inc. v. Hill, 385 U.S. 374 (1967)
Restatement (Second) of Torts § 652E (1976)

See also **Appropriation of Name or Likeness; Defamation and Free Speech; Invasion of Privacy and Free Speech; Right of Privacy**

FALWELL, JERRY (1933–)

Jerry Falwell was born in Lynchburg, Virginia. In 1952, he became a "born again" Christian and earned a Divinity degree from Baptist Bible College in Springfield, Missouri. After his graduation, Falwell returned to Lynchburg and married Macel Pate, with whom he has three children. In 1956, Falwell established the Thomas Road Baptist Church in Lynchburg, which grew quickly. Soon after, he began to preach on television and in 1971, Falwell founded Liberty University in Lynchburg.

In 1976, Falwell staged a series of rallies calling for moral renewal and opposing the U.S. Supreme Court ruling on prayer in public schools, homosexuality, pornography, abortion, and the Equal Rights Amendment. In 1979, Falwell founded Moral Majority Incorporated, a secular group that lobbied for moral values. The Moral Majority played a large role in the election of President Ronald Reagan in 1980 and supported George Bush's run in 1988. Falwell disbanded the organization in 1989.

With the publication of a parody in the November 1983 issue of *Hustler Magazine*, Falwell was thrust into a major debate on the First Amendment. The parody was an advertisement for Campari Liqueur that contained Falwell's name and picture. In the advertisement, Falwell purportedly describes his "first time," intoxicated, in an outhouse, with his mother. The advertisement did contain a disclaimer reading "ad parody—not to be taken seriously" and in the table of contents, the advertisement is listed as "Fiction; Ad and Personality Parody." Still outraged by what he believed was an obscene, false, and vulgar piece, Falwell filed suit against Larry Flynt, the publisher of *Hustler Magazine*, and Flynt Distributing Company for libel, invasion of privacy, and intentional infliction of emotional distress. At trial, the court dismissed the invasion of privacy claim, and the jury ruled against him on the libel count, because they did not believe the advertisement could be reasonably understood as conveying actual facts or events. However, Falwell did prevail on the count of intentional infliction of emotional distress and was awarded $200,000.

On appeal, the court upheld the ruling that the First Amendment did not shield Flynt and *Hustler* from liability. However, Flynt and *Hustler* appealed that decision, and on February 24, 1988, the U.S. Supreme Court reversed the appellate court's decision as inconsistent with the First Amendment. The Supreme Court reasoned that public figures cannot recover under intentional infliction of emotional distress for such a publication unless they can show that the publication contained a "false statement of fact" that "was made with 'actual malice.'" Because the jury held that the advertisement parody was not reasonably believable, Falwell could not meet his burden of proof.

Falwell continues to provoke controversy because of his willingness to address controversial issues and speak candidly about his beliefs. He frequently speaks out against homosexuality, pornography, abortion, and communism and in support of family, morality, human life, voluntary prayer, and the teaching of creationism in schools. Although criticized for not respecting the division between church and state,

Falwell continues to believe that there is a place for God in government.

MARY K. MANKUS

References and Further Reading

D'Souza, Dinesh. *Falwell Before the Millennium: A Critical Biography.* Chicago: Regnery Gateway, 1984.

Falwell, Jerry. *Falwell: An Autobiography.* Lynchburg, Virginia: Liberty House Publishers, 1997.

Hustler Magazine and Larry C. Flynt v. Jerry Falwell, 485 U.S. 46; 108 S.Ct. 876 (1988).

Smolla, Rodney. *Jerry Falwell v. Larry Flynt: The First Amendment on Trial.* Urbana and Chicago: University of Illinois Press, 1990.

See also **Abortion; Equal Rights Amendment; Flynt, Larry; *Hustler Magazine v. Falwell,* 485 U.S. 46 (1988); Prayer in Public Schools**

FAMILY UNITY FOR NONCITIZENS

Family unity for noncitizens originates primarily from family-sponsored immigration, which is one of the mainstays of the federal immigration law system. Recognizing the importance of the family unit, family reunification has been a significant policy of the immigration law system since the early twentieth century. After 1952, when the Immigration and Nationality Act was enacted, the immigration law system contains a comprehensive family-based set of preferences, specifying which noncitizen family members can be reunited with their relatives who are either U.S. citizens or noncitizens who are legal permanent residents of the United States (LPRs). Noncitizens who are parents, spouses, or minor children of adult U.S. citizens are admitted as immediate relatives and are not subject to quotas or waits, only the administrative processing times.

Same sex partners and unmarried cohabitants are not eligible for family-sponsored immigration as spouses. Family unity for noncitizens does not include the right to reunite in the United States with a U.S. citizen spouse if the couple was married abroad and the noncitizen spouse is denied the right to enter the country. Thus, noncitizen families do not enjoy the same level of constitutional protection for the fundamental family unit as recognized by the U.S. Supreme Court in the case of U.S. citizens.

The family-based preferences are limited to the following: first, the unmarried adult sons and daughters of U.S. citizens; second, the spouses or unmarried children of LPRs; third, the married sons and daughters of U.S. citizens, and the fourth and final preference is for brothers and sisters of adult U.S. citizens. There are lengthy waits during which noncitizen families abroad are separated from their U.S.-based relatives, depending on when a visa will become available in each preference category under congressionally mandated quotas and country limits. No other noncitizen relatives are allowed to enter the United States under family-based immigration.

Children of noncitizens born in the United States acquire U.S. citizenship at birth but cannot file a family-sponsored immigration petition for their noncitizen parents until they reach the age of 21. Thus, if a noncitizen parent is subject to removal from the United States, the fact that the noncitizen parent has a U.S. citizen child does not prevent the removal of the parent to his or her country of origin. Scholars have argued that such a child's citizenship should be valued as much as the citizenship of an adult, yet the fact remains that a U.S. citizen child does not have the right to reside in the United States with his or her parents if they are removable noncitizens. International law grants broader rights to family unity that those granted in domestic immigration law in such situations. At least one lower court has ruled that when the non-citizen father of a U.S. citizen child is about to be removed from the United States, the U.S. government must take into account customary international law regarding family unity and consider the best interests of the child.

MARÍA PABÓN LÓPEZ

References and Further Reading

Legomsky, Stephen H. *Immigration and Refugee Law and Policy.* New York: Foundation Press, 2005.

Jastram, Kate (2003). Family unity, in Aleinikoff, T. Alexander, and Vincent Chetail, eds. *Migration and International Legal Norms.* The Hague: T.M.C. Asser Press, pp. 185–201.

Romero, Victor C. *Alienated: Immigrant Rights, the Constitution, and Equality in America.* New York: New York University Press, 2005.

———. *Asians, Gay Marriage, and Immigration: Family Unification at a Crossroads,* Indiana International & Comparative Law Review 15 (2005) 2:337–347.

Cases and Statutes Cited

Adams v. Howerton, 673 F.2d. 1036 (9th Cir. 1982)

Beharry v. Reno, 183 F. Supp. 2d 584 (E.D. N.Y. 2002), vacated on other grounds sub nom, *Beharry v. Ashcroft,* 329 F.3d 51 (2nd Cir. 2003) (NO. 02-2171), as amended (Jul 24, 2003)

Immigration and Nationality Act, P.L. 82-414, 66 Stat. 163 (June 27, 1952), as amended

Hermina Sague v. U.S., 416 F. Supp. 217 (D.P.R. 1976)

Moore v. City of East Cleveland, 431 U.S. 494 (1977)

INA § 201 (b)(2)(A)(i), codified at 8 U.S.C. § 1151 (b)(2)(A) (i) (2000)

INA § 203 (a), (d), codified at 8 U.S.C. § 1153(a), (d) (2000)

FAMILY VALUES MOVEMENT

The family values movement is actually a very loose alliance of different organizations united by the belief that government has a duty to protect both the traditional American family and the moral foundations of society. The central tenet of the various groups that make up the family values movement is that the state has not just a role but a duty to promote a particular type of morality for the good of all its citizens.

There are two main views as to how the state gets its duty to protect morality. Some value morality extrinsically: immorality corrupts every aspect of society and so morality must be promoted to protect all members of society from that corruption. Others see morality as something that's intrinsically important; actions that violate this morality are simply wrong and ought to be stopped. This view is particularly prevalent among more religious groups whose morality rests on Judeo-Christian ethics and other theological justifications. This second position has attracted criticism for ignoring the establishment clause of the First Amendment.

Although the family values movement is often thought of as beginning in the 1980s, it can trace its origin to the reactions against the shift in American politics away from its traditional, broadly conformist, White Anglo-Saxon Protestant roots that began in the 1950s. These changes were aimed at the creation of a secular, pluralistic society that not only understood and fostered differences in life choices between citizens but also protected the rights of its minorities to act without fear of reprisal from the majority. Mass-based social groups began to push against the traditional constraints placed on their members, particularly feminists striving for equality in the workplace, and homosexual rights groups campaigning against state discrimination such as policies preventing homosexuals from working for the federal government.

The impetus for the many of these policy changes came from the courts in a series of decisions that favored the autonomy of the individual over the interests of the state in promoting a particular morality.

Some of these decisions were centered on the right to make choices over their behavior within the privacy of their homes. One example of this would be *Stanley v. Georgia,* which recognized a "right to satisfy emotional needs in the privacy of [one's] own house" that precluded the state from banning the possession of pornography.

Others were centered on the right of the individual to make decisions about their body and intimate aspects of their lives. One example of this would be *Roe v. Wade,* where the Court recognized the importance of a woman's right to choose to have an abortion.

Others were aimed at protecting the rights of minorities from discrimination by the majority motivated by animus and moral differences. An example of this would be *Romer v. Evans,* where the Court struck down a state constitutional amendment prohibiting laws that would protect homosexuals from discrimination.

The family values movement saw these decisions as dangerous and worked in the courts and the legislatures to protect the role of the state in advancing and defending a particular idea of morality to protect society. They achieved many successes in the electoral realm, especially in the southern states, only to have many laws later overturned by the courts. They regarded the interventions of the court as undemocratic intrusions on the ability of the majority to protect their society.

The family values movement thinks that reformers, including the courts, fail to see that some apparently private acts actually have wide-ranging consequences for all of society. Permitting the use of pornography degrades all women, desensitizes the public to sex, and leads to increased sexual violence. Allowing the use of contraceptives decouples sex from reproduction and promotes sex outside of marriage. Abortion involves the termination of another life and can lead to decreased regard for all human life.

The movement is often characterized as being "right wing," religious, and Republican, and some of its most high-profile groups have included the Moral Majority, the Christian Coalition, Concerned Women for America, and the Family Research Council.

The socially conservative views of the movement attract religious groups from across the wider political spectrum. The movement is most associated with the Republican Party, because that party has actively courted them by pursuing family-based moral policies for some time. This link with the movement was most active and important in the 1980s when President Ronald Reagan placed traditional family values at the core of his political philosophy.

The political power of the family values movement has declined since the 1980s, but it remains active through its many organizations. They have not given up attempts to overturn the developments of the last few decades and continue to fight a rearguard action in the face of further socially liberal reforms. At the start of the twenty-first century, the most heated battles involve the expansion of the term marriage to cover same sex unions. This opposition is even more intense when children are involved, and they see same sex adoption as not only giving official recognition to deviant behavior but also potentially affecting the child's sexual orientation by growing up in a home where homosexual behavior is the norm.

Although the culture wars fought by the family values movement show no sign of abating, their political victories of the movement have tended to be either short lived (as *Bowers v. Hardwick* gave way to *Lawrence v. Texas*) or merely limiting the scope of their defeat (as *New York v. Ferber* qualified *Stanley*). Their opponents have been far more successful in challenging the status quo and have radically transformed American society over the past few decades. It seems unlikely that these opponents will win completely, but their advances show no sign of slowing, and it remains to be seen whether the movement can force a retrenchment of traditional family values in American politics.

GAVIN J. REDDICK

References and Further Reading

Formicola, Jo Renee, and Hubert Morken, eds. *Religious Leaders and Faith-based Politics : Ten Profiles*. Lanham, MD: Rowman & Littlefield Publishers, 2001.

Hunter, James D. *Culture Wars: The Struggle to Define America*. New York: Basic Books, 1991.

Kaplan, Esther. "The Religious Right's Sense of Siege is Fueling a Resurgence." *The Nation* July 5, 2004.

Lawler, Michael G. "Family: American and Christian." *America* August 12, 1995.

Walsh, Andrew D. *Religion, Economics, and Public Policy: Ironies, Tragedies, and Absurdities of the Contemporary Culture Wars*. Westport, CT: Praeger, 2000.

Yarnold, Barbara M., ed. *The Role of Religious Organizations in Social Movements*. New York: Praeger Publishers, 1991.

Cases and Statutes Cited

Bowers v. Hardwick, 478 U.S. 186 (1986)
Lawrence v. Texas, 539 U.S. 558 (2003)
New York v. Ferber, 458 U.S. 747 (1982)
Roe v. Wade, 410 U.S. 113 (1933)
Roemer v. Evans, 517 U.S. 620 (1996)
Stanley v. Georgia, 394 U.S. 557 (1969)

See also **Abortion; Abortion Laws and the Establishment Clause; Abortion Protest Cases; Bible in American Law; Birth Control;** *Bowers v. Hardwick*, **478 U.S. 186 (1986);** *Boy Scouts of America v. Dale* **530 U.S. 640 (2000); Child Pornography; Defense of Marriage Act; Gay and Lesbian Rights;** *Griswold v. Connecticut*, **381 U.S. 479 (1965); Homosexuality and Immigration; Marriage, History of; Same-Sex Marriage Legalization;** *Stanley v. Georgia*, **394 U.S. 557 (1969); Right of Privacy;** *Roe v. Wade*, **410 U.S. 113 (1973);** *Romer v. Evans*, **517 U.S. 620 (1996);** *Lawrence v. Texas*, **539 U. S. 558 (2003);** *New York v. Ferber*, **458 U.S. 747 (1982)**

FCC v. LEAGUE OF WOMEN VOTERS, 468 U.S. 364 (1984)

The writers of the Constitution safeguarded the individual right to freedom of speech with the First Amendment, which forbids Congress from making laws abridging freedom of the press. But does the First Amendment also protect television broadcasters, even those established by law and publicly funded? *FCC v. League of Women Voters* (League) is important in shaping the answer: broadcasters, even publicly owned, are protected by the First Amendment.

Educational stations, organized and funded under Public Broadcasting Act of 1967 (PBA), were banned by the PBA from editorializing. A station operator, joined by the League of Women Voters, challenged the ban in a lawsuit against the Federal Communications Commission (FCC), the Regulatory Agency responsible for Broadcast Regulation.

In *League*, the Supreme Court upheld the district court decision that the ban on editorializing violated the First Amendment. The First Amendment rights of broadcasters cannot be taken away, even though they owe their creation and funding to law. The holding relied on the finding in *Red Lion v. FCC*, that broadcasters enjoy the broad First Amendment rights of journalists, limited only as required to accommodate the physical limitations of broadcast spectrum. Finding the right to editorialize fundamental, the Supreme Court suggested that FCC regulations of content on the basis of spectrum scarcity should be closely reviewed. This standard of review was subsequently applied to overrule the Fairness Doctrine, regulations requiring broadcasters to present both sides of an issue.

As a result of the decision in *League*, restrictions on broadcast content are subject to strict scrutiny. Few governmental restrictions remain on television broadcast content. Most important are indecency, as confirmed by the Supreme Court in *FCC v. Pacifica*, and right of response for presidential candidates, specified in the Communications Act of 1934. The particulars of these restrictions are subject to continuing challenge and debate.

KATHLEEN HAWKINS BERKOWE

References and Further Reading

Carter, T. Barton, Marc A. Franklin, and Jay B. Wright. *The First Amendment and the Fifth Estate: Regulation of Electronic Mass Media*. 2nd Ed. Westbury, New York: Foundation Press, 1989.

Corn-Revere, Robert L., *et al. Modern Communication Law*. St. Paul, MN: West Group, 1999.

Russomanno, Joseph. *Speaking Our Minds: Conversations with the People Behind Landmark First Amendment*

Cases. Mahwah: NJ: Lawrence Erlbaum Associates, 2002.

Cases and Statutes Cited

CBS, Inc. v. FCC, 453 U.S. 367 (1981)
FCC v. League of Women Voters of California, 468 U.S. 364 (1984)
FCC v. Pacifica, 438 U.S. 726 (1978)
Red Lion Broadcasting Co. v. FCC, 453 U.S. 367 (1981)
The Public Broadcasting Act of 1967, Pub. L. 90-129, 81 Stat. 365, 47 U.S.C. 390 *et seq.*, 47 U.S.C. 399

See also **Broadcast Regulation; Fairness Doctrine;** *FCC v. Pacifica Foundation*, **438 U.S. 726 (1978); Federal Communications Commission; Government Speech;** *Red Lion Broadcasting Co. v. FCC*, **453 U.S. 367 (1969)**

FCC v. PACIFICA FOUNDATION, 438 U.S. 726 (1978)

George Carlin, a comedian, recorded a famous monologue in which he riffed on "7 Dirty Words"—slang words he claimed could never be uttered on radio or television. Carlin's thesis was proved correct one day when Pacifica's New York radio station broadcast a recording of the monologue during an afternoon program addressing contemporary attitudes on language. A parent driving with his child complained to the Federal Communications Commission (FCC). The FCC found Pacifica had violated "indecency" rules applicable to public broadcasters. Pacifica appealed to the Supreme Court.

The Court found that the First Amendment permits different standards to be applied to the broadcast media, as opposed to print or other public spaces such as taverns. The earlier *Cohen* decision, for example, had overturned the conviction of a war protestor wearing a jacket emblazoned with the words, "F*** the Draft," holding that the government could not sanction offensive words used in public speech because of the risk of censoring ideas.

The key features of broadcasting distinguishing it from other modes of communication reflected the Court's desire to shield "captive audience" members from offensive communications, particularly in the privacy of the home and in other settings in which children might be present. Unlike other contexts in which unwilling listeners may avoid offensive language, on-air listeners cannot so easily predict whether a given program will contain offensive language. The Court also thought that parents could not realistically monitor broadcasts for indecent language to protect children.

JOHN NOCKLEBY

References and Further Reading

Cohen v. California, 403 U.S. 15 (1971).
Red Lion Broadcasting Co. v. FCC, 395 U.S. 367 (1969).
Reno v. ACLU, 521 U.S. 844 (1997).

Cases and Statutes Cited

Cohen v. California, 403 U.S. 15 (1971)
18 U.S.C. § 1464 (1976)

See also **Broadcast Regulation; Captive Audiences and Free Speech;** *Cohen v. California*, **403 U.S. 15 (1971); Federal Communications Commission; Public Vulgarity and Free Speech**

FEDERAL COMMUNICATIONS COMMISSION

The Federal Communications Commission (FCC), a Regulatory Agency established by Congress, implements Broadcast Regulation, Cable Television Regulation, and regulates telecommunications services, and common carriers under the Communications Act of 1934, the Telecommunications Act of 1996, and others.

Guided by the public interest standard, the FCC sets technical standards and operating regulations and monitors and enforces compliance. It assigns broadcast licenses for the television and radio spectrum. Decisions of the five FCC commissioners, appointed by the President, are appealed to federal courts.

FCC regulations affecting broadcast content have provoked challenges that they and the underlying laws abridge the right to free speech under the First Amendment of the U.S. Constitution (First Amendment). As confirmed in *Red Lion v. FCC*, the FCC preserves broadcasters' First Amendment protections as journalists while administering laws that permissibly affect content such as the Communications Act's requirement that broadcasters offer equal time to federal candidates. As special situations justifying the regulations change, the FCC has overturned policies such as the Fairness Doctrine, requiring balanced views in broadcast content.

While FCC regulation of indecency is permissible, as confirmed by the Supreme Court in *FCC v. Pacifica*, the FCC is required to regulate speech of new technologies in the face of successful challenges to underlying legislation such as the Communications Decency Act. The FCC regulates obscenity, a form of Unprotected Speech; however, the definitions and standards are the subject of continuing challenges.

The FCC's Equal Opportunity rules, adopted in 1969 under the public interest standard, required broadcasters to hire minorities and women in proportion to the local population. Federal courts rejected the rules as unconstitutional race-based qualifications violating the equal protection clause of the Fifth Amendment of the U.S. Constitution.

A federal court in *Prometheus Radio Project v FCC* found that limits on cross-ownership of broadcast and cable stations in the same markets may survive First and Fifth Amendment challenges. It remanded the case to the FCC to develop permissible regulations.

Aware that improper regulation can be challenged as a government taking of property under the Fifth Amendment, the FCC has interpreted current laws narrowly as inapplicable to new media and new technologies. The FCC determined that Internet access offered by cable companies is not a regulated telecommunications service, a decision upheld by the U.S. Supreme Court in *National Cable & Telecommunications Association v. Brand X Internet*.

The FCC is the arbiter of first resort balancing First and Fifth Amendment rights against regulations and underlying laws in the areas of mass communications. As technologies continue to develop, the FCC will continue its pivotal role in developing Constitutional law.

KATHLEEN HAWKINS BERKOWE

References and Further Reading

Abernathy, Kathleen Q., *The Role of the Federal Communications Commission on the Path from the Vast Wasteland to the Fertile Plain*, Federal Communications Law Journal 55 (2003): May:435.

Botein, Michael, and Douglas H. Ginsburg. *The Regulation of the Electronic Mass Media: Law and Policy for Radio, Television, Cable and the New Video Technologies*. St. Paul, MN: West Group, 1999.

Carter, T. Barton, Marc A. Franklin, and Jay B. Wright. *The First Amendment and the Fifth Estate: Regulation of Electronic Mass Media*. 2nd Ed. Westbury, NY: Foundation Press, 1989.

Communications Law and Policy Resources, maintained by Justin Brown, Assistant Professor, College of Journalism and Communications, University of Florida, http://www.jou.ufl.edu.faculty/jbrown/lawandpolicy.htm (accessed September 1, 2005).

Corn-Revere, Robert L., *et al. Modern Communication Law, Practitioner's Edition*. St. Paul, MN: West Group, 1999.

Creech, Kenneth C. *Electronic Media Law and Regulation*. Boston, MA: Focal Press, 1996.

Einstein, Mara. *Media Diversity: Economics, Ownership and the FCC*. Mahwah, N.J: L. Erlbaum Associates, 2004.

The Federal Communications Commission website. http://www.fcc.gov (accessed September 1, 2005).

Cases and Statutes Cited

The Communications Act of 1934, Act June 19, 1934, ch. 652, 48 Stat. 1064, 47 U.S.C Sec. 151 *et seq.*

The Communications Decency Act, Pub. L. 104-104, Title V, Sec. 501, Feb 8, 1996, 110 Stat. 133

FCC v. Pacifica, 438 U.S. 726 (1978)

FCC v. League of Women Voters of California, 468 U.S. 364 (1984)

Lutheran Church-Missouri Synod v. FCC, 141 F.3ᵈ 344 (D.C. Cir. 1998)

Miller v. California, 413 U.S. 15 (1973)

Prometheus Radio Project v. FCC, ___F. 3ᵈ ____ (3rd Cir. 2003), *cert. den.* June 13, 2005, 545 U.S. ____

The Telecommunications Act of 1996, Pub. L. No. 104-104

See also **Affirmative Action; Balancing Approach to Free Speech; Bill of Rights: Structure; Broadcast Regulation; Cable Television Regulation; Communications Decency Act (1996); Fairness Doctrine;** *FCC v. League of Women Voters*, **468 U.S. 364 (1984); Government Speech;** *Red Lion Broadcasting v. FCC*, **453 U.S. 367 (1981)**

FEDERALIZATION OF CRIMINAL LAW

Since it first adopted a statute with criminal penalties under the alleged authority of the Commerce Clause in 1884, Congress has increasingly been asserting the power to legislate police powers, first on interstate shipments, later within state territory. Most such legislation has claimed authority under ever-broader constructions of the Commerce Clause and the Necessary and Proper Clause, which have been extended to include almost anything. This criminal legislation would have been deemed unconstitutional in the Founding Era.

The original meaning of "commerce among the states" seems to have been limited to tangible commodities the title and possession of which are transferred from a party outside a state to a party within that state. It did not include services, information, energy, or primary production such as mining, farming, hunting, or fishing. Nor did it include manufacturing, transport, possession, use, or disposal, or the activities of the transacting parties, or anything that might have a "substantial effect" on such transactions.

Furthermore, the original meaning of the power to "regulate" did not include the power to prohibit, or to impose criminal penalties, but only civil penalties, such as fines or confiscation.

The original Constitution delegated authority to the central government to punish as crimes, committed on state territory, only a limited number of subjects: (1) treason (Art. III Sec. 3 Cl. 2); (2) counterfeiting (Art. I Sec. 8 Cl. 6); (3) piracy or felonies on the high seas; (4) offenses against the "laws of nations" (Art. I Sec. 8 Cl. 10); or (5) violations of discipline by military or militia personnel (Art. I Sec. 8 Cl. 14).

This was confirmed in the constitutional ratifying conventions, and again in the Kentucky Resolutions of 1798, authored by Thomas Jefferson, although he omitted the last one in that document.

There have been no subsequent amendments to expand the criminal powers of Congress, other than the Thirteenth (slavery), Fourteenth (violations of rights by state agents), Fifteenth (denial of vote to former slaves), Eighteenth (alcohol prohibition, repealed by Twenty-first), Nineteenth (denial of vote to women), and Twenty-sixth Amendments (denial of vote to those aged 18 or older).

The process has been driven by perceived problems that evoked public demand for solutions, combined with diminished public understanding, from generation to generation, of what is and is not constitutional, and declining public devotion to the strict enforcement of the Constitution.

U.S. criminal statutes that exceeded the bounds asserted by the Kentucky Resolutions of 1798 did occasionally get adopted between 1798 and 1884, but only in minor ways. They were seldom enforced and were not subjected to the test of appellate review until 1906.

The next significant piece of legislation was the Sherman Anti-Trust Act of July 2, 1890, which imposed criminal penalties on monopolistic combinations but was sustained by a 1908 precedent enforcing it not against industrialists but against a call for a boycott by a labor union.

The next significant precedent was in 1911, in which criminal penalties were sustained for violation of regulations by the Secretary of Agriculture, not for regulation of interstate commerce but of grazing rights on federal lands, even though exclusive jurisdiction over them had not been ceded to Congress by a state legislature under U.S. Const. Art. I Sec. 8 Cl. 17. This was also significant in that it breached the nondelegation doctrine that legislative powers could not be delegated to administrative agencies.

The Necessary and Proper Clause was extended by a key 1914 precedent that it may be necessary to regulate "purely" intrastate activities so that the regulation of interstate activities might be fully effectuated. When written, the commerce clause was only intended to authorize what might be required to make the *effort* to exercise a delegated power, not whatever might be convenient to attain an *outcome* for which the power might be exercised. This represented a major departure from the original understanding of what a delegated power is.

In 1917 the U.S. Supreme Court sustained a conviction under a 1910 statute forbidding transport of women across state lines for sexual purposes. This was the first exercise of a "police power" against immoral behavior, and it also introduced the notion that the U.S. government acquired criminal jurisdiction over offenses that involve crossing a state line.

In 1919, the Court sustained a conviction under a 1916 act, a precedent that Congress has criminal jurisdiction over fraud that influences or obstructs interstate commerce. In 1920, there was a precedent that extended "commerce" to include communications, including noncommercial communications, across state lines. In 1925 came a precedent that Congress can exercise a police power by regulating interstate commerce to the extent of forbidding and punishing the use of such commerce as an agency to promote immorality, dishonesty, or the spread of any evil or harm to the people of other states from the state of origin.

The key precedent came in 1942, when the conviction was sustained of a farmer for consuming his own grain, subject to price and production controls, as having a "substantial effect" on interstate commerce. Most federal criminal legislation since then cites this precedent for its authority, including federal criminal drug control statutes, a statute against murdering federal agents, gun control legislation, and more than 4000 other distinct penal provisions.

More federal criminal legislation gets introduced and adopted each session of Congress, with little effective opposition on constitutional grounds. Congress now sees no limit on its powers, other than a few rights expressly protected by the Constitution. From an understanding that "all powers not delegated are prohibited," they have gone to a position that they have "all powers not expressly prohibited," contrary to the Ninth and Tenth Amendments.

It should be noted, however, that none of the precedents or any legislation has actually sought to extend the definition of "commerce." It is all based on ever-broader extensions of the necessary and proper clause, with only tenuous connections to "commerce" as such. From an original understanding of "necessary and proper" to include only the power to make a limited effort to whatever power might be convenient to obtain a desired result.

JON ROLAND

References and Further Reading

Elliot, Jonathan. (1836). "The Debates in the Several Conventions on the Adoption of the Federal Constitution." http://www.constitution.org/elliot.htm.

Meese, Edwin III, chair. "The Federalization of Criminal Law." Report of Task Force of the American Bar Association. http://www.nacdl.org/public.nsf/legislation/overcriminalization/$FILE/fedcrimlaw2.pdf.

Meese, Edwin III and Rhett DeHart. "How Washington Subverts Your Local Sheriff." *Policy Review*, January-February 1996, Number 75; http://www.policyreview.org/jan96/meese.html.

Randolph, J. W., ed. *"The Virginia Report."* Richmond: 1850. Includes writings of Thomas Jefferson and James Madison, the Kentucky Resolutions of 1798 and 1799, and the Virginia Resolution of 1798. http://www.constitution.org/rf/vr.htm.

FEINER v. NEW YORK, 340 U.S. 315 (1951)

Irving Feiner was an undergraduate student at Syracuse University in 1949. As a member of the Young Progressive Party, he had participated in the Party's decision to invite John Rogge, a past Assistant Attorney General of the United States and a member of the American Progressive Party, to give a speech to be held in public school about what he, and the Progressives, thought was the unfair conviction of several young blacks in a New Jersey courtroom. The mayor was enraged about this invitation, as was the chapter of the Syracuse American Legion, and the mayor orchestrated a denial of the permit for Rogge to speak in the school auditorium.

Feiner, and his associates from the Progressives, arranged to have Rogge speak in a private hotel in Syracuse. To publicize this new venue and to advertise some of the themes they expected Rogge to emphasize, Feiner held a street corner rally in downtown Syracuse. Standing on a box and using a microphone, Feiner condemned the Mayor, the local political system, and the American Legion. Quoting from the subsequent trial court record (and Feiner disputed some of these contentions), the judge found that specifically Feiner said: " Mayor Costello is a champagne-sipping bum; he does not speak for the Negro people... The 15th Ward is run by corrupt politicians, and there are horse rooms [betting parlors] operating there.... President Truman is a bum.... Mayor O'Dwyer [of Syracus] is a Nazi Gestapo.... The Negroes don't have equal rights; they should rise up in arms and fight for their rights." A crowd of approximately seventy-five to eighty (the police estimate accepted by the trial judge; twenty-five to thirty were estimated by the defense) gathered on the street corner to hear Feiner's comments. Some in the crowd voiced approval; other objected, some vociferously. Passersby on the sidewalk might also have had their paths partially blocked by the crowd. The police alleged that one spectator (never a witness during trial however) shouted to them: "If you don't get that son of a bitch off, I will go over and get him off there myself." The police judged that the situation was becoming dangerous and asked Feiner to stop speaking. When he ignored them, they asked him to step down from the box and informed him that he was under arrest for disorderly conduct.

Feiner's arrest was upheld in the local court, and he was sentenced to thirty days in jail. The case was appealed (unsuccessfully for Feiner) to two New York courts and finally to the U.S. Supreme Court. The Court in a six to three decision in 1951 also upheld the trial court's decision reasoning that police should have discretion to decide when a local rally was becoming a danger to the community. The Court stressed that Feiner was not arrested for the political content of his speech but for the effects his words were having on the crowd, and the Court thought that the police could legitimately conclude that a disturbance or breach of the peace was imminent. The dissenting justices, in addition to calling into question the "factual" record the trial judge had sustained, also questioned the premise of the majority Supreme Court decision. Specifically, they thought that the police, rather than ask Feiner to stop speaking in the face of a potentially hostile audience, should have asked-insisted that the crowd move aside and allow pedestrians to pass and should have informed any one in the crowd threatening the speaker that this kind of threat was unacceptable, and that if a threat was serious, it could lead to the spectator's arrest. In the dissenters' view, the majority deferred too much to both the police and trial judge version of the events, but even if the view of the police and judge was accepted for the sake of the argument, Feiner's right to speak nonetheless should have been upheld by the majority. The decision, the dissenters maintained, gave the police too much discretion to decide when a speaker's words were likely to lead to a breach of the peace and did not make the dissenters sufficiently responsible for those in a crowd threatening a speaker.

Feiner had been expelled from Syracuse shortly after the trial court's decision but was free on bail pending the final resolution of the case. After the Supreme Court's decision was announced, Feiner served his thirty days in jail.

The Feiner case has become known as the case that supported what has been called the "heckler's veto." The police could legitimately conclude—here by the crowd's demeanor in general, by the "get the son-of-a-bitch" comment in particular—that continued speech would result in a breach of peace.

And so the legal history ends, but the question that remains is "whatever happened to Irving Feiner," what happened to this idealistic student arrested because the courts decided to defer to local police assessments of the consequences of his words. Several years ago, with the help of my students, we tracked Irving Feiner to his home outside of New York City. It was wonderful to learn that he had had a relatively successful business career, ultimately was reaccepted into

Syracuse and earned his college degree, and now stands as a kind of icon for "doing the right thing." He has spoken at several law schools about the case and is an annual speaker in my undergraduate class at Rutgers. Still the fighter for principled issues, two pieces of Irving Feiner's take on *Feiner* are important to include in this entry. First, he notes that his "take up arms" comments were referring to what he had experienced in post-war France, when thousands of citizens walked down the Champs-Elysee "arm in arm" to insist on greater social justice. Second, he thinks the recollection of calling Truman a "bum" was incorrect. Noting that he knows his own rhetorical style, he now invariably tells his audience that he would never have used the word "bum" but instead would have said something more colorful, something that included a reference to Truman's relationship to his mother!

MILTON HEUMANN

References and Further Reading

Barker, Lucius, and Twiley Barker, Jr. *Civil Cases and Commentaries Liberties and The Constitution.* 4th Ed. Englewood Cliffs, NJ: Prentice Hall, 1982, pp. 17–28.
Cushman, Robert. *Cases in Civil Liberties.* New York: Appleton-Century-Crofts, 1968.
Heumann, Milton. *Interview with Irving Feiner.* New Brunswick, NJ: Rutgers University, March 2005.
Konvitz, Milton. *Bill of Rights Reader.* 5th Ed. Revised, Ithaca: Cornell University Press, 1973.

Cases and Statutes Cited

Feiner v. New York 340 U.S. 315 (1951)

See also **Captive Audiences and Free Speech; Fighting Words and Free Speech; Heckler's Veto Problem in Free Speech**

FELON DISENFRANCHISEMENT

Felon disenfranchisement refers to the practice of restricting the voting rights of those convicted of felony-level crimes. The loss of voting rights is a Collateral Consequence of a felony conviction. Almost every state in the United States bars felons from voting for some amount of time. States vary, however, in the classes of felons disenfranchised and the duration of disenfranchisement.

In general, states follow one of four disenfranchisement schemes: (1) disenfranchising prisoners; (2) disenfranchising prisoners and parolees; (3) disenfranchising prisoners, parolees, and probationers; or (4) disenfranchising prisoners, parolees, and probationers, and former felons who have completed their sentences. In the first three categories, voting rights are usually restored automatically on completion of prison, parole, or probation. In the last category, however, persons wishing to vote must receive a pardon or clemency from the state. Some states make further distinctions by restoring rights automatically only to first-time offenders or to those convicted of nonviolent crimes, while requiring recidivists and violent offenders to receive a pardon or clemency. The United States is unusual in restricting the voting rights of non-incarcerated felons, because almost no other democratic nation does so.

Origins and Development of Felon Disenfranchisement Laws in the United States

The practice of limiting the citizenship rights of criminals has ancient origins, and some form of disenfranchisement has been practiced in the United States since colonial times. Earlier forms of disenfranchisement, however, were limited both in scope and duration, because laws typically barred from voting only those convicted of specific crimes and only for a limited time. It was not until the 1800s that states began disenfranchising entire classes of felons without regard to the underlying crime. By 1850, eleven states disenfranchised felons, all of which imposed indefinite disenfranchisement that typically required a gubernatorial or legislative pardon to regain voting rights. The 1860s and 1870s were a period of significant change, during which seventeen states added a felon disenfranchisement law.

Because this period coincided with the end of the Civil War and the passage of the Fourteenth and Fifteenth Amendments, which expanded both definitions of citizenship and the right to vote, many assert that felon disenfranchisement laws are linked to racial conflict. This theory stresses that states used felon disenfranchisement laws as a tool to suppress the voting power of African Americans. Research has found a link between the proportion of African Americans in a state's prison population and passage of a felon disenfranchisement law. Competing views, however, stress that the laws are race-neutral, and any disparate impact is an incidental effect.

Another period of marked change occurred nearly a century later. During the 1960s and 1970s, many states liberalized their disenfranchisement laws, typically by providing for automatic restoration of rights on completion of sentence. This trend toward expanding the voting rights of felons continued throughout the rest of the century, although a few states implemented new restrictions on felon voting rights.

Constitutional Challenges to Felon Disenfranchisement

Although voting attained and confirmed its status as a fundamental right through a series of decisions by the Warren Court, felon disenfranchisement laws are treated differently than other Voting Rights cases. Most challenges to the laws have been unsuccessful. In 1974, the Supreme Court upheld the practice of felon disenfranchisement. In *Richardson v. Ramirez*, the Court interpreted disenfranchisement as an "affirmative sanction" of Section Two of the Fourteenth Amendment, which reduced congressional representation of states disenfranchising males, *unless* that disenfranchisement was for "rebellion or other crimes." Thus, while other restrictions on the right to vote are subjected to judicial "strict scrutiny" under which states must demonstrate a compelling state interest served through narrowly tailored means, felon disenfranchisement laws have not been held to this standard.

In addition to general challenges, others claim that felon disenfranchisement denies the right to vote based on race. In 1985, in *Hunter v. Underwood*, the Supreme Court invalidated an Alabama disenfranchisement law based on an impermissible intent to racially discriminate. Race-based challenges focus on the Fourteenth and Fifteenth Amendments, as well as the Voting Rights Act of 1965. Despite the disproportionate impact of felon disenfranchisement on African Americans, courts have rejected these claims in the absence of establishing a clear discriminatory intent.

The Impact of Felon Disenfranchisement Laws

Although the size of the disenfranchised population varies by state, the laws collectively have a large impact in the United States. In the 2000 presidential election, nearly 4.7 million people—about 2.3 percent of the voting-age population—were disenfranchised because of a felony conviction. Of this group, 1.8 million people were African Americans, representing more than seven percent of the African-American voting-age population.

The size of the disenfranchised population also holds the potential to change the outcomes of closely contested elections, particularly in states with laws that ban voting beyond completion of sentence. Because of the demographic characteristics of disenfranchised felons, these voting restrictions seem to

have provided a small but consistent advantage to Republican candidates in several U.S. Senate and presidential elections.

Despite the prevalence of laws disenfranchising felons across the United States, the restrictions do not enjoy widespread popular support. One national poll indicated that eighty percent of Americans approve of permitting felons to vote after they have completed their sentences, whereas sixty percent approved of allowing felons on probation and parole to vote. Incarcerated felons, however, receive less support, with only one-third believing that prisoners should be permitted to vote.

Conclusion

Felon disenfranchisement laws restrict the voting rights of those convicted of felonies. Although the laws in their contemporary form did not take shape until the mid- to late-nineteenth century, nearly all states eventually adopted a law prohibiting certain classes of felons from voting. Although state laws vary, the laws collectively disenfranchise millions and likely hold the power to change elections. Despite the breadth of felon disenfranchisement laws and their disproportionate impact on African Americans, courts have generally upheld their constitutionality as a restriction on the right to vote.

ANGELA BEHRENS and CHRISTOPHER UGGEN

References and Further Reading

Allard, Patricia, and Marc Mauer. *Regaining the Vote: An Assessment of Activity Relating to Felon Disenfranchisement Laws*. Washington, D.C.: The Sentencing Project, 1999.

Behrens, Angela, Christopher Uggen, and Jeff Manza. "Ballot Manipulation and the 'Menace of Negro Domination': Racial Threat and Felon Disenfranchisement in United States, 1850-2002." *American Journal of Sociology* 109 (2003): 3:559–605.

Chin, Gabriel J., *Rehabilitating Unconstitutional Statutes: An Analysis of* Cotton v. Fordice, *157 F.3d 388 (5th Cir. 1998)*, University of Cincinnati Law Review 71 (2002): 2:421–455.

Clegg, Roger, *Who Should Vote?* Texas Review of Law and Politics 6 (2001): 1:159–178.

Demleitner, Nora V., *Continuing Payment on One's Debt to Society: The German Model of Felon Disenfranchisement as an Alternative*, Minnesota Law Review 84 (2000): 4:753–804.

Ewald, Alec C., *'Civil Death:' The Ideological Paradox of Criminal Disenfranchisement Law in the United States*, University of Wisconsin Law Review 2002 (2002):5:1045–1137.

Fellner, Jamie, and Marc Mauer. *Losing the Vote: The Impact of Felony Disenfranchisement Laws in the United*

States. Washington, D.C.: Human Rights Watch and The Sentencing Project, 1998.

Fletcher, George, *Disenfranchisement as Punishment: Reflections on Racial Uses of Infamia*, UCLA Law Review 46 (1999): 6:1895–1908.

Hench, Virginia, *The Death of Voting Rights: The Legal Disenfranchisement of Minority Voters*, Case Western Law Review 48 (1998): 4:727–798.

Itzkowitz, Howard, and Lauren Oldak, *Restoring the Ex-Offender's Right to Vote: Background and Developments*, American Criminal Law Review 11 (1973): 3:721–770.

Keyssar, Alexander. *The Right to Vote: The Contested History of Democracy in the United States.* New York: Basic Books, 2000.

Manza, Jeff, Clem Brooks, and Christopher Uggen. "Civil Death or Civil Rights? Public Attitudes Toward Felon Disenfranchisement in the United States." *Public Opinion Quarterly* 68 (forthcoming 2004).

Shapiro, Andrew, *Challenging Criminal Disenfranchisement under the Voting Rights Act: A New Strategy*, Yale Law Journal 103 (1993): 2:537–566.

Uggen, Christopher, and Jeff Manza. "Democratic Contraction? The Political Consequences of Felon Disenfranchisement in the United States." *American Sociological Review* 67 (2002): 6:777–803.

United States Department of Justice, Office of the Pardon Attorney. *Civil Disabilities of Convicted Felons: A State-by-State Survey.* Washington, D.C.: United States Government Printing Office, 1996.

Cases and Statutes Cited

Hunter v. Underwood, 471 U.S. 222 (1985)
Richardson v. Ramirez, 418 U.S. 533 (1974)
Voting Rights Act of 1965, Act of Aug. 6, 1965, 79 Stat. 437, codified at 42 U.S.C. § 1973

See also **Collateral Consequences; Fourteenth Amendment; Voting Rights; Voting Rights Act of 1965; Warren Court**

FIALLO v. BELL, 430 U.S. 787 (1977)

Under U.S. immigration law, biological mothers who are citizens or lawful permanent residents may petition their nonmarital offspring to enter the country; similarly, nonmarital children may petition their biological mothers. Biological fathers do not enjoy the same privileges with respect to their nonmarital children. In *Fiallo*, three sets of fathers and unwed children challenged the law as unconstitutional. The Court ruled in the government's favor, holding that Congress's plenary power over the admission of noncitizens precluded the judiciary from second-guessing the legislature's reasons for enacting the law. Citing precedent, the Court noted that immigration laws are closely connected with the political branches' conduct of foreign affairs. Writing for the majority, Justice Powell opined that Congress enacts many laws that

draw distinctions between U.S. citizen and noncitizen—based on age, for example—that, while they may seem arbitrary, are rational. Specifically, he surmised that Congress might have perceived family ties between the biological father and nonmarital child to be less close than those between mother and child. Likewise, Congress may have been concerned about the difficulty in proving paternity in many cases. Powell rejected the argument that the Court more closely scrutinize this law, finding that the effects on U.S. citizens and lawful permanent residents, the gender and illegitimacy discrimination alleged, and the absence of a national security concern did not warrant less deferential judicial review. Although criticized for its deference to Congress, *Fiallo v. Bell* has long been recognized as a key case to support the government's plenary power over immigration.

VICTOR C. ROMERO

References and Further Reading

Satinoff, Debra L., *Sex-Based Discrimination in U.S. Immigration Law: The High Court's Lost Opportunity to Bridge the Gap Between What We Say and What We Do,* American University Law Review 47 (1998): 1353–1392.

See also **Aliens, Civil Liberties of; Citizenship; Equal Protection of Law (XIV); Illegitimacy and Immigration; Sex and Immigration**

FIELD, STEPHEN J. (1816–1899)

One of the most colorful individuals to ever serve on the Supreme Court, Stephen J. Field led major shift in constitutional jurisprudence. He pioneered a broad reading of the Fourteenth Amendment in an effort to define and preserve liberty, and especially economic freedom, by restraining the power of government.

Field was born in Haddam, Connecticut, the sixth child of a Congregationalist minister. Although Field never shared his father's religious commitment, a strong sense of moral certitude permeated his judicial opinions. Reared in Connecticut, Field spent two and a half years in present-day Turkey before beginning study at Williams College. Field graduated first in his class at Williams in 1837. Thereafter, he moved to New York City to study law with his brother, David Dudley Field, a prominent attorney and legal reformer. Field practiced law with his brother in New York City until 1848. A year later he moved to California, where gold had been recently discovered. Field, however, had no intention of prospecting for gold. Rather, he saw the gold rush as a chance to begin a law practice. After brief service as alcalde (an office combining functions of mayor and judge) of Marysville

585

and as a member of the California legislature, Field unsuccessfully sought election to the U.S. Senate. He then developed a lucrative private practice of law in Marysville until he was elected as a Democrat to the California Supreme Court in 1857. The Court heard a large number of disputes over land ownership, and Field helped to develop a consistent body of law in this area. On the outbreak of the Civil War, Field was a Union loyalist.

In 1863, Congress revamped the structure of the federal judiciary and created a new spot on the U.S. Supreme Court for a justice who would have responsibility for the isolated Pacific Coast federal judicial circuit. President Abraham Lincoln was anxious to name a Californian for political and geographical reasons, and he selected Field in part to strengthen California's attachment to the Union. Easily confirmed by the Senate, Field served as a justice for thirty-four years and ranks second among justices for longevity of service.

Although Field generally voted to uphold the actions of the Lincoln administration in the Civil War, he soon demonstrated a libertarian bent. Field joined the opinion in *Ex Parte Milligan* (1866), which invalidated the trial of civilians by the military when civil courts were open. Writing for the Court, Field struck down Civil War loyalty oaths in *Cummings v. Missouri* (1867) and *Ex Parte Garland* (1867). He reasoned that such oaths, designed to keep ex-Confederates out of public offices and certain professions, constituted unconstitutional bills of attainder and ex post facto laws. Field also consistently voted to curtail the confiscation of property owned by Confederate supporters. He authored a number of opinions that held particular confiscations under the Second Confiscation Act to be invalid.

Anti-Chinese sentiments on the West Coast produced numerous laws discriminating against Chinese immigrants. Although not fully consistent in cases involving Chinese immigrants, Field was often sympathetic to their plight. In *Ah Kow v. Nunan* (1879), decided by Field on the federal circuit bench, he invalidated the San Francisco queue ordinance intended to harass the Chinese as discriminatory class legislation barred by the Fourteenth Amendment.

Field is best known for a series of dissenting opinions in which he asserted that the due process clause of the Fourteenth Amendment placed substantive, as well as procedural, checks on state authority. In the *Slaughterhouse Cases* (1873), for example, Field argued in dissent that the Amendment protected the rights of persons to engage in lawful occupations. Field, again in dissent, amplified his views in *Munn v. Illinois* (1877), a case involving state-imposed rate regulation. He vigorously assailed the notion that

government could control the right of owners to charge for the use of their property absent special circumstances. Field also broadly defined liberty as more than freedom from restraint, and as encompassing the right to pursue ordinary trades. During the 1880s Field's views gradually gained ascendancy on the Supreme Court.

Property and liberty were closely linked in Field's jurisprudence. He was primarily concerned to safeguard economic liberties of individuals against state-imposed regulations. In his view, governmental power could not be legitimately used to interfere in the market or redistribute wealth. Voting with the majority in *Pollock v. Farmers' Loan and Trust Co.* (1895) to invalidate the 1894 income tax, Field expressed concern that the levy constituted class legislation, because it imposed burdens based on wealth. In *Allgeyer v. Louisiana* (1897), decided at the end of Field's tenure on the bench, the Court built on his theory that the due process clause Fourteenth Amendment protected the right to pursue lawful callings to recognize the right to make contracts without unreasonable state interference.

Field, however, was never a doctrinaire laissez-fairest or a one-sided champion of business interests. He recognized that states had the authority under the police power to protect the health and safety of their residents. In *Missouri Pacific Railway Company v. Humes* (1885), for instance, he spoke for the Court in an opinion upholding state railroad fencing laws as a means to prevent accidents. Similarly, Field was often supportive of claims of injured industrial workers. He validated state laws that abrogated the fellow-servant rule for railroad employees in *Missouri Pacific Railway Company v. Mackey* (1888). Field also believed that states possessed wide power to promote public morals. He readily sustained laws regulating the sale of alcoholic beverages and controlling lotteries. Writing for the Court in *Davis v. Beason* (1890), he affirmed a territorial law that denied suffrage to those who belonged to a group advocating polygamy and concluded that the First Amendment protected religious beliefs but not conduct.

Field's emphasis on the due process clause of the Fourteenth Amendment as a vehicle to protect property rights and limit government influenced Supreme Court decisions for decades after his retirement. In 1937, however, the Court abandoned the due process review of economic legislation and fashioned a dichotomy between property rights and other personal liberties. Nonetheless, the justices continue to invoke substantive due process to safeguard noneconomic interests, a development that partially reflects Field's jurisprudence.

JAMES W. ELY, JR.

References and Further Reading

Ely, James W., Jr. *The Chief Justiceship of Melville W. Fuller, 1888–1910*. Columbia: University of South Carolina Press, 1995.

Field, Stephen J. *Personal Reminiscences of Early Days in California*. 1877 Reprint, New York: Da Capo Press, 1968.

Kens, Paul. *Justice Stephen Field: Shaping Liberty from the Gold Rush to the Gilded Age*. Lawrence: University Press of Kansas, 1997.

McCurdy, Charles W. "Justice Field and the Jurisprudence of Government-Business Relations: Some Parameters of Laissez-Faire Constitutionalism." *Journal of American History* 61 (1975): 970–1005.

Swisher, Carl Brent. *Stephen J. Field: Craftsman of the Law*. Washington: Brookings Institute, 1930. Reprint: Chicago: University of Chicago Press, 1969.

Cases and Statutes Cited

Ah Kow v. Nunan, 12 F. Cases 252 (C.C.C. Cal. 1879)
Allgeyer v. Louisiana, 165 U.S. 578 (1897)
Cummings v. Missouri, 71 U.S. 277 (1867)
Davis v. Beason, 133 U.S. 333 (1890)
Garland, Ex Parte, 71 U.S. 333 (1867)
Milligan, Ex Parte, 71 U.S. 2 (1866)
Missouri Pacific Railway Company v. Humes, 115 U.S. 512 (1885)
Missouri Pacific Railway Company v. Mackey, 127 U.S. 205 (1888)
Munn v. Illinois, 94 U.S. 113 (1877)
Pollock v. Farmers' Loan and Trust Co., 157 U.S. 429 (1895)
Slaughterhouse Cases, 83 U.S. 36 (1873)

FIGHTING WORDS AND FREE SPEECH

The Supreme Court has held that some speech is not deserving of First Amendment protection—including obscenity, defamation, and fighting words—so that government can regulate it. The Court first articulated the fighting words doctrine in *Chaplinsky v. New Hampshire*, 315 U.S. 568 (1942), upholding a statute that prohibited the use of "offensive, derisive or annoying" language. The *Chaplinsky* decision defined fighting words as "those which by their very utterance inflict injury or tend to incite an immediate breach of the peace," and concluded that statements such as those uttered by Chaplinsky—he called a city marshal a "damned racketeer" and "a damned Fascist"—were of so little value that government could ban them to preserve order and morality. Although the Court continues to reaffirm the fighting words doctrine, it has not upheld any convictions for using fighting words since *Chaplinsky*. In subsequent cases, the Court has either held that the speech in question does not meet the definition of fighting words or concluded that the statute at issue could be construed to be overbroad or underinclusive.

The Court has subsequently narrowed the definition of fighting words to those that are likely to provoke immediate retaliatory violence. In *Terminiello v. Chicago*, 337 U.S. 1 (1949), the Court clarified that speech does not lose First Amendment protection merely because it causes anger. Terminiello's speech enraged a large audience by criticizing various political and racial groups, but the Court held that it was protected unless it was "shown likely to produce a clear and present danger of a serious substantive evil that rises far above public inconvenience, annoyance, or unrest." Similarly, in *Street v. New York*, 394 U.S. 576 (1969), the Court held that the mere offensiveness of speech does not strip it of constitutional protection. Street was convicted of violating a New York state flag desecration statute because, in response to hearing about the murder of civil rights leader James Meredith, he burnt an American flag and said "If they let that happen to Meredith, we don't need an American flag." The Court reversed Street's conviction because, although contemptuous, his speech was not "so inherently inflammatory as to come within that small class of 'fighting words' which are 'likely to provoke the average person to retaliation, and thereby cause a breach of the peace.'"

The Court further narrowed the definition of fighting words and expanded protection for offensive speech in *Cohen v. California*, 403 U.S. 15 (1971). Cohen, a Vietnam War protester, was convicted of disturbing the peace for wearing a jacket bearing the words "Fuck the Draft." The Court held that the words on Cohen's jacket were not fighting words, because they were not directed at an individual and so were not "personally abusive epithets which, when addressed to the ordinary citizen, are, as a matter of common knowledge, inherently likely to provoke violent reaction." The Court also recognized that both the emotive and the cognitive impact of Cohen's expression were deserving of First Amendment protection.

In more recent years, the Court has overturned convictions for using fighting words on the grounds that the statutes prohibiting them were constitutionally overbroad. In *Gooding v. Wilson*, 405 U.S. 518 (1972), the Court cautioned that states must narrowly regulate fighting words so as not to chill protected speech. The *Gooding* court struck down a Georgia statute prohibiting "opprobrious words or abusive language, tending to cause a breach of the peace" because it concluded that the law had been broadly construed to proscribe speech that would not cause an immediate violent response. Similarly, in *Lewis v. City of New Orleans*, 415 U.S. 130 (1974), the Court struck down an ordinance that made it illegal for "any person wantonly to curse or revile or to use obscene or opprobrious language toward or with reference to any member of the city police while in the actual performance of his duty," concluding that the statute could be construed to prohibit offensive, but constitutionally protected, speech. Indeed, in *City of Houston v. Hill*, 482 U.S. 451 (1987), the Court reasoned that the fighting words doctrine "might require a narrower application in cases involving words addressed to a police officer, because 'a properly trained officer may reasonably be expected to exercise a higher degree of restraint than the average citizen, and thus be less likely to respond belligerently to fighting words.'"

In its most recent fighting words case, the Court recognized for the first time that fighting words are not "entirely invisible to the Constitution." In *R.A.V. v. City of St. Paul*, 505 U.S. 377 (1992), the Court struck down as underinclusive a St. Paul, Minnesota, ordinance prohibiting the display of a symbol one has reason to know "arouses anger, alarm or resentment in others on the basis of race, color, creed, religion or gender." The defendants were charged with burning a cross on an African-American family's lawn. Justice Scalia's majority opinion reasoned that government regulation of fighting words cannot be based on hostility or favoritism toward any constitutionally protected message those words contain. Accordingly, even though the ordinance regulated only unprotected speech, it violated the First Amendment for the city to draw a content-based distinction between subsets of fighting words. Four concurring justices, disagreeing with the majority rationale, argued that the ordinance was constitutionally overbroad, because it prohibited expression that "causes only hurt feelings, offense, or resentment."

DENISE C. MORGAN

References and Further Reading

Greenwalt, Kent. *Fighting Words: Individuals, Communities, and Liberties of Speech*. Princeton, NJ: Princeton University Press, 1995.

Hill Collins, Patricia. *Fighting Words: Black Women and the Search for Justice*. Minneapolis: University of Minnesota Press, 1998.

Note, *The Demise Of The Chaplinsky Fighting Words Doctrine: An Argument For Its Interment*, Harvard Law Review 106 (1993): 5:1129–1146.

FIRST AMENDMENT AND PACS

The Political Action Committee, or PAC, is a type of "separate segregated fund" that allows corporations and business entities, long barred from giving directly to candidates for office, to make political contributions. Although some labor organizations and unions had been using PACs before 1971, their legality was questionable. The Federal Election Campaign Act, known as FECA, of that year established rules legalizing and governing PACs. Since that time, PACs have proliferated and have become a primary and, at times, controversial vehicle for candidate financing.

As Congress has progressively strengthened campaign finance regulations over time, PACs have been at the center of the debate over the legality of restricting political giving in light of the Constitutional protection of free speech. Opponents of regulation argue that political contributions amount to political speech and, therefore, merit First Amendment protection from Congressional infringement. Proponents of reform, by contrast, suggest that large campaign contributions such as those from PACs exert undue influence on the political process, whereas regulation of such contributions does not necessarily constitute a check on free speech.

While recognizing that campaign contributions were equivalent to speech and that statutes limiting them would have to withstand strict scrutiny, the Supreme Court affirmed the constitutionality of certain restrictions on political giving in the seminal case *Buckley v. Valeo* (1976). However, the Court later struck down as unconstitutional a provision of FECA which made it illegal for PACs to spend more than $1,000 in "independent expenditures" in *Federal Election Commission v. National Conservative Political Action Committee* (1985). The Supreme Court recognized that speech does not lose constitutional protection merely because it originates from a corporation or union. However, the most recent major campaign finance reform bill, the Bipartisan Campaign Reform Act (2002), has placed additional restrictions on PAC giving. The legislation, which was tested before the Supreme Court in *McConnell v. Federal Election Commission* (2003), affects *inter alia* caps on PAC giving, PAC coordination with candidate committees, and, of course, the main object of the legislation, soft money.

ANDREW FINKELMAN

References and Further Reading

Lowenstein, Daniel H., and Richard L. Hasen, eds. *Election Law: Cases and Materials*. 3rd Ed. Durham, NC: Carolina Academic Press, 2004, pp. 717–750.

Morgan, Anne M. (Note), *Election Law: Limitations on Independent PACs Held Unconstitutional*, Federal Election Commission v. National Conservative Political Action Committee, *105 S. Ct. 1459 (1985)*, Marquette Law Review 69 1985–1986:143.

Cases and Statutes Cited

Buckley v. Valeo, 424 U.S. 1 (1976)
Federal Election Commission v. National Political Action Committee, 470 U.S. 480 (1985)
McConnell v. Federal Election Commission, 540 U.S. 93 (2003)

Cases and Statutes Cited

Boyd v. United States, 116 U.S. 616 (1886)

See also **Boyd v. United States, 116 U.S. 616 (1886); Grand Jury Investigation and Indictment; Self-Incrimination (V): Historical Background**

FISHER v. UNITED STATES, 425 U.S. 391 (1976)

Taxpayers being investigated by the Internal Revenue Service (IRS) provided workpapers prepared by their accountant to their attorney, and the IRS then served a summons on the attorney to obtain the personal records of the clients. While the attorney could not assert the Fifth Amendment Self-Incrimination Privilege on behalf of the client, the Supreme Court found that if the documents would have been protected by the Fifth Amendment in the hands of the taxpayers, then the attorney–client privilege would protect them when the attorney holds the records.

The Court rejected the argument that the Fifth Amendment protects the contents of voluntarily produced documents, largely overturning its 1886 holding in *Boyd v. United States*. The Court changed the Fifth Amendment analysis by holding that the Self-Incrimination Privilege does apply to an individual's act of production in response to a subpoena in a grand jury investigation, which can communicate information about the existence, possession, and authenticity of the records.

A recipient of a grand jury subpoena or an IRS summons may not resist production in every case, however, if the government can show that it will not gain any information from the individual's act of production because the existence, possession, and authenticity of the records is a foregone conclusion. The act of production issue is highly fact-specific and depends on the types of records sought and the scope of the government's knowledge about them. *Fisher* makes clear that the content of the records is not protected by the Self-Incrimination Privilege.

PETER J. HENNING

References and Further Reading

Allen, Ronald J., and M. Kristin Mace, *The Self-Incrimination Clause Explained and Its Future Predicted*, Journal of Criminal Law & Criminology 94 (2004): 2:243–293.

LaFave, Wayne R., Jerold H. Israel, and Nancy J. King. *Criminal Procedure*. 2nd Ed. Vol. 3, St. Paul, MN: Thomson West, 1999, pp. 248–254.

Reitz, Kevin J., *Clients, Lawyers and the Fifth Amendment: The Need for a Projected Privilege*, Duke Law Journal 41 (1991): 3:572–660.

FLAG BURNING

The American flag is a powerful symbol that evokes strong emotions in many citizens. As a result, few methods of political protest are as offensive—or as potentially effective at attracting public attention—as flag burning. Although incidents of flag burning in the United States are relatively rare, law-makers have enacted flag-desecration statutes and even proposed a federal constitutional amendment that would prohibit flag burning. Supporters of these efforts believe they are necessary to preserve the flag as a cherished emblem of national unity. Opponents argue that flag burning constitutes a means of expressing dissent that is, and must remain, fully protected by the First Amendment. In a pair of cases decided in 1989 and 1990, the U.S. Supreme Court held that the First Amendment protects flag burning as a type of Symbolic Speech. Since then, proposals for a flag-desecration amendment to the Constitution have been introduced frequently in Congress, but so far none has gathered the two-thirds support in the Senate needed for passage.

Is Flag Burning "Speech"?

The First Amendment ensures the right to free speech; it does not prohibit the government from regulating behavior. Flag burning certainly communicates a message, but it does so through an act and without the necessity of words. Could the government therefore treat flag burning as illegal conduct, rather than as protected expression?

The Supreme Court dodged the question when it first emerged in the 1960s in *Street v. New York* (1969). In that case, decorated war veteran Sydney Street burned a flag on a Brooklyn street corner after learning that civil rights activist James Meredith had been shot by a sniper in Mississippi. Street told the gathered crowd, "We don't need no damn flag," and explained to a police officer that "If they let that happen to Meredith we don't need an American flag." Street was convicted under a New York statute that criminalized flag desecration, as well as the expression of contemptuous words about the flag.

Although the Supreme Court overturned Street's conviction on First Amendment grounds, the decision rested on the conclusion that Street had been punished for his offensive language, rather than for his act of flag burning.

In related contexts, however, the Court had already recognized that expressive conduct could qualify as speech entitled to a measure of First Amendment protection. For example, in *Stromberg v. California* (1931), the Court overturned a woman's conviction under a California law that prohibited public use or display of a red flag "as a sign, symbol or emblem of opposition to organized government," noting that the ban interfered with free political discussion. And in a famous case involving a war protestor who burned his draft card, *United States v. O'Brien* (1968), the Court outlined a test for determining when government regulation is justified in symbolic speech cases. According to that test, the First Amendment requires that government regulation of symbolic speech be content neutral and narrowly tailored to achieve a valid government interest that is unrelated to the suppression of expression.

Does all behavior that communicates an idea, therefore, constitute speech protected by the First Amendment? Not necessarily. According to the Court in *Spence v. Washington* (1974), expressive conduct will only qualify as symbolic speech if an "intent to convey a particular message was present, and...the likelihood was great that the message would be understood by those who viewed it."

Texas v. Johnson

The Supreme Court finally addressed the flag-burning issue in *Texas v. Johnson* (1989), holding by a five-to-four vote that Gregory Johnson's conviction under a Texas flag desecration statute violated the First Amendment. Johnson had burned an American flag at the 1984 Republican National Convention in Dallas as part of a public protest against Reagan Administration policies and had been tried, convicted, and sentenced to one year in jail and a $2,000 fine. The statute prohibited any physical mistreatment of the flag "that the actor knows will seriously offend one or more persons likely to observe or discover his action."

Writing for the majority, Justice William Brennan began by confirming that Johnson's act qualified as symbolic speech under the First Amendment, noting that flag burning in this context clearly conveyed a particular political message. Justice Brennan then looked to see whether the state could justify its prohibition against flag burning in a content-neutral way.

The state made two arguments to support Johnson's conviction: first, that it was necessary to avert a breach of the peace; and second, that it preserved the flag's unique symbolic value.

With respect to the first argument, Justice Brennan noted that although several onlookers had been offended by Johnson's conduct, no breach of the peace had occurred or had been threatened. According to the Court, the state may not prohibit offensive speech by merely asserting that such speech presents a risk of violence. Nor could the state say that Johnson's conduct fell within the First Amendment exception for Fighting Words, because no bystander could have reasonably regarded Johnson's act as "a direct personal insult or an invitation to exchange fisticuffs."

As for the asserted state interest in safeguarding the flag's value as a national symbol, Justice Brennan concluded that this interest was not content neutral. The Texas flag desecration statute contained an exception that allowed worn, dirty, or torn flags to be burned as a proper method of disposal. Therefore, while the statute allowed respectful, "patriotic" flag burning, it prohibited flag burning as an expression of political protest. "If there is a bedrock principle underlying the First Amendment," Justice Brennan wrote, "it is that the Government may not prohibit the expression of an idea simply because society finds the idea itself offensive or disagreeable."

The Aftermath

The Court's decision in *Texas v. Johnson* touched off what one newspaper termed "a firestorm of indignation" that ultimately resulted in Congressional passage of the federal Flag Protection Act of 1989. The law attempted to prohibit flag desecration in a content-neutral manner by banning all physical harm to the flag (except that caused by disposing of old or soiled flags) regardless of the conduct's effect on bystanders. Nevertheless, the Court in *United States v. Eichman* (1990) struck down the law in a five-to-four decision. Again writing for the majority, Justice Brennan concluded that the federal law violated the First Amendment because it proscribed expression "out of concern for its likely communicative impact." In other words, the statute was content based because it criminalized only those acts that demonstrated disrespect for the flag. "Punishing desecration of the flag dilutes the very freedom that makes this emblem so revered, and worth revering," he wrote. Justice John Paul Stevens authored the dissent, in which he argued that the statute was content neutral, because it prohibited all flag desecration no matter what the actor's intended message.

Since the Court's decision in *Eichman*, the House of Representatives approved a Constitutional amendment in 1995, 1997, 1999, 2001, and 2003 that would have allowed Congress or the states to criminalize "physical desecration of the flag." To date, this proposed amendment has always been defeated in the Senate. Supporters of the amendment argue that the flag is a unique national symbol that deserves special protection against mistreatment or disrespect. Flag burning, according to this view, adds nothing meaningful to the marketplace of ideas and, therefore, has no value as speech. Critics respond that a nation founded on principles of liberty must safeguard its citizens' right to express dissent—even when that expression takes a form that the majority finds offensive. Critics also object to the possible wide array of legislative interpretations under the amendment regarding what constitutes either "desecration" or "the flag."

NICOLE B. CÁSAREZ

References and Further Reading

Goldstein, Robert Justin. *Flag Burning and Free Speech: The Case of* Texas v. Johnson. Lawrence, KS: University Press of Kansas, 2000.

Greenawalt, Kent, *O'er the Land of the Free: Flag Burning as Speech*, UCLA Law Review 37 (1990): 925–947.

Smolla, Rodney A. *Free Speech in an Open Society*. New York: Alfred A. Knopf, Inc., 1992.

Van Alstyne, William W. Freedom of speech and the flag anti-desecration amendment: antinomies of constitutional choice, in Rodgers, Raymond S., ed. *Free Speech Yearbook*, Vol. 29. Carbondale & Edwardsville: Southern Illinois University Press, 1991, pp. 96–105.

Cases and Statutes Cited

Spence v. Washington, 418 U.S. 405 (1974)
Street v. New York, 394 U.S. 576 (1969)
Stromberg v. California, 283 U.S. 359 (1931)
Texas v. Johnson, 491 U.S. 397 (1989)
United States v. Eichman, 496 U.S. 310 (1990)
United States v. O'Brien, 391 U.S. 367 (1968)

See also **Content-Based Regulation of Speech; Draft Card Burning; Fighting Words and Free Speech; Symbolic Speech**

FLAG SALUTE CASES

In 1935, Jehovah's Witnesses in Germany refused to salute the Nazi flag. Ultimately, more than 10,000 German Jehovah's Witnesses would be sent to concentration camps for their affront to Nazi authorities. In 1935, the leader of the Jehovah's Witnesses in

America declared that followers of the faith "do not 'Heil Hitler' nor any other creature." He found scriptural support for this position by arguing that saluting the flag was a form of idolatry. After this speech, American Jehovah's Witnesses refused to take part in flag saluting ceremonies. After this change in their religious practice, Jehovah's Witnesses began to face disciplinary actions in public schools across America. In *Minersville School District v. Gobitis* (1940), the Court upheld the school district's attempt to force students to salute the flag. In *West Virginia State Board of Education, v. Barnette* (1943) the court reversed course, siding with the claims of religious freedom made by the Jehovah's Witnesses.

Minersville School District v. Gobitis (1940)

This case resulted from the refusal of twelve-year-old Lillian Gobitis and her ten-year-old brother William to say the pledge of allegiance in the public schools of Minersville, Pennsylvania. The father of these children, Walter Gobitis, had grown up in Minersville and was raised in a Roman Catholic family and of course saluted the flag as a child. In 1931, Gobitis became a Jehovah's Witness, a faith that regularly denounced the Catholic Church and the Pope. At the time Lillian was eight and William was six. The Gobitis children continued to salute the flag until November 1935, when members of their faith across the nation ceased to salute the flag.

In a more cosmopolitan community, the refusal of the Gobitis children to salute the flag might have gone unnoticed. But, neither Gobitis nor his faith was popular in Minersville, where eighty percent of the population was Roman Catholic. Rather than ignoring what was neither an act of defiance nor a disruption in the schools, the school board adopted a regulation allowing for the expulsion of any students who would not salute the flag. Gobitis then sent his children to a private Jehovah's Witness school.

Eighteen months later, Gobitis sued the school district. The case was first heard by Judge Albert B. Maris, a recent Roosevelt appointee to the federal court. As a Quaker, Maris was probably more sympathetic to the Jehovah's Witnesses than most Americans. Although he had a distinguished military record during World War I, as a member of a faith long persecuted for its pacifism, Maris, doubtless understood the nature of prejudice and religious persecution that the Jehovah's Witnesses faced.

During the trial, the school superintendent was openly hostile toward the Gobitis children and the Jehovah's Witnesses, asserting that the children were "indoctrinated," thereby implying that their actions were not based on sincerely held religions beliefs. Judge Maris rejected Roudabush's contentions. Judge Maris asserted that "To permit public officers to determine whether the views of individuals sincerely held and their acts sincerely undertaken on religious grounds are in fact based on convictions religious in character would sound the death knell of religious liberty." Maris refused to sustain "such a pernicious and alien doctrine" and reminded the school officials that Pennsylvania itself had been founded "as a haven for all those persecuted for conscience' sake." Judge Maris found that "although undoubtedly adopted from patriotic motives," the flag salute requirement "appears to have become in this case a means for the persecution of children for conscience' sake." He noted that "religious intolerance is again rearing its ugly head in other parts of the world" and thus it was of "utmost importance that the liberties guaranteed to our citizens by the fundamental law be preserved from all encroachment." While not central to his decision, Maris's point placed the controversy over the Jehovah's Witnesses in the context of the rise of Nazism, preparation for World War II, and eventually American involvement in the War. In part the cases involving the Jehovah's Witnesses raised important questions about how much dissent a democracy can allow at a time of crisis and international conflict. Maris took the position that such dissent was vital to the democracy and part of its ultimate strength. The Minersville School Board took the position that national unity required submission to the will of the majority, especially on issues involving outward displays of patriotism. This argument would reemerge among before the Supreme Court in both *Gobitis* and *Barnette*.

Having concluded that the flag salute requirement was motivated by a desire to provide "a means for the persecution of children for conscience' sake," Maris ordered the children readmitted to the public schools, and a unanimous panel of the U.S. Court of Appeals affirmed this decision. Minersville school officials did not plan to appeal the Supreme Court, but, patriotic groups, including the American Legion, stepped in to help finance the case. Before the Supreme Court, Harvard Law School Professor George K. Gardner argued Gobitis's case on behalf of the American Civil Liberties Union.

In an eight to one decision, the Supreme Court reversed the two lower court decisions and upheld the right of the Minersville School District to require that students salute the flag. Writing for the Court was Justice Felix Frankfurter, who conceded that "the affirmative pursuit of one's convictions about the ultimate mystery of the universe and man's relation to it is placed beyond the reach of law. Government may not interfere with organized or individual expression of belief or disbelief." However, Frankfurter noted that there were no absolute guarantees of religious freedom. He found that the task of the Court was to "reconcile two rights in order to prevent either from destroying the other." He found that "conscientious scruples have not, in the course of the long struggle for religious toleration, relieved the individual from obedience to a general law not aimed at the promotion or restriction of religious beliefs. The mere possession of religious convictions that contradict the relevant concerns of a political society does not relieve the citizen from a discharge of political responsibilities." Put simply, Frankfurter was arguing that the First Amendment's guarantee of religious freedom only extended to protection from laws that were overtly religious in nature. Frankfurter rejected the findings of the lower court that the enforcement of the pledge was overt religious discrimination.

In a hyperbolic analogy, Frankfurter compared the dilemma of the Jehovah's Witnesses to that of Lincoln's query during the Civil War: "Must a government of necessity be too *strong* for the liberties of its people, or too *weak* to maintain its own existence?" Frankfurter argued that the flag was a "symbol of national unity, transcending all internal differences" and as such he implied that failure to salute it somehow threatened the existence of the nation.

He further argued that the states should be given great latitude in determining how best to instill patriotism in children. He thought judicial review was "a limitation on popular government" that should be used sparingly. Thus, he urged that issues of liberty be fought out in the state legislatures and "in the forum of public opinion" to "vindicate the self-confidence of a free people."

Justice Harlan Fiske Stone dissented, asserting that "by this law the state seeks to coerce these children to express a sentiment that, as they interpret it, they do not entertain, and which violates their deepest religious convictions." Stone dismissed Frankfurter's appeals to patriotism and his unrealistic suggestion that the issue be decided "in the forum of public opinion" by appeals to the wisdom of the legislature. Stone pointed out that "History teaches us that there have been but few infringements of personal liberty by the state which have not been justified, as they are here, in the name of righteousness and the public good, and few which have not been directed, as they are now, at politically helpless minorities." Finally, Stone argued that the Constitution was more than just an outline for majoritarian government, it was "also an expression of faith and a command that freedom of mind and spirit must be preserved, which government must obey, if it is to adhere to that justice and moderation without which no free government can exist."

Stone understood the value of instilling patriotism in future citizens. He declared that the state might "require teaching by instruction and study of all in our history and in the structure and organization of our government, including the guarantee of civil liberty, which tend to inspire patriotism and love of country." But, forcing children to violate their religious precepts was, in Stone's mind, not the way to teach patriotic values. He thought it far better that the schools find "some sensible adjustment of school discipline in order that the religious convictions of these children may be spared" than to approve "legislation which operates to repress the religious freedom of small minorities...."

The *Gobitis* decision helped unleash a wave of political, legal, and physical attacks on Jehovah's Witnesses. Immediately after the decision, there were hundreds of assaults on Jehovah's Witnesses and their property. Throughout the nation, Jehovah's Witnesses were beaten, mobbed, and kidnapped. Their attackers often included police officials. In Odessa, Texas, for example, seventy Jehovah's Witnesses were arrested for their own "protection," held without charges when they refused to salute the flag, and then released to a mob of more than 1,000 people who chased them for five miles, throwing stones at them. In Wyoming some Jehovah's Witnesses were tarred and feathered, in Arkansas some were shot, and in Nebraska one Jehovah's Witness was castrated. In Richwood, West Virginia, the police arrested a group of Jehovah's Witnesses who sought police protection, forced them to drink large amounts of castor oil, tied them up, and paraded them through the town. By 1943 more than 2,000 Jehovah's Witnesses had been expelled from schools in all forty-eight states. This was the nationwide answer to Justice Frankfurter's unrealistic suggestion that the Jehovah's Witnesses appeal to the state legislatures for relief.

The nation's intellectual community responded to *Gobitis* in quite a different way. Overwhelmingly law review articles condemned the decision. The law reviews at Catholic universities, such as Fordham, Georgetown, and Notre Dame, were unanimous in their opposition to *Gobitis*, even though the Jehovah's Witnesses had traditionally vilified the Roman Catholic Church. But, the issue here was civil liberties, not theology, as Catholic scholars clearly understood.

Members of the Supreme Court soon came to doubt the wisdom of *Gobitis*. In another case involving the Jehovah's Witnesses, *Jones v. Opelika* (1942), three dissenting justices who had voted with the majority in *Gobitis* declared they now believe it was "wrongly decided" and that "the historic Bill of Rights has a high responsibility to accommodate itself to the religious views of minorities however unpopular and unorthodox those views may be."

Barnette v. West Virginia State Board of Education

In January 1942, the West Virginia state school board adopted a strict flag salute requirement. The board's resolution, which had the authority of a statute, began with a long preamble that quoted at length portions of Frankfurter's *Gobitis* opinion. The resolution ended by declaring "that refusal to salute the Flag [shall] be regarded as an act of insubordination, and shall be dealt with accordingly." Shortly after the adoption of this resolution, school officials in Charleston expelled a number of Jehovah's Witnesses, including the children of Walter Barnette.

In August 1942, attorneys for Barnette and other Jehovah's Witnesses asked the District Court to convene a three-judge panel to permanently enjoin state school officials from requiring Jehovah's Witnesses to salute the flag. Writing for a unanimous court, Judge John J. Parker, of the Fourth Circuit Court of Appeals, granted the injunction. Parker acknowledged that "ordinarily" the lower court would "feel constrained to follow an unreversed decision of the Supreme Court of the United States, whether we agreed with it or not." However, in the light of the dissents in *Opelika*, Parker expressed doubt that *Gobitis* was still binding. The three-judge panel believed that the West Virginia flag salute requirement was "violative of religious liberty when required of persons holding the religious views of the plaintiffs."

West Virginia's attorney general refused to appeal this decision to the U.S. Supreme Court, so the attorney for the Board of Education appealed the case with an unimaginative argument that relied almost entirely on *Gobitis*, supported by a weak *amicus* brief from the American Legion. Attorneys for Barnette attacked *Gobitis*, comparing it to the *Dred Scott* decision of 1857. Amicus briefs for Barnette came from the American Civil Liberties Union written by Osmond K. Fraenkel and Arthur Garfield Hays and the American Bar Association's Committee on the Bill of Rights written by Harvard Law professor Zachariah Chafee, Jr.

On June 14, 1943, which was Flag Day, Justice Robert Jackson, speaking for a six to three majority upheld the lower court and reversed the *Gobitis* precedent. Justice Frankfurter wrote a bitter dissent.

While the Flag Salute cases are generally seen as involving freedom of religion, that issue is virtually absent from Jackson's majority opinion. He accepts, without question, that the Jehovah's Witnesses sincerely held beliefs that made it impossible for them to conscientiously salute the flag. But, Jackson does not offer any analysis of the importance of that belief or even of the role of religious freedom in striking down the mandatory flag salute. Indeed, he links the freedom to worship with other bill of rights protections, noting that the "right to life, liberty, and property, to free speech, a free press, freedom of worship and assembly, and other fundamental rights may not be submitted to vote; they depend on the outcome of no elections." He finds that the "freedoms of speech and of press, of assembly, and of worship may not be infringed" on "slender grounds."

Rather than grounding his opinion in freedom of religion, Jackson analyzed the case as one of freedom of speech and expression. Jackson argued that the flag salute—or the refusal to salute the flag—was "a form of utterance" and thus subject to standard free speech analysis. He noted that the flag was a political symbol, and, naturally, saluting that symbol was symbolic speech:

> Symbolism is a primitive but effective way of communicating ideas. The use of an emblem or flag to symbolize some system, idea, institution, or personality, is a short cut from mind to mind. Causes and nations, political parties, lodges and ecclesiastical groups seek to knit the loyalty of their followings to a flag or banner, a color or design. The State announces rank, function, and authority through crowns and maces, uniforms and black robes; the church speaks through the Cross, the Crucifix, the altar and shrine, and clerical raiment. Symbols of the State often convey political ideas just as religious symbols come to convey theological ones.

The question for Jackson was rather simple, did the "speech" of the Jehovah's Witnesses threaten the rights of any individuals or the peace and stability of the government. If the answer to either question was yes, then Jackson might have allowed the mandatory flag salute. But, if they did not threaten the rights of others or threaten the government, then there was no valid reason to suppress their expression.

Jackson noted that the conduct of the Jehovah's Witnesses "did not bring them into collision with rights asserted by any other individuals." The Court was not being asked "to determine where the rights of one end and another begin." It was, rather, a conflict "between [governmental] authority and rights of the individual."

Jackson compared the forced flag salute to *Stromberg v. California*, 283 U.S. 359 (1931), which had allowed protestors to carry a red flag. This case and

others supported the "commonplace" standard in free speech cases "that censorship or suppression of expression of opinion is tolerated by our Constitution only when the expression presents a clear and present danger of action of a kind the State is empowered to prevent and publish. It would seem that involuntary affirmation could be commanded only on even more immediate and urgent grounds than silence." But, were there such grounds? No one claimed that the silence of the children "during a flag salute ritual creates a clear and present danger that would justify an effort even to muffle expression." Jackson pointed out the irony of the flag salute requirement, in light of the expanded freedom of speech found in recent decision. "To sustain the compulsory flag salute we are required to say that a Bill of Rights which guards the individual's right to speak his own mind, left it open to public authorities to compel him to utter what is not in his mind."

Jackson's shrewd analysis had turned the case inside out. It was no longer one of freedom of religion, but one that in part took the form of an establishment of religion on the part of the government through its "flag salute ritual." Jackson correctly saw that the Jehovah's Witnesses were not trying to force their views on anyone else, but rather, that the government was trying to force its views and beliefs on the Jehovah's Witnesses. He noted that in *Gobitis* the Court had "only examined and rejected a claim based on religious beliefs of immunity from general rule." But, Jackson pointed out, this was not the correct question to ask. Indeed, Jackson noted that people who did not hold the religious views of the Jehovah's Witnesses might still find "such a compulsory rite to infringe constitutional liberty of the individual." For Jackson the correct question was "whether such a ceremony so touching matters of opinion and political attitude may be imposed upon the individual by official authority ... under the Constitution." In other words, did the government have the power to force anyone, regardless of their religious beliefs, to participate in any ceremony or "ritual." What Jackson might have asked was, did the Constitution allow for the establishment of a secular national religion with the flag as the chief icon? This led him to a discussion, and refutation, of various points in *Gobitis*.

In *Gobitis*, Frankfurter had noted Lincoln's "memorable dilemma" of choosing between civil liberties and maintaining a free society. Jackson had little patience for "such oversimplification, so handy in political debate." He "doubted whether Mr. Lincoln would have thought that the strength of government to maintain itself would be impressively vindicated by our confirming power of the state to expel a handful of children from school." Here Jackson revealed the fundamental weakness of Frankfurter's assertion in *Gobitis* that somehow the safety of the nation depended on whether Jehovah's Witnesses were forced to salute the flag in the public schools.

Along this line, Jackson noted even Congress had made the flag salute optional for soldiers who had religious scruples against such ceremonies. This act "respecting the conscience of the objector in a matter so vital as raising the Army" contrasted "sharply with these local regulations in matters relatively trivial to the welfare of the nation."

This led Jackson to the national security issue raised by Frankfurter in *Gobitis*. At the time of *Gobitis,* the nation was not at war, but war seemed imminent. By the time the Court heard *Barnette,* the nation had been at war for more than a year. Jackson agreed that in wartime "national unity" was necessary and something the government should "foster by persuasion and example."

But, could the government gain national unity by force? Jackson made references to the suppression of the early Christians in Rome, the Inquisition, "the Siberian exiles as a means of Russian unity," and the "fast failing efforts of our present totalitarian enemies." He warned that "those who begin coercive elimination of dissent soon find themselves exterminating the dissenters. Compulsory unification of opinion achieves only the unanimity of the graveyard." During a war against Nazism, Jackson's opinion was a plea for the nation to avoid becoming like its enemies.

Jackson ended his opinion by reminding Americans that the patriotism in a free county could not be instilled by force. Indeed, he argued that those who thought otherwise "make an unflattering estimate of the appeal of our institutions to free minds." America's strength, he argued, was found in diversity. The test of freedom was "the right to differ as to things that touch the heart of the existing order." This led Jackson to a ringing defense of individual liberty: "If there is any fixed star in our constitutional constellation, it is that no official, high or petty, can prescribe what shall be orthodox in politics, nationalism, religion, or other matters of opinion or force citizens to confess by word or act their faith therein."

Justice Felix Frankfurter was unmoved by Jackson's powerful defense of individual liberty and his condemnation of oppressive "village tyrants" who expelled small children from school because of their religious beliefs. At a time when millions of Jews (and thousands of Jehovah's Witnesses) were perishing in German death camps, Frankfurter used his ethnicity to justify his support for the suppression of a religious minority in the United States. He began: "One who belongs to the most vilified and persecuted minority in history is

not likely to be insensible to the freedoms guaranteed by our Constitution." But, he argued that he could not bring his personal beliefs to the Court because, "as judges we are neither Jew nor Gentile, neither Catholic nor agnostic." He then defended judicial self-restraint and recapitulated and elaborated on his *Gobitis* opinion.

Frankfurter argued that "saluting the flag suppresses no belief nor curbs it" because those saluting it were still free to "believe what they please, avow their belief and practice it." In making this point Frankfurter failed to explain how one could "practice a belief" by doing what that belief prohibited. Nor did he explain how forcing children to say and do one thing, while encouraging them to secretly believe that what they were doing was a violation of God's commandments, would inspire patriotism in them.

Frankfurter conceded that the flag salute law "may be a foolish measure," and that "patriotism cannot be enforced by the flag salute." But he argued that the court had no business interfering with laws made by democratically elected legislatures. Frankfurter argued that because a total of thirteen justices had found the flag salute laws to be constitutional, the state laws "can not be deemed unreasonable." Because the state legislators had relied the recent decision in *Gobitis,* Frankfurter thought it unfair to strike down their legislation.

Frankfurter condemned "our constant preoccupation with the constitutionality of legislation rather than with its wisdom...." Yet he refused to strike down the West Virginia law that he conceded was unwise, not because it passed all constitutional tests but because of judicial restraint and respect for *stare decisis.* He argued that the "most precious interests of civilization" were to be "found outside of their vindication in courts of law" that thus he urged that the Court not interfere in the democratic process but to wait for a "positive translation of the faith of a free society into the convictions and habits and actions of the community." What would happen to the Jehovah's Witnesses in the meantime seemed of little concern to Frankfurter.

There was some minor resistance in a few localities to *Barnette.* The Supreme Court heard a few cases in which various local decisions were overturned. On the same day it handed down *Barnette,* the court unanimously overturned a conviction for sedition in *Taylor v. Mississippi,* 319 U.S. 583 (1943). The Jehovah's Witnesses in that case had been convicted for "violating a statute making it an offence to preach, teach or disseminate any doctrine which reasonably tends to create an attitude of stubborn refusal to salute, honor, or respect the Government of the United States or the State of Mississippi." The defendants had been sentenced to remain in jail until the end of the War or for ten years, whichever came first. The Court found the act abridged freedom of speech and press and was "so vague, indefinite, and uncertain as to furnish no reasonably ascertainable standard of guilt." The Mississippi law, and the prosecutions under it, illustrates the extent of official persecution of the Jehovah's Witnesses. After 1946, the Court heard no more cases on the flag salute issue. *Barnette* became an important precedent for other free speech and freedom of religion cases.

PAUL FINKELMAN

References and Further Reading

Manwaring, David. *Render Unto Caesar: The Flag Salute Controversy.* Chicago: University of Chicago Press, 1962.
Peters, Shawn Francis. *Judging Jehovah's Witnesses: Religious Persecution and the Dawn of the Rights Revolution.* Lawrence, KS: University of Kansas Press, 2000.

FLAST v. COHEN, 392 U.S. 83 (1968)

Case litigation requires courts to possess the authority to hear the case ("justiciability"). An important justiciability requirement is that litigants have "standing" (be able to show injury to a protected interest) to sue. One of the most important cases involving standing is *Flast v. Cohen*, where the Supreme Court determined that taxpayers have standing to sue the government to prevent unconstitutional uses of taxpayer funds.

In *Flast*, taxpayers challenged federal legislation financing the purchase of textbooks for religious schools, arguing such use of tax money violated the First Amendment's establishment clause. The issue before the Supreme Court was whether petitioners' status as taxpayers gave them standing to sue in federal courts. Using a two-part test, the Court held (eight to one) that petitioners had standing to pursue the lawsuit.

Flast clarified an earlier ruling in *Frothingham v. Mellon* (262 U.S. 447 [1923]), which prevented taxpayers from having standing to sue the federal government if the only injury was an anticipated tax increase. The Court explained that *Frothingham* did not absolutely bar taxpayer suits but prevented courts from serving as forums for generalized taxpayer grievances. The *Flast* decision allows taxpayer suits against the federal government if the taxpayer can show: (1) a logical relationship between their taxpayer status and the challenged statute; and (2) that the challenged enactment exceeds constitutional limitations imposed on congressional taxing and spending power. Although the Burger and Rehnquist Courts

have restricted standing requirements, taxpayer suits are commonly used today to contest the constitutionality of government actions.

LEE R. REMINGTON

References and Further Reading

Dorf, Michael, ed. *Constitutional Law Stories: Constitutional Law.* New York: Foundation Press, 2004.
Miller, Robert T., and Ronald B. Flowers. *Toward Benevolent Neutrality: Church, State, and the Supreme Court.* 4th Ed. Waco, TX: Markham Press, 1992.
Tribe, Laurence H. *American Constitutional Law.* 3rd Ed. New York: West Publishing Company, 1999.

Cases and Statutes Cited

Flast v. Cohen, 392 U.S. 83 (1968)
Frothingham v. Mellon, 262 U.S. 447 (1923)

FLORIDA STAR v. B.J.F., 491 U.S. 524 (1989)

Florida Star is an important free press case reinforcing the principle that the press can rarely be punished for publishing truthful, lawfully acquired information about a matter of public importance. In *Florida Star*, the Supreme Court refused to punish a weekly newspaper that published the name of a rape victim in violation of a state statute.

The Court agreed that the statute attempted to serve the "highly significant interests" of protecting rape victims' privacy and safety and encouraging victims to report rapes without fear of exposure or reprisal. But the Court majority was unwilling to hold a newspaper liable for publishing truthful information, information in B.J.F.'s case about a matter of "paramount public import: the commission, and investigation, of a violent crime which had been reported to authorities."

The Court did not rule that the press could never be punished for publishing truthful information, but, drawing on *Smith v. Daily Mail Publishing Company*, the Court said only a government interest of the "highest order" would justify such punishment. Once again, the Court left editors to decide what to publish.

The six-member majority was unwilling to hold the press responsible for publishing information that was already public, especially because it was the sheriff's office that released the victim's name. The Court also thought the statute was too broad, automatically punishing the press, whether or not anyone was offended or damaged by the publication.

The three dissenters argued the Court's ruling would "obliterate" the legal protection for a person's "private facts."

KENT R. MIDDLETON

References and Further Reading

Franklin, Mark A., David A. Anderson, and Fred H. Cate. *Mass Media Law: Cases and Materials.* 6th Ed. New York: Foundation Press, 2000, pp. 424–451.

Cases and Statutes Cited

Smith v. Daily Mail Publishing Co., 443 U.S. 97 (1979)

FLORIDA v. JIMENO, 500 U.S. 248 (1991)

Argued March 25, 1991, decided May 23, 1991, by a vote of seven to two, Chief Justice Rehnquist delivered the opinion for the Court, with Justice Marshall and Stevens dissenting. The Court held that a criminal suspect's Fourth Amendment right to be free from unreasonable searches is not violated when, after he gives police permission to search his car, they open a closed container found within the car that might reasonably hold the object of the search.

Police Officer Trujillo followed Jimeno's car after overhearing Jimeno arrange what seemed to be a drug transaction. Jimeno was subsequently stopped for a traffic violation. Officer Trujillo declared he had reason to believe that Jimeno was carrying narcotics in the car and asked permission to search it. Jimeno consented, and Trujillo found cocaine inside a folded paper bag on the car's floorboard. Jimeno argued that his consent to search did not carry the specific consent to open the bag and examine its contents.

Chief Justice Rehnquist opined that the Fourth Amendment was satisfied when, under the circumstances, "it is objectively reasonable for the police to believe that the scope of the suspect's consent permitted them to open the particular container." (p. 250–252). The authorization to search extended beyond the car's interior surfaces to the bag, since Jimeno did not place any explicit limitation on the scope of the search and was aware that Trujillo would be looking for narcotics in the car. Since a reasonable person may be expected to know that narcotics are generally carried in some form of container, it is reasonable for Trujillo to open the bag. There is no basis for adding to the Fourth Amendment's basic test of objective reasonableness a requirement that if police wish to search closed containers within a car, they must separately request permission to search each container.

The dissent argued the distinction between open and closed containers and noted that general consent should not be specific consent as well. "A person who consents to a search of the car from the driver's seat could also be deemed to consent to a search of his person, or indeed of his body cavities, since a

reasonable person may be expected to know that drug couriers frequently store their contraband on their persons or in their body cavities. I suppose (and hope) that even the majority would reject this conclusion, for a person who consents to the search of his car for drugs certainly does not consent to a search of things other than his car for drugs." (p. 256). There are distinct privacy expectations a person has in a car and in closed containers.

AARON R. S. LORENZ

See also **Search (General Definition); Seizures; Warrantless Searches; Automobile Searches**

FLORIDA v. RILEY, 488 U.S. 445 (1989)

Florida v. Riley considered whether helicopter surveillance constituted a search within the meaning of the Fourth Amendment, such that a warrant would be required. In the plurality opinion, the Supreme Court reversed the lower court, holding that the Fourth Amendment did not require police traveling in the public airways (in legal airspace) at an altitude of 400 feet to obtain a warrant to observe what was visible to the naked eye.

After an anonymous tip that respondent was growing marijuana, a sheriff's officer circled over the property in a helicopter flying at 400 feet. With his naked eye, he was able to see through openings in the roof and sides of the greenhouse. After he identified what he thought was marijuana, he obtained a search warrant to confirm his observations.

The Court relied on *California v. Ciraolo*, 476 U.S. 207 (1986), a similar case involving a police inspection from a fixed wing aircraft at 1,000 feet. There, the Court held that the viewing was not a search subject to the Fourth Amendment even though the occupant had a subjective expectation of privacy. A home and its curtilage are not necessarily protected from inspection that involves no physical invasion. "What a person knowingly exposes to the public, even in his own home or office, is not a subject of Fourth Amendment protection." *Ciraolo*, 476 U.S. at 213 (citing *Katz v. United States*, 389 U.S. 347, 351 (1967)). As long as the police are "where [they have] a right to be," *Ciraolo*, 476 U.S. at 213, they need not obtain a warrant.

EMILY FROIMSON

Cases and Statutes Cited

California v. Ciraolo, 476 U.S. 207 (1986)
Katz v. United States, 389 U.S. 347, 351 (1967)

See also **Electronic Surveillance, Technological Monitoring, and Dog Sniffs**

FLORIDA v. ROYER, 460 U.S. 491 (1983)

The nature of a police-citizen encounter determines whether Fourth Amendment rights are implicated and possibly infringed; without a seizure by police, Fourth Amendment protections do not apply. In *Florida v. Royer*, the Supreme Court revisited its stop and frisk doctrine, further clarifying when a consensual encounter becomes a seizure or when a seizure becomes an arrest.

Plainclothes narcotics detectives stopped Royer in the airport, identified themselves, and asked him to speak with them. At their request, Royer gave them his airline ticket and driver's license. Noticing a discrepancy, the detectives told Royer they suspected he was carrying narcotics. Retaining his documents, the detectives asked Royer to come with them to a small room nearby. One detective then retrieved Royer's luggage without his consent. When asked if he would consent to a search of the luggage, Royer simply produced a key and unlocked one bag. Marijuana was found inside, as well as in another bag. Royer was arrested and convicted of felony possession of marijuana.

In a plurality opinion, the Court found the initial encounter had escalated into an unlawful arrest when the detectives moved Royer to a small room while retaining his ticket, license, and luggage. Because Royer's consent was given after the unlawful arrest, it was tainted by this illegality and could not justify the luggage search. Recognizing there was no bright-line marking when an encounter becomes a seizure or an arrest, the Court reiterated that a lawful investigatory detention has to be limited in its scope and duration, considering the specific circumstances justifying its inception.

MARGARET M. LAWTON

References and Further Reading

American Jurisprudence. 2nd Ed., vol. 68 (Searches and Seizures). West Group, 2000, sec. 18–19.

Dressler, Joshua. *Understanding Criminal Procedure*. 3rd Ed. LexisNexis Publishing, 2002, pp. 131–134.

Katz, Lewis R., Terry v. Ohio at Thirty-Five: *A Revisionist View*, Mississippi Law Journal (2004) 74: 423–500.

LaFave, Wayne R., Jerold Israel, and Nancy J. King. *Criminal Procedure: Criminal Practice Series*. vol. 2, Chapter 3, sec. 8. St. Paul, MN: West Group, 1999.

United States v. Mendenhall, 466 U.S. 544 (1980).

Cases and Statutes Cited

Terry v. Ohio, 392 U.S. 1 (1968)

See also **Arrest without a Warrant; Balancing Test; Exclusionary Rule; Race and Criminal Justice; Stop and Frisk**

FLORIDA v. WHITE, 526 U.S. 559 (1999)

How far does the Supreme Court extend the automobile exception to the search warrant requirement? In *Florida v. White*, the court extended the exception in time and place and to new circumstances.

The exception was extended to new circumstances: The defendant's automobile had been searched after it was been seized under a state criminal forfeiture law. Police found drugs inside in the ensuing inventory search.

Police had probable cause to believe that defendant had used the vehicle in a drug transaction, which allowed forfeiture of the vehicle under state law. The court relied on *Carroll v. United States* to declare that police can search without a warrant when they have probable cause to believe that a vehicle contains contraband. In *Florida v. White*, the vehicle did not contain contraband; the vehicle itself was contraband. However, at the time of the seizure defendant was incarcerated and the state proved no immediate need to search.

The exception was also extended in time: The seizure occurred more than two months after defendant was seen using the vehicle in the drug transaction.

And the exception was extended in place: The Court relied on the fact that the vehicle was located in a public place when it was seized. Like seizures of vehicles for taxes in *G.M. Leasing v. United States*, the seizure involved no invasion of privacy because the vehicle was in a public place.

JEFFERSON L. LANKFORD

References and Further Reading

Chilcoat, Kendra H., *The Automobile Exception Swallows the Rule:* Florida v. White, Journal of Criminal Law & Criminology 90 (2000): 917–950.

Dery, George M. III, *Missing the Big Picture: The Supreme Court's Willful Blindness to Fourth Amendment Fundamentals in* Florida v. White, Florida State University Law Review 28 (2001): 571–604.

Cases and Statutes Cited

Carroll v. United States, 267 U.S. 132 (1925)

G.M. Leasing Corp. v. United States, 429 U.S. 338 (1977)

See also **South Dakota v. Opperman, 428 U.S. 364 (1976); Warrantless Searches**

FLYNT, LARRY (1942–)

Born in Kentucky in 1942, Larry Flynt dropped out of school in ninth grade and, lying about his age, joined the army at age fifteen. Discharged at age seventeen, he again lied about his age to get into the navy, where he served as a radar technician. He currently heads the Hustler Publishing Company, which oversees more than twenty sex magazines and sees an annual turnover of a $100 million. In 1974, he started *Hustler* as a working-class magazine. In 1978, an assassination attempt left him paralyzed. Flynt was the defendant in a landmark Supreme Court in 1988 concerning Jerry Falwell in a decision that stipulated that offensive speech aimed at a public figure—Falwell, in this case—was constitutionally protected as long as it did not claim to be fact.

In 1983, when the Defense Department refused to allow American journalists to accompany the U.S. invasion force into Grenada by blockading all news concerning its activities there for two days, Flynt sued the government claiming a constitutionally guaranteed right of access for the media in combat zones under the First Amendment. The case was declared moot, because the Defense Department had lifted the restrictions against coverage by the time to case came to court. That same year, the Flynt-owned *Hustler* magazine ran an advertisement parody in its November issue featuring Jerry Falwell. In response to the parody, Falwell brought a $45 million lawsuit against *Hustler* and its publisher, Larry Flynt. Falwell charged that Flynt and the magazine had appropriated his name and image for advertisement or trade without his consent, that the parody represented libel—written defamation (that false and defamatory statements had been made against Falwell)—and that the parody intentionally inflicted emotional distress on him. According to Falwell and his supporters, constitutionally guaranteed freedoms cannot be understood outside of a moral framework. The First Amendment, in this view, cannot be perverted to mean that the nation must tolerate ideas that the Constitution did not intend to protect and that run counter to the moral truths they believe the Constitution embodies. There is no value in destructive speech, such as appeared in *Hustler,* and thus it does not fall under First Amendment protection. For Flynt and his supporters, the freedom of speech is absolute. In other words, any and all speech that does not physically threaten anyone falls under First amendment protections. Furthermore, Flynt contended that the advertisement was a joke, and any award of damages would be frivolous.

In an opinion written by Chief Justice William Rehnquist on February 24, 1988, the Supreme Court of the United States found that the case presented the question of the First Amendment's limitations on a State's authority to protect its citizens from intentionally inflicted emotional distress. In reversing the judgment of the Court of Appeals, the Supreme Court concluded that public figures cannot recover damages

for emotional distress from issues like the one at issue without also showing that the publication contained a false statement of fact made with actual malice or reckless disregard for its truthfulness. Thus Flynt prevailed in an eight-to-zero opinion.

MELISSA OOTEN

References and Further Reading

Flynt, Larry, with Kenneth Ross. *An Unseemly Man.* Los Angeles: Dove Books, 1996.
Smolla, Rodney. *Jerry Falwell v Larry Flynt: The First Amendment on Trial.* NY: St. Martins Press, 1988.

Cases and Statutes Cited

Hustler Magazine v. Falwell, 485 U.S. 46 (1998)

See also **Falwell, Jerry;** *Hustler Magazine v. Falwell,* **485 U.S. 46 (1998); Obscenity**

FOLLETT v. TOWN OF MCCORMICK, S.C., 321 U.S. 573 (1944)

Mr. Lester Follett, a member of Jehovah's Witness faith, devoted his life to preaching. In this capacity he traveled door-to-door in his hometown of McCormick, South Carolina, and accepted contributions for the sale of religious texts. Follett had no other source of income. The town of McCormick required licensure for book salesmen with a fee amounting to $1.00 per day or $15.00 per year. Mr. Follett claimed the fee imperiled his freedom of religion and refused to remit the licensure fee. Although precedent leaned in his favor, the South Carolina Supreme Court disagreed, narrowly interpreting past cases as only applying to transient booksellers (see *Murdock v. Pennsylvania 319 U.S. 113* and *Jones v. Opelika 319 U.S. 103*).

Justice Douglas delivered for the Court a verdict in favor of Mr. Follett. Noting that similarly to *Murdock* and *Opelika*, Mr. Follett was "engaged in a 'religious' rather than 'commercial' venture," his activities cannot be measured "by the standards governing the sales of wares and merchandise." Justice Douglas narrows the question to whether a license tax is applicable to a preacher in his hometown and concludes that full-time preachers may not be taxed for commercial activities directly related to their evangelism. He writes: "Freedom of religion is not merely reserved for those with a long purse. Preachers of more orthodox faiths are not engaged in commercial undertakings because they are dependant on their calling for a living."

Justices Roberts, Frankfurter, and Jackson dissented, citing two main points. (1) The license tax did not affect only preachers, but all street vendors, and thus did not discriminate against religions expression. (2) The tax exemption would potentially open the door for entire churches to claim tax exemption from their commercial holdings.

JOHN GREGORY PALMER

Cases and Statutes Cited

Murdock v. Pennsylvania, 319 U.S. 113
Jones v. Opelika, 319 U.S. 103

See also **Graham v. Commissioner of Internal Revenue, 490 U.S. 680 (1989)**

FONG YUE TING v. UNITED STATES, 149 U.S. 698 (1893)

In the late nineteenth century, amid a rise in anti-alien sentiment, Congress promulgated a series of Chinese Exclusion Acts. The Act of 1892 required all "Chinese laborers" lawfully resident within the United States to apply for certificates of residence and provided for the deportation of those who did not obtain certificates. Failure to obtain the certificate could be excused by a demonstration of "unavoidable cause" and the testimony of "at least one credible white witness" as to lawful residency. Fong Yue Ting and two other Chinese were arrested in New York City for failure to possess certificates. They challenged the constitutionality of the Exclusion Act.

The question of what limits the Constitution places on Congress's power over aliens had come before the Court before. In *Chae Chan Ping v. U.S*, the Supreme Court held that Congress possessed full and unrestrained power to exclude aliens as an inherent incident of sovereignty. *Fong Yue Ting* presented the further question of whether the Constitution constrained the ability of Congress to expel aliens lawfully present within the country. The Court extended the rule of *Chae Chan Ping*, concluding that the right to expel non-citizens "rests upon the same grounds, and is as absolute and unqualified, as the right to prohibit and prevent their entrance into the country."

The extreme language of *Fong Yue Ting* has been moderated by subsequent cases such as *Wong Yang Sung v. McGrath*, which affirmed that deportation hearings must comport with procedural due process.

KERMIT ROOSEVELT, III

References and Further Reading

Henkin, Louis, *The Constitution and United States Sovereignty: A Century of Chinese Exclusion and its Progeny*, Harvard Law Review 100 (1987): 853.

Neuman, Gerald. *Strangers to the Constitution*. Princeton: Princeton University Press, 1996.
Tribe, Laurence H. *American Constitutional Law*. 3rd Ed. New York: Foundation Press, 2000, pp. 967–977.
Chin, Gabriel J. Chae Chan Ping and Fong Yue Ting: The origins of plenary power, in Martin, David A., and Peter S. Schuck, eds. *Immigrant Stories 7*. Foundation Press, 2005.

Cases and Statutes Cited

Wong Yang Sung v. McGrath, 339 U.S. 33 (1950)
Chae Chan Ping v. U.S., 130 U.S. 581 (1889)

See also **Chae Chan Ping v. U.S., 130 U.S. 581 (1889) and Chinese Exclusion Act; Due Process in Immigration; Undocumented Migrants**

FORCED SPEECH

In times of peril and uncertainty, governments often seek to ensure that all pay obeisance to central tenets of the state. In the 1940s, West Virginia sought to teach school children about democracy and required them to recite the pledge of allegiance. Children of devout Jehovah's Witnesses objected on grounds that their religion forbade such oaths, and school officials expelled them. In *West Virginia v. Barnette*, the Supreme Court reversed in ringing tones: "If there is any fixed star in our constitutional constellation, it is that no official, high or petty, can prescribe what shall be orthodox in politics, nationalism, religion, or other matters of opinion or force citizens to confess by word or act their faith therein."

This principle—that the First Amendment prohibits the government from forcing citizens to feign compliance with state orthodoxy—has been extended. When car owners objected on religious grounds to the slogan, "Live Free or Die," embossed on New Hampshire license plates and covered it, violating state law, the Supreme Court held that the state could not punish the act. Another citizen who wished to distribute literature anonymously was held to have a First Amendment right to do so even though state law required disclosure to avoid anonymous political mud slinging.

Most people recognize the power of social pressure. To one degree or another, we are all pressured to conform to the views and habits of our neighbors, whether those habits consist in wearing fashionable clothes, adhering to implicit codes of behavior (no spitting on the sidewalk; don't eat with your mouth open), or adopting conventional attitudes about other people or policies. Some conformity is essential to civilized society. We adopt laws requiring people to pay taxes, to drive on the right, and to attend schools until age sixteen. And, while the government may require compliance with many rules of behavior, the First Amendment forbids the government from exacting conformity in belief or speech.

Why does our Constitution permit the government to force people to pay taxes but may not force people to salute the flag? The answer lies in a fundamental understanding that individuals must be left free to think their own thoughts, make their own decisions about what and how to express themselves. In addition, a core principle of a functioning democracy is the citizenry's freedom from government coercion in their associations and in developing individual ideas and beliefs. Conflicting perspectives, what *Barnette* called "intellectual individualism," and preservation of the right to dissent are essential characteristics of a democratic society.

In some instances, the principle has protected media outlets from being forced to publish views it opposed. For example, a Florida statute required newspapers to accord equal space to political candidates who the newspaper had criticized. In *Miami Herald v. Tornillo*, the Supreme Court held the statute unconstitutional, because it interfered with editorial judgment about what should be published and essentially punished the paper for criticizing politicians. One might also point to the special favoritism granted political candidates as a further support for the outcome of the decision.

In contrast, in *Turner Broadcasting,* the Court upheld federal law requiring cable operators to carry the signals of local broadcasters. The Court distinguished the Florida case on the ground that the "trigger" for the Florida law was content based—publishing criticism of politicians—whereas here the overriding objective was not to favor one viewpoint over another but the economic one of preserving free television programming regardless of the content of the expression. In enacting the legislation, Congress expressed particular concern that a key communication outlet for large numbers of Americans, local broadcasting, would dry up. The Supreme Court's decision thus recognized the value of preserving multiple channels of communication.

Although the First Amendment prohibits government from coercing speech, different sets of problems arise when the issue concerns government efforts to break up broadcast monopolies or to remove financial barriers to promote diversity among speakers. For example, the Federal Communications Commission, the agency designated to allocate broadcast licenses in the limited spectrum available, sought to promote fairness by requiring broadcasters to allow persons who had been attacked on air a "right of reply" and further required licensees to promote discussion of public affairs. This "Fairness Doctrine" was unanimously upheld in *Red Lion Broadcasting*. The Supreme Court reasoned that the government had selected the broadcasters; because the spectrum was scarce, anyone could be attacked on the air without recourse. Furthermore, much of the public would be unable to access the airwaves without regulations providing for public access rights.

A similar result obtained when California required private shopping centers to permit student protestors to set up a table inside their malls over the owners' objections: California could promote greater diversity of expression in this fashion, and the rule did not infringe the owners' rights not to express ideas since the owners could post a sign disassociating themselves from the petitioners.

Gay rights activists sought to rely on the "access" line of cases to enforce a Massachusetts Human Rights Commission order that allowed them to march in a *privately organized* Irish-American parade. The Supreme Court unanimously held that the Commission rule interfered with the First Amendment right of the organizers to express their own message. Although ostensibly enacted to promote equal treatment of a disfavored minority, the Commission's approach would have supported a ruling by a different agency requiring civil rights marches to include Ku Klux Klan floats.

The distinction between these two lines of cases is that the government may promote access to channels of communication to diversify the voices that may be heard in public spaces provided it neither prescribes the message nor interferes with others' rights to express their own messages or to disavow association with the speech. Indeed, with increasing concentration of media empires, some have argued that it is even more important to democracy for the government to ensure access to media—especially for those who are unable to purchase such access.

A different set of issues arises when the government compels individuals to give financial support to private organizations with whose ideological positions they disagree. In the *Abood* case, for example, public sector employees were represented by a union pursuant to a collective bargaining contract with their employer, the Detroit Board of Education. One provision in the contract required non-union members to pay to the union a service fee equal to union dues as a condition of employment.

Some nonunion employees objected to paying the fee because they disapproved of (1) collective bargaining in the public sector and especially (2) "ideological union expenditures not directly related to collective bargaining." The Supreme Court ruled that mandating fees to support the collective bargaining process was constitutional, but that objecting individuals must be allowed the opportunity to opt out of the "ideological expenditures." The basis of the distinction between the two types of expenditures has proven to be important in subsequent cases as well.

Mandatory fees to support labor negotiations were constitutional, because otherwise the entire system of collective bargaining would be undermined: non-union members could free load off the benefits obtained by the union negotiators without paying for them. On the other hand, fees to support ideological causes unrelated to collective bargaining (for example, lobbying expenses) and that were not germane to the collective bargaining process itself could not constitutionally be imposed on objecting members.

The *Abood* principle was reaffirmed in a case involving mandatory bar dues for lawyers: California could require its attorneys to finance the regulatory apparatus governing lawyers such as bar discipline but could not require objecting attorneys to finance political lobbying by the State Bar organization. But in *Southworth*, the Court held that the First Amendment permits a public university to charge its students an activity fee to support speech activities by extra-curricular student organizations promoting a wide range of ideological views, provided that the program is viewpoint neutral. In contrast to *Abood*, where the Court was concerned to protect dissenters from being forced to subsidize speech they disagreed with, *Southworth* recognized that where the purpose of the fee was to "stimulate the whole universe of speech and ideas" it was implausible that individual students would be permitted to "opt out" of such funding mechanisms.

The First Amendment has also been invoked in cases involving advertising of agricultural products. The federal government and some states finance demand-bolstering advertising for agricultural products such as fruit, vegetables, and beef. In one case, fruit growers objected to mandatory assessments ordered by California agricultural authorities for generic advertising of fruit. They attempted to piggyback off the *Abood* "ideological" branch, arguing that requiring growers to pay for speech they didn't want was unconstitutional "compelled speech." However, in the Court's view, the California marketing arrangement carried no ideological message (which distinguished the case from *Abood*). Moreover, the marketing scheme was part of a broader regulation of the market in fruits.

Nonetheless, when mushroom growers challenged a similar program, the growers cleverly argued that *their* message was that their mushrooms were *superior* to the generic mushrooms. Thus, remarkably, they persuaded the Court that being made to pay for *generic* mushroom advertising by an industry association violated their First Amendment rights not to finance "ideological" messages with which they disagreed.

Many scholars saw the mushroom growers' argument as a smokescreen: the growers simply objected to paying for a government program they disliked, and that funneling the funds through a private association should not have made a difference. However, the mushroom case left open another question: does the First Amendment permit citizens to withhold fees for *government* advertising programs with whose message they disagree? The Court forestalled this possibility in the *Johanns* decision, where the governmental agency responsible for generic beef advertising argued that the government itself was "speaking" about the virtues of beef consumption. The Court ruled that beef producers who objected to government-compelled subsidy of the government's own speech had no valid First Amendment complaint. The mushroom growers case was distinguished on grounds that the growers' money went to a *private* association.

In sum, the government may not force an individual personally to adhere to a message he or she disagrees with; nor may the government generally compel an individual to subsidize an ideological message he or she disagrees with, where the message is expressed by a private entity. However, public universities can require students to pay to support ideologically diverse student organizations. And, individuals have no First Amendment right to challenge compelled subsidies of the government's own message.

JOHN T. NOCKLEBY

References and Further Reading

Cantor, Norman L., *Forced Payments to Service Institutions and Constitutional Interests in Ideological Non-association*, Rutgers Law Review 36 (1983): 3.
Klass, Gregory, *The Very Idea Of A First Amendment Right Against Compelled Subsidization*, University of California at Davis Law Review 38 (2005): 1087.
Jacobs, Leslie Gielow, *Pledges, Parades, And Mandatory Payments*, Rutgers Law Review 52 (1999): 123.
Wasserman, Howard, *Compelled Expression And The Public Forum Doctrine*, Tulane Law Review 77 (2002): 163.

Cases and Statutes Cited

Abood v. Detroit Bd. of Educ., 431 U.S. 209 (1977)
Board of Regents of Univ. of Wis. System v. Southworth, 529 U.S. 217 (2000)
Glickman v. Wileman Bros. & Elliott, Inc., 521 U.S. 457 (1997)
Hurley v. Irish-American Gay, Lesbian & Bisexual Group of Boston, 515 U.S. 557 (1995)

Johanns v. Livestock Marketing Association, 544 U.S. __ (2005)
Keller v. State Bar of California, 496 U. S. 1 (1990)
McIntyre v. Ohio Elections Commission, 514 U.S. 334 (1995)
Miami Herald v. Tornillo, 418 U.S. 241 (1974)
Pruneyard v. Robbins, 447 U.S. 74 (1980)
Red Lion Broadcasting v. FCC, 395 U.S. 367 (1969)
Turner Broadcasting v. FCC, 512 U.S. 622 (1994) (Turner I)
Turner Broadcasting v. FCC, 520 U.S. 180 (1997) (Turner II)
United States v. United Foods, Inc., 533 U.S. 405 (2001)
West Virginia Board of Education v. Barnette, 319 U.S. 624 (1943)

*See also **Abood v. Detroit Board of Education**, 431 U.S. 209 (1977); Anonymity and Free Speech; Broadcast Regulation; Cable Television Regulation; Content-Based Regulation of Speech; Fairness Doctrine; Federal Communications Commission; Forced Speech; Government Funding of Speech; Government Speech; Gay and Lesbian Rights; Miami Herald Publishing Co. v. Tornillo, 418 U.S. 241 (1974); Pledge of Allegiance and First Amendment; Red Lion Broadcasting v. FCC, 395 U.S. 367 (1969); Shopping Centers and Freedom of Speech; Student Activity Fees and Free Speech; Turner Broadcastings Sys., Inc. v. FCC I & II, 512 U.S. 662 (1994); University of Wisconsin v. Southworth, 529 U.S. 217 (2000); West Virginia Board of Education v. Barnette, 319 U.S. 624 (1943)*

FORTAS, ABE (1910–1982)

Abe Fortas is remembered more for the circumstances surrounding his abortive nomination as Chief Justice and his subsequent resignation than for his judicial opinions. This is unfortunate. Trained as a Washington lawyer during the 1930s, and later trusted as a close advisor to President Johnson, Fortas, perhaps more than any other Justice, provided a link between Roosevelt's New Deal and Johnson's Great Society. Although his tenure was brief and controversial, Fortas played a significant role in shaping some of the most important cases to come down from the Warren Court.

Abe Fortas was born on June 19, 1910, in Memphis Tennessee, to Woolfe and Rachel Berzansky Fortas recent Jewish immigrants from Eastern Europe. Theirs was a modest, working class family steeped more in the cultural than the religious tradition of Judaism. From his father, an amateur musician, Fortas inherited a deep and abiding love of music. Fortas himself became an avid violinist, and he later came to count Pablo Casals and Isaac Stern among his friends and clients.

An outstanding student, Fortas won scholarships both to Southwestern College in Memphis and to Yale Law School. At Yale, Fortas served as editor-in-chief of the *Yale Law Journal* and came under the influence of two powerful exponents of legal realism: Thurman Arnold and William O. Douglas. After graduating in 1933, Fortas joined Yale's faculty while also accepting a position with Jerome Frank in Franklin Roosevelt's New Deal Agricultural Adjustment Administration. In 1937, while serving at the Interior Department, Fortas befriended a young Texas Congressman named Lyndon Johnson.

In the 1940s, Fortas left government service but remained in Washington, D.C. and founded a law firm with Thurman Arnold and Paul Porter. Fortas came to exemplify the Washington lawyer of the post-war era. An able and aggressive advocate, trained in the New Deal, he effectively navigated clients through the intricacies of federal policies and programs.

At the outset of the Cold War in the late 1940s, Fortas took a lead role in opposing President Truman's loyalty program. He particularly objected to an incursion of the Executive and Legislative Branches of government into what he perceived as the judicial province of "judging" loyalty. Such incursions threatened to abridge the due process rights of challenged individuals. Soon, loyalty cases occupied a substantial portion of his firm's working hours. Prominent among the cases taken on by Fortas during this time was that of Owen Lattimore, a sinologist who headed the Page School of International Relations at Johns Hopkins University, who was accused by Senator Joseph McCarthy of being the "top Russian espionage agent in the United States." After five years of impassioned and meticulously organized defense by Fortas before investigating committees led both by Senator McCarthy and later, Senator McCarran, Lattimore was finally vindicated in 1955.

In 1962, the U.S. Supreme Court appointed Fortas to represent Clarence Gideon, in what became a landmark case of *Gideon v. Wainright*. Gideon had been convicted of breaking and entering in Florida. He was indigent and could not afford to hire a lawyer at his initial trial. He filed a *pro se* appeal to the Supreme Court asserting that he should be freed because he had been denied effective access to counsel. Fortas argued the case before the Supreme Court and won a unanimous decision. In finding for Gideon, the Supreme Court held that the Sixth Amendment guaranteed anyone accused of a serious crime a right to counsel, and that those too poor to pay would be provided with a lawyer at no cost.

Always drawn to men of power and influence, Fortas maintained his friendship with Lyndon Johnson during the 1950s, serving as his lawyer and close advisor until Johnson, as President, nominated his old friend to the Court in 1965.

On the Court, Fortas developed a reputation as a liberal in civil rights and a conservative in areas involving government regulation of business. "The Courts may be the principles guardians of the liberties of the people," he wrote, but "They are not chiefly the administrators of its economic destiny." Baltimore & Ohio Railroad v. United States, 386 U.S. 372, 478 (1967). His opinions demonstrate an instrumental approach to the law but reveal no coherent legal philosophy. This is not to say Fortas was unprincipled, although some accused him of this, but that, true to his education in legal realism, he saw the law as a tool to achieve specific results.

Fortas' experience as a corporate lawyer led him to take a dim view of government interference in business matters. For example, in *Baltimore & Ohio Railroad v. United States*, 386 U.S. 372 1967, Fortas, in dissent, argued that the Court had no business questioning the informed decision of the Interstate Commerce Commission to allow a merger of two railroads.

Fortas greatest concern, however, lay in protecting the rights of minorities, the disenfranchised, and the powerless. He fiercely championed the rights of criminal defendants, especially their Fifth Amendment right against self-incrimination. In *Re Gault,* 387 U.S. 1 (1967), Fortas wrote a strong opinion that effectively created a "Bill of Rights" for juvenile criminal offenders by extending certain basic Fourteenth Amendment due process rights into juvenile courts. Writing in a realist vein, Fortas relied more on historical, sociological, and psychological studies of the juvenile justice system than on legal precedent to support his holding.

Free speech was an area of special concern for Fortas especially in the era of civil rights and anti–Vietnam War demonstrations. He was not, however, a First Amendment absolutist. To the contrary, he could not abide disruptive civil disobedience or symbolic speech that violated valid laws merely to dramatize dissent. The musician in him cherished harmony and decorum. He allowed for tension and conflict but insisted it be contained or structured. Thus, in *Brown v. Louisiana*, 383 U.S. 131 1966), Fortas found a Louisiana breach of the peace statute unconstitutional as applied to several blacks who conducted a peaceful sit-in of a segregated public library. But in *Street v. new York*, 394 U.S. 576 (1968), Fortas, in a stinging dissent, drew the line at flag burning, declaring that "Protest does not exonerate lawlessness." Id. at 617. Yet in his landmark opinion in *Tinker v. Des Moines School District*, 393 U.S. 503 (609), Fortas held that a school's prohibition on black armbands worn by certain students to protest the Vietnam War was unconstitutional. Echoing his support for juvenile rights enunciated in *Gault*, Fortas declared that students did not surrender their First Amendment rights on entering a school. Wearing armbands, Fortas asserted, was akin to "pure speech" that did not involve "aggressive, disruptive actions" and did not interfere with the school's work. Id. at 508–509, 512.

Fortas also has a very strong commitment to privacy as a constitutional right. Indeed, Fortas saw the right to privacy as a significant limitation to the freedom of the press. Consistent with his free speech cases (and with his deep personal antipathy toward the press), Fortas refused to extend First Amendment protections to press activities he considered to be intrusive or disruptive. Thus, for example, dissenting in *Time v. Hill*, 385 U.S. 374 (1967), Fortas asserted that "There are great and important values in our society, none of which is greater than those reflected in the First Amendment, but which are also fundamental and entitled to the Court's careful respect and protection. Among these is the right to privacy." Id. at 412.

After only three years on the Court, President Johnson nominated Fortas to replace the retiring Earl Warren as Chief Justice. It was an honor from which he never recovered. The confirmation hearings took place after Johnson had become a lame duck by refusing to seek reelection. Fortas soon became the target of a conservative backlash against the activism of the Warren Court and Johnson's Great Society programs. Revelations of his ongoing business connections with millionaire businessman Louis Wolfson didn't help matters any. By October, Johnson was forced to withdraw Fortas' name. One year later, amid further allegations of improper business dealings, Fortas resigned from the Court although he maintained his innocence of any wrongdoing. Back in the private sector he was rebuffed by his old law firm but continued to practice law until his death in 1982.

JONATHAN KAHN

References and Further Reading

Fortas, Abe. *Concerning Dissent and Civil Disobedience.* New York: World Publishing Co., 1968. A fascinating look into Fortas' ideas on the nature and limits of free expression in a civil society, made even more interesting by the fact that he wrote it while sitting on the Supreme Court.

Kalman, Laura. *Abe Fortas: A Biography*. New Haven: Yale University Press, 1990. Kalman's solid study of Fortas' life is the first to be based on complete access to Fortas' private papers. Her work is therefore more complete than Murphy's yet lacks a certain critical distance. Provides a good review of the development of Fortas' legal ideas.

Murphy, Bruce Allen. *Fortas: The Rise and Fall of a Supreme Court Justice.* New York: William Morrow and Co., 1988. An incisive study that concentrates on Fortas' life as a Washington insider. More of a political biography, where Kalman's work is more a mix of the personal and the legal sides of Fortas' life.

Cases and Statutes Cited

Baltimore & Ohio Railroad v. United States, 386 U.S. 372 (1967)
Brown v. Louisiana, 383 U.S. 131 (1966)
In Re Gault, 387 U.S. 1 (1967)
Street v. New York, 394 U.S. 576 (1968)
Time v. Hill, 385 U.S. 374 (1967)
Tinker v. Des Moines School District, 393 U.S. 503 (1969)

FOURTEENTH AMENDMENT

If the standard for the significance of law be its effects on the everyday life of citizens, then the Fourteenth Amendment is one the most significant aspects of American law. This is certainly the case in regard to the Bill of Rights and civil liberties and perhaps in regard to the Constitution itself. In illuminating the impact of this great Amendment, we will first view its evolvement and adoption as a part of post–Civil War reconstruction and then review the history and meaning of the guarantees of its great clauses: privileges and immunities, due process, and equal protection.

The Civil War and Reconstruction

The adoption of the Fourteenth Amendment in 1868 was to change the very nature of America. With the emancipation proclamation of questionable legal merit, the first order of post-war business was the adoption of the Thirteenth Amendment in 1865 and abolishing slavery. The major issue concerning the meaning and intent of the Thirteenth Amendment was whether the amendment could reach "the badges" of slavery—the conditions that the former slaves faced as a result of the bondage and oppression that they had suffered.

That Congress so intended to reach these "badges" is supported by the fact that the Congress adopted civil right's legislation to protect the freed slaves in the South at the same time (Civil Rights Acts of 1865 and 1866) as it adopted the Amendment. Although this evidences the Framers intent that Congress could reach the badges of slavery under its enforcement power, the Framers feared that a still conservative Supreme Court might limit the Amendments and its enforcement power reach to abolition alone. This concern served as the predicate for the adoption, in May and June of 1866, of the most far-reaching

constitutional protection of civil rights and liberties in our nation's history, the Fourteenth Amendment. Of particular relevance and meaning are the self-executing right prohibitions to the states in Section 1, and Section 5's empowering the Congress to enforce the newly creating rights delineated in Section 1.

Amendment XIV (1868)

Section 1. All persons born or naturalized in the United States, and subject to the jurisdiction thereof, are citizens of the United States and of the State wherein they reside. No State shall make or enforce any law which shall abridge the privileges or immunities of citizens of the United States; nor shall any State deprive any person of life, liberty, or property, without due process of law; nor deny to any person within its jurisdiction the equal protection of the laws.

Section 5. The Congress shall have power to enforce, by appropriate legislation, the provisions of this article.

The State Action Limitation

Before we review the rights guaranteed by the noble clauses articulated in Section 1 and Section 5 of the Amendment, one issue begs attention because of its effect on the application of the Amendment as a whole. The Fourteenth Amendment speaks in language directed at state governments, "No state shall make or enforce,...nor shall any state deprive,...nor deny." To what degree did this reference to the states indicate the framers intent that this limit application of the Amendment in regard to private forms of discrimination? This issue has been debated to this very day.

An answer supporting the Amendment's reach to private discrimination is, as noted previously, that the same Congress that adopted the Amendment passed civil rights legislation enforcing the Amendment that was clearly aimed at private conduct. The importance of this question cannot be overstated, since ultimately the fate of freed persons in the South would be decided by their former masters, and if the Amendment could not reach private activity, private racial discrimination would undoubtedly flourish. The answer to this question awaited what the Framers correctly characterized as their major antagonist, the Supreme Court.

The Court faced this issue in the *Civil Rights Cases* in 1883. The onset of "Jim Crow" can be traced to the

Court's creation of the judicial fiction limiting application of the Amendment to affirmative "state action." Affirmative in the sense that inaction, even though a state might allow discrimination by not acting, was not sufficient. It is worthy of note that this was one of a trilogy of cases in which the Court provided threshold interpretations of the Fourteenth Amendment that "watered down" the effect of the Amendments so as to deny its intended benefit not only to the freed persons in the South but to the nation as a whole. The impact of these decisions set back individual rights and liberties until the mid-twentieth century, both doctrinally and substantively. It would be more than 100 years before the noble goals of the post-war era would meet fruition—although, that day would come. The other cases were *Slaughter-House Cases,* 83 U.S. 36 (1872) (Discussed in regard to the privileges and immunities clause, infra.) and *Plessy v. Ferguson,* 163 U.S. 537 (1896) (discussed in regard to the equal protection clause, infra).

The modern "story" of state action emphasizes the ability to reach some forms of what had previously been considered private and unreachable conduct and was closely associated with the rise of the civil rights movements in America in the mid-twentieth century, reaching its zenith in the 1960s and the "Warren Court."

These decisions changed the landscape of the state action doctrine, perhaps bringing it more in touch with the framers intent. Justice Harlan's dissenting opinion in the *Civil Right's Cases,* for example, would be drawn on in this regard. Yet, as the nation turned away from the civil rights era, the more conservative and "privacy" oriented Burger and Rehnquist Courts would limit and retreat from the Warren Court's doctrine liberalizing the ability to reach private activity.

Two concepts have emerged unto which the Court will treat private activity as state action. First, certain private activities are so public in character that they satisfy state action, because they serve a "public function." Note the potential breadth here, since many activities that are in private hands arguably serve a "public function." In recent years, however, the Court has severely limited this doctrine by requiring "the exercise by a private entity of powers traditionally *exclusively* reserved to the State" *Jackson v. Metropolitan Edison Company* (1974). As if to emphasize the limitation of this concept, the Court held in *Flagg Brothers* v. *Brooks* (1978), that, "While many functions have been traditionally performed by governments, *very few* have been "exclusively reserved to the State."

Next, the government may be so involved in regulating private activities that the Court may find state action because of "significant state involvement." Once again, although still a more functional path to reach private activity, the modern Court has limited application of this doctrine as well. Now the state must "significantly encourage private activity," be a "joint actor or participant," or maintain a symbiotic and close relationship with the private activity so that, "there is a sufficiently close nexus between the State and the challenged action of the regulated entity so that the action of the latter may be fairly treated as that of the State itself" *Jackson v. Metropolitan Edison Company* (1974); *Burton v. Wilmington Parking Authority* (1961); *Lugar v. Edmonsdson* (1982).

At what point individual autonomy should end and the protections of the Fourteenth Amendment begin is an important thesis that underlies the concept of state action. In *Moose Lodge v Irivs* (1972), the Court weighed in with its own moral views on this issue by finding that a private club could discriminate against admission of African Americans based on their race, because the activity was private and lacked state action. The Court held, despite liquor licensing by the state, that, "Our holdings indicate that where the impetus for the discrimination is private, the State must have 'significantly involved itself with invidious discriminations,' in order for the discriminatory action to fall within the ambit of the constitutional prohibition."

Since all of the clauses of the Amendment speak to the states, the state action limitation and the issue of private versus public in America are most consequential.

Privileges or Immunities

> . . . No State shall make or enforce any law which shall abridge the privileges or immunities of citizens of the United States.

Incorporation

There is no doubt the first sentence of the Fourteenth Amendment had as its intent overruling the heinous *Dred Scott v. Sanford* (1856) decision. Despite the Court's conclusion in *Dred Scott* that slaves were not "citizens" of the national government because they were mere chattels, now, "All persons born or naturalized in the United States, and subject to the jurisdiction thereof, are citizens of the United States and of the State wherein they reside." The meaning of the second sentence, however, has produced as much debate concerning intent then perhaps any other verbiage in the Constitution: "No State shall make or enforce any law which shall abridge the privileges or immunities of citizens of the United States." What are the "privileges or immunities" of federal citizenship? If the first sentence overruled *Dred Scott*, did the second sentence overrule *Barron v. Baltimore* (1833), where the Supreme Court held that the "bill of rights" was not applicable to the states? Was this "short hand" language for the "Bill of Rights?" If it was, *Baron* would be overruled, the Bill of Rights would be applicable to the states, and the nation would have national protection of civil rights and liberties for the first time in its history. It would seem logical to so conclude based on the language of these two sentences, particularly because the now abolished "slavery" was a major reason for limiting the applicability of the Bill of Rights to the states. Yet, to so conclude would provide a profound change in the power balance between state and federal government, most particularly in the "new" post-war South. Incorporation of the Bill of Rights in the states via the privileges and immunities clause of the Fourteenth Amendment was a question of great meaning, and it awaited application of judicial review by the very Supreme Court the Framers feared.

In the first major post war decision interpreting the Amendment, the Supreme Court faced this most significant issue in the *Slaughter-House Cases* (1872). Despite what seemed to be the framers intent to overrule *Baron*, the Amendment's author had stated the Amendment's intent was, "to arm the Congress,... with the power to enforce the bill of rights" against the states, the Court would not so conclude. Justice Miller, speaking for the Court, refused to "radically change[s] the whole theory of the relations of the State and Federal governments to each other and of both these governments to the people," placed the privileges and immunities clause in the constitutional "waste paper basket," where it still rests today. The Court not only rejected "incorporation" but also provided a limited nature of rights that Miller concluded would be protected—rights already given by some other federal law. Offhand it does not seem likely that the Civil War was fought and the Fourteenth Amendment adopted for access to navigable water, seaports, parks, and to redress the national government *Twining v. State of N.J.* (1908). This rejection of incorporation set the stage for the onset of "Jim Crow" and apartheid that would follow.

For all practical purposes *Slaughter-House* remains "good law" today, and the Court has thus rendered the clause essentially "superfluous." Almost 100 years later the dissents of Field and Bradley in *Slaughter-House* would reach fruition in regard to "fundament rights" incorporation, but by application of the due process clause of the Fourteenth Amendment as opposed to the privileges and immunities clause.

Due Process Of Law

.... nor shall any State deprive any person of life, liberty, or property, without due process of law.

Due Process Incorporation

The mandate that "... Nor shall any State deprive any person of life, liberty, or property, without due process of law," seems to be procedural in character. Although *Slaughter House* was the death knell of "privileges and immunities" incorporation, that finding was not to be the end of the road when it came to the issue of incorporation and national protection of civil rights and liberties. The Court, by the 1930s, would turn to the "due process" clause as a basis for incorporation.

Although due process seems to conjure "procedural" as opposed to "substantive" rights, the use of the term "liberty" in the clause, and the plain and simple "need" for at least some national protection of civil rights and liberties, found it the most likely alternative for "incorporating" rights. By the *Palko v. Connecticut* decision in 1937, there was no longer any doubt that "due process" could embrace not only procedural rights but substantive rights as well. Paramount in this move to "due process" incorporation was the Court applying the free speech protection of the First Amendment to the States on the basis of the due process clause of the Fourteenth Amendment, because freedom of speech was "among the fundamental personal rights and liberties" *Gitlow v. New York* (1925).

If the due process clause was to serve as the basis for incorporation, particularly given the procedural nature of the right, the most significant question was how one would decide which rights were protected? This might have been a less difficult inquiry under the privileges and immunities clause. Recall the argument that the privileges and immunities of national citizenship must have been the Bill of Rights and that the terminology was "short hand" language for such. The "textual" problem of incorporating via due process made this question quite difficult. In the *Palko* and *Adamson v. California* (1937) decisions, the debate between Justices Black, Cardoza, and Frankfurter reached historic proportion as the Justices debated how this process should be invoked.

Ultimately the Court settled on what as been described as fundamental fairness/natural law select incorporation. Natural law because this is an independent Fourteenth Amendment inquiry in regard to the significance and meaning of any particular right. Fundamental fairness because the "trademark" language in both *Palko* (double jeopardy) and *Adamson* (self-incrimination) is whether the right is "implicit in our concept of ordered liberty," "deeply rooted in our civil and political institutions," or a "principal of justice so rooted in the conscience of our people as to be ranked as fundamental."

"Select" because the rights detailed in the first nine amendments are the ones most likely to be deemed "fundamental" via the preceding detailed nomenclature. The Warren Court's active expansion of incorporation looked increasingly to the Bill of Rights to "selectively" incorporate more and more of its specific guarantees via the due process clause of the Amendment. The "fundamental fairness" inquiry would be used to decide which of the protections in the Bill of Rights should be selectively incorporated. To be sure, although selective incorporation centered on the first nine amendments, only those protections of the Bill of Rights deemed fundamental would be so included. Significantly, it was also possible that unarticulated rights not so specified could be deemed "fundamental" and held applicable to the states as well. By *Duncan v. Louisiana* (1968), the present position of the Court in regard to application of fundamental fairness selective incorporation seemed solidified as the Court concluded that the Sixth Amendment right to a jury trial was fundamental to ordered liberty and applicable to the states. By this time almost all of the provisions of the Bill of Rights had been incorporated.

This "fundamental fairness" inquiry, used by the Court to selectively incorporate "fundamental rights," creates and secures rights by a substantive application of the due process clause. Using the due process clause in this sense has been described as "substantive due process." Here the inquiry by which rights are incorporated and made applicable to the states is the approximate inquiry the Court uses to create fundamental rights that are not delineated in the Constitution.

Substantive Due Process

"Substantive due process," John Ely asserted, "sounds like a contradiction in terms—sort of like 'green pastel

redness'" Ely, Democracy and Distrust 18 (1980). "A contradiction in terms" because the concept of due process normally conjures procedural rights, "An established course for judicial proceedings or other governmental activities designed to safeguard the legal rights of the individual" *The American Heritage Dictionary of the English Language*, 4th Ed. 2003.

Although the due process clause has been used to incorporate most of the Bill of Rights to the states, it invokes the greatest controversy when the Supreme Court applies it to create unarticulated rights not specified in the Constitution itself. This we call "substantive" due process. Substantive in the sense that the clause is not applied to protect "process" but to create and secure additional rights against which the government may only intrude with great difficulty.

Much the same as due process incorporation, we apply the fundamental fairness litany to create rights that are not articulated in the Constitution. The creation of unarticulated rights via substantive due process is a most controversial and oft-debated role for the Court.

Those asserting a more clause-bound basis for judicial interpretation, limited to the original intent of the Framers themselves, cite to the repudiation of the Court's creation of the "liberty to contract" as an unarticulated right in *Lochner V. New York* in 1905. The creation of this unarticulated right by the Court's substantive application of the due process clause has been criticized as an example of the danger in allowing the creation of such rights. The activism generated during the "Lochner era," where the Court read "laissez-faire" capitalism as if it were a constitutional mandate, is the traditional armor for those who favor judicial restraint. The application of "substantive due process" to create unarticulated rights that a Court might find "implicit in our concept of ordered liberty and deeply rooted in this Nation's history and tradition," are the controversial tools of this trade.

Nonetheless, and with ongoing controversy, the Court in the modern era has continued to apply substantive due process to create and secure unarticulated constitutional rights. The creation of a right of privacy in *Griswold v. Connecticut* (1965) and its extension to "abortions" in *Roe v. Wade* (1973) are the most notable examples. In the modern era the Court has tended to apply "substantive due process" to conserve traditional social values or to deem privacy interests as fundamental based on a "respect for the teachings of history [and] solid recognition of the basic values that underlie our society" *Moore v. East Cleveland* (1977). Family, for example, is deemed a fundamental privacy interest "precisely because the institution of the family is deeply rooted in this Nation's history and tradition." Ultimately, based on these themes, the Court has extended fundamental right protection "to personal decisions relating to marriage, procreation, contraception, family relationships, child rearing, and education" *Planned Parenthood v. Casey* (1992).

The creation of unarticulated rights rests at the root of a constitutional debate as to how a non-elected Supreme Court, enforcing the supremacy of the Constitution as fundamental law, should interpret the document in light of the framers intent and contemporary needs in a democratic society. Although most citizens today are well aware of the moral controversy extending from the abortion debate, very few are likely aware that among those who study the Court and the Constitution it is the issue of judicially created unarticulated constitutional rights via substantive due process that affords the greatest controversy. The modern Court, for example, has often cited to the word "liberty" in the due process clause to respond to this criticism and to ground these rights in the words of the Constitution. The magnitude of this polemic has been emphasized by the contemporary Senate conformation process of Supreme Court nominees, where nominees' views on the right of privacy have been center stage.

Procedural Due Process

Since due process normally conjures process-based protection, there is no controversy in regard to this application. Procedural due process normally requires some form of individualized hearing before the state can invoke a depravation, for example, employment, license or welfare. It is, however, a right to "process," or how a decision is reached, not the nature of the decision itself. There are two independent inquiries made when the Court applies the procedural protections of the due process clause. First, whether the right to due process protections apply, and second, once process is due, what type of process is required?

The Court has resorted to the specific terminology of the Fourteenth Amendment itself to decide if process is due. A state is required to grant due process if the individual so affected has a sufficient "liberty" and/or "property" interest. Although the interests are often state created and can thus be defined and limited by state law, they have nonetheless been interpreted with some degree of breadth.

A property interest sufficient to invoke due process procedural protection extends beyond "real property." Thus, a welfare benefit, or entitlement, has been held as a sufficient property interest *Goldberg v. Kelly* (1970). The claim to an entitlement is not based on a constitutional right to such a benefit, but rather from a legislative decision by the state to offer the benefit, perhaps subject to certain conditions. A variety of cases after *Goldberg* have extended procedural due process guarantees to a wide range of other claimants: employees, students, prisoners, parolees, debtors, and automobile drivers.

The range of property interests that afford such protection are not "infinite," and the Court has required a "legitimate claim of entitlement," and or a "legitimate expectation to continued employment," to invoke them *Board of Regents v. Roth* (1972).

A liberty interest sufficient to require due process reaches beyond "mere confinement" and may be invoked by a stigma that damages one's reputation *Wisconsin v. Constantineau* (1971). Recently, however, the Court has limited the expansion of a liberty interest that is sufficient to require due process to circumstances where, "more tangible interests such as employment were present," and "that reputation alone, apart from some more tangible interests such as employment," is not "sufficient to invoke the procedural protection of the due process clause" *Paul v. Davis* (1976).

Once a sufficient property and/or liberty interest has been successfully advanced, or "process is due," a court must then decide "what process is due." Here the Supreme Court has made the process due dependent on the factual circumstances and interests in each case. Their guidance for the lower court extends from three criteria, now firmly established in *Mathews v. Eldridge* (1976), "First, the private interest that will be affected by the official action; second, the risk of a erroneous deprivation of such interest through the procedures used, and the probable value, if any, of additional or substitute procedural safeguards; and finally, the Government's interest, including the function involved and the fiscal and administrative burdens that the additional or substitute procedural requirement would entail."

Equal Protection

... nor [shall any state] deny to any person within its jurisdiction the equal protection of the laws.

The Meaning of Equality in an Economically Privileged Society

The Fourteenth Amendment's guarantee that no state shall "deny to any person within its jurisdiction the equal protection of the laws," is perhaps America's greatest anomaly. In a society where privilege abounds, a grant of "equal protection" seems to conflict with our core socioeconomic values. To enforce the equalitarian mandate of this language on our society via judicial review would likely have a revolutionary impact. Consequently, and perhaps much the same as the unequivocal language of the First Amendment, the history of the equal protection clause has been centered around how to limit its meaning and avoid a judicially led reordering of American society.

It is worth noting that almost all laws discriminate. In this regard, for example, a criminal sanction discriminates against the convicted. Here, of course, the argument is that the state has a justified purpose in discriminating against the convicted. Viewed in this sense the clause would be interpreted as allowing a state to deny equal protection, depending on its purpose.

With this in mind, and despite the unequivocal language of the equal protection clause, the Court has interpreted the clause as if it read, "A state *may* deny to any person within its jurisdiction the equal protection of the laws if it has a sufficient purpose." This analysis has at a minimum successfully limited an enforcement of the clause that would challenge the very ethic of privilege that abounds in America. Any study of equal protection is then an analytical inquiry into whether a state has a sufficient purpose to defend its discriminatory classification.

Our review of equal protection will thus center on the degree of scrutiny the Court applies to evaluate a state's purpose. Here the Court, over the years, has devised a method that depends on the classification and/or interest that is discriminated against. The standards the Court applies, particularly how closely they scrutinize a state's purpose in discriminating, are the central issue in the application of equal protection doctrine.

The Rational Purpose Test

The traditional restraint the Court has historically applied in enforcing the equal protection clause has been described as the old equal protection and is identified as the rational purpose test. Here the Court will analyze whether the state has a legitimate purpose and whether or not the means it has chosen to achieve its purpose are rationally related to the attainment of its ends. In practice, this rational purpose review deferred to the legislative process. The application of this minimum scrutiny was so deferential that it was described as "fatal in theory but not in fact." This was the case because *any* rational purpose asserted by the state seemed adequate to defend the constitutionality of its statute *Williamson v. Lee Optical* (1955).

In the modern era, the "lessons of the *Lochner*" have mandated minimal scrutiny of a state's purpose in cases concerning "socio-economics" *Dandridge v. Williams* (1970). Although application of minimum scrutiny in regard to socioeconomics issues continues unto this day, the Court has recently applied the rational purpose test with what it describes as "teeth," so that in some circumstances the test may be "fatal in theory and in fact." Where parties can prove the means chosen by the state are "arbitrary and/or irrational" in relation to its ends, statutes have been held unconstitutional even under minimum scrutiny. Thus, in *Cleburne v. Cleburne Living Center* (1985), the Court applied the rational purpose test in striking down a state statute that discriminated against the disabled and reached much the same result in *Romer v. Evans* (1996) in striking Colorado's Amendment 2, because it "classifies homosexuals not to further a proper legislative end but to make them unequal to everyone else."

In a meaningful review of the present status of the rational purpose test, the majority in *Romer* commented, "In the ordinary case, a law will be sustained if it can be said to advance a legitimate government interest, even if the law seems unwise or works to the disadvantage of a particular group, or if the rationale for it seems tenuous," and that even though Amendment 2 failed this inquiry, "if a law neither burdens a fundamental right nor targets a suspect class, we will uphold the legislative classification so long as it bears a rational relation to some legitimate end."

The Compelling Purpose Test: Strict Judicial Scrutiny

If the rational purpose inquiry was the only standard applied in equal protection analysis, the impact of the clause and its powerful verbiage would likely have become meaningless. Perhaps because of such and by the onset of the "Warren Court," a dual standard, two-tier approach, referenced in the *Romer* opinion above, provided a basis for judicial activism in regard to the clause. The level of judicial scrutiny applied to a state's legislative purpose now depended on *who* was classified and *what* rights the legislation discriminated against. If the "old" equal protection was the deferential rational purpose test, this dual standard test became the "new" equal protection. If a state discriminated against a racial classification or denied a fundamental right the Court would apply strict scrutiny, and the state would be required to prove a compelling purpose. Application of this dual standard seemed to mean that a state's successful defense of its legislation became all but impossible. The compelling purpose test of the new equal protection was thus "strict in theory but *fatal* in fact."

Much the same as our discussion of the current application of the rational purpose test, the Court in the modern era has applied a compelling purpose test that is strict in theory *but not* fatal in fact. A review of the application of strict scrutiny and the present means of analysis is best served by viewing the evolvement of the two conduits to compelling purpose review—race-based classifications and the denial of fundamental rights.

Race-Based Classifications

That the Supreme Court has closely scrutinized race-based discrimination should come as no surprise given the Civil War and the primary purpose of the Fourteenth Amendment and the equal protection clause. The Court's opinion in *Strauder v. West Virginia* (1880) certainly exemplified such, "[What is equal protection] but declaring, [in] regard to the colored race, for whose protection the amendment was primarily designed, that no discrimination shall be made against them by law because of their color? [That] the West Virginia stature respecting juries [is] such a discrimination ought not to doubted."

Based on this premise, the Court has traditionally treated all disadvantaged racial classifications as inherently suspect, mandating close judicial scrutiny and requiring the state to prove a compelling purpose. Traditionally, the closest scrutiny has been applied to what the Court has described as discrete (easily identifiable) and insular (isolated) minorities who have a history of being discriminated against and disadvantaged in the majoritarian process. The degree to which this approach would be applied to any racial group, as opposed to a "discrete and insular" racial minority, awaited the modern civil rights era and the onset of affirmative action.

How, given this history, could Jim Crow and apartheid flourish in the South for some 100 years after the adoption of the clause? The answer rests in the conclusion of the Court in *Plessy v Ferguson* (1896), that racial segregation imposed by the force of state law satisfied the mandate of the equal protection clause. Viewed in this sense, *Brown v. Board of Education* (1954) was of greatest import as an

antiapartheid case, holding that separate but equal was unconstitutional and inherently unequal. Even a determination that apartheid was unconstitutional, however, did not rid us of racial discrimination. In postapartheid America, the Court faced two significant issues in this regard.

Life and discrimination are subtle. It is possible, for example, to discriminate even though a statute is neutral on its face. In postapartheid America, this was a major issue of consequence in regard to race-based discrimination. What resolution when there was a racially discriminatory effect, yet the statute itself was neutral? To require affirmative proof that a state "intended" to discriminate in such a circumstance would be an extremely difficult, if not impossible, burden. This is the case in regard to proving anyone's intent.

Yet, the Supreme Court, as it withdrew from the leadership it had exercised in the civil rights arena, precisely so held. In *Washington v. Davis* (1976), the Court found that "official action will not be held unconstitutional solely because it results in a racially disproportionate impact," and that, "proof of racially discriminatory intent or purpose is required to show a violation of the Equal Protection Clause" *Arlington Heights v. Metropolitan Housing Development Corporation* (1977).

The next issue of constitutional and social significance was whether discrimination against a racial majority should be treated the same as discrimination against a disadvantaged racial minority? Many state programs voluntarily attempted to offer "affirmative action" to remedy the past discrimination suffered by disadvantaged racial minorities. Although it hardly seems odious for a racial majority to discriminate against itself, the concept of discriminating against the majority stirred extensive political controversy. Given such, the standard of review to be applied by the Court was contentiously debated *Regents of The University Of California v. Bakke* (1978).

By 1995, the Court definitively resolved this issue and held, "that all racial classifications, imposed by whatever federal, state, or local governmental actor, must be analyzed by a reviewing court under strict scrutiny." Yet, this was not a compelling purpose test that was always "fatal in fact." For a state could constitutionally advance affirmative action programs if such classifications were, "narrowly tailored measures that further compelling governmental interests" *Adarand Constructors, Inc v. Pena* (1995).

To be "narrowed tailored" and constitutional the Court has indicated that the program must not just remedy the general nature of past societal discrimination but be supported by facts that "identify prior discrimination" in the area challenged. In *City of*

Richmond v. Croson (1989), for example, this meant a history of identified discrimination in the Richmond construction industry itself. In the 2003 term, in *Grutter v. Bollinger*, the Court reaffirmed the *Bakke* decision and held that a law school's admission program that favored racial minority candidates to further the goal of "diversity" was constitutional. This was the case because the program was narrowly tailored in that it did not, "unduly burden individuals who are not members of the favored racial and ethnic groups," and, "because the Law School considers "all pertinent elements of diversity," it can (and does) select nonminority applicants who have greater potential to enhance student body diversity over underrepresented minority applicants."

The Supreme Court has also included classifications based on "religion and national origin" as inherently suspect and requiring application of strict scrutiny. The Court in *Bernal v. Fainter* (1984), made this clear in holding that "a state law that discriminates on the basis of alienage can be sustained only if it can withstand strict judicial scrutiny." The Court cited to a "narrow exception" to this rule that has been labeled the "political function" exception and applies to laws that exclude aliens from "positions intimately related to the process of democratic self-government."

Fundamental Rights

The second conduit to the application of strict scrutiny under equal protection analysis is rights that are deemed fundamental. When a fundamental federal right is denied, strict scrutiny is applied no matter what the discriminatory classification. Thus, although deference is applied to wealth-based classifications, strict scrutiny will be applied if a fundamental federal right is denied to the poor as against the wealthy.

This makes a determination of what rights are deemed fundamental of consequence. With "explicit" constitutional rights most likely deemed "fundamental," the more particularized issue is once again what nonarticulated rights are deemed fundamental as well. Despite the inherent controversy of this process, the fact that a right to vote is not expressly articulated in the Constitution and is most certainly necessary for the democratic government mandated by the document makes it almost impossible not to conclude that there are "implicit, nonarticulated" fundamental rights. Just as our discussion concerning the "implicit" fundamental right of privacy, so we now make a similar inquiry as to other such rights.

The Supreme Court's conclusion that education was not a fundamental right in *San Antonio Independent School District v. Rodriguez* in 1973 articulated reluctance on behalf of the Court to expand implicit fundamental rights. The Court's conclusion in *Rodriquez* that only rights "explicit and implicitly" in the Constitution could be deemed fundamental was, in fact, quite limiting in nature. The conclusion that education was not such a right, and the history since the opinion, indicates the Court's reluctance to expand implicit fundamental rights.

Beyond the explicit detailing of rights in the Constitution, most notably, of course, the Bill of Rights, the following implicit rights have been deemed fundamental and subject to strict judicial scrutiny: vote, privacy, access to courts, and the right to interstate travel.

Heightened Review: The Middle Scrutiny Test

Although the Constitution hasn't changed, the role of women in our society certainly has. Whatever individual justices might have to say about a "living constitution," in *Craig v. Boren* in 1975, the Supreme Court retuned its positional analysis when it came to gender-based discrimination. The Court revolutionized its "two-prong" method and gave birth to "middle scrutiny" or heightened review when it came to gender. Under this increased scrutiny of gender-based classification, the Court held that "[To] withstand constitutional challenge, previous cases establish that classifications by gender must serve important governmental objectives and must be substantially related to achievement of those objectives." As opposed to a legitimate governmental objective, the objective must now be "important," and not just rationally related to its ends, but "substantially."

The Court has, since *Boren*, continued to emphasize this increased scrutiny when it comes to gender. They have put state legislatures on notice that any gender-based classifications "must be applied free of fixed notions concerning the roles and abilities of males and females. Care must be taken in ascertaining whether the statutory objective itself reflects archaic and stereotypic notions" *Mississippi University for Women v. Hogen* (1982). The Court now references the application of middle scrutiny as requiring an "exceedingly persuasive justification" for any gender-based classification. It has described its review as "skeptical scrutiny," rejecting "overbroad generalizations about the different talents, capacities, or preferences of males and females" that "perpetuate the legal, social, and economic inferiority of women" *J.E.B. v. Alabama* (1994). Gender today finds the Supreme Court applying a heightened review that is very close to strict scrutiny.

The application of middle scrutiny review has not been limited to gender. In *Clark v. Jeter* (1988), after some confusion in previous cases, the Court indicated that "intermediate scrutiny" would be applied to any state classification of nonmarital children. The Court has also applied intermediate scrutiny on a case-by-case basis when the nature of the facts may require such. Thus, in *Plyler v. Doe* (1982), the Court found Texas' denial of an education to children who had not been legally admitted into the United States an unconstitutional denial of equal protection, noting the "discrete" nature and "innocence" of the children and carefully limiting the application of middle scrutiny to the facts at hand.

The Enforcement Power

The Congress shall have power to enforce, by appropriate legislation, the provisions of this article.

Finally, and of particular significance given the framers intent of adopting the Fourteenth Amendment to support the constitutionality of post-war civil rights legislation, the Framers granted to Congress the "power to enforce, by appropriate legislation, the provisions of this article." The post-war Congress exercised their enforcement power to adopt legislation that is significant even until today. Notable among this legislation are two statutes offering federal criminal protection: 18 U.S.C. § 241 (Derived from § 6 of the 1870 Act): Conspiracy against rights; 18 U.S.C. § 242 (Derived from § 2 of the 1866 Act); Deprivation of rights under color of law; and their civil law counterparts: 42 U.S.C. § 1983 (Derived from § 1 of the Civil Rights Act of 1871): Civil action for deprivation of rights.; 42 U.S.C. § 1985(3) (Derived from Civil Rights Act of 1871): Conspiracy to interfere with civil rights. Section 1983's deprivation of fundamental rights under color of law has been a major source of litigation in the modern era, because it can be used to protect against the deprivation of all rights protected by the Fourteenth Amendment. This is quite expansive given that most of the Bill of Rights is incorporated by means of the Amendment.

Although most all of this legislation was "remedial" in character, the dominant issue in regard to the enforcement power is whether or not Congress could substantively enforce the Amendment to reach beyond the Court's own definitions of the Amendment's clauses. The first arguments that surfaced addressed whether or not Congress could reach private activity that the Court held the Amendment itself could not (the state action limitation). Although the fact that Section 241 and its civil parallel, Section 1985, seems to address private activity, and despite affirmative nuances by the Warren Court, the Court has essentially settled this question in the negative, and the Fourteenth Amendment's enforcement has been limited to at least some involvement of the state, or state action.

Within the same context, the issue as to whether or not Congress can extend the substantive reach of the Amendment, based on its enforcement power, has also generated much debate. In reviewing one of the most significant pieces of civil rights legislation, the Voting Rights Act of 1965, the Warren Court affirmed its sweeping mandate that extended well beyond the Court's own interpretation of Section 1 *Katzenbach v. Morgan* (1966).

But by the late twentieth century, the Rehnquist Court "put the brakes" on the *Katzenbach* rationale in finding that the Court could not modify substantive rights *City of Boerne v. Flores* 1997. Although they would conclude that Congress could abrogate the states Eleventh Amendment immunity from suit by the enforcement clause, they nonetheless scrutinized congressional purpose and limited legislation to remedies that were "proportional and congruent" to the alleged discrimination *United States v. Morrison* (2000). In fact, as if to make its point in regard to limits on the modern enforcement power, the Court held that in areas where the Court itself provided a higher degree of scrutiny (gender, fundamental rights), they would allow Congress greater leeway in legislating under its enforcement power *Nevada Department of Human Resources v. Hibbs* (2003), *Tennessee v. Lane* (2004).

MARTIN L. LEVY

References and Further Reading

Amar, *The Bill of Rights and the Fourteenth Amendment*, Yale Law Journal 101 (1992): 1193.
The American Heritage Dictionary of the English Language. 4th Ed. 2003.
Charles and Mary Beard. *The Rise of American Civilization.* 2 vols. 1927.
Corwin, E. *The Constitution of the United States of America* 965, 1953.
Currie, *The Constitution in the Supreme Court: Limitations on State Power, 1865–1873*, University of Chicago Law Review 51 (1983): 329, 348.
Ely. *Democracy and Distrust.* 18, 1980.
Fairman, *Does the Fourteenth Amendment Incorporate the Bill of Rights? The Original Understanding*, Stanford Law Review 2 (1949): 5, 132, 137–139.
Graham, *Our "Declaratory" Fourteenth Amendment*, Stanford Law Review 7 (1954): 3, 23, 25.

Reich. "The New Property." *Yale U.* 73 (1964): 733.
Tribe, L. *American Constitutional Law.* 1978.
Tussman and tenBroek, *The Equal Protection of the Laws,* California Law Review 37 (1949): 341.

Cases and Statutes Cited

Adamson v. California, 332 U.S. 46 (1947)
Adarand Constructors, Inc v. Pena, 515 U.S. 200 (1995)
Arlington Heights v. Metropolitan Housing Development Corp., 429 U.S. 252 (1977)
Barron v. Baltimore, 32 U.S. 243 (1833)
Bernal v. Fainter, 467 U.S. 216 (1984)
Board of Regents v. Roth, 408 U.S. 564 (1972)
Brown v. Board of Education, 47 U.S. 483 (1954)
Burton v. Wilmington Parking Authority, 365 U.S. 715 (1961)
City of Boerne v. Flores, 521 U.S. (1997)
City of Richmond v. Croson, 488 U.S. 469 (1989)
Civil Rights Cases, 109 U.S. 3 (1883)
Clark v. Jeter, 486 U.S. 456 (1988)
Cleburne v. Cleburne Living Center, 473 U.S. 432 (1985)
Craig v. Boren, 429 U.S. 190 (1976)
Dandridge v. Williams, 397 U.S. 471 (1970)
Dred Scott v. Sanford, 60 U.S. 393 (1856)
Duncan v. Louisiana, 391 U.S. 145 (1968)
Flagg Brothers v. Brooks, 436 U.S. 149 (1978)
Gitlow v. New York, 268 U.S. 652 (1925)
Goldberg v. Kelly, 397 U.S. 254 (1970)
Griswold v. Connecticut, 381 U.S. 479 (1965)
Grutter v. Bollinger, 1236 S. Crt. 2325 (2003)
Jackson v. Metropolitan Edison Company, 419 U.S. 345 (1974)
J.E.B. v. Alabama, 511 U.S. 127 (1994)
Katzenbach v. Morgan, 984 U.S. 641 (1966)
Lockner v. New York, 198 U.S. 45 (1905)
Lugar v. Edmondson, 457 U.S. 922 (1982)
Mathews v. Eldridge, 424 U.S. 319 (1976)
Mississippi University For Women V. Hogen, 458 U.S. 718 (1982)
Moore v. East Cleveland, 431 U.S. 494 (1977)
Moose Lodge v. Irivs, 407 U.S. 163 (1972)
Nevada Department of Human Resources v. Hibbs, 528 U.S. 721 (2003)
Palko v. Connecticut, 302 U.S. 319 (1937)
Paul v. Davis, 424 U.S. 693. (1976)
Planned Parenthood v. Casey, 505 U.S. 833 (1992)
Plessy v. Ferguson, 163 U.S. 537 (1896)
Plyler v. Doe, 457 U.S. 202 (1982)
Regents of The University Of California v. Bakke, 438 U.S. 265 (1978)
Roe v. Wade, 410 U.S. 113 (1973)
Romer v. Evans (1996), 517 U.S. 620 (1996)
San Antonio Independent School District V. Rodriguez, 411 U.S. 1 (1973)
Slaughter-House Cases, 83 U.S. 36 1872)
Strauder v. West Virginia, 100 U.S. 303 (1880)
Tennessee v. Lane, 124 S.Crt. 1978 (2004)
Twining v. State of N.J., 211 U.S. 78 (1908)
United States v. Morrison 529 U.S. 598 (2000)
Washington v. Davis, 426 U.S. 229 (1976)
Williamson v. Lee Optical, 348 U.S. 483 (1955)
Wisconsin v. Constantineau, 400 U.S. 433 (1971)

44 LIQUORMART v. RHODE ISLAND, 517 U.S. 484 (1996)

Freedom of speech is not unlimited in the case of "commercial speech," such as advertising. A 1942 Supreme Court decision upheld an ordinance that prohibited distribution of advertising leaflets on the street, saying that purely commercial advertising was not entitled to any First Amendment protection.

The Court later retreated from that position. Beginning in 1975, the Court said that an ordinance could regulate the manner of distribution but not its content. In a series of decisions the Court struck down prohibitions of specific types of advertising, where the commercial message also involved a matter of "public interest"—advertisements for abortion clinics, prescription drug prices, lawyers, optometrists, contraceptives, and electrical appliances.

A Rhode Island statute prohibited the advertising of liquor prices. 44 Liquormart's newspaper ad stated that "State law prohibits advertising liquor prices"—but claimed that that 44 Liquormart had low prices for potato chips, peanuts, and sodas. 44 Liquormart filed for a declaratory judgment, challenging the statute's validity.

The Court said that a statute that bans truthful, nonmisleading advertising must be subjected to strict scrutiny. The Court applied two of the four *Central Hudson* tests and overturned the statute. The Court said the prohibition did not directly advance the state's interest in promoting temperance, seeing no evidence that liquor price advertising and alcohol consumption were related. The Court also said that the state could reduce the consumption of alcohol by means other than abridging speech.

Rhode Island also argued that since the state could ban the sale of alcohol, it could ban or regulate the advertising of alcoholic beverages. The state cited, as authority for this proposition, a 1986 Supreme Court decision upholding a Puerto Rico statute limiting advertising of Puerto Rico gambling casinos. *44 Liquormart* overturned that decision.

ELI C. BORTMAN

Cases and Statutes Cited

Central Hudson Gas & Electric Corp. v. Public Service Commission of New York, 447 U.S. 557 (1980)
Posadas De Puerto Rico Assocs. v. Tourism Company of Puerto Rico, 478 U.S. 328 (1986)

See also **Commercial Speech; Lawyer Advertising; Professional Advertising**

FRANCE v. UNITED STATES, 164 U.S. 676 (1897)

This case involved a charge of conspiracy for violating an act of Congress intended to suppress interstate lottery traffic. A lottery drawing of three random numbers was held in the city of Covington, Kentucky, located immediately across the Ohio River from Cincinnati, Ohio. Lottery agents in Cincinnati recorded the numbers chosen by players. At a certain time before the lottery was to be drawn in Covington, the agents in Cincinnati sent messengers with a paper showing the various numbers chosen, the amounts of the bets, and the money to the office in Covington. The messengers would return with "hit slips," which were slips of paper with the winning numbers and the amounts payable to those who won in the last drawing. On their return to Cincinnati, some of the messengers were arrested and charged with conspiracy for carrying these hit slips. This was a violation of the statute prohibiting papers or instruments relating to lotteries across state lines.

Justice Peckham delivered the opinion of the Court and ruled that the words "concerning any lottery" must be strictly construed to mean a current or future lottery. Because the lottery had already been drawn, the hit slips carried by the messengers were not dependent on a current lottery and, therefore, did not violate the law. Furthermore, because the hit slips did not contain any particular person's name, did not have signatures, and were not addressed to any person, they did not represent a ticket, share, or interest in the event of any lottery. Thus, a strict interpretation of the language of the statute required that the judgment against the messengers be reversed.

LYNNE GARCIA

References and Further Reading

Carlisle v. United States, 517 U.S. 416 (1996): a case involving the power of an appellate court to reverse a district court's denial of a motion for a directed verdict.

Millan Couvertier v. Gil Bonar, United States Court of Appeals for the First Circuit, No. 98-1997 (1999): a case involving lotteries in Puerto Rico.

United States v. Halseth, 342 U.S. 277 (1952): case that affirms strictly construing the meaning of "concerning any lottery" when information concerning lotteries is sent through the mail.

FRANCIS v. FRANKLIN, 471 U.S. 307 (1985)

Francis v. Franklin expanded on the Court's earlier decision in Sandstrom v. Montana, 442 U.S. 510 (1979), by holding that jury instructions that create an unconstitutional burden-shifting presumption in a criminal trial could not be cured by informing the jury that the presumption was rebuttable. During an escape from custody, Franklin killed a man with a pistol. Franklin's sole defense was that the firing of the gun was unintentional. The judge charged the jury that a person's acts were presumed to be the product of his will and that a person was presumed to intend the natural and probable consequences of his acts, then the judge charged that these presumptions could be rebutted. The jury convicted Franklin of murder, and he was sentenced to death. After exhausting state remedies through unsuccessful appeals in Georgia, Franklin sought federal habeas corpus relief.

Franklin argued that the jury charge violated the due process clause, because it relieved the State of its burden to prove the element of intent beyond a reasonable doubt, and the Court agreed. Justice Brennan found that a reasonable juror could have understood that the disputed instructions created a mandatory presumption that shifted to Franklin the burden of persuasion on the element of intent once the state had proven the act of firing the pistol. Justice Brennan also found that neither the use of rebuttable language nor the jury instructions read as a whole cured the error.

Franklin affirmed the basic constitutional principle that the State has the burden to prove every element of a crime beyond a reasonable doubt, and the jury must be so charged.

EARL F. MARTIN

Cases and Statutes Cited

Sandstrom v. Montana, 442 U.S. 510 (1979)

See also Capital Punishment; Capital Punishment: Due Process Limits; Capital Punishment: History and Politics; Proof beyond a Reasonable Doubt

FRANK, JOHN P. (1917–2002)

John Frank was a twentieth century legal practitioner, scholar, teacher, mentor, and author who most assuredly lived "a life in the law." As a law professor and practicing lawyer, he participated in a number of the major Supreme Court cases of the modern era.

After earning degrees at the University of Wisconsin and Yale Law School, Frank began his legal career in 1942 as a clerk for Supreme Court Justice Hugo Black. He subsequently taught law at Indiana University and at Yale. In 1954, when health problems pushed him to the southwestern United States, he joined the Phoenix, Arizona, law firm of Lewis and Roca in 1954 and practiced there for almost fifty years.

During his faculty tenure at Yale, Frank, who had met Thurgood Marshall at Indiana, joined in the NAACP Legal Education and Defense Fund assault on segregated education. In 1949 in *Sweatt v. Painter,* the Fund challenged the State of Texas for providing inadequate law school facilities for African Americans. At Marshall's request, Frank and two Yale Law School colleagues submitted an *amicus* brief, eventually signed by 187 law professors, supporting the NAACP suit. The brief in *Sweat v. Painter* went far beyond Marshall's argument, suggesting a complete end to segregation. Frank argued that racial classifications intrinsically violated the Fourteenth Amendment. Although the Court did not at the time accept the academics' argument, the justices did acknowledge that the plaintiff had been denied equal educational opportunity. Ultimately, the constitutional argument was addressed in the 1954 *Brown v. Education* litigation in which Frank also advised Thurgood Marshall.

During his time in private practice in Phoenix, Frank's accomplishments were many and varied. He became an expert on civil procedure and participated in a major revision of those rules. He was noted for his extensive *pro bono* work and represented Ernesto Miranda in *Miranda v. Arizona* in which the United States Supreme Court declared that the Fifth Amendment requires suspects be informed by law enforcement authorities that they have the right to an attorney during questioning. Frank was noteworthy, as well, for his mentoring of aspiring lawyers and was instrumental in encouraging the opening up of law practice to women. As a nationally respected lawyer, he testified in support of Richard Nixon's controversial nomination of Clement Haynsworth to the Supreme Court in 1970 but testified in opposition to Ronald Reagan's Robert Bork nomination in 1987. He also advised Anita Hill in her appearance before the Senate Judiciary Committee in 1991 in the contentious Thomas–Hill confirmation hearings.

Frank remained an active legal scholar until the end of his career, publishing eleven books that included a portrait of Abraham Lincoln as lawyer, a study of the Supreme Court, and last, an examination of the Haynsworth nomination process. His most important legacy, however, was summed up best by a former protégé, Leon Higginbotham, an African-American student of Frank's at Yale who later became chief judge for the U.S. Court of Appeals for the Third Circuit, himself a noted jurist. Higginbotham, in an address to young lawyers thanked Frank for the lesson he had learned from him at Yale—"that the pursuit of justice was not an inappropriate profession for a lawyer."

KAREN BRUNER

References and Further Reading

Barrett, John Q., *Symposium: John Frank, Leon Higginbotham, and One Afternoon at the Supreme Court—Not a Trifling Thing,* Yale Law and Policy Review 20 (2002): 311–323.

Cardena, José A., *John P. Frank: A Life of Socially Useful Work,* Arizona Attorney 39 (November 2002): 22.

Entin, Jonathan L., *In memoriam: John P. Frank,* Case Western Reserve Law Review 53 (Fall 2002): 238–242.

Kluger, Richard. *Simple Justice: The History of Brown v. Board of Education and Black America's Struggle for Equality.* New York: Vintage Books, 1977.

Sperry, Lisa, *John Frank's Mark of Excellence,* Arizona Attorney 36 (December 1999): 40–45.

FRANKFURTER, FELIX (1882–1965)

Felix Frankfurter—law professor and associate justice of the U.S. Supreme Court—had been known as one of the country's leading reformers when Franklin Roosevelt named him to the high court in early 1939. By the time he retired, forced off the bench by a debilitating stroke in 1962—he had become the *bête noire* of most judicial liberals and the most conservative member of the Warren Court. There is an irony here, because the two men—the supposedly "liberal" Professor Frankfurter and the supposedly "conservative" Justice Frankfurter—did not differ that much. Both adhered to a single judicial philosophy—judicial restraint—but whereas that view made a man a liberal in the 1930s, by the 1950s, at least in terms of civil liberties, it stood for the notion that the Bill of Rights could be restricted by the government provided it could offer a minimalist justification.

Born in Austria, Frankfurter came to the United States as a child. His ambitious mother dominated his young life, urging him to excel so he could rise up in the world; she fully believed in the American dream, and it was her drive that got the family out of the immigrant slums and into a better neighborhood. The brilliant Frankfurter easily excelled in public school and at City College, and then went to the Harvard Law School. There he learned a very important lesson, namely, that intelligence did matter, that there was a world in which those who could think clearly, logically, and quickly could do well. At Harvard, he later claimed, he discovered the democracy of merit, an idea that to him epitomized what America was all about.

After graduation he worked briefly—and unhappily—in a private law firm, and then eagerly accepted an offer to become an assistant to U.S. Attorney Henry L. Stimson. The patrician New Yorker would be an important influence in Frankfurter's life, opening to him the possibility of how exciting and rewarding a career in public service could be. He followed Stimson to Washington during the administrations of Theodore Roosevelt and William Howard Taft. Stationed in the War Department, the gregarious Frankfurter soon met all the movers and shakers in the capital. He lived in a house on "I" Street with other young men, where people like Oliver Wendell Holmes, Jr., and Louis D. Brandeis would stop by to visit at what soon became known as the House of Truth. Both Holmes and Brandeis would become mentors to the young Frankfurter, and it was the latter who convinced him to accept an appointment at the Harvard Law School.

From the time Frankfurter joined the Harvard Law faculty in 1914 through the constitutional crisis of 1937, conservatives on the courts used the notion of substantive due process to strike down economic reform legislation they did not like. Led by Holmes and Brandeis, liberals called for judicial restraint, that is, for allowing legislatures wide discretion in policy-making provided no specific constitutional bar prohibited it. Frankfurter stood as the leading academic champion of judicial restraint, and at the time of his appointment, his friends expected—correctly—that he would not allow his personal economic views to thwart legislative will.

But what Frankfurter never understood—and Holmes and Brandeis had made very clear—was that whereas judges ought not to thwart legislative policy in economic matters, they had a special role to play in protecting individual liberties. This showed up in its most explicit form in the famous Footnote Four in the *Carolene Products* case, in which Harlan Fiske Stone said the courts should impose much higher scrutiny on legislation affecting civil rights and civil liberties than on economic regulation. Despite his great reverence for Holmes and Brandeis, Frankfurter did not absorb this lesson.

Frankfurter's earlier reputation is well deserved. Brandeis called him the "most useful lawyer in America." He had opposed A. Mitchell Palmer's Red Scare after World War I; he had taken over Brandeis's role as chief litigator for the Consumer's Union in defending protective legislation for workers; he had been the chief advocate in the most sensational case of the 1920s, the trial of two Italian immigrants, Sacco and Vanzetti, for payroll robbery and murder. Although there is still controversy over whether or not the two men were guilty, it was clear at the time that the two men had been arrested because they were immigrants and anarchists, and the trial was marked by gross prejudice on the part of the presiding judge. Frankfurter thought the entire episode a travesty of justice, and in his view either there should be a new trial with a fair and impartial judge or the two men should be pardoned. His defense of the two men made him a hero to liberals, but many misunderstood his position. The real crime, he believed, had been the perversion of the justice system; to some extent the guilt or innocence of the two men was secondary.

With the arrival of Franklin Roosevelt in the White House in 1933, he became one of the president's closest advisors and a one-man personnel agency stocking New Deal agencies with his former students from Harvard. He had been a member of the American Civil Liberties Union, as well as the National Association for the Advancement of Colored People, and he had used the columns of the *New Republic* to attack judges deciding cases on personal predilection rather than the law.

Yet during most of this time Frankfurter had said little and written less about issues such as freedom of speech. In part this is understandable, since the Supreme Court's agenda through the early 1930s consisted mainly of economic matters; that agenda changed at about the time Frankfurter went on the Court, and so neither he nor his admirers would have expected the types of cases he would confront. However, one might get an idea of his views on this from a letter he wrote to Ellery Sedgewick, the editor of the *Atlantic Monthly,* regarding the attacks on him during the Sacco and Vanzetti controversy. He believed that his criticism of the judge and other public officials opened him to charges of seditious libel. He argued that while it would probably be politically unwise for the state to do so, he believed that it had the right and the power to act against those who attacked the actions of the state.

While on the Court, Frankfurter engaged in a running battle with Hugo Black for more than twenty years on two issues key to civil liberties—the incorporation of the Bill of Rights through the Fourteenth Amendment to apply to the states and the preferred position of the First Amendment, especially freedom of speech in the constitutional pantheon.

Brandeis had first suggested the Fourteenth Amendment's Due Process Clause included noneconomic liberties, and by 1939, the Court had made freedom of speech and press, as well as counsel in capital cases, applicable to the states. Then in *Palko v. Connecticut* (1938), Justice Cardozo had suggested that not all of the protections in the Bill of Rights should be incorporated, but only those that were fundamental to a free society. Frankfurter, who succeeded Cardozo on the Court, took up this theme and thus fought against any notion that all of the Bill of

Rights applied to the states. In part, this belief stemmed not only from conservatism but also from a strong belief in federalism, and that under a federal system states ought to be given as much leeway as possible. Just as judicial restraint meant that judges did not interpose their economic views against Congress and state legislatures, so it also meant that states had the authority to limit rights in a manner denied to the national government.

In 1942, Frankfurter joined with a majority of the Court in declining to extend the right of counsel in *Betts v. Brady* and continued to oppose incorporation of that right throughout his years on the Court. Not until after he retired did the Court unanimously overrule *Betts* in the landmark decision of *Gideon v. Wainwright* (1963).

In 1947, the Court was asked to over rule *Twining v. New Jersey* (1908), in which it had held that a state law permitting comment on a defendant's refusal to testify did not violate procedural due process. Since that time, the Court had begun to incorporate parts of the Bill of Rights to apply to the states, and Frankfurter, in *Adamson v. California,* argued that the Fifth Amendment protection against testifying against oneself, or having the prosecution comment on it, did not apply to the states. The right against self-incrimination, he declared, did not constitute one of those fundamental principles inherent in "the concept of ordered liberty." In a concurring opinion that defined the notion of selective incorporation for the next two decades, Frankfurter spelled out his ideas of federalism, judicial restraint, and the notion that even in the areas of individual liberties courts should not second-guess the legislature.

Opposing him was Hugo Black, who after initially agreeing with Cardozo's *Palko* opinion, had come to the conclusion that the due process clause of the Fourteenth Amendment incorporated totally all of the protections in the first eight amendments. The Court nominally followed the Cardozo–Frankfurter notion of "selective" incorporation, but in the end it was Black who triumphed, because the Court incorporated practically every protection in the Bill of Rights. In 1964, the Court overturned *Adamson* and incorporated the right against self-incrimination in *Malloy v. Hogan* and then a few years later carried it to even greater length in *Miranda v. Arizona* (1966).

Even when Frankfurter was willing to incorporate a provision, he did so in as restricted a manner as possible. He wrote the majority opinion in *Wolf v. Colorado* (1949), which in effect applied the warrant clause to the states but did so in as crabbed a manner as possible. Refusing to come right out and declare the Fourth Amendment protection incorporated, he found that unreasonable searches and seizures on the part of state officials violated the sue process clause of the Fourteenth Amendment. Although that clause was the basis of incorporation, here Frankfurter emphasized the procedural process elements. He also refused to apply the exclusionary clause, the only means of truly enforcing the warrant clause, against the states. Here again, his view was eventually rejected by the Court in *Mapp v. Ohio* (1961).

In terms of free speech, Frankfurter rarely voted to support the individual against efforts by the state to restrict it. In *Carpenters' and Joiners' Union v. Ritter's Café* (1942), he held that peaceful picketing enjoyed no immunity from state regulation, although the Court had earlier extended free speech protection in labor disputes. In what is perhaps his most notable speech opinion, he concurred with the majority in *Dennis v. United States* (1941), a case that has been universally condemned ever since. The Court convicted Communist Party leaders not of attempting to overthrow the government of the United States by force but of conspiring to teach about the idea of overthrowing the government. Although he personally abhorred the McCarthy witch hunt and the various loyalty programs, he believed that the First Amendment posed no barrier to Congress and the executive putting such programs into place.

Unlike Hugo Black and William O. Douglas, who took an absolutist view of the First Amendment Speech Clause, Frankfurter in effect saw no difference between the government's right to regulate economic activity and the regulation of expression. When Black suggested that the First Amendment held a "preferred position," Frankfurter wrote to Stanley Reed "Please tell me what kind of sense it makes that one provision of the Constitution is to be 'preferred' over another? The correlative of 'preference' is 'subordination,' and I know of no calculus to determine when one provision of the Constitution must yield to another."

To Frankfurter, as William O. Douglas correctly observed, the First Amendment was little more than a caution for moderation. This can be seen when a friend reminded him that during the 1920s, Frankfurter had voiced extremely unpopular opinions in defense of Sacco and Vanzetti. Frankfurter shot back that while it would have been poor policy for the Commonwealth of Massachusetts to have put him in jail for what he did, it was clear to him that the state did in fact have the power to do so.

Although Frankfurter strongly believed in separation of church and state, and voted accordingly in *Everson v. Board of Education of Ewing Township* (1947), *Illinois ex rel. McCollum v. Board of Education* (1948), and *Zorach v. Clausen* (1952), he apparently had little interest in the free exercise clause, as he displayed in the series of cases launched by Jehovah's Witnesses in the early 1940s.

In these cases, Frankfurter is best known for his opinions in the two flag salute cases. In *Minersville School District v. Gobitis* (1940), he ruled for an eight-to-one Court that the state could force school children to salute the American flag, even if it went against their religious principles. He dismissed the free exercise argument out of hand, and in a telling phrase wrote: "To the legislature no less than to courts is committed the guardianship of deeply cherished liberties." In essence, courts should accept that legislatures were rights-protective and defer to their judgment. There has been a great deal of comment over this case, and a number of scholars have suggested that the real key to understanding Frankfurter's position is the fact that he was an immigrant and a super-patriot. America had been good to him; in Europe his brilliance would have done him little good, and doors would have been closed to him solely for the reason that he was a Jew. He had had his innate patriotism reinforced in his public school days, and he saw no reason why schools should not continue to do so, especially with the chances so high that the United States would soon be involved in another war. The so-called religious rights of a small and insignificant sect mattered little when balanced against the needs to promote love of country.

The resulting uproar over the *Gobitis* case, the increase on attacks on Witnesses, and the determination of the Witnesses to fight for their civil liberties brought one case after another to the high court, and in every one of them Frankfurter voted against the free exercise claim. Then in *Jones v. Opelika* (1942), Black, Douglas, and Murphy indicated that they had voted wrongly in *Gobitis*, and the following year the Court reheard the flag salute issue, this time finding for the Witnesses in *West Virginia Board of Education v. Barnette* (1943). Justice Jackson wrote a ringing endorsement of the right of free thought, and Frankfurter wrote an anguished dissent noting that, although he belonged to "the most vilified and persecuted minority in history," the courts had no special business protecting minorities. The Framers of the Bill of Rights, he said, "knew that minorities may disrupt society."

Twenty years later Frankfurter still had no sympathy for minorities and voted against making exemption for religious Jewish merchants from Sunday closing laws in *Braunfeld v. Brown* (1961) and *Gallagher v. Crown Kosher Market* (1961).

Frankfurter was not a complete enemy of civil liberties, and even while opposing incorporation of the Fourth Amendment often wrote opinions denouncing the police for going too far in their zeal.

A good case in point is *Rochin v. California* (1952), in which he chastised the police for forcibly pumping a suspect's stomach to get incriminating evidence of drugs. And in the notorious *Rosenberg* case, Frankfurter throughout the ordeal was the only member of the Court to consistently argue that the two had not had a fair trial, and that the Court should review the proceedings.

Frankfurter was also a champion of civil rights and voted in every case that came before the Court during his tenure in support of the rights of black Americans. He named the first African-American clerk to the Court and worked out the strategy that led the Court to reconsider the *Brown* case so that Chief Justice Earl Warren would be able to develop a unanimous opinion. Unfortunately, Frankfurter also imposed the "all deliberate speed" formula on *Brown II*, although it is clear that by it he did not mean it to serve as an excuse for delay. And in *Gomillion v. Lightfoot* (1960), Frankfurter wrote the opinion striking down an Alabama gerrymandering scheme designed to deny black voters their rights.

That opinion, however, led to the overturn of an earlier Frankfurter opinion and in the end marked his departure from the Court with one of the great reversals of his career. In 1946, the Court heard a case challenging the failure of the State of Illinois to reapportion its election districts as required under the state constitution. The result was that although there had been great population shifts into the cities and their suburbs, the now under-populated rural areas still controlled the legislature, and refused to reapportion. In *Colgrove v. Green* (1946) Frankfurter, for a bare four to three majority, held the issue to be a "political question," and therefore not amendable to judicial resolution. He warned the courts to stay out of "the political thicket." In fact, four of the seven justices who heard the case did believe the matter justiciable, but Wiley Rutledge joined Frankfurter's opinion, because he did not believe there was sufficient time before the next election to resolve the case.

Then Frankfurter wrote the *Gomillion* opinion, and now people wondered why it was all right to strike down laws that discriminated against African Americans but not against urban residents. For Frankfurter the answer was clear—the Fifteenth Amendment addressed the issue specifically. But with the Warren Court's attack on segregation (in which Frankfurter joined) and the beginning of its due process revolution, it was only a matte of time before the question of apportionment came up before the high court again.

In *Baker v. Carr* (1962), the Court agreed that the question of mal-apportionment was justiciable and set the case down for argument on its merits in the following term. Frankfurter entered a bitter dissent, accusing the majority of going where it should not go. The answer, he said, lay with the legislature, completely ignoring the fact that a majority of the people could not get their way because the minority controlled the legislature and would not yield that power. What must have made his defeat even more galling was the fact that the majority opinion was written by his one-time student, William Brennen, who with great skill and craftsmanship completely demolished Frankfurter's argument in *Colgrove*.

Frankfurter had a stroke later in the year and was off the Court when it heard the apportionment cases and handed down a series of decisions requiring the states to reapportion on the basis of "one person, one vote." Frankfurter had warned that there was no judicially manageable formula by which courts could oversee reapportionment, but his longtime foe on the Court, William O. Douglas, came up with the catch phrase that not only garnered public support but also provided the judicial formula necessary.

Frankfurter's place in the history of civil liberties is mixed at best. A prisoner of the idea of judicial restraint that he and other reformers championed before the Court crisis of 1937, Frankfurter could never grasp the fact that rights belonging to the people, be they civil rights or civil liberties, are in a different class than simple economic regulations. Practically all of Frankfurter's opinions concerning incorporation and the Bill of Rights—especially relating to the First Amendment—have been overruled or otherwise discarded. Even conservative jurists now agree that, even if they do not use the phrase, the First Amendment does occupy a preferred position and that courts have to be vigilant in the protection of people's liberties. Frankfurter's great heroes—Holmes and Brandeis—understood that; regrettably he never did.

MELVIN I. UROFSKY

References and Further Reading

Hirsch, Harry N. *The Enigma of Felix Frankfurter*. New York: Basic Books, 1981.
Kurland, Philip H., ed. *Felix Frankfurter on the Supreme Court: Extrajudicial Essays on the Court and the Constitution*. Chicago: University of Chicago Press, 1971.
Parrish, Michael E. *Felix Frankfurter and His Times: The Reform Years*. New York: Free Press, 1982.
Silverstein, Mark. *Constitutional Faiths: Felix Frankfurter, Hugo Black, and the Process of Judicial Decision-Making*. Ithaca: Cornell University Press, 1984.
Simon, James F. *The Antagonists: Hugo Black, Felix Frankfurter, and Civil Liberties in Modern America*. New York: Simon & Schuster, 1989.
Urofsky, Melvin I. *Felix Frankfurter: Judicial Restraint and Individual Liberties*. Boston: Twayne, 1992.

Cases and Statutes Cited

Adamson v. California, 332 U.S. 46 (1947)
Baker v. Carr, 369 U.S. 186 (1962)
Betts v. Brady, 316 U.S. 455 (1942)
Braunfeld v. Brown, 366 U.S. 599 (1961)
Brown v. Board of Education of Topeka I, 347 U.S. 483 (1954)
Brown v. Board of Education of Topeka II, 349 U.S. 294 (1955)
Carpenters' and Joiners' Union v. Ritter's Café, 315 U.S. 722 (1942)
Colgrove v. Green, 328 U.S. 549 (1946)
Dennis v. United States, 341 U.S. 494 (1951)
Everson v. Board of Education of Ewing Township, 330 U.S. 1 (1947)
Gallagher v. Crown Kosher Supermarket, 366 U.S. 617 (1961)
Gideon v. Wainwright, 372 U.S. 335 (1963)
Gomillion v. Lightfoot, 364 U.S. 339 (1960)
Illinois ex rel. McCollum v. Board of Education, 333 U.S. 203 (1948)
Jones v. Opelika, 316 U.S. 584 (1942)
Malloy v. Hogan, 378 U.S. 1 (1964)
Mapp v. Ohio, 367 U.S. 643 (1961)
Minersville School District v. Gobitis, 310 U.S. 586 (1940)
Miranda v. Arizona, 384 U.S. 436 (1966)
Palko v. Connecticut, 302 U.S. 319 (1938)
Rochin v. California, 342 U.S. 165 (1952)
Rosenberg v. United States, 346 U.S. 273 (1955)
Twining v. New Jersey, 211 U.S. 78 (1908)
United States v. Carolene Products Co., 304 U.S. 144 (1938)
West Virginia Board of Education v. Barnette, 319 U.S. 624 (1943)
Wolf v. Colorado, 338 U.S. 25 (1949)
Zorach v. Clausen, 343 U.S. 306 (1952)

FRANKLIN, BENJAMIN (1706–1790)

Well-known as a printer, scientist, and inventor, Benjamin Franklin is less well-known as a civil rights champion. There was no more committed proponent of freedom of the press than Franklin, and he was active in the protest movement that began with the Stamp Act Crisis. It is often forgotten that Franklin held certain natural rights sacred, insomuch as he explained in 1759, "They that can give up essential liberty to obtain a little temporary safety deserve neither liberty nor safety."

Long an advocate of such Lockean ideas as the state of nature, the social contract, and natural law, Franklin particularly embraced Locke's reverence for life, liberty, and property. His actions during the Stamp Act Crisis and the Revolutionary period show that Franklin fully embraced the citizen's right to petition the government when government became tyrannical and to initiate revolution when all other means of reform failed. And Franklin's own writings indicate a particular respect for property and equality before the law. Although he was generally not given to profound political theory, and instead embraced the ideas of Locke and other theorists without expounding on them, he did feel compelled to write about property and equality (although he believed Parliament wrong for passing the Intolerable Acts after the Boston Tea Party, Franklin insisted that the activists should pay for the tea they had destroyed, because it was private property).

As a printer, Franklin also had a profound reverence for freedom of speech and the press. And his concern that citizens remain able to express thoughts, ideas, even criticisms through speech and media were well founded. James Franklin, Benjamin's older brother, had been jailed for a month when Franklin was sixteen for printing a piece that was critical of the Pennsylvania Assembly. Furthermore, he was forced to shut down his newspaper. To avoid actually closing the paper down, James transferred responsibility to young Benjamin, who published the *New England Courant* under his own name. So Franklin's concern was not merely academic.

Franklin was also assigned to Thomas Jefferson's committee to draft a Declaration of Independence. While Jefferson wrote the first draft himself, Franklin, John Adams, and the other members of the committee read it and offered suggestions before presenting it to the entire Continental Congress for further editing. It may be assumed, because Franklin left no explicit comment, that he approved of Jefferson's ideas of life, liberty, and the pursuit of happiness.

And it should not be forgotten that Franklin was a framer of the Constitution, as well. Indeed, he argued against property requirements of officeholders; he believed property qualifications would "debase the spirit of the common people." As the convention drew to a close and the time came for delegates to sign the document, Franklin stood and gave a speech. He expressed his belief that the document was not perfect and that he had some reservations but that he believed it better than any other government he knew of. He signed it, of course, and supported its ratification.

JAMES HALABUK, JR.

References and Further Reading

Morgan, Edmund S. *Benjamin Franklin*. New Haven: Yale University Press, 2002.
Wright, Esmond, ed. *Benjamin Franklin, A Profile*. New York: Hill and Wang, 1970.

FREE EXERCISE CLAUSE (I): HISTORY, BACKGROUND, FRAMING

Along with the establishment clause, the free exercise clause is located at the beginning of the First Amendment: "Congress shall make no law respecting an establishment of religion, or *prohibiting the free exercise thereof....*" This article will provide a general guide to understanding the free exercise clause by describing the historical context in which it was drafted, the process by which it was drafted, and an overview of its interpretation and application.

Historical Background

During the time that North America was being explored and settled, England was grappling with the Protestant Reformation's extremely disruptive impact on English society and government. Henry VIII had broken with Rome and established an official Protestant Church of England, but when his eldest child, the devout Roman Catholic Mary Tudor, came to power, she began persecuting Protestants vigorously and drove their leaders into exile. The outright persecution of Mary's reign came to end when she was succeeded by her half-sister Elizabeth, who reestablished the Protestant identity of the Church of England. Queen Elizabeth I continually had to guard, however, against being overthrown by Mary Queen of Scots, who was intent on turning the nation back to Roman Catholicism.

Despite that Elizabeth had reestablished Protestantism in England, many Protestants, known as "Puritans," believed that the Church of England still needed to be cleansed of the residues of Roman Catholic belief and practice. When James I succeeded Elizabeth on her death in 1603, he resolved to suppress and drive the Puritans out. To avoid persecution under James I and his successor, Charles I, by the 1640s as many as 20,000 Puritans had sought refuge by fleeing to North America. Most of these Puritan emigrants congregated in New England; others spread as far south as the West Indies.

When Parliamentary leaders overthrew Charles I in the English Civil War, they ostensibly granted religious freedom to the entire nation, but this actually extended only to conformist Protestants. Catholics were excluded; Baptist ministers were imprisoned; and Protestant clergy who insisted on using the Anglican prayer book were ejected during this period. The official persecution of Protestant dissenters did not end until 1688, and Catholics remained subject to restrictions on political and military office throughout the eighteenth century.

Meanwhile, in the North American colonies, four distinctive approaches to resolving this extremely divisive question of the civil status of religion had been developing. As described by religion clause historian Michael McConnell, these four approaches ranged from the near theocracy of New England, at one end of the continuum; to the southern colonies where the state used religion as a means of social control; to the benign neglect of religion in New York and New Jersey; and finally to the four colonies founded as havens for religious dissenters, at the opposite end of the continuum.

In the New England colonies that the Puritans had founded, civil authorities suppressed any dissenters in an effort to force them to conform to Puritan beliefs and expectations. This approach led to Baptists being banished, dissenters being whipped or jailed, and four Quakers (who had returned after having been expelled) being hanged. Puritans continued to suppress dissenters until 1679, when, in response to a letter from King Charles II expressing support for "freedom and liberty of conscience" for all non-Catholic Christians, Puritan authorities halted the practice of imposing criminal punishments on those who refused to conform to Puritan beliefs and practices.

In most of the southern colonies, the Church of England had been established by order of the Crown and was financed and tightly controlled by the government. Although New England and the southern colonies were alike in maintaining religious establishments, in a more profound sense, as McConnell points out, these two types of systems are better understood as opposites. Whereas in New England the Puritans used government to make society conform to religious ideals, in the south the governing authorities and local gentry used religion to maintain their social status and control. This second approach is thus characterized by state domination of the church. By the eighteenth century, Virginia had become the most intolerant of all of the colonies. Georgia differed from the other southern colonies in that the authorities exhibited a remarkable degree of tolerance toward non-Anglican Protestants and Jews, although Catholics were detested and banned from the colony.

In New York and New Jersey, the official attitude toward religion was one of what McConnell describes as "benign neglect." The populations of these two colonies were religiously quite diverse, and a de facto policy of religious toleration emerged, even in the four counties of metropolitan New York, where majorities had voted to establish the Church of England. In these areas, Protestants were free to live and worship as they chose, and Quakers and Jews were for the most part left alone.

Four colonies were intentionally founded as havens for religious dissenters. Maryland, the first of these, was founded by a Catholic proprietor as a haven from the persecution that Catholics were facing in England. Its founder, Lord Calvert, is credited with the first use of the term "free exercise" in an American legal document. In 1648, he instructed Maryland's new Protestant governor and its councilors to promise to make sure that no Christian, "and in particular no Roman Catholic," is disturbed in the "free exercise" of religion. The proprietor had previously used the term "free liberty of religion" in his attempts to attract Boston-area colonists to resettle in Maryland, but Massachusetts Governor John Winthrop had responded to the effect that no Bostonians were interested in religious "liberty."

In 1649, Maryland's Assembly followed Lord Calvert's lead by enacting a statute that contained the phrase "free exercise." This was North America's first free exercise clause. The security of Catholics in Maryland changed radically, however, after the Glorious Revolution of 1688, which brought about the replacement of England's Catholic King James II with the Protestants William and Mary and sparked a wave of anti-Catholicism in Maryland that led to the establishment of the Church of England there. Soon thereafter Maryland would come to rival Virginia for its lack of tolerance for religious dissenters.

Rhode Island was originally settled by Roger Williams in 1536, just to the south of the Massachusetts Bay Colony, from which Williams had been expelled for his differences with the Puritan authorities. The Rhode Island Charter of 1663 described the colony as a "lively experiment" with a "full liberty in religious concernments." The Charter prohibited the infringement of civil liberty on the basis of "any differences in opinion in matters of religion," and declared that residents may "freely and fully have and enjoy his and their own judgments and consciences, in matters of religious concernments." Religious freedom in Rhode Island had its limits, however. Jews were barred from citizenship and Catholics from public office. Although in later times, many would come to admire Rhode Island's "lively experiment" in religious liberty, during the colonial period neighboring New England colonists tended to see Rhode Island as an embarrassment, "the licentious Republic" and the "sink hole of New England."

Despite Rhode Island's negative reputation, its Charter of 1663 seems to have served as a model for the religious freedom provisions that were included in the original agreements between the proprietors and the prospective settlers of Carolina and New Jersey. These documents contained wording that was almost identical to the religious freedom provisions of the Rhode Island Charter of 1663. These provisions were later superseded by more limited religious freedom provisions for the colonies of North Carolina, South Carolina, and New Jersey, but after the Revolution, many of the new state constitutions seem to have drawn on the Rhode Island model.

In practice, it was probably the middle colonies that were the most influential examples of religious freedom on the later development of the free exercise clause. They established no church (except in the four counties of metropolitan New York), and welcomed persons from a wide range of religious traditions. Under William Penn's Charters of Privileges of 1701, Pennsylvania and Delaware provided for the religious freedom of all theists, while confining the holding of public office to Christians. Pennsylvania's reputation for religious tolerance contributed to the high level of immigration that it enjoyed, which was accompanied by widespread prosperity.

Following the Revolution, several of the states that had established the Church of England as colonies took swift steps to sever their official ties with the church. The new state constitutions of Georgia, New York, North Carolina, and South Carolina eliminated the provisions that had granted the Church of England special status and benefits. Going forward, South Carolina "established" the Protestant religion but provided churches no financial support; Georgia authorized a tax that would go to support the individual taxpayer's own denomination; and New York and North Carolina joined the middle colonies and Rhode Island with no establishment of religion.

Virginia and Maryland moved more gradually toward disestablishment after the Revolution. In 1776, the Virginia Declaration of Rights was adopted, which guaranteed for all the right to "the free exercise of religion," and the Virginia legislature suspended the collection of the compulsory taxes that had been supporting the Church of England. In 1779, these taxes were repealed, but the Church of England was not formally disestablished in Virginia until 1785. Virginia's post-Revolutionary free exercise protections, in practice, were not extended to Anglican clergy, who when they had been ordained in England were required to take an oath of allegiance to the crown. Anglican clergy who refused to violate their oaths after the Revolution were mobbed, beaten, and driven from their pulpits.

The Maryland Declaration of Rights of 1776 disestablished the Church of England, but it also authorized the legislature to impose a general tax "for the support of the Christian religion." The legislative battle over whether such a tax would be imposed lasted throughout the 1780s. Those who supported such an assessment were never able to prevail.

In 1786, the Virginia Statute of Religious Freedom, authored by Thomas Jefferson, was enacted, which prohibited any form of compulsory support of religion and guaranteed the rights of all to worship freely. By 1789, every state, with the exception of Connecticut, had enacted some form of protection for religious freedom, but Maryland and Delaware limited such protection to Christians, and five other states limited it to theists. According to McConnell, "These state constitutions provide the most direct evidence of the original understanding" of what would later be adopted as the Free exercise clause, "for it is reasonable to infer that those who drafted and adopted the first amendment assumed the term 'free exercise of religion' meant what it had meant in their states" (McConnell, 1456).

All of these state constitutional provisions contemplated the protection not only of belief but also of one's freedom to participate in religious activity. Four states described the scope of protection for religious activity in broad terms, but eight states limited such protection to acts of "worship." The First Amendment's Free exercise clause seems to have followed these four states' broader approach by not limiting the protection that it offers to "worship" activities. It also bears noting, however, that the limitation to "worship" in these eight states does not seem to have had any actual impact on the scope of free exercise protection in them.

Drafting

The federal free exercise clause emerged from the debate that surrounded the ratification of the Constitution of 1787 regarding whether or not that document should contain specific guarantees of individual liberties. The Federalists, proponents of the draft Constitution, contended that the inclusion of certain specific guarantees might be interpreted to mean that the other rights that the Constitution had sought to respect by carefully spelling out and limiting the scope of federal power should not also be protected. Their opponents, distrustful of federal power, insisted that specific guarantees were necessary.

Patrick Henry, among others, was concerned that the religious freedoms that had been forged at the state level might be overridden by the emerging federal government. John Leland, the leader of Virginia's Baptists, opposed ratification, because in his view religious freedom was not adequately protected by the Constitution in the form that it had been proposed. Rhode Island decided that it could not support ratification until an accompanying Bill of Rights had been drafted and put forward. Those in several other states who called for explicit constitutional guarantees of individual liberties eventually accepted the promise that a Bill of Rights would be drafted later in exchange for their votes for ratification.

James Madison had initially opposed the addition of specific guarantees of individual liberties in the new Constitution, but he came to accept them as a necessary compromise to ensure ratification. When he announced his candidacy for the first Congress under the new Constitution and learned that local Baptists were planning to support his opponent, James Monroe, Madison responded by pledging his support for express guarantees of all individual rights, including one that would fully protect religious liberty. This won the support of the Baptist leadership and tipped the election in his favor. Having helped Madison to get elected, Virginia's Baptists did not hesitate to remind him of their interest in religious liberty as he headed off to take his place in the first House of Representatives.

On arrival, Madison kept his word. He emerged as the foremost spokesperson for religious freedom in the first session of Congress. More than 200 state-sponsored proposals for constitutional guarantees of individual liberties had been received. Of these, which included five state-sponsored religious freedom proposals, Madison culled nineteen and added one of his own. Initially, he planned to work these amendments into the body of the existing Constitution rather than append them to it in the form of a Bill of Rights.

Madison chose not to put forward any of the religious freedom proposals submitted by the states. Instead, he advanced his own approach by suggesting that in Article I, section 10, the states should be prohibited from violating "the equal rights of conscience." With respect to the federal government, Madison proposed that to Article I, section 9, be added, "The civil rights of none shall be abridged on account of religious belief or worship, nor shall any national religion be established, nor shall the full and equal rights of conscience be in any manner, or under any pretext infringed."

Madison's initial formulation of what would become the First Amendment's religion clauses did not include the term "free exercise" of religion. Rather, in keeping with the laws of his own state and with three of the five state-submitted proposals, he favored protection for the freedom of "belief" and "worship" and of one's "rights of conscience."

Little was said during the recorded debates when the House took up the issue of religious freedom. Most of the controversy centered about what would become the establishment clause. To gain insight into the meaning that the drafters may have intended the free exercise clause to have, one must carefully analyze the wording of successive drafts of the religion clauses.

The House Select Committee that took up Madison's proposals initially shortened the religion clauses to read, "no religion shall be established by law, nor shall the equal rights of conscience be infringed." The reference to protecting freedom of belief and worship was deleted. The phrase "free exercise of religion" made its first appearance in the amended version, as passed by the House and sent to the Senate: "Congress shall make no law establishing religion, or prohibiting the free exercise thereof, nor shall the rights of conscience be infringed."

To this point, the phrases "rights of conscience" and "free exercise of religion" seem to have been used interchangeably. The inclusion of both in the version passed by the House suggests that some thought it necessary to use both terms.

The version that was sent to the Senate used a form of the verb "prohibit" rather than "infringe," as the prior drafts had used. Because this change was made after the close of recorded debate, we have no direct evidence of the reason for it. In a contemporary case, *Lyng v. Northwest Indian Cemetery Protective Association* (1988), the Supreme Court interpreted this switch from protection against *infringements* of free exercise to a ban on *prohibitions* of religious activity to mean that only laws that make the practice of religion unlawful or impossible are forbidden under the free exercise clause. According to the Court in *Lyng,* the free exercise clause is not violated if the practice of religion is merely made more difficult. McConnell has concluded, however, on the basis of the available evidence, that the *Lyng* Court's narrow interpretation of "prohibiting" is not justified, and that the verb should be given approximately the same meaning as "infringing."

In the Senate, Madison's idea about prohibiting the states from violating equal rights of conscience was not supported, presumably out of deference to states' rights. This effectively ended the First Congress' consideration of that possibility. Turning to the House's proposal pertaining to the federal government, the Senate initially amended it to refer only to the "rights of conscience," but then settled on a version that referred to the "free exercise of religion" instead: "Congress shall make no law establishing articles of faith or a mode of worship, or prohibiting the free exercise of religion...."

Without direct evidence of the rationale for this change, since it occurred after the close of recorded debate, one could infer that "rights of conscience" was deleted because it was viewed as redundant, or (as a few expressed during the recorded portions of debate) that some were concerned to avoid establishing protection for claims of conscience based on something other than religion. Although the distinction in Free Exercise law between religiously based and non-religiously based rights of conscience has been criticized in academic circles, as McConnell points out, it makes no difference whether "rights of conscience" was deleted because it was redundant or because of concern about the extension of protection to nonreligious matters of conscience. Neither explanation offers any support for the view that the free exercise clause protection must be provided in secular matters of conscience. Either the scope of "free exercise of religion" is coextensive with that of "rights of conscience," or it is not. Either way, by settling on "free exercise of religion," Congress eliminated any textual support for the view that secular rights of conscience should be protected under the free exercise clause.

A conference committee, which included James Madison, then reconciled the differences between the House and Senate versions. The only change pertaining to the free exercise clause was that the Conference Committee eliminated the Senate version's references to "articles of faith" and "a mode of worship" and replaced them simply with "religion." This meant that the Senate's ban on "prohibiting the free exercise of religion" could be shortened to "prohibiting the free exercise thereof." The conference committee's version was passed by Congress in 1789 and ratified by the states in 1791: "Congress shall make no law respecting an establishment of religion, or prohibiting the free exercise thereof."

The First Congress had developed a constitutional guarantee for religious freedom that contains two complementary clauses: the establishment clause, which seeks to prevent governmental imposition *of* religion; and the free exercise clause, which seeks to prevent governmental imposition *on* religion. Or as John Witte describes it in *Religion and the American Constitutional Experiment,* the establishment clause prohibits the government from *pre*scribing religion, and the free exercise clause prohibits the government from *pro*scribing religion.

Interpretation and Application

Prior to 1940, courts interpreted the religion clauses of the First Amendment as limitations on federal power only, not applicable to the states. It was not until its 1940 decision in *Cantwell v. Connecticut* that the United States Supreme Court held the free exercise clause to apply to the states through the Fourteenth Amendment.

Even after *Cantwell,* virtually all cases finding a free exercise violation involved governmental restrictions on religious *speech* or *belief.* The distinction between a high level of free exercise protection for

religious belief, versus a much lower level of protection for the *practice* of those beliefs in terms of religious *conduct,* originated in the Court's very first free exercise clause case, *Reynolds v. United States* (1879). In *Reynolds,* the Court refused to grant free exercise protection to a Mormon who had been convicted under a federal statute that made polygamy a crime. Although a number of Free exercise scholars, including McConnell (1998), have come to view the *Reynolds* decision as wrongly decided, its emphasis on the distinction between religious belief and conduct would be reaffirmed as recently as the Court's 1990 decision in *Employment Division, Department of Human Resources v. Smith,* which is discussed later.

It was not until 1963 that the Court found a general government regulation of *conduct,* enacted for secular purposes, to violate the free exercise clause in circumstances in which such a regulation conflicted with the freedom to exercise one's faith. In *Sherbert v. Verner* (1963), the Court upheld the unemployment compensation rights of a Seventh Day Adventist factory worker who was discharged for engaging in religiously motivated conduct, by refusing to work on Saturday, in accordance with her beliefs.

In so doing, the Court applied what has come to be known as the "strict scrutiny" test for free exercise claims. The Court first asked whether some "compelling state interest" justifies the governmental infringement of religious freedom. Even if such a compelling interest were found, under this test the state would still have to demonstrate that "no alternative forms of regulation would combat such abuses without infringing First Amendment rights."

The "high water mark" for free exercise clause protection, according to constitutional scholar Jesse Choper, came in *Wisconsin v. Yoder* (1972), when the Court used the strict scrutiny test outside the context of an unemployment compensation dispute (Choper, 657). In *Yoder,* the Court found that the state had no compelling interest in enforcing its compulsory public education laws on Amish children whose parents did not want to expose their children to the influence of public education beyond the eighth grade. The decision in *Yoder* reaffirmed the *Sherbert* rule, that the strict scrutiny test is to be applied even when alleged free exercise violations result from the application of a religiously neutral governmental regulation that was enacted for secular reasons.

In the wake of *Sherbert* and *Yoder,* however, the Court rejected nearly all of the free exercise claims it considered. Then, in *Employment Division, Department of Human Resources v. Smith* (1990), the Court ruled the strict scrutiny test inapplicable to challenges brought against generally applicable regulations, enacted for secular reasons, that restrict the freedom to exercise one's faith. *Smith,* like *Sherbert,* arose in the context of an unemployment compensation dispute. In *Smith,* two Native American drug counselors were dismissed from their employment for having ingested peyote as a part of a Native American religious ceremony. They argued that the sacramental use of peyote should not disqualify them from receiving unemployment benefits as work-related "misconduct." Justice Blackmun agreed, in dissent, finding that Oregon had not advanced any state interest compelling enough to meet the demands of the strict scrutiny test.

Justice Scalia's opinion for the Court, however, asserted that the strict scrutiny test had been applied in challenges to generally applicable laws only when the free exercise clause was implicated along with other constitutional protections, such as freedom of speech. Justice Scalia thus refused to apply the strict scrutiny test to the drug counselors' claims. Justice Scalia conceded that, as a result of the Court's decision in *Smith,* accommodation of free exercise interests would need to be sought through the political process, which "may fairly be said ... [to] place at a relative disadvantage those religious practices that are not widely engaged in...." Smaller, less influential religious groups are not protected by the free exercise clause against the risk of being subjected to legislation that seriously restricts their freedom to practice their beliefs.

Justice Scalia's opinion in *Smith* did not, however, undermine the availability of free exercise protection against intentional discriminatory measures aimed by government at regulating the conduct of specific religious groups. Accordingly, in *Church of the Lukumi Babalu Aye v. City of Hialeah* (1993), the Court struck down a city ordinance targeted at prohibiting the ritual sacrifice of animals according to the Santeria religion.

Congress has attempted to restore the type of free exercise protection offered by the strict scrutiny test to the extent that to do so lies within its power. In 1993, it enacted the Religious Freedom Restoration Act (RFRA), which would have reestablished strict scrutiny protection for free exercise claims. In *City of Boerne v. Flores* (1997), however, the Supreme Court struck RFRA down, on the grounds that in enacting RFRA Congress had violated federalism and separation of powers principles. In 2000, Congress responded by enacting the Religious Land Use and Institutionalized Persons Act (RLUIPA). More narrowly focused than RFRA, RLUIPA reestablishes strict scrutiny protection for free exercise claims arising in the context of land use regulations and the treatment of institutionalized persons. To date, RLUIPA's constitutionality has been upheld.

DAVID T. BALL

References and Further Reading

Choper, Jesse, *The Rise and Decline of the Constitutional Protection of Religious Liberty*, Nebraska Law Review 70 (1991): 651–688.

Cobb, Sanford H. *The Rise of Religious Liberty in America: A History*. New York: Macmillan, 1902.

Hutson, James H. *Religion and the Founding of the American Republic*. Washington, D.C.: Library of Congress, 1998.

Lupu, Ira C., *Where Rights Begin: The Problem of Burdens on the Free Exercise of Religion*, Harvard Law Review 102 (1989): 933–990.

McConnell, Michael W. What would it mean to have a 'First Amendment' for sexual orientation? in Olyan, Saul M., and Martha C. Nussbaum, eds. *Sexual Orientation & Human Rights in American Religious Discourse.* New York: Oxford University Press, 1998, p. 249.

———, *The Origins and Historical Understanding of Free Exercise of Religion*, Harvard Law Review 103 (1990): 1409–1517.

McLoughlin, William G. *New England Dissent, 1630–1833: The Baptists and the Separation of Church and State.* 2 vols. Cambridge, MA: Harvard University Press, 1971.

Witte, John, Jr. *Religion and the American Constitutional Experiment: Essential Rights and Liberties.* Boulder, CO: Westview Press, 2000.

Cases and Statutes Cited

Cantwell v. Connecticut, 310 U.S. 296 (1940)

Church of the Lukumi Babalu Aye v. City of Hialeah, 508 U.S. 520 (1993)

City of Boerne v. Flores, 521 U.S. 507 (1997)

Employment Division, Department of Human Resources v. Smith, 494 U.S. 872 (1990)

Lyng v. Northwest Indian Cemetery Protective Association, 485 U.S. 439 (1988)

Reynolds v. United States, 98 U.S. 145 (1879)

Sherbert v. Verner, 374 U.S. 398 (1963)

Wisconsin v. Yoder, 406 U.S. 205 (1972)

See also **Baptists in Early America; Establishment Clause (I): History, Background, Framing**

FREE EXERCISE CLAUSE DOCTRINE: SUPREME COURT JURISPRUDENCE

The free exercise clause of the First Amendment provides that Congress shall "make no law...prohibiting the free exercise" of religion. The application of the free exercise clause to a person's religious beliefs is relatively noncontroversial, because the United States Supreme Court has held that the state cannot penalize a person on account of his or her beliefs. For example, in *Torcaso v. Watkins* (1961), the Court held that the state of Maryland could not condition the right to hold public office on whether a person believed in God. More controversial has been the application of the free exercise clause to religiously motivated conduct. In recent years, the Supreme Court has made clear that if the state prohibits certain conduct for the *purpose* of disadvantaging a particular religion, then it violates the free exercise clause. In *Church of the Lukumi Babalu Aye v. City of Hialeah* (1993), for example, the Court considered the constitutionality of several municipal ordinances that prohibited the slaughtering of animals in certain circumstances. The City of Hialeah, Florida, had promulgated these ordinances in response to an increase in the number of practitioners of the Santeria religion who engaged in a variety of practices and rituals, including animal sacrifice, that many non-Santerians found offensive. The Santerians argued that the ordinances violated their free exercise clause rights. The Court agreed, concluding "that suppression of the central elements of the Santeria worship service was the object of the ordinances." Because the ordinances were not "neutral" in their purpose with respect to religion, the Court found that they violated the free exercise clause.

More controversial—indeed, the most frequently litigated free exercise clause issue at the Supreme Court during the past half century—has been the question whether the state is obliged to give exemptions from neutral and generally applicable regulatory laws to individuals for whom those laws burden the exercise of their religion. The question whether an "accommodation"—an exemption from a regulatory provision—is sometimes *required* has dominated free exercise clause jurisprudence for much of the past half century.

The Supreme Court first considered the question of exemptions from generally applicable regulatory statutes in *Reynolds v. United States* (1878), a case involving the constitutionality of a congressional statute governing the Territory of Utah that made it a crime for a person to have more than one spouse. This criminal prohibition conflicted with the religious obligations of members of the Church of Jesus Christ of Latter-Day Saints (the Mormons) whose church doctrine at that time provided that it was a "duty of male members of said church, circumstances permitting, to practise polygamy." Reynolds, a Mormon who had engaged in plural marriage, was convicted of violating that statute.

The question for the Court in *Reynolds* was whether "religious belief can be accepted as a justification of an overt act made criminal by the law of the land." In holding that enforcement of the criminal prohibition on polygamy against Reynolds did not violate his free exercise clause rights, the Court, with Chief Justice Morrison Waite writing, cited Thomas Jefferson for his "belief-action" distinction: religious beliefs and opinions enjoy greater protection from governmental

interference than do religiously motivated actions. In his Bill for the Establishment of Religious Freedom, Jefferson had written that to permit "the civil magistrate to intrude his powers into the field of opinion, and to restrain the profession or propagation of principles on supposition of their ill tendency, is a dangerous fallacy which at once destroys all religious liberty," but that it was legitimate for the magistrate "to interfere when principles break out into overt acts against peace and good order." Moreover, in his famous 1802 letter to the Danbury Baptists, Jefferson had written that "[b]elieving with you that religion is a matter which lies solely between man and his God;... the legislative powers of the government reach actions only, and not opinions." The *Reynolds* Court placed great weight on the views of Jefferson: "Coming as this does from an acknowledged leader of the advocates of the [free exercise clause], it may be accepted almost as an authoritative declaration of the scope and effect of the amendment thus secured. Congress was deprived of all legislative power over mere opinion, but was left free to reach actions which were in violation of social duties or subversive good order....To permit [an exemption] would be to make the professed doctrines of religious belief superior to the law of the land, and in effect to permit every citizen to come a law unto himself." Accordingly, the Court enforced the criminal sanction against Reynolds.

The Court in *Reynolds* concluded that the free exercise clause did not compel an exemption from regulatory statutes for religiously motivated conduct. Because the free exercise clause restrained only Congress, few cases arose under the clause, and the Court had limited opportunity to revisit its decision in *Reynolds*. After the Court incorporated the free exercise clause against the states through the due process clause of the Fourteenth Amendment in *Cantwell v. Connecticut* (1940), free exercise clause claims became far more common on the Court's docket. Since its decision in *Cantwell*, the Court's position on the application of the free exercise clause to religiously motivated conduct has ebbed and flowed.

In *Cantwell*, some Jehovah's Witnesses in New Haven, Connecticut, had been convicted of, among other things, soliciting without a license and "inciting a breach of peace" by playing an anti-Catholic phonograph record on the street in a Catholic neighborhood. Citing *Reynolds*, the Court, with Justice Owen Roberts writing, reasserted the distinction between "freedom to believe and freedom to act." The Court noted that "the first is absolute but, in the nature of things, the second cannot be. Conduct remains subject to regulation for the protection of society." But the Court went on to say that "the power to regulate must be so exercised as not, in attaining a permissible end, unduly to infringe the protected freedom." In suggesting that some prohibitions on religiously motivated conduct might "unduly infringe" free exercise clause rights, the Court invited a "weighing of two conflicting interests": the state's interest "in the preservation and protection of peace and good order" and the Jehovah's Witnesses' interest in "free communication of views, religious or other." The Court, on weighing these interests, ruled in favor of the Jehovah's Witnesses.

During the 1960s and 1970s, the Court extended the constitutional protection of religiously motivated conduct in two landmark cases. In *Sherbert v. Verner* (1963), the Court considered whether the free exercise clause compelled an exemption from a neutral and generally applicable regulatory statute for a person's religiously motivated conduct. Sherbert, a Seventh-Day Adventist employed at a South Carolina textile mill, refused to work on Saturday, her church's Sabbath, when her employer rearranged her schedule requiring such work. As a result, the textile mill terminated her employment. Sherbert applied for unemployment benefits, but refused all job opportunities that required her to work on Saturday. The state Employment Security Commission denied her benefits claim because she had failed "without good cause, to accept available suitable work when offered."

The Supreme Court, with Justice William Brennan writing, held that the denial of unemployment benefits to Sherbert violated the free exercise clause as applied to the states through the Fourteenth Amendment. The Court found that the South Carolina unemployment scheme imposed a burden on Sherbert by forcing her "to choose between following the precepts of her religion and forfeiting benefits, on the one hand, and abandoning one of the precepts of her religion to accept work, on the other hand. Government imposition of such a choice puts the same kind of burden on the free exercise of religion as would a fine imposed against appellant for her Saturday worship." Having found that the unemployment system imposed a burden on Sherbert's free exercise right, the Court then considered whether the government had a "compelling state interest" for imposing this burden. The Court stated that in this "highly sensitive constitutional area," only "the gravest abuses, endangering paramount interests, give occasion [to the government] for permissible limitation." The government justified the denial by asserting an interest in preventing "the filing of fraudulent claims by unscrupulous claimants feigning religious objections to Saturday work" that might "not only dilute the unemployment compensation fund but also hinder the scheduling by employers of necessary Saturday work." The Court concluded, however, that there was no evidence

questioning the sincerity of Sherbert's motives and that "even if the possibility of spurious claims did threaten to dilute the [unemployment insurance] fund and disrupt the scheduling of work, it would be plainly incumbent upon [the state] to demonstrate that no alternative forms of regulations would combat such abuses without infringing First Amendment rights."

In dissent, Justice John Harlan, joined by Justice Byron White, rejected such a broad reading of the free exercise clause. Justice Harlan concluded that those "situations in which the Constitution may require special treatment on account of religion are, in my view, few and far between." He rejected "the conclusion that the State is constitutionally compelled to carve out an exception to its general rule of eligibility in the present case." Thus, for Justices Harlan and White, the resolution of the question of accommodating religious practices by granting exemptions from neutral and generally applicable regulatory laws should be left to the discretion of the political branches. Almost thirty years later, a majority of the Supreme Court would come to agree with them.

Nine years after *Sherbert*, the Supreme Court reconsidered the question of constitutionally compelled exemptions for religiously motivated conduct. In *Wisconsin v. Yoder* (1972), the Court considered the refusal of Yoder, a member of the Old Order Amish, to send his children to school after they completed the eighth grade. Wisconsin required school attendance until age sixteen and refused to grant Yoder's two children an exemption from that requirement. (Yoder's children, although they had completed eighth grade, had not yet reached age sixteen.) Yoder objected to the formal education of his children beyond the eighth grade on religious grounds, contending that high school emphasized "intellectual and scientific accomplishments, self-distinction, competitiveness, worldly success, and social life with other students" as opposed to the Amish emphasis on "informal learning-through-doing," "wisdom, rather than technical knowledge," and "community welfare, rather than competition." The Supreme Court, with Chief Justice Warren Burger writing, acknowledged the state's "interest in universal education," but concluded that that interest did not outweigh the Amish's religiously motivated desire to direct the education of their children as they saw fit.

After *Sherbert* and *Yoder*, the government was constitutionally compelled to grant an exemption from neutral, generally applicable regulatory statutes to persons claiming an infringement on their free exercise rights unless the government had a compelling interest in uniform enforcement and there was no less restrictive means of fulfilling the government's interest. Thereafter, in a few unemployment benefit cases in which a person had quit his or her job for religious reasons, the Court required an exemption. For example in *Thomas v. Review Board* (1981), the Court held that a state could not deny unemployment benefits to an employee who quit his job rather than accept a transfer to a section of the employer's factory that produced armaments when the employee had religious objections to that type of work. Similarly, in *Hobbie v. Unemployment Appeals Commission* (1987), the Court held that a state could not deny unemployment benefits to an employee who was fired for refusing to work on her Saturday Sabbath— similar to the employee in *Sherbert v. Verner*. Two years later, in *Frazee v. Illinois Department of Income Security* (1989), the Court held that a state could not deny unemployment benefits to an employee who refused to work on Sunday because of a religious objection to such work.

In all other free exercise clause cases that it considered during the 1970s and 1980s, however, the Court refused to grant exemptions from neutral and generally applicable regulatory laws, despite the burden the enforcement of such laws placed on religiously motivated persons. For example, in *United States v. Lee* (1982), the Court rejected a challenge by an Amish taxpayer to the required payment of Social Security taxes. The Amish taxpayer argued that the Amish believe it "sinful not to provide for their own elderly and therefore are religiously opposed to the national social security system." The Court held that mandatory participation in the social security system was "indispensable" to its fiscal vitality and that burdening the free exercise rights of the Amish taxpayer was therefore "essential to accomplish an overriding governmental interest."

In *Bob Jones University v. United States* (1983), the Court held that the federal government's refusal to grant tax exempt status to a private religious college that engaged in racial discrimination did not violate the free exercise clause, even though the college's racially discriminatory policies were motivated by its religious beliefs. The Court noted that "the Government has a fundamental, overriding interest in eradicating racial discrimination in education" that "substantially outweighs whatever burden denial of tax benefits places on petitioners' exercise of their religious beliefs." The Court further held that the elimination of racial discrimination was a "compelling government interest" and that "no less restrictive means are available to achieve the government interest."

Other free exercise clause claimants also lost their challenges to generally applicable governmental regulations. In *Goldman v. Weinberger* (1986), the Court refused to grant an Orthodox Jew who wished to wear a yarmulke an exemption from an Air Force dress code requirement that barred members of the Air Force from wearing headgear indoors, citing the military's need for uniformity. In *Bowen v. Roy* (1986), the Court rejected a free exercise clause challenge to a requirement that individuals must provide Social Security numbers to receive welfare benefits. The Court emphasized that the "free exercise clause simply cannot be understood to require the Government to conduct its own affairs in ways that comport with the religious beliefs of particular citizens." In *O'Lone v. Estate of Shabazz* (1987), the Court rejected a prisoner's free exercise clause challenge to a neutral prison work policy that impeded the ability of Muslim prisoners to attend certain religious exercises. The Court relied on the prison's articulated need for the policy to reject the free exercise clause claim. As the Court had deferred to the military in *Goldman*, so the Court deferred to prison officials in *O'Lone*.

In *Lyng v. Northwest Indian Cemetery Protective Association* (1988), the Court considered a variation on the traditional free exercise claim to an exemption from a regulatory statute. In *Lyng*, the government proposed the construction of a road and the harvesting of timber in a portion of a National Forest that was a sacred religious site for three Native American tribes. The tribes claimed that the traffic, noise, and logging threatened to render impossible the exercise of their religion on the sacred land in question. The Court rejected the claim, holding that the free exercise clause rights of the tribes "do not divest the Government of its right to use what is, after all, its land."

In the meantime, both Congress and various state legislatures granted literally hundreds of statutory exemptions from generally applicable regulatory laws for individuals whose otherwise prohibited conduct was religiously motivated. But some critics questioned whether religiously motivated individuals should receive exemptions from regulatory laws that would be denied to persons motivated by non-religious reasons. Why, for example, should a person retain eligibility for unemployment benefits on refusing Saturday work for religious reasons, whereas a person who refuses such work to spend time with his family is denied benefits? Some argued that the granting of exemptions for persons whose conduct is religiously motivated constituted an unconstitutional state preference for religion in violation of the establishment clause.

The Court addressed this question in *Corporation of Presiding Bishop v. Amos* (1987). In *Amos*, a Mormon owned-and-operated gymnasium fired a worker because he failed to secure a "temple recommend"—a necessary endorsement from the Mormon. The worker alleged a violation of Title VII of the Civil Rights Act of 1964 that prohibits, among other things, employment discrimination based on religion. The church defended on the grounds that the Civil Rights Act expressly granted religious organizations an exemption from the prohibition on religious discrimination. The question for the Court was whether this statutory exemption, which gave preferential status to religious organizations, violated the establishment clause. The Court held that it did not. First, the Court found that the exemption did not have the *purpose* of advancing religion; rather, it had the secular purpose of allowing religious groups to carry out their mission unfettered by government regulation. Second, the Court found that the exemption did not have the *effect* of advancing religion. (Justice Sandra Day O'Connor, in her concurrence, argued that the exemption *did* have the effect of advancing religion, but that the exemption did *not* constitute an "endorsement" of religion and hence was not unconstitutional.) After *Amos*, both Congress and state legislatures were free to grant statutory exemptions to religious organizations or to religiously motivated individuals from neutral and generally applicable regulatory laws without offending the establishment clause.

Three years later, in *Employment Division v. Smith* (1990), the Court revisited the question whether a religiously motivated person had a *constitutional right* under the free exercise clause to an exemption from a neutral and generally applicable regulatory law. At issue in Smith was whether the state of Oregon properly withheld unemployment benefits from two Native Americans who were discharged from their jobs because they smoked peyote—a substance prohibited under Oregon law. The Native Americans, who had smoked the peyote as part of a religious ceremony, argued that the denial of unemployment benefits violated their rights under the free exercise clause. The Court rejected their claim, concluding that the free exercise clause afforded no such exemption from laws that were neutral and generally applicable and that did not infringe any other constitutional right—even if such laws imposed a substantial burden on the free exercise of religion for certain persons. The *Smith* decision constituted an important shift in the Court's free exercise clause doctrine, foreclosing constitutional claims for an exemption from neutral and generally applicable regulatory laws that interfered with a person's religiously motivated conduct. After *Smith*, such persons would need to appeal to the legislative process for relief from a regulatory statute.

The Court's decision in *Smith* sparked a significant political fight eventually capturing congressional attention. In 1993, Congress enacted the Religious Freedom Restoration Act (RFRA) by an overwhelming margin in response to the *Smith* decision. In this statute, Congress provided that "Government may substantially burden a person's exercise of religion only if it demonstrates that application of the burden to the person (1) is in furtherance of a compelling governmental interest; and (2) is the least restrictive means of furthering that compelling governmental interest." In doing so, Congress made clear that it sought to restore the legal landscape that existed prior to the Court's decision in *Smith*. Specifically, Congress found that "in *Employment Division v. Smith*, the Supreme Court virtually eliminated the requirement that the government justify burdens on religious exercise imposed by laws neutral toward religion." Congress stated that its purpose in enacting RFRA was "to restore the compelling interest test as set forth in *Sherbert v. Verner* and *Wisconsin v. Yoder* and to guarantee its application in all cases where free exercise of religion is substantially burdened."

But in *City of Boerne v. Flores* (1997), the Court found RFRA to be an unconstitutional exercise of congressional power to the extent that it applied to state and local governments. (Lower courts have found RFRA constitutional as applied to the federal government.) Congress had justified RFRA's limitation on state and local governments by relying on its power under Section 5 of the Fourteenth Amendment that gave Congress authority to enact legislation for the purpose of preventing state violations of Section 1 of that amendment. Because the Supreme Court had previously held that state restraints on the free exercise of religion violated the due process clause of Section 1 of the Fourteenth Amendment, Congress concluded that it had power under Section 5 to prohibit state and local governments from burdening the free exercise of religion unless they could justify such burdens by reference to a compelling state interest. The problem was that Congress in RFRA defined free exercise rights more expansively than had the Court in *Smith*. As a result, in *City of Boerne*, the Court found RFRA unconstitutional as applied to state and local governments. To the Court, Section 5 permitted Congress to redress free exercise clause violations as defined by the Court—not to define free exercise rights more expansively than the Court had done in *Employment Division v. Smith*. Accordingly, the Court concluded that Congress had exceeded its Section 5 power.

In response to *City of Boerne*, Congress took further action. Relying on its constitutional power to regular interstate commerce, Congress in 2000 enacted the Religious Land Use and Institutionalized Persons Act (RLUIPA) that provided that land use regulations (such as zoning) and regulations governing institutionalized persons (primarily in prisons and mental hospitals) may not "substantially burden" the exercise of religion unless the state has a "compelling interest." Although RLUIPA is more limited in its scope than is RFRA, it restored some of the protections that Congress had provided in the earlier statute.

Today, if a person or religious organization seeks an exemption from a neutral and generally applicable law that prohibits its religiously motivated conduct, it must appeal to the legislative process because the free exercise clause no longer affords relief (unless the statute in question infringes another constitutional protection, such as the Free Speech Clause). Rather, the free exercise clause provides protection from outright restraints on religious belief or restraints on conduct that are motivated by a desire to disadvantage a particular religion.

DAVISON M. DOUGLAS

References and Further Reading

Duncan, Richard F., *Free Exercise is Dead; Long Live Free Exercise: Smith, Lukumi, and the General Applicability Requirement*, University of Pennsylvania Journal of Constitutional Law 3 (2001): 850–884.
Gordon, James D., *The New Free exercise clause*, Capital University Law Review 26 (1997): 65–92.
Hamilton, Marci A., *The First Amendment's Challenge Function and the Confusion in the Supreme Court's Contemporary Free Exercise Jurisprudence*, Georgia Law Review 29 (1994) 81–135.

Cases and Statutes Cited

Bob Jones University v. United States, 461 U.S. 574 (1983)
Bowen v. Roy, 476 U.S. 693 (1986)
Cantwell v. Connecticut, 310 U.S. 296 (1940)
Church of the Lukumi Babalu Aye v. City of Hialeah, 508 U.S. 520 (1993)
City of Boerne v. Flores, 521 U.S. 507 (1997)
Corporation of Presiding Bishop v. Amos, 483 U.S. 327 (1987)
Frazee v. Illinois Department of Income Security, 489 U.S. 829 (1989)
Goldman v. Weinberger, 475 U.S. 503 (1986)
Hobbie v. Unemployment Appeals Commission, 480 U.S. 136 (1987)
Lyng v. Northwest Indian Cemetery Protective Association, 485 U.S. 439 (1988)
O'Lone v. Estate of Shabazz, 482 U.S. 342 (1987)
Reynolds v. United States, 98 U.S. 145 (1878)
Sherbert v. Verner, 374 U.S. 398 (1963)
Thomas v. Review Board, 450 U.S. 707 (1981)
Torcaso v. Watkins, 367 U.S. 488 (1961)
United States v. Lee, 455 U.S. 252 (1982)
Wisconsin v. Yoder, 406 U.S. 205 (1972)

See also **Accommodations of Religion; Free Exercise Clause (I): History, Background, Framing**

FREE PRESS/FAIR TRIAL

Under the United States Constitution, there has always been tension between the right of a criminal defendant to a fair trial, untainted by excessive and prejudicial publicity, and the press' right to report on criminal proceedings.

The landmark decision is *Sheppard v. Maxwell*, 383 U.S. 333 (1966). That case involved Dr. Sam Sheppard who was convicted of murdering his wife and children under sensational circumstances, and who claimed that he was unfairly convicted based on excessive and prejudicial pretrial publicity. In reviewing Sheppard's conviction, the Court began by emphasizing the importance of a free press to society, as well as to the criminal justice process, noting that the "press does not simply publish information about trials but guards against the miscarriage of justice by subjecting the police, prosecutors, and judicial processes to extensive public scrutiny and criticism." However, the Court also recognized that every criminal defendant is entitled to a fair trial and that freedom of speech (especially excessive reporting) has the potential to subvert the criminal justice process. The Court held that the criminal justice process is subverted when there is a violation of the "requirement that the jury's verdict be based on evidence received in open court, not from outside [sources]." In other words, defendant was entitled to have his or her case tried by the jury without the effect of excessive and prejudicial pretrial publicity. In *Sheppard*, the Court found that defendant's rights had not been sufficiently protected, because "bedlam reigned at the courthouse during the trial and newsmen took over practically the entire courtroom, hounding most of the participants in the trial, especially Sheppard." Throughout the preindictment investigation and the nine-week trial, "circulation-conscious editors catered to the insatiable interest of the American public in the bizarre." In this atmosphere of a "'Roman holiday' for the news media, Sam Sheppard stood trial for his life."

After *Sheppard*, even though the courts had the duty and obligation to mitigate the effects of publicity on the criminal justice process, it was unclear how that objective was to be accomplished. In *Nebraska Press Association v. Stuart*, 427 U.S. 539 (1976), in a highly sensational murder case, the trial judge became concerned that "because of the nature of the crimes charged in the complaint that there is a clear and present danger that pretrial publicity could impinge upon the defendant's right to a fair trial." In an effort to limit the impact of the publicity on the trial, the judge entered a gag order restraining the press from publishing or broadcasting accounts of confessions or admissions made by the accused or facts "strongly implicative" of the accused. However, the U.S. Supreme Court concluded that the trial court had gone too far. The Court emphasized the importance of the press to the criminal justice process, noting that a "responsible press has always been regarded as the handmaiden of effective judicial administration, especially in the criminal field.... The press does not simply publish information about trials but guards against the miscarriage of justice by subjecting the police, prosecutors, and judicial processes to extensive public scrutiny and criticism." In addition, the Court emphasized the importance of a free press noting that it had "learned, and continue to learn, from what we view as the unhappy experiences of other nations where government has been allowed to meddle in the internal editorial affairs of newspapers. Regardless of how beneficent-sounding the purposes of controlling the press might be."

In *Nebraska Press*, the Court did not rule out the possibility of a gag order in a criminal case. However, it concluded that a much stronger showing of necessity must be made. In deciding whether to grant a gag order, the trial court must consider three factors: "(a) the nature and extent of pretrial news coverage; (b) whether other measures would be likely to mitigate the effects of unrestrained pretrial publicity; and (c) how effectively a restraining order would operate to prevent the threatened danger." Although the Court concluded that the *Nebraska Press* case involved significant danger of excessive pretrial news coverage, it concluded that there was insufficient evidence regarding whether alternatives to a gag order might not be sufficient.

After the holding in *Stuart*, it has been widely recognized that courts should avoid entering gag orders restricting trial coverage and should instead use other means for protecting defendants against the possible adverse impact of prejudicial trial publicity. These other measures, originally cataloged in *Sheppard* but reaffirmed in *Stuart*, include the following. First, the trial court can order a change of venue when the glare of publicity is too great. In a locale that is removed from the publicity, the court is more likely to be able to seat an unbiased jury, and the defendant is more likely to receive a fair trial. Second, the court can postpone a defendant's trial until press interest is less intense and public attention has sufficiently subsided. Third, as part of the *voir dire* process, the trial judge and the attorneys can ask searching questions of prospective jurors in an effort to screen out jurors who have been unduly prejudiced by pretrial publicity. Fourth, and additionally, a trial judge can provide the jury with clear and emphatic instructions regarding their duty to disregard media

speculation and to decide the case based only on evidence presented in open court. Fifth, in an appropriate case, the trial court can sequester jurors to insulate them against the effects of publicity. In other words, courts must strive to maximize the possibility of press coverage while using other methods to protect the defendant's right to a fair trial.

RUSSELL L. WEAVER

References and Further Reading

Weaver, Russell L., and Arthur E. Hellman. *The First Amendment: Cases, Materials & Problems.* LexisNexis (2002): 747–761.
Weaver, Russell L., and Donald E. Lively. *Understanding the First Amendment.* LexisNexis, (2003): 217–229.

FREE SPEECH IN PRIVATE CORPORATIONS

Writers and speakers are often dependent on corporate publishers or corporate-owned locales to be heard. Business corporations use their economic power to participate in the political process through lobbying, news media, contributions, and political campaigns.

The Tillman Act (1907) barred corporate contributions to federal candidates, expressing a view that corporations were not legitimate political actors. The courts restricted the ban and its state equivalents to a limited core. The current statute specifically permits corporations to use corporate money to staff political action committees so long as the funds transferred to candidates are derived from employee contributions (FECA, 2 U.S.C. § 441[b]).

Generally, First Amendment law does not distinguish between corporate and human speakers. Thus, governmental restriction of corporate funds used for lobbying, "public education" and even referenda campaigns seems to be fully barred by the First Amendment (*First National Bank v. Bellotti* (political lobbying); *New York Times v. Sullivan* ["editorial advertisement"]). However, corporate law typically requires corporate decisionmakers to cause the corporation to use its resources (including its employees' voices) on behalf of the limited, legally constructed interests of the institution itself, not any human affiliated with it. Accordingly, granting free speech rights to corporations probably does not further free speech values of political self-governance or freedom of expression even of corporate participants.

Dissident speakers within the corporation (for example, employees who disagree with official corporate positions or shareholders who seek to change corporate policies) have no First Amendment rights against business corporations, because the Amendment extends only to state action.

DANIEL J. H. GREENWOOD

References and Further Reading

Greenwood, Daniel J. H., *Essential Speech: Why Corporate Speech Is Not Free*, Iowa Law Review 83 (1998): 5:995–1070.

Meir, Dan-Cohen. *Rights, Persons, and Organizations: A Legal Theory for Bureaucratic Society*. Berkeley: University of California Press, 1986.

Winkler, Adam, *McConnell v. FEC, Corporate Political Speech and the Legacy of the Segregated Fund Cases*, Election Law Journal 3 (2004): 2:361–369.

Cases and Statutes Cited

First National Bank v. Bellotti, 435 U.S. 765 (1978)
McConnell v. FEC, 124 U.S. 619 (2003)
Federal Elections Campaign Act (FECA), 2 U.S.C. § 441(b)
Tillman Act (1907), Ch. 420, 34 Stat. 864

FREEDOM OF ACCESS TO CLINIC ENTRANCES (FACE) ACT, 108 STAT. 694 (1994)

Originally introduced in 1992 by then House members Charles Schumer (D-NY), Constance Morella (R-MD), and Senator Ted Kennedy (D-MA), it gained impetus for passage only after the first death of an abortion provider, Dr. Paul Gunn of Florida, killed by anti-abortion extremists in 1993. The FACE Act was passed in 1994.

The FACE Act prohibits the intentional use of force, threat, or physical obstruction to either attempt or actually to injure, intimidate, or interfere with somebody providing or obtaining reproductive health services. It also punishes anyone found to be intentionally damaging or destroying a reproductive health facility (www.prochoice.org, National Abortion Federation website, 12/17/2005). This legislation protects not only facilities at which abortions are actually provided but also those providing "medical, surgical, counseling, or referral services related to pregnancy (or the termination of pregnancy). It covers facilities located in hospitals, clinics, doctors' offices or "any other facility providing" such health services (NAF website). Those protected at both pro-choice and pro-life "pregnancy crisis centers" include security guards, maintenance staff, patients, and their escorts.

As with other attempts to limit the presence of anti-abortion activity at reproductive health clinics, two sets of constitutional challenges have been brought. The first concerns the assertion of a First Amendment freedom of speech right to tell clients about opposing views outside clinics. Most states have dealt with this question through constitutionally protected "buffer zones" of a certain radius outside clinics. The FACE Act does not prohibit constitutionally protected speech, only those threatening or intimidating activities designed to prevent clients from reaching the clinic.

The second constitutional question that has been raised in response to this Act has been that of Congress' authority to affect the private sector (the operation of clinics). In 1997 and 2005, the Fifth Circuit Court of Appeals ruled that the FACE Act was constitutional, based on Congressional authority to "regulate commerce among the states" as granted by the commerce clause in Article I. Those opposing this view argue that those who interfere with reproductive clinics are not engaging in "commercial or economic" activity as required by the statute. This argument has been successfully used to continuously appeal judgments against Joseph Scheidler of the Pro-Life Action League and Randall Terry of Operation Rescue under the RICO statute, passed in the 1970s to curtail racketeering. However, it has not damaged the FACE Act. The FACE Act was written specifically for reproductive health facilities and thus does not suffer the constitutional problems of trying to apply an "overly broad" statute. Each of the eight federal appeals courts that has heard challenges to FACE have upheld its constitutionality, and the Supreme Court has been asked but chosen not to review these cases (unlike the RICO statute cases regarding abortion clinics). Similarly, federal appeals courts have upheld Congress' right to enact FACE through its commerce clause powers. The Alan Guttmacher Institute reports that as of December 2005, thirteen states and the District of Columbia have enacted state FACE statutes specifically with respect to abortion providers.[1]

The FACE Act provides for criminal and civil penalties. Only the federal government can file criminal charges, whereas federal and state governments or any person harmed by a prohibited act under FACE can file a civil lawsuit against a violator. Criminal penalties include one year in prison and a fine of $100,000 for a first-time offender and penalties up to $250,000 and three years in prison for subsequent offenses. For offenses that are nonviolent in nature (yet still constitute physical obstructions of facilities), the penalties begin at 6 months' jail time and a fine of

[1] Alan Guttmacher Institute, www.guttmacher.org, "State Policies in Brief: Protecting Access to Clinics," as of December 1, 2005; website accessed 12/17/05.

$10,000 (both of which are increased on subsequent offenses). The maximum sentence contained in the legislation is ten years in prison for bodily injury and life imprisonment for causing death (NAF website, 12/17/2005). Civil penalties may include fines of $10,000 or $15,000 and also the potential of getting an injunction against further actions by the protesters.

The National Abortion Federation website, www. prochoice.org, states that FACE prosecutions have been extremely successful in deterring "hard-core" violence at reproductive clinics. This is important, because some actions have included the gluing of locks or spraying of butyric acid (rendering a facility unusable): a woman in 1996 who threatened a doctor by shouting, "remember what happened to Dr. Gunn; this could happen to you," and a man who parked a Ryder truck outside a clinic shortly after the Oklahoma City bombings. In 1994, at the time of the act's passage, half the clinics (fifty-two percent) reported some type of violence directed against them that would be actionable under FACE (such as bombing, arson, stalking, gunfire, or physical violence). That percentage had been reduced by more than half (to twenty percent total) by 2000, usually attributed to the legislation's enforcement. On the other hand, violence directed at clinics has not totally ceased. For example, in the two months after the September 11, 2001, attacks, 500 reproductive and women's rights facilities reported anthrax threats. Similarly, in 2004, the Feminist Majority Foundation stated that about one in every five reproductive care facility in the United States reports that it continues to experience violence.

MELISSA HAUSSMAN

References and Further Reading

Planned Parenthood. National Abortion Federation and Alan Guttmacher websites: www.plannedparenthood. org, www.prochoice.org, www.guttmacher.org.

See also **Abortion**

FREEDOM OF ASSOCIATION

After the American Revolution, neither the U.S. nor the state constitutions protected the freedom of association. They protected the freedom of assembly, which encompassed the right of "the people" collectively to protest against an unjust government but did not protect minorities from majorities.

States limited the freedom of association to protect the majority from minorities. Political parties were considered "factions" that put private interests ahead of the common good. Labor unions were

treated as illegal "conspiracies" in common law, because they promoted the interests of one class over the public interest. The ability to form a corporation was strictly limited. Corporations were considered public institutions that must serve the common good. In New England, states denied corporate privileges to many churches until disestablishment in 1818 in Connecticut, 1819 in New Hampshire, and 1833 in Massachusetts. Virginia refused to grant any churches corporate privileges, denying them the ability to hold property and govern their own institutional affairs. The status of corporations changed when the Supreme Court, in the *Dartmouth College* (1819) decision, ruled that corporate charters were contracts protected by the Constitution. *Dartmouth* transformed many corporations from public agencies to private ones. After *Dartmouth*, corporations gained new rights vis-à-vis the state. Moreover, as the number of corporations expanded, more and more citizens demanded the right to form one to pursue their own commercial and charitable purposes. States responded with general incorporation laws allowing any group of persons to associate and receive corporate privileges under certain guidelines.

Philanthropic trusts followed a similar path as corporations. Americans, especially Thomas Jefferson, worried that trusts placed too much wealth beyond the people's control. Many states denied their courts equity jurisdiction for trusts. In the *Girard Will* case (1844), however, the U.S. Supreme Court ruled that federal common law recognized trusts, granting them legal rights and privileges.

Laborers continued to struggle for the right to organize. Not until the early 1810s in New York, and then in the 1844 Massachusetts case of *Commonwealth v. Hunt*, did laborers gain the freedom to associate. When laborers sought collective bargaining or closed shops, however, courts continued to define their activities as coercive and illegal.

After the Civil War, associations and corporations faced new challenges and limits. Labor unions continued to seek collective bargaining rights, whereas courts used new techniques, such as the injunction, to limit them. Catholics faced a challenge to their freedoms when Oregon passed a law requiring all children to attend public schools. With the KKK's support, Oregonians hoped to teach Catholics Protestant values. In *Pierce v. Society of Sisters* (1925), the Supreme Court ruled that the law violated religious liberty, permitting religious minorities to associate for educational purposes.

During the Gilded Age, business corporations expanded beyond any one state's control and threatened the welfare of workers and consumers. Politicians and reformers pressed for new regulations, but federal courts struck down state laws interfering with economic freedom. In the Progressive and New Deal eras, reformers turned to the federal government. Starting with the Sherman Anti-Trust Act, the federal government committed itself to ensuring a free market by challenging corporate monopolies. Ironically, the Sherman Act was also used against unions until the Wagner Act legalized collective bargaining and set up procedures to recognize unions in return for allowing the federal government to oversee and regulate their activities. The subsequent Taft–Hartley Act weakened Wagner by permitting states to pass "right to work" laws limiting closed shops. Today, labor unions are again threatened. Many of the rights gained in the New Deal are routinely violated. In addition, important categories of workers, including agricultural workers, still do not have a guaranteed right to unionize.

From the 1920s through the 1950s, political minorities faced limits to their freedom to associate when their goals supposedly threatened the public interest. In the early 1920s, ten states passed laws to limit the activities of the Ku Klux Klan. Louisiana and New York also required KKK members to register with the state. These laws were upheld in *Bryant v. Zimmerman* (1928). The 1917 Espionage Act, passed during World War I, prohibited associating with groups hostile to the government. During the Red Scare, the Supreme Court in *Gitlow* v. *New York* (1925) upheld convictions for publishing communist propaganda. (*Gitlow* also incorporated the freedom of speech as a nationally protected right of all American citizens under the due process clause of the fourteenth amendment. As a result, the federal government became the major arbiter in future freedom of association cases.) The Alien Registration (or Smith) Act (1940) extended the ban to peacetime. In 1947, President Truman issued Executive Order 9835 requiring all civil servants to declare loyalty to the government and prohibiting membership in any association the Attorney General determined to be "totalitarian, fascist, communist, or subversive."

Gilded Age money established new philanthropic foundations, including those founded by Rockefeller and Carnegie. Many progressives echoed Jefferson's fears that the foundations would enhance the power of the rich through permanent foundations beyond the people's control. In fact, foundations proved supportive of many progressive causes and it was the Right that turned against them. In the early 1950s, Congressional leaders in the House Select Committee to Investigate Tax-Exempt Foundations launched a broad probe into whether foundations were promoting communist ideas within the United States.

The emergence of constitutional protection for the freedom of association was tied to the civil rights revolution of the twentieth century. In the 1950s, southern states sought to check the NAACP by forcing members to register their names. In *NAACP v. Alabama* (1958), the Supreme Court ruled that the freedom to associate is protected by the Constitution. According to Justice John M. Harlan, "It is beyond debate that freedom to engage in association for the advancement of beliefs and ideas is an inseparable aspect of 'liberty' assured by the Fourteenth Amendment due process clause." The freedom of association was not absolute, however. The Court distinguished *NAACP* from *Bryant* by noting that the KKK, unlike the NAACP, promoted violence and illegal activity.

Although *NAACP* raised the bar for limiting associations, the Supreme Court continued to allow the government to monitor, and to limit, the activities of associations deemed threatening. In *Dennis v. United States* (1951) and *Yates v. United States* (1957), the Court upheld convictions under the Smith Act for advocating the violent overthrow of the U.S. government. Two cases concerning the membership clause of the Smith Act were decided in 1961. The first, *Scales v. United States*, sustained the conviction of a member of the Communist Party, because party membership proved commitment to overthrow the government. In *Noto v. United States* (1961), the Court limited the Smith Act to cases in which violence against the government was clearly intended, providing greater protection for the freedoms of expression and association.

The McCarran Subversive Activities Control Act (1950) and the Communist Control Act (1954) passed in the McCarthy era required Communist groups to register members with the Attorney General. The McCarran act was upheld in *Communist Party v. Subversive Activities Control Board* (1961). Moderating the act in *Albertson v. Subversive Activities Control Board* (1965), a unanimous Supreme Court ruled that the Board could not force a person to register if he invoked the Fifth Amendment. Congress subsequently repealed the mandatory registration clause. Finally, in *Boorda v. Subversive Activities Control Board* (1969), the Supreme Court let stand a D.C. Circuit Court ruling that Party members cannot be exposed unless it can be proved that they shared the Party's violent goals, bringing some of the protections promised in *NAACP* to Communists.

The Supreme Court also limited the scope of loyalty oaths such as those required under EO 9835. *Adler v. Board of Education* (1952) allowed state governments to refuse to hire public employees who belonged to the Communist Party or similar associations. In *Elfbrandt v. Russell* (1966) and *Keyishian v. Board of*

Regents (1967), the Court changed course and ruled that such actions amounted to guilt by association.

Recent cases have continued to balance the freedom of association against the public interest. In *Moose Lodge no. 107 v. Irvis* (1972), the Court decided that private social clubs could refuse to admit a member because of his race without violating the Fourteenth Amendment. But in *Bob Jones University v. United States* (1983), the Court ruled that Bob Jones University could not receive nonprofit status, meaning that it must pay taxes, if it discriminates against African Americans. In *Roberts* v. *U.S. Jaycees* (1984), the Supreme Court ruled that the Jaycees of Minnesota must admit girls. The Court determined that admitting girls would not alter the association's core mission and that the state's interest in eradicating gender discrimination outweighed the Jaycees' associative freedom. The Court reinforced these principles: *Board of Directors of Rotary International v. Rotary Club of Duarte* (1987). On the other hand, in *Boy Scouts of America v. Dale* (2000), the Supreme Court ruled that the Boy Scouts' religious beliefs permitted them to discriminate against homosexuals despite a New Jersey law protecting gay citizens. The Court argued that compelling the Boy Scouts to admit homosexuals violated the core purposes of the association and thus imposed an unconstitutional burden. Together, *Jaycees* and *Boy Scouts* expose the difficult balance the state has tried to maintain in the post-*NAACP* era.

After the attacks of September 11, 2001, new questions arose about how to balance the freedom of association with national security. These debates are nothing new. For better or for worse, Americans have always sought to balance the freedom of association with national security and the common good.

JOHANN N. NEEM

References and Further Reading

Bresler, Robert J. *Freedom of Association: Rights and Liberties under the Law*. Santa Barbara, CA: ABC-CLIO, 2004.

Cole, David, and James X. Dempsey. *Terrorism and the Constitution: Sacrificing Civil Liberties in the Name of National Security*. New York: Norton, 2002.

Compa, Lance. *Unfair Advantage: Workers' Freedom of Association in the United States under International Human Rights Standards*. Ithaca: ILR Press, 2004.

Fellman, David. *The Constitutional Right of Association*. Chicago: University of Chicago Press, 1963.

Gutmann, Amy, ed. *Freedom of Association*. Princeton: Princeton University Press, 1998.

Hall, Peter Dobkin. *Inventing the Nonprofit Sector and Other Essays on Philanthropy, Voluntarism, and Nonprofit Organizations*. Baltimore: Johns Hopkins University Press, 2001.

Hammack, David C., ed. *Making the Nonprofit Sector in the United States: A Reader*. Bloomington: Indiana University Press, 1998.

Katz, Stanley, Barry Sullivan, and C. Paul Beach, *Legal Change and Legal Autonomy: Charitable Trusts in New York, 1777–1893*, Law and History Review 03 (1985): 1:51–89.

Neem, Johann N. "Freedom of Association in the Early Republic: The Republican Party, the Whiskey Rebellion, and the Philadelphia and New York Cordwainers' Cases." *Pennsylvania Magazine of History and Biography* 127 (2003): 3:259–290.

———. "The Elusive Common Good: Religion and Civil Society in Massachusetts, 1780-1833." *Journal of the Early Republic* 24 (2004): 3:381–417.

Novak, William J. "The American Law of Association: The Legal-Political Construction of Civil Society." *Studies in American Political Development* 15 (Fall 2001): 163–188

Tomlins, Christopher L. *The State and the Unions: Labor Relations, Law, and the Organized Labor Movement in America, 1880–1960*. New York: Cambridge University Press, 1995.

———. *Law, Labor, and Ideology in the Early American Republic*. New York: Cambridge University Press, 1993.

Wyllie, Irvin G. "The Search for an American Law of Charity." *Mississippi Valley Historical Review* 44 (1959): 2:203–221.

Cases and Statutes Cited

Dartmouth College v. Woodward, 17 U.S. 518 (1819)

Commonwealth v. Hunt, 4 Metcalf 111 (1842)

Vidal v. Girard's Executors, 43 U.S. 127 (1844)

Pierce v. Society of Sisters, 268 U.S. 510 (1925)

Gitlow v. New York, 268 U.S. 652 (1925)

Bryant v. Zimmerman, 278 U.S. 63 (1928)

Dennis v. United States, 341 U.S. 494 (1951)

Adler v. Board of Education, 342 U.S. 485 (1952)

Yates v. United States, 354 U.S. 298 (1957)

NAACP v. Alabama, 357 U.S. 449 (1958)

Scales v. United States, 367 U.S. 203 (1961)

Noto v. United States, 367 U.S. 290 (1961)

Communist Party of the United States v. Subversive Activities Control Board, 367 U.S. 1 (1961)

Albertson v. Subversive Activities Control Board, 382 U.S. 70 (1965)

Elfbrandt v. Russell, 384 U.S. 11 (1966)

Keyishian v. Board of Regents, 385 U.S. 589 (1967)

Boorda v. Subversive Activities Control Bd., 421 F.2d 1142 (D.C. Cir.1969)

Moose Lodge No. 107 v. Irvis, 407 U.S. 163 (1972)

Bob Jones University v. United States, 461 U.S. 574 (1983)

Roberts v. United States Jaycees, 468 U.S. 609 (1984)

Board of Directors, Rotary International v. Rotary Club of Duarte, 481 U.S. 537 (1987)

Boy Scouts of America v. Dale, 530 U.S. 640 (2000)

FREEDOM OF CONTRACT

The right to liberty of contract is not found in the text of the Constitution but has its origins in Anglo-American common law and natural rights ideology.

Beginning in the 1880s, American courts began to assert that a right to contract free from unreasonable government regulations is protected by the due process clause of the Fourteenth Amendment. The U.S. Supreme Court first invalidated a law as a violation of liberty of contract in the infamous 1905 case of *Lochner vs. New York.*

Lochner, however, was something of an anomaly until the 1920s, because the Court almost always deferred to the states' assertion of their regulatory powers, the so-called police power. Between 1923 and 1934, however, the Court aggressively policed the boundaries of the states' regulatory powers, invalidating a wide range of laws as violations of liberty of contract that had no valid police power rationale. For example, in 1923 in *Adkins v. Children's Hospital*, the Court, in a controversial five-to-four decision, invalidated a law mandating minimum wages for women workers.

Ultimately, the doctrine of liberty of contract could not survive the Great Depression and of the pro regulatory sentiment that accompanied it. In the late 1930s, the Supreme Court announced that henceforth it would defer to government regulations of economic activity and the longer enforce the right to liberty of contract. Since then, Americans' right to make and enforce contracts has largely been at the mercy of legislative majorities.

DAVID E. BERNSTEIN

References and Further Reading

Bernstein, David E., *Lochner Era Revisionism Revised: Lochner and the Origins of Fundamental Rights Constitutionalism*, Georgetown Law Journal 92 (2003):1–67.
Gillman, Howard. *The Constitution Besieged: The Rise and Demise of* Lochner *Era Police Powers Jurisprudence*. Durham and London: Duke University Press, 1993.

Cases and Statutes Cited

Lochner v. New York, 198 U.S. 45 (1905)
Adkins v. Children's Hospital, 261 U.S. 525 (1923)

FREEDOM OF EXPRESSION IN THE INTERNATIONAL CONTEXT

The First Amendment's protection of freedom of expression became part of the U.S. Constitution in 1791. The French Declaration of the Rights of Man and of the Citizen, adopted by the French National Assembly in 1789, provides that "No one shall be disquieted on account of his opinions" (Article 10) and "That the free communication of ideas and opinions is one of the most precious of the rights or man.

Every citizen may, accordingly, speak, write and print with freedom, but shall be responsible for such abuses of this freedom as shall be defined by law" (Article 11). Otherwise, provisions for protecting freedom of expression have mostly come through the principal human rights documents that have been adopted or that have come into force only since World War II. This does not mean that countries without explicit rights documents have always failed to protect of freedom of expression. This is also not to suggest that freedom of expression has been universally honored since World War II by counties with explicit protective provisions. Indeed, either with or without rights documents, the number of national governments with serious breaches of freedom of expression no doubt has far exceeded the number of governments that has consistently protected that freedom. Nonetheless, it is important to remember that the great movement toward formal documentation of human rights after World War II began with the Universal Declaration of Human Rights (adopted in 1948). The freedom of expression provision of the Universal Declaration is contained in Article 19: "Everyone has the right to freedom of opinion and expression; this right includes the right to hold opinions without interference and to seek, receive and impart information and ideas through any media and regardless of frontiers." Other post–World War II human rights documents with provisions protecting freedom of expression include the International Covenant on Civil and Political Rights (Article 19, came into force in 1976), the American Declaration of the Rights and Duties of Man (Article 4, adopted 1948), the European Convention for the Protection of Human Rights and Fundamental Freedoms (Article 10, came into force in 1953), the American Convention on Human Rights (Article 13, came into force in 1978), and the African Charter of Human and Peoples' Rights (Article 9, came into force in 1986). These provisions, mostly from the second half of the twentieth century, usually include qualifications or conditions set out in a separate paragraph, for example, the European Convention's qualifications are set out in paragraph (2) of Article 10: "The exercise of these freedoms, since it carries with it duties and responsibilities, may be subject to such formalities, conditions, restrictions or penalties as are prescribed by law and are necessary in a democratic society, in the interest of national security, territorial integrity or public safety, for the protection of health or morals, for the protection of reputation or rights of others, for preventing the disclosure of information received in confidence, or for maintaining the authority and impartiality of the judiciary." Taken together, these qualifications represent what is known in the decisions of the

European Court of Human Rights as the "margin of appreciation." The margin has been described by Judge R. St. J. Macdonald of the European Court as involving the "delicate task of balancing the sovereignty of Contracting Parties (member-states of the Council of Europe) with their obligations under the [European] Convention." As we shall see in the following, this balancing act has required the recurring attention of the European Court of Human Rights.

After proclaiming freedom of expression in Article 19(2), Article 19(3) of the International Covenant on Civil and Political Rights contains the proviso that: "The exercise of these rights provided for in paragraph 2 of this article carries with it special duties and responsibilities. It may therefore be subject to certain restrictions, but these shall only be such as are provided by law and are necessary." Thus, Article 19(3)(a) provides, "For respect of the rights and reputations of others," and 19(3)(b) provides, "For the protection of national security or of public order, or of public health or morals." Also Article 20 provides that "any propaganda for war shall be prohibited by law" and also for the prohibition by law of, "Any advocacy of national, racial, ore religious hatred that constitutes incitement to discrimination, hostility or violence."

It should be noted that in the United States, although the First Amendment's protection of freedom of speech seems on its face to be absolute ("Congress shall make no law abridging freedom of speech"), the balance between freedom of speech and other values or interests has been worked out in decisions of the Supreme Court of the United States. In U.S. practice none of the first Amendment freedoms are absolute. The rights documents adopted after World War II all contain explicit provisos, perhaps recognizing both the recent excesses and outrages that led to World War II and to the tensions of the cold war, as well as the experience of the Supreme Court of the United States in working out the limits of freedom of expression.

International Institutions

What institutions are responsible for enforcing human rights in the international context? The most active and influential institution has been the European Court of Human Rights, which has ultimate responsibility for interpreting the European Convention on Human Rights. While that Convention first came into force in 1953, the first judges of the European Court of Human Rights were not appointed until 1959, when fifteen European Countries were obligated to

follow the European Convention. Its first decision on the merits was not made until 1961. The European Convention now applies to forty-four member-states with an aggregate population of more than 800 million people. Contrasting to the European Court, the Inter-American Court that applies the American Declaration and the American Convention on Human Rights is a fledging institution, having become active in 1979, whereas the African Commission on Human and Peoples Rights, responsible for interpreting the African Charter is even more recent, being fully staffed only in 1989.

The freedom of expression articles of the Universal Declaration of Human Rights and the International Covenant on Civil and Political Rights (ICCPR) are broadly within the responsibilities of the United Nations Commission on Human Rights and the United Nations High Commissioner for Human Rights, and, in the instance of the ICCPR, the UN Human Rights Committee, but there is no United Nations agency or court with the authority to adjudicate cases involving alleged violations of freedom of expression and the direct or indirect power to enforce its decisions. The International Criminal Court, although not a UN agency was proposed under UN auspices at the conference that adopted what is known as the 1998 Rome Statute for the International Criminal Court. That court came into force on July 1, 2002, but it has exclusively criminal jurisdiction to try war crimes, crimes against humanity, genocide, and other crimes defined by the Rome Statute, rather than comprehensive authority of human rights.

Freedom of Expression under the European and American Conventions

As noted previously, the first substantive decision of the European Court of Human Rights was not made until 1961. The first Article 10 case before the European Court of Human was the 1976 *Handyside* case in which the prosecution of a publisher for having in his possession obscene books for publication for gain was upheld as having a legitimate aim of the protection of morals that was necessary in a democratic society. Among the other early Article 10 cases was *Sunday Times v. United Kingdom* (1979), the first case in which a violation of Article 10 was found by the European Court of Human Rights. That case is notable for our purposes because its shares its English common law origins with the United States and because its key issue, the legitimacy of an injunction (prior restraint) against publication of a newspaper article, also had been the subject of a case before the

Supreme Court of the United States in the 1971 Pentagon Papers cases (*New York Times v. U.S.*).

The *Sunday Times* case involved a conflict between freedom of the press and the contempt powers of British courts applied to the press through an injunction to prevent the publication of an article that would have tended to "obstruct, prejudice or abuse the administration of justice." The article that *The Sunday Times* proposed to publish was about the development, sale, and prescription of the drug thalidomide, which had resulted in the birth of a number of children with serious deformities. One feared consequence of the proposed article was that it would influence the payment of damages offered by the defendant pharmaceutical company for the suffered deformities. The House of Lords Appellate Committee, the court of last resort for the United Kingdom, sustained an injunction against *The Sunday Times* in 1973. It was this injunction that was held by the European Court of Human Rights (ECHR) in 1979 (by 11 votes to 9) to violate Article 10 of the European Convention on Human Rights. This was the first violation of Article 10 found by the ECHR.

The five law lords who had ruled against *The Sunday Times* had concluded that prejudgment of important issues through trial by newspaper should be prevented. While it was clear to all of the judges of the ECHR that the injunction was a violation of Article 10(1), the key issue was whether the injunction had a legitimate aim ("maintaining the authority and impartiality of the judiciary" was included in Art. 10 [2]) that was "necessary in a democratic society." Eleven members of the ECHR found that the injunction did not represent a pressing social need sufficient to outweigh the right to freedom of expression, whereas nine members disagreed. Their differences were over the "margin of appreciation" to be allowed national authorities by a transnational institution. The majority concluded that the exceptions to the freedom of expression protected by Article 10(1) must be narrowly interpreted. Freedom of expression was the primary concern. This "presumption" in favor of freedom of expression is like that expressed by the Supreme Court of the United States when it assesses intrusions on "preferred or fundamental freedoms" (*U.S. v. Carolene Products Co.*).

The second case in which the ECHR found a violation of freedom of expression was in 1986. It also involved a journalist who was sued in a private prosecution for defamation brought by Bruno Kreisky, then the outgoing Chancellor of Austria and President of the Austrian Socialist party. Austrian law provided for criminal punishment for any who "accuses another of possessing a contemptible character or attitude or of behavior contrary to honour or morality of such a nature as to make him contemptible or otherwise lower him in public esteem." The defendant, Peter Lingens, had accused Kreisky, in a series of articles, of protecting former members of the SS for political reasons and of being too accommodating toward former Nazis, as well as citing his lack of tactful treatment of the victims of the Nazis. When, after extensive litigation in Austria, Lingens was found guilty and fined for his articles, he appealed to the ECHR. Once again, the violation of Article 10 (1) was clear, so the margin of appreciation the issue. Austria claimed that the prosecution was justified under the express provision of Article 10(2) to protect the "rights and reputations of others." In holding that the criminal prosecution of Lingens was not "necessary in a democratic society," and was "disproportionate to the legitimate aim pursued" (the protection of the reputation of others), the ECHR concluded that, "The limits of acceptable criticism are...wider as regards a politician as such than as regards a private individual. Unlike the latter, the former inevitably and knowingly lays himself open to close scrutiny of his every word and deed by both journalists and by the public at large, and he must consequently display a greater degree of tolerance." As was true with the *Sunday Times Case*, the *Lingens* case has a U.S.-relevant U.S. precedent, *New York Times v. Sullivan* (1964), with much the same outcome.

The second *Sunday Times Case* (1991), along with its companion cases for the *Guardian* and the *Observer,* was another prior restraint case, this one involving the proposed publication by the three newspapers of articles about or excerpts from *Spycatcher*, Peter Wright's book about his work as a senior member of the British Security Service (MI5). The House of Lords had first voted to continue a preliminary injunction against publication of the articles, pending a trial on the facts of the confidentiality and security issues involved. That was followed by the judgment in the House of Lords Legal Committee that *The Sunday Times* had breached a duty of confidentiality by publishing extracts from the book and was liable to account for its profits from the publication. No permanent injunction was issue because by the time of judgment, global dissemination of *Spycatcher* had destroyed any element of confidentiality. When *The Sunday Times* took its case to The European Court of Human Rights, that court noted that "the dangers inherent in prior restraint are such that they call for the most careful scrutiny on the part of the Court." Consistent with its concern, the ECHR found, by a vote of fourteen to ten, that although confidentiality and national security justified an injunction against publication for the first year, after that the injunctions were no longer justifiable under Article 10(2). Once confidentiality had been lost by publication outside the United Kingdom, the only purpose in continuing the injunctions was to deter others who might choose to emulate Peter Wright or to demonstrate that the Security Service would not "countenance authorized publication." Neither of these justifications was seen as sufficient to support a continuation of the injunction. It is interesting that the dissenters expressed even stronger protection for freedom of expression and even greater suspicion of prior restraints than the majority.

Consistent with its strong protection for freedom of expression, in 1992 the European Court of Human Rights in the case of *Castells v. Spain* wrote that, "Freedom of the press affords the public one of the best means of discovering and forming an opinion of the ideas and attitudes of their political leaders," whereas the 1994 decision in *Jersild v. Denmark,* the ECHR held that punishing a journalist for assisting another person in the dissemination of information violated Article 10.

Among the most recent decisions of the European Court of Human Rights, the case of *Hirico v. Slovakia* (2004) involved a publisher and editor of a weekly publication that published a series of articles concerning a prosecution for defamation brought by a government minister against a poet who had claimed that the minister was a fascist. The articles included accusations against the judge who tried the defamation case, and the judge then brought proceedings against the publisher and editor of the weekly claiming that the articles had impugned his civil and professional honor and his authority as a judge. The publisher claimed the protection of Article 10, and once again the issue was the appropriate margin of appreciation. The judge's position was complicated by the fact that he also was a political candidate on the list of the Christian-Social Union, a party that had well-known views on issues involved in the defamation case that had been discussed in the series of articles. In a very brief opinion, the ECHR found for the publisher, holding that the limits of acceptable criticism are larger when a judge enters political life. Moreover, it held that Article 10's protection extends journalistic freedom to include the expression of opinions that may "shock or offend" and even "possible recourse to a degree of exaggeration." The articles commented on issues "of general concern on which a political debate existed." Presumably the European cases involving freedom of expression have focused on press freedom, because that is where the critical issues have arisen

To aid in the enforcement of Article IV of the American Declaration of Human Rights and Article 13 of the American Convention on Human Rights, the Office of the Special Rapporteur on Freedom of Expression of the Inter-American Commission on Human Rights developed a Declaration of Principles on Freedom of Expression that were approved by the Inter-American Commission in October 2000. These thirteen principles were especially concerned with access to information and prior censorship and with the use of violence or threats of violence to intimidate or prevent social communications.

Also, in a 1985 Advisory Opinion (OC-5-85), the Inter-American Court of Human Rights wrote that: " [F]reedom of expression is a cornerstone upon which the very existence of a democratic society rests....It represents, in short, the means that enable the community, when exercising its options, to be sufficiently informed. Consequently, it can be said that a society that is not well informed is not a society that is truly free."

It is not surprising that Inter-American institutions should place such an emphasis on free access to information, when we take into account that one of the first substantive decisions of the Inter-American Court of Human Rights case in the 1988 case of Velásquez Rodríguez involving the disappearance of a journalist. The Inter-American court there stressed that the investigation into his disappearance must be objective and effective. In its 1998 Annual Report, the Inter-American Commission of Human Rights wrote that threatening, intimidation, abduction or murder of journalists "seek to silence the press in its watchdog role, or render it an accomplice to individuals or institutions engaged in abusive of illegal actions."

National Courts

Nihal Jayawickrama's excellent review of contemporary application of human rights law, while focusing chiefly on the work of the European Court of Human Rights and the UN Human Rights Committee, reviews cases from Canada, India, Nigeria, Lithuania, and from the High Court of St. Vincent and the Grenadines that have viewed freedom of expression as being "indispensable to the operation of a democratic system." These precedents suggest that the jurisprudence of the Supreme Court of the United States will be only part of the story of the protection of freedom of expression in the future. It will be a good thing if other countries have more success stories for the protection of freedom of expression through their own processes.

DONALD W. JACKSON

References and Further Reading

Inter-American Commission on Human Rights. *Report on Terrorism and Human Rights.* Washington, DC, 2002.

Jackson, Donald W. *The United Kingdom Confronts the European Convention on Human Rights.* Gainesville: The University Press of Florida, 1997.

Jayawickrama, Nihal. *The Judicial Application of Human Rights Law: National, Regional and International Jurisprudence.* Cambridge: Cambridge University Press. 2002.

Cases and Statutes Cited

Castells v. Spain, 14 E.H.R.R. 445 (1992)

Handyside v. United Kingdom, 24 Eur. Ct. H.R. (ser. A) (1976)

Hirico v. Slovakis, 41 E.H.R.R. 300 (2004)

Jersild v. Denmark, 19 E.H.R.R 28 (1994)

Lingens v. Austria, 103 Eur. Ct. H.R. (ser. A) (1986)

New York Times v. Sullivan, 376 U.S. 254 (1964)

New York Times v. U.S., 403 U.S. 703 (1971)

Sunday Times v. United Kingdom, 30 Eur. Ct. H.R. (ser. A) (1979)

U.S. v. Carolene Products Co., 394 U.S.144 (1938)

FREEDOM OF INFORMATION ACT (1966)

The First Congress charged executive departments of the federal government with "housekeeping," or maintenance, of their own records. Neither the Constitution nor any comprehensive law required disclosure of government records until the Administrative Procedure Act of 1946 (APA). However, access under the APA was severely limited. Agencies could regulate access, and only "persons properly and directly concerned" with records were entitled to see them.

Dissatisfaction with secrecy in government, especially on the part of the press, grew in the 1950s. Bills were introduced in Congress as early as 1957, but none gained traction until 1963, when the APA came subject to overhaul. After back and forth between House and Senate, resolute dissent from federal agencies, and a threatened White House veto, President Lyndon B. Johnson signed into law the Freedom of Information Act (FOIA) on July 4, 1966.

The FOIA, as since amended, mandates publication by executive authorities of materials such as rules and procedures and mandates disclosure of any executive branch record on request, regardless of the requester's motive. However, the FOIA enumerates nine exemptions, including classified national security matters, trade secrets, agency memoranda, certain law enforcement records, matters of personal privacy, and records exempted by other statutes.

Though often touted as a journalist's tool, the FOIA is used more widely by businesses and individuals. The FOIA has been litigated extensively, especially as to the scope of its exemptions. Since the terrorist attacks of September 11, 2001, the scope of the FOIA's national security exemption has been fiercely contested.

RICHARD J. PELTZ

References and Further Reading

Hammitt, Harry A., David L. Sobel, and Mark S. Zaid, eds. *Litigation Under the Federal Open Government Laws 2004.* 22nd Ed. Washington, D.C.: EPIC Publications, 2004.

O'Reilly, James T. *Federal Information Disclosure.* 3rd Ed. St. Paul: West Group, 2000.

Cases and Statutes Cited

Administrative Procedure Act, 5 U.S.C. §§ 551–706, Act of June 11, 1946, c. 324, 60 Stat. 237

Freedom of Information Act, 5 U.S.C. § 552, Act of July 4, 1966, Pub. L. No. 89-487, 80 Stat. 250

See also **Access to Government Operations Information; Classified Information; Freedom of Information and Sunshine Laws; Media Access to Information; United Nations Subcommission on Freedom of Information and of the Press**

FREEDOM OF INFORMATION AND SUNSHINE LAWS

Although the First Amendment to the Constitution provides a freedom to speak and publish information that a person possesses, especially about government, the Constitution has not been construed to provide a freedom to obtain information. Thus the extent to which government must conduct business in public view or in secret is chiefly a matter for federal statutory and state law. Still, openness has long been recognized as a critical component of democracy. Louis D. Brandeis famously observed in 1914, "Sunlight is said to be the best disinfectant." Laws ensuring public access to government have thus been termed "sunshine" laws.

At the federal level, the principal sunshine laws are the Freedom of Information Act (FOIA) and the Privacy Act, which provide access to government records, and the Federal Advisory Committee Act and Government in the Sunshine Act, which provide access to government meetings. All but the FOIA (1966) were enacted in the 1970s, when the Vietnam War and the Watergate scandal strained public confidence in government.

The federal laws were mirrored at the state level and made sunshine an entrenched feature of state government, although many states had sunshine laws dating to the early twentieth century. Today every state has an open meetings law and an open records law. They vary dramatically in their particulars. Some states, such as Florida and North Dakota, have sunshine laws in their state constitutions. Some states, such as Connecticut and Virginia, have established freedom of information councils to facilitate sunshine law compliance.

RICHARD J. PELTZ

References and Further Reading

Leslie, Gregg, and Rebecca Daugherty, eds. *Tapping Officials' Secrets*. 4th Ed. Arlington, VA: Reporters Committee for Freedom of the Press, 2001.
O'Reilly, James T. *Federal Information Disclosure*. 3rd Ed. St. Paul: West Group, 2000.

Cases and Statutes Cited

Fla. Const. Art. I, § 24
N.D. Const. Art. 11, §§ 5-6
Federal Advisory Committee Act, 5 U.S.C. app. 2, Act of Oct. 6, 1972, Pub L. 92-463, 86 Stat. 770
Freedom of Information Act, 5 U.S.C. § 552, Act of July 4, 1966, Pub. L. No. 89-487, 80 Stat. 250
Government in the Sunshine Act, 5 U.S.C. § 552b, Act of Sept. 13, 1976, Pub. L. No. 94-409, 90 Stat. 1241
Privacy Act, 5 U.S.C. § 552a, Act of Dec. 31, 1974, Pub. L. No. 93-579, 88 Stat. 1896
Conn. Gen. Stat. §§ 1-205 to -205a
Va. Code §§ 30-178 to -181

See also **Access to Courts; Access to Government Operations Information; Access to Judicial Records; Access to Prisons; Brandeis, Louis Dembitz; Classified Information; Congressional Protection of Privacy; Freedom of Information Act (1966); Media Access to Information; Media Access to Judicial Proceedings; Media Access to Military Operations; Nixon, Richard Milhous; Right of Access to Criminal Trials**

FREEDOM OF SPEECH AND PRESS UNDER THE CONSTITUTION: EARLY HISTORY, 1791–1917

When reading this, it is important to remember that most of the First Amendment law concerning freedom of speech and press came after the period covered here. Nonetheless, 1791 was important as the year when the U.S. Bill of Rights (the first ten amendments to the U.S. Constitution) came into effect through ratification, whereas 1917 is the year the U.S. Espionage Act, which was designed to punish certain political speech (seen as being dangerous during World War I) was passed. So, the end of our period was just before the first important free speech decision of the Supreme Court of the United States in 1919, *Schenck v. United States*, which interpreted the scope of freedom of political speech under that act by adopting the "clear and present danger test."

When we consider the freedoms protected by the First Amendment to the U.S. Constitution during the first 125 years of American constitutional history, our first task is to set aside our contemporary understanding of what the word "freedom" means to us. To be sure, First Amendment "freedom language" is mostly a product of the years since 1917, beginning, as noted previously, with several important cases involving political speech that were decided in the immediate aftermath of World War I. Our task is made somewhat easier by the fact that the seminal early book on freedom of speech, Professor Zechariah Chafee's *Freedom of Speech*, was first published in 1920, just after the period that we consider here. Chafee's update, *Freedom of the Speech in the United States,* was published in 1941, but, as he notes in his preface to that edition, the substantive material that was covered and first published in 1920 (Part I of the 1941 update) was mostly unchanged. Thus Chafee's work can help us understand how freedom of speech was seen in 1920.

In Chafee's 1941 update, from a book of more than 500 pages, only Chapter I (just more than thirty pages) deals with the pre-1918 period, so the first thing we realize is that for most purposes freedom of speech law developed with the prosecutions of political dissidents that followed World War I. It is true that the historical precedent to the Espionage Act of 1917 was the U.S. Sedition Act of 1798, through which the Federalist Party of John Adams sought to prosecute their political opponents, but that act led to no important Supreme Court decisions. Instead, the Act lapsed in March 1801, just before Thomas Jefferson's inauguration as president. An excellent book, James Morton Smith's *Freedom's Fetters*, covers the relevant events of those years.

We need to note that one reason why a bill of rights was not included in the original U.S. Constitution was based on the view that the U.S. Congress had no power to enact legislation on the subjects eventually covered by the Bill of Rights of 1791. That point was belied by the Sedition Act of 1798, which was predicated on the view that Congress had the power to punish unlawful conspiracies or combinations that might impede the efforts of the federal government. Without knowing that he was beginning a tradition of exceptions, President John Adams called the Alien and Sedition Acts war measures justified by a perceived emergency (because of the possibility of war with France). The Sedition Act created the possibility of prosecution of anyone who "shall write, print, utter or publish...scandalous and malicious writing or writings against the government of the United States, or either House of the Congress...or the President...with the intent to defame...or to bring them...into contempt or disrepute; or to excite against them...the hatred of the good people of the United States." It is important to note that freedom of speech and freedom of the press were treated in much the same manner at this time, and freedom of the press was probably the more important of the two because then the only way to reach a large audience was through print media.

Elkins and McKitrick's *The Age of Federalism* describe the Federalists' resort to prosecution of its opponents. Their narrative relies in part on Madison's *Federalist 10* in which he argued against political parties and factions as being usually contrary to the public interest. The ideal was that, instead of factions, enlightened and virtuous leaders should transcend narrow interests and seek the higher public good. When this ideal was applied in practice by the Federalists, the outcome was that when men of such good will and reason (as the Federalists saw themselves) were attacked by others who were insolent, vulgar, self-interested, and demagogic (as they saw their opponents), the Sedition Act of 1798 was the reasonable consequence. Madison, however, was not part of this outcome.

Indeed, in 1800 Madison reported to the Virginia legislature on the Alien and Sedition Acts. He argued that the Sedition Act was unconstitutional, because the federal government had no jurisdiction under its enumerated or implied powers over conduct that may have been criminal under English common law (political sedition) and that the First Amendment replaced the common law on freedom of speech and press. As to the federal government, freedom of speech and press were absolute, because there was no authority on the part of the federal government to legislate on those subjects. As to the notion that the common law had only prevented previous restraints against publications and did not prohibit post-publication criminal liability, as quoted by Leon Levy, Madison argued that, "It would seem a mockery to say that no laws should be passed preventing publications from being made, but that laws might be passed for punishing them in case they should be made." In the United States, Madison argued, the people, rather than the king, were sovereign and they granted to the government only the powers that they had spelled out in the Constitution of the United States. Another compelling argument in Madison's report was the fact

that the First Amendment also prohibited an establishment of religion by the federal government, whereas there was clearly such an establishment (the Church of England) under the common law. The logical implication was that the common law was modified by the Bill of Rights when the two conflicted, as they did with respect to the establishment of religion. In this context it must be recognized that this logical implication did not apply to the states, although this was not explicitly decided by the Supreme Court until 1833 in the case of *Barron v. Baltimore,* which held that the Bill of Rights was written to limit the national government. The adoption of provisions protecting freedom of speech and press in state constitutions, however, possibly raised the same logical implication. Although Levy concludes that Madison's *Report* was not necessarily indicative of the intended meaning of the Bill of Rights in the period of 1789–1791, it certainly represented the evolution of Madison's thinking by 1800.

There were fourteen prosecutions under the Sedition Act. Elkins and McKitrick argue that these cases, while marked with "brutal highhandedness," were more striking for the "almost comic clumsiness, the sheer political ineptitude with which the Federalists went about their work of trying to silence the opposition press." Nonetheless only one defendant was acquitted under the Sedition Act of 1798. Because the Sedition Act expired in 1801, coupled with the fact that the U.S. Supreme Court did not exercise the power of judicial review until its decision in *Marbury v. Madison* in 1803, there was no constitutional review of these cases.

Although political sedition had been part of the common law of England, whether it had been, in effect, repealed by the First Amendment's protection of freedom of speech was a question that never reached the Supreme Court in our early history. An interesting book on that question is Leon Levy's *Legacy of Suppression.* Levy argues that the Federalist leaders, who contributed to the drafting and ratification of the U.S. Constitution, and later the Bill of Rights, did not understand freedom of speech to have broad scope, especially in the instance of political expression. Levy concluded that we know relatively little about the original understanding of the meaning of freedom of speech or of the press within the First Amendment. He notes that, "The phrase, 'freedom of speech' used in connection with the right of a citizen to speak his mind was extremely rare in the seventeenth century." Freedom of the press and of religion were of much greater concern, but even so, under English law prosecutions for seditious libel were the means by which the press could be controlled. Greater tolerance of political criticism and a libertarian understanding of freedom of speech, he suggests, did not come until the Jeffersonians took power. However, Justice Holmes took a contrary position in *Abrams v. U.S.* (1919), when he concluded that the First Amendment's protection for freedom of speech was intended to prohibit prosecutions for political sedition, as it was then understood in English common law. Chafee affirms that position in the first chapter of *Freedom of Speech in the United States*. Whichever view is right, it is necessary to first understand at least the basic elements of the English law of seditious libel (political sedition).

Seditious Libel

The English common law of seditious libel criminalized speech that might have the tendency to bring the government into disrepute, even if the content of the speech was true. According to Chafee, the law of seditious libel in England through the close of the eighteenth century was "the intentional publication without lawful excuse or justification, of any written blame of any public man, or of the law, or of any institution established by law." Under this definition, freedom of speech and of the press consisted chiefly of the absence of prior censorship, whereas the publication of information tending to disparage public officials or institutions was usually punishable. The early common law rule was that the only question for a jury was whether the defendant had indeed published the material; all other issues were questions of law to be determined by judges. Thus, liberty of the press in particular was simply the absence of a government censor to which publications had to be submitted prior to publication. As reported by Levy, the result was that in prosecutions for criminal libel—those libels against the state—"a man might be arrested on a general warrant, prosecuted on an information without the consent of a grand jury, and convicted for his political opinions by judges appointed by the government he had aspersed."

Probably the most famous early prosecution for political sedition in the American colonies was the trial in 1735 of John Peter Zenger, printer of the *New York Weekly Journal*. Zenger attacked the administration of colonial Governor William Cosby. Cosby assumed his office in 1731 and promptly achieved widespread unpopularity. Zenger, who was associated with the Popular Party that opposed Cosby, was defended by Alexander Hamilton, who argued that truth should be a defense to prosecution for seditious libel. As noted in the website cited in the references, the prosecution accused Zenger of "being

a seditious person and a frequent printer and publisher of false news and seditious libels" who had "wickedly and maliciously" sought to "traduce, scandalize and vilify" Governor Cosby and his cabinet. Hamilton argued that the law of New York colony need not be the same as the common law of England. The presiding judge ruled that Hamilton could offer no proof of the truth of Zenger's publication and instructed the jury that its duty was clear; it was not to judge or alter the law. However, when the question of his guilt was submitted to a jury, Zenger was acquitted. That single, although famous, outcome did not establish the universal principal of truth as a defense, but it did reveal and offer the prospect for enhancing the power of American juries. Yet, Levy concludes that one of the reasons for the fame of the Zenger case was its singularity. Today such verdicts are known as *jury nullification,* that is, when a jury simply refuses to enforce the extant law. Even given such occasional victories as Zenger's, Levy argues that to consider the American colonies as "a society in which freedom of expression was cherished is a hallucination of sentiment that ignores history."

Levy reports that the first instance of freedom of speech being protected by a constitution came in Pennsylvania in 1776, when its first constitution said "That the people have a right to freedom of speech, and of writing, and publishing their sentiments; therefore the freedom of the press ought not to be restrained."

Despite those words, Pennsylvania failed to protect Loyalist (pro-English) speech during the American Revolution, and Quakers were often the objects of official persecution.

The Cushing-Adams letters of 1789, reviewed by Levy, are often cited for their relatively broad understanding of freedom of speech and press. Cushing was then the Chief Justice of Massachusetts. In his letter to John Adams, Cushing sought Adams confirmation of his view that the free press clause of the Massachusetts constitution guaranteed "freedom to discuss all subjects and characters 'within the bounds of truth.'" Adams' reply was that he agreed the provision that Cushing relied on supported the view that a jury ought to determine the truth of accusations and if they found that they were published for the "Public good," they would acquit. This standard was indeed contained in the Sedition Act of 1798, but the acquittals did not follow. Indeed, Cushing, who became a Justice of the Supreme Court of the United States in 1789, after his letter to Adams was written, presided over some of the trials brought under the Sedition Act of 1798 and viewed that act as constitutional. Since the Sedition Act came only seven years after the First Amendment became part of the U.S. Constitution, the conclusion that Federalists, who then held power, did not see that amendment as a bar to prosecutions for seditious libel seems inescapable.

Story's Commentaries

In the absence of early judicial precedents interpreting the scope of freedom of speech and press in the United States, we must consider instead the work of notable nineteenth century scholars. Joseph Story's *Commentaries on the Constitution of the United States* was published in three volumes in 1833 and dedicated to then Chief Justice John Marshall. In the last volume of his treatise, when discussing freedom of the press, Story emphasized responsibility rather than freedom. He wrote that absolute freedom was a "supposition too wild to be indulged by any rational man."

Instead he wrote that:

> It is plain then, that the language of this amendment imports no more, than that every man shall have a right to speak, write, and print his opinions upon any subject whatsoever, without any prior restraint, so always, that he does not injure any other person in his rights, person, property or reputation; and so always that he does not thereby disturb the public peace, or attempt to subvert the government. (Section 1874)

And he added that:

> Every freeman has an undoubted right to law what sentiments he pleases before the public; to forbid this is to destroy the freedom of the press. But, If he publishes what is improper, mischievous, or illegal, he must take the consequences of his own temerity. (Section 1878).

Story's position was consistent with Blackstone's narrative of the English common law as prohibiting "previous restraints" but not subsequent prosecution. Blackstone's *Commentaries,* published in a readily portable format, probably was the single most important law book on the American frontier.

Cooley's Constitutional Limitations

In his famous book, first published in 1871, Thomas Cooley also concluded that the English law of libel was not abolished by the First Amendment, citing as precedent the opinion of Chief Justice Parker of Massachusetts, who, writing in 1825 in *Commonwealth v. Blanding* about his own state constitution's protection of liberty of the press, argued that such liberty should be distinguished from licentiousness and that all that was prohibited by liberty of the

press was previous restraints on publication. Thus, prosecutions for publication of material of a blasphemous, obscene, or a scandalous character were not protected. However, Cooley did review at some length the exceptions to the general common law rule against seditious libel that had in England sustained prosecution of publications that had a tendency to defame the government or to subject public officials or institutions to disrepute.

As to common law prosecutions for seditious libel in federal courts, Cooley argued that they could not be maintained, because those courts had no common law jurisdiction, their only jurisdiction being prescribed by Article III of the U.S. Constitution. Reviewing the Sedition Act of 1798, Cooley argued that it was counterproductive, because he thought all such extreme measures might be among a democratic populace. In the abstract he ventured an exception of the discussion of "constitutional questions"—that they ought to be privileged "if conducted with calmness and temperance"— and that they ought not to be indictable unless beyond the "bounds of fair discussion." But then he noted the indeterminacy of words like calmness and temperance.

As to state prosecutions, if the American states are the receptors and standard bearers of English common law, Cooley urged that prosecution for seditious libel, because those had been brought in England, were "unsuited to the condition and circumstances of the people of America, and therefore ought never to be adopted in the several states." Thus, in considering whether there might be liability for criticizing public officials, Cooley reviewed several cases from the American states. For example, a case from New York upheld such criticism as, "the most sacred and unquestionable rights of free citizens; rights essential to the very existence of a free government; rights necessarily connected with the relations of constituent and representative; the right of petitioning for the redress of grievances and the right of remonstrating to the competent authority against the abuse of official functions." However, when the criticism involved the allegation of the commission of a crime or of corrupt practices, another case from New York held that the proof of justification, chiefly the truth of the allegations, rested on the person making such charges. Finally, when the charges against a public official or candidate concerned only his or her qualifications for office, and did not impugn personal character, there was no basis for recovery of damages. These state cases seem to have offered somewhat greater protection for freedom of speech and press than previously had been the rule under the English common law—because truth was accepted as a defense—as it had not previously been under criminal prosecutions for libel in

England. Under the English rule there arose a common law maxim: "The greater the truth, the greater the libel," as Cooley reports. Nonetheless, newspapers were presumed to have been guilty of malice when their published words were untrue and damaging to individuals. They had the burden of rebutting that presumption. Still, Cooley reported that publishers could not be liable for exemplary or "vindictive" damages without proof of actual malice or of negligence. Cooley's first edition was published in 1871. It was not until the case of *New York Times v. Sullivan* (1964) that the U.S. Supreme Court required greater First Amendment protection for the press.

Cooley also reported that several American state constitutions provided that in libel cases the jury had the right to determine both the law and the facts of the case. The limited role of juries in libel cases under the common law of England led to the enactment of what was known as Mr. Fox's Libel Act in 1792 and, it seems, to the insertion of these provisions in state constitutions. Levy reports that after the Libel Act of 1792, juries were, with few exceptions, as repressive as judges had been. Levy reports that "There are more trials for seditious utterances reported in the *State Trials* for the two years after Fox's Libel Act than the total number reported for the whole of the eighteenth century before that time." These included the conviction of Tom Paine for publishing *The Rights of Man.* American state constitutional provisions made truth a defense, but only if published with good motives and justifiable ends. Cooley reported that the meaning of those conditions had not been settled by judicial precedents.

In the views of Levy and other scholars, it was the Sedition Act of 1798 that provoked the Jeffersonian Republicans to support a more libertarian understanding of freedom of speech and press and to repudiate the law of seditious libel, chiefly as their defense to Federalist oppression. Jefferson's Kentucky Resolutions against the Alien and Sedition Acts were introduced in the Kentucky legislature in 1799. It is clear that the resolutions were motivated by fear of Federalist support for greater power for the national government and by Federalist repression of their enemies. That the supporters of the resolutions also favored state nullification of acts of Congress and possibly the right of secession from the union had even greater interest in the events leading to the Civil War.

Lincoln and the Civil War

Certain steps taken by military authorities during the civil war intruded on freedom of speech. A recent book, Daniel Farber's, *Lincoln's Constitution,* does an excellent job of reviewing the Lincoln years. The most famous of these was *Ex parte Vallandingham* (1864), which involved an order by General Burnside proclaiming that the "habit of declaring sympathies for the enemy will not be allowed in this Department" (Ohio). In 1863, Vallandingham, a former congressman who opposed the war, was arrested for violating Burnside's order.

Farber reports that Vallandingham had given a speech in which he referred to the war as "wicked, cruel and unnecessary," and although he said that he would not counsel civil disobedience, he urged his audience to turn Lincoln out of office through use of the ballot box. Although Vallandingham was ordered to be detained for the duration of the war, Lincoln instead ordered that he be expelled into rebel territory. As to the constitutionality of Vallandingham's treatment, Farber quotes Lincoln's argument that Vallandingham had been properly prosecuted because he "avows his hostility to the war on the part of the Union; and his arrest was made because he was laboring, with some effect, to prevent the raising of troops; to encourage desertions from the army, and to leave the rebellion without an adequate military force to suppress it." Whether Lincoln was right or wrong was not determined by the federal courts. The Supreme Court concluded that it had no jurisdiction to review the decisions of the military tribunal that had tried Vallandingham, so it did not rule on the legality of his treatment. Indeed, it ruled on issues like these only after World War I, after the period covered in this article.

One other incident was even more problematic. Lincoln seized the premises of the *New York World,* a newspaper he suspected of being involved in a Confederate conspiracy, and ordered the arrest of those responsible for its publication. This violates even the guarantee affirmed by Blackstone and others as being protected by the common law: the prohibition against previous restraint.

Lincoln's defense of his actions was extra-legal: that he acted in response to the necessity of preserving the union and consistent with his oath as president to see that the laws are faithfully executed.

In his 1999 book, *All the Laws But One,* Chief Justice William Rehnquist reviewed Lincoln's conduct as well, but as part of his book's overall review of civil liberties in wartime. Because Lincoln's wartime policies were never effectively challenged in the federal courts, Rehnquist infers that Lincoln's policies became the "benchmark for future wartime presidents. Referring to Vallandingham, Rehnquist repeats Lincoln's famous question: "Must I shoot a simple-minded soldier boy who deserts while I must not touch a hair of a wily agitator who induces him to desert?" The Chief Justice's comments on Lincoln's policies focus on the fact that Lincoln, and the military authorities who acted under his executive powers, acted alone, that is, without explicit congressional authorization, yet there was no challenge of his policies as violations of the First Amendment. Although Rehnquist does not adopt the Latin maxim, *Inter arma silent leges* (the law is silent in wartime), he concludes that although the laws may not be silent in time of war, "they will speak with a somewhat different voice." It was not until 1919 that the U.S. Supreme Court seriously attempted to set the tone for that different voice.

DONALD W. JACKSON

References and Further Reading

Blackstone, Sir William. *Commentaries on the Laws of England (1765–1769)*. Chicago: University of Chicago Press, 1979.

Chafee, Zechariah, Jr. *Freedom of Speech*. Cambridge, MA: Harvard University Press, 1920.

———. *Freedom of Speech in the United States*. Cambridge, MA: Harvard University Press, 1941.

Cooley, Thomas M. *Treatise on the Constitutional Limitations Which Rest on the Legislative Powers of the States of the American Union*. Boston: Little Brown, 1890.

Elkins, Stanley, and Eric McKitrick. *The Age of Federalism: The Early American Republic, 1788–1800*. New York: Oxford University Press, 1993.

Farber, Daniel. *Lincoln's Constitution*. Chicago: University of Chicago Press, 2003.

Levy, Leonard W. *Legacy of Suppression: Freedom of Speech and Press in Early American History*. Cambridge: Harvard University Press, 1960.

Madison, James. Federalist No. 10 in Hamilton, Alexander, John Jay and James Madison, *The Federalist Papers*. New York: The Modern Library Edition, 1937.

Rehnquist, William. *All the Laws But One: Civil Liberties in Wartime*. New York: Vintage Books, 1998.

Smith, James Morton. *Freedom's Fetters: The Alien and Sedition Laws and American Civil Liberties*. Ithaca, NY: Cornell University Press, 1956.

Story, Joseph. *Commentaries on the Constitution of the United States*. (Reprint of the 1833 edition in 3 volumes). New York: Da Capo Press, 1970.

On the trial of John Peter Zenger: www.law.umkc.edu/faculty/projects/ftrials/zenger/zengeraccount.html (accessed July 26, 2005).

Cases and Statutes Cited

Abrams v. U.S., 250 U.S. 616 (1919)
Barron v. City of Baltimore, 7 Pet. 243 (1833)
Commonwealth v. Blanding, 3 Pick. 304 (Mass. 1825)
Ex parte Vallandingham, 68 U.S. 243 (1864)

FREEDOM OF SPEECH AND PRESS: NINETEENTH CENTURY

The nineteenth century is notable for the inactivity of the Supreme Court in matters of freedom of speech and freedom of the press. The century began with these freedoms enumerated in the Bill of Rights, but when interpreted with their common law understandings, proved to offer little protection for individual liberty. A more libertarian and protective notion of freedom of speech and freedom of the press would not emerge in Supreme Court doctrine until the twentieth century. Because provisions of the First Amendment were not incorporated into the Fourteenth Amendment until the twentieth century as well, speech and press were subject to the state-level determination of public order that superseded liberty claims. Given that states and local governments in early America relied on the police power to maintain social order, the criminalization of written material that was offensive or mischievous to public peace was permissible and expected under the common law standards. Nevertheless, the nineteenth century occasioned the development for the construction of modern free speech theory outside the courts. In the interplay that ensued between the exercise of public ordering and the resultant resistance from affected individuals who invoked freedom of speech and freedom of the press in more protective versions, a constitutional discourse did take place in American political culture. In these extrajudicial venues, activists articulated modern conceptions of speech. These included the theory of the marketplace of ideas, which encouraged the proliferation of all ideas in the expectation that truth would emerge; the notion of the liberty of speech and liberty of press as prepolitical rights that are not subject to governmental creation or denial; the notion of freedom of speech and freedom of press as instrumental and necessary for a self-governing people to assess their public officials; and the identification of free speech and a free press as essential to the development of human autonomy. Although these theories did not inform the Court's doctrine in the nineteenth century, the ongoing discourse allowed for a dissemination of these theories in political culture, laying the groundwork for acceptance of the Supreme Court's later modern free speech doctrine.

Earlier Legacies

The century began with the predominance of the common law conception of freedom of speech and freedom of press and the aftermath of the Sedition

Act of 1798. In his exposition of the common law, the eighteenth-century British jurist Sir William Blackstone explained freedom of the press as consisting of the absence of no prior restraint. Liberty of the press meant that the government could not censor material before it was published; once it was printed, however, the writer had to accept the consequences of his words if the government found the expression to be criminal. In this tradition, the Sedition Act was a legitimate exercise of government power. The product of a majority Federalist legislature designed to restrict criticism from the Jeffersonian Republicans in the impending election of 1800, however, this partisan measure invited opposition. Detractors developed arguments against the federal government's restriction of speech and press and articulated positive arguments for the role of freedom of speech and freedom of the press in self-governance by the people. As President, Jefferson pardoned those who had been convicted under the Sedition Act. The outrage against the Sedition Act did not render illegitimate the federal government's criminalization of sedition—it would pass a Sedition Act again in World War I—but it did set the tone of free speech discourse that would occur time and again in the nineteenth century in inviting the dynamic of repression and resistance.

Free Speech Theory outside the Courts

The common law doctrine gave way to more libertarian theories in a pattern of repression and response from radical groups. In stated efforts to maintain public peace and social order, state governments and the federal government passed laws and policies that restricted, silenced, and censored the expressions of groups that threatened the social order, whether they were challenges to slavery, gender norms, or employment law. In response, as affected individuals and groups sought free speech and free press in the public sphere, they mustered arguments that defended their right to freedom of speech and press against government suppression.

As tensions over slavery mounted in the nineteenth century, the federal government sought to avoid deciding on the issue of slavery and to avoid talking about it altogether. Congress, federal agencies, state governments—both north and south—and citizen groups repressed the expression of the ideas that issued from the abolitionist movement. When technological advances allowed for a proliferation of newspapers and pamphlets, abolitionists printed their own literature and attempted to mail it to slave states to reach slaves. The Postmaster General deferred to slaveholding states that prohibited the dissemination of literature for fear of slave insurrection. The federal government supported these state laws with the Post Office Act of 1836, which held that the post office would refuse to deliver mail that was rendered criminal by state law. In the same year, abolitionist groups inundated Congress with petitions requesting it to address the abolition of slavery in the District of Columbia. The House of Representatives received the petitions but failed to discuss them in the notorious gag rule that was finally ended in 1844 after the persistent efforts of Rep. John Quincy Adams. Abolitionist newspapers were targets of anti-abolitionist mobs. The office of the Cincinnati newspaper, *Philanthropist,* was beset by mobs, and the printer Elijah Lovejoy lost his life defending his presses from mobs in Illinois in November 1837. In response to the multiple forms of suppression of speech, abolitionists responded with defenses of their right to the discussion of slavery in speech and in print. In addition to defending the liberty of slaves, they defended the liberty of abolitionists to express their positions. Abolitionists declared freedom of the speech and the press as natural rights, never relinquished to government, and necessary political rights for participating in self-government. The free exchange of ideas in newspapers, they argued, would allow for a flourishing of positions and the possibility of arriving at the truth. Although public opinion was initially against the abolitionists regarding the issue of slavery, public sentiment turned more sympathetic as the issues of freedom of speech and freedom of press emerged, altering the position of the abolitionist movement in American politics and centrally positioning protective theories of free speech and the press in the public discourse.

The abolitionist movement welcomed women in its ranks, providing them with a forum in the public sphere. Laws denied women the political rights of voting and jury service, whereas social norms dictated that they not speak in public. The practices of the abolitionist movement challenged those norms, with abolitionist meetings seating men and women, blacks and whites, together. Abolitionist women were enlisted as public speakers, violating the stricture against women speaking in public, provoking the charge that women were speaking in front of "promiscuous audiences." Forerunners included Frances "Fanny" Wright, who conducted a lecture series to much controversy in 1829. Maria Stewart, a freeborn black woman, was a well-known speaker in the early years of the abolitionist movement. In response to a public speaking tour by Sarah Grimke and Angelina Grimke, members of the Massachusetts Congregational clergy publicly expressed their chastisement.

The Grimke sisters responded with the development of a theory that recognized women's right to speech. In her letters written on the equality of the sexes, Sarah Grimke outlined women's equal rights with men by developing a rights theory in which all rights were granted by God. A government could not create or deny those rights that were between a woman and God. In making the case, Grimke asserted a place for women in free speech theory, but she also advanced modern free speech theory in arguing that freedom of speech was prepolitical and could not be denied to a citizen because of her gender. The common law doctrine, with its repression of speech for the purpose of public order, could not come between the natural rights of any individual and the Creator. A less visible development took place in the practices of women who collected signatures for petitions and sewed goods for sale, opportunities for women to redefine their political identity and to claim a space in political life.

The Civil War occasioned the deprivation of civil liberties of the abolitionists' opponents—those northern Democrats who declared themselves to be against the war and President Lincoln's policies. Clement Vallandingham, a former Ohio politician, was arrested in May 1863 for an antiwar speech he delivered at a political rally. A civilian, he was arrested by the United States military and denied habeas corpus, which had been suspended by Lincoln in 1861. Other Democrats were arrested for their dissent, and the military closed or threatened to close newspapers. In response, the Democratic newspaper, *Chicago Times,* claimed the freedom of the press, a right that preceded the Constitution that the federal government had no right to suppress. U.S. soldiers destroyed copies of the *Chicago Times,* an act that was reported by the *New York Tribune* as government suppression of the press. A series of newspaper stories, protest meetings, and party conventions pointed to the recognition that even opponents to abolition deserved the right to speak their opinion. Despite the government's explanation that civil liberties deserved less protection in time of rebellion, members of the public, abolitionists, and Democrats alike acknowledged the importance of the speech, even speech of the opposition, to democratic governing.

Free speech controversies also occupied the social reformers involved in the free love movement, which originated in the utopian communities of the 1820s and 1830s. Free love advocates challenged the conventions of gender norms and marriage. Early leaders Frances Wright and Robert Dale Owen worked for equality within marriage and reform in divorce laws. The later free love activist Victoria Woodhull provoked a free press controversy in 1872 when *Woodhull*

and Claflin's Weekly publicized the Beecher-Tilton Scandal, revealing an affair between Reverend Henry Ward Beecher and the wife of his friend, Theodore Tilton. Anthony Comstock had Woodhull arrested for sending obscene material through the mails, but a judge dismissed the charge, noting that the federal statute did not apply to newspapers. The Comstock Act (1873), which suppressed the trade and circulation of obscene literature and items deemed for immoral use, would subsequently target a wide variety of material considered obscene. The Comstock Act included literature about birth control in its prohibitions, a feature that would be fought out in the twentieth century. It was also instrumental in banning books such as *Lysistrata, The Canterbury Tales, Moll Flanders,* and *The Arabian Nights* from the mails. The National Defense Association, founded in 1878, provided a libertarian defense for those convicted under the Comstock Act, but the surveillance of the Comstock Act would linger into the twentieth century, and the Act remains part of American law. Prosecuted under the Comstock Act, Ezra Heywood, author of *Cupid's Yokes* (1876), claimed freedom of speech to be essential to the development of human autonomy. He sought to associate the earlier abolitionist movement with the free love and anarchy movements of his own time. His prosecution indicates the disconnect between the various radical movements of the nineteenth century. Although the radical social reform and workers' movements further contributed to the development of modern free speech theory, their theories of free speech became less sympathetic in the eyes of the law and the larger public.

Labor unions in the later decades of the nineteenth century exercised their right to speak. At the Haymarket rally in Chicago on May 4, 1886, in the midst of a nationwide strike over the eight-hour workday, various speakers spoke out for workers' rights and against the death of two workers at the hands of police at a strike the previous day. Members of anarchist groups distributed fliers for the rally, and Samuel Fielden, a member of the Socialist Labor Party, issued a speech urging workers to challenge and defy the law. Following his speech, a bomb was thrown into the crowd. Eight police officers would eventually die of wounds resulting from the bomb, and a riot ensued, with attendees killed and injured, as the police dispersed the crowd. Eight men were charged, not with throwing the bomb, but with criminal conspiracy. Four of them were eventually hanged. The Supreme Court foreclosed any question of the free speech rights of the speakers when it dismissed the petition for writ of error in *Spies v. Illinois* (1887).

The disputes over freedom of speech and freedom of the press at the end of the nineteenth century indicated that the struggle between the government's perceived need for order would continue to conflict with individuals' stated liberty requirements. Although these struggles would continue into the twentieth century, they would, eventually, fall under the purview of the courts. The nineteenth century remains notable for the public participation in defining and defending rights of speech and press.

KATHLEEN S. SULLIVAN

References and Further Reading

Curtis, Michael Kent. *Free Speech: 'The People's Darling Privilege': Struggles for Freedom of Expression in American History*. Durham: Duke, 2000.
Rabban, David M. *Free Speech in Its Forgotten Years*. New York: Cambridge University Press, 1997.
Zaeske, Susan, *Signatures of Citizenship: Petitioning, Antislavery, and Women's Political Identity*. Chapel Hill: The University of North Carolina Press, 2003.

Cases and Statutes Cited

Spies v. Illinois 123 U.S. 131 (1887)

See also **Abolitionist Movement; Comstock, Anthony**

FREEDOM OF SPEECH EXTENDED TO CORPORATIONS

Since 1791, the First Amendment's text has protected "the press." Today, the press often is owned by large corporations whose speech rights are protected by the First Amendment as if they were people rather than legally created, artificial entities.

The doctrine of corporate personhood dates back to 1886, when the U.S. Supreme Court held in *Santa Clara v. Southern Pacific* that the Fourteenth Amendment equal protection clause protects corporations just as it does persons. In 1936, the Court held in *Grosjean v. American Press Co.* that the corporate press was a "person" within the meaning of the Fourteenth Amendment equal protection and due processes clauses and that the tax at issue in the case "abridged the freedom of the press." Then, in 1978, the Court ruled in *First National Bank of Boston v. Bellotti* that corporations possess a First Amendment right of free speech. It wrote that speech about government affairs is "indispensable to decisionmaking in a democracy, and this is no less true because the speech comes from a corporation rather than an individual." It added that "[i]n cases where corporate speech has been denied the shelter of the First Amendment, there is no suggestion that the reason

was because a corporation rather than an individual or association was involved." Corporate speech in the form of truthful advertising about lawful products/services receives protection today under the commercial speech doctrine.

Corporate speech is now a "dominant discourse," as Herbert Schiller wrote. Corporations control the marketplace of ideas and, some argue, use the protection of free speech to ward off government attempts to regulate the content they propagate.

CLAY CALVERT

References and Further Reading

Allen, David S. "The First Amendment and the Doctrine of Corporate Personhood: Collapsing the Press-Corporation Distinction." *Journalism* 2 (2001): 255–278.
Schiller, Herbert I. *Information Inequality: The Deepening Social Crisis in America*. New York: Routledge, 1996.

Cases and Statutes Cited

First National Bank of Boston v. Bellotti, 435 U.S. 765 (1978)
Grosjean v. American Press Co., 297 U.S. 233 (1936)
Santa Clara County v. Southern Pacific Railroad Corp., 118 U.S. 394 (1886)

FREEDOM OF SPEECH IN BROADCASTING

Broadcasters enjoy free speech rights under the First Amendment, but not to the same degree as their colleagues in the print or online media.

One rationale for the differential treatment is that broadcasting—unlike other media in the United States—is licensed by the federal government. When Congress first addressed the licensing issue in the 1920s, it was decided that the government should not own the broadcast system in this country but instead should regulate it to ensure that broadcasters operate in the "public interest, convenience, and necessity."

At that time, broadcasters asked the government to intervene because the spectrum of available frequencies was limited, and amateurs too often usurped the airwaves space others had occupied. This scarcity of available spectrum space was another reason for government to step in and create some system of order. As the industry developed throughout the twentieth century, however, broadcasters grew weary of the government's interference in their operations. In the 1980s, Congress and the courts relaxed a number of the programming requirements on broadcasters, but some controversial content restrictions remain.

Broadcasters, for instance, may not air *indecent* material between 6:00 a.m. and 10:00 p.m. The United States Supreme Court has upheld that rule as it affects broadcasting, but has struck down a similar restriction as applied to the Internet. Print media face no such restrictions.

Likewise, in the political arena, broadcasters are required to provide equal opportunities for candidates to appear on the air. Print and online media have no similar space requirements.

ROBERT D. RICHARDS

References and Further Reading

Carter, T. Barton, *et al. The First Amendment and the Fifth Estate*. New York: Foundation Press, 1999.

Cases and Statutes Cited

Federal Communications Commission v. Pacifica, 438 U.S. 726 (1978)
Miami Herald Pub. Co. v. Tornillo, 418 U.S. 241 (1974)
Reno v. ACLU, 521 U.S. 844 (1997)
Communications Act of 1934, 47 U.S.C. § 315(a)
Radio Act of 1927, 44 Stat. 1162

See also **Broadcast Regulation; Cameras in the Courtroom; Communications Decency Act (1996); Fairness Doctrine; Federal Communications Commission;** *Miami Herald Publishing Co. v. Tornillo*, **418 U.S. 241 (1974);** *Red Lion Broadcasting Co. v. FCC*, **395 U.S. 367 (1969);** *Reno v. ACLU*, **521 U.S. 844 (1997)**

FREEDOM OF SPEECH: MODERN PERIOD (1917–PRESENT)

Introduction

The U.S. Supreme Court did not decide a case presenting a significant First Amendment free speech question until 1919. Since that time, however, the Court has decided a substantial number of free speech cases and in the process has developed a vast and complex array of legal doctrine that delineates the contours and dimensions of expression protected by the First Amendment. But not all of this doctrine is of equal importance. Consequently, the most prominent and significant doctrinal developments contained in the Court's post-1919 free speech decisions will be analyzed here.

In particular, the essay examines case law in which the Supreme Court developed doctrines that allow the government, in limited circumstances, to use the

criminal law to punish individuals for engaging in certain types of expression—especially that which is harshly critical of the current government and its policies. How protective the law is toward such speech is, in many respects, an accurate barometer of how protective the law is of expression in general. As Farber (2003, p. 57) explains: "[e]ver since governments have existed, they have used force to suppress their opponents and quell criticism. Tolerance for enemies of the established order, then, is the acid test for free speech."

In addition, this essay examines how the Court has developed what might be labeled a neutrality theory of the First Amendment—a theory premised on the idea that a democratic government should be significantly restricted from favoring particular ideas or viewpoints. The neutrality theory posits that constitutional democracies governed by free speech principles should be limited from coercing individuals into subscribing to government-endorsed ideas or views, as well as from enacting policies that systematically favor the private expression of such ideas and views. Nearly all aspects of the Court's current free speech doctrine—particularly that pertaining to time, place, and manner regulations—have been strongly influenced by the Court's deep aversion to content- and viewpoint-biased policies. Indeed, one could easily argue that content and viewpoint neutrality theory has become the central cog in the modern Supreme Court's understanding of the First Amendment—and that Amendment's place in the broader American constitutional regime.

Expression and the Incitement of Criminal Activity

The World War I Era

In the wake of WWI, the U.S. Supreme Court heard several cases involving First Amendment free speech issues. Not surprisingly, these cases dealt with left-wing, anti-war activists who had criticized foreign and defense policies of the U.S. government during WW I. In the first (and most famous) of these cases, *Schenck v. United States* (1919), the Court addressed whether the free speech clause prohibited the government from prosecuting the expressive activities of anti-war protesters pursuant to the Espionage Act of 1917. Charles Schenck had been charged with "attempting to cause insubordination...in the military and naval forces of the United States" (ibid) by mailing circulars critical of the draft to men who recently had been drafted. The document, which drew on the Thirteenth Amendment's prohibition against involuntary servitude, asserted that a conscript was "little better than a convict" and constituted "despotism in its worst form and [was] a monstrous wrong against humanity in the interest of Wall Street's chosen few" (ibid). However, although the document asked its recipients to "not submit to intimidation" and to "assert [their] rights," it did not specifically ask anyone to act violently or to violate the law (ibid).

A unanimous Supreme Court held, in an opinion written by Justice Oliver Wendell Holmes, that Schenck's conviction did not violate the First Amendment. Although the First Amendment does more than simply prohibit prior restraints on private speech, the Court concluded that it does not provide absolute freedom to expressive activity. Instead, the Court held that the government could regulate speech that presents a "clear and present danger" of bringing "about the substantive evils that Congress has a right to prevent" (ibid). Justice Holmes, having had significant experience with the criminal law as a judge on the Massachusetts Supreme Judicial Court, compared Schenck's expressive activities to the law of criminal attempts. He explained that the government has a right to intervene and punish individuals for expressive activities if those activities are dangerously close to eliciting illegal activities (such as refusing to report for duty when drafted). Justice Holmes noted that it "is a question of proximity and degree" (ibid) as to when the government can intervene and punish individuals on the grounds that they are inciting criminal activity. Moreover, whether the government's intervention is constitutional will depend on the context in which the expression occurs. As Justice Holmes explained, "the character of every act depends upon the circumstances in which it is done," and that Schenck's expression would have been protected by the First Amendment "in many places and in ordinary times" (ibid).

One week after the *Schenck* decision was announced, the Court handed down decisions in *Frohwerk v. United States* and *Debs v. United States*, both of which also involved prosecutions under the Espionage Act of 1917. In *Frohwerk,* a unanimous Court upheld the defendant's conviction of conspiring to disrupt the war effort by disseminating material critical of the national government's draft policy in a Missouri-based German language newspaper. Similarly, a unanimous Court upheld the conviction of Eugene Debs on the grounds that a speech he had delivered to the 1918 state convention of the Ohio Socialist Party constituted a clear and present danger to the nation's war effort. Justice Holmes approvingly explained in *Debs* that the trial judge had instructed the jury to convict Debs only if "the words used had as their natural tendency and reasonably probable effect to obstruct the recruiting service...and unless the defendant had the specific intent to do so in his mind." Although the Court interpreted the statute to impose a *scienter* requirement, this and later cases often assumed that such requirements were satisfied if the speech in question had a reasonable tendency to produce the substantive harm that the government wanted to prevent.

In both *Frohwerk* and *Debs* the Court concluded that the government had satisfied the requirements of the clear and present danger test. However, as the quote from Justice Holmes' *Debs* opinion illustrates, it is certainly questionable whether the Court was sufficiently demanding in its evaluation of the nexus between the speech act for which the defendants were convicted and the illegal action (that is, substantive harm) that the government was seeking to prevent. For example, Justice Holmes indicates that the nexus was satisfied in *Frohwerk* because "it is impossible to say that it might not have been found that the circulation of the paper was in quarters where a little breath would be enough to kindle a flame." Quite simply, this language does not have much in common with the notion that the expression must present a "clear and present danger" of producing illegal activities.

It was not until the Court decided *Abrams v. United States* (1919) that we find a member of the Court casting a dissenting vote in favor of free speech. In *Abrams*, seven members of the Court cited *Schenck* and its progeny and concluded that Abrams could be punished under the amended Espionage Act of 1918. Abrams had distributed circulars on the streets of New York City and was charged with acting to "'incite, provoke, and encourage resistance to the United States' during World War I, and of conspiring 'to urge, incite, and advocate curtailment of production [of] ordnance and ammunition, necessary [to] the prosecution of the war'" (Sullivan and Gunther, 2003, p. 19). The *Abrams* majority concluded that Abrams intended to disrupt the U.S. military forces because that would be the natural tendency of his expression, and that "[m]en must be held to have intended, and to be accountable for, the effects which their acts were likely to produce." So much for the idea that a *scienter* requirement would be a major impediment to government prosecutions of speech acts.

The dissenting votes in *Abrams* were cast by Justices Brandeis and Holmes. In this instance, we see the justices heretofore most responsible for the development of the clear and present danger test conclude that the majority erred in its application. First, Holmes and Brandeis argued that the majority's conception of what constitutes the requisite level of intent under the statute was not sufficiently demanding. Instead, Holmes argued that intent to disrupt the war effort by curtailing the production of munitions is satisfied only if the "aim to produce it is the proximate motive of the specific [expressive] act." Second, the dissenters argued that the government could prosecute only those expressive acts that "present danger of immediate evil or an intent to bring it about," neither of which, they believed, was present in this case. As Holmes explains, "Nobody can suppose that the surreptitious publishing of a silly leaflet by an unknown man, without more, would present any immediate danger that its opinions would hinder the success of the government arms or have any appreciable tendency to do so" (*Abrams*). Some scholars argue that Holmes modified his views about the requirements of the clear and present danger test—by requiring that the danger be immediately and dangerously proximate to the substantive harm targeted by the statute—between the time the Court decided *Schenck*, *Frohwerk*, and *Debs* and the time it decided *Abrams* (Sullivan and Gunther, 2003, p. 23–24).

As the Supreme Court was developing the clear and present danger test, lower federal court judge Learned Hand was developing his own test for when the government could prosecute individuals for inciting illegal activity. According to Hand, such convictions could occur only in those instances when the speaker "directly advocated" illegal activity (*Masses Publishing Co. v. Patten*). Hand rejected contextual tests that allowed the government to regulate expression that had a tendency to incite others to engage in illegal activity. Hand did not think that the Justice Holmes's *Abrams* version of the clear and present danger test provided adequate protection for expression. Hand feared that contextual tests of the ilk used in *Schenck* and *Abrams* were too easily manipulated by prosecutors and judges, especially during periods of social and political unrest. Instead, Hand believed that direct advocacy of law violation was the appropriate standard. Hand explained that as long as "one stops short of urging upon others that it is their duty or their interest to resist the law, [then] it seems to me one should not be held to have attempted to cause its violation" (*Masses*). This test, which came to be known as "Hand's 'incitement' approach" (Sullivan and Gunther, 2003, p. 28), was not used by the Supreme Court until 1969, when the Court incorporated it into the modern test for incitement of illegal activity.

The Red Scare Era

During the red scare period of U.S. history, the Court decided several additional cases involving speech and

criminal attempts and conspiracies. The most famous of these is *Gitlow v. New York* (1925). Benjamin Gitlow, who was involved with the publication of *The Left Wing Manifesto,* was prosecuted for violating a New York statute that, in part, authorized the criminal punishment of one who "advises or teaches the duty necessity, or propriety of overthrowing or overturning organized government by force or violence" (Sullivan and Gunther, 2003, p. 29). Although the majority opinion explained that "[t]here was no evidence of any effect resulting from the publication and circulation of the *Manifesto*" (ibid), the Court nevertheless upheld Gitlow's conviction. The Court noted that this case was different from the 1919 free speech cases, because Gitlow was charged with violating a state law that expressly forbade the use of certain language and the expression of certain ideas. In contrast, the 1919 cases involved prosecutions under statutes that only prohibited certain actions (for example, disrupting the war effort or the production of munitions); unlike the law involved in *Gitlow*, the 1919 statutes did not codify certain language or ideas that could not be articulated. The defendants in the 1919 cases were prosecuted because their expression was deemed to constitute an attempt to complete one of the acts prohibited by the criminal law.

As a result of this difference, the Court argued that it should be deferential toward the state legislature and its decision to statutorily proscribe certain types of expression. Consequently, the *Gitlow* majority rejected the notion that the clear and present danger test was applicable, and instead developed what came to be known as the "bad tendency test." In language quite similar to that used by Justice Holmes in *Debs*, the majority explained that a "single revolutionary spark may kindle a fire that, smoldering for a time, may burst into a sweeping and destructive conflagration," and that the government can legitimately punish the defendant's "specific utterance...if its natural tendency and probable effect was to bring about the substantive evil which the legislative body might prevent" (*Gitlow*). The Gitlow majority did not require the government to provide evidence demonstrating that the *Left Wing Manifesto* caused anyone to take steps toward overthrowing the government by force and violence or that the publication created a clear and present danger of inciting individuals to take such steps. The fact that Gitlow had engaged in expression that the state legislature considered dangerous was enough to sustain his conviction. Indeed, given Gitlow's expression, his conviction probably would have been upheld by the Court if it had used Judge Learned Hand's direct advocacy test—a test that Hand thought was more protective of speech than the clear and present danger test. In any event, *Gitlow* did expand speech protections in the United States by holding—for the first time—that free speech was a fundamental right entitled to protection from state governments by the Fourteenth Amendment.

In their dissenting opinion in *Gitlow*, as well as their concurring opinion in *Whitney v. California* (a 1927 case in which the Court upheld convictions pursuant to a California statute similar to the one involved in *Gitlow*), Justices Holmes and Brandeis argued that the Court should apply the clear and present danger test in all free speech cases involving the incitement of criminal activity. The two justices, who had worked since *Abrams* to strengthen the speech protective capacities of the clear and present danger test, believed that only that speech that had a high probability (clear) of producing imminent (present) violations of serious laws (danger) could be subjected to criminal punishment by the government. In his concurring opinion in *Whitney*, Justice Brandeis explained that "[w]henever the fundamental rights of free speech and assembly are alleged to have been invaded, it must remain open to a defendant to present the issue whether there actually did exist at the time a clear danger; whether the danger, if any, was imminent; and whether the evil apprehended was one so substantial as to justify the stringent restriction interposed by the legislature."

The World War II and McCarthy Era

Despite the economic and military crises faced by the United States in the two decades after *Gitlow*, the Supreme Court became, somewhat surprisingly, more protective of free speech. For example, in *De Jonge v. Oregon* (1937) and *Herdon v. Lowry* (1937) the Court reversed, on free speech grounds, convictions under state laws prohibiting individuals from organizing to incite or attempting to incite others to violate the law (Sullivan and Gunther, 2003, p. 39). In those cases, as well as others (see *Thornhill v. Alabama* and *Cantwell v. Connecticut*), it seemed that the Court was using a test similar to the clear and present danger test. What is not clear is whether this shift toward speech protection was because the ideological predispositions of the justices toward free speech issues were becoming more liberal or whether the Court was beginning to see its role as one revolving around the protection of rights essential for democratic government (see footnote four, *Carolene Products Co. v. United States*). Whichever the case, free speech reached a new high water mark in the late 1930s and throughout the 1940s.

The case that best captures this libertarian perspective toward freedom of speech came near the end of

this period in *Terminiello v. Chicago* (1949). Father Arthur Terminiello, a Catholic priest who one might characterize as a Christian nationalist, was charged by municipal authorities for disturbing the peace as a result of a speech he delivered to a capacity crowd of 800 sympathizers in a Chicago auditorium. Terminiellos's speech was filled with negative references to racial, ethnic, religious, and political groups, and for these and other reasons relating to his views, a hostile crowd of more than 1,000 people had convened in the streets outside the auditorium. The crowd, which Terminiello on several occasions disparaged in his speech, soon grew restive and began throwing stones, bricks, and stink bombs. The police feared that they were losing control of the situation and arrested Terminiello for inciting the crowd to act disorderly.

Over four dissenting votes—and a passionate dissenting opinion from Justice Jackson—five members of the Supreme Court overturned Terminiello's conviction. Writing for the majority, Justice Douglas argued that speech is "protected against censorship or punishment, unless shown likely to produce a clear and present danger of a serious substantive evil that rises far above public inconvenience, annoyance, or unrest." Given the circumstances of this case, especially the fact that violent acts had already begun to occur—seemingly as a result of Terminiello's speech—the majority's conclusion demonstrates that its members subscribed to something akin to Justice Holmes and Brandeis's *Abrams-Gitlow-Whitney* conceptualization of the clear and present danger test. Thus, entering the 1950s, it seemed that the Court was poised to be very protective of free speech claims.

But that was not to be. As a result of rapid turnover in the Court's membership, and the rise of Joseph McCarthy's efforts to expose alleged Communist sympathizers within the United States, the Court became much less inclined to question government regulation of expressive activities. For example, in 1952, the Court upheld a disorderly conduct conviction for expressive behavior that, compared with the circumstances in *Terminiello*, seemed quite tame (*Feiner v. New York*, 1951). Soon thereafter, the Court indicated that it was in no mood to protect individuals who were critical of the government and who were expressly advocating that it be violently overthrown and replaced with a socialist state.

The preeminent case of this era is *Dennis v. United States* (1952). In *Dennis,* the Court upheld the *Smith Act* prosecution of Eugene Dennis and other upperechelon members of the U.S. Communist Party. The *Smith Act*, passed by Congress in 1940, was similar to the New York statute upheld by the Court in *Gitlow*. However, the one distinction was that the Smith Act made it "unlawful for any person to *attempt* to commit, or to *conspire* to" advocate—or organize for the purpose of advocating—the overthrow of the U.S. government by force and violence (*Dennis*). Because criminal attempts and conspiracies are incomplete offenses in which the substantive harm has not yet occurred, this is not a trivial distinction. Indeed, as Justice Black noted in his *Dennis* dissent:

> At the outset I want to emphasize what the crime involved in this case is, and what it is not. These petitioners were not charged with an attempt to overthrow the Government. They were not charged with overt acts of any kind designed to overthrow the Government. They were not even charged with saying anything or writing anything designed to overthrow the Government. The charge was that they agreed to assemble and to talk and publish certain ideas at a later date: The indictment is that they conspired to organize the Communist Party and to use speech or newspapers and other publications in the future to teach and advocate the forcible overthrow of the Government. No matter how it is worded, this is a virulent form of prior censorship of speech and press, which I believe the First Amendment forbids.

Unfortunately for Black, six members of the Court did not see it this way.

Instead, the Court upheld the *Smith Act* prosecutions by purportedly relying on the clear and present danger test. In reality, however, the Court used on a watered-down version of the clear and present danger test that has subsequently become known as the "clear and probable danger" test. This test, first articulated by Judge Learned Hand when the *Dennis* case was before the Court of Appeals for the Second Circuit, posited that the government could punish conspiracies that organize to advocate the violent overthrow of the government if "the gravity of the 'evil,' discounted by its improbability, justifies such invasion of free speech as is necessary to avoid the danger" (183 F.2d at 212). Hand's clear and probable danger test is, like the Holmes/Brandeis clear and present danger test, one that is based on context. However, Judge Hand's clear and probable danger test allows judges and prosecutors to balance—or trade-off—the serious danger, high probability, and imminence prongs of the clear and present danger test. In other words, if the danger is severe enough (for example, overthrow of civil government by force), then it does not need to be something that is likely to imminently occur. Similarly, if the danger that the government wants to avoid is likely to imminently occur, then the danger does not need to be serious. In contrast, Holmes and Brandeis argued that the government had to meet each element (severity, probability, imminence) of the clear and present danger test in their strictest forms.

From the 1960s to the Present

Beginning in the late 1950s and throughout the 1960s, the Court became less inclined to uphold convictions of individuals either because they advocated (or were organizing to advocate) the overthrow of the government by force and violence or because they expressed support for violating the criminal law (see, Sullivan and Gunther, 2003, pp. 47–50). But during this period the Court was unable (or unwilling) to articulate a test to govern First Amendment challenges to such prosecutions. In most cases it engaged in a form of ad hoc balancing, whereby it examined the government's interests vis-á-vis the speaker's interests and ruled in favor of that party whose interests were deemed greater.

This situation came to an end, however, when the Court announced in *Brandenburg v. Ohio* (1969) that the government could not punish individuals for speech advocating illegal activity "except where such advocacy is directed to inciting or producing imminent lawless action and is likely to incite or produce such action." Some have argued that this test combines elements of the Holmes/Brandeis clear and present danger test with Hand's direct advocacy test (Sullivan and Gunther, 2003). The test requires that individuals advocate law violation (direct advocacy) and that the danger be probable/likely and imminent (the latter two being two of the three elements of the clear and present danger test). It is unclear, however, whether any advocacy of law violation qualifies, or whether the law violation must be one that poses a serious and substantial danger (which was deemed necessary under the Holmes/Brandeis conception of the clear and present danger test). Although the *Bradenburg* test has been used by the Court for the past thirty-six years in incitement cases, the number of such cases has been sparse. As a result, it is not fully clear how the current Court conceptualizes the test, how protective it is of free speech, or how firmly entrenched it is in First Amendment law.

Freedom of Expression, Democratic Theory, and Government Neutrality

The Relation of Free Speech to Democratic Government

Another crucial doctrinal development since 1919 is the Court's conclusion that the First Amendment's free speech clause imposes content and viewpoint neutrality requirements on the government. In a plethora of cases decided since the mid-twentieth century, the Court has argued that free speech is integrally related to democratic government. For democracy to work correctly—for the citizenry to engage in effective self-rule—the people must be afforded ample freedom to discuss the merits and demerits of all types of political, social, and economic ideas. In most instances, public policies will be tailored around those ideas that, in the end, are endorsed by the largest segment of the population. Democracy does not mean much, and probably does not truly exist, if the citizenry is not allowed to debate ideas and then enact policies that are consistent with the views garnering majority support. Of course, democracy does not mean the majority should be allowed to ensconce its views into public policy in all instances, but it does mean that in most situations there is a presumption in favor of allowing such a result. To be sure, democracy is often defined as majority rule with minority rights. But clearly there must be significant latitude for the former if a regime is going to be considered democratic.

However, allowing free and fair debate often comes hard to those in power. After all, those in power typically do not want to lose their grip on the levers of government control. Therefore, dominant groups—and their representatives in government—often have an incentive to maintain their authority by preventing others from criticizing their policies, actions, and agendas. Indeed, these tendencies are what led to the long line of cases pertaining to the incitement of illegal activity that was discussed earlier. Current laws normally represent the choices of those in power, and it is a potential threat to their status if outsiders are allowed to advocate that those laws be intentionally violated.

But there are more subtle techniques available to those in power to prolong their control. More subtle methods, that is, than crushing those who advocate illegal activity. For example, the dominant governing coalition could decide to enact policies that directly promote the ideological worldview and political orthodoxy to which it subscribes. These policies, if successful, will persuade members of the citizenry—perhaps even those who were initially not supportive of the dominant coalition's ideology—that the current regime's ideology is correct and (as a corollary) that its representatives in government ought to be retained at the next election. In *West Virginia State Board of Education v. Barnette* (1943), a majority of the Supreme Court argued that the state of West Virginia was engaging in just such an effort and that it had contravened core principles underlying the First Amendment.

The West Virginia state school board had enacted a policy requiring students, at the commencement of each day's public school classes, to rise and recite the pledge of allegiance while offering a stiff-arm salute to the American flag. Students who refused to engage in this activity could be suspended from school, and their parents could be subjected to fines. In *Barnette*, the parents of two school children challenged the state's pledge policy by arguing that it violated the tenets of their religious beliefs—and thus the First Amendment's free exercise clause. However, rather than relying on the free exercise clause, the Supreme Court—which at the time was a staunch supporter of the First Amendment—concluded that the state's policy violated the free speech interests of the school children.

In a stirring opinion for the Court, Justice Robert Jackson argued that the free speech clause protects a person's right to both speak and to remain silent. The government, according to Jackson, cannot force individuals to articulate support for or subscribe to any particular beliefs, ideologies, or orthodoxies. This principle, Jackson explained, is one of the primary differences between democratic and totalitarian governments, and that the latter have frequently resorted to extreme measures in their efforts to induce political consent. In his *Barnette* opinion Justice Jackson wrote that "[t]hose who begin coercive elimination of dissent soon find themselves exterminating dissenters. Compulsory unification of opinion achieves only the unanimity of the graveyard." In subsequent decisions, the Supreme Court has affirmed its commitment to prevent the government, in most circumstances, from forcing individuals to express their support for particular political, social, religious, or economic viewpoints (see *Wooley v. Maynard*, 1977, where the Court upheld the right of a New Hampshire resident to cover the motto "Live Free or Die" on his vehicle's license plate).

First Amendment First Principles: Content and Viewpoint Neutrality

One can argue that the *Barnette* case constitutes the earliest doctrinal foundations for the Supreme Court's conclusion that the First Amendment requires government regulations touching on private expression be content and viewpoint neutral. What the Court feared in *Barnette*, and what it fears in the presence of any content- and viewpoint-biased regulations of expression, is the possibility that the government is attempting to tilt the free speech playing field so that the government's preferred views will "win" the battle in the marketplace of ideas. If such behavior is allowed, then the ruling majority coalition can tailor government policies to inculcate its ideological worldview among members of the public—thus orchestrating its continued political support and, ultimately, perpetuating its rule of the regime. Such machinations smell more of fascism than democracy.

To challenge such efforts, the Supreme Court has developed the content and viewpoint neutrality doctrines. The former looks unfavorably on speech regulations that limit the types of subjects and topics that can be discussed in a particular setting. For example, in *R.A.V. v. City of St. Paul* (1992), the Supreme Court concluded that a St. Paul, Minnesota, hate speech ordinance was unconstitutional, because it was content biased. The *R.A.V.* majority noted that the ordinance only prohibited hate speech pertaining to "race, color, creed, religion, or gender." The law was content biased because it did not prohibit all types of hate speech. However, during that same Term the Court upheld a law that the each justice agreed was content biased. The policy being challenged in *Burson v. Freeman* (1992) prohibited individuals from soliciting votes or displaying and distributing campaign paraphernalia within 100 feet of a polling place entrance. The law was upheld because the Court concluded that the state had a compelling state interest in promoting the integrity, fairness, and accuracy of elections, as well as in protecting the citizen's fundamental right to vote. Moreover, the policy was narrowly tailored to further those objectives.

Viewpoint neutrality doctrine is concerned with regulations that favor particular viewpoints about a particular subject or topic. For example, a regulation that allowed supporters (but not opponents) of the nation's defense policy speak in a public park would be a prime example of a viewpoint-biased law. Similarly, in 1989 and 1990, the Supreme Court concluded that state and federal flag desecration laws were viewpoint biased—and thus unconstitutional (see *Texas v. Johnson*, 1989 and *United States v. Eichman*, 1990). The Court argued that the only government interests being furthered by these laws were those pertaining to the sanctity and image of the flag and the government's desire to prohibit its disrespectful treatment. After all, neither law punished those who burned a flag in a respectful and dignified manner (for example, to dispose of a soiled flag). Punishment only resulted if the flag's desecration was disrespectful and likely to anger those who witnessed the event. Clearly, the application of the laws hinged on the views being conveyed by the person burning the flag.

The Supreme Court considers problematic both content- and viewpoint-biased regulation of expressive activities, and the presence of either typically results in the policy being declared unconstitutional. However, the justices consider viewpoint bias the worst of the two, because in that instance the government is openly seeking to promote one side of a political debate. Consequently, as of 2005, the Supreme Court has never upheld a viewpoint-biased regulation of expressive activity. In fact, even in those instances when the government is regulating a form of expression not considered entitled to significant First Amendment protection (for example, obscenity, libel, fighting words), or when it enacts an otherwise legitimate time, place, and manner regulation (for example, constraints on the use of sound trucks), the government will normally encounter insurmountable First Amendment obstacles if it has created a content- or viewpoint-biased regulatory scheme. The content and viewpoint neutrality doctrines, along with the Court's larger effort to curb government attempts to manipulate the chorus of voices in the marketplace of ideas, represent bedrock principles of the Supreme Court's interpretation of the First Amendment in the modern era.

MARK KEMPER

References and Further Reading

Farber, Daniel A. *The First Amendment*. 2nd Ed. New York: Foundation Press, 2003.

Sullivan, Kathleen, and Gerald Gunther. *First Amendment Law*. 2nd Ed. New York: Foundation Press, 2003.

Cases and Statutes Cited

Abrams v. United States 250 U.S. 616 (1919)
Brandenburg v. Ohio 395 U.S. 444 (1969)
Burson v. Freeman 504 U.S. 191 (1992)
Cantwell v. Connecticut 310 U.S. 296 (1940)
Carolene Products Co. v. United States 304 U.S. 144 (1937)
De Jonge v. Oregon 299 U.S. 353 (1937)
Debs v. United States 249 U.S. 211 (1919)
Dennis v. United States 341 U.S. 494 (1951)
Feiner v. New York 340 U.S. 315 (1951)
Frohwerk v. United States 249 U.S. 204 (1919)
Gitlow v. New York 268 U.S. 652 (1925)
Herdon v. Lowry 301 U.S. 242 (1937)
Masses Publishing Co. v. Patten 244 Fed. 535 (S.D.N.Y., 1917)
R.A.V. v. City of St. Paul 505 U.S. 377 (1992)
Schenck v. United States 249 U.S. 47 (1919)
Terminiello v. Chicago 337 U.S. 1 (1949)
Texas v. Johnson 491 U.S. 397 (1989)
Thornhill v. Alabama 310 U.S. 88 (1940)
United States v. Eichman 496 U.S. 310 (1990)
West Virginia State Board of Education v. Barnette 319 U.S. 624 (1943)
Whitney v. California 274 U.S. 357 (1927)
Wooley v. Maynard 430 U.S. 705 (1977)

FREEDOM OF THE PRESS: MODERN PERIOD (1917–PRESENT)

Freedom of the press is a work in progress. The U.S. Constitution's First Amendment provides that the U.S. Congress shall make no law abridging freedom of the press. State constitutions predating the adoption of the Bill of Rights in 1791 provide similar protection. Nevertheless, press freedom had limited scope and meaning when the United States entered World War I in 1917. At the time, courts and the vast majority of legal scholars held the view that the press clause protected only against government censorship, or prior restraint. Government, however, could rightfully punish after publication, as English jurist Sir William Blackstone (1723–1780) noted in his influential *Commentaries on the Laws of England*.

In June 1917, Congress passed the Espionage Act. The Act targeted, among other activities, the mailing of materials advocating treason, insurrection, or resistance to U.S. laws. The following year, Congress amended it with the Sedition Act of 1918. The Sedition Act criminalized statements intended to provoke or encourage resistance to the war effort. Many states passed similar statutes, resulting in more than 2,000 prosecutions and more than 1,000 convictions under federal and state laws. The repressive laws were part of the overall government attack on civil liberties during our nation's first red scare (1917–1920).

Sometimes, government repression breeds unanticipated results. Because several defendants appealed their convictions to the U.S. Supreme Court, some of the justices—notably Oliver Wendell Holmes, Jr. (1841–1935) and Louis D. Brandeis (1856–1941)—reexamined their theories about dissent and national security. (Similarly, during this era, which included the Palmer Raids, the American Civil Liberties Union was formed.)

But post-WWI defendants did not benefit from the justices' emerging theories on free press and free speech. The Court upheld the convictions of defendants in cases involving leafleting and periodicals: *Schenck v. U. S.*, 249 U.S. 47 (1919), *Frohwerk v. U. S.*, 249 U.S. 204 (1919), *Abrams v. U.S.*, 250 U.S. 616 (1919), and *Gitlow v. New York*, 268 U.S. 652 (1925). (At the same time, in *Schenck*, Holmes, writing for a unanimous court, said a person might be convicted of a conspiracy to obstruct recruiting by mere words of persuasion. He said, "free speech would not protect a man in falsely shouting fire in a theater and causing a panic," a now well-worn phrase. He also used the phrase clear and present danger, an expression that has found a place in popular culture.

Holmes also delivered the opinion in *Frohwerk v. U.S.* He acknowledged that the circulation of the German-language newspaper in question was too small to have an impact on recruiting. Nevertheless, he said, the paper posed a threat to national security because it "represented a little breath that could 'kindle a flame' in the 'tinder box'" of the Germany community…"

A Clear and Present Danger

That summer, intellectuals whom Holmes respected took issue with his view of the appropriate limits of government authority to punish subversive advocacy. Law professors Zechariah Chafee (1885–1957) at Harvard and Ernst Freund (1864–1932) at the University of Chicago and political scientist Harold Laski (1893–1950), also at Harvard, sharply criticized Holmes' reasoning in *Schenck* and *Frohwerk* in articles published in the *New Republic* and *Harvard Law Review*, letters and in conversation. Laski, Chafee, and Holmes met for tea and discussion on July 23. It is not known what they said, but Holmes' First Amendment position took a libertarian turn that October in *Abrams v. United States*. Seven justices upheld the convictions of Russian immigrant Jacob Abrams and others for circulating leaflets urging opposition to the war. Their writings posed a clear and present danger, the majority found.

But Holmes and Brandeis dissented, setting the Court on a decades-long search to establish a test to judge the point at which inflammatory words posed a danger to national security and community safety sufficient to justify state punishment. In *Abrams*, Holmes contended that the First Amendment protected the expression of political opinions "unless they so imminently threaten immediate interference with the lawful and pressing purposes of the law that an immediate check is required to save the country." Holmes also first articulated what he said was a core value of the First Amendment, the marketplace theory of ideas, "that the best test of truth is the power of the thought to get itself accepted in the competition of the market…." The free expression theory undergirded much of the Court's free press-free speech rulings in the 1960s and 1970s and has been invoked by proponents of broadcast deregulation.

Congress repealed parts of the espionage and sedition laws in 1921. Much of the Espionage Act remains in Title 18 U.S.C. 793, 794. (Fifty years later, the federal government unsuccessfully argued before the Court that the *New York Times* violated Title 18 U.S.C. 793, 794 by publishing the Pentagon Papers in *New York Times Co. v. United States*, 403 U.S. 713 (1971).

In the 1930s, a majority of the Court clung to the bad tendency test. By the early 1950s, however, a majority applied various incarnations of the clear and present danger test. Finally, in *Brandenburg v. Ohio*, 395 U.S. 444 (1969), the justices developed a doctrine combining Holmes and Brandeis's immediacy component with a requirement that expression must incite unlawful action to justify government restriction. The serious and imminent threat test is substantially more protective of subversive expression than any of the clear and present danger variants; some scholars contend it is yet another variation of the clear and present danger test. In the first decade of the twenty-first century, the *Brandenburg* serious and imminent doctrine remains the test for determining the constitutional limits on laws that punish political speech.

For the most part, the *Brandenburg* test also has protected the entertainment media against liability in incitement lawsuits—wrongful death and other kinds of negligence actions seeking monetary damages. Starting in the mid-1970s, such incitement lawsuits contended, for example, that disk jockey banter, sexually and violently explicit Rock lyrics, on-air stunts, and graphically vicious movie scenes instructed, urged, or inspired a family member to commit crimes leading toward death. The overwhelming number of the suits failed because appeals courts required that plaintiffs show specific intent to promote criminal activity and a direct causal link between exposure to words and resulting deaths.

But the U.S. Circuit Court of Appeals for the Eleventh Circuit allowed a jury award to stand against a magazine publisher in *Braun v. Soldier of Fortune Magazine*, 968 F.2d 1110 (1992). The appeals court ruled that an advertisement placed in *Soldier of Fortune Magazine* by a gun-for-hire offering his services to kidnap and murder was an obvious offer of criminal activity. The Court declined to review the ruling. In *Rice v. Paladin*, 128 F. 3d 233 (4th Circuit 1997), cert. denied, 523 U.S. 1074 (1998), the U.S. Circuit Court of Appeals for the Fourth Circuit reversed a grant of summary judgment favoring a book publisher and sent an aiding and abetting lawsuit back to trial. The appeals court said the publisher had stipulated that he had intended that "the book would immediately be used by criminals and would-be criminals in the solicitation, planning, and commission of murder...." The Court declined to hear the publisher's appeal....

Prior Restraint

Government may impose prior restraints under certain conditions. In *Near v. Minnesota*, 283 U.S. 697 (1931), the leading Court ruling on prior restraint, Chief Justice Charles Evans Hughes held that prior restraints are legitimate to prevent the obstruction of military recruiting, the dissemination of troop locations, transport dates and numbers, incitements of violence, and publication of obscenity. In the Pentagon Papers case, the *Near* doctrine protected the right of the *New York Times* to continue to publish classified government papers. Journalists and civil libertarians hailed *Near* and the *Pentagon Papers* rulings as major victories for press freedom.

In *Snepp v. U.S.*, 444 U.S. 507 (1980), the Court ruled that nondisclosure agreements requiring former CIA agents from publishing without government approval were legitimate prior restraints. The Court also ruled that public school officials have the authority to impose prior restraints on student newspapers in *Hazelwood School District v. Kuhlmeier*, 484 U.S. 260 (1988). Government's authority to license broadcasters; to limit public protest by time, place, and manner; and court injunctions to prevent violation of copyright laws are other forms of permissible prior restraints.

Sexual Expression

When does sexual expression become obscene? In 1917, such a determination was based on the *Hicklin* rule established in a British Parliamentary measure in 1868 and adopted by courts in the United States. The rule imposed a version of the highly restrictive bad tendency test; materials that had a tendency to deprave and corrupt minds open to immoral influences could be banned as obscene. *Hicklin* remained the leading test of obscenity until U.S. Judge John Woosley's ruling in U.S. v. *One Book Called "Ulysses,"* 5.Supp. 182 (S.D.N.Y.1933) A book is obscene, the judge said, only when it arouses lust in a person with average sexual instincts, rather than to minds open to immoral influences such as abnormal adults and children as the *Hicklin* rule required. Woosley ruled that James Joyce's *Ulysses*, now acclaimed as a literary masterpiece, was not obscene.

In 1959, the Court handed down its first opinion on obscenity in *U.S. v. Roth*, 354 U.S. 476 (1957), establishing a nationwide standard. Justice William Brennan (1906–1997) fashioned the following test for obscenity: "whether to the average person, applying contemporary standards, the dominant theme of the material taken as a whole appeals to prurient interest." Brennan also declared that obscenity enjoys no protection under the law because it is "devoid of redeeming social importance."

Over the course of sixteen years, the Court wrestled with its definition of obscenity until it reached consensus in *Miller v. California*, 413 U.S. 15 (1973). Under the *Miller* guidelines—still the predominate test for obscenity—a judge or jury must weigh whether the "average person, applying contemporary community standards" would find that a work in its entirety appeals to prurient interests; whether the work depicts patently offensive sexual conduct; and whether it lacks serious literary, artistic, political, or scientific value.

Miller did not put to rest legal efforts to redefine obscenity. Feminists led by novelist Andrea Dworkin and law professor Catharine McKinnon waged an assault on pornography, persuading the Indianapolis–Marion County City–County Council to pass an ordinance banning pornography as sex-based discrimination. The U.S. Court of Appeals for the Seventh Circuit struck down the ordinance as unconstitutional in *American Booksellers Association, Inc. v. Hudnut*, 771 F.2d 323 (1985). In *New York v. Ferber*, 458 U.S. 747 (1982), the Court placed the production and sale of child pornography outside the First Amendment's protection.

Starting in the mid-1990s, the U.S. Congress pursued several mostly unsuccessful efforts to censor adult entertainment in cyberspace. The Court, for example, struck down two provisions of the Communications Decency Act (CDA) in *Reno v. ACLU*, 521 U.S. 844 (1997), ruling that the Internet was entitled to a level of First Amendment protection historically enjoyed by print. Two decades after *Ferber*, the Court—acknowledging that computer technology allows one to make realistic human images without the use of live models—ruled the Child Pornography Prevention Act of 1996 unconstitutional. In *Ashcroft v. Free Speech Coalition*, 535 U.S. 234 (2002), Justice Anthony M. Kennedy ruled that child sexual abuse recorded in child pornography is not the same as the expression of the idea of child sexuality created by digital technology.

In *American Civil Liberties Union v. Ashcroft*, 535 U.S. 564 (2004), the Court affirmed a lower court finding that the Child Online Protection Act (COPA) violated the First Amendment. Earlier, the Court ruled the Children's Internet Protection Act (CIPA) constitutional in *U.S. v. American Library Association*, 539 U.S. 194 (2003). CIPA requires public libraries to place filters on computers to prevent children from accessing adult content.

Meanwhile, by one count, the number of pornographic Web pages grew from fourteen million in 1998 to 420 million within five years. In 2004, it was estimated that Americans spent $10 billion a year on adult entertainment.

Libel

For 173 years, courts considered libel—defamatory statements that harm reputation—outside the protection of the First Amendment. Consequently, citizens and journalists risked criminal prosecution and civil liability by accusing government officials of misconduct. Under most states' seditious libel laws, truth was no defense. Under most states' civil libel laws, truth was a defense, but a statement's minor inaccuracies rendered an entire news report untrue. Thus, public officials could and did use such laws to intimidate or punish critics and muckrakers. In the early 1960s, the threat of such suits dampened news coverage of the civil rights movement.

That changed after the Court handed down its ruling in *New York v. Sullivan*, 375 U.S. 254 (1964), one of the Court's most significant free press rulings. The ruling stemmed from a libel action brought by L. B. Sullivan, a public affairs commissioner in Montgomery, Alabama. Inaccurate and false statements published in a political advertisement in the *New York Times* in 1960 falsely defamed him, Sullivan charged. Sullivan won a $500,000 judgment against the *Times*.

Overturning the judgment, Brennan sought to create breathing space for the erroneous statements that are inevitably part of political debate and journalism reportage by creating a test for defamatory statements targeting public officials in their public capacity. The First Amendment, Brennan declared, required a public official to show with clear and convincing evidence that a defamatory statement about an official's public conduct was made with actual malice or with knowing or reckless disregard for the truth. The ruling also declared the Sedition Act of 1798 unconstitutional, deemed that advertisements addressing social issues were political speech worthy of full First Amendment protection, and made libel law a federal constitutional matter. In following years, the Court required nongovernmental, public figures to meet the same standard in libel actions.

The ruling had an immediate impact beyond the legal sphere; it is widely believed that soon after, news coverage of the civil rights struggle increased. It has had long-term consequences. The Media Law Resource Center, for example, reports that since 1980, the annual average number of trials in each decade declined, and media defendants' win percentage has increased during the same period.

Free Press v. Privacy

The press's right to report on matters of public concern may be checked by an individual's right to privacy, the right to be left alone. In 1890, Brandeis, then a Boston lawyer and Samuel Warren, also a lawyer, proposed a theory of a right to privacy to check what they saw as the press's excessive gossip mongering. Their theory gave rise to civil actions (torts) in which plaintiffs sued for the emotional and physical harm resulting from invasion of privacy. In the early 1900s, the New York legislature and Georgia Supreme Court were the first to recognize such legal actions.

In 1960, another law review article sparked renewed interest in invasion of privacy torts. In that article, legal scholar William L. Prosser defined four types of invasion of privacy torts: intrusion, false light, appropriation, and publication of private matters. Most states allow plaintiffs to sue based on Prosser's four legal actions.

Free press advocates are troubled by the intrusion and publication of private torts because, unlike libel, truth is not necessarily a defense in such cases. In the 1990s, plaintiffs recast intrusion complaints and other allegations of wrongdoing such as fraud and misrepresentation into news-gathering torts. Such new legal theories threatened to handcuff the press's ability to gather news, particularly to conduct undercover investigations.

News-Gathering Torts

In its landmark ruling in *Cohen V. Cowles Media Co.*, 501 U.S. 663 (1991), the Court held that journalists must obey laws that apply to everyone—laws of general applicability. In *Cowles Media*, the general applicable law was contract. Two newspaper reporters broke their promise of confidentiality to a source. As a result, the source lost his job.

Within a few years after *Cowles Media*, plaintiffs—mostly corporations—targeted journalists for alleged wrongs committed during news gathering. In the mid-1990s, a lawsuit brought by the Food Lion, Inc. supermarket company against Capital Cities/ABC Inc. threatened to make investigative reporting too costly to pursue. Food Lion sued ABC-TV's *Prime Time Live* for fraud, trespass, misrepresentations, and breach of loyalty stemming from the television magazine shows' undercover probe of food preparation at a Food Lion store. The allegations of unsanitary food preparation were apparently true; they were caught on camera. Nevertheless, a jury awarded the company an astounding $5,545,750 in punitive damages and $1,400 in actual damages in 1997.

The size of the punitive damage award, many in the media argued, posed a grave threat to freedom of the press. Two years later, however, an appeals court reduced the award to a mere two dollars. The court ruled that undercover journalists did not defraud the company in *Food Lion, Inc. v. Capital Cities/ABC, Inc.*, 194 F.3d 505 (4th Cir. 1999).

As a general rule, the First Amendment does not license journalists to break the law to obtain information. The Court, however, held in *Bartnicki v. Vopper*, 532 U.S. 514 (2001) that the First Amendment protects news media outlets that disseminate information about a matter of public significance when a stranger breaks a law to obtain the information.

A small minority of state courts also allow a journalist to mount a substantive First Amendment defense during a criminal trial; that is, a judge allows a journalist to argue to a jury that he broke the law solely to publicize a publicly significant matter, did not benefit from the illegal act, or cause the harm the statute was designed to prevent. Typically, however, courts reject the notion that the First Amendment provides a defense to a criminal charge.

Access

It is almost universally accepted that governments have a legitimate interest in keeping sensitive military, espionage, and diplomatic information from the public. In the United States, laws establishing federal departments called "housekeeping statutes," passed as early as 1789, allowed such departments to keep certain information secret. Even so, it was not until the cold war period that the news media and government clashed over public access to government documents.

Such conflicts led to the formation of a Special Subcommittee on Government Information, more popularly know as the Moss subcommittee after its chair, California Democratic Representative John E. Moss (1915–1997) in 1955. Meanwhile, prominent journalists and the American Society of Newspaper Editors (ASNE) spearheaded efforts to fight government secrecy. The ASNE formed the Freedom of Information Committee. Their combined efforts led to the passage of the Federal Public Records Law, known as the Freedom of Information Act (FOIA) in 1966.

The act provides a right of access to government information, although it provides nine categories of exemptions. The 1972 Federal Advisory Committee Act requires executive branch federal advisory committees to be open. The 1976 Government in the Sunshine Act requires public access to federal boards, commissions, and councils subject to the nine exemptions provided by FOIA. The 1996 Electronic Freedom of Information Act requires access to electronically stored databases. States and the District of Columbia have passed similar acts and Sunshine Laws requiring open access to public meetings.

The First Amendment, however, does not guarantee the press or the public a right to government information or access to meetings and places. From a free press advocate's view, such lack of constitutional protection weakens the right to know, because statute-guaranteed rights are quite vulnerable to politics. Such advocates also argue that FOIA exemptions are so broad as to make the disclosure requirements almost meaningless.

In its September 2004 edition of *Homefront Confidential: How the War on Terrorism Affects Access to Information and the Public's Right to Know,* the Reporter's Committee for Freedom of the Press claimed the Bush Administration's post-9/11 security measures severely threatened public access to government-held information. The committee identified Attorney General John Ashcroft's 2001 memo, instructing agency heads on how to use FOIA exemptions to deny access by claiming invasion of privacy or breach of national security and new federal laws and regulations that override state open records laws as part of the effort limiting access. The committee, however, noted that the highly controversial USA Patriot Act had not had an impact on news gathering.

In the 1990s, the popularity of personal computers, allowing anyone access to the Internet, launched the Information Age. But quick and easy access to a wealth of government-collected data and information raised concerns about invasion of privacy. Privacy right advocates argued that the universal and almost effortless access to public records containing information such as social security numbers that the Internet provides posed a threat to privacy that did not exist when the same public records were stored in files in government buildings. Acting on that logic, access to driver's license information that the public and press enjoyed for many decades was restricted under the federal Drivers Privacy Protection Act of 1994 and similar state statutes.

Fair Trial–Free Press

A presumption that local and federal trials are open to the public and the press predates the U.S. Constitution. Of course, the Founding Fathers did not contemplate photography cameras or radio and television broadcast equipment. But during the first four decades of the twentieth century, many judges allowed reporters to use photography cameras and radio transmission equipment at criminal trials. In 1937, the American Bar Association (ABA) adopted Judicial Canon 35 and spurred the federal government and all states to ban cameras and broadcasting equipment from courtroom proceedings. The ABA adopted Canon 35 in response to what many saw as the largely media-created chaos of the Bruno Hauptmann trial of 1937.

No court has held that the news media have a First Amendment right to televise courtroom proceedings. The Court, however, ruled in *Chandler v. Florida*, 449 U.S. 560 (1981) that states may televise trials as long as a defendant's right to a fair trial is protected. Under Federal Rules of Criminal Procedure 53, only the Court and Congress have the authority to permit cameras at federal criminal trials. The Court exercised that authority when it declined to allow the oral arguments of *Bush v. Gore*, 531 U.S. 98 (2000) to be televised.

Although some reporter's tools might be banned, the Court has held that reporters and the public have a First Amendment right to attend pretrial proceedings, jury selection, and trials. Lower federal and state courts have held that reporters have a right to attend other proceedings such as bail and plea hearings.

The constitutional right of access does not extend to civil proceedings nationwide. Only a handful of federal appeals courts have ruled that reporters and the public have a constitutional right of access to such proceedings. Since the late 1980s, reporters and free press advocates have been highly critical of the practice by some judges of sealing files to prevent news of filings and settlements of lawsuits and the practice of deleting opinions from the public record.

Under the Constitution, judges have the authority to impose gag orders—another form of prior restraint—on reporters to protect a defendant's right to a fair trial. But judges are required to adhere to a balancing test established in *Nebraska Press Association v. Stuart*, 427 U.S. 539 (1976). Can court-imposed injunctions effectively work as prior restraints in the Internet era? Any one with a website, access to e-mail, or access to chat groups can disseminate confidential government and court documents to thousands within minutes. The risk remains, however, that courts may use their contempt power to punish after publication.

Electronic Media

Radio did not start as a mass medium. In its earliest incarnation in 1900, mostly shipping vessels used radio wave transmitters and receivers to communicate ship to ship. Even then, governments recognized the need to regulate the airwaves, particularly for maintaining safety on the high seas. The radio wave spectrum is limited, and a frequency is useless when more than one entity transmits on or near it simultaneously. Consequently, the U.S. government started to regulate use of the airwaves in 1910.

By 1923, radio had become a mass medium; there were 556 broadcasting stations operating and 550,000 radio receivers that year. With the growing popularity of radio broadcasting, interference problems resurfaced. In response, Congress passed the Radio Act of 1927, which established the Federal Radio Commission. The Act authorized the commission to issue and revoke licenses to ensure clear radio transmission, to regulate programming for the public interest, convenience, and necessity, but not to censor broadcasters.

In 1934, Congress passed the Communications Act, folding the FRC and its authority into the newly created Federal Communications Commission (FCC). But the Act failed to clarify whether the authority to regulate in the public interest infringed on a broadcaster's right to control its programming. The Court issued its first response to that question in *National Broadcasting Co. v. U.S*, 319 U.S. 190 (1943), noting that potential broadcasters far outnumbered the availability of radio frequencies and, consequently, government regulation was necessary. Under that rationale—otherwise known as spectrum scarcity—radio and television broadcasters do not enjoy the full First Amendment rights accorded print journalists.

The Court reaffirmed the doctrine's legitimacy in *Red Lion Broadcasting Co. Inc. v. FCC*, 395 U.S. 367 (1969). In its ruling, the Court upheld the FCC's fairness doctrine that requires radio and television outlets to allow targets of on-air personal or political attacks to reply. The Court also noted that the public's First Amendment rights are paramount to broadcasters'. The FCC eliminated the fairness doctrine in 1987. Nevertheless, it is still constitutionally valid, having never been struck down by the Court. In contrast, the Court struck down a similar right-to-reply imposed on newspapers in *Miami Herald Publishing Co. v. Tornillo*, 418 U.S. 241 (1974).

The Court held in *FCC v. Pacifica Foundation*, 438 U.S. 726 (1978), that the uniquely pervasive presence of broadcasting in the home justifies FCC authority to fine licensees for indecent broadcasting. In contrast, print publishers and writers of sexually explicit expression are subject only to prosecution for obscenity.

Civil libertarians and free market advocates argue that spectrum scarcity is not a valid rationale for government regulation of broadcast because cable and satellite television, the Internet, and the technological capability to splice the spectrum have dramatically increased consumers' choices of electronic media. In the 1970s and 1980s, the Court seemed as though it was open to reexamine its spectrum scarcity-public trustee rationale in its ruling in *CBS, Inc. v. Democratic National Committee*, 412 U.S. 94 (1973) and *FCC v. League of Women Voters of California*, 468 U.S. 364 (1984). Yet as of 2005, the Court had not abandoned the spectrum rationale.

It has, however, ruled that spectrum scarcity does not provide a rationale for government licensing of cable TV outlets, communication satellites in *Turner Broadcasting System, Inc. v. FCC*, 512 U.S. 622 (1944), and or the Internet in *Reno v. ACLU*, 521 U.S. 844 (1997). Under *Reno v. ACLU*, the Court held that the Internet enjoys the substantial First Amendment protections afforded the print media.

The Court has not made clear the precise contours of cable's First Amendment protections. The government, for example, has the authority to require some cable operators to set aside channel capacity for local broadcasters as the Court held in *Turner Broadcasting System v. FCC*, 520 U.S. 180 (1997). On the other hand, in *U.S. v. Playboy Entertainment Group*, 529 US 803 (2000), the Court declined to apply the restrictions of *FCC v. Pacifica Foundation* on cable television.

Reporter's Privilege

The press argued that reporters should be shielded from forced testimony as early as 1848 when the U.S. Senate put *New York Herald* reporter John Nugent under arrest, the first recorded jailing of a journalist for refusing to identify a confidential source. Nugent refused to reveal the identity of the source who gave him a copy of a secret draft treaty between the United States and Mexico. After a month, the Senate released Nugent. Most historians believe then-Secretary of State James Buchanan was the source of the leak.

In 1957, the same newspaper—then the *New York Herald Tribune*—engaged in another dispute over the reporter's privilege to remain silent. The newspaper argued in *Garland v. Torre*, 259 F. 2d 545 (1958), that journalists enjoy a reporter-source privilege under the First Amendment. The *Herald Tribune* was the first to make a First Amendment argument for such a testimonial privilege for journalists, but to no avail. A federal appeals court rejected the argument.

Twelve years later in *Branzburg v. Hayes*, 408 U.S. 444 (1969), the Court declined to find a testimonial privilege for an agreement a journalist makes with a source to conceal information. The ruling was five to four, and a plurality opinion said prosecutorial bad-faith investigations amounted to impermissible harassment. A concurring opinion noted that courts would protect journalists "where legitimate First Amendment interests require protection." In addition, Justice Potter Stewart's (1915–1985) dissent offered a rationale for striking the proper balance between freedom of the press and the general obligation to respond to a subpoena.

By the early years of the twenty-first century, eleven of twelve federal appeals courts recognized some form of qualified reporter's privilege, with the Eighth Circuit as the exception. Courts and legislatures in forty-nine states and the District of Columbia also recognized a qualified reporter's privilege. Most used Stewart's balancing test. Statutes that provide protection against forced testimony by reporters are called shield laws, and in response to the scandal stemming from the outing of Valerie Plame, a CIA operative, by a newspaper columnist, federal legislators proposed two versions of a federal shield law in 2005.

In 1791, few doubted that freedom of the press entitled pamphleteers to protection under the newly adopted Bill of Rights. Yet in the first decade of twenty-first century, bloggers—the modern-day counterpart to pamphleteers—had yet to earn the full protections and privileges enjoyed by traditional reporters. In 2005, for example, a California appeals judge in *Apple Computer, Inc. v. Doe*, 1-04-CV-032178 (2005), declined to address whether bloggers were qualified to invoke the reporter's privilege to remain silent. Freedom of the press is a work in progress.

ARTHUR S. HAYES

References and Further Reading

Blackstone, William. *Commentaries on the Laws of England.* Chicago: University of Chicago Press. 1991.

Cornwell, Nancy C. *Freedom of the Press: Rights and Liberties under the Law.* Santa Barbara: ABC-CLIO, Inc. 2004.

Reporters Committee for Freedom of the Press. *Homefront Confidential: How the War on Terrorism Affects Access to Information and the Public's Right to Know,* http://www.rcfp.org/homefrontconfidential, (2005).

Cases and Statutes Cited

Abrams v. U.S., 250 U.S. 616 (1919)

American Booksellers Association, Inc. v. Hudnut, 771 F.2d 323 (1985)

American Civil Liberties Union v. Ashcroft, 322 F. 3d 240 (3d Cir. 2003)

Apple Computer, Inc. v. Doe, 1-04-CV-032178 (2005)

Ashcroft v. Free Speech Coalition, 535 U.S. 234 (2002)

Bartnicki v. *Vopper*, 532 U.S. 514 (2001)

Brandenburg v. Ohio, 395 U.S. 444 (1969)

Braun v. Soldier of Fortune Magazine, 968 F.2d 1110 (1992)

Bush v. Gore, 531 U.S. 98 (2000)

CBS, Inc. v. Democratic National Committee, 412 U.S. 94 (1973)

Chandler v. Florida, 449 U.S. 560 (1981)

Cohen V. Cowles Media Co., 501 U.S. 663 (1991)

FCC v. League of Women Voters of California, 468 U.S. 364 (1984)

FCC v. Pacifica Foundation, 438 U.S. 726 (1978)

Food Lion, Inc. v. Capital Cities/ABC, Inc., 194 F.3d 505 (4th Circ. 1999)

Frohwerk v. U.S., 249 U.S. 204 (1919)

Garland v. Torre, 259 F. 2d 545 (2d Cir., 1958)

Gitlow v. New York. 268 U.S. 652 (1925)

Hazelwood School District v. Kuhlmeier, 484 U.S. 260 (1988)

Miami Herald Publishing Co. v. Tornillo, 418 U.S. 241 (1974)

Miller v. California, 413 U.S. 15 (1973)

National Broadcasting Co. v. U.S. 319 U.S. 190 (1943)

Nebraska Press Association v. Stuart, 427 U.S. 539 (1976)

Near v. Minnesota, 283 U.S. 697 (1931)

New York v. Ferber, 458 U.S. 747 (1982)

New York Times Co. v. United States, 403 U.S. 713 (1971)

New York v. Sullivan, 375 U.S. 254 (1964)

Red Lion Broadcasting Co. Inc. v. FCC, 395 U.S. 367 (1969)

Reno v. ACLU, 521 U. S. 844 (1997)

Rice v. Paladin, 128 F. 3d 233 (4th Circ.1997), cert. denied, 523 U.S. 1074 (1998)

Turner Broadcasting System, Inc. v. FCC, 512 U.S. 622 (1994)

Schenck v. U.S., 249 U.S. 47 (1919)

Snepp v. U.S., 444 U.S. 507 (1980)

U.S. American Library Association, 539 U.S. 194 (2003)

U.S. v. Playboy Entertainment Group, 529 U.S. 803 (2000)

U.S. v. One Book Called "Ulysses," 5.Supp. 182 (S.D.N.Y.1933)

U.S. v. Roth, 354 U.S. 476 (1957)

FREUND, PAUL A. (1908-1992)

Paul A. Freund, an eminent constitutional law scholar at Harvard Law School, was born in St. Louis, Missouri on February 16, 1908. After graduating from Washington University in 1928 and receiving his L.L.B and S.J.D. from Harvard Law School in 1931 and 1932, he served as law clerk to Justice Louis D. Brandeis (1932–1933). He spent most of the next dozen years serving in the executive branch of the federal government—in the Treasury Department, Reconstruction Finance Corporation, and twice in the Solicitor's General's office. He joined the Harvard Law School faculty first in 1939, and then permanently in 1946, where he taught until his retirement in 1976. Freund declined the entreaty of President John

F. Kennedy to serve as Solicitor General in December 1960. Kennedy later considered, but passed over, Freund for two Supreme Court appointments in 1962. Freund died February 5, 1992.

Freund wrote widely on the Supreme Court and its justices and the constitutional issues of the era, including those relating to civil liberties. He frequently testified before Congressional committees considering such matters.

Freund generally supported the Warren Court's decisions that took on expansive view of civil liberties. He thought they made America more participatory and less hierarchical. He did not usually embrace the absolute tests of many of those opinions, believing that the cases often involved competing principles. He tended to strike the balance in a way that protected civil liberties but thought the Warren Court sometimes prescribed one approach when a range of solutions would protect the constitutional norm.

Freund defended the Court's decisions in the early 1960s that banned organized school prayer and classroom Bible reading. He thought these outcomes reflected a proper balance between the claims of the establishment and free exercise clauses consistent with the concept of religious voluntarism implicit in American traditions. The classroom presented an area where psychological pressures to conform were most likely to be coercive. Freund did not view the establishment and free exercise clauses as absolutes. They must yield at times to public concerns and to each other.

Freund helped develop and defend the constitutional basis for the public accommodations section of the Civil Rights Act of 1964. In a 1963 brief requested by the Senate Committee on Commerce, Freund argued that Congress had power under the Commerce Clause to outlaw racial discrimination in places of public accommodation. He thought that resting the legislation on § 5 of the Fourteenth Amendment was riskier and more problematic jurisprudentially. Congress adopted Freund's rationale, and the Supreme Court upheld the legislation on that basis.

Freund gave early defense to race conscious remedies to address past discrimination against African Americans. In 1964, when affirmative action was in its infancy, he argued that the Constitution did not preclude transitional measures to provide favored treatment to racial minorities to correct for past disadvantage. The Constitution mandated equal protection of the law, not color blindness. The latter was simply a metaphor, and a misleading one at that.

JOEL K. GOLDSTEIN

References and Further Reading

Freund, Paul A. *On Law and Justice.* Cambridge: The Belknap Press of Harvard University Press, 1968.
———. *The Supreme Court of the United States: Its Business, Purposes, and Performance.* Cleveland: World Publishing Company 1961.
In Memoriam: Paul A. Freund. (Essays by Hon. William J. Brennan, Jr., Hon. Lewis F. Powell, Jr., Archibald Cox, James Vorenberg, and Anthony Lewis) Harvard Law Review 106 (1992): 1–18.

See also **Affirmative Action; Brandeis, Louis Dembitz; Civil Rights Act of 1964; Establishment and Free Exercise Clauses; Warren Court**

FRISBIE v. COLLINS, 342 U.S. 519 (1952)

Frisbie v. Collins involved the forcible capture of Collins in Illinois by Michigan law enforcement agents and his subsequent murder conviction in that state. Collins alleged that "Michigan officers forcibly seized, handcuffed, blackjacked and took him to Michigan" in violation of the Fourteenth Amendment and the Federal Kidnapping Act, thus voiding his conviction. The Supreme Court, with Justice Black writing for the majority, rejected Collins' argument that the illegal nature of his apprehension denied the Michigan Court jurisdiction, thus reaffirming a position first articulated in the 1886 case *Ker v. Illinois. Frisbie* reified the concept of *male captus bene detentus*, otherwise known in Court jurisprudence as the *Ker-Frisbie* rule, applying it to cases of domestic and extraterritorial abduction. Despite lower court attempts to limit the rule's scope and application, the precept seems to have survived later constitutional development unscathed.

The Court in *Ker* affirmed the conviction of a defendant who had been forcibly abducted in Peru by a U.S. agent acting *ultra vires* and brought back to the United States to stand trial. In *Frisbie*, Justice Black announced that the Court had "never departed from the rule announced in *Ker v. Illinois*," which allowed law enforcement officers personal jurisdiction over an accused, despite the commission of illegal acts in bringing him or her to trial. Had Congress added a sanction to the Kidnapping Act denying states' jurisdiction to prosecute defendants brought to Court in violation of one of its provisions, a different result the Justices concluded, might obtain. Nor do such abductions enhance the State's case at trial, as would be the case with illegally seized evidence, for example. But Black's opinion focused on the fairness of the trial as the critical issue in the due process analysis, finding no Fourth or Fourteenth Amendment violations in the presumably illegal rendition of the defendant across state lines. "Due process of law" wrote the Court, "is satisfied when one present in court is convicted of crime after having been fairly apprised the charges against him and after a fair trial in accordance with constitutional procedural safeguards."

The U.S. Court of Appeals for the Second Circuit leveled the first major attack on Ker-Frisbie in *United States v. Toscanino*, holding that recent Supreme Court decisions expressed an "expanded and enlightened" interpretation of due process to cover the pretrial treatment of a defendant. Toscanino had allegedly been tortured by American officials, among others, enroute to trial in the United States from Uruguay. The Second Circuit held that the Constitution would require the Court to divest itself of jurisdiction in the face of "unreasonable invasion of the accused's constitutional rights" where such conduct "shocked the conscience." However, the demise of *Ker-Frisbie* in the wake of *Toscanino* proved illusory. The Fifth, Seventh, and Eleventh Circuit Courts of Appeals have been unreceptive to such an interpretation, whereas the Supreme Court later refused to void a conviction due to "illegal arrest or detention" in *Gerstein v. Pugh*.

The continuing vitality of the rule does prevent it from being challenged by publicists who argue that it condones detainee abuse by law enforcement officials. But the *Ker-Frisbie* rule will likely remain relevant, especially in so far as it concerns extraterritorial abduction, because the United States prosecutes its war on terrorism and combats drugs abroad.

ANDREW FINKELMAN

References and Further Reading

Campbell, Andrew, *The Ker-Frisbie Doctrine: A Jurisdictional Weapon in the War on Drugs*, Vanderbilt Journal of Transnational Law 23 (1990–1991): 385.
Semmelman, Jacques, *Due Process, International Law, and Jurisdiction over Criminal Defendants Abducted Extraterritorially: The Ker-Frisbie Doctrine Reexamined*, Columbia Journal of Transnational Law 30 (1992): 513.
Torcia, Charles, ed. *Wharton's Criminal Procedure*. 13th Ed. Rochester, NY: Lawyers Co-Operative Publishing Co., 1989.

Cases and Statutes Cited

Gerstein v. Pugh, 420 U.S. 103 (1975)
Ker v. Illinois, 119 U.S. 436 (1886)
United States v. Toscanino, 500 F.2d 267 (2d Cir. 1974)

FRISBY v. SCHULTZ, 487 U.S. 474 (1988)

A town enacted an ordinance prohibiting picketing "before or about" any residence. Abortion foes who wished to picket on the public street outside the residences of abortion providers brought suit, contending that the ordinance was invalid on its face. Substantial precedent supported their position: all public sidewalks, streets, and parks are considered traditional public forums—presumptively open for peaceful marches and protests. The town, however, urged that the Court treat residential picketing differently.

The initial question was the exact reach of the ordinance. Did it prohibit *all* picketing in residential areas? Or just "targeted" picketing—that is, directed to a particular residence? Because it preferred to avoid addressing substantial constitutional difficulties raised by the broader interpretation, the Court reviewed only the narrower "targeted picketing."

Place regulations may be upheld only if "narrowly tailored to serve a significant government interest" and must "leave open ample alternative channels of communication." Here, other "channels" remained open: protesters could solicit door-to-door, by phone, or through the mails. Moreover, preserving residential privacy and the tranquility of the home justified the restriction on targeted residential picketing. In public spaces, one can often avert ones eyes or avoid the controversy. This becomes difficult when one is targeted at home.

The Court's holding effectively protects residential picketing, yet acknowledges the capacity of government to reduce the din outside a target's home. Picketers have a right to cycle throughout residential neighborhoods, including in front of a "target's" home, but the government may prohibit picketing focused on a specific residence.

JOHN NOCKLEBY

See also **Public Forum Doctrines**

FRUIT OF THE POISONOUS TREE

When the police seize evidence in violation of a defendant's constitutional rights, the courts have historically applied an exclusionary evidence rule that prevents the prosecutor from using the evidence to convict the defendant (See *Mapp v. Ohio*, 367 U.S. 643 [1961]). They apply this rule to deter the police from violating citizen's constitutional rights. A corollary to the exclusionary evidence rule is provided by the "fruit of the poisonous tree" doctrine (a/k/a the "derivative evidence" rule). The fruit of the poisonous tree doctrine provides that, not only is the prosecution prohibited from introducing evidence obtained "directly" from illegality (the poisonous tree), they are also prohibited from using evidence "derived" from the illegality (the fruit) (See *Brown v. Illinois*, 422 U.S. 590 [1975]).

Although the derivative evidence rule has been applied in a variety of contexts, it frequently arises in several contexts. One is when the police illegally interrogate a suspect and obtain a confession from which they are able to locate and seize other evidence (for example, a murder weapon). Because the confession was illegally obtained, it constitutes the "poisonous tree," and the weapon constitutes derivative evidence because the police learned of its existence only because of the illegally obtained confession. A second context in which the derivative evidence rule applies is when the police illegally seize a defendant and obtain a confession as a result of the seizure. For example, suppose that the police illegally stop a motorist who they take to the police station for questioning. The initial seizure may be illegal if the police lacked adequate grounds to make the stop (the police generally must have a "reasonable suspicion" that the motorist was involved in criminal activity), and the decision to take the suspect to the police station may be illegal if the police lacked probable cause. As a result, both the decision to seize and the decision to transport the suspect to the police station constitute "poisonous trees." If the suspect is then interrogated at the police station and confesses, the confession might be regarded as a "fruit" of the poisonous tree. A third context is when the police illegally stop a motorist (again, perhaps, without a reasonable suspicion of criminal activity) and then develop probable cause to search the motorist's vehicle, which leads them to find contraband. The illegal search might be regarded as a "fruit" of the illegal stop.

Although the derivative evidence rule is an important part of modern criminal procedure, it is important to realize that it is not slavishly or routinely applied. If the police can show that the fruit of the illegal conduct would have "inevitably" been discovered, or that they have an "independent source" for the information, the courts will sometimes allow it into evidence.

RUSSELL L. WEAVER

References and Further Reading

Weaver, Russell L., et al. *Principles of Criminal Procedure*. Thomson/West, 2004, pp. 253–258.
Weaver, Russell L., et al. *Criminal Procedure: Cases, Problems & Exercises*. 2nd Ed. Thomson/West, 2001, pp. 662–671.

See also **Exclusionary Rule; Probable Cause; Search (General Definition); Seizures**

FULLER COURT (1888–1910)

The Supreme Court under the leadership of Melville W. Fuller (1888–1910) decided more constitutional controversies than all previous Courts combined. From a contemporary perspective, however, the Fuller Court's jurisprudence was flawed in a number of respects. For example, it decided *Plessy v. Ferguson*, which adopted "separate but equal" as an interpretation of the equal protection clause. In the field of civil liberties, it was not an aggressive champion of the noneconomic rights protected by the Constitution but instead a defender of property rights. Even so, the Fuller Court decided a number of significant civil liberties cases and laid much of the groundwork for contemporary constitutional doctrine. Twenty justices served during the Fuller Court, including justices nominated by presidents from Lincoln to Taft and such important figures as John Marshall Harlan I, David Brewer, and Oliver Wendell Holmes, Jr.

The Fuller Court was the first to use the theory of substantive due process to invalidate state legislation. In 1905, it decided the case that often provides the name for this entire period in Court history, *Lochner v. New York*. The Fuller Court's substantive due process decisions were largely limited to economic rights, but these cases laid the fundamental-rights groundwork for much of the Court's later civil liberties jurisprudence. Perhaps most importantly, the Fuller Court's substantive due process jurisprudence established, despite great controversy, judicial enforcement of fundamental rights as part of the Supreme Court's role. Many members of the Court believed that this included protection of unenumerated rights against government invasion. Commentators have traced the origins of modern Privacy decisions to the Fuller Court's substantive due process jurisprudence.

At the same time as it was protecting unenumerated economic rights, however, the Fuller Court consistently rejected incorporation of the criminal procedural protections found in the Bill of Rights into the due process clause of the Fourteenth Amendment. The Fuller Court, in other words, resisted the various efforts of litigants to federalize state criminal procedure, often over dissents by the first Justice Harlan. It rejected incorporation of the guarantee against cruel and unusual punishment in *O'Neil v. Vermont* and *In re Kemmler*, the confrontation clause in *West v. Louisiana*, the right to a twelve-member jury in criminal cases in *Maxwell v. Dow*, and the privilege against self-incrimination in *Twining v. New Jersey*. But its legacy here is complicated. In *Chicago, Burlington, and Quincy Railroad Co. v. Chicago*, the Fuller Court held for the first time that a provision in the Bill of Rights applied to the states. That case involved, not surprisingly, property rights protected by the Takings Clause; indeed, this was just one of many significant Takings Clause cases during this period. In addition, *Twining*, decided in 1908, clarified the fundamental-rights analysis that would be applied in deciding whether to apply Bill of Rights safeguards to the states in future cases.

The Fuller Court did decide some important cases of first impression involving constitutional safeguards in federal criminal cases. Few such cases reached the Supreme Court before extension of its appellate jurisdiction in criminal cases in 1889 and 1891. In two cases, the Fuller Court was the first to address the constitutionality of immunity statutes in light of the Fifth Amendment privilege against self-incrimination, although it is worth noting that both involved business prosecutions. In *Counselman v. Hitchcock*, a unanimous Court held that the privilege against self-incrimination applies to grand jury witnesses and that immunity statutes must provide at least as much protection as the constitutional privilege. *Counselman* was not very clear, however. In its immediate aftermath, Congress adopted an immunity statute providing transactional immunity for compelled testimony in federal proceedings. In *Brown v. Walker*, a narrowly divided Court upheld this statute. But the Court has since held, most significantly in *Kastigar v. United States*, that the Fifth Amendment only requires use/derivative use immunity, the *Kastigar* majority concluding that the broad transactional-immunity language in *Counselman* was merely dicta. The Fuller Court also applied the protection against unreasonable searches and seizures to corporations, while rejecting application of the privilege against self-incrimination to corporations in *Hale v. Henkel*. The *Insular Cases* held that constitutional guarantees did not apply in territories acquired in the Spanish-American War. Finally, in *Weems v. United States*, the Court inserted a proportionality standard into the protection against cruel and unusual punishment.

In religion cases, in *Bradfield v. Roberts*, the Court rejected a taxpayer's Establishment Clause challenge to a contract between the District of Columbia and a Roman Catholic hospital, holding that institutions with secular purposes may receive governmental aid, as long as they are not pervasively sectarian. The Fuller Court's most notable free-exercise cases, both decided in 1890, involved laws burdening the practice of plural marriage among members of the Church of Jesus Christ of Latter-day Saints. In *Davis v. Beason*, the Court upheld an Idaho territory law denying voting rights to members of the church, following the 1878 precedent *Reynolds v. United States*. A closely divided Court upheld a federal law abolishing the Utah church and expropriating its property in *Late Corporation of the Church of Jesus Christ of Latter-day Saints v. United States*. In the latter case, involving property rights, Chief Justice Fuller and three other members of the Court dissented.

The Fuller Court decided two early speech cases, both against speech rights. In *Turner v. Williams*, the Court upheld the deportation of an English anarchist based on his political beliefs. In *Patterson v. Colorado*, in an opinion by Justice Holmes, the Court upheld a conviction for criminal contempt based on criticism of the state high court.

The Fuller Court's greatest contribution to civil liberties jurisprudence arguably came in *Ex Parte Young*, which held that the Eleventh Amendment does not bar suits to enjoin state officials from violating the Constitution and federal law. The legal fiction created in this case has been used by litigants seeking to protect civil liberties and other rights in a great number of cases.

EMERY G. LEE, III

References and Further Reading

Bernstein, David E., *Lochner Era Revisionism, Revised: Lochner and the Origins of Fundamental Rights Constitutionalism*, Georgetown Law Review 92 (2003): 1:1–60.

Currie, David P. *The Constitution in the Supreme Court: The Second Century 1888–1986.* Chicago: University of Chicago Press, 1990.

Ely, Jr., James W. *The Chief Justiceship of Melville W. Fuller, 1888–1910.* Columbia: University of South Carolina Press, 1995.

Fiss, Owen M. *History of the Supreme Court of the United States, Volume 8: Troubled Beginnings of the Modern State, 1888–1910.* New York: Macmillan, 1993.

King, Willard L. *Melville Weston Fuller: Chief Justice of the United States 1888–1910.* Chicago: University of Chicago Press, 1967.

Yarbrough, Tinsley E. *Judicial Enigma: The First Justice Harlan.* New York: Oxford University Press, 1995.

Cases and Statutes Cited

Bradfield v. Roberts, 175 U.S. 291 (1899)

Brown v. Walker, 161 U.S. 591 (1896)

Chicago, Burlington, and Quincy R. Co. v. Chicago, 166 U.S. 226 (1897)

Counselman v. Hitchcock, 142 U.S. 547 (1892), overruled by *Kastigar v. United States*, 406 U.S. 411 (1972)

Davis v. Beason, 133 U.S. 333 (1890), overruled by *Romer v. Evans*, 517 U.S. 620 (1996)

Ex Parte Young, 209 U.S. 123 (1908)

Hale v. Henkel, 201 U.S. 43 (1906), overruled by *Murphy v. Waterfront Commission*, 378 U.S. 52 (1964)

In re Kemmler, 136 U.S. 436 (1890)

Kastigar v. United States 406 U.S. 411 (1972)

Late Corp. of Church of Jesus Christ of Latter-day Saints, 136 U.S. 1 (1890)

Lochner v. New York, 198 U.S. 45 (1905)

Maxwell v. Dow, 176 U.S. 581 (1900), overruled *by Williams v. Florida*, 399 U.S. 78 (1970)
O'Neil v. Vermont, 144 U.S. 323 (1892)
Patterson v. Colorado 205 U.S. 454 (1907)
Reynolds v. United States, 98 U.S. 145 (1878)
Turner v. Williams 194 U.S. 279 (1904)
Twining v. New Jersey, 211 U.S. 78 (1908), overruled by *Malloy v. Hogan*, 378 U.S. 1 (1964)
Weems v. United States, 217 U.S. 349 (1910)
West v. Louisiana, 194 U.S. 258 (1904), overruled by *Pointer v. Texas*, 380 U.S. 400 (1965)

See also **Incorporation Doctrine; Mormons and Religious Liberty; Substantive Due Process; Waite Court; White Court**

FURMAN v. GEORGIA, 408 U.S. 238 (1972)

Furman v. Georgia began the modern era of Capital Punishment jurisprudence in the United States. The broad issue in the case was whether the death penalty was unconstitutional, but the narrower issue concerned capital sentencing procedures. A majority of the Justices did not resolve the first issue, but the Court held that the procedures used to impose the death penalty violated the constitution.

At the time of *Furman*, death penalty statutes gave juries complete discretion on the issue of whether or not to impose the death penalty. The previous year, in *McGautha v. California*, the Supreme Court held that such systems do not violate the due process clause of the Fourteenth Amendment. However, in *Furman*, the Court in a five-to-four decision held that these discretionary systems do constitute cruel and unusual punishment in violation of the Eighth and Fourteenth Amendments.

Furman left open several issues because there was no clear consensus among the Justices. In addition to the short per curiam opinion striking the death penalty in the cases at issue, each of the nine Justices wrote a separate opinion, creating the longest decision ever issued by the Court.

Two of the Justices in the majority concluded that the death penalty itself is unconstitutional, but the other three Justices in the majority did not go so far, focusing on the arbitrariness and racial discrimination resulting from the process. *Furman* ended the death penalty in the United States until the Court approved of new death penalty statutes approximately four years later in *Gregg v. Georgia*.

JEFFREY L. KIRCHMEIER

References and Further Reading

Kirchmeier, Jeffrey L., *Another Place Beyond Here: the Death Penalty Moratorium Movement in the United States*, Colorado Law Review 73 (2002): 1:1–116 (article available at http://www.colorado.edu/law/lawreview/issues/summaries/73-1.htm).
Woodward, Bob, and Scott Armstrong. *The Brethren: Inside the Supreme Court* 260. New York: Avon Books, 1981.
Zimring, Franklin E., and Gordon Hawkins. *Capital Punishment and the American Agenda*, New York: Cambridge University Press, 1989.

Cases and Statutes Cited

Furman v. Georgia, 408 U.S. 238 (1972)
Gregg v. Georgia, 428 U.S. 153 (1976)
McGautha v. California, 402 U.S. 183, 196 (1971)

See also **Capital Punishment;** *Gregg v. Georgia*, **428 U.S. 153 (1976)**

FW/PBS, INC. v. CITY OF DALLAS, 493 U.S. 215 (1990)

Young v. American Mini-Theatres (1976) and *Renton v. Playtime Theatres* (1986) upheld the constitutionality of zoning ordinances regulating the locations of movie theaters specializing in sexually explicit films to counter the theatres' negative secondary effects on adjacent neighborhoods or nearby places of worship or schools. In the wake of these decisions, localities adopted more comprehensive regulations, including licensing schemes as well as zoning restrictions that focused on a wider array of "adult businesses."

Dallas, Texas, the respondent in this case, adopted a regulatory regime involving zoning, licensing, and inspections of sexually oriented businesses that included adult arcades, bookstores, video stores, cabarets, motels, theaters, and, before the Supreme Court reviewed the ordinance, escort agencies, nude model studios, plus "sexual encounter centers." Three separate lawsuits were filed by an array of businesses in federal district court that upheld most of the ordinance. The cases were subsequently appealed to the Fifth Circuit Court of Appeals, which affirmed the lower court, viewing it as a content-neutral time, place, and manner regulation under *Renton*.

Critical to the Supreme Court's review was the circuit court's conclusion that, despite the absence of the procedural safeguards mandated in the film censorship case, *Freedman v. Maryland* (1965), the ordinance was constitutional. Brennan's majority opinion in *Freedman* struck down Maryland's law because the procedures for censoring and licensing the presentation of films created the risk of delay while lacking prompt judicial review of decisions censoring or banning films. Prompt judicial review was needed whenever "unduly onerous" procedures for judicial review mean the "censor's determination may, in practice, be final."

Brennan proposed three procedural protections in *Freedman*. First, a censorship scheme must assure the exhibitor, "by statute or authoritative judicial construction, that the censor will, within a specified brief period, either issue a license or go to court to restrain showing the film." Second, the censorship scheme must "assure a prompt final judicial decision" after a refusal to license because, Brennan reasoned, "only a judicial determination in an adversary proceeding ensures the necessary sensitivity to freedom of expression." Third, "the burden of proving that the film is unprotected expression must rest on the censor."

FB/PBS, Inc. v. City of Dallas resulted in a complex, divided ruling that affirmed in part, reversed in part, and vacated in part with the cases remanded for further consideration. One issue dividing the Court was whether the Dallas ordinance constituted a censorship regime with regard to the regulation of adult businesses. Another issue, if the Dallas law was a censorship regime, was whether *Freedman* applied and if so whether all three parts of Brennan's test were also applicable.

O'Connor authored the fractured opinion. Stevens and Kennedy joined her opinion declaring the Dallas ordinance unconstitutional because it constituted a prior restraint on protected expression. According to O'Connor, a regulatory regime placing "unbridled discretion in the hands of a government official or agency" with respect to the location, licensing, or inspection of adult businesses "constitutes a prior restraint." Such restraints are not unconstitutional per se, but "any system of prior restraint...comes to this Court bearing a heavy presumption against its constitutional validity."

Brennan, Marshall, and Blackmun agreed with O'Connor that the ordinance was unconstitutional, giving her six votes on this question. The three justices, however, balked at her conclusion that because the Dallas ordinance did not pose the "grave 'dangers of a censorship system'" that only *Freedman's* first two elements, particularly "the possibility of prompt judicial review," were applicable. The three justices argued the burden of proof element also applied.

White and Rehnquist, agreeing with the Fifth Circuit Court, felt the ordinance as a time, place, and manner restriction was not subject to strict scrutiny and thus *Freedman* was inapplicable. Scalia dissented from the judgment and developed an alternative argument that the Dallas ordinance legitimately regulated the "pandering" activity of adult businesses, consistent with *Ginzburg v. Unites States* (1966).

The difficulties the decision in *FW/PBS* created for the lower courts surfaces in the litigation leading to *City of Littleton v. Z.J. Gifts* (2004).

ROY B. FLEMMING

References and Further Reading

Hixson, Richard F. *Pornography and the Justices: The Supreme Court and the Intractable Obscenity Problem*. Carbondale, IL: Southern Illinois University Press, 1996.
Mackey, Thomas C. *Pornography on Trial: A Handbook with Cases, Law, and Documents*. Santa Barbara, CA: ABC-Clio, 2002.

Cases and Statutes Cited

City of Littleton v. Z.J. Gifts D-4, L.L.C., 2003-058 (2004)
City of Renton v. Playtime Theatres, Inc., 475 U.S. 41 (1986)
Freedman v. Maryland, 380 U.S. 51 (1965)
FW/PBS, Inc. v. City of Dallas, 493 U.S. 215 (1990)
Ginzburg v. United States 383 U.S. 463 (1966)
Young v. American Mini Theatres, Inc., 427 U.S. 50 (1976)

INDEX

Bullying, homosexuality and, 1398
Bunting v. Oregon, 1596
   White Court and, 1777
Burch v. Louisiana, 803
Burdeau v. McDowell, 195
Burden of proof, 195–197
  Batson v. Kentucky and, 225
  Sandstrom v. Montana and, 1410
Bureau of Alcohol, Tobacco and Firearms (BATF)
  Branch Davidian Church, 1731
  Ruby Ridge and, 1384–1385
Bureau of Catholic Indian Missions, 1253
Bureau of Drug Abuse Control, 1743
Bureau of Indian Affairs, 1253
Bureau of Investigation, 774
Bureau of Land Management, 51
Bureau of Narcotics and Dangerous Drugs, 1743
Bureau of Prisons, 1625
Bureau of Prohibition, 64
Bureau of Refugees, Freedmen and Abandoned Lands, 964
Burger Court, 198–202
  civil rights and, 1544, 1545
  effect of, 206
  Emerson and, 499
  Francis v. Henderson and, 325
  habeas corpus and, 233–234, 727
  judicial review and, 865
  Marshall, T., and, 972
  Rehnquist Court and, 1286–1287, 1288
  Roe v. Wade and, 198, 1367–1368
  Wainwright v. Sykes and, 325
Burger, Warren, 203–206, 1416
  Aguilar v. Felton and, 32–33
  bail and, 98
  Bivens v. Six Unknown Names Agents of Federal Bureau of Narcotics and, 149
  Board of Education, Kiryas Joel Village School District v. Grumet and, 158
  Board of Education v. Pico and, 157
  Bowen v. Roy and, 168
  Bowers v. Hardwick and, 169
  Buckley v. Valeo and, 194
  Cain v. Kentucky and, 212
  Coker v. Georgia and, 386
  death of, 205
  equal protection and, 517
  First Amendment and, 206, 1299–1300
  Hudson v. Palmer and, 781
  Hutchinson v. Proxmire and, 788
  legislative chaplains and, 267
  Lemon test and, 918
  Marsh v. Chambers and, 966
  Miami Herald Publishing Co. v. Tornillo and, 1003–1004
  Miller v. California and, 1012–1013, 1283
  New York Times v. United States and, 1090
  Nixon, R. and, 203–204, 1384
  NLRB v. Catholic Bishop of Chicago and, 1100, 1301–1302
  nomination of, 204
  obscenity and, 1118, 1124
  Pell v. Procunier and, 1151
  Philadelphia Newspapers, Inc. v. Hepps and, 1158
  Planned Parenthood of Central Missouri v. Danforth and, 1173
  Powell, Lewis, and, 1194

  on proportionality, 245
  Rabe v. Washington and, 1255
  Regents of the University of California v. Bakke and, 206, 1284
  religious accommodation and, 23
  on religious symbols, 938
  retirement of, 10
  Rowan v. United States Post Office Department and, 1384
  sexual orientation and, 1223
  Wallace v. Jaffree and, 1737
  Walz v. Tax Commission and, 1738–1739
  Wisconsin v. Yoder and, 628, 1788
  Wolman v. Walter and, 1790
  Zablocki v. Redhail and, 1811
Burgh, James
  Jefferson and, 847
  wall of separation and, 1735
Buritica v. United States, 296
Burke, Edmund, 207
Burks, David, 207–208
Burks v. United States, 207–208, 1655
  Hudson v. Louisiana and, 781
Burleson, Albert
  free speech and, 1794
  Wilson, W., and, 1784
Burling, John, 842
Burnett, Henry L., 146
Burns Baking Company v. Bryan, 209
Burns v. Wilson
  military law and, 1007
Burnside, Ambrose, 646
  Ex parte Vallandigham and, 552–553
Burr, Aaron
  Hamilton and, 733
  Marshall, J., and, 970
  treason and, 1664–1665
Burroughs, Wellcome, 26
Burroughs, William S., 1051
Burson v. Freeman
  hate speech ordinances and, 657
  Mills v. Alabama and, 1014
Burstyn v. Wilson
  Code of 1930 and, 756
  obscenity and, 1123
Burton, Harold, 208
  Vinson Court and, 1721
Burton, Richard, 1039
Burton v. Wilmington Parking Authority, 606
Bush, George H.W.
  Diversity Immigrant Visa Program and, 427
  drugs and, 1744
  Falwell and, 575
  mandatory minimum sentences and, 954
  NAACP and, 1064
  NRA and, 1070
  Public Health Service Act and, 674
  Souter and, 1495
  Supreme Court and, 1287
Bush, George W., 1318
  abortion and, 10–11
  Amnesty International and, 60
  Ashcroft and, 84
  AUMF and, 731
  birth control and, 148

INDEX

INDEX

INDEX

National Right to Life Committee
  Eagle Forum and, 1134
  Operation Rescue and, 1133–1134
National security, 1071
  antidiscrimination and, 789–790
  classified information and, 310–311
  dissent and, 36, 658
  exclusion and deportation and, 789–792
  free speech and, 1072–1074
  indefinite detention and, 805
  injunctions and, 1212–1213
  legislation and, 1765
  prior restraints and, 1074–1076
  Schlafly and, 1421
  United States v. United States District Court and, 1696
  West Virginia State Board of Education v. Barnette and, 595
  wiretapping and, 856
National Security Act of 1947, 257
  Intelligence Identities Protection Act and, 817
  USA PATRIOT Act and, 1149
National Security Agency (NSA), 1520
National Security Council (NSC)
  CIA and, 257
  Meese and, 996–997
National Security Entry-Exit Registration System (NSEER), 1053
National Sex Offender Public Registry, 997
National Treasury Employees Union v. Von Raab, 1076–1077,
    1480, 1746
  drug testing and, 452–453
National Victims' Constitutional Amendment network, 1711
National War Labor Board, 1601
National Woman Suffrage Association, 65, 1522
National Women's Party, 520
Nationalism
  Marshall, J., and, 1557
  Stevens and, 1557
Nationality Act of 1965, 1070
Nationalization Act of 1940, 562
Native American Church (NAC), 24, 92–93, 807, 1818
  AIRFAA and, 501
  defining religion and, 410
  *Employment Division, Department of Human Resources of Oregon
    v. Smith* and, 500–501
  peyote and, 454, 1263, 1305
Native American Church v. Navajo Tribal Council, 807
Native Americans, 1411–1412
  AIRFA and, 51
  American Revolution and, 53
  Bill of Rights and, 1254, 1258
  citizenship clause and, 293
  criminal justice and, 1258
  cultural defense and, 391
  double jeopardy and, 441
  *Employment Division, Department of Human Resources of Oregon
    v. Smith* and, 500–501, 630
  free exercise and, 119–120, 626
  Friedman v. Board of County Commissioners and, 371
  ICRA and, 806–809
  Indian Civil Rights Act and, 1258
  Indian Removal and, 833
  Jackson, A. and, 832–833
  La Follette and, 901
  lynching and, 243
  Lyng v. Northwest Indian Cemetery Protective Association and,
    629, 939, 1470

Madison and, 946
  marriage and, 963
  as mascots, 1188
  miscegenation laws and, 1022
  Mormons and, 1036–1037
  police and, 1258
  property and, 1538
  Quick Bear v. Leupp and, 1253–1254
  racial discrimination and, 1256
  religious liberty and, 1077–1079
  religious practices of, 1470
  RLUIPA and, 1308
  Social Security and, 168
  sovereign immunity of, 1411
  sovereignty of, 807
  Storey and, 1570
  tribal courts of, 808–809
Nativity scenes, 1439
  County of Allegheny v. ACLU and, 42, 1313
  Lemon test and, 918
  Lynch v. Donnelly and, 937–938, 1312, 1314
Natural Born Killers, 210
Natural Law, 1079–1081, 1535
  Locke and, 930
  privacy and, 1225
Natural rights
  Declaration of Independence and, 401
  freedom of contract and, 636–637
  as human rights, 1325
  as liberty rights, 1326
  Locke and, 930–931, 1357
  natural law and, 1080–1081
Natural Theology (Paley), 377
Naturalization, 293–294
  Gillette v. United States and, 1143
  Girouard v. United States and, 1142
  illegal, 413
  pacifists and, 1141–1143
  revocation of, 413
  U.S. Constitution and, 353
Naturalization Act of 1798, 37
Naturalization Act of 1906, 1141
Naturalization Act of 1952, 1141
Naturalization Law of 1790, 796
Nature, 313
Nature of the Judicial Process, The (Cardozo), 248
Nauvoo, 1037–1038
Nauvoo Expositor, 1038
Navajo Nation
  autopsies and, 93
  ICRA and, 807
  tribal courts and, 808
Navajo Nation v. Crockett, 808
Navigation Acts, 1803
Navy, homosexuals in, 885
NAWSA. *See* National American Woman Suffrage Amendment
NAWU. *See* National Agricultural Workers' Union
Nazis. *See also* Neo-nazis
  ACLU and, 50
  Baldwin and, 103
  book banning and, 162
  citizenship and, 1390
  Communist Party and, 339
  eugenic sterilization and, 546
  freedom of expression and, 639

Hoover and, 775
Hughes Court and, 782
internment and, 496
Jackson, R. and, 833
Japanese internment and, 418, 839, 1373–1374
judicial review and, 864–865
military tribunals and, 1008
Murphy and, 1047
NAACP and, 1064
New Deal and, 1082–1085, 1564
powers of, 1801
Rauh and, 1269
Roosevelt, T., and, 1372
Rutledge, W., and, 1389
Soviet Union and, 150
spying and, 1518
Supreme Court and, 1373–1374
suspect categories and, 518
Vinson and, 1718
Wilson, W., and, 134, 1372, 1374
World War II and, 1372–1373
Roosevelt, Theodore, 770
antitrust and, 1471–1472
birth control and, 147
on dual citizenship, 456
eugenic sterilization and, 545–546
Frankfurter and, 617
Hand and, 736
"In God We Trust" and, 1066–1067
La Follette and, 902–903
McReynolds and, 992
Roosevelt, F., and, 1372
Taft and, 1601
Roper v. Simmons, 224, 386
California v. Ramos and, 216
Cardozo and, 248
Kennedy, A., and, 885
O'Connor and, 1127
proportionality and, 246
Stevens and, 1558
Rorty, Richard, 1374–1375
Rosales-Lopez v. United States, 1376
voire dire and, 873
Rose v. Clark, 1410
Rose v. Locke, 1376
Rosebud Reservation, 1253
Rosen v. United States, 1286, 1689
Rosenberg espionage trial, 322
Frankfurter and, 619
Rosenberg, Ethel, 322, 1377–1378, 1721
Communist Party and, 1377, 1378
Douglas, William, and, 1378
electric chair and, 485
FBI and, 1377
HUAC and, 780, 1377
Kaufman and, 883, 1377–1378
Vinson and, 1722
Rosenberg, Julius, 322, 1377–1378, 1721
Communist Party and, 1377, 1378
Douglas, William, and, 1378
FBI and, 1377
HUAC and, 780, 1377
Kaufman and, 883, 1377–1378
Vinson and, 1722
Rosenberg v. Board of Education of the City of New York, 163

Rosenberg v. United States, 1721
Rosenberger v. Rector and Visitors of the University of Virginia, 1298, 1379–1380, 1496, 1574
balancing and, 100
Breyer and, 183
Lamb's Chapel v. Center Moriches Union Free School District and, 907
limited public forum and, 922
National Endowment for the Arts v. Finley and, 1065
public forum doctrine and, 1229, 1244
religious organizations and, 699, 1379
religious speech and, 1229
student newspapers and, 1699
Thomas and, 1650
viewpoint discrimination and, 1715, 1717
Rosenbloom v. Metromedia, Inc., 1243
Rosie the Riveter, 965
Ross v. Moffitt, 1380–1381
Rossiter, Clinton, 1801
Rostker v. Goldberg, 698
Rostow, Eugene, 258
on Japanese internment, 840
ROTC
conscientious objection and, 349
Roth test
A Book Named "John Cleland's Memoirs of a Woman of Pleasure" v. Massachusetts and, 1
Ginzburg v. United States and, 688, 1282
Jacobellis v. Ohio and, 835–836
pandering and, 689
Roth v. United States, 1382–1383, 1521
A Book Named "John Cleland's Memoirs of a Woman of Pleasure" v. Massachusetts and, 1–2
Brennan in, 1382–1383
Cain v. Kentucky and, 212
Douglas and, 447, 1382
First Amendment and, 1382
Ginzburg v. United States and, 688
Harlan, I, in, 1382–1383
low value speech and, 937
Miller test and, 1012–1013
Miller v. California and, 1012
Mishkin v. New York and, 685, 1023
obscenity and, 659–660, 1117, 1123, 1228, 1382–1383
Paris Adult Theatre v. Slaton and, 1147, 1148
Pope v. Illinois and, 1191
Rabe v. Washington and, 1255
Stewart, P., and, 1560
United States v. Reidel and, 1690–1691
Warren Court and, 1755
Warren in, 1382–1383
Rousseau, Jean-Jacques
civil religion and, 297
civil rights and, 1638–1639
Meiklejohn and, 999
Roviaro v. United States, 1384
Rowan v. United States Post Office Department, 1384–1385
captive audiences and, 247
solicitations and, 829
Roy, Stephen, 168
Royce, Josiah, 735
Royer, Mark, 598
Rubber stamp objection, 1439
Rubin, Jerry, 278
Rubin v. Coors Brewing Co., 332

INDEX

Stevens, John Paul (*cont.*)
  44 Liquormart, Inc. v. Rhode Island and, 216
  Gardner v. Florida and, 675
  Hudson v. Palmer and, 781
  Jurek v. Texas and, 866
  Kyllo v. United States and, 900
  Madsen v. Women's Health Center and, 949
  Moore v. East Cleveland and, 1033
  O'Connor and, 1126
  Payton v. New York and, 1151
  Philadelphia Newspapers, Inc. v. Hepps and, 1158
  Planned Parenthood of Central Missouri v. Danforth and, 1173
  proportional punishment and, 1241
  R.A.V. v. City of St. Paul and, 1271
  Regents of the University of California v. Bakke and, 1284
  Reno v. ACLU and, 1316
  Rhode Island v. Innis and, 1331
  sexually explicit materials and, 1120
  United States v. Eichman and, 590
  vulgar speech and, 1248
  Wallace v. Jaffree and, 1029, 1737
  Webster v. Reproductive Health Services and, 11, 1770
  Wolman v. Walter and, 1790
  Zablocki v. Redhail and, 1811
Stevens, Robert, 1773
Stevens, Thaddeus, 146
  Thirteenth Amendment and, 1648
Stevenson, Adlai
  Goldberg and, 697
Steward Machine Co. v. Davis, 209
Stewart, Iain, 1032
Stewart, Jimmy, 775
Stewart, Lynne, 1625
Stewart, Maria, 648
Stewart, Potter, 1559–1561
  Abington Township School District v. Schempp and, 2
  Branzburg v. Hayes and, 179
  Burger Court and, 198
  Chimel v. California, 284–285
  Coolidge v. New Hampshire, 365
  on death penalty, 245
  Engel v. Vitale, 502, 1298
  Furman v. Georgia, 233
  Godfrey v. Georgia, 691
  Gregg v. Georgia, 223, 710
  on Jewish Sabbath, 852
  Katz v. United States and, 882, 1433
  Kingsley International Pictures Corporation v. Regents of the University of New York and, 892
  Lucas v. Forty-Fourth General Assembly of Colorado and, 1276
  Meiklejohn and, 1000
  Monroe v. Pape and, 1031
  NAACP v. Button and, 1058
  New York Times v. United States and, 1090
  North Carolina v. Pearce and, 1112
  obscenity and, 1118, 1123
  Pell v. Procunier and, 1151
  Planned Parenthood of Central Missouri v. Danforth and, 1173
  Poe v. Ullman and, 1183
  prison interviews and, 1415
  privacy and, 1219
  Redrup v. New York and, 1282
  on reporter's privilege, 664
  wall of separation and, 1736

  Wolman v. Walter and, 1790
  Zablocki v. Redhail and, 1811
Stewart, Raymond, 315
Stewart, Tom, 1426
Stewart, William, 145
  Bingham and, 146
Stimson, Henry L., 617
Sting, 59. *See also* Entrapment
Stockton, Julia, 1387
Stockton, Richard, 1387
Stogner v. California
  Breyer and, 183
  ex post facto laws and, 554
Stone Court, 1561–1563
Stone, Geoffrey R., 37
  Sedition Act and, 39
Stone, Harlan Fiske, 175, 1564–1566, 1802
  equal protection and, 515
  Girouard v. United States and, 1142
  Hirabayashi v. United States and, 839
  Hughes Court and, 782
  martial law and, 494
  Minersville School District v. Gobitis and, 591–593, 1630
  preferred position rule and, 1199, 1200
  on rational basis test, 251
  spying and, 1518
  United States v. Carolene Products Co. and, 515, 784
Stone, Lucy, 1522
  women's suffrage and, 1793
Stone, Oliver, 210
Stone, Sydell, 1563
Stone v. Graham, 3, 90, 1314, 1438, 1439, 1563–1564
  Burger and, 206
  Burger Court and, 200
  Lemon test and, 533, 538, 1313
  Ten Commandments and, 1314
Stone v. Powell
  exclusionary rule and, 555
  habeas corpus and, 556
  habeas corpus restrictions and, 728
Stonewall riot, 677, 1566–1567
Stoolies, 757
Stop and frisk doctrine, 275, 1015, 1431, 1445, 1567–1570. *See also* Frisking; Stops
  Florida v. Royer and, 598
  need *vs.* intrusion test and, 1752
  as seizure, 1627
  Warren Court and, 1757
Stop and identify statutes, 894
Stops
  intrusiveness of, 1568
  seizures and, 1445–1446, 1568
Storey, Moorfield, 1570–1571
  Buchanan v. Warley and, 191
Storrs Lectures, 248
Storrs v. Holcomb, 1401
Story, Joseph, 409, 1572
  establishment clause and, 532
  freedom of speech and, 645
  Marshall Court and, 968
  personal liberty laws and, 1154
  privileges and immunities and, 1231
  Vidal v. Girard's Executor and, 1712
  in *Wilkinson v. Leland*, 477
Story of My Life, The (Darrow), 394

INDEX

INDEX

Y

Yablonski, Jock, 1270
Yahweh, 1035
Yakus v. United States, 1391, 1801
Yale College
    Calhoun and, 214
Yale Law and Policy Review
    Emerson and, 499
Yale Law Journal
    ERA and, 521
    fair use doctrine and, 572
    Fortas and, 603
Yale Law School
    Bork and, 165
    Douglas and, 443
    Emerson and, 497
    Fortas and, 603
    Frank and, 615
    Griffiths and, 812
    Kunstler and, 898
    Rostow and, 258
Yale University, 1374
    Griswold v. Connecticut and, 712
Yalta Conference, 765
Yamashita, Tomoyuki, 1390
Yamataya v. Fisher
    due process and, 460
Yang v. Sturner, 93
Yarmulkes
    Goldman v. Weinberger and, 852
    in military, 1007
Yasui, Minoru, 839
    litigation of, 841–842
Yasui v. United States, 839–840
Yates v. United States, 68, 110, 1807
    Burks v. United States and, 858
    Clark, T., and, 309
    freedom of association and, 635
    Harlan, II, and, 741
    national security and, 1073
    Smith Act and, 1488
Yee, Johnny, 1792
Yellow dog contracts
    Adair v. United States and, 465
    Coppage v. Kansas and, 465
    White Court and, 1777
Yellow fever, 1387
Yick Wo v. Hopkins
    discriminatory prosecution in, 423
    equal protection clause and, 228
    Fourteenth Amendment, 515
Yippies, 898
YMCA. *See* Young Men's Christian Association
Yoder, Jonas, 1787
Yoo, John Choon, 1096
Young, Brigham, 72, 1330
    Mormons and, 1038
    polygamy and, 396
Young Earth creationism, 1616
Young Lawyer for the New Deal: An Insider's Memoir of the Roosevelt Years (Emerson), 498
Young Men's Christian Association (YMCA), 1592
    Comstock and, 341
Young Republicans, 204

Young v. American Mini-Theatres, 1318, 1418, 1436, 1807–1808, 1820
    content-neutral regulation and, 364
    Stevens and, 1556
    viewpoint discrimination and, 1714
    zoning laws and, 669, 1121
Youngberg v. Romeo, 282
Younge, Samuel, 161
Younger abstention, 1809
Younger, Evelle, 1809
Younger v. Harris, 1808–1809
    good faith exception and, 868
Youngs Drug Productions Corporation, 160–161
Youngstown Sheet & Tube Co. v. Sawyer, 495
    executive powers and, 731
    Jackson, R. and, 835
    Vinson Court and, 1720
Yousef, Ramzi, 1622
Youth International Party, 278
Yurok Indians, 939
Yutzy, Adin, 1787
YWCA, 520

Z

Zablocki v. Redhail, 1479, 1811–1812
Zacchini v. Scripps-Howard Broadcasting Co., 77, 1812
Zadvydas v. Davis, 460, 1530
    Breyer and, 183
    material witnesses and, 981
Zant v. Stephens, 237
Zaps, 26
Zellman v. Simmons-Harris, 31–32, 167, 422, 1298, 1416, 1528, 1812–1814
    ADL and, 69
    Americans United and, 57
    Breyer and, 183
    Charitable Choice and, 270
    Committee for Public Education and Religious Liberty v. Nyquist and, 334
    government funding and, 542
    Locke v. Davey and, 929
    Mueller v. Allen and, 1045–1046
    non-funding provisions and, 153
    O'Connor and, 1127
    school vouchers and, 1424
    Souter and, 1496
    Witters v. Department of Services and, 1789
    Wolman v. Walter and, 1791
    Zobrest v. Catalina Foothills School District and, 1817
Zenger, John Peter, 644, 705, 1440, 1814–1816
    Bishop's Case and, 1667
    free speech law and, 815
    freedom of press and, 1202, 1207
    Hamilton and, 734
    jury nullification and, 869
    national security and, 1072
Zeno, James, 940
Zeran, Ken, 45
Zeran v. America Online, 45
Ziang Sung Wan v. United States, 1018
Zimbalist, Efrem, Jr., 775
Zion, 1035
Z.J. Gifts, 926